A SHORT HISTORY OF RUGBY LEAGUE IN AUSTRALIA

WILL EVANS

Front cover: Queensland captain Wally Lewis (right) and halfback Allan Langer rejoice after the Maroons' 12-6 defeat of New South Wales in the second match of the 1987 State of Origin series at the SCG.

Back cover: Canberra captain Mal Meninga (right) and halfback Ricky Stuart share in the elation of the Raiders' maiden Grand Final victory—a 19-14 extra-time defeat of the Balmain Tigers in the 1989 decider.

The Slattery Media Group
1 Albert Street, Richmond
Victoria, Australia, 3121
visit slatterymedia.com

Text copyright © Will Evans, 2012
Images copyright © Newspix (2012) and Newtown Jets RLFC
First published by the The Slattery Media Group, 2012

All records and statistics current to the end of 2011

National Library of Australia Cataloguing-in-Publication entry
    Title: A short history of Rugby League in Australia / Will Evans ; Nick Tedeschi
    Author: Evans, William John, 1981-
    ISBN: 9781921778728 (pbk.)
    Subjects:Rugby League football--Australia--History.
    Other Authors/Contributors: Tedeschi, Nick.
    Dewey Number: 796.3338

Group Publisher: Geoff Slattery
Author: Will Evans
Editor: Nick Tedeschi
Creative Director: Guy Shield
Designers: Kate Slattery and Beck Haskins
Typesetting: Stephen Lording

Printed in China through Everbest Printing

FOR TUMS—1980-2007

'GOOD GAME BRO'

CONTENTS

FOREWORD

The history of Rugby League is something I've come to appreciate much more since my retirement as a player. When I was playing, it felt like it was never going to end. But since my career ended, the game's history—and the place I've been fortunate enough to occupy within Rugby League's story—has become a whole lot more important to me.

I always appreciated the chances I had to meet and talk with former players and prominent Rugby League figures during my career, whether casually or at those times when they would come to speak to us before a big game. Primarily, I was (and am!) incredibly grateful for the contribution of the players that went before me in keeping Rugby League growing—and giving blokes like me the chance to live the life that I have.

The players that I idolised through my growing up years were predominantly from the local A grade competition in western Sydney. Tony Cosatto—who played for Ashcroft before going on to a lengthy first grade career with Parramatta, Wests and Easts—was a particular favourite. I was very taken with Manly as a youngster in the late-1970s, while I have vivid memories of travelling all over Sydney with a mate and his father in support of Souths for a couple of seasons. I marvelled at the attacking mastery of Sea Eagles half Phil Blake, who went on to become one of the code's greatest try-scorers during his nomadic premiership career.

I began following the Panthers after I moved to Penrith at the age of 13 and started playing for the club's junior representative teams, before coach Ron Willey blooded me in first grade as a 17-year-old schoolboy in 1989. Willey, a no-nonsense mentor from the old school, never made an issue out of my age, which instilled me with a great deal of confidence. It was a great buzz to run out for the Panthers in front of my mates.

In hindsight, I realise how fortunate I was to come into such a tough, aggressive side with established internationals such as Greg Alexander and Royce Simmons guiding us. To win the premiership in 1991 with a group of guys that I had known since I was 15 or 16 was a massive thrill and something I will always treasure. Winning another Grand Final with the Sydney Roosters as captain in 2002 provided similar feelings of pride and elation despite my veteran status then. Today, I have a deep connection with both clubs as a result of those team achievements.

Touring Britain and France with the Kangaroos in 1990 was an amazing experience—a trip I learnt from on and off the field, leading to a much more successful tour form-wise in '94. While it was an enormous honour to take on the

New South Wales and Australian captaincy during the divisive Super League war years—following in the footsteps of some of Rugby League's great names—it probably came before I was ready and presented some huge challenges. But as time progressed I felt like I had earned it and deserved it, and accordingly I became more comfortable in the role.

I was influenced by some great coaches during my career: I played under Phil Gould for nine seasons at the Panthers and the Roosters, and during six State of Origin campaigns; Bob Fulton at Test level; and my former NSW and Australian teammate Ricky Stuart towards the end of my club career. My career was also touched briefly, but unmistakably, by the ARL Coach of the Century, the late Jack Gibson. I made my NSW debut in 1990 under Jack (when he famously provided me with the nickname 'Freddy') and a couple of simple things he said stuck with me. He said: "You can never kick the ball high enough", which came in handy later in my career. He also advised against ever playing tennis or squash on the grounds that you'd inevitably twist your ankle—a suggestion I wish I'd followed before having a game of tennis and consequently carrying an ankle injury through the 2000 finals series. Jack would often come into the changing rooms after Roosters games later in my career and I always enjoyed his company.

There were certainly changes in Rugby League from when I started out to when I retired in 2004—training became more specific, the emphasis on defence became more pronounced. But I didn't notice too many differences when I was in the thick of it; I still saw the same head in the mirror every day. The most obvious change in the game since I hung up the boots has been the lamentable slowing down of the play-the-ball and the emergence of the notorious 'wrestle.' I used to love training, genuinely looked forward to it. But I don't know how eager I would have been if I knew I was going to be rolling around with sweaty blokes all day! I think we will see that area of the game cleaned up in the future and Rugby League will return to its natural speed.

I've always loved the game and felt comfortable around the footy field and around its people. Being able to continue my involvement with Rugby League in a media capacity has been fantastic. I know I was lucky to have played with some of the best to have ever played the game—I value that greatly and it will always stay with me. My gratitude to the players and officials who 'dug the well,' and built Rugby League to the stage where it became fully professional, cannot be understated. I feel unbelievably fortunate to have spent virtually my whole life in Rugby League.

A Short History of Rugby League in Australia, covering the story of the century-plus of Rugby League so far, is a comprehensive and entertaining account of how the code arrived at the point it has reached, and provides a fitting tribute to all those people who made Rugby League the great game it is.

Brad Fittler, August 2012

INTRODUCTION

The 1989 Grand Final between Canberra and Balmain is widely regarded as the greatest decider in Australian Rugby League history, but it is also fondly recalled as the match that kick-started a Rugby League revolution in New Zealand. With the match beamed live into New Zealand for the first time, I have vague memories of my dad's animated cheering—probably when 'Chicka' Ferguson's famous late try sent the match into extra-time—and the overwhelming response of Australia's easterly neighbours to the epic contest saw premiership matches shown in New Zealand regularly from 1990.

My real introduction to Rugby League came as an eight-year-old during that 1990 season, a telecast of a modern-day classic at Lang Park, won 22-20 by the Broncos over defending premiers the Raiders. The following season introduced me to State of Origin football—in the legendary Wally Lewis' last series—as Queensland defeated New South Wales in what remains the tightest series on record. That was it for me. Born on the Gold Coast to Kiwi parents, I moved to New Zealand aged two. Rugby union runs deep in my heritage (my great-grandfather played a Test for the All Blacks in 1921), but despite growing up in Queenstown, situated in the 15-a-side heartland of Otago in New Zealand's South Island, I traded in the All Blacks and the Highlanders for the Broncos and the Maroons (although I still fiercely support the Kiwis against the Kangaroos).

I realised two things when I bawled my eyes out after the Broncos were eliminated by North Sydney from the 1994 finals. Firstly, it confirmed that even the historic admission of the Auckland Warriors to the premiership in 1995 was not going to be enough to shift my club allegiances (not immediately, anyway), regardless of Dad's unwavering loyalty to the Warriors from day one. Secondly, it became clear that the game of Rugby League was not just a following for me, but an obsession.

Soon enough, I found myself delving headlong into Rugby League's rich history. I soaked up the writings of Ian Heads, David Middleton, Malcolm Andrews and Gary Lester, and got my hands on any old (and new) copies of *Rugby League Week* and *Big League* magazines that I could. Immersing myself in tales of the players of yesteryear—Burge, Churchill, Carlson, Gasnier, Beetson *et al*—and the great games and stories that are entwined in the tapestry of the game's narrative, I felt compelled to write about Rugby League's past and present.

I have ridden the highs and lows of being a Rugby League supporter in the 18 years since my awakening, through Origin victories, euphoric premiership triumphs and World Cup upsets to last-minute defeats, heartbreaking finals exits and Grand Final losses. But my passion for Rugby League and the story it encompasses has endured at a constant peak—and has intensified after moving to Brisbane in 2008—a fascination I have shared on these pages.

A Short History of Rugby League in Australia is the manifestation of a two-decade love affair with the game. The aim of this book is to enlighten and enthral with the characters, anecdotes, anomalies and lesser-known aspects of Rugby League's history, while also presenting a broad spectrum of Rugby League's key elements, from the code's origins through to the modern era. It's obsessive in its detail, offering a personal and quirky viewpoint on an extraordinary history that is constantly evolving. One of Rugby League's most endearing qualities is its capacity to change and progress, and this book depicts the influences, pathways and occasional revolutions that have led to those changes. I hope these stories assist the reader to understand where Rugby League is now, how it got there, and the direction it might be headed.

Will Evans, August 2012

CHAPTER I
THE GAME

The foundations for Rugby League in Australia were laid in 1907, courtesy of a breakaway movement rebelling against the amateur ideals of rugby union. The inaugural premiership and representative fixtures were staged in 1908, and the code has navigated its way through a plethora of soaring highs and potentially crippling challenges to continue to thrive in 2012. A detailed account of the game's birth in Australia and the important events, matches and players from each of Australian Rugby League's 104 seasons is contained in this section. The game's most phenomenal premiership matches, the influential coaches, and the prominent officials and media identities are also profiled in this section, along with the history of Indigenous Rugby League, the introduction of golden point and the unfortunate teams that have been stripped of competition points.

THE PIONEERING YEARS

Rugby League's origins lie in England, and in rugby union, which—as legend has it, despite limited evidence—began at Rugby School in Warwickshire in 1823. During a game of traditional football, student William Webb Ellis allegedly picked up the ball and ran with it, planting the seeds for a new code. Rules for the fledgling sport were drawn up at Rugby School during the 1840s and rugby football was played widely in Britain from the 1860s, before spreading to Australia and New Zealand soon afterwards.

The game was popular throughout England, but a schism developed in the 1890s when the predominantly working-class northern clubs lobbied the Rugby Football Union to allow 'broken time payments'—effectively compensation to players who had to take time off work to play. The controlling body and the largely upper- and middle-class players and officials from the affluent southern clubs vehemently opposed this challenge to the amateur ethos of the sport. The RFU voted resoundingly against the northern clubs' move towards financial compensation. In 1895, a meeting at the George Hotel in Huddersfield resulted in the establishment of a breakaway movement involving 21 clubs from Yorkshire and Lancashire— the Northern Rugby Football Union.

The rebel clubs originally had no intentions of starting a new game and initially played under the traditional rugby rules. But line-outs and loose rucks were eradicated in 1897, while the scoring system was also altered (reducing penalty and drop goals to two points), and professionalism was allowed from 1898. The number of players in each team was reduced from 15 to 13 in 1906.

The birth of Rugby League in Australia was based on similar principles. The first rugby clubs were established in Sydney in the 1860s and a formal metropolitan competition began in the 1870s. Rugby became established as the dominant football code in Sydney during the early-1900s, while the governing body was prosperous due to gate-takings from burgeoning crowd numbers. In March 1907, arrangements were made for a professional rugby team from New Zealand to tour Britain. The tour by a squad largely made up of prominent amateur rugby union players was organised by the man recognised as the founding father of Rugby League in New Zealand—Wellington postal worker Albert Henry Baskerville. News filtered through to Australia in July that the team—derisively dubbed the 'All Golds' (as opposed to the amateur New Zealand national team known as the All Blacks)—would be playing games in Sydney en route to Britain.

The announcement coincided with a shoulder injury suffered by prominent Sydney forward Alec 'Bluey' Burdon in a match on New South Wales' north coast. Burdon's injury has traditionally been put forward as the leading catalyst for the rise of a breakaway movement, although leading historians generally concur that it was just one of series of incidents and factors that led to Rugby League beginning in Australia. Nevertheless, it was an important and iconic event indicative of the cashed-up rugby union establishment's lack of concern for its players, refusing to compensate players for medical costs incurred or time lost at work due to injury, or time taken off work to play, declaring it an 'act of professionalism.'

The three men regarded as being most responsible for the breakaway Rugby League movement in Sydney were entrepreneur James Joseph Giltinan, prominent Australian Labor Party member Henry Hoyle, and the finest cricketer of the era, legendary batsman Victor Trumper. The trio of founding fathers—along with prominent rugby union players—met regularly in Trumper's sports store on Sydney's Market Street to discuss the rough deal footballers were receiving. On August 8 1907, at Bateman's Hotel in George Street, a meeting shrouded in secrecy was held and the NSW Rugby League was formally established. Hoyle became president, Giltinan secretary and Trumper treasurer of the organisation. Players present at the meeting signed a document declaring their intent to, if selected, play in three scheduled matches against the New Zealand 'All Golds' later in the month. The rebel group had secured the use of Sydney's Royal Agricultural Ground for the staging of the matches.

Days later, Giltinan, Hoyle and Trumper secured the signature of an outstanding player, in an event that was as important as any to Rugby League's fledgling success. Herbert Henry 'Dally' Messenger was the preeminent Australian footballer of the time—a genuine rugby superstar. Messenger's mother Annie famously negotiated on Dally's behalf, accepting the NSWRL founders' offer in a meeting at her Double Bay home. Prominent players that had been involved in the get-togethers at Trumper's store or were at the inaugural meeting at Bateman's Hotel included Burdon, Peter Moir, Arthur Hennessy, Sid 'Sandy' Pearce, Albert Rosenfeld, Billy Cann and 'Tedda' Courtney—all of whom played against the 'All Golds' and would have a major impact during Rugby League's pioneering seasons.

Threats of life bans from rugby union did little to halt the momentum and the three matches between New Zealand and New South Wales went ahead. Played under rugby union rules (rulebooks from the Northern Union in England were not available), the matches were well-received, attracted healthy crowds and—more importantly—turned a tidy profit. Messenger was the undoubted star for New South Wales, and was consequently asked to tour Britain with the 'All Golds,' where he was again the standout.

Rugby League encountered widespread criticism from sections of the media and the public, lambasting the supposedly greedy move towards 'professionalism.' But the breakaway movement was not about a desire to be professional, but to provide equity to players—particularly those from the lower-middle and working classes—that had been financially disadvantaged by the strictly amateur philosophy of rugby union.

Arthur Hennessy was integral to drumming up support for the new code, encouraging rugby union clubs to join the breakaway movement. Glebe became the first Australian Rugby League club on January 9 1908, while Newtown, South Sydney, Balmain, Eastern Suburbs, Western Suburbs and North Sydney followed suit in the ensuing weeks. In April—less than nine months after that historic meeting at Bateman's Hotel—a premiership competition involving the seven clubs and a team from Newcastle got underway, while Cumberland joined just after the commencement of the inaugural competition.

Attracted by the same ideals that led to the NSWRL's formation, officials in Queensland including Sidney Boland and Alf Faulkner, and leading players Mickey Dore and the founding father of Rugby League in the Sunshine State, Jack Fihelly, helped form the Queensland Rugby Association in March 1908. Giltinan's and Trumper's input was also influential to the code's tentative first steps in Queensland.

Rugby League's formative seasons were exciting, arduous and tumultuous as the game attempted to find its feet. The Sydney premiership strived for recognition, while overseas tours and international Test matches quickly became a regular part of the calendar. The premiership witnessed great club sides—the inaugural champions South Sydney, Eastern Suburbs' three-time premiers, and the Balmain dynasty that won five titles in six years—and a plethora of marvellous players that would still be regarded as some of the greatest to lace on a boot a century later, such as Harold Horder, Frank Burge, Howard Hallett, Charles 'Chook' Fraser, Jimmy Craig, Arthur 'Pony' Halloway, Chris McKivat and, of course, the great Dally Messenger. The NSWRL controversially opted to forge on with premiership competition during World War I, a decision that was ultimately vital to Rugby League swiftly surpassing rugby union as the dominant football code in New South Wales and Queensland.

1908

The breakaway movement gathered momentum and made its play for public acceptance with the staging of an eight-team premiership. Crowds during the initial first grade season were underwhelming, while the competition lacked continuity as representative fixtures took precedence. Although the season did not meet the NSWRL's financial expectations—finishing the year £500 in the red—and the prospects for the fledgling code were far from certain, the events of 1908 laid a foundation, albeit a shaky one, for eventual success.

THE PREMIERSHIP

The inaugural NSWRL premiership commenced with the eight existing teams playing on Easter Monday, April 20 1908. Newtown centre Jack Scott scored the first try of the premiership (from an intercept), but Eastern Suburbs became the first club to register a win by overwhelming the Bluebags 32-16 in front of 3,000 supporters at Wentworth Oval, with winger Johnno Stuntz crossing for four tries. Glebe defeated Newcastle 8-5 in the other match at Wentworth Oval, while Balmain thrashed Western Suburbs 24-0 and South Sydney defeated North Sydney 11-7 at Birchgrove Oval with a 3,000-strong crowd in attendance. The Cumberland club formed a day after the first premiership matches and made its debut in round two. Souths won the first minor premiership with a superior for-and-against to Easts, after both clubs lost just one of nine matches. With the cream of the competition's players en route to Britain on the first Kangaroo Tour, Easts subdued Norths 23-10 and Souths despatched Glebe 16-3 to advance to the foundational premiership final. South Sydney was crowned the NSWRL's first champions after overcoming Eastern Suburbs 14-12 in a worthy decider at Sydney's Agricultural Ground.

- **Biggest win:** North Sydney d. Cumberland 45-0 at Wentworth Oval, round nine
- **Top Point-scorer:** Horrie Miller (Eastern Suburbs) 47
- **Top Try-scorer:** Horrie Miller (Eastern Suburbs) 15

THE REPRESENTATIVE SCENE

The touring New Zealand 'All Golds' side (on their way back from a trailblazing trip to Britain) won the first trans-Tasman Test series after winning the opening two encounters against Australia in Sydney and Brisbane (with Souths forward Arthur Hennessy as captain), before Norths forward Dinny Lutge led Australia to its maiden Test victory in the third match, 14-9 in Sydney. Albert Baskerville, New Zealand Rugby League's founding father, scored a try in the first Test but developed pneumonia en route to Brisbane and died *(see Tragic Figures)*. A Maori side toured soon afterwards and proved competitive against New South Wales and Queensland, while Australia defeated the Maori 20-10. New South Wales comfortably defeated Queensland in the inaugural interstate matches; Souths winger Tommy Anderson scored four tries for NSW in the 43-0 result in the first clash. A 35-strong representative squad embarked on a gruelling seven-month tour of Britain. Although the tour was a financial disaster, the pioneering Kangaroos—captained by Dinny Lutge and featuring the dazzling talents of Dally Messenger—established what would become a revered tradition. The first Anglo-Australian Test was drawn 22-all, but England prevailed in the remaining two encounters to claim a series victory.

STANDOUT PLAYER

Former Wallaby star Dally Messenger was the inaugural premiership's biggest drawcard. The Easts centre excelled for his club and in the domestic representative fixtures, but his contribution on the Kangaroo Tour was the lasting memory of the pioneering legend's 1908 season. He scored 155 points in 31 tour matches—a mark which stood as a tour record for 25 years.

MEMORABLE MATCH

The premiership final provided a gripping conclusion to the disjointed inaugural NSWRL season. Souths scored four tries, while winger Horrie Miller crossed for both of Easts' touchdowns. Souths led 8-7 at halftime and 14-9 late in the match, until Miller's second try narrowed the margin, but forward Herb Brackenberg was unable to level the scores with his conversion attempt.

1909

The second season of Rugby League in Australia was marked by controversy within the game's officialdom and a flailing financial position that threatened to terminate the fledgling code. Kangaroo Tour manager James J. Giltinan, who secured a loan to bankroll the trip and was so vital to the code's establishment in Australia, was unceremoniously dumped from his post as NSWRL secretary due to the fiscal failings of the ground-breaking tour. President Henry Hoyle and treasurer Victor Trumper were also dismissed from office. Entrepreneur and philanthropist James Joynton Smith alleviated the League's problems, however, by bankrolling a series of matches between the rugby union Wallabies and the Kangaroos. While the series only just covered Joynton Smith's costs (after the staging of a fourth match that had significations ramifications for the premiership), several Wallabies stars—most notably captain Chris McKivat—switched codes for 1910, providing Rugby League with desperately needed new drawcards and considerably weakening its major competitor. The game made great advancements in Queensland, with the staging of the inaugural Brisbane premiership, won by Valleys. Tweed Heads became the first country Rugby League club established in Australia.

THE PREMIERSHIP

The second NSWRL premiership was reduced to eight teams after Cumberland folded. Embarrassingly small crowds prevailed throughout the season, while the Kangaroos' absence until May (and the decision of several squad members to link with English clubs) starved the competition of star quality. Souths finished clear atop the competition ladder at the end of the regular season, and won through to the final along with Balmain. But Balmain sensationally forfeited the final in protest of the match's scheduling as a curtain-raiser to the fourth Wallabies v Kangaroos match (see Bizarre Matches). South Sydney was consequently declared premiers after fronting up for the final.

- **Biggest win:** Newcastle d. Western Suburbs 34-0 at Newcastle Showgrounds, round seven
- **Top Point-scorer:** Stan Carpenter (Newcastle) 46
- **Top Try-scorer:** Tommy Anderson (Souths) 11

THE REPRESENTATIVE SCENE

Australia came from a Test down to defeat the touring New Zealand side 2-1 to record its maiden series victory. A Maori squad toured again in 1909, defeating New South Wales in all four matches and upsetting Australia in the first of three contests. No interstate matches were played.

STANDOUT PLAYER

South Sydney winger Tommy Anderson was superb following his return from the Kangaroo Tour, scoring hat-tricks in consecutive weeks against Glebe and Wests, before crossing for two tries in Souths' 20-0 semi-final defeat of Newcastle.

MEMORABLE MATCH

Balmain's 24-15 defeat of Easts in the penultimate round featured wild brawling, resulting in five players being sent off—including Easts forward and Australian Test captain Larry O'Malley, for kicking.

1910

The coup of 1909 which brought a bevy of Wallaby stars to Rugby League sealed the new game's ascension to the forefront of Sydney's sporting landscape. James Joynton Smith was elected president of the NSWRL, beginning a 19-year reign at the helm of the organisation. Newcastle pulled out of the premiership and formed a local competition which quickly thrived, while Annandale emerged to keep the number of teams in the Sydney competition at eight. The inaugural tour of an England Northern Union side monumentally boosted the NSWRL's coffers.

THE PREMIERSHIP

Newtown edged Souths for the minor premiership, winning 11 and drawing one of its 14 matches in the extended regular season. No semi-finals were played, with the NSWRL premiership decided by a final between the top two teams. Newtown was crowned champions after grinding out a 4-all draw against Souths in the final on account of its superior regular season record.

- **Biggest win:** South Sydney 53 d. North Sydney 4 at the Agricultural Ground, round nine
- **Top Point-scorer:** Dally Messenger (Eastern Suburbs) 71
- **Top Try-scorer:** Arthur McCabe (South Sydney) 18

THE REPRESENTATIVE SCENE
England, led by James Lomas, secured the first Anglo-Australian Test series on Australian soil with 27-20 and 22-17 victories over the Dally Messenger-captained hosts. NSW swept Queensland 3-0 in the Brisbane-based interstate series.

STANDOUT PLAYER
Souths pivot Arthur McCabe crossed for four hat-tricks among his 18 premiership tries, setting a still-standing season total record for a five-eighth (equalled by Trent Barrett and Ben Walker during the NRL era). The former Wallaby scored two tries for NSW in each of the first two interstate matches against Queensland.

MEMORABLE MATCH
Newtown secured a premiership-winning draw in the tense final at the Agricultural Ground with a famous late goal to captain Charles 'Boxer' Russell. Trailing 4-2 in the dying minutes, Bluebags centre Albert Hawkes marked the ball on halfway and Russell opted to kick for goal (as the rules of the day allowed), successfully landing the long-range attempt.

1911

The game's rapid expansion throughout New South Wales and Queensland, along with a prosperous Sydney premiership and burgeoning junior club numbers, solidified Rugby League's standing as the premier winter code. The game was played at the Sydney Cricket Ground and the Sydney Sports Ground for the first time, while the 'Australasian' Kangaroos ventured to Britain.

THE PREMIERSHIP
Glebe won the 1911 minor premiership with 11 wins from its 14 regular season games, but the Dirty Reds' best opportunity for premiership glory in their 22-season existence fell by the wayside with consecutive defeats to second-placed Easts, 22-9 in the final and 11-8 in the resultant challenge final (afforded to Glebe as minor premiers).

- **Biggest win:** Eastern Suburbs 30 d. Annandale 3 at the Agricultural Ground, round one
- **Top Point-scorer:** Dally Messenger (Eastern Suburbs) 148
- **Top Try-scorer:** Dave Garlick (Glebe) 13

THE REPRESENTATIVE SCENE
NSW decimated Queensland three times in the space of eight days in the 1911 interstate series in Sydney—65-9, 49-0 and 32-8. New Zealand toured Australia but did not play any Tests, while the Kiwis were defeated in all three matches against NSW. The 'Australasian' Kangaroos (so named because of the inclusion of four New Zealand players) made a triumphant tour of Britain, winning the Test series against England with victories in the first and third Tests and a draw in the second encounter—Australia's last Ashes success on British soil for 52 years.

STANDOUT PLAYER
The great Dally Messenger was in spectacular form throughout 1911. He topped the competition with 148 points—a mark that stood for 24 years—and racked up 72 points

in the interstate series, including a record 32 points in the first encounter. Messenger scored a remarkable 20 points (two tries, seven goals) in Easts' 23-10 semi-final defeat of Souths before captaining the Tricolours to their maiden premiership success. He declined the invitation to make his second Kangaroo Tour.

MEMORABLE MATCH
Glebe led the challenge final 8-4 on the back of two wonderful tries to winger Charles Cubitt. But Easts snatched the lead 13 minutes from fulltime after Charlie Lees scored his side's only try and Messenger converted. Skipper Messenger added a field goal for an 11-8 triumph and was chaired from the Agricultural Ground by his elated teammates.

1912

A first-past-the-post system was instigated to decide the champion club of Sydney in 1912, with the minor premiers awarded the title at the end of the regular season unless a tie for first place necessitated a final. The City Cup knockout competition, staged at the conclusion of the premiership season, made its debut; Souths defeated Glebe 30-5 in the inaugural City Cup final.

THE PREMIERSHIP
Losing just one of its 14 regular season games, Eastern Suburbs successfully defended the premiership by finishing atop the competition ladder. Chris McKivat's Glebe side finished runners-up for the second straight year. The season also saw the emergence of 18-year-old Souths winger Harold Horder, who scored a legendary 90-yard try in a match against Glebe to set in motion a 13-season career of remarkable tryscoring excellence.

- **Biggest win:** Eastern Suburbs 35 d. Balmain 0 at Birchgrove Oval, round seven
- **Top Point-scorer:** Dally Messenger (Eastern Suburbs) 80
- **Top Try-scorer:** Roy Algie (Glebe) 12

THE REPRESENTATIVE SCENE
The interstate matches were again alarmingly lopsided—NSW racked up another 65-9 victory in the first encounter, then prevailed 32-4 with an all-new line-up two days later. NSW won eight of nine matches on a tour of New Zealand—including an 18-10 victory over the national side—while the Kiwis toured Australia and lost two of their three matches against NSW.

STANDOUT PLAYER
Dally Messenger turned down a spot on NSW's tour of New Zealand, but dominated Rugby League domestically once more in 1912. 'The Master' topped the premiership's pointscoring again and spearheaded Easts' title victory as captain. He scored 21 points in NSW's 65-9 thrashing of Queensland and starred for his state in the home fixtures against the touring Kiwis.

MEMORABLE MATCH
Easts effectively sealed the premiership with a gripping, try-less 6-4 victory over fellow front-runners Glebe in round 11. The combatants traded penalty goals, before Messenger provided the clutch play, slotting a magnificent field goal with time running out.

1913

The 1913 season heralded the end of the career of Australian Rugby League's first superstar, Dally Messenger. After initially retiring prior to the start of the season, Messenger was enticed to play on, leading Easts to a third straight title and dominating representative fixtures yet again. A wet Sydney winter dictated the first grade season was played on almost exclusively muddy pitches, but that did not deter the crowds and Rugby League's popularity continued to skyrocket. Young official Harry Sunderland was appointed secretary of the struggling Queensland Rugby League in what would be one of the most significant developments for the code in the Sunshine State. Glebe won Sydney's City Cup.

THE PREMIERSHIP

Easts captured the outright competition lead in round five and maintained top spot on the ladder until the end of the season to claim a hat-trick of premierships. The Tricolours' dynasty boasted several pioneering greats, including Dally Messenger and his younger brother Wally, halfback Arthur 'Pony' Halloway, hooker Sid 'Sandy' Pearce, winger Dan Frawley, former Test captain Larry 'Jersey' O'Malley and future Kangaroos captain Les Cubitt. Newtown finished runners-up, three competition points adrift of Easts.

- **Biggest win:** Glebe 29 d. Annandale 0 at Wentworth Oval, round three
- **Top Point-scorer:** Harold Horder (South Sydney) 65
- **Top Try-scorer:** Harold Horder (South Sydney) 13

THE REPRESENTATIVE SCENE

Newtown forward Paddy McCue captained NSW on a tour of New Zealand for the second successive season. NSW was unbeaten in 11 matches and crushed the New Zealand Test side 33-19 and 58-19. The Kiwis toured Australia and lost the four-match series against NSW 3-1. A second-string NSW side won two hard-fought matches against Queensland in Brisbane while the first-choice squad was on tour across the Tasman.

STANDOUT PLAYER

Teenage winger Harold Horder led the premiership in terms of tries and points in his initial full first grade season, crossing the stripe 13 times for Souths in 1912. Horder toured New Zealand with the NSW squad, scoring five tries in the 58-19 drubbing of the national side.

MEMORABLE MATCH

Easts' unbeaten start to the season was halted in round eight by a 14-11 loss to Newtown with a 23,000-strong crowd in attendance at the SCG. In the premiership's finest contest of 1913, the Bluebags took an early 8-2 lead before the Messenger brothers kicked Easts back to level. Penalty goals to 'Boxer' Russell kept Easts at bay 12-11 after Dan Frawley scored and Newtown hung on for a three-point win courtesy of Russell's fourth goal.

1914

The 1914 season was dominated by the feverishly anticipated return of England's Northern Union team. Massive crowds met the Lions at almost every turn as

Rugby League proved it had comprehensively dwarfed rugby union in popularity. Complementing the rapid expansion of the code in country NSW, the Townsville Rugby League was formed as a Rugby League heartland began to develop in North Queensland. Foundation Easts winger Horrie Miller took over as fulltime secretary of NSWRL, a post he would hold for 32 years. The outbreak of World War I on July 28, 1914 signalled a new set of challenges for Rugby League and presented the game's authorities with some difficult decisions.

THE PREMIERSHIP

South Sydney broke Easts' three-year stranglehold on the premiership by winning 11 and drawing one of its 14 matches to finish first-past-the-post—just one competition point ahead of Newtown. The premiers were captained by Arthur Butler and coached by the team's revered fullback, Howard Hallett.

- **Biggest win:** Balmain 39 d. Western Suburbs 8 at Birchgrove Oval, round 13
- **Top Point-scorer:** Harold Horder (South Sydney) 87
- **Top Try-scorer:** Harold Horder (South Sydney) 19

THE REPRESENTATIVE SCENE

England, captained by the great centre Harold Wagstaff, won the first Test convincingly 23-5, before the Sid Deane-led Australians levelled the series 12-7. The tourists won the decider 14-6 despite seemingly insurmountable odds in the shape of a shocking injury toll; England's heroic Ashes-winning victory would forever be known as the 'Rorke's Drift' Test *(see Courageous Performances)*. Wally Messenger kicked nine goals as Metropolis thrashed the Lions 38-10 in front of a then-world record Rugby League crowd of 50,300. No interstate fixtures were played in 1914.

STANDOUT PLAYER

Souths custodian Howard Hallett was awarded the 'Greenstripe Whisky silver belt' following a public vote on the premiership's outstanding player. The preeminent fullback of Australian Rugby League's formative years, Hallett's peerless catching and tackling at the back and outstanding kicking were at their zenith in 1914, while he played in all three Tests against England.

MEMORABLE MATCH

An exhibition match between England and NSW was staged in Melbourne at the conclusion of the Ashes Test series. But the match descended into a violent affair marked by serious injuries, brawling and send-offs. England initially refused to return to the field after halftime, but the tourists were eventually persuaded out and prevailed 21-15.

1915

The NSWRL's controversial and frequently debated decision to proceed with Rugby League competition during World War I exacerbated the balance of power that had shifted from rugby union to the professional code. Rugby union suspended competition during the war—largely due to the fact the majority of its (predominantly middle- and upper-class) playing ranks had enlisted for service. Rugby League's mainly working-class players were, on the whole, less fervent for the British Empire's war cause. But several prominent identities lost their lives overseas, including Newtown's 1908-09 Kangaroo Frank Cheadle, ex-Easts and 1909 Australian representative Johnno Stuntz, Easts and 1914 Test winger Bob Tidyman, New Zealander and 1911-12 'Australasian' Kangaroo tourist Charles Savory and respected former NSWRL secretary Ted Larkin (who died on the fields of Gallipoli). Meanwhile, the NSWRL donated £3,440 to patriotic funds during 1915. The League's first treasurer and celebrated Test cricketer Victor Trumper died of Bright's disease in June at the age of 37, sadly, without having reconciled with the NSWRL after his sacking in 1909.

THE PREMIERSHIP

Balmain started one of the all time great club dynasties by becoming the first club to go through a season unbeaten, winning 12 and drawing two of its 14 matches. 'The Watersiders', captain-coached by former New Zealand and Australian Test representative Bill Kelly, boasted two-time Kangaroo Arthur 'Pony' Halloway, 1911-12 Kangaroo Charles 'Chook' Fraser, dual international Bob Craig and future Kangaroo Reg 'Whip' Latta. Glebe, who racked up a then-record 59-3 defeat of Norths during the season, finished runners-up—the Dirty Reds lost just two matches in 1915, both to Balmain.

- **Biggest win:** Glebe 59 d. North Sydney 3 at Wentworth Oval, round 10
- **Top Point-scorer:** Charles 'Chook' Fraser (Balmain) 74
- **Top Try-scorer:** Frank Burge (Glebe) 20

THE REPRESENTATIVE SCENE

World War I halted Test football for five years, but interstate matches were played in 1915. NSW won the two match series played in Sydney with resounding 53-9 and 39-6 defeats of Queensland.

STANDOUT PLAYER

The tryscoring potency of Glebe forward Frank Burge, a Test debutant during the 1914 Ashes series, began to be realised in 1915. Burge scored a then-record 20 tries in the 14 premiership rounds, including two hat-tricks—the start of an extraordinary run for arguably the most destructive attacking forward the game has seen.

MEMORABLE MATCH

Burge scored three tries for Glebe in a round 12 clash with fellow high-flyers Newtown, but the Dirty Reds still trailed by three points in the closing minutes of the SCG thriller. Future Test forward Bert Gray crossed for the match-winner to snatch a 22-20 win for Glebe.

1916

Rugby League provided a welcome respite for the Sydney public encompassed by the grim spectre of war and Australian casualties overseas, but crowds dwindled as the realities of international conflict began to take its toll on the home front. At a January meeting, the NSWRL deferred a decision on staging a competition in 1916, before eventually voting to forge ahead—although interstate competition ceased for the ensuing three seasons. Growing numbers of enlistments significantly reduced playing stocks in NSW and Queensland, but domestic competitions in both states carried on. The League contributed 10 per cent of gate receipts to the war effort.

THE PREMIERSHIP

Balmain pipped Easts—previously unbeaten in the second half of the season—8-7 in the final round to draw level with Souths at the top of the table. In a dour final where the standard was of a below-par standard, a penalty goal by Charles 'Chook' Fraser was the difference after tries to Balmain captain-coach Arthur 'Pony' Halloway and Souths winger Gordon Vaughan. The halftime scoreline of 5-3 remained until fulltime and Balmain was crowned premiers for the second year in a row.

- **Biggest win:** Eastern Suburbs 53 d. Western Suburbs 0 at Sydney Sports Ground, round 12
- **Top Point-scorer:** Charles 'Chook' Fraser (Balmain) 94
- **Top Try-scorer:** Frank Burge (Glebe) 22

STANDOUT PLAYER

Frank Burge's phenomenal attacking prowess saw him extend his premiership record to 22 tries, while the powerful forward scored an unprecedented six tries in a 36-7 defeat of Norths.

MEMORABLE MATCH

Balmain's 24-match unbeaten streak was halted by Newtown in round four. The Bluebags led 6-2 at halftime of the SCG clash, and although Halloway scored the only try of the match in the second stanza, the Watersiders went down 8-7.

1917

Extensive recruitment to the armed services cut into Rugby League's playing stocks further and resulted in a mid-May start to premiership. But the 1917 season was dominated by a furore surrounding Glebe player Dan 'Laddo' Davies, who joined the club from Newcastle Wests prior to the start of the season. Annandale lodged a protest after Davies starred in Glebe's 26-5 win over the Dales in the opening round, and it was found that he failed the NSWRL's residential requirements (stating that a player must reside in the district of the club he played for). Glebe had its competition points stripped, while Davies was banned for life—an incredible decision that had far-reaching implications for the local Newcastle competition after Davies returned (*see Points Docked*). The Dirty Reds were involved in further tumult with the NSWRL after the first grade side went on strike in protest over lengthy suspensions dished out to two of their lower-grade players (*see Extinct Clubs*).

THE PREMIERSHIP

Balmain claimed a hat-trick of premierships in emphatic fashion, losing just one match in the 14 rounds—a 16-9 loss to Newtown in round eight—to finish eight points clear of its rivals at the top of the table. South Sydney was distant runners-up with nine victories.

- **Biggest win:** Balmain 37 d. North Sydney 3 at Birchgrove Oval, round two
- **Top Point-scorer:** Charles 'Chook' Fraser (Balmain) 67
- **Top Try-scorer:** Harold Horder (South Sydney) 17

STANDOUT PLAYER

South Sydney wing marvel Harold Horder scored a club record five tries in a match on two occasions in 1917 as he pushed his case as arguably the era's finest player.

MEMORABLE MATCH

A Kangaroos v The Rest of NSW exhibition match was staged in August at the conclusion of the premiership. The Kangaroos line-up—predominantly made up of 1908-09 and 1911-12 Kangaroo tourists—featured the one-game comeback of retired legend Dally Messenger. The 34-year-old produced a couple of familiar twinkles of attacking spark, but the younger Rest side prevailed 20-13, while former Test captain Sid Deane and Balmain back Lyall Wall were sent off for fighting.

1918

The events of the Rugby League season paled in comparison to the news from abroad on the 11th of November that the Great War had ended. The NSWRL had stoically defended its decision to continue competition for the duration of the war—despite ardent opposition from some sections of the community—consequently broadening the gap between Rugby League and the adjourned rugby union code, while contributing financially to Australia's war effort.

THE PREMIERSHIP

South Sydney surged to take its fourth premiership, holding off runners-up Western Suburbs by a solitary win to finish on top of the competition ladder. Captained by Howard Hallett and coached by pioneering player Arthur Hennessy, Souths dropped just two matches and ended the season on an eight-match winning streak. Three-time premiers Balmain finished fourth in an aberration during the club's period of overwhelming dominance. Annandale became the first club to fail to register a win in a season, losing all 14 of its matches. Wests, led by brilliant dual international centre Herb Gilbert, claimed the first major trophy in the club's history with victory in the City Cup.

- **Biggest win:** Balmain 43 d. Annandale 0 at Birchgrove Oval, round five
- **Top Point-scorer:** Harold Horder (South Sydney) 87
- **Top Try-scorer:** Frank Burge (Glebe) 24

STANDOUT PLAYER

The greatest 'Dirty Red,' Frank Burge, scored a premiership record season total of tries for the third time. Burge bagged two hat-tricks and two hauls of four tries among 24 in just 14 premiership rounds—three touchdowns ahead of Harold Horder, whose 21 tries was the third-highest season total at the time.

MEMORABLE MATCH

Souths embarked on a three-match tour of Queensland after winning the Sydney premiership, defeating Merthyrs (who was leading the Brisbane premiership at the time) and Toowoomba, before drawing 19-all with the Queensland state side in front of a bumper crowd of 13,000 at the Brisbane Cricket Ground.

1919

The disruption of the war was followed hot on the heels by the Spanish influenza pandemic—from which approximately 12,000 people perished after its spread to Australia—threatening the staging of the 1919 premiership. The Government considered closing football grounds to stop further spreading of the disease, but the proposed preventative measure did not eventuate and Rugby League flourished.

Interstate football resumed, while Australia played its first Test matches in five years on a tour of New Zealand.

THE PREMIERSHIP

Balmain was restored to its pedestal as the dominant club in Sydney, despite surrendering the competition lead with just two rounds remaining. Glebe's 21-12 upset of Balmain allowed Easts to leapfrog the Watersiders into top spot. But Easts succumbed to Souths a week later and Balmain overcame the Tricolours 13-4 in a final round showdown that was effectively a play-off for the premiership. Norths registered just one win to finish last, showing few signs of the amazing success that awaited the club in the near future.

- **Biggest win:** Balmain 37 d. Annandale 2 at Birchgrove Oval, round three
- **Top Point-scorer:** A. McPherson (Western Suburbs) 89
- **Top Try-scorer:** Gordon Wright (Eastern Suburbs) 17

THE REPRESENTATIVE SCENE

NSW won all four interstate clashes with Queensland, but the northerners proved far more formidable opposition than they had in pre-war seasons—a precursor to the dominance they would enjoy in the 1920s. Australia won the first trans-Tasman Test series staged in New Zealand 3-1; the second Test loss was Australia's only defeat on the nine-match tour. Arthur 'Pony' Halloway and Albert 'Ricketty' Johnston captained Australia during the Test series. The Kiwis made a disappointing tour of Australia, losing all six matches against the NSW and Queensland state sides.

STANDOUT PLAYER

Brilliant centre Les Cubitt scored 11 tries for second-placed Easts—including seven in the opening four rounds—before starring on Australia's tour of New Zealand. Cubitt played all four Tests, scoring four tries, and racked up an incredible 17 touchdowns in the last three tour matches. He finished the nine-match tour with the mind-blowing tally of 24 tries.

MEMORABLE MATCH

The unparalleled brilliance of Souths winger Harold Horder severely dented Easts' premiership bid. A week after snatching the competition lead in round 12, the Tricolours were upset by sixth-placed Souths 15-12; Horder landed a goal to level the scores at 12-all, before scoring a late match-winning try.

THE 1920s

The 1920s witnessed two remarkable club combinations in the Sydney premiership—the North Sydney side of the early part of the decade, and the South Sydney dynasty that dominated from 1925. The competition also welcomed two new clubs in the shape of University and St. George, but witnessed the demise of Annandale and Glebe. Anglo-Australian Test football flourished, while Queensland enjoyed its greatest era in interstate football prior to the advent of State of Origin.

Prominent players from the game's early years forged on into the 1920s, including Harold Horder, Frank Burge, Jimmy Craig and Charles 'Chook' Fraser. A new set of budding all time greats emerged, most notably Duncan Thompson, George Treweek and Eric Weissel, and in Queensland, Herb Steinohrt and Tom Gorman.

1920

The return of Harold Wagstaff's Lions squad from England provided the shimmering highlight of the 1920 season. In the first Anglo-Australian series since 1914, Australia regained the Ashes—its last series victory against the 'Old Enemy' for three decades. A fully amateur club from Sydney University joined the premiership; the Students won just one match in their debut season, against Annandale. The winless Dales folded at the end of the season, while the St. George club formed in November 1920, in preparation for its entry to the Sydney competition in 1921.

THE PREMIERSHIP
Balmain blitzed the competition to clinch its fifth premiership in six seasons, finishing seven competition points clear of the field after winning 11 and drawing one of its 13 matches. South Sydney finished runners-up, edging Glebe on for-and-against. The NSWRL halted the competition with three rounds to play due to Balmain's unassailable competition lead. After a dismal 1919 campaign, Norths climbed to fifth spot following the acquisition of star South Sydney wing duo Harold Horder and Cec Blinkhorn (a Norths junior who had moved to Souths). Blinkhorn scored a club record five tries in a victory over Annandale.
- **Biggest win:** Western Suburbs 52 d. Annandale 3 at Pratten Park, round 11
- **Top Point-scorer:** Frank Burge (Glebe) 110
- **Top Try-scorer:** Gordon Wright (Eastern Suburbs) 18

THE REPRESENTATIVE SCENE
Australia secured the Ashes with victories in the opening two Tests—8-4 in Brisbane and 21-8 in Sydney. England restored pride with a 23-13 result in the third Test. Albert 'Ricketty' Johnston captained Australia in the first Test, while Herb Gilbert led the side in the remaining two clashes. Queensland continued to close the gap on New South Wales; the scoreline was not a true indicator of the hard-fought one-off interstate clash, with a late NSW scoring blitz blowing it out to 40-18.

STANDOUT PLAYER
Glebe marvel Frank Burge rewrote the record books once again, crossing for a premiership record eight tries in a 41-0 defeat of University—a mark that stands unchallenged more than 90 years later. He added four goals in the rout for a total of 32 points to establish a first grade record that stood for 15 years, and finished as the premiership's top point-scorer. Burge was a tower of strength in Australia's Ashes triumph, scoring tries in the first and third Tests, and kicking a goal in the series-sealing second Test victory.

MEMORABLE MATCH
The mighty Balmain side—led by captain-coach Arthur 'Pony' Halloway in his last season in Sydney—suffered its only defeat in round nine. Easts, in third place

at the time, caused a 30-13 boilover at the Agricultural Ground, with winger Gordon Wright scoring five tries. Remarkably, Easts enjoyed just one more win and slumped to sixth.

1921

The domestic season was shortened to a mere nine premiership rounds due to the departure of the Kangaroos, but 1921 heralded a maiden first grade title for a North Sydney side brimming with class. While the Ashes was lost in a desperately close Test series on English soil, the feats of Australia's freakish individual stars ensured the 1921-22 Kangaroos would hold a treasured place in the annals of Rugby League history.

THE PREMIERSHIP
Norths went through the abbreviated season undefeated, winning six and drawing one of its seven games (the teams each had one bye). Coached by former Kangaroos captain Chris McKivat, the Shoremen line-up boasted captain Harold Horder, wing partner Cec Blinkhorn, wonderful centre combination Herman Peters and Frank Rule, the great halfback Duncan Thompson (a Queensland product who rejoined Norths for his second stint in 1921) and forward Clarrie Ives. All six were chosen in the Kangaroo Tour squad, although Rule withdrew due to injury. Easts finished runners-up after losing just one and drawing one its matches.

- **Biggest win:** Balmain 57 d. University 0 at Birchgrove Oval, round one
- **Top Point-scorer:** Rex Norman (Eastern Suburbs) 75
- **Top Try-scorer:** Gordon Wright (Eastern Suburbs) 11

THE REPRESENTATIVE SCENE
NSW prevailed in two matches against Queensland, and smashed the touring Kiwis 56-9. New Zealand also lost two of its three matches against Queensland and went down to Toowoomba. The Kangaroo squad was captained by Easts centre/five-eighth Les Cubitt, but injury restricted him to just four matches and Charles 'Chook' Fraser—a veteran of the 1911-12 tour—captained Australia in the Tests. After going down 6-5 in the first encounter, Australia levelled the series with a 16-2 second Test victory. But a broken leg suffered by Fraser (with no replacements allowed) cruelled the tourists' chances in a 6-0 loss in the decider.

STANDOUT PLAYER
It is impossible to separate the remarkable Kangaroo Tour deeds of Norths' premiership-winning wing pairing Horder and Blinkhorn, and Glebe forward Frank Burge. Blinkhorn scored 39 tries in 29 appearances, Horder amassed 35 tries in 25 matches (and led the squad with 127 points) and Burge crossed 33 times in 23 matches—the top three try totals in Kangaroo Tour history.

MEMORABLE MATCH
A then-record crowd of 48,818 packed the SCG for Norths' round three encounter with Easts, and the competition heavyweights produced a thriller. A last-minute try to Norths hooker George Green secured an 8-all draw in one of the finest premiership matches of Rugby League's early decades.

1922

North Sydney's stellar line-up became recognised as one of the greatest club combinations of all time following a second straight premiership success in the extended 18-round 1922 season. The year also heralded Queensland's maiden victory over New South Wales in the 21st interstate clash—a momentous result for the northerners, who were entering a halcyon era marked by the emergence of some of the state's best-ever players. Meanwhile, British authorities followed the lead of Australia by changing the name of their controlling body from the Northern Rugby Football Union to the Rugby Football League—the code would henceforth be known as Rugby League around the world.

THE PREMIERSHIP

South Sydney was the early front-runner, but Norths and Glebe quickly pushed to the head of the table and staged a fascinating duel for the title. Norths led the competition by four points with six rounds remaining, but dropped three straight matches to allow the Dirty Reds to draw level. Both sides held their nerve to finish equal-first at the end of 18 rounds, necessitating the first final since 1916. But Frank Burge's Glebe side was blown off the muddy SCG by the rampant 'Shoremen.' Frank Rule, Cec Blinkhorn and Harold Horder each crossed for two tries (Horder also added seven goals for a 20-point haul) in Duncan Thompson-led Norths' 35-3 drubbing of title-less Glebe.

- **Biggest win:** St. George 45 d. University 2 at Hurstville Oval, round eight
- **Top Point-scorer:** Harold Horder (North Sydney) 151
- **Top Try-scorer:** Cec Blinkhorn (North Sydney) 20

THE REPRESENTATIVE SCENE

Queensland's historic 25-9 defeat of NSW in Sydney was particularly stirring given halfback Cyril Connell was forced off the field injured, forcing the perennial whipping boys to play a man short for much of the second half. A star-studded NSW squad embarked on an unbeaten tour of New Zealand at the conclusion of the premiership, playing exclusively against provincial representative sides.

STANDOUT PLAYER

The linchpin of North Sydney's remarkable side was undoubtedly captain Duncan Thompson. Arguably the finest halfback the game had seen, Thompson's peerless playmaking ability was the perfect foil for the attacking brilliance of the club's outstanding three-quarter line. In a match against Glebe, Thompson famously swung around his own goalpost while being pursued by Frank Burge to set up Harold Horder for a length-of-the-field try.

MEMORABLE MATCH

In its sophomore season in the premiership, University sprung two major upsets in the space of eight days. The Students, boosted by the one-season stay of captain-coach and Kangaroo star Jim Craig, defeated third-placed Balmain 24-14 in round 13 and rolled competition leaders Norths 7-6 a week later, among just five wins for the season for Varsity.

1923

The 1923 edition of the premiership was overshadowed by the season-ending suspension meted out to Norths captain Duncan Thompson for kicking. It is generally accepted that he was harshly dealt with—Thompson, with an unblemished record of fair conduct, accidentally caught a Glebe opponent in the face with his boot while struggling to break free from his clutches. But the evidence of a touch judge saw the suspension handed down, and a disillusioned Thompson left Sydney football to add another remarkable chapter to a magnificent career in his native Toowoomba. The balance of interstate power continued to swing the way of Queensland following the arrival of Test star 'Mr. Versatile' Jimmy Craig, who captained the Maroons to a 2-0 series win over NSW. Craig had moved to Ipswich after being an integral part of Balmain's 1915-20 dynasty and spending a season with University.

THE PREMIERSHIP

Thompson's suspension cruelled Norths' bid for three straight titles—the Shoremen had a share of the competition lead after 11 rounds, but lost their last six matches to fade to fifth. Norths' sharp decline signalled the beginning of the most notorious title drought in premiership history. Inner-city rivals Easts and Souths finished equal-first after losing just three games apiece during the regular season. Centre and captain Harry Caples scored two tries (including a late match-winner) in the Tricolours' 15-12 victory over Souths in a magnificent final.

- **Biggest win:** Balmain 45 d. Newtown 3 at Birchgrove Oval, round three
- **Top Point-scorer:** Arthur Oxford (Eastern Suburbs) 113
- **Top Try-scorer:** Herman Peters (North Sydney) 16

THE REPRESENTATIVE SCENE

Queensland backed up a 23-14 victory over an international-laden Sydney Metropolis line-up with an 18-10 defeat of NSW in Sydney, and an emphatic 25-10 result in the return clash at the Brisbane Exhibition Ground.

STANDOUT PLAYER

South Sydney winger Benny Wearing's dazzling talents came to the fore in 1923. Wearing scored 15 tries and came within an ace of spearheading a premiership victory, scoring all of Souths' points (from two tries and three goals) in the 15-12 loss in the final.

MEMORABLE MATCH

Leading the competition by two points heading into the final round, Easts needed only a draw against Balmain to secure the premiership, but the in-form Watersiders pipped Easts 12-11. Souths defeated embattled Norths 17-13 to force a mid-week premiership final.

1924

The visit of Jonty Parkin's Lions was the pinnacle of the 1924 season, but Australia could not wrest the Ashes from England in another hard-fought Test series. North of the border, Duncan Thompson's arrival was a catalyst for Queensland's continued interstate dominance and the all-conquering performances of one of the great representative combinations—'The Galloping Clydesdales' from Toowoomba. The Australian Rugby League Board of Control was established at the end of the year to provide the game with a separate entity to handle international Rugby League matters.

THE PREMIERSHIP

The premiership season was shortened to just nine rounds, while the Lions tour resulted in long interruptions to the competition. Balmain and Souths finished equal-first at the end of the disjointed regular season, five points clear of Glebe after winning six and drawing one of eight games respectively. The final was the first Rugby League game to be broadcast on Australian radio, with veteran Charles 'Chook' Fraser captain-coaching Balmain to a 3-0 victory over Souths. Reg 'Whip' Latta's try was the only score in the match; Balmain survived a late attacking raid from Souths wing pairing Harold Horder and Benny Wearing to claim its sixth title.

- **Biggest win:** Balmain 29 d. St. George 2 at Birchgrove Oval, round two
- **Top Point-scorer:** Jack Courtney (North Sydney) 42
- **Top Try-scorer:** Tommy Kennedy (Balmain) 10

THE REPRESENTATIVE SCENE

England sealed its Ashes defence with a 22-3 victory in the opening Test, and a 5-3 result in the second clash courtesy of a try to skipper Parkin 10 minutes from fulltime. Jim Craig's Australian side achieved a consolation 21-11 victory in the third Test. Queensland defeated NSW 3-0 in the interstate series. Toowoomba, featuring the 'Downs Fox' Duncan Thompson, along with the nucleus of the state side and Test stars Tom Gorman, Vic Armbruster, Herb Steinohrt, Edwin 'Nigger' Brown, Mick Madsen and Dan Dempsey, defeated all comers in 1924. 'The Galloping Clydesdales' upset England 23-20, defeated Jim Craig's Ipswich side 3-0 in an intercity series, shut out NSW 16-0 and thrashed Victoria 47-18.

STANDOUT PLAYER

Jim Craig's influence as one of Rugby League's great leaders reached its apex in 1924, leading Queensland to a series whitewash of NSW before being chosen to captain Australia for the first time against the touring Lions. The multitalented Craig led his country from halfback in the first Test before reverting to the centres for the remaining two matches.

MEMORABLE MATCH

Toowoomba's victory over England ranks as one of the most memorable tour matches played on Australian soil. Inspired by Duncan Thompson, the home side shot to a 10-0 lead and held off a spirited comeback by the Lions, prevailing 23-20 to spark jubilant scenes in the Darling Downs country town.

1925

South Sydney began an era of premiership domination that would only be bettered by one club in Australian Rugby League history, but a lacklustre standard of football and corresponding crowds resulted in a financially disastrous season for the NSWRL. Meanwhile, the glory days continued unabated for Queensland, welcoming back the influential visionary Harry Sunderland as QRL secretary and extending its interstate reign over New South Wales to four seasons. The Australian Board of

Control made the decision that future Australian teams would wear the traditional green and gold national colours; previously, Test and touring sides wore maroon and blue hooped jumpers.

THE PREMIERSHIP

Captained by five-eighth Alf 'Smacker' Blair and coached by the legendary fullback Howard Hallett, who retired from playing at the end of 1924, Souths capitalised on the last season of the first-past-the-post system of deciding the premiership. The Rabbitohs were undefeated with an unassailable 10 point-lead on the field after 13 rounds, prompting the NSWRL to call an end to the premiership five rounds early. Wests finished runners-up with the modest record of six wins and five losses.

- **Biggest win:** South Sydney 31 d. Glebe 8 at the Sydney Cricket Ground, round six
- **Top Point-scorer:** Benny Wearing (South Sydney) 80
- **Top Try-scorer:** Benny Wearing (South Sydney) 12

THE REPRESENTATIVE SCENE

Queensland's phenomenally talented side won four of the five interstate matches contested with NSW in 1925, in what was to be Duncan Thompson's final series for the Maroons. He was at the forefront as Toowoomba swept aside Brisbane and Ipswich to claim the inaugural Bulimba Cup, before defeating New Zealand and NSWRL premiers South Sydney. Jim Craig led Queensland on a tour of New Zealand, losing just one of 11 matches. After going down to New Zealand 25-24, Queensland regrouped with a 35-14 thrashing of the national side and crushed its provincial opposition. Jim Craig top-scored with 126 points, while Test winger Cec Aynsley crossed for an incredible 34 tries.

STANDOUT PLAYER

Tom Gorman's burgeoning reputation as arguably the decade's finest centre was enhanced by his consistently brilliant performances for the dominant Toowoomba and Queensland combinations throughout 1925.

MEMORABLE MATCH

In one of the few matches Souths was challenged in 1925, the eventual premiers held off a stirring comeback by Wests. The Rabbitohs led 23-7 heading into the final quarter though doubles to winger Benny Wearing and mobile forward Ernie Lapham, but the Fruitpickers piled on three late tries to set up a thrilling finish.

1926

The reintroduction of a finals series and the clean-up of the play-the-ball rules enhanced the premiership product and drew the crowds back to the football in 1926. South Sydney carved out a powerful premiership victory, while University were shock runners-up in the greatest season of the amateur club's 18-season history that garnered little success. Queensland ruled the interstate roost again in a season north of the border that signalled the end of the career of the great Harold Horder, who spent two seasons in Brisbane following his record-breaking tenure with Souths and Norths. Britain's Rugby Football League invited New Zealand to tour in the 1926-27 northern winter—at the expense of Australia, after both countries sought an invitation. The Kiwis tour was a disaster, with player strikes and suspension providing a bleak backdrop to dismal on-field results, while the decision extended the eventual gap between Kangaroo Tours to eight years.

THE PREMIERSHIP

The Rabbitohs streeted their premiership rivals to finish nine points clear at the top of the table. Souths duly advanced to the final with a 21-5 semi-final victory over Easts, but University stunned the Sydney Rugby League public by thumping second-placed Glebe 29-3 in the other semi. In a brave showing, the Alby Lane-led Students went down 11-5 to Alf Blair's star-studded South Sydney side that featured luminaries of the era Benny Wearing, Eddie Root and George Treweek.

- **Biggest win:** South Sydney 36 d. University 8 at the Sydney Cricket Ground, round 18
- **Top Point-scorer:** Jack Courtney (North Sydney) 104
- **Top Try-scorer:** Benny Wearing (South Sydney) 14

THE REPRESENTATIVE SCENE

NSW challenged Queensland's recent supremacy by winning the first two interstate clashes in Sydney. But the Maroons rallied with a 26-11 victory in Newcastle and claimed another series victory with comfortable results in two Brisbane-hosted matches, including a record 38-0 defeat in the fourth encounter.

STANDOUT PLAYER

Queensland centre Tom Gorman again emphasised his class after moving from Toowoomba to Brisbane, captaining Past Brothers to the BRL premiership and the Brisbane representative side to a famous 16-15 victory over Jim Craig's Ipswich side in a Bulimba Cup match. He was similarly influential in Queensland's come-from-behind interstate series victory.

MEMORABLE MATCH

In the premiership's first great comeback victory, also-rans Newtown reeled in an 18-0 deficit to defeat frontrunners Souths 25-24. The Rabbitohs scored a last-minute try, but 'Smacker' Blair's missed conversion attempt sealed a remarkable win for the Bluebags.

1927

Glebe legend Frank Burge was lured to St. George as captain-coach in 1927 for the princely sum of £200, and the phenomenal tryscoring forward transformed the previous year's wooden spooners into premiership contenders. But Burge's charges were unable to topple the might of South Sydney. The lifting of international transfer bans by Britain sparked a flurry of offers to Australian stars from English clubs, and a clutch of outstanding players were enticed overseas—an indicator of what was to follow in the ensuing two decades.

THE PREMIERSHIP

The Rabbitohs secured the minor premiership after losing just two matches in 18 rounds, with the revitalised Saints finished three points adrift in second. A last-round scramble resulted in Wests and Easts qualifying for the finals at the expense of Newtown, but both sides were comprehensively beaten at the semi-final stage by Souths and St. George respectively. Captain-coach Alf Blair led Souths to a third consecutive premiership courtesy of a 20-11 victory over St. George in the final, signalling the end of Burge's extraordinary playing career.

- **Biggest win:** South Sydney 42 d. University 11 at Earl Park, round 17
- **Top Point-scorer:** Alf 'Smacker' Blair (South Sydney) 94
- **Top Try-scorer:** Benny Wearing (South Sydney) 19

THE REPRESENTATIVE SCENE

NSW reversed a five-year trend with a 3-1 victory over Queensland in one of the finest interstate series on record, sealing the result with a 15-11 triumph in the fourth encounter in Brisbane.

STANDOUT PLAYER

Alf 'Smacker' Blair combined the dual responsibilities of captaining and coaching the Rabbitohs with aplomb to guide the club to its third straight title, while finishing as the premiership's top point-scorer. The influential five-eighth played a key role in NSW's drought-breaking interstate series success.

MEMORABLE MATCH

Tries to winger Tony Redmond and forward Frank Matterson, and a goal to mercurial captain and fullback Frank McMillan propelled Wests to a last-minute 8-6 victory over third-placed Easts in the final round. The nail-biting result saw the Fruitpickers avoid a fourth-place play-off with Newtown.

1928

The 1928 season heralded another eventful tour by the Jonty Parkin-led Lions squad, the inaugural City v Country NSW clash and an infamous club match between Balmain and St. George, forever to be known as 'The Earl Park Riot.' The NSWRL's coffers continued to skyrocket on the back of tremendous crowd figures.

THE PREMIERSHIP

St. George and Easts dominated the 14-round regular season, losing just one game apiece—while three-time premiers Souths finished eight competition points off the pace in third. But the Rabbitohs stormed to a record fourth straight premiership by despatching minor premiers St. George 13-5 in the semi-final and subjecting the Tricolours to a 26-5 drubbing in the final at the Agricultural Ground (a dispute over 'unreasonable terms' between the NSWRL and the SCG saw major premiership fixtures shifted from the hallowed venue for six seasons).

- **Biggest win:** Balmain 42 d. Eastern Suburbs 17 at Birchgrove Oval, round three; South Sydney 39 d. Newtown 14 at Sydney Sports Ground, round 14.
- **Top Point-scorer:** Benny Wearing (South Sydney) 94
- **Top Try-scorer:** Tony Redmond (Western Suburbs) 9

THE REPRESENTATIVE SCENE

England's successful retention of the Ashes came in the shape of victories over the Tom Gorman-led hosts in the opening two encounters—15-12 in Brisbane and a grinding 8-0 result at the SCG—before Test debutant Benny Wearing inspired the hosts to a 21-14 win in the third encounter. Riverina five-eighth Eric Weissel played his way into the Test team by leading Country Firsts to a 35-34 victory in the inaugural match with City Firsts, while Queensland regained interstate supremacy with a 3-1 series win over NSW.

STANDOUT PLAYER

Benny Wearing's spectacular debut for Australia proved the folly of selectors' continual snubbing of the Rabbitohs winger. He scored two tries and kicked three goals in the victory, but incredibly, was never selected to play for his country again (*see One-Game Wonders*). Wearing led the premiership in pointscoring and was integral to the continuation of Souths' title-winning streak.

MEMORABLE MATCH

Frontrunners St. George's 21-3 late-season defeat of lowly Balmain at Earl Park was soured by on-field violence that quickly descended into full-scale rioting by the incensed crowd. Among other flare-ups, Tigers forward Tony Russell allegedly kicked the Saints' former Kangaroos centre George Carstairs in the head, but was not sent off. Supporters took matters into their own hands, ripping palings from the fence and storming the pitch in pursuit of Russell. Police had their hands full containing the chaos of 'The Earl Park Riot' as a seemingly innocuous first grade game etched its place in Australian Rugby League folklore (*see Bizarre Matches*).

1929

Souths rolled on to another premiership victory—extending its record streak to five straight—but another foundation club, Glebe, was axed from the competition at the end of the year. Glebe's declining on-field performances, its lack of a home ground and perceived poor organisation off the paddock contributed to the NSWRL narrowly voting out Australian Rugby League's first club. The Kangaroos—led by a Queenslander for the first time—toured Britain after an eight-year gap, but their Ashes challenge was thwarted by the most famous no-try decision in the code's history. The moniker 'The Greatest Game of All' was used for the first time, emblazoned on the front page of the Rugby League News.

THE PREMIERSHIP

The Rabbitohs secured the minor premiership four points ahead of second-placed St. George, and won through to the Final with a courageous 22-10 semi-final victory over Wests. Fourth-placed Newtown upset St. George 8-7 in the other semi, but the Bluebags were swamped 30-10 in the final, with Souths captain Alf Blair and winger Reg Williams collecting hat-tricks.

- **Biggest win:** South Sydney 31 d. Glebe 4 at the Sydney Sports Ground, round 11
- **Top Point-scorer:** Jim Craig (Western Suburbs) 86
- **Top Try-scorer:** Alan Brady (Western Suburbs) 11

THE REPRESENTATIVE SCENE

The interstate pendulum swung dramatically back in NSW's favour courtesy of a 5-0 series defeat of Queensland. The Tom Gorman-led Kangaroos were desperately unlucky to not return with the Ashes after winning the first Test 31-8 and going down 9-3 in the second encounter. Easts halfback Joe 'Chimpy' Busch had a seemingly fair try disallowed by a touch judge's ruling, and the third Test finished in a 0-0 draw. An unprecedented fourth Test was staged to decide the series, but England prevailed 3-0 to retain the symbol of Anglo-Australian Rugby League supremacy.

STANDOUT PLAYER

Easts winger Bill Shankland scored 10 tries for the Tricolours in 1929, before winning a place in the Kangaroo Tour squad—his maiden national call-up. Shankland scored two tries on Test debut in the 31-8 victory at Headingley, and scored Australia's only try in the second Test loss, finishing as the squad's top try-scorer with 24 in just 23 games. After a stint in the Riverina, Shankland returned to England with Warrington as one of the 1930s' finest Australian imports.

MEMORABLE MATCH

Souths' semi-final victory over the Jim Craig captain-coached Wests outfit was achieved despite having winger Alan Righton sent off in the opening 10 minutes. Wests leapt out to a 10-0 lead, but the Rabbitohs trailed by just two at the break after a Oscar Quinlivan double and piled on four second half tries to triumph 22-10.

THE 1930s

The 1930s began with the Great Depression and ended the onset of the Second World War, but Rugby League pressed on through the hardships. Ashes competition was fierce, but ultimately dominated by England, while NSW restored the natural order in interstate competition. The NSWRL premiership welcomed Canterbury-Bankstown and farewelled University, while Wests and Canterbury won maiden titles and Eastern Suburbs—spearheaded by the magnificent Dave Brown—won a hat-trick of premierships. Other champions of the decade included Vic Hey, Wally Prigg, Frank McMillan and Ray Stehr, but many Australian stars were lured to England by big-spending British clubs.

1930

The harsh grip of the Great Depression began to wreak its devastating impact on Australian society, and Rugby League was not immune. Attendances fell away and Sydney players departed for country clubs that could offer more attractive packages—impossible to resist in the tough economic conditions of the time. Western Suburbs, the last existing foundation club yet to win a first grade title, finally broke through to win the 23rd NSWRL premiership under inspirational captain-coach Jimmy Craig. Pioneer Easts and Kangaroo hooker Sid 'Sandy' Pearce passed away in November at the age of 47. Future Easts legend Dave Brown made his first grade debut aged just 16.

THE PREMIERSHIP

Wests took possession of the competition lead in round five and maintained top spot for the remainder of the regular season to edge second-placed Easts by a solitary win. Defending five-time premiers Souths finished third and the club's phenomenal run came to an end with a 9-5 semi-final loss to the minor premiers. St. George upset Easts 11-10 in the other semi, and rolled Wests 14-6 in the final to force the premiership's first official Grand Final (minor premiers reserved the right of challenge if beaten during the finals until compulsory Grand Finals were introduced in 1954). Wests swamped the plucky Dragon Slayers 27-2 in the Grand Final, with winger Alan Brady scoring three tries.

- **Biggest win:** Eastern Suburbs 43 d. North Sydney 11 at the Agricultural Ground, round 14
- **Top Point-scorer:** Jim Craig (Western Suburbs) 86
- **Top Try-scorer:** Morrie Boyle (Eastern Suburbs) 15

THE REPRESENTATIVE SCENE

Country Firsts defeated City Firsts 35-26 at the Sydney Sports Ground, while NSW won its second straight series against Queensland. The Blues won the first encounter in Sydney 16-11, before Queensland levelled the series 25-11. NSW prevailed 15-12 in a hard-fought decider. New Zealand embarked on a disappointing tour of Australia, winning just five of 12 games and succumbing twice to each of the NSW and Queensland state sides (no Test matches were scheduled).

STANDOUT PLAYER

Temora five-eighth Eric Weissel scored 17 points (one try, seven goals) as captain of Country's 35-26 victory over City. The Kangaroos star was chosen to captain NSW in the first interstate encounter, but declined to play in a Jack Hore Gold Cup match for Temora instead. When advised that he would be prevented from playing anywhere if he refused state selection, Weissel famously led NSW to victory over Queensland in Sydney on the Saturday and drove to Canowindra (stopping at Bathurst overnight) to spearhead Temora's crucial victory on the Sunday.

MEMORABLE MATCH

St. George's 14-6 boilover against Wests in the final was largely thanks to two intercept tries to winger Eric Freestone. The Saints led 9-0 soon after halftime following Freestone's first try, but Wests hit back to trail by just three and appeared set to level the scores in the closing minutes, before the flanker snaffled his second intercept and ran the length of the field to seal the upset.

1931

While Australia battled the rigours of the Great Depression, Eastern Suburbs and South Sydney provided some light amidst the gloom with the staging of one of the great premiership deciders. The Rabbitohs collected their sixth title in seven years in the Grand Final, but it was a painful missed opportunity for the table-topping Tricolours. Queensland regained interstate bragging rights in another gripping series with NSW, bringing a sense of unity north of the border to help alleviate the financial and political quarrelling between the QRL and the BRL which threatened to derail the code in Queensland.

THE PREMIERSHIP

Boasting budding stars Dave Brown, Ernie Norman, Ray Stehr and Sid 'Joe' Pearce, Easts lost just two regular season matches to finish six points clear of Souths and Wests. The Magpies upset Easts 10-8 at the semi-final stage, and Souths won the right to face the Tricolours in the Grand Final after defeating Wests 17-2 in the final under the peculiar post-season system of the era. Souths' big-match experience told in the Grand Final as the Paddy Maher-captained Rabbitohs overcame Easts 12-7.

- **Biggest win:** Eastern Suburbs 52 d. North Sydney 4 at the Sydney Sports Ground, round 14
- **Top Point-scorer:** Jack Lynch (Eastern Suburbs) 124
- **Top Try-scorer:** Jack Lynch (Eastern Suburbs) 16

THE REPRESENTATIVE SCENE

Easts captain Norm Pope led City Firsts to a narrow 17-15 victory over Country. In a tit-for-tat interstate series, NSW won the first clash 39-17 in Sydney before Queensland struck back in a 23-20 thriller. The Blues emphatically won the third match 28-6, and the series moved on to Brisbane. Captain-coached by veteran forward Herb Steinohrt, Queensland won the interstate crown with 15-8 and 4-3 victories in the remaining two matches.

STANDOUT PLAYER

Veteran Souths winger Benny Wearing scored 13 tries and 107 points in 1931—second in the premiership on both counts—and scored a try and a goal in the Rabbitohs' Grand Final victory. The 30-year-old crowd favourite proved he had lost little of his crowd-pleasing magic.

MEMORABLE MATCH

Easts led the Grand Final 4-0 at halftime, before Wearing propelled underdogs Souths to the lead with a try and a superb goal. A long-range try to Easts winger Fred Tottey and a penalty goal to Souths set up a 7-all stalemate, but Souths five-eighth Harry Eyers scored a blistering try from deep inside his own territory with only seconds remaining to steal a dramatic premiership victory.

1932

The tour of Jim Sullivan's Lions was the glowing focal point of the 1932 season, drawing massive crowds and providing respite and unity in a year that Australia's unemployment rate peaked at 29 per cent. England's visit and the Ashes series dwarfed interest in all other Rugby League competition, including Queensland's unbeaten interstate victory and yet another premiership draped in myrtle and green.

THE PREMIERSHIP

Souths lost its opening match of the season, but embarked on an unbeaten 14-match run on the way to claiming its 11th title—and the club's seventh in eight years. The Rabbitohs disposed of Easts 26-8 to advance to the final, where they were upset by second-placed Wests 23-8. The George Treweek-led South Sydney side regrouped with a 19-12 Grand Final defeat of the Magpies.

- **Biggest win:** Eastern Suburbs 40 d. Newtown 0 at Marrickville Oval, round 10; Balmain 45 d. North Sydney 5 at Pratten Park, round 10
- **Top Point-scorer:** Les Mead (Western Suburbs) 104
- **Top Try-scorer:** Alan Ridley (Western Suburbs) 18

THE REPRESENTATIVE SCENE

Queensland opened the interstate series with a 23-15 victory over NSW in Sydney. After a 9-all draw in the second encounter, the Maroons secured a 2-0 series triumph with a 19-9 result at the new home of Queensland Rugby League, the Brisbane Cricket Ground (more commonly known as the 'Gabba). England won the first Test

8-6 in front of a 70,204-strong SCG crowd, before Australia achieved a famous 15-6 victory in the 'Battle of Brisbane,' so-called after the home side battled on with numerous injury problems and Eric Weissel defied an ankle injury to set up a long-range try for Hec Gee. England's 18-13 success in the third Test locked up the Ashes for the fifth straight series.

STANDOUT PLAYER

The 1932 season provided crowning achievements for two all time great veteran forwards. Toowoomba's Herb Steinohrt captained Queensland's series victory before leading Australia in the Ashes series, making the last of his nine Test appearances. The peerless attacking second-rower George Treweek was inspirational as captain in Souths' emphatic premiership triumph.

MEMORABLE MATCH

The premiership was not decided until the final moments of the Grand Final. Wests kept pace with minor premiers Souths all day, twice coming from behind to level the scores at 12-all. The Rabbitohs had two tries disallowed inside the final quarter, before Benny Wearing piloted a wonderful penalty goal through the posts in the dying minutes. Wearing made a long break in the shadows of the siren to set up a try for lock Eric Lewis, capping a 19-12 result.

1933

The 1933 season flitted between triumph and tragedy, high achievement and ultimate disappointment. Newtown won its first premiership in 23 years, while the previous year's runners-up Wests slumped to a wooden spoon. Easts prodigy Dave Brown set Kangaroo Tour records never to be challenged, but the Australians' spirited journey through Britain and France was swathed in sadness after three-quarter Ray Morris—the first and only player to be selected for national honours from the University club—contracted an ear infection en route to England and died after being hospitalised in Malta while his teammates sailed on (see Tragic Figures).

THE PREMIERSHIP

The Kangaroos' departure dramatically altered the trajectory of the Sydney competition—Wests' slide to the bottom of the table can be attributed to five players being selected in the Australian squad (including five-eighth Vic Hey and captain Frank McMillan); and Easts finished second, but crashed out in the semi-final 13-10 to fourth-placed St. George after four stars departed. Newtown won the minor premiership and brushed Souths aside in the semi-final (ending the magnificent career of Rabbitohs winger Benny Wearing). Captained by Keith Ellis and coached by the club's 1910 premiership-winning skipper, Charles 'Boxer' Russell, the Bluebags took out their second title with an 18-5 defeat of St. George in the final.

- **Biggest win:** University 42 d. St. George 8 at the Sydney Sports Ground, round nine
- **Top Point-scorer:** Syd Christensen (Balmain) 86
- **Top Try-scorer:** Jack Gray-Spence (University) 11

THE REPRESENTATIVE SCENE

NSW overturned the interstate dominance Queensland had enjoyed for the better part of a decade with a 3-1 series win, starting a trend that would only be broken sporadically in the ensuing 50 years. McMillan's Kangaroos became the first to lose an Anglo-Australian series 3-0, but the 4-0, 7-5 and 19-16 scorelines in favour of Jim Sullivan's England side told a story of a close-fought Ashes campaign. Dave Brown's pointscoring exploits were the inevitable talking point of the tour, while new ground was broken when Australia and England played the first Rugby League match in France—an international won 63-13 by the Kangaroos.

STANDOUT PLAYER

Remarkably, Easts' devastating centre Brown was not a recognised goalkicker before the Kangaroos departed, but he returned with the phenomenal tally of 285 points (19 tries, 114 goals) in 32 games—including a 27-point haul in the international in Paris.

MEMORABLE MATCH

The second semi-final was witness to an extraordinary and controversial finish. St. George led for the majority of the contest, but Easts fought back to level the scores at 10-all. The fulltime siren sounded and Saints centre Norm Tipping skewed a field goal attempt, but Jim Rutherford swooped through on the unsuccessful kick to score a try, despite the Tricolours' protests that the backrower was offside.

1934

In a significant year of advancement for Australian Rugby League, crowd numbers made an upward turn to counter the spiralling trend of the Depression years. Western Suburbs' rollercoaster decade reached an apex with a magnificent premiership triumph to send a champion out as a winner, while the authorities prepared an early prototype for State of Origin football with the staging of an interstate match under lights in Sydney. The Country Rugby League was established, and the NSWRL displayed overdue gratitude to James J. Giltinan's contribution to the birth of Rugby League in Australia, with the Kangaroos v The Rest clash doubling as a testimonial for the pioneering figure.[1]

THE PREMIERSHIP

Easts and Wests finished the regular season tied for first with 12 wins apiece. The Magpies won a play-off for the minor premiership 7-2, and advanced to a final rematch with the Tricolours. Wests became the first and only team to win the premiership a year after collecting the wooden spoon after subduing star-studded Easts 15-12 in the final, which was postponed for a week due to heavy rain and ground conditions—the first time a first grade match had been deferred because of weather. Wests' wonderful captain and fullback, the 1933-34 Kangaroos skipper Frank 'Skinny' McMillan, retired after the match (he made an eight-game comeback in 1935).

- **Biggest win:** South Sydney 45 d. University 3 at Leichhardt Oval, round three
- **Top Point-scorer:** Dave Brown (Eastern Suburbs) 121
- **Top Try-scorer:** Dave Brown (Eastern Suburbs) 11; Fred Gardner (St. George) 11;
  Vic Hey (Western Suburbs) 11

---

1 Ian Heads and David Middleton, *A Centenary Of Rugby League.* Sydney, 2008

THE REPRESENTATIVE SCENE

The five-match interstate series was drawn 2-all—NSW, captained by 20-year-old Dave Brown, won the first two Sydney-based clashes comfortably, before Queensland prevailed in the floodlit third match. The series advanced to Brisbane and two 'Gabba thrillers: a 25-all draw and a 22-20 victory to the Dan Dempsey-led Maroons.

STANDOUT PLAYER

McMillan was the sentimental hero, but the linchpin of Wests' premiership was unrivalled five-eighth Vic Hey. Regarded by many as Australia's greatest-ever pivot, Hey scored 11 tries in 1934 and represented NSW before spearheading the Magpies' title charge.

MEMORABLE MATCH

The 1934 final was a worthy premiership decider. Bulldozing Wests winger Alan Ridley scored the only try of the first half to set up a 7-2 lead at the break, before halfback Viv Thicknesse levelled for Easts. Ridley completed a double to put the Magpies out to 15-7 and they held on despite a late try to Easts lock Andy Norval.

1935

Canterbury-Bankstown was admitted to the Sydney premiership. The season also heralded the return of trans-Tasman Test football after a 16-year absence, and the emergence of a club combination that ranks alongside any the code's history. Queensland lost the interstate series 4-1, but the game was revitalised in the Sunshine State by Wests and Kangaroos five-eighth Vic Hey's lucrative move to Toowoomba. Past Brothers won a thrilling Grand Final 11-9 over Valleys in extra-time, while the spiritual home of Queensland Rugby League, Lang Park, was used for the first time.[2]

THE PREMIERSHIP

Easts lost just one match all season, winning 11 straight to emphatically take out the premiership. Coached by Arthur 'Pony' Halloway and captained by 'The Bradman of League' Dave Brown, the Tricolours' luminous line-up defeated Wests in the semi-final and thrashed Souths 19-3 in the final—despite losing Brown to injury before the decider. As they would for the following two seasons, every other side in the competition was playing for second place behind dominant Easts. At the other end of the table, University lost all 16 of its matches.

- **Biggest win:** St. George 91 d. Canterbury 6 at Earl Park, round five (premiership record)
- **Top Point-scorer:** Dave Brown (Eastern Suburbs) 244
- **Top Try-scorer:** Dave Brown (Eastern Suburbs) 38 (premiership record)

THE REPRESENTATIVE SCENE

NSW thumped Queensland 4-1 in the interstate series, including a 51-8 drubbing in the third encounter. Former All Black Bert Cooke led New Zealand to a shock 22-14 win at Auckland's Carlaw Park in the first Test against Australia since 1919, but the Dave Brown-led tourists won the remaining two Tests at the same venue comprehensively, 29-8 and 31-8. City defeated Country 20-5 on the back of a four-try haul to Wests winger Alan Ridley.

---

2 Max and Reet Howell, *The Greatest Game Under The Sun*. Brisbane, 1989

STANDOUT PLAYER

Dave Brown's season ranks among the most dominant by a single player in the game's history. The brilliant centre smashed the record for most points in season (244), and set new marks for tries in a season (38) and points in a match (45) that still stand. Australia's youngest-ever Test captain at 22 in the series win over New Zealand, Brown scored 38 points in the series, while he also dominated for NSW. Injury robbed Brown of his place in the final, but his contribution to the Tricolours' premiership victory was enormous.

MEMORABLE MATCH

Fledgling Canterbury was subjected to the two biggest defeats in premiership history—91-6 by St. George in round six and 87-7 by Eastern Surburbs a week later. Saints winger Les Griffin scored a record 36 points (two tries, 15 goals), only to be bested the following weekend by Brown, who scored a phenomenal 45 points (five tries, 15 goals). The 'Cantabs' conceded 660 points in their debut season, but two wins against University was enough to avoid the wooden spoon.

1936

The Eastern Suburbs juggernaut rolled on to an unbeaten premiership season. The Lions tour proved to be a boon for the Australian Rugby League, attracting massive crowds to alleviate the hardships of the Depression-era years. The Ashes series was as closely fought and rugged as ever, but Jim Brough's England side maintained the Old Enemy's dominion over Anglo-Australian Rugby League.

THE PREMIERSHIP

Easts won 11 and drew two of its 13 regular season games for a resounding minor premiership success. The Tricolours downed Canterbury—who surged from an arduous debut season to third spot in 1936—25-13 in the semi-final. Balmain defeated Norths 16-3 in the other semi, but was trounced 32-12 by Easts in the final.

- **Biggest win:** Canterbury 41 d. University 0 at Belmore Sports Ground, round 11
- **Top Point-scorer:** Syd Christensen (Balmain) 123
- **Top Try-scorer:** Fred Tottey (Eastern Suburbs) 25

THE REPRESENTATIVE SCENE

NSW swept the interstate series 3-0 despite the presence of Vic Hey at five-eighth for Queensland. Alan Ridley (who bagged six tries in a match for Wests during the premiership season) again starred for City Firsts, scoring three tries in a 41-8 defeat of Country. Captain Dave Brown inspired Australia to a resounding 24-8 victory in the first Ashes Test, but England grasped a series win with identical 12-7 scorelines in the remaining two clashes. Easts enforcer Ray Stehr became the first and only player to be sent off twice in the same Ashes series, receiving his marching orders in the first and third Tests along with England rivals Nat Silcock and John Arkwright respectively.

STANDOUT PLAYER

Dave Brown scored 15 tries for Easts in captaining the club to a decisive premiership triumph. After leading Country and NSW to convincing successes, Brown's 14-point haul (two tries, three goals) spearheaded Australia's first Test victory over England and was reliably outstanding in the hosts' gallant series loss.

MEMORABLE MATCH

Canterbury held a shock 11-9 halftime lead over Easts in its finals debut. But a broken collarbone suffered by prop Eddie Burns decimated the Berries' pack and Dave Brown scored a masterful hat-trick in the minor premiers' second half rush to prevail 25-13.

1937

The impending departure of the Kangaroos took precedence over the Sydney premiership, which was shortened to just nine rounds and was the last to operate under the first-past-the-post system. Easts notched its third consecutive title, but it was the end of the line for the University club—the Students voluntarily withdrew from the premiership after another winless season. Newcastle lock Wally Prigg was chosen as captain and became the first player to make three Kangaroo Tours, but more Ashes heartache awaited the 'colonials' in England, while a historic Test series was staged in France. Dave Brown had already been lured to England by Warrington and Vic Hey left for Leeds mid-season from Ipswich. Both Australian superstars lined up against the Kangaroos.

THE PREMIERSHIP

The Tricolours won six and drew two of their eight games, stretching their unbeaten streak to 34 matches (it ended at a record 35 matches in round two of 1938) and claiming the premiership under the captaincy of halfback Viv Thicknesse. South Sydney was runners-up with five wins and a draw.

- **Biggest win:** South Sydney 63 d. University 0 at the Sydney Sports Ground, round one
- **Top Point-scorer:** Jack Beaton (Eastern Suburbs) 56
- **Top Try-scorer:** Fred Tottey (Eastern Suburbs) 10

THE REPRESENTATIVE SCENE

NSW wrapped up a second straight 3-0 series whitewash over Queensland. The Kangaroos played a two-Test series in New Zealand en route to Britain, drawing 1-all with the Kiwis. Australia's Ashes bid came undone with a 5-4 loss in the series-opener and a 13-3 loss in the second encounter. The tourists achieved a morale-boosting 13-3 victory in the third Test, before winning the first Franco-Australian Test series 2-0.

STANDOUT PLAYER

The captaincy of the Kangaroos was just reward for Wally Prigg, one of Australia's greatest forwards. Prigg's leadership in seven Tests abroad was outstanding, and his durability was emphasised in making the equal-most appearances (29) and scoring the equal-most tries (13)—the first time a forward had topped the try count on a Kangaroo Tour.

MEMORABLE MATCH

Former All Black legend George Nepia—playing in his only Rugby League Test—inspired New Zealand to a famous 16-15 upset of Australia in the second Test at Carlaw Park. The 32-year-old fullback, who also starred in New Zealand Maori's 16-5 defeat of the tourists, kicked two goals and was magnificent in defence and with ball in hand.

1938

Canterbury-Bankstown ended Eastern Suburbs' reign with a thrilling premiership triumph in just the club's fourth season—an achievement bettered only by the champions of the first three years of the competition, Souths and Newtown, and the Melbourne Storm 61 years later. Queensland's interstate series loss was exacerbated by the retirement of the great prop Mick Madsen, and QRL secretary Harry Sunderland's departure to England. A charismatic, controversial, industrious and groundbreaking administrator, Sunderland's influence on Australian Rugby League's first three decades was profound. He took on the manager position at Wigan and garnered a treasured place in the fabric of the English game.

THE PREMIERSHIP

Coached by the legendary Jim Craig and captained by former Wests three-quarter Alan Brady, the young Canterbury club soared to the minor premiership by winning 11 and drawing two of its 14 regular season matches. The Berries advanced to the final via a high-scoring semi-final victory, 31-24 over Balmain. Second-placed Souths fell 19-10 to three-time defending premiers Easts in the other semi, but a second half charge by Canterbury secured a 19-6 final success over the gallant Tricolours.

- **Biggest win:** Balmain 57 d. Western Suburbs 11 at Pratten Park, round three
- **Top Point-scorer:** Tom Kirk (Canterbury) 94
- **Top Try-scorer:** Don Manson (South Sydney) 13

THE REPRESENTATIVE SCENE

NSW won the interstate series-opener 20-19 courtesy of a late goal by Souths centre Fred Felsch that hit the upright and dropped over the crossbar, before swamping Queensland (who played the majority of the match with 12 men after hooker Jack Little was sent off) 44-7 in the second clash. Queensland restored pride with a 36-22 win in Brisbane. An understrength Kiwis side made a tour of Australia but did not play any Tests, and struggled against the state representative sides.

STANDOUT PLAYER

Brisbane lock Eddie 'Babe' Collins starred on the club and representative scenes in 1938. He scored a try in Queensland's 37-17 defeat of the touring New Zealand side, and was outstanding in the state side's narrow loss in the interstate series opener. Collins' absence contributed to the Maroons' heavy defeat in the second game, but he returned with a try in a 36-22 success in the third encounter. The 1937-38 Kangaroo was brilliant in Norths' 16-10 defeat of Valleys, attracting the title of 'the greatest Brisbane loose forward of all time.'[3]

MEMORABLE MATCH

Canterbury held a 4-3 lead at halftime of the final after a dour, forward-dominated opening 40 minutes. Lock Dick Dunn scored to put Easts in front, but five-eighth Jim Duncombe's try reclaimed the advantage for Canterbury and the club's first title was sealed 19-6 on the back of two dazzling tries to winger Joe Gartner.

---

3   *The Courier Mail*, 5 September 1938

1939

On the day of the 1939 premiership final came the news that changed the world forever. Balmain's first title in 15 years faded into the background as the Australian public grappled with the potential impact of Germany's invasion of Poland. Prime Minister Robert Menzies announced the following day that Australia was joining Great Britain's declaration of war against Hitler's Nazi Gemany and Rugby League gritted its teeth for another period of hardship.

THE PREMIERSHIP

Balmain edged the previous season's wooden spooners St. George and defending champions Canterbury for the minor premiership. The Tigers eliminated the Berries 13-9 in the semi-final, while fourth-placed Souths knocked off the second-placed Saints 23-10 in the other semi. The 'Prince of Coaches,' Bill Kelly, and captain Sid Goodwin guided Balmain to a 33-4 trouncing of the Fred Felsch-led Rabbitohs in the Final. Winger Tom Bourke scored two tries, while Frank Hyde—a talented centre who later became the doyen of Rugby League radio commentators—also crossed for the Tigers.

- **Biggest win:** South Sydney 53 d. North Sydney 0 at the Sydney Sports Ground, round 14
- **Top Point-scorer:** Neville Smith (St. George) 97
- **Top Try-scorer:** Sid Goodwin (Balmain) 18

THE REPRESENTATIVE SCENE

The 1939 interstate series was truly a tale of two cities. NSW won the first two matches, both played in Sydney, 50-15 and 54-13. But back in Brisbane, the Jack Reardon-led Queenslanders prevailed 29-13 and 23-13 to draw the four-match series 2-all. City Firsts defeated Country Firsts 38-17 in Newcastle great and former Kangaroos captain Wally Prigg's final appearance for the bush boys.

STANDOUT PLAYER

Balmain captain and prolific winger Sid Goodwin topped the competition with 18 tries, including a double in the semi-final defeat of Canterbury. He scored a try for City Firsts and starred for NSW, scoring an interstate record six tries in the 54-13 thrashing of Queensland. The premiership-winning skipper was denied a certain Australian jumper during a stellar career by the World War II-enforced embargo on Test football.

MEMORABLE MATCH

Balmain secured the minor premiership outright with a gripping 11-10 victory over second-placed St. George in the final round. Tigers captain Sid Goodwin scored two tries in the SCG thriller described as 'one of the greatest club struggles in years' by the Herald.[4]

---

4 Steve Haddan, *The Finals* (third edition). Sydney, 2008

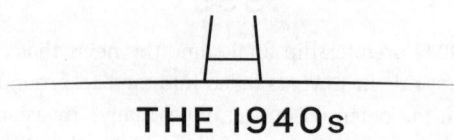

THE 1940s

Rugby League in Australia carried on through the adversity of World War II and flourished afterwards. St. George broke through for the club's maiden premierships, while Eastern Suburbs and Balmain also claimed multiple titles. South Sydney experienced its first period in the doldrums, but recovered by the end of the decade with a young fullback named Clive Churchill leading the club's charge. Parramatta and Manly joined the premiership, and international football resumed after a wartime embargo.

1940

Rugby League took a backseat as Australia focussed on the war effort. But as it did during the Great War of 1914-18, the premiership forged on through World War II, providing the public with a welcome distraction from the spectre of overseas conflict and raising funds for Australia's war coffers. Easts returned itself to the premiership pedestal, while Queensland achieved a stunning interstate series success.

THE PREMIERSHIP
Easts captain-coach Dave Brown, who returned from Leeds the previous season, led the Tricolours to the minor premiership. But injury ruled Brown out of the finals and veteran prop Ray Stehr skippered Easts to a 10-3 semi-final defeat of St. George. Newtown repeated the Saints' 1939 effort by finishing second a year after collecting the wooden spoon, but succumbed to fourth-placed defending premiers Canterbury 19-11 in the semi-final. In a rematch of the 1938 decider, the result was reversed after a late surge propelled Easts to a 24-14 victory over the Berries in the final.
- **Biggest win:** Eastern Suburbs 38 d. South Sydney 7 at the Sydney Sports Ground, round 11
- **Top Point-scorer:** Tom Kirk (Newtown) 99
- **Top Try-scorer:** Jack Lindwall (St. George) 19

THE REPRESENTATIVE SCENE
Queensland overturned an eight-year series-winning drought, and a 52-11 defeat at the hands of NSW in the opening clash of 1940, to regain interstate supremacy. The Maroons pipped NSW 19-16 in the second Sydney match and crushed the Blues 45-8 in the third match in Brisbane, with winger Dan O'Connor landing a Queensland record 12 goals. Queensland maintained its irresistible momentum to take the series 23-15 in the fourth and final match.

STANDOUT PLAYER
St. George three-quarter Jack Lindwall led the competition with 19 tries, including four hat-tricks. Lindwall—the brother of St. George teammate and future cricketing great Ray—bagged trebles in consecutive SCG wins against Canterbury, Souths and Newtown, beginning a decade as one of the premiership's most prolific try-poachers in fine style.

MEMORABLE MATCH

The grinding, forward-dominated final was in the balance until the late stages. Easts held just a two-point advantage at halftime, before a late rush of tries confirmed a 24-14 triumph. The Tricolours' backrow triumvirate of Harry Pierce (two tries), Sid 'Joe' Pearce and Joe Clarke (one each) scored four of Easts' six tries. Test forward Pearce, the son of pioneering Easts great Sid 'Sandy' Pearce, produced a towering display in the decider.

1941

St. George, the only club in the competition without a first grade title next to its name, carved out a stirring maiden premiership triumph. NSW overcame Queensland with a 3-1 result in a tight series, before interstate football went on a three-season hiatus. The year was tinged with sadness as 1911-12 Kangaroos captain Chris McKivat and QRL president John Graham Stephenson passed away.

THE PREMIERSHIP

In a phenomenally close minor premiership race, Easts finished in top spot on for-and-against from Balmain and Canterbury, with St. George a solitary competition point adrift. Easts edged the Berries 24-22 in the first semi-final and the Saints thumped the Tigers 32-8 in the other semi. The final delivered an exhilarating exhibition of attacking Rugby League. Captain-coached by second-rower Neville Smith, St. George scored seven tries to Easts' four in a 31-14 triumph, while rival forwards Bill Tyquin (St. George) and Jack Arnold (Easts) were sent off during a physical opening half.

- **Biggest win:** Western Suburbs 40 d. South Sydney 9 at the Sydney Sports Ground, round 14
- **Top Point-scorer:** Neville Smith (St. George) 84
- **Top Try-scorer:** Sel Lisle (Eastern Suburbs) 13; Percy Dermond (Eastern Suburbs) 13

THE REPRESENTATIVE SCENE

Led by Souths centre Fred Felsch, NSW wrapped up the interstate series with victories in the first three games—a 44-10 drubbing in the second encounter was bookended by close results. Jack Reardon captained Queensland to a 27-21 win in the fourth match. In a unique occurrence, brothers Lin and Dick Johnson were opposing fullbacks in the City v Country representative fixture. Canterbury custodian Lin's City side prevailed 44-21 over Country and Cessnock fullback Dick.

STANDOUT PLAYER

Saints skipper Neville Smith was inspirational in the club's historic victory in the final, scoring a try and five goals in the 31-14 success, which also lifted him to the top of the competition's pointscoring table. The respected second-rower, a Queensland representative from Valleys in 1938, played for City and NSW with distinction in 1941.

MEMORABLE MATCH

Easts and Canterbury had developed a keen rivalry in the previous few seasons, contesting two of the previous three premiership deciders. It was the Tricolours that won the 1941 bragging rights with two crucial regular season victories and a thrilling 24-22 result in the semi-final. Dave Brown scored a try and five goals in a man of the match performance in the semi, before playing the last match of an extraordinary career in the final two weeks later.

1942

Wartime Rugby League marched ahead, despite enlistments placing a drain on player numbers and the inevitable financial impact of war on Australia as a whole. Several clubs utilised different jumper designs due to wartime shortages *(see Club Colours)*, while New South Wales confronted the threat of war on the home front after Japanese submarine attacks on Sydney and Newcastle just weeks after the premiership's May kick-off. Canterbury claimed its second first grade title courtesy of a dramatic late goal on an SCG quagmire.

THE PREMIERSHIP

A play-off was required to decide the minor premiership, with winger Edgar Newham scoring a club record five tries as Canterbury outlasted Balmain 26-20. Fresh from a weekend off, St. George defeated the Berries 25-10 in the semi-final and Easts 18-5 in the final, setting up a Grand Final rematch with Canterbury, who exercised its right of challenge as minor premiers. A downpour sparked memorable scenes on Grand Final day as thousands of drenched supporters stampeded the grandstand and members area of the SCG during the reserve grade decider. The Grand Final—the first required in a decade—was won by a penalty goal from close range by Berries fullback Lin Johnson in the dying seconds. Johnson lost his footing in the hazardous conditions and the ball skimmed over the crossbar for an 11-9 victory *(see Unlikely Heroes)*.

- **Biggest win:** St. George 44 d. North Sydney 17 at Hurstville Oval, round 12
- **Top Point-scorer:** Ray Lindwall (St. George) 143
- **Top Try-scorer:** Jack Lindwall (St. George) 16

THE REPRESENTATIVE SCENE

Country Firsts defeated City Firsts 14-11 at the SCG in the season's only top-level representative fixture—just the bush boys' fifth victory in 18 clashes against their Sydney-based rivals.

STANDOUT PLAYER

St. George's Lindwall brothers, fullback Ray and winger Jack, were in dazzling form in 1942. Ray kicked 10 goals in a match against Norths on his way to a then-club record 143 points, while Jack scored four tries in a vital late-season win over Easts. The pair scored all of the Saints' points in the Grand Final—Jack scored a try and Ray kicked three goals. Ray also scored a try and kicked a goal in City's loss to Country.

MEMORABLE MATCH

Country's 14-11 upset of City was marked by former Canterbury winger Merv Denton's magnificent double, featuring a length-of-the-field effort regarded as one of the greatest tries seen at the SCG. Denton was based in Young, before returning to Sydney with Balmain in 1943. The official crowd figure reached 39,884, but was said to be a few thousand higher after returned servicemen were granted free entry to the match.

1943

Despite the gloomy presence of war hovering ominously at all times, the Sydney premiership enjoyed a fruitful season of record-breaking crowd numbers and exhilarating football. Two teams that had struggled in recent seasons produced historic campaigns: Newtown won its last first grade title by defeating North Sydney, who was appearing in the only Grand Final in the club's history. At the other end of the scale, Canterbury became the only defending premiers to finish a season with the wooden spoon. One of Australian Rugby League's founding fathers and preeminent administrators, Sir James Joynton Smith, passed away at the age of 85.

THE PREMIERSHIP

Newtown pipped Balmain 11-10 in a play-off for the minor premiership, before being upset 21-16 by Norths in the semi-final. Norths overcame St. George 25-19 in the final for the opportunity to take on the Bluebags again in the Grand Final. The decider set an attendance record of 60,992 at the SCG. Norths, captained by NSW representative centre Frank Hyde, suffered a setback before kick-off when star lock Harry Taylor did not arrive at the SCG—unbeknownst to his teammates, army man Taylor was in camp near Brisbane preparing to ship out to Papua New Guinea. The Frank Farrell-led Bluebags smashed the unsettled Norths side 34-7 in an eight-try drubbing. Former Balmain winger Sid Goodwin crossed for a double, while fullback Tom Kirk kicked five goals.

- **Biggest win:** South Sydney 39 d. Eastern Suburbs 5 at the Sydney Sports Ground, round 13
- **Top Point-scorer:** Tom Kirk (Newtown) 116
- **Top Try-scorer:** Kelly McMahon (North Sydney) 12

THE REPRESENTATIVE SCENE

Merv Denton, the star of Country's upset win in 1942, scored three tries in City Firsts' 37-25 defeat of Country Firsts played before 33,000 supporters at the SCG. Denton's Balmain teammate Tom Bourke kicked five goals.

STANDOUT PLAYER

The great forward Herb Narvo, who toured with the 1937-38 Kangaroos from Newtown before returning to Newcastle the following season and serving in the Royal Australian Air Force during World War II, played for the Bluebags in 1943 while stationed in Sydney. Narvo's presence provided Newtown's pack with an intimidating edge and the future Australian heavyweight boxing champion scored a try in a powerhouse Grand Final display.

MEMORABLE MATCH

Illegal betting and bribery crept into the game as horseracing was scaled back during wartime. South Sydney's Jack Walsh knocked back a bribe to throw a match against Easts during 1943, informing club management of the situation prior to the match. Ironically, Walsh bombed what would have been a match-winning try in the dying moments when he stumbled and fell just short of the tryline, with Easts holding on to win 8-6.[5]

---

5   Ian Heads and David Middelton, *A Centenary Of Rugby League*. Sydney, 2008

1944

Balmain's triumph in the 1944 premiership was overshadowed by allegations that minor premiers Newtown threw the final against the Tigers for the purpose of procuring extra gate-takings via the staging of Grand Final a week later. An investigation by the NSWRL upheld the integrity of the Newtown players, while Balmain went on to upset the Bluebags again in the Grand Final. The game in Queensland basked in a revival after the arduous first few years of World War II; the Brisbane and Toowoomba competitions flourished, while the Bulimba Cup— won by Toowoomba—was revived after a two-season absence.

THE PREMIERSHIP
Newtown topped the table and crushed St. George by 55-7 in the semi-final. Balmain disposed of Souths 15-6 in the other semi to advance to the final, where the Bluebags surrendered an 11-0 lead after 20 minutes to go down 19-16 in the wake of a listless second half display—sparking calls of a rort. The combatants returned to the SCG a week later for the Grand Final and the Arthur Patton-led Tigers prevailed 12-8; the four-point winning margin was the biggest of the match in a close-fought decider.

- **Biggest win:** Balmain 64 d. Western Suburbs 2 at Pratten Park, round 12
- **Top Point-scorer:** Tom Kirk (Newtown) 185.
- **Top Try-scorer:** Sid Goodwin (Newtown) 22

THE REPRESENTATIVE SCENE
Balmain captain Arthur Patton led City Firsts to a three-tries-to-none, 17-10 victory over Country.

STANDOUT PLAYER
Former Tigers premiership-winning skipper Sid Goodwin represented City Firsts, while his 22 tries for Newtown took him past the century mark in first grade. A stellar year ended in disappointment when the Bluebags went down to Goodwin's former club in the Grand Final.

MEMORABLE MATCH
Newtown's 55-7 demolition of St. George still stands as a finals record, while centre Len Smith's four tries and fullback Tom Kirk's 25 points (one try, 11 goals) were individual scoring records for a finals match at the time. Frank Farrell's Bluebags led just 15-2 at halftime, before piling on the misery for the Saints in the second stanza.

1945

The end of World War II brought unbridled joy to Australians, and Rugby League could be satisfied that it had provided an outlet to the wider community burdened by the conflict, while contributing £25,000 the war effort. Interstate football returned in 1945 and Eastern Suburbs claimed its ninth premiership on the strength of a towering individual performance by Dick Dunn, but all other events in Rugby League were overshadowed by the Bill McRitchie ear-biting incident. St. George prop McRitchie reeled out of a scrum against Newtown at Henson Park, with his ear badly severed. Bluebags enforcer Frank Farrell was fingered as the likely culprit, but he was cleared by an NSWRL enquiry (15 votes to 12) and maintained his innocence until he died in 1985, while McRitchie spent 22 weeks in hospital. The matter was never resolved; Farrell made his Test debut the following season, but McRitchie never played again. Country Rugby League recovered after struggling through the wartime years, expanding from three active groups a year earlier to 12 in 1945.

THE PREMIERSHIP

Easts finished as minor premiers, just one point ahead of Newtown. The Tricolours eliminated Wests Magpies (who were making their first finals appearance in 10 years) 28-13 in the semi-final, advancing to meet Balmain in the Final after the Tigers upset Newtown in the other semi. A stunning 19-point haul by lock Dick Dunn carried Easts to a 22-18 triumph at the SCG. South Sydney came last for the first time in the club's history after winning just one of its 14 matches.

- **Biggest win:** Newtown 44 d. St. George 10 at Henson Park, round seven
- **Top Point-scorer:** Dick Dunn (Eastern Suburbs) 150
- **Top Try-scorer:** Charles Cahill (Newtown) 13

THE REPRESENTATIVE SCENE

New South Wales won the two-match interstate series—the first since 1941—two games to nil. The Herb Narvo-led Blues won the first encounter in Sydney 37-12 and backed it up with a 30-19 victory in second match in Brisbane. Balmain winger Keith Parkinson scored three tries as City Firsts, captained by Newtown forward Herb Narvo, defeated Country Firsts 41-12.

STANDOUT PLAYER

Dick Dunn—unwanted by Easts a year earlier—produced one of the great big-match performances in the game's history in the final. Dunn scored a second half hat-trick and kicked five superb goals to drive the Tricolours to a gripping victory (*see Unlikely Heroes*).

MEMORABLE MATCH

The final balanced on a knife's edge throughout—Balmain led 10-2 during the first half and 13-5 soon after the break. Back-to-back tries to Dick Dunn propelled Easts to a 17-13 advantage, but halfback Stan Ponchard's second try restored the Tigers' lead with eight minutes remaining. Dunn landed a 45-yard penalty in the closing minutes before icing a remarkable performance with his third try on fulltime, and a 22-18 final score. Renowned prop and Easts captain-coach Ray Stehr retired after the victory.

1946

Anglo-Australian Test competition resumed after a nine-year absence with the visit of Gus Risman's 'Indomitables'—named after the aircraft carrier that transported the squad to Australia—from England. The Lions achieved the unique feat going through a series in Australia unbeaten as the green-and-golds attempted to adapt to Test football (none of the Australian players had represented their country prior to the series). Balmain won the premiership for the second time in three seasons, and NSW retained the interstate crown. NSWRL secretary Horrie Miller was dumped from the position he had held for 32 years due to money that had allegedly gone missing, bringing a sad end to the career of one of Australian Rugby League's most prominent pioneers and administrators.

THE PREMIERSHIP

The proud South Sydney club's plight worsened with a winless season in 1946. St. George won the minor premiership, but was upset in the semi-final by third-placed Balmain. The Tigers edged out Canterbury 8-7 two weeks later to face off against St. George again in the Grand Final, and used their momentum to defeat the Dragons 13-12 in a controversial decider; two Balmain tries appeared to come from blatant forward passes.

- **Biggest win:** Newtown 38 d. South Sydney 0 at the Sydney Sports Ground, round eight
- **Top Point-scorer:** Tom Kirk (Newtown) 122
- **Top Try-scorer:** Jack Lindwall (St. George) 16

THE REPRESENTATIVE SCENE

NSW swept the interstate series 3-0, but Queensland took great pride from a euphoric 25-24 over the touring England side. After an 8-all draw in the first Ashes Test, England retained the trophy with 14-5 and 20-7 victories in the subsequent two clashes. Centres Joe Jorgensen and Ron Bailey captained Australia during the series.

STANDOUT PLAYER

Balmain centre Joe Jorgensen starred on the club and representative scene in 1946. His performances for City and NSW saw him selected as Australia's captain for the first and third Ashes Tests, while his second half double in the Grand Final was integral to Balmain's tight victory.

MEMORABLE MATCH

St. George led the Grand Final 6-0 after two early tries, before Balmain clawed back to 6-3 by halftime after a contentious try to veteran winger Arthur Patton. Jack Lindwall nudged the Saints 9-5 ahead in the second half, but Joe Jorgensen's second try with seven minutes remaining—after referee George Bishop missed another forward pass—saw the Tigers lead 13-9. Lindwall scored in the corner with two minutes on the clock, but his brother Ray (playing in his last Rugby League game before concentrating fulltime on cricket) narrowly missed with what would have been a title-winning conversion.

1947

Sydney welcomed two new premiership clubs—Manly and Parramatta—but farewelled a host of England-bound stars, headlined by Test players Lionel Cooper and Arthur Clues. Another player who had had only a limited impact in first grade, Easts winger Brian Bevan, also left and became the greatest try-scorer in Rugby League history over the ensuing two decades in Britain. Harry Bath and Pat Devery joined English clubs after helping Balmain to a second straight premiership. South Sydney's revival began with the acquisition of rugged forward Jack Rayner, and Newcastle duo Clive Churchill and Johnny Graves. The competition was extended to 18 rounds.

THE PREMIERSHIP

Fledgling Manly and Parramatta occupied the two bottom spots on the ladder, while Canterbury finished as minor premiers three points clear of Balmain.

The Berries and Tigers won through to the final, and the black-and-golds prevailed 25-19 (with Devery scoring 16 points from two tries and five goals) to force a Grand Final. For the second straight season, Tom Bourke's Balmain side defeated the minor premiers twice to take out the title, winning the decider 13-9 against the Henry Porter-led Berries. Joe Jorgensen, a hero of the 1946 premiership victory, was on the outer for most of 1947 and spent the majority of the season playing country football. He was recalled to Balmain's line-up for the Grand Final—his first appearance for the season—and remarkably scored all of the Tigers' points, from a try and five goals.

- **Biggest win:** St. George 61 d. Manly 11 at Hurstville Oval, round four
- **Top Point-scorer:** Pat Devery (Balmain) 142
- **Top Try-scorer:** Bobby Lulham (Balmain) 28

THE REPRESENTATIVE SCENE
Captain Pat Devery scored three tries as City Firsts defeated Country Firsts (who were captained by Test halfback Clem Kennedy) convincingly 31-10. Devery also led NSW to a 2-1 victory over Queensland in the four-match interstate series, after the final match in Brisbane was drawn 13-all.

STANDOUT PLAYER
Balmain winger Bobby Lulham arrived from Newcastle as a 20-year-old in 1947 and crossed for an astonishing 28 tries—the second-highest season total in premiership history at the time. The total included a club record-equalling five tries against Parramatta, while Lulham celebrated in the Tigers' Grand Final victory. He represented NSW in all four interstate matches and was named Player of the Year in E.E. Christensen's *Official Rugby League Yearbook*.

MEMORABLE MATCH
Manly endured a harrowing initiation to premiership football at the hands of St. George in round four. The Dragons racked up 13 tries in a 61-11 drubbing, which remained a record defeat for the Sea Eagles for 57 years. Saints winger Jack Lindwall cashed in with a phenomenal 36-point haul from six tries and nine goals.

1948

The 1948 season signalled the return of trans-Tasman Test football and Kangaroo Tours after an 11-year break, but the year is inevitably remembered for the most shameful selection controversy in Australian Rugby League history. Incumbent Test captain-coach Len Smith was left out of the Kangaroo Tour squad altogether; theories put forward by the disbelieving Rugby League community suggested the Newtown centre's non-selection was religion-based, but it emerged years later that the desire of selector Norm 'Latchem' Robinson to coach the side was behind the injustice *(see Bolters, Controversial Selections and Shock Omissions)*. Western Suburbs won its first premiership in 14 years as Sydney's clubs battled through the latter part of the season without their Kangaroos stars. South Sydney adopted Redfern Oval as its home ground, while the club's star fullback Clive Churchill was denied the opportunity to take up a lucrative £10,000 contract with Workington Town by the resumption of an international transfer ban.

THE PREMIERSHIP

Wests, captained by veteran forward Jack Walsh, stormed to the minor premiership after dropping just two matches in the 18 regular season rounds. Balmain scored a finals win over the minor premiers for the third straight season, pipping the Magpies 8-7 in the semi-final. Newtown finished in second spot, but dipped out at the semi-final stage 20-8 to St. George. The Tigers beat the Dragons 13-12 in the final to book a rematch with Wests, but the minor premiers grinded out an 8-5 Grand Final victory to halt Balmain's title streak.

- **Biggest win:** South Sydney 38 d. Parramatta 5 at Redfern Oval, round 10
- **Top Point-scorer:** Jack Lindwall (St. George) 101
- **Top Try-scorer:** Norm Jacobson (Newtown) 27

THE REPRESENTATIVE SCENE

NSW powered to a 3-1 interstate series victory, while Australia drew the two-Test series against the touring Kiwis 1-all. Wests centre Col Maxwell was the surprise choice to captain the Kangaroos, but injury restricted him to just one Test appearance on tour. Easts pivot Wally O'Connell and Queensland forward Bill Tyquin also led Australia in the 3-0 Ashes series loss, while Tyquin skippered the tourists in the 2-0 series win against France.

STANDOUT PLAYER

E.E. Christensen paid tribute to the snubbed Len Smith by naming him as the 1948 NSW Player of the Year in the *Official Rugby League Yearbook*—scant consolation, but due recognition for NSW's series-winning skipper and the captain-coach of the drawn Test series against New Zealand.

MEMORABLE MATCH

The Grand Final was a physical, close-fought affair. Veteran Balmain captain Tom Bourke—playing in his final game before retiring—set up a 5-3 halftime lead for the Tigers with a try and a goal. The premiership-winning play came 25 minutes into the grinding second half, when Magpies second-rower Kevin Hansen busted the line and ran 40 yards to score. Wests fullback Bill Keato converted for an 8-5 final score.

1949

Australia toured New Zealand for the first time in 12 years, while NSW's domination of Queensland in the interstate series raised concerns about the shape of the game north of the border. Souths' resurgence—spearheaded by Kangaroos Clive Churchill, Johnny Graves and Jack Rayner—continued with the capture of the minor premiership just three years after the winless 1946 season. But the Rabbitohs were overwhelmed by an outstanding St. George line-up that timed its run perfectly to claim the club's second premiership. The once-powerful Easts slumped to collect the first wooden spoon in club history, while the young Parramatta outfit was unlucky to miss out on a maiden finals berth after recording draws in its final three matches and finishing two points shy of fourth spot.

THE PREMIERSHIP

Souths thumped St. George 22-4 in the last regular season round, but the third-placed Dragons upset the minor premiers 16-12 in the semi-final a week later.

The Saints conquered Balmain 18-7 in the final, and powered to a 19-12 triumph over the Rabbitohs in the Grand Final. Kangaroos centre Johnny Hawke captained the Saints from five-eighth in his first season in Sydney after joining from Canberra.

- **Biggest win:** South Sydney 48 d. Eastern Suburbs 6 at Redfern Oval, round 14
- **Top Point-scorer:** Bill Keato (Western Suburbs) 163
- **Top Try-scorer:** Ron Roberts (St. George) 25

THE REPRESENTATIVE SCENE

NSW swept to a 4-0 series whitewash of Queensland, at an average margin of more than 22 points per game. Australia embarked on a 10-game tour of New Zealand, incurring just one loss—26-21 in the first Test. The visitors levelled the two-Test series with a 13-10 victory in the second encounter. Johnny Graves starred with 12 tries in seven appearances.

STANDOUT PLAYER

Newtown halfback Keith Froome was the named the inaugural *Sun Herald* Player of the Year in 1949 and was a central figure on the representative scene, captaining City Firsts to a 23-2 defeat of Country and leading NSW to series victory. The 1948-49 Kangaroo capped a fine year by winning selection as captain-coach for Australia's tour of New Zealand, scoring a try and kicking a goal in the second Test win.

MEMORABLE MATCH

St. George led Souths in the Grand Final 11-5 at halftime and powered to a 12-point lead in the second half, before a late Rabbitohs try finished the scoring at 19-12. The Dragons' outstanding three-quarter line scored all five of their tries—wingers Ron Roberts and Noel Pidding crossed for doubles, while centre Matt McCoy also scored. Pidding and McCoy each kicked a goal.

THE 1950s

The beginning of Australian Rugby League's 'Golden Age' was marked by a drought-breaking Test series victory over Great Britain, but Ashes glory on English soil still proved elusive. World Cup tournaments were introduced, while New Zealand and France developed into formidable Test opponents. Souths dominated the first half of the decade, before St. George commenced the greatest dynasty in the code's history. Clive Churchill and Keith Holman spearheaded Australia's successes in the early part of the 1950s, the likes of Keith Barnes and Norm Provan rose to prominence during the middle stages, Brian Carlson was magnificent throughout, while the close of the decade heralded the introduction of extraordinary talents Reg Gasnier, Johnny Raper and Ken Irvine.

1950

The halfway point of the 20th Century was marked by a Lions tour and a historic Test series victory for Australia. The country's first Ashes success in 30 years, and the dramatic Test victory that secured the treasured trophy, ranks as one of the highest peaks in Australia's Rugby League narrative. After an 18-year title drought, Souths began the second of its three golden eras with a memorable premiership triumph. One of the game's founding fathers, James Joseph Giltinan, passed away in September at the age of 84.

THE PREMIERSHIP

In Jack Rayner's first season as captain-coach, Souths secured the minor premiership two points clear of Fred de Belin's Balmain side. The Rabbitohs trounced Newtown 30-4 in the first semi-final, before fourth-placed Wests upset the Tigers 28-10 in the second semi on the back of eight goals to fullback Bill Keato. A Grand Final was not required for the first season since 1945 after Souths subdued Wests, who boasted Test halves pairing Keith Holman and Frank Stanmore, 21-15 in the final. Johnny Graves scored two tries and prolific pointscoring forward Bernie Purcell landed five goals in the triumph.

- **Biggest win:** South Sydney 45 d. Manly 11 at Redfern Oval, round eight
- **Top Point-scorer:** Bill Keato (Western Suburbs) 180
- **Top Try-scorer:** Jack Troy (Newtown) 16

THE REPRESENTATIVE SCENE

NSW won the three-match interstate series 2-0; the 9-all draw in the second clash in front of a dismal 6,000-strong SCG crowd was bookended by resounding Blues victories in Sydney and Brisbane. The Ernest Ward-led Great Britain side won the first Ashes Test 6-4, before Churchill's Australians squared the series 15-3. The SCG decider was played in quagmire-like conditions and a lengthy 2-all stalemate ensued. The Ashes-winning sequence—rated the greatest moment in the game's history in a 1980s *Rugby League Week* poll—came with 14 minutes remaining. A sweeping passing movement allowed 19-year-old Norths centre Keith Middleton to put Ron Roberts into space. The rangy St. George winger powered 25 yards through the sludge to score in the corner, and Australia grimly hung on for a euphoric 5-2 result.

STANDOUT PLAYER

Clive Churchill is rated by many as Australia's greatest player, and few seasons in the magnificent fullback's career can compare to 1950. As captain, the 23-year-old was superb in NSW's series victory and was the linchpin of Australia's joyous Ashes triumph. His influence was equally apparent in Souths' premiership success.

MEMORABLE MATCH

Great Britain's matches against the main state sides were memorable occasions. In front of a then-SCG record crowd of 70,419, the Lions prevailed 20-13 over NSW. But Queensland produced a 15-14 upset of the tourists at the 'Gabba. Halfback and captain Bill Thompson scored a brilliant 70-yard solo try, while the Maroons' pack featured Duncan Hall, Brian Davies and Harold 'Mick' Crocker.

1951

Clive Churchill's Ashes-winning Australian side was brought back to earth by the unforgettable maiden visit of the French touring team, 'Les Chanticleers.' Queensland ended more than a decade of NSW dominance with a stunning interstate series victory. Manly came of age by qualifying for the Grand Final in just the club's fifth season, but the Sea Eagles ran into a South Sydney juggernaut that subjected them to a devastating defeat in the decider. The marvellous J.J. Giltinan Shield was inaugurated in 1951, awarded to each season's premiers for the next 46 years, after which it became the coveted prize for the NRL's minor premiers.

THE PREMIERSHIP

Souths lost just one regular season match to finish 11 points clear of second-placed Manly—a record margin for a minor premiership. But the Rabbitohs were stunned by third-placed St. George to the tune of 36-8 in the semi-final, with Noel Pidding scoring 17 points for the victors. Manly, after eliminating Wests in the other semi, overwhelmed the Dragons 18-8 in the final. Souths regrouped for the Grand Final and savaged the green Sea Eagles 42-14. Winger Johnny Graves scored a Grand Final record four tries, while Bernie Purcell landing seven goals in the eight-try drubbing. Hapless North Sydney collected its third wooden spoon in four seasons.

- **Biggest win:** Manly 57 d. Parramatta 10 at Brookvale Oval, round 14
- **Top Point-scorer:** Ron Rowles (Manly) 220
- **Top Try-scorer:** Johnny Graves (South Sydney) 28

THE REPRESENTATIVE SCENE

Captained by Duncan Hall, Queensland won its first interstate series since 1940. The Maroons won the first encounter 29-18 in Sydney, before NSW squared the series 31-8 four days later. The decider was played in Brisbane, and a week after securing a 22-all draw against France, Queensland trumped the Blues 39-23. France and the enigmatic genius of skipper and fullback Puig-Aubert snatched a stirring series victory over Australia. The combatants won a Test each to force an SCG decider, where the tourists swept to a 35-14 boilover.

STANDOUT PLAYER

Johnny Graves' magnificent Grand Final haul took his season tally to 28—the equal-second highest in history to that point, which included three regular season hat-tricks. A fine goalkicker, the temperamental Graves also landed 31 goals for a total of 146 points. Graves scored two tries in City Firsts' 24-6 defeat of Country, represented NSW and scored a try in Australia's first Test loss to France, his only appearance of the series.

MEMORABLE MATCH

Australia was confident of victory in the decider against France after a 23-11 second Test result. But the contest was effectively over at halftime as 'Les Chanticleers' charged to a 20-4 advantage. Halfback Jo Crespo scored three tries and Puig-Aubert kicked seven goals in the 35-14 triumph, to give him 18 for the series from as many attempts.

1952

With the heyday of international Rugby League in full swing, 1952 brought a tour of Australia by the New Zealand Kiwis and a Kangaroo Tour of Britain and France—but little success for Clive Churchill's Australian side. NSW regained interstate supremacy with a series whitewash, while Wests' triumph in the Sydney premiership was overshadowed by a refereeing performance that has been shrouded in controversy and suspicion ever since.

THE PREMIERSHIP

Wests won the minor premiership—three points clear of St. George—but suffered an 18-10 upset at the hands of Souths in the semi-final. Fourth-placed Norths rolled the Dragons in the club's first finals appearance since the 1943 Grand Final, but succumbed to the Rabbitohs in the final. The Magpies claimed their last first grade title with a 22-12 win over Souths in a Grand Final tainted by the questionable refereeing of George Bishop. In a violent decider, rival forwards Hec Farrell (Wests) and Bryan Orrock (Souths) were sent off in the second half, while a crucial Magpies try from an obvious forward pass was at the forefront of Souths' sentiments of being cheated. Heavy betting on the match and rumours Bishop placed a £400 wager on Wests—combined with Bishop's immediate retirement after the match—have unfortunately clouded the Magpies' achievement in the annals of history.

- **Biggest win:** Balmain 59 d. Eastern Suburbs 8 at Leichhardt Oval, round 18
- **Top Point-scorer:** Ron Rowles (Manly) 178
- **Top Try-scorer:** Peter O'Brien (North Sydney) 20

THE REPRESENTATIVE SCENE

NSW won the interstate series 3-0, courtesy of a last-minute try to Noel Pidding for an 18-17 win in the first match, before prevailing by comfortable margins in the remaining clashes. Australia defeated New Zealand 25-13 in the first Test, but Travers Hardwick's Kiwis stunned the hosts by a record 49-25 scoreline in the second Test and won the decider 19-9. Consequently, Churchill's Kangaroos were labelled the worst touring team to leave Australia's shores. Great Britain regained the Ashes with victories in the first two Tests. The Kangaroos achieved a morale-boosting 27-7 result in the third Test, but lost the series against France 2-1.

STANDOUT PLAYER

Captain Clive Churchill's superlative performances were a welcome constant throughout Australia's disappointing international schedule. 'The Little Master' was duly recognised as Player of the Year in E.E. Christensen's *Official Rugby League Yearbook*.

MEMORABLE MATCH

Controversy aside, the 1952 Grand Final was a gripping encounter. Both sides were missing their Kangaroos stars, while Souths led 7-5 at halftime and 12-10 with 10 minutes remaining. But the Peter McLean-led Magpies rushed in four late tries (including Dev Dines' contentious three-pointer) to seize the premiership.

1953

The 1953 season witnessed the unique—if unsuccessful—tour of the American All-Stars, a team of US gridiron players and college athletes led by promoter and all-round sportsman Mike Dimitro. Winning just three of 18 games, the tour was described as a farce by critics—the most vocal of which was the always outspoken former Test prop Ray Stehr—but history has come to view the All-Stars as a colourful experiment and a welcome curiosity within Rugby League's historical narrative.

Australia embarked on a tour of New Zealand, but was foiled in its bid to restore the natural trans-Tasman pecking order. Souths' resounding triumph was the last in which a final decided the premiership—the minor premiers' 'right of challenge' system was replaced and mandatory Grand Finals introduced in 1954.

THE PREMIERSHIP

Easts' last-round victory over Norths lifted the Tricolours into the finals and cost the Shoremen the minor premiership, allowing Souths and St. George to slip into the top two spots. The Rabbitohs eliminated Norths 5-4 in a dour semi-final, while St. George despatched Easts 25-7. Brilliant winger Ian Moir scored a hat-trick in Souths' emphatic 31-12 victory over the Saints in the final, which saw rival forwards Martin Gallagher (Souths) and Billy Wilson (St. George) sent off for fighting.

- **Biggest win:** Manly 36 d. St. George 0 at Brookvale Oval, round eight
- **Top Point-scorer:** Ron Rowles (Manly) 152
- **Top Try-scorer:** Ian Moir (South Sydney) 23

THE REPRESENTATIVE SCENE

Country Firsts pipped City Firsts 28-27, propelling Country skipper Bob Bartlett to the NSW captaincy ahead of Clive Churchill. The Blues won the opening two interstate matches in Sydney, but the Ken McCaffery-led Queenslanders squared the series with two victories in Brisbane. Churchill captained Australia on a tour of New Zealand, but the hosts wrapped up the series with victories in opening two Tests, before a face-saving 18-16 Australian win in the third clash.

STANDOUT PLAYER

Gifted 20-year-old Brian Carlson—top try-scorer on the previous year's Kangaroo Tour with 29—again starred on the representative scene in 1953. He scored a try in Country's victory over City, represented NSW and toured New Zealand with the Australian side, playing two Tests and scoring an incredible nine tries in a 98-7 thrashing of Northland. Carlson also featured in Northern Suburbs' premiership victory in the Newcastle competition.

MEMORABLE MATCH

Norths' semi-final loss to Souths on a heavy SCG track was contentious. Leading 2-0 at halftime and 4-3 with four minutes remaining after two Allan Arkey penalty goals, Norths prop Cec Waters was penalised for taking too long to play the ball. Clive Churchill, who scored the only try of the match, piloted a superb goal through from near the sideline for a 5-4 victory.

1954

International competition took precedence again in 1954 with an Ashes series in Australia and the staging of the inaugural World Cup in France. But the Lions tour and Australia's Test series triumph was overshadowed by the disgraceful Great Britain v NSW tour match, a vicious and brawling encounter that was abandoned by referee Aub Oxford after 54 minutes (*see Bizarre Matches*). Souths again reigned supreme over Sydney, NSW swept the interstate series, while Australians Harry Bath and Brian Bevan featured for Warrington in the Challenge Cup Final replay against Halifax in front of a world record crowd of 102,569 at Odsal Stadium, Bradford.

THE PREMIERSHIP

Newtown lost just one regular season match to take out the minor premiership. The structure of the finals was changed, with the top two teams facing off in a semi for a spot in the Grand Final. The third- and fourth-placed teams played an elimination semi, with the winner advancing to the preliminary final. Second-placed Souths knocked off the Bluebags 24-14, while St. George eliminated Norths 15-14. Newtown rallied to defeat the Dragons 27-13 in the preliminary final (with winger Kevin Considine crossing for four tries), but Souths again proved too formidable in the inaugural mandatory Grand Final, prevailing 23-15. Newtown's wingers Ray Preston (34 tries, the second-highest total in history) and Considine (22 tries) scored a combined 54 tries in 1954, while Souths flankers Les Brennan (29 tries, a club record and the third-highest total of all time) and Ian Moir (21 tries) chalked up 50—the two highest totals by a wing pairing in premiership history.

- **Biggest win:** Manly 45 d. Canterbury 7 at Brookvale Oval, round 14
- **Top Point-scorer:** Ron Rowles (Manly) 221
- **Top Try-scorer:** Ray Preston (Newtown) 34

THE REPRESENTATIVE SCENE

Clive Churchill led NSW to a 4-0 interstate series whitewash over Queensland, which featured three narrow victories and a 46-7 thrashing in the third clash. Australia opened the Ashes series with an emphatic 37-12 victory, but Great Britain squared the ledger 38-21 in the second Test. Australia won the decider 20-16, and the captain and coach combination of Churchill and Vic Hey had again delivered an Ashes triumph. But Australia failed to make the final of the inaugural World Cup in France after losing two of its three preliminary matches. Great Britain defeated France in the tournament decider.

STANDOUT PLAYER

Manly prop Roy Bull was named Player of the Year in E.E. Christensen's *Official Rugby League Yearbook* for his outstanding contribution at club and representative level, providing the front-row muscle in Australia's Ashes success.

MEMORABLE MATCH

St. George led the semi-final against Norths 10-7 at halftime. Two penalties nudged Norths into the lead, but the Dragons held a four-point advantage after a converted try to winger Kevin Hole. New Zealand centre George Martin kicked ahead to score a try for Norths with less than two minutes on the clock, but Allan Arkey's missed conversion consigned the long-suffering club to a season-ending 15-14 loss.

1955

South Sydney produced a remarkable sudden-death run of victories—which subsequently became known as the 'Miracle of '55'—to claim its fifth premiership in six seasons. The interstate series was drawn, while France repeated the heroics of the tourists of four years earlier with a third successive series triumph over Australia. A controversial selection robbed Clive Churchill of a significant milestone—he was left stranded on 99 consecutive representative appearances when selectors opted to rest Churchill and halfback Keith Holman from the Sydney v France fixture.

THE PREMIERSHIP

The Rabbitohs sat just one win off the bottom of the table at the halfway mark of the competition, before winning their last eight regular season games to scrape into fourth spot. Souths eliminated Manly and St. George on the way to another Grand Final appearance against minor premiers Newtown. In a fitting climax, Rabbitohs halfback Col Donohoe scored a try in the closing minutes and Bernie Purcell landed the conversion to win the decider 12-11. It was a heartbreaking conclusion for the Dick Poole-led Newtown side—minor premiers in consecutive seasons with no title to show for their consistency.

- **Biggest win:** Manly 46 d. Western Suburbs 0 at the Sydney Cricket Ground, round three
- **Top Point-scorer:** Doug Fleming (St. George) 185
- **Top Try-scorer:** Brian Allsop (Eastern Suburbs) 18; Ian Moir (South Sydney) 18

THE REPRESENTATIVE SCENE

In a tit-for-tat four-match interstate series, NSW won the opening clash in Sydney before Queensland squared up four days later. The rival states won one match apiece in Brisbane for a 2-all series stalemate. Despite brilliant skipper Puig-Aubert's injury-enforced absence from the series, France came from a Test down to win the series 2-1 under the captaincy of outstanding centre Jacques Merquey.

STANDOUT PLAYER

St. George captain-coach Ken Kearney was named E.E. Christensen's Player of the Year after leading the Dragons to a second-place finish in the minor premiership and playing all three Tests against the touring French at hooker.

MEMORABLE MATCH

The most famous win of Souths' streak came in the penultimate round against Manly, when Clive Churchill played through the agony of a broken arm suffered during the first half to kick a sideline conversion on fulltime for a 9-7 triumph to keep the club's premiership dream alive (see Courageous Performances). The injury ruled Churchill out of the Rabbitohs' finals charge.

1956

St. George returned to the premiership dais, but few would have predicted the unprecedented period of domination the club's 18-12 Grand Final victory over Balmain began. Australia gained retribution for recent series losses to New Zealand with a whitewash of the touring Kiwis. The departure of the Kangaroos—led by Ken Kearney—brought fresh hope of a drought-breaking Ashes triumph on English soil. But another 2-1 series loss unfolded, while the tour signalled the end of the great Clive Churchill's Test career as he was usurped by Newtown fullback Gordon 'Punchy' Clifford.

THE PREMIERSHIP

The Saints finished one point ahead of Balmain at the top of the table ahead of a high-scoring finals series. Souths eliminated Wests 45-7, St. George advanced to the Grand Final with a 30-25 win over Balmain, and the Tigers booked a rematch with the Dragons by prevailing 36-33 in a preliminary final masterpiece against the Rabbitohs. St. George was forced to play all but 13 minutes of the Grand Final with 12 men after centre Merv Lees was forced off with a shoulder injury, but Ken Kearney's charges grinded out an 18-12 win.

- **Biggest win:** St. George d. Eastern Suburbs at Kogarah Oval, round six
- **Top Point-scorer:** Doug Fleming (St. George) 189
- **Top Try-scorer:** Tommy Ryan (St. George) 19

THE REPRESENTATIVE SCENE

NSW won a tight interstate series 3-1, with the margin in each match not exceeding eight points. Tom Baxter's Kiwis defeated both state sides, but were comprehensively outplayed in the 3-0 Test series loss. The Kangaroos forced a decider in the Ashes series before going down 19-0 in the third Test. A disappointing tour finished on a bright note as Australia ended five years of Test torment by sweeping France 3-0.

STANDOUT PLAYER

Determined halfback Keith Holman captained Wests to the finals and featured in eight of Australia's nine Tests in 1956, earning E.E. Christensen's Player of the Year accolade and the *Sun Herald* Best and Fairest for his consistent efforts. Holman became the first Australian to play Tests in seven consecutive years.

MEMORABLE MATCH

Balmain and Souths produced 13 tries in the preliminary final, which stood as the highest-scoring finals match of all time until 2003. Souths lock Les 'Chicka' Cowie crossed for four tries and Balmain centre Kevin Mosman notched a hat-trick, but the difference was nine goals from Tigers fullback Keith Barnes after the Rabbitohs scored seven tries to six.

1957

Australia hosted—and won—the World Cup for the first time in 1957. It was the highlight of a representative schedule that featured the worrying decline of Queensland, with NSW winning all four interstate clashes by big margins. Ken Kearney resumed as captain-coach of St. George (former Dragons player Norm Tipping coached the side to the title in 1956), and led his team to a successful and emphatic premiership defence.

THE PREMIERSHIP

The Saints won the minor premiership seven points clear of Manly and advanced to the decider with a 21-7 semi-final defeat of the Sea Eagles. Third-placed Souths eliminated Wests, but succumbed 15-11 to Manly in the preliminary final, bringing the marvellous career of five-time premiership-winning Rabbitohs captain-coach Jack Rayner to an end. Veteran forward Harry Bath, who returned from a celebrated tenure in English club football in 1957, kicked a Grand Final record eight goals in St. George's 31-9 thrashing of Manly.

- **Biggest win:** Western Suburbs 49 d. South Sydney 9 at Pratten Park, round one; South Sydney 50 d. Parramatta 10 at Redfern Oval, round seven
- **Top Point-scorer:** Darcy Russell (Western Suburbs) 169
- **Top Try-scorer:** Tommy Ryan (St. George) 26

THE REPRESENTATIVE SCENE

NSW's 4-0 series sweep included a record 69-5 demolition at the SCG, in which five-eighth Greg Hawick kicked 15 goals. The City v Country fixture had become increasingly one-sided; Ian Moir scored four tries and Keith Barnes kicked 10 goals as City Firsts prevailed 53-2. Captain-coached by Newtown centre Dick Poole, Australia won the World Cup without the need for a final after dominating New Zealand, Great Britain and France in the round-robin matches. Australia capped the successful campaign with a 20-11 defeat of a Rest of the World combination.

STANDOUT PLAYER

Norm Provan was adjudged Player of the Year in E.E. Christensen's *Official Rugby League Yearbook*; the respected journalist lauded his elevation to the top echelon of Australia's greatest second-rowers.[6] The 1956-57 Kangaroo tourist featured prominently in St. George's premiership victory and Australia's World Cup success.

MEMORABLE MATCH

South Sydney led the preliminary final 11-2, but veteran Test prop Roy Bull inspired a Manly fight-back. Bull scored two second half tries to snatch the lead with eight minutes remaining, and the Sea Eagles qualified for their second Grand Final courtesy of the 15-11 result.

1958

The St. George juggernaut collected its third premiership in succession, while another set of heroes in red and white—the touring Lions—left Australia's shores with the Ashes for the first time in 12 years after a brave series triumph. Clive Churchill's playing career in Sydney came to an abrupt end when Souths, for reasons unknown, halved the captain-coach's season bonus. 'The Little Master' departed to play in Brisbane in 1959.

THE PREMIERSHIP

The dominant Dragons finished the regular season eight points clear of second-placed Wests, but the big-spending Magpies stunned the champs with a 34-10 defeat in the semi-final. Forced to qualify for the Grand Final the hard way, St. George overcame Balmain (who scraped into the finals via a fourth-place play-off) 26-21 in the preliminary final. The Saints rectified the balance of power with a comprehensive 20-9 victory over Wests in the Grand Final. Norm Provan scored two tries, while Harry Bath—who set a premiership record for points in a season by a forward with 225—kicked four goals.

- **Biggest win:** Western Suburbs 52 d. North Sydney 4 at the Sydney Cricket Ground, round five
- **Top Point-scorer:** Harry Bath (St. George) 225
- **Top Try-scorer:** Eddie Lumsden (St. George) 18

THE REPRESENTATIVE SCENE

NSW achieved another comfortable series victory by winning all three interstate matches, while City Firsts swamped Country 55-14. Queensland forward Brian

6　Ian Heads and David Middleton, *A Centenary Of Rugby League*. Sydney, 2008

Davies captained Australia to a 25-8 first Test victory at the SCG, but Great Britain squared the series 25-18 as captain Alan Prescott famously battled on after breaking his arm in the first half *(see Courageous Performances)*. The momentum was with the tourists and Great Britain racked up a record 40-17 result in the decider back in Sydney.

STANDOUT PLAYER
Brian Carlson, who joined North Sydney from Wollongong the previous season, terrorised Country Firsts with four tries and five goals in City's big win. The attacking genius starred for NSW and scored a try in each of the first two Ashes Tests, while he top-scored for the Bears with 146 points (including a team-high 10 tries).

MEMORABLE MATCH
Great Britain led the deciding Ashes Test just 14-12 at halftime, but a dazzling second half display thrust the tourists to a 23-point victory. Prolific winger Mike Sullivan scored three tries and fullback Eric Fraser landed eight goals in the staggering 40-17 triumph.

1959

The St. George machine surged to an even higher plane of excellence with an unbeaten season in collecting a fourth straight title, while the club unveiled two players that would become regarded as the greatest Dragons—local junior Reg Gasnier and Newtown recruit Johnny Raper. The arrival of Clive Churchill inspired Queensland to its first interstate series victory in eight years, Australia toppled New Zealand and embarked on a memorable Kangaroo Tour, but the year was tinged with sadness. The pioneering legend Herbert Henry 'Dally' Messenger—Rugby League's first superstar—passed away in Gunnedah on November 24, aged 76.

THE PREMIERSHIP
Ken Kearney's Saints won 17 and drew one of their 18 regular season games, before brushing Wests aside 35-25 in the semi-final and completing a truly dominant season with a 20-0 shutout of Manly in the Grand Final. Raper played centre in the decider in the place of the injured Gasnier, while powerhouse winger Eddie Lumsden scored three tries. Harry Bath was sent off in the last match of a celebrated career, along with Manly's dual international front-rower Rex Mossop. St. George's 1959 model is the last team to have finished a season undefeated.
- **Biggest win:** St. George 61 d. Parramatta 4 at Cumberland Oval, round 12
- **Top Point-scorer:** Darcy Russell (Western Suburbs) 206
- **Top Try-scorer:** Ken Irvine (North Sydney) 19

THE REPRESENTATIVE SCENE
Injury prevented Churchill from turning out in the interstate series, but he coached Queensland to a memorable 2-1 series triumph over NSW. Australia wrapped up the home trans-Tasman Test series inside two matches, before the Kiwis pegged a win back in the third encounter. Balmain fullback Keith Barnes led the Kangaroos through Britain and France—an exciting squad featuring the burgeoning talents of Gasnier, Raper, Norths winger Ken Irvine and Queensland forward Noel Kelly—but

after a superb first Test victory, Australia narrowly lost the remaining two matches. The tourists swept the Test series in France 3-0.

STANDOUT PLAYER

Reg Gasnier's awe-inspiring rookie season earned him E.E. Christensen's Player of the Year honour. Although injury ruled him out of the Grand Final, the 20-year-old centre scored 13 tries for the Dragons and bagged three tries in Australia's emphatic second Test victory over New Zealand. He crossed for another hat-trick in his Ashes debut among 20 tries in 19 Kangaroo Tour appearances.

MEMORABLE MATCH

Western Suburbs built a 10-3 first half lead against Manly in the preliminary final. But the Sea Eagles' vaunted forward pack wore the Magpies down and Manly surged to an 11-10 advantage. Wests made one last lunge for a Grand Final berth when former Souths winger Ian Moir crossed for his second try with eight minutes remaining, but Manly hit back immediately via winger George Hugo's second try to secure a nail-biting 14-13 victory.

THE 1960s

The St. George machine powered on to set records for posterity, but the introduction of limited tackle football changed the face of Rugby League and coincided with South Sydney's emergence as the premiership's dominant force. Australia assumed Great Britain's mantle as the Rugby League world's preeminent power. Reg Gasnier, Johnny Raper, Ken Irvine, Ian Walsh and Noel Kelly fulfilled the promise they showed at the end of the 1950s to become all time greats of the game, while the premiership was inundated with an unprecedented volume of young superstars, including Graeme Langlands, Les Johns, Ron Coote, Bob Fulton, Arthur Beetson, Bob McCarthy and Ken Thornett.

1960

The season after Dally Messenger passed away, Australian Rugby League lost another of its most influential figures. Australian Board of Control Chairman and NSWRL President Harry 'Jersey' Flegg died at the age of 82, ending the 31-year reign of the pioneering Easts forward. Flegg was replaced by another unbending old-stager, former Newtown hooker and veteran administrator Bill Buckley. The controversial residential rule was mercifully ditched, and a transfer fee system was introduced—which caused just as much consternation as the previous regime. France made another characteristically enigmatic tour Down Under, while Australia was unable to defend its World Cup crown. St. George was as dominant as at any stage of its 11-season premiership streak.

THE PREMIERSHIP

St. George won the minor premiership six points clear of four clubs tied for second place, forcing an elaborate play-off system to decide finals spots. The Dragons advanced to the Grand Final with a 31-7 defeat of Wests, while Easts toppled the Magpies to qualify for the decider. But the Tricolours—captained by future coaching great Jack Gibson—were exposed by the relentless Saints, who powered to a 31-6 triumph and a fifth straight title.

- **Biggest win:** St. George 52 d. Parramatta 0 at the Sydney Cricket Ground, round one
- **Top Point-scorer:** Brian Graham (St. George) 193
- **Top Try-scorer:** Reg Gasnier (St. George) 25

THE REPRESENTATIVE SCENE

Led by five-eighth Bob Banks, Queensland drew the interstate series with NSW 2-all. Australia and France drew the first Test 8-all, before the Keith Barnes-captained hosts amassed a record 56-6 scoreline in the second encounter. But the inscrutable 'Les Chanticleers' staged an incredible turnaround to win the third Test and draw the series. Australia's World Cup defence came undone courtesy of a 10-3 loss in the final round-robin match against hosts Great Britain.

STANDOUT PLAYER

Johnny Raper was named Player of the Year in E.E. Christensen's *Official Rugby League Yearbook* for his stellar performances during 1960. The 21-year-old lock represented NSW, featured prominently in Australia's international schedule and starred in St. George's premiership success.

MEMORABLE MATCH

St. George's 23-match unbeaten streak—stretching back to the 1958 finals series—was halted by Manly in round two of the 1960 season. Winger George Hugo crossed for a hat-trick in the Sea Eagles' emphatic six-tries-to-two, 22-10 victory at the SCG.

1961

Australian Rugby League made its first tentative, clumsy steps into the medium of television, broadcasting games on a weekly basis from 1961. The quality of the coverage rapidly improved in the ensuing seasons, with colourful callers such as former dual international forward Rex Mossop leading the way. St. George set a new premiership record with its sixth consecutive premiership, while Australia's nine-match tour of New Zealand was the sum total of a low-key international schedule.

THE PREMIERSHIP

Despite a knee injury that ended Ken Kearney's career (he remained till the end of the season as coach), St. George powered to another title—but Wests pipped the all-conquering Dragons for the minor premiership on for-and-against. Wests—dubbed the 'Millionaires'—had recruited far and wide, boasting a team containing Queensland Test forwards Noel Kelly and Kel O'Shea, former Wallaby half Arthur Summons, and Illawarra pair Harry Wells and Peter Dimond. But the big-match hardened Saints beat the Magpies 9-4 in the semi-final and 22-0 in the Grand Final. Veteran enforcer Billy Wilson captained St. George in Kearney's absence, while winger Eddie Lumsden scored three tries in the shutout, which marked the end of the career of the magnificent Wests and Australian halfback Keith Holman. Parramatta collected its sixth wooden spoon in succession, but astute recruitment ensured a ground-breaking season was just around the corner.

- **Biggest win:** St. George 65 d. Newtown 9 at Kogarah Oval, round 15
- **Top Point-scorer:** Bob Landers (Eastern Suburbs) 164
- **Top Try-scorer:** Johnny King (St. George) 20

THE REPRESENTATIVE SCENE

Country Firsts, captained by Tony Paskins, broke an eight-year drought by defeating the Brian Carlson-led City Firsts line-up 19-5. Halfback Barry Muir skippered Queensland to a 2-all interstate series draw, fighting back after NSW won the opening two matches. Carlson captained the Australian squad to New Zealand and in the 12-10 first Test loss, before Muir led the tourists to a 10-8 victory in the second and final Test with Carlson sidelined.

STANDOUT PLAYER

Tenacious Brisbane Wests halfback Barry Muir inspired Queensland throughout a superb interstate campaign as captain, while his performances since succeeding Keith Holman as Australia's Test halfback in 1959 saw him chosen as vice-captain for the tour of New Zealand. Muir's leadership was vital to Australia's series-levelling second Test victory in Auckland.

MEMORABLE MATCH

A spectacular individual try to Wests second-rower Kel O'Shea and a three-pointer to Balmain centre Gil MacDougall (who joined Wests the following season) set up a 5-3 scoreline in favour of the Magpies at halftime of the gripping preliminary final. A penalty goal to each side advanced the score to 7-5, and Balmain was awarded a penalty in the dying minutes. But captain Keith Barnes—one of the great goalkickers —was unable to convert the opportunity and the Tigers dipped out of the title race.

1962

The arrival of the Lions was the centrepiece of the 1962 season, an event-packed tour led by veteran centre Eric Ashton. Six players were sent off in a wild match against New South Wales; Great Britain crushed the mighty St. George side 33-5; and young fullback Les Johns inspired Newcastle to a 23-18 upset of the tourists. But when the dust settled, Great Britain again departed with the Ashes. Despite the demoralising defeat to the Lions and the departure of captain-coach Ken Kearney, the Saints marched on to a seventh successive title with Norm Provan at the helm and a new star in the shape of Kangaroos hooker Ian Walsh, who linked with the club from country NSW.

THE PREMIERSHIP

The Dragons regained the minor premiership, one point ahead of Newtown. Reg Gasnier scored three tries in St. George's 30-9 semi-final thumping of the Bluebags, while Wests defeated Newtown in the preliminary final to set up a rematch of the previous season's decider. The Saints prevailed 9-6 in a desperately close Grand Final. Parramatta qualified for its maiden finals series in the club's 16th season. Kearney had come on board as coach, while Ken Thornett returned to Australia from England (Leeds had lured Thornett from rugby union) and became known as 'The Mayor of Parramatta.' Thornett was absent with injury from the Eels' finals debut, a 6-0 loss to Wests.

- **Biggest win:** Manly 38 d. North Sydney 12 at Brookvale Oval, round seven
- **Top Point-scorer:** Don Parish (Western Suburbs) 123
- **Top Try-scorer:** Eddie Lumsden (St. George) 21

THE REPRESENTATIVE SCENE

The 1962 series marked the start of a grim period for Queensland in interstate competition; NSW won the four-match series 3-0 after the final match was drawn. Young Wollongong fullback Graeme Langlands starred in Country's 18-8 upset of City, a precursor to his move to St. George in 1963. Great Britain wrapped up the Ashes series with victories in the first two Tests, before Australia snatched a famous late win in the third clash. Australia used three different captains during the series—Reg Gasnier (Australia's youngest-ever Ashes captain), Keith Barnes and Arthurs Summons.

STANDOUT PLAYER

Arthur Summons was E.E. Christensen's pick as Player of the Year and he also won the *Sun Herald* Best and Fairest. A brilliant tactician, half/five-eighth Summons led Wests to the Grand Final and was superb during the Ashes series, leading to his elevation to captain for the third Test victory.

MEMORABLE MATCH

Great Britain winger Mike Sullivan, and opposing forwards Derek Turner and Dud Beattie were sent from the field during the third Test. Despite the one-man disadvantage, the tourists led 17-11 late in the game. But Australian winger Ken Irvine kicked a penalty and scored a try in the dying moments. Irvine landed the sideline conversion after famously taking advice from referee Darcy Lawler regarding the positioning of the ball to steal an 18-17 result.

1963

A muddy, controversial SCG Grand Final epic produced a photograph that went on to become the symbol of Rugby League supremacy—John O'Gready's shot of rival captains Norm Provan and Arthur Summons was dubbed 'The Gladiators' and has been the basis for every premiership trophy since 1982. South Africa made a ground-breaking tour of Australia, while the Kiwis also visited and the Kangaroos set off for Britain and France during a jam-packed season.

THE PREMIERSHIP

Minor premiers St. George faced the sternest test of its 11-year reign; second-placed Wests was responsible for the Dragons' only two regular season defeats and advanced to the decider with a 10-8 semi-final victory over the Saints. Parramatta eliminated Balmain 9-7 but could not overcome the Dragons, who won the preliminary final 12-7. St. George prevailed 8-3 on an SCG quagmire in a Grand Final tainted by the controversial decisions of referee Darcy Lawler that went against Wests. Rumours have persisted that Lawler had placed a wager on the Dragons—exacerbated by the referee's immediate retirement—but Norm Provan's charges had nevertheless secured their eighth title in a row. St. George won premierships in all three grades in 1963, the fourth and last club to achieve the feat.

- **Biggest win:** St. George 51 d. Parramatta 2 at the Sydney Cricket Ground, round one
- **Top Point-scorer:** Fred Griffiths (North Sydney) 136
- **Top Try-scorer:** Reg Gasnier (St. George) 24

THE REPRESENTATIVE SCENE

NSW decimated Queensland 4-0 in a series intersected by Australia's Test campaigns against New Zealand and South Africa, won 2-1 and 2-0 respectively. Arthur Summons was chosen as captain-coach of the Kangaroos but injury kept him out of the Ashes series. The honour of leading Australia to its first series victory on English soil since 1911-12 went to Saints hooker Ian Walsh; the Kangaroos secured the Ashes with a 28-2 victory in the first Test and a record 50-12 triumph in the second encounter, which became known as the 'Swinton Massacre.' Summons returned to lead Australia to a 2-1 series defeat of France.

STANDOUT PLAYER

Johnny Raper's display in the Swinton Test ranks as one of the great individual displays in the game's history, featuring in nine of Australia's 12 tries. The virtuoso lock was typically superb in St. George's premiership campaign (winning the *Sun Herald* Best and Fairest gong) and played in 10 of Australia's 11 Tests during 1963.

MEMORABLE MATCH

Parramatta trailed Balmain 7-4 as the elimination semi-final moved into the final quarter. But a freakish try secured the club's maiden finals victory and a preliminary final berth—a 40-metre penalty goal attempt by Eels halfback Bob Bugden hit the goalpost and captain Ron Lynch charged through to catch the ball and score the match-winning try.

1964

The sad news that legendary administrator Harry Sunderland had died in Manchester at the age of 74 came in January. Such an important figure in the rise of Rugby League in Queensland and France, a Kangaroo Tour manager and an influential manager at Wigan after leaving Australian shores, the charismatic Sunderland's memory was honoured by the striking of a medal for the best Australian player in a Test series and a trophy for man of the match in England's premiership final (later the Super League Grand Final)—both of which are still awarded almost five decades later. The continued drain of Queensland's players to the Sydney clubs enriched by poker machine profits ensured the Maroons' interstate series misery continued, but Australia finally broke its home series duck against a woeful French touring side. St. George extended its premiership streak to nine seasons, while in Brisbane, Northern Suburbs collected its sixth straight title under legendary coaching figure Bob Bax.

THE PREMIERSHIP

Another season, another St. George minor premiership. Wests' slide out of finals contention left the Dragons without any genuine threats to their supremacy, robbing the 1964 competition of its zeal. Graeme Langlands scored a then-finals record 27 points in the Saints 42-0 semi-final demolition of Parramatta. Keith Barnes' young Balmain side showed plenty of fight in the Grand Final, but St. George grinded out an 11-6 win. North Sydney, captain-coached by South African import Fred Griffiths, qualified for the finals after a decade-long absence, but succumbed to the Tigers 11-9.

- **Biggest win:** North Sydney 49 d. Eastern Suburbs 10 at the Sydney Sports Ground, round 17
- **Top Point-scorer:** Fred Griffiths (North Sydney) 160
- **Top Try-scorer:** Reg Gasnier (St. George) 18

THE REPRESENTATIVE SCENE

The Johnny Raper-led NSW side won all four interstate matches comfortably against Barry Muir's Queenslanders, with Ken Irvine crossing for seven tries in the series. France was badly outclassed, crashing to a 3-0 series loss against Australia—20-6, 27-2 and 35-9.

STANDOUT PLAYER

Reg Gasnier topped the premiership's tryscoring table for the third time in five years for the St. George juggernaut, and captained Australia in the series whitewash of France, scoring a hat-trick in the second Test thrashing. The centre nonpareil was named joint Player of the Year in E.E. Christensen's *Official Rugby League Yearbook* with Saints teammate Johnny Raper.

MEMORABLE MATCH

Norths' first finals appearance since 1954 ended in heartbreak against the Tigers. Trailing 11-9, skipper Fred Griffiths lined up a long-range penalty goal after the fulltime siren. But the season's top point-scorer's attempt to send the match into extra-time fell agonisingly short and the Bears were eliminated.

1965

St. George racked up a perfect 10 sequence of premierships in 1965, but the rise of an exciting young South Sydney outfit electrified the Rugby League public and set the scene for a record-breaking day at the Sydney Cricket Ground. Australia embarked on an eight-match tour of New Zealand—taking a squad containing just three Queenslanders after the Maroons were given another 4-0 bath by NSW in the interstate series.

THE PREMIERSHIP

The Dragons finished six points clear of second-placed Norths in the minor premiership, while the hopeful Bears were spanked 47-7 by the merciless Saints in the semi-final. Fourth-placed Souths eliminated Ken Thornett's Parramatta side 17-2 and Norths 14-9 on the way to a Grand Final showdown with St. George. An official record SCG crowd figure of 78,056 was given for the decider, but many more thousands crammed into the ground and lined the grandstand roofs as unprecedented demand outstripped the hallowed venue's capacity. The Saints held off the plucky Rabbitohs 12-8 in a enthralling climax to the season—a fitting exit from the game for second-row legend Norm Provan, who featured in all 10 of the club's streak of Grand Finals and captain-coached the 1962-65 sides. Captained by Test pivot Jim Lisle, Souths possessed budding greats Ron Coote, John Sattler, John O'Neill and Bob McCarthy, who formed the nucleus of the side that eventually halted mighty St. George's run.

- **Biggest win:** St. George 41 d. Balmain 0 at the Sydney Cricket Ground, round 16
- **Top Point-scorer:** Fred Griffiths (North Sydney) 181
- **Top Try-scorer:** Johnny King (St. George) 15

THE REPRESENTATIVE SCENE

Queensland were well and truly mired in the slump that eventually gave rise to State of Origin football, conceding 105 points and scoring just 35 in four losses to the powerful NSW line-up that contained several Queensland-bred stars. Ian Walsh led Australia on the tour across the Tasman; the visitors won the first Test 13-8, but New Zealand levelled the two-Test series with a 7-5 upset in the second clash.

STANDOUT PLAYER

Superlative fullback Ken Thornett captain-coached Parramatta to the finals in 1965 and was honoured by E.E. Christensen as NSW's Player of the Year, despite playing no part in the representative schedule. Thornett's outstanding performances at club level also garnered the *Sun Herald* Best and Fairest award.

MEMORABLE MATCH

Billy Smith, playing in the centres but later one of Australia's finest halfbacks, scored the only try in the first half of the Grand Final. But the long-range penalty kicking of fullback Kevin Longbottom kept Souths in the contest. Saints held a tenuous 9-6 lead with 13 minutes remaining when winger Johnny King blazed over in the corner, stretching his incredible streak of scoring at least one try in the Grand Final to six successive seasons. Another penalty, to Rabbitohs winger Eric Simms, finished the scoring at 12-8.

1966

The Lions tour was packed with the requisite drama and excitement, while Australia clinched its first ever successful Ashes defence. A gripping series swung on the first half performance of a debutant second-rower named Arthur Beetson. The 21-year-old Indigenous Queenslander had arrived at Balmain at the start of the season via Roma and Redcliffe, starring as the Tigers again established themselves as the strongest contender to end St. George's dominance. But Norm Provan's retirement and a season-ending knee injury to champion centre Reg Gasnier did little to slow the Saints' momentum—hooker Ian Walsh carried on the great tradition of club captain-coaches to lead the Dragons to the last of 11 straight titles. Manly made its first finals appearance in five years, sparked by rookie teenage five-eighth Bob Fulton, while Easts became the last club to produce a winless season.

THE PREMIERSHIP

St. George finished three points clear of Balmain at the top of the table and duly defeated the Tigers 10-2 in the semi-final. Balmain booked a Grand Final rematch with an 8-5 preliminary final victory over the Sea Eagles, who were captained by Queensland Test forward Ken Day. But the Dragons employed their customary ruthlessness in the decider to keep the Tigers try-less, surging to a 23-4 result on the back of a seven-goal haul by Graeme Langlands.

- **Biggest win:** Manly 53 d. Eastern Suburbs 0 at the Sydney Sports Ground, round 14
- **Top Point-scorer:** Bob Lanigan (Newtown) 185
- **Top Try-scorer:** Ken Irvine (North Sydney) 13

THE REPRESENTATIVE SCENE

Queensland's 4-0 interstate series loss was reflected in the apathy of supporters, with crowd numbers for the clashes dwindling in Sydney and Brisbane. Great Britain won the first Test 17-13, before Keith Barnes kicked Australia to victory 6-4 in a try-less second Test. Two pieces of Beetson magic set up an 8-2 halftime lead for Australia, and although the youngster went off injured at halftime (spawning the derogatory nickname 'Half-a-game Artie'), the green-and-golds secured the coveted Ashes trophy 19-14.

STANDOUT PLAYER

Test halfback Billy Smith belatedly assumed the No.7 at club level from George Evans (Smith played in the centres in the Dragons' 1963-65 Grand Finals). He was outstanding in the Saints' premiership victory and won the Harry Sunderland Medal as the best player in Australia's Ashes triumph. Smith also collected the *Sun Herald* Best and Fairest and E.E. Christensen's NSW Player of the Year honours.

MEMORABLE MATCH

A bumper crowd of 55,934 piled in for the introduction of Sunday football at the SCG. In a top of the table clash, Keith Barnes' five goals outstripped British forward Dick Huddart's solitary try in Balmain's 10-3 defeat of St. George.

1967

The 1967 season was a watershed year for Rugby League. The game changed forever as the unlimited tackle era came to an end and the four-tackle rule was introduced. Sydney had new premiers for the first time since 1956 as St. George was finally toppled from the premiership pedestal it had occupied for 11 seasons. Cronulla and Penrith joined the premiership, expanding the NSWRL competition to 12 teams. The international schedule featured Australia's series whitewash of the Kiwis, and a successful Kangaroo Tour that was ultimately viewed with mixed sentiments after widespread reports of off-field player misbehaviour and a career-ending injury suffered by one of the game's greats.

THE PREMIERSHIP

The competition was extended to 22 regular season rounds. Under the tutelage of rugged former first grade prop Jack Gibson, Easts recovered from its winless 1966 campaign to qualify for the finals in one of the premiership's greatest-ever turnarounds. St. George claimed the minor premiership for the 11th time in 12 seasons, but was subdued by the Rabbitohs 13-8 in the semi-final. Canterbury, in the club's first finals series in seven years, ended the Dragons' world record run 12-11 in a dramatic preliminary final. Souths won an equally gripping Grand Final 12-10 over Kevin Ryan's Berries, with a long-range intercept try to Rabbitohs second-rower Bob McCarthy the game-turning play. Firebrand prop John Sattler had been the surprise choice to skipper Souths at the start of the season, while the premiership victory was a triumph for club legend Clive Churchill, who returned in 1967 as coach.

- **Biggest win:** South Sydney 39 d. Penrith 0 at Penrith Park, round nine
- **Top Point-scorer:** Eric Simms (South Sydney) 233
- **Top Try-scorer:** Les Hanigan (Manly) 16

THE REPRESENTATIVE SCENE

Test pivot John Gleeson led Queensland in a vastly improved interstate series performance; after losing the two Sydney matches, the Maroons secured a draw and a narrow win in Brisbane. Reg Gasnier captain-coached Australia to a 3-0 home series defeat of New Zealand and led the Kangaroos to Britain. The omission of Bob McCarthy, Bob Fulton and Arthur Beetson caused controversy before the squad departed, and player misbehaviour—most notably the infamous 'Man in the Bowler Hat' incident—provided an unsavoury backdrop to Australia's Ashes series victory (see Kangaroos, Lions and the Ashes). The Kangaroos lost Gasnier to injury in the first Test loss, but Queensland prop Peter Gallagher and Saints lock Johnny Raper skippered Australia to wins in the subsequent Tests. Gasnier's incomparable career ended in a manner unbefitting of a player of his stature, limping off with a recurrence of a knee injury in his comeback match in a low-key tour game in France.

STANDOUT PLAYER

Brilliant golden-haired fullback Les Johns starred in Canterbury's historic 1967 campaign and played all six Tests on the Kangaroo Tour, forcing Graeme Langlands to centre. He was named E.E. Christensen's Player of the Year.

MEMORABLE MATCH

Competition newcomers Penrith scored a king-sized upset to christen its new home ground, Penrith Park. The Panthers overwhelmed 11-time premiers St. George 24-12 in round four, scoring four tries to two in euphoric victory that proved to be a false dawn for the long-suffering club.

1968

St. George's era of dominance had been quelled, and South Sydney set about building its own dynasty. The four-tackle rule continued to provoke vigorous debate—some campaigned for the return of unlimited tackles, while others more sagely suggested extending it to six tackles. But the changes appeared to have the blessing of the fans, who set a new season attendance record in 1968. The World Cup made a return after eight years on ice, with Australia hosting—and dominating—the tournament. The tobacco company-sponsored Rothmans Medal, voted on by the game's referees, became the premiership's official player of the year award; Cronulla halfback Terry Hughes was the surprise inaugural winner, edging out Saints lock Johnny Raper for the award. The premiership farewelled two of its greatest-ever fullbacks—Balmain's Keith Barnes and Parramatta's Ken Thornett.

THE PREMIERSHIP

The Rabbitohs won its first minor premiership in 15 years, with Manly hot on their heels in second spot. The Sea Eagles booked the first Grand Final berth courtesy of a 23-15 semi-final upset of the Souths. The Saints remained competitive—despite the retirement of Reg Gasnier and Ian Walsh—and Raper led them to the preliminary final, where their season was extinguished 20-8 by Souths. The decider finished one try apiece, but five goals to Souths fullback Eric Simms proved the difference in the 13-9 triumph over the Sea Eagles, who were captained by 20-year-old Bob Fulton.

- **Biggest win:** Parramatta 48 d. Canterbury 9 at Cumberland Oval, round 17
- **Top Point-scorer:** Eric Simms (South Sydney) 212
- **Top Try-scorer:** Stan Gorton (St. George) 22

THE REPRESENTATIVE SCENE

Queensland's 15-8 victory in the second interstate clash was bookended by heavy defeats as NSW won the three-match series 2-1. Coached by Harry Bath and captained by Johnny Raper, Australia swept aside Great Britain, New Zealand and France in the preliminary rounds of the World Cup, before thumping France 20-2 in the final.

STANDOUT PLAYER

Indigenous sharpshooter Eric Simms displayed the form that would see him become—if only for a few years—the most prolific point-scorer in premiership history. Topping the 200-point mark for the second straight season with Souths, Simms made his only interstate appearance for NSW (scoring 14 points) and was the leading point-scorer at the World Cup with 50 in four matches.

MEMORABLE MATCH

Parramatta racked up a stunning 48-9 victory over the previous season's grand finalists Canterbury in round 17. Former Test forward Dick Thornett scored four tries, while future Manly stalwart Peter Peters kicked nine goals.

1969

South Sydney's bid for three straight premierships was thwarted by arguably the greatest Grand Final upset of all time, as Balmain employed contentious but savvy 'go-slow' tactics to throw the Rabbitohs' momentum. A proposed 'World Championship' tournament was scrapped and Australia's international schedule consisted of a disappointing tour of New Zealand. After hints of a Queensland revival in the previous two series, NSW crushed the Maroons four games to nil. Australia's greatest lock forward, the irrepressible Saint Johnny Raper, retired at the end of the season.

THE PREMIERSHIP

Minor premiers Souths advanced to the Grand Final with a 14-13 eclipse of second-placed Balmain. Raper's magnificent career ended in St. George's semi-final loss to Manly, but the Sea Eagles were sunk by a last-minute try to Tigers winger George Ruebner in the preliminary final. Peter Provan, a premiership-winner with the Saints, emulated the feat of his illustrious brother Norm by captaining Balmain to a stunning 11-2 defeat of Souths in the decider, while former Tigers winger Leo Nosworthy had achieved a remarkable premiership victory in his maiden season as a first grade coach.

- **Biggest win:** South Sydney 43 d. Cronulla 4 at Redfern Oval, round three
- **Top Point-scorer:** Eric Simms (South Sydney) 265
- **Top Try-scorer:** Ken Irvine (North Sydney) 17

THE REPRESENTATIVE SCENE

NSW outscored Queensland 113 points to 42 in the four-match interstate series whitewash. Newcastle winger Father John Cootes scored a memorable try in Country Firsts' spirited 26-20 loss to City Firsts, and subsequently became the first priest to represent NSW and Australia later in the season. Australia's hectic six-match tour of New Zealand was crammed into 13 days. John Sattler led the side in a 1-all Test series draw against the Kiwis, while the tourists were also upset by Auckland 15-14.

STANDOUT PLAYER

Ron Coote was named E.E. Christensen's NSW Player of the Year in the *Official Rugby League Yearbook* for his outstanding performances for Souths, City, NSW and Australia. He finally took ownership of the Australian lock jersey, after playing the majority of his Test career to that point in the second-row to accommodate Johnny Raper.

MEMORABLE MATCH

The lead changed hands six times in the second half of an extraordinary semi-final between Souths and Balmain. The Tigers trailed 7-2 at halftime, but South African fullback Len Killeen kicked them to an 8-7 advantage. Wingers Paul Cross (Balmain) and Michael Cleary (Souths) traded tries for the Rabbitohs to hold a tenuous 12-11 lead, before Killeen landed his fifth goal with four minutes remaining to nudge the Tigers in front. But Eric Simms—who broke Dave Brown's 34-year-old premiership record with 265 points in 1969—slotted a 45-yard penalty goal inside the two-minute mark to snatch a dramatic 14-13 win.

THE 1970s

South Sydney's last golden era progressed into the early part of the decade, before the club was pitched into a harrowing battle for financial survival. Manly finally won its maiden premiership and claimed three more before the 1970s were out, bookending a magical two-season reign by the Jack Gibson-coached Eastern Suburbs outfit. Parramatta fell agonisingly short of a breakthrough title, but St. George surged at the back end of the decade to add two more premierships to the club's tally. But for a couple of aberrations, Australia thoroughly dominated international Rugby League competition, which was in a worrying state of decline in Great Britain, New Zealand and France. Stars of the 1960s including Bob Fulton, Arthur Beetson, Graeme Langlands and Ron Coote extended their excellence into the 1970s, while the emergence of the likes of Steve Rogers, Mick Cronin, Graham Eadie and Ray Price ensured Australia stayed ahead of the game as Rugby League hurtled toward the professional era.

1970

The decade began with a season marked by brutal matches and blatant thuggery at club and international level. Great Britain regained the Ashes in an upset during the Lions tour, before Australia gained revenge with a World Cup triumph on English soil in a violent final. Balmain forward Dennis Tutty's challenge resulted in the Supreme Court ruling aspects of the NSWRL's transfer system invalid and a restraint of trade. A martyr for his cause, Tutty sat out the 1969-70 seasons and endured financial and personal ruin after the Tigers blocked him from joining another club—despite his contract having expired. Tutty represented Australia in 1967, but his lasting legacy is as a man of principle that singlehandedly made a significant advancement for player rights. Norths captain Ken Irvine was accused of sensationally leading a walk-off in his side's match against Canterbury in protest of Keith Page's refereeing *(see Bizarre Matches)*. Queen Elizabeth II was in attendance for the round six Grand Final rematch between Souths and Balmain at the SCG on the Queen's Birthday weekend, won 14-5 by the Rabbitohs. But the lasting impression of the 1970 season is of a courageous captain in myrtle and green that led his team to Grand Final glory—the 'broken jaw hero' John Sattler.

THE PREMIERSHIP
Souths won a third straight minor premiership and defeated second-placed Manly 22-15 in the semi-final to progress to the decider. Manly overcame St. George 15-6 in the preliminary final to secure a rematch with the Rabbitohs. Sea Eagles forward John Bucknall savagely smashed Sattler's jaw in the early minutes of the Grand Final, but the skipper played out the match under extreme duress in Australian sport's most famous act of courage. The Rabbitohs forwards doled out their retribution to Bucknall, while the minor premiers converted a 12-6 halftime lead to a 23-12 triumph over the John McDonald-led Sea Eagles. Eric Simms kicked a Grand Final record four field goals in the victory.

- **Biggest win:** Manly 44 d. Balmain 10 at Brookvale Oval, round one
- **Top Point-scorer:** Eric Simms (South Sydney) 244
- **Top Try-scorer:** Ken Irvine (North Sydney) 16

THE REPRESENTATIVE SCENE
After a 16-15 upset result in the opening match, Queensland slumped to a 3-1 loss to NSW in the interstate series. Sparked by brilliant young stars Roger Millward and Malcolm Reilly, the Lions came from a Test down to win back the Ashes 2-1. In another famous, spiteful instalment of Anglo-Australian rivalry, Australia and Great Britain met in a violent World Cup final at Leeds, where the Ron Coote-led Australian side soaked up an astonishing amount of punishment to prevail 12-7.

STANDOUT PLAYER
In his first season as club captain, Graeme Langlands guided St. George to a preliminary final appearance, and won the *Sun Herald* Best and Fairest and E.E. Christensen's Player of the Year honours. Langlands captained Australia in the 37-15 first Test victory, but injury forced him out of the remainder of the series.

MEMORABLE MATCH
Easts and St. George produced one of the great regular season matches on the Labour Day holiday—a 14-try classic won 37-23 by the Roosters. Breathtaking attack was the order of the day as the Dragons led 16-12 at halftime, before being overrun by Easts and a hat-trick from powerhouse winger Bill Mullins.

1971

The six-tackle rule was introduced in Australia (a rule that was not adopted internationally until 1975), while the overreliance on the field goal as a scoring option saw its value halved to one point. The South Sydney dynasty claimed its fourth premiership in five seasons, unknowing that it would herald the beginning of a drought for Australian Rugby League's most successful club that would extend four decades and counting. The presence of British players in Sydney stepped up a gear after Manly handed over an exorbitant $30,000 transfer fee to Castleford for the services of lock Malcolm Reilly. In the quietest season of international football since World War II, New Zealand shocked Australia in the one-off Test in Auckland.

THE PREMIERSHIP

Manly broke Souths' stranglehold on the minor premiership by losing just three regular season games, but fell to Souths 19-13 in the semi-final and 15-12 to St. George in the preliminary final. The Saints, coached by Jack Gibson, were gallant in their 16-10 Grand Final loss to the Rabbitohs. Souths led by the unprecedented score of 1-0 at halftime courtesy of an Eric Simms field goal, before extending out to 11-0 during the second half. But a Dragons fight-back reduced the deficit to just one point and the result was not sealed until a Bob McCarthy try inside the final 10 minutes.

- **Biggest win:** Western Suburbs 55 d. Canterbury 12 at Lidcombe Oval, round one; Manly 48 d. North Sydney 5 at Brookvale Oval, round 16
- **Top Point-scorer:** Graeme Langlands (St. George) 196
- **Top Try-scorer:** Paul Cross (Balmain) 18

THE REPRESENTATIVE SCENE

Another series cleansweep to NSW exacerbated the decline of interstate competition, reflected by dismal crowd numbers in Sydney. Roy Christian's New Zealand side stunned the Rugby League world with 24-3 dismantling of a star-studded Australian line-up at Carlaw Park—the Kiwis' last trans-Tasman victory for 12 years.

STANDOUT PLAYER

Despite the disappointment of Grand Final and Test defeats as captain, Graeme Langlands was again outstanding in 1971. He topped the premiership with 196 points and was named Player of the Year by E.E. Christensen.

MEMORABLE MATCH

Langlands and halfback Billy Smith spearheaded St. George's 15-12 upset of Manly in the preliminary final. Trailing 7-4 at halftime, Smith laid on two tries for Langlands to lift the Dragons to the lead. Langlands added three goals in the match for a 12-point haul, while Smith kicked three field goals.

1972

Manly's premiership quest was finally realised in the club's 26th season as the aggressive recruitment drive that brought British lock Malcolm Reilly, North Sydney legend Ken Irvine, and Souths pair John O'Neill and Ray Branighan to the club bore fruit. The Rabbitohs' gradual deterioration was expedited by Ron Coote's departure to Easts, while captain John Sattler left for Queensland at the end of the year. Premiership crowds continued to decline in an apparent reaction to the contentious six-tackle rule. Australia gained revenge over New Zealand with a comprehensive 2-0 series victory on home soil, but the France-hosted World Cup ended in a controversial victory to Great Britain after a dramatic drawn final. An Australian Schoolboys side embarked on a trailblazing tour of England, decimating all opponents in 12 matches and beginning a fine tradition. The squad was coached by Roy Masters—later a first grade coach with Wests and St. George—and contained future internationals Royce Ayliffe, Les Boyd, Ian Schubert and Craig Young.

THE PREMIERSHIP

Manly finished the minor premiership one win clear of Eastern Suburbs and thumped the Roosters 32-8 to advance to the Grand Final. The Ron Coote-captained Easts side regrouped to edge out St. George 8-6 in the preliminary final, but the Sea Eagles' maiden Grand Final triumph was more emphatic than the 19-14 scoreline suggests. Manly, captained by hooker Fred Jones and coached by former Kangaroos fullback Ron Willey, led 19-4 with less than 10 minutes remaining before Easts scored two late tries.

- **Biggest win:** Eastern Suburbs 50 d. Parramatta 12 at the Sydney Sports Ground, round four
- **Top Point-scorer:** Allan McKean (Eastern Suburbs) 220
- **Top Try-scorer:** Bob Fulton (Manly) 19

THE REPRESENTATIVE SCENE

NSW's commanding 29-5 and 27-6 wins over Queensland resulted in an interstate Colts match (won 11-10 by the Maroons) replacing the third encounter. Graeme Langlands led Australia to 36-11 and 31-7 thrashings of the touring Kiwis. But a magnificent try by the skipper in the World Cup final was incorrectly disallowed, and Great Britain won the trophy on account of a superior preliminary round record after the scores were tied 10-all at the end of extra-time (*see World Cups*).

STANDOUT PLAYER

Tenacious Western Suburbs halfback Tom Raudonikis captained New South Wales in the opening interstate clash and made his Test debut against the Kiwis, before winning the Rothmans Medal for his inspirational efforts at club level for the Magpies.

MEMORABLE MATCH

A bumper year of attendances in Brisbane finished with a fitting climax in a BRL Grand Final thriller. Easts and Valleys were tied 15-all in the dying minutes of a see-sawing decider in front of a 40,000-strong Lang Park crowd, before Easts lock Jeff Fyfe kicked the first field goal of his career to win the premiership for Des Morris' Tigers.

1973

Manly secured back-to-back premierships with a victory in the most brutal of all Grand Finals against the Cronulla Sharks, who qualified for their first decider after seven seasons in the competition. A five-team finals series was introduced in 1973, while South missed the finals for the first time in eight years and dwindling crowds and financial problems threatened the famous club's very existence. NSWRL president Bill Buckley passed away in April aged 66; he was replaced by former Balmain front-rower and club secretary Kevin Humphreys, who steered

Australian Rugby League into the modern era. The Kangaroos toured Britain and France for the first time in six years and reclaimed the Ashes, but interstate competition continued to flounder.

THE PREMIERSHIP

Manly finished just one point ahead of Cronulla at the end of the regular season, and as minor premiers under the five-team finals system, received a week's rest. Captain-coached by aggressive and astute British halfback Tommy Bishop, the Sharks trounced 'big brother' St. George 18-0 in their finals debut in a battle of the southern Sydney clubs. The Jack Gibson-coached Newtown eliminated Canterbury in the fourth- and fifth-place showdown, while the Bluebags required a replay to defeat St. George after the minor semi-final ended in a 12-all draw. Manly progressed to the Grand Final with a 14-4 major semi victory over the Sharks, who subsequently downed Newtown 20-11 to join the Sea Eagles in the decider. The Grand Final was marked by violent clashes and wild brawling in the first half, but a brilliant individual try in each half to gun centre Bob Fulton propelled the Sea Eagles to a 10-7 victory. Legendary winger Ken Irvine—the greatest try-scorer in Australian Rugby League history—retired after the match.

- **Biggest win:** Manly 70 d. Penrith 7 at Penrith Park, round 19
- **Top Point-scorer:** Graeme Langlands (St. George) 183
- **Top Try-scorer:** Bob Fulton (Manly) 18

THE REPRESENTATIVE SCENE

Queensland failed to register a point in three losses to NSW. The Kangaroos set off under captain-coach Graeme Langlands and regrouped after a loss in the first Test to regain the Ashes. Langlands was injured in the opening clash, with Bob McCarthy and Tom Raudonikis leading Australia to victory in the second and third Tests respectively, while 20-year-old Manly custodian Graham Eadie replaced Langlands at fullback.

STANDOUT PLAYER

Bob Fulton was named E.E. Christensen's Player of the Year for the second straight season. The premiership's top try-scorer for the second season running, Fulton's two-try display ranks as one of the great individual Grand Final performances. He played all five Tests in Britain and France alternating between five-eighth and centre, and was the Kangaroo Tour's undisputed star with 20 tries in just 14 appearances.

MEMORABLE MATCH

Newtown defeated St. George by the unique score of 1-0 in round eight at the SCG; a rule change halving the value of field goals only made the scoreline possible two seasons prior. Bluebags utility-back Ken Wilson slotted the match-winner (see Bizarre Matches).

1974

Another all time great club combination emerged under the tutelage of Jack Gibson in 1974. Eastern Suburbs' supremely talented line-up—with peerless ball-playing prop Arthur Beetson as skipper—emphatically knocked the Sea Eagles off their perch. St. George missed the finals for the first time since 1950, while Balmain slumped to its first wooden spoon in the club's 67-season history. Australia was forced to work hard to retain the Ashes against a Lions side rated as the worst to leave Britain, and international Rugby League welcomed another country with the addition of Papua New Guinea as a full member. Dave Brown, the record-breaking Easts and Kangaroos centre of the 1930s, and the Tricolours' 1921-22 Kangaroos lock Jack 'Bluey' Watkins both passed away in 1974. Western Division, coached by former Test winger Johnny King, added colour to the season by winning the inaugural Amco Cup midweek competition involving the Sydney premiership clubs, defeating Penrith 6-2 in the final.

THE PREMIERSHIP

Easts streeted the competition in the regular season, finishing the minor premiership eight points clear of Manly. The defending premiers were bounced from the finals via consecutive losses to Canterbury and Wests, while the Roosters were also stunned by the Berries in the major semi, 17-14. The Tricolours rallied to despatch Wests 25-2 in the preliminary final and kept their tryline intact again in a commanding 19-4 defeat of Canterbury in the Grand Final, ending a 29-year premiership drought.

- **Biggest win:** Western Suburbs 62 d. Balmain 5 at Lidcombe Oval, round one
- **Top Point-scorer:** Graham Eadie (Manly) 216
- **Top Try-scorer:** Bill Mullins (Eastern Suburs) 23; Kevin Junee (Manly) 23

THE REPRESENTATIVE SCENE

In a rare display of Queensland competitiveness in the 1970s, the Barry Muir-coached Maroons salvaged draws in the second and third interstate clashes after NSW—captained by Tom Raudonikis in all three games—won the series-opener 22-13. Widely panned after a meek display in a 12-6 first Test loss, Great Britain levelled the Ashes series with a shock 16-11 result in the second clash. Captain-coach Graeme Langlands (who was reinstated after being dumped for the second Test) enjoyed one of his greatest days in the decider, inspiring Australia to a 22-18 triumph.

STANDOUT PLAYER

Arthur Beetson won the *Rugby League Week* Player of the Year award following a season of unprecedented consistency at club level, before captaining Easts to a resounding title triumph. He was magnificent throughout the Ashes series, leading Australia in the second Test, and was named E.E. Christensen's Player of the Year.

MEMORABLE MATCH

Manly and underdogs Wests produced a classic minor semi-final contest, featuring a tremendous duel between rival linchpins Bob Fulton and Tom Raudonikis. The defending champs led 15-4 at halftime, but the Magpies staged a rousing comeback and back-to-back Raudonikis tries saw Wests surge to a 23-15 lead. A Fulton try reduced the deficit to three points to set up a grandstand finish, but Wests hung on 23-20.

1975

The 1975 season is synonymous with an ill-fated Grand Final display by one of the game's champions, and the infamous set of footwear he wore in the match. Easts charged to a second straight title, producing one of the most dominant seasons in premiership history before tearing St. George apart by a Grand Final record 38-0. Saints skipper Graeme Langlands—wearing white boots (a novelty in the 1970s) as part of a sponsorship deal—carried a leg injury into the match, and was a virtual passenger in the second half after a painkilling injection at halftime struck a nerve. Australia won the World Series tournament, which was completed in two stages on a home and away basis. Bill Kelly, a New Zealand and Australian international of the 1910s that went on to garner the tag of 'The Prince of Coaches,' passed away at the age of 83.

THE PREMIERSHIP

Easts strung a premiership record 19-match winning streak together during 1975 and finished the regular season a staggering 10 points clear of second-placed Manly. But the third-placed Dragons upset the Sea Eagles and Roosters on their way to booking the first Grand Final berth. Easts brushed Manly aside 28-13 in the preliminary final and racked up eight tries in the 38-0 Grand Final demolition of the Saints, after leading just 5-0 at halftime. Seasoned international forwards Arthur Beetson, Ron Coote and Elwyn Walters combined wonderfully with emerging backline talent Ian Schubert and astute halves John Peard and Johnny Mayes to form one of the great club sides.

- **Biggest win:** Canterbury 50 d. North Sydney 6 at North Sydney Oval, round nine
- **Top Point-scorer:** Graham Eadie (Manly) 242
- **Top Try-scorer:** Johnny Mayes (Eastern Suburbs) 16

THE REPRESENTATIVE SCENE

Former Test prop Jim Morgan captained Country Firsts to a 19-9 upset of City Firsts—the bush boys' first win over the city slickers in eight years. Barry Muir coached Queensland to a 14-8 win over NSW in the opening interstate encounter to break a five-year drought, before the Ron Coote-led Blues won the remaining two matches. Graeme Langlands led Australia through the home stage of the World Series mid-season, before Arthur Beetson took over from the injured Langlands (who remained with the team as coach) at the end of the year in Europe as the green-and-golds finished top of the table to be crown world champions.

STANDOUT PLAYER

Steve Rogers won the Rothmans Medal, despite his Cronulla side finishing in the bottom half of the table. The brilliant 20-year-old centre scored 156 points for the Sharks and was selected in Australia's World Series squad at the end of the season, combining in the centres with Mick Cronin for the first time and starring with two tries against France.

MEMORABLE MATCH

Parramatta entered their minor preliminary semi-final match-up with Canterbury on the back of three games in the previous week. The Eels overcame Wests and Balmain in a three-way midweek play-off for fifth spot, before eclipsing the Berries 6-5 in a precursor to the low-scoring finals the clubs would produce a decade later. Canterbury centre Mick Ryan scored the only try of the match in the first half, but second-rower Keith Campbell's third penalty secured a valiant victory for Parramatta.

1976

After the disappointments of the 1974-75 finals series, Manly returned to the premiership penthouse at the expense of fellow 1947 entrants the Parramatta Eels, who marked their 30th season with a maiden Grand Final appearance. Attendances continued to climb after the downturn of the early-1970s, while jersey sponsorship became widespread in the premiership. Graeme Langlands retired after six rounds of the premiership, unable to eradicate the memories of his Grand Final nightmare from the previous season, but leaving the legacy of a career of rare brilliance. Manly captain Bob Fulton—the club's greatest player—shocked the Rugby League fraternity by joining Easts after leading the Sea Eagles to premiership glory. For the first time since 1945, Australia had no international fixtures scheduled.

THE PREMIERSHIP

Manly pipped Parramatta for the minor premiership, before being outgunned by the Eels 23-17 in the major semi. Canterbury captain Bob McCarthy, who joined the club in 1976 after 13 seasons with Souths, scored a hat-trick as his side eliminated St. George in the minor semi. Manly regrouped to defeat Canterbury 15-12 in the preliminary final and won a dramatic decider against the Eels 13-10. Led by Queensland forward Ray Higgs, Parramatta hit the front 10-7 early in the second half, but Manly fullback Graham Eadie's magnificent goalkicking edged the Sea Eagles in front. An infamous dropped pass with the tryline beckoning by winger Neville Glover saw the Eels' chances of a breakthrough title slip away.

- **Biggest win:** Manly 57 d. Newtown 6 at Henson Park, round nine
- **Top Point-scorer:** Graham Eadie (Manly) 233
- **Top Try-scorer:** Bob Fulton (Manly) 21

THE REPRESENTATIVE SCENE

Powerhouse Souths winger Terry Fahey scored three tries and Graham Eadie amassed 20 points in City Firsts' 47-0 demolition of Country Firsts. City captain Tom Raudonikis subsequently led NSW to a 3-0 series cleansweep against Queensland.

STANDOUT PLAYER

Rugged Parramatta forward Ray Higgs, who joined the club from Nambour in 1975, skippered the Eels to the Grand Final and represented NSW against his native Queensland. His consistent performances were recognised with the Rothmans Medal-*Rugby League Week* Player of the Year double in 1976.

MEMORABLE MATCH

Although both clubs finished outside of finals reckoning, foundation clubs Wests and Souths staged a Sunday afternoon classic at a packed Lidcombe Oval in round seven. Tom Raudonikis' Magpies led 12-8 late in the second half, before Souths hooker George Piggins scored one of the decade's most famous individual tries, bulldozing through several Wests defenders to snatch a one-point lead. But Wests remained composed and forward Geoff Foster crossed for his second try to win the match in the dying seconds, 17-13.

1977

A historic drawn Grand Final was the dramatic high point of the 1977 season. But Parramatta was still searching for its maiden premiership after an anti-climatic 22-0 drubbing at the hands of the aggressive young St. George side in the replay. Australia and New Zealand hosted the World Cup, which Australia won despite a selection storm at the beginning of the tournament when Arthur Beetson was left out of the squad to travel to Auckland *(see Bolters, Controversial Selections and Shock Omissions)*. NSWRL president Kevin Humphreys was charged with fraud and misappropriation of more than $50,000 while he was secretary-manager of the Balmain Leagues club. The charges were dismissed, but sensationally resurfaced six years later in one of the most dramatic administration events in the game's history.

THE PREMIERSHIP

Boosted by the arrival of Gerringong Test centre Mick Cronin, Parramatta won its first minor premiership, losing just three regular season games. The Eels were upset 10-5 by the second-placed Saints in the major semi, but booked a rematch with the Steve Edge-captained Dragons courtesy of a 13-5 preliminary final victory over Bob Fulton's Easts line-up. St. George led the Grand Final 9-0 after a brilliant individual try to fullback Ted Goodwin, but Parramatta clawed back and levelled the scores through a try to winger Ed Sulcowicz with three minutes remaining. Cronin's conversion swung wide to leave the scores at 9-all at fulltime, while 10 minutes each way of extra-time failed to produce an addition to the scoreboard. 'Bath's Babes'— named after Saints coach Harry Bath—dominated the replay a week later, employing roughhouse tactics of questionable legality to unsettle the Eels. Goodwin kicked six goals and a field goal in the 22-0 thumping.

- **Biggest win:** Manly 50 d. Newtown 2 at Brookvale Oval, round 21
- **Top Point-scorer:** Michael Cronin (Parramatta) 225
- **Top Try-scorer:** Russell Gartner (Manly) 17

THE REPRESENTATIVE SCENE

The two-match interstate series was staged exclusively in Brisbane. NSW, captained by Arthur Beetson, won the first encounter 19-3. Queensland was on the verge of a rare victory in the second encounter, until veteran halfback Tom Raudonikis came off the bench to replace Blues rookie Steve Mortimer, who had been terrorised by opposing No.7 Greg Oliphant in a torrid debut. In a famous cameo, Raudonikis ripped into Oliphant and spurred NSW to a 14-13 win with a vital try. Queensland forward Greg Veivers captained Australia to a tournament-opening win over New Zealand in Auckland, before Beetson was restored to the side as skipper and led the green-and-golds to a World Cup triumph in his international farewell, defeating Great Britain 13-12 in the SCG final.

STANDOUT PLAYER

In his long-awaited first season in Sydney, Mick Cronin topped the premiership's pointscoring charts and won the Rothmans Medal and the *Rugby League Week* Player of the Year award. Cronin top-scored in Australia's World Cup success and was named Player of the Year in E.E. Christensen's *Official Rugby League Yearbook*, the last recipient of the honour before it was discontinued.

MEMORABLE MATCH

A dramatic major preliminary semi-final unfolded between keen rivals Easts and St. George at the SCG. The fiery contest was locked 7-all at halftime, before Easts' key forward Arthur Beetson was sent off for elbowing Saints magic man Ted Goodwin. The Roosters nosed in front 14-9 with a try to Kevin 'Stumpy' Stevens, but the Dragons gradually capitalised on the one-man advantage, hitting the front via Rod Reddy's second try to win 19-14. Beetson was suspended for the incident and missed the remainder of the Roosters' finals campaign.

1978

A pre-season exhibition match in Melbourne between Manly and Wests descended into a violent, brawling affair that sparked one of the most intense club rivalries in Australian Rugby League history—the 'Fibros' v the 'Silvertails' *(see Rivalries and Local Derbies)*. The Sea Eagles were again at centre of controversy during the finals, surviving a chain of dramatic sudden-death clashes and two replays—against the backdrop of a series of contentious performances by referee Greg Hartley—to achieve one of the most remarkable premiership triumphs of all time. The Kangaroos made their first tour of Britain and France in five years, retaining the Ashes but suffering a shock series loss to France. Just a year after his magnificent wing partner Cec Blinkhorn passed away, the Souths, Norths and Kangaroos 'Wonder Winger' of the 1910s and 1920s Harold Horder died, aged 84. In the decade's most poignant incident, rookie Penrith prop John Farragher was left a quadriplegic after a scrum collapsed against Newtown at Henson Park *(see Tragic Figures)*.

THE PREMIERSHIP

The rugged Magpies—under rookie first grade coach and motivator extraordinaire Roy Masters—won the minor premiership three points clear of the Norm Provan-coached Cronulla Sharks, who were the first side through to the Grand Final with wins over Manly and Wests. Parramatta and Manly drew the minor semi-final 13-all; the Sea Eagles won the replay 17-11 after a notorious display by referee Hartley, which included a seventh-tackle try to Manly and a plethora of miscounted sets. Manly defeated arch-enemies Wests 14-7 in an equally explosive preliminary final. In an uninspiring Grand Final, the Sea Eagles and Sharks were locked at 11-all after 80 minutes. With no provisions for extra-time, a replay was played just three days later due to the impending departure of the Kangaroos. A dominant display by fullback Graham Eadie spearheaded Manly's 16-0 shutout of the Sharks—the Sea Eagles' fifth match in 17 days. The stunning achievement represented the second title in three years for Manly coach Frank Stanton and the first as captain for hooker Max Krilich.

- **Biggest win:** North Sydney 55 d. Penrith 3 at North Sydney Oval, round 17
- **Top Point-scorer:** Michael Cronin (Parramatta) 282
- **Top Try-scorer:** Larry Corowa (Balmain) 24

THE REPRESENTATIVE SCENE

NSW won the interstate series 3-0 and Australia was similarly dominant in a three-Test home series whitewash of New Zealand. Bob Fulton led the Kangaroos to Britain and France in his farewell international campaign. Australia retained the

Ashes 2-1, but the French side—in a steady decline since the early-1960s—won both Tests against the tourists.

STANDOUT PLAYER

Mick Cronin won the coveted Rothmans Medal for the second straight season. His world record of 547 points in calendar year included a premiership record 282 points for the Eels and a tour-high 142 points for the Kangaroos, while Cronin's general play in the centres was characteristically outstanding.

MEMORABLE MATCH

The major semi between Wests and Cronulla had wider ramifications for the remainder of the premiership race after Sharks captain Greg Pierce was sent off and suspended for four matches. Cronulla led 10-4 at halftime, but Magpies sharpshooter Peter Rowles kicked three straight penalties to level the scores. Despite Pierce's dismissal for fighting with Wests firebrand John Donnelly, Cronulla booked a Grand Final berth 14-10 after two late goals to the mercurial Steve Rogers.

1979

The most dismal Lions tour in Anglo-Australian Test history to that point painted a grim picture of the future of international Rugby League, becoming the first Great Britain or England side to lose a Test series to Australia 3-0. A NSW side including Sydney-based Queensland products Kerry Boustead and Rod Reddy trounced the Maroons as the push for a 'State of Origin' interstate format gathered momentum. 'Bath's Babes' bounced back from missing the 1978 finals to claim their second premiership in three years as the Sydney competition provided 1979's spark in the wake of a languid representative season. Easts captain-coach Bob Fulton called time on one of the great playing careers, succumbing to a shoulder injury early in the season.

THE PREMIERSHIP

St. George won the minor premiership and progressed through to the Grand Final with a 15-11 major semi defeat of Parramatta. Fifth-placed Canterbury was the Dragons' surprise opponent for the decider, sweeping aside Wests, Cronulla and Parramatta in a sudden-death run. The Craig Young-captained Saints led the Grand Final against George Peponis' Bulldogs 17-2, before a second half comeback created an exciting finish. But St. George held on 17-13 to claim the club's 15th title—its last as a single entity.

- **Biggest win:** Parramatta 41 d. North Sydney 3 at Cumberland Oval, round 19
- **Top Point-scorer:** Michael Cronin (Parramatta) 253
- **Top Try-scorer:** Mitch Brennan (St. George) 16; Tom Mooney (Manly) 16

THE REPRESENTATIVE SCENE

Queensland, featuring teenage BRL stars Wally Lewis and Mal Meninga, conceded 96 points in NSW's 3-0 series cleansweep. The George Peponis-led Australia side was similarly dominant in the Ashes series, racking up 85 points to Great Britain's 16.

STANDOUT PLAYER

Inspirational Parramatta lock and dual international Ray Price won just about every accolade on offer in 1979. He collected the Rothmans Medal-*RLW* Player of the Year double for his performances at club level, and was awarded the Harry Sunderland

Medal as Australia's outstanding player in the Ashes series after being named man of the match in the first and third Test thrashings.

MEMORABLE MATCH

The records continued to tumble for Mick Cronin. In a wonderful individual display, Cronin racked up a club record 27 points from three tries and nine goals in Parramatta's 48-17 demolition of hapless North Sydney in round eight. Cronin tormented the Bears again with a 20-point haul in a 41-3 drubbing in round 19.

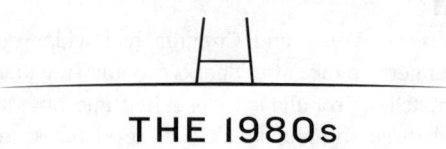

THE 1980s

The 1980s heralded an interstate Rugby League revolution in the shape of State of Origin, while Australia further asserted itself as the preeminent force on the international scene—highlighted by two unbeaten Kangaroo Tours of Britain and France. The premiership welcomed the addition of five new teams and witnessed the demise of one of its treasured foundation clubs. Parramatta and Canterbury dominated the decade with four titles each, Balmain provided the hard-luck story of the 1980s with twin Grand Final defeats, while a new force dressed in lime green emerged at the close of the decade with a victory in the greatest decider of them all. The 1980s were illuminated by the talents of Parramatta stars Peter Sterling, Brett Kenny and Eric Grothe; Canterbury halves Steve Mortimer and Terry Lamb; Balmain's Wayne Pearce, Garry Jack, Steve Roach and Ben Elias; and a host of Queenslanders as the Maroons controlled the Origin arena, including Gene Miles, Allan Langer and the decade's undisputed No.1 player, 'The King' Wally Lewis. A president fell on his sword, causing the biggest administration shake-up the game had seen in Australia and providing a platform for Rugby League to become more professionally governed as it hurtled towards the commercial age.

1980

State of Origin competition between Queensland and New South Wales became a reality in 1980. Largely thanks to the tireless campaigning of QRL president Ron 'The Senator' McAuliffe (and the cooperation of NSWRL counterpart Kevin Humphreys), a match was staged with players selected based on where they played their first senior football. Queensland, captained by 35-year-old former Test great Arthur Beetson and featuring a host of other Sydney-based stars, carved out a stirring 20-10 upset of NSW at Lang Park. An interstate Rugby League revolution was born. 'Gentleman' Jim Comans began his clean-up of the game in his position as judiciary chief, dishing out the most severe suspensions in premiership history in the ensuing seasons to help eradicate the blight of violent acts in Rugby League. Canterbury's 'Entertainers' ended the club's 38-year premiership drought, with two sets of three brothers—the Mortimer and the Hughes clans—spearheading the triumph. Two of Australian Rugby League's greatest players were mourned in 1980: legendary halfback of the 1910s and 1920s Duncan Thompson died in May, aged

85, and Newcastle great and three-time Kangaroo lock Wally Prigg passed away in September, aged 71. The Dally M Awards were held for the first time, a player of the year honour voted on by the game's media while also recognising the best player in each position, the best coach and the game's outstanding rookie. Souths pivot Rocky Laurie was the surprise winner of the inaugural Dally M Medal.

THE PREMIERSHIP

Under the coaching of Bob Fulton, Easts claimed the minor premiership on for-and-against from Canterbury. The Roosters went down to the Bulldogs 13-7 in the major semi, but qualified for the Grand Final with an emphatic 41-5 preliminary final thrashing of Wests. An uninspiring decider was lit up by a brilliant try to Canterbury winger Steve Gearin, who latched onto a high centring kick from fullback Greg Brentnall and dived over for a spectacular try, typifying the enterprise that garnered the Ted Glossop-coached Bulldogs the 'Entertainers' tag. George Peponis captained the 18-4 victory, while halfback Steve Mortimer was the linchpin—a relentless competitor and a brilliant attacking No.7 that would be integral to the club's impending successes.

- **Biggest win:** South Sydney 59 d. Penrith 5 at Redfern Oval, round seven
- **Top Point-scorer:** Steve Gearin (Canterbury) 220
- **Top Try-scorer:** John Ribot (Western Suburbs) 17; Wayne Wigham (Balmain) 17

THE REPRESENTATIVE SCENE

NSW won two residency-based interstate clashes by comfortable margins before Queensland's euphoric Origin victory. Peponis capped a decorated year by leading Australia to a convincing 2-0 series defeat of the Kiwis in New Zealand.

STANDOUT PLAYER

Rugged halfback Kevin Hastings was superb in Easts' charge to the minor premiership and Grand Final, winning the first of three straight *Rugby League Week* Player of the Year awards. He was also named Dally M Halfback of the Year and finished second in the Dally M Medal count.

MEMORABLE MATCH

Arthur Beetson's last match of a 15-season career in Sydney was as part of Parramatta's reserve grade Grand Final side. The 35-year-old forward great had lost little of his playmaking guile, but could not prevent a Canterbury victory, 18-16 in extra-time. Beetson was nevertheless chaired from the SCG—a venue he had lit up on dozens occasions in Grand Finals and Tests—before returning to Redcliffe to finish his career in 1981.

1981

Few maiden triumphs can compare with the euphoria and pandemonium that followed Parramatta's breakthrough success in the 1981 Grand Final. A line borrowed from *The Wizard of Oz* was the sum total of coach Jack Gibson's victory speech—'Ding Dong, the witch is dead'—while overzealous fans burned the grandstand at the club's Cumberland Oval base to the ground. Another successful one-game State of Origin experiment laid the foundation for a permanent departure from residency-based interstate clashes. The sin-bin was introduced to the premiership; Newtown hooker Barry Jensen was sat down for five minutes by referee Kevin Roberts for repeated scrum infringements in the opening round to create a novel slice of history. A *Rugby League Week* competition honoured the game's four greatest post-World War II players and introduced a sacred term to the Rugby League vernacular when Clive Churchill, Reg Gasnier, Johnny Raper and Bob Fulton were named the original 'Immortals.'

THE PREMIERSHIP

Easts won its second straight minor premiership, but dipped out of the finals with consecutive losses to Parramatta and Newtown. Rebranded as the Jets a few years earlier, Newtown was featuring in its first finals series since 1973 with burgeoning coaching talent Warren Ryan and veteran former Wests halfback Tom Raudonikis calling the shots. Captain Raudonikis scored a determined try just after halftime to give Newtown an 11-7 lead in the Grand Final, but three tries in the final 15 minutes delivered Parramatta's long-awaited title. Hooker Steve Edge captained the Eels to become the first player to captain two clubs to Grand Final victory; he was ably backed by young stars Peter Sterling, Brett Kenny (who scored two tries) and Steve Ella, and experienced campaigners Mick Cronin, Ray Price and Bob O'Reilly.

- **Biggest win:** Canterbury 52 d. Balmain 13 at Leichhardt Oval, round four
- **Top Point-scorer:** Steve Rogers (Cronulla) 194
- **Top Try-scorer:** Terry Fahey (Eastern Suburbs) 15

THE REPRESENTATIVE SCENE

NSW won the last two interstate clashes played under the traditional residency-based format. Queensland, under the captaincy of young five-eighth Wally Lewis, fought back from 15-0 down to win the one-off Origin match 22-15. Lewis and Canterbury halfback Steve Mortimer formed a debutant halves pairing in Australia's 2-0 Test series victory over the dismal French touring side.

STANDOUT PLAYER

Cronulla champion Steve Rogers captained the NSW Origin side and Australia's Test series success against France from centre, but displayed his outstanding versatility by collecting the Dally M Medal after a season at lock for the Sharks.

MEMORABLE MATCH

The infamous minor semi-final between Newtown and Manly featured one of the ugliest brawls ever seen at the SCG. The melee erupted in the first minute, with rival enforcers Steve Bowden (Newtown) and Terry Randall (Manly) receiving an early shower. The underdog Jets led 16-0 soon after halftime, before a surging comeback by star-studded Manly reduced the deficit to just four points with 10 minutes remaining. Newtown hung on 20-15 after Ken Wilson slotted a late field goal, but Bowden's subsequent suspension ruled him out of the club's Grand Final side.

1982

The NSWRL added two new clubs to the premiership as it began a push towards decentralisation. The Illawarra Steelers (based in the NSW South Coast city of Wollongong) and the Canberra Raiders expanded the competition to 14 teams as the only clubs not situated in Sydney. But the expansion and Australian Rugby

League's 75th anniversary celebrations clouded the worrying decline of crowd numbers and financial crises developing at several clubs. The game received a massive sponsorship injection from tobacco company Rothmans, however, with the premiership rebranded as the Winfield Cup. Tobacco sponsorship would be outlawed in the mid-1990s, but it proved to be a prosperous partnership for the League for more than a decade. Parramatta forged ahead towards a dynasty with its second straight title, while judiciary chairman Jim Comans' crusade continued as he outed Wests forward Bob Cooper for 15 months after a violent brawl in a match against Illawarra. State of Origin became established as a three-match series, while the year-ending Kangaroo Tour widened the gap between Australia and Great Britain as the squad returned unbeaten, lavished with the glorious tag 'The Invincibles.'

THE PREMIERSHIP
The added teams saw the competition stretched to 26 weeks to allow two full home and away rounds. Parramatta finished as minor premiers, eight points clear of second-placed Manly. Norths made a return to the finals after a 17-year absence, but dipped out with consecutive losses to Manly and Easts, while the Sea Eagles advanced to the Grand Final with a 20-0 major semi shutout of the Eels. Parramatta whipped Easts 33-0 in the preliminary final, however, and overwhelmed Manly 21-8 in the Grand Final. Five-eighth Brett Kenny scored another double to spearhead the Eels' comprehensive victory. The Raiders collected a debut-season wooden spoon, while the Steelers finished second-last.

- **Biggest win:** Parramatta 54 d. Canberra 3 at Belmore Sports Ground, round seven
- **Top Point-scorer:** Michael Cronin (Parramatta) 279
- **Top Try-scorer:** Steve Ella (Parramatta) 23

THE REPRESENTATIVE SCENE
Queensland overcame a loss in the first encounter to take out the inaugural Origin series 2-1 over the Max Krilich-led NSW side, vindicating the shift away from residency-based interstate matches. Krilich led Australia in a 2-0 Test series win against New Zealand, and in a 38-2 win in the maiden Test against Papua New Guinea in Port Moresby en route to a flawless tour of Britain and France. The Kangaroos scored 99 points and conceded just 18 in the Ashes series against Great Britain to establish themselves as one of the great Australian sides.

STANDOUT PLAYER
Big, strong and fast, Brisbane Souths centre Mal Meninga terrorised defenders at all levels and racked up points with reckless abandon in 1982. He was named man of the match on a losing side for Queensland in the Origin series-opener and featured in the Maroons' victory in the decider, made his Test debut against New Zealand and top-scored for the Kangaroos with 166 points—including 48 points in the Ashes series as one of Australia's dominant players.

MEMORABLE MATCH
Canterbury and Newtown played out the only scoreless draw in premiership history in round four at Henson Park. The Bulldogs' 'Entertainers' tag appeared to be misplaced, while 1981 grand finalists Newtown were equally inept in a truly unique afternoon *(see Bizarre Matches)*.

1983

The most sensational administration controversy in Australian Rugby League history saw NSWRL president Kevin Humphreys stand down from his post in 1983. The ABC's *Four Corners* program and journalist Chris Masters (brother of St. George coach Roy) uncovered high-level corruption stemming from Humphreys' 1977 acquittal on charges of misappropriating funds during his term as secretary-manager of the Balmain Leagues Club. Humphreys resigned as president two days after the program aired (he quit as ARL chairman the day before the program aired, citing poor health) as the Rugby League world watch in stunned disbelief at what had unfolded. Neville Wran stood down as NSW Premier after the program revealed he had tried to influence the magistracy during Humphreys' committal six years earlier, while former Chief Stipendiary Magistrate Murray Farquhar was jailed in 1985 for perverting the course of justice. The structure of the game's administration was given a facelift in the wake of the debacle; Tom Bellew became NSWRL president, while former Manly secretary Ken Arthurson was installed as chairman of the ARL, John Quayle was appointed to the newly created role of general manager of the NSWRL and a nine man board of directors was instituted. On the field, Parramatta became the first side since the St. George line-ups of the 1950s and 1960s to win three premierships in a row, and the value of a try was increased from three points to four. Several clubs faced extinction; Cronulla players reluctantly accepted a 50 per cent pay cut ease the club's dire financial situation, while debt-ridden Newtown and Western Suburbs were agonisingly cut from the premiership at the end of the year. The Magpies took their fight to the Supreme Court and were reinstated for the 1984 season, but it was the end of the line for Newtown's proud 76-season first grade history.

THE PREMIERSHIP

Coached by Bob Fulton for the first time, Manly emphatically took out the minor premiership, eight points clear of defending champs Parramatta. The Sea Eagles duly advanced to the Grand Final with a 19-10 major semi defeat of the Eels, but Jack Gibson's charges rallied to eliminate Canterbury 18-4 in the preliminary final and overwhelmed Manly 18-6 in the decider. Brett Kenny scored two tries in the Grand Final for the third year in succession, while the Sea Eagles were left to lament another listless performance in a decider. Balmain—featuring young stars Steve Roach, Ben Elias, Garry Jack and captain Wayne Pearce—returned to the finals after a six-year absence; St. George and Canterbury also qualified after disappointing 1982 campaigns.

- **Biggest win:** Parramatta 54 d. Newtown 4 at Belmore Sports Ground, round 15
- **Top Point-scorer:** Mike Eden (Eastern Suburbs) 256
- **Top Try-scorer:** Phil Blake (Manly) 27

THE REPRESENTATIVE SCENE

Queensland triumphed 2-1 in an Origin series that was overshadowed by NSW and Manly firebrand forward Les Boyd's vicious elbow that left Maroons prop Daryl Brohman with a broken jaw. Boyd was suspended for 12 months over the incident. Max Krilich's Australian side defeated New Zealand 16-4 in the first encounter of a two-Test series, but the Graham Lowe-coached Kiwis pulled off a stunning

19-12 upset at Lang Park to square the ledger—New Zealand's first victory over Australia since 1971.

STANDOUT PLAYER
Versatile former Test back Phil Sigsworth enjoyed his best season in his first year at Manly, winning the *Rugby League Week* Player of the Year award and finishing second in the Dally M Medal count. Sigsworth represented NSW for the last time in 1983, alternating between centre and five-eighth throughout the season at club level and scoring the Sea Eagles' only try in the Grand Final.

MEMORABLE MATCH
In a high-scoring major preliminary semi-final between Parramatta and Canterbury, the Eels leapt out to a 24-10 lead before a Steve Mortimer-inspired comeback cut the deficit to two points. Parramatta eventually held on to prevail 30-22, but the highlight of the match was a barnstorming first half try to the Eels' destructive winger Eric Grothe, who powered through five Bulldogs defenders and scored in the tackle of Mortimer.

1984

The disturbing decline of the British game uncovered by the 'Invincibles' was exacerbated by the Lions' dreadful performances Down Under in 1984—the 90th year of Rugby League in England. Canterbury's 'Entertainers' became a distant memory as new coach Warren Ryan's 'Dogs of War' ended Parramatta's premiership reign. The talented but ill-disciplined Les Boyd's tumultuous career in Australia came to an abrupt end when he received a 15-month ban for gouging Bulldogs hooker Billy Johnstone in just his third game back from a 12-month suspension. But the year belonged to brilliant and abrasive young Queenslander—'The King' Wally Lewis.

THE PREMIERSHIP
Souths returned to the finals under coach Ron Willey, denying Canberra a maiden post-season appearance by eliminating the Raiders in a fifth-place play-off. Canterbury finished as minor premiers and qualified for the Grand Final via a 16-8 defeat of Parramatta. The Eels—coached by John Monie after Jack Gibson departed at the end of 1983—subsequently edged out St. George 8-7 with a late Eric Grothe try in a dramatic preliminary final, but their title sequence came to an end 6-4 in the decider. Steve Mortimer captained the Bulldogs in the grinding triumph, while brother Chris kicked the goal that proved the difference between the two sides.

- **Biggest win:** Manly 56 d. North Sydney 4 at North Sydney Oval, round 21
- **Top Point-scorer:** Steve Gearin (St. George) 190
- **Top Try-scorer:** Terry Lamb (Canterbury) 17; Steve Morris (St. George) 17

THE REPRESENTATIVE SCENE
In Arthur Beetson's fourth straight year as state coach, the Wally Lewis-led Maroons wrapped up the Origin series in the first two matches, before Steve Mortimer captained NSW to a face-saving game three victory. The Blues' skipper in the first two clashes, Ray Price, retired from representative football after the Ashes series, which intersected the interstate contests. Great Britain was comprehensively outplayed in the 3-0 Test series whitewash at the hands of Australia.

STANDOUT PLAYER

Wally Lewis' 1984 season incorporated an extraordinary amount of success. 'The King' won two man of the match awards in skippering Queensland to series glory; captained Australia for the first time in the Ashes series and was named man of the match in the series opener; led Combined Brisbane to victory in the final of the midweek Amco Cup over Sydney's Eastern Suburbs; and starred in Wynnum-Manly's 42-8 BRL Grand Final triumph against Southern Suburbs. Lewis was named the inaugural winner of the Golden Boot award after a phenomenal year of achievement.

MEMORABLE MATCH

Playing in their first finals match in four years, the Rabbitohs overcame an early 14-0 deficit to defeat the star-studded Manly side 22-18 in the minor preliminary semi-final. Souths' astute use of the 'bomb' paved the way for the rousing comeback victory, with second-rower Bill Hardy bagging two tries *(see Finals Magic)*.

1985

Rugby League's 'Little Master,' the South Sydney legend and record-breaking Australian captain Clive Churchill, lost his battle with cancer in August, aged 58. He was farewelled at St. Mary's Cathedral in one of Sydney's biggest sporting funerals. Canterbury's rugged and relentless style netted back-to-back premiership triumphs for the first time in the club's history. In a year packed with important milestones, Penrith qualified for its maiden finals series after 19 seasons of first grade; Parramatta's Mick Cronin became the competition's greatest point-scorer, overtaking Manly fullback Graham Eadie's mark of 1,917; New South Wales belatedly broke through for its maiden State of Origin series success; and Monday Night Football was introduced. In Queensland, Ron McAuliffe—one of the state's great Rugby League administrators and the man most responsibility for the birth of Origin football—retired as QRL chairman, while 35-year-old coach Wayne Bennett steered Souths to the BRL premiership by overcoming Wynnum-Manly 10-8 in the Grand Final, overturning the 34-point loss suffered against the Seagulls in the 1984 decider.

THE PREMIERSHIP

St. George won the minor premiership, with the exciting Frank Stanton-coached Balmain Tigers second and the Bulldogs third. The Panthers qualified in fifth after defeating Manly 10-7 in extra-time in the fifth-place play-off, but were destroyed 38-6 by Parramatta in their finals debut. Canterbury also needed extra-time to defeat Balmain in the major preliminary semi, while the Tigers dipped out with a heavy 32-4 loss to the Eels. The Dragons advanced to the Grand Final first courtesy of a convincing 17-6 major semi win over Canterbury, but the Bulldogs hammered Parramatta 26-0 in the preliminary final and edged out the Saints 7-6 in a dour decider. Tough centre Andrew Farrar's field goal was the difference, but Canterbury was in control for most of the match, until a late Steve Morris try set up a tight finish.

- **Biggest win:** Canterbury 52 d. Western Suburbs 0 at Lidcombe Oval, round 13
- **Top Point-scorer:** Michael Cronin (Parramatta) 204
- **Top Try-scorer:** Steve Linnane (St. George) 17

THE REPRESENTATIVE SCENE

Steve Mortimer captained NSW to the breakthrough Origin series victory with wins in the opening two matches, before Queensland pegged a game back in the third encounter. Australia won the opening two Tests against New Zealand, requiring an at-the-death try to winger John Ribot in each encounter to snatch victory. NSW and Australian coach Terry Fearnley controversially dropped four Queenslanders for the third Test, replacing them with NSW players. Howls of protest came from north of the border, and the derision appeared to be vindicated as the unsettled green-and-golds were thrashed 18-0 by a rampant Kiwi side led by bruising backrower Mark Graham.

STANDOUT PLAYER

Brett Kenny was awarded the Golden Boot for 1985 after starring at club level for Parramatta, winning the Lance Todd Trophy for a stellar performance in Wigan's Challenge Cup final triumph at Wembley, and outpointing opposing No.6 Wally Lewis in the Origin series, scoring the historic series-sealing try for NSW.

MEMORABLE MATCH

A crowd of almost 100,000 was in attendance for the 1985 Challenge Cup final between Wigan and Hull, a match regarded as the greatest of all Cup finals and referred to in some quarters as 'Australia Day at Wembley.' Wigan featured man of the match Kenny and two-try hero and Easts winger John 'Chicka' Ferguson, while Peter Sterling was magnificent for Hull alongside Parramatta and Kangaroos teammate John Muggleton. Captained by New Zealand's Graeme West, Wigan prevailed 28-24.

1986

Parramatta and Canterbury—the only premiership-winning clubs of the first six seasons of the 1980s—faced off for premiership supremacy in the Grand Final, producing a dramatic try-less classic that saw two of the era's greatest players celebrate a fitting farewell. The representative scene was more clear-cut: New South Wales recorded the first Origin series whitewash; Australia crushed New Zealand 3-0 to reassert its trans-Tasman dominance; and Wally Lewis' Kangaroos— the 'Unbeatables'—repeated the feat of their predecessors in Britain and France. Parramatta Stadium was officially opened by Queen Elizabeth II and Prince Philip, and the Eels christened their new home with a 36-6 thrashing of St. George 11 days later, while the Sydney Sports Ground closed its gates after 75 years of Rugby League competition for construction to begin on the game's new headquarters—the Sydney Football Stadium. The drowning death at Byron Bay of former Wests and Australian Test forward John 'Dallas' Donnelly, one of the game's great characters and genuine cult heroes, was the saddest moment of 1986 *(see Tragic Figures)*.

THE PREMIERSHIP

Parramatta won the minor premiership and South Sydney was the surprise packet in second place, just one point adrift of the Eels in George Piggins' first season as coach. But the Rabbitohs slipped out the back door of the finals with losses to Canterbury and Balmain. The Tigers stormed from a fifth-place play-off to the preliminary final, where their run was halted by the Bulldogs 28-16. Departing

Parramatta veteran Mick Cronin landed two penalty goals to Terry Lamb's one for Canterbury in a decider of spine-tingling proportions, won 4-2 by the Eels—the only try-less decider in Grand Final history. The gripping victory represented one of the most famous triumphant farewells the game has witnessed, with Cronin and captain Ray Price retiring after the match. Halfback Peter Sterling was awarded the inaugural Clive Churchill Medal as man of the match.

- **Biggest win:** Canterbury 54 d. Western Suburbs 4 at the Sydney Cricket Ground, round 16
- **Top Point-scorer:** Terry Lamb (Canterbury) 210
- **Top Try-scorer:** Phil Blake (Manly) 13; Garry Schofield (Balmain) 13

THE REPRESENTATIVE SCENE

NSW's series cleansweep was close-fought—Wayne Pearce's Blues won by margins of six, four and two. Australia dominated the three-Test series against New Zealand, winning by an average margin of 17 points, with Brett Kenny accumulating five tries. The Wally Lewis-led Kangaroos thrashed Papua New Guinea 62-12, before sweeping Great Britain 3-0 and decimating France in a two-Test series to finish the tour unbeaten. Former Wallaby Michael O'Connor top-scored with 190 points on tour and set a host of Test matches records.

STANDOUT PLAYER

Terry Lamb was outstanding for Canterbury, topping the premiership with 210 points and collecting the Dally M Players' Player and Five-eighth of the Year gongs, while finishing third in the Dally M Medal count. He played two matches for NSW and showed his versatility by creating the unique record of playing all 20 matches on the Kangaroo Tour—including all five Tests. Lamb led the squad with 19 tries.

MEMORABLE MATCH

Balmain, weary from a fifth-place play-off just four days earlier, overcame an early 12-0 deficit to defeat Manly in the minor preliminary semi. The Tigers surged to lead 19-12 at halftime, before the send-off of Manly five-eighth Cliff Lyons sparked a Sea Eagles fight-back. But Balmain eventually subdued the 12-man Sea Eagles 29-22 to advance.

1987

The 1987 premiership represented a changing of the guard in many ways. The two heavyweights of the decade, Parramatta and Canterbury, missed the finals; Easts returned to the top-five for the first time since 1982; and the Canberra Raiders qualified for their maiden finals series, and subsequently their first Grand Final. The decider debutants were overwhelmed by runaway minor premiers Manly in the last Grand Final played at Sydney Rugby League's spiritual home, the Sydney Cricket Ground. The premiership's decentralisation continued with the announcement that Brisbane, Gold Coast and Newcastle would be admitted in 1988, expanding the competition out of NSW for the first time. A nominal international schedule featured another Lang Park upset by New Zealand, a change to the structure of City v Country fixtures, and the arrival on the Origin stage of a diminutive blonde-haired halfback from Ipswich. The back pages were dominated by the feud that boiled over between Bulldogs coach Warren Ryan and his skipper Steve Mortimer; the halfback initially sought a release to join Manly, but it was Ryan that departed at the end of an unhappy year for the club. Brothers won the 1987 BRL premiership—a competition that would be severely weakened the following season after the advent of the Brisbane Broncos.

THE PREMIERSHIP

Manly finished six points clear of Easts at the top of the table. The Arthur Beetson-coached Roosters downed third-placed Canberra 25-16, but succumbed 10-6 to Manly in a bruising major semi. The Raiders rallied to smash Souths 46-12 in a match best-known for the notorious performance of flamboyant Rabbitohs three-quarter Steve Mavin *(see Minties Moments)*, before the shock return of Mal Meninga from a broken arm spearheaded Canberra's 32-24 triumph over Easts in the preliminary final. The Sea Eagles were a class above, however, winning the Grand Final 18-8 over the Dean Lance-led Raiders. Veteran Queensland and Australian backrower Paul 'Fatty' Vautin skippered the victorious Manly side, while Michael O'Connor netted 14 points and ball-playing pivot Cliff Lyons won the Clive Churchill Medal.

- **Biggest win:** Eastern Suburbs 44 d. St. George 2 at the Sydney Cricket Ground, round four
- **Top Point-scorer:** Ross Conlon (Balmain) 196
- **Top Try-scorer:** Terry Lamb (Canterbury) 16

THE REPRESENTATIVE SCENE

City's and Country's elite sides were chosen on a 'Place of Origin' basis from 1987—Wayne Pearce's City Origin side defeated the Peter Sterling-led Country Origin 30-22 in the inaugural clash. Allan Langer's outstanding debut for Queensland in the opening Origin clash could not prevent NSW's last-gasp victory courtesy of a Mark McGaw try, but 'Alfie' was brilliant throughout the campaign and was man of the match in the series-deciding third match. A fourth match Origin match—an exhibition clash not included as part of the series—was staged in Long Beach, California, won 30-18 by NSW. The inexperienced New Zealand side—captained by Roosters skipper Hugh McGahan—caused a 13-6 boilover in the one-off Test against Australia in Brisbane.

STANDOUT PLAYER

Despite Parramatta's slide down the ladder, Peter Sterling's performances reached a new plane of excellence in 1987. He became the first player to win the Dally M Medal-Rothmans Medal double, while he was also crowned *Rugby League Week* Player of the Year. Sterling captained Country Origin and NSW, winning two man of the match awards in the four interstate matches, and played in Australia's Test loss to the Kiwis. The accolades continued to flow with 'Sterlo's' naming as the joint Golden Boot recipient (with McGahan).

MEMORABLE MATCH

Wooden spooners Wests came agonisingly close to knocking off dominant eventual premiers Manly, but eventually went down by a point. The lowly Magpies led the table-topping Sea Eagles 25-12 with 16 minutes remaining in the round 16 clash at Brookvale Oval. But the home side flashed in for three tries, including a last-minute match-winner to young winger David Ronson, to complete a great escape 26-25.

1988

The NSWRL unveiled its shiny new headquarters, the Sydney Football Stadium, in Australia's Bicentenary year, and three new premiership clubs in the shape of the star-studded Brisbane Broncos, the confident Gold Coast-Tweed Giants and the fanatically supported Newcastle Knights. The Broncos stunned the Rugby League world with a 44-10 dismantling of defending premiers Manly in the opening round and led the competition unbeaten after six weeks, but the weekly grind of the premiership took its toll and the club faded to finish seventh. The Knights and Giants finished 14th and 15th in the 16-team competition respectively. The inaugural 'Super Sevens' seven-a-side tournament was staged at Parramatta in the pre-season, featuring 15 premiership clubs (Easts declined the invitation) and a Combined Brisbane side. Souths—inspired by custom-made sevens star and player of the tournament Phil Blake—won the tournament. The Lions showed signs of a Great Britain revival on their tour of Australia, the green-and-golds hoodwinked New Zealand in the World Cup final, and the Maroons secured their first Origin series whitewash just two months before the passing of influential Queensland administrator Ron McAuliffe, aged 70.

THE PREMIERSHIP

After seven years out of finals contention, the Cronulla Sharks were surprise minor premiers, but exited the finals via back-to-back losses to second-placed Canterbury in the major semi and the Balmain juggernaut in the preliminary final. The Warren Ryan-coached Tigers surged from a fifth-place play-off defeat of Penrith to eliminate Manly, Canberra and Cronulla on their way to a remarkable Grand Final appearance. The Bulldogs were too strong in the decider, prevailing 24-12 after the Tigers' star player—brilliant British import Ellery Hanley—was knocked senseless in an alleged high tackle by Canterbury pivot Terry Lamb. Test prop Peter Tunks captained the side after Steve Mortimer relinquished the post earlier in the season. Mortimer, one of Canterbury's greatest players, retired after the Grand Final victory—he played a bit-part role off the bench after coming back from a broken arm injury late in the season.

- **Biggest win:** Manly 64 d. Parramatta 12 at Parramatta Stadium, round three
- **Top Point-scorer:** Gary Belcher (Canberra) 218
- **Top Try-scorer:** John Ferguson (Canberra) 20

THE REPRESENTATIVE SCENE

In Wayne Bennett's third season as coach, Queensland blitzed NSW 3-0—despite being without Wally Lewis for the first time in an Origin match (Paul Vautin replaced the injured Lewis as captain). The Lions showed plenty of fight in a 17-6 loss in the first Test played at the SFS—the 100th Anglo-Australian Test match—and despite Australia sealing the series in the second encounter in Brisbane 34-14, Great Britain won its first Ashes encounter in a decade (and the first on Australian soil since 1974) 26-12 in the third clash. After talking up New Zealand's favouritism for the World Cup final played at Auckland's Eden Park, Australia thumped the Kiwis 25-12 despite losing captain Wally Lewis at halftime with a broken arm. The World Cup was a complicated home-and-away series played over four years incorporating matches from Test series to determine which two teams contested the final (*see*

World Cups). The green-and-golds also thrashed Papua New Guinea by a then-Test record 70-8 and defeated a Rest of the World combination 22-10 as part of Australia's Bicentennial celebrations.

STANDOUT PLAYER

Cronulla's ball-playing backrower Gavin Miller won the Dally M Medal after spearheading the Sharks' drive to the minor premiership. Miller earned a maiden national call-up, representing Australia against Papua New Guinea and Rest of the World, before scoring a try in the World Cup final triumph against New Zealand.

MEMORABLE MATCH

In just his second match since his infamous nightmarish performance against Canberra in the 1987 finals series, South Sydney winger Steve Mavin scored the match-winning try in a round two nail-biter against Easts. Trailing 14-12 after Roosters centre David Smith kicked his fifth goal, the Rabbitohs furiously threw the ball around searching for an opening, before the enigmatic Mavin crashed over in the corner with only seconds to spare. The 16-14 victory doubled as the Rabbitohs' first appearance at their new home ground, the Sydney Football Stadiuim, after leaving Redfern Oval at the end of 1987. The Roosters were the SFS's other permanent tenants.

1989

The season began with a rousing season launch that presented Australian Rugby League as a genuinely marketable entertainment package, and finished with the greatest premiership decider in the game's history. The NSWRL unveiled a glamorous, slick television advertisement featuring American rock star Tina Turner singing her 1987 hit *What You Get is What You See* interspersed with on-field action and flashy sequences of the game's statuesque stars away from the playing fields. The campaign proved exceedingly popular and signalled Rugby League's growth as a professional sport, capitalising on the ever-increasing media saturation of the game. But Turner's song that was used for the 1990 season and beyond—*Simply the Best*—could have been an ode to the 1989 Grand Final between Canberra and Balmain. Meanwhile, underperforming seasons by heavyweight clubs resulted in captaincy upheavals at Brisbane and Manly. Broncos coach Wayne Bennett stripped Test skipper Wally Lewis of the club captaincy (replacing him with Gene Miles) after Brisbane's season ended with a fifth-place play-off loss to Cronulla; and Manly informed premiership-winning captain Paul Vautin he was no longer wanted at the club after a dismal 12th-place finish, and the popular Origin and Test backrower joined Easts in 1990.

THE PREMIERSHIP

South Sydney stormed to the minor premiership after just three losses in 22 regular season matches, five points clear of second-placed Penrith. But the Rabbitohs and Panthers both exited the finals courtesy of back-to-back losses to Balmain and Canberra. The Tigers entered the Grand Final as favourites and led the Raiders 12-2 at halftime, but Tim Sheens' Green Machine clawed their way back in the second half and trailed 14-8 after Gary Belcher scored their first try. A number of chances to seal the Grand Final slipped through Balmain's grasp and a memorable try to Canberra winger John 'Chicka' Ferguson sent the decider into extra-time. The Raiders had harnessed irresistible momentum and nudged in front early in the added period via a Chris O'Sullivan field goal, before replacement forward Steve Jackson bumped and spun his way to one of the great Grand Final tries *(see Unlikely Heroes)* to clinch Canberra's maiden title 19-14. The game is routinely referred to as the premiership's best-ever decider, and arguably the greatest match in the code's history. Raiders lock Bradley Clyde, just 19 years of age, was awarded the Clive Churchill Medal.

- **Biggest win:** Eastern Suburbs 48 d. Illawarra 6 at Henson Park, round five
- **Top Point-scorer:** Andy Currier (Balmain) 146; Ricky Walford (St. George) 146
- **Top Try-scorer:** Gary Belcher (Canberra) 17

THE REPRESENTATIVE SCENE

Queensland—with Arthur Beetson returning as coach—carved out the most emphatic series victory of State of Origin's first decade, decimating the Blues (who had installed Jack Gibson as coach) 3-0 for the second year in a row. The Maroons racked up 36 points in each of the first and third games, while they produced a famous backs-to-the-wall victory in the second encounter in Sydney despite a host of injuries *(see Courageous Performances)*. Wally Lewis led Australia on a tour of New Zealand, winning all three Tests comfortably but falling to the Auckland provincial side 24-22.

STANDOUT PLAYER

Mal Meninga overcame four broken arm injuries in the 1987-88 seasons to achieve spectacular success in 1989. Playing in his first Origin match since 1986, Meninga scored two tries and four goals (for a then-Maroons record 16 points) in Queensland's record 36-6 victory in the series-opener, before starring on Australia's tour of New Zealand, starting the third Test in the unfamiliar position of second-row. The giant centre assumed the Canberra captaincy midway through the season and led the club to a euphoric premiership triumph. Meninga was named the 1989 Golden Boot winner.

MEMORABLE MATCH

Cellar-dwellers Wests staged the upset of the season in round 13 against eventual premiers Canberra. Languishing in second-last spot, the Mapgies trailed the Raiders—who were entrenched in the top-five—18-6 at the half-hour mark. But British imports Ellery Hanley and Garry Schofield inspired Wests in a stirring comeback, with the Magpies scoring four tries to three in a thrilling 25-22 result.

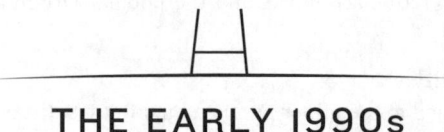

THE EARLY 1990s

Australian Rugby League capitalised on the advancements it made in the 1980s, progressing towards fulltime professionalism in the first half of the 1990s. The code's burgeoning popularity reflected the outstanding standard of football, and a new crop of superstars lit up the premiership and representative spheres. Superpowers

Canberra and Brisbane battled for the mantle of the game's dominant club, with the likes of Manly and St. George offering stern challenges, while Penrith broke through for a euphoric maiden title. Drugs, drafts, salary caps and rule changes ensured that Australian Rugby League and its purveyors were constantly on their toes during the early-1990s, which could be viewed as the tail-end of the game's innocence as the looming Super League war changed the sport forever in 1995.

1990

The unbridled commercial success of the end of the 1980s took a mild hit in the shape of a recreational drugs scandal at South Sydney in 1990. Nine unnamed players tested positive to marijuana, while 19-year-old utility-back Scott Wilson was sacked by the club after traces of cocaine were found in his drug test sample. In one of the most spectacular turnarounds in first grade history, the Rabbitohs finished last with just two wins—only 12 months after winning the minor premiership. Despite the negative publicity, the on-field product remained as strong as ever and Canberra claimed back-to-back titles despite the brazen challenges of Penrith and Brisbane. NSW reclaimed the Origin crown for the first time in four years, while Australia's successful Kangaroo Tour was preceded by the controversial omission of Test skipper Wally Lewis after he failed a team medical on a recovering broken arm, denying him the record of becoming the first player to lead two tours to Britain and France. A horror year for Lewis was exacerbated by the Broncos effectively cutting him loose by offering the game's highest-profile player a minimal contract for 1991, and he joined the Gold Coast. A contentious draft system was introduced in 1990—despite stiff opposition from the Players' Association—and 23 players switched clubs via the draft at the end of the year. Western Suburbs prop Pat O'Doherty was the first player signed from the draft, picked up by the Gold Coast.

THE PREMIERSHIP

Canberra edged out Brisbane for the minor premiership on for-and-against, but third-placed Penrith—under new coach Phil Gould—trumped the heavyweight pair to claim the first Grand Final berth. The Panthers upset the Broncos 26-16, and defeated the Raiders 30-12 in extra-time after the scores were locked 12-all at the 80-minute mark. Graham Lowe's Manly side eliminated Balmain, ending the decorated career of Tigers captain Wayne Pearce, before the Sea Eagles were halted 12-4 by Brisbane. Canberra regrouped to crush the Broncos 32-4 in the preliminary final and overcame Grand Final debutants Penrith 18-14 to secure back-to-back titles. Halfback Ricky Stuart won the Clive Churchill Medal, while club stalwarts John 'Chicka' Ferguson, Dean Lance and Chris O'Sullivan retired after the triumph.

- **Biggest win:** Canberra 66 d. Eastern Suburbs 4 at Bruce Stadium, round five
- **Top Point-scorer:** Mal Meninga (Canberra) 212
- **Top Try-scorer:** Mal Meninga (Canberra) 17

THE REPRESENTATIVE SCENE

With Jack Gibson as coach and Balmain rake Ben Elias as captain, NSW won the Origin series for the first time since 1986, two games to one. Australia thumped France 34-2 in the NSW country centre of Parkes and overwhelmed New Zealand 24-6 in Wellington. Great Britain carved out a stunning 19-12 upset at Wembley in the first Ashes Test, but the Kangaroos levelled the series with a 14-10 victory after Ricky Stuart conjured a long-range injury-time try for captain Mal Meninga. Australia retained the Ashes 14-0 in the third Test of the closest-fought Ashes series in 16 years and decimated France in the subsequent two-Test series.

STANDOUT PLAYER

Master ball-playing five-eighth Cliff Lyons produced the most consistent season of his career to collect Dally M Player of the Year honours, leading Manly's charge to the finals and winning his maiden national call-up with Kangaroos selection. Lyons was elevated to the Test side after Australia's first Test loss and was outstanding as the Kangaroos fought back to win the series.

MEMORABLE MATCH

In what then shaped as a Grand Final preview, a sell-out Lang Park crowd witnessed a top-shelf clash between Brisbane and Canberra. The Broncos raced out to an 18-2 lead after 22 minutes, before the Raiders clawed back with three tries to lead 20-18. But the home side rallied and snatched a 22-20 victory with a brilliant try to rookie fullback Paul Hauff, giving Brisbane the outright competition lead.

1991

Shedding the 'Chocolate Soldiers' tag forever, Penrith broke through for the club's first premiership, winning the Grand Final against a Canberra side that was mired in a financial crisis. The two-time premiers had exceeded the 1990 salary cap by over $85,000 and were staring down the barrel of a $6 million debt. The club survived the turmoil, but not before several high-profile stars were forced to join rival teams to help alleviate the massive overspend. The Federal Court ruled the contentious player draft was a restraint of trade late in 1991 and it was consequently abolished; in the short-lived draft's most publicised case, young Souths centre Terry Hill was forced to join Easts after the club picked him in the draft, despite desperately wanting to join Wests. The draft's demise allowed Hill to join the Magpies in 1992 after spending the 1991 season with the Roosters. State of Origin's greatest player was appropriately farewelled in triumph after arguably the best interstate series ever staged, while Australia stamped its authority in a series win over New Zealand—despite a shock win by the Kiwis in the opening Test.

THE PREMIERSHIP

Penrith finished as minor premiers six points clear of Manly and Norths in a thrilling regular season race; Canberra finished outright fourth, while Wests defeated Canterbury in a play-off for fifth. Brisbane, Illawarra and St. George finished just one win adrift of a finals appearance. Norths beat neighbours and archrivals Manly 28-16 to record the club's first finals win in 39 years, but an elusive Grand Final appearance was agonisingly out of reach for the long-suffering Bears, succumbing to Penrith and Canberra in the major semi and the preliminary final respectively. The embattled Raiders, hit hard by injury to compound their financial woes, embarked on a valiant sudden-death run with wins over Wests, Manly and Norths to reach their third straight decider. But the Greg Alexander-led Panthers broke their premiership duck in a euphoric 19-12 triumph over Canberra in the

Grand Final, overhauling a 12-6 halftime deficit. Departing club legend and former Test hooker Royce Simmons scored two tries in one of the great farewells.

- **Biggest win:** Illawarra 46 d. Gold Coast 4 at Wollongong Showgrounds, round eight
- **Top Point-scorer:** Daryl Halligan (North Sydney) 196
- **Top Try-scorer:** Alan McIndoe (Illawarra) 19

THE REPRESENTATIVE SCENE

Queensland captain Wally Lewis departed the Origin arena in glory after the closest and most dramatic interstate series of all time. Each match was decided by two points; the Maroons won the series-opener 6-4, before NSW levelled the series 14-12 with a late Michael O'Connor sideline conversion at the SFS in an explosive clash that featured a memorable stoush between Lewis and Penrith firebrand Mark Geyer. Queensland won a see-sawing decider 14-12. New Zealand scored a stunning 24-8 upset of Australia in the first Test in Melbourne, ending Wally Lewis' international career, but the green-and-golds crushed the Kiwis 44-0 and 40-12 in the remaining matches. Australia made a historic five-match tour of Papua New Guinea at the end of the season, winning both Test matches handsomely.

STANDOUT PLAYER

Assuming the club captaincy from Royce Simmons in 1991, Greg Alexander was the linchpin of Penrith's breakthrough title success. The gifted playmaker was named Dally M Halfback of the Year and finished third in the Dally M Medal count, before spearheading the Panthers' Grand Final victory with a long-range field goal and a sideline conversion late in the game. Alexander played two matches for NSW at fullback during the Origin series.

MEMORABLE MATCH

A phenomenal performance by Welsh dual international Jonathan Davies inspired 1991's most remarkable comeback and catapulted Canterbury into a play-off for fifth spot. Also-rans Cronulla led the Bulldogs 16-0 in the first half of the final-round clash, but two dazzling individual tries and five goals to Davies (for an 18-point haul) pegged Canterbury back into the contest. A try to former Test prop Bruce McGuire sealed a 24-16 victory described by chief executive Peter Moore as the greatest performance of his 22-season tenure at the club.

1992

The Brisbane Broncos came of age in 1992 with an emphatic premiership triumph. The Wayne Bennett-coached side employed an exhilarating brand of attacking football and were a class above their rivals, while the Broncos added to their aura with a World Club Challenge defat of all-conquering English club Wigan at the end of the year. Wigan had ventured to Australia in the pre-season and took out the World Sevens competition, defeating Brisbane in the final. Canberra faded out of finals contention in the wake of the financial crisis that gripped the club in 1991, while defending premiers Penrith failed to recover from the devastating death of young utility Ben Alexander—brother of captain Greg—in a car accident, and missed the top-five *(see Tragic Figures)*. Fellow 1991 heavyweights Norths and Manly also dipped out of the finals race. Parramatta legend Peter Sterling retired early in the season due to a recurring shoulder injury, while 'The King' Wally Lewis hung up his boots after captain-coaching the Gold Coast to the wooden spoon. The NSWRL announced mid-season that a team from Auckland would be admitted to the competition in 1995, while confirmation sides from Perth and Townsville, and another team based in Brisbane, would also join came at the end of the year.

THE PREMIERSHIP

Brisbane won its first minor premiership, six points clear of second-placed St. George. The Illawarra Steelers and the Newcastle Knights both qualified for maiden finals appearances and recorded their first post-season victories on finals debut against the Saints and Wests respectively. But the Dragons recovered to eliminate the Knights (3-2) and Steelers (4-0) in low-scoring contests to join the Broncos in the Grand Final. Brisbane had advanced to its maiden decider courtesy of a 22-12 major semi defeat of Illawarra. The Broncos claimed their first title with a resounding 28-8 defeat of the Brian Smith-coached Dragons and the premiership went to Queensland for the first time.

- **Biggest win:** Eastern Suburbs 56 d. South Sydney 16 at the Sydney Football Stadium, round 22
- **Top Point-scorer:** Daryl Halligan (North Sydney) 168
- **Top Try-scorer:** Mark Bell (Western Suburbs) 16; Tim Brasher 16 (Balmain)

THE REPRESENTATIVE SCENE

Laurie Daley captained Country Origin to its maiden win over City Origin, 17-10. Buoyed by the new captain and coach combination of Daley and Phil Gould, NSW won an engrossing Origin series 2-1 against Queensland in Mal Meninga's first series as skipper of the Maroons. The touring Lions stunned Australia by levelling the Ashes series with a Garry Schofield-inspired 33-10 victory in the second Test in Melbourne, but Meninga magnificently led the home side to a tense 16-10 result in the decider to retain the hallowed trophy. Australia defeated a spirited Papua New Guinea side 36-14 in Townsville later in the season. The green-and-golds retained the World Cup trophy with a gripping 10-6 victory over Great Britain in a spiteful clash at Wembley at the end of the year. Brisbane centre Steve Renouf scored the decisive try in the tense triumph.

STANDOUT PLAYER

Installed as Brisbane captain following the departure of Gene Miles, Allan Langer won the Rothmans Medal in leading the Broncos to the minor premiership, and was a resounding choice as Clive Churchill medallist after scoring two tries in the club's Grand Final triumph. The diminutive 'Alfie' kicked the match-winning field goal in Queensland's 5-4 victory in the second Origin encounter, and was superb throughout Australia's successful Ashes campaign.

MEMORABLE MATCH

Illawarra's blossoming into finals contenders after a barren decade in the premiership continued with a gripping 10-8 defeat of front-runners Brisbane at Lang Park. The Steelers won their first trophy—the pre-season Tooheys Challenge—with a try-less 4-2 victory over the Broncos, and doubled up with another two-point win in round seven. Young guns Paul McGregor and John Cross scored the tries in a victory that showcased the Steelers' burgeoning maturity under coach Graham Murray.

1993

The International Board made the bold decision to instigate the 10-metre rule in 1993, stipulating the defensive side must be back 10 metres from the play-the-ball instead of the previously regulated five metres. The rule came into effect midway through the Australian season and immediately increased the amount of points scored in premiership matches. But the changes did not impact on Brisbane's premiership defence—after a patchy regular season, the Broncos embarked on a history-making charge through the finals to claim back-to-back titles. Tina Turner—the voice and face of the NSWRL's successful advertising campaigns for five seasons—performed at the 1993 Grand Final and celebrated with the Broncos on-field after the decider.

THE PREMIERSHIP

After a five-year finals absence, Canterbury won a desperately close minor premiership race, earning a week off due to a superior for-and-against to St. George after both teams finished on 17 wins. But the Dragons advanced to the Grand Final with comprehensive defeats of Canberra and the Bulldogs, while defending premiers Brisbane charged to the decider by sweeping aside Manly, Canberra and Canterbury. The Broncos created history with their dour 14-6 Grand Final victory over the highly fancied Saints, becoming the first team to win the competition from fifth spot.

- **Biggest win:** Canberra 68 d. Parramatta 0 at Bruce Stadium, round 21
- **Top Point-scorer:** Daryl Halligan (North Sydney) 180
- **Top Try-scorer:** Noa Nadruku (Canberra) 22

THE REPRESENTATIVE SCENE

NSW retained the Origin crown by winning the opening two Origin clashes, including a 16-12 game two victory at the SFS that ranks as one of the great interstate encounters. The Maroons restored pride and sent veteran lock Bob Lindner out a winner with a 24-12 win at Lang Park in the dead-rubber third match. Australia won the three-Test trans-Tasman series 2-0 after the first Test at Auckland's Mt. Smart Stadium was drawn 14-all.

STANDOUT PLAYER

The Raiders were late-season premiership favourites, but a broken leg suffered by brilliant halfback Ricky Stuart in the penultimate round curtailed their title bid. Stuart was in irresistible form for Canberra and was the linchpin of NSW's Origin series success. He collected the Dally M Medal and Rothmans Medal on crutches following his heartbreaking injury.

MEMORABLE MATCH

The impact of Canberra's Fijian winger Noa Nadruku on the 1993 premiership was best exemplified in a heavyweight clash with Manly in round 10. The former rugby union international scored a crucial try and produced two try-saving tackles as the Raiders overtured a 10-0 deficit to prevail 21-10 at Brookvale Oval. Nadruku scored a hat-trick against Souths a week later and finished as the competition's top try-scorer with 22 in just 21 games.

1994

Modern giant Mal Meninga's impending departure provided the backdrop to the 1994 season. Queensland was unable to send its skipper out with a series victory but still provided an Origin highlight to live on for posterity. Meanwhile, Meninga led Canberra on a stunning surge to the premiership and the Kangaroos on another successful tour of Britain and France. Newcastle halfback Andrew Johns captured the imagination of the Rugby League public with a club record 23-point haul in his starting debut in the opening round of the season against Souths, showing but a glimpse of the ability that would carry him to the mantle of the game's best-ever No.7. The initial whispers of the rebel movement that would tear Rugby League in half a year later emerged early in 1994, as *Rugby League Week*'s Tony Durkin revealed constant bickering between the NSWRL and the Brisbane Broncos was potentially going to lead to the forming of a breakaway competition.

THE PREMIERSHIP

Canterbury's consistency was rewarded with its second straight minor premiership, finishing one point ahead of second-placed North Sydney. Terry Lamb's Bulldogs advanced to the Grand Final with a heart-stopping 19-18 extra-time defeat of Canberra in the major semi, just a day after the Bears eliminated two-time premiers Brisbane 15-14 in another thriller. The Raiders accounted for luckless Norths 22-9 in a dramatic preliminary final that saw rival forwards John Lomax (Canberra) and Gary Larson (Norths) sent off in separate incidents. Canberra blitzed the Bulldogs 36-12 in the Grand Final, sending retiring skipper Mal Meninga out with a dream premiership farewell. The Bulldogs failed to recover after knocking on from the kick-off and conceding the first four tries, while the Raiders' vaunted attack was in devastating touch.

- **Biggest win:** Manly 61 d. St. George 0 at Brookvale Oval, round 14
- **Top Point-scorer:** Daryl Halligan (Canterbury) 270
- **Top Try-scorer:** Steve Renouf (Brisbane) 23

THE REPRESENTATIVE SCENE

Queensland produced the greatest finish in Origin history in the series-opener to win 16-12 in Sydney, conjuring a long-range try finished off by St. George centre Mark Coyne. NSW levelled the series in front of a then-record crowd for a Rugby League match in Australia of 87,161 at the MCG with a 14-0 shutout, and spoiled Mal Meninga's Origin farewell with a 27-12 victory in the decider at Lang Park. Australia hammered the touring French side 58-0 in a one-off Test at Parramatta Stadium, before Meninga—embarking on a record fourth tour as the first player to captain two Kangaroo Tours—led the green-and-golds to Ashes glory in England. A 12-man Great Britain side upset Australia in the first Test at Wembley, but the tourists rallied to win the remaining clashes comfortably. Australia crushed France 74-0 in the last match of the tour—a fitting valediction for retiring legend Meninga.

STANDOUT PLAYER

Although surrounded by superstars, Canberra halfback Ricky Stuart carried the Raiders' fate in his hands. Stuart was at his most dominant in 1994, winning the NSW Rugby League Writers' award and finishing second in the *Rugby League Week* Player of the Year standings before steering the Raiders to premiership glory. He spearheaded NSW's third straight Origin series success and, in a remarkable repeat of the 1990 Ashes series, replaced Allan Langer after the Kangaroos' first Test loss and was the linchpin as Australia recovered to win the series.

MEMORABLE MATCH

North Sydney maintained its unbeaten start to the season with high-quality 11-10 win over defending premiers Brisbane in round six at Stadium Australia. The Bears raced to a 10-0 halftime lead, but the home side hit back to set up a grandstand finish. A field goal to Norths halfback Jason Taylor proved the difference in an eerie precursor to the clubs' finals showdown five months later.

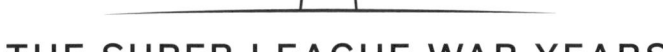

THE SUPER LEAGUE WAR YEARS

The News Limited-backed Super League's brazen and aggressive attempt to wrest control of Australian—and subsequently world—Rugby League from the ARL turned the game on its head on the 31st of March, 1995. The days, weeks and months that followed were packed with inflated contracts, secret negotiations, signings and counter-signings, propaganda and broken promises—all of which contributed to the biggest split in Australian sport since the NSWRL formed to create a rebellion against rugby union in 1908.

Premiership heavyweights Brisbane and Canberra were viewed as the figurehead clubs of Super League's breakaway movement, and that pair of clubs' involvement encouraged Cronulla, Penrith, the Sydney Bulldogs, and the only recently admitted Auckland, North Queensland and the Western Reds to get on board within a week of the upheaval. The remaining 12 clubs eventually sided with the ARL. The majority of the defecting clubs' players signed with Super League, but the ARL rallied with the influence of media magnate Kerry Packer and pay-television operator Optus Vision providing the establishment with a fighting chance.

The ARL demanded that all 20 clubs sign a loyalty agreement, with the Super League clubs' reluctant acceptance of this mandate forming the basis of the ARL-Super League court case. Astronomical sums were being thrown at players, coaches and even referees to align with one side or the other, creating an extraordinary windfall—with the money provided by Rupert Murdoch's News Limited (Super League) and Kerry Packer's media empire (ARL). The irony of Packer's staunch support of the ARL was that the breakaway movement possessed many similarities with the World Series Cricket revolution of the 1970s, of which Packer was founder.

Representative coaches Phil Gould and Bob Fulton were drafted in to negotiate with players and coaches on behalf of the ARL, which secured the signatures of hundreds of players to ensure the traditionalists maintained a strong and sizeable pool of talent. Super League—and its visibly prominent chief executive, ex-Test winger John Ribot—proclaimed to have signed the world's best players to form a higher-quality competition boasting Origin-style intensity. But 11 of the 28 Kangaroo tourists from the previous season stayed loyal to the ARL, while Bulldogs internationals Dean Pay and Jason Smith (along with star clubmates Jim Dymock and Jarrod McCracken) reneged on their Super League contracts to side with the establishment in one of the ARL's most significant victories of 1995.

International heavy-hitters Great Britain and New Zealand, and virtually every smaller nation in world Rugby League, joined the Super League movement, effectively cutting off the ARL from the international Rugby League community. The Federal Court case between the warring factions began during the 1995 finals series and continued through the summer. The initial verdict early in 1996 blocked Super League from getting underway, but an appeal overturned that decision to well and truly split the game in two. After just one fractured, discontented year of rival competitions being run, the game was thankfully united again in 1998. The bitter Super League-ARL war was unmistakably hostile, regularly vitriolic and always passionate, in many cases ending close friendships and lengthy associations. But despite the purveyors' strength of their convictions, their respective love for Rugby League eventually saw the bridges mended for the greater good of the game.

1995

The expanded 20-team premiership began with the excitement of having games staged in the Rugby League outposts of Auckland, Townsville and Perth in the opening round. The Auckland Warriors were gallant in a 25-22 loss to superpower Brisbane, while the Western Reds upset St. George 28-16 at the W.A.C.A. ground. But the North Queensland Cowboys and South Queensland Crushers were given a glimpse of the tough debut-season road ahead in big losses to heavyweights the Sydney Bulldogs and Canberra respectively. On the eve of round four, the landscape of the code changed dramatically as Super League aggressively began signing players, coaches and clubs. The ARL responded in kind and Rugby League descended into an all-out bidding war as the on-field action took a backseat. The exclusion of Super League signees from the representative schedule left both Origin squads depleted, but more so Queensland, which was forced to call upon several unheralded reserve graders and rookies. The under-strength sides produced one of the most memorable chapters in interstate history, however, as Paul 'Fatty' Vautin's Maroons claimed a seemingly impossible series cleansweep. Similarly disadvantaged, the Australian Test team achieved remarkable success, blitzing New Zealand 3-0 in the Test series and surging to World Cup glory under 23-year-old captain Brad Fittler. The quality of the premiership had not been undermined despite the upheaval, with the Super League-aligned Bulldogs—who were in turmoil during the year when star quartet Jason Smith, Jim Dymock, Dean Pay and Jarrod McCracken reneged on contracts with the rebel outfit to sign with the ARL and Parramatta—storming to an unlikely Grand Final triumph. Tobacco company sponsorship's impending ban dictated that the 1995 premiership would be the 14th and last Winfield Cup.

THE PREMIERSHIP

The Bob Fulton-coached ARL figureheads Manly produced the best start to a season in premiership history with 15 straight wins, and finished minor premiers on for-and-against from Canberra after both teams lost just two regular season matches. The expanded eight-team finals series witnessed a succession of thrilling contests;

top-four sides Brisbane and Cronulla dipped out of the finals with consecutive losses, while fifth-placed Newcastle earned a maiden preliminary final date with the Sea Eagles, valiantly going down 12-4. The sixth-placed Bulldogs eliminated St. George, Brisbane and Canberra on a stunning run to the Grand Final, and outplayed overwhelming favourites Manly 17-4 in the decider. One of the great Grand Final upsets, the Bulldogs' triumph under adversity simultaneously sent retiring club legend and captain Terry Lamb out with a fairytale premiership and dismissed the notion that a team could not win the competition from outside the top-four under the new eight-team finals format (Lamb later returned to aid the undermanned Bulldogs in 1996, extending his premiership appearances record to 349 games).

- **Biggest Win:** Sydney Bulldogs 66 d. North Queensland 4 at Belmore Sports Ground, round 22
- **Top Point-scorer:** Matthew Ridge (Manly) 257
- **Top Try-scorer:** Steve Menzies (Manly) 22

THE REPRESENTATIVE SCENE

Vautin's ragtag Queensland line-up caused the biggest boilover in Origin history by defeating NSW 2-0 in the series-opener—the only try-less match in the concept's 32 seasons. But the Trevor Gillmeister-captained Maroons went on to win the next two matches to complete an unfathomable series whitewash. Despite featuring a staggering 14 Test debutants during the series, Australia dominated the full-strength New Zealand side in a 3-0 series destruction. A handful of Canberra players lodged an appeal against their exclusion from the mid-season Tests, and the court found in their favour that they must be considered for the end-of-year World Cup. But the ARL defiantly picked a squad of exclusively loyal players. After losing the World Cup tournament-opener to hosts England, Australia rallied by defeating New Zealand in an extra-time classic 30-20 in the semi-final and outlasted England 16-8 in the final. The green-and-golds rode the brilliance of captain Brad Fittler and international rookie Andrew Johns to World Cup glory.

STANDOUT PLAYER

Newcastle's 21-year-old halfback Andrew Johns emerged as one of the premiership's dominant players, scoring 194 points and finishing equal-third in the Rothmans Medal and equal-second in the Dally M Medal counts, while taking out the Dally M Halfback of the Year gong. He debuted for NSW in the halves alongside older brother and clubmate Matthew, before claiming player of the tournament honours at the World Cup. Playing at hooker but predominantly occupying a first-receiver role (with halfback Geoff Toovey at dummy-half), Johns scored a world record-equalling 30 points (two tries, 11 goals) on Australian debut against South Africa and starred in the final triumph over England, finishing with a tournament-high 62 points.

MEMORABLE MATCH

Trailing 14-6 at halftime of its round 13 clash against lowly Parramatta, Brisbane staged a blistering second half turnaround and unveiled a future superstar. The Broncos piled on nine tries in the second stanza to amass a 60-14 scoreline, while 18-year-old five-eighth Darren Lockyer was injected late into the game, marking his first grade debut off the bench with a hand in several four-pointers.

1996

While Super League staged a soggy World Nines competition in Fiji (won by New Zealand) and the ARL forged ahead with its World Sevens competition (with Newcastle emerging victorious), the warring factions awaited a court decision on the game's fate. Justice Burchett's decision in February put the kybosh on the proposed 1996 Super League premiership, banning the rebel competition until 2000 and slamming the men behind the breakaway movement for their dishonesty and deception. Super League launched an immediate Federal Court appeal, while the rebel players initially refused en masse to participate in an ARL-run competition. Seven of the eight clubs forfeited opening-round matches (Auckland received two competition points after stating their willingness to field a side against forfeiting Brisbane), but everyone was back on deck for round two. Several Super League players were forced back to ARL clubs: Anthony Mundine and Nathan Brown returned from Canterbury and Cronulla respectively, while Auckland-bound Matthew Ridge initially resisted before returning to Manly and playing a vital role in the club's premiership victory. But Gorden Tallis defiantly sat out the season ahead of an impending move to the Broncos, refusing to play for St. George, while ex-Manly forward Ian Roberts also took a year out before joining North Queensland. After almost folding and undergoing a plethora of ownership, coaching and administration changes in the off-season, the Gold Coast club was rebranded as the Chargers and fielded a team against the odds in 1996 (see Extinct Clubs). The premiership's quality was not compromised by the game's uneasy holding pattern caused by the court appeal, while less than a week after the Grand Final, Justice Burchett's decision was overturned and Super League was given the go-ahead to form its own competition in 1997.

THE PREMIERSHIP

Manly collected its second straight minor premiership, one win ahead of the Broncos—who again flaked out of the finals with consecutive losses, to Norths and Cronulla. Phil Gould's Sydney City Roosters, spearheaded by Test captain Brad Fittler, finished fourth (after earlier heading the competition unbeaten after 10 rounds) to compete in their first post-season since 1987. But after a pulsating 16-14 loss to Manly in the quarter-finals, the Roosters were trounced 36-16 by St. George. The Dragons, who lost new coach Rod Reddy to the Super League cause in the off-season and brought in David Waite, finished seventh before edging out Canberra 16-14 with a late sideline conversion by lock Wayne Bartrim, eliminating the Roosters and smashing the hapless Bears 29-12 in the preliminary final. Manly eased into the Grand Final with a 24-0 preliminary final defeat of Cronulla and claimed an emphatic premiership victory with a 20-8 win over the Saints in the Grand Final. Ridge's performance in the decider was pivotal, while courageous captain Geoff Toovey won the Clive Churchill Medal just a week after suffering a fractured eye socket in the preliminary final.

- **Biggest Win:** Sydney City 62 d. South Sydney 0 at the Sydney Football Stadium, round six
- **Top Point-scorer:** Jason Taylor (North Sydney) 238
- **Top Try-scorer:** Noa Nadruku (Canberra) 21

THE REPRESENTATIVE SCENE

Super League players were eligible for Origin selection in 1996, which favoured Queensland on the surface, but it was NSW that swept to a convincing 3-0 series triumph. A full-strength Australian squad was selected to play in a proposed Test against New Zealand, but the NZRL refused to sanction the match and threatened bans against players that took part. The Super League-aligned Australian players refused to play in a match not sanctioned by the NZRL and the match was scrapped, with an ARL-loyal Test squad decimating Fiji 84-14 instead. Andrew Johns scored a then-world record 32 points in the romp. Geoff Toovey captained Australia to a 52-6 victory over a Papua New Guinea side, captained by Adrian Lam and consisting of ARL-aligned players, a week after the Grand Final in Port Moresby.

STANDOUT PLAYER

Brisbane captain Allan Langer's status as one of Rugby League's premier match-winners was enhanced in a Dally M Medal-winning 1996 campaign. The brilliant halfback was Queensland's best player in a disappointing Origin series, assuming the Maroons' captaincy for the last two matches.

MEMORABLE MATCH

A resurgent Parramatta and second-placed Sydney City staged a magnificent 20-all draw in round 18. Widely panned after a dismal first half of the season, the big-spending Eels were on the cusp of a late-season challenge for a finals spot (which was ultimately unsuccessful). The match reached a thrilling conclusion when Parramatta halfback-cum-winger Chris Lawler launched a towering field goal attempt as the fulltime siren sounded that fell just under the crossbar to leave the combatants with a competition point each.

1997

The court ruling in favour of Super League in October 1996 was a precursor to the most unique season in the game's history. Two competitions ran concurrently in a Rugby League year unlike any other, but one that ultimately left all involved feeling unfulfilled. Mercifully, the warring parties—after 993 days of bitter fighting—came to an agreement late in the year, announcing on December 19 that a unified National Rugby League competition would be initiated in 1998. The Rugby League world was also united in mourning former Test centre/five-eighth Peter Jackson in November. A gifted player and a larger-than-life personality, 'Jacko' died of a heroin overdose after a long battle with severe depression.

AUSTRALIAN RUGBY LEAGUE

The 12-team Optus Cup premiership provided its share of regular season highlights, but the year's standout moments were predominantly delivered by an electrifying finals series followed by the greatest finish to a Grand Final in Rugby League's history. Not to be outdone by Super League's rule innovations, the ARL introduced the exceedingly popular 40/20 rule, giving teams a scrum feed if they found touch inside the opposition 20-metre zone after kicking from inside their own 40-metre line. ARL head honchos John Quayle and Ken Arthurson resigned in quick succession early in the year, worn down from the tumult of the Super League conflict after making significant advancement for Rugby League in Australia since the early-1980s.

THE PREMIERSHIP

Manly won the minor premiership three points ahead of Newcastle and Parramatta, with Norths and Sydney City a win further back. Illawarra and finals debutants the Gold Coast secured the last two spots in the ARL's painfully confusing seven-team finals series system. Despite the baffling format, some of the great finals contests were staged in 1997. The Roosters defeated Norths 33-21 in an extra-time epic, a day before the Eels—in their first finals match since the 1986 Grand Final—surrendered an 18-0 lead to go down 28-20 to Newcastle. The Chargers upset Illawarra 27-14 in their maiden finals match, but were eliminated by the Roosters a week later, while the Bears despatched Parramatta. In a heart-stopping preliminary final weekend at a soggy SFS, a late Matthew Johns field goal propelled Newcastle to a 17-12 defeat of Norths, while Manly pipped the Roosters 17-16 in another thriller. In one of the greatest matches in the game's history, Newcastle fought back from a 16-8 halftime deficit against Manly in the Grand Final, drawing level when Clive Churchill medallist Robbie O'Davis scored his second try with five minutes remaining. A blindside burst by Knights linchpin Andrew Johns opened up a gap for winger Darren Albert to race over for arguably the premiership's most famous try with seven seconds remaining, sparking scenes of joyous pandemonium at the SFS and back in Newcastle in the wake of the Knights' 22-16 victory.

- **Biggest Win:** Sydney City 42 d. South Sydney 0 at the Sydney Football Stadium, round eight; Parramatta 52 d. South Queensland 0 at Parramatta Stadium, round 13
- **Top Point-scorer:** Jason Taylor (North Sydney) 242
- **Top Try-scorer:** Terry Hill (Manly) 22

THE REPRESENTATIVE SCENE

Geoff Toovey captained New South Wales to a 2-1 series victory after securing tight wins in the first two encounters; Queensland scored a morale-boosting 18-12 result in the third match. With virtually no international opposition available, Australia played a Test against a Rest of the World line-up made up of ARL-loyal international players. Australia defeated the Adrian Lam-led combination 28-8 in Brisbane.

STANDOUT PLAYER

Although injury ruled him out of NSW's Origin campaign, Sydney City captain Brad Fittler was a resounding winner of the ARL's official premiership player of the year award, the Provan-Summons Medal (which became a people's choice award from 1998).

MEMORABLE MATCH

Norths led the minor qualifying final against Sydney City 13-0 at halftime, before a double to brilliant fullback Andrew Walker pulled the Roosters back to level at 14-all. Jason Taylor nudged the Bears in front with a field goal, but his opposing No.7 Adrian Lam snapped a one-pointer from dummy-half to send the match into extra-time. Lam scored one of three Roosters tries in the added 20 minutes as they surged to a 33-21 victory.

SUPER LEAGUE

For the all the glitz, glamour and promises of 'Origin-quality' premiership matches on a weekly basis, the Super League season ultimately fell flat. Brisbane was streets ahead of the field in the premiership, with Cronulla and Canberra the only clubs offering genuine resistance. Expansion teams Adelaide and the Newcastle-based Hunter Mariners performed admirably, but the likes of Auckland, North Queensland the Perth Reds were extremely disappointing. The premiership was disjointed due to extended breaks for the staging of the ill-fated and costly World Club Challenge competition involving the European Super League clubs, which featured embarrassingly lopsided results and was also won easily by the Broncos *(see World Club Challenge)*. Positive legacies from the Super League competition included the introduction of the video referee (despite some teething problems) and the 'zero tackle' from an opposition mistake, but the rule change of the scoring side kicking off to restart play found little favour and American-style innovations of players choosing their own numbers at each club was also criticised.

THE PREMIERSHIP

Brisbane finished as minor premiers, five points clear of Cronulla, with Canberra a win further back in third. Canterbury and Penrith made up the top-five finals series; the Panthers upset the Bulldogs 15-14, but were comprehensively eliminated by Canberra. The Sharks and Raiders staged two gripping finals encounters in the major preliminary semi-final and the preliminary final—both won by the Andrew Ettingshausen-led Cronulla side. But Brisbane was a class above, decimating the Sharks 34-2 in the major semi and repeating the dose 26-8 in the Grand Final, which was staged at Brisbane's Stadium Australia and included a hat-trick to Broncos centre Steve Renouf.

- **Biggest Win:** Brisbane 54 d. Penrith 12 at Stadium Australia, round 16; Canberra 58 d. Adelaide 16 at Bruce Stadium, round 17
- **Top Point-scorer:** Ryan Girdler (Penrith) 197
- **Top Try-scorer:** Matthew Ryan (Canterbury) 17

THE REPRESENTATIVE SCENE

The Tri-Series competition between New South Wales, Queensland and New Zealand (a non-Test side) lacked the atmosphere of State of Origin, but provided high-quality football nonetheless. NSW thumped Queensland 38-10 in the series-opener, prior to the Anzac Day Test between Super League Australia and New Zealand, which the Laurie Daley-led Australians won 34-22. Queensland defeated New Zealand 26-12 when the Tri-Series resumed and advanced to the final after the Kiwi side was controversially denied a late try in a 20-15 loss to NSW. The NSW side won the final in a golden point classic, 23-22. Matthew Ridge inspired the New Zealand Test side to a 30-12 boilover against Australia at the end of the season, before Australia embarked on a tour of England, winning the Test series 2-1 against Great Britain.

STANDOUT PLAYER

Laurie Daley was named the Super League premiership's Player of the Year, while he captained the NSW and Australian Super League line-ups superbly, scoring three tries in the 38-14 first Test victory against Great Britain and crossing for another four-pointer in the 37-20 win in the deciding third Test.

MEMORABLE MATCH

The Tri-Series final at Brisbane's Stadium Australia produced a 104-minute epic between NSW and Queensland; the scores were locked 22-all (with Brett Mullins scoring a hat-trick for NSW) after 80 minutes and no points were added in 20 minutes of extra-time. NSW halfback Noel Goldthorpe slotted a golden point field goal to win the final 23-22, capping one of the great games and undoubtedly the finest encounter of Super League's sole season.

THE NRL ERA

Australian Rugby League chief executive Neil Whittaker and Super League counterpart Ian Frykberg brokered a peace deal between the warring factions to set up a unified competition under the 'National Rugby League' banner in 1998. The inaugural 20-team competition featured 11 ARL clubs and eight Super League clubs, with the addition of the fledgling News Limited-owned Melbourne Storm. The ARL-loyal South Queensland Crushers and Super League sides the Perth Reds and Hunter Mariners were disbanded at the end of 1997, while the NRL pledged to reduce the number of teams to 14 by the year 2000 as the game attempted to remedy the financial and social losses incurred during the bitter three-year upheaval. With Whittaker at the helm, and later David Moffett and David Gallop, the NRL took Rugby League in Australia into a bold new era. The game endured its share of hardships in the first 14 years of the NRL and weathered crippling controversies. Three mergers took place—two of which went on to win premierships, while one folded to effectively signal the end of North Sydney's involvement in the premiership. Adelaide and the Gold Coast folded after the NRL's first season, but a new club was established on South-East Queensland's holiday strip in 2007. South Sydney was axed from the competition and readmitted two years later in a stirring example of 'people power.' The competition witnessed an unprecedented turnover of premiers, with no club claiming back-to-back titles to date in the NRL era. Heroes of the early-to-mid-1990s pressed on, such as Brad Fittler, Allan Langer, Laurie Daley, Andrew Johns and Stacey Jones, while the likes of Darren Lockyer, Nathan Hindmarsh, Brett Kimmorley, Billy Slater, Cameron Smith, Greg Inglis, Johnathan Thurston and Benji Marshall provided the code with new superstars to marvel at. New South Wales and Queensland wrestled evenly for interstate supremacy, before the Maroons pieced together an unprecedented period of Origin dominance. Australia remained the preeminent force on the international scene, but New Zealand emerged as a brazen challenger during the 2000s with a string of triumphs in high-powered tournament finals. Constant and ever-present challenges confronted Rugby League, but the game clawed itself back to a powerful position after the harrowing days of the Super League war.

1998

The reunification of the game under the NRL banner was a welcome relief after the turmoil of the previous three seasons, but was not without unease as war wounds took time to heal over. The game was hit with unrelated controversy in the shape of a performance-enhancing drugs scandal. Melbourne front-rower Rodney Howe and Newcastle Grand Final trio Robbie O'Davis, Wayne Richards and Adam MacDougall tested positive to banned substances. Howe, O'Davis and Richards (who was also sacked by the Knights) were handed the maximum 22-week suspensions, while MacDougall had his ban reduced to 11 weeks on the grounds of his complicated medical history. The NRL's rationalisation plan to reduce the number of teams in the premiership to 14 by 2000 (based on a rigorous performance criteria outline) put most clubs—particularly those in Sydney—under intense pressure. Several clubs entertained the idea of entering into a joint venture after the NRL's offer of multi-million dollar cash injection for newly merged entities. St. George and Illawarra announced the formation of the game's first joint venture during Grand Final week, while Adelaide and the Gold Coast folded at the end of the season. The unified representative season provided some glowing highlights, while the Brisbane Broncos proved themselves as the best of the best with a decisive premiership triumph. The hastily assembled Melbourne Storm was one of 1998's supreme success stories, keeping pace with the NRL's front-runners in a phenomenal debut season.

THE PREMIERSHIP

Respective champions of the rival 1997 competitions, Brisbane and Newcastle finished tied at the top of the table after 24 rounds, with the Broncos' superior for-and-against securing the minor premiership. First-year club Melbourne was the surprise packet in third, while St. George was the only club in the 10-team finals series that did not qualify for the post-season in 1997. The feature of the finals was Canterbury's phenomenal charge from ninth spot, eliminating the Saints and Norths, before advancing to the Grand Final with consecutive extra-time triumphs over Newcastle and Parramatta. The Broncos were upset by the Eels in their first finals match, but rebounded with emphatic defeats of Melbourne and Sydney City to reach the decider. Despite trailing 12-10 at halftime of the inaugural NRL Grand Final, the star-studded Broncos stampeded to a 38-12 victory over the gallant but weary Bulldogs.

- **Biggest Win:** North Sydney 62 d. North Queensland 0 at North Sydney Oval, round 24
- **Top Point-scorer:** Ivan Cleary (Sydney City) 284
- **Top Try-scorer:** Darren Smith (Brisbane) 23

THE REPRESENTATIVE SCENE

Queensland claimed the interstate crown in a thrilling 2-1 series result, winning the first match 24-23 with a last minute try reminiscent of the 1994 series-opener, before NSW levelled the series 26-10 in game two. The Maroons won the decider 19-4 against a Blues outfit decimated by injuries. New Zealand won its first Test against a full-strength Australian team since 1991 with a 22-16 boilover at North Harbour Stadium early in the season, while future great Darren Lockyer made a disastrous, error-prone debut off the bench in the only blot on a brilliant season for the 21-year-old fullback. A Broncos-stacked Australian side won two post-season Tests against the Kiwis comprehensively.

STANDOUT PLAYER

Veteran halfback Allan Langer was at his game-breaking best in captaining Brisbane to the premiership, Queensland to Origin glory and Australia to Test series success—an unprecedented feat that has only been matched by Darren Lockyer (2006) since.

MEMORABLE MATCH

The pulsating last-round clash between Illawarra and Canterbury at Wollongong doubled as the Steelers' last match before their merger with St. George. The first half featured a sizzling 85-metre try to 18-year-old Illawarra fullback and future Bulldogs great Luke Patten, helping the Steelers to a 16-12 lead at the break. The lead changed hands several times in the second half and the scores were locked 24-all heading into the final 10 minutes. Five-eighth Craig Polla-Mounter slotted a field goal with 30 seconds remaining to secure a finals berth for the Bulldogs 25-24.

1999

Rugby League had a new headquarters in 1999, officially opening the new Olympic venue, Stadium Australia, with a double-header in front of a world record 104,583-strong crowd in round one. That mark was extended to 107,999 for the Grand Final at the end of the year—between surprise qualifiers, the first-year joint venture St. George Illawarra and second-year club Melbourne. What transpired was the most extraordinary finish to a premiership decider in the game's history. It became apparent during the year that several clubs were not going to meet the NRL's performance criteria to survive beyond 1999, leading to Western Suburbs and Balmain announcing a merger in July. North Sydney's rapid decline in 1999, after an ill-fated relocation to Gosford hit a snag with construction delays to their new stadium, backed the club into a corner and the Bears reluctantly entered a joint venture with arch-rivals Manly at the end of the year. But the year's most heart-rending development was the axing of South Sydney from the competition at the end of the year. Led by obstinate chairman George Piggins, the Rabbitohs defiantly refused to consider merging, and the premiership's most famous and successful club's unbroken 92-season history was halted. The NRL also imposed a $3.25 million salary cap on all clubs for 1999, bringing to an end the outlandish salaries players commanded during the Super League upheaval. The McIntyre finals system was introduced, a controversial format that remained in place until overturned at the beginning of 2012. NRL chief executive Neil Whittaker stood down from the role at the end of the year and was replaced by former New Zealand Rugby Football Union supremo David Moffett. Wally Lewis and Graeme Langlands were added to the ranks of the 'Immortals' by *Rugby League Week*.

THE PREMIERSHIP

Cronulla finished as minor premiers, and advanced to the preliminary final with a 42-20 qualifying final defeat of eighth-placed Brisbane. The Broncos' title defence got off to a disastrous start—the perennial heavyweights sat in outright last after 12 rounds, while captain and club legend Allan Langer retired abruptly after an indifferent start to the season. But the club staged one of the great in-season turnarounds, piecing together an 11-match winning streak to scrape into the finals. Second-placed Parramatta qualified for the preliminary final by eliminating Newcastle, but the highly fancied Eels and Sharks were upset one game short of the Grand Final by Melbourne and St. George Illawarra respectively. Riding the brilliance of unpredictable five-eighth Anthony Mundine to the decider, the Dragons were installed as warm favourites due to their 34-10 qualifying final thrashing of the third-placed Storm three weeks earlier. The Paul McGregor-captained Saints led 14-0 at halftime of the Grand Final, but Melbourne clawed back and trailed only 18-14 heading into the final five minutes. Storm winger Craig Smith looked set to score out wide after claiming a Brett Kimmorley cross-field kick, but he was felled in the in-goal by opposing winger Jamie Ainscough's high tackle and dropped the ball. The premiership hung on the decision of video referee Chris Ward, who sensationally but correctly ruled a penalty try. Matt Geyer's resultant conversion from in front of the posts secured an outlandish 20-18 triumph in just the Storm's second season. Captain Glenn Lazarus retired after the victory as the only player to win premierships with three different clubs, while halfback Kimmorley won the Clive Churchill Medal.

- **Biggest Win:** Newcastle 60 d. South Sydney 0 at Marathon Stadium, round 23
- **Top Point-scorer:** Matt Geyer (Melbourne) 242
- **Top Try-scorer:** Nathan Blacklock (St. George Illawarra) 24

THE REPRESENTATIVE SCENE

A grinding, hard-fought Origin series ended in a historic draw. Queensland won the first match 9-8, before NSW levelled 12-8 in game two. The decider finished 10-all in a match that marked the end of the interstate careers of opposing five-eighth greats Laurie Daley and Kevin Walters. The Maroons retained the Origin shield as the previous series' winners. Australia regained the Bill Kelly Cup with a hard-fought 20-14 victory over the Kiwis in the early-season Test. A Tri-Nations series was held for the first time between Australia, New Zealand and Great Britain. The British side was thrashed by both of the Southern Hemisphere teams, while the Kiwis upset the Kangaroos 24-22. Australia turned the tables on its plucky trans-Tasman rivals 22-20 in a heart-stopping final.

STANDOUT PLAYER

Andrew Johns collected the Dally M Medal-*Rugby League Week* Player of the Year double for the second successive season in another year of consistent brilliance that saw the 25-year-old Newcastle No.7 lauded as potentially the best halfback ever.

MEMORABLE MATCH

The 11th match of Brisbane's amazing winning streak was the closest-fought—a 9-8 victory over equal ladder leaders Sydney City. Played on a wet Friday night at the SFS, the Roosters clung to their 8-4 halftime lead until the final 10 minutes, when young Broncos interchange Shaun Berrigan stretched out to level the scores. Ben Walker's conversion was waved away, but fullback Darren Lockyer kept Brisbane's finals bid on track with field goal five seconds from fulltime.

2000

The NRL season started in early-February due to the September staging of the Sydney Olympics. But the surprise results and close finishes that marked club and representative Rugby League in 1999 was replaced by overwhelming dominance. Brisbane streeted the NRL field; NSW recorded the most dominant series victory in Origin history; and Australia was a class above its international competition at the year-ending World Cup. The Wests Tigers appeared destined for a first-season finals appearance sitting in second spot after 16 rounds, but lost eight of their last 10 games to slump to 10th. The Northern Eagles' debut year was marked by backroom bickering and poor on-field performances in a 12th-place finish. St. George Illawarra—grand finalists in 1999—missed the top-eight, rocked by the early-season walkout of star five-eighth Anthony Mundine, who left abruptly and acrimoniously to pursue a career in professional boxing. The Auckland Warriors' diabolical financial situation and dismal results led to calls for their exclusion from the NRL, but the purchase of the franchise by millionaire businessman Eric Watson at the end of 2000 turned the embattled club around. Cronulla great Andrew Ettingshausen retired after 328 games for the Sharks—a premiership appearance record for one club. The NRL voted to scrap the unlimited interchange rule—used so effectively by coach Wayne Bennett and the powerful Broncos—from 2001, introducing a maximum of 12 interchanges per game for each team.

THE PREMIERSHIP

Brisbane finished six points clear of the Sydney Roosters at the end of the regular season, and for the first time since 1992 in a unified competition, the top two teams squared off in the Grand Final. The Kevin Walters-captained Broncos grinded out a 16-10 preliminary final win over the young Parramatta outfit, which had surged to the penultimate weekend of the competition from seventh. Brad Fittler's Roosters overcame a 14-point halftime deficit in the preliminary final against Newcastle to advance 26-20. But the relentless Broncos forward pack overpowered their counterparts in a dour 14-6 Grand Final victory, with rival fullbacks Darren Lockyer and Luke Phillips providing the rare glimpses of brilliance in the match. Lockyer was named the Clive Churchill medallist, while Walters retired with a fairytale premiership win—his sixth with Canberra and Brisbane.

- **Biggest Win:** Melbourne 70 d. St. George Illawarra 10 at the Melbourne Cricket Ground, round five
- **Top Point-scorer:** Joel Caine (Wests Tigers) 224
- **Top Try-scorer:** Nathan Blacklock (St. George Illawarra) 25

THE REPRESENTATIVE SCENE

NSW scored the most emphatic series victory in its Origin history; after a controversial 20-16 comeback win in the series-opener that saw Queensland firebrand Gorden Tallis sent off for dissent, NSW wrapped up the series 28-10 in game two and set a host of records in a 56-16 demolition of the shell-shocked Maroons in the dead-rubber clash. Australia blitzed a shambolic New Zealand outfit 52-0 in the Bill Kelly Cup Test, and charged to an emphatic World Cup triumph at the end of the year, defeating the Kiwis 40-12 in the final.

STANDOUT PLAYER

Brad Fittler captained NSW and Australia to resounding successes, while his game-breaking class was the key component of the Sydney Roosters' drive to the NRL Grand Final. The five-eighth leader was 2000's Golden Boot recipient.

MEMORABLE MATCH

The passing of Canterbury club patriarch Peter 'Bullfrog' Moore provided an emotional backdrop to the round 23 match between the Bulldogs and defending premiers Melbourne just three days later. Moore was the father-in-law of opposing coaches Steve Folkes (Canterbury) and Chris Anderson (Melbourne). Out of finals contention, the Bulldogs channelled their emotions to upset the third-placed Storm 31-22, with Folkes dedicating the two points to the 'Bullfrog.'

2001

The shock return of veteran halfback Allan Langer from England to play for Queensland in the State of Origin decider, and South Sydney's successful Federal Court appeal against the club's exclusion from the NRL paving the way for its return in 2002, provided glowing highlights in a year speckled with unsavoury controversy. Newcastle's stunning Grand Final upset of runaway minor premiers Parramatta, too, was a high point, although the NRL's decision to break with tradition and play the match at night was met with mixed reviews. The Wests Tigers were rocked by star players Kevin McGuinness and Craig Field testing positive to cocaine early in the season; the pair spent 11 weeks on the sideline. Shortly afterward, hothead Tigers winger John Hopoate was outed for 12 matches and dumped by the club after being found guilty of contrary conduct for poking his finger into the backsides of opposing North Queensland players, earning international notoriety. The Bulldogs' supporter base was put under the microscope after repeated crowd disturbances at the club's matches. The now-professional rugby union's reversal of a 90-year-old trend stepped up a gear with the poaching of Australian Test wingers Wendell Sailor and Mat Rogers. Parramatta halfback Jason Taylor broke Daryl Halligan's premiership record for career points; the former Wests, Norths and Northern Eagles sharpshooter retired after the Eels' Grand Final loss with 2,107 points to his name.

THE PREMIERSHIP

Parramatta surged to the minor premiership with 20 wins and two draws from its 26 matches, five points clear of the Bulldogs, who were eliminated from the finals courtesy of consecutive losses to St. George Illawarra and Cronulla. The Eels crushed the rebranded New Zealand Warriors 56-12 in the qualifying final, but it was a watershed year for the Auckland-based club, reaching the finals for the first time after six seasons of underachievement and administrative calamity. Wendell Sailor scored four tries in Brisbane's 44-28 semi-final elimination of the Dragons, but the Broncos' campaign ended in a gallant 24-16 preliminary final loss to Parramatta. Third-placed Newcastle flew under the radar with rookie coach Michael Hagan at the helm, despatching the Sydney Roosters and Cronulla on its way to the Grand Final, and subsequently stunned the Eels in a first half ambush, racing to a 24-0 lead at the break. Captain Andrew Johns pulled the strings while destructive forward Ben Kennedy provided the grunt as the Knights held off a spirited Parramatta comeback 30-24. The Eels had amassed a premiership record 942 points in 2001, but their unparalleled consistency during the season did not translate to an elusive title for Brian Smith's charges.

- **Biggest Win:** Melbourne 64 d. Wests Tigers 0 at Docklands Stadium, round 18
- **Top Point-scorer:** Ben Walker (Northern Eagles) 279; Andrew Johns (Newcastle) 279
- **Top Try-scorer:** Nathan Blacklock (St. George Illawarra) 27

THE REPRESENTATIVE SCENE

The City Origin v Country Origin fixture returned after a four-year absence, resulting in a record 42-10 win to the bush boys. Queensland's stunning turnaround was achieved with a hungry batch of Origin rookies, and in spite of captain Gorden Tallis' season-ending injury before the second game. Fullback Darren Lockyer led the Maroons brilliantly for the remainder of the series, spearheading the 40-14 victory in the decider in conjunction was shock returnee Allan Langer. Australia swept aside New Zealand and Papua New Guinea in Test clashes, but the proposed Kangaroo Tour was put on hold after the events in New York on September 11. A shortened tour was eventually undertaken, with Australia rebounding from a series-opening loss to take the first Ashes series since 1994 2-1 in captain Brad Fittler's international swansong.

STANDOUT PLAYER

Andrew Johns scored a club record 279 points—the equal-third highest season total ever at the time—while a late-season suspension cost him a third Dally M Medal. Johns captained Newcastle to the premiership with a Churchill Medal-winning performance in Grand Final upset of Parramatta, and was Australia's chief destroyer in the Ashes victory, scoring 20 points in the series-saving second Test win.

MEMORABLE MATCH

Canterbury's decision to move its home game against the Warriors to the New Zealand capital of Wellington paid dividends with a bumper crowd of 27,724 turning out for the match, and appeared certain to leave with two competition points at 24-8 in front with 10 minutes remaining. But the flamboyant Warriors ran in three quick-fire tries to lock up the scores. Faced with a relatively simple conversion to win the match after Clinton Toopi's late four-pointer, Kiwi halfback Stacey Jones sprayed the kick to consign the match to a draw.

2002

The joyous return of South Sydney to the premiership was quickly followed by the harsh reality of week-to-week competition for a club with a limited playing roster and modest finances. The Rabbitohs won just five games in their first season back, but were saved from the wooden spoon by the revelations of salary cap rorting by runaway competition leaders the Bulldogs with only three rounds of the season remaining. A *Sydney Morning Herald* investigation into the proposed 'Oasis' property development—which the Bulldogs were found to be a partner in—subsequently uncovered the club's secret payments to players that resulted in a $750,000 overspend in 2001, while they had exceeded the salary cap by almost $900,000 in 2002. NRL CEO David Gallop, who only came into the role in February, announced the heartbreaking decision that the Bulldogs would be stripped of all competition points accrued in 2002, effectively consigning them to last place, and fined $500,000. The Bulldogs had pieced together a 17-match winning streak during the year and were overwhelming title favourites. The club's board, chief executive Bob Hagan and Leagues Club chairman Gary McIntyre all resigned in the wake of the furore. The disastrous Northern Eagles joint venture slumped to new depths as the Manly faction effectively assumed the running of the club, ending North Sydney's 94-season involvement in the premiership. The joint venture fully disbanded at the end of 2002 and the Manly Sea Eagles fielded a team in the 2003 season.

THE PREMIERSHIP

The Bulldogs' demise threw the premiership race wide open. New Zealand took out its maiden minor premiership on for-and-against from Newcastle, with Brisbane one point back in third. The Knights' campaign hit the skids when Andrew Johns suffered a season-ending back injury in the upset 26-22 qualifying final loss to seventh-placed St. George Illawarra, crashing 38-12 to the Sydney Roosters a week later. The in-form Roosters advanced to the Grand Final with their eighth straight win in a gripping 16-12 preliminary final defeat of the Broncos, ending the decorated career of Allan Langer, who returned to Brisbane for a wonderful swansong season in 2002. On the other side of the draw, the Warriors despatched Canberra 36-20 and outlasted Cronulla 16-10 in another preliminary final thriller. The Daniel Anderson-coached Warriors snatched an 8-6 lead early in the second half of the decider, but captain Brad Fittler inspired the Roosters to a resounding 30-8 triumph—the club's first Grand Final victory in 27 years, and a rookie-season premiership for coach Ricky Stuart.

- **Biggest Win:** Parramatta 64 d. Penrith 6 at Parramatta Stadium, round one; New Zealand 68 d. Northern Eagles 10 at Ericsson Stadium, round five
- **Top Point-scorer:** Hazem El Masri (Bulldogs) 254
- **Top Try-scorer:** Nigel Vagana (Bulldogs) 23

THE REPRESENTATIVE SCENE

Queensland recovered from a 32-4 pasting at the hands of NSW in the series-opener to force a drawn series, consequently retaining the Origin shield. The Maroons won the second encounter 26-18 (despite a notorious debut from young three-quarter Justin Hodges), before Dane Carlaw scored a 50-metre last-minute try to draw the decider 18-all. The tied result sparked howls of disapproval from south of the border and led to introduction of golden point in Origin matches in 2003. Andrew Johns led Australia to a record 64-10 dismantling of Great Britain mid-season, while Gorden Tallis captained the Kangaroos in a hard-fought 32-24 win over New Zealand at the end of the year.

STANDOUT PLAYER

New Zealand talisman Stacey Jones' match-winning prowess was at its zenith in 2002. Taking over as captain of the Warriors after an early-season injury to Monty Betham, Jones led the club to the minor premiership and a maiden Grand Final appearance, scoring one of the great individual tries in the spirited 30-8 loss. Jones finished fifth in the Dally M Medal count and became just the second Kiwi to win the Golden Boot, which he collected after captaining his country in five post-season Tests.

MEMORABLE MATCH

Brisbane scored one of the most famous wins in its history against the Wests Tigers at Campbelltown. Missing 15 regular first grade players due to injuries and Origin duty, along with Queensland coach Wayne Bennett, the 'Baby Broncos' defied the odds to down the Tigers 28-14. Assistant coach Craig Bellamy prepared the squad that contained six debutants and boasted an average age of just 21 (including five teenagers) as the Broncos dipped heavily into the ranks of Queensland Cup feeder club Toowoomba.

2003

The burgeoning rivalry between 2002 champions the Sydney Roosters and would-be premiers the Bulldogs dominated the majority of title favouritism talk during 2003, but an unfancied team from Sydney's west trumped both heavyweights to carve out one of the modern era's most memorable premiership victories. Penrith—wooden spooners just two years earlier and 12th in 2002—swept to the minor premiership and a stirring Grand Final triumph marked by an incredible covering tackle. Golden point was introduced to decide drawn NRL and State of Origin encounters, receiving a mixed reaction from the game's coaches. A bitter industrial dispute between the NRL and the Rugby League Players' Association over the negotiations of a new collective bargaining agreement led to NRL chief executive David Gallop making his second difficult decision in as many seasons in charge, announcing the cancellation of the Dally M Awards night. Arthur Beetson was named as the seventh Immortal by *Rugby League Week*.

THE PREMIERSHIP

Penrith won 18 regular season games to finish top of the table two points ahead of the Roosters, with the Bulldogs one win further back. Competition front-runners after 17 rounds, Brisbane lost its last eight games to slump to eighth spot, and was promptly eliminated by the Panthers 28-18. The sixth-placed New Zealand Warriors staged a stunning 46-22 upset of the Bulldogs in the first week of the finals (with winger Francis Meli scoring a finals record five tries) and advanced to the preliminary final with a pulsating 17-16 semi-final defeat of much-improved Canberra, but their run was halted by the Panthers 28-20. The showdown Rugby League supporters had been gagging for occurred in the other preliminary final, with the Roosters outlasting the Bulldogs 28-18. Clive Churchill medallist Luke Priddis set up two tries for winger Luke Rooney and scored one himself in the Panthers' 18-6 defeat of the Roosters in an engrossing Grand Final. But the turning point came midway through the second half with the scores locked at 6-all—Roosters winger Todd Byrne set off on a long run down the touchline with only open pasture in front of him, but Penrith lock Scott Sattler sprinted across in cover and bundled the flyer into touch with a textbook tackle to etch his name into Grand Final folklore.

- **Biggest Win:** Parramatta 74 d. Cronulla 4 at Parramatta Stadium, round 24
- **Top Point-scorer:** Hazem El Masri (Bulldogs) 294
- **Top Try-scorer:** Rhy Wesser (Penrith) 25

THE REPRESENTATIVE SCENE

Andrew Johns was in irresistible form as NSW wrapped up the Origin series in the first two matches, before Queensland racked a record-equalling 36-6 victory in the dead-rubber clash. Australia decimated New Zealand 48-6 mid-season but was upset 30-16 by the Kiwis en route to England at the end of the year. Darren Lockyer led the injury-hit Kangaroos to a spectacular Ashes series whitewash of hosts Great Britain, winning all three matches in heart-stopping late comebacks.

STANDOUT PLAYER

Darren Lockyer handled the responsibility of being the chief playmaker for Brisbane and Queensland from fullback with customary class and outstanding consistency. An injury to Andrew Johns handed the Test captaincy to Lockyer, and he was phenomenal in getting Australia out of jail in the first and third Ashes Tests in England, garnering the Golden Boot award in his final season wearing the No.1 jersey ahead of a switch to five-eighth in 2004.

MEMORABLE MATCH

Eventual premiers Penrith looked anything but contenders after losses in the opening two rounds, but the Panthers' stirring 23-22 defeat of defending champs the Sydney Roosters in round three provided the impetus they needed to start their charge. Trailing 16-6 early in the second half, the Panthers piled on three tries and fullback Rhys Wesser completed his hat-trick to set up a 22-16 lead. A field goal to captain Craig Gower with eight minutes remaining sealed the victory.

2004

The NRL was rocked by allegations emanating from the Bulldogs' stay at Coffs Harbour for a pre-season trial. Six Bulldogs players were alleged to have gang-raped a 23-year-old woman, sparking a major police investigation that put the club and the game as a whole under the microscope. No charges were laid after prosecutors found insufficient evidence. The club asserted the outcome vindicated its players and there were suggestions the Bulldogs had been unfairly treated, but Rugby League had undoubtedly had its image severely tarnished. Player misbehaviour was in the headlines again in the lead-up to the State of Origin series-opener, when Mark Gasnier and Anthony Minichiello were dumped from the NSW squad for leaving an obscene message on the voicemail of a 27-year-old Sydney woman during a drunken team 'bonding' session, while five other players were fined. Both players returned later in the series, but the debacle led to coaching guru Phil Gould announcing he would step down from the Blues' post at the conclusion of the series. Meanwhile, Queensland winger Chris Walker was punted after being ejected from a Brisbane nightclub and capsicum sprayed by police. Newcastle captain Andrew Johns suffered a serious knee injury in just round three—the third year in a row his season had been cut short by injury. The Australian Rugby Union courted Johns during his layoff and for a time it appeared Rugby League's No.1 player would switch codes, but he eventually decided to remain in the NRL.

THE PREMIERSHIP

The battle between the Sydney Roosters and the Bulldogs for title of the NRL's dominant club raged on as the bitter rivals finished equal first at the end of the regular season, with the Roosters claiming the minor premiership on for-and-against. Brisbane finished five points adrift in third, while the Broncos' season was terminated by back-to-back finals losses to Melbourne and North Queensland (in retiring captain Gorden Tallis' last game). The seventh-placed Cowboys had shocked the Bulldogs 30-22 in their finals debut a week earlier, and their rousing charge was finally halted by the Roosters 19-16 in a gripping preliminary final. The Bulldogs regrouped to qualify for the Grand Final via comprehensive wins over Melbourne and Penrith. Under siege off the field just a few months earlier, the Bulldogs overcame a 13-6 halftime scoreline in favour of the Roosters to triumph 16-13 in a worthy decider. Bulldogs forward Willie Mason's powerful display was rewarded with the Clive Churchill Medal, while Roosters captain and modern great Brad Fittler retired on a losing note.

- **Biggest Win:** Penrith 72 d. Manly 12 at Penrith Stadium, round 22
- **Top Point-scorer:** Hazem El Masri (Bulldogs) 342 (premiership record)
- **Top Try-scorer:** Amos Roberts (Penrith) 23

THE REPRESENTATIVE SCENE

NSW five-eighth Shaun Timmins kicked a field goal to win the first ever golden point Origin match 9-8 in the series-opener, before an unforgettable double to Billy Slater propelled Queensland to a series-levelling 22-18 win in game two. Brad Fittler received a fitting Origin farewell after coming out of representative retirement, helping the Blues to a 36-14 victory in the decider. The Kangaroos asserted their dominance of the international game with a 37-10 Anzac Test win over New Zealand and a devastating 44-4 defeat of Great Britain in the England-hosted Tri-Nations final.

STANDOUT PLAYER

Danny Buderus was named the Dally M Player of the Year despite his Newcastle side missing the finals for the first time in eight years, while a season-ending injury to Andrew Johns thrust the tenacious hooker into the captaincy at club and representative level. He skippered NSW in its series victory, before an injury to Test captain Darren Lockyer saw Buderus lead Australia in two Tri-Nations matches against Great Britain.

MEMORABLE MATCH

The annual Anzac Day showdown between the Sydney Roosters and St. George Illawarra provided one of the season's highest-quality encounters. The Roosters led 2-0 at halftime after a thrilling try to Dragons centre Mark Gasnier was controversially vetoed by the video referee. The Saints posted the first try to lead 8-2 in the second half, but the match swung on a magical try to 32-year-old Roosters skipper Brad Fittler, who busted the defensive line on halfway and stepped off both feet to bamboozle Dragons fullback Ben Hornby and score. Fittler's charges grafted out an 11-8 result.

2005

In the wake of the off-field tribulations of the previous season, the primary focus on the outstanding quality of the football produced in 2005 was as much of a relief as it was invigorating. It was described as "The Game's Most Sensational Season" on the cover of David Middleton's *Official Rugby League Annual*—a glowing assessment of a year boasting countless reversals of fortune, astonishing firsts, drought-breaking results and some of the modern era's finest matches. Parramatta won the minor premiership on for-and-against from St. George Illawarra after both teams won 16 and lost eight games—the most losses by a minor premier in the competition's history. Brisbane appeared certainties for top spot, piecing together a 10-match winning streak and heading the table for 16 weeks, before a familiar late-season fadeout saw the club drop to third on the back of five straight losses. At the other end of the table, Newcastle lost its first 13 games in the worst start to a season since Easts winless 1966 campaign. But the Knights won eight of their last 11 games to finish the regular season as the NRL's form team—despite collecting the wooden spoon (their eight wins was the most ever in a season by a last-placed team). The premiers of the previous three seasons—the Sydney Roosters, Penrith and the Bulldogs—all flaked out of finals contention, while Manly made a return after seven-year post-season absence. In the middle of it all were two exhilarating and unheralded teams—finals debutants the Wests Tigers and second-time finalists North Queensland—that soared to contest the Grand Final. The 2005 instalment of Origin included a golden point series-opener and an individual display for the ages by Andrew Johns, while the season-ending Four Nations featured several high-quality contests culminating in a shock defeat in the final for the long-dominant Australian side.

THE PREMIERSHIP
The Wests Tigers crushed North Queensland 50-6 in the qualifying final clash between the fourth and fifth, with Tigers fullback Brett Hodgson scoring a post-season record 30 points (three tries, nine goals). But both sides advanced to the preliminary final stage by eliminating Brisbane and Melbourne respectively. The Tigers thwarted premiership favourites the Dragons 20-12, while the Cowboys stunned minor premiers Parramatta 29-0 to set up a Grand Final rematch. In an entertaining decider, the Tim Sheens-coached Tigers proved too strong in a 30-16 triumph, highlighted by young five-eighth Benji Marshall's scorching run and audacious flick pass for long-striding winger Pat Richards to score a long-range try—a fitting finale to the most unpredictable premiership ever staged. Halfback and captain Scott Prince was a worthy Clive Churchill Medal recipient.

- **Biggest Win:** Cronulla 68 d. Manly 6 at Shark Park, round 24
- **Top Point-scorer:** Brett Hodgson (Wests Tigers) 308
- **Top Try-scorer:** Matt Bowen (North Queensland) 21

THE REPRESENTATIVE SCENE
A golden point intercept try to Matt Bowen delivered a 24-20 win to Queensland in a series-opening thriller, but Andrew Johns' electrifying return spearheaded NSW's retention of the crown. Australia continued its mid-season dominance of New Zealand with a 32-16 result in Brisbane, but after trans-Tasman honours were shared in the two preliminary Tri-Nations clashes, the Kiwis produced a shock 24-0 shellacking of the Kangaroos in the final at Elland Road, Leeds—Australia's first loss in a Test series since 1978.

STANDOUT PLAYER
Despite playing just 16 games for the NRL's wooden spooners, Andrew Johns almost pulled off the most extraordinary win in Dally M history. A cracked jaw ruled him out for seven weeks in the first half of the season, but he polled 28 points out of a possible 36 in the last 12 rounds as the Knights made a late-season surge to finish just one point adrift of winner Johnathan Thurston. Johns' unbelievable streak of form came after producing the most dominant individual performance in NSW's Origin history in game two—earning comparisons to Wally Lewis—to spearhead the Blues' series victory.

MEMORABLE MATCH

The Wests Tigers upset defending champs the Bulldogs in a fluctuating round three thriller. The Bulldogs led the Tigers 18-6, before a second half avalanche of tries catapulted the Tigers to 36-18 in front with 13 minutes remaining. But the Bulldogs produced three quick-fire tries—all converted by Hazem El Masri—in the space of eight minutes to draw level. Despite surrendering the momentum, the Tigers worked the ball into position and halfback Scott Prince slotted a field goal with just 20 seconds on the clock. The Bulldogs' total of 36 points equalled the premiership record for most points in a match by a losing side.

2006

The 2006 season heralded the emergence of a new powerhouse in the shape of the Craig Bellamy-coached Melbourne Storm, a relentlessly consistent team whose surge to an emphatic minor premiership was led by burgeoning superstars Cameron Smith, Greg Inglis, Billy Slater and Cooper Cronk. The New Zealand Warriors started the season on minus four competition points after admitting to salary cap breaches, a penalty that ultimately cost the club a finals berth (see Points Docked). A new collective bargaining agreement was reached to increase the salary cap increased to $4 million from 2007, while Andrew Johns became the premiership's greatest point-scorer by overhauling Jason Taylor's mark of 2,107. But 2006 belonged to inspirational captain Darren Lockyer—under fire at the start of the season for his teams' repeated failures—after spearheading spectacular triumphs at club, state and international level.

THE PREMIERSHIP

Melbourne finished eight points clear of the second-placed Bulldogs in top spot. Brisbane was two wins further back in third, but was upset by the sixth-placed side—on this occasion St. George Illawarra, 20-4—for the third straight season. The Broncos recovered to decimate Newcastle 50-6 in the semi-final and fought back from a 20-6 halftime scoreline to overrun the Bulldogs 37-20 in the preliminary final in one of the great post-season turnarounds. On the other side of the draw, the Dragons eliminated Manly 28-0 in the semi-final, but their title bid was impeded by the ruthless Storm courtesy of a 26-10 preliminary final defeat. Melbourne entered the Grand Final as favourites, but the experience and guile of the Broncos—and in particular skipper Lockyer—laid the platform for a tense 15-8 boilover in retiring Brisbane front-row great Shane Webcke's last match.

- **Biggest Win:** New Zealand 66 d. South Sydney 0 at Stadium Australia, round 16
- **Top Point-scorer:** Hazem El Masri (Bulldogs) 296
- **Top Try-scorer:** Nathan Merritt (South Sydney) 22

THE REPRESENTATIVE SCENE

Under new coach Mal Meninga, Queensland bounced back from a one-point series-opening loss to clinch its first series win since 2001, courtesy of a late try to skipper Darren Lockyer in a dramatic decider. Following Australia's crunching 50-12 win in the one-off Test against New Zealand earlier in the year, the Kangaroos and Kiwis staged one of the great Test matches in the Tri-Nations final at the end of the year. A golden point try to Lockyer saw Australia regain the crown it had relinquished 12 months earlier, 16-12.

STANDOUT PLAYER

Darren Lockyer enjoyed one of the greatest individual seasons in the game's history, captaining Brisbane to the NRL title, Queensland to Origin glory and Australia to Tri-Nations success. He scored the winning try in both representative triumphs, while his consummate display in the Grand Final was unlucky not to be rewarded with the Churchill Medal. The Dally M Five-eighth and Representative Player of the Year won his second Golden Boot award at the end of an incomparable season.

MEMORABLE MATCH

Newcastle and Brisbane exchanged the lead five times in a high-scoring round nine thriller at EnergyAustralia Stadium. Rival captains and linchpins, Andrew Johns and Darren Lockyer, duelled spectacularly in the 11-try classic. Lockyer had a hand in four Broncos tries and scored a 50-metre four-pointer himself, but it was not enough to prevent a 32-30 loss.

2007

The 100th premiership season witnessed the retirement of arguably Rugby League's greatest-ever player after just two rounds. Newcastle halfback Andrew Johns suffered a serious neck injury and called time on an extraordinary career after it was revealed he risked permanent and 'catastrophic' damage if he returned to the playing field. But he was in the news again on the eve of the finals after being arrested in London for possession of an ecstasy tablet, before revealing he had battled drug and alcohol problems throughout his career, and had been diagnosed with bipolar disorder. The revelations tarnished his legacy in the eyes of many, but his earnest confession was lauded in some quarters and shed light on the prevalence and pain of mental illness in modern society. The Gold Coast Titans made an impressive entry to the NRL, finishing 12th but just one win away from finals reckoning. Meanwhile, the contentious purchase of South Sydney by actor Russell Crowe and businessman Peter Holmes à Court (and the club's subsequent recruitment drive) paid immediate dividends: the Rabbitohs qualified for their first finals series in 18 years. But the 2007 premiership developed into a somewhat predictable two-horse race between Melbourne and Manly as the two big dogs of the year cleared out on their rivals.

THE PREMIERSHIP

Minor premiers Melbourne despatched injury-ridden defending premiers Brisbane 40-0 in the qualifying final, while second-placed Manly ended seventh-placed Souths' fairytale 30-6. The Storm and the Sea Eagles advanced to a Grand Final showdown by defeating Parramatta and North Queensland respectively in the preliminary finals. But the decider was a fizzer—Melbourne eased to a commanding 34-8 victory on the back of a brilliant two-try performance by Clive Churchill medallist Greg Inglis, a Test three-quarter controversially shifted to five-eighth at the start of the season by triumphant Storm coach Craig Bellamy.

- **Biggest Win:** Brisbane 71 d. Newcastle 6 at Suncorp Stadium, round 11
- **Top Point-scorer:** Hazem El Masri (Bulldogs) 210
- **Top Try-scorer:** Matt Bowen (North Queensland) 22

THE REPRESENTATIVE SCENE

Queensland wrapped up the Origin series inside two matches for the first time since 1995, coming back from a 12-point deficit to win the first match 25-18 and grinding out a 10-6 victory in the second encounter. NSW restored pride with a hard-fought 18-4 result in the dead-rubber clash. In a light international schedule ahead of the 2008 World Cup, Australia comfortably accounted for New Zealand 30-6 in April, while a Kangaroos line-up featuring eight Test debutants destroyed the Kiwis by a record 58-0 in Wellington at the end of the season.

STANDOUT PLAYER

Melbourne captain Cameron Smith finished third in the Dally M Medal count, while his performances in the Origin series garnered the Wally Lewis Medal and the Ron McAuliffe Medal, as well as Dally M Representative Player of the Year honours. Smith led the Storm to a second straight minor premiership and an emphatic Grand Final victory and captained Australia's post-season hammering of New Zealand in the injury-enforced absence of Darren Lockyer.

MEMORABLE MATCH

The resurgent Sydney Roosters and the finals-bound New Zealand Warriors fought out a golden point draw that was heralded as one of the modern era's greatest matches in round 21 at the SFS. The Warriors fought back from 16-0 down to lead 18-16 at halftime and had charged to a 30-18 lead by the time their centre Simon Mannering was controversially sin-binned. The Roosters scored twice to level the scores while the Warriors were a man short, before Braith Anasta nailed a 38-metre field goal to edge the home side in front in the dying minutes. But the Warriors regained possession from a one-on-one strip and five-eighth Michael Witt landed an equalising one-pointer with 17 seconds on the clock. The golden point period failed to produce a scorer and the classic encounter finished 31-all.

2008

Australian Rugby League's Centenary season featured a glorious celebration of the game's 100 years, with various Teams of the Century and the ARL's 100 Greatest Players honouring the code's finest. The game mourned the passing of recently named Coach of the Century Jack Gibson, just hours before the Centenary Test between Australia and New Zealand at the SCG in May, at the age of 79. The NRL premiership featured a gripping finals series, culminating in the biggest victory in Grand Final history. The Australia-hosted Centenary World Cup witnessed a string of dominant performances by the Kangaroos—before a final upset for the ages. But the year was frequently tainted by the undercurrent of unsavoury off-field incidents involving the game's stars as player misbehaviour reached inglorious new levels. Incumbent Australian and NSW pivot Greg Bird was stood down after being charged with glassing his girlfriend (he was later acquitted); Brisbane representative trio Karmichael Hunt, Sam Thaiday and Darius Boyd were questioned by police over an alleged nightclub sexual assault during the finals series; and Canberra star Todd Carney was sacked for the latest in a string of drunken off-field misdemeanours. Superstar New Zealander Sonny Bill Williams sensationally walked out on the Bulldogs mid-season, joining French rugby union club Toulon in the year's biggest controversy, while St. George Illawarra Test centre Mark Gasnier defected to union at the end of the season with Stade Français, giving up a certain Kangaroos World Cup berth. The embattled Bulldogs slumped to the wooden spoon, bringing coach Steve Folkes' 11-year tenure at the club to an end.

THE PREMIERSHIP
Melbourne won a third straight minor premiership on for-and-against from Manly and Cronulla. But the Storm became the first minor premiers to be defeated by the eighth-placed team under the McIntyre finals system, succumbing 18-15 to the New Zealand Warriors courtesy of a spectacular long-range try in the dying minutes. The in-form Warriors despatched the Sydney Roosters a week later, but their run was halted 34-6 by Manly in the preliminary final. The Storm were thrust into a sudden-death semi-final against Brisbane at Suncorp Stadium; in one of the most explosive finals matches of all time, Melbourne snatched a 16-14 victory with a last-minute Greg Inglis try *(see Finals Magic)*. The result brought coach Wayne Bennett's record 21-season reign at the Broncos to an end ahead of his move to the Dragons, while Storm captain Cameron Smith was controversially suspended for the remainder of the finals for an ugly tackle of Sam Thaiday. A depleted Melbourne line-up swept aside the Sharks 29-0 in the preliminary final, but was overwhelmed by the Sea Eagles in the Grand Final by an unprecedented 40-0 scoreline. Winger Michael Robertson scored three tries for the Des Hasler-coached Manly outfit, while departing club great Steve Menzies—the game's most prolific tryscoring forward and equal-appearances record-holder—was sent out a winner.
- **Biggest Win:** Canberra 74 d. Penrith 12 at Canberra Stadium, round 22
- **Top Point-scorer:** Luke Covell (Cronulla) 206
- **Top Try-scorer:** Brett Stewart (Manly) 22

THE REPRESENTATIVE SCENE
After a lacklustre 18-10 loss to NSW in game one, Queensland secured a hat-trick of series triumphs with wins in the remaining two clashes. Melbourne's Cameron Smith captained the Maroons in the injury-enforced absence of Darren Lockyer, while opposing hooker and skipper Danny Buderus played his last Origin game before heading to England. Australia won the Centenary Test against New Zealand at the SCG 28-12 early in the season and blazed through the preliminary rounds of the World Cup, but the Kiwis pulled off a stunning 34-20 upset in the final of the tournament at Suncorp Stadium.

STANDOUT PLAYER
Electrifying Melbourne fullback Billy Slater made his belated Test debut in 2008 and scored the winning try in Queensland's victory in the Origin decider. A one-match suspension late in the year robbed Slater of the Dally M Medal, but he was named the Golden Boot recipient and the inaugural RLIF Player of the Year after scoring seven tries in Australia's World Cup campaign.

MEMORABLE MATCH
The magic of Sunday afternoon football at a suburban ground delivered another glorious encounter courtesy of the Wests Tigers' 20-18 victory over the Gold Coast at Leichhardt Oval in round 11. The 17,493-strong crowd provided the customary electric atmosphere as the Tigers held off a late comeback by the NRL ladder

leaders after earlier building a 20-6 advantage. Tigers hooker Robbie Farah collected maximum Dally M points, but Titans fullback Preston Campbell was the star of the day with mesmerising attacking display.

2009

Negative publicity plagued the NRL on the eve of the season after defending premiers Manly's disastrous season launch. Star fullback Brett Stewart—who had been unveiled as the face of the NRL's advertising campaign just days earlier— was charged with the sexual assault of a 17-year-old girl outside his North Manly apartment block. The NRL controversially stood Stewart down for five weeks for public drunkenness, sparking a long-running feud between the fullback and the game's CEO David Gallop, while he was eventually acquitted of the charges in 2010. Incoming coach Wayne Bennett immediately turned St. George Illawarra into a consistent premiership powerhouse, steering the club to the minor premiership on for-and-against from the Bulldogs, who enjoyed a spectacular turnaround under new mentor Kevin Moore after finishing last in a tumultuous 2008 season. The Gold Coast Titans qualified for their maiden finals series in third place. Cronulla and the Sydney Roosters suffered alarming falls from grace after top-four finishes in 2008; both clubs were mired in off-field atrocities while dismal performances consigned the Roosters to the wooden spoon and the Sharks to second-last. Parramatta lit up the premiership in the second half of the year, riding the brilliance of fullback Jarryd Hayne from 14th spot with 10 rounds remaining, to an improbable Grand Final appearance. Meanwhile, two referees were appointed to control NRL matches from the beginning of 2009, attracting mixed reviews.

THE PREMIERSHIP

Parramatta upset minor premiers St George Illawarra 25-12 in the first week of the finals, before advancing to the decider by eliminating the Gold Coast and defeating Canterbury 22-12 in a pulsating preliminary final played in front of a non-Grand Final post-season record crowd of 74,549. The gallant loss ended the admirable career of popular winger and goalkicker extraordinaire Hazem El Masri, who retired with a premiership record 2,418 points to his name. Brisbane advanced to the preliminary final under new coach Ivan Henjak after impressive wins over the Titans and Bennett's Dragons, but Melbourne ruthlessly despatched the Broncos 40-10 one game short of the decider. The Storm led from the front in the Grand Final, ultimately holding off a thrilling late comeback by the Eels to prevail 23-16.

- **Biggest Win:** Canberra 56 d. Brisbane 0 at Canberra Stadium, round 21
- **Top Point-scorer:** Hazem El Masri (Bulldogs) 248
- **Top Try-scorer:** Brett Morris (St. George Illawarra) 25

THE REPRESENTATIVE SCENE

Queensland's record-breaking fourth straight series triumph was achieved on the back of comfortable wins in the opening two matches, before NSW won arguably the most hostile Origin match of the decade 28-16 in game three. Reasserting itself as the international Rugby League kingpin, Australia trounced the world champion New Zealand side 38-10 in May. Despite escaping with a lucky 20-all draw against the Kiwis in the opening match of the inaugural Four Nations, the Kangaroos scored two convincing victories over hosts England to win the tournament, including a 46-16 result in the final.

STANDOUT PLAYER

Jarryd Hayne produced one of the most electrifying form streaks in premiership history to take out the Dally M Medal. The Parramatta fullback took the maximum three points from six straight matches during the club's phenomenal late-season charge, while his individual try to cap the finals upset of St. George Illawarra ranks as one of the great post-season tries. Hayne was NSW's best player by the length of the straight during the Origin series and collected the Brad Fittler Medal, while he won a Test recall on the wing for Australia's Four Nations campaign.

MEMORABLE MATCH

Parramatta's Jarryd Hayne and Wests Tigers' playmaker Benji Marshall starred as the NRL's two form teams produced one of 2009's most pulsating encounters in round 24. Marshall's mesmerising flick pass for a Blake Ayshford try was trumped by Hayne's chip-and-chase try that sealed the Eels' 26-18 victory.

2010

The NRL season was turned on its head after one of the most dramatic developments in premiership history in April. Defending premiers Melbourne had its 2007 and 2009 titles and three minor premierships stripped, while the club was fined $500,000 and ordered to repay $1.1 million in prize-money after revelations of deliberate and systematic salary cap breaches over five seasons—peaking at an estimated $850,000 in 2010 alone. The final crushing blow to the Storm was the NRL's decision that they would not be eligible to earn competition points in 2010, effectively consigning the club to the wooden spoon. St. George Illawarra shed the 'chokers' tag and earned its first premiership as a joint venture, warding off the challenges of the Wests Tigers and the Sydney Roosters. Brisbane's 18-season finals streak came to an end after an NRL season-ending rib injury to Darren Lockyer sparked a late-season collapse. Canberra, New Zealand and second-placed surprise packets Penrith joined the Roosters and Tigers as finals returnees. The pre-season featured the inaugural Indigenous All-Stars v NRL All-Stars match on the Gold Coast—the brainchild of Indigenous Titans star Preston Campbell—with players selected via a public vote. The Indigenous All-Stars prevailed 16-12 after a late try to Jamie Soward.

THE PREMIERSHIP

The Tigers and Roosters staged one of the all time great games in the qualifying final, producing the first-ever golden point finals match. A stunning field goal to Roosters captain Braith Anasta as the siren sounded sent the match into extra-time, and a 100th-minute try to centre Shaun Kenny-Dowall secured a 19-15 victory for the Bondi boys, who subsequently cruised to the Grand Final with handsome wins over top-four sides Penrith and the Gold Coast. The Tigers were pitched into a semi-final date with Canberra, holding on for a nerve-jangling 24-22 victory, but their season ended with a heartbreaking 13-12 loss to minor premiers St. George Illawarra. The Ben Hornby-led Saints overwhelmed the Roosters 30-8 in the Grand Final after trailing by two points at halftime, bringing three decades of torment to an end for long-suffering supporters of the famous 'Red V' jersey. The gallant Roosters, under new coach Brian Smith, had become the first club to reach a Grand Final after finishing last the previous season, while bad boy five-eighth Todd Carney was the club's linchpin and claimed a remarkable Dally M Medal victory after spending 2009 with country Queensland club Atherton.

- **Biggest Win:** Canterbury 60 d. Sydney Roosters 14 at Stadium Australia, round three; Melbourne 58 d. North Queensland 12 at Dairy Farmers Stadium, round 15
- **Top Point-scorer:** Michael Gordon (Penrith) 270
- **Top Try-scorer:** Shaun Kenny-Dowall (Sydney Roosters) 21; Akuila Uate (Newcastle) 21

THE REPRESENTATIVE SCENE
Queensland capped a fifth consecutive series victory by achieving its first series whitewash in 15 years as NSW's interstate woes worsened. Australia won the Bill Kelly Cup contest with New Zealand for the 12th straight season, but the Kiwis repeated their World Cup heroics with a euphoric 16-12 victory in the Brisbane-hosted final of the Four Nations against the Kangaroos, courtesy of a spectacular long-range try finished off by Nathan Fien in the dying minutes.

STANDOUT PLAYER
Wests Tigers five-eighth Benji Marshall produced his most consistent season to finish fourth in the Dally M Medal count, while regularly producing his customary off-the-cuff attacking genius to spearhead the club's top-four finish. But it was his spellbinding performance as captain in New Zealand's Four Nations final triumph that sealed his status as arguably the game's premier match-winner and garnered the Golden Boot award.

MEMORABLE MATCH
The Sydney Roosters held off a barnstorming Brisbane comeback in a round 20 Monday night thriller at Suncorp Stadium. The visitors racked up a 28-6 lead early in the second half, but the Broncos piled on four converted tries to snatch a 30-28 advantage with 10 minutes remaining. The Roosters stemmed the flood of points, however, and centre Shaun Kenny-Dowall scored his fourth try of the night to seal a 34-30 victory.

2011

A considerable proportion of media attention and public sentiment focussed on the impending retirement of champion Brisbane, Queensland and Australian captain Darren Lockyer. The talismanic five-eighth was afforded fitting Origin and Test farewells, but while a fairytale premiership eluded him, Lockyer still had one last piece of magic for the Broncos' faithful. After the soul-destroying salary cap ordeal of 2010, Craig Bellamy performed a coaching miracle by steering his depleted, new-look Melbourne squad to the minor premiership. The 2011 finals featured a stunning sudden-death surge by the New Zealand Warriors, while Manly's emphatic title triumph was quickly soured by the impending disintegration of the club's premiership-winning set-up. St. George Illawarra supercoach Wayne Bennett ended weeks of speculation early in the season by announcing he would join Newcastle at the end of the year. Continuing delays in the establishment of the long-awaited independent commission put expansion plans on hold until 2015; bid teams from the Central Coast, Perth, Brisbane, Central Queensland, Papua New Guinea and Wellington had entered the race for the NRL's projected increase to 18 clubs. The proposed independent commission—after more than three years of negotiations—was set to supersede the partnership of the ARL and News Limited in the running of the game under the NRL banner in 2012.

THE PREMIERSHIP
New Zealand, coached by Penrith-bound coach Ivan Cleary, was thumped 40-10 by the third-placed Broncos in the qualifying final. But the Warriors overcame a 12-point halftime deficit to pip the Tigers 22-20 courtesy of a freakish Krisnan Inu try in the dying minutes, before upsetting Melbourne in the preliminary final with a 20-12 victory of the highest quality. Brisbane eliminated the Dragons 13-12 in a dramatic semi-final; the Broncos led for most of the contest, but a late converted try to the Saints consigned the match to golden point. Darren Lockyer, who only 10 minutes earlier suffered a fractured cheekbone in an accidental clash with teammate Gerard Beale, snapped a field goal in the second minute of added time to spark jubilant scenes at Suncorp Stadium. It was to be Lockyer's final act of a premiership record 355-game career, as the injury kept him out of the following week's preliminary final. The plucky young Broncos were gallant in their 26-14 loss to Manly. The Sea Eagles proved too strong for the Warriors in the Grand Final, prevailing 24-10 despite a spirited final-quarter fight-back by the New Zealanders. But the celebrations turned to despair in the following days and weeks after coach Des Hasler announced his departure to Canterbury, with key off-field staff following him and the spectre of several high-profile stars also leaving the club looming.

- **Biggest Win:** South Sydney 56 d. Parramatta 6 at Stadium Australia, round 22
- **Top Point-scorer:** Benji Marshall (Wests Tigers) 211
- **Top Try-scorer:** Ben Barba (Canterbury) 23; Nathan Merritt (South Sydney) 23

THE REPRESENTATIVE SCENE
The NRL All-Stars defeated the Indigenous All-Stars 28-12 in the concept's second instalment to kick of the season. The return of Ricky Stuart as coach resulted in a much-improved NSW campaign; the Paul Gallen-led Blues were pipped late in a 16-12 series-opening loss, before grinding out a deserved 18-8 game two win. But a first half avalanche of tries provided the impetus for Queensland's 34-24 victory in the decider, which doubled as an interstate farewell to retiring Maroons skipper Darren Lockyer in his record 36th appearance. Australia dominated New Zealand in Tests on the Gold Coast and in Newcastle, while Darren Lockyer bid adieu to Rugby League in the Kangaroos' resounding Four Nations triumph in England, defeating the hosts 30-8 in the final.

STANDOUT PLAYER
Billy Slater's climb to the top echelon of Rugby League's greatest-ever fullbacks continued in 2011, claiming the unique treble the Dally M Medal, the Golden Boot and the RLIF Player of the Year award as his performances soared to an even higher plane.

MEMORABLE MATCH
Brisbane and New Zealand delivered a round 22 classic at Suncorp Stadium befitting of the clubs' title contender status. The Warriors led 12-8 at halftime on the back of

two of 2011's best tries—a sizzling 70-metre individual effort to rookie halfback Shaun Johnson, and a magnificent try finished off by fullback Kevin Locke after a chip-and-chase by No.6 James Maloney. The combatants traded tries in a pulsating second half and were locked 20-all in the dying minutes. Golden point beckoned, but a field goal to Brisbane halfback Peter Wallace with one minute on the clock snatched a 21-20 victory for the home side.

GREAT ESCAPES, INCREDIBLE COMEBACKS AND THRILLING FINISHES

This chapter chronicles the most stirring comebacks and remarkable conclusions witnessed in regular season premiership matches.

BLUEBAGS RUN DOWN RABBITOHS FOR FAMOUS WIN Newtown staged the first great comeback in premiership history in 1926. Down to 12 men after losing a player to injury and with no replacements allowed, Newtown trailed premiers Souths 18-0 in the late-season Sydney Cricket Ground clash. But five tries—all converted by fullback Tommy Ellis—catapulted the Bluebags to a 25-21 advantage. The victory was not yet assured, however. A late try brought the Rabbitohs back to within a point of Newtown, but captain Alf 'Smacker' Blair was unsuccessful with the conversion attempt and the Bluebags secured a celebrated victory 25-24.

LAST-GASP VICTORY SECURES MINOR PREMIERSHIP FOR SOUTHS Defending champs South Sydney entered the final regular season round of 1968 on top of the ladder, with a chasing pack of three clubs just one competition point adrift—including the Rabbitohs' last-round opponents, Eastern Suburbs. The inner-city rivals produced a classic encounter in front of a bumper 39,933-strong Sydney Cricket Ground crowd. Chasing their first minor premiership since 1945, the Jack Gibson-coached Roosters led the Rabbitohs 22-19 as the clock wound down on the back of four goals to Allan McKean and two field goals to Kevin Ashley. But Souths five-eighth Dennis Pittard crossed for his second try in the dying minutes to level the scores, and fullback sharpshooter Eric Simms slotted the conversion on fulltime to confirm a heart-stopping 24-22, four-tries-to-two victory—and the all-important minor premiership.

CROWD SPARKS REMARKABLE TURNAROUND Defending premiers Parramatta left the field to a chorus of boos at halftime in its 1987 clash with Canberra at Parramatta Stadium, a disparaging acknowledgement of a dismal 40 minutes that saw the Eels trail 22-0. But the Eels piled on five unanswered second half tries, including a double to man of the match Bob Lindner, to seal a remarkable 30-22 victory. It ranked as the biggest comeback in 80 seasons of premiership football.

TWIN LAST-MINUTE DEFEATS FOR SEA EAGLES IN TRYING
SEASON A pair of agonising losses was ultimately the difference between a finals spot and an early offseason for Manly in 1992. The Sea Eagles took an early-season home game against Newcastle to Auckland's Carlaw Park—the first premiership match to be played outside Australia—due to the club's large following in New Zealand and a prominent Kiwi presence within the side, including Matthew Ridge (who missed the match with injury), Kevin and Tony Iro, Darrell Williams and coach Graham Lowe. But the trailblazing trip ended in heartbreak for the Sea Eagles. Despite holding a slender lead in the final minute, the Sea Eagles went down 16-13 after a miracle try to Knights winger Ashley Gordon. The final pass from another Kiwi, Newcastle centre Tony Kemp, was clearly forward.

In the penultimate round of the season—with Manly clinging to a slim chance of making the five-team finals series—the club's hopes were dashed by another loss at the death, this time to Illawarra. The match doubled as a Brookvale farewell to retiring club champion Michael O'Connor, who scored a dream runaway try to give the Sea Eagles an 8-4 advantage in the second half. But in the dying stages, Steelers centre Brett Rodwell made a bust and linked with Test winger Rod Wishart, who stepped inside Ridge to score. Wishart slotted the conversion from close range to consign the home side to a 10-8 loss, ending their finals bid.

BEARS SNATCH UNLIKELY WIN WITH EIGHT-POINT TRY
Famous for finding new ways to lose matches throughout a hapless 92-season history, North Sydney defeated competition leaders Canterbury in improbable fashion in 1993. Behind 17-0 after just 23 minutes, the Bears pegged their way back to trail by five points with three unanswered tries. Norths winger David Hall raced over for his second try with six minutes remaining, and referee Bill Harrigan controversially ruled an eight-point try when Bulldogs halfback Craig Polla-Mounter dived on Hall after he had scored. The Bears' other winger, Craig Makepeace, who had missed his previous three attempts at goal, hooked the first conversion attempt of the eight-point try from a relatively simple position. But he made no mistake with the second shot from in front of the posts to seal a momentous 18-17 victory.

TIGERS SURGE TO STEAL DRAW
The 1993 Canberra Raiders had every reason to approach their Round 18 Bruce Stadium clash against Balmain with confidence. The Raiders were on a five-match winning streak, had lost just one of their previous 10 games and had assumed outright premiership favouritism. The Tigers, meanwhile, had won just five of their 17 matches and were inundated with off-field turbulence. The match was going to script with little more than 15 minutes on the clock with the home side leading 32-12. But the Tigers put the final act through the shredder with four quick-fire tries in the space of 10 minutes. Former NSW Origin winger Graham Lyons' second try in the corner shaved the deficit to two points, leaving Tim Brasher to convert for a draw. Brasher fired a booming attempt from the touchline, and the ball hit the upright before dropping over the crossbar to complete one of the most spectacular turnarounds ever produced.

THE BIGGEST COMEBACK North Queensland's 1998 season unfolded in the same vein as the club's previous three since joining the premiership—poorly, finishing 16th out of 20 teams. But in Round 12 of the unified NRL competition, the Cowboys staged a comeback unmatched in Australian Rugby League history. Penrith ran five first half tries past the Cowboys at Penrith Stadium to head to the sheds 26-0 in front, but North Queensland coach Tim Sheens worked a halftime miracle. Fijian flyer Noa Nadruku opened the Cowboys' account three minutes into the second half and sparked an avalanche of points. When the dust settled, the Cowboys had scored seven tries—including a hat-trick to Nadruku and two tries to five-eighth Andrew Dunemann—to record a 36-28 turnaround. The Panthers players left their home turf to a cacophony of crowd ridicule, taking possession of the record for the worst collapse in premiership history.

WARRIORS WIN AFTER MAD SCRAMBLE The 1998 Auckland Warriors were an inconsistent bunch, but they conjured a chaotic match-winning try to consign NRL debutants Melbourne to one of just two home defeats midway through the season with an after-the-buzzer stunner. The Warriors led 14-4 at the break, but squandered their lead as the Storm rolled in for three quick tries in the second half. Melbourne No.7 Brett Kimmorley appeared to wrap up the tense contest with a field goal two minutes from fulltime, giving his side a 21-18 advantage. But on the last play of the game, the Warriors swung the ball from one sideline to the other, before Stacey Jones launched a bomb after the siren sounded. Despite a horde of Storm players waiting at the kick's destination, the Warriors managed to bat the ball back, and centre Nigel Vagana fired it out for an unmarked Tony Tatupu to score. After an agonising wait for the video referee's decision as he dissected the myriad of fumbles and rebounds in the movement, the try was awarded, handing victory to Auckland—a rare highlight in a dismal season for the club.

ALBERT DOES IT AGAIN The scorer of the most famous last-gasp try in Grand Final history reprised his match-winning role less than two years later in a dramatic Newcastle victory in 1999 at the Sydney Football Stadium. St. George Illawarra looked to have snatched a late victory in a see-sawing round 24 clash against the Knights when hooker Nathan Brown crossed for try with three minutes on the clock. Trailing 20-18, the Knights recovered the ball from a short kick-off. With only seconds remaining, centre Matthew Gidley slipped a brilliant trademark pass (*see Signature Moves*) to winger Darren Albert, who tiptoed down the sideline to win the game 22-20. Albert scored the buzzer-beating try in the 22-16 Grand Final defeat of Manly at the same venue in 1997 that delivered Newcastle's first premiership.

PANTHERS STUN TIGERS WITH PHENOMENAL COMEBACK Perhaps spurred on by the memory of the debacle against North Queensland two years earlier, Penrith produced an equally miraculous comeback against the Wests Tigers during the 2000 season. Fielding a side containing seven players from that disastrous night against the Cowboys, the Panthers trailed the Tigers 31-8 with half an hour to play after the first-season joint venture had scored three quick tries. But the Panthers rallied to score back-to-back tries and reduce the scoreline to 31-20 heading into the last quarter of the match. New Zealand backrow giant Tony Puletua was running roughshod over the Tigers' defence, and when he scored two tries in quick succession, the Panthers found themselves just one point behind. Chris Hicks nailed the conversion of Puletua's second touchdown from wide out *(see Unlikely Heroes)* to put Penrith in front 32-31 and confirm one of premiership history's great comebacks. The incredible result had even greater ramifications for the finals race— Penrith surged into the top-four, while the Tigers dropped from second to sixth and eventually missed the finals.

WESTS TIGERS REEL IN EVENTUAL PREMIERS The Wests Tigers, in turn, produced a sensational revival of their own the following season against heavyweights Newcastle. In the NRL cellar late in 2001, the Tigers had already suffered a 50-point hiding at the hands of the Knights earlier in the year. A hat-trick to Newcastle lock Ben Kennedy had helped open up a 32-12 advantage just after halftime in the round 23 encounter and another rout seemed inevitable. But when Owen Craigie and Ben Galea scored in the space of three minutes, the Tigers had discovered irresistible momentum. Joel Caine crossed with 15 minutes remaining to reduce the deficit to two points, before livewire centre Kevin McGuinness found the tryline to put the Tigers in front for the first time. The partisan Campbelltown crowd had to endure a heart-stopping final 10 minutes until they could celebrate the momentous 36-32 result.

BLACKLOCK SPECIAL GETS DRAGONS HOME St. George Illawarra winger Nathan Blacklock was an excitement machine and a bona fide game-breaker during his career, scoring 121 tries in 142 first grade appearances. But arguably his best touchdown came in the shadows of fulltime against the Wests Tigers in 2001. The Dragons played from behind all day at Leichhardt Oval, pegging their way back from 14-0 down to trail 22-21 with less than a minute to play. Blacklock, who had already scored two tries, collected the ball inside his own quarter for the Dragons' last opportunity of the match, and beat the Tigers' chasing contingent to break into open spaces down the left flank. Confronted by fullback Joel Caine, Blacklock placed a perfect chip kick back towards the posts and regathered to score the scintillating match-winner. Blacklock celebrated with a trademark back-flip and the ensuing conversion gave the Dragons a last-gasp 27-22 victory.

EL MAGIC FINISHES AMAZING FIGHT-BACK A surging comeback from the Bulldogs in front of a parochial Newcastle crowd was capped by one of the most famous pressure kicks in premiership history. At the tail-end of a 17-match winning streak in 2002, the Bulldogs trailed an Andrew Johns-inspired Newcastle side 19-0 at halftime. Bulldogs five Braith Anasta sparked the revival—two of his kicks led to tries, while a superb long pass resulted in another. A no-try ruling against workhorse forward Steve Reardon with four minutes left appeared to cruel the Bulldogs' comeback with the score at 21-16. But when the Knights ran out of defenders in the final minute, Bulldogs fullback Luke Patten slid over in the corner to leave Hazem El Masri with an opportunity to win the match after the siren. Setting the ball up metres from a baying pro-Knights crowd and with a swirling breeze to contend with, 'El Magic' stepped up and curled a spine-tingling conversion through the posts to snatch a legendary victory.

TALLIS HEROICS GET BRONCOS OUT OF JAIL A rampaging performance by skipper Gorden Tallis saved Brisbane from an embarrassing early-season loss to lowly Souths in 2003. Tallis had scored a powerful second half try in an attempt to inspire his lacklustre team-mates, but the Rabbitohs looked set to produce a major boilover when they led 20-12 inside the final 10 minutes. But Tallis intervened again, putting through a superb grubber kick that took a freakish bounce and resulted in a try to Michael De Vere. Souths held out a late Brisbane attacking raid and only had to ruck the ball out for the few remaining seconds to claim a famous two-point victory. Tallis was intent on producing a trifecta of big plays, however. Reliable prop Paul Stringer carted the ball forward off his own line, before Tallis wrenched the ball free in a one-on-one strip. Shaun Berrigan swung the ball wide for Brent Tate to score his second try in the corner and secure one of the NRL's great escapes 22-20.

DRAGONS CONJURE BROOKVALE MIRACLE St. George Illawarra looked anything but premiership contenders for the first hour of their round 25 clash against 13th-placed Manly in 2004. The fifth-placed Dragons trailed 34-10 with little more than 20 minutes remaining. But a quick double to Nathan Blacklock and tries to Ben Hornby and Matt Cooper in the space of 13 minutes reduced the margin to four points. The Sea Eagles were rattled, but grimly defended their slender lead, until Saints prop Justin Poore powered over to score with three minutes on the clock. Hooker Mark Riddell gave his familiar warm-up salute before slotting the angled conversion to give the Dragons a 36-34 victory in front of a delirious Oki Jubilee Stadium crowd.

COWBOYS PREVAIL IN EPIC BROOKVALE ROLLERCOASTER North Queensland's 26-24 defeat of Manly at Brookvale Oval in round 21 of 2005 was undoubtedly one of the most entertaining and topsy-turvy clashes of the NRL era. The Sea Eagles surged to an 18-6 halftime lead, but the visitors clawed back to trail by just two points, before hitting the front with one of the great regular season tries. The Cowoboys' mercurial fullback Matt Bowen was surrounded deep in his own in-goal, but threw an audacious pass to Ty Williams. The Queensland Origin winger sped out of danger and into open territory, then beat the challenge of Manly fullback Brett Stewart (who earlier scored a sizzling try of his own) and dotted down for a 108-metre special. A try and conversion to Sea Eagles winger Chris Hicks looked to have grabbed victory for the home side with two minutes remaining, but the Cowboys reclaimed the ball from a short kick-off and an Aaron Payne grubber to the Manly in-goal allowed Williams to collect his third try with only centimetres and seconds to spare.

MAD MONTH OF CLIFFHANGERS St. George Illawarra's 8-1 defeat of Parramatta (see Bizarre Matches) at the start of June in 2006 sparked a month of nailbiting Friday night finishes. Seven days after the Dragons' victory, Manly pipped Wests Tigers with a spectacular last-minute try. The Sea Eagles trailed 12-10 in the dying stages, before halfback Matt Orford found open space with a banana kick (see Signature Moves). Brilliant fullback Brett Stewart snatched the awkward, high-bouncing ball from the clutches of Tigers five-eighth Benji Marshall to score under the posts and steal a 16-12 victory. The try earned a nomination for the Dally M Headline Moment of the Year award.

The Dragons featured again a week later with a heart-stopping 18-16 victory over the Broncos at Suncorp Stadium. Brisbane had six players backing up from the State of Origin clash two nights earlier, and displayed tremendous endurance and resolve to overturn a four-point halftime deficit and lead 16-12 in the closing minutes. But a last-ditch try to rookie Saints winger Brett Morris set the scene for hooker Aaron Gorrell to win the game after the siren with a magnificent sideline conversion.

Competition front-runners Melbourne completed an astonishing month of finishes with the most spectacular of the bunch in round 16. The Storm's 11-match winning streak at Olympic Park was in jeopardy when they trailed the Bulldogs 12-6 late in the second half, but a superb pass from second-rower Ryan Hoffman put Jake Webster over in the corner with a couple of minutes remaining. Cameron Smith's conversion attempt hit the post, however, leaving Melbourne two points adrift. In the final minute of play, Storm halfback Cooper Cronk put in a beautifully weighted cross-field kick from inside his own half, which was picked up by a wide-ranging Hoffman on the first bounce. Despite the attention of Bulldogs Trent Cutler and Luke Patten, Hoffman again found Webster with a brilliant one-handed pass, and the Kiwi winger powered away for the match-winner in the shadows of the post.

LOCKYER PRODUCES BUZZER-BEATING CLASSIC Brisbane captain Darren Lockyer produced one of 2008's most unforgettable moments against Parramatta in round 12—his only match during a 10-week period battling a knee injury that would eventually keep him out of the entire Origin series. The Broncos were cruising at 26-18 in front with just nine minutes remaining on the back of a hat-trick to young winger Denan Kemp. But enigmatic Eels winger Krisnan Inu scored two brilliant tries in the space of three minutes (both unconverted) to level the scores. The entertaining clash was headed for a golden point conclusion as the Broncos worked the ball out from their own half in the dying seconds, but Lockyer scooped up a loose pass as the siren sounded and headed across field, before putting an angled chip kick over the heads of the Parramatta three-quarters. The ball popped up for a flying Kemp, who outsprinted the Eels cover defence in a 30-metre run to the corner for the spectacular match-winner. Kemp's fourth try equalled the Brisbane club record, while providing one of the greatest finishes in the history of the premiership.

BUNNIES THE COMEBACK KINGS OF 2008 The 2008 season was deflating for South Sydney after breaking through for the club's first finals appearance in 18 years the previous season, winning just one of their first 11 games. But the Rabbitohs provided some memorable highlights in the second half of the season, proving themselves as the 'heart-attack' team of the NRL with a series of stunning comebacks and late victories.

The Rabbitohs began the trend against the Warriors in round 13, recovering from a 14-0 deficit to win 35-28—largely on the back of debutant halfback Chris Sandow's brilliance.

A Sandow field goal was the difference three weeks later as Souths recorded the equal-second biggest comeback of all time against the North Queensland. Trailing

28-4 with less than half an hour to play, the Rabbitohs stormed back to level with four quick tries, before Sandow snapped a one-pointer in the final minute.

Just nine days later, Souths recovered from an 18-point deficit against the Bulldogs to send the match into extra-time. The Dogs led 24-6 early in the second stanza, but the match was levelled at 30-all when Rabbitohs winger Fetuli Talanoa scored with seven minutes remaining. Craig Wing sent Luke Capewell over for a try in the second period of golden point to clinch a memorable 34-30 victory.

The Rabbitohs went achingly close to producing another miracle comeback in the penultimate round of the season. Falling behind 22-0 against arch-rivals and top-four side the Sydney Roosters, Souths ran in four unanswered tries in the final 25 minutes to reduce the margin to two points. Chris Sandow's wide conversion attempt of the last of those four-pointers thudded into the upright, denying the plucky Rabbitohs a chance to win the match in golden point.

COURAGEOUS LOCKE PLUCKS ROOSTERS
New Zealand winger Kevin Locke was the hero in the most spectacular finish of 2010. In rainy, freezing conditions at Christchurch's AMI Stadium, the Sydney Roosters led the Warriors 18-8 with five minutes to go, but a powerhouse try to Manu Vatuvei kept the Warriors alive. Locke had already scored a memorable first half double, and toed a Lance Hohaia grubber kick ahead from near halfway in the final minute of play. Displaying electrifying pace, Locke narrowly won the race to the ball ahead of Roosters speedster Phil Graham and planted the ball as his torso simultaneously collided with the goalpost. Replays showed Locke had successfully scored the gutsy leveller, and James Maloney added the simple conversion after the siren to win a thrilling encounter 20-18. Locke's bravery cost him two weeks on the sideline with injury, but earned a place in club folklore, while the precociously talented youngster became recognised as one of the NRL's best fullbacks in 2011.

BENJI THWARTS COUNTRYMEN IN MIRACULOUS FIGHT-BACK
The New Zealand Warriors boasted six straight wins when they hosted a round 14 clash against the patchy Wests Tigers, who had strung together consecutive wins just once in 2011. The match followed the form guide for more than an hour; the Warriors piled on five tries—including two tries to giant winger Manu Vatuvei and a blistering 50-metre touchdown to second-game halfback Shaun Johnson in the second half—to lead 22-4 with just 18 minutes on the clock. But the Tigers' five-eighth magician and Kiwi Test captain Benji Marshall sprung into action scoring two stunning tries and putting a towering bomb up for ex-Warriors fullback Wade McKinnon to cross for another; Marshall converted all three touchdowns to level the scores at 22-all with seven minutes remaining. Marshall then employed trademark sleight of hand to conjure the match-winner, floating a pass over the Warriors' defence for winger Beau Ryan to score in the corner with inches to spare. But the pivot's dramatic night was not finished—in the dying seconds he ran behind his own tryline and over the dead-ball line to run down the clock, before being shoved into the advertising hoardings by Warriors utility Lewis Brown, sparking a heated push-and-shove. But it was Marshall that had the last laugh in his homeland after engineering a remarkable comeback victory.

BIZARRE MATCHES

Rugby League's most unique and peculiar matches and incidents are recalled in this chapter—a tribute to some of the code's most off-the-wall occurrences.

THE FORFEITED FINAL Balmain's forfeit of the 1909 final was arguably the biggest controversy of the Sydney premiership's formative seasons. Minor premiers South Sydney and second-placed Balmain won through to the final with semi-final victories over Newcastle and Eastern Suburbs respectively, before the finals series was suspended for a month due to the staging of a three-match cross–code series between the Kangaroos and the Wallabies. But the League and financier James Joynton Smith faced a large cash deficit after the series, and decided to stage a fourth match to recover the shortfall—with the premiership final to be played as the curtain-raiser. Balmain was furious with the demotion of the year's biggest match to secondary status and the club's committee refused to field a team. Souths, led by Arthur Conlin, fronted up for the clash while Balmain formed a picket line outside the Agricultural Ground. Farcically kicking off to a non-existent opponent, South Sydney picked up the ball to score a try and was declared premiers via forfeit. The Watersiders would have to wait another six seasons to clinch their maiden first grade title.

THE EARL PARK RIOT One of the most infamous matches in premiership history was staged in round 11 of the 1928 season, between St. George and Balmain. Played at the Saints' home ground—the now-defunct Earl Park in Arncliffe—the contest degenerated into a running brawl. St. George won comfortably 21-3, despite having forward Harry Flowers sent from the field for foul play, while the referee's reluctance to send any Balmain players from the field for repeated acts of thuggery incensed the partisan crowd. The tenuous situation reached fever pitch when Balmain forward Tony Russell allegedly kicked St. George's former Test centre George Carstairs in the head. In the dying moments, Balmain's future Kangaroo George Bishop chased after veteran St. George clubman Arnold Traynor, sparking the crowd into action. Irate spectators stormed the field brandishing fence palings, seeking retribution on Russell. Police had to use force to subdue the frenzied crowd, making several arrests, while they handcuffed a transgressor to the goalposts... and forgot about him, leaving him there for three hours. In one of the more dramatic accounts, future prominent St. George administrator Alex Mackie recalled seeing a man behind the grandstands swinging an axe, while Russell was attacked by spectators and suffered injuries. He was then put into an ambulance—with Carstairs! Legend has it that the pair resumed their battle en route to the hospital, having to be restrained by ambulance staff. Fighting at the ground continued for several hours, while Russell and Bishop had to front Kogarah court charged with inciting a riot, charges that were subsequently dropped. It was a unique day in Australian Rugby League—its very own brand of soccer hooliganism, forever to be recalled as the Earl Park Riot.

THE ABANDONED INTERNATIONAL The unthinkable happened in Great Britain's clash with New South Wales on the Lions' tour Down Under in 1954. Unable to contain incessant brawling between the two sides, referee Aub Oxford declared the match a no-contest and walked off the field after 56 minutes. The match was played in the lead-up to the deciding third Ashes Test, and while NSW picked a strong line-up containing eight members of the eventual Australian side, Great Britain fielded just three Test players and named several players out of position. The prevailing notion was that the makeshift Lions line-up—which featured several bruising forwards in the backline—was intended to put a few of the Blues' Test players out of commission. The match—played in front of 27,000 supporters at the Sydney Cricket Ground—exploded after halftime, with a succession of melees breaking out involving most players from both sides. Oxford quit refereeing after the regrettable international, which has been officially recorded in the Rugby League annals as 'Match abandoned'.

KEN IRVINE LEADS WALK-OFF North Sydney's greatest player, ARL Team of the Century winger Ken Irvine, almost sparked one of the most sensational incidents in premiership history in 1970. Captain Irvine and Bears backrower John McDonnell were sent off in the opening-round clash with Canterbury at Belmore Sports Ground by referee Keith Page. Marched for using foul language, Irvine allegedly attempted to lead his team from the field in protest of Page's treatment of his players. Several Bears were prepared to back their skipper's stance, but the club's English coach Roy Francis dissuaded them from taking the drastic measure. The depleted Bears remained on the field and Canterbury went on to win the match 16-14, but the scoreline seemed irrelevant in the wake of the afternoon's scandalous events. Irvine was later subject to a lengthy inquiry but was not censured. Ironically, McDonnell later captained Canterbury to a Grand Final in 1974.

NEWTOWN INVOLVED IN LANDMARK SCORELINES Before being excluded from the premiership at the end of 1983, the Newtown club was part of two unique pockets of Rugby League history. The Bluebags defeated St. George with a solitary field goal at the SCG in 1973, providing the code with its first-ever 1-0 final score. The scoreline had not been possible until two years earlier, when the value of a field goal was reduced from two points to one, but no match has ended 1-0 since. Utility-back Ken Wilson, the highest point-scorer in the club's history, kicked the historic one-pointer.

Wilson returned to Newtown—who adopted the Jets moniker in the late 1970s—in 1979 after a stint with Penrith, and was captain of the club in 1982 when it participated in the premiership's only scoreless draw, against Canterbury at Henson Park in 1982. Despite a myriad of opportunities for both sides in the early-season clash, the combatants gave the scoreboard attendant the day off, and history was made. Remarkably, Newtown was victorious in the first of just three 2-0 scorelines in premiership history (against Easts in 1914), and in the maiden 3-0 result (against Glebe in 1910)—a score that has been repeated just five times.

CHISHOLM POLEAXES WEEKES, GETS 10 WEEKS South Sydney forward Wayne Chisholm made arguably the most infamous contact with a referee in premiership history during a 1991 match against Newcastle. Former All Black John Schuster had just taken an intercept and Chisholm moved across in his direction, but instead of cutting off the Knights' New Zealand centre, he crunched referee Geoff Weekes in a heavy tackle. The bizarre incident cost Chisholm more than two months on the sidelines courtesy of a 10-week suspension, charged with trying to gain an advantage by physically interfering with the referee. The former City Origin representative departed Souths at the end of the year after 109 first grade games with the club and retired following a disappointing season with Norths in 1992.

TEST FARCE IN PALMERSTON NORTH The second Test of the 1993 series between New Zealand and Australia was hotly anticipated after a first-up 14-all draw in Auckland. But the second encounter, staged in the central North Island city of Palmerston North, ended in farcical circumstances. Australia won the match 16-8 with a fine display in freezing, wet conditions, but the game was marred by crowd behaviour—balls that were kicked into touch were stolen by spectators, delaying the game for several minutes when the last ball was pilfered. Kiwi captain Gary Freeman attempted a walk-off after Australian five-eighth Laurie Daley was hit with a bottle thrown from the crowd. But Australian skipper Mal Meninga kept his men out on the field with the game in their keeping, eager to avoid the match being abandoned and forced into a replay. The soaked players were eventually able to finish the match, but despite the unsavoury ordeal, Palmerston North hosted subsequent Tests against France, Papua New Guinea and Great Britain in the 1995-96 seasons.

WILD WEATHER IN BATTLE FOR FINALS SPOTS Western Suburbs and Newcastle were locked in a tense battle for the last top-eight spot going into the final round of the 1996 regular season, but the rival teams had more than their respective opponents to contend with. Torrential rain and gale-force winds plagued the Magpies' clash with Illawarra, who were out of contention, and the Knights' tough away assignment against finals-bound Cronulla. Running with a powerful gale in the first half so strong it blew a kick-off back past the halfway line, Wests could only build a 12-6 advantage at halftime. But Tom Raudonikis' side defended stoically in the second stanza in the face of the driving wind to tough out a 12-8 victory and leapfrog Newcastle into eighth spot. The Knights' destiny was in their own hands—an upset over Cronulla would see the club qualify for the finals. But the weather was even more abhorrent at Shark Park. Incredibly, after choosing to run into the wind in the first half, the Sharks defied the stormy conditions to lead 16-0 at the break. Newcastle had no counter in the second half and went down 22-0, its finals hopes blowing away in one of the worst weather days witnessed in premiership football during the 1990s.

SIMPKINS MANHANDLED BY AUCKLAND INTERNATIONALS Arguably the most controversial match of the 1999 NRL season resulted in three Auckland players receiving a total of nine weeks suspension after the Warriors' 17-8 loss to Balmain. Auckland led 8-4 at halftime at Leichhardt Oval, but was helpless to stop the Tigers piling on 13 unanswered points after the break. After Balmain pivot Ben Duckworth slotted a crucial field goal, Warriors captain Matthew Ridge and fellow New Zealand Test player Nigel Vagana rushed at referee Paul Simpkins, arguing that the ball had been touched in-flight. Unfortunately, the fired-up Warriors were not aware the rule had been changed during the off-season, instead grabbing Simpkins to launch their protest. Ridge and Vagana were suspended for three weeks apiece for placing their hands on a referee, while Kiwi and Samoan Test lock Tony Tuimavave joined them on the sidelines after being cited for a reckless high tackle.

SNOW FALLS IN THE CAPITAL The only Australian premiership match to be played in the snow occurred in 2000, with Canberra hosting the Wests Tigers. Inclement weather and plummeting temperatures resulted in a blanket of snow for the Bruce Stadium surface by the time the first grade fixture kicked off, setting the scene for one of the most unique first grade matches ever staged. In conditions more commonly sighted in the frosty north of England, the Raiders won a see-sawing clash 24-22, but the score hardly seemed important while players attempted to keep frostbite at bay. A resilient 7,000-strong crowd turned out to see the match which sealed Canberra's reputation as one of the NRL's least desirable road trips.

RAIDERS SEEK RESTITUTION AFTER FULLTIME FARCE The round nine encounter between St. George Illawarra and Canberra at WIN Stadium in 2002 produced one of the most extraordinary finishes in premiership history. The Dragons fought back from a 21-8 halftime deficit to trail by just one point, before their hooker Mark Riddell was sent off for a high tackle in the 77th minute. The 12-man Saints continued to press for the win, however, and Brent Kite was held up over the line in the dying seconds. Referee Steven Clark called time off with the clock showing zero seconds, and awarded the Dragons a differential penalty from the scrum, ruling Raiders halfback Brett Finch was offside in charging down opposing No.7 Willie Peters' field goal attempt. Unable to kick for goal from a differential penalty, the Dragons took a tap and Peters landed a one-pointer to draw the game 21-all. Canberra's coach Matthew Elliott and his players were livid with the outcome, while Raiders chief executive Simon Hawkins sought to have the result overturned—a demand that was unsurprisingly laughed off by NRL counterpart David Gallop.

HARRIGAN DUMPED AFTER SIN-BIN MADNESS Newcastle accounted for Parramatta 28-14 midway through 2002 in a replay of the previous year's Grand Final, with referee Bill Harrigan hammering the Eels 7-3 in the penalty count. The fiery clash—which featured an all-in brawl, Parramatta captain Nathan Cayless being cautioned for dissent and Eels centre David Vaealiki copping a five-week striking suspension—set the scene for an explosive rematch just three weeks later in Newcastle, with Harrigan again manning the whistle. After warning Parramatta's players for repeatedly holding down in the ruck during the first half, Harrigan despatched Michael Buettner to the sin-bin 15 minutes into the second stanza. Backrower Nathan Hindmarsh followed three minutes later, and the hapless Eels were reduced to 10 men for a short time after five-eighth Adam Dykes was also marched. The Knights rallied from a four-point deficit to lead 20-18 during this period, and Buettner made his second trip to the sin-bin for abusing a touch judge when his opposing centre Mark Hughes scored the match-sealing try in the 74th minute. Harrigan was stood down for round 18 of the NRL for his controversial display, but he returned a week later and eventually controlled the 2002 Grand Final.

CRAZY FINISH CAPS FIELD GOAL SHOOT-OUT St. George and Parramatta produced quite possibly the most bizarre match of the modern era at Oki Jubilee Oval in 2006. The match was played in atrocious conditions and the score remained at 0-0 for 70 minutes. Eels five-eighth John Morris broke the impasse with a field goal 10 minutes from fulltime, creating the first 1-0 scoreline since North Sydney halfback Clayton Friend opened the scoring with a one-pointer against Newcastle in 1989, before the Bears went down 14-1. Morris' field goal triggered a frenetic finish to the contest. Ben Hornby kicked back-to-back field goals for the Dragons in the final five minutes, and at 2-1 the match was headed for the lowest-scoring result in a premiership match since the scoreless draw between Newtown and Canterbury 24 years earlier. But in the dying seconds Parramatta had a scrum feed near their own tryline, and Eels halfback Jeremy Smith stopped after feeding the scrum when he heard referee Sean Hampstead's whistle. But Hampstead was signalling time on, and Saints centre Matt Cooper scooped up the loose ball for the match-sealing try. A frustrated Smith shoved Hampstead in the back, later receiving a four-week suspension for contrary conduct, adding a confounding post-script to a truly bizarre night. The final score: St. George Illawarra 8 Parramatta 1.

POINTS DOCKED

There have been several instances of competition points being deducted for breaking the rules. Breaching replacement and interchange regulations, the salary cap or the old residential rules have carried costly ramifications for the offending teams.

CHAOS AFTER GLEBE BREACH RESIDENTIAL RULE The residential rule, which dictated terms in the premiership until 1959, required players to live in the area represented by their club. In 1917, Annandale protested after a 26-5 loss to a Glebe side containing Newcastle product Dan 'Laddo' Davies, who was residing in Annandale. Incredibly, the NSWRL not only stripped Glebe of the two competition points—they suspended Davies from the game for life. The furore had far-reaching ramifications for the game in Sydney and Newcastle. In conjunction with further incidents that resulted in bans for Glebe lower grade players, the Davies case resulted in strike action by several Dirty Reds first graders—who were also subsequently slapped with lengthy suspensions. A similarly explosive situation developed in Newcastle, where Davies had returned to play for Wests in the local competition. The NSWRL had forbidden Davies to play anywhere in the state, and when Norths agreed to play Wests, the entire Northern Branch of the Newcastle competition was disqualified. Two competitions ran in Newcastle for the next two years, until the formation of the Newcastle Rugby League in 1920 saw the region reunited. Meanwhile, the bans on Glebe's striking players were rescinded by the NSWRL and they were free to play in the 1918 premiership.

MAGPIES FIRST TO BREACH REPLACEMENT RULE A replacement breach cost Western Suburbs dearly in the context of the club's 1975 finals bid. Mick Liubinskas was brought off the bench during the Magpies' late-season 7-all draw with Canterbury, but under the rules of the era a first grade replacement was required to play at least half a game in reserve grade earlier in the day— a prerequisite the centre/forward had not fulfilled. The Magpies were stripped of the competition point they had earned for the draw, and eventually tied for fifth spot with Parramatta and Balmain. The Eels won through to the finals with fifth-place play-off victories over the Magpies and Tigers, leaving Wests to lament the lost point that would have given the club the last spot in the finals series outright.

WILSON MAKES INAUSPICIOUS DEBUT Talented journeyman utility-back Scott Wilson had a colourful career on and off the field—beginning with his first grade debut for Souths in 1988. The Rabbitohs recorded a stirring 28-14 Anzac Day defeat of arch-rivals and defending premiers Manly, with 17-year-old Wilson sent on late in the contest by coach George Piggins. But Wilson had played in the President's Cup earlier in the afternoon, breaching a new rule stating players could not be used in higher grades after playing in the Under-21s match on the same day. The NSWRL was loath to take the hard-fought two points off Souths, but were left with little choice after the rule breach.

REPLACEMENT BUNGLE CONSIGNS SEAGULLS TO WOODEN SPOON Gold Coast was denied true reward for one of the finest victories in the club's short history in 1992. The reigning wooden spooners upset Illawarra 18-8 in an early-season match despite having New Zealand Test prop Brent Todd sent off— a major boilover considering the Steelers were pre-season champions and on their way to a maiden finals berth. But the gritty win, under the guidance of captain-coach Wally Lewis, was soured by the realisation the 12-man Seagulls had used five replacements. The two competition points, which would have been enough to see the Seagulls leapfrog Parramatta and avoid another wooden spoon at the end of the season, were subsequently docked.

FIFTH MAN COSTS TIGERS Shayne Boyd's only appearance for Balmain was an unfortunate one—the former Penrith prop had the indignity of being the Tigers' fifth replacement in a stirring 28-12 upset of his old club, breaching the interchange rules. It was one of the lowly Tigers' best efforts of 1993, but three weeks after the match, the NSWRL officially stripped Balmain of the two points. The decision resulted in the Tigers dropping below Souths into 15th place at the end of the season, while Boyd did not feature in first grade again.

EXTRA REPLACEMENT DENIES AUCKLAND MAIDEN WIN A premiership club was docked two competition points for fielding a fifth replacement for the third time in four seasons in 1995. This time it was competition newcomers the Auckland Warriors who inadvertently broke the rules in a round three thrashing of

Wests, denying the club its first competition points. The Warriors had dominated from start to finish, with Phil Blake scoring four tries in a 46-12 drubbing. But former New Zealand representative Jason Mackie was sent into the fray late in the game, tipping the Warriors over the allowed four interchange players. The initial disappointment had an even more bitter postscript. Auckland missed out on a finals spot to Norths on for-and-against—the win would have given the Warriors eighth spot outright.

INTERCHANGE CALAMITY ADDS TO COWBOYS' SEASON OF WOE North Queensland was denied its first competition points of a disastrous 2000 campaign for having 14 players on the field against heavyweights Parramatta. The Cowboys held off a late charge by the Eels to win 26-18 in the round four match-up, but celebrations turned sour when it was revealed Tim Sheens' hapless side had played with an extra man for four of the final 10 minutes of the match. The club's protests were to no avail, and the Cowboys eventually finished with the wooden spoon three wins adrift of Auckland and the Northern Eagles.

THE BULLDOGS' 2002 SALARY CAP RORT The 2002 NRL season was shaping as a watershed year for the Bulldogs—the club had pieced together a phenomenal 17-match winning streak during the season and were overwhelming title favourites with a five-point break on the rest of the field in the minor premiership race with three rounds remaining. But revelations the Bulldogs had flagrantly exceeded the salary cap by $1.5 million in 2001 and 2002 turned the competition on its head. NRL CEO David Gallop—in his first season as the game's boss—summed up the feelings of Rugby League fans across the country. "The game has had its heart broken in an unexpected and tragic way," he said, before fining the club $500,000 and stripping all 37 competition points the Bulldogs had accrued so far in 2002—effectively consigning the blue-and-whites to the wooden spoon.

BRONCOS DODGE A BULLET Brisbane was stripped of two competition points for fielding an illegal replacement in an early-season clash with the Wests Tigers in 2004, but later had them restored on appeal. The Broncos had been awarded a penalty and subsequent free interchange for a high tackle on their prop Shane Webcke. But Corey Parker came off the bench and onto the field before Webcke had been assisted off and scored a crucial try. The Broncos eventually won 32-24, but were livid when a breach notice was issued by the NRL. The points were stripped less than a week later, but a successful appeal saw the Broncos regain the spoils of their victory and escape with a fine.

WARRIORS' HONESTY CRUELS 2006 CAMPAIGN Upon realising they had inadvertently breached the salary cap by almost $1 million prior to the 2006 season, the New Zealand Warriors owned up to their bookkeeping error by informing the NRL. As commendable as the club's admission was—particularly in light of the Bulldogs' rorting four years earlier—it ultimately cost the Warriors a spot in the finals. The NRL docked four competition points from the Warriors prior to the opening round, meaning the club started 2006 with minus four points on the premiership ladder. The Warriors, in coach Ivan Cleary's first season with the club, won two of their first four games to get back to zero and stormed home with eight victories in their last 12 matches to finish 10th. In a frustrating reminder of their interchange nightmare during their debut season, the Warriors finished four points outside the top-eight—the docked points would have been enough for them to clinch eighth spot on for-and-against from Parramatta.

GRANDMA-GATE Ancestral confusion cost the New Zealand Test side points during the 2006 Tri-Nations competition. Warriors half Nathan Fien, a Mount Isa-bred former Origin representative, was selected in the Kiwis squad on the basis of a supposedly New Zealand-born grandmother. Controversy surrounded Fien's selection throughout the opening weeks of the tournament, and the camp plunged into turmoil when it was revealed that it was in fact his great-grandmother that had been born in the Shaky Isles. Fien was immediately released from the squad and the Kiwis had the two points they had earned with an 18-14 defeat of Great Britain in Christchurch deleted. New Zealand still qualified for the final of the tournament, however, with a 34-4 thumping of the Lions two weeks later in Wellington, before going down in golden point to Australia in the decider. Fien, meanwhile, was selected for the Kiwis again in 2007, qualifying on residential grounds, and played halfback in the nation's historic defeat of Australia in the 2008 World Cup final. He won a premiership with St. George Illawarra and scored the winning try in New Zealand's 2010 Four Nations final triumph against the Kangaroos, and had racked up 19 Test appearances for the Kiwis by the end of 2011.

BULLDOGS SLIP-UP COSTS MINOR PREMIERSHIP A bench bungle marginalised the Bulldogs' last-gasp victory over Penrith in the second round of 2009. Bulldogs five-eighth Ben Roberts crossed for a try in the final minute to level the see-sawing contest at 26-all, with Hazem El Masri's sideline conversion after the buzzer giving the blue-and-whites a thrilling victory. But an NRL investigation confirmed reports the Bulldogs had 14 men on the field at the time of the winning try. Club officials had mistakenly sent skipper Andrew Ryan back into the action while an injured teammate remained on the field receiving attention. The penalty cost the club a minor premiership—the Bulldogs finished second to St. George Illawarra on points differential at the end of the regular season.

MELBOURNE DYNASTY STRIPPED OF PREMIERSHIPS Shocking details of the Melbourne Storm's systematic rorting of the salary cap—dating back to 2006—came to light early in the 2010 season, provoking an unprecedented response from the NRL and CEO David Gallop. The cap breaches, which peaked at an estimated $850,000 for the 2010 season alone, resulted in the Storm having the 2007 and 2009 NRL titles and the 2006-08 minor premierships stripped, while they were ordered to pay back $1.1 million in prizemoney and were slapped with a $500,000 fine. The Storm also had the competition points they had accrued to that point in 2010 stripped and were denied the opportunity to play for points in 2010—effectively consigning the club to the wooden spoon. Former CEO Brian Waldron (who had joined fledgling Super Rugby franchise the Melbourne Rebels) emerged as the villain of the piece, endorsing a series of illegal payments to star players. The players and coaching staff were cleared of any wrongdoing. Melbourne stoically fought on and finished the season with 14 wins—which would have been enough to qualify for the finals in fifth place—but had no option other than to dismantle the powerful squad that had been built on false pretences, with high-profile players Greg Inglis, Brett Finch, Ryan Hoffman, Brett White, Jeff Lima and Aiden Tolman moving on at the end of 2010 to alleviate the club's salary cap situation. But Craig Bellamy performed a coaching miracle in 2011, steering his new-look side to the minor premiership in one of the great club performances in the game's history, before being bundled out by the Warriors in the preliminary final.

GOLDEN POINT

Golden point extra-time was introduced by the NRL in 2003 to add another element of excitement to matches tied after 80 minutes of regulation time. Despite opposition from some figures within the game—most pointedly Brisbane coach Wayne Bennett—the bold rule change, consisting of five minutes each way of sudden death, first-scorer-wins extra-time, was ratified after first being mooted late in 2002. The rule stipulated that if no team had scored after 10 minutes of golden point time the match would be declared a draw, with each side receiving a competition point.

Rugby League's introduction to golden point football came six years earlier, in the epic Super League Tri-Series final between New South Wales and Queensland. The enthralling match was tied 22-all at the end of 80 minutes, with neither side able to add to their scores in 20 minutes of extra-time. The showdown headed into an unprecedented golden point period, and Hunter Mariners halfback Noel Goldthorpe finally clinched the result for New South Wales with a sweetly struck field goal in the 104th minute—the longest game of top-level Rugby League ever played.

Fans had to wait until round 10 of the 2003 season to witness the premiership's first golden point encounter: a controversial 36-34 victory to Manly over Parramatta at Brookvale Oval. The Sea Eagles were awarded a contentious 88th minute penalty, which was converted by five-eighth Ben Walker. Ironically, Manly coach Peter Sharp had been a vocal critic of golden point's introduction. Penrith's Tony Puletua had the distinction of scoring the first-ever golden point try three weeks later, snatching a 28-24 victory over the Cowboys. A stirring comeback from 24-6 down by the New Zealand Warriors against Souths in Round 16 was the precursor to golden point's maiden field goal, slotted by mercurial Kiwi halfback Stacey Jones for a 31-30 victory.

One of the most common criticisms in the lead-up to golden point's introduction (along with player burnout) was that deadlocked matches would descend into a field goal shoot-out, but statistics show that a one-pointer is not the overwhelming match-winning play that was predicted. Of the 60 golden point games staged to the end of 2010, 30 have ended with a field goal being kicked. A try has decided the result on 14 occasions, a penalty goal has been the winning score seven times, while nine games have finished as a draw after 10 minutes of added time. The figures are exaggerated by 2011's contribution to the golden point story—eight of the 10 extra-time matches staged during the season ended with a field goal, while one game finished via a penalty goal and one game was drawn.

Penrith have appeared in the most golden point matches, winning five, losing three and drawing two of 10 encounters. South Sydney and Cronulla are next with nine appearances, while Brisbane, Wests Tigers and the Warriors follow closely with eight. Despite winning the first golden point game, Manly has made the fewest appearances, going into extra-time just once more—a loss to Newcastle in 2008.

The Canberra Raiders were the undisputed champions of golden point, emerging victorious in the first five extra-period matches they contested, including four games in 2006. But the Green Machine succumbed in two golden point matches in 2011 to halt their unbeaten extra-time streak. The Wests Tigers have proved to be the 'bunnies' of golden point, winning just one from eight, including two losses to the Raiders in 2006. St. George Illawarra, meanwhile, is yet to record a golden point victory—the club has lost five of the six games it has been involved in, and the other was drawn.

The 2011 NRL season was the most prolific golden point season to date with 10 matches, followed by the 2004 and 2007 seasons with nine matches. Incredibly, three matches in round 22 of the 2007 went into golden point: some Braith Anasta brilliance saw the Roosters home 26-22 against the Tigers; the Sharks snapped a seven-match losing streak to defeat the Eels 25-24; and North Queensland centre Ashley Graham's third try sunk the Panthers 30-26. At the other end of the scale, just two golden point matches occurred in 2005—the lowest total of matches tied at the end of regulation time since 1993 (not including the 1997 Super League season, which was contested by only 10 teams).

Two NRL finals matches have gone into golden point. The qualifying final between the Tigers and Roosters in 2010 *(see Finals Magic)* was also the first final in 12 years to go into extra-time, and was decided by a 100th-minute long-range intercept try to Roosters centre Shaun Kenny-Dowall for an epic 19-15 triumph. In 2011, Darren Lockyer kicked a dramatic field goal in the second minute to lift Brisbane to a 13-12 semi-final defeat of St. George Illawarra *(see Finals Magic and Courageous Performances)*. Golden point was required to decide both curtain-raisers to the 2008 NRL Grand Final. Twenty minutes of extra-time was unable to separate Wentworthville and Newtown in the NSW Cup decider, but a try to Wentworthville winger Iwi Hauraki in the 104th minute clinched the title after both sides missed a myriad of field goal opportunities. In the following match, the inaugural Toyota Cup Under-20s Grand Final saw the young Raiders and Broncos tied at 24-all after 80 minutes, but a spectacular try to second-rower Jarrad Kennedy in the eighth minute of golden point secured the NYC premiership.

GOLDEN POINT AT REPRESENTATIVE LEVEL The call for extra-time or golden point in State of Origin football began long before its NRL launch, particularly south of the border. The deciders of the 1999 and 2002 Origin series ended in draws; Queensland retained the shield both times as the winner of the previous year's series. With golden point also allocated to drawn Origin matches from 2003, the first interstate match to go into an extra period was the first clash of 2004. In a typically tight Origin contest the scores were locked 8-all at the end of 80 minutes, before Blues five-eighth Shaun Timmins nailed a 37-metre field goal in the third minute of golden point time to win the series-opener.

Remarkably, the corresponding match of the 2005 series also went into golden point. NSW fought back from a 19-0 deficit to lead by a point in the dying minutes, until Johnathan Thurston kicked a field goal on debut to level up for Queensland. A daring attacking raid from deep inside their own territory came unstuck for the Blues in golden point when Brett Kimmorley fired a cut-out pass. The ball was plucked out of the air by Queensland interchange Matt Bowen, who waltzed in for the 40-metre match-winner after just three and a half minutes of added time; the try gave the Maroons a 24-20 victory.

The only international match to require golden point extra-time was the 2006 Tri-Nations final between Australia and New Zealand. Despite the Kiwis scoring two tries to Australia's one, the match was locked at 12-all at the end of regulation time. Both sides missed with field goal attempts during the golden point period, and it took a trademark 'show-and-go' from Johnathan Thurston to break the stalemate. Thurston dummied his way through the tiring Kiwi defensive line and found his skipper Darren Lockyer looming in support. Lockyer capped a magical year by scoring under the posts to regain the Tri-Nations trophy for the Australia.

THE BEST OF GOLDEN POINT Remarkably, South Sydney was involved in the first three golden point draws—against North Queensland and Brisbane in 2004, and against the Bulldogs in 2005. The 34-all deadlock against the Broncos equalled the premiership record for the highest-scoring draw. Souths twice came from behind to eventually lead 34-28, but a sideline conversion from Brisbane forward Corey Parker of a Neville Costigan try saw the match head into an extra period. Rabbitohs halfback Joe Williams hit the post with a field goal attempt during golden point, and a series of missed one-point chances by both sides consigned the match to a draw.

Clinton Schifcofske proved to be a golden point specialist during 2004 and 2006 for the Raiders. In Canberra's first golden point fixture in 2004, Schifcofske sent the round 20 clash against New Zealand into extra-time with a last-minute field goal, only a minute after Stacey Jones had put the Warriors 29-28 in front with a one-pointer of his own. Schifcofske nailed his second field goal less than two minutes into golden point to steal a remarkable 30-29 victory. He was at it again early in 2006 as the club's captain, kicking a late sideline conversion to send a match against Penrith into golden point at 20-all, before kicking a field goal in the second period of extended time to win the game. Late in 2006 the ice-cool fullback kept the Raiders' finals hope on track by landing a penalty goal in golden point to defeat the Tigers 20-18.

Demonstrating that Schifcofske wasn't the only Raider capable of taking a golden point game by the scruff of the neck, teenage five-eighth Todd Carney won two matches for Canberra in 2006 with long-range field goals in extra-time. Against North Queensland in round 12, Carney nailed a 40-metre attempt in the 87th minute, before sealing the Raiders' finals spot with a 38-metre field goal to down the Tigers in controversial circumstances in round 23. Carney appeared to be offside in charging down field goal attempts by Tigers skipper Scott Prince prior to his own match-winning strike.

Darren Lockyer conjured twin victories for his Broncos over neighbourly newcomers Gold Coast in golden point fixtures in 2007 and 2008, both at Suncorp Stadium. Lockyer kicked one of the great field goals from 40 metres out against the Titans in 2007—the ball bounced off each post before dropping over the crossbar to snatch a thrilling 19-18 victory in the 81st minute. In the corresponding derby the following season, Lockyer crafted arguably the finest golden point try after spending much of the week battling a virus. The match was tied 21-all at fulltime, but after three minutes of extra-time Lockyer shifted the ball to Joel Moon on halfway after the Titans rushed up to shut down a field goal attempt. Moon found space and Lockyer backed up on the inside to send Kiwi back-rower Greg Eastwood over for a sensational match-winner.

Playing just his fourth NRL game, Bulldogs half Ben Roberts produced a memorable golden point play against the Warriors in 2006. The scores were tied 18-all at fulltime after a second half arm-wrestle. Roberts looked set to take a shot at field goal in third minute of golden point, but scythed through a tiny gap in the Warriors' line and found burly prop Mark O'Meley with a flick pass on the inside. O'Meley dived over for a rare try to clinch two vital competition points.

Nursing a heavy injury toll, South Sydney was desperate for a win against the Wests Tigers to keep their finals hopes alive late in 2010. But at 28-12 behind 10 minutes into the second half, the Rabbitohs looked dead and buried. A stirring fightback dragged them back into the match, however, and a try to John Sutton tied the game at 30-all with three minutes to go. Seven field goal attempts went astray in extra-time, including an attempt from halfway by Tigers star Benji Marshall that fell just under the crossbar, and the match appeared destined for a draw. Enter Rhys Wesser. The veteran Rabbitohs fullback beat four tackles to break into the clear and fired a speculative pass on his outside when confronted by the cover defence. The pass hit Jason Clark on the chest, and Clark got an offload back on the inside to debutant Dylan Farrell *(see Unforgettable Debuts)*, who scored in the corner as the siren sounded.

South Sydney halfback Chris Sandow landed arguably the best golden point field goal and undoubtedly one of the greatest of all time against arch-rivals the Sydney Roosters in 2011. Greg Inglis scored a try five minutes from fulltime and Sandow converted to force the 80-minute tie. Seven minutes into added time, Sandow stepped up to pilot an extraordinary 49-metre field goal to win the match 21-20. The game-breaking No.7's strike was one of the longest one-pointers kicked in the NRL era.

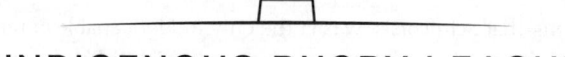

INDIGENOUS RUGBY LEAGUE

The contribution of Indigenous Australians holds a significant and special place in the Rugby League narrative. While many Indigenous players rank among the modern-day greats of the game, no Indigenous players were selected for Australia before 1960. Throughout the game's history, Indigenous players have faced the same prejudices and discrimination from administrators, fellow players and the general public that have plagued most aspects of Australian society. Rugby League has represented an accessible mode of social mobility for Indigenous Australians to gain acceptance in wider society, but it has been a long and arduous road to eradicate racism and inequality from the game and create a level playing field.

Although his exact heritage is still uncertain, North Sydney forward George Green is generally recognised as the first Indigenous Australian to play first grade Rugby League. Green made 91 appearances for Norths between 1912 and 1922, playing hooker in the club's 1921-22 premiership-winning sides, regarded as one of the all time great club combinations. But leading historians such as Andrew Moore question the authenticity of his Aboriginality, asserting that his dark skin was more likely due to Afro-Carribean ancestry, while Green himself told people he was Maori or Polynesian—possibly a by-product of the prejudices invariably faced by Indigenous Australians in an unenlightened era.[7] Nevertheless, the NRL struck the George Green Medal in 2008, awarded to the game's outstanding rising Indigenous star.

Glen Crouch's status as an Indigenous pioneer is more assured—he scored seven tries on Queensland's tour of New Zealand in 1925, becoming the first Aboriginal footballer to tour overseas. But Aboriginal Rugby League legend Frank Fisher was denied the chance to play abroad. Great Britain captain Jim Brough described Fisher, the star of the Wide Bay representative side that took on the 1936 Lions, as the best player the tourists had encountered in Australia. English club Salford offered Fisher a contract on the strength of Brough's glowing appraisal, but Fisher's application to travel was denied by the Queensland Government.[8] Born in Townsville, Fisher developed his skills in Cherbourg, a rich Rugby League breeding ground that has produced modern stars Steve Renouf, Willie Tonga and Chris Sandow. A contemporary—and occasional teammate—of famed Aboriginal cricketer Eddie Gilbert, Fisher is the grandfather of Australian Olympic athletics great Cathy Freeman. His attempts to join the Australian Imperial Force in World War II were also blocked on racial grounds.[9]

Where Fisher had been refused the opportunity, Northern Territory-born winger Wally McArthur flourished. McArthur initially played Rugby League in South Australia and Western Australia, before venturing to England and racking up 165 appearances for Rochdale, Blackpool Borough, Salford and Workington. But the speedster was by no means free from discrimination—it has been suggested by prominent historians that he was left out of Australia's track-and-field team for the 1952 Helsinki Olympics because of his Aboriginal heritage.[10]

Made up predominantly of Indigenous players, club sides such as the Tweed Heads All Blacks and Redfern All Blacks formed during the 1930s. Although indicative of the prejudice and separatism that abounded during that time, the teams proved to be extremely formidable opposition for established clubs.

Brothers Dick and Lin Johnson were among the few Indigenous players to turn out in the Sydney premiership during the 1930s and 1940s, while their brother Stan was a prominent jockey.[11] Dick Johnson played 90 games for Newtown, Souths, Wests and Canterbury, and represented NSW 11 times between 1938 and 1945. A NSW rep in 1940, Lin Johnson was a goalkicking fullback in 91 games for Canterbury, landing

---

7   Andrew Moore, "The Wrong Man", *Sydney Morning Herald,* 8 November 2008
8   Colin Tatz, *Obstacle Race: Aborigines In Sport.* University of New South Wales, 1995
9   *Courier Mail,* "4 Aborigines Not Allowed To Join A.I.F.", 3 July 1940
10   Sean Fagan, "First Indigenous Footballers"
11   John Maynard, *Aboriginal Stars Of The Turf: Jockeys Of Australian Racing History.* ACT, 2001

a famous late goal to clinch an 11-9 victory in the 1942 Grand Final victory over St. George (*see Unlikely Heroes*). In a unique occurrence, the brothers were opposing fullbacks in the annual City Firsts v Country Firsts clash in 1941—Canterbury's Lin for City and Newcastle-based Dick for Country.

Wynnum-Manly winger Lionel Morgan made a major breakthrough in 1960 when he became Australia's first Indigenous Test player. Morgan scored two tries on debut in Australia's 56-6 demolition of France at the Brisbane Cricket Ground and was retained for the shock 7-5 loss two weeks later. He toured England at the end of the year with the World Cup squad, again playing against France in his only appearance at the tournament. The trailblazing flyer scored 11 tries and kicked 19 goals in 12 interstate matches for Queensland between 1960 and 1963.

Indigenous footballers began to make a substantial impact in Sydney during the 1960s. Wollongong front-rower Bruce Olive represented NSW in eight interstate matches from 1958-62 and played 71 games in four seasons after joining Newtown (1964-67). Goalkicking fullbacks Kevin Longbottom and Eric Simms established a legacy of Indigenous Rugby League excellence at South Sydney that extends to the present day. Longbottom played 105 games for the Rabbitohs (1961-69), landing three trademark long-range goals in the club's famous 12-8 Grand Final loss to St. George in front of a record SCG crowd in 1965 before celebrating in Souths' 1967 premiership success. Simms played on the wing in the 1965 decider and at centre in 1967 to accommodate Longbottom, before slotting in at fullback for the 1968-71 Grand Finals. A brilliant goalkicker and phenomenal field goal exponent, Simms amassed a then-premiership record 1,843 points in a then-club record 206 games for Souths. He played eight games during Australia's 1968 and 1970 World Cup successes, top-scoring at each tournament.

Redcliffe pair Arthur Beetson and Kevin Yow Yeh, BRL Grand Final-winners in 1965, joined Balmain in 1966. Brilliant three-quarter Yow Yeh played in the Tigers' Grand Final loss to St. George in 1966, but struggled to adapt to life in Sydney and the racism he was subjected to. A tortured soul, Yow Yeh left Balmain at the end of 1967 and tragically died in police custody in Mackay in 1975 (*see Tragic Figures*). His great-nephew, Brisbane Broncos flyer Jharal Yow Yeh, made his Test and Origin (Queensland) debuts in 2011.

Beetson, meanwhile, carved out one of the great Rugby League careers over the next 15 years. He made his Test debut in 1966—a year before Australians voted to give Indigenous Australians full residential rights in a referendum—and overcame a reputation early in his career for being lazy to become Australia's greatest ball-playing forward. After missing Balmain's 1969 Grand Final victory through suspension, 'Big Artie' skippered Easts to consecutive titles in 1974-75. Beetson was a genuine trailblazer, becoming the first Indigenous sportsperson to captain an Australian national sporting team when he led the Kangaroos against France in 1973, while he skippered his country in a total of eight Test and World Cup games until his international swansong in 1977. A pivotal figure in the State of Origin story as Queensland's inaugural captain in 1980, Beetson smashed down more barriers by coaching the Maroons in 16 matches, and coaching Australia in 1983. He was a tireless and vocal supporter for the advancement of his people until his death in 2011.

A first grade opponent of Beetson's and a teammate during the prop's first season at Easts, centre Ron Saddler captained NSW against Queensland in 1967 and toured with the 1967-68 Kangaroos while making 118 first grade appearances for the Tricolours. Saddler is thought to be one of the first Indigenous players to captain a state side—if not the first. Another prominent Indigenous player, Bruce 'Larpa' Stewart, turned out for the Roosters alongside Saddler in the late 1960s.

Thursday Islander George Ambrum, a Cairns product, became a crowd favourite in nine seasons with North Sydney (1966-74), scoring 54 tries in 157 games on the wing for the Bears and representing Australia in two Tests in 1972. Nicknamed the 'Black Flash,' Larry Corowa lit up the premiership with Balmain in the late-1970s and early-1980s, representing Australia in two Tests in 1978-79 and topping the premiership with 24 tries in 1978. An Aboriginal squad made a whirlwind visit to New Zealand in 1973, playing nine games in 10 days, winning seven. The team was captained by Penrith's Ron Mason.

The advent of State of Origin football elevated many Indigenous players to the highest level of Rugby League, particularly Queenslanders. Colin Scott, Tony Currie, Dale Shearer and Sam Backo used their performances at Origin level for the Maroons as a springboard to Australian Test honours. Queensland and Australian great Mal Meninga's Aboriginality has long been a source of ambiguity (he was even named in an Indigenous Team of the Century in 2001) but he has stated publicly that he is a South Sea Islander, although he has worked extensively with Indigenous youth in Australia.

Electrifying winger John 'Chicka' Ferguson was the most prominent NSW Indigenous player to emerge during the mid-1980s, playing three Origin matches and three Tests for Australia in 1985 while at Easts. Moving to Canberra, Ferguson represented the Blues five more times, was the premiership's top try-scorer in 1988, scored the famous try for the Raiders that sent the 1989 Grand Final into extra-time and scored another try as he farewelled the game with a premiership victory in the 1990 decider. Destructive forward 'Rambo' Ron Gibbs combined with Shearer, hooker and 1986 Rothmans medallist Mal Cochrane and reserve Paul Shaw in Manly's 1987 Grand Final victory, while five-eighth Cliff Lyons was named the Clive Churchill Medal winner, emphasising the increased presence of Indigenous players in the premiership.

Lyons debuted for NSW earlier in 1987 and represented the Blues again the following season. Indigenous players were often pigeonholed as 'enigmatic'—a tag that Lyons often had to contend with during his career. But as one of the modern era's great ball-players with incomparable sleight of hand, Lyons won the Dally M Medal in 1990 and 1994—a reward for consistently brilliant performances—and starred for Australia on the 1990 Kangaroo Tour. Lyons played in three more Grand Finals for the Sea Eagles (1995-97) and came out of retirement to play for the club in 1999 at the age of 37. Canberra great Laurie Daley bumped Lyons to lock in the Indigenous Team of the Century named in 2008; Daley rates as one of the all time greats of the game, but his Indigenous heritage was not widely publicised during his playing career.

An 'Australian Aborigines' team competed in the 1990 Pacific Cup staged in Tonga—a squad bolstered by premiership stars Ron Gibbs (who had joined the Gold Coast), and NSW Origin wingers Ricky Walford and Graham Lyons—and again in 1992 and '94. The premiership in first half of the 1990s featured a growing base of Indigenous playing talent: Easts' Origin and Test prop Craig Salvatori; Illawarra's two-time Dally M Lock of the Year Ian Russell; livewire Souths halfback Darrell Trindall; Canterbury's 1991 Rothmans Medal-winning halfback Ewan McGrady; Canberra's NSW Origin winger Ken Nagas; brilliant Brisbane backline stars Steve Renouf and Wendell Sailor; St. George youngsters Gorden Tallis and Anthony Mundine; and prolific three-quarter Matt Sing.

Renouf developed into one Rugby League's greatest attacking centres, scoring 142 tries in 183 games for the Broncos with his unstoppable combination of speed, footwork and a devastating fend. The Murgon product represented Queensland in 11 Origins and Australia in 10 Tests, touring with the 1994 Kangaroos along with clubmate and Thursday Islander Wendell Sailor, a potent try-scorer and one of the game's genuine personality players who was regarded as the game's best winger from 1995 until his switch to rugby union at the end of 2001. Tallis later joined the pair in Brisbane and captained the Broncos, Queensland and Australia in an illustrious career as arguably the most destructive forward of the modern era.

Central Queensland product Sing began his first grade career with Penrith, making his Origin and Test debuts after signing with the ARL in 1995 before linking with the Roosters. His career enjoyed a spectacular second wind as a mercurial tryscoring winger for the Cowboys from 2002-06, finishing with 159 tries in 275 games.

Mundine and contemporaries, Roosters fullback/five-eighth Andrew Walker, Cronulla No.1 David Peachey and Dragons winger Nathan Blacklock emerged as some of the competition's foremost match-winners in the mid-to-late-1990s. St. George rode five-eighth magician Mundine's brilliance to the 1996 Grand Final, while he combined with the incredible tryscoring talents of Blacklock in St. George Illawarra's drive to the decider in 1999.

A wonderful No.6 in a golden era of five-eighths that included Daley, Brad Fittler and Kevin Walters, Mundine's regular public outbursts against representative selectors—accusing them of racism for not picking him—were ill-conceived. The son of one of Australia's most prominent trailblazing Indigenous sportspeople, boxing champ Tony Mundine, Anthony walked out on the Dragons and the NRL in 2000, later citing his representative snubbing as a factor (three interchange appearances for the Blues in 1999 was the sum total of his representative achievements). The outspoken Mundine followed in his father's footsteps to carve out a successful boxing career.

The constant representative rejection of Blacklock, however, was bewildering. The NRL's top try-scorer from 1999-2001, the Tingha product finished his career with 121 tries in just 142 games, but made only two Test appearances for Australia and could not break into the Origin arena with NSW. Likewise, Peachey made just one Origin appearance for NSW, although his fullback competition was stiffer than Blacklock encountered as a winger.

An incident involving Mundine during the 1998 finals underlined the NRL's commitment to stamping out racism in the game that would have been swept under the carpet or ignored in another era. Canterbury prop Barry Ward was fined $10,000 for racially vilifying the Dragons five-eighth in a landmark ruling. In 2005, South Sydney skipper Bryan Fletcher received an identical penalty and was stripped of the club captaincy for abusing Parramatta's Dean Widders. To his credit, Fletcher apologized unreservedly and undertook Indigenous community work with Widders to add a positive footnote to the unsavoury incident.

In 1999, an Australian Aborigines combination played two 'Tests' against Papua New Guinea, winning 58-12 and 32-10. Coached by Arthur Beetson and managed by Ricky Walford, the squad contained veteran captain Cliff Lyons, prominent NRL players Widders, Mark Tookey, Kevin McGuinness and Owen Craigie, and future Queensland Origin forwards Carl Webb, John Buttigieg and John Doyle. Following the naming of an Indigenous Team of the Century line-up in 2001, Beetson called for an Aboriginal side's inclusion in future World Cup competitions.

Ball-playing backrower Widders won the Ken Stephen Medal in 2004 as recognition for his work in the community, joining previous winners Walford, Blacklock and Peachey—indicative of the positive influence of Rugby League on the Indigenous community. The increased pathways and guidance had made progressing to top-level Rugby League much smoother, and the proportion of Indigenous players in the NRL increased exponentially during the 2000s.

A plethora of Indigenous players emerged as some of the NRL's most dominant stars. Half/fullback Preston Campbell won the Dally M Medal with Cronulla in 2001, won a premiership with Penrith in 2003 and starred for the fledgling Gold Coast Titans from 2007 (winning the Ken Stephen Medal in 2008). Volatile centre Justin Hodges left the Broncos and won a premiership with the Roosters in 2002, before returning to Brisbane and becoming established as arguably the game's best centre, winning a title with the Broncos in 2006. North Queensland fullback Matt Bowen set the NRL alight as one of the game's finest attacking talents, while Cowboys teammate Johnathan Thurston won Dally M Medals in 2005 and 2007, and remained the NRL's preeminent halfback at the end of 2011—the linchpin of the Queensland and Australian representative sides. Melbourne and later South Sydney centre Greg Inglis was lauded as potentially the best player ever; there is little doubt he is one of the most freakish athletes Rugby League has ever seen. Halfback Scott Prince captained the Wests Tigers to the 2005 premiership and represented Queensland and Australia, before becoming the Titans' foundation co-captain and marquee player. Sam Thaiday developed from an explosive impact player into one of the NRL's most valuable and durable forwards, an automatic selection for Queensland and Australia, the successor to Darren Lockyer as Brisbane club captain and—keeping in line with Indigenous players' outstanding contribution to their community—the 2011 Ken Stephen Medal recipient.

The talents of recent and current Indigenous stars such as Rhys Wesser, Nathan Merritt, Willie Tonga, Chris Sandow, Ben Barba, Jharal Yow Yeh, Jamie Soward and Jamal Idris are worthy of their own chapter.

The 'All-Stars' concept, which debuted in 2010, was the brainchild of Preston Campbell and is destined to be the brilliant 267-game veteran's greatest legacy. The Gold Coast Titans and in particular CEO Michael Searle put their weight behind bringing the idea to fruition. The players selected in the Indigenous All-Stars and NRL All-Stars teams were based on a public vote, with the game staged at the Titans' Skilled Park in February. The Indigenous All-Stars' jerseys were designed by former Brisbane and Penrith Indigenous centre/backrower Sid Domic, and featured traditional Aboriginal artwork. Winning a spot in either side carried a great deal of prestige, enhanced by the unique public selection process. The Australian and New Zealand captains and vice-captains were automatic selections for the NRL All-Stars, while the remainder of the squad was made up by the highest-polling player from each club.

The inaugural clash featured one of the season's great moments. Recently retired from the NRL, Wendell Sailor scored the opening try for the Indigenous All-Stars from a Scott Prince kick, before pulling the corner-post out and playing it like a didgeridoo as his teammates danced around him. In a hard-fought and high-intensity clash, the Neil Henry-coached Indigenous All-Stars prevailed 16-12 courtesy of a late Jamie Soward try. The Indigenous side's captain, concept founder Campbell, had a man of the match medal struck in his honour, which was claimed by Johnathan Thurston in 2010.

The old firm of Wayne Bennett and Darren Lockyer teamed up as coach and captain of the NRL All-Stars in the 2010-11 clashes, and they turned the tables in the second instalment, defeating the Laurie Daley-coached and Thurston-captained Indigenous All-Stars 28-12. Canberra and NRL All-Stars fullback Josh Dugan was a resounding Preston Campbell Medal recipient.

As well as being a celebration of Indigenous culture and raising awareness of Indigenous issues, the match acts as a valuable fundraiser. The first match alone raised over $2 million earmarked for community programs for Indigenous health and education, and the match has quickly become a popular starting point of each season. The All-Stars innovation is a prominent example of the contribution of Rugby League to the advancement of Indigenous communities, which is becoming increasingly enthusiastic and significant. The ever-increasing pool of Indigenous talent that has thrilled the Rugby League world in the modern era is reflective of that successful partnership.

THE COACHES

The role of the coach in Rugby League has increased exponentially since the code's inception. Coaches were regarded as somewhat of a luxury at some clubs during the game's formative decades, while employing a captain-coach was commonplace until the end of the 1970s. But coaches in the modern era are regarded as arguably the most important figure—and one of the highest-paid—at every club. Often a thankless vocation, and most certainly one for only the most dedicated and resilient characters, the buck stops with the coach. Rugby League's most successful, controversial and influential mentors are profiled in this chapter.

ARTHUR HENNESSY A pivotal figure in Rugby League becoming established in Australia as one of the original rugby union defectors in 1907, revered pioneer Arthur 'Ash' Hennessy is regarded as the founding father of South Sydney and became Australia's first Test captain in 1908, leading his country against New Zealand. Hennessy guided Souths in the inaugural 1908 NSWRL premiership season as captain-coach, famously issuing the 'no kicking' edict that was the backbone of the club's success during the code's early seasons. He toured with the first Kangaroos (meaning he missed Souths' premiership final victory against Easts) and joined Easts for a season upon his return, skippering the Tricolours to the finals. Hennessy retired after playing for Souths in the 1910-11 seasons, but returned for a season as coach in 1918 and led the club to a first-past-the-post premiership triumph—the only title between 1915 and 1920 not won by the Balmain dynasty. The former front-rower came back on board as Souths coach in 1946 at the age of 69, but the stint lasted just one season as the Rabbitohs created unwanted club history by failing to win a match.

BILL KELLY Outstanding centre Bill Kelly, a New Zealand dual international before immigrating to Australia and representing his adopted country in a Test against the touring Lions in 1914, became known as the 'Prince of Coaches.' Kelly captain-coached Balmain to its maiden premiership in a ground-breaking unbeaten 1915 season, beginning a club dynasty of five premierships in six seasons. He served in World War I and injuries suffered in Belgium curbed his playing career.[12] But he returned to the Sydney premiership as coach of the University club for the 1923-24 seasons, in which the Students garnered characteristically low table positions with just two wins in each season. Kelly coached Newtown in the 1936 and '37 seasons, guiding the Bluebags to fifth- and fourth-place finishes respectively, before a Balmain homecoming from 1938-43. He steered the Tigers to another title in 1939 with a 33-4 hammering of Souths in the final and led the club to finals appearances in 1938 and 1941-43. Kelly took St. George to the finals in 1944 and wound up a celebrated coaching career with a disappointing sixth-place finish as Canterbury's mentor in 1945.

ARTHUR 'PONY' HOLLOWAY Pioneering halfback Arthur 'Pony' Halloway was a giant of Australian Rugby League's pioneering years despite his diminutive frame, and boasts one of the most impressive coaching résumés in premiership history. Halloway toured with the 1908-09 and 1911-12 Kangaroos while playing for Glebe and Balmain respectively, before winning three straight titles as halfback for Easts (1911-13). He returned to Balmain in 1914, and succeeded Bill Kelly (who guided the club to its maiden premiership in 1915) as captain-coach in 1916. Halloway steered the club to premiership glory in 1916-17 and 1919-20 as the Watersiders carved out a phenomenal dynasty, while he represented Australia for the final time against New Zealand in 1919. After retiring as a player after the 1920 success, Halloway coached Newtown to the wooden spoon in 1923, but enjoyed a glorious tenure with Easts in the 1930s. Halloway led the club to the finals in 1930-31 and 1933-34 (Frank Burge coached the club in 1932), before overseeing the Tricolours' glorious premiership hat-trick of 1935-37. Departing after Easts' loss to Canterbury in the 1938 final, Halloway took over for a disappointing two-year stint with North Sydney (1940-41), but a one-season return to Easts garnered another premiership in 1945. Halloway's last season as a first grade coach was in 1948, leading Canterbury to a fifth-place finish. As coach of two of the all time great club combinations, Halloway won a total of eight first grade titles—a premiership record that stands more than 60 years after he retired from coaching. Halloway's 12 premierships as a player and coach is also an all time record.

---

12   Alan Whiticker and Glen Hudson, *The Encyclopedia Of Rugby League Players*. Sydney, 2006

CHARLIE LYNCH Charlie Lynch assumed the coaching reins of three-time defending premiers South Sydney in 1928 and was at helm as the club's dominance continued into the early-1930s. The Rabbitohs surged to titles in 1928-29 and 1931-32 under Lynch—a disciple of the Arthur 'Ash' Hennessy school of attacking football. He departed the club after a runner-up finish in 1934, but returned for four seasons from 1937-40, guiding the Rabbitohs to the finals in 1938-39, but another premiership was out of reach. He coached St. George for a single season in 1947, which ended with a loss to Wests in a fourth-place play-off. Lynch's 11 seasons with Souths remained a record for most seasons as coach of one club until the 1990s, when he was surpassed by Bob Fulton (Manly) and Wayne Bennett (Brisbane). His four premierships as a non-playing coach was a jointly held record (with Arthur Halloway) that was finally bettered by Jack Gibson in 1983.

NORM 'LATCHEM' ROBINSON Norm Robinson was an immensely influential figure as a player, coach and administrator in almost six decades of association with the Balmain club. He made his first grade debut in 1924 and represented NSW in five interstate matches from 1925-26, playing 71 games for the Tigers before his retirement as a player in 1933. 'Latchem' Robinson captain-coached Balmain to a sixth-place finish in 1930, before returning as coach for the club's golden era of the 1940s. He took over in 1944 and guided the Tigers to four straight Grand Finals, winning premierships in 1944 and 1946-47. But his role as the villain in the infamous Len Smith non-selection in the 1948-49 Kangaroo Tour squad has left an unfortunate blemish on Robinson's reputation. Incumbent Test captain-coach Smith was incomprehensibly left out of the Kangaroos side altogether; selector Robinson, it has been alleged, was behind the move to oust the Newtown centre as he had ambitions to coach the Kangaroos himself (as it happened, Robinson did not get the coaching gig, with Wests centre Col Maxwell the shock choice as captain-coach). Nevertheless, Robinson co-managed the 1952-53 Kangaroos and managed the Australian side during its maiden World Cup triumph in 1957, slotting in another stint as Tigers coach in between (1954-56) and steering the club to the 1956 Grand Final—an 18-12 loss to St. George. He also assisted the American All-Stars touring side in 1953, helping the squad of Rugby League novices grasp the finer points of the game. Robinson finally received his chance as Australian coach in the home Ashes series in 1958, but the touring Great Britain side came from a Test down to claim a courageous 2-1 series victory. Balmain appeared in three Grand Finals and won its last premiership in 1969 with Robinson as club secretary, before he embarked on a decade-long stint as Tigers president. He passed away in 1980, aged 80, and the ARL Life Member was honoured by Balmain with the naming of the 'Latchem' Robinson Stand at Leichhardt Oval.

FRANK BURGE Glebe legend Frank Burge, the tryscoring phenomenon and the greatest forward of Australian Rugby League's pioneering decades, carved out a respected coaching career after his retirement. Burge was lured to St. George as captain-coach in 1927, guiding the previous year's wooden spooners to the Grand Final in his first season, which the Dragon Slayers lost 20-11 to the South Sydney dynasty. His incomparable playing career concluded in the defeat, but he remained as coach of the Saints for three more seasons, steering the club to a maiden minor premiership in 1928 and another Grand Final in 1930 (a 27-2 loss to Wests).

The remainder of 'Chunky' Burge's coaching career consisted of one-season stints, but he achieved an extraordinary strike-rate of qualifying for the finals. He led Easts to third place in 1932 and returned Norths to the finals in 1935 after a seven-year absence, before taking second-year club Canterbury—subjected to the two biggest defeats in premiership history in its 1935 debut—to the 1936 finals. Burge returned to St. George in 1937, garnering a third-place finish in the shortened 'first-past-the-post' decided season. Enhancing his reputation as something of a coaching miracle worker, Burge broke Newtown's seven-year finals drought in 1940—just 12 months after the Bluebags finished last. His second stint at Norths ended with a loss in a play-off for fourth in 1945, before he guided Wests to victory in the corresponding match in 1947 to qualify for the finals—Burge's last season as a first grade coach. Burge finished with an enviable 59 per cent win rate in 183 first grade matches at the helm.

VIC HEY Rated by many as Australia's greatest five-eighth, 1933-34 Kangaroo Vic Hey enjoyed a career of rare quality with Western Suburbs and in Queensland, before starring on the English club scene. He returned to Sydney as captain-coach of fledgling Parramatta in 1948. Injuries restricted Hey to just 10 games as a player for the club before his retirement in 1949, but he remained as Parramatta's coach until 1953, achieving modest results with the limited talent at his disposal. He coached Australia for the first time in 1950, guiding his country to a historic home series victory over Great Britain—Australia's first Ashes success in 30 years. Hey was at the helm for Australia's Ashes series triumph at home in 1954, but suffered series losses in Australia against France in 1951 and 1955. The latter defeat brought Hey's tenure as national coach to a controversial end—he was responsible for centre Darcy Henry's sensational dumping from the side shortly before kick-off in the deciding Test *(see Bolters, Controversial Selections and Shock Omissions)*.

Hey coached Canterbury in 1955-56 and steered Wests to a Grand Final in 1958 (his first season in charge of the Magpies, the club he won a premiership with as a player in 1934), before stepping down following the Magpies' preliminary final exit in 1959. One of the most influential figures in Australian Rugby League history, Hey's lasting legacy as a coach was masterminding the drought-breaking Ashes series triumphs in the first half of the 1950s.

CLIVE CHURCHILL South Sydney fullback Clive Churchill is an unquestionable contender for the title of Australia's greatest-ever Rugby League player. But 'The Little Master' also carved out a career in later years as one of the game's most successful coaches. Churchill captain-coached the 1952-53 Kangaroos and assumed that role for the Rabbitohs following the retirement of Jack Rayner at the end of 1957. But a pay dispute saw Churchill move to Queensland in 1959, and although injury prevented him from playing in the interstate matches, he coached the Maroons to their first series victory in 19 years in his first season in the Sunshine State. Churchill toured with the 1959-60 Kangaroos as non-playing coach, fulfilled that role for NSW in 1960 and coached country club Moree in 1961. He returned to the Sydney premiership as coach of Canterbury in 1963 but departed after the Berries collected the 1964 wooden spoon, while his role as Test coach in series wins over New Zealand and South Africa in 1963 was not enough to prevent him from being ousted by Wests captain Arthur Summons as coach of the Kangaroos at the end of the year.

The Newcastle product rejoined South Sydney as first grade coach in 1967 and steered his beloved club during its last golden era. Churchill's charges won premiership's in 1967-68 and 1970-71, a streak of triumphs broken only by an upset loss to Balmain in the 1969 Grand Final. Souths reached the finals in 1972 and 1974 under Churchill, but the inspirational figure stood down from his post after the club's poor start to 1975 and Bob McCarthy stepped into a captain-coach role for the remainder of the season. Churchill's four premierships as non-playing coach equalled the record of Souths' mentor of the late-1920s and early-1930s Charlie Lynch, while his death after a battle with cancer at the age of 58 in 1985 prompted an unprecedented outpouring of emotion from the Rugby League community.

RON WILLEY Ron Willey was an outstanding goalkicking fullback for Canterbury, Manly and Parramatta, scoring 1,288 points in a 201-game first grade career that spanned 17 seasons (1948-64). He toured with the 1952-53 Kangaroos, but Clive Churchill's presence thwarted his Test aspirations. Willey captain-coached in Rockhampton in 1955 and fulfilled the same role with Manly in 1962, finishing seventh. He succeeded George Hunter as Sea Eagles coach in 1970 and led the club to its maiden premierships in 1972-73. Willey departed Brookvale after Manly's finals exit in 1974, before resurfacing as head coach of Balmain in 1977. After guiding the Tigers to the finals in his first season (the club's first post-season appearance in eight years), Willey's remaining two seasons were disappointing and he came under fire for the roughhouse tactics employed by his Balmain side.

Continuing his drought-breaking first grade coaching career, Willey took over at Norths in 1980 and steered the long-suffering Bears to their first finals series in 17 years in 1982. But he was inexplicably dumped at the behest of club secretary (and Willey's former Kangaroo teammate) Ken McCaffery due to Norths' defence-oriented style under the hard-nosed Willey. His services were snapped up by South Sydney for 1983 and he led the Rabbitohs to the finals the following season, but was replaced by George Piggins at the end of 1985. Willey assumed the reins of the NSW Origin side in 1986, culminating in a historic series cleansweep triumph at his first attempt, before the Blues narrowly went down in the 1987 series.

Willey was the controversial choice to replace Tim Sheens at Penrith in 1988 (ahead of lower grade mentor Graham Murray), but brought several young players through that would form the nucleus of the club's maiden premiership side. Penrith was bundled out in the fifth-place play-off in 1988, but finished the regular season second in 1989. Willey made the brave but bewildering decision to start 17-year-old prodigy Brad Fittler at five-eighth ahead of cast-iron veteran and former international Chris Mortimer in the Panthers' two finals matches, both of which they lost. The veteran mentor was replaced by Phil Gould at the end of the year. A subsequent stint with English club Bradford-Northern—his last high-profile appointment—ended with Willey's sacking during his first season. Willey's total of 403 games as a first grade coach eclipsed Jack Gibson's mark and remained as a premiership record until broken by his former superstar charge at Manly, Bob Fulton, in 1999.

JACK GIBSON Jack Gibson's naming as the coach of Australian Rugby League's Team of the Century in 2008—just weeks before his death at the age of

79—was warmly received and widely expected. Gibson is undoubtedly the most revolutionary and innovative coaching figure in the code's history, paving the way for the status of the modern coach as arguably the most important person in a football club. A strict disciplinarian, a tactical pioneer, and infinitely quotable with a dry sense of humour, Gibson is one of the most popular and original characters Rugby League has known. A clever and tough prop-forward in his playing days, Gibson represented NSW in 1954 and played 154 first grade games from 1953-64 for Easts, Newtown and Wests. He captained the Tricolours in the 1960 Grand Final loss to St. George, while he endured another decider defeat to the mighty Dragons in 1963 with the Magpies, and was unlucky not to achieve higher representative honours during his career.

Gibson took over as coach of Easts in 1967, taking the previous season's winless wooden spooners to the finals in one of the great 12-month turnarounds in premiership history. Famously issuing all of his teams with a 'no fighting' edict (beginning with the Roosters), Gibson guided Easts to the finals again in 1968 before taking a year out. He returned to the premiership as St. George's coach following the retirement of captain-coach Johnny Raper at the end of 1969. Gibson led the Dragons, the club that graded him in the early-1950s, to a gallant Grand Final loss to Souths in 1971. After another year-long spell, Gibson coached unfancied Newtown to the 1973 preliminary final in the club's first post-season appearance for seven years. Rejoining Easts the following season, Gibson moulded one of the great club combinations, steering the Roosters to emphatic premiership triumphs in 1974 and '75. Gibson borrowed heavily from the philosophies and methods of American gridiron coaches during the 1970s. Among the innovations he brought to Australian Rugby League were the use of video and computers to analyse team performance; the analysis of statistics such as tackle counts, that are part and parcel of the modern game; and training and fitness regimes previously unseen in Australia. He became the first coach to effectively harness the use of the 'bomb' as a tactical attacking weapon—most prominently via Easts five-eighth John 'Bomber' Peard—while other more gimmicky but equally memorable innovations included players putting mascara under their eyes for night games to supposedly reduce glare from the lights.

Gibson left Easts after the club's exit in the first week of the 1976 finals, but resurfaced as coach of South Sydney in 1978. His two-season stint with a Rabbitohs squad short on star quality brought little success, but his tenure at Parramatta was arguably the crowning achievement of his career. Gibson guided the Eels to their maiden premiership in 1981 and followed it up with Grand Final victories in the ensuing two seasons before handing the reins over to John Monie at the end of 1983. The brevity of his Grand Final victory speech in 1981—'Ding, dong, the witch is dead'—has passed into the game's folklore. Gibson's ability to communicate with players, and improve and nurture rookies and veterans alike, is perhaps his greatest legacy, introducing the notion of the 'manager' style of coaching. In a curious nuance of his coaching career, Gibson never stayed at a club for longer than three seasons and always took a year's sabbatical in between clubs. Gibson coached Cronulla to three mid-table finishes from 1985-87, but laid the foundation for a fruitful period at the club in the late 1980s under Allan Fitzgibbon. Retiring from club coaching, Gibson belatedly entered the representative realm, coaching NSW in the 1989-

90 Origin series. The first campaign ended in a 3-0 drubbing at the hands of the Maroons, but he helped the Blues regain the interstate crown for the first time in four years in 1990. A true Rugby League original, John Arthur 'Jack' Gibson's legacy is destined to live on through generations.

BOB BAX Bob Bax is a Queensland coaching legend. A fine player in Mount Isa before arriving in Brisbane in 1947 and playing for Brothers, Bax captain-coached Goondiwindi and Rockhampton Fitzroys to local premierships during intermittent stints in country Queensland. Following his retirement as a player, Bax took over as coach of Brothers in 1955 and guided the 'Brethren' to five consecutive BRL Grand Finals, winning premierships in 1956 and 1958. Bax joined defending premiers Norths in 1960 and was at the helm as the club won another five straight BRL premierhsips. He steered the dominant club to four more Grand Finals and two titles before stepping down at the end of 1970. Bax coached the Queensland state side in the early-1970s with little success as interstate football entered a dark era that eventually led to the birth of State of Origin. Bax's disappointing return to the coaching post at Norths in 1978 garnered a last-place finish, but he oversaw the club's premiership triumph in 1980 (with New Zealander Graham Lowe coaching the side) as president.

FRANK STANTON Talented centre/halfback Frank 'Biscuits' Stanton played 129 games for Manly from 1961-69 and toured with the 1963-64 Kangaroos, playing 18 minor matches in Britain and France. But he achieved a greater legacy as a coach at club and representative level after succeeding Ron Willey at Manly in 1975. With his 1968 Grand Final teammate Bob Fulton as captain, Stanton steered the Sea Eagles to a premiership in 1976, before leading the club on a dramatic finals charge in 1978 that culminated in a Grand Final replay triumph. Stanton took the reins as Australian Test coach in 1978, and oversaw a series whitewash of New Zealand before taking the Kangaroos to Britain and France (reacquainting with captain Fulton, who had moved to Easts)—a mixed tour that saw the retention of the Ashes and a shock 2-0 series loss to France. Stanton relinquished his role at Manly after the defending premiers failed to make the finals in 1979, spending the 1980 season with Brisbane club Redcliffe. He retained the national post for an Ashes whitewash at home in 1979, and 2-0 defeats of New Zealand and France in 1980 and 1981 respectively. Accepting the first grade coaching role at Balmain in 1981, Stanton lifted the Tigers from a wooden spoon in his first season to finals appearances in 1983 and 1985-86.

But arguably his greatest achievement was as coach of the 1982 Kangaroo Tour. The Australian side returned from Britain and France unbeaten, and were subsequently dubbed 'The Invincibles,' with Stanton's rigorous training regimen ultimately viewed a crucial element of the success after early criticism. Stanton stepped down as Test coach in 1983, but returned to lead Australia to a third consecutive Ashes series cleansweep in 1984, finishing with 23 wins from a then-record 26 Tests as coach. Stanton linked with North Sydney in 1987 but his three-season stay brought little success. He later moved into club administration, occupying the role of chief executive at Manly, the ill-fated Northern Eagles and North Queensland (in a caretaker role).

HAROLD HORDER, the 'Wonder Winger' of Australian Rugby League's formative seasons, scored 152 tries in just 136 games for Souths and Norths from 1912-26.

Rival captains **FRANK HYDE** (Metropolitan) and **RAY STEHR** (Combined Services) shake hands before a representative fixture in 1942.

BRIAN CARLSON striding out for Australia against Great Britain. The naturally gifted Newcastle product was equally devastating at fullback, centre or wing in 23 Test appearances between 1952 and 1961.

CLIVE CHURCHILL redefined the role of the fullback. 'The Little Master' is seen here in familiar attacking form for South Sydney against Newtown during the 1950s. The Newtown defender is forward hard-man **VIC CARTER**.

DICK POOLE, the dashing Newtown centre, making a break against South Sydney. Poole captained the Bluebags to a Grand Final appearance in 1955 and became Australia's inaugural World Cup-winning skipper in 1957.

KEITH 'YAPPY' HOLMAN, the tenacious halfback, resplendent in the Australian jersey he wore with distinction in 35 Tests from 1950-58. Holman toured twice with the Kangaroos and played 200 first grade games for Western Suburbs.

Canterbury captain-coach **KEVIN RYAN** (left) and St. George halfback **BILLY SMITH** after a match in 1967. Enforcer Ryan won seven Grand Finals with the Dragons, before leading the Berries to a historic victory over the Saints in the 1967 preliminary final, halting the club's run of 11 consecutive premierships.

BOB McCARTHY making a trademark bust against Parramatta in 1972. The blockbusting South Sydney forward was a revolutionary attacking figure as a wide-running second-rower. The Eels players in pursuit are **JOHN VINCENT** (left) and **JOHN WILSON.**

Commentator **RAY 'RABBITS' WARREN** (left) and Manly secretary **KEN ARTHURSON** (right) flank former Kangaroo **KEN McCAFFERY** at a function in 1973. Warren became the voice of Rugby League in the modern era, Arthurson later served as NSWRL and ARL president, while McCaffery was a prominent administrator.

Five-eighth **JOHN 'BOMBER' PEARD**, coach **JACK GIBSON**, second-rower **BARRY 'BUNNY' REILLY** and captain **ARTHUR BEETSON** (from left to right). Four great characters celebrating Eastern Suburbs' 19-4 defeat of Canterbury in the 1974 Grand Final.

GRAEME 'CHANGA' LANGLANDS, the legendary Australian captain, scores a spectacular try during the 1975 World Series against Wales—the 43rd of his then-record 45 appearances in the green and gold. Blockbusting three-quarter **MARK HARRIS** (left) is in support of his skipper.

HARRY BATH One of the great Rugby League forwards, Brisbane Souths junior Harry Bath won two premierships with Balmain (1946-47) but was lured to England before he had the chance to represent his country. Bath became a legend of the British game in a decade with Warrington, before returning to Australia at the age of 32 and sharing in three Grand Final victories with St. George (1957-59). The retired Bath took over as coach of Balmain in 1961, steering the club to Grand Final appearances in 1964 and 1966. The Tigers were subdued by the Saints in each decider, and Bath left the club following the latter defeat. Bath coached Newtown from 1969-71, garnering underwhelming lower-table results. He coached Australia to an Ashes series loss in 1962, and later mentored the national team in three World Cup tournaments; Bath guided Australia to triumphs in the 1968 and 1970 tournaments, and a controversial countback loss in 1972 after the final against Great Britain was drawn.

But Bath's coaching legacy was immortalised by his stint at St. George after captain-coach Graeme Langlands' retirement in 1976. 'Bath's Babes'—so-called because of the youthfulness of his squad—swept to premiership glory in 1977 after a 22-0 defeat of Parramatta in the historic Grand Final replay. The Dragons slumped to eighth in 1978, but rallied to win another title in 1979 by downing Canterbury 17-13 in the decider. Bath imparted his abundant wisdom of tough and skilful forward play to the likes of Rod Reddy and Craig Young, which provided the impetus for the Saints' twin premiership victories. He left the coaching game at the end of 1981 after 318 first grade games in charge of the Tigers, Bluebags and Dragons.

ROY MASTERS Roy Masters was a rarity among high-profile coaches—he did not have a playing career of any note—but he enjoyed a fascinating decade-long tenure as a first grade mentor, and was unlucky not to add a premiership to his résumé. A high school teacher in Tamworth by occupation, Masters led the inaugural Australian Schoolboys side on an unbeaten tour of Britain in 1972. The squad contained four future internationals and decimated their opposition, scoring 402 points and conceding just 17 in their 12 matches. Masters was appointed Western Suburbs first grade coach in 1978 and was the man most responsible for propagating the 'Fibros' v 'Silvertails' war between his Magpies and the Manly club (see From Millionaires to Fibros). An expert motivator that used psychology as a potent coaching weapon, Masters steered his aggressive and skilful charges to the minor premiership in 1978. Wests dipped out of the finals with consecutive losses to Cronulla and bitter adversaries Manly, but the Magpies remained a force under Masters' tutelage despite consistently losing star players to richer rival clubs. He led Wests to the finals again in the 1979-80 seasons and a respectable sixth in 1981, before succeeding dual premiership-winning coach Harry Bath at St. George in 1982. After finals appearances in 1983 and '84, Masters was named Dally M Coach of the Year in 1985 after the Dragons stormed to the minor premiership. They were the first team through to the Grand Final after beating defending champs Canterbury in the major semi-final, but the Bulldogs regrouped to beat Masters' Saints 7-6 in the decider, and his tenure as coach ended with two seasons out of finals contention in 1986-87. Masters commenced a highly successful career as a journalist following his retirement as a Rugby League coach, most notably with the *Sydney Morning Herald*, while he penned the seminal book Inside League, which was released in 1990.

NORM PROVAN ARL Team of the Century second-rower Norm Provan famously featured in 10 consecutive Grand Final victories for the mighty St. George side from 1956-65. Provan captain-coached the Dragons' 1962-65 premiership triumphs, retiring after the 1965 Grand Final victory over Souths. Following his successor as captain-coach Ian Walsh's retirement in 1967, Provan became the Dragons' first non-playing coach since 1956 when he guided the club through the 1968 season. The Saints reached the preliminary final under Provan, but reverted to the captain-coach policy with Johnny Raper taking over in 1969. Provan coached Parramatta for a season in 1975, steering the Eels through an arduous three-way play-off for fifth spot before their admirable sudden-death run came to an end in the minor semi-final. He was installed as Cronulla coach in 1978, achieving a second-place regular season finish and guiding the Sharks to the Grand Final, but the club's bid for a maiden premiership was thwarted by a 16-0 loss to Manly in the Grand Final replay after the decider ended in an 11-all draw. The Sharks finished third in 1979 but exited the finals with back-to-back losses in the iconic Provan's last season as a first grade.

TERRY FEARNLEY Front-rower Terry Fearnley made his first grade debut in 1954 and amassed 139 first grade appearances in 11 seasons with Eastern Suburbs. He represented NSW in 1960 and captain-coached Easts in 1961, missing the finals by a solitary point. After serving a valuable coaching apprenticeship under former Easts teammate Jack Gibson at the Roosters in the 1970s, Fearnley took over from Norm Provan as Parramatta's first grade coach in 1976, guiding the Eels to their maiden Grand Final appearance in his first season at the club. Parramatta lost the '76 decider 13-10 to Manly and succumbed to St. George 22-0 in the historic Grand Final replay under Fearnley's tutelage in 1977. Fearnley coached Australia to a World Cup triumph in 1977, but he left the Eels after the preliminary final defeat at the hands of Canterbury in 1979. He resurfaced as Wests' coach in 1982 and guided the financially embattled Magpies to a finals appearance in his sole season at the club, before joining another beleaguered outfit—the cash-strapped Cronulla Sharks. Fearnley's two-season stint resulted in a ninth- and 10th-place finishes in 1983 and '84 respectively. Re-entering representative coaching in 1985, Fearnley led New South Wales to its maiden State of Origin series victory after Queensland had dominated the first five years of the concept. But he courted controversy in his simultaneous role as Australian Test coach in 1985; after the green-and-golds narrowly won the first two Tests of the series against New Zealand with last-minute John Ribot tries, Fearnley dropped four Queensland players from the squad for the third encounter in Auckland and replaced them with NSW stars, causing a furore north of the border. Australia was thrashed 18-0 by the Kiwis at Carlaw Park and Fearnley was replaced as state and national coach in 1986, while the only coach to hold Origin and Test posts simultaneously since was Queensland's Wayne Bennett in 1998. Fearnley's last first grade coaching appointment was a one-season stay with Illawarra in 1988. After a promising start which garnered five wins a draw in the opening 10 rounds, the Steelers lost 11 straight to finish 13th and Fearnley was replaced by his former Parramatta charge Ron Hilditch for 1989.

TED GLOSSOP Ted Glossop played 15 first grade games as a halfback for St. George during the 1950s, but found fame as Canterbury's premiership-winning coach in 1980. Glossop was granted his initial first grade coaching opportunity by

Cronulla in 1977, but despite guiding the Sharks to a much-improved sixth-place finish, he was replaced by Norm Provan after just one season. He was installed as Canterbury coach in 1978, however, and restored the club to the finals in his first year at Belmore. Glossop guided the Bulldogs to the Grand Final in 1979—a 17-13 loss to St. George—before the club broke a 38-year premiership drought under Glossop's guidance with an 18-4 triumph over Easts in the 1980 decider. The exhilarating attacking style employed by Glossop saw Canterbury dubbed 'The Entertainers,' and he remained at the club until the end of 1983, when he was replaced by Warren Ryan despite taking the Bulldogs to the preliminary final.

Glossop coached NSW in the inaugural State of Origin match in 1980 and the one-off clash in 1981. He was recalled to the post in 1983, coaching the Blues to a 2-1 series loss. His last high-profile coaching appointment was as St. George's first grade mentor in 1988. The Dragons won the midweek Panasonic Cup under his tutelage, but the club's disappointing 10th-place finish in the premiership resulted in Glossop being shown the door at the end of the year. 'Gentleman' Ted Glossop died in 1998 after a battle with cancer.

ARTHUR BEETSON Australia's greatest ball-playing forward, Arthur Beetson developed into a respected coach at club and representative level, but it was in the Origin arena that 'Big Artie' achieved his greatest success in a non-playing capacity. Beetson skippered Easts to consecutive titles in 1974-75 under the coaching of Jack Gibson, and succeeded his mentor to captain-coach the Roosters in the 1977-78 seasons. He led the club to the finals in 1977 in his dual role, but was sent off in Easts' loss to St. George in the major preliminary semi-final and suspended for the remainder of the finals series. The Roosters finished just outside of finals reckoning in 1978 and Beetson joined Parramatta in 1979, before captaining Queensland to a 20-10 victory in the inaugural State of Origin clash in 1980 as a 35-year-old. Beetson returned to his home state in 1981 and captain-coached Redcliffe in his final season as a player; injury kept him out of Queensland's playing squad for the one-off Origin clash, but he coached the Maroons to a stirring 22-15 comeback victory, while he guided the Dolphins to the BRL Grand Final—a 13-9 loss to Souths. He coached Queensland to three straight series triumphs from 1982-84, and guided Australia to a 1-all series result against New Zealand in 1983 before Easts lured him back to Sydney as Laurie Freier's first grade coaching replacement in 1985.

Beetson was named Dally M Coach of the Year after steering the Roosters to second in the minor premiership in 1987—a campaign that ended with a preliminary final loss to Canberra. He departed the club after a disappointing 12th-place finish in 1988. Returning to the helm of Queensland's Origin side, Beetson led the Maroons to an emphatic 3-0 series whitewash in 1989 and a 2-1 loss in 1990, both years facing off against his great mate and Blues coach Gibson. Beetson took over at struggling Cronulla in 1992, but could not turn the club's fortunes around during a two-year stint with the financially embattled Sharks. He fulfilled a caretaker-coach role for Easts in the latter rounds of the 1994 season after the club dumped Mark Murray— Beetson's last high-profile coaching appointment.

WARREN RYAN An astute, strong-headed mentor, Warren Ryan ranks with the modern era's finest Rugby League thinkers after a successful and controversial first grade coaching career that spanned 22 seasons. After representing Australia in the shot put at the 1962 Commonwealth Games, Ryan played first grade football for St. George and Cronulla. He joined Wollongong Wests in 1969 and captain-coached the club in 1972-73, before coaching Collegians in the Illawarra competition in 1974 and getting a Sydney coaching grounding in Western Suburbs' lower grades. Ryan was installed as Newtown's first grade coach in 1979. The Jets had collected the previous two wooden spoons, but within three years Ryan had guided the club to its last Grand Final appearance. Newtown was gallant in the 20-11 loss to Parramatta in the 1981 decider, while Ryan departed the financially struggling club after a respectable seventh-place finish in 1982. Ryan was lured to Canterbury in 1984 and transformed the 'Entertainers' from the early part of the decade into a ruthless, grinding defensive outfit. His 'Dogs of War' claimed back-to-back premierships in 1984-85, before a 4-2 loss to Parramatta in the epic try-less Grand Final of 1986. An uncompromising character, Ryan was often at loggerheads with the Bulldogs' administration and had a highly publicised feud with captain Steve Mortimer, culminating in Ryan's departure at the end of 1987.

'Wok' Ryan linked with Balmain and steered the club to consecutive Grand Finals in 1988-89. He was widely—and somewhat unfairly—criticised for his decision to replace international forwards Steve Roach and Paul Sironen with defensive specialists Kevin Hardwick and Michael Pobjie in an attempt to close out the 1989 decider against Canberra. After leading 12-2 at halftime, the Tigers were run down by the Raiders, succumbing 19-14 in a gut-wrenching extra-time defeat. Ryan joined Wests in 1991 after taking Balmain to the finals for the third successive season. He was named Dally M Coach of the Year in his first season as Magpies mentor, guiding the club to its first finals appearance in nine years with a clutch of his former Canterbury charges playing key roles. Another finals appearance eventuated in 1992—the eighth time in nine seasons Ryan had coached a team to the top-five—but his stint with the Magpies ended with his resignation prior to the end of the 1994 season. Ryan took five years out from coaching and delved into a Rugby League media career, but returned as the surprise choice to replace Malcolm Reilly at Newcastle in 1999. He led the Knights to seventh in 1999 and a preliminary final appearance the following season, but his two-season stay in the Hunter Valley was sullied by conflict with senior players at the club and he retired at the end of 2000. Ryan broke Bob Fulton's premiership record for first grade games as coach in his last season, finishing with 415—a mark that was bettered by Tim Sheens in 2001. His representative coaching experience consisted of five seasons in charge of Country Origin (1987-91).

JOHN MONIE Former Cronulla five-eighth John Monie served his coaching apprenticeship under the great Jack Gibson, before carving out a reputation as an astute and successful mentor in his own right. After 48 first grade games for the Sharks from 1968-70, Monie played in the Newcastle competition and began his coaching career as captain-coach of NSW Central Coast club Woy Woy. Monie joined Parramatta as an assistant to Gibson and stepped into the first grade post after the legendary coach stepped down at the end of 1983. The 37-year-old Monie took the three-time premiers to the 1984 Grand Final (a 6-4 loss to Canterbury) and the preliminary final in 1985, before guiding the Eels to their last premiership to date in 1986 with a 4-2 triumph in the dramatic try-less decider against the Bulldogs. Parramatta's fortunes dwindled for the remainder of the decade and Monie departed at the end of 1989. He immediately succeeded Manly-bound New Zealander Graham Lowe as coach of the powerful Wigan club in England, steering the 'Riversiders' to four consecutive championship-Challenge Cup doubles—an unprecedented coaching feat. Bringing several Wigan stars with him, Monie was lured to Auckland as the Warriors' inaugural coach for the club's 1995 entry into the premiership. His acquisition was viewed as a major coup for the club, but Monie's tenure quickly unravelled. Auckland achieved a promising 10th-placed finish in 1995, but an interchange bungle—which Monie took responsibility for—cost the Warriors a debut-season finals berth *(see Points Docked)*. A disastrous start to the 1997 Super League premiership season resulted in Monie standing down midway through the campaign; reserve grade coach and Kiwi Test mentor Frank Endacott stepped into the breach for the embattled Warriors. Monie returned to Wigan and guided the club to victory in the 1998 Super League Grand Final, but a fifth double eluded him after the Sheffield Eagles scored a stunning 17-8 upset of Wigan in the Challenge Cup final. In his last club appointment, Monie coached the London Broncos in a dismal 2000 campaign. He took over as France's Test coach in 2005 and led the rebuilding national side until the end of the 2008 World Cup.

BOB FULTON His status as one of Rugby League's all time great players assured, Bob 'Bozo' Fulton crafted one of the finest coaching careers in the game's history with Easts, Manly and Australia. The centre/five-eighth wizard won three premierships with Manly in the 1970s (including one as captain in 1976), before joining Easts in 1977 and succeeding Arthur Beetson as the Roosters' captain-coach in 1979. A knee injury forced Fulton's retirement midway through 1979 but he remained at Easts as a non-playing coach and guided the club to back-to-back minor premierships in 1980-81 (he was named as one of the four original 'Immortals' in the latter season). The Roosters lost the 1980 Grand Final to Canterbury and dipped out of the 1981 finals with consecutive defeats. After another post-season appearance in 1982 with Easts, Fulton returned to Manly in 1983, but again endured Grand Final heartache after winning the minor premiership in his first season in charge of the Sea Eagles—this time at the hands of Parramatta. Manly stalled somewhat in the ensuing seasons, but the club stormed to an emphatic minor premiership success in 1987, culminating with an 18-8 triumph over Canberra in the Grand Final.

Fulton stood down as coach following the Sea Eagles' exit from the 1988 finals (he remained at the club in a coaching coordinator role), focussing on his duties as Australia's new Test coach from 1989. Fulton became Australia's longest-serving and most successful Test coach, guiding the green-and-golds to 30 wins and a draw in 37 matches, including Ashes triumphs on consecutive Kangaroo Tours (1990 and 1994), and two World Cup successes (1992 and 1995). He relinquished the post during 1998 after a remarkable decade in charge. Fulton returned as Manly coach in 1993 after Graham Lowe resigned due to poor health, and led his beloved club into a golden era. Finals appearances in 1993-94 were followed by three straight minor premierships and Grand Finals from 1995-97. But the Sea Eagles won just one title during their period of dominance—courtesy of a 20-8 defeat of St. George in the 1996 decider—after being upset in the 1995 and 1997 Grand Finals by the Sydney

Bulldogs and Newcastle respectively. Fulton was one of the ARL's staunchest and most vocal supporters during the Super League conflict, remaining true to Rugby League's traditional ideals as coach of the ARL's figurehead club and the depleted Australian Test side (the 1995 World Cup triumph was achieved without the aid of Super League-aligned players). Manly scraped into the 10-team finals series in the inaugural 1998 NRL season and started 1999 poorly, leading to Fulton standing down early in the season after a then-record 405 games as a first grade coach. He remains one of the most revered playing and coaching figures in the game's history.

DON FURNER Don Furner toured with the 1956-57 Kangaroos while playing for Toowoomba Souths, making one Ashes Test appearance. The tough forward, born in Condobolin and originally a Balmain junior, represented Queensland in seven interstate appearances, but a back injury curtailed his playing career. Furner moved into coaching and cut his teeth in first grade with a three-season stint in charge of Eastern Suburbs, joining the club in 1970 and steering the Roosters to the 1972 Grand Final—a 19-14 loss to Manly.

He moved to Queanbeyan and coached locally, sporadically taking charge of the Country Firsts representative side during the 1970s, before becoming the foundation coach of the Canberra Raiders in 1982. Success was limited in the fledgling club's early seasons, but with Wayne Bennett as co-coach in 1987 (Furner predominantly handled the media duties, while Bennett's speciality was the football side of operations), Furner was an integral part of the Raiders' charge to a maiden Grand Final appearance. The 18-8 loss signalled the end of Furner's club coaching career.

He assumed the Australian Test coaching position from Terry Fearnley in 1986 and led the Kangaroos on their second consecutive unbeaten tour of Britain and France. The awesome achievements of the 'Unbeatables' seemed a world away for Furner when New Zealand caused a 13-6 boilover at Lang Park in 1987, but the amiable mentor's 15-Test tenure concluded with a home Ashes series victory and an emphatic 25-12 World Cup final triumph in 1988. Furner later fulfilled roles as chairman of selectors for the NSWRL and the ARL, and as interim chief executive of the embattled Gold Coast Seagulls, while his last significant coaching appointment was taking Fiji to the 2000 World Cup. His son David was a goalkicking backrower and a Canberra club great, emulating his father's achievements by touring with the 1994 Kangaroos. David Furner took over as coach of the Raiders in 2009, with his brother, Don Jr., as CEO of the club.

TIM SHEENS A hard-working prop-forward and valuable clubman in 177 first grade games (and a club record of 258 games in all grades) for Penrith from 1973-82, Tim Sheens went on to become the longest-serving coach in premiership history— and one of the most successful. Sheens captain-coached Campbelltown to a Group 6 premiership in 1983, before returning to Penrith as first grade coach in 1984. After a vastly improved seventh-place finish in 1984 (just one point adrift of the finals) that saw Sheens achieve Dally M Coach of the Year honours, the long-suffering Panthers qualified for their maiden finals series under his guidance in 1985. The club was unable to capitalise on that breakthrough achievement in the 1986-87 seasons, but that did not discourage Canberra from snapping up Sheens' services for 1988 after Wayne Bennett left the club to become Brisbane's foundation coach.

Sheens oversaw Canberra's maiden premiership triumph in 1989 courtesy of an unforgettable Grand Final defeat of Balmain in extra-time. He was named Dally M Coach of the Year again after guiding the club to its first minor premiership in 1990, followed by another Grand Final victory against his former club Penrith. After coaching NSW to a desperately close Origin series loss in 1991, Sheens helped the Raiders weather the financial crisis that gripped the club. Canberra lost the 1991 Grand Final to the Panthers and missed the finals the following season after being forced to shed several key players to fit under the salary cap, but Sheens remodelled his squad and celebrated in a stunning title success in 1994 after the Raiders thrashed minor premiers Canterbury 36-12 in the Grand Final. Sheens was lured to North Queensland in 1997, but his tenure in Townsville was the low point of his career and threatened to tarnish his legacy. The Cowboys finished last in the 1997 Super League season and in the 2000 NRL; despite having several seasons to run on his contract, Sheens was farcically forced to stand down for 'health reasons' by the club during 2001 and he resigned mid-season. But the Wests Tigers signed Sheens to take over from Terry Lamb in 2003 and the veteran mentor guided the effervescent and unheralded young squad to a spectacular NRL title success in 2005, while also collecting his third Dally M Coach of the Year gong. Sheens remained at the club despite missing the finals from 2006-2009, returning the Tigers to heavyweight status with third-place finishes in the 2010-11 minor premierships—and agonising finals exits in each season. He had coached a record 645 games in first grade by the end of 2011, 12 games ahead of Bennett. Sheens took the reins as Australian Test coach in 2009, leading the green-and-golds to Four Nations success in 2009 and 2011—bookending a loss to a New Zealand side inspired by his Wests Tigers linchpin Benji Marshall in the final of the 2010 tournament.

WAYNE BENNETT Beneath his gruff exterior, Wayne Bennett is a master man manager and possesses one of the greatest minds Rugby League has ever known. The long-serving Brisbane mentor's ranking as one of the top two coaches in the game's history is almost unanimous, while his recent feats with St. George Illawarra have elevated him above the great Jack Gibson in the eyes of many. Hailing from the tiny Darling Downs town of Allora in Queensland, Bennett was a talented winger, representing his state in seven matches (1971-73) and touring New Zealand with the Australian squad in 1971. Bennett played in two minor tour matches across the Tasman. His first senior coaching role came as captain-coach of Brisbane Souths in 1977, aged just 27, before joining Brothers as a non-playing coach in 1980. Bennett coached the 'Brethren' for three seasons, and after a year away from the BRL, returned to Souths in 1984. Guiding the Magpies to the BRL Grand Final in his first season back at the club, Bennett's charges were humiliated 42-8 by a Wynnum-Manly side featuring Wally Lewis and Gene Miles, but he led Souths to a stirring 10-8 victory over the Seagulls in the 1985 decider.

Bennett joined the Canberra Raiders as Test mentor Don Furner's co-coach in 1987, with a view to taking over as head coach the following season. The duo steered the club to the Grand Final in 1987—an 18-8 loss to Manly—but Bennett sought a release from his contract to join the fledgling Brisbane Broncos for their 1988 debut, after the Broncos (and in particular charismatic director Paul 'Porky' Morgan) refused to take no for an answer. Bennett also had extenuating family reasons for wanting to return to Brisbane, and the Raiders graciously granted his request. He endured many trials and tribulations during the star-studded Broncos' formative seasons, including stripping Test skipper Wally Lewis of the captaincy at the end of 1989 and effectively ousting 'The King' from the club a year later. Single-minded and self-assured in his focus, Bennett endured a barrage of public criticism in the wake of each event involving Lewis, but the contentious decisions ultimately proved the making of the club. With brilliant halfback Allan Langer as captain, Bennett led the Broncos to back-to-back premierships in 1992-93 with a side that played an attractive and expansive attacking brand of Rugby League.

A visible proponent of Super League, Bennett's support and influence were integral to the rebel movement as coach of the organisation's figurehead club. The Broncos won the Super League premiership in 1997 under his tutelage, before emphatic title victories in the 1998 and 2000 unified NRL seasons. Bennett reinvented the Broncos as a relentless, forward-oriented machine in the 2000 season to combat changes to his squad and to the way the game was played. After a series of late-season fadeouts in the first half of the 2000s, Bennett achieved what he regarded as his most satisfying success as the underdog Broncos won the 2006 Grand Final with a 15-8 result against minor premiers Melbourne. Bennett had agreed to terms to replace Ricky Stuart as coach of the Sydney Roosters commencing at the end of 2006, but he backed out of the deal after details became public against his wishes. Bennett extended his premiership record tenure at the Broncos to 21 straight seasons before joining St. George Illawarra at the end of 2008. The Sydney media salivated over Bennett's arrival at the Dragons, but his three-season stint was so successful that they rarely had any ammunition to get under the skin of the notoriously curt supercoach. Bennett guided the perennially underachieving club to consecutive minor premierships in 2009-10 and to its first Grand Final victory as a joint venture in the latter season—his seventh premiership victory as a coach to close to within one of Arthur 'Pony' Halloway's all time record. He ended weeks of speculation early in the 2011 season by announcing he would be joining Newcastle the following season, sparking feverish excitement in the Hunter Valley as several high-profile players also joined the club in the wake of the acquisition of Bennett.

Bennett has coached extensively at representative level, first coaching Queensland in a 3-0 series loss to NSW in 1986. But he retained the post and helped the Maroons regain the interstate crown with a 2-1 series victory, while he stepped down after the emphatic 3-0 series victory in 1988. Bennett returned as Queensland coach in 1998, guiding the state side to its first triumph in a unified series for seven years, while also leading Australia to two post-season Test wins against New Zealand. Following the Maroons' embarrassing 3-0 series loss in 2000, Bennett was enlisted to turn their fortunes around in 2001. He pulled off the greatest selection ruse in Origin history by bringing veteran Warrington-based halfback Allan Langer back to Australia for the decider; it proved a masterstroke, with Langer playing a vital role in the Queensland's 40-14 boilover victory. Bennett stayed on for two more series— a drawn result in 2002 that saw Queensland retain the shield, and a 2-1 loss in 2003. He took over as Australian coach for two seasons, helping the Test side to Tri-Nations success in 2004, but his tenure came to an unhappy end after the Kiwis stunned the Kangaroos 24-0 in the final of the corresponding tournament in 2005—Australia's first loss in a Test series since 1978. Much to the consternation of the more patriotic among

Australia's Rugby League fraternity, Bennett was an advisor to the Stephen Kearney and the New Zealand Test side in 2008, celebrating on Suncorp Stadium with the Kiwis after their shock victory in the World Cup final. Regarded as a father figure by scores of his players, Bennett's success has been built on discipline and belief in the strength of his convictions as much as his tactical nous, while his total of 633 first grade games as coach is second only to Tim Sheens in premiership history. Undoubtedly, Wayne Bennett is one of the most influential men in the history of Rugby League.

PHIL GOULD Tactically superb, outspoken, controversial and a master motivator, Phil 'Gus' Gould is a giant among modern coaches. Gould was a talented and versatile ball-playing backrower in an 11-season first grade playing career with Penrith, Newtown (where he played in the 1981 Grand Final), Canterbury and Souths. But Gould was always destined for a coaching career. After his retirement as a player at the Rabbitohs in 1986, Gould was installed as Canterbury's reserve grade coach under his former Jets and Bulldogs mentor Warren Ryan in 1987, and was elevated to the first grade role following Ryan's departure at the end of the year. Aged just 30, Gould became the youngest-ever premiership-winning coach and just the second (after Balmain's Leo Nosworthy in 1969) to win a title in his maiden first grade season after the Bulldogs accounted for Balmain 24-12 in the 1988 Grand Final. But Gould was on his way to Penrith—the club he captained as a 20-year-old in 1976—just 12 months later after falling out with the Bulldogs' hierarchy.

He steered the Panthers to their first Grand Final in 1990, an 18-14 loss to Canberra, and oversaw the club's long-awaited maiden premiership courtesy of a 19-12 defeat of the Raiders in the 1991 decider. His motivational discourse and psychological approach to coaching was a perfect match for the high-intensity Origin arena, and Gould took over as NSW coach in 1992, leading the Blues to a then-record three straight series victories. But the fortunes of the Panthers plummeted from 1992 and Gould quit the club midway through the 1994 season—just weeks after being banished from the sideline by referee Bill Harrigan during a match against Cronulla (see Bizarre Matches)—and linked with Eastern Suburbs, stepping in for the last round of the season (the Roosters had sacked coach Mark Murray and Arthur Beetson had been occupying a caretaker role). Gould was among the most vehemently vocal opponents of Super League, while he was at the helm of the NSW side humbled 3-0 by Paul Vautin's unheralded Queensland squad in the 1995 Origin series. He exacted revenge by guiding the Blues to a series cleansweep of their own the following season before relinquishing the post. Gould took the Roosters to their first finals series in nine years in 1996 and the club was a perennial contender under his tutelage, but after a fourth straight post-season failure in 1999, the mastermind retired from club coaching.

Gould concentrated on media endeavours in print, radio and television, but maintained his ties with the Roosters and took on the role of coaching director at the club. He returned as coach of NSW for the 2002 series, which was drawn, and helped the Blues regain the Origin crown with a 2-1 victory in 2003. Flagrant off-field player misbehaviour prior to the 2004 series-opener led to Gould stepping down from the role at the end of the series, despite NSW's 2-1 success. He became one of the game's most prominent television commentators in subsequent seasons, before accepting the role of football manager with Penrith during 2011—an appointment that quickly instigated many positive changes at the club, not the least of which was the acquisition of high-rated New Zealand Warriors mentor and a former player under Gould at the Roosters, Ivan Cleary, as coach for 2012. A polarising figure in many respects, Gould ranks as one Rugby League's most influential figures of the modern era.

GRAHAM LOWE One of the great motivators, New Zealander Graham Lowe enjoyed great coaching success in his homeland as well as in England and Australia. He guided Auckland club Otahuhu to victory in the Fox Memorial Shield—New Zealand's most prestigious club prize—in 1977 and joined Brisbane Norths in 1979. Lowe took Otahuhu backrower Mark Graham with him and the pair combined to help Norths win the 1980 BRL premiership with a 17-15 upset of Souths in the Grand Final.

Lowe remained at Norths until accepting the New Zealand Test coaching position in 1983. In a memorable four-season stint in the national post, Lowe guided the Kiwis to rare Test wins over Australia in 1983 and 1985, and a 3-0 series whitewash of the touring Lions in 1984. After the Kiwis' drawn series against Great Britain in England in 1985, Lowe's tenure came to a disappointing end with a 3-0 series defeat to Australia and a maiden Test loss to Papua New Guinea in 1986. Lowe signed with English powerhouse Wigan and oversaw the beginning of one of Rugby League's most dominant club eras. He steered Wigan to championship glory in 1987 and to consecutive Challenge Cup victories in 1988 and '89—the first two of eight straight Wembley final victories the club would enjoy. Lowe expertly harnessed the eclectic and prodigious talents of Ellery Hanley, Andy Gregory, Shaun Edwards, Joe Lydon and Kiwis Dean Bell, and Kevin and Tony Iro.

He linked with the embattled Manly club in 1990, luring the Iro brothers Down Under and poaching All Black fullback Matthew Ridge from rugby union. The Sea Eagles endured a disastrous 1989 season on and off the field, but Lowe restored them to the finals at his first attempt. Manly's 1990 and '91 campaigns ended with spirited minor semi-final defeats. Lowe was controversially chosen to coach Queensland's Origin side in 1991, but carved a niche in interstate Rugby League folklore by guiding the Maroons to a thrilling series victory in Wally Lewis' farewell to the Origin arena—despite spending time in hospital with a blood clot in his leg in the lead-up to the decider. Queensland went down narrowly in the 1992 series under Lowe's tutelage, while Manly faded out of finals contention. Lowe's declining health saw him step down from the club (he was replaced by Bob Fulton) and he moved into commentary. He returned to the clipboard to coach Western Samoa at the 1995 World Cup in England and led North Queensland to an improved 17th-place in 1996 after the club had collected the wooden spoon in its first season.

After an ill-fated period as co-owner of the Warriors (which included installing Mark Graham as coach), Lowe faded from the Rugby League spotlight. He coached the Bay of Plenty Stags in the 2008 Bartercard Premiership, before being appointed as Manly's CEO late in 2009. Lowe stepped down from his role with the Sea Eagles during 2011, again citing health reasons. He remains a revered coaching figure in the New Zealand Rugby League narrative, improving the Kiwis' international standing during the 1980s and contributing to the Australian premiership's spike in popularity across the Tasman as coach of Manly in the 1990s.

BRIAN SMITH Brian Smith's record of four Grand Final losses from as many appearances with three different clubs has seen him pigeonholed as the perennial coaching bridesmaid, but he remains one of the most enduring and fascinating mentors in premiership history. A former first grade halfback with St. George and Souths, Smith interrupted his playing career to coach James Cook High in 1977-78, but returned to the Rabbitohs as a player in 1979. Smith moved into coaching with the club and guided Souths' Under-23s side to a premiership in 1981, before taking on the first grade role at Illawarra in 1984. His four-season stint with the Steelers garnered two wooden spoons, but after guiding English club Hull to a premiership final appearance, Smith returned to Australia as coach of St. George in 1991.

Smith steered the club to consecutive Grand Finals in 1992-93, but Brisbane proved the Dragons' nemesis in each decider, starting an intense and long-running rivalry with Broncos coach Wayne Bennett. St. George faded to miss the finals in 1994 and he departed the club at the end of 1995 to spend another season in England with Bradford. Smith joined big-spending Parramatta in 1997 and led the club to its first post-season appearance in 11 years. His 10 consecutive seasons with the Eels is a record bettered only by Bennett at Brisbane, and by Canterbury's Steve Folkes in premiership history. Parramatta was a persistent heavyweight during Smith's term, but a title eluded the club. After three consecutive preliminary final exits (1998-2000), the Eels charged to the minor premiership in 2001, but were upset 30-24 in the Grand Final by Newcastle courtesy of a first half ambush. Another minor premiership season in 2005 ended with a shock preliminary final loss to North Queensland, and Smith left Parramatta midway through 2006 after an indifferent start to the year and the announcement that his 2001 Grand Final conqueror Michael Hagan was to replace him in 2007. Ironically, Smith assumed the position Hagan vacated at Newcastle. He was responsible for a massive player cleanout in 2007, raising the ire of Knights supporters as several club favourites departed. Smith left Newcastle with three rounds of the 2009 season remaining after he announced he would taking over as the Sydney Roosters coach in 2010. In a remarkable coincidence, caretaker coach Rick Stone steered the Knights to the 2009 finals after Smith's departure, as Jason Taylor did with the Eels following Smith's premature exit in 2006—the only two times a club has qualified for the finals after the mid-season departure of its coach.

Smith guided the previous year's wooden spooners on a remarkable run to the Grand Final in 2010 and was named Dally M Coach of the Year for the second time (after previously winning with the Eels in 2001), but St. George Illawarra—coached by Bennett—was too strong, subduing the Roosters 32-8 in the decider. The Roosters slipped off the finals radar in 2011 under Smith's tutelage. His total of 577 first grade games as coach is behind only Tim Sheens and Bennett.

CHRIS ANDERSON A two-time Kangaroo tourist and club great winger with 94 tries in 14 seasons for Canterbury (1971-84), Chris Anderson's initial foray into coaching resulted in a memorable Challenge Cup final victory as captain-coach of Halifax. Anderson coaxed fellow Test veteran Graham Eadie out of retirement and the pair spearheaded the club's gripping 19-18 defeat of St. Helens at Wembley in 1987. After returning to the Bulldogs as a lower grade mentor, Anderson succeeded Phil Gould as first grade coach in 1990. He was named Dally M Coach of the Year in 1993 and steered Canterbury to consecutive minor premierships in 1993-94 (also coaching Country Origin in each season), but the Bulldogs exited the 1993 finals with back-to-back losses and were hammered 36-12 in the 1994 Grand Final by Canberra. Not one to tolerate perceived disloyalty, Anderson dropped Queensland Origin regular Darren Smith in 1994 for negotiating with rival clubs (Smith failed to make it back into the line-up for the decider), before dumping Jason Smith, Dean Pay, Jim Dymock and Jarrod McCracken the following season after the star quartet reneged on Super League contracts to sign with the ARL. Anderson galvanised the besieged Super League-aligned Bulldogs in 1995, guiding the club to a phenomenal premiership victory on the back of a stirring finals charge and a 17-4 Grand Final boilover against Manly (with Jason Smith, Pay and Dymock back in the side).

Anderson became the foundation coach for the fledgling Melbourne Storm in 1998 and achieved remarkable success immediately, taking the infant club to top-four finishes in its first two seasons and securing the NRL premiership in 1999 with a famous 20-18 comeback victory over St. George Illawarra in the decider. During the Storm's finals charge, Anderson made the tough decision to drop his son, five-eighth Ben, from the side. It proved to be an inspired choice as converted winger Matt Geyer starred in the premiership victory in the No.6. He took over as Australian coach in 1999 and enjoyed a highly successful five-season tenure, leading the national side to glory in the 1999 Tri-Nations, the 2000 World Cup and in two Ashes series in England—a 2-1 victory in 2001 (despite suffering a heart attack and being rushed to hospital during the deciding third Test), and a 3-0 whitewash in 2003 with a Kangaroos squad decimated by injury. Anderson copped heavy criticism for drafting in St. Helens-based 34-year-old Darren Smith to the team for the dead-rubber third Test in 2003, despite having a fit international rookie in Luke Lewis to call upon. Nevertheless, Anderson finished with the enviable record of 21 wins in 24 Tests as coach.

Following a dismal start to 2001 and a falling out with Melbourne powerbrokers John Ribot and Chris Johns, the hard-nosed Anderson resigned from his post at the Storm seven rounds into the season, before replacing John Lang at Cronulla in 2002. Although the man known as 'Opes' led the Sharks to a preliminary final in 2002, his two-year stint with the club was controversial. He lured former Melbourne halfback Brett Kimmorley to the club, shunting 2001 Dally M medallist Preston Campbell (who joined Penrith in 2003) from the No.7 spot, and demoted fellow club favourites Nick Graham and Dean Treister. He persisted with another son, goalkicking winger Jarrad, during 2003 at the expense of future Test player and Melbourne star Matt King. Anderson was sacked by Cronulla at the end of 2003. He spent a season with Welsh rugby union club Newport Gwent Dragons in 2004 prior to a return to the NRL with the Sydney Roosters in 2007. But Anderson stood down after the Roosters won just five games in the first 16 rounds of his first season at Bondi—a disappointing end to the career of one of the modern era's most influential and succesful coaches.

GRAHAM MURRAY Graham Murray played 89 games for Parramatta and Souths from 1977-79, captaining the Eels to reserve grade premierships in 1977 and 1979, and garnering the nickname 'Little Artie' (after the great forward Arthur Beetson) for his ball-playing panache. But it was with clipboard in hand that Murray made a lasting impression on Rugby League. After captain-coaching Lismore, Murray cut his teeth in Penrith's lower grades and won a reserve grade title in 1987.

He left the Panthers after being overlooked for the first grade role when Tim Sheens joined Canberra in 1988, and coached Balmain's reserve grade side before joining Illawarra as Ron Hilditch's assistant.

Murray's belated first head coaching role came in 1991 as Hilditch's replacement at Illawarra. In his second year with the club, Murray steered the Steelers to victory in the Tooheys Challenge pre-season competition and the first finals series in their 11-season history. Illawarra was ousted 4-0 in the 1992 preliminary final by St. George, but Murray collected the Dally M Coach of the Year award in the wake of the ground-breaking season. But while the club shaped as an emerging heavyweight, the Steelers failed to qualify for the finals in 1993-94. Murray was sacked by club management in 1995 after signing a Super League contract, and was installed as coach of the rebel outfit's Newcastle-based club the Hunter Mariners.

Super League was prevented from starting its own competition in 1996—putting Murray's coaching career on ice for a year—but he moulded the Mariners into a competitive side under difficult circumstances in the 1997 season. Hunter finished sixth in the Super League premiership and qualified for the final of the World Club Challenge competition, but the club folded after the formation of the NRL ensured only one competition would be staged from 1998. Murray took over as coach of English club Leeds for two seasons and guided the Rhinos to a Super League Grand Final loss in 1998, before succeeding Phil Gould at the Sydney Roosters in 2000. The unassuming mentor led the Roosters to their first Grand Final appearance in 20 years at his first attempt—a plucky 14-6 loss to Brisbane—but was unceremoniously dumped after the club's disappointing seventh-place finish in 2001.

He replaced Murray Hurst as North Queensland coach during 2002 after the Cowboys' dismal start to the season and led the underperforming club to unprecedented success. Murray harnessed the brilliance of emerging stars such as Matt Bowen and—as he did at Illawarra—took the Cowboys to their maiden finals series, in 2004. After a gallant post-season run that ended in the preliminary final in 2004, Murray's charges qualified for the 2005 Grand Final, where they were overwhelmed 30-16 by the Wests Tigers.

Coach of City Origin from 2001-05, Murray was installed as Ricky Stuart's successor as NSW Origin coach in 2006 (Stuart had accepted the Kangaroos post). But the Blues lost their first series since 2001 in Murray's first campaign at the helm, and his tenure as state coach finished with another 2-1 series loss in 2007. The affable mentor took North Queensland to another preliminary final appearance in 2007, but Murray was informed by management that his contract would not be extended beyond 2008 after a poor start to the following season and he stepped down after 10 rounds despite initially vowing to see out the season. Still possessing one of the finest football brains in Australia, Murray was appointed to incoming Newcastle coach Wayne Bennett's staff for 2012.

MALCOLM REILLY Renowned Castleford and Great Britain enforcer Malcolm Reilly was well-known to Australian Rugby League supporters after his magnificent performances at lock for the victorious 1970 Lions and in five seasons for Manly—including Grand Final victories in 1972-73. Reilly was a long-serving captain-coach of Castleford until his playing retirement in 1986. He took over as coach of Great Britain in 1987 and the team achieved renewed respectability under his stewardship in the wake of a disastrous decade. Reilly led the Lions on spirited tours to Australia in 1988 and 1992 (losing each series 2-1), and came agonisingly close to an Ashes series victory on English soil against the 1990 Kangaroos. He combined his national duties with club coaching roles for Leeds and Halifax, but finished as Great Britain coach with a record of 29 wins in 42 Tests prior to the Kangaroos' 1994 visit after accepting the position of coach of the Newcastle Knights for 1995.

The terse British mentor was an ideal fit for the Knights and harnessed the burgeoning talent of halves combination Andrew and Matthew Johns superbly, while maintaining Newcastle's trademark forward grunt, as the club qualified for its maiden preliminary final in 1995. Reilly's fitness and competitiveness was legendary among his Knights squad, and he brought a new level of professionalism to the club. Following an underwhelming 1996 campaign, Reilly guided the Knights to a euphoric Grand Final triumph over Manly in the 1997 ARL Grand Final, becoming the first overseas coach to win a premiership and sealing his place in Newcastle folklore. Reilly navigated a tumultuous 1998 season at Newcastle—which included three Knights players being suspended for testing positive to banned substances— to a second-place finish in the minor premiership of the inaugural NRL season, but returned to England after the injury-ravaged Knights' finals exit. His last professional coaching appointment was in 1999, enduring a disappointing season with Huddersfield as the club collected the Super League wooden spoon.

JOHN LANG Brisbane Easts stalwart John Lang was one of the finest hookers of the 1970s, representing Australia in eight Tests and touring with the Kangaroos in 1973. Lang spent a season in Sydney with Eastern Suburbs, helping the club to a Grand Final appearance and starring in Queensland's victory in the inaugural State of Origin match in 1980. He returned to Brisbane to coach Easts the following season, guiding the Tigers to a BRL premiership triumph in 1983 during a four-season stint. After a break from the game, Lang took the reins at Easts again in 1990, leading the club to another title the following season and BRL Grand Final losses in 1992 and '93. Lang signed on as Cronulla coach and immediately turned the Sharks' fortunes around; after a much-improved seventh-place finish in 1994, Lang guided his effervescent young squad to a top-four berth in 1995 and a preliminary final appearance in 1996. The Sharks qualified for the Super League Grand Final under Lang's tutelage (a 26-8 loss to Brisbane), while the unassuming mentor coached Super League's Australian representative side in all five Tests during 1997—a win and a loss against New Zealand, and a 2-1 series win against Great Britain on English soil.

Lang's Sharks took out the NRL minor premiership in 1999 before crumbling in the preliminary final 24-8 to St. George Illawarra. He left the club after another preliminary final loss in 2001 (18-10 to Newcastle), joining reigning wooden spooners Penrith. Lang rebuilt the flailing Panthers and after an improved 12th-place result in 2002, he steered the club to a stunning premiership victory in 2003 with an 18-6 boilover against the star-studded Sydney Roosters in the Grand Final. The Panthers reached the preliminary final stage in 2004, but Lang's contract was not renewed after finishes in the bottom half of the table in 2005-06 and he was replaced by Matthew Elliott. Lang rekindled his long-term relationship with former Cronulla and Penrith chief executive Shane Richardson at Souths, joining the club in a football consultant role. Rabbitohs coach Jason Taylor's sacking for a 'Mad Monday' altercation with forward David Fa'alogo at the end of 2009 saw Lang return to the clipboard in 2010. Souths narrowly missed the 2010 and '11 finals during Lang's two-season tenure; he retired at the end of the latter year. An animated character during games, Lang was one of the few modern mentors to spend matches on the bench—the traditional position, but uncommon in the NRL era as most coaches prefer to be situated high above in the box.

MAL MENINGA Mal Meninga was one of Rugby League's most decorated and devastating players in a remarkable career with Brisbane Souths, Canberra, Queensland and Australia. Meninga set a plethora of records at representative level and captained the Raiders to three premierships, while the centre was selected in the ARL Team of the Century in 2008. It initially appeared as though Meninga's greatness as a player was not going to translate to the coaching sphere during a trying five-season stint as Canberra's mentor, but he later guided Queensland to unprecedented success at Origin level to add to his enormous legacy. Meninga hung up his boots at the end of 1994 and succeeded his former mentor Tim Sheens at Canberra two years later. A vocal supporter of the Super League movement, Meninga's first season in charge of the Raiders was the 1997 Super League season. He steered the heavyweight club to the preliminary final of the rebel competition, and to the NRL finals in 1998 and 2000, but his tenure was generally considered a failure and he stepped down after the Raiders came 11th in 2001—the club's worst finish since 1992. Nevertheless, Meninga finished with a respectable 53.6 per cent win record.

After a few years away from the game, Meninga was installed as Queensland's State of Origin coach in 2006, replacing Newcastle's Michael Hagan. The former Origin great galvanised the underdog Maroons, guiding them from a game down to their first series victory in five years. Queensland won the next five series straight under Meninga (a streak still unbroken heading into 2012), equalling NSW's Phil Gould's record of six series wins as coach—but the Maroons' six consecutive years on top doubled the previous Origin record. His rivalry with NSW coach and former teammate Ricky Stuart was a feature of the hard-fought 2011 series, while Meninga's stunning spray aimed at the NSW team, the Sydney media and the judiciary after the series added a tense post-script. Clubs in England clambered to sign Meninga in the wake of his representative success, but he re-signed with the QRL for another four seasons at the end of 2011.

MICHAEL HAGAN Clever half Michael Hagan represented Queensland in five Origin matches (1989-90) and won premierships with Canterbury in 1985 and 1988, before joining Newcastle and captaining the club to its maiden finals series in 1992. Hagan coached Canberra's President's Cup and First Division sides under NRL coach Mal Meninga during the late-1990s before returning to Newcastle as First Division coach in 2000. He was elevated to the Knights' first grade role at the end of the year following the departure of Warren Ryan, and joined a select band of coaches to win a premiership in their debut season of first grade with a 30-24 defeat of Parramatta in the 2001 NRL Grand Final. Hagan guided the Knights to the finals in 2002-03, but late-season injuries to captain Andrew Johns derailed each campaign. Becoming

Queensland coach after Wayne Bennett stepped down from the role, Hagan led the Maroons to spirited 2-1 series losses in the 2004-05 campaigns before relinquishing the post to Meninga. Newcastle finished with the wooden spoon in 2005 and Hagan signed a deal with Parramatta early in 2006, joining the Eels after a top-four finish in his last season as Knights mentor. Hagan replaced Brian Smith (who ironically joined Newcastle) at Parramatta and steered the club to a preliminary final appearance in 2007, but he stepped down from first grade coaching at the end of the Eels' disappointing 2008 season, citing health and family reasons. He rejoined the Queensland Origin camp as Meninga's assistant in 2010.

RICKY STUART One of the shrewdest tacticians of the modern era as a player, coaching in the NRL was a natural progression for Ricky Stuart. The pugnacious halfback was the linchpin of Canberra's 1989-90 and 1994 premiership sides, toured twice with the Kangaroos and ranks among the most influential players in NSW's Origin history. After retiring as a player in 2000 while at Canterbury, Stuart's ascension to the top echelon of the game's coaches was phenomenally swift. He coached the Bulldogs' Jersey Flegg side to a premiership in 2001 and was fast-tracked into the first grade role at the Sydney Roosters for the following season. Stuart's passion, sound strategies and emphasis on aggressive defence were key components in the Roosters' stirring charge to their 2002 premiership triumph, seeing him become just the fourth rookie first grade coach to win a Grand Final after Leo Nosworthy at Balmain (1969), Stuart's mentor and confidant Phil Gould at Canterbury (1988), and Michael Hagan at Newcastle (2001). He guided the club to Grand Finals in the subsequent two seasons, but the Roosters were upset by Penrith and the Bulldogs in the 2003 and 2004 deciders respectively.

The Roosters faded out of finals contention in the 2005-06 seasons and Stuart was terminated by the club one week from the end of the latter campaign. It emerged later that Wayne Bennett had agreed to terms with the Roosters for 2007 prior to Stuart's axing, but the Brisbane coach pulled the pin on the deal after details became public against his wishes, while Stuart was snapped up by Cronulla. Stuart led the gritty, defence-oriented Sharks to an equal share of first place at the end of the 2008 regular season (third on for-and-against), but an admirable campaign came to an end with a preliminary final defeat to Melbourne. He held the club together during Cronulla's disastrous 2009 campaign that included a plethora of off-field incidents involving players and administrators, a drug ban for star recruit Reni Maitua and dismal results on the paddock. Despite having 18 months to run on his contract, Stuart announced during 2010 that he would be leaving the Sharks at the end of the season, and eventually stepped down with seven rounds remaining.

Stuart has achieved significant success at representative level. After overseeing Country Origin's 22-18 victory over City in 2004, Stuart succeeded Phil Gould as NSW Origin coach in 2005 and steered the Blues to a third consecutive series triumph. He took over from Wayne Bennett as Australian Test coach the following season, guiding the Kangaroos as they reclaimed the Tri-Nations title in 2006 and in a record 58-0 defeat of New Zealand in 2007. Australia was on target for an emphatic World Cup victory under Stuart in 2008, but New Zealand pulled off a shock 34-20 win in the final at Suncorp Stadium, and Stuart was forced to resign from his post for abusing referee Ashley Klein in the team hotel after a series of contentious calls went against the Kangaroos. With no club commitments on his plate, Stuart returned as coach of the Blues (who had not won a series since his 2005 stint) in 2011. The new-look NSW side narrowly lost the series-opener and forced a decider for the first time since 2008 with an emphatic victory in the second encounter. Queensland won the third match comfortably to extend its Origin dominance to six straight seasons, but the Blues' steely resolve under the passionate motivator Stuart raised hopes of a drought-breaking series victory in the not too distant future.

STEVE FOLKES Canterbury stalwart Steve Folkes was a tireless backrower in his playing days, touring with the 1986 Kangaroos and making five Test appearances for Australia. He retired in 1991 and spent several seasons as a conditioner and lower grade coach for the Bulldogs. After steering the club's reserve grade side to a premiership in the 1997 Super League season, Folkes was elevated to the first grade role after the departure of another Canterbury favourite son, Chris Anderson. Folkes was one of the fittest players and most dedicated trainers during his career, and that ethos filtered through to his charges in 1998. Canterbury stormed from ninth spot in the inaugural NRL season's 10-team finals series all the way to the Grand Final, on the back of consecutive 100-minute extra-time victories over Newcastle and Parramatta. The Bulldogs succumbed 38-12 to the rampant Broncos in the Grand Final, but the loss could not diminish Folkes' superb achievement in becoming the first rookie coach to guide a team to a decider since 1988.

Folkes withstood the salary cap scandal that scuppered the Bulldogs' premiership dream in 2002 and player misconduct in the 2004 pre-season at Coffs Harbour that threatened to derail another campaign, steeling his squad for a memorable surge to the 2004 NRL premiership. The 16-13 Grand Final victory over arch-rivals the Sydney Roosters was a testament to Folkes' determination, excellent game-plans and his man-management skills under adversity, meanwhile shying away from the media histrionics of his high-profile coaching rivals.

The Bulldogs' Grand Final squad gradually disintegrated over the ensuing seasons and Folkes was let go following the club's disastrous 2008 wooden spoon season, with his job made exceedingly difficult by Sonny Bill Williams' shock mid-season walkout. Folkes' 11 consecutive seasons as coach of one club is second in premiership history only to Wayne Bennett's 21-year tenure at Brisbane. After a stint as a conditioner for the West Indies cricket team, Folkes joined Wests Tigers in a similar role on Tim Sheens' staff, remaining hopeful of a return to the ranks of NRL first grade coaching.

CRAIG BELLAMY Craig Bellamy emerged from a long apprenticeship under legendary Brisbane mentor Wayne Bennett to become one of the NRL era's dominant coaching figures. A tough and versatile player, Bellamy was a foundation Canberra Raider, playing 148 first grade games for the club from 1982-92 and coming off the bench in the 1990 Grand Final victory over Penrith. Bellamy quickly moved into coaching with the Raiders and guided the club's President's Cup side to premiership success in 1995. He joined the Broncos as performance coordinator and was Bennett's assistant coach from 1998-2002, encompassing NRL Grand Final triumphs in 1998 and 2000. Bellamy replaced Mark Murray as head coach at the Melbourne Storm in 2003 and immediately improved the club's position.

After finals appearances in his first three seasons in the Victorian capital, Bellamy steered his squad—largely moulded from young stars he had nurtured such as Cameron Smith, Billy Slater, Cooper Cronk and Greg Inglis—to an emphatic minor premiership in 2006. The Storm were upset 15-8 by Bennett's Broncos in the Grand Final, but Bellamy's charges were galvanised from the defeat and blitzed Manly 34-8 in the 2007 decider. Bellamy was linked to a return to Brisbane after Bennett announced he would be joining St. George Illawarra at the end of 2008, but he remained at Melbourne and steered the club to a third straight minor premiership in 2008 (followed by a record 40-0 Grand Final loss to the Sea Eagles) and a second Grand Final triumph against Parramatta in 2009 the first coach since Clive Churchill (1967-71) to qualify for four deciders in a row.

Bellamy held the club together during the devastating salary cap scandal of 2010 that saw the Storm's two premierships under his tutelage stripped. Despite going through the gut-wrenching process of playing for no competition points in 2010, Bellamy's tight-knit group won 14 matches. He performed a coaching miracle in 2011 by steering his new-look squad (the club was forced to shed several stars to fit under the salary cap) to the minor premiership. Although the campaign ended with a preliminary final defeat to the New Zealand Warriors, Melbourne's fight-back from the horrors of 2010 ranks as one of the great club achievements, while Bellamy was named Dally M Coach of the Year for the third time after previous wins in 2006-07. A savvy tactician with a remarkable ability to transform average players into outstanding first grade contributors, Bellamy's reputation as an intense character precedes him but he forms close bonds with his players in the same manner that coaching luminaries Bennett and Jack Gibson are renowned for. Bellamy took over as NSW Origin coach in 2008 but was unable to overturn Queensland's interstate dominance in three seasons at the helm, standing down from the post after the Blues' 3-0 whitewash at the hands of a Maroons squad boasting several of his Storm stars.

DES HASLER One of the most versatile players in Rugby League history, Des Hasler toured with the 1986 and 1990 Kangaroos in a 12-Test career and made 287 first grade appearances for Penrith, Manly and Western Suburbs. Hasler won premierships with the Sea Eagles playing halfback (1987) and hooker (1996) as one of the club's finest servants, but was even more influential at the club during an eight-season coaching tenure.

Hasler coached Manly's First Division side in 2001 and '02, before stepping up as an assistant to Sea Eagles first grade coach Peter Sharp in 2003 after the Northern Eagles joint venture dissolved. He was also on Phil Gould's staff during NSW's 2003 State of Origin series victory. Hasler was installed as Manly's head coach for 2004 and gradually rebuilt the fallen superpower. He guided the club to its first finals appearance in seven years in 2005, and after an impressive campaign the following season, Hasler's side qualified for the Grand Final in 2007—a 34-8 defeat to Melbourne. The Sea Eagles gained sweet revenge over the Storm with a Grand Final record 40-0 demolition in the 2008 decider, with Hasler's reputation as one of the NRL's finest mentors soaring. Hard-nosed, meticulous and technically excellent, Hasler developed a close bond with his players that has been a trademark of all time great coaches such as Gibson, Bennett and Bellamy.

Manly won the World Club Challenge early in 2009, but the club's ensuing two NRL seasons finished with first-week finals exits, while the disappointing 2010 campaign—in which the Sea Eagles finished eighth—was marked by Hasler infamously ripping the dressing-room door off its hinges at Parramatta Stadium in a post-match spray after his side surrendered a 20-0 lead against the Eels. But Hasler and his squad regrouped in 2011 to craft a magnificent premiership season, combining rugged defence with swarming attack to blitz their finals competition, culminating in a resounding 24-10 defeat of New Zealand in the Grand Final. But his 27-year association with the Sea Eagles came to an abrupt end just five days after the decider. Largely due to an ongoing pay dispute, Hasler announced he would be joining Canterbury in 2013. Manly sacked Hasler a month later for "serious breaches of contract," and the Bulldogs fast-tracked him into the head coach role for 2012.

OFFICIALS AND MEDIA

Rugby League's administrators, referees and media identities have added plenty of colour and controversy since the code's humble beginnings, and their enormous contribution to the game should not be overlooked. This chapter pays tribute to the best and most well-known men of the boardroom, the whistle, the pen and the microphone.

THE ADMINISTRATORS

JAMES J. GILTINAN One of Australian Rugby League's founding fathers, famed entrepreneur Giltinan was the inaugural secretary of the NSWRL—a post he was controversially dumped from upon his return as manager of the historic but financially disastrous 1908-09 Kangaroo Tour. The J.J. Giltinan Shield was inaugurated after his death in 1950 and awarded to each year's premiers until 1997, after which it became the symbol of winning the minor premiership *(see also The Pioneering Years)*.

HENRY HOYLE The NSWRL's inaugural president, Hoyle is regarded as one of the game's founding fathers with James Giltinan and Victor Trumper. A prominent politician, Hoyle chaired the meeting at Bateman's Hotel in 1907 that led to the breakaway Rugby League movement in 1908. Along with Giltinan and Trumper, Hoyle was dumped as president after the financial failings of the code's first season *(see also The Pioneering Years)*.

VICTOR TRUMPER Legendary Australian batsman Victor Trumper was the preeminent cricketer of the early part of the 20th century and a vital figure in the advent of Rugby League in Sydney. The early meetings held in his sports store that sparked the breakaway movement have passed into the game's folklore, while he became the NSWRL's first treasurer, being sacked along with fellow founding fathers James Giltinan and Henry Hoyle *(see also The Pioneering Years)*.

S. GEORGE BALL One of the men most responsible for the formation of the South Sydney club, S.G. Ball was one of the code's most famous administrators. The club's first treasurer, Ball served as Souths' secretary for more than 50 years. Named in his honour, the SG Ball Cup is the premier competition for Under-18 players in NSW and has been operating since 1965.

HARRY 'JERSEY' FLEGG Arguably the most famous administrator in Australian Rugby League history, Flegg was integral to forming Eastern Suburbs and was the club's captain in the inaugural premiership final against Souths in 1908. He was a NSW and Australian Test selector before becoming the NSWRL's fifth president in 1929, a role he occupied concurrently with the chairmanship of the Australian Board of Control from 1941 until his death in 1960. The H 'Jersey' Flegg Memorial Trophy was inaugurated a year later for under-20s competition in NSW; it ceased in 2008 after the introduction of the National Youth Competition, the Toyota Cup.

HORRIE MILLER Pioneering Easts winger Miller scored two tries in the club's 14-12 loss to Souths in the inaugural 1908 premiership final. Miller became Easts' secretary in 1909 before taking over as NSWRL secretary in 1914. Attributed with coining the phrase 'The Greatest Game of All' to describe Rugby League, Miller was also appointed to the dual role of secretary of the Australian Board of Control, but was sacked from his posts in 1946 when £80 could not be accounted for in a sad postscript from one of the pre-World War II period's most prominent off-field figures.

HARRY SUNDERLAND Born in Queensland, Sunderland was integral to the growth of Rugby League in the state as a long-serving secretary for the QRL from 1913. Enthusiastic, tireless, strong-minded and controversial, Sunderland did not always win universal approval, but he was nothing if not forward-thinking. He was vital to the game starting in France, when as manager of the 1933-34 Kangaroos he set up an international between Australia and England in Paris. Sunderland also made ambitious—if unsuccessful—attempts to promote the game in Victoria and the United States. He left Australia in 1938 to become secretary-manager of English club Wigan, where he was equally revered. The larger-than-life character is honoured by the Harry Sunderland Medal for the best Australian player in a Test series, and with the awarding of the Harry Sunderland Trophy for the man of the match in the Super League Grand Final in England.

HAROLD MATTHEWS Matthews' association with the NSWRL began in 1924 when he became Balmain's delegate to the League, before serving as the club's secretary for more than two decades from 1929. He became NSWRL secretary in 1951 before relinquishing the post in 1966 citing poor health. The Under-16s Harold Matthews Cup has operated since 1970.

W.G. 'BILL' BUCKLEY Newtown forward Buckley's brief first grade career was ended by a broken leg in 1928, but he had a marked impact on the code as an administrator. He served as the Bluebags' delegate to the NSWRL, before co-managing the 1948-49 Kangaroos. Buckley succeeded Harry 'Jersey' Flegg as

NSWRL president and ARL chairman upon Flegg's death in 1960. An equally hard-nosed character, Buckley passed away while still in office in 1973.

FRANK FACER A rugged front-rower in 11 seasons for North Sydney and St. George, 'Fearless' Frank Facer played hooker in Norths' 1943 Grand Final loss and featured in the Dragons' 1949 Grand Final triumph. But he became better known as an influential administrator, becoming secretary of St. George in 1956 as the club began its record run of 11 premierships. One of the first fulltime club secretaries, Facer was viewed as an integral part of the Dragons' monumental success, and was responsible for the astute recruitment that brought Saints legends such as Johnny Raper, Brian Clay, Graeme Langlands and Ian Walsh to the club. He oversaw another premiership victory in 1977, before passing away in 1978.

PETER MOORE Canterbury patriarch Peter 'Bullfrog' Moore was at the helm of the club as secretary and later chief executive from 1969-95 and one of the code's foremost administrators. Becoming known as 'the family club' under Moore's stewardship, Canterbury won five premierships during his reign. The 'Bullfrog's' recruitment nous was top-shelf and he brought some of the greatest players to don the blue and white jersey to the club, while he also managed NSW and Australian representative teams. Moore passed away in 2000. His son, former Bulldogs halfback Kevin, coached the club from 2009-11.

KEN STEPHEN Stephen played for Balmain and Souths and represented NSW in 1948 in a career that was cut short by injury, but he made a lasting contribution as an administrator, succeeding Harold Matthews as NSWRL secretary in 1967. The Ken Stephen Medal was struck in his honour following his death at the age of 62 in 1988, and awarded annually for services to Rugby League and the community

KEVIN HUMPHREYS Humphreys assumed the dual roles of NSWRL president and ARL chairman in 1973 after the death of Bill Buckley. The former Balmain prop had served as Tigers secretary since 1965. As an administrator, Humphreys guided Rugby League into the modern era and oversaw many important changes, including working with QRL counterpart Ron McAuliffe to establish State of Origin in 1980. But he resigned in 1983 after an investigation by ABC's *Four Corners* program exposed high-level corruption in his 1977 acquittal on charges of misappropriation of funds during his tenure as Balmain secretary *(see also The 1980s)*.

KEN ARTHURSON Manly's Grand Final halfback in 1951, Ken Arthurson's playing career ended after fracturing his skull playing in Parkes two years later. He coached the Sea Eagles to Grand Finals in 1957 and '59, before entering officialdom and becoming club treasurer in 1961 and secretary in 1963. Along with St. George's Frank Facer, Arthurson was one of the first secretaries appointed fulltime by a Sydney club. His shrewd approach was reflected in the players he helped bring to the club that saw the Sea Eagles break their premiership duck and win four titles in the 1970s. 'Arko' became the ARL chairman after Kevin Humphreys resigned in 1983 and became the ninth president of the NSWRL in 1986, overseeing an unprecedented era of prosperity and advancement for the game in Australia. He was at the coalface of the ARL's fight against Super League from 1995 and, wearied from the upheaval, stood down in 1997.

JOHN QUAYLE Rugged backrower Quayle played nine seasons of first grade with Easts and Parramatta (1968-76), representing Australia during the 1975 World Series tournament. A shoulder injury forced Quayle's retirement, but he moved into administration with Easts before becoming the inaugural general manager of the ARL and NSWRL in the 1980s. Working in tandem with Ken Arthurson, Quayle was at the forefront of the code's rise in popularity and commercial success in the late-1980s and early-1990s. He took the fight to Super League in 1995-96, but stood down early in 1997 to help expedite the reunification of the game.

RON McAULIFFE Ron 'The Senator' McAuliffe—so named because of a decade-long term in as a Senator for the Australian Labor Party in Parliament—was a prominent Rugby League administrator in Queensland for more than three decades. He became secretary of the QRL in 1953 and was the man most responsible for the advent of State of Origin football. Tributes flowed following his death in 1988, recognising his enormous contribution to the game in Queensland and Australia. The Ron McAuliffe Medal was struck in 2004 and is awarded to Queensland's players' player after each Origin series.

JOHN RIBOT Powerhouse Queensland winger Ribot scored nine tries in as many Tests (1981-85) and played for Newtown, Wests and Manly during six seasons in Sydney. Moving into administration, Ribot served as QRL development manager before becoming the Brisbane Broncos' inaugural chief executive, regularly clashing with the NSWRL. He became chief executive of the Super League movement and was the public face of the rebel group, which eventually established its own competition for one season in 1997. Ribot, a vilified figure for his role in the game's split, stepped down from his post to help set up the fledgling Melbourne Storm in 1998.

NEIL WHITTAKER Durable hooker Whittaker played 119 games for Balmain from 1979-85. He was involved with club administration at the Tigers during the 1990s, before taking over from John Quayle as ARL chief executive in 1997. After helping broker a peace deal with News Limited and Super League, Whittaker became the CEO of the newly formed National Rugby League, overseeing the NRL's rigorous rationalisation process before resigning at the end of 1999.

DAVID MOFFETT Former New Zealand Rugby Union supremo Moffett succeeded Neil Whittaker as NRL chief executive at the end of 1999. After two years with the NRL, Moffett departed to take up the role as CEO of Sport England early in 2002 and later with the Welsh Rugby Union.

DAVID GALLOP Gallop served as the Director of Legal and Business Affairs for the newly formed National Rugby League in the late-1990s, before succeeding David Moffett as NRL chief executive in 2002. Gallop has faced down several challenges during his decade in charge, handling the salary cap scandals involving the Bulldogs (2002) and Melbourne (2010), the dispute between the NRL and the Rugby League Players' Association that led to the cancellation of the 2003 Dally M Awards night, and a plethora of severe cases of off-field player misbehaviour. Well-spoken and unflappable, Gallop was named the Australian Sports Administrator of the Year in 2006.

THE REFEREES

TOM J. McMAHON Rugby League's first great referee, 'Gentleman' Tom McMahon controlled top-level matches from 1908-26. McMahon refereed Anglo-Australian Tests in Australia between 1910 and 1924 and remains a revered figure from the code's formative years.

WILLIAM 'WEBBY' NEILL A foundation Souths player and 1911-12 Kangaroo, 'Webby' Neil was a top-flight referee for 17 years and officiated in the 1932 Ashes series.

LAL DEANE Former Norths player (14 first grade games) and brother of Test captain Sid Deane, Lal Deane controlled each premiership decider from 1928-32 and five Ashes between 1928 and 1936.

TOM P. McMAHON No relation to the pioneering referee of the same name, McMahon was a dominant whistle-blower from 1933-51. He controlled 246 first grade games and seven Tests matches in an illustrious career.

JACK O'BRIEN Much admired, O'Brien refereed seven Grand Finals from 1942-54, but his Catholic faith prevented him from a promotion to Test level at a time when the Mason v Catholic religious division in the game was at its most ardent. O'Brien controlled a then-record 262 games.

GEORGE BISHOP A long-serving Balmain hooker and 1929-30 Kangaroo tourist, Bishop refereed at Test level and controlled four Grand Finals. But his controversial handling of Wests' defeat of Souths in the 1952 decider—exacerbated by his immediate retirement—remains arguably his most prominent legacy to the game, with allegations he bet on the Magpies abounding. Bishop later served as a Test selector.

DARCY LAWLER A hard-headed, cantankerous but respected character, Lawler controlled a then-record seven Grand Finals and is one of the most famous and controversial referees in Rugby League history. Routinely criticised by touring Great Britain sides, Lawler's contentious performance in the 1963 Grand Final between St. George and Wests—followed by his retirement after the match—has been shrouded in claims he placed a wager on the Dragons ever since. Lawler refereed 19 Test and World Cup games.

COL PEARCE The quiet, genial character to Darcy Lawler's authoritative flamboyance, Pearce was a highly respected official and controlled a then-record 343 first grade games—including five straight Grand Finals (1964-68). Rarely embroiled in the controversy that has routinely hounded the game's top officials, the popular Pearce refereed 12 Test and World Cup games before retiring in 1969.

AUB OXFORD Oxford played two first grade games for Newtown in 1935 and became a graded referee in 1942. His name is entrenched in Rugby League folklore after abandoning the infamous NSW v Great Britain match at the SCG in 1954 due to persistent fighting. Oxford walked away from refereeing after the match.

KEITH PAGE Criticised by Souths for his performance in the club's 1969 Grand Final loss to Balmain, Page nevertheless controlled subsequent deciders in 1972-73 and was one of the most prominent whistle-blowers of his era.

KEITH HOLMAN Among Australia's greatest-ever halfbacks, 35-Test veteran and Wests great Holman moved into refereeing after his playing retirement. 'Yappy' Holman was equally flamboyant and opinionated with the whistle in hand, while he controlled the 1971 Grand Final and two Test matches in 1972.

GREG HARTLEY Undoubtedly the most controversial referee of all time, Hartley's performances during the 1978 finals series have gone down in infamy. Injury ended the Newtown halfback's career aged 22, but he rose to the highest ranks of refereeing and despite his outrageous flamboyance and histrionics, Hartley was recognised as an excellent official. Hartley raised the ire of many a club coach, but retained his status as the game's top whistle-blower to control four straight Grand Finals (1978-81).

BARRY GOMERSALL Affectionately known as the 'Grasshopper,' Gomersall was a prominent State of Origin referee during the 1980s, controlling nine games. He was a much-loved character in his native Queensland, but NSW frequently accused him of bias—pointing to the fact that the Blues won just two games under his control.

MICK STONE Cut from the Col Pearce-mould, Stone controlled the 1986-88 Grand Finals and four Origin matches—provoking a hail of beer cans in 1988 when he sin-binned Queensland pair Greg Conescu and Wally Lewis in an infamous Lang Park incident.

GREG McCALLUM McCallum was the premiership's top referee during the early-1990s, officiating in the 1992-94 Grand Finals. The bearded whistle-blower also controlled five Origin matches and 13 Tests during his career, while in retirement he has served as the Executive Director of the RFL in Britain and has been the NRL's match review committee chairman since 2004.

BILL HARRIGAN The record-holder for most first grade games (393), Grand Finals (10), State of Origins (21) and Tests (21) for a referee, Harrigan is generally recognised as the game's best-ever referee, but also one of the most controversial. 'Hollywood' Harrigan was criticised for perceived arrogance, but was undeniably the fittest referee the game had seen. He infamously had long-running feuds with

Manly coach Bob Fulton and Queensland firebrand Gorden Tallis (who he sent off for dissent in the 2000 Origin series-opener), while he sided with Super League during the split with the ARL and was forced to sit out two seasons from officiating. Harrigan's legacy to current-day refereeing is undeniable, while he retains a prominent role in the game as referees coach.

DAVID MANSON Queenslander Manson's friendly demeanour rendered him one of the most popular referees of the 1990s. Manson controlled 10 Origin matches (including the infamous Wally Lewis-Mark Geyer halftime stoush during the 1991 series) and the 1996-97 ARL Grand Finals.

TIM MANDER Hailing from Queensland, Tim Mander controlled first grade matches in the NSWRL premiership from 1992 and refereed the 2004-05 Grand Finals after the retirement of Bill Harrigan. Mander was one of the most prominent Super League-defecting referees.

STEVE CLARK Strong in his convictions and notoriously hard on player dissent, Clark was fated to never control a Grand Final in his 16-season career (1992-2007), but was one of the modern era's top whistle-blowers.

TONY ARCHER Archer has become established as the No.1 referee in the game, controlling the 2007-08 Grand Finals solo and the first three deciders since the two-referee system was introduced (2009-11). Debuting in 1999, Archer controlled 268 NRL games, 11 Origins and nine Tests to the end of 2011. He was named International Referee of the Year at the RLIF awards in 2008 and 2010-11, and won the Col Pearce Medal as the top Australian whistle-blower in 2007-08 and 2010.

THE MEDIA

CLAUDE CORBETT Corbett was a highly respected sports journalist who wrote, and was the sporting editor for Sydney's *Sun* newspaper in the early 20th century. A prolific sportsman himself, Corbett set the standard for all Rugby League writers to follow.

TOM GOODMAN Goodman covered cricket and Rugby League with trademark passion and integrity with the *Evening Herald* (1916-31) and the *Sydney Morning Herald* (1932-67) for more than 50 years.

ERNIE 'TIGER' BLACK A diminutive hooker that played two first grade games for St. George in 1940, 'Tiger' Black was a pioneering figure of Rugby League broadcasting. A much-loved character calling matches on radio station 2KY, Black's geniality and humour won him many fans.

FRANK HYDE An outstanding centre with Newtown, Balmain and Norths from 1936-44, Hyde represented NSW five times (1938-39) and captained Norths in the 1943 Grand Final loss to the Bluebags. But as a radio caller, Hyde became one of Rugby League's most well-known and exceedingly popular characters. Hyde began calling matches for 2SM in 1953 and his colourful manner became entrenched in the fabric of the game for over three decades. He called 33 straight Grand Finals until his retirement in 1986, while he was honoured with the Dally M Life Achievement Award in 1982. His trademark "It's high enough, it's long enough, it's straight between the posts" is one of Rugby League's best-known phrases.

GEORGE CRAWFORD Incredibly knowledgeable and passionate, Crawford was a veteran Rugby League reporter for the *Daily Telegraph*. His meticulous recording of facts and figures was a forerunner to more recent statistical and historical experts such as David Middleton.

E.E. CHRISTENSEN Christensen was a prominent reporter on a number of sports, but his contribution to Rugby League was monumental. He compiled the *Official Rugby League Yearbook* from 1946-77, while his naming of the NSW Player of the Year with each edition ranked as one of the game's highest individual honours. Christensen covered Rugby League for the *Sun*, while his death in 1980 the day he returned from the Moscow Olympics saddened the Australian sporting fraternity.

RAY STEHR Opinionated, forthright and always entertaining, all time great Easts front-rower Ray Stehr was almost as formidable in retirement as he was on the field. The two-time Kangaroo became a popular radio caller and a pioneer of Rugby League television (calling the first ever commercial television broadcast on Channel 9 in 1961) with his trademark "Easts to win" catchcry.

REX MOSSOP A dual international forward and Manly great of the 1950s and 1960s, 'The Moose' became even better known as the voice of Rugby League on television for almost three decades. Mossop became a legend of the fledgling medium, his forthright opinions and unique twisting of the English language is a treasured part of Rugby League's media history.

GEORGE LOVEJOY Nicknamed 'Mr. Football,' Lovejoy was the doyen of Rugby League callers in Queensland during the 1950s and 1960s, becoming a household name in the Sunshine State with radio station 4BH. A plaque commemorating his colourful career was unveiled in Suncorp Stadium's Sports Media Hall of Fame.

GEOFF PRENTER Cutting his teeth as a soccer reporter for the *Daily Telegraph* and later the *Sun*, Prenter began reporting on his first love—Rugby League—with the *Sun* before taking a punt and becoming the first editor of the fledgling *Rugby League Week* magazine in 1970. Prenter's belief and tireless efforts saw the publication flourish. Keeping true to a promise he made in the late-1970s, Prenter stepped aside after circulation of *RLW* hit 100,000 copies in 1980 and was replaced by Ian Heads.

IAN HEADS A giant of Rugby League's literary field, Heads was a reporter for the *Daily* and *Sunday Telegraph* (1969-81) before joining *Rugby League Week* as managing editor (1981-87). Heads is a prolific author, writing several club histories and a plethora of biographies on the game's greats. He released the seminal *True Blue: The Story of the NSW Rugby League* in 1992 and co-wrote *A Centenary of Rugby*

League with David Middleton, which was released in 2008. Heads' love for the game shines through in his thorough and spirited writing.

PETER FRILINGOS Frilingos was one of Rugby League's best-known journalists, beginning his career with the *Daily Mirror* in 1962. He became the paper's chief Rugby League reporter and continued in the role after its merger with the *Daily Telegraph*. Affectionately known as 'Chippy,' Frilingos died of a heart attack in 2004 aged 59; the Peter Frilingos Memorial Dally M Headline Moment of the Year Award was instigated in 2006.

DARREL EASTLAKE What Eastlake lacked in knowledge of the finer points of Rugby League, he made up for with unbridled enthusiasm and high-decibel excitability. His approach to television commentating was a good match for the high-octane State of Origin clashes of the 1980s and early-1990s.

RAY WARREN 'Rabbits' began calling Rugby League on television in the 1970s, was one of the code's most prominent commentators in the early-1980s with Network Ten and has been the undisputed voice of the game since the early-1990s with Channel 9. Possessing a famously distinctive voice and wonderfully excitable tones, Warren's passionate commentary has seen him become one of Rugby League's favourite characters. His verbal jousting with co-commentator Phil Gould has been a feature of NRL television coverage during the last decade. Warren has an extensive background in horseracing commentating, calling three Melbourne Cups in the early-1980s, and has become synonymous with Australia's Olympic swimming coverage. A statue of 'Rabs' was unveiled in his home town of Junee in 2011.

RAY HADLEY Hadley became the most prominent Rugby League radio commentator since Frank Hyde, fronting 2UE's 'Continuous Call Team' from 1987. An overwhelming ratings success during the 1990s, Hadley joined 2GB in 2001. Passionate, opinionated and often courting controversy, Hadley was awarded a Medal of the Order of Australia in the Queen's Birthday Honours List in 2002 for his services to Rugby League as a broadcaster.

ROY MASTERS Former Western Suburbs and St. George coach Roy Masters became one of the game's most prominent newspaper columnists with the *Sydney Morning Herald* after his tenure with the Dragons finished in 1987. Also covering several other sports, Masters was awarded a Medal of the Order of Australia in the Queen's Birthday Honours List in 2012 for his services to sports and journalism. Master penned the successful book Inside League (1990).

GRAEME HUGHES A skilful backrower for Canterbury and NSW, and a state representative cricketer, Hughes was a leading television commentator with Network Ten in the late-1980s and early-1990s until the network lost the broadcasting rights at the end of 1991. Slick, insightful and with a voice custom-made for broadcasting, Hughes called premiership games beamed into New Zealand prior to and after the Auckland Warriors' 1995 entry to the competition, alongside co-commentator and prominent coach Graham Lowe.

PAUL VAUTIN Outstanding backrower 'Fatty' Vautin played 13 Tests for Australia and represented his beloved Queensland side in 22 Origin matches from 1982-90, and captained Manly to the premiership in 1987. A natural funny-man, Vautin quickly moved into a career in the Rugby League media as a commentator with Channel 9 after his retirement as a player. He also became host of the exceedingly popular television program *The Footy Show* in 1994 and remained in the role as it entered its 19th season in 2012.

PETER STERLING One of the game's most decorated halfbacks during a 15-season career with Parramatta that garnered four premierships, 18 Test appearances and a plethora of individual awards, 'Sterlo' began appearing as a television commentator while still his playing career was still active. He was a natural in the role with his insightful analysis and obvious love of the game he played so proficiently. Co-hosting *The Footy Show* with 'Fatty' Vautin for many years, Sterling remained on the Channel 9 commentary team more than two decades after his debut at the microphone.

DAVID MIDDLETON Since compiling *Rugby League Week's Book of Records* as a schoolboy in the 1980s, Middleton has become the doyen of the game's statisticians—a walking encyclopedia of Rugby League and a highly respected authority on the game. Middleton has chronicled each season with the *Official Rugby League Annual* since 1987, while he worked as a reporter for *Rugby League Week* for several seasons. Referred to as 'The Guru,' Middleton has a number of publications to his name, including 2008's *A Centenary of Rugby League*, co-written with Ian Heads.

WARREN SMITH Warren Smith came to prominence as a Rugby League television commentator with Fox Sports during the NRL era, becoming increasingly popular with an enthusiastic calling style and distinctive booming voice. Smith has hosted the Dally M Awards night and the traditional Grand Final breakfast for several seasons.

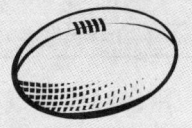

CHAPTER 2
THE GLORY

The goal for every Rugby League player and club is to win a premiership—partaking in a Grand Final victory lap is routinely rated as a career highlight for those fortunate enough to be part of a title-winning team. But it is a long and difficult road to get there. After navigating the trials and tribulations of the regular season and the mad scramble for finals spots, teams have had to navigate a minefield of play-off matches to decide table positions, and a series of finals matches just to reach the Grand Final. The matches and moments that have decided premierships are ingrained in the Australian Rugby League narrative—the most memorable are recalled in this section.

FINAL ROUND CHAOS

The mad scramble for finals spots and jostling for position among the competition's front-runners routinely ramps up the intensity of the premiership during the closing rounds. Minor premierships and finals series berths have frequently been decided on the last weekend—and often the very last match—of the regular season, producing some of the most memorable and desperately fought matches in first grade history.

1911 Glebe and South Sydney were co-leaders of the 1911 premiership with one round remaining, followed by Eastern Suburbs just one win behind. The Dirty Reds thumped lowly Wests 24-0 to confirm at least an equal-first regular season finish, while a Dally Messenger try was the only scoring play as Easts kept their season alive by defeating Norths 3-0. Souths stumbled with a 9-3 loss to last-placed Balmain, forcing the club into a play-off for second against Easts. The Tricolours subsequently won the play-off 23-10 before defeating minor premiers Glebe twice to take out their maiden first grade title.

1916 Defending premiers Balmain approached the final regular season round of 1916 on top of the ladder. But with Souths equal with them on 20 competition points and drawn to play lowly Annandale, the Watersiders knew victory over in-form Easts—barring a major boilover—was required to qualify for the Final. Souths duly defeated Annandale 11-3 to guarantee at least a share of the competition lead, before Balmain ended Easts' six-match unbeaten streak 8-7 at the Agricultural Ground to take out the minor premiership on for-and-against and force a final with Souths. Balmain held on for a 5-3 win after a scoreless second half, securing premiership victories in all three grades for the second straight season.

1919 Balmain led the 1919 competition by a single point from Eastern Suburbs with one round remaining, and Sydney Rugby League supremacy boiled down to a showdown between the season's two best teams on the last weekend of August. Balmain held a slender 4-2 advantage at halftime in front of a 20,000-strong crowd at the Agricultural Ground, before powering away to a 13-4 victory to clinch the club's fourth first grade premiership in five seasons. Fullback Lyall Wall's five goals were vital to the title-sealing win.

1942 Canterbury and Balmain were tied for the competition lead after the penultimate round of the 1942 season, with St. George and Easts trailing one win behind in equal third. Souths remained in contention for the finals a further two competition points back. The prolific Jack Lindwall scored four tries as Saints confirmed third position by defeating Easts 21-12, a result that left the Tricolours teetering. Souths required victory over Newtown to force a play-off with Easts, but could only muster a 16-all draw with the Bluebags, who had won only two games all season. Former NSW centre Fred Felsch scored all of the Rabbitohs' points, but it was to no avail as the club's finals bid fell one point short. Canterbury and Balmain both recorded comfortable last-round victories, necessitating a play-off for the minor premiership, which the Berries won 26-20 before going on to win the premiership.

1943 The 1943 minor premiership was still up for grabs heading into the last weekend of the regular season—Newtown and Balmain were locked on 19 competition points at the top of the table. Meanwhile, North Sydney, South Sydney and St. George were engaged in a three-way battle for the remaining two finals spots, tied on 16 points apiece. Clouding the post-season picture was the final round schedule: Newtown was drawn to play Souths, while Norths and Saints faced off in the weekend's most vital clash. Incredibly, Norths and St. George played out a 9-all draw, leaving the Rabbitohs in a must-win situation. But the Bluebags prevailed 22-9 over Souths to maintain a share of the competition lead with the Tigers, who defeated Wests 10-5. A Dragons loss would have been enough for the Rabbitohs to exercise the right to play off for fourth spot. Two tries to winger Bruce Ryan spearheaded Newtown's 11-10 defeat of Balmain in a play-off for the minor premiership, before the Bluebags progressed to thrash Norths 34-7 in the Grand Final and claim the club's last first grade title.

1953 A dramatic final regular season round drastically shook up the premiership table heading into the finals. Norths headed the ladder on for-and-against from Souths (both 21 points), with St. George and Canterbury one point behind in third-equal. Easts (19 points) and Newtown (18 points) were still clinging to a finals chance. The Berries choked 16-10 against bottom-placed Manly before the Bluebags joined them on 20 points with a 19-5 win over Parramatta. Saints kept their top-two chances alive with a 19-9 defeat of Wests, consigning the Magpies to the wooden spoon, and Souths guaranteed at least second spot by accounting for Balmain 19-11. Easts upset top-ranked Norths 14-11 to leapfrog Canterbury and Newtown into fourth, while Norths' loss saw the club slide to third and handed the minor premiership to the Rabbitohs, who went on to win their third title in four years and atone for their controversial loss in the 1952 decider.

1960 The congestion in the top half of the 1960 premiership table was compounded by a manic final regular season round. St. George had already wrapped up the minor premiership, with Balmain in outright second (22 points) and Wests, Easts, Manly and Canterbury in equal-third (all 20 points). The logjam was complicated by the dominant Dragons' 13-9 defeat of Balmain. Wests beat Souths 22-7, Canterbury accounted for Newtown 17-10 and Easts collected the points 20-8 over wooden spooners Parramatta to each join the Tigers on 22 points in second place. Manly's 10-7 loss to neighbours North Sydney foiled the previous year's grand finalists of back-to-back deciders. The four-way tie for second necessitated an unprecedented series of play-off matches (*see The Play-offs*). But the chasing pack was a class below the mighty Saints, who thumped Easts 31-6 in the Grand Final to take out their fifth straight premiership.

1966 Balmain led premiers for the previous 10 years St. George by a solitary competition point with one round remaining in the 1966 competition, while Manly, Souths and Newtown were locked on 18 points in third place, battling it out for the remaining two finals berths. The Bluebags upset the Tigers 8-6 to ensure a play-off opportunity, as did Manly with a 16-12 defeat of Parramatta. St. George simultaneously snatched its fifth straight minor premiership and eliminated Souths from finals calculations through a merciless 33-5 thrashing, with Eddie Lumsden claiming three tries and wing partner Johnny King a double.

1967 St. George and Canterbury recorded comfortable wins over also-rans in the final round of 1967 to cement first and third place respectively, but a dogfight for fourth spot developed over the course of the weekend. Balmain began the round in fourth on for-and-against from Easts, with Manly one win in arrears. The Tigers went down 11-10 to second-placed Souths after sharpshooter Eric Simms snapped two field goals for the Rabbitohs, before the Sea Eagles moved into fourth on points differential following their 26-11 disposal of Wests. Easts needed to beat Parramatta to claim fourth outright, while a loss would have forced a three-way tie. The Tricolours, who were winless the previous season, shattered the finals ambitions of Manly and Balmain by edging the Eels 15-14. The Roosters were outscored two-tries-to-one, but field goals again played a key role, with second-rower Kevin Ashley slotting two. Souths went on to win the premiership after Canterbury ended the Dragons' record run off 11 straight titles.

1975 Runaway minor premiers Easts, and heavyweights Manly and St. George had comfortably secured the top three positions on the ladder heading into the last round of 1975, but five clubs remained in contention for the other two finals spots. Canterbury sat in fourth on 22 points, with Balmain one point behind in fifth and the desperate trio of Wests, Cronulla and Parramatta clinging to slim hopes of a post-season appearance on 19 points. The Magpies doused the Sharks' finals bid and simultaneously kept their own alive with a 31-17 victory in the first game of the weekend, before Parramatta stayed in the race by defeating Norths 28-13. The make-up of the final five hinged on the last game of the regular season—Canterbury against Balmain at Belmore. Canterbury squeaked home 17-16 in front of a bumper home crowd to seal fourth place, while the Tigers were plunged into a three-way play-off for fifth with the Eels and Magpies. The Eels snatched the last available finals spot with consecutive midweek victories over their play-off adversaries, while the Magpies could only bemoan a competition point they had stripped for fielding an illegal replacement earlier in the season (*see Points Docked*).

1983 The top four spots were virtually locked in heading into round 26 of the 1983 season, but the last finals place remained up for grabs—Easts began the weekend in fifth spot on 29 points, with the chasing pack of St. George and Norths tied for sixth on 27 points. The Bears bowed out with a hard-fought 16-12 loss to fourth-placed Balmain, while the Dragons stayed in the hunt with a 32-2 demolition of Parramatta. The Eels, assured of second spot on the ladder, rested several internationals, including Peter Sterling, Ray Price and Eric Grothe, allowing the Dragons to cruise to a six-tries-to-none victory. The Roosters had the opportunity to clinch a finals spot outright, but instead sunk to their fourth straight loss, 33-12 to eighth-placed Souths. Saints hammered the Roosters 44-16 in the subsequent fifth-place play-off.

1986 The make-up of the 1986 finals rested on the results of a dramatic series of last-round regular season clashes. Souths entered round 26 on top of the table on 37 competition points, one point ahead of Parramatta, while Balmain, St. George and Norths were tied for fifth place on 28 competition points. British import Garry Schofield scored a hat-trick as Balmain confirmed at least an equal-fifth finish with a 38-20 upset of the Rabbitohs, who were subsequently leapfrogged by Parramatta for the minor premiership following the Eels' Peter Sterling-inspired 22-6 defeat of fourth-placed Manly. St. George blew a fifth-place play-off berth with an 18-all draw against Canberra at the SCG, finishing one point adrift of the Tigers. The Dragons scored four tries to three, but star centre Michael O'Connor—playing in his last game for the club before joining Manly—could only manage one goal from four attempts to leave his side agonisingly short of the finals. Norths booked a play-off date with Balmain courtesy of a 17-10 victory over Cronulla.

1987 Two blockbuster matches forced a reshuffle near the top of the table in the last round of 1987, while surprise Sunday afternoon results made for a nail-biting battle for fifth spot. The Sea Eagles had already wrapped up the minor premiership, and accounted for third-placed Balmain 26-8 to confirm their title favouritism. Canberra sealed its first finals appearance and squeezed past the Tigers into third spot with a come-from-behind 22-18 victory over the second-placed Roosters, who were resting several stars. South Sydney went into round 26 in fifth place—one point ahead of Canterbury—but was left vulnerable after faltering 22-14 to the 10th-placed Bears. With a finals berth at their mercy, the Bulldogs were pipped 16-14 by the inconsistent Dragons at the SCG. Canterbury had qualified for the Grand Final in the previous three seasons, but despite fighting back from a 14-point deficit against Saints, coach Warren Ryan's successful and tumultuous tenure at the club ended on a disappointing note.

1988 Cronulla and Canterbury were locked on 32 points at the top of a congested premiership ladder heading into the final round of 1988, with Penrith in outright third on 30 points. Canberra, Manly, Balmain and Brisbane were tied for fourth on 28 competition points to set up a riveting weekend of critical encounters. The Bulldogs were upset 18-14 by eighth-placed Souths on the Friday night, and Cronulla duly sealed the minor premiership with a 16-14 eclipse of St. George two days later. Canberra hammered Gold Coast 24-4, before Manly downed Penrith 18-4 to catapult the Raiders and Sea Eagles into third- and fourth-place respectively, relegating Penrith to fifth on for-and-against. The Tigers extinguished the Broncos' bid for a finals appearance in their debut season with a 20-10 victory, setting up a midweek play-off for fifth spot with Penrith. After taking care of the Panthers, Balmain eliminated Manly, Canberra and Cronulla on an extraordinary charge to the Grand Final.

1993 The five teams to contest the 1993 finals series were already locked in going into the last regular season round, but a bottleneck at the top of the table and two blockbuster clashes ensured plenty was at stake in round 22. Canberra headed into the weekend in top spot, but the premiership favourites' title bid was thrown into disarray by a broken leg suffered by star playmaker Ricky Stuart a week earlier in the record 68-0 annihilation of Parramatta. Brisbane, Canterbury and St. George were tied for second, one competition point adrift of the Raiders, while Manly sat a win further back in outright fifth. The Dragons upset the Broncos 16-10 on Friday night in front of a 58,593-strong crowd at Stadium Australia in Brisbane—a record attendance for a regular season match—to temporarily occupy first position on the ladder. The Bulldogs overpowered the rudderless Raiders 32-8 the next day to take out the minor premiership, consigning defending premiers Brisbane to a sudden-death minor preliminary semi-final showdown with the Sea Eagles, who leapfrogged the Broncos into fourth spot on percentages with a comfortable 26-12 victory over Wests. The Bulldogs were subsequently bundled out of the finals courtesy of consecutive losses, while the Broncos became the first club to take out the premiership from fifth on the back of four straight finals victories.

1995 A frenzied grab for post-season berths developed on the eve of the inaugural eight-team finals series in 1995. The top six teams were assured of finals spots heading into the last round, but the seventh and eighth positions were still being hotly contested. St. George and premiership debutants Auckland were locked on 24 competition points, with North Sydney one point off the pace in ninth and the Roosters still in the hunt on 22 points. The Dragons accounted for the Western Reds 36-18 to confirm their place in the finals, while a Jason Taylor sideline conversion in the dying minutes saw the Bears escape with a 14-all draw against cellar-dwellers Gold Coast to slide past the Warriors into eighth on for-and-against. The Warriors' destiny remained in their own hands—but the red-hot Broncos and a packed Stadium Australia stood in their way. Steve Renouf scorched over for four tries as the home side extinguished Auckland's campaign 44-6, leaving the newcomers to rue two competition points stripped for fielding an illegal replacement in a win over Wests early in the season (*see Points Docked*). Norths' scratchy draw also thwarted the Roosters, who cleaned up the Tigers 44-6 but finished in ninth due to the Bears' superior points differential.

1997 The Tom Raudonikis-coached Magpies appeared destined for the ARL's seven-team finals series in 1997, despite heading into the final round in ninth spot on 20 competition points. Illawarra and Gold Coast, drawn to play each other in the last round, were tied on 21 points in sixth-equal on the ladder; eighth-placed Balmain (20 points) faced the daunting task of taking on heavyweights Newcastle, while Wests squared off against wooden spooners South Queensland. The Steelers prevailed 28-6 to leave the Chargers' bid for a maiden finals berth on tenterhooks, before the Tigers bowed out of the race with a 34-10 loss to the Knights. The last place in the finals was there for the Magpies' taking, but the lowly Crushers sprung a Suncorp Stadium upset to streak away 39-18—a record victory in the club's last-ever match, and just its fourth win of the season. The unlikely result gifted Gold Coast seventh spot, and the perennial minnows turned the tables to eliminate Illawarra in the first week of the finals.

2002 The late-season stripping of 37 competition points from runaway NRL leaders the Bulldogs *(see Points Docked)* threw the race for the 2002 minor premiership wide open. Newcastle occupied top spot by one point from Brisbane heading into the final round, with the Warriors a point further back. The Warriors accounted for the Wests Tigers 28-12 to keep their chances of a maiden minor premiership alive, while the Broncos fell 25-18 to the still-brooding Bulldogs to drop to third spot just hours later. The Knights needed to beat eighth-placed St. George Illawarra or lose by less than 10 points to secure first position, but were swamped 40-22 by the desperate Saints at the SFS on the last Sunday of the regular season, handing the minor premiership to the Warriors. The Dragons snatched seventh spot after their upset win and Canberra prevailed 25-16 in an eighth-place shootout with Melbourne. Saints and the Raiders leapfrogged Northern Eagles, who were seventh heading into the weekend before inexplicably crumbling 68-28 to also-rans Penrith.

2007 A finals berth went begging for the Wests Tigers following a last-minute loss to bottom-placed Newcastle in the final round of the 2007 NRL season. The Tigers needed a victory and Brisbane to lose to Parramatta two days later to claim eighth spot. But after leading 12-6 at the break, the Tigers' season finished in gut-wrenching defeat—Knights fullback Kurt Gidley slotted a 30-metre penalty goal in the dying seconds to snatch a 24-22 victory. Newcastle consequently offloaded the wooden spoon to Penrith courtesy of the boilover result. Guaranteed at least eighth spot, the Broncos had the opportunity to climb up to fifth and a likely second life in the finals with a win over the Eels. The defending premiers led 14-6 early, but collapsed in the face of a Jarryd Hayne- and Krisnan Inu-inspired avalanche to go down 68-22, garnering unwanted club records for most points conceded in a match and equal-biggest defeat. Brisbane scraped into eighth ahead of the Tigers on for-and-against, before being despatched from the finals 40-0 by minor premiers Melbourne a week later.

2008 Intriguing struggles developed at both ends of the top-eight as the 2008 regular season reached its climax. Manly, Melbourne and Cronulla entered the final round tied for first spot—the Sea Eagles boasted a +272 points differential, the Storm stood on +264, while the Sharks were well back on +61. Manly took the Sharks—who defeated North Queensland 28-22—out of the equation by comfortably putting away Penrith 34-16 on Saturday night, leaving the fate of the J.J Giltinan Shield in the hands of Melbourne. Needing to win by 27 points to clinch their third consecutive minor premiership, the Storm mauled Souths 42-4 at Olympic Park, taking out top spot. More was at stake lower down the ladder as Newcastle and New Zealand jostled for the last place in the finals. Locked on 28 competition points, the Knights sat in eighth going into the weekend with a 139-point healthier for-and-against than the Warriors. Brisbane did the Warriors a favour by shutting out Newcastle 24-2, and the Auckland-based club capitalised with a 28-6 defeat of Parramatta on the back of a Manu Vatuvei hat-trick. The Warriors subsequently became the first eighth-placed club to beat the minor premiers under the McIntyre system, toppling Melbourne 18-15 *(see Finals Magic)*.

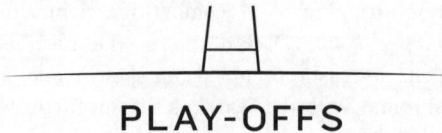

PLAY-OFFS

Points for-and-against are currently used to decide places in the top-eight if two or more teams are tied on the same total of competition points. But prior to 1995, with fewer finals spots up for grabs, a midweek play-off would be staged to break the deadlock.

The first play-off took place in 1911. With the post-season scheduled to consist of only a final between the two top teams, a play-off was required to separate two teams tied for second place—Eastern Suburbs and South Sydney. Easts, captain-coached by the legendary Dally Messenger, defeated Souths 23-10 before downing minor premiers Glebe in the final and the subsequent challenge final (in the days before mandatory Grand Finals, the minor premiers reserved the right to challenge if they lost the final).

The following three play-offs were to decide the minor premiership. Wests beat Easts 7-2 in 1934, Canterbury accounted for Balmain 26-20 in 1942 and Newtown pipped Balmain 11-10 in 1943. All three play-off victors went on to claim that season's premiership.

Balmain (1945 and 1958), Wests (1947 and 1956) and Norths (1952) each advanced to the four-team final series after winning fourth place play-offs, before an extraordinary logjam in 1960 necessitated an elaborate play-off series. Wests, Easts, Balmain and Canterbury all tied for second spot behind runaway minor premiers St. George. In a double-header at the Sydney Sports Ground, Wests defeated Balmain and Easts beat Canterbury. Four days later Wests denied Easts 18-7 in a play-off for second spot, while Canterbury ended Balmain's season with an identical scoreline in a play-off for fourth. Taking advantage of their exhausted opponents, the Dragons hammered Wests 31-7 to advance to the Grand Final, before subjecting the Tricolours to a 31-6 flogging in the decider.

Newtown thrashed Wests 20-5 in the last play-off for fourth place in 1966, before the five-team final series was introduced in 1973. In 1975, Wests, Parramatta and Balmain tied for fifth spot. Parramatta eliminated Wests 18-13 and Balmain 19-8 to snag the last available spot in the finals, and kept the momentum going to beat Canterbury 6-5 before succumbing to Manly in the minor semi. The Magpies were particularly unlucky—earlier in the year they had a competition point deducted for fielding an illegal replacement, which would have been enough to give them fifth place outright (see Points Docked).

After a seven-year break from play-offs for finals spots, a sequence of four seasons requiring a play-off was set in motion. Winger Steve Gearin scored 20 points as St. George pummelled the Roosters 44-16 in the 1983 fifth-place play-off. The Dragons went on to defeat the fourth-placed Tigers in extra-time, before narrowly going down to Canterbury in the minor semi; Souths denied the Raiders a maiden finals appearance in just their third season with a 23-4 defeat in 1984; perennial strugglers Penrith qualified for the club's first post-season with a tense 10-7 victory over Manly after two pressure goals from Greg Alexander in extra-time in 1985; and Balmain bundled Norths out 14-7 in 1986, with Scott Gale's majestic individual try—featuring two kick-and-regathers—proving the difference, before advancing all the way to the preliminary final, where they were beaten by the Bulldogs.

Following a clear-cut final five in 1987, another four-year streak of fifth-place play-offs ensued. Balmain went one better than their 1986 effort as the Ellery Hanley-inspired Tigers thumped Penrith 28-8 in a play-off in 1988. Rival forwards Steve Roach (Balmain) and Matt Goodwin (Penrith) were sent off for head-butting, but it was Roach's high tackle that rubbed Panthers five-eighth Chris Mortimer out of the game that had the most significant ramifications for the Tigers' finals campaign. The Tigers subsequently won sudden-death finals against Manly, Canberra and Cronulla to advance to the Grand Final—a 24-12 defeat, again to Canterbury. The following season, Cronulla quashed the star-studded Broncos' bid for a finals debut with a resounding 38-14 play-off triumph. The match was delicately poised at 14-all early in the second half, before the guile of ball-playing backrower Gavin Miller spearheaded a four-try blitz.

Brisbane qualified for the finals in 1990, but fellow 1988 premiership entrants Newcastle went down in a gallant 12-4 loss to a Wayne Pearce-inspired Balmain in the fifth place play-off at Parramatta Stadium. Plagued by a knee injury, captain Pearce scored a vital try and defended doggedly. The Tigers led by just two points when a late Steve O'Brien intercept try sealed their finals spot. The Knights had pipped the Tigers (who were without the injured Pearce) just two days earlier in the final regular season round to force the midweek showdown. The last play-off occurred in 1991. Wests defeated Canterbury 19-14 in a thrilling grudge match—the Magpies' line-up included four former Bulldogs players and was coached by the Bulldogs' 1984-85 premiership-winning mentor Warren Ryan. Canterbury halfback and 1991 Rothmans Medallist Ewan McGrady inspired a second half comeback, before a late try to Wests winger Wayne Simonds appeared to clinch victory and fifth spot. But Magpies No.7 Jason Taylor's sideline conversion attempt cannoned off the upright to off the Bulldogs a glimmer of hope. After some frantic passing, Canterbury's brilliant Welsh import Jonathan Davies charged into open spaces as the siren sounded, but referee Bill Harrigan controversially blew fulltime as the crowd invaded Parramatta Stadium.

The premiership's expansion and the advent of an eight-team finals series in 1995 saw play-offs abolished in favour of for-and-against differentials to decide any deadlocks. In that first season, a superior for-and-against allowed Norths to grab eighth spot ahead of the Roosters and luckless debutants Auckland (*see Points Docked*). But, incredibly, for-and-against has decided the last place in the finals just once since, with the Broncos edging out Wests Tigers in 2007.

FINALS MAGIC

With the stakes significantly raised at the conclusion of the regular season, teams competing in the finals series have consistently produced matches and moments that are ingrained in the Australian premiership's century-old narrative. The outstanding team and individual performances, and epic contests from the finals are recalled in this chapter.

EASTS THWART DIRTY REDS Foundation club Glebe's best opportunity to win a premiership during its 22-season existence was in 1911. The Dirty Reds claimed their only minor premiership after winning 11 of their 14 regular season matches, and awaited the victor of a second-place play-off between South Sydney and Eastern Suburbs to confront in the final. The Dally Messenger-led Tricolours defeated Souths 23-10 and carried that momentum into the showdown with Glebe, swamping the top-ranked side 22-9. Messenger kicked five goals and winger Eddie White crossed for a double in the four-tries-to-one upset. As minor premiers, Glebe enacted its right to play Easts again in a challenge final to decide the premiership. But Easts was primed for the task, extending its winning streak to seven matches and securing its first premiership with a hard-fought 11-8 victory. Glebe winger Charles Cubitt scored two tries, while brother Les—a future Kangaroo centre/five-eighth and Easts great—kicked a field goal, but Messenger's boot again proved decisive for Easts, landing four goals to complement Charlie Lees' try.

TRICOLOURS PREVAIL IN CLASSIC FINAL The finals were abandoned between 1912 and 1925 in favour of a 'first-past-the-post' system of awarding the premiership to the club that finished the regular season on top of the ladder. But a deadlock between Easts and Souths at the conclusion of the premiership rounds in 1923 necessitated a final to decide Sydney Rugby League supremacy. Champion Souths winger Benny Wearing opened the scoring with an unconverted try, before centre Les Steel crashed over for Easts' first try to level the scores. Wearing nudged Souths two points in front with a penalty, but Easts took a 7-5 lead into halftime on the back of two Arthur Oxford goals. Wearing hared after a kick to claim his second try and converted for a 10-7 advantage, and despite Easts skipper Harry Caples snatching the ascendancy back with a converted try, Wearing squared the ledger with another penalty to set up a grandstand finish. Five-eighth Caples broke the impasse with his second try. Easts defended grimly to hang on for a 15-12 victory and the club's fourth premiership.

TWELVE-MAN RABBITOHS OUTLAST WESTS Minor premiers of 1929 Souths—first grade champions in the previous four seasons—faced a daunting task in the semi-final against third-placed Western Suburbs after winger Alan Righton was sent off just 10 minutes into the Sydney Sports Ground encounter. Wests took immediate advantage of its one-man surplus with tries to prop Frank Spillane and centre Cliff Pearce, but only led 10-8 at the break following a quick-fire double to Rabbitohs three-quarter Oscar Quinlivan. Despite being a player short, Alf 'Smacker' Blair's charges piled on 14 unanswered points in the second half. Souths forward and future Kangaroo Frank O'Connor crossed for two tries, while star winger Benny Wearing also bagged a three-pointer in one the finest wins of the club's spectacular dynasty. The Rabbitohs brushed aside Newtown 30-10 in the final to clinch their fifth straight premiership.

BALMAIN FALLS SHORT DESPITE STIRRING COMEBACK

Emphatic minor premiers after losing just one match during the 1938 regular season, Canterbury-Bankstown was coasting to a comfortable victory over Balmain in the semi-final at the SCG. Canterbury piled on five tries in the first half—including a double to Frank McCormack—before Balmain finally posted its first three-pointer through centre Darcy Kearney just before halftime, trailing 21-7. But the Frank Hyde-led Balmain side launched a valiant comeback in the second half; forwards George Watt and Jimmy Quealey crossed for tries, before Hyde set up Kearney's second with five minutes remaining and Bill Johnson took his match tally to six goals. Canterbury's advantage had been shredded to 28-24, but the minor premiers extinguished brave Balmain's season when halfback Ted Anderson dotted down for his second try of the half. After just four seasons in the competition, Canterbury wrapped up its maiden premiership with a comprehensive 19-6 defeat of Easts in the final two weeks later.

NEWTOWN PUTS ST GEORGE TO THE SWORD IN RECORD WIN

Minor premiers of 1944 Newtown racked up the biggest finals win in premiership history, subjecting St. George to a 55-7 semi-final thrashing at the SCG. Ahead 15-2 at the break, the Bluebags cut loose in the second half to finish 11-tries-to-one victors. Centre pairing Len Smith and Lin McLean crossed for seven tries between them for the defending premiers, with Smith scoring a then-finals record four tries, while fullback Tom Kirk scored 25 points (one try, 11 goals), also a post-season record at the time. The 48-point drubbing ranks as the second-biggest defeat in St. George's proud 78-year history before the club's merger with Illawarra in 1999. Newtown was defeated 12-8 by Balmain in the Grand Final three weeks later.

INNER-CITY RIVALS PRODUCE 13-TRY EPIC Four tries to lock Les 'Chicka' Cowie was not enough to propel South Sydney into the 1956 Grand Final, with Balmain holding on for an incredible 36-33 result in the preliminary final at the SCG. The Rabbitohs led 15-14 at the break and outscored the Tigers seven tries to six, but the boot of Balmain's legendary fullback Keith Barnes was eventually the difference—'Golden Boots' slotted nine goals from 11 attempts. Centre Kevin Mosman scored a hat-trick for the Tigers, who withstood a late fight-back from Souths after leading 36-25 inside the final 10 minutes. Cowie's haul was unmatched by a forward in a finals match for 35 years, while it was the highest-scoring finals match until the Warriors' 48-22 defeat of the Bulldogs in 2003.

LANGLANDS' RECORD HAUL St. George was on its way to a ninth consecutive premiership in 1964 and young fullback Graeme Langlands was beginning to stamp himself as one of the most exhilarating talents in the game. Parramatta represented merely a speed-bump in the major semi for the dominant Dragons, who orchestrated an eight-try, 42-0 demolition at the SCG. Langlands was the chief destroyer, scoring three tries and nine goals for a finals record 27 points—a mark that stood for 41 years.

END OF AN ERA The unthinkable happened in 1967, the first year of the limited tackle-era—St. George's world record run of 11 premierships was broken by Canterbury in the preliminary final. The Berries were competing in their first finals series in seven years, and twice came from behind to record one of the great September victories. The Dragons cruised to a 9-0 lead, but were reeled in and trailed 10-9 at halftime. Saints winger Dennis Preston kicked his fourth goal to snatch back the lead in the second half, but a towering penalty goal from Canterbury second-rower George Taylforth put his side in front 12-11 and the Berries desperately hung on to bring a remarkable era to a close. Canterbury's progression to the club's first Grand Final in two decades was spearheaded by front-row enforcer and captain Kevin Ryan, who had played in the last seven of St. George's premierships.

TIGERS PIP SEA EAGLES AT THE DEATH Balmain's defeat of Souths in 1969 rates as the biggest upset in Grand Final history, but the Tigers required a try in the dying minutes of the preliminary final against Manly just to qualify for the decider. The lead changed hands several times in the preliminary final, with the Sea Eagles leading 14-12 inside the final two minutes. Balmain's English five-eighth Dave Bolton set for a levelling field goal but fumbled the ball, before rookie fullback Bob Smithies fired it wide to his winger George Reubner, who powered through the tackle of Manly custodian Bob Batty to score the match-winner.

REPLAY REQUIRED AFTER ST. GEORGE AND NEWTOWN DRAW

The introduction of a five-team finals series in 1973 provided Rugby League fans with an extra two post-season matches, but they received another bonus in the first year of the new format when Newtown and St. George could not be separated in the minor semi. The Dragons led 12-10 with a minute to play before their second-row Graeme Sams conceded a ruck penalty. Newtown five-eighth John Bonham kicked his third goal of the afternoon as the hooter sounded to send the match into extra-time. The scoreboard remained unchanged at 12-all during the added period and the combatants returned to the SCG two days later. Saints led 5-3 at halftime of the replay on the back of a try to pivot John Peard, but Bluebags halfback Steve Hansard scored his fourth try of the 1973 finals with 25 minutes remaining and Newtown held firm for an 8-5 victory. The battle-weary Bluebags exited the premiership with a gallant 20-11 loss to Cronulla in the preliminary final four days after the replay.

SEA EAGLES' REMARKABLE RUN FULL OF CONTROVERSY

Manly's 1978 finals charge ranks as one of the great team feats in Rugby League history—and one of the most contentious title victories of all time. The Sea Eagles played five games in 17 days and survived two replays to take out the premiership. A 17-12 loss to Cronulla in the major preliminary semi-final pitched the Sea Eagles into a sudden-death battle with archrivals Parramatta a week later. Despite trailing 13-3 with half an hour to play, Manly stormed home to level the scores on the back of a 7-1 second half penalty count against the Eels from referee Greg Hartley. With no extra-time scheduled for drawn results in the 1978 finals, the combatants were forced to return the following Wednesday to replay the match. 'Hollywood' Hartley's performance in the replay would go down in the refereeing hall of infamy. Parramatta led 11-2 when Hartley sent Eels lock Ray Price from the field five minutes before halftime, but Manly's English hooker John Gray followed him 10 minutes after the resumption. With both sides a man short, the Sea Eagles seized control, scoring three tries to advance to the preliminary final with a 17-11 victory.

Parramatta, so incensed at the officiating, attempted to have the result annulled due to several glaring errors by Hartley—Manly half Steve Martin's try came on the seventh tackle and Hartley missed two other seven-tackle counts with the Sea Eagles in possession, while the Eels were subjected to three short counts of five tackles. The Eels' appeal was rejected, and with Hartley again manning the whistle, Manly displayed incredible fortitude to overcome the Magpies 14-7 in the preliminary final. The Sea Eagles' clash with Cronulla in the Grand Final was a dour affair, ending 11-all with just one try scored by each team, necessitating a replay of the decider for the second year in a row—and Manly's second replay in two weeks. Defying their fatiguing fortnight, the Sea Eagles dominated the Sharks in the replay, winning 16-0 to clinch the club's fourth premiership. Much of the post-finals debate focussed on Hartley's role in Manly's winning run (he also controlled the Grand Final and the replay), but even the widespread outcry from rival clubs and fans could not diminish the club's marvellous achievement.

CONTRASTING FORTUNES FOR DRAGONS IN CONSECUTIVE THRILLERS
St. George was involved in two of the most tense finals matches of the 1980s in the space of a week. The Dragons bundled Balmain out of the finals with an extra-time victory in the 1983 minor preliminary semi, coming from 14-6 behind to level the scores after a magnificent team try finished off by Richie Jones and a penalty goal from sharpshooter Steve Gearin. A field goal to first-year rugby union convert Michael O'Connor, and another calmly potted Gearin penalty with two minutes of added time on the clock, sealed an epic 17-14 win.

But Gearin missed a chance to send the showdown with his former club Canterbury into extra-time seven days later. Graeme Wynn scored two tries to help peg the Dragons back to 20-all in a see-sawing battle, but an in-goal error from the towering second-rower allowed the Bulldogs' teenage lock Paul Langmack to score in the 70th minute. Saints winger Steve Morris crossed in the corner with three minutes remaining, but Gearin's conversion attempt was off target and Canterbury advanced to a preliminary final date with the Eels 26-24.

PARRAMATTA GET OUT OF JAIL
One of the strongest challenge to Balmain's 1969 cliff-hanger victory over Manly for the greatest-ever preliminary final escape act came from Parramatta in 1984. Trailing St. George 7-4 inside the final five minutes of a dramatic arm-wrestle, the three-time premiers were hammering the Dragons' line. Referee Kevin Roberts repeatedly blew penalties for the Eels as Saints desperately hung on, stopping halfback Peter Sterling centimetres from the line. But composed backline play from Brett Kenny and Mick Cronin provided Eric Grothe with space on the outside, and the powerhouse winger crashed over in the corner despite Steve Rogers' copybook tackle. The Eels' 8-7 victory propelled them into a fourth consecutive Grand Final.

SOUTHS REEL IN SEA EAGLES TO RECORD FAMOUS WIN
The Rabbitohs staged a stirring comeback to defeat archrivals Manly 22-18 in the 1984 minor preliminary semi-final—Souths' third sudden-death victory in the space of six days. After a final-round win over Norths and a fifth-place play-off defeat of Canberra, the Rabbitohs found themselves on the back foot against the Sea Eagles,

who raced to a 14-0 lead after 15 minutes through tries to Test backs Chris Close and Kerry Boustead. Souths' revival in the fiery clash was largely due to their expert use of the bomb. Second-rower Bill Hardy scored a double and captain and winger Ziggy Niszczot also crossed, with each try coming as a result of a high attacking kick. Souths held off a late rally to eliminate the star-studded Manly side.

FARRAR CLASSIC WINS EXTRA-TIME BEAUTY Balmain transformed from emerging force to genuine contender in 1985—finishing the regular season in second place—and defending premiers Canterbury required every scrap of their grit and guile to subdue the Tigers in the major preliminary semi. The Tigers led 6-0 at halftime courtesy of a try to brilliant Brit Garry Schofield, but the Bulldogs squared the ledger shortly after the break with a superb team try finished off by Terry Lamb. The Canterbury pivot nudged his side in front 8-6 with a 51st-minute penalty goal, before Balmain's former Test winger Ross Conlon sent the match into extra-time with a calmly taken penalty in the last minute of regulation time. But neither combatant was able to capitalise on a myriad of opportunities during a frenetic added period. The match seemed destined for a replay until the 100th minute, when Bulldogs fullback Mick Potter put Andrew Farrar into a hole on the Canterbury side of halfway. The rugged centre shrugged off Conlon and outpaced John Davidson to score in the corner despite the desperate challenge of Tigers fullback Garry Jack. Lamb slotted the sideline conversion after the siren to ice the heart-stopping 14-8 result.

SUDDEN-DEATH SPECIALISTS Balmain's unbeaten run from a fifth-place play-off to the Grand Final in 1988 ranks as one of the greatest achievements of the five-team finals series era. The Tigers prevailed in must-win clashes in the final two rounds against fellow contenders Penrith and Brisbane to qualify for a play-off against the Panthers. Balmain thumped the weary Panthers 28-8 in a spiteful clash at Parramatta Stadium that had significant ramifications for the club's unlikely title quest—Test prop Steve Roach was sent off for an ugly tackle on Chris Mortimer and subsequently suspended for four weeks. Showing no signs of the fatigue incurred from three gruelling matches in eight days, the Tigers disposed of defending premiers Manly 19-6 in the minor preliminary semi-final, with brilliant English import Ellery Hanley scoring two tries.

Hanley was crucial to the Tigers' defeat of Canberra a week later as the black-and-golds teetered along the finals tightrope. Trailing 6-2 at halftime, the Tigers completed a defensive shutout of the dangerous Raiders in the second half and hit the front through a brilliant Hanley try out wide. Kiwi halfback Gary Freeman sealed the 14-6 victory with a try two minutes from fulltime. The Balmain wave then barrelled minor premiers Cronulla in the preliminary final. The Tigers led 3-2 in a try-less opening 70 minutes, before Hanley yet again proved the match-winner by finishing off a superb movement, booking a Grand Final berth with a 9-2 victory.

Balmain's remarkable charge had captured the Rugby League public's imagination, but a fairytale Grand Final win was not in the script. Hanley was knocked out the first half of the decider by a controversial Terry Lamb tackle. Despite Balmain hooker Ben Elias scoring the opening try, the Bulldogs outlasted the Tigers 24-12.

BRANDY INSPIRES PANTHERS TO MAIDEN GRAND FINAL

Maligned earlier in his career for failing to take control in big games, the greatest Panther Greg Alexander truly came of age in the 1990 major semi against Canberra. Despite upsetting the Broncos a week earlier to record the club's first win in a finals match, Penrith went into its clash with the defending premiers as distinct underdogs, but prevailed 30-12 after an extra-time blitz. Alexander combined brilliantly with teenage centre Brad Fittler to score in the first half and kicked a pressure penalty goal near the end of regulation time to send the match into an extra 20 minutes at 12-all. 'Brandy' scored a sneaky dummy-half try in extra-time, before Fittler wrapped up a historic Grand Final berth by breaking the tiring Canberra defence to score. Alexander's haul of 22 points (from two tries and seven goals) was the highest individual tally in a finals match in 26 years.

CANBERRA AND MANLY PRODUCE MATCH FOR THE AGES

Two wounded teams produced one of the all time great finals matches in the 1991 minor semi-final. Manly, coming off a loss to Norths a week earlier, was missing internationals Michael O'Connor, Des Hasler, Tony Iro and Ian Roberts through injury, while several of 1989-90 premiers Canberra's stars were carrying injuries. The Sea Eagles' problems were compounded when they lost Geoff Toovey with an eye injury early in the first half and Test prop Martin Bella finally succumbed to a hip problem at halftime. Undeterred, the combatants turned on 80 minutes of attacking mastery. Canberra gained the early ascendancy with a try to Gary Belcher and a first-half double to second-row workhorse Gary Coyne. But Manly responded with a try to Kevin Iro, before Iro combined brilliantly with Cliff Lyons to send winger Frank Stokes away for a long-range try. The Raiders appeared to have a preliminary final berth wrapped up at 28-14 when Mark Bell scored a thrilling 80-metre try from a scrum win and Coyne crashed over for his third touchdown, but the battered Sea Eagles refused to concede defeat. Darrell Williams handled twice in conjunction with David Ronson to put Owen Cunningham in the clear for a sensational try, before Iro grabbed his second to reduce the deficit to two points with 10 minutes on the clock. The epic struggle was settled inside the final five minutes when the Raiders, with Bell in the sin-bin, took a quick tap from a penalty and caught Manly's weary defence napping. Coyne crashed over for another try—the first time a forward had scored four in a finals match since Souths' Les Cowie in 1956—and placed the match out of reach at 34-26. It was a cruel way for the season to end for emotional coach Graham Lowe's courageous Sea Eagles, who would have taken little comfort from the fact they had participated in one of Australian Rugby League's finest contests.

STEEL CITY TEAMS WIN ON FINALS DEBUT
The Knights and Steelers each qualified for their first finals series respectively in 1992 and posted their maiden post-season victories on the same weekend. Illawarra upset 'big brother' St. George 18-16 at the SFS, with young home-grown stars Paul McGregor, Brett Rodwell and John Simon starring. A day later at the same venue, the Newcastle knocked Wests out the premiership race with a 21-2 thumping, highlighted by a brilliant Robbie O'Davis double. Both sides were eventually bundled out of the premiership race in dour losses to the Dragons.

BRONCOS FIRST TO WIN FROM FIFTH The Broncos were runaway minor premiers on the way to winning their maiden title in 1992, but were engaged in a much tighter finals race the following season. A last-round loss to St. George saw the Broncos slide to fifth place, instead of a second-place finish and an all-important second life. But the Broncos made history during a memorable charge in which they became the first team to win the premiership from fifth spot. After ruthlessly despatching Manly 36-10 and Canberra 30-12, Brisbane took on minor premiers Canterbury in a classic preliminary final. The Broncos grabbed an early lead through tries to Steve Renouf and Michael Hancock, but trailed 16-10 at halftime as skipper Terry Lamb's brilliance swung the momentum the way of the Bulldogs. Kerrod Walters sent captain Allan Langer over for the equalising try in the second stanza, before Langer calmly potted a field goal to snatch the lead. A rampaging solo try to nuggetty second-rower Alan Cann sealed the 23-16 win and another Grand Final berth for the Broncos. Brisbane beat a confident St. George side in the decider for the second year in a row, taking out the 1993 Winfield Cup with a dour 14-6 victory.

WHAT A WEEKEND! North Sydney and Brisbane played out a gripping minor semi-final at the SFS in 1994, only for Canterbury and Canberra to trump it with an extra-time thriller in the major semi 24 hours later at the same venue. The Bears led hot favourites Brisbane 14-4 midway through the first half after a barrage of tries down Michael Hancock's wing, but a double to youngster Wendell Sailor and a try to five-eighth Kevin Walters brought the defending premiers back to level shortly after halftime. The Broncos dominated much of the second half but ignored a myriad of deadlock-breaking field goal opportunities. Norths capitalised during a rare foray into Brisbane's half—sharpshooter No.7 Jason Taylor drilled a 30-metre field goal down the middle with five minutes remaining. Desperate attempts by the two-time premiers to save their season in the dying stages came up empty, with Norths holding on for a famous 15-14 victory.

The following day, Canterbury took an early 6-0 lead after a terrible mistake from Canberra winger Noa Nadruku presented a try to Jarrod McCracken inside two minutes. But the Raiders hit back with a breathtaking try to Brett Mullins from a perfectly executed scrum move. A brilliant offload from Bulldogs second-rower Jason Smith sent winger Jason Williams over in the corner, before Mal Meninga stormed over for a try for Canberra, reducing the halftime deficit to 14-12. The Bulldogs led 18-12 for most of the second half after a Steven Hughes try, but a break by David Furner inside the final minute saw interchange forward David Westley score under the posts for the Raiders to send the match into extra-time. A frantic 20 minutes of added time ensued, until Williams unleashed a giant step to evade opposing winger Ken Nagas and race 50 metres up the sideline. Two plays later, fellow Kiwi flanker Daryl Halligan potted a field goal from close range with two and a half minutes remaining to book Canterbury's spot in the Grand Final 19-18.

BESIEGED BULLDOGS COME FROM THE CLOUDS The year 1995 was set to go down in history as the most tumultuous season in Canterbury's 60-year history, but instead played witness to one of the club's greatest triumphs. The Bulldogs sided with Super League—as did most of their players—but Jim Dymock, Jason Smith, Dean Pay and Jarrod McCracken reneged on their contracts with the rebel outfit, causing great consternation within the club. The Bulldogs—minor premiers in the previous two seasons—finished sixth after a patchy regular season, but advanced to the second week of the finals with a gripping 12-8 victory over St. George in the wet at the SFS. The Bulldogs booked a preliminary final showdown with the Raiders by trouncing heavyweights Brisbane 24-10. Canberra, the defending premiers, had lost just twice all season, but could not halt the Bulldogs' momentum in a 25-6 boilover. The rain fell in Sydney again, but the Bulldogs were in sparkling touch, with veterans Terry Lamb and Simon Gillies leading the charge. 1995 heralded the inaugural eight-team finals series and many experts predicted it would be impossible to win the premiership from outside the top-four. But the Bulldogs put paid to that theory by downing red-hot favourites Manly 17-4 in the Grand Final, capping a finals campaign that ranks among the most remarkable in the game's history.

DRAGONS CHARGE TO UNLIKELY GRAND FINAL BERTH

With a squad decimated by the Super League upheaval and a new coach, St. George started 1996 as rank outsiders for the title. The Dragons were struggling in 13th place after 12 rounds, but lost just one of their last 10 matches to qualify for the finals in sixth spot. Wayne Bartrim was the hero of the Saints' quarter-final defeat of Canberra. After scoring a scintillating 50-metre individual try in the first half, Bartrim converted Mark Bell's late try with a booming sideline kick for a 16-14 victory. A relentless air-raid formed the basis of a stunning 36-16 defeat of favourites Sydney City in the semi-final a week later. Kicks led to all but one of the Dragons' six tries, with wingers Bell and Adrian Brunker collecting two tries apiece. St. George went into the preliminary final against Norths as clear-cut underdogs, but brilliant pivot Anthony Mundine was untouchable in a shock 29-12 result. Saints led just 7-6 at halftime, but a four-try second half blitz—including a blistering 60-metre try to Mundine and yet another four-pointer to Bell—booked the club its third Grand Final in five seasons. The sentimental favourites could not match Manly in the decider, going down 20-8 to the dominant minor premiers, but the Dragons' memorable stampede through the finals was one of the highlights of 1996.

BACK-TO-BACK EXTRA-TIME CLASSICS MARK ANOTHER CANTERBURY CHARGE

Channelling the club's 1995 breed, the Bulldogs embarked on another incredible finals charge in 1998. The club scraped into the 10-team finals series in ninth spot after winning its last four games in the NRL's inaugural season and, in a repeat of 1995, advanced past the first week of the finals with a tight and controversial 20-12 victory over the Dragons. The Bulldogs pegged back an early 12-0 deficit with contentious tries to Daryl Halligan and Rod Silva, before Saints forward Jeff Hardy had a second half try denied by the video referee. A 23-2 shutout of Norths a week later saw Canterbury progress to an ominous assignment against Newcastle, and at 16-0 down in the first half, the Bulldogs' season was on the ropes. But in a stirring fightback, the Bulldogs levelled the scores with 10 minutes remaining when the Hughes brothers, Glen and Corey, combined for the latter to score. Canterbury almost snatched victory on fulltime, but warhorse Tony Grimaldi lost the ball over the tryline. The Bulldogs had built unstoppable momentum, however, and launched themselves into a preliminary final showdown against archrivals with two extra-time tries.

Canterbury's predicament was even more dire the following Sunday against the Eels—18-2 behind with 11 minutes to go—before staging arguably the greatest finals comeback of all time. Halfback Craig Polla-Mounter scored in the 70th minute to give the Bulldogs a glimmer of hope. They closed to within six points shortly afterwards when second-rower Robert Relf slipped a magical ball to facilitate Rod Silva's thrilling 50-metre dash to the line, followed by a booming Daryl Halligan conversion. Fullback Silva's guile gave Kiwi centre Willie Talau enough room to crash over in the corner with three minutes to go and Halligan stepped up to kick a famous goal from the sideline and level the scores at 18-all. Incredibly, enigmatic Eels fullback Paul Carige provided the Bulldogs with a chance to win the game on fulltime when he kicked from deep inside his own territory as the siren sounded, and Polla-Mounter launched a towering field goal attempt from halfway. The kick fell under the crossbar by a mere few inches, requiring video replays to confirm whether it had missed. The rattled Eels had no answer for a swarming Bulldogs outfit in extra-time. Polla-Mounter kicked two field goals and scored his second try, before Travis Norton ploughed over to seal a phenomenal 32-20 result and a Grand Final berth. Canterbury's dramatic winning streak ended in the decider despite leading 12-10 at halftime, going down to the rampant Broncos 38-12.

INFANT STORM WALK THE FINALS TIGHTROPE Melbourne's epic Grand Final victory over the Dragons in just its second season is one of the finest club achievements in Rugby League history. But the Storm's nerve-wracking road to the 1999 decider is often overlooked. After finishing the regular season in third spot, Melbourne were humbled 34-10 in the qualifying final by the sixth-placed Dragons at Olympic Park. But the Storm resuscitated their premiership dream with a heart-stopping 24-22 victory over the Bulldogs. The lead changed hands several times in a fluctuating contest; Melbourne came from behind to establish an 18-12 halftime lead, before Canterbury hit back with consecutive tries to lead 22-18. A misdirected kick from Bulldogs halfback Ricky Stuart proved decisive as Matt Geyer, who had been switched to the unfamiliar position of five-eighth, fielded the ball and raced 80 metres for the match-winning try. Melbourne's effort the following weekend demonstrated even greater portions of grit and poise after trailing Parramatta 16-6 at halftime of the preliminary final. Clawing their way back with tries to Aaron Moule and Richard Swain from Brett Kimmorley kicks, the Storm clung to an 18-16 lead for the final 16 minutes to reach the Grand Final. Melbourne famously overhauled a 14-0 halftime deficit in a rematch with the Dragons in the decider, winning the premiership 20-18 after a late penalty try.

MUNDINE MAGIC FOILS SHARKS The year 1999 shaped as the season Cronulla finally broke through for the club's maiden premiership after 32 fruitless attempts. The minor premiers had defeated defending champs Brisbane 42-20 in the qualifying final to earn a week off and confidently awaited the victor of St. George Illawarra's clash with the Roosters. The Dragons prevailed 28-18, but entered the preliminary final as underdogs. It appeared to be the Sharks' day when they scored the only try of a dour first half—through David Peachey from a Nathan Blacklock error—to lead 8-0 at the break. But Dragons five-eighth Anthony Mundine threw the script out the window, scoring a second half hat-trick that oozed individual brilliance. He climbed over Peachey to take a high ball for one try, but his third touchdown—featuring a devastating step and a thrilling 30-metre dash to the corner—sealed a spot in the Grand Final 24-8 and saw Mundine and Blacklock unleash a somersault show in front of the adoring Dragons Army.

DE JA COCK-A-DOODLE VU FOR KNIGHTS Andrew Johns' Newcastle side built up sizeable leads against the Roosters during the 1998 and 2000 finals, only to be run down by the Brad Fittler-inspired Tricolours on both occasions. The Knights had earned a break for the first weekend of the 1998 NRL finals after finishing in second spot, waiting for the Roosters to win their way through to a Marathon Stadium showdown a week later. The energised home side leapt out to a 15-0 halftime lead with three tries. But a second half blitz stunned the parochial crowd as an endless procession of Roosters ran in tries—six in total. The Roosters advanced to the preliminary final with the 26-15 victory, while the Knights' season ended a week later with an extra-time loss to the Bulldogs.

The story was eerily similar in the 2000 preliminary final—the Knights raced away to a 16-2 halftime lead, with Andrew Johns scoring a try and setting up two more. But a five-minute three-try spree by the Roosters—including an intercept try to Fittler from a Johns pass—had Newcastle reeling at 20-16 down. A Shannon Hegarty try extended the lead to 10 points before Timana Tahu struck back for the Knights to peg the score back to 26-20. But the Knights' last-ditch drives at the Roosters' line were thwarted by magnificent defence, and the Novocastrians were left to lament another lost opportunity as they farewelled club greats Matthew Johns and Tony Butterfield.

BABY EELS KNOCK ROOSTERS OFF PERCH Parramatta, one of the youngest first grade sides ever to appear in finals football, defied experience, reputation and table position to upset the highly fancied Roosters at the qualifying final stage of 2000 post-season. With the seventh-placed Eels averaging just 21 years of age, it was NRL novices Pat Richards, Jamie Lyon, Dennis Moran and PJ Marsh that starred in a 32-8 upset. The star-studded Roosters, containing superstar captain Brad Fittler and nine current or future internationals, led 8-0 in the first half and trailed by only two at halftime. But a gaffe from fullback Luke Phillips *(see Minties Moments)* led to an opportunist try to Parramatta's young Kiwi centre David Vaealiki just after the break, handing the Eels a 16-8 lead. The Parramatta pack cramped the Roosters' attacking armoury and laid the platform for further tries to Moran and Richards, completing the memorable rout.

2002 PRELIMINARY FINALS The penultimate weekend of the 2002 NRL season produced two classic preliminary final battles. On Saturday night, perennial heavyweights the Broncos were pipped 16-12 by the in-form Roosters, who entered the game on a seven-week winning streak. The Roosters leapt out to an 8-0 advantage early on, with winger Anthony Minichiello scoring from a scrum move and Craig Fitzgibbon adding two goals. But a long-range try to Brent Tate and an individual effort from fullback Darren Lockyer saw Brisbane head for the sheds at halftime with a 12-8 lead in their keeping. Proving Rugby League is often a cruel game, an error from retiring Broncos legend Allan Langer ultimately proved the difference. Langer's wayward pass in the 51st minute was scooped up by Roosters winger Brett Mullins, who raced 50 metres to score. Another Fitzgibbon penalty soon after completed the scoring, but the Roosters had to survive a nerve-tingling final quarter to maintain their lead and advance to the Grand Final.

The Warriors made history the following afternoon by qualifying for their maiden Grand Final with a thrilling 16-10 defeat of the Sharks. Backed by a large contingent of Kiwi fans amongst the 45,702-strong crowd at Telstra Stadium (after club owners gave away thousands of tickets to any supporters that held a New Zealand passport) the Warriors skipped to a 6-0 lead through an opportunist try to Motu Tony. The Sharks struck back just after halftime with a try to Matthew Rieck, but the minor premiers refused to wilt. Young centre Clinton Toopi showcased his burgeoning talent to score a brilliant try for a 10-4 scoreline, before Sharks linchpin Brett Kimmorley levelled the scores heading into the final quarter with an individual try of his own. A closing 20 minutes equally as tense as the previous night's ensued, and the deadlock was not broken until the 76th minute, when No.7 maestro Stacey Jones threaded through a beautiful grubber for John Carlaw to score a history-making try.

MELI'S HANDFUL IN WARRIOR AMBUSH The sixth-placed Warriors were clear-cut underdogs going into their qualifying final showdown with the Bulldogs, who finished the regular season third, at the Sydney Showground. But New Zealand produced one of the most devastating finals performances of the modern era, defeating the highly fancied Bulldogs 48-22. The Warriors led 16-4 at halftime and were at their razzle-dazzle best after the break, piling on another six tries. Fullback Brent Webb, who racked up a personal tally of 18 points (two tries, five goals), centre Clinton Toopi and halfback Stacey Jones cut the dazed Bulldogs to ribbons, but Francis Meli was the main beneficiary—the powerhouse winger scored a finals record five tries in the drubbing.

DEFENDING PREMIERS HOLD OFF FAST-FINISHING DRAGONS The Panthers appeared to have wrapped up the fourth v fifth qualifying final inside the opening quarter when they opened up a 24-0 lead over the Dragons, with halfback Craig Gower and backrower Trent Waterhouse terrorising the Saints' defence. Gower laid on two tries for Waterhouse in the first six minutes, before the Test pair combined to put Preston Campbell over for a try. The Dragons rallied to post two tries for a 24-12 halftime scoreline, but Campbell's second try, a 90-metre intercept effort right after the break, halted the visitors' comeback momentarily. St. George Illawarra refused to submit, however, reducing the deficit to six points with tries to backrowers Shaun Timmins and Lance Thompson. But a Gower field goal put the result beyond doubt for the 2003 champs, despite a converted try to Saints second-rower Dean Young in the dying minutes. The final score: Penrith 31 St. George Illawarra 30.

COWBOYS RIDE HIGH IN DEBUT FINALS SERIES Qualifying for the first finals series in club history in their 10th season was a monumental achievement for perennial cellar-dwellers North Queensland. But the NRL's northern-most team captured the imagination of the Rugby League public with two king-sized upsets during the 2004 finals, before narrowly bowing out at the preliminary final stage.

After finishing seventh in the regular season, North Queensland was odds-on to be eliminated by the powerful second-placed Bulldogs. But the Cowboys shocked the Dogs, racing to a 26-6 lead midway through the second half. The Bulldogs fired back with three tries to set up a nail-biting finish, until Cowboys winger Matt Sing scored from a spectacular leap—his third try for the match—to seal a 30-22 boilover. The Cowboys' match the following week, against 'big brother' Brisbane, was scheduled for Sydney, but the Broncos graciously volunteered for the match to be relocated to Townsville. North Queensland ground out a tense 10-0 shutout of the star-studded Broncos in front of a 24,989-strong home crowd, who created an electrifying atmosphere from start to finish. The Cowboys' triumph brought to an end the career of Townsville-bred Broncos great Gorden Tallis. North Queensland's dauntless finals run was halted in a gripping 19-16 loss to heavyweights the Sydney Roosters in the preliminary final. The sentimental favourites scored three tries to two and the scores were level with a quarter of the match remaining, but the relieved Roosters managed a penalty and a field goal to qualify for their third decider in a row.

TIGERS AND BRONCOS AWESOME IN RECORD VICTORIES

The Wests Tigers and Brisbane, premiers in 2005 and 2006 respectively, both recorded 50-6 finals victories on their way to Grand Final glory. The fourth-placed Tigers dismantled the Cowboys, who finished fifth, in devastating fashion at Telstra Stadium. Ahead only 14-6 at halftime, the Tigers piled on six unanswered tries after the break. Fullback Brett Hodgson was the chief beneficiary, scoring a finals record 30 points from three tries and nine goals amidst a complete team performance. Incredibly, the Cowboys rallied to qualify for the Grand Final three weeks later, where the Tigers prevailed with a harder-fought 30-16 result.

The Broncos were staring down the barrel of a straight-sets exit from the finals for the third season in a row in 2006 after going down to the Dragons in the qualifying final. But with captain Darren Lockyer at his talismanic best, Brisbane responded with a merciless eight-try demolition of Newcastle at the SFS. The Knights missed suspended star hooker Danny Buderus and injured forward Steve Simpson, but it is doubtful the Test duo's presence could have altered the result, such was the comprehensive nature of the Broncos' performance. The eventual premiers scorched to a 50-0 lead and were on track to for the biggest finals win of all time, until fullback Kurt Gidley put the Knights on the board with a try two minutes from fulltime.

BRONCOS' COMEBACK STUNS BULLDOGS Brisbane's 2006 finals campaign was on tenterhooks at halftime of its preliminary final showdown with the Bulldogs, down 20-6 at the break after conceding three first half tries. But the Broncos produced one of the greatest second half performances in finals history to book a spot in the Grand Final and leave the shell-shocked Bulldogs reeling. The onslaught began when stand-in fullback Justin Hodges carried the ball off his own line and embarked on a sizzling 40-metre run. He found the support of hooker Shaun Berrigan, who sprinted all the way to the corner, expertly planting the ball despite the desperate attention of Bulldogs giant Willie Mason. A determined try to Dane Carlaw and brilliant support play resulting in a four-pointer to Darius Boyd saw the Broncos hit the lead 22-20 with a quarter of the match remaining. Skipper Darren Lockyer characteristically took control from that point, combining with

Tonie Carroll to score a try that covered 50 metres, before setting up Brent Tate for a touchdown, and finally slotting a field goal to wrap the game up at 33-20. Corey Parker completed the 31-0 second half rout with a last-minute try, icing one of the most spectacular fight-backs ever seen in September football.

WARRIORS CREATE HISTORY WITH SHOCK WIN In 2008, New Zealand became the first eighth-placed club to beat the minor premiers at the qualifying final stage since the introduction of the controversial McIntyre System nine years earlier. The Warriors won eight of their last 10 regular season matches to scrape into the last finals spot, but rolled defending champs Melbourne with a sensational long-range try in the dying moments. The Storm had only been defeated once in all games at Olympic Park since the Warriors scored an upset win there in 2006, and scored the first try through Origin winger Anthony Quinn. But the Warriors hung tough for Jerome Ropati to plunge over for their first four-pointer just before halftime. Michael Witt's sideline conversion levelled the scores at 8-all. The visitors took the lead when man-mountain winger Manu Vatuvei latched onto a Grant Rovelli grubber, but the scoreboard was locked up after a powerful try to Israel Folau and a penalty goal from skipper Cameron Smith. The Warriors' plucky bid for finals survival was on life support when Greg Inglis nailed a field goal in the 68th minute, but a last-ditch attacking raid by the underdogs instantaneously turned the finals series on its head. Ropati stood up Folau on the Warriors' 30-metre line and slipped a wonderful offload to Vatuvei. Big Manu stepped inside Cooper Cronk and powered up the sideline and, despite being ankle-tapped by countryman Jeremy Smith, threaded a brilliant one-hander between Storm defenders Billy Slater and Scott Anderson to send Witt on a 20-metre run to the corner, sealing a miraculous 18-15 victory. Witt gave coach Ivan Cleary and Warriors fans palpitations by bizarrely holding up the ball in celebration before dotting down, only just avoiding the lunging foot of Melbourne captain Smith.

INGLIS BREAKS BRONCOS HEARTS IN DRAMA-CHARGED EPIC Melbourne kept its premiership defence alive a week later with an equally heart-stopping last-minute victory in one of the modern era's most gripping finals matches. The scene was already set for a classic showdown with Brisbane, with the bitter rivalry between the two clubs to be played out in front of 50,000-plus fans at Suncorp Stadium in potentially Wayne Bennett's final game in charge of the Broncos. The Broncos were also under siege after three of their rep stars became embroiled in a public furore surrounding an alleged sexual assault just days earlier. But the home side showed no signs of their torrid build-up by powering to a 12-0 halftime lead over the favourites. The three players at the centre of the allegations—Karmichael Hunt, Sam Thaiday and Darius Boyd—combined to open the scoring, with Boyd finishing off some superb lead-up work, before fellow winger Denan Kemp scored Brisbane's second try after a brilliant team movement.

Melbourne was on the board after halftime when Israel Folau—bound for the Broncos in 2009—set Michael Crocker up for a try, but tempers frayed soon after, when Cameron Smith and Jeremy Smith enacted an ugly grapple tackle on Thaiday. The pair subsequently received two and one match bans respectively, while Storm prop Jeff Lima was sin-binned two minutes later for a late challenge on Michael

Ennis, allowing Corey Parker to boot the Broncos to a 14-6 lead. Boyd was denied a second try by the video referee, and when Billy Slater scored next to the posts, the deficit was cut to two points. The Broncos appeared to have wrapped up a famous upset in the dying minutes when prop Ben Hannant crashed over, invoking a rare display of emotion from the usually stony-faced Bennett, but the video referee ruled Hannant was held up. With a minute and a half to play and the home side working the ball out of their own territory, a crunching tackle by Storm forward Sika Manu on Broncos counterpart Ashton Sims jolted the ball free. Melbourne utilised a blindside overlap in the ensuing possession and Greg Inglis, who was earlier denied a freakish try by the video ref, crossed in the corner to steal the match 16-14. Brisbane captain Darren Lockyer's anguished scream while standing among his devastated troops was one of the year's most poignant images.

TITANS FALL TO 'BIG BROTHER' IN FINALS TRY-FEST The Southeast Queensland derby that had flourished since the Titans' 2007 arrival in the NRL was thrust onto the finals stage in 2009. Third-placed Gold Coast hosted Brisbane, who finished sixth, in its finals debut and opened the scoring in front of 27,227 fans with a try to Preston Campbell. The Broncos snatched the lead with tries to Andrew McCullough and Israel Folau, before the Titans narrowed the margin to 12-10 through winger David Mead. But the visitors skipped to an 18-point halftime lead courtesy of Folau's second touchdown and further tries to rookie Jharal Yow Yeh and skipper Darren Lockyer. Far from being overawed by the enormous task that confronted them, the Titans exploded with the first three tries of the second stanza— two of them to lightning-quick winger Kevin Gordon. The second of rookie Gordon's tries was a thrilling 95-metre intercept effort that pegged the score back to 28-26 in favour of the Broncos. But Folau plucked an intercept of his own to complete his hat-trick and temporarily dampen the spirits of the frenzied pro-Titans crowd. Mead's second try, from a Scott Prince kick, again cut the deficit to two points. Brisbane finally put away the plucky finals newcomers five minutes from fulltime when giant forward Dave Taylor intercepted a Prince pass and charged 30 metres to score. The 40-32 result represented the highest-scoring finals match of all time, while the Titans' total was second only to Souths' 33 points against Balmain in 1956 as the most points scored by a losing side in a final.

EELS RIDE HAYNE BRILLIANCE TO GRAND FINAL Parramatta's incredible charge to the Grand Final was the story of 2009. Sitting in 14th place after round 18, the Eels pieced together a seven-match winning streak to scrape into eighth spot, largely on the back of the awesome form of fullback and Dally M Player of the Year Jarryd Hayne. The blue-and-golds' winning run was snapped 37-0 by minor premiers St. George Illawarra in the final round, setting up a rematch with the Dragons at WIN Jubilee Oval in the first week of the finals. The Eels scored the first two tries of the qualifying final, building a 12-8 halftime lead over the nervous Saints, before winger Eric Grothe scored to extend the visitors' lead to 10 points. Grothe's opposite number Brett Morris pegged it back to 18-12 with a 71st-minute try, but a booming 43-metre field goal to Luke Burt put the result beyond doubt. The coup de grace was provided by Hayne with three minutes to go. The explosive No.1 received the ball 20 metres out from the Dragons line and beat eight defenders with a combination of footwork and power to score one of the great individual finals tries.

The Eels breezed through to the preliminary final with a commanding 27-2 defeat of the Titans at the SFS, booking a date with archrivals the Bulldogs. The bumper crowd of 74,549 was a finals record for a non-Grand Final, and it was the Bulldogs who gave their fans reason to cheer first after Bryson Goodwin scored a wonderful try in the corner from a Hazem El Masri kick after just four minutes. A potential eight-point try was awarded after Hayne dived in with his knees in an attempt to prevent the try, connecting with Goodwin's head and leaving the winger unconscious. Hayne rallied to kick a crucial 40-20 and set up Joe Galuvao for the Eels' first try, but was bamboozled by a Ben Roberts grubber later in the half and Josh Morris pounced to give the Bulldogs a 12-6 halftime lead. But two months of virtual sudden-death football held Parramatta in good stead during a torrid second stanza. Luke Burt's 100th NRL try and Tim Mannah's first presented the Eels with their first lead, and a sizzling team try finished off by rookie half Daniel Mortimer cemented a Grand Final berth 22-12. The match was widely heralded as one of the great finals encounters. But the Eels' charmed run finished in heartbreak—a gallant 23-16 loss to Melbourne in the decider.

ROOSTERS PIP TIGERS IN GOLDEN POINT MASTERPIECE

In a match that earns the author's vote for the best match of the last 20 years, the Sydney Roosters staged a remarkable comeback at the SFS to force the Wests Tigers into the first-ever golden point finals match. Todd Carney opened the scoring for the Roosters with a penalty goal, but it was the Tigers who were on the front foot during the first half. Five-eighth magician Benji Marshall set up tries for wingers Lote Tuqiri and Beau Ryan, but earlier cost his side a four-pointer when he was involved in a punch-up with Roosters halfback Mitchell Pearce after playing the ball. The Tigers' British second-rower Gareth Ellis latched onto a kick to dot down while the melee unfolded, but the video referee ruled no-try and a penalty against Marshall. It was the third time in the first 10 minutes Ellis was denied a try—he earlier had it knocked from his grasp by Carney as he was about to score, and then was held up over the tryline in the space of two minutes.

But the Tigers were in control 10-2 at halftime, and extended their lead after the break when young centre Blake Ayshford snatched an intercept and scored after a thrilling 70-metre run to the line, despite a valiant Carney chase. A coolly taken field goal by captain Robbie Farah stretched the lead beyond two converted tries in the 54th minute. But Carney, perhaps tired of being upstaged by his opposite number Marshall, produced the Roosters' first try six minutes later with a terrific chip-and-regather before sending his skipper Braith Anasta over. Crowned 2010's Dally medallist earlier in the week, Carney then made a searing break on halfway and positioned Pearce beautifully to score under the posts, slicing the margin to one point with six minutes on the clock. Meanwhile, Marshall left the field nursing a knee injury. The sixth-placed Roosters forced a dropout inside the final two minutes, knowing that a loss could mean an early finals exit if other results went against them.

Despite the high-octane nature of the match to this point, the weary combatants conjured more drama and excitement in the final passage than most games produce in 80 minutes. The Tigers looked to be home when backrower Simon Dwyer reeled off one of the biggest hits seen in decades to force the ball loose from giant young Kiwi forward Jared Warea-Hargreaves with less than 60 seconds remaining. But, unbelievably, with the Tigers just needing to win the scrum and ruck the ball out for victory, the Roosters came up with a controversial win against the feed. The Roosters appeared to abandon the opportunity to attempt a levelling field goal by spreading the ball wide but, after some frantic passing, Anthony Minichiello found Anasta, who drilled a one-pointer from out wide and beyond the 30-metre line as the siren sounded.

Both sides missed field goal attempts in a frenetic golden point period, but the deadlock was finally broken in the 100th minute of the match when Shaun Kenny-Dowall intercepted a Liam Fulton pass on the Roosters' 40-metre line. The much-improved Kiwi centre evaded several tired Tigers defenders and outpaced Lote Tuqiri in an exhilarating sprint to the corner. It was regrettable that a team had to finish as losers after such an epic contest, but the Tigers could only take solace from the fact they had fought gallantly in one of the best games of Rugby League ever played.

LOCKY'S LAST STAND Darren Lockyer's final game at Suncorp Stadium attracted a 48,474-strong crowd for the Broncos' sudden-death semi-final showdown with the Dragons in 2011. In a further twist, the match doubled as potentially former Brisbane mentor Wayne Bennett's last game in charge of St. George Illawarra. The hosts dominated the first half, but could only muster a 6-0 lead at the break through a Ben Te'o try. Brisbane backrower Corey Parker slotted a penalty goal early in the second stanza before Saints landed on the scoreboard with a try to interchange forward Adam Cuthbertson. Rookie winger Dale Copley restored the Broncos' six-point advantage with a try in the corner, but a Jamie Soward bomb turned the final on its head. Broncos fullback Gerard Beale leapt to mark the ball and his knee collided with Lockyer's face. The skipper sat dazed on the hallowed turf for an extended period before re-entering the fray with what was later revealed to be a fractured cheekbone. The Dragons sent the match into golden point with a 77th-minute try to Darius Boyd and a magnificent pressure conversion from out wide by Soward. But Soward's fourth-tackle kick in the Dragons' first possession of the extra period proved fatal for their season. Brisbane returned the ball in handy field position and a clearly inconvenienced Lockyer stepped up to slot the winning field goal with little room to move. It was a phenomenal final performance by Lockyer on his home ground, and his field goal proved to be his last act in a Broncos jersey. The nature of Lockyer's injury dictated he could not fly via aeroplane to Sydney, so he was flown south by a helicopter at low altitude. But it was to no avail as he was forced to make the agonising decision to pull out of the preliminary final and hope the Broncos won through to the Grand Final. The under-strength Brisbane side was courageous in going down 26-14 to eventual premiers Manly.

WARRIORS JUGGERNAUT RECOVERS FROM WEEK ONE THRASHING The Warriors were staring done the barrel of a straight-sets exit from the 2011 finals after a dismal 40-10 qualifying final loss to the Broncos. Entering the post-season with seven wins from their last nine games, the Warriors dropped their bundle in the Suncorp Stadium debacle, highlighted by strike winger Manu Vatuvei's error-riddled performance. The Auckland-based club was expected to be semi-final cannon-fodder for Wests Tigers—who were riding high on a nine-match winning streak—and accordingly, Tim Sheens' charges shot out to a 12-0 lead. A sizzling dummy-half run and breathtaking offload from fullback Kevin Locke sent James Maloney over for the Warriors' first try, before the Tigers established an 18-6 halftime lead with a soft try to skipper Robbie Farah.

But Ivan Cleary's men returned to the field with a steely resolve that would carry them through their next 120 minutes of football. Rookie halfback Shaun Johnson put Feleti Mateo over eight minutes into the second half with a wonderfully disguised short ball, and Lance Hohaia scampered over from dummy-half to slash the deficit to two points with 15 minutes remaining. The Warriors snatched an improbable victory with an even more unlikely try—Johnson launched a cross-field bomb, Tigers winger Lote Tuqiri was unable to control the loose ball and it popped into the hands of enigmatic Warriors centre Krisnan Inu, who was on the ground after contesting the bomb. Inu needed two lunges to plant the ball over the line, before the video referee correctly adjudicated that he was not held and put up the green light for a try—and the Warriors' progression to a shock preliminary final date with Melbourne.

Storm forward Sika Manu powered over for the first try at AAMI Park inside five minutes, but the Warriors responded shortly after from another Johnson high kick, with winger Bill Tupou picking up the loose ball to score. Michael Luck served up a superb pass for five-eighth Maloney to cross in the 16th minute, but the hosts drew level five minutes before halftime when centre Beau Champion punched through a gap and ran 70 metres to score. A Maloney penalty on halftime provided the Warriors with a two-point buffer and the scoreboard remained at 14-12 for the first 36 minutes of the second half, until Johnson set off on a spellbinding cross-field run before offloading for centre Lewis Brown to score in the corner. Maloney landed a towering sideline conversion to seal the Warriors' Grand Final berth at the end of arguably the most complete and controlled performance in the club's history. New Zealand's memorable charge ended with a gallant 24-10 loss to Manly in the decider.

GRAND FINAL MOMENTS

Grand Final day is the most hallowed on the Rugby League calendar and the moments that define each year's decider become ingrained in the constitution of the game's history. The great tries, heroic efforts, controversies and blunders that have characterised the season's biggest game since the advent of mandatory Grand Finals in 1954 are recalled in this chapter.

1954—SOUTH SYDNEY 23 DEFEATED NEWTOWN 15 The first mandatory Grand Final was delicately poised at 12-10 in favour of defending premiers Souths heading into the last 10 minutes. But dynamic lock Les 'Chicka' Cowie, one of the finest tryscoring forwards of all time, crossed for a double in the space of two minutes to place Souths on a trajectory to premiership glory.

1955—SOUTH SYDNEY 12 DEFEATED NEWTOWN 11 The Rabbitohs had won a string of nail-biting regular season and finals matches for the opportunity to meet minor premiers Newtown in the decider, and needed a late try to win the Grand Final and complete the 'Miracle of '55'. Trailing 11-7 in the dying minutes, Souths skipper Jack Rayner toed the ball through twice before halfback Col Donohoe pounced on the loose ball to score. Bernie Purcell's conversion nudged Souths a point in front.

Newtown fullback Gordon Clifford had a chance to win the Grand Final for the Bluebags in the dying seconds with a long-range penalty attempt. But Clifford, who had already kicked three penalties and a field goal, was off-target. South Sydney had secured its 16th—and most remarkable—premiership.

1956—ST. GEORGE 18 DEFEATED BALMAIN 12 The Dragons won the first of their world record 11 consecutive Grand Finals under duress, with a shoulder injury to centre Merv Lees leaving Saints a man short for all but 13 minutes of the decider. Playing in the days of no replacements, St. George soldiered on in front of a then-record SCG crowd of 61,987, putting the result beyond doubt with a quarter of the match remaining when Norm Provan sent Harry Melville on a 30-yard run to the line to open up an 18-5 lead.

1957—ST. GEORGE 31 DEFEATED MANLY 9 Overwhelming favourite St. George was locked 4-all with Manly after a try-less opening 35 minutes. But powerhouse Dragons winger Tommy Ryan snapped up a loose pass from Manly forward Rex Mossop and sprinted 80 yards to score a thrilling try and snatch a 9-4 halftime lead. The try was Ryan's 26th of 1957, breaking Ron Roberts' club record.

Legendary Saints forward Harry Bath booted Manly out of the contest in the second half, finishing the match with eight goals from as many attempts—a Grand Final record that still stands.

1958—ST. GEORGE 20 DEFEATED WESTERN SUBURBS 9 Two tries in the vital 10 minutes before halftime to towering second-rower Norm Provan turned a 5-0 deficit into a 10-5 lead at the break for the Dragons. In one of the toughest Grand Finals on record, Saints rebuffed the determined second half challenge of the Magpies, who had thrashed the Dragons 34-10 in the major semi to be the first side through to the decider Provan combined in the backrow with younger brother Peter, a late inclusion in the St. George side and a future premiership-winning captain with Balmain.

1959—ST. GEORGE 20 DEFEATED MANLY 0 A fiery encounter that saw referee Darcy Lawler dish out a spate of cautions in the opening exchanges exploded again in the second half. A stoush between rival forwards Harry Bath and Rex Mossop resulted in an all-in brawl, and Lawler sent the influential enforcers from the field.

Powerful Dragons winger Eddie Lumsden, a try-scorer in the 1957-58 deciders, scored the final try of the match to complete a superb hat-trick in the shutout. St. George became just the sixth (and last) club to finish a season undefeated.

1960—ST. GEORGE 31 DEFEATED EASTERN SUBURBS 6 Featuring in his first Grand Final, future Immortal centre Reg Gasnier bagged a magnificent double for the Dragons, effectively sealing Easts' fate after the underdogs had kept pace with the four-time premiers for the first quarter of the match. Saints scored seven tries in all, while the Tricolours failed to breach their opponents' tryline.

Referee Darcy Lawler sent off two players in a Grand Final for the second year in a row, despatching forward combatants Kevin Ryan (St. George) and Brian Wright (Easts) 15 minutes into the second half for fighting.

1961—ST. GEORGE 22 DEFEATED WESTERN SUBURBS 0 Eddie Lumsden scored his second Grand Final hat-trick, crossing for three of his side's four tries as the Dragons wrapped up their sixth title in a row with a dominant display against minor premiers Wests.

1962—ST. GEORGE 9 DEFEATED WESTERN SUBURBS 6 St. George was genuinely tested for the first time of its winning run in one of the tightest of all Grand Finals. The defending champs' cause was not aided by the send-off of 1961 Grand Final captain Billy Wilson, who was marched by referee Jack Bradley for levelling young Wests second-rower Jim Cody in a get-square.

The Dragons' desperate 12-man defence secured the club's seventh consecutive premiership as they clung to a 7-6 lead for much of the second half. Fullback Kevin McDonald kicked his second penalty to edge Saints further in front with just two minutes remaining.

1963—ST. GEORGE 8 DEFEATED WESTERN SUBURBS 3 The SCG, resembling a quagmire, played host to one of the most controversial Grand Finals of all time as a record 69,860-strong crowd witnessed what would become known as the 'Mudbath' Grand Final. Western Suburbs was denied a seemingly fair try late in the first half by referee Darcy Lawler, but the most contentious moment came 15 minutes from fulltime when Saints winger Johnny King was brought down by Wests fullback Don Parish near the touchline. Wests players claimed they heard Lawler call held, but King leapt up and darted the remaining 30 yards to score in the corner and the try was awarded. Wests front-rower and future coaching great Jack Gibson claimed to have information that Lawler, who retired after the match, was part of a £600 wager on a St. George victory. The match has been shrouded in mystery since.

Australian Rugby League's most iconic photograph was taken in the aftermath of the 1963 decider when John O'Gready snapped a magnificent shot of mud-caked rival captains Norm Provan and Arthur Summons. The photograph became known as 'The Gladiators' and has adorned the premiership's various trophies since 1982.

1964—ST. GEORGE 11 DEFEATED BALMAIN 6 The only try of another close Grand Final was scored 10 minutes into the second half. Dragons fullback Graeme Langlands reeled in a penalty kick from Balmain forward Bob Boland which failed to find touch, and set off from halfway, eventually linking with halfback Billy Smith on the Tigers' quarter-line. Smith found Johnny King, who raced in to finish off the brilliant movement and score a Grand Final try for the fifth year in a row.

1965—ST. GEORGE 12 DEFEATED SOUTH SYDNEY 8 The enduring image of a pulsating decider was the sight of hundreds of supporters lining the rooftops and staircases of the SCG, with the iconic venue unable to accommodate the unprecedented demand. The official crowd figure was announced as an SCG-record 78,056, but it was speculated many more thousand piled into the ground amidst the chaos.

Slick backline play resulted in both St. George tries to Billy Smith and Johnny King, who extended his tryscoring run to six consecutive Grand Finals, while the plucky young Souths side kept in touch via the superb long-range goalkicking of fullback Kevin Longbottom. The victory was an appropriate farewell for St. George legend Norm Provan, who featured in all 10 of the club's consecutive Grand Final victories to that point, captain-coaching the indomitable side from 1962.

1966—ST. GEORGE 23 DEFEATED BALMAIN 4 Three superb tries and the goalkicking of Graeme Langlands were the features of the last of St. George's 11 straight Grand Final victories. Billy Smith put centre Bruce Pollard over for the opener, before captain-coach Ian Walsh set up English forward Dick Huddart for a try before halftime. Enforcer Kevin Ryan sealed the result in the 54th minute with a fine try in his last match in the Red-V, while Langlands booted seven goals—one short of Harry Bath's Grand Final record.

1967—SOUTH SYDNEY 12 DEFEATED CANTERBURY 10 St. George's incredible streak came to an end in the first season of limited-tackle football, going down to Canterbury in the preliminary final. The Berries led Souths 8-5 in the Grand Final after three penalties to George Taylforth and a long-range field goal by Ron Raper. But the key moment of the decider arrived four minutes before halftime. Canterbury hooker Col Brown's looping pass out wide was intercepted by Souths backrower Bob McCarthy, who raced three-quarters of the field to score one of the most famous of all Grand Final tries.

With the scores locked at 10-all, Eric Simms landed a superb pressure penalty goal with just three minutes remaining to deliver the Rabbitohs' 17th premiership and usher in another golden era for 'The Pride of the League.'

1968—SOUTH SYDNEY 13 DEFEATED MANLY 9 Manly upset minor premiers and defending champs Souths in the major semi to advance to the Grand Final first, but the Rabbitohs stormed to an 11-2 halftime lead after Test winger Mike Cleary scooped up a loose ball and dashed 80 metres to score.

The second stanza featured a stirring Manly comeback. A try in the corner to second-rower John Morgan, converted by veteran fullback Bob Batty, was followed by an expertly taken field goal by 20-year-old skipper Bob Fulton to set up a grandstand finish. The Rabbitohs hung on to claim their 18th title, however, leaving Manly to continue their chase for a maiden premiership after four Grand Final losses.

1969—BALMAIN 11 DEFEATED SOUTH SYDNEY 2 Balmain, with captain Peter Provan and first-year coach Leo Nosworthy at the helm, outfoxed Souths to pull off the biggest Grand Final upset of all time. The Tigers led 6-0 at halftime and scored the only try of the match through replacement winger Syd Williams in the second half, while their go-slow tactics thwarted Souths' attempts at a comeback.

English import Dave Bolton's sweetly struck field goal with 15 minutes to go—his second of the match—established a nine-point lead and sealed Balmain's last premiership victory.

1970—SOUTH SYDNEY 23 DEFEATED MANLY 12 In one of the most infamous Grand Final moments, Manly forward John Bucknall callously smashed Souths skipper John Sattler's jaw with a savage elbow in the opening five minutes of the decider. But in an effort that ranks amongst the most courageous and oft-recalled in the code's history, Sattler saw out the match with a badly shattered jaw to lead his side to victory, while Bucknall was forced from the field before halftime courtesy of brutal retribution from the Rabbitohs' forwards.

The individual brilliance of halfback Bob Grant was a telling factor in Souths' victory. Grant scored two superb tries and laid on another with a looping pass to winger Ray Branighan. Fullback Eric Simms booted a Grand Final record four field goals, along with three goals, in the 11-point win.

1971—SOUTH SYDNEY 16 DEFEATED ST. GEORGE 10 Rabbitohs super-boot Eric Simms kicked the first one-point field goal in a Grand Final (following a rule change before the start of the season) to set up an unusual 1-0 halftime scoreline. Determined tries after the break to Ray Branighan and Ron Coote put the Rabbitohs 11-0 in front in the first Grand Final of the six-tackle era.

The Jack Gibson-coached Saints staged a mighty comeback in the final quarter, with converted tries to Barry Beath and Ted Walton pegging the deficit back to a point. But superb lead-up work from Coote laid on a try for Bob McCarthy with two minutes remaining to put the Grand Final to bed, sealing Souths' fourth premiership in five years—and their last to date.

1972—MANLY 19 DEFEATED EASTERN SUBURBS 14 The Grand Final was locked at 4-all at the end of a try-less first half after the Roosters failed to capitalise on a series of gilt-edged scoring opportunities. Contentious tries to Manly captain Fred Jones and Souths recruit Ray Branighan, who also finished with six goals, set up a match-winning 19-4 lead to secure the Sea Eagles' maiden premiership in their sixth Grand Final.

Two tries in the final 10 minutes added some respectability to the scoreline for Easts. The highlight was a miraculous through-the-legs pass from Arthur Beetson that led to a try to powerful winger Bill Mullins.

1973—MANLY 10 DEFEATED CRONULLA 7 The first half of the most brutal Grand Final on record was marked by a procession of brawling and thuggery. Referee Keith Page struggled to maintain control as fighting broke out with alarming regularity, but he refrained from ordering any players from the field.

The individual brilliance of Bob Fulton was the difference on a day when mayhem reigned. Fulton's acceleration netted him spectacular tries in each half to propel Manly to an 8-2 lead with quarter of the match remaining. The Sea

Eagles hung on to secure their second successive title, despite a converted try to Cronulla replacement Rick Bourke.

1974—EASTERN SUBURBS 19 DEFEATED CANTERBURY 4
Under the tutelage of master motivator Jack Gibson, the Roosters won their first premiership in 29 years with a three-tries-to-nil defeat of Canterbury. Captain Arthur Beetson scored the only try of the first half for Easts to go into the break ahead 7-4, where the score remained until the 66th minute. Beetson created space for a rampaging Mark Harris to score, before Bill Mullins finished off a fine backline movement in the dying moments to ice a superb victory.

1975—EASTERN SUBURBS 38 DEFEATED ST. GEORGE 0
The 1975 Grand Final is synonymous with the white boots St. George skipper Graeme Langlands wore and the champion fullback's indifferent display in the decider. Although coloured boots are almost mandatory in modern times, Langlands' white boots (worn to promote a footwear company) caused a stir and in a terrible irony 'Changa' turned in the worst performance of his decorated career after a misdirected painkilling injection at halftime rendered his injured right leg virtually useless.

A superb runaway effort to halfback Johnny Mayes was the only try of the first half, but the enduring memory of the opening 40 minutes was a spectacular head clash between young superstars Ian Schubert and Ted Goodwin. Saints centre Goodwin was chasing through on a kick and collided head-on with Roosters fullback Schubert, leaving both players strewn on the SCG pitch.

Despite leading only 5-0 at halftime, Easts racked up the biggest win in Grand Final history (a record that stood until Manly's 40-0 decimation of Melbourne in 2008) with a blistering seven-try assault in the second half, including a superb touchdown to a recovered Schubert, who was just 18 years of age.

1976—MANLY 13 DEFEATED PARRAMATTA 10
Parramatta qualified for its maiden Grand Final in the club's 30th season, defeating star-studded rivals Manly in the major semi. A gripping rematch ensued two weeks later in the decider. The scores were tied 7-all at halftime; Parramatta scored when winger Jim Porter climbed to take a trademark John Peard bomb, before Manly responded with a try in the corner to superb English import Phil Lowe.

Manly fullback Graham Eadie's goalkicking form negated a try to Eels forward Geoff Gerard, edging the Sea Eagles 11-10 in front with two penalties, but the crucial moment of the match came seven minutes from fulltime. Deep on attack in Manly's quarter, the Eels created an overlap with some slick backline passing, but centre John Moran's pass was dropped by unmarked winger Neville Glover with a free passage to the tryline in front of him (*see Minties Moments*). Eadie added another penalty goal and the Sea Eagles closed out the match to claim their third title in club legend Bob Fulton's last match in maroon and white.

1977—ST. GEORGE 9 DREW WITH PARRAMATTA 9
The confident young Dragons side, coached by Harry Bath, led minor premiers Parramatta 9-0 at halftime of the Grand Final, largely thanks to the brilliance of enigmatic fullback

'Lord' Ted Goodwin. He landed two penalty goals before scoring one of the finest individual tries in Grand Final history right on halftime, splitting the defence, chipping over the fullback and forcing the ball inches before the dead-ball line.

The Eels edged their way back into the contest with three penalty goals to Mick Cronin in the second half, before Cronin and Price combined superbly to send centre Ed Sulcowicz in for the score-levelling try three minutes from fulltime. But Cronin sprayed the conversion attempt and for the first time the Grand Final was drawn at the end of 80 minutes. Saints missed two penalty goal attempts during the 20 minutes of extra-time and the stalemate necessitated a replay for the following weekend.

REPLAY—ST. GEORGE 22 DEFEATED PARRAMATTA 0 Strong-arm tactics from St. George's forwards laid the platform for a crushing victory in the Grand Final replay. Rod Reddy received four cautions in the first half from referee Gary Cook after relentlessly terrorising Eels backrower Ray Price, but the tactics worked and Saints took a 7-0 halftime lead when John Jansen scored from a questionable pass.

Ted Goodwin kicked six goals and a field goal in the thrashing, which finished with a penalty try awarded to St. George halfback John Bailey on the cusp of fulltime.

1978—MANLY 11 DREW WITH CRONULLA 11 The Sea Eagles and Sharks scored identical tries in the 1978 decider—bombs that were allowed to bounce by the defence resulted in three-pointers to rival wingers Tom Mooney (Manly) and Steve Edmonds (Cronulla). Manly fullback Graham Eadie and Cronulla centre Steve Rogers each kicked four goals, and with no extra-time scheduled this time around, the Grand Final was consigned to a draw for the second straight year.

REPLAY—MANLY 16 DEFEATED CRONULLA 0 The replay was played just three days later on the following Tuesday due to the imminent departure of the Kangaroos to England. The match was dominated by the Sea Eagles, who were playing their fifth match in 17 days, including two replays *(see Finals Magic)*. Eadie and centre Russell Gartner were particularly devastating; Eadie scored a powerful try and kicked three goals, while Gartner collected a superb double.

1979—ST. GEORGE 17 DEFEATED CANTERBURY 13 'Bath's Babes' won their second premiership in three years on the back of a magnificent first half display. Superb tries to Brian Johnson, Mitch Brennan and Rod Reddy set up a 17-2 lead at the break.

The youthful Canterbury side, featuring three Mortimer brothers and three Hughes brothers, responded with three fine tries of their own in the second half, but ultimately left its run too late.

1980—CANTERBURY 18 DEFEATED EASTERN SUBURBS 4 Ted Glossop's Bulldogs led 7-4 at the break, with the only try of the half going to winger Chris Anderson. Steve Gearin landed three penalty goals in the second half to effectively wrap up the decider, but his place in Grand Final folklore was sealed five minutes before fulltime. Canterbury backrower Graeme Hughes put fullback Greg Brentnall into space and the Test custodian hoisted a high kick, 40 metres out from Easts' line. Gearin outpaced the Roosters chasers to spectacularly mark the ball on the full and crash over for arguably the most famous of all Grand Final tries. The victory clinched Canterbury's first premiership in 38 years.

1981—PARRAMATTA 20 DEFEATED NEWTOWN 11 Newtown, playing in its first Grand Final in 26 years, scored two tries to one in the first half but trailed 7-6 at halftime thanks to the accurate boot of Eels centre Mick Cronin and a great try to Brett Kenny. But Jets fans dared to dream when veteran halfback Tom Raudonikis scored a typically dogged try from a scrum win to snatch an 11-7 advantage.

The Eels had too much left in the tank, however, running down the brave battlers from Newtown in the final 15 minutes of the first decider played on a Sunday. Winger Graeme Atkins finished off a long-range movement to put Parramatta back in front, before Cronin's conversion of a superb Steve Ella try gave the Eels an unassailable lead. The icing on the cake was provided by Kenny, who grabbed a deflected kick on halfway and threw an audacious dummy to run in his second try—the long-suffering Eels had finally claimed their first premiership after 34 fruitless attempts.

1982—PARRAMATTA 21 DEFEATED MANLY 8 Manly entered the Grand Final as favourites after disposing of defending premiers Parramatta in the major semi, and scored the first try of the decider when teenage halfback Phil Blake pounced on a loose ball to score after the Eels spilled a bomb. But Parramatta's backline cut Manly to ribbons to establish a 16-3 halftime lead through superb tries to Brett Kenny, Steve Ella, Eric Grothe and Neil Hunt.

Brett Kenny's bagged a double for the second Grand Final in succession, reaching out for the final try to seal the result for Parramatta in a dour second half.

1983—PARRAMATTA 18 DEFEATED MANLY 6 The 1983 Grand Final was a carbon copy of the previous year—the Sea Eagles qualified for the decider first by beating Parramatta in the major semi, but the Eels raced to a formidable halftime lead through the class of their backs. Great hands netted Brett Kenny the first try and a powerful four-pointer to winger Eric Grothe set up a 12-0 advantage at the break. Kenny grabbed a brace of tries for third consecutive Grand Final just after halftime as Parramatta became the first club since St. George's world record premiership streak to snare a hat-trick of Grand Final victories.

1984—CANTERBURY 6 DEFEATED PARRAMATTA 4 The 1984 decider started a sequence of three low-scoring Grand Finals and wrested the crown of Rugby League supremacy from the brilliant Eels. A try to Mick Cronin provided Parramatta with a 4-0 halftime lead, which was nullified just after the break when Canterbury hooker Mark Bugden charged through a yawning gap from dummy-half. Chris Mortimer's conversion edged the Bulldogs two points in front.

Mick Cronin had an opportunity to send the match into extra-time when he lined up a penalty goal with three minutes on the clock, but the prolific point-scorer was off-target.

1985—CANTERBURY 7 DEFEATED ST. GEORGE 6 Warren Ryan's 'Dogs of War' ground out another Grand Final with victory over minor premiers

St. George. Peter Mortimer scored the only try of the first half and the score remained at 6-0 for over 40 minutes until Andrew Farrar's field goal afforded the Bulldogs a seven-point buffer.

A dreary decider was set alight in the final minutes when Dragons winger 'Slippery' Steve Morris scored a brilliant solo kick-and-chase try to reduce the deficit to a point. The club's two lower grade sides had come from behind to win Grand Finals earlier in the day, but St. George's first grade outfit had left its run too late.

1986—PARRAMATTA 4 DEFEATED CANTERBURY 2 Despite producing the only try-less decider in Grand Final history, Parramatta and Canterbury turned on a thriller that was high on drama and incident. Brett Kenny had one try in each half disallowed—both efforts showcased Kenny's sublime talent and were difficult, line-ball calls for referee Mick Stone that could have easily gone Parramatta's way

Canterbury fullback Phil Sigsworth, who on the day became the first player to lose Grand Finals with three clubs, was the first player in 24 years to be sent off in a decider. He was unlucky to be marched after his high tackle on Brett Kenny.

Parramatta clung to a 4-2 lead in the nerve-jangling final minutes, with Canterbury narrowly missing out on a try in the corner and Terry Lamb misdirecting a penalty goal attempt that would have sent the match into extra-time. The fulltime whistle blew with the Bulldogs hammering the Eels' tryline.

1987—MANLY 18 DEFEATED CANBERRA 8 The spark in the Sea Eagles' clinical display in the decider—the last played at the SCG—was provided by Churchill medallist Cliff Lyons and brilliant centre Michael O'Connor. Five-eighth Lyons fended off opposite number Chris O'Sullivan and stepped inside Raiders fullback Gary Belcher to score a wonderful solo try, the only touchdown of the first half.

The match was effectively wrapped up with 25 minutes remaining; Manly fullback Dale Shearer lobbed a pinpoint cross-field kick over Canberra's replacement winger Kevin Walters and O'Connor raced through to collect the bouncing ball for a try to add to his five goals for the day.

1988—CANTERBURY 24 DEFEATED BALMAIN 12 Balmain qualified for the Grand Final following an incredible sudden-death run from a fifth-place playoff (*see Finals Magic*), largely on the back of the efforts of Great Britain captain and Rugby League aristocrat Ellery Hanley. But the decider swung on Hanley's exit from the match 13 minutes before halftime. After scoring the first try through hooker Ben Elias, the Tigers were rocked when an alleged swinging arm from Canterbury five-eighth Terry Lamb left Hanley unconscious on the SFS turf and unable to continue. The Bulldogs scored their first try soon after when halfback Michael Hagan backed up a long break by winger Glen Nissen.

Canterbury extended its 10-8 halftime lead with a sensational try to hitman David Gillespie that exclusively involved forwards. Picking the ball up from dummy-half just a metre out, prop and captain Peter Tunks switched play to a short blindside. Quick hands from lock Paul Langmack and second-rower Steve Folkes found Gillespie lurking on the wing; he stretched out to score a memorable try in the corner as the converging Balmain cover defence arrived.

With the match well within Canterbury's keeping, club legend Steve Mortimer, who spent much of the season injured, made his way onto the field wearing jersey No.18 for his final appearance in premiership football. Fittingly, the 1984-85 Grand Final-winning skipper finished with the ball as the siren sounded to mark the Bulldogs' emphatic victory.

1989—CANBERRA 19 DEFEATED BALMAIN 14 The 1989 Grand Final is generally regarded as the greatest decider in Australian Rugby League history. Packed with drama, brilliance and moments frozen in time, it is the only Grand Final to be decided in extra-time. But the first half was all the Tigers, who scored the opening try through an intercept to winger and former Wallaby James Grant. Balmain's second four-pointer was a Grand Final try for the ages. Clever work from prop Steve Roach released Andy Currier down the right-hand touchline on the Tigers' side of halfway, before the British centre launched a speculative centring kick when he ran out of room. The ball took a wicked bounce and finished the hands of Grant, who found Currier backing up on the inside just before being bundled into touch. Currier headed in-field and passed to a rampaging Paul Sironen. The giant backrower charged 20 metres and palmed off Raiders lock Bradley Clyde to score beside the posts just on halftime.

Raiders fullback Gary Belcher's try and a penalty goal to Currier advanced the scoreboard to 14-8 in favour of Balmain, but the Tigers were unable to convert a plethora of match-sealing opportunities: Canberra captain Mal Meninga ankle-tapped tryline-bound Tigers five-eighth Mick Neil; Balmain skipper Wayne Pearce coughed up the pill deep on attack with a massive overlap beckoning; and Ben Elias' field goal attempt from close range cannoned off the crossbar. To add to the drama, in Rugby League's most infamous substitution decision, Tigers coach Warren Ryan replaced Test forwards Sironen and Roach with defensive specialists Kevin Hardwick and Michael Pobjie in an attempt to close out the match.

Canberra's last throw of the dice came in the final 90 seconds—Canberra five-eighth Chris O'Sullivan hoisted a bomb towards Balmain's goalposts and teenage centre Laurie Daley came up with the ball. Daley fired an overhead pass to John 'Chicka' Ferguson, and the veteran winger evaded three defenders with three left-foot steps and carried two more Tigers over the line to plant the ball down. Mal Meninga's simple conversion sent the Grand Final into extra-time.

O'Sullivan edged the Raiders into the lead with a well-taken field goal from a scrum win in the first period of extra-time, but Balmain's fire was not extinguished until Steve Jackson scored as the game approached its 100th minute. Meninga scooped up a misdirected kick ahead from Currier and offloaded to unheralded reserve forward Jackson, who swerved, bumped, spun and charged his way through five Tigers defenders to score a try that would become one of the most replayed Grand Final passages of all time.

1990—CANBERRA 18 DEFEATED PENRITH 14 Playing in his final match of an admirable career, 36-year-old winger and 1989 Grand Final hero 'Chicka' Ferguson scored the first try of the 1990 decider—a trademark effort featuring two jinks off his left foot and blinding acceleration to finish. Panthers winger Alan

McIndoe had pulled down his opposite Paul Martin in a brilliant try-saving tackle on the previous passage.

After conceding the opening two tries, Penrith hit back through 18-year-old centre Brad Fittler. The Panthers prodigy, who was named as the youngest-ever Kangaroo tourist hours later, stormed onto a pass by Greg Alexander and busted the tackles of hardened Canberra forwards Dean Lance and Glenn Lazarus to score.

The Panthers closed the gap to 12-10 soon after the break. Their second try came after the rare occurrence of one winger passing to his teammate on the other wing—McIndoe doubled around fullback David Greene to feed Paul Smith with a superb overhead pass. Smith stepped inside Mal Meninga and powered through Ferguson and Ricky Stuart for the try.

Canberra's crossed for the sealer five minutes from fulltime. Penrith prop Joe Vitanza coughed up the ball on the Raiders' side of halfway and Laurie Daley immediately put Mal Meninga away for a 30-metre charge. The skipper offloaded back to Daley, who embarked on a searching run across field before finding unmarked replacement winger Matthew Wood to score in the corner.

1991—PENRITH 19 DEFEATED CANBERRA 12 Veteran Penrith hooker Royce Simmons launched one of the great Grand Final farewells with the opening try of the 1991 decider. Receiving the ball flat-footed 10 metres out from Canberra's line, Simmons put a wonderful spin move on fullback Gary Belcher and steamrolled hulking prop Glenn Lazarus to score just the 14th try of his career.

The hobbled Raiders snatched a 12-6 halftime lead with two brilliant Matthew Wood four-pointers. In the 10th minute, Ricky Stuart's searching kick over the head of Penrith winger Paul Smith bounced up into the hands of Wood for a sensational try in the corner. The winger's second was even better. Stuart and Laurie Daley spread the ball virtually the width of the field in two passes, before Mal Meninga put Bradley Clyde into a yawning gap with a deft offload. Clyde summed up the situation perfectly to draw Penrith fullback Greg Barwick and send Wood in for his brace.

The Panthers' quest for their maiden title was on tenterhooks when Mark Geyer was sin-binned for abusing touch judge Martin Weekes. But the firebrand second-rower made amends with 10 minutes of the match remaining, popping a brilliant offload to give Brad Fittler space on Canberra's 40-metre line. Fittler stepped through two tackles and slipped an exquisite no-look, around-the-corner pass to Brad Izzard, who ran 20 metres untouched to tie up the scoreboard.

Penrith captain Greg Alexander put his side in front four minutes later with a magnificent 38-metre field goal—arguably the finest field goal ever seen in a Grand Final.

The killer blow was delivered after the Raiders attempted a short drop-out with time running out. Geyer snatched the bouncing ball out of the air and found Simmons in support, and the departing hero crossed in the corner to score the first double of his 234-game career. Alexander's majestic conversion from the sideline put the result beyond doubt, transporting the premiership trophy to the foot of the Blue Mountains for the first time and denying Canberra a historic treble.

1992—BRISBANE 28 DEFEATED ST. GEORGE 8 Skipper Allan Langer and nuggetty second-rower Alan Cann each scored a brace of tries for the dominant

Broncos. Brilliant No.7 Langer scored Brisbane's first two tries, opening the scoring after a superb wrap-around manoeuvre with prop Gavin Allen, before burrowing over from dummy-half for the first try of the second half. Cann accepted a superb offload from Trevor Gillmeister and displayed power, determination and a massive step to score his first try, while excellent footwork sealed Cann's double and the last of the Broncos' five tries.

In a rare highlight for the Dragons, veteran winger Ricky Walford finished off a fabulous movement to restrict the halftime score to 6-4 in favour of Brisbane. Second-rower Scott Gourley produced a brilliant offload for Michael Beattie; the skipper found Peter Coyne in support and the five-eighth floated a magnificent pass out wide for Walford to cross in the corner.

After Broncos winger Willie Carne sensationally evaded a wave of chasers to escape from the in-goal, Langer swept the ball wide to Steve Renouf. The electrifying centre stepped inside Saints replacement Rex Terp and scorched 98 metres, outlasting Walford in a thrilling chase to the tryline, effectively wrapping up Brisbane's maiden title.

1993—BRISBANE 14 DEFEATED ST. GEORGE 6 The confident Dragons' hopes of overturning the previous year's Grand Final result suffered a major blow in the opening minute of the 1993 decider, when boom rookie prop Jason Stevens broke his thumb in the first tackle of the match. The rattled Saints never recovered as they bumbled their way to a disappointing loss.

The 1993 decider is regarded as arguably the dourest Grand Final of the modern era, but Broncos five-eighth Kevin Walters provided two touches of class in the first 40 minutes. Dummying on halfway, Walters shot through an opening and positioned centre Chris Johns on his inside for the first four-pointer of the match after 21 minutes. Walters was at it again nine minutes later, using expert sleight of hand to send Terry Matterson over for Brisbane's second try with another inside ball. Walters was an obvious choice for the Clive Churchill Medal, but the honour surprisingly went to St. George backrower Brad Mackay.

1994—CANBERRA 36 DEFEATED CANTERBURY 12 It became apparent it was not Canterbury's day during the opening seconds of the 1994 decider. The Bulldogs failed to take Canberra's kick-off on the full and burly veteran front-rower Martin Bella fumbled the bobbling ball in the in-goal, conceding a dropout. It set the tone for a tough afternoon for Terry Lamb's Dogs.

Veteran prop Paul Osborne, a late inclusion in the side for suspended Kiwi John Lomax, laid on the first two tries for David Furner and Ken Nagas with brilliant offloads in one of the great Grand Final cameos (see Unlikely Heroes).

Laurie Daley scored a brilliant solo try in the first half after David Furner popped a superb pass on halfway. The dynamic five-eighth sprinted through an opening and outpaced fullback Scott Wilson to plant the ball in the corner.

Canterbury clung to a glimmer of hope when Kiwi winger Jason Williams intercepted a Daley pass and outlasted Jason Croker and Brett Mullins on an 80-metre chase to the tryline to open the Bulldogs' account.

Retiring Canberra skipper Mal Meninga capped a dream premiership farewell with the last of the Raiders' seven tries, intercepting a long pass from Bulldogs backrower Jason Smith and sprinting 30 metres to score one of the most popular of all Grand Final tries.

1995—CANTERBURY 17 DEFEATED MANLY 4 The Bulldogs were rank outsiders to defeat minor premiers Manly, and they were put under intense pressure after just six minutes when referee Eddie Ward sin-binned 34-year-old skipper Terry Lamb. Sea Eagles fullback Matthew Ridge opened the scoring with two points from the resultant penalty, but the 12-man Bulldogs held firm during the next 10 minutes, giving them the confidence to produce one of the great Grand Final upsets.

Five minutes after Lamb returned, Canterbury scored the first try through young forward Steve Price. The try was controversial—the 'money' ball from lock Jim Dymock was arguably forward. To make matters worse for the indifferent Sea Eagles, the second Bulldogs try—scored by Glen Hughes in the second half— took place on the seventh tackle due to a miscount by Ward.

Retiring captain Lamb effectively sealed the unlikely victory with a 69th-minute field goal to provide the Bulldogs with a seven-point buffer, before fullback Rod Silva scored next to the posts in the final two minutes.

1996—MANLY 20 DEFEATED ST. GEORGE 8 Astute fullback Matthew Ridge produced the big play of the 1996 Grand Final as the Sea Eagles made amends for their horror display in the previous year's decider. St. George had opened their account leading into halftime with a penalty goal, pegging the score back to 8-2 in favour of Manly. But Ridge spied an opportunity from the ensuing restart, kicking off short and regathering the ball. He was tackled by Nathan Brown but was controversially ruled not held, and scampered another 20 metres. Nik Kosef put Steve Menzies over for a try after the next ruck on the stroke of halftime to set up a match-winning lead.

1997—NEWCASTLE 22 DEFEATED MANLY 16 (ARL GRAND FINAL) A savage first half was marked by several heated clashes between rival enforcers Paul Harragon and Mark Carroll. Pint-sized Manly captain Geoff Toovey was knocked unconscious and stumbled several times as he attempted to re-enter the fray, before having his face stomped by Newcastle winger Adam MacDougall in the second half.

The Sea Eagles set up an imposing 10-2 lead by cutting the Knights' right-side defence ribbons. Three-quarters John Hopoate and Craig Inness scored tries on the back of superb lead-up work from Toovey and Cliff Lyons.

Fullback Robbie O'Davis scored Newcastle's first try from a scrum win, embarking on a majestic cross-field run and dummying his way over for a vital four-pointer. A try to his Manly counterpart Shannon Nevin after the Sea Eagles won a scrum against the feed extended the scoreline to 16-8 at halftime.

An Andrew Johns penalty was the only score of the first 33 minutes of the second half, but a long break by unheralded Newcastle backrower Troy Fletcher put the underdogs deep on attack. O'Davis stepped and spun in the despairing tackle of Nevin to plant the ball under the posts. Johns' conversion locked up the scores at 16-all. Matthew Johns' angled 78th-minute field goal attempt from the 20-metre line seemed to hang in the air for an eternity before bouncing off the upright.

Andrew Johns tried for a one-pointer with 30 seconds remaining but was charged down; the tackle count was restarted and Knights winger Darren Albert went to ground with the ball. Ignoring another field goal opportunity, Andrew Johns ran blindside from dummy-half and found Albert on the inside. The snowy-haired flyer split the exhausted Manly defenders to run around behind the posts to secure Newcastle's first premiership with seven seconds on the clock. Albert was mobbed by his jubilant teammates as scenes of ecstatic pandemonium broke out around the Sydney Football Stadium.

1997—BRISBANE 26 DEFEATED CRONULLA 8 (SUPER LEAGUE GRAND FINAL) With the inaugural (and only) Super League Grand Final delicately poised at 10-8 in favour of the Broncos after 54 minutes, renowned hitman Peter Ryan busted the game wide open. Chasing through on a Darren Lockyer bomb, the Brisbane backrower crunched Cronulla fullback David Peachey in a devastating tackle, forcing the ball loose. A superb pass from Lockyer on the next play sent Steve Renouf over for his second try.

Lockyer produced another superb pass for man-of-the-match Renouf 10 minutes later, turning the brilliant centre inside to complete his hat-trick and effectively wrap up the premiership at Brisbane's cavernous Stadium Australia (formerly QEII Stadium).

1998—BRISBANE 38 DEFEATED CANTERBURY 12 Coming off two gruelling extra-time finals matches (see Finals Magic), the courageous Bulldogs snatched a 12-10 halftime lead thanks to Steve Price. The soon-to-be Test prop stepped through the Brisbane defensive line, beat the tackle of Kevin Walters and superbly drew fullback Darren Lockyer to put centre Willie Talau over for Canterbury's second try.

It was all one-way traffic after the break though, and it took the Broncos just two minutes to hit the front. Rampaging lock Tonie Carroll, who many thought should have taken out Clive Churchill Medal honours, powered through three defenders to score beside the posts and begin a 26-0 second half run.

Faced with one of the most daunting tasks in 1990s Rugby League—defending one-on-one against a runaway Steve Renouf—Bulldogs fullback Rod Silva pulled off a magnificent textbook try-saver on the brilliant Broncos centre. Silva's efforts were in vain, however, as Darren Smith and Walters combined to send Wendell Sailor over in the corner on the next play.

The Broncos put an exclamation point on a flawless 40 minutes with an 80-metre try in the dying minutes. Allan Langer put Carroll through a hole and into open pastures, before Smith loomed in support and accepted an inside pass to score his 23rd try of 1998, equalling the Brisbane club record. Darren Lockyer's conversion propelled the Broncos to the highest Grand Final score in 23 years.

1999—MELBOURNE 20 DEFEATED ST. GEORGE ILLAWARRA 18 Brilliant Dragons winger Nathan Blacklock scored one of Grand Final history's most memorable individual tries. Standing at fullback late in the first half, Blacklock attacked a dangerous chip kick by Storm No.7 Brett Kimmorley, collecting the ball at full pace and galloping 60 metres to score, extending Saints' halftime lead to 14-0.

The turning point arrived with half an hour to play. Ahead 14-2, the Dragons had set up camp in Storm territory for the opening passages of the second half. Melbourne failed to clean up an Anthony Mundine grubber, and the dazzling No.6 regathered, only to cough up the ball over the tryline in the tackle of Craig Smith when a four-pointer seemed certain. Centre Tony Martin scored Melbourne's first try three minutes later after running off a dubious Matt Geyer pass.

In a remarkable period of quick-fire action, Saints captain Paul McGregor responded with a try just two minutes later, before backrower Ben Roarty hit back for the Storm almost immediately.

After a tense final quarter in front of a world record crowd of 107,999 at Stadium Australia, one of the most sensational incidents in Grand Final history unfolded. Trailing 18-14 with four minutes on the clock, Melbourne halfback Brett Kimmorley put up a cross-field bomb. Storm winger Smith caught the ball on the full but was felled in a high tackle by Jamie Ainscough as he was about to plant the ball for the equaliser. As Smith *(see Unlikely Heroes)* lay unconscious on the turf, video referee Chris Ward eventually awarded a penalty try to Melbourne. The conversion attempt was consequently taken in front of the posts, handing Melbourne a dramatic premiership win in the club's second NRL season.

2000—BRISBANE 14 DEFEATED SYDNEY ROOSTERS 6 In a dour
decider reminiscent of the Broncos' 1993 Grand Final victory over the Dragons, it was the opposing fullbacks that provided the highlights. After having an early try disallowed, Brisbane custodian Darren Lockyer displayed guile and pace to get around Roosters centre Ryan Cross and send Lote Tuqiri over the for the opening four-pointer. Roosters No.1 Luke Phillips was inspirational throughout, pulling off four try-saving tackles in the first half and providing attacking thrust from the back. Lockyer was later awarded the Clive Churchill Medal, while Phillips would have been a shoe-in for the gong had the Roosters won.

The Broncos led 14-2 heading into the final stages courtesy of a Wendell Sailor try earlier in the second half, but the match sprung into life when Roosters backrower Craig Fitzgibbon crashed over in the corner. Fitzgibbon attempted the conversion that would have reduced the deficit to a converted try but, agonisingly, the ball thudded into the crossbar, confirming Brisbane's fifth premiership triumph.

2001—NEWCASTLE 30 DEFEATED PARRAMATTA 24 Andrew
Johns was the puppeteer of a first half ambush, but it was Newcastle's enthusiastic forwards dominating the scoreboard as the Knights shot to a 24-0 lead over the shell-shocked Eels after 32 minutes. Bill Peden bagged a double, and Steve Simpson and Ben Kennedy scored tries, all from close range.

The Knights' desperate cover gave them a defensive clean sheet in the first half. Simpson miraculously held Andrew Ryan up over the line, before Sean Rudder and Matt Gidley bundled a tryline-bound Luke Burt over the sideline.

Despite the massive deficit, the introduction of PJ Marsh off the bench gave the Eels a glimmer of hope in the second half. A brilliant break from dummy-half by Marsh and an excellent Andrew Ryan offload allowed fullback Brett Hodgson to sprint 30 metres for Parramatta's first try. Another teasing Marsh run out of dummy-half turned into a break and Jamie Lyon backed up on the inside to peg the score back to 30-18 with eight minutes on the clock.

2002—SYDNEY ROOSTERS 30 DEFEATED NEW ZEALAND 8

A powerful break by captain Brad Fittler from deep inside Roosters' territory laid the platform for the first try. Bryan Fletcher released Brett Mullins down the left flank after the ensuing ruck, and Mullins popped a one-handed offload back on the inside for Shannon Hegarty to streak away and open the scoring.

Warriors skipper Stacey Jones' try five minutes after halftime ranks as one of the great individual touchdowns. Accepting a pass from PJ Marsh on the Roosters' 40-metre line, Jones dummied his way past Craig Wing and displayed brilliant footwork to step around forwards Bryan Fletcher and Jason Cayless, swerved around fullback Luke Phillips and outpaced Fittler and Craig Fitzgibbon to put the Warriors 8-6 in front.

The Roosters led 12-8 heading into the final quarter when Warriors interchange forward Wairangi Koopu shoulder-charged Fittler as he was shaping to kick. Tempers frayed when Richard Villasanti dived on the dazed Roosters skipper, clashing heads with him and opening up a gash above Fittler's eye. Fittler was ruled to have knocked on, but a few tackles later the Roosters gained retribution courtesy of a thunderous Adrian Morley hit on Fittler's assailant Villasanti. The incident—and a subsequent 40-20 kick from Fittler—proved the catalyst for the Roosters to run away with the Grand Final, scoring three late tries.

2003—PENRITH 18 DEFEATED SYDNEY ROOSTERS 6 Panthers

hooker Luke Priddis produced an emphatic Churchill Medal-winning performance, displaying guile and ball-playing brilliance to lay on two tries for winger Luke Rooney and score the other himself.

With his father having already left an indelible mark on Grand Final folklore in 1970, Penrith lock Scott Sattler carved out his own piece of history on the game's biggest stage with the most famous cover tackle of all time on Roosters winger Todd Byrne (see Unlikely Heroes).

2004—BULLDOGS 16 DEFEATED SYDNEY ROOSTERS 13

The Roosters sailed to a 13-6 halftime lead following an Anthony Minichiello try four minutes before the break. Explosive rookie backrower Anthony Tupou made a powerful bust on halfway and positioned the Test fullback beautifully for a try under the posts.

The Bulldogs took the lead for the first time in the 53rd minute via super-boot winger Hazem El Masri's 100th first grade try. Halfback Brent Sherwin, who laid on a first half try for his other winger Matt Utai with a wonderful long ball, expertly drifted across the field and turned El Masri on the inside. El Masri crashed over the line in the tackle of Ryan Cross to claim the decisive score.

The last throw of the dice for the Roosters came inside the final 30 seconds. Halfback Brett Finch put Michael Crocker into a hole with a cut-out pass, but stand-in skipper Andrew Ryan (regular captain Steve Price was injured in the preliminary final) ankle-tapped Crocker 30 metres out from the Bulldogs line and the ball spilled free. Ryan became the first player since Easts' Ray Stehr in 1935 to win a premiership on his captaincy debut. Opposing skipper Brad Fittler retired after the loss, bringing down the curtain on one of the great careers.

2005—WESTS TIGERS 30 DEFEATED NORTH QUEENSLAND 16

North Queensland linchpins Johnathan Thurston and Matt Bowen handled twice in a helter-skelter movement that produced the opening try of the Grand Final to Bowen in the eighth minute.

Cowboys captain Paul Bowman offered the Tigers' their first try on a platter with an ill-conceived in-goal pass over the head of fullback Bowen; young Tigers forward Bryce Gibbs pounced on the ball to open his side's account.

With the scores locked at 6-all and five minutes remaining before halftime, Tigers fullback Brett Hodgson fielded a Thurston kick five metres out from his own line and passed to Benji Marshall. The precocious Kiwi five-eighth skipped through the tackles of Thurston and Matt Sing before accelerating and crossing the halfway. Faced with Bowen and the sideline, Marshall popped an audacious flick pass on the inside for Pat Richards. The long-striding winger palmed off Cowboys utility Rod Jensen and dived over to score. The try and Marshall's pass have become embedded in modern Rugby League folklore.

The Tigers led 24-12 after tries to Anthony Laffranchi and Daniel Fitzhenry, but a brilliant cut-out pass by Thurston gave Sing a free passage to the tryline with three minutes to go and provided the Cowboys with a glimmer of hope. But sharpshooter Josh Hannay hooked the conversion, effectively confirming victory for the Tigers. Burly forward Todd Payten scored from a Brett Hodgson grubber in the dying seconds to cap a euphoric maiden title for the Wests Tigers.

2006—BRISBANE 15 DEFEATED MELBOURNE 8
Playing in his 200th and final first grade game before heading to Super League, Melbourne five-eighth Scott Hill set up both of his side's tries with trademark ball-playing wizardry. Hill bumped out of two tackles and popped a magnificent around-the-body pass for winger Steve Turner to score the first try of the decider, before sending centre Matt King over with a marvellous short ball to lock the game up at 8-all early in the second half.

Hill's opposite and Brisbane skipper Darren Lockyer provided several moments of inspiration for the underdog Broncos, but his hand in the match-winning try to Brent Tate stands out. Running the ball on the last tackle in the 61st minute, Lockyer linked with Corey Parker, who in turn found Casey McGuire. The utility threw a speculator over his head which was scooped up by Lockyer. The captain released Tonie Carroll into space, and Carroll drew Billy Slater for Brent Tate to score in the corner, finishing a 45-metre movement and setting up a 14-8 lead. Lockyer nailed a field goal with six minutes remaining to seal a memorable Grand Final boilover.

2007—MELBOURNE 34 DEFEATED MANLY 8
The decisive moment of the 2007 Grand Final occurred four minutes after halftime. Melbourne held a tenuous 10-4 lead when five-eighth Greg Inglis piloted a towering bomb towards Manly fullback Brett Stewart. The game-breaking No.1 took a superb catch, but Storm enforcer Michael Crocker arrived simultaneously and flattened Stewart with

a legitimate and punishing tackle. Stewart, the Sea Eagles' main attacking weapon, left the field with concussion, taking his side's premiership hopes with him.

Inglis put the exclamation point on a Clive Churchill Medal-winning performance with a brilliant solo try in the second half. Coach Craig Bellamy was maligned during 2007 for shifting the free-running Inglis to pivot, but his blistering Grand Final display silenced the knockers. Inglis ran 70 metres and dismissed Manly winger Michael Robertson with a trademark 'don't argue' on the way to his second try in the 56th minute.

2008—MANLY 40 DEFEATED MANLY 0 Michael Robertson scored a magnificent winger's hat-trick, crossing for three of the Sea Eagles' first four tries with only inches to spare on each occasion. He scored in the first half from a beautiful Brett Stewart cut-out pass, latched onto a Matt Orford kick for his second try and completed the treble by finishing off a sweeping Manly movement in the corner.

Brent Kite—the first prop to win the Clive Churchill Medal since Canterbury's Paul Dunn 20 years earlier—crashed over under the posts after a seven-pass interchange to effectively put the match out of Melbourne's reach at 24-0.

With the premiership trophy well within Manly's keeping, departing club legend Steve Menzies returned from the bench for the closing period of the Grand Final. Within minutes, Menzies put Robertson into space down the sideline and was the recipient of a return pass from the hat-trick hero to score a fairytale try reminiscent of his former Kangaroo skipper Mal Meninga's effort in 1994.

2009—MELBOURNE 23 DEFEATED PARRAMATTA 16 Melbourne led the 2009 decider 22-6 after 55 minutes—forwards Ryan Hoffman and Adam Blair scored barnstorming first half tries; Greg Inglis spectacularly claimed an attacking bomb on the run to score in the 49th minute, nullifying a powerful four-pointer to Eels winger Eric Grothe; and Clive Churchill medallist Billy Slater finished off a superb bust by Blair to score the Storm's fourth try.

A try to centre Joel Reddy catapulted Parramatta back into the contest, and the Eels trailed by just six when cult hero prop Fuifui Moimoi scored one of the most memorable individual tries in Grand Final history three minutes later. Receiving the ball 20 metres from Melbourne's line, Moimoi brushed off Will Chambers and Cooper Cronk before steamrolling Slater and Steve Turner to score in the corner in the 72nd minute.

The Eels' brave comeback was thwarted by a contentious refereeing decision with four minutes on the clock. Slater appeared to lose possession trying to play the ball on Melbourne's side of halfway, but Parramatta was penalised for interference in the ruck. The Storm worked their way into position for Inglis to slot a field goal and seal the southerners' second Grand Final win in three years.

2010—ST. GEORGE ILLAWARRA 32 DEFEATED SYDNEY ROOSTERS 8 The Dragons scored first when veteran centre Mark Gasnier soared to claim a pinpoint Jamie Soward kick. But the try was controversial—replays revealed Saints winger Brett Morris had stepped into touch on the previous play.

Roosters skipper Braith Anasta spearheaded a fight-back by diving on a loose ball to score his side's first try, before second-rower Mitch Aubusson displayed excellent footwork to get rid of Dragons centre Matt Cooper and score in the corner three minutes later. The Roosters led 8-6 at the break but were unlucky to not be ahead by more when a contentious forward pass ruling denied rookie winger Joseph Leilua a try.

Kiwi winger Jason Nightingale turned the Dragons' two-point deficit into an 18-8 lead before the hour mark, showcasing his excellent finishing skills to score twice in the space of 13 minutes.

The Dragons emphatically secured their first premiership since 1979 (and their first as a joint venture) with close-range tries to Dean Young and Nathan Fien, sparking emotional scenes as the club shed the 'chokers' tag.

2011—MANLY 24 DEFEATED NEW ZEALAND 10 Churchill medallist Glenn Stewart supplied the critical play of a quality Grand Final shortly before halftime. The dynamic Manly backrower threaded an audacious grubber through on the Sea Eagles' 20-metre line for his winger Michael Robertson, who embarked on a run of 50 metres. Warriors hooker Aaron Heremaia appeared to be obstructed by Daly Cherry-Evans in attempting a tackle on Robertson, but play was allowed to continue and hooker Matt Ballin was eventually halted just five metres out from New Zealand's line. Rookie halfback Cherry-Evans crashed over from the ensuing ruck to set up an imposing 12-2 halftime advantage.

Nineteen-year-old Will Hopoate, playing his last game before embarking on a two-year Mormon mission, conjured a piece of magic to extend Manly's lead. Heading into touch at a rapid rate near the Warriors' tryline, Hopoate produced a one-handed flick-pass back on the inside, hitting Glenn Stewart on the chest for an easy passage to score the third try of the afternoon.

Preliminary final hero and halfback whiz-kid Shaun Johnson sparked a valiant New Zealand comeback in the last quarter of the match. Drifting across the park in a run reminiscent of his mesmerising effort from a week earlier (see Finals Magic), Johnson fired a long ball to hulking winger Manu Vatuvei, who worked a narrow corridor to plant the ball in the corner. Johnson found makeshift centre and fellow rookie Elijah Taylor with another lofted pass on the opposite side of the ground five minutes later, and Taylor brushed off Manly's Kiwi Test centre Steve Matai to crash over for the Warriors' second try. Brilliant pivot James Maloney missed with both conversion attempts from out wide, however, leaving the Warriors eight points in arrears before Manly captain Jamie Lyon scored in the dying minutes to cap an emphatic victory.

CHAPTER 3
THE CLUBS

The Australian Rugby League premiership has played host to 31 clubs during its 104-season history. Each club boasts a colourful history—all of which are profiled in-depth in this section, including the triumphs, troughs, outstanding players and momentous events in every club's tale. A full history of the 16 current clubs, plus memorable eras of former clubs North Sydney, Western Suburbs and St. George are contained in the following pages, along with a detailed overview of the 15 clubs no longer fielding a first grade team.

THE PRIDE OF THE LEAGUE

South Sydney is Australian Rugby League's most successful and most famous club. Producing an endless line of champion players and building some of the most dominant club eras in the game's history, Souths won 20 first grade titles between the premiership's 1908 foundation season and 1971, and bred generations of supporters whose feverish passion was reflected in the exploits of their heroes in cardinal red and myrtle green jerseys. 'The Pride of the League'—a label coined by renowned Rugby League writer Claude Corbett during the 1920s—epitomises the club's importance to the Australian game's story.

Arthur 'Ash' Hennessy is regarded as the South Sydney club's founding father, instigating meetings in 1907 and being elected as one of Souths' delegates to the New South Wales Rugby League after the club was officially formed at a meeting at the Redfern Town Hall on January 17, 1908. Hennessy was also named as captain-coach for the inaugural premiership season, while he vehemently enforced his edict of not kicking the ball upon his South Sydney side—a vital ingredient to the club's early success. S. George Ball was also instrumental in the formation of the club and held the post of treasurer until 1966. The SG Ball Cup Under-16s competition was named in honour of one of Rugby League's foremost administrators.

South Sydney claimed the 1908 premiership with a 14-12 victory over Eastern Suburbs in the final, despite missing six players—Hennessy, Billy Cann (who was also heavily involved in establishing the club), Tommy Anderson, Jim Davis, Arthur Butler and Johnny Rosewell—who were en route to England with the pioneering Kangaroos. Hennessy became Australia's first Test captain earlier in the season when he led his country against New Zealand. After finishing atop the competition table in 1909 and winning through to the final with a 20-0 semi-final defeat of Newcastle, South Sydney was crowned champions again when Balmain sensationally forfeited the final in protest of the match being played as a curtain-raiser to a Kangaroos vs. Wallabies exhibition match *(see Bizarre Matches)*.

The club won its next title in 1914, finishing outright first on the ladder (no finals were played between 1912 and 1925 except in the event of a tie for first place). The side was led by Howard Hallett, the champion fullback of the code's formative years who played 155 games in 16 seasons for Souths and toured with the 1911-12 Kangaroos. But the undeniable star of Souths' line-up was 'Wonder Winger' Harold Horder. A future great from the moment he scored a length-of-the-field try on first grade debut in 1912, Horder crossed for 19 tries in the club's 1914 premiership season and finished his career with 152 tries in 136 games for Souths and Norths (including 102 in just 86 games in red and green). Horder scored 11 tries in 13 Tests and 35 tries in 25 games on the 1921-22 Kangaroo Tour, and is regarded by many as the greatest winger Australia has produced.

SOUTH SYDNEY'S FIRST DYNASTY Souths' 1918 premiership provided a brief respite from an era of Balmain dominance (Balmain won titles from 1915-17 and 1919-20), while the club was on the cusp of its own dynasty. After finishing runners-up with losses in the 1923 and '24 premiership finals (the latter season witnessing the retirement of Horder and Hallett), Souths won five consecutive first grade titles—a feat bettered only by St. George's run of 11 premierships from 1956-66. Hallett remained at the club as coach for 1925-26, while the side was captained superbly by five-eighth Alf 'Smacker' Blair, who debuted for the club in 1917 and made his only Test appearance against England in 1924. Souths' phenomenal line-up included all time great second-rower George Treweek; wonderful front-row forward Eddie Root; brothers and outstanding forwards Alf and Frank O'Connor, who made their Test debuts in home Ashes series in 1924 and 1932 respectively; and versatile back Harry 'Mick' Kadwell.

But the standout was another incredible wingman—the electrifying Benny Wearing. He scored a club record 144 tries and a then-record 836 points in 172 games between 1921 and 1933, but despite his status as one of the premiership's preeminent superstars, he was bewilderingly overlooked for representative selection throughout his career. Wearing made just one Test appearance (starring with two tries and three goals in Australia's only win of the 1928 Ashes series) and the constant snubbing of the wing luminary is one of the great mysteries in the history of representative football.

Souths won the 1925 premiership in the last season played under the 'first-past-the-post' system, before winning four straight premiership finals from 1926-29, with Blair as captain-coach in 1927 before Charlie Lynch embarked on a long coaching tenure (1928-34 and 1937-40). After finishing a distant third in the 1928 regular season, Souths upset minor premiers St. George 13-5 in the semi-final and crushed second-placed Easts 26-5 in the final. The club's run culminated in the selection of Treweek, Root, Kadwell, winger Harry Finch and centre Paddy Maher, who was chosen as vice-captain in 1929-30 Kangaroo Tour squad—but, again, Wearing was a shock omission.

Maher captained the Rabbitohs to another title in 1931 with a 12-7 victory over minor premiers Easts in the Grand Final, while Treweek led the club to a 19-12 defeat of Wests in the 1932 Grand Final, giving Souths the astonishing record of seven premierships in eight seasons. But following a period of such unbridled success, the club endured a lengthy drought during the 1930s and 1940s. After runner-up finishes in 1935, '37 and '39, the Rabbitohs slipped down the ladder and finished last in the 1945-46 seasons, failing to win a match in the latter campaign.

THE GOLDEN FIFTIES But the club was building towards another glorious era. Tough forward Jack Rayner joined Souths in 1946, while brilliant fullback Clive Churchill and devastating winger Johnny Graves arrived from Newcastle in 1947, as did tryscoring lock and Rockhampton product Les 'Chicka' Cowie. The quartet toured with the 1948-49 Kangaroos. Goalkicking forward Bernie Purcell linked with the Rabbitohs in 1949 and the club won the minor premiership, before succumbing 19-12 to St. George in the Grand Final.

Churchill assumed the Test captaincy in 1950 and led his country to a famous series victory over Great Britain—Australia's first Ashes success since the 1911-12 Kangaroos returned with the hallowed prize. A scintillating attacking fullback and a magnificent defender, Churchill's incomparable career saw him come to be regarded as arguably the greatest Rugby League player of all time, as his nickname 'The Little Master' attests. He was chosen as one of the four original Immortals in 1981, while he was posthumously named as the No.1 Australian player ever in expert polls conducted in 1992 and 2000. The Clive Churchill Medal—awarded to the best player in each year's Grand Final—was struck in his honour in 1986, a year after his death.

As Horder and Wearing had been in the early decades, Churchill was the superstar of Souths' 1950s line-ups, but Rayner was the Rabbitohs' captain-coach, ruling with an iron fist. Rayner's leadership was integral to the club's premiership triumphs in 1950-51 and 1953-55, embedding his name in the fabric of Australian Rugby League history as one of the game's greatest skippers. He played a then-record 194 games for Souths before retiring in 1957.

Souths snapped an 18-year title drought by defeating Wests 21-15 in the 1950 premiership final and hammered Manly 42-14 in the 1951 Grand Final, with Graves crossing for four tries. But the Rabbitohs' bid for a hat-trick of premierships was halted by a 22-12 loss to Wests in the 1952 Grand Final, a match shrouded in controversy after a series of contentious decisions by referee George Bishop went against Souths. Rumours that Bishop had bet on the outcome of the Grand Final were rife, and the plume of allegations was exacerbated by the fact he retired after the match.

Nevertheless, the Rabbitohs reclaimed supremacy with a 31-12 thrashing of St. George in the 1953 premiership final and back-to-back Grand Final victories over Newtown in 1954 and 1955. The club's last title triumph in the sequence subsequently became known as 'The Miracle of '55.' Languishing near the bottom of the ladder with just three wins in the opening 10 rounds, Souths embarked on a virtual sudden-death run of regular season matches, the most dramatic of which was in the penultimate round against Manly. Churchill broke his arm after five minutes, but soldiered on (with the cover of an exercise book forming a makeshift splint) and sent Cowie over for a last-minute try to lock up the scores at 7-all. Churchill stepped up to kick arguably the most famous goal in premiership history from the sideline as the siren sounded to win the match. While Churchill played no further part in the 1955 season, his courageous display is among the game's most well-known stories and kept the Rabbitohs on course for a miraculous premiership. Souths scraped into fourth place and pipped Manly and St. George in tight finals matches, before eclipsing the Bluebags 12-11 in the Grand Final—the Rabbitohs' 11th straight win. The club boasted several champions of the 1950s, including versatile 1952-53 Kangaroo Greg Hawick and prolific try-scorer Ian Moir (105 tries in 110 games), a blistering winger who toured with the 1956-57 Kangaroos.

THE RABBITOHS' LAST GREAT ERA Souths' gifted line-up qualified for consecutive preliminary finals in 1956-57 as St. George began its rule of the premiership roost, but the gradual disintegration of the Rabbitohs' squad led to the club missing the finals in the ensuing seven seasons, including a wooden spoon in 1962. Jack Rayner retired at the end of 1957 and was replaced by Clive Churchill as captain-coach. But Churchill's magnificent playing tenure at the club ended in unfortunate circumstances; Souths halved Churchill's season bonus and the fullback nonpareil departed for Queensland prior to the 1959 season. The Rabbitohs surged again in the mid-1960s with a youthful team stacked with future greats. Bernie Purcell returned to coach the club in 1964 and steered the Rabbitohs to the Grand Final the following season, with five-eighth Jim Lisle as captain and fellow dual international Michael Cleary starring on the flank. Future internationals including goalkicking winger/fullback Eric Simms, outstanding backrowers Ron Coote and Bob McCarthy, and forward enforcers John Sattler, John O'Neill and Jim Morgan lined up against the mighty St. George side in the 1965 decider, going down 12-8 in a gallant display in front of a Sydney Cricket Ground record 78,056-strong crowd.

Churchill made a triumphant return to Redfern as coach in 1967, guiding Souths to the first premiership of the limited-tackle era and simultaneously breaking the Dragons' 11-year stranglehold on the competition. The Rabbitohs defeated Canterbury 12-10 in the Grand Final, with a famous long-range intercept try to McCarthy proving pivotal. McCarthy was a revolutionary figure—a powerful, wide-running second-rower who scored 100 tries in a club record 211 games and ranks as one of Australia's greatest forwards. But he was left out of the 1967-68 Kangaroos squad that included Souths stars Coote, Sattler and Elwyn Walters, a tenacious hooker who had just completed his debut season in first grade.

Sattler was a surprise selection as captain of Souths, due to his notoriously volatile temperament. But the Newcastle product proved an inspired choice. The ferocious prop/second-rower joined Alf Blair and Jack Rayner in the realms of South Sydney's—and Rugby League's—greatest-ever skippers, leading the Rabbitohs to four Grand Final victories in five seasons. Coote, meanwhile, carved out a magnificent career that sees him ranked behind only his 1960s contemporary and St. George legend Johnny Raper as the best lock-forward of all time. A formidable ball-runner and magnificent cover defender, Coote's brilliance was utilised in the second-row in Australia's Test side until Raper retired; and so it was when the ARL's Team of the Century was announced in 2008, with Raper at lock and Coote named in the second-row. Coote featured in nine Grand Finals (for six premiership victories) in a 257-game career for Souths and Easts.

South Sydney defeated Manly 13-8 in the 1968 Grand Final to take out its second straight premiership, but the Rabbitohs were outfoxed by Balmain in the 1969 decider. The Tigers' stifling go-slow tactics frustrated Souths and were the catalyst for an 11-2 result in one of the biggest upsets in Grand Final history. Souths reclaimed the premiers' tag with a 23-12 Grand Final triumph over Manly in 1970, made famous by Sattler's heroic performance of playing out the entire match after having his jaw brutally smashed by Sea Eagles prop John Bucknall in the opening minutes. More than any other match, the 1970 Grand Final sealed Sattler's legacy.

Fullback Simms kicked three goals and four field goals in the defeat of Manly, and his prowess contributed to the value of field goals being reduced to one point in 1971. The Indigenous sharpshooter scored 1,843 points for Souths, including 265 in 1969—both unassailed club marks that stood as premiership records until 1983 and 1978 respectively. Simms represented Australia at the 1968 and 1970 World Cups, top-scoring at both tournaments. McCarthy, O'Neill, halves Dennis Pittard and Bob Grant, exceptional three-quarters Ray Branighan and Bob Honan, and centre/lock Paul Sait each made their international debuts in 1969 or 1970, while second-row hard-man Gary Stevens won his first Australian guernsey in 1972.

Souths overcame minor premiers Manly 19-13 in the 1971 major semi, before outlasting St. George 16-10 in the Grand Final to secure the club's 20th first grade title. Whether it was apparent at the time or not, the victory represented the end of an era as the Rabbitohs' playing stocks were plundered and the club descended into a difficult period clouded by fiscal uncertainty.

SWIFT DECLINE AND 1980s REVIVAL After such a magical period of dominance, South Sydney's deterioration during the 1970s beggared belief. More affluent rival clubs picked apart the Rabbitohs' champion line-up as Souths began to struggle financially due to substandard facilities at Redfern Oval and subsequent dwindling gate takings, mismanagement of the leagues and football clubs, and the changing demographics of the South Sydney district. Manly won the 1972 Grand Final with John O'Neill and Ray Branighan in its line-up, defeating an Eastern Suburbs outfit captained by Ron Coote, while Sattler left Souths for Queensland at the end of 1972. The club still provided four players to the 1973 Kangaroo Tour squad—McCarthy, Sait, Stevens and Walters—despite missing the finals for the first time in seven years. Walters joined Easts in 1974, opening the door for loyal clubman George Piggins, who played in the 1971 Grand Final win in Walters' absence, to finally assume the first grade hooking role.

McCarthy skippered the Rabbitohs to the finals in 1974, but was lumbered with captain-coach duties after Churchill stepped down amid Souths' dreadful start to the 1975 season, ending 'The Little Master's' nine-year tenure as coach. The Rabbitohs collected their first wooden spoon in 13 years and McCarthy joined Canterbury at the end of the year (he returned to finish his career with Souths in 1978). Rare bright spots in a dismal season were O'Neill's return to the club and Piggins' international debut during Australia's World Series campaign. Former Test winger Johnny King (1976), a retired O'Neill (1977) and even 'supercoach' Jack Gibson (1978-79) could not revive the Rabbitohs' fortunes during coaching stints.

Souths' largely unheralded squad—captained by future Australian team doctor Nathan Gibbs, and headlined by NSW prop Gary Hambly and inaugural Dally M Player of the Year Rocky Laurie—returned to the finals under rookie first grade coach Bill Anderson in 1980. Former Kangaroo fullback and two-time premiership-winning Manly coach Ron Willey took over in 1983 and steered Souths to its next finals appearance the following season. With Newcastle product and former NSW Origin winger Ziggy Niszczot as captain of a plucky side driven by passionate local juniors Mario Fenech, Craig Coleman and David Boyle, Souths came back from 14-0 down to upset archrivals Manly 22-18 in the minor preliminary semi—the Rabbitohs' first finals win since the 1971 Grand Final. Souths exited a week later in a fiery loss to St. George, but the club entered a fruitful period following George Piggins' return to Redfern as coach in 1986.

Temperamental hooker/prop Fenech was handed the captaincy, cheeky livewire Coleman became one of the premiership's most dominant halfbacks, and dynamic 20-year-old Ian Roberts emerged as the game's most exciting forward prospect. Aided by the experience of recruits Phil Gould and Neil Baker, the Rabbitohs finished the 1986 season in second place—just one point shy of minor premiers Parramatta—before bowing out with consecutive finals losses to Canterbury and Balmain. Aggressive forward Les Davidson was chosen in the 1986 Kangaroo Tour squad, becoming the club's first Australian representative since powerhouse winger Terry Fahey played against Great Britain in 1979.

Souths finished fifth in 1987 and eliminated the Tigers, but the season ended with a 46-12 minor semi capitulation to Canberra, highlighted by a nightmarish display from flamboyant Rabbitohs three-quarter Steve Mavin *(see Minties Moments)*. The 1989 season represented the club's last gilt-edged chance to win a title to date.

Souths secured its first minor premiership since 1970, losing just three regular season games. Skipper Fenech was in career-best form, representing NSW for the first time, while only a broken hand prevented him from touring New Zealand with the Australian side; former Manly prodigy Phil Blake, who joined the club in 1987, was brilliant at five-eighth and also debuted for the Blues; and 17-year-old hooker Jim Serdaris was crowned Dally M Rookie of the Year. But the Rabbitohs were skittled in consecutive finals by the Tigers (20-10) and the Raiders (32-16)—a deflating conclusion to the club's best season in almost two decades.

A DECADE OF DESPAIR Ian Roberts' controversial departure to Manly at the end of 1989 coincided with a dramatic fall from grace for South Sydney. The Rabbitohs won just two of their first nine games in 1990, before enduring a 13-match losing streak and collecting the wooden spoon. Meanwhile, a recreational drugs scandal rocked the club. Piggins stood down as coach, while the club's tenuous financial position led to the departure of Fenech, Davidson and Blake. Winger Graham Lyons represented New South Wales, while aggressive front-rower Mark Carroll made his Test debut and toured with the Kangaroos in rare highlights of a demoralising season.

Frank Curry took over as coach in 1991 as Souths relied on emerging talents such as diminutive fullback Rod Maybon, and livewire halves Darrell Trindall and Craig Field to lead the club into its next phase. Curry departed after three consecutive 14th-place finishes. The Rabbitohs enjoyed a mini-revival under Ken Shine in 1994 (after co-coach Bob McCarthy stood down early in the year, citing health reasons), defeating two-time premiers Brisbane 27-26 in the final of the pre-season Tooheys Challenge and piecing together a seven-match winning streak in the middle of the season. But Souths faded badly to miss the finals and floundered near the bottom of the table for the remainder of the decade, despite regular injections of representative recruits such as Craig Salvatori, Julian O'Neill and Tim Brasher.

With Piggins as club president, South Sydney sided with the ARL during the Super League war, but became a victim of the National Rugby League's rationalisation program. The Rabbitohs shunned potential merger partners and were subsequently excluded from the 2000 NRL premiership. Piggins led a passionate crusade for readmission—backed by outraged supporters numbering in the tens of thousands—with massive public rallies and high-profile court cases. After initially failing in its bid for readmission in 2000, South Sydney won a High Court appeal in 2001 and the NRL agreed to include the Rabbitohs in the following season's competition. Craig Coleman—the Rabbitohs' coach in 1999—retained the role for the club's comeback season, while only utility Chris Caruana and towering forward Paul McNicholas played in Souths' 1999 and 2002 seasons.

FROM THE ASHES Despite the euphoria of the club's readmission to the NRL and the acquisition of former internationals Adam Muir and Russell Richardson, and high-profile first grade veterans Owen Craigie and Jason Death, the Rabbitohs wallowed in the premiership cellar for several seasons. Only the Bulldogs' salary cap scandal saved Souths from the wooden spoon in 2002, and coach Coleman was dumped for Paul Langmack at the end of a season that yielded just five wins. Test backrower Bryan Fletcher arrived the following season to assume the captaincy from the retired Muir, but the Rabbitohs finished last in 2003 and 2004. Arthur Kitinas replaced Langmack midway through the latter season, before Shaun McRae took over in 2005. Souths improved to 13th with nine wins and a draw, before slumping to another wooden spoon in 2006 with a dismal three victories. The Rabbitohs were devoid of consistent performers, with the exception of ex-Broncos lock Ashley Harrison, who was installed as captain during 2005 and became the club's first Queensland Origin representative since Mitch Brennan in 1982. The most significant development at South Sydney in 2006 was the club member vote allowing 75 per cent purchase of the club by Australian movie star Russell Crowe, a Souths supporter since childhood, and businessman Peter Holmes á Court. The high-profile duo's involvement provided a much-needed financial boost, while Crowe's passion for the club saw him personally procure top-line playing talent.

Crowe spearheaded an aggressive recruitment drive for 2007 on and off the field. Jason Taylor was originally scheduled to come on board with the Rabbitohs as McRae's assistant in 2007, but was installed as head coach after steering Parramatta to the 2006 finals as caretaker coach. Meanwhile, the playing ranks were bolstered by New Zealand Test stars Roy Asotasi, David Kidwell and Nigel Vagana, along with ball-playing backrower Dean Widders from the Eels. Five wins in the last seven rounds propelled Souths to a seventh-place finish and its first finals series in 18 years. Although the Rabbitohs were swiftly eliminated courtesy of a qualifying final defeat to Manly, the post-season appearance set expectations soaring for success in the ensuing seasons.

Souths developed brilliant Queensland halfback Chris Sandow, mercurial tryscoring winger Nathan Merritt, livewire Kiwi hooker Isaac Luke and enigmatic Maroubra junior five-eighth/lock John Sutton, and lured (again with Crowe heavily involved) internationals Michael Crocker, Sam Burgess and Greg Inglis, and boom Broncos forward David Taylor to the club. But the Rabbitohs could not shake their inconsistent habits and missed the finals in the ensuing four seasons. Taylor was controversially sacked as coach after a 'Mad Monday' altercation with departing backrower David Fa'alogo at the end of 2009; former Cronulla and Penrith mentor John Lang took the reins for 2010-11, before highly rated ex-Melbourne assistant and Wigan coach Michael Maguire arrived ahead of the 2012 season.

South Sydney was still yearning for the glory days that the club had enjoyed so regularly throughout its first 64 seasons. But the passion of the Rabbitohs' supporter base, combined with the financial clout of the likes of Crowe, has ensured the ongoing presence in the premiership—which was devastatingly taken away for two years—of the Australian game's most successful club, 'The Pride of the League.'

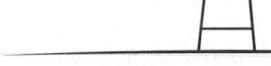

HEARTBREAK IN BEARS' FINAL DECADE

North Sydney won its only first grade titles in consecutive seasons, 1921-22, with a side regarded as one of the great premiership combinations of all time. Featuring wing immortals Harold Horder and Cec Blinkhorn, and legendary halfback Duncan Thompson, the club's powerhouse status rescinded as quickly as it had risen. The club qualified for the finals just twice in the next two decades. North Sydney was crushed 34-7 in its only Grand Final appearance, the 1943 decider against Newtown.

After collecting three wooden spoons in four seasons, Norths, spearheaded by forwards Peter Diversi and Norm Strong, made the finals in three consecutive seasons in the early 1950s. The club's greatest player, ARL Team of the Century winger Ken Irvine, and South African captain-coach Fred Griffiths steered the Bears to post-season appearances in 1964-65. But another extended period in the premiership cellar ensued: the club's only finals appearance in the following quarter of a century was in 1982.

The rot finally stopped in 1991 under the coaching of former international Steve Martin. Veteran forward recruits Pat Jarvis and Mario Fenech added starch to a potential-packed engine-room featuring tyros David Fairleigh, Gary Larson and Billy Moore—all of whom had played State of Origin football by 1992. Test five-eighth Peter Jackson and 1990 rookie of the year Jason Martin formed a brilliant halves combination, while club stalwarts Greg Florimo and captain Tony Rea blossomed with long overdue quality personnel supporting them.

The Bears finished the regular season in third spot with 14 victories and upset bitter rivals Manly 28-16 in the major preliminary semi-final, guaranteeing two shots at the club's first Grand Final berth in 48 seasons. Coming up against minor premiers Penrith, errant goalkicking from the season's top point-scorer, Kiwi rugby union convert Daryl Halligan, cost Norths victory in the major semi. The red-and-blacks scored three tries to the Panthers' two, but Halligan managed just one goal from five attempts—including a missed penalty shot with three minutes remaining—in the 16-14 defeat. The Bears squandered their second chance in the preliminary final. Leading 12-0 early against injury-ravaged two-time premiers Canberra, the hapless Bears were swamped 30-14 by their big-match hardened opponents.

Despite the lost opportunity, there was sufficient cause for optimism. But Norths finished 11th in 1992. The often prickly Martin's style had become stale and the coach resigned at the end of the season. Peter Louis arrived to guide the Bears into the next phase and produced immediate results. Norths landed just outside the finals in sixth spot, accumulating the same tally of wins as in 1991, including a 40-20 pasting of defending premiers Brisbane.

Astute recruiting and the emergence of outstanding young talent catapulted the Bears to the pointy end of the premiership table in 1994. Halfback general Jason Taylor joined from Wests and became one of the club's best-ever signings; Kiwi winger Sean Hoppe scored 15 tries in a one-season cameo in North Sydney colours; and fullback dynamo Matt Seers was one of the finest discoveries of 1994, taking out the Norwich Rising Star award. The club's formidable backrow triumvirate of Larson, Moore and Fairleigh had become established rep stars, while Fairleigh won the 1994 Rothmans Medal.

Finishing the regular season in second with a club record 17 wins, Norths' finals assault hit a speed-bump in the shape of the star-studded Raiders, who disposed of the Bears 26-12 in the preliminary major semi. But the Bears recouped to eliminate 1992-93 premiers Brisbane 15-14 in a classic minor semi the following weekend. Taylor, who had smashed the club pointscoring record during the season, was the hero with a late field goal. Approaching the preliminary final rematch with Canberra as underdogs, the Bears were poised to finally break the drought when Raiders prop John Lomax was marched for a high tackle. Norths already led 6-2 at the time of the 23rd minute send-off, but the ledger was inexplicably squared when Larson joined Lomax in the early-shower brigade with a spear tackle four minutes later. Despite hanging on to a 7-6 lead at the break, the Bears were overrun 22-9 by the Raiders in a devastating repeat of their loss on the season's penultimate weekend three years earlier.

The 1994 Kangaroo Tour squad announcement provided a bright footnote to a bitter end to the season for the club, with Fairleigh and Florimo chosen to tour England and France. Taylor, Moore and especially Larson were considered unlucky to miss out. The Bears failed to capitalise on their success in 1995, however—a last-round draw with lowly Gold Coast saw the club scrape into the finals, where they were promptly eliminated by Newcastle. Personal achievement supplied the brightest highlights for the club, with seven Bears participating in the State of Origin series and Larson and Moore making their Test debuts for Australia.

The 1996 season featured arguably the Bears' most regrettable lost opportunity. The injection of backline stars Brett Dallas, Ben Ikin and Michael Buettner helped propel the club to third spot at the end of the regular season. Captain Jason Taylor was the competition's top point-scorer and won the last Rothmans Medal, ahead of second-placed teammate David Fairleigh. Norths upset Brisbane at Suncorp Stadium to advance to the preliminary final stage, facing underdogs St. George after a week's rest. But after keeping pace with the Dragons to trail just 7-6 at halftime, North Sydney was blown off the park by an Anthony Mundine-led assault. Finding themselves in the unusual position of favourites in a finals match, the Bears had self-destructed to 29-12 defeat. It was a gilt-edged Grand Final opportunity lost for the hapless club.

North Sydney was one of the ARL-loyal heavyweights, and justified that status with a top-four finish in the 1997 Optus Cup during the game's great divide, receiving another preliminary final chance. After a gut-wrenching 33-21 extra-time loss to the Roosters in week one of the finals, the Bears rebounded to eliminate Parramatta 24-14 seven days later and claim the right to take on Newcastle for a spot in the decider. Norths hit back from a 12-4 halftime deficit against the Knights, but in a cruel reminder of Halligan's off day with the boot six years earlier, sharpshooter Taylor could manage just two goals from five attempts and the drama-charged match was locked at 12-all with five minutes to play. Matthew Johns nailed a 35-metre field goal to edge Newcastle in front, before Owen Craigie finished off a long-range try from the ensuing short kick-off to consign the Bears to a 17-12 defeat. It was another bitter pill to swallow for the club—easily the closest of its four preliminary final defeats during the 1990s.

Although the Bears finished fifth in the unified NRL competition in 1998, telltale signs of a club in decline were beginning to appear. The Bears were hammered 60-6 by Brisbane—a record score conceded by a North Sydney side—but the club was cautiously confident heading into the finals on the back of six straight wins. But after being bullied 25-12 by the aggressive Eels in the opening week of the finals, the Bears slipped out the back door when they were trounced 23-2 by Canterbury. It was to be the club's last finals appearance.

There is no question that 1999 was an unmitigated disaster for Norths. The proposed relocation of the club to the Central Coast of NSW—to enhance the club's chances of standing alone in the rationalised 2000 NRL competition—stalled when the construction of a purpose-built new stadium was delayed due to an horrendous run of wet weather. Poor gate receipts at alternative venues—including Suncorp Stadium in Brisbane and the cavernous Stadium Australia in Sydney—compounded the Bears' spiralling financial woes, while in-fighting and poor results saw coach Louis depart mid-season. The proud club lost eight matches in a row late in the season, before its 92-season heritage came to a close with victories over Melbourne and North Queensland. Norths' hands were tied, and the club reluctantly entered into an ill-fated merger with Manly. The Northern Eagles lasted just three seasons— and by 2002 Manly had assumed total control of the joint venture, which by that stage contained just two players who had played first grade for the Bears.

The Northern Eagles reverted to the Manly Sea Eagles in 2003, leaving Bears supporters without a club affiliation for the first time since the premiership's inception. Norths continued to field lower grade sides—reaching the Grand Final of the 2007 Premier League competition—but renewed hope emerged with the proposed Central Coast Bears firming as leading contender to become one of the NRL's mooted expansion teams in 2015. The Gosford-based entity retains several links to the North Sydney club, with former Bears greats Greg Florimo and David Fairleigh installed as the inaugural chief executive and coach respectively. The spectre of the Central Coast Bears represents a fresh chance to ease the pain for long-suffering Norths supporters.

For a complete North Sydney club history, see The Extinct Clubs

FROM MILLIONAIRES
TO FIBROS

The last two great eras in the history of the Western Suburbs Magpies club were built on two contrasting foundations. The image and ethos of big-spending Wests' star-studded 'Millionaires' side of the late-1950s and early-1960s was poles apart from the rough-and-tumble, working-class 'Fibros' team of the late-1970s and early-1980s which, ironically, had many of its best players poached by rival clubs.

After winning the 1952 premiership, the Magpies wallowed in the competition cellar for three years, collecting the wooden spoon in 1953 and 1955. But the club embarked on an aggressive recruitment drive to climb the ladder again in 1956. With abundant revenue from a newly purchased leagues club, Wests lured all time greats Kel O'Shea and Harry Wells from Queensland and Wollongong respectively, and fellow Test representatives Darcy Henry and Ian Johnstone from NSW country centres.

The tactic paid immediate dividends: the Magpies returned to the finals in 1956 after beating Newtown in a play-off for fourth place, before claiming outright fourth spot in 1957. Eliminated in the finals by Souths in each season, Wests finished second in the minor premiership in 1958 and hammered the mighty St. George Dragons in the major semi to advance to the Grand Final. The Magpies were overwhelmed 20-9 in the decider as the Dragons claimed their third consecutive title, but the black-and-whites had asserted themselves as a premiership heavyweight. Wests had acquired the services of former Test centre Rees Duncan and Dapto teenager Peter Dimond in 1958, with the bulldozing winger making his Test debut in his first year with the club.

The Magpies finished second in the 1959-60 regular seasons, but were beaten in consecutive preliminary finals by Manly and Easts respectively, while the club's big-spending ways continued unabated. Criticised for inflating player payments and inciting bidding wars for players throughout the Sydney premiership, the Magpies nonetheless signed Test three-quarters Dick Poole (Newtown) and Ian Moir (Souths) from rivals clubs for the 1959 season. Former Wallaby half Arthur Summons joined the club in 1960, while Test fullback Don Parish (Dubbo) and Kangaroo hooker/prop Noel Kelly (Ipswich) followed suit in 1961.

Wests claimed its fourth minor premiership in 1961, but was beaten 9-4 by St. George in the major semi and swamped 22-0 by the dominant Dragons in the Grand Final. After finishing third in 1962, the Magpies defeated Balmain and Parramatta to advance to another Grand Final against St. George, where they were narrowly beaten 9-6 in a tense decider. But Wests came even more tantalisingly close to ending the Dragons' run in 1963. The Magpies defeated St. George three times during the season, including a 10-8 victory in the major semi, but went down 8-3 in one of the most controversial Grand Finals of all time. Rumours of referee Darcy Lawler placing a large wager on the Dragons have shrouded the 'Mudbath' Grand Final ever since, with two contentious calls singled out by proponents of rort claims. Peter Dimond was denied a seemingly fair try, while St. George winger Johnny King leapt up and ran in for a try after Wests players vehemently asserted they had heard Lawler call for King to play the ball 20 metres further back.

The contentious loss brought an end to a golden period for the club. Despite retaining 1963 Kangaroos Dimond, Kelly and captain Summons, the Magpies finished seventh out of 10 teams in 1964 and did not return to the finals for another decade. The steady flow of Test players and up-and-coming stars the club relentlessly recruited had dried up, and Wests returned to also-ran status.

The Magpies began to build a formidable line-up again in the mid-1970s, led by tenacious halfback Tom Raudonikis, who captained Australia in the Ashes-deciding third Test on the 1973 Kangaroo Tour among 29 Test appearances. Future Test players John Dorahy and Les Boyd linked with the club in the mid-1970s, while cult hero forward John Donnelly joined from Gunnedah in 1975 and represented Australia in his first season in Sydney. The unfancied Magpies made the finals in 1974, but the arrival of coach Roy Masters in 1978 saw the club reach—and arguably exceed—its potential.

Tapping into the working-class psyche of his Wests team, Masters developed an 'us-against-them' mentality within the squad which corresponded with their aggressive, take-no-prisoners style of play. Wests' adoption of the 'Fibros' moniker during this period was attributable to puppeteer Masters. It was a reference to the fibro (short for Fibrous Asbestos Cement) sheets that were a popular building material at the time, particularly for inexpensive housing in working-class areas—

such as Sydney's western suburbs. Masters stirred his players up before a pre-season match against Manly's 'Silvertails,' as he called them, a wealthy club based on Sydney's northern beaches.

The promotional match, staged in Melbourne, erupted into a series of wild brawls and a bitter feud was born. The 'Fibros' vs. 'Silvertails' fixtures over the next few seasons provided some of the premiership's most brutal and ferociously contested clashes. Another tactic employed by Masters involved his players firing themselves up by engaging in vigorous face-slapping sessions with each other in the changing rooms before matches. The novel method attracted controversy when it was aired as part of a story on top-rating current affairs program 60 Minutes.

On the back of this passion and fire, Wests won the minor premiership in 1978 after posting a club record 16 regular season victories. But the Magpies were rolled 14-10 by Cronulla in the major semi and succumbed 14-7 to arch-nemesis Manly in an explosive preliminary final. Wests finished fourth in 1979, before being eliminated by Canterbury on the first weekend of the finals, after which rival clubs pillaged the Magpies' playing stocks. Test stars John Dorahy and Les Boyd, along with NSW hooker Ray Brown (a non-playing reserve for Australia in the 1979 Ashes series), signed with Manly, exacerbating the ill feeling between the two clubs. The cash-strapped Magpies also watched club legend Tom Raudonikis and future NSW Origin rep Graeme O'Grady depart to play for Newtown.

Undeterred, Masters found a new batch of players to enforce his fire-and-brimstone approach. John Ribot joined from the Jets and was transformed from a hard-working lock into one of the game's most damaging wingers; Jim Leis was the inaugural Dally M Rookie of the Year in 1980 and represented Australia; determined five-eighth Terry Lamb was another eye-catching newcomer; and 'Lord' Ted Goodwin, a former international and superstar St. George fullback, enjoyed a late-career renaissance as a forward with Wests.

Masters was named Dally M Coach of the Year for his efforts in taking his new-look Wests side to within one victory of the 1980 minor premiership. After a dogged campaign, the Magpies were eventually eliminated in the preliminary final by Easts. But the club's strongarm tactics came into conflict with the NSWRL's efforts to clean up the game in the early-1980s. 'Dallas' Donnelly was slapped with a 14-match ban against the Sea Eagles in the first match of 1981, and Wests finished sixth to miss the finals for the first time Masters' term as coach.

Terry Fearnley, who steered Parramatta to consecutive Grand Finals in 1976-77, replaced the St. George-bound Masters in 1982. Discipline still proved a problem, however, with Bob Cooper receiving an unprecedented 15-month suspension for his role in a vicious brawl in a match against Illawarra. Against the odds, Fearnley guided the Magpies to the finals in 1982, but the coach and several key players departed at the end of the season as the club's financial situation deteriorated. Wests' exhilarating 'Fibro' era had abruptly come to a close and the Magpies finished last under coach Len Stacker in 1983.

The club was excluded from the 1984 premiership along with Newtown, but was reinstated following a court appeal. The remainder of the 1980s offered few highlights for the Magpies, before they enjoyed a brief comeback with consecutive finals appearance in 1991-92 with shrewd coach Warren Ryan at the helm and a host of former Bulldogs players, including internationals David Gillespie, Paul Langmack and Andrew Farrar, in great form. Raudonikis returned to coach the club in its last five seasons, taking Wests to the 1996 finals, but standing alone in a 14-team NRL competition was not a viable option and the Magpies entered a merger with Balmain in 2000 after collecting consecutive wooden spoons in 1998-99.

The Magpies, who retain a direct presence with a side in the NSW Cup, maintained a solid identity within the Wests Tigers joint venture and rejoiced in the club's 2005 premiership triumph. The rich history of each club is celebrated and remembered, including those talented and colourful teams of yesteryear with contradicting cultures—'The Millionaires' and 'The Fibros.'

For a complete Western Suburbs club history, see The Extinct Clubs

TRICOLOURS' UNBROKEN HISTORY

Eastern Suburbs—later known as the Sydney Roosters—are the only club to field a team in every premiership season. One of only two foundation clubs remaining (with South Sydney), the Tricolours have endured deep troughs during their existence, but their enduring legacy is some of the greatest club combinations in Rugby League history.

The Eastern Suburbs Rugby League Club was formed at a meeting on January 24, 1908, with Harry 'Jersey' Flegg appointed as club secretary. Flegg was Easts' inaugural captain, but his most significant contribution to the game was as an administrator, serving as the NSWRL president from 1929 until his death in 1960. Easts fielded many of the finest rugby union converts and pioneering luminaries, including centre Dan Frawley, revered hooker Sid 'Sandy' Pearce and the great winger Albert Rosenfeld (who became a marvel of the English club scene after leaving Australia in 1909)—all of whom were named in the ARL's 100 Greatest Players in 2008. But the major coup—for the club and Rugby League in general—was the signing of Herbert Henry 'Dally' Messenger. The preeminent rugby union player of his time, Messenger became Rugby League's first superstar and his influence was vital to the code's success in Australia.

Easts qualified for the first premiership final in 1908, going down to Souths 14-12. The club was without its galaxy of stars that were on en route to England with the first Kangaroos—Messenger, Frawley, Rosenfeld, Pearce and forward Larry 'Jersey' O'Malley, who became Easts' second Test captain (after Messenger) when he led Australia in two Tests against New Zealand in 1909.

The club secured its first premiership in 1911, beating minor premiers Glebe in the final 11-8 despite missing Frawley, halfback Arthur 'Pony' Halloway and front-rower Bob Williams, who were chosen in the Kangaroo Tour squad. Easts set about creating the first Australian Rugby League dynasty, winning the ensuing two first grade titles. With the premiership awarded on a 'first-past-the-post' system from 1912-25, the Messenger-led Eastern Suburbs side was crowned champions after finishing atop the ladder at the end of the 1912 and 1913 seasons. Messenger, whose brother Wally featured in the 1912-13 premierships and represented Australia in two Tests against England in 1914, retired at the conclusion of Easts' hat-trick of titles.

Easts finished as runners-up in 1919 and 1921, while brilliant centre Les Cubitt captained the 1921-22 Kangaroo Tour squad, which contained clubmates 'Sandy' Pearce, Jack Watkins, Rex Norman and Harry Caples. The club finished equal-first with Souths in 1923 and won its fourth premiership with a 15-12 result over the Rabbitohs in the final, with skipper Caples scoring his second try late in the match to snatch victory. Featuring esteemed Test stars such as halfback Joe 'Chimpy' Busch, goalkicking forward Arthur Oxford and outside back Nelson Hardy, Easts finished runners-up in 1928, and again in 1931 and 1934 with a batch of new standouts that would spearhead another Tricolours dynasty.

EASTS' DECADE OF DOMINANCE Under the guidance of coach 'Pony' Halloway, Easts moulded a team of extraordinary ability. The side contained magnificent fullback/centre Jack Beaton; Test centre Ross McKinnon; incomparable halves pairing Ernie Norman and Viv Thicknesse; prolific tryscoring wingers Fred Tottey and Rod O'Loan; all time great lock Andy Norwal; international second-rowers Sid 'Joe' Pearce (son of Sandy) and Harry Pierce; and Kangaroos prop enforcer Ray Stehr. Beaton, Norman, Thicknesse, Norval, Pearce and Stehr would later be named in the ARL's 100 Greatest Players in 2008—along with the undeniable star of an incredible line-up: freakish centre Dave Brown.

Dubbed 'The Bradman of League,' Brown set a mark never to be bettered by scoring 285 points on the 1933-34 Kangaroo Tour, before slashing his way into the premiership record books in 1935. Easts' captain scored 38 tries (including six in a match twice) for the season and amassed 45 points in an 87-7 thrashing of Canterbury (he also scored 38 points against the competition newcomers later in the season)—both all time first grade records which still stand—amongst a then-record season total of 244 points. Easts lost just one of its 16 regular season games and, despite losing Brown to injury in the semi-final defeat of Wests, downed Souths 19-3 in the premiership final with Stehr as skipper.

In 1936, Easts became the fourth side to go through a season undefeated, winning 11 and drawing two of its 13 regular season games and swamping Balmain 32-12 in the premiership final. The club repeated the feat in 1937, winning six and drawing two of eight games in a season shortened due to the departure of the Kangaroos (no finals matches were played), sealing a hat-trick of premierships. Between 1935 and 1938 Easts went undefeated in 35 matches, but Canterbury ended the Tricolours title streak with a 19-6 defeat in the 1938 final.

Brown returned as captain-coach in 1940 after a stint with English club Leeds, and guided the club to the minor premiership. A leg injury ruled him out of the final, but Stehr deputised again and led Easts to a 24-14 defeat of the Berries. Stehr captain-coached the club to a runner-up finish in 1941 following a 31-14 loss to St. George in the final, but skippered another premiership-winning side when 'Pony' Halloway returned for one last season as coach in 1945. Easts defeated Balmain 22-18 in an epic final that is best remembered for lock Dick Dunn's career-defining performance, scoring 19 points from three tries and five goals to propel the Tricolours to their ninth title (see *Unlikely Heroes*).

LITTLE TO CROW ABOUT After a period of brilliant success, the Tricolours struggled for much of the next three decades. Powerhouse winger Lionel Cooper and hooker George Watt represented Australia in the 1946 home Ashes series (Cooper left at the end of the season and became a legend of the British game), while fullback Vic Bulgin and Wally O'Connell, who became Easts' fourth Test captain, toured with the 1948-49 Kangaroos. But Easts languished mid-table from 1946-48 and finished last for the first time the club's history in 1949. Halfback Col Donohoe and second-rower Ferris Ashton went on the 1952-53 Kangaroo Tour, and spearheaded Easts' return to the finals in 1953—although it ended abruptly with a 25-7 defeat to St. George in the semi-final. Also in the Tricolours' side was a tough front-rower that would later have a monumental impact on the club in a coaching capacity—Jack Gibson.

But the remainder of the decade brought little joy—the club finished no higher than sixth and came second-last twice—despite the return of Dave Brown as coach from 1957-59. Dick Dunn came onboard as coach in 1960 and steered Easts to equal-second on the ladder. Following an elaborate play-off series, Easts won through to the Grand Final, despite not having a past, current or future international in its playing ranks. But the Gibson-led side was thumped 31-6 by St. George as the Dragons chalked up their fifth straight title, while the club's lowest ebb was still to come.

Easts collected the wooden spoon in 1965, and were anchored to the bottom of the ladder the following season after losing all 18 regular season matches. It was the first time a club had failed to win a match in 20 years, while no team has finished a season winless since.

MASTER COACH INITIATES GOLDEN PERIOD Jack Gibson returned to the club as coach in 1967 and, in one of the great club turnarounds, the Roosters qualified for the finals. Although Easts was eliminated 13-2 by Canterbury in the semi-final, the embattled club had made a spectacular recovery from the depths of the winless 1966 season. Centre Ron Saddler and nippy halfback Kevin Junee toured with the 1967-68 Kangaroos. Gibson departed after leading Easts to the finals again in 1968, but the club faded again with South African Louis Neumann as captain-coach in 1969 and in the first two seasons of former Queensland and Kangaroos forward Don Furner's stint as coach. Furner guided the Roosters to the Grand Final at the end of a much-improved 1972 season, however, with South Sydney and Test great Ron Coote as skipper of a side containing Australian prop Arthur Beetson (who joined from Balmain in 1971), powerhouse three-quarters Bill Mullins and Test star Mark Harris, former Wallaby five-eighth John Ballesty and goalkicking fullback Allan McKean, who played an Ashes Test in 1970. The second-placed Roosters succumbed 19-14 in the Grand Final to minor premiers Manly.

Former Easts, Manly and NSW five-eighth Tony Paskins coached Easts to a sixth-place finish in 1973, before Gibson took the reins again following fruitful stints with St. George and Newtown. He installed Beetson—the club's only 1973 Kangaroos representative—as captain in 1974, and the legendary ball-playing front-rower responded by taking his game to another level and becoming one of the great leaders. Bolstered by the acquisition of Souths and Kangaroo hooker Elwyn Walters, rugby union stars Russell Fairfax and John Brass, and the return of pivot John Peard, halfback Johnny Mayes and hard-hitting forward Barry 'Bunny' Reilly from stints with rival clubs, the Roosters claimed the minor premiership and broke a 29-year title drought with a 19-4 defeat of Canterbury in the Grand Final.

The Tricolours were even more dominant in 1975 as they established a legacy as one of the great club sides of all time, piecing together a premiership record 19-match winning streak to emphatically take out top spot on the ladder. Despite being upset 8-5 in the major semi by St. George, Easts swept aside Wests 25-2 in the preliminary final before annihilating the Dragons 38-0—a Grand Final record that stood for 33 years. Leading just 5-0 at halftime, the Roosters piled on seven second half tries in the decider equally remembered for Saints' injury-hampered captain Graeme Langlands' infamous 'white boots' performance after a painkilling injection went wrong. Beetson, Brass, Peard, Mayes, teenage fullback/winger Ian Schubert, and forwards Ian Mackay and John Quayle featured in Australia's successful World Series campaign at the end of the season, with Beetson (three matches) and Brass (one) each captaining the side.

Gibson departed after the fourth-placed Roosters were bundled out in the minor preliminary semi-final by Canterbury in 1976, with Beetson taking over as captain-coach in 1977. He was joined at the club by Manly and Australian Test superstar Bob Fulton, who captained the Roosters during the 1977 finals in the injury-enforced absence of Beetson. Fulton was partnered in the halves by a young Kevin Hastings, a tenacious No.7 who went on to win the Rothmans Medal in 1981 and three consecutive Dally M Halfback of the Year gongs (1980-82) on his way to a then-club record 228 appearances for Easts. The Roosters' 1977 season ended with preliminary final defeat to Parramatta, while Beetson joined the Eels in the wake of Easts' disappointing 1978 season. Fulton, captain of the 1978 Kangaroo Tour squad, assumed the captain-coach role for the club.

'Bozo' retired due to a shoulder injury early in 1979, but remained as coach and guided the Roosters to consecutive minor premierships in 1980 and '81. Captained by Test prop Royce Ayliffe and featuring electrifying winger Kerry Boustead and wily hooker John Lang—both Queensland and Kangaroos representatives—Easts lost the 1980 Grand Final 18-4 to the Bulldogs, while the club dipped out of the 1981 finals with back-to-back losses to Parramatta and Newtown. Fulton's association with the club ended after he took the Roosters to the 1982 preliminary final, where they lost 33-0 to the Eels.

EASTS IN THE DOLDRUMS After the Gibson-Beetson-Fulton sequence concluded at the end of 1982, Easts qualified for the finals just once in the ensuing 13 seasons. Former Roosters forward Laurie Freier took over as coach and Hastings assumed the captaincy, guiding the club to a fifth-place play-off loss to St. George, while Mike Eden scored a then-club record 256 points. Beetson replaced the sacked Freier following the Roosters' disastrous second-last finish in 1984, while the period was marked by a glut of short-lived, ill-fated signings. But valuable acquisitions such as potent ex-St. George winger and Test halfback Steve Morris, New Zealand Test backrower Hugh McGahan, North Queensland halfback Laurie Spina and brilliant British outside-back Joe Lydon spearheaded the club's 1987 season. Eastern Suburbs, skippered by McGahan, finished second in the minor premiership, but was overrun 32-24 by Canberra in the preliminary final.

Russell Fairfax endured a dreadful stint as Roosters coach after replacing former teammate Beetson at the end of 1988. During a horror 1990 campaign, Easts copped a 66-4 hammering from defending champs Canberra, Test veteran Paul Vautin was dropped to reserve grade in his first season after joining the club from Manly, and Faifax was sacked before the end of the season. McGahan filled in as captain-coach ahead the arrival of former Kangaroo halfback Mark Murray. Ball-playing prop Craig Salvatori made his Test debut for Australia in 1991 and Kiwi Test captain Gary Freeman joined the club in 1992 as the club displayed signs of improvement under Murray. Halfback Freeman, who became the first overseas player to win the Dally M Medal in 1992, immediately established himself as the Roosters' go-to player. But mid-season slumps in 1992 and 1993 cruelled Easts' bid to return to the finals, while Freeman was punted a month before the end of the latter season after signing with Penrith for 1994, allegedly going back on an agreement he made with club management. Freeman's abrupt departure pre-empted a return to the premiership cellar. Murray was shown the door before the end of 1994, with Beetson seeing out the season in a caretaker role.

ROOSTER REVIVAL The club changed its name to the Sydney City Roosters in 1995 and began its resurgence under the direction of dual premiership-winning coach Phil Gould. The Roosters sided with the ARL during the Super League upheaval and consequently acquired Test captain Brad Fittler and fellow Penrith international Matt Sing in 1996 (both of whom played under Gould at the Panthers), along with goalkicking fullback/centre Ivan Cleary from North Sydney. Fittler and Adrian Lam—the linchpin of Queensland's 3-0 Origin series triumph in 1995— formed one of the premiership's most dominant halves combinations. Meanwhile, fullback/five-eighth Andrew Walker emerged as a brilliant—if enigmatic—match-winner and the arrival of representative forwards David Barnhill, Scott Gourley and Terry Hermansson transformed the club into a genuine heavyweight.

The Roosters qualified for the finals in 1996—their first post-season appearance in nine years—but bowed out with consecutive losses to Manly and St. George. The club's 1997-98 seasons ended one week short of the Grand Final courtesy of preliminary final defeats to Manly and Brisbane respectively, and Gould stepped down as coach following a straight-sets exit from the 1999 finals. Ex-Illawarra and Hunter Mariners mentor Graham Murray took over a line-up that was built around Fittler's inspirational captaincy and game-breaking excellence. Again renamed in 2000, this time as the Sydney Roosters, the club attained its best regular season finish since taking out the 1981 minor premiership. The second-placed Roosters advanced to the Grand Final with a stirring come-from-behind preliminary final triumph over Newcastle, but were subdued 14-6 by Brisbane in the decider. Valuable No.7 Lam departed to English club Wigan at the end of 2000, while Murray was unceremoniously axed after the Roosters limped into the 2001 finals in seventh place before being eliminated 40-6 in a qualifying final demolition at the hands of the Knights.

Rookie first grade coach Ricky Stuart took the reins in 2002, and the Roosters emerged from a patchy start to enter the finals as the NRL's form team in fifth spot. The Roosters accounted for the Sharks, Knights and Broncos on their way to a Grand Final showdown with New Zealand. The Roosters' comprehensive 30-8 victory in the decider was the club's ninth win in succession and broke a 27-year premiership drought. Fittler was the key to the title success, but was ably backed in the leadership department by club stalwart and lock Luke Ricketson and Test backrower Bryan Fletcher. Ricketson, goalkicking backrower Craig Fitzgibbon, winger-cum-fullback Anthony Minichiello, ultra-versatile hooker-half Craig Wing, elusive three-quarter Shannon Hegarty and fiery forward Michael Crocker all subsequently debuted for Australia by the end of 2003.

Established as the NRL's glamour team, the Roosters endured twin Grand Final defeats in the ensuing two seasons. The Roosters were upset 18-6 by Penrith in 2003, before the club's first minor premiership in 23 years was nullified by a 16-13 loss to archrivals the Bulldogs in the 2004 decider. The latter defeat marked the end of Fittler's nine-season tenure at the club, bringing down the curtain on one of the great Rugby League careers.

ROOSTERS RIDE THE ROLLERCOASTER Ricketson assumed the captaincy in 2005 and brought up 300 first grade appearances for the club before retiring at the end of the season. But the Roosters missed the finals for the first time in a decade and Stuart was dumped after the club finished second-last in 2006. Dual premiership-winning coach Chris Anderson replaced Stuart after the club botched the signing of Wayne Bennett—the Brisbane supercoach reneged after the deal became public knowledge against his wishes. Anderson's 2007 stint was disastrous— he stood down after just 17 games, with the Roosters languishing in 15th place following a 56-0 loss to Manly. But a gratifying late-season revival under caretaker coach Brad Fittler lifted the club to 10th and the former captain was offered the role fulltime in 2008. Representative recruits Braith Anasta, Nate Myles and Willie Mason continued the revival alongside outstanding young talents Mitchell Pearce and Shaun Kenny-Dowall in 2008. Fittler's charmed run continued with a top-four finish in the 2008 minor premiership, although his side was bundled out of the finals with consecutive losses to the Broncos and Warriors.

But a change of calendar heralded a stunning reversal of fortune for Fittler and the Roosters. A string of alcohol-fuelled off-field atrocities in 2009—the most notable involving Queensland Origin forward Myles and coach Fittler in separate incidents—were mirrored by disastrous results on the paddock. The club was condemned to its first wooden spoon since the winless 1966 season after recording just five victories. It was an unbefitting end to the NRL career of Roosters great Craig Fitzgibbon, who departed with a club record 1,454 points from 228 games in 10 seasons for the club.

The 2010 season brought another dramatic turnaround. Veteran coach Brian Smith joined the Roosters and the club threw troubled playmaker Todd Carney a lifeline. The result: Carney was named Dally M Player of the Year and Smith Coach of the Year, while Anasta claimed the Captain of the Year gong. The Roosters surged to the Grand Final on the back of a heart-stopping golden point victory over Wests Tigers in the qualifying final, and comfortable wins over Penrith and Gold Coast. Despite being overwhelmed 32-8 by St. George Illawarra in the decider, the Roosters had nevertheless become the first club in premiership history to collect the wooden spoon and play in a Grand Final 12 months later. Yet again the recovery proved to be a false dawn as the Roosters slumped to 11th in 2011—thanks in no small part to further indiscretions that led to Carney's departure from Bondi. But with quality youngsters emerging and its cheque book at the ready, the only club to feature in every premiership season remains a prominent part of the Rugby League landscape.

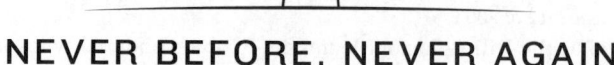

NEVER BEFORE, NEVER AGAIN

St. George's feat in winning 11 consecutive Grand Finals between 1956 and 1966 dwarfs every other club achievement in Rugby League history. After winning their first premierships in 1941 and 1949, Saints finished runners-up to South Sydney in 1953. But nobody could have predicted the period of unparalleled dominance the Kogarah-based club was about to enjoy. Boasting unmatched professionalism off the field in the form of famed secretary 'Fearless' Frank Facer and president Len Kelly—both premiership-winners with St. George as players during the 1940s—the club constructed a phenomenal empire. Sharply astute recruitment and nurturing of outstanding junior talent was at the centre of the Dragons' success, assembling a phenomenally talented squad that was consistently joined by outstanding players that became established as all time greats. Former Wallaby Ken Kearney linked with St. George in 1952 after switching codes and honing his craft with English club Leeds. He captain-coached the club to the finals in 1954-55, but Norm Tipping—a former St. George fullback and the club's coach in 1953—was reintroduced as coach in 1956, with the intimidating Kearney as skipper.

1956 St. George collected the third minor premiership in the club's history in 1956 on the strength of a magnificent second half of the regular season. Sitting in fourth at the halfway mark of the competition, the Dragons lost just one of their remaining nine games to top the ladder—a solitary point in front of Balmain. A second half surge propelled the Saints to a 30-25 victory over the Tigers in the major semi, booking the first Grand Final berth. The J.J. Giltinan Shield made its way to Kogarah for the third time following St. George's gritty 18-12 defeat of Balmain a fortnight later. The Dragons played most of the decider with 12 men after centre Merv Lees left the field with a shoulder injury in the opening 20 minutes. Skipper Ken Kearney captain-coached Australia to a 3-0 series whitewash of New Zealand during the season, and retained the role for the Kangaroo Tour at the end of the year, joined in the touring squad by clubmates Norm Provan and Kevin O'Brien. Winger Tommy Ryan topped the premiership's tryscoring stakes in 1956 with 19; centre O'Brien was equal-second with 15 touchdowns. Fullback Doug Fleming led the competition by racking up 189 points.

1957 Kearney replaced Norm Tipping as coach in 1957, heralding the club's policy of strictly employing captain-coaches that would last for over a decade. The defending premiers also welcomed three key additions to their playing ranks—legendary forward Harry Bath returned from a stellar career in English club football, ex-Manly winger Eddie Lumsden pulled on the Red V for the first time and former Newtown Grand Final centre Brian 'Poppa' Clay joined the Dragons after a season in Griffith, becoming a highly influential five-eighth/lock for the club. The Saints streeted the field in the regular season, finishing seven points clear of second-placed Manly. After accounting for the Sea Eagles 21-7 in the major semi, St. George trounced them 31-9 in the decider. Bath kicked eight goals for 16 points—both Grand Final records. Tommy Ryan headed the premiership with a club record 26 tries (including three hauls of four tries), while Lumsden crossed 18 times. Clay, Kearney and Provan featured in Australia's inaugural World Cup success earlier in the year.

1958 Saints lost just two matches during the 1958 regular season—an opening-round defeat to Manly and a shock mid-season loss at the hands of wooden spooners Parramatta—to finish eight points ahead of the field. But the two-time premiers were humbled 34-10 by second-placed Western Suburbs in the major semi. Finding themselves in an unfamiliar sudden-death situation in the preliminary final a week later, the Dragons regrouped to advance to the Grand Final with a hard-fought 26-21 victory over Balmain. Wests entered the decider as favourites on the strength of its win a fortnight earlier, but St. George prevailed 20-9 to secure a hat-trick of first grade titles. Norm Provan scored two first half tries to establish a 10-5 lead at the break, before late tries to halfback Bobby Budgen and winger Lumsden in a torrid second stanza sealed victory. Bath led the competition's point-scorers with 225 points—an all time St. George record and a premiership record for a forward which still stands. Lumsden yielded another 18 tries in 1958 to finish atop the premiership. Kearney, Provan and winger Ross Kite represented Australia in the 2-1 Ashes series loss against the touring Lions.

1959 St. George became the sixth (and, to date, last) club to go through a season undefeated in 1959. A 10-match winning streak to start the year was halted by a 20-all draw with Balmain, before the Dragons won another nine straight to seize an emphatic premiership triumph. During a particularly savage eight-day period, St. George ran 60 points past both Parramatta and Canterbury. Saints overcame Wests 35-25 in another high-scoring major semi, before shutting out Manly 20-0 in the Grand Final. Lumsden crossed for three of the Dragons' six tries, while Harry Bath (playing in his last game) and Manly enforcer Rex Mossop were sent off for fighting. The 1959 season was equally significant for the club debuts of a pair of teenagers that would become arguably the two greatest Saints—promising Newtown lock John Raper, and centre Reg Gasnier, a St. George junior (Gasnier missed the Grand Final victory with injury). Gasnier, Raper, Lumsden and veteran front-rower Billy Wilson debuted for Australia in the home series against the Kiwis, and were joined on the 1959-60 Kangaroo Tour by 'Poppa' Clay, halfback Bugden and centre Johnny Riley (who also missed the Grand Final due to injury). Bath scored 205 points in 1959 (a premiership record for points in a season by a prop) to finish just one point behind the competition leader, Wests' Darcy Russell. North Sydney's Ken Irvine (19 tries) was the top try-scorer, followed by three Saints—winger Brian Messiter (18), Bugden (16) and Lumsden (15). St. George's dominance garnered its fifth straight club championship.

1960 The Dragons swept to their fifth straight premiership with consummate ease, equalling the record of the South Sydney side of 1925-29. The minor premiers posted more than 50 points in regular season wins over Parramatta and Newtown, before crushing Wests 31-7 in the major semi. Eastern Suburbs was similarly outclassed in the Grand Final as Saints stormed to a 31-6 victory. Reg Gasnier scored a double in his maiden Grand Final appearance to take his season try tally to 25—just one shy of the club record, and nine clear of his premiership rivals. Winger Johnny King, an 18-year-old newcomer to the St. George line-up in 1960, also crossed twice in the decider to start a phenomenal streak of scoring tries in six consecutive Grand Finals. Kevin Ryan was lured to the club in 1960 and immediately became established as one of the premiership's most feared enforcers. The former Wallaby was sent off in the Grand Final along with Easts rival Brian Wright. Saints fullback Brian Graham was the premiership's top point-scorer with 193. Bobby Bugden scored three tries on Test debut against France, while Gasnier, Raper, Provan and Lumsden also featured in the drawn home series. The 1960 premiership win marked Ken Kearney's last as captain-coach; injury ended his playing career during the following season.

1961 Western Suburbs broke St. George's five-season stranglehold on the minor premiership, securing the honour with a points differential a mere nine points superior to the Dragons' after both sides finished equal with 15 wins. It was the only season during the Saints' 11-year domination that they did not couple Grand Final victory with the minor premiership. Honours were shared one win apiece in matches between the heavyweight rivals during the regular season, but Saints won a hard-fought major semi 9-4, before romping home 22-0 over the Magpies in the Grand Final. Billy Wilson skippered the Dragons to victory in the absence of Kearney, who claimed his fifth premiership as coach. Powerhouse winger Eddie Lumsden scored another Grand Final hat-trick in the comprehensive defeat of the big-spending, star-studded Wests outfit. King's second season in first grade yielded a competition-high 20 tries, while Graham's 153 points placed him second in the premiership. In an anomaly of St. George's world record premiership run, just two of the club's stars represented Australia—Reg Gasnier and Eddie Lumsden played both Tests in the drawn series with New Zealand.

1962 Norm Provan succeeded Ken Kearney as captain-coach in 1962, and the St. George machine was further strengthened by the acquisition of Eugowra's Kangaroo hooker Ian Walsh and robust Test second-rower Elton Rasmussen from Queensland. The Dragons reclaimed the minor premiership, finishing the premiership rounds one point ahead of Newtown. Reg Gasnier scored three tries in a 30-9 thrashing of the Bluebags in the major semi, but the Magpies were a much tougher proposition in the tightest-scoring Grand Final of the Dragons' run. In his last match for the club, Billy Wilson was sent off for decking Wests forward Jim Cody (in an apparent act of retribution after Saints skipper Provan was poleaxed during the first half), leaving the Dragons a man short. St. George's resilient defence formed the basis of a tense 9-6 victory, and the club's seventh straight title. Eddie Lumsden was the premiership's top trycorer with 21 touchdowns, while Johnny King (16) finished second and Reg Gasnier (15) equal-third. Gasnier became Australia's youngest Ashes captain when he led his country in the first Test of the home series, and he was joined during the 2-1 series loss by clubmates Walsh, Rasmussen, Raper and Lumsden (the side was coached Harry Bath). But the Saints' pride took a rare battering when they were thumped 33-5 by the touring Lions in front of a bumper midweek crowd of 57,744 at the Sydney Cricket Ground. St. George reclaimed the club championship for the first time since 1959 after winning just the second reserve grade premiership in the club's history.

1963 St. George's awe-inspiring defensive curtain achieved new levels of excellence in 1963, conceding just 95 points in 18 premiership rounds at a miserly 5.28 points per game. The Dragons lost only two regular season matches—both to Western Suburbs. The Magpies pipped the minor premiers for a third time in the major semi, scoring a last-minute try to snatch a 10-8 win and the first Grand Final berth. Required to play a preliminary final for just the second time in the club's title-winning streak, St. George outlasted Parramatta 12-7 to book a rematch with Wests. Saints prevailed over the Magpies 8-3 on an SCG quagmire, but Darcy Lawler's controversial refereeing performance dominated post-match debate. Nevertheless, St. George had secured its eighth straight title, while opposing captains Norm Provan and Arthur Summons were captured after the game by photographer John O'Gready in the famous 'Gladiators' shot—a photo that has formed the basis for every premiership trophy since 1982. The Dragons won the reserve grade and third grade Grand Finals, becoming the fourth—and last—club to win premierships in all three grades in one season. Wollongong sensation Graeme Langlands was brought to the club in 1963 and immediately starred at fullback, scoring 15 tries. Reg Gasnier topped the premiership again with 24 tries, and crossed for a hat-trick in St. George's 22-7 defeat of the touring New Zealand side. Another future club great debuted in 1963—St. George junior Billy Smith, who later became one of the finest halfbacks the game had seen, featured in the Grand Final victory as a centre. Langlands made his Test debut during 1963 and was chosen in the Kangaroo Tour squad at the end of the year alongside Saints teammates Gasnier, Raper, Walsh and Kevin Ryan. Walsh skippered Australia to its first Ashes series victory in England in over half a century (tour captain-coach Summons was sidelined with injury); Langlands top-scored with 207 points, including 17 tries; and the great Raper produced a career-defining performance in the 'Swinton Massacre,' the Kangaroos' series-sealing 50-12 victory in the second Test.

1964 The St. George dynasty rolled on in 1964, winning 15 of 18 regular season matches to lock up another minor premiership. One of the Dragons' losses was to Parramatta, but the Eels were devastatingly outclassed by the champs in the major semi. Graeme Langlands scored 27 points (a finals record which stood for 41 years) as St. George unleashed an eight-try, 42-0 thrashing. Balmain led St. George 4-2 at halftime of the Grand Final two weeks later—the only time during the Dragons' reign that they trailed at the break of a decider—but a Johnny King try and three goals to Langlands propelled Saints to an 11-6 victory over the Keith Barnes-led Tigers. Hooker Peter Armstrong, who deputised for Ken Kearney in the 1961 decider, won his second Grand Final medal after filling in for the injured Ian Walsh. Reg Gasnier's 18 tries yielded his third tryscoring title, while he captain-coached Australia to a 3-0 series whitewash of France, with Billy Smith making his Test debut at halfback.

1965 St. George made it a perfect 10 in 1965 to farewell club legend Norm Provan with a memorable Grand Final triumph. Captain-coach Provan, the last survivor from the dynasty-heralding 1956 premiership success, led Saints to a 12-8 defeat of a plucky Rabbitohs side (on the verge of their own golden era) in the Grand Final. The Dragons won the minor premiership six points clear of the field, before crushing second-placed North Sydney 47-7 in the major semi, with Johnny King crossing for a hat-trick. In front of an SCG-record 78,056 supporters, King scored the pivotal try with 13 minutes remaining as St. George outlasted Souths 12-8 in the decider. King's finals haul saw him top the premiership with 15 tries, while Langlands was second in the competition's pointscoring race with 161. Ian Walsh captain-coached Australia in the drawn two-Test series in New Zealand during 1965; it was a precursor to the wonderful hooker assuming the role at club level.

1966 The last of St. George's world record sequence of premierships was achieved in typically emphatic and calculated fashion. The Dragons topped the table yet again in 1966 and qualified for the Grand Final with a 10-2 defeat of Balmain. Saints held the Tigers try-less again in the decider, scoring three of their own while Graeme Langlands booted seven goals in a 23-4 success. Reg Gasnier missed the Grand Final with injury, while Test halfback Billy Smith finally shifted from the centres to oust George Evans for the No.7 jersey at club level. The Grand Final victory was the first for revered Great Britain Test forward Dick Huddart. He was lured to the club in 1964, but injuries kept him out of the previous two deciders. Ian Walsh's expert leadership extended into Australia's euphoric Ashes series success over Great Britain, captain-coaching his country to a 2-1 victory alongside Saints teammates Langlands, Smith, Raper, and Johnny King, who made a belated Test debut. King was also the equal-top try-scorer in the premiership with a modest 11 tries. St. George claimed its fifth straight club championship in 1966.

St. George won 184, lost just 33 and drew five of 222 matches between 1956 and 1966—including 22 victories from 24 finals matches. The dominant Dragons amassed 5,103 points while conceding just 2,153 during the 11-season period. The club's reign came to an end in 1967, coinciding with the introduction of the four-tackle rule, but the innovation was not necessarily responsible for the fall of the St. George empire. Saints won the 1967 minor premiership—their sixth in succession and 11th in 12 years—before going down narrowly to Souths (13-8) and Canterbury (12-11) in consecutive finals matches. The regular season was extended to 22 matches, and the ageing Dragons faded at the end of the season against their younger, fresher rivals. Enforcer Kevin Ryan, a winner of seven premierships with St. George, captained the Berries' preliminary final defeat of his former club. Captain-coach Ian Walsh, champion centre Reg Gasnier and eight-time premiership-winner Brian Clay retired ahead of the 1968 season, while Eddie Lumsden had hung up the boots 12 months earlier.

The club's astonishing accomplishment of 11 straight premierships was a world record for top-level championships in any football code. It eclipsed Fremantle's 10 consecutive titles in the Western Australia Football League (1887-96) and Bulgarian soccer club CDNA Sofia's nine championships in a row between 1954 and 1962. St. George's mark stood until 2002, when Latvian soccer club Skonto Riga won its 12th consecutive Virsliga championship (the club's run ended at 14 titles in 2004).

While Saints' world record was eventually toppled, the likelihood of their unprecedented period of dominance being replicated by another Australian Rugby League club is remote. The Dragons' phenomenal success can also be measured by the honours lavished on the players from the era. Reg Gasnier and Johnny Raper were named as two of the original Immortals in 1981, while the hallowed tag was bestowed upon Graeme Langlands in 1999. The esteemed trio was joined by Norm Provan in the Australian Rugby League Team of the Century in 2008; all four were included in the New South Wales Team of the Century, while Langlands, Eddie Lumsden and Ian Walsh won selection in the NSW Country Team of the Century. Named in 2007 and 2006 respectively, Gasnier, Raper and Provan were chosen in the Team of the 1950s, while Gasnier, Raper, Langlands, Walsh, Billy Smith and Johnny King were selected in the Team of the 1960s. The eight aforementioned greats, plus Ken Kearney, Brian Clay and Harry Bath, were named in the ARL's 100 Greatest Players during the 2008 Centenary celebrations.

For a complete St. George club history, see The Extinct Clubs

BERRIES TO BULLDOGS

The history of the Canterbury-Bankstown club is one of an inauspicious start and early success, a long title drought preceding a tremendous era of accomplishment, and the emergence through a series of crippling controversies to again scale the highest of Rugby League's heights. Through it all, Canterbury has remained a proud club—the 'family' club—and boasts a colourful 77-year narrative. Possessing a rich junior nursery, the south-western Sydney club became the ninth in the NSWRL premiership in 1935. Local mayor Stan Parry's pledge to build a football field at Belmore Sports Ground clinched the club's admission and Canterbury-Bankstown called the ground home from 1936 through until 1998.

But the blue-and-whites endured an arduous debut season in the premiership. Coached by former international 'Tedda' Courtney, the newcomers were decimated 91-6 by St. George and 87-7 by Eastern Suburbs in consecutive weeks—the two biggest defeats in premiership history. Canterbury also conceded 65 points twice in the last three weeks of the season, but beat winless University twice during the year to stave off the wooden spoon. The legendary Frank Burge took the coaching reins in 1936 and steered the club to the finals in third place. Easts eliminated Canterbury in the semi-final, but the Berries had already arrived as a premiership force—an inconceivable notion just 12 months earlier.

PREMIERSHIP GLORY COMES EARLY In just its fourth season, Canterbury-Bankstown claimed its maiden premiership. The Berries lost just one regular season match and clinched the title with a commanding 19-6 defeat of Easts—premiers in the previous three seasons—in the 1938 premiership final. Only foundation clubs South Sydney, the inaugural premiers, and 1910 champions Newtown had achieved title success earlier, while just Melbourne (NRL premiers in

1999, the club's second season) has since. Revered former Test great Jimmy Craig was coach of the trailblazing side, while former New South Wales representative three-quarter Alan Brady had the honour of becoming the club's first premiership-winning captain. The legendary combination of props Eddie Burns and Henry Porter, and hooker Roy Kirkaldy, arguably the greatest club front-row trio of all time with 501 combined appearances for the Berries, teamed up for the first time in 1938. Local junior Frank Sponberg, a NSW representative with Western Suburbs in 1933-34, was integral to Canterbury's inaugural premiership, while winger Joe Gartner (whose son Ray and nephews Jim, Clive and Keith went on to play for the club in the 1950s and 1960s) scored two tries in the final.

The Berries made the finals in the ensuing three seasons, losing the 1940 final 24-14 to Easts, before celebrating their second premiership in 1942. Canterbury beat Balmain in a play-off for the minor premiership, and after being upset by St. George in the semi-final, recovered to pip the Saints 11-9 on a sodden Sydney Cricket Ground with a famous late penalty goal to fullback Lin Johnson *(see Unlikely Heroes)*. Centre Ron Bailey—captain-coach in 1941—skippered the successful side, with former Wests, St. George and NSW halfback Jerry Brien as coach. Newcastle product Bailey became Canterbury's first Test player during the 1946 home Ashes series and captained Australia in the second clash with England.

THE LONG DROUGHT Canterbury-Bankstown became the first defending premiers to finish last in 1943, and collected another wooden spoon the following season. The Berries returned to the finals under the coaching of former Easts international Ross McKinnon in 1946 and finished as minor premiers in 1947, but lost the final (25-19) and the Grand Final (13-9) to Balmain in consecutive weeks. Goalkicking halfback Bruce Hopkins became the club's first Kangaroo representative when he toured with the 1948-49 squad. Prolific pointscoring fullback Ron Willey was the first Canterbury junior to represent Australia, touring with the 1952-53 Kangaroos, but he was kept out of the Test side by Clive Churchill and left to captain-coach Rockhampton in 1955 before a highly successful stint with Manly.

The club wallowed in the premiership cellar throughout the 1950s, never finishing higher than sixth and coming second-last (ninth) five times despite enlisting a succession of high-profile coaches. Former Test stars Vic Bulgin, Vic Hey and Col Geelan (as captain-coach) failed to turn the Berries' fortunes around. Three of famed former Easts and Test winger Lionel Cooper's brothers played for Canterbury in the 1950s—Cec, Reg and Col wore the blue and white during the decade, while Cec coached the club in 1958-59. The great Queensland forward Brian Davies joined Canterbury in 1959 at the conclusion of his 33-Test career and captained the club to its first finals appearances for 13 years in 1960. Club legend Eddie Burns had returned as coach and the Berries finished in a four-way tie for second, before eventually being eliminated by Easts in the minor semi following an elaborate series of play-offs. Davies was joined in the front-row by hooker Fred Anderson, who appeared in 197 first grade games in 12 seasons with Canterbury and played Test football as a guest player for South Africa against New Zealand in 1963 (technically becoming the first Canterbury junior to play Test football).

Newcastle fullback Les Johns joined Canterbury in 1963 and became one of the club's greatest players. Although injury restricted the blonde-haired custodian to 103 first grade games in nine seasons, he carved out a career as one of the best of all time in his position during a golden era of fullbacks, playing 14 Tests and touring twice with the Kangaroos. St. George centre Johnny Greaves joined the club in 1964 and debuted for Australia in the 1966 Ashes series. But the Berries still languished near the bottom of the ladder for most of the 1960s (including a wooden spoon in 1964 with Clive Churchill as coach), until dual international enforcer Kevin Ryan arrived as captain-coach in 1967. Ryan, a seven-time Grand Final-winner with St. George, masterminded the end of the Dragons' run of 11 consecutive premierships by guiding Canterbury to an epic 12-11 victory in the 1967 preliminary final. The Berries went down to South Sydney 12-10 in a gripping Grand Final a week later, with a famous intercept try to Rabbitohs second-rower Bob McCarthy from a pass by Canterbury hooker Col Brown—one of four brothers to play for the club—swinging the match. The Canterbury side also contained Queensland's former Test centre Bob Hagan, former Great Britain Test prop Merv Hicks and goalkicking backrower George Taylforth, who landed four goals in the decider. Johns, Greaves and industrious forward Kevin Goldspink toured with the Kangaroos at the end of the year. Brisbane winger Johnny Rhodes joined the Berries in 1968 and represented Australia at the World Cup in the first of his five seasons for the club.

One of the most significant developments in the club's history occurred when Ryan and Peter Moore forced a backroom shake-up late in 1969. 'Bullfrog' Moore was voted club secretary and remained at the helm of Canterbury-Bankstown as chief executive until 1995, ranking as one of the most influential administrators the game has seen. Aggressive recruitment brought Test forward Ron Costello and a bevy of New Zealand and Great Britain internationals to Belmore, while astute talent scouting brought the likes of NSW country youngsters Chris Anderson and Garry Dowling to the club in the early 1970s. Malcolm Clift assumed the first grade coaching role in 1973, restoring the Berries to the finals in his first season and steering the club to the 1974 Grand Final, where they succumbed to Jack Gibson's magnificent Eastern Suburbs side 19-4.

THE ENTERTAINERS The Hughes brothers—second-rower Graeme, five-eighth Garry and centre/pivot Mark—each made their first grade debut for Canterbury in 1974. The Mortimer brothers, halfback Steve (1976), winger Peter (1977) and centre Chris (1978) debuted for the club in successive seasons. Together, the two sets of siblings spearheaded a new era of unprecedented success for Canterbury. Clift was replaced by former St. George halfback and Cronulla coach Ted Glossop in 1978. Glossop was named Coach of the Year in 1978 after guiding the club—now known as the Bulldogs—back to the finals by employing an exhilarating brand of attacking football. The side contained former Test five-eighth Tim Pickup, who represented Australia in the 1975 World Cup in his first season at Canterbury, future Test fullback Greg Brentnall, and hooker and captain George Peponis. Peponis became the first Canterbury junior to represent Australia in Test football while still playing for the club in 1978, and became Canterbury's first home-grown Test skipper the following season. Peponis and prolific tryscoring winger Chris Anderson toured with the Kangaroos at the end of 1978.

The Bulldogs became the first side to reach the Grand Final from fifth spot in 1979, rolling Wests, Cronulla and Parramatta on their way to the decider. Canterbury trailed St. George 17-2 at halftime of the Grand Final, but fought back gamely to eventually go down 17-13. 'The Entertainers' sealed their legacy by securing the club's first premiership in 38 years in 1980. Canterbury advanced to the decider with a 13-7 major semi defeat of minor premiers Easts, and ground out an 18-4 win over the Roosters in the Grand Final. Winger Steve Gearin scored one of the most famous Grand Final tries of all time by latching on to a towering kick by Brentnall at full pace to dive over and seal the victory. Gearin, who scored a then-club record 242 points the previous season, also added five goals in the 1980 decider and went on to rack up 1,006 points during two stints with Canterbury.

The six members of the Hughes and Mortimer clans featured in the Grand final win. The linchpin of the premiership success, however, was brilliant No.7 Steve Mortimer. Tenacious, an attacking livewire and a wonderful cover defender, Mortimer made a belated Test debut in 1981 and toured with the 1982 Kangaroos— along with clubmates Anderson and Brentnall—although he was displaced in the Test side by young Parramatta rival Peter Sterling in England.

DOGS OF WAR Canterbury sank to disappointing lower-table finishes in 1981 and 1982, and Glossop departed at the end of 1983 despite guiding the Bulldogs to a preliminary final appearance. Warren Ryan, a former St. George and Cronulla forward who coached Newtown to the 1981 Grand Final, supplanted Glossop and transformed Canterbury into a relentless defensive outfit. Dubbed the 'Dogs of War,' their style was in direct contrast to 'The Entertainers,' but heralded an even more successful era for the club. Ryan recruited rugged forwards Peter Tunks, Peter Kelly and Mark Bugden, along with determined Wests five-eighth Terry Lamb, a Canterbury junior. Tough centre Andrew Farrar and tireless backrower Steve Folkes blossomed under Ryan's tutelage, while he developed teenage lock Paul Langmack and young fullback Michael Potter into first grade stars.

Ryan shook things up at Canterbury, dropping skipper Chris Anderson and long-serving pivot Garry Hughes, but his methods yielded impressive results. Captained by Steve Mortimer, the Bulldogs claimed the club's first minor premiership in 37 years in 1984, and eclipsed 1981-83 champions Parramatta 6-4 in a dour, grinding Grand Final victory. Lamb won the Rothmans Medal, while 20-year-old Potter was named Dally M Player of the Year.

The Bulldogs secured back-to-back titles for the first time in the club's history in 1985, disposing of the Eels 26-0 in the preliminary final before prevailing 7-6 over minor premiers St. George in the Grand Final. A Farrar field goal proved the difference, but the tight scoreline belied the Bulldogs' control throughout the decider. Canterbury's bid to emulate Parramatta's 'three-peat' was foiled by the Eels in the 1986 Grand Final—the only try-less Grand Final ever played—4-2 in a riveting contest. The 1986 Kangaroo squad contained five Bulldogs: Chris Mortimer, Lamb and forward trio Langmack, Folkes and Paul Dunn.

Ryan's strained relationship with skipper Steve Mortimer reached breaking point during 1987 and the conflict contributed to the Bulldogs' disappointing sixth-place finish. Phil Gould, who played for Newtown and coached Canterbury's reserve grade side under Ryan, replaced the controversial mentor in 1988. The 30-year-old Gould steered the club to its fourth premiership of the decade in his first season in charge, defeating Ryan's Balmain side 24-12 in the Grand Final. Mortimer stepped down as captain in his final season, and a broken arm injury saw arguably the club's greatest player come off the bench in the decider after returning late in the year. Test prop Peter Tunks assumed the captaincy, while Queenslander Michael Hagan—younger brother of former Berries centre and coach Bob—formed a formidable halves combination with Lamb. While maintaining their aggressive approach, the presence of Queensland and Australian three-quarter Tony Currie and young fullback Jason Alchin promoted a more expansive attacking approach. Dunn won the Clive Churchill Medal and featured in Australia's subsequent World Cup Final victory over New Zealand alongside fellow Bulldogs Lamb, Farrar and hard-hitting forward David Gillespie, who made his international debut in the match.

REBUILDING THE FAMILY CLUB The defending premiers finished a dismal ninth in 1989 and Phil Gould left for Penrith at the end of the season after falling out with club supremo Peter Moore. By 1992, Lamb—who assumed the captaincy in 1990—was the only remnant of the Bulldogs' premiership-winning sides in the playing group. Favourite son Chris Anderson returned to the club in 1990 as Gould's replacement and finally led the club back to finals with consecutive minor premierships in 1993-94. More astute recruitment from 'Bullfrog' Moore brought brothers Darren and Jason Smith, halfback Craig Polla-Mounter and teenage winger Brett Dallas to the club from Queensland; raw Kiwi centre Jarrod McCracken joined the club after being spotted in Port Macquarie; former Test prop Martin Bella, front-rower Darren Britt, phenomenal goalkicking Kiwi winger Daryl Halligan and ball-playing lock Jim Dymock arrived from rival clubs; and the Bulldogs developed hardworking forwards such as Dean Pay and Simon Gillies after bringing them to Belmore from NSW country centres.

But the Bulldogs dipped out of 1993 finals race with consecutive defeats, before qualifying for the 1994 Grand Final with a thrilling 19-18 extra-time win over Canberra in the major semi. A knock-on by Bella from the kick-off and a heavy hit by Raiders captain Mal Meninga on Bulldogs counterpart Lamb, limiting his effectiveness, painted just part of the picture as Canterbury capitulated 36-12 to a rampant Canberra in the decider. Jason Smith and Pay gained some solace from the crushing loss by starring on the subsequent Kangaroo Tour.

The Super League war arguably affected the Sydney Bulldogs—as they were rebranded for the 1995 season—more than any other club. The Bulldogs sided with the rebel organisation, but Dallas signed with the Australian Rugby League and made his Test debut, while star quartet Jason Smith, Dymock, Pay and McCracken reneged on Super League deals to sign ARL contracts (the foursome joined Parramatta in 1996). Anderson dropped all five players, but all bar McCracken fought their way back into first grade, while Dallas was injured during the finals.

In spite of the fallout, the Bulldogs staged an incredible run to claim the unlikeliest of premiership triumphs. Finishing sixth ahead of the inaugural eight-team finals series, the Bulldogs eliminated St. George and heavyweights Brisbane and Canberra on their way to the Grand Final. Red-hot favourites Manly crumbled in the decider against the battle-hardened Dogs, who grafted out a 17-4 boilover victory. The Bulldogs' try-scorers were rookie forward Steve Price, dazzling fullback Rod Silva, a mid-season recruit from the Roosters, and Glen Hughes, one of Garry Hughes' three sons to enjoy long and fruitful careers with the club. Centre Steven

Hughes played in the 1994 decider, while Corey played in the 1998 Grand Final as a rookie halfback and went on to become a long-serving hooker for the Bulldogs, winning a premiership in 2004. Inspirational veteran Terry Lamb retired as a premiership-winning captain, but ultimately returned to assist the depleted Bulldogs the following season.

The club understandably struggled in its 1996 title defence and produced an uninspiring campaign in the 1997 Super League season. Chris Anderson departed at the end of the year to coach the fledgling Melbourne Storm and was replaced by another club favourite in Steve Folkes, Moore's son-in-law and Anderson's brother-in-law. Canterbury scraped into the inaugural NRL season's bloated 10-team finals series in ninth place, but embarked on another spellbinding finals run to reach the Grand Final. The Darren Britt-led Bulldogs cast aside St. George and Norths, before producing extraordinary comebacks to defeat Newcastle and Parramatta in extra-time. After leading minor premiers Brisbane 12-10 at halftime of the decider, the Bulldogs' streak ended with a 38-12 loss as the Broncos dominated the second half.

BULLDOGS COMBAT MULTIPLE CRISES After second-week finals exits in 1999 and 2001, the Bulldogs were on target for an emphatic premiership victory in 2002. Captained by Test prop Steve Price, the club had built an elite, youthful squad containing boom five-eighth Braith Anasta, a Kangaroo in his 2001 rookie season; crafty halfback Brent Sherwin; pointscoring wizard Hazem El Masri, also a prolific try-scorer, who assumed the goalkicking duties from Halligan and arguably became better than the Kiwi maestro; New Zealand three-quarter trio Nigel Vagana, Willie Talau and Matt Utai; valuable fullback Luke Patten; and fearsome future Australian Test forwards Willie Mason and Mark O'Meley. The Bulldogs pieced together a 17-match winning streak—the second-longest in premiership history—but their title hopes crumbled around them three weeks out from the finals amid revelations the club had exceeded the salary cap by upwards of $1.5 million. CEO Bob Hagan, leagues club president Gary McIntyre and the entire football club board resigned; Steve Mortimer came in as chief executive, but NRL boss David Gallop handed down the gut-wrenching punishment of stripping the Bulldogs of all of their competition points (as well as slapping the club with a $500,000 fine), effectively consigning the club to the wooden spoon.

Dr George Peponis headed the new football club board in 2003 as the Bulldogs attempted to claim the premiership they believed was rightfully theirs the previous season, but eventually came up short, going down 28-18 to archrivals and defending premiers the Sydney Roosters in the preliminary final. The club was mired in an even more damaging controversy during the 2004 pre-season, when a trip to Coffs Harbour resulted in several Bulldogs players becoming the target of rape allegations. Lack of evidence eventually saw the case against the unnamed players dropped, but the furore led to more backroom bloodshed, with club stalwarts Mortimer and Garry Hughes ousted from their roles as CEO and football manager respectively.

But the Bulldogs rallied to mount a premiership challenge and qualified for the Grand Final with comfortable finals victories over Melbourne and Penrith after a shock qualifying final loss to North Queensland. Bolstered by former Eels forward Andrew Ryan (who captained the Bulldogs in the decider after Steve Price sustained a knee injury in the preliminary final, his captaincy debut), and emerging talents Sonny Bill Williams, Willie Tonga, Reni Maitua and Roy Asotasi, the Bulldogs came back from a seven-point halftime deficit to triumph 16-13 over the Roosters in the Grand Final. Matt Utai scored a powerful double, while El Masri crossed for a try and kicked three goals to take his premiership record season tally to 342 points. The victory capped a tumultuous three-season period that threatened to tear the family club apart.

Another dismal premiership defence in 2005 was followed by a preliminary final collapse against the Broncos in 2006 and a meek exit from the 2007 finals. But worse was to follow. Mason, the Clive Churchill Medallist in the 2004 Grand Final, departed in acrimonious circumstances at the end of 2007, before Williams sensationally walked out on the club just 18 months into a five-year deal to sign with French rugby union club Toulon midway through 2008. The Bulldogs slumped to their first wooden spoon since 1964, while the only members of the club's most recent premiership success to front for the 2009 season were skipper Ryan, El Masri and Patten.

The club recruited decorated halfback Brett Kimmorley, outstanding Dragons outside back Josh Morris and Broncos quartet Ben Hannant, Michael Ennis, Greg Eastwood and David Stagg, while Folkes—the Bulldogs' longest-serving coach—was replaced by long-time assistant Kevin Moore, a former Canterbury halfback and son of club patriarch Peter Moore. He was duly named Dally M Coach of the Year in 2009 after steering the Bulldogs to second on the ladder (the club would have claimed the minor premiership if not for an early-season interchange bungle that cost the Bulldogs two competition points), while Stagg, Ennis, Hannant and Morris bagged positional gongs. The Bulldogs' wonderful turnaround culminated in a gallant 22-12 loss to the Parramatta juggernaut in the preliminary final.

Failing to build on that platform, Canterbury faded out of finals contention in the ensuing two seasons, while Moore stood down mid-season in 2011. Assistant coach and the club's 1995 Churchill medallist Jim Dymock filled in admirably in a caretaker role for the remainder of the season, earning a one-season deal ahead of Manly's dual premiership-winning coach Des Hasler's 2013 arrival at Canterbury. Hasler split from Manly a year early, however, and was immediately installed as the Bulldogs' head coach for 2012, with Dymock as his assistant. The two-time Kangaroo tourist was hailed as Canterbury's saviour upon his arrival—a revered coach capable of leading the club into its next great era.

MANLY'S DOMINANT ERAS

Manly-Warringah had its original bids to field a first grade Rugby League side in the premiership rebuffed in 1937 and 1944 by the NSWRL. But the establishment finally relented and the club made its entry in 1947, playing out of Brookvale Oval from its debut season. Based in the suburbs on Sydney's northern beaches, Manly-Warringah came from humble beginnings and waited for what seemed an eternity to achieve premiership success, but eventually became the most affluent—and consequently the most successful and most hated—team in the competition.

Former Souths player Harold Johnson was Manly's inaugural coach, but was dumped only five matches into the club's first season and replaced by Easts and Kangaroos front-row great Ray Stehr. Former North Sydney forward Max Whitehead was the foundation captain, while another player from Manly's neighbours, winger Johnny Bliss, represented New South Wales in 1947. Prop Roy Bull became the club's first international when he toured New Zealand with the Australian side in 1949 and played the first of 25 Tests. But Manly struggled initially, finishing in the bottom-three in its first four seasons.

Kangaroo five-eighth Wally O'Connell arrived as captain-coach in 1950 (although he was restricted to a non-playing role in his first season as Easts appealed against O'Connell joining the club on residential grounds), while Manly also recruited Test hooker Kevin Schubert from Wollongong and goalkicking winger Ron Rowles from Newcastle. O'Connell returned to the playing field in 1951 and featured in Australia's series against France, along with Schubert, Bliss and three-quarter Gordon Willoughby. The club finished the regular season in second spot and advanced to the Grand Final with finals victories over Wests and St. George, but was decimated 42-14 in the decider by Souths.

After a three-season lull, former Test five-eighth Pat Devery coached Manly to the finals in 1955, with Bull (who made his second Kangaroo Tour the following season) as captain. The club's 1951 Grand Final halfback Ken Arthurson, whose career was ended prematurely after fracturing his skull while captain-coaching in Parkes in 1953, took over as coach in 1957 and guided the Sea Eagles to two Grand Finals in his first three seasons in charge. Stalwart backrower George Hunter captained Manly to a 31-9 defeat to St. George in the 1957 decider, while former Kangaroo and prolific pointscoring fullback Ron Willey led the Sea Eagles in a 20-0 loss to the dominant Dragons two seasons later. Halfback Peter Burke, prop Bill Delamere and outstanding dual international forward Rex Mossop toured with the 1959-60 Kangaroos from the club. Arthurson, meanwhile, had a massive influence on the club as secretary for two decades from 1963, before becoming president of the ARL and NSWRL during the 1980s.

The Sea Eagles meandered through the 1960s without a great deal of success, qualifying for the finals in 1961 under Mossop's captaincy, before beginning their surge to perennial heavyweight status in 1966. O'Connell returned as coach of a side featuring 1963-64 Kangaroos halfback Frank Stanton, Queensland Test forwards Ken Day and Mick Veivers, backrowers John Morgan and Bill Bradstreet (who represented Australia in 1965 and 1966 respectively), NSW centre Alec Tennant and goalkicking fullback Bob Batty, an outstanding clubman. Manly reached the preliminary final in 1966, losing 8-5 to Balmain. The Sea Eagles' try-scorer that day was 18-year-old five-eighth Bob Fulton, a Rugby League prodigy starting out on his path to greatness. The club missed the finals in 1967, however, and its only Kangaroos representative was Wollongong winger Les Hanigan, the premiership's top try-scorer in his first season with the club. Fulton was a shock omission.

The brilliant Fulton, just 20, captained Manly to the Grand Final in 1968 (with George Hunter as coach) following a 23-15 major semi upset of minor premiers and defending champs Souths. Taking on the star-studded Rabbitohs again in the decider, the Sea Eagles gamely fought back from 13-2 down early in the second half, before eventually falling four points short. Fulton belatedly won Australian selection for the 1968 World Cup, along with Sea Eagles hooker Fred Jones. Queensland three-quarter John McDonald and Newcastle forward Allan Thomson, both 1967-68 Kangaroos, joined the club in 1969, but the Sea Eagles were eliminated in the preliminary final by Balmain courtesy of a last-minute try to Tigers winger George Reubner.

Ron Willey returned to the club as coach in 1970. Captained by McDonald, Manly won through to the decider, but the club suffered its fifth loss in as many Grand Final appearances, 23-12 to Souths in a match principally remembered for Rabbitohs captain John Sattler soldiering on after having his jaw savagely broken by Sea Eagles prop John Bucknall. Fred Jones assumed the captaincy in 1971 and Manly won its first minor premiership. But consecutive losses to Souths and St. George cost the Sea Eagles another bite at the Grand Final cherry.

PREMIERSHIP SUCCESS AT LAST Ken Arthurson set about strengthening Manly's squad in the early-1970s with an aggressive recruitment strategy. The great winger Ken Irvine was lured to Brookvale from neighbouring Norths in 1971, and the brutal and brilliant Great Britain lock Malcolm Reilly joined the same season. South Sydney Test stars, prop John O'Neill and three-quarter Ray Branighan, linked with Manly in 1972. Combined with superstar Fulton, who was predominantly playing in the centres, emerging talents such as rugged defender Terry Randall in the second-row and teenage fullback Graham Eadie, and Ron Willey's hard-nosed coaching, Manly had all bases covered to finally break through for its first title.

The Sea Eagles became the decade's dominant club, winning four premierships in the space of seven seasons and leading the way in regards to recruitment and professionalism off the field. Manly compensated for the departure of champions such as Fulton, Irvine, Reilly and O'Neill, while Frank Stanton picked up where Willey left off as coach and became an outstanding mentor in his own right.

- 1972—Manly claimed the minor premiership for the second straight season with 18 regular season wins and qualified for the Grand Final with a comprehensive 32-8 major semi defeat of second-placed Easts, with centre Bob Fulton scoring two tries. In a tense rematch in the decider, Manly and the Roosters were locked at 4-all at halftime, but second half tries to skipper Fred Jones and Ray Branighan, who also landed six goals, propelled the Sea Eagles to a 19-4 lead and the club's maiden premiership. Two late Easts tries narrowed the final scoreline to 19-14. Fulton, Jones, Branighan, O'Neill and halfback Dennis Ward toured with Australia's World Cup squad at the end of the season. Fulton topped the premiership with 19 tries, while veteran Irvine crossed 13 times.
- 1973—The 1973 season followed a similar script: the Sea Eagles claimed their third consecutive minor premiership with 17 wins (including a club record 70-7 demolition of Penrith) and advanced to the decider with a comfortable major semi win—this time 14-4 against Cronulla. What followed two weeks later against the Sharks was the most brutal Grand Final ever witnessed, featuring a first half of violent clashes and savagery. Bob Fulton scored two blistering individual tries—one in each half—to clinch a 10-7 victory and back-to-back premierships. Fullback Graham Eadie emerged as one of the competition's deadliest goalkickers with 152 points (third in the

premiership), while Fulton finished atop the field again with 18 three-pointers. Fulton, Eadie, Branighan, hard-hitting second-rower Terry Randall and front-rowers O'Neill and Bill Hamilton toured with the 1973 Kangaroos. Ken Irvine, Australia's greatest try-scorer and arguably its finest ever winger, retired at the end of the season.

- 1974—The Sea Eagles finished the regular season in second place, but were bundled out of the finals with consecutive upset losses to Canterbury (20-14) and Wests (23-20). Graham Eadie was the competition's top point-scorer with 216 and won the Rothmans Medal, while halfback Kevin Junee finished as equal-top try-scorer with Easts' Bill Mullins, crossing for a then-club record 23 tries. Fulton, Eadie, Branighan and O'Neill featured in Australia's retention of the Ashes in the home series win over Great Britain.

- 1975—After another second-place finish in Frank Stanton's initial season as coach, Manly secured a preliminary final berth, but was outplayed 28-13 by defending and eventual premiers Eastern Suburbs. British lock Malcolm Reilly left at the end of the year after five superb seasons with the club. Eadie topped the premiership with 242 points—a club record that would stand for 20 years—while Eadie and Fulton scored 14 tries apiece, behind only Easts' Johnny Mayes. Eadie, Fulton and Randall featured in Australia's successful World Series campaign.

- 1976—Manly took out the 1976 minor premiership and advanced to the Grand Final with a 15-12 preliminary final defeat of Canterbury, after being upset 23-17 by Parramatta in the major semi. The Sea Eagles prevailed in the rematch with the Eels, who were playing in their first Grand Final, winning a tense decider 13-10. English lock Phil Lowe scored Manly's only try, while Eadie landed five goals. The victory provided a triumphant farewell for captain and club legend Fulton, who joined Easts the following season. Fittingly, Fulton was the premiership's top try-scorer with 21, and Eadie led the competition again with 233 points.

- 1977—The Sea Eagles, captained by stalwart five-eighth/lock Ian Martin, struggled initially in the post-Fulton era. But they recovered from a four-game losing streak early in 1977 to qualify for the finals in fifth spot, only to be eliminated in the minor preliminary semi-final 23-15 by Balmain. Centre Russell Gartner topped the premiership with 17 tries and made his international debut during Australia's World Series campaign, teaming up with clubmates Eadie and Randall.

- 1978—Hooker Max Krilich assumed the captaincy in 1978 and led Manly to a third-place finish in the minor premiership before the club embarked on arguably the most spectacular and controversial finals campaign in the game's history. The Sea Eagles went down to Cronulla 17-12 in the major preliminary semi; drew the sudden-death minor-semi 13-all with Parramatta, and advanced with a 17-11 victory in the replay three days later that was overshadowed by a series of contentious decisions by referee Greg Hartley; defeated archrivals and minor premiers Wests 14-7 in the preliminary final following another questionable performance by Hartley; drew the Grand Final 11-all against Cronulla, before claiming the premiership with 16-0 shutout of the Sharks in the replay. Gartner scored two tries in the replay, while Eadie crossed for a try and kicked three goals in a man of the match display. Manly's remarkable triumph was shrouded in the fallout from Hartley's refereeing, but the Sea Eagles' effort to play five do-or-die finals matches in 17 days ranks as one of the great club achievements. Krilich, Eadie, five-eighth Alan Thompson, rookie halfback Steve Martin, livewire half Johnny Gibbs (who was injured in the minor semi and missed the Grand Final), and forwards Bruce Walker and Ian Thomson jetted to Britain with the Kangaroos following the premiership victory.

Manly's premiership defence culminated with the club missing the finals for the first time since 1967. The Sea Eagles finished seventh in 1979 and 1980, with the emergence of young Queensland backrower Paul Vautin one of the few highlights for the rebuilding side. The 'Fibros' vs. 'Silvertails' rivalry stepped up a gear when Manly signed internationals Les Boyd and John Dorahy, and NSW hooker Ray Brown from Wests.

The Sea Eagles returned to the finals in fifth spot in 1981 under the coaching of former Manly and Australian World Cup winger Ray Ritchie, but were eliminated 20-15 by Newtown in an infamous, brawling minor semi. Premiership glory was tantalisingly close during the early-1980s; Manly finished the 1982 regular season in second, and won the 1983 minor premiership (with Bob Fulton returning as coach), advancing through to the Grand Final with major semi victories over Parramatta in each season. But the dominant Eels cruised to 21-8 and 18-6 wins in the 1982 and '83 deciders respectively.

The Sea Eagles' squad was bolstered by Queensland and Australian stars Kerry Boustead, Chris Close, John Ribot and Paul McCabe, former internationals Geoff Gerard, Phil Sigsworth and Ian Schubert, explosive second-rower/centre Noel Cleal and teenage halfback Phil Blake, who scored a club record 27 tries in 1983 (also a premiership record for a halfback). Max Krilich captained the 1982 Kangaroos—dubbed 'The Invincibles' after going through Britain and France undefeated—containing fellow Manly stars Boyd, McCabe and Brown.

Club greats Krilich and Eadie retired at the end of 1983 and Manly worked through another rebuilding period. Cleal, halfback Des Hasler, prop Phil Daley, Queensland outside back Dale Shearer and brilliant dual international three-quarter Michael O'Connor toured with the 1986 Kangaroos. Along with skipper and Test backrower Vautin and ball-playing five-eighth Cliff Lyons, the tourists were crucial to Manly's 1987 premiership victory. The Sea Eagles streeted their rivals in the minor premiership before defeating Canberra 18-8 in the Grand Final; O'Connor scored a try and kicked five goals, while Lyons crossed for Manly's other try and won the Clive Churchill Medal.

Fulton departed after Manly's minor preliminary semi exit against Balmain in 1988 to concentrate on coaching the Australian Test side. The club descended into a nightmarish 1989 season under club great Alan Thompson, who was punted after the Sea Eagles finished a dismal 12th, while Vautin and Shearer left in acrimonious circumstances. Former New Zealand Test coach Graham Lowe, fresh from a decorated stint with all-conquering British club Wigan, took over in 1990, luring All Black fullback Matthew Ridge and Kiwi internationals Tony and Kevin Iro to the club. Manly also recruited representative forwards Martin Bella and Ian Roberts. O'Connor was installed as captain. Geoff Toovey emerged as a top-shelf halfback, with the ultra-versatile Hasler moving to lock, and Manly returned to the finals in 1990 and 1991. Hasler, Lyons and Bella toured with the 1990 Kangaroos, while Toovey made his Test debut on the 1991 tour of Papua New Guinea.

Manly finished eighth in 1992—O'Connor's last season before retiring—and Lowe resigned due to ill health prior to the 1993 season. Fulton returned as coach and took the Sea Eagles to back-to-back fourth-place finishes in 1993-94 with Toovey stepping up to the captaincy, but each finals campaign ended with minor preliminary semi defeat to Brisbane. Fulton attracted representative players David Gillespie, Mark Carroll and Terry Hill to the club in 1994, and unearthed exceptional Dally M Rookie of the Year Steve Menzies. Hill, Menzies and Roberts were chosen in the 1994 Kangaroo Tour squad (with Fulton as coach), while the evergreen Lyons won his second Dally M Player of the Year Award, after winning previously in 1990.

MANLY DOMINATE THE MID-1990s The Manly Sea Eagles were the undisputed premiership heavyweights of the mid-1990s, but twin Grand Final failures prevented the side from Sydney's northern beaches from being ranked alongside the great club sides of all time. The Sea Eagles were minor premiers in the 20-team ARL competition in 1995 and 1996, and the 1997 ARL premiership during the game's great split. Manly accounted for St. George in the 1996 Grand Final to claim the club's sixth title, but was upset by the Bulldogs and Knights in the 1995 and 1997 deciders respectively. The club's dominance was built around relentless defence and brilliant, calculated attack. The shrewd coaching of Fulton, Toovey's gutsy leadership, Lyons' playmaking guile, the forward grunt of Carroll and Gillespie, phenomenal backrow trio Menzies, Nik Kosef and Daniel Gartner, Kiwi general Ridge's judicious fullback play and goalkicking excellence, and the backline strike-power provided by Hill, Craig Innes, John Hopoate, Danny Moore and Craig Hancock made putting those plans into practice a much easier proposition.

- 1995—The Sea Eagles rebuffed almost every challenge put to them in the 1995 regular season, losing just two of 22 matches and remaining unbeaten away from home. Putting aside the pressure of being the ARL's figurehead club during the season's divisive Super League upheaval, the Sea Eagles won their first 15 games— the best start to a season in premiership history, and the third-longest winning streak of all time.

  Menzies (22 tries) and 1995 Norwich Rising Star award winner John Hopoate (21) were the competition's top two try-scorers as the Sea Eagles totalled a club record 124 touchdowns. Ridge was the competition's top point-scorer with a club record 257 points amongst a team total of 727—at the time second only to the 1994 Raiders in first grade history. The Super League upheaval placed a greater representative strain on the ARL-loyal Sea Eagles, who provided seven players to the Origin series and nine players to the Australian and New Zealand Test sides.

  Manly was ambushed by a youthful Cronulla outfit in the first week of the finals and trailed 20-8 during the second half, before Cliff Lyons inspired a stirring comeback and a 24-20 victory. After outlasting Newcastle 12-4 in a gruelling preliminary final, the Sea Eagles entered the Grand Final showdown with the Bulldogs as overwhelming favourites. But Manly turned in its worst performance of the season and, combined with refereeing blunders that led to two Bulldogs tries, crumbled to lose 17-4. The Sea Eagles were held try-less for the first time in two and a half years, ending a near-perfect season on a bitter note.

- 1996—The Super League split robbed the club of fearsome Kangaroo forward Ian Roberts and inspirational fullback Ridge, although the court decision preventing the rebel competition from starting up in 1996 saw Ridge return two months into the season—a decision that proved crucial to Manly's title aspirations. Kangaroo hooker from 1994 Jim Serdaris and former All Black centre Craig Innes also headed to Brookvale in 1996 to bolster an already enviable roster.

Emulating the club's first premiership-winning sides of 1972-73, Manly was unbeaten at home in 1996 and finished the season as minor premiers for the second straight season. The Sea Eagles booked another Grand Final appearance with a narrow 16-14 victory over the Roosters on the opening weekend of the finals before crushing a confident Sharks outfit 24-0 in the preliminary final. This time they would not be denied Grand Final victory—the Sea Eagles led the Dragons 14-2 at halftime and closed out the match 20-8 in the second half of a clinical display. Skipper Toovey produced a courageous Churchill Medal-winning performance despite fracturing his eye socket in the preliminary final, before captaining Australia against Papua New Guinea at the end of the season. Manly provided six players to Australia's Test sides during 1996 and Ridge captained New Zealand, while Menzies was second on the premiership's tryscoring table with 20.

- 1997—Manly was without Super League defectors Ridge, Solomon Haumono and Owen Cunningham in 1997, but acquired Rabbitohs halfback Craig Field. Despite the departures, the Sea Eagles were heavily favoured to take out the 12-team ARL competition. And they played accordingly to sit comfortably atop the ladder at the end of the regular season—the first time a team had claimed three consecutive minor premierships since the Manly side of 1971-73. Terry Hill scored 22 tries to top the competition, while the club provided seven Origin players, five Australian Test players and Rest of the World representative Innes. The script for back-to-back titles was playing out perfectly with a commanding 27-12 defeat of Newcastle in Manly's first finals match and a gripping 17-16 preliminary final victory over the Roosters on a soggy Sydney Football Stadium, setting up a rematch with the Knights in the Grand Final. But the Sea Eagles' reign as Australian Rugby League's kingpin had a heartbreaking conclusion. Manly had beaten Newcastle in the last 11 clashes between the bitter rivals and scored three first half tries to lead 16-8 at halftime in the decider. The Knights produced one of the great Grand Final revivals, however, and held Manly scoreless in the second half. Newcastle winger Darren Albert scored the match-winning try in the shadows of the fulltime siren to consign the era's dominant club to another gut-wrenching Grand Final defeat.

The Sea Eagles of the mid-1990s deserve to be classed alongside the finest sides in the club's 65-season history, including the great teams that broke through for the club's first four premierships during the 1970s. Manly won 60 games in seasons 1995-97, an achievement topped previously in a three-season period by only Parramatta's 61 victories between 1981 and 1983. Defeat in two Grand Finals they should have won has undeniably deprived Fulton's and Toovey's Sea Eagles the recognition they deserve historically.

Manly's descent from the top in the reunified National Rugby League competition in 1998 was swift. Installed as one of the early premiership favourites after three consecutive Grand Final appearances, the Sea Eagles were thumped by Super League champs Brisbane in the first match of the NRL era and mustered just four wins in the opening 14 rounds to languish in 16th place. The club's revival was spectacular, winning nine of its remaining 10 games to snatch the last spot in the 10-team finals series. But Manly was the first team eliminated—17-4 by Canberra—and started 1999 with a seven-match losing streak, while coach Fulton simultaneously stood down, citing health reasons. Peter Sharp took over and achieved moderate results, but Manly ended the year in 13th place before merging with neighbours and bitter rivals North Sydney.

The Northern Eagles merger was a disaster—both financially and on-field— and after three seasons the joint venture disbanded, with the Manly Sea Eagles fronting up for the 2003 NRL season. Manly finished second-last in its return to the premiership as a single entity, and Sharp was replaced by Des Hasler, one of the club's greatest servants as a player, in 2004. The Sea Eagles' climb was gradual—they finished 13th (but only two wins outside the top-eight) in 2004, before returning to the finals in eighth spot in 2005. The acquisition of representative forwards Ben Kennedy and Brent Kite, and the emergence of young stars Brett Stewart and Anthony Watmough spearheaded the club's revival. Former Northern Eagles and Melbourne halfback general Matt Orford arrived in 2006 and his signing proved pivotal. The Sea Eagles rose to fifth in 2006, and despite dipping out of the finals with consecutive losses, success was not far away.

RETURN TO THE TOP Manly recovered from the dark days of the Northern Eagles merger, and the laborious journey of re-establishing the club as a competitive outfit, to craft another marvellous era. Astute recruiting in the shape of players such as Test centre Jamie Lyon and the club's peerless development of young talent helped coach Hasler mould a formidable squad. Three Grand Final appearances and two emphatic premierships added a glorious chapter to the club's story. The Sea Eagles (with Brisbane) are one of only two clubs to boast multiple premierships in the NRL era.

- 2007—Manly led the competition for several weeks during the first half of the season. Victories over the previous year's Grand Finalists Brisbane and Melbourne in consecutive weeks staked the Sea Eagles' claim as a premiership contender, and they finished the regular season in second spot after racking up 18 wins. Manly advanced to the Grand Final with convincing defeats of Souths (30-6) and North Queensland (28-6), but was outclassed 34-8 by the rampant Storm in the decider. After trailing just 10-4 at halftime, the Sea Eagles lost their main strike weapon when fullback Brett Stewart was ironed out by Melbourne forward Michael Crocker, effectively cruelling any chance of a comeback.

  Stewart scored 19 tries (including three during the finals) and was chosen to make his Test debut for Australia three weeks after the Grand Final—Manly's only representative in the Kangaroos side to take on New Zealand (aggressive centre Steve Matai was in the Kiwis' line-up, but was sent off for a high tackle on Mark Gasnier as Australia romped to a 58-0 win). Jamie Lyon and Brent Kite featured in Australia's 30-6 defeat of the Kiwis earlier in the season. Lyon, Kite and Stewart represented NSW, while Steve Bell starred in Queensland's Origin series victory.

- 2008—The Sea Eagles recovered from a slow start in 2008 to finish equal-first on the ladder at the end of the regular season, missing out on the minor premiership on for-and-against to Melbourne by a mere 12 points. After despatching St. George Illawarra 38-6 in the qualifying final, Manly halted the in-form Warriors' run in the preliminary final with a commanding 32-6 victory. Manly's chances of Grand Final revenge were boosted by Melbourne skipper Cameron Smith's suspension, but few would have predicted the scale of the Sea Eagles' dominance in the decider. The 40-0 scoreline represented the biggest winning margin in Grand Final history. After leading 8-0 at halftime, the Sea Eagles ran in six second half tries, with winger Michael Robertson collecting a hat-trick and departing club legend Steve Menzies scoring a late try in a fairytale farewell. Brett Stewart led the NRL with 22 tries, while captain Matt Orford was equal-third in pointscoring (169 points) and won the Dally M Player of the Year Award. Clive Churchill Medallist Brent Kite was selected in Australia's World Cup squad at the end of the season, along with clubmates and Test debutants Glenn Stewart, David Williams, Anthony Watmough and Josh Perry.

- 2009—Despite becoming the first NRL club to win the World Club Challenge in six years by defeating Leeds 28-20 at Elland Road, Manly endured a disastrous start to its premiership defence. The club attracted a substantial fine from the NRL after several reports of public drunkenness at the Sea Eagles' season launch, while Brett Stewart—who had just been unveiled as the face of the NRL's 2009 advertising campaign—was charged with sexual assault. The NRL suspended Stewart for five weeks (for his drunkenness bringing the game into disrepute) sparking a feud between the star fullback and NRL CEO David Gallop that was still bubbling three years later, while he succumbed to a season-ending knee injury after just five appearances. The Sea Eagles opened their campaign with four straight losses, but scrambled to finish the minor premiership in fifth place. Billy Slater scored four tries as Melbourne thumped Manly 40-12 in the qualifying final, and the reigning champs became a victim of the McIntyre System, exiting the finals race on the opening weekend as other results went against them.

- 2010—It appeared as if the Sea Eagles' star was on the wane in 2010. The club won only half of its 24 games to limp into the finals in eighth place, before making a swift exit courtesy of a 28-0 loss to minor premiers St. George Illawarra. Jamie Lyon and Jason King, who made his Origin debut for NSW in 2010 and won his second straight club player of the year award, were installed as co-captains following Matt Orford's departure to Bradford. Rookie Trent Hodkinson enjoyed a fine rookie season as Orford's halfback replacement, but he departed for Canterbury at the end of the season. New Zealand five-eighth Kieran Foran—a Kiwi Test debutant after only a handful of NRL appearances in 2009—emerged as a budding superstar with a magnificent season. Brett Stewart was ruled out for the season after suffering another knee injury in the opening round, while late-season suspensions to Glenn Stewart and Steve Matai contributed to the Sea Eagles' meek end to 2010.

- 2011—Manly rallied in 2011 to rejoin the NRL's frontrunners. Entrenched in the top-four from round nine, the Sea Eagles finished the regular season in second spot. They trailed the Cowboys 8-0 at halftime of the qualifying final, before romping to a 42-8 victory, breaking the premiership record for most points scored in a half of a finals match in the process. Manly overwhelmed an injury-hit Brisbane side 26-14 in the preliminary final and Jamie Lyon lifted the NRL trophy a week later following the Sea Eagles' comprehensive 24-10 defeat of the Warriors in the Grand Final. Lock Glenn Stewart, who made his return in the Grand Final from a three-match suspension stemming from an infamous brawl against Melbourne, won the Churchill Medal at the end of a career-best season, before being named Manly's player of the year. Rookie halfback Daly Cherry-Evans and bulldozing backrower Tony Williams were bolters in Australia's Four Nations squad, joining clubmate Anthony Watmough for the tour to

England, while Glenn and Brett Stewart pulled out with injury. The Stewart brothers were involved in a post-Grand Final media storm after an alleged terse exchange with NRL CEO David Gallop on the victory dais regarding the suspension imposed on Brett in 2009.

The club's well-deserved premiership triumph was quickly overshadowed by off-field tumult, with Hasler—now regarded as one of the modern era's finest coaches—announcing he had signed with Canterbury for 2013 less than a week after the Grand Final. Amid rumblings of extensive poaching of the playing group by the Bulldogs and the signing of key staff such as recruitment manager Noel Cleal, Manly sacked Hasler in November and installed assistant and club great Geoff Toovey as his replacement for 2012.

There is a strong correlation between outsiders' hatred of the Sea Eagles and the club's position among the premiership's heavyweights at the time; needless to say, Manly's unpopularity was at fever pitch in 2011. But the Sea Eagles are happy to play the part of the villain. Manly has won premierships in each of the last five decades—a feat unmatched in Australian Rugby League history—while the club's eight titles in the last 40 seasons trumps all of its rivals (Canterbury and Brisbane are next with six). The game needs its villains as much as it needs its heroes, and the Manly-Warringah Sea Eagles will preserve a treasured place in the premiership as they forge ahead to their next triumphant era.

PARRAMATTA'S GOLDEN ERA
SHINES THROUGH

The proud history of the Parramatta Eels encompasses some deep troughs and is littered with missed premiership opportunities. The club's stellar run during the 1980s sparkles brightly amidst the blue-and-golds' 65-season narrative, but has also served as an unattainable peak for every Parramatta side since to strive for.

Parramatta was admitted to the NSWRL competition along with Manly-Warringah in 1947, providing the district with its first premiership club since Cumberland's sole 1908 season (see Extinct Clubs). Parramatta teams previously played in the Western Suburbs junior competition, and the promoted club contained a strong influence from its neighbouring 'big brother.' Wests great and 1933-34 Kangaroo Tour captain Frank McMillan was installed as Parramatta's foundation coach, while former Magpies centre Bob Andrews became the fledgling club's inaugural captain.

But the club finished last in its first season, winning just three games. All time great five eighth Vic Hey returned from an illustrious decade in England to captain-coach Parramatta in 1948. Although injuries restricted Hey to just 10 games in two seasons, he remained as coach of the club until 1953. Parramatta missed the finals by just two competition points in 1949, lamenting three consecutive draws to end the regular season. Goalkicking utility-back Ian Johnston became the club's first Test player in 1949, playing centre in the first Test loss to New Zealand in Wellington, while winger Mitchell Wallace emerged as a prolific try-scorer. Wallace crossed 18 times in 1949 and 1951 among 57 career tries—both club records that stood until the early-1980s.

After a respectable sixth-place finish in 1951, Parramatta became the competition's whipping boys, collecting the wooden spoon in eight of the next 10 seasons, including a premiership record six straight from 1956. Parramatta's squad, made up predominantly of local juniors, was unable to consistently compete with the longer-established clubs. But the club underwent a startling transformation in 1962. The main catalysts for the change in fortune were the arrival of fullback Ken Thornett, a rugby union convert who returned to Australia from a stint with Leeds, and the acquisition of revered St. George captain-coach Ken Kearney in a non-playing capacity. Captain Ron Lynch was joined in a formidable forward pack by fellow Test representatives Brian Hambly, Billy Rayner and Ron Boden, while Ken's brother and Wallaby international Dick Thornett joined the club in 1963. Former St. George and Kangaroos halfback Bobby Budgen also linked with Parramatta in 1962. The perennial cellar dwellers qualified for four straight finals series (1962-65), reaching the preliminary final stage in 1963 and 1964.

Ken Thornett was the star, however, earning the nickname 'The Mayor of Parramatta' for his magnificent deeds in becoming one of Rugby League's greatest custodians. He played 12 Tests despite competing with Les Johns, Keith Barnes and Graeme Langlands for the Australian fullback role. Ken and Dick Thornett became the first brothers to appear in a Test together for over half a century, while the pair was joined in the 1963-64 Kangaroo Tour party by clubmate Brian Hambly, and Lithgow centre Barry Rushworth, who joined the Eels upon the squad's return.

The club slipped back to mid-table finishes during the latter part of the 1960s, while the gradual retirement of its Test representatives eventually consigned the Eels to the wooden spoon in 1970. Ken Thornett came out of retirement in 1971 for one season and restored the Eels to the finals for the first time in six years, but a wooden spoon in 1972 and two subsequent second-last finishes in 1973-74 followed. A positive development was the rise of ball-playing prop Bob O'Reilly, who became Parramatta's first local junior to play for Australia in 1970. O'Reilly left the club for an ill-fated stint at Penrith in 1976, missing out on the Eels' maiden Grand Final appearances.

Parramatta qualified for the 1976 Grand Final in coach Terry Fearnley's first season, defeating Manly in the major semi, only to be pipped 13-10 by the Sea Eagles in a gripping decider. The club had been boosted by the arrival of international pivot John Peard and former Wallaby forward Ray Price, while Kangaroo centre and goalkicking sensation Mick Cronin was finally lured from Gerringong in 1977. Parramatta claimed its first minor premiership in 1977, but after playing out the first drawn Grand Final with St. George, 9-all, the Dragons smashed the Eels 22-0 in a one-sided replay. Following a heartbreaking and controversial finals exit at the hands of Manly in 1978 (in another replay), the advent of the Eels as a heavyweight was emphasised by the selection of Price, Cronin, and forwards Geoff Gerard, Ron Hilditch and Graeme Olling in the Kangaroo Tour squad, while Peard, Ray Higgs, John Quayle, John Kolc, Jim Porter, Denis Fitzgerald and Neville Glover (who infamously dropped a pass with the tryline open in the 1976 Grand Final) represented Australia from the club during the mid-to-late-1970s.

THE GOLDEN ERA Fearnley departed after Parramatta's preliminary final loss in 1979, and after missing the finals under John Peard in 1980, the club acquired the services of revered coach Jack Gibson. The exceptional young talent of halfback Peter Sterling, brilliant five-eighth Brett Kenny, dazzling centre Steve Ella and devastating winger Eric Grothe complimented the experience and guile of Price and Cronin, the leadership of ex-St. George hooker Steve Edge, and veteran forward hard-heads Hilditch, Bob O'Reilly (who returned to the club from Easts) and Kevin 'Stumpy' Stevens. Under Gibson's expert tutelage, Parramatta broke its premiership hoodoo with a 20-11 defeat of Newtown in the 1981 Grand Final. Overzealous fans burned down the grandstand at the club's home ground, Cumberland Oval, after the momentous triumph, forcing the Eels to play out of Canterbury's Belmore Sports Ground for the next four seasons.

Despite losing consecutive major semi-finals to Manly in 1982-83, the Eels won through to the Grand Final in each season and trounced the Sea Eagles—21-8 and 18-6 respectively—to claim three straight premierships. Kenny scored two tries in each of the three Grand Final victories, while Parramatta remains the only club since the mighty St. George side of the 1950s and 1960s to win a hat-trick of first grade titles. The Eels contributed six players to the unbeaten 1982 Kangaroo Tour squad—Sterling, Kenny, Ella, Grothe, Price and second-rower John Muggleton (Cronin declined to tour); and a New South Wales-record eight players from the club turned out for the Blues in the second Origin match of 1983. Gibson stood down at the end of the season and was replaced by former Cronulla halfback John Monie.

Parramatta's run was halted by a tense 6-4 loss to minor premiers Canterbury in the 1984 Grand Final. The Bulldogs proved the Eels' bogey again in 1985 courtesy of a 26-0 thrashing in the preliminary final. The club unveiled its new headquarters in 1986, the impressive Parramatta Stadium, and won another minor premiership en route to its fifth Grand Final in six years. In the only try-less decider in history, the Eels prevailed 4-2 over Canterbury in a dramatic showdown between the heavyweight rivals. Sterling, who was named the season's Dally M Player of the Year, won the inaugural Clive Churchill Medal, while the victory was a fitting send-off for retiring club greats Cronin and skipper Price. With Sterling and Kenny at the peak of their powers and the likes of Ella and Grothe still in their mid-20s, the Eels remained confident the veterans' departures would not curtail the club's dominance.

EELS IN THE DOLDRUMS Parramatta's decline was swift. The side that carried the Eels to such phenomenal success in a six-year period rapidly disintegrated. Ella and Grothe retired before the decade was out after a succession of injury-hampered seasons, and former Test lock Peter Wynn hung up the boots at the end of 1990. Sterling retained his status as one of the premiership's elite performers, collecting the Dally M-Rothmans Medal double in 1987 and winning the Rothmans Medal again in 1990, but a recurring shoulder injury forced him into retirement early in 1992 after playing just four games in the previous 18 months. Kenny, who also endured his share of injury problems during the late-1980s, was the last remnant of the club's glory days. He retired at the end of 1993 after setting new club records for career tries (110) and appearances (265) (since broken by Luke Burt and Nathan Hindmarsh respectively).

High-profile recruits such as Test lock Bob Lindner (1987-88) failed to fire, while local juniors such as Jason Bell, David Penna and Glenn Liddiard did not kick on after impressive starts that suggested they would fill the void created by the departed greats. Monie left the club at the end of 1989 to join all-conquering English side Wigan, but club favourites Mick Cronin (1990-93) and Ron Hilditch (1993-96) were unable to reverse the Eels' flagging fortunes. After hovering mid-table for four seasons, the Eels slumped to second-last in 1991 and '92 and fared little better in the ensuing two seasons. Boasting precious little star quality—young centre/five-eighth Michael Buettner and former Canterbury and Kangaroos forward Paul Dunn were notable exceptions—Parramatta sunk to a new low in 1995, finishing 19th out of 20 teams in the expanded competition.

The club stuck solid with the ARL during the 1995 Super League upheaval and embarked on a lavish spending spree. Parramatta controversially snapped up Bulldogs quartet Jason Smith, Jim Dymock, Dean Pay and Jarrod McCracken; World Cup hooker Aaron Raper and his Cronulla teammate, boom prop Adam Ritson; and former Kiwi Test captain and halfback Gary Freeman. Smith, Dymock and Pay became the club's first Origin representatives since 1988, and although they finished an unflattering 13th in 1996, the Eels proved they could once again be competitive with the heavyweight sides.

SO CLOSE, SO FAR Brian Smith's decade-long tenure as coach began in 1997 and he immediately returned the Eels to the finals after a 10-season absence. The rise of outstanding young talent such as Nathan Hindmarsh, Nathan Cayless, Luke Burt and Jamie Lyon pointed to future premiership glory, but Smith's reign was peppered with finals heartache. After being bundled out of the ARL finals with consecutive losses in 1997, Parramatta reached the preliminary final in the inaugural 1998 NRL season. The Eels led Canterbury 18-2 with 11 minutes remaining, but crumbled to a 32-20 extra-time defeat in the most celebrated finals collapse in premiership history. Parramatta made another preliminary final appearance in 1999, building a 10-point halftime lead over Melbourne before fading to go down 18-16. The inexperienced Eels line-up exceeded expectations by navigating their way to a third consecutive preliminary final in 2000, a gallant 16-10 loss to Brisbane.

Everything clicked for Parramatta in 2001, however, as the club powered to its first minor premiership since 1986 and entered the Grand Final showdown with Newcastle as comfortable favourites. But Newcastle ambushed the shell-shocked Eels to establish a 24-0 halftime lead in the decider. Despite a spirited second half fightback, the Eels were never in the hunt and succumbed 30-24, with all time premiership records for most points (943) and tries (159) in a season little more than stinging reminders of the club's missed opportunity.

Parramatta slumped again during the next three seasons; after being eliminated in the first week of the 2002 finals, the club missed the top-eight in 2003 and '04. NSW representatives Brett Hodgson (Wests Tigers) and Andrew Ryan (Canterbury) departed for rival NRL clubs, while 2001 Kangaroo Jamie Lyon stunned the Eels by walking out on the club in early-2004. The Eels rallied to take out the minor premiership in the topsy-turvy 2005 NRL season, but an inexplicable preliminary final performance saw the Eels eliminated 29-0 at the hands of the Cowboys. The arrival of international three-quarter Timana Tahu, the Test debut of powerhouse winger Eric Grothe Jr., the emergence of Dally M Rookie of the Year halfback Tim Smith and the unwavering consistency and commitment of Nathan Hindmarsh were individual highlights of a 2005 season that promised much more for the club. Hindmarsh has been the Eels' heart and soul during the NRL era, winning an extraordinary seven Ken Thornett Medals as the club's player of the year and racking up 307 first grade appearances to the end of 2011, as well as playing 22 Tests and 17 Origins.

Brian Smith departed mid-season after the Eels' indifferent start to 2006, before Premier League coach and the club's 2001 Grand Final halfback Jason Taylor stepped into the breach and guided the team to an unlikely finals berth. Parramatta, with ex-Knights coach Michael Hagan at the helm and scintillating new talents Jarryd Hayne and Krisnan Inu leading the charge on the field, was among the contenders again in 2007, but an admirable campaign ended with a brave 26-10 loss to Melbourne in the preliminary final after holding the minor premiers to 10-all at halftime. Hagan stepped down after the Eels' disappointing 2008 season and was replaced by former New Zealand Warriors and St. Helens mentor Daniel Anderson, a lower grade coach with Parramatta before heading to Auckland.

The club seemed to be in disarray in 2009, with the upheaval surrounding the mid-year departure of outspoken chief executive Denis Fitzgerald after three decades in charge compounded by poor on-field results. But on the back of a phenomenal run of performances from virtuoso fullback Jarryd Hayne, Parramatta recovered from 14th position after 14 rounds to scrape into the finals, before winning through to the Grand Final. The Eels lost few admirers in the wake of their hard-fought 23-16 loss to the Storm in the decider, but the club failed to capitalise on that momentum and Anderson was sacked after a dismal 2010 season, while record-breaking skipper Nathan Cayless retired. Highly regarded Kiwi Test coach Stephen Kearney took the reins in 2011, but only narrowly avoided the wooden spoon. The club's bizarre recruitment policy for 2011—consisting of luring ageing ex-NRL stars from Super League—was mercifully abandoned, and the Eels recruited Test centre Willie Tonga and brilliant halfback Chris Sandow for 2012. CEO Paul Osborne met the same fate as Fitzgerald at the end of 2011 as off-field bumbling once again interfered with Parramatta's bid to end its premiership drought.

CHOCOLATE SOLDIERS
TO MOUNTAIN MEN

Penrith was promoted to the NSWRL premiership along with Cronulla in 1967. But for almost two decades, the club's ordinary on-field results—combined with its brown and white playing strip—saw the hapless Panthers derisively dubbed 'The Chocolate Soldiers.' The team from the foot of the Blue Mountains in far western Sydney came of age in the early-1990s, however, and achieved memorable premiership victories in 1991 and 2003.

The Panthers recruited impressively from rival clubs in their formative seasons; Newtown's former Test five-eighth Tony Brown was the club's inaugural captain, while goalkicking NSW representative winger Bob Landers joined from Easts for Penrith's maiden season. Foundation coach Leo Trevena lasted just one season and veteran Balmain forward Bob Boland came on board as captain-coach in 1968. Although the club won the pre-season Wills Cup in 1968, the Panthers' results in the premiership were underwhelming, finishing no higher than eighth before Boland was axed early in the 1973 season (he had retired as a player in 1970 but remained as coach) and replaced by Trevena. Captained by ex-Parramatta and veteran Test lock Ron Lynch, Penrith slumped to a wooden spoon finish in 1973 and was humiliated 70-7 by Manly late in the season—the most points conceded by a first grade team in 38 years.

Due to the affluent leagues club that funded the Panthers football club, cash-flow was not an issue and Penrith outlaid massive transfer fees to recruit English stars Mike Stephenson and Bill Ashurst in 1974. Both imports added value—ultra-professional and determined hooker Stephenson was installed as captain-coach in 1975, while brilliant but petulant backrower Ashurst provided the Panthers with a genuine match-winner in the pack. But Stephenson's captain-coach experiment lasted just a season as the club finished second-last (he stayed on as skipper until 1978), and Ashurst secretly walked out on the club and returned to England prior to the 1977 season. The club's ambitious, big-spending ways was very much a hit-and-miss proposition: ex-Balmain forward Dennis Tutty proved an excellent buy, but a two-season stint at Penrith almost ruined Parramatta Test forward Bob O'Reilly's career, while former All Black prop Kent Lambert made just one first grade appearance.

Two players that would later have a sizeable impact on the club in a coaching capacity made significant on-field contributions during the 1970s. Tim Sheens, originally a second-rower before gravitating to the front-row later in his career, played a then-record 177 first grade games for the Panthers between 1970 and 1982. Versatile ball-playing backrower Phil Gould became the youngest captain in the club's history, leading the Panthers as a 20-year-old in 1978 (in just his second first grade game) following Stephenson's retirement. Penrith's extensive junior catchment area was emphasised by the Panthers' Under-23s side capturing the club's first premiership in 1978, but the lower-grade success did not translate to future first grade prosperity—Penrith collected another wooden spoon in 1980 under the coaching of Len Stacker. John Peard assumed the coaching position in 1982 but his two years in charge produced ordinary results.

The Panthers were not devoid of fine playing talent during this trying period. Dazzling fullback Kevin Dann represented New South Wales in an interstate (non-Origin) match against Queensland in 1980; burly ball-playing forward Daryl Brohman became the club's first Queensland State of Origin representative in 1983 (a broken jaw suffered in that match cost him an almost certain Test jumper); Gooloogong hooker Royce Simmons debuted for the club in 1980 and assumed the captaincy from an injured Brohman during 1983, holding the post for seven subsequent seasons; goalkicking utility-back Mark Levy starred for the club during the first half of the 1980s; and teenage centre Brad Izzard became the club's first Origin representative when he debuted for NSW as a first grade rookie in 1982, before amassing 209 games as an integral and versatile component of Penrith's first premiership side.

Penrith's belated push for credibility gathered momentum in 1984. Among a batch of forward-thinking initiatives off the football field was Tim Sheens' return to the club as first grade coach. Meanwhile, the playing ranks were bolstered by the emergence of a 19-year-old local junior named Greg Alexander, who claimed Dally M Rookie of the Year honours. The Panthers finished seventh, but the season could so easily have garnered a maiden finals berth. Sitting in fifth spot with two rounds remaining, Penrith succumbed to Canberra and Parramatta to miss out by a single competition point. In another individual milestone, captain Simmons made his Origin debut for New South Wales.

The 18-year wait concluded the following season, however, with Penrith finishing the regular season equal-fifth before defeating Manly 10-7 in extra-time in a play-off for the last finals spot. Despite being thrashed by Parramatta in their finals debut—a 38-6 minor preliminary semi-final exit—the Panthers had broken a long-standing threshold. Winning three matches in the closing four rounds just to draw level with the Sea Eagles was a sign of the burgeoning maturity and stability within the club. Astute recruitment brought former Test forward Geoff Gerard and veteran St. George five-eighth Tony Trudgett to the club in 1985, complementing the determined leadership of Royce Simmons, and Greg Alexander's attacking brilliance. The precocious halfback was named Dally M Player of the Year, while he set a club record for most points in a season (196) and equalled Glenn West's mark for tries in a season (14).

The Panthers failed to capitalise on their progress in the ensuing two seasons—the club finished eighth in 1986 and 12th (of 13 teams) in 1987. Penrith was on track for the finals in the former year, but just one win in the last seven rounds cruelled its bid. But individual achievements and the rise of outstanding junior talent kept the Panthers' pot boiling during the two-season backslide. Royce Simmons became the club's first Test player during the 1986 series against New Zealand, and was joined on the year-ending Kangaroo Tour by the versatile Alexander. Promising forwards John Cartwright, Mark Geyer and Col Van der Voort broke into first grade in 1986 and were at the forefront of Penrith's ascension to contender status in the ensuing seasons—the trio cemented backrow starting spots in 1988.

Coach Sheens took up the Canberra post vacated by Brisbane-bound Wayne Bennett in 1988, and was replaced at the foot of the Blue Mountains by Manly's inaugural premiership-winning coach, Ron Willey. The club also welcomed experienced Canterbury duo Chris Mortimer and Peter Kelly, and goalkicking utility-back Neil Baker. Willey's old-school values gelled with the rugged and willing Panthers, but after sharing the competition lead with two rounds remaining, consecutive losses plunged Penrith into a fifth-place play-off with Balmain. The Panthers were swamped 28-8 to miss out on the finals when a maiden minor premiership was in the offing just 10 days earlier.

Alexander, Geyer, Cartwright and Kelly debuted for NSW in 1989, while Alexander made his Test debut on Australia's subsequent tour of New Zealand. The Panthers finished the regular season in outright second, but the club's finals inexperience seeped through in consecutive losses to eventual Grand finalists Balmain (24-12) and Canberra (27-18). Illawarra international and Queensland Origin winger Alan

McIndoe proved an excellent buy for the club, while teenage half Steve Carter bustled his way into first grade. But it was 17-year-old centre/five-eighth Brad Fittler that created the biggest stir the schoolboy star debuted late in the regular season and was chosen as starting pivot for both of the Panthers' finals matches. Fittler became the youngest-ever Origin player when he debuted off the bench in 1990 (a record beaten by Queensland's Ben Ikin five years later), while he settled into the centres at first grade level.

Feeling their way through the realm of the competition heavyweights during the previous few seasons finally bore fruit for the Panthers under former club captain and Canterbury's 1988 premiership-winning coach Phil Gould, who replaced Willey at the end of 1989. Penrith claimed third spot on the ladder and its maiden finals win with a 26-16 upset of Brisbane in the major preliminary semi.

Faced with defending champs and minor premiers Canberra a week later, the Panthers booked a Grand Final berth by forcing the major semi into extra-time and storming to a 30-12 victory on the back of the brilliance of Alexander and Fittler. Alexander racked up 22 points from two tries and seven goals. But the enormity of the occasion hampered Penrith in the decider rematch with the Raiders—the Grand Final debutantes fought valiantly but played from behind on the scoreboard all day and eventually went down 18-14. Consolation came in the form of Kangaroo Tour selection for Alexander, Geyer, Cartwright and Fittler (the youngest Kangaroo tourist in history).

Alexander replaced Simmons as captain in 1991 and Penrith lost just four regular season games to secure its first minor premiership, six points clear of the field. Penrith's squad was strengthened by powerhouse winger Graham Mackay, who scored a club record 16 tries, and former Kangaroo prop Paul Dunn. A gripping 16-14 major semi victory over North Sydney booked the Panthers a Grand Final spot, where they again met the Raiders. After trailing 12-6 at halftime of the decider, a surge in the final quarter of the match thrust Penrith into the lead. Club great Simmons' second try in his farewell match and Alexander's sideline conversion sealed a euphoric 19-12 triumph.

Penrith's patchy premiership defence went into freefall following the death of versatile 21-year-old Ben Alexander—younger brother of skipper Greg—in a car accident in June 1992. The Panthers won just one of their last six games to slide out of finals contention, while fiery backrower Mark Geyer experienced a bitter split with the club and joined Balmain in 1993. The club slumped to 12th in 1993 and although the arrival of Kiwi Test halfback Gary Freeman in 1994 spearheaded an improved eighth-place finish, Greg Alexander left Penrith to become a foundation Auckland Warrior. Meanwhile, Gould departed before the end of the season and was replaced as coach by Royce Simmons. Penrith sided with Super League in 1995, but Brad Fittler became an ARL figurehead—the brilliant five-eighth was installed as Test skipper and linked with Gould at the Sydney City Roosters in 1996.

Mired amongst the premiership's also-rans in 1995 and '96, the Panthers qualified for the Super League finals in 1997 after being boosted by Alexander's return, and the rise of young stars such as teenage half/hooker Craig Gower, goalkicking centre Ryan Girdler and fullback-cum-backrower Matt Adamson. All three represented the Super League Australian Test side. Geyer also rejoined the club in 1998, while Gower and Girdler made full Test debuts in 1999, but the Panthers finished 14th and 10th in the first two NRL seasons respectively. The Steve Carter-led Panthers returned to the finals in 2000—their first post-season appearance in a full competition since the 1991 Grand Final—but the club finished as dismal wooden spooners in 2001.

Former Cronulla coach John Lang took over from Simmons in 2002 and a batch of outstanding youngsters led the Panthers' charge to an unlikely minor premiership the following season. Potent three-quarters Luke Lewis and Luke Rooney, electrifying fullback Rhys Wesser, explosive backrowers Tony Puletua and Joe Galuvao, and livewire five-eighth Preston Campbell joined forces with linchpin halfback and captain Gower, former NSW hooker Luke Priddis, and veterans Girdler and Scott Sattler to top the ladder in 2003. After accounting for Brisbane and the Warriors to advance to the decider, Penrith upset defending premiers the Sydney Roosters 18-6 with a clinical and committed Grand Final performance. Priddis set up both of Rooney's tries and scored one himself to claim Clive Churchill Medal honours. Lewis and tyro forwards Joel Clinton and Trent Waterhouse went on the subsequent Kangaroo Tour (although Lewis controversially did not play a Test), while Lewis, Rooney, Waterhouse (all NSW), Wesser and prop Ben Ross (both Queensland) made their respective Origin debuts in 2004.

Following a preliminary final appearance in 2004, the Panthers missed the top-eight in the ensuing two seasons and Lang departed at the end of 2006. Raiders coach Matthew Elliott's first season in charge at Penrith garnered a wooden spoon and he narrowly avoided the sack after disappointing 2008-09 campaigns. Brisbane great and veteran Kangaroo prop Petero Civoniceva joined the club in 2008 and assumed the captaincy, while the versatile Lewis (now playing predominantly in the backrow) and quicksilver centre Michael Jennings made their Test debuts in 2009. With fullback Lachlan Coote and goalkicking three-quarter Michael Gordon leading the youth brigade, the Panthers surged to a surprise second-place finish in the 2010 minor premiership. But consecutive finals losses to Canberra and the Roosters brought the renaissance to a disappointing conclusion. Phil Gould accepted the position of general manager of the Panthers during 2011 and Elliott was punted midway through the year as the club fell back into its inconsistent ways. Gould lured highly rated Warriors coach Ivan Cleary to take over the reins in 2012, but the departure of Civoniceva and club stalwart Waterhouse placed the Panthers squarely into a rebuilding phase.

CRONULLA'S ETERNAL PREMIERSHIP STRUGGLE

Despite reaching three Grand Finals, winning two minor premierships and producing outstanding players such as Steve Rogers, Greg Pierce, Andrew Ettingshausen, David Peachey and Paul Gallen, Cronulla-Sutherland remains the oldest club to have not won a premiership. The Sharks have bounced back from dire financial positions on several occasions to resurface as a genuine title contender, but have fallen agonisingly short time and again in 45 seasons.

Promoted from the NSWRL's Second Division competition to the premiership in 1967 (along with Penrith), the southern Sydney club entered the big time with a strong influence from neighbouring 'big brother' club St. George—former premiership-winning forward Monty Porter was Cronulla's inaugural captain, while legendary Saints captain-coach Ken Kearney was the club's coach for its first three seasons. The Sharks finished last in two of their first three seasons (the only wooden spoons in the club's history), but the arrival of Great Britain halfback Tommy Bishop midway through 1969 proved a turning point. Bishop took over as captain-coach the following season and guided the Sharks to respectable mid-table finishes from 1970-72. Meanwhile, hooker Ron Turner became Cronulla's first Australian representative during the 1970 World Cup.

The 1973 season was a watershed year for the club. The 32-year-old Bishop, ably backed by former St. Helens and Test teammate Cliff Watson (who linked with the Sharks in 1971), Rothmans Medallist Ken Maddison, and local juniors Greg Pierce and 18-year-old rookie centre Steve Rogers, led Cronulla to second on the ladder at the end of the regular season. The Sharks qualified for their maiden Grand Final in their first finals series following emphatic victories over St. George and Newtown. Facing Manly in the decider, Cronulla went down 10-7 in a notorious match marred by savage violence in the first half and regarded as the most brutal Grand Final of all time. There was some consolation for Pierce, Maddison and Rogers, who were selected for the subsequent Kangaroo Tour.

Cronulla was unable to come to contractual terms with Bishop and Watson for 1974 and the pair left the club, consigning the Sharks to a 10th-place finish. Legendary St. George lock Johnny Raper replaced Noel Thornton as coach in 1975, but the future Immortal's two-season stint garnered disappointing on-field results. The Sharks enjoyed a revival under Ted Glossop in 1977—finishing just one win adrift of the finals—but he was replaced as coach by yet another St. George luminary, Norm Provan, for the following season. Showing Glossop the door was a controversial decision given Cronulla's vast improvement in his sole season in charge, but Provan's arrival produced immediate results.

Industrious lock Pierce became Cronulla's first Test captain in 1978, leading Australia to a 24-2 thumping of New Zealand, while Rogers was established as one of the game's elite players. With Steve Kneen and Kiwi Test enforcer Dane Sorensen adding starch to the pack, the Sharks finished second in the minor premiership, before becoming the first side through to the Grand Final with wins over Manly and Wests. Pierce and Sorensen were both absent from the decider due to suspension. After the Grand Final showdown with Manly finished in an 11-all draw, the Sea Eagles again proved Cronulla's nemesis with a 16-0 shutout in the replay three days later, with Sharks stars Mick Mullane, Barry Andrews and John McMartin forced to withdraw from the replay injured. Rogers, Pierce and Kneen departed with the 1978 Kangaroos shortly afterwards, a bittersweet reward after letting a gilt-edged title chance against the weary Sea Eagles slip away.

Rugged forward Kurt Sorensen—brother of Dane and a fellow Kiwi Test star—joined Cronulla in 1979 and the club won the midweek Amco Cup before qualifying for the finals in third place, but exited following consecutive losses to Parramatta and Canterbury. Provan departed and was replaced by Tommy Bishop, but a dismal 1980 campaign saw the recently retired Pierce take the coaching reins in 1981. He restored the Sharks to the finals, while Rogers captained Australia against France and won the Dally M Player of the Year award. But both club greats departed at the end of a disappointing 1982 season (Rogers joined St. George), and a host of stars—including the Sorensen brothers, the Mullane brothers (Mick and Greg) and ball-playing backrower Gavin Miller—followed a year later after the club's grim finances sparked a player payment fiasco.

Highly regarded ex-Eels coach Terry Fearnley lasted just two seasons with Cronulla and was replaced by the great Jack Gibson in 1985. The Sorensen brothers and Rogers returned that season, but Rogers' comeback lasted just one game after having his jaw smashed by Bulldogs hooker Mark Bugden, while Miller came back to the club in 1986. Cronulla's table position failed to improve in three seasons under Gibson, but the foundations had been laid for a prosperous end to the decade. Allan Fitzgibbon assumed the coaching position in 1988 and steered the Sharks to their maiden minor premiership, while Miller and outstanding young three-quarters Andrew Ettingshausen and Mark McGaw made their Test debuts. But Cronulla squandered two chances to qualify for the Grand Final courtesy of back-to-back losses to Canterbury (26-8) and Balmain (9-2), and another premiership opportunity fell by the wayside.

Miller became the fifth Cronulla player to claim the Rothmans Medal in 1989 (sharing the award with Newcastle's Mark Sargent), won the Dally M Player of the Year award for the second straight year and captained NSW. The Sharks scraped into the finals with a 38-14 thrashing of the star-studded Broncos in the fifth-place play-off, but were eliminated four days later following a 31-10 loss to eventual premiers Canberra.

The Sharks slipped back to also-ran status in the early-1990s. Arthur Beetson replaced Allan Fitzgibbon in 1992, but the all time great front-rower's two-season stint was overshadowed by more financial difficulties, while a lack of genuine star quality (Ettingshausen aside) on Cronulla's roster made significant on-field improvements difficult. Former Test hooker John Lang arrived as coach in 1994 from Brisbane Easts, bringing with him outstanding halfback Paul Green and blooding a clutch of talented youngsters. Cronulla finished a much-improved seventh in Lang's first season in charge, while the club's reserve grade and President's Cup sides collected premierships.

Lang guided the effervescent young Sharks, who were skippered by Ettingshausen, to a top-four regular season finish in 1995. Green won the Rothmans Medal and formed a superb combination with five-eighth Mitch Healey, while Mat Rogers (son of Steve), David Peachey, Paul Donaghy and Kiwi Richie Barnett established themselves as stars of the future. But the club's season of progress came to an end with successive finals losses to Manly (24-20) and Newcastle (19-18). Cronulla, along with its coach and the majority of its key playing personnel, aligned with Super League earlier in 1995.

The Sharks qualified for the finals in fifth spot in 1996 and won their way through to the preliminary final by accounting for Wests and Brisbane, but they again discovered Manly to be an impregnable opponent in a demoralising 24-0 defeat. Emerging as a heavyweight in the 10-team Super League premiership in 1997, Cronulla finished the regular season in second spot and approached the finals with confidence after smashing the table-topping Broncos 32-4 during the year.

But Brisbane was a class above during the finals, crushing the Sharks 34-2 in the major semi-final and repeating the dose 26-8 in the Grand Final a fortnight later. Six Cronulla players won selection in the Super League Australian Test side.

A sub-par 1998 campaign saw the Sharks miss the finals, but Lang's charges rebounded to secure the club's second minor premiership in 1999. Cronulla booked a preliminary final berth with a 42-20 decimation of defending NRL premiers Brisbane in the first week of the finals. But a Grand Final appearance slipped away when a second half capitulation against St. George Illawarra a fortnight later consigned the Sharks to a gut-wrenching 24-8 loss, terminating a season that represented perhaps the club's best chance to break its premiership duck. Cronulla had firmed as title favourites and led the Dragons 8-0 at halftime, but had no answer to a blistering Anthony Mundine hat-trick in the second 40.

The Sharks limped into the 2000 finals in eighth place and were swiftly despatched by minor premiers Brisbane. The season brought down the curtain on the career of Andrew Ettingshausen after 328 games—a then-premiership record tally for one club—and 165 tries. Livewire halfback Preston Campbell continued the Sharks' excellent track record of producing individual award-winners, taking out the 2001 Dally M Player of the Year gong. Despite a top-four regular season finish and a hard-fought 18-10 preliminary final loss to Newcastle, Lang was replaced by dual premiership-winning coach Chris Anderson at the end of 2001 (Lang led the Panthers to a title two years later).

Anderson brought his former Melbourne halfback Brett Kimmorley with him, and after a rocky start to 2002, the Test No.7 became the Sharks' key player. Kimmorley guided the club to another preliminary final appearance, where the Sharks were eclipsed 16-10 by the Warriors in a thriller—the third time in four seasons the club had fallen one game short of the Grand Final. The following season was a disaster, however, and Test coach Anderson departed after the Sharks slumped to 11th and were humiliated 74-4 by Parramatta in a club record defeat. John Raper's son Stuart, who coached Cronulla to lower grade premierships in the mid-1990s, replaced Anderson in 2004. A finals berth in 2005 was the highlight of Raper's three-season tenure, but that mild success was followed by a dismal 13th-place finish in 2006 and Raper made way for Australian coach Ricky Stuart.

The Sharks punched well above their weight in 2008 under passionate mentor Stuart. Despite possessing a low-profile squad with a lack of scoring firepower (Cronulla had the NRL's second-worst attacking record), Stuart guided the club to an equal share of the competition lead at the end of the regular season, instilling a gritty defensive steel in his side. Cronulla reached the preliminary final, but was thumped 29-0 by Melbourne. The 2009 season heralded an unceremonious fall from grace for the club; dreadful results and a seemingly endless procession of off-field atrocities saw the Sharks narrowly avoid the wooden spoon, although the 15th-place finish was the lowest in Cronulla history.

Fiscal problems sparked familiar calls for the Sharks to be relocated or dumped from the NRL, while Stuart left the club midway through 2010. Long-time assistant Shane Flanagan assumed the role and while the Sharks remained well out of finals contention, they built a reputation as a determined outfit and began to attract quality playing talent in 2011 and 2012. Captain and club stalwart Paul Gallen took over as NSW skipper in 2011, and the workhorse lock became established as one of the NRL's elite performers.

But the reality cannot be avoided that the Sharks are no closer to breaking through for a maiden premiership. Three Grand Final losses, two minor premierships and six preliminary final defeats are all the club has to show for 45 years of first grade toil. As Jack Gibson once famously quipped, waiting for Cronulla to win a premiership is like leaving the porch light on for Harold Holt.

RAIDERS DEFY THE CRITICS

In the wake of Canberra's fruitless early seasons after being admitted to the premiership in 1982, the nation's capital seemed an unlikely location for a Rugby League dynasty. But the Raiders were an ever-present force in the late-1980s and the first half of the 1990s, featuring in five Grand Finals, winning three premierships and missing the finals just once between 1987 and 1994. Players that would be recognised amongst the all time greats in their respective positions wore the lime green—Mal Meninga, Laurie Daley, Bradley Clyde, Ricky Stuart, Steve Walters, Glenn Lazarus and Gary Belcher ranked among the era's dominant figures.

But when club stalwarts and esteemed internationals Daley, David Furner and Brett Mullins departed at the end of 2000, few remnants of Canberra's golden period remained. Unable to attract star players to the city as they had in the mid-1980s, the Raiders relied on solid veterans, underrated recruits from rival clubs and home-grown talent to fill a modest roster. Consequently, Canberra was perennially panned in critics' pre-season predictions for much of the next decade and had few friends among punters—if the Raiders were not wooden spoon favourites then they were tipped to finish near the foot of the ladder. But, as they did by building one of the great club combinations of the modern era, the Raiders regularly exceeded expectations during the 2000s. The 'Green Machine' qualified for the top-eight six times between 2002 and 2010, keeping alive the club's remarkable record of not missing the finals two seasons in a row since 1986.

Canberra was admitted to the 1982 NSWRL competition along with Illawarra. The premiership's most isolated club, the Raiders foundation coach was former Kangaroo forward Don Furner, who coached Easts to a Grand Final appearance in 1972. The '13 import rule' dictating that a club could only recruit 13 players from outside its junior area—combined with Canberra's remoteness made it difficult for the fledgling club to attract quality playing talent. Ex-Balmain forward David Grant was the Raiders' inaugural captain and, along with former Queensland representative hooker Jay Hoffman, was one of the club's only notable acquisitions.

The club's debut season was a trying exercise. Thumped 54-3 by defending premiers Parramatta, which remains a club record defeat, and succumbing 45-0 to fellow newcomers Illawarra, Canberra collected the wooden spoon in 1982 after winning just four games. In a precursor to the difficulty opposition teams would have travelling south in the future, all four of the Raiders' victories came at their home ground, Seiffert Oval in Queanbeyan.

Half Chris O'Sullivan and centre/five-eighth Craig Bellamy, a versatile duo recruited from the Newcastle competition, were two of the Raiders' best in 1982, and flourished the following season with the addition of goalkicking centre Ron Giteau and former Test winger Terry Fahey, and the rise of young Crookwell lock Ashley Gilbert. Canberra finished 10th in 1983 and qualified for a fifth-place play-off in 1984 after recording 13 regular season wins, but the Raiders were denied a maiden finals berth after being humbled 23-4 by South Sydney.

The Raiders languished in the bottom half of the table in 1985 and 1986, but an influx of representative stars in the latter season laid the foundation for vast future success. Powerhouse Kangaroo centre Mal Meninga was joined by fellow Queenslanders and future Australian representatives Gary Belcher, Steve Walters and Gary Coyne, while the Raiders also recruited electrifying Test winger John 'Chicka' Ferguson from Eastern Suburbs. Kevin Walters and Queensland Origin centre Peter Jackson added to the Raiders' Maroon contingent—which included club stalwart and future Test prop Sam Backo—in 1987, while New Zealand Test front-rower Brent Todd also made his debut for the club.

Canberra's new-look side stormed to third place in the 1987 minor premiership, and after going down 25-16 to Easts in its finals debut, the Dean Lance-led club despatched South Sydney (46-12) and the Roosters (32-24) to advance to a maiden Grand Final appearance. Although the Raiders went down to the crack Manly side 18-8 in the decider, their spirits were not dampened after a season of substantial achievement. Highly regarded Queensland Origin coach Wayne Bennett co-coached the club with Furner in 1987 and was being groomed to take the reins fulltime in 1988, but personal circumstances and an offer too good to refuse from the fledgling Brisbane Broncos combined to lure Bennett away from Canberra, leaving the Raiders in need of a new mentor. Canberra settled on Penrith coach Tim Sheens.

Teenage centre Laurie Daley and giant Queanbeyan front-rower Glenn Lazarus were blooded in 1987 and, along with rugby union convert halfback Ricky Stuart and Belconnen junior Bradley Clyde, headed a wave of rising Raiders stars in 1988. The club finished third again but exited the finals with consecutive narrow losses to Canterbury and Balmain. Ferguson topped the premiership's tryscoring table and became the club's first New South Wales representative, while Backo, Jackson and 1986 Kangaroo Belcher rose to Test status, but the Raiders missed the services of marquee centre Meninga for much of 1987-88 due to a succession of broken arm injuries.

But Meninga made an inspirational return in 1989 and assumed the club captaincy from Lance mid-season. Meanwhile, Kevin Walters, Coyne (Queensland), Daley, Lazarus and Clyde (NSW) all made their State of Origin debuts. The 19-year-old Clyde was selected in the Australian squad for the subsequent tour of New Zealand. Canberra only secured a finals spot with a come-from-behind victory over also-rans St. George in the final round, but embarked on a run that saw the club become the first to win the premiership from fourth spot. The Raiders swept aside Cronulla, Penrith and minor premiers Souths for the right to meet Balmain in the Grand Final. In the greatest—and most-documented—decider of all time, Canberra recovered from a 12-2 halftime deficit to send the match into extra-time with a 'Chicka' Ferguson try 90 seconds from fulltime. The shell-shocked Tigers had no counter to the resurgent Raiders in the added period; a Chris O'Sullivan field goal and a famous individual try to interchange forward Steve Jackson delivered the Winfield Cup to the capital 19-14.

After moving its home base from Seiffert Oval to the newly built Bruce Stadium in 1990, Canberra secured its maiden minor premiership and rolled on to a second straight title. Despite being upset by Penrith in extra-time in the major semi, the Raiders crushed the Broncos 32-4 in the preliminary final and held off the Panthers 18-14 in the Grand Final. Meninga was subsequently chosen as skipper of the Kangaroo Tour squad and was joined by teammates Belcher, Daley, Stuart and Lazarus for the ultimately successful retention of the Ashes. Clyde would have been an automatic inclusion but for a knee injury that also ruled him out of the Grand Final, while rake Steve Walters was desperately unlucky to miss selection.

A potentially crippling salary cap drama shrouded the two-time premiers in controversy in 1991, with NSWRL auditors reporting that the Raiders had exceeded the $1.8 million cap by $120,000. In spite of the financial crisis and a burgeoning injury toll, Canberra qualified for the finals in fourth spot and grafted to its fourth Grand Final in five seasons by outlasting Western Suburbs, Manly and Norths. But the Panthers proved too big a hurdle in the decider. After leading 12-6 at halftime, the Raiders were overrun by the minor premiers, who prevailed 19-12.

Front-rowers Lazarus (Brisbane) and Todd (Gold Coast), along with a host of promising fringe players, departed Canberra at the end of the season to help ease the fiscal strain on the club. Combined with long-term injuries to Belcher and Daley, the Raiders slumped to a 12th-place finish. Regrouping in 1993, the Raiders assumed title favouritism and were on track for the minor premiership until linchpin halfback Ricky Stuart broke his ankle in the penultimate round. It was a cruel blow for Stuart (who picked up the rare Dally M/Rothmans Medal double while on crutches) and the Raiders; the rudderless side was dumped from the finals courtesy of consecutive heavy defeats to St. George and Brisbane.

The 1994 Raiders were arguably the finest vintage of the club's halcyon days. Supporting the superstar quintet of Meninga, Daley, Stuart, Clyde and Walters, was New Zealand Test front-row duo Quentin Pongia and John Lomax, boom fullback Brett Mullins, potent wing duo Ken Nagas and Noa Nadruku, the phenomenally versatile Jason Croker, powerhouse Kiwi centre Ruben Wiki and dynamic second-rower David Furner. Mullins and Croker equalled the club record set by Fijian star Nadruku the previous season by crossing for 22 tries apiece. The Raiders qualified for the Grand Final with twin defeats of North Sydney, and reversed an extra-time major semi loss to Canterbury with an emphatic 36-12 demolition of the Bulldogs in the decider. The result was a fitting farewell for retiring skipper Meninga, who subsequently set unprecedented marks by embarking on his fourth Kangaroo Tour and captaining the squad for the second time, while the Raiders equalled the record for most players on a Kangaroo Tour from a single club. Daley and Stuart were chosen to make their second trips, and were joined by Clyde, Walters, Mullins and Furner.

Despite Meninga's retirement and the distraction of the club being used as a figurehead for the Super League movement, Canberra lost just two regular season games to claim second spot, missing out on another minor premiership due to Manly's superior for-and-against. But after accounting for the Broncos 14-8 in a high-quality quarter-final, the Raiders were stunned 25-6 by the in-form Bulldogs in a preliminary final boilover. A season-ending knee injury to Stuart after just three rounds derailed the club's 1996 campaign. Although the Raiders rallied from an indifferent start to the season to finish sixth, they were eliminated by St. George in the first week of the finals.

Coach Sheens' nine-season reign ended with his departure to North Queensland for the 1997 Super League season, taking senior players Walters and Lomax with him. With club legend Meninga taking over the coaching duties, Canberra was one of the rebel competition's heavyweights, but a pair of finals losses to Cronulla prevented a Grand Final appearance.

The rationalisation of the game under the National Rugby League banner—including a strict salary cap reduction for each club—saw Raiders greats Stuart and Clyde controversially released by the Raiders at the end of 1998 in an attempt to shore up the young talent coming through the ranks, including the likes of Dally M Rookie of the Year Mark McLinden. Canberra finished seventh in the inaugural NRL season and bowed out in the second week of the 10-team finals series with a loss to Melbourne. The outflow of experience contributed to the Raiders missing the finals in 1999, albeit by a single competition point, as the club finished ninth.

Canberra surprised the sceptics with a top-four finish in 2000, followed by a 34-16 qualifying final defeat of Penrith in the last home match for revered skipper Daley and club stalwarts Furner and Mullins. The Raiders were eliminated a week later, 38-10 by the Roosters. Widespread predictions of a swift tumble down the ladder appeared to be coming to fruition in 2001. The club won just nine games (its lowest total since 1986) to finish 11th and Meninga left his coaching post.

But after a disastrous start to 2002 that yielded just one win in their first seven matches, the Raiders steadied the ship to qualify for the finals in eighth spot despite fielding one of the NRL's most inexperienced sides under new coach Matthew Elliott. Veteran centre-cum-forward leader Ruben Wiki was in outstanding touch, while rookie three-quarter Phil Graham scored 13 tries in 16 games to announce himself as one of the season's best discoveries. Canberra's run came to an end with a spirited 36-20 loss to minor premiers New Zealand in Auckland on the first weekend of the finals.

Most pundits predicted Canberra, bereft of marquee players, to slip into also-ran status as a matter of course in 2003. But the club finished the regular season in fourth place—just two wins behind minor premiers Penrith—after recording 16 victories. Although their campaign finished with a 30-18 defeat to Melbourne and a heartbreaking 17-16 loss to the Warriors in the finals, the Raiders were lauded as the NRL's undisputed overachievers. Goalkicking fullback Clinton Schifcofske was the club's best, while versatile stalwarts Wiki and Jason Croker continued to give the club excellent value. Another three-quarter star was unearthed—future international Joel Monaghan scored 21 tries in 22 matches in his second full season of first grade.

Although Canberra's 2004 season was marred by inconsistency—winning three games in a row once and recording back-to-back victories just one other time—the Raiders still managed to qualify for the finals for the third consecutive season. A late-season losing streak threatened their chances, but the Raiders scraped into eighth spot with an emphatic 62-22 last-round thrashing of Souths. Minor premiers the Sydney Roosters predictably snuffed out Canberra's season with a comprehensive

38-12 qualifying final defeat. Ryan O'Hara became just the second Raider of the decade to play Origin for NSW (after Croker in 2001), underlining the club's lack of star quality. A spate of injuries to key personnel cruelled the Raiders' progress in 2004, while the departure of Wiki, Monaghan and livewire half Mark McLinden prompted the doomsayers to forecast a bleak 2005.

But the acquisition of veteran ball-player and former Test star Jason Smith from Super League saw the Raiders grab an early competition lead, unbeaten after five rounds of the 2005 season. On track for another finals berth, Canberra suffered another wretched run with injuries (only two players started in more than 20 matches). The club's depth was severely strained and the Raiders crumbled to finish second-last, losing their last seven matches. But so even was the 2005 NRL season, Canberra finished just three wins outside the top-eight, leaving the club to lament tight late-season defeats at the hands of the Warriors, Brisbane and North Queensland.

Again absent in the player market, another year anchoring the NRL ladder loomed in 2006 for Canberra following the retirement of representative backrowers Matt Adamson and Tyran Smith and the departure of fellow frontline forwards Ian Hindmarsh, Ben Cross and Ryan O'Hara. But, with an eager young pack laying the platform for Clinton Schifcofske, Alan Tongue and teenager Todd Carney to unleash their brilliance, Canberra returned to the finals with a seventh-place finish. The Raiders won 13 of their 24 regular season games—just two shy of the second-placed Bulldogs—but consistency was a bugbear once again, unable to string three wins together more than once. Canberra's expertise in the pressure-cooker atmosphere of golden point proved the difference between a top-eight berth and finals oblivion. The Raiders won all four of their matches that required extra-time, with Schifcofske and Carney the match-winners on two occasions apiece (see Golden Point).

Canberra exited the finals with a 30-12 loss to the Bulldogs, but September football was well out of the club's reach in 2007. A massive 551 games worth of experience in the lime green jumper left the club in the shape of Jason Croker and Simon Woolford, while captain Schifcofske switched to rugby union—a combined void of experience the Raiders were unable to compensate for despite the acquisition of Colin Best, Neville Costigan and 2007 player of the year Scott Logan. Carney was undoubtedly the club's most capable match-winner, but a ban for off-field indiscretions limited his appearances and the Raiders finished 14th, just two points ahead of last-placed Penrith.

The Raiders overcame Carney's eventual sacking, season-ending injuries to young guns Phil Graham and William Zillman, and a mediocre first half of the season to thunder into the 2008 finals. On the back of a rich vein of form from five-eighth Terry Campese, Canberra won seven of its final nine games, establishing itself as the form team of the NRL as it clinched sixth position on the ladder. The Raiders clocked the club's highest-ever score (and the equal-third highest team total of all time) with a 74-12 demolition of Penrith, with Campese compiling 36 points—the most points by a player in a first grade match since Canberra legend Mal Meninga scored 38 against Easts in 1990. Although the Raiders exited the finals with a meek 36-10 loss to Cronulla, Campese and returning flyer Joel Monaghan became the club's first Australian representatives since Jason Croker in 2000 when they won selection for the World Cup. Also boding well for the future was the performance of Canberra's

Under-20s side, who won the inaugural Toyota Cup competition with a golden point victory over Brisbane in the Grand Final.

Josh Dugan, Jarrod Croker, Daniel Vidot and Shaun Fensom were part of that 2008 NYC side, and went on to become some of the NRL's brightest young stars over the next two seasons. The emergence of rookie talent was the highlight of a disappointing 2009 campaign that saw the Raiders slump to 13th with just nine wins. Brave and brilliant fullback Dugan tied with nuggetty forward Josh Miller for the club's player of the year award; slashing centre Croker was Canberra's top try-scorer with 12, including four in a 56-0 hammering of Brisbane; and powerful winger Vidot scored six tries in eight late-season games, producing some of the season's most miraculous tryscoring plays. The Test selection of former Roosters prop David Shillington and Origin debuts for Shillington (Queensland), Campese and Tom Learoyd-Lahrs (both NSW) were also cause for optimism.

A giant forward pack fed the consistent brilliance of second-year stars Dugan, Croker and Vidot along with marquee pivot Campese in a watershed 2010 season. Shillington and Learoyd-Lahrs developed into bona fide representative props, and their rotation at NRL level with fellow man-mountains Dane Tilse and Scott Logan bent opposing defensive lines back at will. But the Raiders looked anything but finals contenders sitting in 12th spot with just five wins after 17 rounds. The situation was desperate, before the Raiders responded with eight wins in the last nine rounds—including a stirring 32-16 victory over eventual premiers St. George Illawarra—to scrape into the finals in seventh spot. To put Canberra's form during this period in perspective in such an even NRL competition, Sydney Roosters, Gold Coast, New Zealand and Wests Tigers—all teams in the top-six—were the next best performed sides over the last nine weeks of the season, with just six wins apiece.

The Raiders continued the streak with a heart-stopping 24-22 defeat of the Panthers at CUA Stadium—the Green Machine's first finals win in 10 years, and their first post-season victory away from home since 1995. The Raiders' charge captured the imagination of a Rugby League supporter base in the nation's capital that had dwindled since the glory days of the early-1990s. A record Canberra Stadium crowd turned out for the semi-final showdown with Wests Tigers a week later. But the match ended in heartbreak for the Canberra faithful and the young Raiders. Canberra pegged back a 12-point deficit to trail 26-24, but a distraught Jarrod Croker, who had landed his previous 13 attempts at goal, missed a relatively easy penalty attempt in the dying stages that would have sent the match into golden point. Shillington and Learoyd-Lahrs won Australian selection for the year-ending Four Nations campaign, while train-on squad members Dugan and Croker could be considered unlucky omissions. Campese would have been a strong contender to make a return to the national squad, but he suffered a terrible knee injury late in the finals loss to the Tigers—a misfortune that would have grave ramifications for Canberra's 2011 campaign.

More than any other season, 2010 won the Raiders respect from the Rugby League media and public. The re-signing of Dugan despite a host of lucrative offers from rival clubs was a boon for a tight-knit Canberra side finally building a roster brimming with star quality, despite the humiliating exit of former Test star Monaghan after the club's ill-fated 'Mad Monday' session. Canberra Stadium remained a fortress—even in the leaner seasons of the 2000s, the Raiders finished with at least a 50 per cent home record and peaked with nine wins from 12 home games in 2008.

The sound of critics scoffing at the Raiders' now-genuine premiership chances had faded to a whisper as the exciting new crop strived to emulate the deeds of the club's heroes of yesteryear. But Canberra was not finished confounding the pundits. Tipped as a likely top-four contender, the Raiders finished 15th in 2011 after recording just six wins (the club's worst performance since its 1982 debut season), and only avoided the wooden spoon on account of their superior for-and-against to the Titans. The acquisition of former Manly premiership-winning captain and halfback Matt Orford was a disaster, while Campese played less than half a game due to injury and Dugan also spent extended periods on the sideline. The experts' expectations of Raiders in 2012 were lowered to a familiar lower-ladder position, but the plucky, consistently underrated club has a habit—for better or worse—of proving popular opinion wrong.

BRONCOS SET THE PACE

The Brisbane Broncos have set the standard for Rugby League clubs to follow since being admitted to the competition in 1988. Mixing unprecedented off-field professionalism with on-field results unmatched in the modern era, the Broncos are the prototype for success in the Australian game, and arguably Australian sport in general. The Broncos immediately usurped Manly as the club opposition fans loved to hate—and the team opposition sides lifted against. The club had a ready-made, star-studded roster gleaned from Brisbane's local competition upon entering the premiership, but one of the most impressive aspects of the Broncos' dominance has been their ability to nurture, develop and retain their own talent—an accomplishment largely owing to long-serving master coach Wayne Bennett, recruiters such as the late Cyril Connell, and a succession of top-class officials. The salary cap has made it increasingly difficult to stay near the top of the NRL, but the Broncos' ability to reinvent themselves and turn unheralded youngsters into star players almost overnight was the backbone of an extraordinary 18 consecutive finals series run, which was eventually broken in 2010.

THE EARLY YEARS Queensland Origin coach Bennett—fresh from a Grand Final appearance with Canberra—became the Broncos' foundation coach. Australian captain Wally Lewis, Test teammates Gene Miles, Greg Dowling, Bryan Niebling, Greg Conescu and Colin Scott, and brilliant Maroons halfback Allan Langer formed the basis of Brisbane's formidable 1988 squad. The Broncos immediately lived up to the hype, trouncing defending premiers Manly 44-10 in their premiership debut at Lang Park. Lock Terry Matterson scored 24 points (a club record which stood for 14 years), while the incomparable Lewis scored two tries. Brisbane won its first six games, but the weekly grind of the premiership and the taxing representative period—which would become a familiar theme in the club's existence—saw the Broncos fade to finish seventh following a final-round loss to Balmain (it should be noted that the club's 14 wins would have been enough to qualify for the finals in any subsequent season except 1993). Langer finished third in the Dally M Medal count, made his Test debut against Papua New Guinea and starred in Australia's World Cup Final defeat of New Zealand at the end of the season alongside skipper Lewis.

Dynamic hooker Kerrod Walters usurped Greg Conescu at club, state and international level in 1989, while teenage winger Michael Hancock broke into the Queensland and Australian sides. Both youngsters claimed Dally M positional awards in 1989. Matterson and Chris Johns became the club's first New South Wales representatives, while Test stars Tony Currie (Canterbury), Peter Jackson and Sam Backo (Canberra) returned to Queensland with the Broncos. Leading the 1989 competition after 10 rounds, Brisbane faltered during the representative season—exacerbated by a broken leg suffered by Langer and injury layoffs for Lewis and Miles—but surged late in the season to qualify for a fifth-place play-off with Cronulla. The Sharks trounced the weary Broncos 38-14, however, and Bennett caused a state-wide sensation by dumping Lewis as skipper ahead of the 1990 season, replacing him with Gene Miles.

Lewis' 1990 season was cruelled by a broken arm, restricting him to just nine appearances. With a ready-made five-eighth replacement in Raiders recruit Kevin Walters, the Broncos' miserly contract offer virtually forced Lewis out of the club at the end of 1990. But it was a breakthrough year on the field for the Broncos; an 11-match winning streak pitched the club into second spot on the table (on for-and-against behind minor premiers Canberra). After being upset 26-16 by Penrith in their finals debut, the Broncos eliminated Manly 12-4 but were crushed 32-4 by the Raiders in the preliminary final. Langer, Hancock, Johns, twins Kerrod and Kevin Walters, and Test veteran Dale Shearer (who joined the Broncos from Manly in 1990) toured with the Kangaroos at the end of the season. Lewis' arm injury saw him controversially ruled out of the squad after he failed a team medical.

The decision to effectively move on the highest-profile player in the game and arguably Queensland's greatest-ever player drew heavy criticism, but Bennett's gamble proved the making of the club, despite a disappointing seventh-place finish in 1991. A host of young Broncos emerged on the representative scene—Willie Carne, Paul Hauff and Andrew Gee made their Australian debuts, while Steve Renouf and Gavin Allen did likewise for Queensland holding the club in good stead for the future. Miles, Dowling and Shearer departed at the end of the season, but the acquisition of Kangaroo prop Glenn Lazarus from Canberra for 1992 was pivotal. Lazarus became the cornerstone of Brisbane's pack and provided an attacking platform for the genius of Langer and the Walters brothers, and dazzling three-quarters Carne, Hancock, Renouf and Johns.

PREMIERSHIP SUCCESS Langer assumed the captaincy in 1992 and his performances reached new heights. He won the Rothmans Medal as Brisbane claimed an emphatic minor premiership, while his two-try effort in the Broncos' 28-8 Grand Final victory over St. George was rewarded with the Clive Churchill Medal. Brisbane's maiden premiership sparked euphoric scenes north of the border as the trophy headed north of Sydney for the first time. Teenage fullback Julian O'Neill and second-row hitman Trevor Gillmeister became key members of the Broncos' line-up, and the club underlined its dominance by defeating the all-conquering Wigan side

22-8 in the World Club Challenge at Central Park at the end of the year—just a week after Langer, Kerrod and Kevin Walters, Hancock, Renouf, Carne and Lazarus had spearheaded Australia's 10-6 World Cup Final victory over Great Britain at Wembley. The club farewelled Lang Park at the end of 1992, moving to the higher-capacity Stadium Australia (formerly QEII Stadium)—the home of the 1982 Commonwealth Games—the following season and setting a host of regular season attendance records.

The Broncos' bid for back-to-back titles hit a speed-bump when a final-round loss to the Dragons relegated them to fifth heading into the 1993 finals. But Brisbane created history by becoming the first club to win the premiership from fifth spot, disposing of Manly, Canberra and Canterbury on its way to a Grand Final rematch with St. George. In a dour decider, the Broncos outplayed the nervous Dragons and cruised to a 14-6 win. The club attempted to repeat the effort in 1994 after a patchy regular season—including a heavy injury toll and a string of suspensions that fuelled a siege mentality within the Brisbane camp against the NSWRL—consigned it to another fifth-place finish. The Broncos again eliminated Manly, but were pipped 15-14 by North Sydney in the second week of the finals. Renouf's exhilarating attacking class garnered a club record 23 tries in 1994—first in the premiership—and he toured with the 1994 Kangaroos alongside clubmates Langer, Kevin Walters, Hancock, Lazarus and wing sensation Wendell Sailor.

THE SUPER LEAGUE YEARS Brisbane was a figurehead club for the Super League movement and the club's players signed en masse with the rebel organisation (effectively eliminating the representative drain on the club in 1995 after Super League-aligned players were blacklisted from selection). But despite top-four finishes leading into the eight-team finals series in 1995 and 1996, the Broncos made early exits in both seasons on the back of consecutive losses.

The Broncos swept all before them during the 1997 Super League season. Runaway minor premiers, Brisbane thumped Cronulla 34-2 in the major semi and again 26-8 in the Grand Final. The club added to the triumph with a low-key victory in the ill-fated World Club Challenge competition, defeating Hunter Mariners 36-12 in the final. Several future superstars were unearthed during this tumultuous period, including fullback Darren Lockyer, props Shane Webcke and Petero Civoniceva (compensating for Lazarus' departure to Melbourne in 1998), towering second-rower Brad Thorn and hard-running, big-hitting centre/lock Tonie Carroll. St. George recruit Gorden Tallis developed into the game's most destructive forward with the Broncos after sitting out the 1996 season when the Dragons refused to grant him a release.

BRONCOS REASSERT DOMINANCE Hell-bent on proving themselves as the best of the best, the Broncos launched a devastating assault on the inaugural NRL premiership in 1998. Boasting easily the best attacking and defensive figures in the competition, the minor premiers encountered a hiccup when they were upset 15-10 by Parramatta in their opening finals match, but proceeded to the Grand Final with 30-6 and 46-18 drubbings of Melbourne and Sydney City respectively. Despite trailing Canterbury 12-10 at halftime of the decider, Brisbane's ruthlessness came to the fore as it carved out a convincing 38-12 result. The Broncos' dominance showed no signs of subsiding, but a horror start to 1999 saw the club languishing in last place with one win from the opening 10 rounds, while club legend Langer shocked the Rugby League world by announcing his retirement less than two months into the season, citing a lack of desire. But in one of the club's finest achievements, the Broncos rallied with a club record-equalling 11-match winning streak to scrape into the finals in eighth place. The defending premiers had run their race, however, and were promptly despatched 42-20 by Cronulla in the qualifying final.

The end of the season heralded a changing of the guard, with club greats Steve Renouf and Andrew Gee joining English clubs and backrow hit-man Peter Ryan switching to rugby union. But Bennett reformulated the Broncos as a relentless, forward-oriented outfit, and the club streeted the field in the 2000 minor premiership. Brisbane ground out a 14-6 Grand Final victory over the Roosters to farewell captain Kevin Walters with a premiership. Brilliant No.1 Darren Lockyer was an obvious choice for the Clive Churchill Medal, while wing giants Wendell Sailor and Lote Tuqiri crossed for tries—each player's 18th touchdown for the season respectively.

FIVE YEARS OF FADEOUTS Future internationals Shaun Berrigan, Dane Carlaw, Justin Hodges, Corey Parker, Brad Meyers and Carl Webb emerged to take the club into the next era alongside seasoned internationals Lockyer, Webcke and new captain Tallis. But late-season fadeouts plagued the Broncos in the ensuing five seasons. A career-threatening neck injury to Tallis headlined a horrific injury toll in 2001, contributing to a six-match losing streak. Led by Lockyer, the Broncos rallied to reach the preliminary final, bravely going down to minor premiers Parramatta 24-16. Sailor defected to rugby union at the end of the season, and was joined by Tuqiri a year later. The Bulldogs' salary cap scandal presented a gilt-edged opportunity for Brisbane to claim its sixth title in 2002. Langer returned to the club at the age of 35 for one last season in 2002 and was typically inspirational, but a gut-wrenching 16-12 preliminary final defeat to the Roosters ended the Broncos' campaign.

The club returned to the remodelled Suncorp Stadium (formerly Lang Park) in 2003, boasting arguably the finest Rugby League stadium in the world. But the Broncos lost their last seven regular season games in 2003 to finish eighth, before being bounced out of the competition at the qualifying final stage by minor premiers Penrith. Darren Lockyer (who assumed the Australian captaincy in 2003) was established as one of the all time great fullbacks, but switched to five-eighth the following season—purely for the benefit of his club side—and immediately became the game's premier No.6, moving to pivot at Test and Origin level. New Zealand-born 17-year-old Karmichael Hunt was Lockyer's replacement at fullback for the Broncos. A courageous and dynamic custodian, Hunt made his debuts for Australia and Queensland in 2006 while still a teenager. But the Broncos' late-season woes continued in 2004 and 2005; after finishing the regular season third in each season, Brisbane bowed out of the finals with consecutive losses in both years. Tallis retired at the end of 2004 and Lockyer, in his first full season as club skipper, bore the brunt of the criticism for Brisbane's 2005 failure. Incredibly, the Broncos led the competition at some stage in each season between 2001 and 2005, as late as round 15 in 2001; round 10 in 2002; round 17 in 2003; round seven in 2004; and round 24 in 2005 (the Broncos headed the table for 15 weeks, but lost their last five matches to gift the minor premiership to the Eels).

THE GREATEST SUCCESS A similar fate loomed in 2006. The Broncos were on top of the table at the halfway mark of the season, but a five-match losing streak looked set to derail another campaign. But coach Bennett refused to concede his side was in a slump and Brisbane hit form at the right time, securing third spot with three impressive wins to end the regular season. A 20-4 qualifying final loss to St. George Illawarra was merely an aberration; the Broncos demolished Newcastle 50-6 a week later, before overcoming a 14-point halftime deficit to stun the Bulldogs 37-20 in the preliminary final in one of the great post-season comebacks. Entering the Grand Final bearing the unfamiliar underdog tag, the Broncos outfoxed runaway minor premiers Melbourne 15-8. Lockyer's composed display was vital to the triumph, while converted hooker Shaun Berrigan—a former Test centre and Origin half—collected Churchill Medal honours. Bennett labelled the success as Brisbane's finest premiership victory, while veteran front-rower Shane Webcke retired in deserving fashion.

The season was a personal vindication for under-fire captain Lockyer. He was the skipper and linchpin of Brisbane's premiership victory, Queensland's first Origin series win in five years, and Australia's retrieval of the Tri-Nations crown from New Zealand. Lockyer scored the winning try in the nail-biting Origin and Test deciders, while he laid on two tries and kicked the match-sealing field goal in the Grand Final. He won the Golden Boot for the second time (after winning the award in 2003 while still playing fullback) and sealed his rightful place as one of the greatest to ever play the game. He was joined in Australia's victorious squad by Berrigan, Hodges, Hunt, Civoniceva and outstanding three-quarter Brent Tate, while dynamic second-rower Sam Thaiday made his Test debut during the tournament.

PREMIERSHIP HANGOVER The Broncos' premiership defence was cruelled by a mammoth casualty list. By the end of round 21, season-ending injuries had claimed Lockyer, Tate, Hunt and Berrigan. Brisbane limped into the finals in eighth after a 68-22 loss to Parramatta in the final round denied them a fifth-place finish. A red-hot Melbourne side despatched the Broncos courtesy of a 40-0 qualifying final drubbing. Broncos greats Berrigan, Tate, Civoniceva, Thorn and Carlaw left the club at the end of the season—the Test quintet boasted 896 combined appearances for the club. Veteran prop Civoniceva's split with the club was particularly unpleasant, with a meagre contract offer from the Broncos at the heart of his move to Penrith.

Despite Lockyer's ongoing knee problems, the Broncos somehow plugged the gaps with eager youngsters yet again in 2008. Penrith recruit Peter Wallace became the Broncos' most dominant No.7 since Langer and debuted for NSW; Ben Hannant made his debut for Queensland and assumed Civoniceva's role as the cornerstone of Brisbane's pack; winger Darius Boyd broke into the Queensland and Australian sides; and speedster Denan Kemp scored 19 tries in his first full season of first grade. Lockyer, meanwhile, remained the consummate match-winner, engineering a heart-stopping victory on fulltime against Parramatta, and a golden point win over Gold Coast for the second straight season. The Broncos hit the finals in fifth spot and outmuscled the Roosters 24-16 in the qualifying final, before suffering a gut-wrenching 16-14 loss to Melbourne a week later at Suncorp Stadium, with a last-minute try stealing victory for the Storm (*see Finals Magic*). The defeat brought father figure Wayne Bennett's 21-year tenure at the Broncos to an end—the master coach had agreed to terms with St. George Illawarra for 2009.

CONFRONTING LIFE WITHOUT WAYNE Tonie Carroll retired, Boyd followed Bennett to the Dragons, Kemp was snapped up by the Warriors, while Hannant, Kiwi Test forward Greg Eastwood, former Origin backrower David Stagg and dynamic hooker Michael Ennis joined the Bulldogs. Bennett's replacement was long-time assistant Ivan Henjak, who played 185 first grade games for St. George, Canberra and Wests, before joining the Broncos' coaching staff in 1994. Melbourne's Test and Origin three-quarter Israel Folau linked with the club in 2009, but Brisbane was tipped to struggle in its first season without Bennett at the helm. The Broncos started strongly before enduring a horror mid-season slump—including a record 56-0 loss to also-rans Canberra—that prompted crisis talks and Carroll to come out of retirement. But Henjak's charges won their last five regular season games to qualify for the finals in sixth, and rolled the Titans 40-32 in a qualifying final try-fest. Brisbane muscled up a week later to bully Bennett's minor premiership-winning Dragons out of the finals 24-10, but a fractured ankle suffered by Wallace stymied the Broncos' momentum. Melbourne eliminated the Broncos for the third straight season, 40-10 in the preliminary final. Inspirational fullback Hunt defected to fledgling AFL club Gold Coast Suns at the end of the season, while giant forward Dave Taylor joined Souths.

After a dismal start to 2010 that netted just two wins in the opening eight rounds, the Broncos set their sights on the finals with a wonderful mid-season run. But disaster struck in a victory over lowly North Queensland—Lockyer suffered a rib cartilage injury and Brisbane lost its final four regular season fixtures to blow out to a tenth-place finish, ending the club's 18-season streak of qualifying for the finals. The club's cause was not aided by a hamstring injury that ruled gun centre Justin Hodges out for the entire season. Folau scored 20 tries in as many games, before the Broncos again became a victim of the AFL's expansion program—Folau signed a rich deal with 2012 AFL entrant Greater Western Sydney.

FAREWELL TO A LEGEND Brisbane welcomed back Test prop Ben Hannant from the Bulldogs in 2011 but appeared to be a club in disarray when Ivan Henjak was shown the door just a fortnight out from the first match of the season. Exacerbating the confusion was Melbourne superstar Greg Inglis' decision to renege on a deal with the Broncos to instead join Souths.

Under-20s coach Anthony Griffin was thrust into the hot-seat, and the Bennett-like character handled the step up with aplomb. Several of Griffin's Toyota Cup protégés had progressed to the NRL, including freakish winger Jharal Yow Yeh, who made his Test and Origin debuts in 2011; fullback Josh Hoffman, the club's 2010 player of the year and very much in the Karmichael Hunt mould; Alex Glenn, at home at second-row or centre and a New Zealand Test debutant in 2011; Gerard Beale, who also broke into the Kiwis' squad in 2011, a sensation at fullback, centre or wing; and clever hooker Andrew McCullough. These youngsters, along with versatile 2010 Dally M Rookie of the Year Matt Gillett, and centre sensation Jack Reed, an England international by the end of his 2011 rookie season, represented the future of the Broncos and combined seamlessly with the old firm of Lockyer, Hodges, Thaiday, Parker and Hannant.

The impending retirement of the great Darren Lockyer was inescapable throughout 2011. But the young side defied the pundits' predictions and overcame the constant media glare to finish the regular season third—the club's best finish in five years—and thumped the Warriors 40-10 and edged out the Dragons 13-12 in a golden point thriller to advance to the preliminary final stage. But Lockyer—who broke the all time premiership appearance record a few weeks earlier—fractured his cheekbone in an accidental collision with Beale late in the win over the Dragons. He kicked the winning field goal in extra-time, but was eventually forced to withdraw from the clash against Manly a week later. The Broncos were brave against the Sea Eagles, but could not peg back a poor start and succumbed 26-14.

Entering the post-Lockyer era represented arguably the biggest challenge in the club's history. Petero Civoniceva returned for a Brisbane swansong in 2012, while Thaiday became just the seventh club captain of the Broncos. Finding a five-eighth to succeed the maestro would surely prove a taller order, but typically the Broncos vowed to find a replacement from within.

Brisbane's aura has entrenched the club as a perennial powerhouse of the premiership, which is only enhanced by the bare facts and figures:

- Brisbane has won six premierships since their inception in 1988—twice as many as Canberra, Canterbury, Manly and Melbourne (who had two titles stripped in 2010 for breaching the salary cap) during the same period.
- With six Grand Final appearances, the Broncos—along with Manly—have appeared in more deciders than any other club since 1988. Melbourne and the Roosters have reached five Grand Finals apiece, while the Raiders and Bulldogs have qualified for four deciders each. Brisbane's remarkable record of emerging victorious in all six of their Grand Final appearances is unequalled in premiership history. Newcastle (two from two) and Wests Tigers (one from one) are the only other clubs with flawless Grand Final records.
- Brisbane's percentage of first grade titles per seasons in the premiership is better than any team in the game's history (six premierships in 24 seasons—25 per cent).
- The club won consecutive titles in 1992-93 and 1997-98. The only other team to win two premierships in a row during the Broncos' era is the Raiders of 1989-90.
- Four minor premierships rank the Broncos alongside Melbourne and ahead of Manly (three) since 1988—and the Storm had three (2006-08) stripped amidst the 2010 salary cap drama. More remarkably, Brisbane went on to win the Grand Final in each of their minor premiership-winning seasons.
- Qualifying for 20 finals series in 24 seasons sets the Broncos apart from their premiership rivals. Canberra (17), Manly (16), the Bulldogs (13), Newcastle (12), Cronulla and the Roosters (11 each) are the next best performers since 1988.
- Brisbane's incredible run of 18 consecutive finals series appearances (1992-2009) is second only to the all-conquering Dragons' 23 straight appearances (1951-1973) in premiership history. The Broncos' achievement in the era of the salary cap is put into perspective by the next best club efforts since 1988—the Roosters (1996-2004) qualified nine times in a row, while Newcastle (1997-2003), Melbourne (2003-2009) and Manly (2005-11) made the finals in seven straight seasons. Brisbane eventually missed the finals in 2010, for the first time since 1991—but every other club in the NRL had missed the finals at least once since 2004.
- Finishing 10th in 2010 was the club's worst result in 24 seasons. Every other club that has played more than one season since 1988 has finished at least as low as 13th.

Prior to 2010, eighth-place finishes in 1999, 2003 and 2007 were the Broncos' worst results—still good enough to qualify them for the finals.

- Brisbane's ability to hang onto players during the high-pressure salary cap era is reflected by 10 players bringing up 200 first grade games for the club. Canberra, with seven 200-gamers since 1988, is next. Five Broncos players have advanced their total to 250 games (compared to one Raider), while Darren Lockyer (355 games) holds the premiership's all time appearance record.
- The Broncos have produced a record 54 State of Origin representatives, despite not forming until the interstate series' ninth season. The Sea Eagles have provided 46 players to Origin football—15 of them before Brisbane's inception.
- Brisbane has provided 11 players to a single Origin match five times—another Origin record.
- The club has produced 40 Australian representatives—behind Souths, the Roosters, Manly, St. George, Canterbury, Wests, Parramatta and Balmain, clubs who are at least 40 years older than the Broncos. But Brisbane is well in front since 1988—the Bulldogs are next with 27 representatives.
- Brisbane's four Australian Test captains is behind only the Roosters (7), St. George (6), Wests and Balmain (5 apiece), and better than any other club since 1988.
- The Broncos set an all time record when nine of the club's players were selected for Australia to face the Kiwis in a post-season Test in 1998, beating the previous mark of seven set by St. George in 1968 and equalled by Canberra in 1994.
- Wayne Bennett coached the Broncos from 1988 until 2008—a premiership record 21 consecutive seasons in charge of the same club, 10 seasons ahead of his nearest rival, Steve Folkes, who coached the Bulldogs for 11 straight seasons (1998-2008).

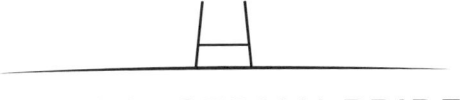

NOVOCASTRIAN PRIDE

Almost eight decades after a Newcastle side participated in the first two premiership seasons, the Newcastle Knights were admitted to the 1988 Winfield Cup along with Brisbane and Gold Coast. Content to stage a local premiership during the interim—a strong competition that spawned some of the all time greats of the game—tentative plans to re-enter the NSWRL premiership had been afoot since the 1970s. Newcastle's foundation coach was former World Cup winger Allan McMahon, while the fledgling club delved heavily into the local competition for playing talent. The Knights also had a strong Kiwi flavour, including inaugural captain and New Zealand Test forward Sam Stewart, and current or future internationals Tony Kemp, Adrian Shelford, George Mann, Tea Ropati and James Goulding. Ex-Penrith prop Tony Butterfield immediately became a reliable cornerstone of the Knights' pack and played a then-record 229 games for the club before his retirement in 2000. The Knights finished 14th of 16 teams in their inaugural season, recording just five wins.

An aggressive recruitment drive for their sophomore season netted clever half Michael Hagan and Mark Sargent from Cantebury, and highly rated Easts fullback Gary Wurth. Hagan debuted for Queensland in 1989 to become the club's first Origin representative, Wurth played for Country Origin, and Sargent was a surprise joint-winner of the Rothmans Medal with Cronulla second-rower Gavin Miller. The Knights won half of their games in 1989 to finish a respectable seventh, while the club boasted easily the best home crowd averages in the competition—in excess of 20,000—in its first two seasons. The devastating earthquake that hit Newcastle in December 1989, killing 13 people, bound the community tighter and the Knights became even more of a focal point for the embattled Hunter Valley region.

The Knights responded with a superb 1990 season, embarking on an eight-match winning streak before defeating 1988-89 grand finalists Balmain in the final round to snare an equal-fifth finish. The Tigers regrouped to oust Newcastle 12-4 in the fifth-place play-off, but the loss could not diminish the Knights' sense of progress. The club attracted a reputation as a dour, forward-oriented team in its formative seasons, but Dally M Winger of the Year Ashley Gordon was the regular season's equal-top try-scorer with Canberra captain Mal Meninga, while livewire halfback Steve Fulmer finished third in the 1990 Rothmans Medal count. Sargent became the Knights' first New South Wales Origin representative, before winning selection for the 1990 Kangaroo Tour.

Newcastle was unbeaten after five rounds of the 1991 season—winning two and incredibly drawing three matches—but mustered just four more victories and finished a dismal 13th. Coach McMahon stood down mid-season and was replaced by assistant David Waite, a former Test winger and 1973 Kangaroo tourist. The arrival of brilliant former All Black John Schuster was a rare positive—Schuster was a devastating attacking centre, scoring 11 tries and topping a century of points for the Knights in 1991. He scored a club record 152 points in 1992 (broken by Andrew Johns two years later).

The 1992 season was a watershed year for the club. Fearsome prop Paul 'Chief' Harragon burst onto the representative scene with NSW and Australia, and fellow foundation Knight Robbie McCormack—previously a half or centre—debuted for the Blues in his first season at hooker, claiming Newcastle's player of the year award. Winger Adrian Brunker represented the Maroons, while fellow Queenslander Robbie O'Davis ousted Ashley Gordon from the Knights' other flank to carve out a superb rookie season. Halfback Matthew Rodwell scooped the rookie awards pool with the Dally M gong and the Norwich Rising Star Award, forming a potent combination with skipper Hagan. Newcastle's pack boasted international prop Sargent and hardworking backrowers Marc Glanville, Paul Marquet and David Boyd (injury restricted Tony Butterfield to just three games).

The Knights qualified for their maiden finals series in fourth place and thumped Western Suburbs 21-2 in their first post-season appearance, with O'Davis scoring a sensational double. But their landmark campaign came to an end a week later with an agonising 3-2 defeat to St. George. The loss was tempered by the selection of Sargent and fullback bolter Brad Godden in Australia's World Cup squad (Harragon was unavailable due to injury). Sargent featured in Australia's 10-6 triumph at Wembley in the Final, but Godden was restricted to minor tour appearances and failed to play representative football again. The Knights' strong performance across all three grades resulted in the club's first (and, to date, only) club championship.

Newcastle did not capitalise on its breakthrough season, however, stumbling to a ninth-place finish in 1993. The club's highlights came in the form of the emergence of rookie five-eighth Matthew Johns, dynamic backrower Adam Muir, and former Wests three-quarter Jamie Ainscough, who led the Knights with 14 tries. Meanwhile, Hagan, Schuster and Kemp departed at season's end. Matthew Johns' younger brother Andrew scored a then-club record 23 points against South Sydney in the opening round of 1994—the halfback's initial first grade start—and carried the Knights' fortunes on his shoulders in the ensuing 14 seasons, becoming one of the greatest players in Rugby League history in the process. The Knights seemed destined for another finals appearance in 1994, but lost their last seven regular season matches and slid to 10th. Harragon was Newcastle's sole representative on the Kangaroo Tour.

Waite was replaced by former Great Britain coach Malcolm Reilly at the end of the year, heralding a bold new era for the club. The Knights maintained their trademark forward pack dominance through Harragon (who took over the captaincy from Sargent) and Butterfield, but the brilliant Johns brothers' instinctive halves combination saw Newcastle become recognised as one of the premiership's most exciting attacking outfits. The club sided with the ARL during the Super League upheaval in 1995. The bulk of the Knights' key players signed en masse with the establishment, but Sargent, McCormack and several officials (most notably football manager Robert Finch) and fringe first grade players eventually linked with Super League hometown rivals the Hunter Mariners.

The subsequent blacklisting of Super League-aligned players from representative football elevated Matthew Johns, Andrew Johns and Muir to the NSW side, while O'Davis turned out for the depleted Maroons. The quartet—along with Ainscough, who broke the club record with 17 tries for the Knights—all made their Test debuts by the end of 1995. Beginning the season with a club record nine-match winning streak, the Knights qualified for the inaugural eight-team finals series in fifth spot, eliminating North Sydney 20-10 and Cronulla 19-18 to advance to a preliminary final date with minor premiers Manly. Newcastle was valiant in the 12-4 loss to the Sea Eagles at a soaked Sydney Football Stadium and shaped as a heavyweight club of the ensuing seasons, while the club secured its first premiership courtesy of the Brett Kimmorley-inspired reserve grade side's Grand Final victory over Cronulla. Andrew Johns starred in Australia's against-the-odds World Cup triumph at the end of the year, collecting player of the tournament honours, while Harragon became the club's first Test skipper when he led Australia to an 86-6 victory over South Africa.

Entrenched in the top-four at the halfway point of the 1996 season, Newcastle suffered a dramatic form slump to miss the finals by one win. Home crowds dwindled to an average of 14,257—the lowest in the club's history—during the 1997 ARL season, but the Knights were about to launch the biggest party in the city's history. Newcastle finished second in the 12-team competition as rising stars Matthew Gidley, Owen Craigie and Darren Albert came to the fore. An ankle injury suffered in the pre-season sidelined Andrew Johns for the first half of the year, but former Brisbane reserve grade half Leo Dynevor was magnificent in his absence, combining superbly with Matthew Johns and assuming the goalkicking duties. Andrew Johns' performance in the first week of the finals pegged the Knights back from an 18-point deficit to defeat Parramatta 28-20, but he sustained a painful rib injury in the match, while Gidley suffered a broken leg. Johns sat out the following weekend's match—a 27-12 loss to minor premiers Manly that held little consequence, with both heavyweights advancing to the preliminary final stage. Newcastle led Norths 12-4 at halftime in the preliminary final at a muddy SFS, but the Bears fought back to level the scores. With his brother off the field, Matthew Johns kicked a dramatic 35-metre field goal in the dying minutes to edge the Knights in front, before teenage centre Craigie sealed a Grand Final berth with a runaway try on the fulltime siren to take the final score to 17-12.

Andrew Johns' playing status was in doubt throughout Grand Final week, but he eventually took the field and played a leading hand in the euphoric victory over Manly. Trailing 16-8 at halftime, the Knights clawed their way back to level when Robbie O'Davis scored his second try with five minutes remaining. After a Matthew Johns field goal attempt hit the upright, Andrew Johns went on a blindside foray from dummy-half and found snowy-haired flyer Albert on the inside to cross for the premiership-winning try with seven seconds on the clock. Scenes of pandemonium broke out from the SFS all the way back to Newcastle in the wake of the spellbinding triumph. Fullback O'Davis won the Clive Churchill Medal for his mesmerising display.

But the 1998 National Rugby League season turned sour for the club when O'Davis, backrower Wayne Richards and blockbusting winger Adam MacDougall (who had recently made his Origin debut for NSW) tested positive to performance enhancing drugs. The trio was banned for 22 weeks, while MacDougall's appeal (based on needing the prescribed medication to treat an ongoing condition) was denied. Newcastle rallied though—largely on the back on Dally M medallist Andrew Johns' inspirational efforts—to finish the season in second spot, behind minor premiers Brisbane on for-and-against. The Knights eventually ran out of steam under a mounting injury toll, surrendering a 15-point lead to go down to Sydney City in the second week of the finals before being eliminated 28-16 in an extra-time classic by Canterbury, despite earlier leading 16-0.

Coach Reilly stepped down and was replaced by veteran mentor Warren Ryan, who the club had originally courted to be its foundation coach more than a decade earlier. But the 1999 season did not live up to expectations. Skipper and primary enforcer Harragon retired mid-season due to a chronic knee injury, and the Knights finished seventh before promptly being despatched at the qualifying final stage. Andrew Johns' burgeoning status as the world's best player was aided by his second straight Dally M Player of the Year Award, while Matt Gidley debuted for Australia. The following season was dominated by rumoured infighting between the coach and star players, while the decision to not offer favourite son Matthew Johns a contract beyond 2000 angered the club's playing ranks and supporters alike. Nevertheless, the Knights finished the regular season third and advanced to a preliminary final date with the Roosters, but again coughed up a big advantage, leading 16-2 before succumbing 26-20. The abrasive Ryan was replaced by former captain Michael Hagan for 2001.

With captain Andrew Johns in typically irrepressible form, a new supporting cast provided the impetus for the Knights' second premiership triumph. Ben Kennedy became one of the NRL's most destructive forwards after joining from the Raiders in 2000, former utility Danny Buderus developed into the game's best hooker and Timana Tahu emerged as a top-shelf finisher. Newcastle placed third in the 2001 regular season and accounted for the Roosters and Sharks on the way to the

Grand Final, where the Knights ambushed runaway minor premiers Parramatta to lead 24-0 at halftime. Unsung backrower Bill Peden scored a first half double, while Kennedy was at his defence-scattering best. Johns pulled the strings in the 30-24 upset and was awarded the Clive Churchill Medal. He went on to spearhead Australia's Ashes series victory on the 2001 Kangaroo Tour, combining with clubmates Buderus, MacDougall and Kennedy.

The Knights' fortunes swung on NSW and Australian skipper Johns' health in subsequent seasons. Mounting a compelling premiership defence in 2002, a back injury suffered by Johns—awarded his record-breaking third Dally M Medal just days earlier—in the qualifying final loss to St. George Illawarra saw second-placed Newcastle bounced out 38-12 by eventual premiers the Sydney Roosters a week later, with the inexperienced John Morris thrust into the No.7. A bulging disc in Johns' neck ended the maestro halfback's season a month out from the 2003 finals, consigning the Knights to a qualifying final exit. A knee injury in just the third match of his comeback in 2004 ruled Johns out for the remainder of the year, while a lengthy casualty list that included Test players Tahu, Kennedy and Steve Simpson saw Newcastle miss the finals for the first time in eight years. The emergence of the versatile Kurt Gidley—younger brother of Matt—was an overwhelming positive during a trying few seasons. Gidley was routinely thrust into the hot-seat when Johns was injured, and eventually assumed the role of Newcastle's marquee player after the legend's eventual retirement. Buderus, meanwhile, took over the NSW captaincy from the injured Johns and skippered Australia in the intermittent absence of Darren Lockyer during 2004-05.

Tahu (Parramatta) and Kennedy (Manly) moved on at the end of 2004, while former Test fullback O'Davis retired. Compounding the high-profile departures was a cracked jaw sustained by Johns in the Knights' fifth game of 2005, sidelining their linchpin for several weeks as they lost their first 14 matches—the worst start to a season since Eastern Suburbs' winless 1966 campaign. The Gidley brothers also spent extended injury-enforced periods out of action. Although Newcastle slumped to the first wooden spoon in the club's history, it was the form team in the NRL late in the season, piecing together a six-match winning streak. Meanwhile, Johns incredibly finished just one point behind winner Johnathan Thurston in the Dally M Medal count despite making just 16 appearances in 2005. Johns' masterful performances in the Blues' series victory (under Buderus' captaincy) were also season highlights.

The Knights secured a top-four finish in 2006 and their average home crowds exceeded 20,000 for the first time in seven years. Newcastle defeated Manly in the first week of the finals, but with Buderus (suspended) and Simpson (injured) missing from the semi-final clash against Brisbane, the Knights were swamped 50-6 by the eventual champs. Matt Gidley joined Super League club St. Helens at the end of 2006, before Johns was forced into retirement by a recurrence of a neck injury just three rounds into the 2007 season, bringing down the curtain on the career of the Knights' greatest-ever player. Although his heir apparent, Jarrod Mullen, debuted for NSW that season, Newcastle only narrowly avoided the wooden spoon. New coach Brian Smith alienated several players and scores of supporters by overseeing the release of club favourites Clint Newton, Kirk Reynoldson and former Origin prop Josh Perry amongst a thorough playing roster cleanout. Johns' arrest for possession of an ecstasy tablet in London and subsequent revelations of years of drug and alcohol abuse and his silent battle with bipolar disorder also rocked the club.

Kurt Gidley made his Test and Origin debuts in 2007 as he gained recognition as one of the NRL's elite performers, and assumed the Knights' captaincy following Danny Buderus' departure to English club Leeds at the end of 2008—a season that saw Newcastle come within one win of a finals appearance. Brian Smith abruptly departed the club late in the 2009 season after announcing he would be joining the Roosters at the end of the year, but caretaker coach Rick Stone steered the club to a qualifying final appearance with three wins in his first four matches in charge. Stone retained the role in 2010 and did an admirable job with a modest roster at his disposal, despite a recreational drug scandal that saw key forwards Danny Wicks and Chris Houston arrested. Wicks was later was later charged with distribution, while Houston returned to the club in 2011 after he was found to have no case to answer. Stone navigated the embattled club to a respectable 11th-place finish in 2010 before again taking the Knights to the finals in 2011. Fijian winger Akuila Uate emerged as one of the game's best wingers, topping the NRL with an equal-club record 21 tries in 2010 before making his NSW and Australian debuts in 2011.

Billionaire mining magnate Nathan Tinkler purchased a controlling interest in the club during 2011 in one of the most important off-field developments in the club's history. Tinkler lured 'supercoach' Wayne Bennett to Newcastle for 2012, which in turn attracted St. George Illawarra's marquee fullback Darius Boyd, and Test prop Kade Snowden (who made his NRL debut for the Knights) from Cronulla, while veteran Knights greats Buderus and Tahu returned to the Hunter Valley. The developments saw average crowds hit a five-year high in 2011 as an air of expectation engulfed the city. With the Knights' identity so deeply entwined with its community, the prospect of a third premiership had the Newcastle region abuzz.

WARRIORS TURN THE CORNER

The Auckland Warriors' admission to the 1995 ARL premiership was the most significant development in the history of Rugby League in New Zealand, and represented bold new territory for the Australian game. Moves had been afoot since the late-1980s for a first grade team to be based across the Tasman, and Auckland's bid was accepted in 1992. Impressive crowds for three premiership matches staged at Carlaw Park—the spiritual home of the code in New Zealand—in 1992 and 1993 instilled confidence for the fledgling club's viability in a rugby union-mad country.

Ericsson Stadium—the home of the 1990 Commonwealth Games (as Mt. Smart Stadium)—was secured as the club's home ground, ahead of the dilapidated Carlaw Park. In a major coaching coup, former Parramatta premiership-winner and all-conquering Wigan mentor John Monie was signed as foundation coach, while Wigan captain Dean Bell—32 years of age and a veteran of 26 Tests for New Zealand—came on board as the Warriors' inaugural skipper. Star Great Britain and Wigan forwards Dennis Betts and Andy Platt also made the move to Auckland, while the 'Riversiders' connection was complete with the acquisition of Wigan's goalkicking genius and former All Black Frano Botica. Greg Alexander and Phil Blake headlined the Australian recruits, while Kiwi Test stars Sean Hoppe, Stephen Kearney and Gene Ngamu returned to New Zealand from Winfield Cup stints. The impressive squad was rounded out by established (Tea Ropati, Duane Mann) and emerging (Stacey Jones, Syd Eru, Joe Vagana) Kiwi talent.

High debut season expectations were fuelled by Auckland's superb display in its first match, an epic 25-22 loss to perennial powerhouse Brisbane at a sold out Ericsson Stadium in the opening round of 1995. But the Warriors won just one of their first five games—a 46-12 thrashing of Western Suburbs—and had those competition points stripped for fielding an illegal replacement, a bungle that proved costly *(see Points Docked)*. After winning 11 of their next 13 matches, a late-season slump saw the Warriors narrowly miss the finals. Hoppe top-scored for the Warriors with 19 tries, while 19-year-old halfback Jones confirmed his status as a future superstar. Earlier in the year, the club followed the lead of the NZRL and signed with the Super League movement. Alexander replaced the retired Bell as captain in 1996, but another patchy regular season and a four-game losing streak to end the year consigned the club to an 11th-place finish.

Auckland welcomed Kiwi skipper Matthew Ridge from Manly for the 1997 Super League season, but Monie stood down mid-season amid a terrible run of form and was replaced by New Zealand and Warriors reserve grade coach Frank Endacott. The Warriors finished seventh of 10 teams, with the club's gallant 22-16 loss to the Broncos in the World Club Challenge semi-final a rare highlight. Worse was to follow as the Warriors descended into a downward spiral on and off the field.

The Warriors won just nine games in the 1998 NRL competition, while the 36 clubs that made up the Auckland Rugby League voted to sell their 100 per cent stake in the club. A consortium fronted by former New Zealand, Wigan and Manly coach Graham Lowe joined forces with the wealthy Tainui Tribe to purchase the club. Lowe replaced Endacott with Mark Graham—a legendary Kiwi player with an association with Lowe that stretched back more than two decades—as coach, but prominent Kiwi internationals Stephen Kearney, Kevin Iro and Quentin Pongia left the club.

The Warriors were controversially granted a seven-year license by the NRL, guaranteeing the beleaguered club's survival in a rationalised competition. But crowds dwindled and results failed to improve during Graham's two-season tenure. Ridge's suspension- and injury-ravaged stint in Auckland finished at the end of 1999, while the Warriors' ordinary performances and tenuous financial situation prevented the club from landing high-profile talent, instead restricted to recruiting journeymen and fringe first graders—an arduous hit and miss process. Hookers Jason Death and Robert Mears were two of the Warriors' best throughout the disastrous 1999 and 2000 seasons, but speedsters Lee Oudenryn and Scott Pethybridge and former-NSW halfback John Simon produced their best form only in brief patches.

The farcical off-field conditions came to a head during 2000 when the scope of the club's financial position threatened player payments, and the NZRL entered into a partnership with millionaire businessman Eric Watson to purchase the Warriors, effectively establishing a new club. Rebranded as the New Zealand Warriors in 2001 and with Watson's brother Mick providing the rebuilding club with a savvy chief executive, the transformation was almost instantaneous. Parramatta lower grade coach Daniel Anderson replaced Mark Graham and steered the club to its maiden finals series. Australian recruits Ivan Cleary, Kevin Campion (who was installed as co-captain with Jones) and Mark Tookey proved valuable purchases, while dazzling Kiwi juniors Clinton Toopi, Ali Lauiti'iti, Francis Meli and Henry Fa'afili set the NRL alight with their explosive, intuitive brilliance. Although the eighth-placed Warriors were trounced 56-12 in their finals debut by minor premiers Parramatta, the 2001 season represented a distinct turning point in every aspect of the club.

Talismanic No.7 Stacey Jones—so often the Warriors' only saviour during the club's tumultuous infancy—remained at the heart of the team's on-field success, and assumed the captaincy in 2002 when injury ended new skipper Monty Betham's season after just two games. Jones' ever-improving supporting cast grew with the emergence of teenage five-eighth Lance Hohaia and livewire utility Motu Tony, and the astute recruitment of youthful Australian talent such as Eels half PJ Marsh and Cairns utility-back Brent Webb. Marsh was moved to hooker and broke into the Queensland side as a No.9 (the Warriors' second Origin representative after Campion), while the brilliant Webb became a long-serving Kiwi Test fullback after fulfilling residential requirements. The Warriors' instinctive brand of attacking football won plenty of admirers from the Australian media and public—the majority of who had vehemently protested the club's presence in the NRL a few short seasons earlier—and attracted a groundswell of support in their homeland.

New Zealand finished 2002 as minor premiers in the wake of the Bulldogs' salary cap scandal and advanced to the Grand Final by defeating Canberra 36-20 in the qualifying final, and edging out the Sharks 16-10 in a gripping preliminary final, with the club offering free tickets to the match to anyone holding a New Zealand passport. An entire nation rode on the shoulders of diminutive skipper Stacey Jones as he put the Warriors 8-6 ahead of the Sydney Roosters with a blistering individual try early in the second half of the Grand Final. But the in-form Roosters overwhelmed the Warriors 30-8 with a final-quarter surge. Jones was awarded the Golden Boot at the end of the year.

Although they were less consistent in 2003, the Warriors peaked at the right time of the year and qualified for the finals in sixth spot. New Zealand blitzed the third-placed Bulldogs 48-22 in a spellbinding qualifying final performance, with Francis Meli scoring a finals record five tries, and Toopi and Webb running riot. Jones lifted the Warriors to a 17-16 semi-final victory over the Raiders with a late field goal, before their run was halted by Penrith in a gallant 28-20 preliminary final defeat.

The Warriors' euphoric rise to contender status was brought undone by a disastrous 2004 season. Coach Anderson stood down and star backrower Lauiti'iti walked out on the club early in the year, while the Warriors finished second-last with a dismal six wins under former New Zealand Test centre Tony Kemp. In a double-coup, the Warriors lured Bulldogs skipper and Kangaroo veteran prop Steve Price and Kiwi legend Ruben Wiki to Auckland in 2005 (Wiki signed as a foundation Warrior a decade earlier, but reneged on the deal to remain in Canberra). Despite a vast improvement on their 2004 campaign, the Warriors were mired in inconsistency and bade farewell to Super League-bound Stacey Jones with an 11th-place finish. Kemp was replaced by assistant Cleary—who had won a Premier League title with the Roosters after retiring as a player—for 2006.

Cleary began his rookie season as an NRL coach behind the eight-ball when the club admitted to salary cap breaches and started 2006 on minus four competition points, ultimately costing the Warriors a spot in the finals (see Points Docked). Low-profile signings such as Cowboys backrower Michael Luck provided excellent value, while a batch of Kiwi juniors that would form the basis of the club's next golden era—blockbusting winger Manu Vatuvei, centre/backrower Simon Mannering, dynamic three-quarter Jerome Ropati and intimidating prop Sam Rapira—flourished under the leadership of Price and Wiki. Supporters bemoaned Brent Webb's departure to Leeds at the end of 2006, but ex-Parramatta fullback Wade McKinnon proved equally devastating in 2007, while stalwart backrower Logan Swann returned to the club after three seasons in England. The Warriors secured a top-four berth in 2007 after winning nine and drawing one of their last 12 regular season games, but were bounced out of the finals courtesy of consecutive losses to Parramatta and North Queensland.

A similar late-season run propelled the Warriors into the finals in eighth spot in 2008. Boasting superb new recruits in ex-Broncos Test centre Brent Tate and unheralded hooker Ian Henderson, New Zealand became the first eighth-placed team to topple the minor premiers under the McIntyre Finals System. The Warriors secured a heart-stopping 18-15 triumph with a Michael Witt try in the dying minutes (see Finals Magic) and advanced to the preliminary final with a convincing 30-13 defeat of the Roosters. Manly was too good in the preliminary final, however, disposing of the Warriors 32-6 in Wiki's swansong appearance. A luminous highlight of the 2008 season was the blossoming of Manu Vatuvei into arguably the game's premier winger. Derided as a liability earlier in his career—particularly after an error-riddled performance against the Eels in 2007—Vatuvei scored 16 tries in 17 games in 2008 and was named as one of David Middleton's Five Players of the Year in his Official Rugby League Annual.

Stacey Jones made a shock NRL return with the Warriors in 2009 and they were installed as one of the premiership favourites. But the tragic drowning of boom backrower/centre Sonny Fai during the pre-season shattered the club. In a luckless year, a knee injury sidelined Tate after just three games, Price missed 10 matches with various injuries, and prized wing recruit Denan Kemp and utility Nathan Fien were released mid-season due to indifferent form as the broken hearted Warriors crumbled to a 14th-place finish. Jones showed glimpses of his match-winning best and extended his club record to 261 appearances, but the season was more significant for the rise of youngsters Kevin Locke, Ben Matulino, Lewis Brown, Russell Packer and Aaron Heremaia—all of whom would be New Zealand Test representatives by the end of 2011.

Mannering was controversially promoted to the captaincy at Price's expense in 2010, although the veteran prop failed to take the field due to a foot injury and was forced into retirement. The arrival of unheralded James Maloney from the Storm finally provided the Warriors with a dominant figure in the halves for the first time since Jones' heyday. Equalling coach Cleary's club record with 28 points in a 48-16 drubbing of the Broncos at Suncorp Stadium early in 2010, Maloney spearheaded New Zealand's drive to the finals. Meanwhile, Vatuvei was at his destructive best, scoring 20 tries in just 19 games to be named the club's player of the year. But after qualifying in fifth, a 28-16 defeat to the fourth-placed Titans ended the Warriors' compelling premiership bid after other results conspired against them under the fickle rules of the McIntyre System.

The Warriors' Under-20s side claimed an emphatic Toyota Cup premiership in 2010, and the club reaped the benefits in the 2011 NRL season. The captain of the side, backrower Elijah Taylor, handled the step up to first grade with ease and was amongst the Warriors' most consistent forwards before making his Test debut at the end of the year. Halfback Shaun Johnson exploded onto the NRL scene mid-season and became an immediate superstar. With sleight of hand and footwork reminiscent of compatriot Benji Marshall, Johnson's blistering speed garnered several long-range tries in 2011, while his scintillating four-pointer against the Broncos was the undisputed individual try of the season. Maloney produced an even better follow-up season and formed an irresistible halves combination with Johnson. Kevin Locke cemented the club's fullback spot and drew comparisons with Billy Slater for his blinding speed, brilliant ball skills and bravery. An off-season recruitment drive netted dynamic—if enigmatic—Eels duo Feleti Mateo and Krisnan Inu, while former Kangaroos utility Shaun Berrigan's versatility proved valuable before injury ruled him out of the Warriors' finals campaign. Former North Queensland backrower Jacob Lillyman (who joined the Warriors in 2009) developed into one of the NRL's best and most underrated props, winning a recall to the Queensland Origin side.

Finishing the regular season in sixth spot, the McIntyre System worked in the Warriors' favour in 2011 when they received a second life despite bumbling their way to a 40-10 qualifying final loss to the Broncos. New Zealand overcame a 12-point halftime deficit against Wests Tigers a week later, fighting back to snatch a heart-stopping 22-20 victory with a freakish try to Inu in the dying minutes. With New Zealand's massive expat population enthusiastically mobilised, the Warriors travelled to Melbourne and upset the Storm in the preliminary final. The 20-12 victory was arguably the finest in the club's 17-season history. A supreme defensive effort kept the home side at bay in a tense second half, before Johnson's now-famous, mesmerising cross-field run and offload set up the winning try for centre Lewis Brown. The Warriors' enchanting run to the Grand Final temporarily knocked the Rugby Union World Cup—being staged concurrently in New Zealand—off the back pages across the Tasman. A glut of errors, bad luck and some questionable calls thwarted the Warriors in the decider against Manly. Down 18-2 with a quarter of the match remaining, Johnson inspired a comeback by laying on tries for Vatuvei and Taylor with trademark ball-playing wizardry. But Maloney's sideline conversion attempts veered agonisingly wide and a maiden premiership slipped out of reach, although the Warriors were praised for their gallant performance in the 24-10 defeat.

The club was represented in all three matches on Grand Final day—the Under-20s sealed back-to-back Toyota Cup titles with a golden point triumph over the Cowboys, while feeder team the Auckland Vulcans suffered a last-minute loss to Canterbury in the NSW Cup Grand Final. The Warriors farewelled veteran Lance Hohaia— a wonderful performer at fullback, hooker or in the halves in 185 games for the club—along with Heremaia and Berrigan, but the flock of outstanding youngsters progressing through the ranks puts the club in an enviable position for the future. Cleary was poached by Penrith for 2012, with former Leeds and New Zealand Test coach Brian McLennan coming on board as coach. From the club's promising beginnings, to its calamitous formative years and subsequent revival in the new millennium, the Warriors are now better placed than ever to take the NRL trophy out of Australia for the first time.

COWBOYS RIDE HIGH
AFTER LONG DROUGHT

The NSWRL granted a license to a consortium of eight Townsville businessmen in 1993 for inclusion in the expanded 20-team premiership two year later, providing the Rugby League heartland of North Queensland with its own team in an elite, national competition. The region had produced esteemed Australian representatives Kel O'Shea, Bob Banks, Kerry Boustead, Dale Shearer and Greg Dowling. Despite healthy crowd support and a succession of high-profile playing and coaching recruits, the North Queensland Cowboys struggled for on-field success for almost a decade. But the emergence of some outstanding junior talent and a more astute recruitment strategy transformed the club into a genuine title contender in the mid-2000s.

The Cowboys enlisted a local in Grant Bell as the club's foundation coach, while Innisfail-bred former Test winger Boustead was installed as chief executive. The club lured several North Queensland products back to their home region, including Test and State of Origin veteran prop Martin Bella (Mackay) and former Norths, Easts and Cronulla halfback Laurie Spina (Ingham). Queensland Origin representative Adrian Vowles, former Illawarra skipper Dean Schifilliti, 1990 Dally M Rookie of the Year Jason Martin, 1991-92 Dally M Lock of the Year Ian Russell and Welsh wizard Jonathan Davies added significant experience and class to the fledgling franchise.

But North Queensland won just two matches in 1995—against Illawarra and Wests—and was subjected to 60-point floggings at the hands of Norths and the Bulldogs en route to a debut-season wooden spoon. The club struggled for stability, using six different captains during the season, while Bella and creative half Noel Solomon were sacked for alleged breaches of discipline. Coach Bell was replaced by former New Zealand and Manly mentor Graham Lowe for 1996. The Cowboys improved moderately in their sophomore season to finish 17th, winning six games and claiming the scalps of finalists St. George and Cronulla.

Aligning with the Super League movement, the Cowboys attracted three-time premiership-winning Canberra coach Tim Sheens to the club for the rebel competition's 1997 season. The revered mentor took high-profile Raiders pair, Kangaroo hooker Steve Walters and New Zealand Test prop John Lomax, with him, while former Australian Test forward Ian Roberts and Queensland Origin backrower Owen Cunningham joined from Manly. But North Queensland finished last in the 10-team Super League premiership. The Cowboys also fared poorly in the inaugural 1998 NRL season, placing 16th of 20 teams despite sharing the competition lead after five wins in the opening six rounds and staging the biggest comeback in premiership history (defeating Penrith 36-28 after trailing 26-0 at halftime) later in the season.

Cronulla linchpin Paul Green and ex-St. George Grand Final No.7 Noel Goldthorpe were lured to the club in 1999 to provide experience and class in the halves. While Green became the Cowboys' first Origin representative when he debuted for Queensland in 1999, his tenure at the club was less than favourable; Sheens preferred Goldthorpe and Mount Isa teenager Scott Prince in the key positions and Green was controversially sacked by the Cowboys in 2000 for negotiating with other clubs while still under contract. Despite guiding the club to a second-last finish with just four wins in 1999, Sheens signed a five-year extension to remain in Townsville.

Foundation player and Proserpine junior Paul Bowman debuted in the centres for Queensland in 2000, while Green and new recruit Julian O'Neill also turned out for the Maroons. Another high-profile acquisition, brilliant fullback Tim Brasher, became the Cowboys' first New South Wales representative in the same series. Although North Queensland racked up a club record seven wins—including a shock 50-4 thrashing of 1999 Grand Finalists St. George Illawarrra—the wooden spoon made its way to Townsville for the third time in six seasons. In another blow for the Cowboys, Prince left the club to link with the powerful Brisbane Broncos.

Prop John Buttigieg, hooker John Doyle and halfback Nathan Fien debuted for Queensland alongside clubmate Bowman in the Maroons' euphoric 2001 series success, but Cowboys coach Tim Sheens announced his resignation mid-season after another dismal start to the year. He was replaced by assistant coach Murray Hurst for the remainder of the season, and the club narrowly staved off a fourth wooden spoon with a last-round upset of finals-bound New Zealand, finishing above Penrith on points differential.

In spite of a lack of on-field success, the Cowboys never lacked local support. Healthy crowd averages—including thousands of fans travelling from country centres several hours from Townsville—were the lifeblood of the club. And the diehards were given reason for optimism following Hurst's sacking early in 2002 after conceding 130 points in the opening three rounds of the season. Former Illawarra, Hunter and Sydney Roosters coach Graham Murray was installed as the Cowboys' new boss and lifted his promising charges to 11th on the ladder with eight wins. Representative three-quarter Matt Sing set a club record with 16 tries in his first season for the Cowboys, second-year fullback Matt Bowen gave a taste of the skills that would light up the NRL over the next decade with 12 tries, and Innisfail winger Ty Williams crossed for 13 tries in his rookie season.

Sing made a comeback to the Queensland side in 2003 after a three-year absence, scoring an Origin record-equalling three tries in game three, with clubmates Bowen and goalkicking centre Josh Hannay making their state debuts in the same match. Sing subsequently became the Cowboys' first Australian representative, scoring two tries in the 48-6 thrashing of New Zealand in his first Test appearance since 1999. The winger extended his North Queensland season tryscoring record to 21 tries in 2003, while the astute acquisition of representative forwards Kevin Campion and Paul Rauhihi was critical to the club's rapid improvement. Posting 10 wins to again finish 11th, the Cowboys were left to rue a golden point loss to Penrith and a last-minute defeat to Parramatta that would have had the long-suffering club knocking on the door of a finals berth. Murray, ably assisted by former Canterbury hooker and renowned trainer Billy Johnstone, had awakened a slumbering giant.

The Cowboys' faithful did not have to wait long to see their team partake in the September action. After a dismal start to 2004 netted just one win in their opening six games, the Cowboys won six of their last eight to qualify for the finals for the first time in seventh place. The club was boosted by the off-season recruitment of Queensland Origin lock Travis Norton, who assumed the Cowboys' captaincy during 2004, and aggressive backrower Luke O'Donnell. North Queensland was expected to make a swift exit, but the finals newcomers stunned the second-placed Bulldogs 30-22 in the qualifying final. Matt Sing crossed for a memorable hat-trick after spending much of the season sidelined with injury. The Cowboys were drawn to play 'big brother' Brisbane in Sydney a week later, before the Broncos graciously suggested relocating the semi to Townsville. A crowd of 24,989 created an electrifying atmosphere as the Cowboys completed a gripping 10-0 shutout of the star-studded Broncos, a match that marked the end of Brisbane captain and Townsville product Gorden Tallis' decorated career. North Queensland's stirring charge was arrested 19-16 by the Sydney Roosters in a spine-tingling preliminary final. The underdogs matched the heavyweight Roosters every step of the way; the scores were locked at 16-all with less than 10 minutes remaining, before a field goal and penalty got the Roosters home. The Cowboys out-scored the Roosters three tries to two and a Grand Final appearance was tantalisingly within reach, but coach Murray was proud and satisfied in the knowledge that the club had arrived as an NRL force. Matt Bowen became the first Cowboys junior to represent Australia when he made his debut against France on the Tri-Nations tour at the end of 2004.

Bulldogs half Johnathan Thurston and fiery Broncos forward Carl Webb arrived in Townsville in 2005 to complete the Cowboys' line-up, while Townsville junior Aaron Payne established himself as one of the NRL's finest hookers. A club record was established in the first two Origin encounters of 2005 when six North Queensland players lined up for the Maroons; Thurston and Ty Williams made their debuts, and were accompanied by Bowman, Sing, Bowen and Webb. The Cowboys won 14 of their 24 regular season games to qualify for the finals in fifth. A 50-6 qualifying final thrashing at the hands of Wests Tigers left the Cowboys reeling, but they rallied to eliminate Melbourne 24-16 a week later and swept minor premiers Parramatta aside 29-0 in an astonishing preliminary final upset. Bowen scored the opening try of the Grand Final against the Tigers, but the Cowboys trailed 12-0 at halftime and eventually succumbed 30-16. Complementing a historic season of achievement for the club, Thurston was named Dally M Player of the Year, Bowen scored a club record-equalling 21 tries to top the NRL's tryscoring table, and O'Donnell was selected to make his Test debut, playing in all five matches of Australia's Tri-Nations campaign.

Picking up from where they left off, the Cowboys led the NRL by four competition points after winning their first six matches in 2006. But the club lost eight of its next nine games and eventually finished two points shy of a finals berth in ninth spot. Thurston's Test debut against New Zealand, O'Donnell breaking into the NSW side (with Murray as coach), and the participation of six Cowboys—Thurston, Bowen, Webb, Hannay, and young forwards Matthew Scott and Jacob Lillyman—in Queensland's first series victory since 2001, provided rare highlights in a season of lost opportunity.

North Queensland rebounded in 2007 to secure its maiden top-four berth with a club-best 15 regular season victories. The Cowboys' club record winning streak of seven matches extended into Dairy Farmers Stadium finals victories over the Bulldogs (20-18) and Warriors (49-12), catapulting the Thurston-led side into a preliminary final showdown with Manly. The 28-6 loss to the Sea Eagles was a disappointing end to a season of unprecedented consistency for the Cowboys, but their efforts in 2007 bode well for the future. Thurston won his second Dally M Medal, while Bowen polled fourth on the back of a dazzling season that garnered a North Queensland record 22 tries to head the NRL's try-scorers for the second time.

But the club languished near the foot of the ladder for the next three seasons. Graham Murray's six-year reign ended just two months into the 2008 season, departing after the Cowboys mustered only three wins in the opening 10 rounds. Ian Millward stepped in as caretaker-coach for the remainder of the year, but North Queensland slumped to a club record 13 consecutive defeats and finished second-last. Knee surgery restricted Bowen to just six games, while Thurston also battled injury problems, curtailing the impact of North Queensland's two best weapons. Highly regarded Canberra coach Neil Henry—Murray's former assistant in Townsville—returned to the Cowboys in 2009, but the club struggled during the first two seasons under the new regime. Despite the arrival of Test centre Willie Tonga, who topped the Cowboys' tryscoring charts in 2009 and 2010, the club returned 12th- and 15th-place finishes respectively. Matthew Scott's Test debut in 2010 was a rare bright spot in a bleak period for the club.

With Henry's head on the block, the Cowboys staged an impressive revival in 2011. An aggressive recruitment campaign brought veteran Test centre Brent Tate, former Queensland Origin lock Dallas Johnson, destructive rookie backrower Tariq Sims and flamboyant Kiwi winger Kalifa Faifai Loa to Townsville. Combined with the rejuvenated old firm of Thurston and Bowen, and Scott's emergence as the NRL's dominant prop, the acquisitions kept North Queensland in the top-four for most of the season, before a late-season slump dropped the club to seventh place. After grinding out an 8-0 halftime lead, the Cowboys were blitzed 42-8 by eventual premiers Manly in the qualifying final. But a return to the finals was a significant advancement for the club. Thurston was a runaway leader in the Dally M Medal count until an injury layoff saw the brilliant halfback finish equal-fourth, while Bowen was just two points back in equal-sixth. The balance within the Cowboys' squad, the potential of the their youth (North Queensland's Under-20s squad lost the 2011 Toyota Cup Grand Final to the Warriors in golden point), and the class of Bowen and co-captains Thurston and Scott holds the NRL's northern-most club in good stead for the future, minimising the chances of a return to the cellar-dwelling days of the 1990s and early-2000s.

STORM'S IMMEDIATE SUCCESS

Rugby League's powerbrokers began testing the waters in Melbourne—the Australian Rules-mad capital of Victoria—with the staging of representative and first grade fixtures in the first half of the 1990s. The hastily assembled Melbourne Storm, formed in the chaotic wake of the Super League war and subsequent establishment of the National Rugby League in 1998, was tipped to struggle initially. But the club qualified for the finals in its debut season, before seizing a shock premiership triumph in just its second year. Melbourne became the NRL's preeminent superpower within a decade—despite a salary cap scandal that threatened to rip the heart out of the club—and produced some of the modern era's greatest players under the passionate and meticulous coaching of Craig Bellamy.

A State of Origin match in 1990, a Trans-Tasman Test in 1991 and an Ashes Test in 1992 were staged in Melbourne, while St. George and Western Suburbs clashed in the city's first premiership match in 1993. Balmain took two of its 1994 home games to Melbourne's Princes Park, but the 87,161-strong crowd that attended the second Origin clash that season at the Melbourne Cricket Ground—a then-record for a Rugby League match in Australia—best illustrated the potential for a first grade side in the AFL heartland. The MCG hosted another Origin match in 1995, drawing a crowd of 52,994, while the warring ARL and Super League factions both declared intentions to set up a franchise in Melbourne during the game's split. Super League chief executive John Ribot was behind the successful establishment of the Melbourne Storm, while Brisbane's former Test centre Chris Johns was the other vital cog of the backroom brains trust as the club's inaugural CEO.

Melbourne shrewdly picked the carcasses of the defunct Hunter Mariners and Perth Reds Super League clubs to form the basis of its 1998 squad. Super League internationals Robbie Ross (the club's first major signing), Brett Kimmorley and Scott Hill, plus Richard Swain, Paul Marquet and John Carlaw joined after the Newcastle-based Mariners folded; meanwhile, Super League Australia representative forwards Rodney Howe and Robbie Kearns, along with Perth teammates Matt Geyer, Wayne Evans and Paul Bell, headed east after the Reds' demise.

All time great prop Glenn Lazarus signed on as foundation captain and was joined in the pack by intimidating New Zealand Test lock Tawera Nikau, while Chris Anderson departed Canterbury to coach the fledgling club. Melbourne exceeded even the most optimistic expectations with a stunning debut season; leading the competition after 15 rounds, the Storm qualified for the finals in third spot. A first-up finals loss to Sydney City was followed by a sudden-death victory over Canberra, before the Storm exited at the hands of eventual premiers Brisbane. But the excellent results, superb individual performances and reasonable home crowds at Olympic Park set the club on a path to glory. Lazarus, Kearns and Howe represented New South Wales and Australia, although Howe received a 22-week ban after testing positive to anabolic steroids and did not return until midway through 1999. Papua New Guinean winger Marcus Bai—an acquisition from the Gold Coast Chargers—scored 14 tries and was named Dally M Winger of the Year, while Nikau picked up the Lock of the Year gong. Halfback Kimmorley established himself as one of the NRL's best No.7s, forming a brilliant halves combination with Scott Hill.

The Storm's engine-room was bolstered by Auckland's Test forward Stephen Kearney and fellow Kiwi Matt Rua in 1999, while Matt Geyer and Robbie Ross debuted at Origin level for the Blues. Melbourne finished the regular season in third spot again, but was overrun 34-10 by sixth-placed St. George Illawarra in the first week of the finals. Scaling the September tightrope, the Storm staged come-from-behind sudden-death victories over Canterbury (24-22) and Parramatta

(18-16) to qualify for an unlikely Grand Final rematch with the Dragons—themselves a first-year joint venture. Saints, warm favourites after their convincing win three weeks earlier, charged to a 14-0 halftime lead. But a stirring revival in the second stanza reached an extraordinary climax, with Melbourne winger Craig Smith being awarded a penalty try in the dying minutes after being knocked unconscious by Dragons winger Jamie Ainscough as he was about to ground the ball. The resultant conversion from in front of the posts put the Storm in front for the first time 20-18 and delivered a second-year premiership to Melbourne—the earliest success achieved by a club since Souths won the inaugural 1908 competition. Clive Churchill medallist Kimmorley made his Test debut during Australia's subsequent Tri-Nations campaign, and was joined by clubmates Ross and Howe, while Anderson had taken the reins as national coach.

Melbourne's premiership defence opened with four losses, but its first win of 2000 was a memorable one—the Storm annihilated the Dragons 70-10 at the MCG, a particularly sweet result given outspoken Saints five-eighth Anthony Mundine's comments that the premiers were 'nothing but pretenders.' The Storm recovered to qualify for the finals in sixth, but exited the finals after a 30-16 loss to Newcastle in the qualifying final. Kimmorley and Hill debuted for the Blues alongside Kearns and Howe, while Kimmorley, Hill and Kearns celebrated in Australia's World Cup Final victory over New Zealand in England at the end of the season. But the announcement that Kimmorley would be joining the Northern Eagles in 2001 was a bitter blow for Melbourne.

Anderson departed midway through 2001 and was replaced by former Roosters and Queensland Origin coach Mark Murray, but the Storm's failure to make the finals in 2001 and '02 resulted in Murray making way for long-time Broncos assistant Craig Bellamy. With Matt Orford calling the shots at halfback, a solid base of experience remaining from the club's title-winning squad, astute purchasing in the form of Kiwi Test forward David Kidwell, and feeder side Brisbane Norths grooming outstanding young talent such as Cameron Smith, Billy Slater and Steven Bell, Melbourne finished fifth in 2003. The Storm was eliminated in the second week of the finals by the Bulldogs. Melbourne secured sixth-place finishes in 2004 and 2005, and upset heavyweights Brisbane in the qualifying final in each season, before suffering second-week exits at the hands of the Bulldogs and North Queensland respectively. Wily hooker Smith debuted for Queensland in 2003, while exhilarating fullback Slater joined him in the Maroons side the following season. Matt King's rapid rise to first grade stardom in 2004 garnered NSW and Australian debuts for the tall three-quarter in 2005.

Orford's departure to Manly at the end of 2005 was met with similar dismay to that of Kimmorley's five years earlier, but handy utility Cooper Cronk stepped into the breach in 2006 and developed into one of the modern era's finest halfbacks. Gifted teenage flyer Greg Inglis debuted in the second half of 2005, before exploding into the consciousness of every Rugby League supporter with his extraordinary talents in 2006. Inglis debuted for Queensland in 2006, as did clubmates Steve Bell, an elusive and potent tryscoring centre, and workhorse lock Dallas Johnson. Ex-Penrith winger Steve Turner cemented a first grade spot and scored 18 tries in 2006 to tie with Inglis as the club's top try-scorer. Rangy backrower Ryan Hoffman announced himself as a future representative player with an outstanding season, while mobile prop Antonio

Kaufusi, Country Origin front-rower Brett White, and Kiwis Jeremy Smith and Adam Blair further reinforced Melbourne's formidable pack.

The Storm secured an emphatic maiden minor premiership, losing just four regular season games to finish eight points clear of the field. Bellamy's clinical and ultra-consistent side pieced together a club record 11-match winning streak, which was broken by the Warriors in their only loss at Olympic Park in 2006. Advancing to the Grand Final with finals wins over the Eels (12-6) and Dragons (24-10), Melbourne started favourites against Brisbane in the decider. But the squad's Grand Final inexperience told on the night (Matt Geyer was the only Melbourne player to have appeared in a decider) as the Darren Lockyer-led Broncos ground out a 15-8 victory over the Storm.

It was a heartbreaking end to a season a of high achievement for Melbourne, and it was particular poignant for departing veteran Scott Hill, who missed the 1999 Grand Final triumph through injury. Hill laid on both of Melbourne's tries in the Grand Final, his 200th first grade appearance, before linking with Super League club Harlequins. Further individual honours did little to ease the pain of defeat, but Test debuts for Cameron Smith, Inglis, Kaufusi (Australia) and Blair (New Zealand), and Smith's Dally M Player of the Year Award victory (plus the naming of Cronk as Halfback of the Year and Bellamy as Coach of the Year) was nevertheless well-received recognition for a phenomenal season.

Melbourne wrapped up the minor premiership again in 2007—this time incurring only three losses—before decimating Brisbane 40-0 in the qualifying final, overwhelming Parramatta 26-10 in the preliminary final, and claiming its second Grand Final success with a convincing 34-8 defeat of Manly. Bellamy had been criticised for moving the free-running Inglis to five-eighth following Hill's departure, but received the ultimate justification courtesy of Inglis' two-try, Churchill Medal-winning performance in the decider. Another Queensland star was blooded by the Storm in 2007; powerful 17-year-old three-quarter Israel Folau broke the club's season tryscoring record with 21 touchdowns on the way to a debut-season premiership. He became Australia's youngest-ever Test player at the end of the season, with clubmates Johnson, Hoffman and Cronk also making their Kangaroo debuts in the 58-0 demolition of New Zealand in Wellington. Cameron Smith captained the side in the absence of Lockyer, while Inglis and Michael Crocker also featured for Australia. Storm forwards Jeff Lima and Jeremy Smith made their Test debuts for the Kiwis in the heavy defeat. Fiery backrower Crocker, who joined Melbourne in 2006 but missed the Grand Final loss to Brisbane with injury, produced the crucial play of the 2007 decider when he forced Sea Eagles fullback and strike weapon Brett Stewart from the field with a punishing tackle.

The J.J. Giltinan Shield headed to Melbourne for the third straight season after the Storm topped the table on for-and-against from Manly and Cronulla in 2008. But a shock qualifying final loss to the Warriors (the first time the minor premiers had lost to the eighth-placed team under the McIntyre system) and Cameron Smith's suspension in the drama-charged semi-final victory over Brisbane ultimately cruelled the Storm's bid for back-to-back premierships. After cruising to a 29-0 preliminary final victory over the Sharks, Melbourne was caned by a Grand Final record 40-0 scoreline at the hands of the Sea Eagles. Billy Slater gained a belated Australian debut in the Centenary Test against New Zealand, and became established as the game's premier fullback. A suspension robbed him of the Dally M Player of the Year Award (won by Manly captain Orford), but he won the 2008 Golden Boot and was named the inaugural Rugby League International Federation Player of the Year. Wingers Steve Turner and Anthony Quinn joined 2007 debutants Brett White and Ryan Hoffman in the NSW side, Folau was an automatic selection to make his Queensland debut, while explosive forward Sika Manu earned his Test stripes for New Zealand. Manu and Jeremy Smith celebrated in the Kiwis' World Cup Final boilover against an Australian side containing Cameron Smith, Slater, Inglis and Folau.

Folau joined the Broncos in 2009 and Crocker linked with South Sydney, but Brett Finch's impromptu arrival from Parramatta early in the season allowed Inglis to revert to his more natural role in the centres. Melbourne's 2009 model appeared to come back to the field—finishing fourth and losing nine regular season games—but the squad's big-match experience came to the fore during the finals series. Slater scored four tries as the Storm despatched Manly 40-12 in the qualifying final, before an Inglis hat-trick provided the impetus for a 40-10 preliminary final thrashing of the Broncos. Melbourne led Jarryd Hayne's Parramatta juggernaut from go to whoa in a tense and hard-fought Grand Final, eventually closing the decider out 23-16. The accolades continued to flow for Slater as he collected the Churchill Medal, while Inglis was awarded the Golden Boot.

With their status as one of the great club combinations of all time assured after four consecutive Grand Final appearances and two premierships, the Storm's empire fell about them when the 2010 season was just six rounds old. Revelations of systematic salary cap breaches dating back to 2006, totalling $3.78 million of payments made to players outside the cap, rocked the Rugby League fraternity. Arguably the biggest scandal in the sport's history attracted undoubtedly the greatest punishment ever meted out by the game's authorities—the NRL stripped Melbourne of its 2007 and 2009 premierships, and its 2006-08 minor premierships. The club was slapped with a $500,000 fine and ordered to repay all prize-money. Just as devastatingly, the Storm was consigned to the wooden spoon as the NRL decreed no competition points would be awarded for matches the club won in 2010 (and the eight points already earned were also stripped). Former CEO Brian Waldron, who left the club at the start of the year to join fledgling Super 15 Rugby Union club the Melbourne Rebels, was identified as the main culprit. Melbourne's players and coaching staff were absolved from any blame.

The club's character shone through during the inconceivably tumultuous period. Melbourne finished the season with 14 wins—which would have been enough to earn fifth spot had the team been playing for competition points—and remained one of the NRL's most formidable sides. The Storm moved their home base from Olympic Park to the brand new AAMI Park during 2010—a rare positive in a soul-destroying year. The inevitable purging of players to fit under the salary cap for 2011 saw superstar centre Inglis and front-rowers Brett White and Aiden Tolman join rival NRL clubs, while Brett Finch, Ryan Hoffman and Jeff Lima linked with English heavyweights Wigan. Although Inglis' departure was a particularly bitter blow, the club thankfully retained the other members of the so-called 'Big Four'—Slater, Smith and Cronk (who finally made his Queensland Origin debut in 2010).

In what surely ranks as one of the most extraordinary achievements in premiership history, Bellamy's revamped squad lost just five regular season games to take out the 2011 minor premiership. With a batch of youngsters and unfashionable recruits stepping into the breach of the departed stars, Melbourne maintained its status as an NRL powerhouse. Slater made up for the disappointment of 2008 by taking out the Dally M Player of the Year Award (with Cronk finishing third and Smith equal-ninth), before collecting his second Golden Boot and RLIF Player of the Year gongs. After accounting for Newcastle in the qualifying final, the Storm were outgunned 20-12 by bogey team New Zealand in the preliminary final, denying Melbourne the ultimate retribution for the horrors endured in 2010. But the club's strength under adversity and ability to reinvent itself was the real story to come out of Melbourne in 2011, ensuring a significant Rugby League presence in the home of the AFL for many seasons to come.

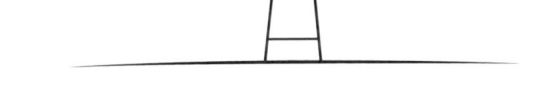

DRAGONS SHED THE 'CHOKERS' TAG

The St. George Dragons and Illawarra Steelers merged at the end of 1998 to form the National Rugby League's first joint venture. Retaining a place in the rationalised NRL competition—which was scheduled to be cut to 14 teams by 2000—was no certainty for the financially embattled Steelers. The strong historical link between the clubs (Saints legends Graeme Langlands and Craig Young hailed from the Illawarra region) rendered the club obvious partners. It was a smooth transition. Cynics sneered that the St. George Illawarra Dragons merger was little more than a takeover; the new club assumed St. George's nickname and the famous 'Red V' jumper. But home games were split between Wollongong (WIN Stadium) and Kogarah Oval, while the Steelers contributed a clutch of vital players to the joint venture's inaugural squad and many Illawarra juniors went on to make a sizeable impact for the Dragons.

St. George's David Waite was installed as foundation coach, with Steelers mentor Andrew Farrar named as his assistant. The first issue confronting the duo was accommodating brilliant five-eighths Anthony Mundine (St. George) and Trent Barrett (Illawarra) in the same side. While still a wonderful individual talent with an incisive running game, Barrett's ability to play a more structured style saw him moved to halfback to compliment Mundine's off-the-cuff genius. St. George's veteran Test centre Mark Coyne was awarded the captaincy, but he lost his first grade spot late in the 1999 season as the odd man out in a three-quarter line contingent that included Paul McGregor, Shaun Timmins, Rod Wishart (Illawarra), Jamie Ainscough and Nathan Blacklock (St. George)—all former or future internationals. Gun centre McGregor took over as skipper after Coyne's demotion.

The Steelers also contributed New Zealand Test front-rower Craig Smith, teenage fullback Luke Patten, goalkicking backrower Craig Fitzgibbon and giant prop Chris Leikvoll to the joint venture's inaugural squad, while 12-Test veteran Brad Mackay donned the 'Red V' again after three seasons for Illawarra. St. George stars included playmaking hooker Nathan Brown, lock Wayne Bartrim (a former Test rake), second-rowers Lance Thompson and Darren Treacy, and experienced props Colin Ward and Corey Pearson.

St. George Illawarra floundered in 11th place after 11 rounds of its debut season as combinations slowly took shape, before piecing together a seven-match winning streak to qualify for the finals with a wet sail in sixth spot. The Dragons thumped third-placed Melbourne 34-10 in the qualifying final, and despatched Sydney City 28-18 a week later. Mundine's virtuosity propelled the club to a stunning 24-8 defeat of minor premiers Cronulla in the preliminary final—the sublimely skilled No.6 scored a second half hat-trick after his side trailed 8-0 at halftime. Saints entered the Grand Final showdown with the Storm as warm favourites on the back of their scintillating run of form, and opened up a 14-0 halftime lead in the decider, with a sizzling runaway try to Nathan Blacklock the highlight.

But the Dragons collapsed in the second half as a patient Storm worked their way back into the contest. Clinging to a four-point advantage in the dying minutes, St. George Illawarra's premiership dream evaporated when Jamie Ainscough—the club's official player of the year—knocked opposing winger Craig Smith unconscious with a high tackle in the Dragons' in-goal as Smith was about to score. A penalty try was awarded and the consequent conversion from in front of the posts consigned St. George Illawarra to a heart-breaking 20-18 loss in front a world record 107,999-strong crowd at Stadium Australia. No team had surrendered as big a lead in Grand Final history, setting in a motion a 'chokers' reputation that followed the club for more than a decade. St. George's losses in its previous four decider appearances—1985, 1992-93 and 1996—contributed to the unwelcome tag.

Mundine was the joint venture's first Origin representative, coming off the bench in all three games for New South Wales during the drawn 1999 series, while Timmins made his Test debut in the Tri-Nations tournament at season's end to become the club's first Australian player. Nathan Brown replaced the retired McGregor as skipper, while Waite and Farrar were named as co-coaches as the Saints attempted to bury the memories of their missed opportunity. Seemingly a frontline contender leading into the 2000 season, the Dragons endured a disastrous start by losing five of their first six games—including a 70-10 debacle in a Grand Final rematch at the MCG, made all the more ignominious by Mundine's pre-match claims that premiers Melbourne were 'nothing but pretenders.' Mundine sensationally walked out on the club just two months into the competition to take up a career in professional boxing. In the midst of the controversy, the Dragons slumped to a humiliating 50-4 loss to eventual wooden spooners North Queensland, before hammering Auckland 54-0 a week later in an incredible turnaround. But a late-season surge was not enough to prevent St. George Illawarra from missing the finals. Trent Barrett provided most of the club's highlights in 2000, claiming the Dally M Player of the Year Award and starring in Australia's victorious World Cup side at the end of the year.

A neck injury prematurely ended Brown's career at the age of 27 during the 2001 pre-season. Suspension-prone prop Craig Smith was named captain, while Waite parted ways with the club and Farrar took over as sole head coach. St. George Illawarra finished seventh in 2001 and 2002 (with Barrett as captain in the latter season following Smith's departure to Super League), but upset the second-placed team in the qualifying final in each season—the Bulldogs and Newcastle respectively—before succumbing in the second week of the post-season.

Although the Dragons were seen as the NRL's great underachievers, the period was significant for the young talent that emerged through the club's junior systems. Precociously talented centre Mark Gasnier (nephew of the Immortal Reg Gasnier), robust hooker Mark Riddell, and Illawarra juniors Jason Ryles, Luke Bailey, Matt Cooper and Ben Hornby debuted in first grade during 2000. Gasnier and Ryles toured with the 2001 Kangaroos (along with Barrett and Blacklock), while Ryles and fellow front-rower Bailey debuted for NSW in 2002. Blacklock topped the NRL's tryscoring charts for the third straight season in 2001 and his Kangaroos selection ended a long period of being snubbed by representative sides. The magnificent winger left the Dragons midway through 2002 for a short-lived Super Rugby stint, however, but returned the following season and finished his career with the Saints in 2004. Blacklock retired with 100 tries in just 114 games for the joint venture.

Brown replaced Farrar as coach in 2003 and blooded future internationals Dean Young and Ben Creagh. But Saints finished a disappointing 10th and Brown's rookie coaching season is infamously remembered for slapping his skipper Barrett during a sideline tirade in a loss to Manly. Gasnier, Cooper and Hornby made their NSW debuts in 2004 and the Dragons won five of their last six regular season fixtures to qualify for the finals in fifth place—the joint venture's best finish in its six seasons. But after going down to defending premiers Penrith 31-30 in the qualifying final (the Dragons trailed 24-0 in the first half), St. George Illawarra became a victim of the McIntyre Finals System, making a first-week exit after other results went against them.

The 2005 season entrenched St. George Illawarra's 'chokers' reputation. The Dragons finished the minor premiership second with 16 wins—including seven on the trot to end the regular season—and assumed title favouritism going into the finals. Saints accounted for Cronulla 28-22 in the qualifying final, but were rolled 20-12 in a soul-destroying preliminary final defeat by the Wests Tigers juggernaut. A five-match losing streak in the second half of 2006 (directly following on from seven straight wins) saw the Dragons finish in sixth spot, but their bid for a long-awaited premiership gathered momentum with a 20-4 qualifying final upset of Brisbane and a comprehensive 28-0 elimination of Manly in the semi-final. St. George Illawarra was rated an excellent chance of toppling minor premiers Melbourne in the preliminary final, but succumbed 24-10 to the methodical Storm.

Captain Barrett joined Super League club Wigan at the end of the season and the Dragons faced a rebuilding period in 2007. New skipper Gasnier suffered a torn pectoral muscle on the eve of the season and did not play until round 19; Hornby and Ryles assumed co-captain duties, while the club posted consecutive wins just once and finished a dismal 13th. A terrible start to 2008 pointed to another disappointing season, but a seven-match winning run enabled the Dragons to nab seventh spot. They were promptly bounced from the finals by Manly, however, and captain Gasnier immediately took up a deal with French Rugby Union side Stade Francaise. Ryles also left for France, joining Super League club Catalans, while coach Brown had been told his services would not be required beyond 2008.

In a major coup, the Dragons signed revered coach Wayne Bennett, who left Brisbane after 21 seasons and six premierships in charge of the Broncos. The transformation was instant. The previously erratic Saints became a consistent, relentless defensive machine. Bennett named Hornby as captain and permanently moved the former Origin custodian to halfback. He instilled five-eighth Jamie Soward with the confidence to become one of the NRL's most dominant playmakers and Soward responded by finishing third in the 2009 Dally M Medal count. The master motivator turned props Justin Poore and Michael Weyman, long-striding winger Brett Morris (who topped the competition with 25 tries in 24 games) and centre/backrower Beau Scott into representative players. Former Broncos winger Darius Boyd matured into one of the game's top fullbacks, while veteran winger Wendell Sailor enjoyed a career renaissance under his former Brisbane mentor after returning to the NRL from a rugby union stint and two-year recreational drug ban. The club secured its maiden minor premiership, but was upset 25-12 by the resurgent eighth-placed Eels in the qualifying final and made a premature exit after being outmuscled 24-10 by the Broncos a week later. Becoming the first minor premiers to dip out of a top-eight finals series with consecutive losses did little to alleviate the 'chokers' taunts.

But the critics were just a year away from being silenced. The Dragons cruised to a second straight minor premiership in 2010 and advanced to the preliminary final after thrashing Manly 28-0 in the qualifying final. The much-maligned Saints thwarted the death-riders and held their nerve to pip the Tigers 13-12 in the preliminary final courtesy of a late Soward field goal. Despite trailing the in-form Roosters 8-6 at halftime in the Grand Final, St. George Illawarra emphatically clinched its first premiership 32-8. Mark Gasnier, who returned from France mid-season, scored the Dragons' first try, New Zealand Test winger Jason Nightingale bagged a double, and Nathan Fien—the Mount Isa-bred Kiwi Test utility who linked with the club after being discarded by the Warriors midway through 2009—burrowed over for the final four-pointer. It had been 31 years since St. George won its last Grand Final under the captaincy of Craig Young; his son Dean played a key role in the Dragons' drought-breaking victory and the pair hugged on the pitch in a poignant post-match moment. The relief amongst the St. George Illawarra players was as palpable as the elation.

There was no denying the enormous contribution of 'Saint Benny' to the triumph, and with the job completed, Bennett ended intense speculation early in the 2011 season by announcing a move to Newcastle for 2012. But the prospect of back-to-back premierships firmed in favouritism as the Dragons lost just one game in the first half of the season. The representative season inflicted a heavy toll, however, and the Saints could only muster two wins in their next 10 games (the club contributed eight players to the Origin series, including NSW debutants Soward, Young and prop Trent Merrin). The Dragons recovered to finish the regular season fifth, but went down 21-12 to the Tigers in the qualifying final before Bennett's tenure finished with a gallant 13-12 golden point semi-final defeat at Suncorp Stadium to Brisbane. Gasnier retired at the end of the season, while invaluable No.1 Darius Boyd followed Bennett to Newcastle. Highly rated assistant coach Steve Price (who guided the Dragons to a gritty 21-15 World Club Challenge victory over Wigan early in 2011 with Bennett remaining in Australia due to a family illness) was named as Bennett's replacement as the club entered a new era, but one without the 'chokers' tag hanging ominously overhead.

WESTS TIGERS MERGED FOR SURVIVAL AND SUCCESS

The Wests Tigers joint venture was formed by two foundation clubs with proud histories that had struggled—financially and on the paddock—during the 1990s. The Balmain Tigers and Western Suburbs Magpies faced uncertain futures by going it alone during the NRL's rationalisation period, and the clubs guaranteed a presence in the 2000 competition and beyond by voting overwhelmingly to merge at the end of 1999. The former rivals split virtually every aspect of the joint venture 50/50—home grounds, club colours, seats on the board—while the NRL's $6 million funding injection provided the new club with a fiscally secure position Balmain and Wests were unaccustomed to as standalone entities. The result was a harmonious partnership that garnered a premiership after just six seasons, success Balmain had not enjoyed since 1969 and Western Suburbs since 1952. In one of the only critical decisions where one partner had to concede to the other, Balmain and New South Wales coach Wayne Pearce ousted colourful Magpies mentor (and Pearce's Blues predecessor) Tom Raudonikis as Wests Tigers' foundation coach.

Representative stars Terry Hill, Jarrod McCracken, Matt Seers and John Hopoate were lured to the new club, along with livewire halfback Craig Field and enigmatic Newcastle centre Owen Craigie. The high-profile recruits complemented the Balmain and Western Suburbs players retained by the joint venture, including experienced Tigers forwards Mark O'Neill and Darren Senter, New Zealand Test representatives Jason Lowrie and Tyran Smith, goalkicking winger/fullback Joel Caine, Magpies brothers Ken and Kevin McGuinness, rugged prop John Skandalis, veteran utility Steve Georgallis and former Country Origin hooker Ciriaco Mescia. Kiwi second-rower McCracken was chosen as the club's inaugural skipper, but a spear tackle by Melbourne duo Stephen Kearney and Marcus Bai ended his career mid-season, and abrasive No.9 Senter took over as skipper.

Wests Tigers snatched a stirring 24-all draw with heavyweights Brisbane in their premiership debut at Campbelltown and stunned their NRL rivals to occupy second spot after 17 rounds. But a late-season collapse saw the Tigers win just two of their last 10 matches, consigning the fledgling outfit to a 10th-placed finish. Joel Caine finished the season as the NRL's top point-scorer with 224, while Terry Hill became the club's first Origin representative by turning out for the Blues during the 2000 series.

Pearce stepped down as coach at the end of the season and was replaced by Terry Lamb, who endured a horror introduction to NRL coaching. Kevin McGuinness and Craig Field were suspended after testing positive to cocaine a month into the 2001 premiership, before John Hopoate's infamous finger-poking antics made worldwide headlines just two weeks later. The disgraced winger was eventually punted by the club. After a promising start, the Wests Tigers slumped to 12th on the table by season's end.

It was a similar story in 2002: the Tigers won five of their first seven matches, but recorded just three further victories. Tim Sheens took the coaching reins the following season and blooded a batch of youngsters that would form the basis of the club's maiden premiership-winning side. Anthony Laffranchi became a permanent fixture in the backrow, local juniors Robbie Farah and Chris Heighington were introduced off the bench, while dazzling schoolboy half Benji Marshall debuted late in the season.

The acquisition of brilliant halfback Scott Prince, former Origin fullback Brett Hodgson (who played for the Magpies in the late-1990s before joining Parramatta), long-striding winger Pat Richards and mobile forward Todd Payten in 2004 put more pieces of the puzzle into place. A last-round loss to Newcastle cost the Tigers a maiden finals berth, but the club was on the cusp of a landmark season.

The Tigers languished in 11th spot at the halfway point of the 2005 season, before piecing together a club record winning streak on the back of their brilliant halves. Five-eighth Marshall made his Test debut for the Kiwis early in the season and formed an irresistible combination with the scheming Prince. Marshall's spellbinding footwork and phenomenal ball-skills cultivated from a touch football background set the NRL alight as the Tigers won eight consecutive games to storm into the finals in fourth place.

The club's premiership credentials were further boosted by its 50-6 demolition of North Queensland on finals debut—including an all time finals record haul of 30 points by Hodgson—before eliminating the Broncos 34-6 at the semi-final stage. Marshall inspired a 20-12 preliminary final boilover against title favourites St. George Illawarra, and the Tigers advanced to their maiden Grand Final— a rematch with the rejuvenated Cowboys.

Marshall's break and audacious flick-pass for Pat Richards to streak away for a famous long-range try gobbled up countless newspaper column inches in the aftermath of the Tigers' 30-16 victory in the decider, while captain Prince was awarded the Clive Churchill Medal. But the euphoric premiership triumph was a magnificent team effort by one of the least-heralded title-winning sides in the game's history. Farah emerged as one of the game's most dynamic hookers; brave custodian Hodgson scored 308 points, the second-highest season total in premiership history; Kiwi internationals Paul Whatuira and Dene Halatau played key roles at centre and lock respectively; young forwards Laffranchi, Heighington, Liam Fulton and Bryce Gibbs defied reputations and the critics that claimed the Tigers' pack was too small; and outside-backs Daniel Fitzhenry and Shane Elford, and underrated backrower Ben Galea all made telling contributions.

Hodgson, Skandalis (both Magpies), Galea and Mark O'Neill (both Tigers) all made their respective first grade debuts for either Western Suburbs or Balmain before the two clubs merged, and celebrated in the Grand Final success. Prince became Wests Tigers' first Australian representative by winning selection for the subsequent Tri-Nations tour, ousting Queensland halfback and Cowboys linchpin Johnathan Thurston. The unlikely premiership sealed Tim Sheens' status as one of the all time great coaches, adding to a list of achievement that included steering Penrith to its maiden finals series and winning three Grand Finals with Canberra.

The Wests Tigers' premiership defence was plagued by injury and inconsistency. A fractured cheekbone and a recurring shoulder complaint restricted Marshall to just nine starts, while Hodgson—NSW's fullback in 2006—was limited to 15 appearances. Hodgson was installed as captain in the wake of Prince's pre-season announcement that he would be joining the fledgling Gold Coast Titans in 2007. The Tigers won consecutive games just once in 2006 and consequently finished 11th.

Marshall played just half a season in 2007, and in a devastating repeat of three years earlier, the Tigers missed the finals after a final-round loss to the Knights— this time courtesy of a last-minute penalty goal. But there were positive signs for the club. Robbie Farah emerged as one of the NRL's dominant players, finishing second behind Johnathan Thurston for the Dally M Medal after appearing certain to take out the award. Meanwhile, teenage centre Chris Lawrence announced himself as a star of the future with 16 tries in 18 appearances.

Skipper Hodgson departed for Super League club Huddersfield at the end of 2008—another lamentably inconsistent season for the Tigers—and Farah assumed the captaincy. The ball-playing No.9 earned Origin and Test debuts in 2009 and finished equal-fourth in the Dally M Medal, but the patchy Tigers finished ninth for the third time in six seasons, missing the finals by a single competition point. Great Britain and England Test veteran Gareth Ellis was added to the club's roster and immediately gained recognition as one of the NRL's premier backrowers, winning the first of three consecutive club player of the year awards in 2009. Giant, bulldozing Kiwi winger Taniela Tuiaki scored 21 tries in 22 games and scooped the Dally M Winger of the Year gong, but his career was tragically cut short by a terrible broken ankle suffered late in the season.

Putting his injury woes well behind him, Marshall unleashed his jaw-dropping talents on the Tigers' NRL rivals with a career-best season in 2010, spearheading the club's long overdue return to the finals in tandem with the consistently brilliant Farah. Farah finished second in the Dally M count again, while Marshall came fourth. The Tigers secured third place in the minor premiership with a club record 15 wins, before embarking on an extraordinarily nerve-jangling finals campaign. The Tigers coughed up a 15-2 second half lead (and a one-point advantage as the fulltime siren sounded) to go down 19-15 to the Roosters in the first-ever golden point finals encounter. Regrouping six days later, the Tigers absorbed a Canberra comeback to hold on for a 24-22 semi-final victory. But a late Jamie Soward field goal sunk the Tigers in the preliminary final as they let yet another second half lead slip as the Dragons advanced to the Grand Final 13-12. Lote Tuqiri's return to the NRL after seven seasons in rugby union was one of the season's highlights— the big winger scored 18 tries, culminating in a recall to the Australian side. Chris Lawrence joined Tuqiri in the Four Nations squad and made his Test debut against New Zealand.

Marshall was awarded the 2010 Golden Boot after captaining New Zealand to a stunning Four Nations Final triumph over Australia. The five-eighth magician was again at the forefront of the Tigers' premiership assault in 2011. Unfounded rumours of in-fighting at the club and the shedding of players such as props Gibbs and Andrew Fifita to accommodate the 2012 arrival of marquee Melbourne forward Adam Blair fuelled familiar inconsistency on the field. The Tigers were floundering on the fringe of the top-eight after 18 rounds, but won their last eight regular season matches—including rousing come-from-behind victories in high-powered clashes with heavyweights Manly and St. George Illawarra—to claim another top-four berth. Marshall was pipped by Billy Slater for the Dally M Medal, just days before the Tigers overwhelmed the Dragons again 21-12 in the qualifying final for a club record ninth consecutive win. But the Tigers were run down by the Warriors in a heart-breaking semi-final defeat a week later, squandering an 18-6 halftime lead to be eliminated courtesy of a freakish Krisnan Inu try in the dying minutes. Despite the shattering finals exits of 2010-11, the Wests Tigers had finally arrived as a regular title contender hell-bent on emulating the club's phenomenal maiden premiership triumph.

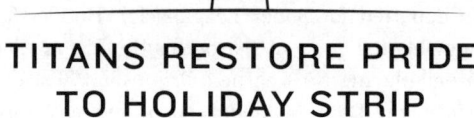

TITANS RESTORE PRIDE
TO HOLIDAY STRIP

Heeding the lessons of the original Gold Coast club's succession of catastrophes between 1988 and 1998 (see Extinct Clubs), the Gold Coast Titans' off-field drive and professionalism transferred into success on the paddock after their 2007 inception, finally providing the burgeoning Rugby League heartland with a team to be proud of.

The push for a premiership team to be based on the Gold Coast again began almost immediately after the Chargers' demise at the end of the inaugural National Rugby League season. With astute businessman Michael Searle (a foundation Gold Coast Giant forward and veteran of 55 games for the club) and Paul Broughton, a former Sydney first grade player and coach described as the 'godfather of Gold Coast Rugby League,' at the helm, the bid was accepted by the NRL in 2005 after initially being rejected a year earlier.

The Queensland Government's pledge to build a $100 million state-of-the-art stadium at Robina was a major factor in the Gold Coast consortium's successful bid, while the club set about assembling a squad that would be instantly competitive from its 2007 NRL debut. Chief executive Searle and chairman Broughton signed John Cartwright as the Titans' foundation coach. The former Penrith and Test forward had been a highly regarded assistant to Ricky Stuart at the Sydney Roosters, and was part of Phil Gould's New South Wales coaching staff in 2004.

The Titans recruited shrewdly, bringing together a squad consisting of proven experience and class, combined with outstanding emerging talent. Former Dally M medallist and Panthers premiership-winner Preston Campbell was the club's first signing, and was followed by two marquee recruits—Wests Tigers Grand Final-winning halfback and captain Scott Prince, and veteran NSW and Australian prop Luke Bailey. Dual international Mat Rogers returned from rugby union to join the Titans, while former Test forward Brad Meyers, New Zealand Test three-quarter Jake Webster, former Queensland State of Origin winger Chris Walker, and backrowers Anthony Laffranchi and Mark Minichiello gave the new squad an impressive balance.

There were disappointments, however; Melbourne winger Steve Turner reneged on a contract with the Titans after playing in the 2006 Grand Final with the Storm, and popular Irish winger and Great Britain Test star Brian Carney had a change of heart about his stint on the Gold Coast, announcing he would be returning home two months out from the Titans debut.

Co-captained by Prince and Bailey, Gold Coast was extremely competitive during 2007, winning 10 games and finishing 12th. The Titans defeated Brisbane 28-16 in the first derby between the clubs, while a golden point loss to 'big brother' ultimately proved the difference between a debut-season top-eight berth and finals oblivion—the club finished just one win adrift of the eighth-placed Broncos. The extra-time loss came in the midst of a five-match losing streak during the second half of the season that began when the Titans were occupying a top-four spot. Bailey became the club's first Origin and Australian Test representative, and shared the club's player of the year award—the Paul Broughton Medal—with Laffranchi. Gold Coast played out of Suncorp Stadium and Carrara Stadium during its debut season before unveiling the brand new Skilled Park in the opening round of 2008.

The Titans headed the NRL ladder after 10 rounds of the 2008 season on the back of mesmerising No.7 Prince's brilliant form. But Prince, who simultaneously became the club's first Queensland representative with Ashley Harrison, broke his arm in the Origin decider. Gold Coast won just one of seven games while its injured linchpin was sidelined, finishing 13th with 10 victories. Courageous fullback Preston Campbell was appropriately award the Paul Broughton Medal, while Prince and Laffranchi (who also debuted for NSW in 2008) won selection in Australia's World Cup squad at the end of the season, with Cartwright joining the Kangaroos' coaching staff as an assistant. The Titans' home crowds averaged 21,618 in their first season at Skilled.

The club came of age in 2009, emphatically qualifying for its maiden finals series in third spot on the ladder. The Titans' new-found consistency was built around the guile and brilliance of veterans Prince, Campbell and Rogers; the forward grunt of Bailey, Laffranchi, Meyers and Minichiello; the canny dummy-half work of hooker and player of the year Nathan Friend; and the backline speed of youngsters Kevin Gordon and David Mead. Occupying a top-four position for all but five weeks of the regular season, the Titans made their finals debut against archrivals Brisbane, but succumbed 40-32 after trailing 28-10 at halftime in a high-scoring thriller at Skilled. Gold Coast's season of immense progress reached a deflating conclusion courtesy of a 27-2 defeat at the hands of the Jarryd Hayne-led Parramatta juggernaut.

Cartwright installed Prince as sole captain in 2010 and the dexterous No.7 responded with another fine season, claiming Dally M Halfback of the Year honours and leading Gold Coast to another top-four finish. The club had allegations of financial misappropriation levelled at it early in the year regarding unpaid bills from the construction of the club's Centre of Excellence, while Prince was under the microscope amid rumours a club sponsor had agreed to build a house for him for free. But the Titans prevailed in court, while Prince and the club were cleared by the NRL's salary cap auditor Ian Schubert.

The Titans were among the NRL's front-runners throughout 2010 and won six of their last seven regular season games to secure a home qualifying final, where they accounted for the in-form New Zealand Warriors 28-16. Upset results in the first week of the finals catapulted the Titans directly into the club's first preliminary final. But the resurgent Roosters ended Gold Coast's season with a 32-6 drubbing at Suncorp Stadium. After trailing just 12-6 at halftime, the Titans produced their worst 40 minutes of the season to let a Grand Final berth slip through their fingers.

Greg Bird's NRL return via the Titans in 2010 was a significant boost for the club; the controversial lock/five-eighth added an extra dimension to the team and his outstanding form was rewarded with recalls to the NSW and Australian sides.

The increasingly highly regarded Cartwright extended his contract with the club until the end of 2016, but the Titans' worst fears were realised in 2011. Gold Coast's ageing squad—minus retired veteran utility-back Mat Rogers—won just six games and collected the wooden spoon. It was a season reminiscent of the original Gold Coast club's dark days in the early-1990s rather than a side that was coming off back-to-back top-four finishes. Injuries were a mitigating factor—Friend and Gordon played just four and two games respectively due to season-ending injuries, while Prince, Bird, Campbell and Harrison also spent extended periods on the sideline. Rogers' late-season comeback lasted just one game after the 35-year-old broke a bone in his foot. The timing could not have been worse for the Titans—cross-code rivals the Gold Coast Suns made their AFL debut in 2011, averaging 19,169-strong crowds to the Titans' 15,428. Veteran front-rower Luke 'Bull' Bailey's form was a rare highlight, collecting his second Paul Broughton Medal in a row (and third overall), while electrifying Papua New Guinea international David Mead broke the club's season tryscoring record with 16 touchdowns, including one of the season's most freakish individual efforts against Cronulla.

The old guard that had been so vital to Gold Coast's surge up the ladder was dismantled ahead of the 2012 season. Campbell, Meyers and former Kiwi Test centre Clinton Toopi retired, Laffranchi joined English club St. Helens, and Friend linked with the Warriors. The most aggressive recruitment drive since the club's debut season netted NSW and Kangaroo representative Jamal Idris from Canterbury, the Roosters' Origin and Test forward Nate Myles, ironman Cronulla front-rower Luke Douglas, and slick City Origin centre Beau Champion from Melbourne. Desperate to avoid the slumps and off-field calamities that engulfed the Giants, Seagulls and Chargers two decades earlier, the Titans proactively sought a solution that the club is confident will return it to contender status, and eventually deliver a maiden premiership to the holiday strip.

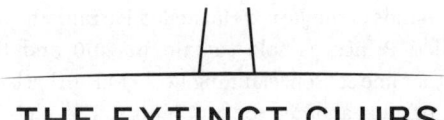

THE EXTINCT CLUBS

There are 17 Rugby League clubs to have graced the premiership that are no longer in existence. The proud and colourful histories—of varying success and duration—of these clubs are detailed in the following pages.

CUMBERLAND (1908) The Cumberland Plain is a region is Sydney's west, taking its name from Cumberland County—the cadastral land division that encompasses most of metropolitan Sydney—conferred in honour of Ernest Augustus, Duke of Cumberland, by Governor Phillip in 1788. In April 1908, a discontented breakaway group within the Western Suburbs Rugby Union Club named themselves 'Central Cumberland' and approached the NSWRL for admission to the premiership, which was in its inaugural season. Originally instructed by the NSWRL to integrate with the already existing Western Suburbs club, the group persisted and Cumberland became the ninth premiership club, debuting in round two of the 1908 season against South Sydney. Cumberland was defeated 23-2 by Souths at the Royal Agricultural Ground in a curtain-raiser to the first Test between Australia and New Zealand. Taking the field in the royal blue and gold colours that would later be adopted by Parramatta, Cumberland copped a 37-0 hiding at the hands of Newcastle the following weekend and lost its first six matches. Cumberland recorded its only victory in round eight, accounting for neighbours Wests 14-6, with versatile back Harry Bloomfield contributing a club record 11 points. Bloomfield and A. Harris were selected for New South Wales during the 1908 interstate series with Queensland, becoming Cumberland's first and only representative players. North Sydney thumped Cumberland 45-0 in the penultimate round—easily the biggest defeat in the Sydney premiership's maiden season—consigning Cumberland to the wooden spoon with an inferior for-and-against record to Wests, who also won just one game. Cumberland was disbanded at the end the season and it would be another 39 years before the district was represented in the premiership again in the shape of the Parramatta club.

NEWCASTLE (1908-09) Eighty years prior to the advent of the Knights, Newcastle entered a team in the first two seasons of the Sydney premiership. The Rugby League rebellion spread north from Sydney and made its way to the Hunter Valley, largely thanks to the efforts of James Giltinan and Henry Hoyle. Despite staunch opposition from pro-rugby union factions amongst the district's footballers, Giltinan and Hoyle persevered and Newcastle became the eighth club admitted to the inaugural NSWRL premiership—just 10 days before the April 20 commencement of the 1908 season. Known as 'The Rebels' and playing in red and white jumpers, Newcastle lost its first match 8-5 to Glebe at Wentworth Oval, but opened its account in style with a nine-try, 37-0 flogging of Cumberland in its next match. Facing the disadvantage of playing every match in Sydney, Newcastle finished a creditable fifth—just outside finals reckoning—with four wins in its nine matches.

Newcastle played three games at home in 1909—recouping some of the financial losses the club incurred in its debut season—and finished the regular season in third place after winning half of its 10 games. South Sydney was too strong in the major semi, defeating Newcastle 20-0 to advance to the final. The club produced four Australian representatives during its short existence; Pat Walsh and Bill 'Jerry' Bailey toured with the 1908-09 Kangaroos, and Ernie Patfield and captain Stan Carpenter played against the New Zealand Maoris in 1909. Winger Bailey was Newcastle's most prolific try-scorer, crossing for nine in each year, while forward Carpenter was the club's top point-scorer with 80 over two seasons.

At the instigation of the NSWRL, the district formed its own four-team competition in 1910 and pulled its Newcastle side from the Sydney premiership. The local competition proved itself as one of the toughest in Australia over the next eight decades until the Knights' 1988 premiership debut. The region produced Test greats such as Clive Churchill, Brian Carlson, Wally Prigg, Les Johns, Johnny Graves, Eddie Lumsden, Herb Narvo and John Sattler, while the Newcastle representative side recorded many famous victories over international touring sides.

ANNANDALE (1910-20) The Annandale club was introduced to the NSWRL premiership in 1910 to maintain an eight-team competition, following Newcastle's decision to form its own local competition at the end of 1909. Originally a working-class suburb, Annandale's inclusion in the premiership created a high concentration of clubs in Sydney's inner west, an area which already boasted teams from Glebe and Balmain. 'The Dales' were formed by a group of disgruntled Rugby Union players from the area, while the impetus for the club's promotion to the premiership was provided James Giltinan, one of the code's founding fathers. The former honorary secretary of the NSWRL, Giltinan successfully lobbied the game's governing body to include a team from Annandale. But the club enjoyed little success in 11 seasons of competition.

Sharing Wentworth Park with Glebe as its home ground, Annandale took the field in amber and gold hooped jerseys featuring a capital 'A' on the chest. The Dales won five and drew one of their 14 games in 1910 to finish sixth, while an identical performance in 1911 garnered fifth spot on the ladder—the highest finishing position the club achieved. The club finished with the wooden spoon in 1914, 1918 and 1920, while it came second-last in 1912-13, 1916-17 and 1919. Annandale became the first team to go through a season winless in 1918 and repeated the feat in 1920, a season which garnered the club's worst loss—52-3 against Wests at Pratten Park. Annandale recorded its biggest win in 1911, thumping North Sydney 31-11.

Mobile forward Bob Stuart was the club's only Australian representative; the Annandale-born former Wallaby became a dual international with selection in the 1911-12 Kangaroo Tour squad, but played just two minor matches on tour and never appeared in a Test. Ted Burdett became the club's first representative player after winning selection for New South Wales in 1911, while winger Bill Lindsay, five-eighth Ray Norman and forward Walter Haddock represented the state side in 1912. Norman played alongside brothers Rex and Roy for Annandale—Ray went on to debut for Australia in 1914 while playing for Souths and Rex toured with the 1921-22 Kangaroos from Easts, becoming just the second set of brothers to represent Australia. Haddock set a record for most appearances for Annandale, playing 80 games for the club. Wal Palmer, who played two games for NSW in 1915 before joining Wests, was Annandale's only other state representative. The Dales managed to attract one high-profile player during their brief existence: pioneering Glebe fullback and 1908-09 Kangaroo Charles Hedley played in Annandale's first two seasons, kicking 19 goals.

Annandale's increasingly poor results, combined with University's promotion to the premiership in 1920 and St. George's proposed inclusion the following season, saw the club axed at the end of its winless 1920 campaign by the NSWRL. Neighbouring rivals Glebe, Balmain, Newtown and Wests benefitted from the reallocation of Annandale's territory under the residency rules of the day.

GLEBE (1908-29) Glebe lays claim to being the first Rugby League club formed in Australia. Despite failing to win a premiership and folding after 22 seasons, the Dirty Reds hold a cherished place in the game's history. Glebe rugby union player Alex Burdon's denied compensation claim after breaking his arm was a catalyst for the advent of Rugby League on these shores. On 9 January 1908 at the Glebe Town

Hall, the working-class, inner-city Sydney club became the first to hold a meeting and affiliate with the New South Wales Rugby League.

A powerhouse of the inaugural 1908 premiership, Glebe—sporting dark red jerseys and white shorts—finished the regular season third after winning seven of its nine games. Glebe went down to eventual premiers South Sydney 16-3 in the semi-final; six of the club's players were en route to England with the pioneering Kangaroos at the time—club captain Burdon, fullback Charles Hedley, five-eighth Albert Conlon, forwards Peter Moir and Tom McCabe, and halfback Arthur 'Pony' Halloway, who went on to become one of the code's all time greats with Easts and Balmain.

The second wave of Wallaby defections at the end of 1909 delivered halfback Chris McKivat and centre Jack Hickey to the club, and the pair represented Australia in the first home Test series against England in 1910. McKivat was named captain of the 1911-12 'Australasian' Kangaroos—a squad that contained clubmate Peter Burge. In the absence of the Kangaroo duo, Glebe finished the 1911 season as minor premiers, but was defeated twice by Easts—in the final and the subsequent challenge final—and the club's best premiership chance fell by the wayside.

The Burge name is entrenched in Glebe's narrative; Peter's brother Alby 'Son' Burge captained the 1911 side, alongside Frank, who broke into first grade as a 16-year-old earlier in the season. A fourth brother, Laidley, debuted in 1916. But it is phenomenal tryscoring forward Frank Burge's career that is most closely entwined with Glebe's history. An unlucky omission from the 1911-12 Kangaroos squad, he played 13 Tests and toured with the 1921-22 Kangaroos (with clubmate Bert Gray). Burge dominates Glebe's record books, setting every conceivable mark for appearances, tries and points in a match, season and career. Among 137 tries for the club, Burge scored a premiership record eight tries in a match against University in 1920, while he scored 24 tries in 1918—an all time record for tries in a season by a forward that still stands. He left the club at the end of 1926 to captain-coach St. George and was named as a reserve in the ARL's Team of the Century in 2008.

Glebe finished runners-up in 1912 and 1915 in the era of no finals matches and came third in 1918 and 1920-21. The club endured a tumultuous 1917 season that was shaping as the year it broke its premiership duck. Table topping Glebe was stripped of two competition points when opponents Annandale later protested the residential qualifications of Glebe player Dan 'Laddo' Davies (see Points Docked). Later in the year, Glebe players boycotted a match against Balmain after the NSWRL moved it from the SCG to Birchgrove Oval (therefore attracting a far smaller gate). Balmain thrashed a reserve grade-strength Glebe line-up 40-9, and the players that sat out the match were suspended for a year by the NSWRL (the bans were lifted by the start of the 1918 season).

Finishing the 1922 season tied for first place with defending champs North Sydney, Glebe's last great chance to win a first grade title was thwarted by a 35-3 defeat at the hands of the Shoremen in the premiership final. The Dirty Reds landed in second place at the end of the 1926 regular season, but were eliminated in the finals by University.

Following three seasons near the bottom of the table, Glebe was narrowly voted out (13 votes to 12) of the competition by the NSWRL's delegates.[13] Poor on-field results, a lack of a home ground and perceived poor organisation within the club contributed to Glebe's demise. Although Glebe was unable to win a first grade premiership, the club claimed five reserve grade titles and took out the third grade premiership once. The working-class suburb's population stagnated during the period as factories and warehouse made inroads into the residential areas. A petition boasting 3,000 signatures and a submission by the club to be granted territory from Souths, Balmain and Newtown to bolster its player catchment area was not enough to budge the NSWRL from its stance. Gentrification in recent decades has turned the suburb into a trendy, vibrant inner-city suburb with a distinct multicultural and bohemian vibe with an abundance of restaurants and artisans. Few remnants remain of one of the great pioneering Rugby League clubs—Australia's first.

UNIVERSITY (1920-37) Rugby union clubs in Australia ceased competition during World War I and were slow to regroup at its conclusion. The NSWRL capitalised by establishing a premiership club at Sydney University—a traditional bastion of the amateur code. Its players were to compete strictly as amateurs, and despite criticism and opposition from amateur sporting officials, the University club was formed following a meeting in February, 1920. Understandably, the club lacked experience and star quality during its existence and collected 10 wooden spoons in 18 seasons, despite boasting the services of a string of Rugby League luminaries as coach.

Known as 'The Students,' the club was coached by pioneering greats Arthur Hennessey, Alex Burdon and Paddy McCue in its maiden 1920 season, but returned just one win, a 13-8 defeat of soon-to-be-axed Annandale to stave off the wooden spoon. University conceded 40-plus points in eight of its 13 debut-season matches, and finished winless in 1921. In a major coup, Test utility Jimmy Craig arrived as captain-coach in 1922—fresh from touring with the Kangaroos—and steered the club to five victories. But Craig departed after one season and 'Varsity' finished last again in 1923, followed by lower-table finishes in the ensuing two campaigns.

Bill Kelly, a New Zealand dual international and Australian Test centre before captain-coaching Balmain to the 1915 premiership, took over the coaching reins at University and qualified for the 1926 finals in fourth spot with nine regular season wins. University swamped second-placed Glebe 29-3 in a semi-final upset to snare a place in the premiership final against South Sydney. The Students lost few admirers in a hard-fought 11-6 loss to the Rabbitohs, who claimed the second of five straight first grade titles.

The premiership final appearance proved to be the pinnacle of University's existence; the club slumped to wooden spoon finishes in 1927 and 1929-31. The Students achieved their biggest win in 1933, trouncing St. George 42-8 at the Sydney Sports Ground, with Jack Gray-Spence crossing for a hat-trick on his way to topping the premiership with a club record 11 tries.

---

13   Ian Collis and Alan Whiticker, *The History Of Rugby League Clubs*. Sydney, 2004

The year ended in tragedy, however, following one of the proudest achievements in the club's history. Three-quarter Ray Morris joined University from Wests in 1933, making the last of his eight appearances for NSW in his first season for the Students before becoming the first player from the club to win selection for Australia. But Morris developed an ear infection while en route to England with the 1933-34 Kangaroos and died after being hospitalised in Malta *(see Tragic Figures)*.

The club boasted some fine playing talent during its stint in the premiership: A.S. 'Georgie' Lane, University's captain in the 1926 final, played eight matches for NSW and captained the state side in 1926; centre Frank O'Rourke represented NSW eight times before heading to England and carving out a fine career with Leeds; and Ross McKinnon, another outstanding centre, who debuted for NSW from University in 1933, but became a Test star after joining the all-conquering Eastern Suburbs club in 1935 alongside fellow former Student, prolific tryscoring winger Rod O'Loan. University was unable to retain its best players for any great length of time, no doubt contributed to by the club's admirable commitment to the amateur ethos. Five-eighth Ernest 'Sammy' Ogg was a rare exception, racking up a club record 116 first grade appearances—46 clear of his nearest clubmate.

University finished last in each of its final four seasons (1934-37). After winning its opening-round match against Norths in 1934, the Students lost a premiership record 42 consecutive games, finally halting the undesirable streak with a 13-11 defeat of St. George in the last round of 1936. It was to be University's last victory—the club lost every match in the shortened 1937 season (including 63-0 and 65-5 defeats to Souths and St. George respectively). The club voluntarily pulled out of the premiership competition at the end of the year, leaving a colourful—but ultimately unsuccessful—18-season legacy behind.

NEWTOWN (1908-83) The history of the Newtown club is a proud narrative of working-class, inner-city battlers that doggedly strived for every victory that came its way. Some of the game's great names and memorable characters wore the blue and white of Newtown, but while the club claimed three premierships, post-World War II success eluded it. Newtown became the first team in 56 years to be excluded from the competition as the realities of financial strife and the area's changing social and cultural landscape took hold at the end of 1983.

Newtown was long thought to be the first Rugby League club to form in Australia, but it is now generally accepted that the minutes of the inaugural meeting in 1908 were incorrectly dated 8 January. The meeting at the Newtown Town Hall has been revealed to have taken place on 14 January, thus referring the honour of being the first club to Glebe.[14] But Newtown was nevertheless a vital component of the NSWRL premiership's formative years. The Bluebags finished seventh of nine teams in 1908, with just a win and a draw to show from their nine games, and the club fared little better the following season. But Newtown finished as minor premiers in 1910 after winning 11 of its 13 matches, and faced off in a dramatic final against 1908-09 champions South Sydney to decide the premiership. Captain Charles 'Boxer' Russell piloted a famous pressure goal from out wide near halfway late

---

14   Ian Collis and Alan Whiticker, *The History Of Rugby League Clubs*. Sydney, 2004

in the piece to secure a 4-all draw; Newtown was awarded the premiership on account of finishing the regular season with more competition points.

The Bluebags provided three players to the pioneering 1908-09 Kangaroo Tour— centre Frank Cheadle (who became Newtown's first Test player in the series against New Zealand during 1908), and forwards 'Tedda' Courtney and Bill Noble. Noble had been integral to the formation of the club, and captained Newtown during the 1910 premiership season before missing the final through injury. Newtown benefitted greatly from the wave of rugby union defections ahead of the 1910 season, with Russell, 'Paddy' McCue and the Farnsworth brothers Bill and Viv switching codes to play for the Bluebags. Seven Newtown players were selected for the 1911-12 'Australasian' Kangaroo Tour—a record that was equalled by rival clubs, but never bettered. Russell, McCue, Noble, Bill and Viv Farnsworth (who became the first brothers to represent Australia), forward Joe Murray and fullback William 'Webby' Neil set sail for England with the Kangaroos.

During the years where no semi-finals were staged, Newtown finished runners-up in 1913 and 1914, but struggled throughout the 1920s. Despite employing a steady stream of esteemed former internationals as coach—'Pony' Halloway, 'Ricketty' Johnston, Bill Farnsworth—the Bluebags slumped to wooden spoons in 1924-25 and 1928. Newtown turned its fortunes around in 1929 to qualify for the final, before being outclassed 30-10 by South Sydney. 'Boxer' Russell returned to the club as coach in 1933 and steered the Bluebags to the minor premiership in a season shortened due to the impending departure of the Kangaroos. Newtown—captained by Keith Ellis with his brother, club stalwart Tom, at fullback—defeated Souths in the semi-final and accounted for St. George 18-5 in the final to claim its second first grade title. Remarkably, the Bluebags were running last after losing their opening four matches of the season, but won 11 of their remaining 12 games to record a remarkable premiership triumph.

The ensuing decade brought little in the way of on-field success (an emphatic 57-5 victory in the final of the City Cup over premiership powerhouse Eastern Suburbs in 1937 was a notable exception), but the club unveiled a clutch of players that would be vital to its last premiership triumph. Powerful forward Herb Narvo debuted for Newtown in 1937 and toured with the Kangaroos at the end of the season, before returning to his native Newcastle for several seasons; front-row enforcer and local junior Frank Farrell hit the first grade scene in 1938 and went on to become arguably the greatest Bluebag, playing a club record 204 first grade games; and prolific pointscoring fullback Tommy Kirk joined the club from Canterbury in 1940. Narvo came back to Newtown in 1943 and the Farrell-captained side took out the minor premiership, before crushing North Sydney 34-7 in the Grand Final. Former Balmain Test winger Sid Goodwin, who joined the Bluebags in 1943, scored two tries in the emphatic victory, while Kirk landed five goals. Newtown was coached by Arthur Folwell, who played 84 games for the Bluebags and toured with the 1933-34 Kangaroos. Ironically, Frank Hyde was captain of Norths—Hyde had made his first grade debut for Newtown in 1936, before being forced to play for Balmain when it was discovered he had been supplied with a fake address to turn out for the Bluebags.

The club was shrouded in controversy the following season, however. After securing the minor premiership again in 1944, the Bluebags demolished St. George

55-7 in the semi-final—a premiership record win in a finals match. But Newtown was accused of 'throwing' the premiership final following its 19-16 loss to Balmain, with an alleged ruse to obtain a better price with the bookies in the consequent Grand Final a week later at the centre of the furore. The Bluebags went down 12-8 in the decider, but that did little to silence the sceptics. Controversy was never far away from the club and its players during the 1940s. Farrell was implicated in the infamous Bill McRitchie 'ear-biting' incident against St. George at Henson Park in 1945—although Farrell was narrowly cleared by a NSWRL inquiry, it is widely believed he was guilty and only cleared due to a lack of evidence. Farrell gave differing accounts professing his innocence, from his argument during the inquiry that he had left his false teeth in the dressing room, to the tongue-in-cheek claim shortly before his death in 1985 that he could not have been the culprit as he was 'at home crook in bed.'[15] Despite the unsavoury episode, Farrell made his Test debut the following season and captain-coached Newtown from 1946 until his retirement in 1951. In 1948, Australia's incumbent captain-coach Len Smith was inexplicably left out of the Kangaroo Tour squad after appearing to be a certainty to lead the squad. Theories on Newtown centre Smith's omission range from religious prejudice to a power struggle for the coaching role.

The 1950s provided great promise but nothing in the way of premiership rewards for the Bluebags. Newtown lost just one match in the 1954 regular season, but was overwhelmed 23-15 by South Sydney in the Grand Final. Minor premiers again in 1955, Newtown was pipped 12-11 in the decider, again by bogey team Souths. The club possessed a playing group arguably more talented than at any stage of its history. Winger Jack Troy scored a club record six tries against Easts in 1950 (the last time the feat has been achieved in a first grade game), and featured in Australia's historic Ashes series win that year. Local junior Col Geelan played eight Tests at centre and five-eighth in the early 1950s while at Newtown; Ray Preston (whose 109 tries is a club record) scored 34 tries and Kevin Considine 22 during the club's watershed 1954 season—a premiership record for a wing pairing; goalkicking fullback Gordon 'Punchy' Clifford played eight Tests for Australia, unseating the great Clive Churchill, and scored a then-record 919 points for the club; future St. George great Brian Clay played at centre in Newtown's 1954-55 Grand Final losses; five-eighth Tony Brown debuted for the club in 1956 and toured with the 1959-60 Kangaroos; and second-rower Henry Holloway played three Tests against France in 1955. Brilliant centre Dick Poole, another local junior, debuted for Newtown as a teenager in 1950, captain-coaching the club to the 1955 Grand Final and Australia to its maiden World Cup success in 1957, before being lured to big-spending Western Suburbs in 1959.

Success was scarce for Newtown during 1960s and 1970s—preliminary finals in 1962 and 1973, and a semi-final appearance in 1966 were the club's only forays into September football in a two-decade period. The venerable Jack Gibson—a front-rower in Newtown's 1962 preliminary final side—guided the club to the penultimate weekend of the 1973 season, his only year as coach of the club before achieving greatness with Easts in the ensuing two seasons. Newtown also secured the club championship for the only time in the club's history and won the pre-season Wills

15 Tony Adams, *Hit Men*. Sydney, 1994

Cup in 1973. Newtown's standout performers during this period included 1963-64 Kangaroo forward Graham Wilson, Test forward Paul Quinn, outstanding clubman and 1967-68 Kangaroo centre Brian 'Chicka' Moore, and Queensland winger and 1973 Kangaroo tourist Lionel Williamson.

In the late-1970s, prominent businessman John Singleton pumped a considerable amount of money into reinvigorating the club he had followed since childhood, which was now nicknamed the Jets. He received little return for his investment, but his efforts were integral to Newtown's last grab for glory. Warren Ryan took over as coach in 1979 and Singleton enticed Wests' veteran Test halfback Tom Raudonikis to the club the following season. Goalkicking utility-back Ken Wilson returned to the club, while the aggressive recruitment drive in the late-1970s and early-1980s included the acquisition of ball-playing Penrith forward Phil Gould, future Test winger John Ferguson and former New Zealand Test enforcer Bill Noonan. The Raudonikis-led Jets stormed to second place in the 1981 regular season and—after losing to Parramatta in the major semi—defeated Manly and minor premiers Easts to qualify for a Grand Final rematch with the Eels. Newtown was gallant in the 20-11 loss, but the club's downward spiral and eventual exclusion from the premiership was rapid.

Raudonikis and Ryan moved on at the end of 1982, with club stalwarts 'Chicka' Moore and Ken Wilson installed as coach and captain respectively the following season (Wilson became the first Newtown player to top 1,000 career points for the club in 1983). The Jets' dire financial position and substandard facilities at Henson Park saw the club axed from the 1984 premiership, along with Wests (the Magpies were later reinstated). A proposed relocation to Campbelltown to gain readmission was aborted. Newtown made a comeback via the Metropolitan Cup in 1991, winning four titles in that competition during the 1990s, before fielding teams in the various second-tier competitions to the NRL—the now-defunct Premier League competition and currently the NSW Cup. The Jets have acted as a feeder club to NRL sides the New Zealand Warriors, Cronulla, and most recently, the Sydney Roosters.

SOUTH QUEENSLAND (1995-97) The South Queensland Crushers became the second premiership club based in Brisbane, joining the competition in 1995 along with the Warriors, Cowboys and Reds, but became a casualty of the Super League war after just three seasons. Hometown rivals the Brisbane Broncos perceived the Crushers' admission as a ploy by the ARL to curb their dominance— the license was granted just two months after the Broncos' maiden Grand Final victory. Playing out of Suncorp Stadium, the Crushers received generous crowd support during their debut season, while they were the only one of the four expansion clubs to side with the ARL during the Super League conflict. But home crowds dwindled over the ensuing two seasons and the Crushers Leagues Club's crippling debt forced the club to fold at the end of 1997 after Gold Coast declined the offer of a merger.

Bill Gardner was installed as the club's inaugural coach, but was replaced by former Test lock Bob Lindner prior to the Crushers' premiership entry. Lindner was at the helm for two seasons before being replaced by reserve grade coach Steve Bleakley for 1997. The club's playing roster consisted of several high-profile players at the tail-end of their careers—Mario Fenech was the Crushers' first captain, but was swiftly replaced by Trevor Gillmeister. Maroons stalwart Gillmeister became the club's only Australian Test player after skippering a depleted Queensland side containing clubmates Dale Shearer, Mark Hohn, Terry Cook and Craig Teevan to a 3-0 series boilover. Front-rowers Tony Hearn and Clinton O'Brien represented the Maroons from the club during the next two seasons, while Tony Kemp was recalled to the Kiwi Test side in 1995. The Crushers also blooded future stars Clinton Schifcofske, Danny Nutley, Mark Tookey and Aaron Moule.

South Queensland's on-field results were dismal during its three-season existence. The Crushers finished 16th of 20 teams in their 1995 debut season with six wins, including victories over finals sides North Sydney (the club's maiden success) and Newcastle. But the club collected consecutive wooden spoons after recording a total of just seven wins in the 1996-97 seasons. The Crushers' finest hour came in their last match, a 39-18 thrashing of finals hopefuls Western Suburbs in the final round of the 1997 ARL premiership. South Queensland won its only piece of silverware with victory in the 1996 President's Cup Grand Final.

WESTERN REDS (1995-97) The NSWRL premiership went international in 1995 with the advent of the Auckland Warriors, but it ventured further afield with the admission of the Perth-based Western Reds—1,000 kilometres further from Sydney than Auckland. Boasting a solid junior base and with some astute recruitment, powerbrokers were optimistic of the Reds attracting a sizeable following in the Rugby League outpost and becoming a premiership force. But the Super League war broke out a month after the club's debut, an upheaval that eventually resulted in the Reds' demise after just three seasons.

Great Britain and France played tour matches in Western Australia during the 1950s and 1960s, but the possibility of fielding a team in the premiership only gathered momentum when the NSWRL began staging first grade fixtures in Perth from 1989. After the famed W.A.C.A. cricket ground hosted a game in four straight seasons, a team from the state capital was accepted as an expansion club in November, 1992. The team was dubbed the Western Reds—after the state's native 'Great Red' kangaroo—and enlisted North Sydney lower grade mentor Peter Mulholland as its inaugural coach. Former Test firebrand Mark Geyer was the club's first high-profile recruit, and was later joined on the roster by foundation captain and Australian Test lock Brad Mackay, dual Dally M-winning fullback Michael Potter, Kiwi Test forward Brendon Tuuta and 1992 rookie of the year Matthew Rodwell, along with a host of emerging fringe first graders and mid-level players. Former All Black centre Craig Innes joined from Leeds mid-season.

The Reds debuted with a euphoric 28-16 defeat of St. George in front of 24,392 fans at the W.A.C.A., but were brought back to earth courtesy of a 54-14 thrashing at the hands of Newcastle a week later. The club was just four games into its existence when Super League turned the Rugby League world upside down, and the Reds quickly jumped onboard with the rebel organisation. But the move proved divisive—Mackay and Innes sided with the ARL, while CEO Gordon Allen resigned mid-season and was replaced by ex-Knights CEO Brad Mellen. The club's on-field performances were satisfactory, however, winning half of its 22 games in 1995 to finish 11th. The Reds remained in finals contention until the penultimate round of the regular season.

But 1996 was a disaster for the club, despite recruiting Queensland Origin fullback Julian O'Neill from Brisbane and future Test forward Robbie Kearns from Cronulla. Supporter discontent with the direction the club was headed under Super League saw crowd support dwindle, while on the paddock the Reds mustered just one win in the opening 12 rounds. Although they broke a 10-match losing streak with an 11-8 boilover against eventual premiers Manly and recorded five wins and a draw in the remaining 10 weeks of the competition, the Reds finished a dismal 16th. Mulholland was shown the door (he joined the UK Super League's French club Paris St. Germain) and replaced by ex-Raiders captain Dean Lance for the 1997 Super League season, while the Reds were mired in an extremely difficult financial position.

Renamed the Perth Reds, the club yielded just seven wins in 18 games to finish eighth of 10 teams in the Super League premiership, while it was the worst-performed Australian club in the ill-fated World Club Challenge. There were some individual highlights in 1997; Julian O'Neill and Rodney Howe represented the Super League Australia Test side, and Scott Wilson turned out for NSW's Tri-Series side, but the tempestuous O'Neill was cut loose by the Reds midway through the year for disciplinary breaches. The reunification of the game under the NRL banner sounded the death knell for Perth—neither the ARL nor Super League were willing to shoulder the club's crippling debt and the Reds folded less than two weeks after the Super League Grand Final. Along with several ex-Hunter Mariners (who also folded at the end of 1997), a number of Reds players (most notably Kearns, Howe and Matt Geyer) formed the nucleus of the fledgling Melbourne Storm in 1998. The NRL's recent push for expansion has revived the possibility of a Perth-based team in the premiership, with a bid from Western Australia strongly favoured to get the nod for a 2015 entry.

HUNTER MARINERS (1997) Super League's desire to base a team in the Rugby League stronghold of Newcastle after the Knights sided with the Australian Rugby League in 1995 led to the formation of the Hunter Mariners. The Super League franchise licence was initially accepted by the affluent Newcastle Wests Leagues Club, but the club pulled out just months later after a hostile response from its largely pro-ARL supporter base. News Limited effectively assumed the financial responsibility of running the Mariners.

In a cruel irony, Justice Burchett's court ruling in February 1996, preventing the Super League competition from commencing, came on the same day as the Hunter Mariners' season launch. It would be another 12 months before the fledgling club played its first official match. The Mariners' nucleus—on and off the field—was formed by recruiting players and officials from the Knights. Football manager Robert Finch was the first to come on board, assuming the same role with the Mariners.

Several former Knights stars joined Hunter, including ex-Test prop Mark Sargent (although he retired from playing before the Mariners took the field and moved into an administration role), former NSW hooker Robbie McCormack, outstanding young fullback Robbie Ross (who spent 1996 with the Broncos after the court ruling delayed the Mariners' debut), former Australian international Brad Godden, underrated backrower Paul Marquet and winger Keith Beauchamp. Fringe first graders Brett Kimmorley, Richard Swain, Tim Maddison and John Carlaw—all members of the Knights' 1995 reserve grade Grand Final-winning side—also linked with the Mariners in search of an opportunity.

Former Illawarra mentor Graham Murray was recruited as the club's coach, while the squad was bolstered by New Zealand Test brothers Kevin and Tony Iro; promising Canterbury five-eighth Scott Hill; halfback Noel Goldthorpe, prop Troy Stone and winger Nick Zisti from St. George's 1996 Grand Final side; and highly rated Steelers backrower Neil Piccinelli.

With Tony Iro, Goldthorpe, McCormack and Stone sharing the captaincy, the Mariners lost five of their first six games in the 1997 Super League season before staging a mid-season revival. Hunter recorded six wins in eight matches, including consecutive victories over heavyweights Brisbane and Canberra. The Mariners' stunning 24-6 upset of a full-strength Broncos side lifted hopes of a finals appearance, but four straight losses to end the regular season saw the first-year club come up two wins short. Hunter was a tough proposition at Topper Stadium (sharing the facility with soccer club the Newcastle Breakers), winning seven of nine matches at home, but remained winless on the road.

The Mariners' travel blues did not extend to the World Club Challenge, however, defeating Paris-St. Germain, Castleford and Sheffield on their Northern Hemisphere leg of the tournament. Hunter won all three return clashes in Newcastle against its European rivals to top the pool of lower seeded Australian sides, before winning through to the final with a quarter-final upset of English powerhouse Wigan and a semi-final defeat of premiership Grand finalists Cronulla by identical 22-18 scorelines. But Brisbane proved too powerful in the final, subduing the Mariners 36-12.

The club faced widespread hostility from Knights- and ARL-loyal members of the Newcastle community, which was reflected by average home crowds of 5,413 during the Super League premiership. But the Mariners were resilient and arguably exceeded expectations in 1997.

Noel Goldthorpe and Robbie Ross represented New South Wales during the Super League Tri-Series, with Goldthorpe kicking a 104th-minute golden point field goal to clinch victory over Queensland in an epic final. But he was ousted for the Mariners' halfback spot in the second half of the season by burgeoning star Brett Kimmorley, who became the club's only Super League Australian Test player. Tony and Kevin Iro, and Tyran Smith—a mid-season recruit from North Queensland—represented the New Zealand Test side.

The reconciliation between Super League and the ARL that resulted in the establishment of the National Rugby League spelt the end of the Hunter Mariners at the end of 1997—the impending 20-team NRL competition could not accommodate two teams based in Newcastle. A proposed merger with the Gold Coast Chargers fell down when the Gold Coast club opted to go it alone (before folding 12 months later), officially bringing down the axe on the Mariners. The fledgling Melbourne Storm benefitted substantially from the Mariners' demise—Kimmorley, Ross, Hill, Swain and Marquet were integral to the Victorian club's early success.

ST. GEORGE (1921-98) Second only to South Sydney as the most successful club in Australian Rugby League history, the St. George Dragons and their famous 'Red-V' jumper is synonymous with pride and power, and its record 11 consecutive first grade premiership from 1956 to 1966 provides a unattainable yardstick for which every great side must be compared. St. George's 78-season occupancy in the premiership ended in its original form at the end of 1998, when the club entered into a joint venture with Illawarra as part of the National Rugby League's rationalisation program in the wake of the Super League split.

The St. George district in southern Sydney encompasses the suburbs of Kogarah, Hurstville, Rockdale and Arncliffe, and the area was granted a first grade team in the NSWRL premiership in 1921. Illustrious dual international and Test centre Herb Gilbert was recruited as captain-coach for the club's maiden season. Saints finished second-last with just two wins in 1921, but provided Albert 'Ricketty' Johnston and local junior George Carstairs to the Kangaroo Tour squad at the end of the year. The club's formative years were a hard slog, finishing no higher than fifth and yielding two wooden spoons in its first six seasons.

The arrival of Glebe legend and all time great forward Frank Burge as captain-coach in 1927 heralded St. George's first fruitful period. Featuring internationals Arthur 'Snowy' Justice, Percy Fairall and Harry 'Mick' Kadwell, St. George qualified for the finals in five straight seasons, finishing runners-up in 1927 and 1930. The club claimed its first minor premiership in 1928, but was bundled out of the finals courtesy of a loss to third-placed Souths in the semi-final. The 1928 season was also highlighted by the infamous 'Earl Park Riot' after a game between St. George and Balmain at the Dragons' home ground (see Bizarre Matches).

Saints garnered two more second-placed finishes in 1933 and 1937, before free-falling to last in 1938. Despite missing the finals in 1935, the Dragons demolished first-year club Canterbury 91-6 at Earl Park—setting premiership records for most points in a match and biggest winning margin that still stand.

St. George's 21st season reaped the club's maiden premiership. After finishing the regular season in fourth, the Dragons—captain-coached by Neville Smith, a Queensland and New South Wales representative forward—overwhelmed Balmain 32-8 in the semi-final and Eastern Suburbs 31-14 in the final. The history-making line-up included Herb Gilbert Jnr., future club president Len Kelly and 1948-49 Kangaroo Bill Tyquin. St. George remained a force throughout the 1940s, narrowly losing Grand Finals in 1942 and 1946 to Canterbury and Balmain respectively. The Lindwall brothers, tryscoring freak Jack and fullback Ray, who later took 228 Test wickets as one of Australian cricket's greatest fast bowlers, starred for the Dragons during their seasons of near misses.

But an influx of backline talent later in the decade propelled Saints to their second premiership in 1949. Captained by Test five-eighth Johnny Hawke, St. George boasted international backs Doug McRitchie, Matt McCoy, Noel Pidding and future Ashes hero Ron Roberts. Complimented by Test prop Jack 'Dutchy' Holland and tough hooker Frank Facer (whose greatest contribution to the club came later as an administrator), the Dragons defeated minor premiers Souths 19-12 in the Grand Final.

St. George was among the competition's front-runners during the early-1950s, going down to the Rabbitohs in the 1953 premiership final. But with Facer pulling the strings as club secretary, and players such as Ken Kearney and Norm Provan leading the charge on the field, the Dragons were on the verge of a dynasty that would dwarf every other club achievement in Australian Rugby League history and rank as one of the finest accomplishments in world sport. St. George won 11 consecutive Grand Finals from 1956 to 1966, shattering Souths' previous record of five premierships in a row (1925-29). The Dragons also won 10 minor premierships, 10 club championships, went through the 1959 season undefeated and won Grand Finals in all three grades in 1963.

A team built around unprecedented defensive ruthlessness coupled with dazzling attack, St. George's astute recruitment and fostering of junior talent allowed the club to field an unbeatable line-up for over a decade. John Raper and Brian Clay were lured from rivals Newtown; Harry Bath returned to Australia with the Dragons after a revered career in England; Eddie Lumsden, Johnny King and Ian Walsh came to the club from country NSW centres; Elton Rasmussen and former Wallaby Kevin Ryan arrived from Queensland; and Graeme Langlands joined from Wollongong. Local juniors Reg Gasnier and Billy Smith are two of the club's most famous names, while halfback Bobby Bugden was brought to the club as a teenager from Murwillumbah.

St. George's phenomenal reign was halted in 1967, losing consecutive finals clashes with Souths and Canterbury after winning another minor premiership. But the Dragons remained a force under the captaincy of future Immortals Raper and Langlands. 'Changa' Langlands skippered Saints to a gallant 16-10 loss to Souths in the 1971 decider (with Jack Gibson as coach), before the club's premiership record streak of 23 consecutive seasons qualifying for the finals was broken in 1974. Captain-coach Langlands led the Dragons to another decider in 1975, but in what became known as the 'white boots' Grand Final (Langlands wore conspicuous white boots in the match, while a painkilling injection to his leg at halftime rendered the skipper virtually a passenger for the remainder of the match), Saints were decimated by Eastern Suburbs to the tune of 38-0.

Langlands retired early in 1976, but the return of Harry Bath as coach of the club a year later heralded another golden period. Captained by hooker Steve Edge and featuring brilliant former Test star Ted Goodwin at fullback, and future Kangaroo forwards Rod Reddy and Craig Young, the Dragons participated in the first drawn Grand Final against Parramatta in 1977. The match remained 9-all after 20 minutes of extra-time, but Bath's youthful, rugged side blitzed the Eels 22-0 in the replay a week later. 'Bath's Babes' won another title in 1979, with Young installed as captain, and Test halfback Steve Morris and future international backrower Graeme Wynn in their first seasons with the club. The Dragons outlasted Canterbury 17-13 in the Grand Final.

Roy Masters arrived as coach in 1982 and took the club agonisingly close to another premiership, with representative stars Michael O'Connor and Pat Jarvis complimenting the experience of Young and Morris. After a last-gasp defeat to Parramatta in the 1984 preliminary final, the minor premiership-winning Dragons were eclipsed 7-6 by the Bulldogs in the 1985 Grand Final. But St. George sank to also-ran status almost instantaneously, languishing in a six-season finals hiatus that encompassed short-lived coaching stints by Ted Glossop and Craig Young.

Brian Smith assumed the reins in 1991 and guided the Dragons to consecutive Grand Finals in 1992-93. Kangaroo forward Brad Mackay and Queensland Origin centre Mark Coyne combined with representative forwards Scott Gourley and David Barnhill, and experienced campaigners Michael Beattie and Michael Potter, but both deciders ended in demoralising defeat to Brisbane. Forced into a rebuilding phase after a dismal 1994 season and the departures of Mackay and coach Smith, the ARL-loyal Dragons rose from oblivion to qualify for the 1996 Grand Final. Driven by brilliant youngsters Anthony Mundine and Nathan Brown, the Mark Coyne-led Saints embarked on a memorable finals charge from seventh spot, but were humbled 20-8 by Manly in the decider. Former Test winger and Newcastle mentor David Waite had been rushed into the coaching hot-seat after the Super League defection of Rod Reddy, making the Dragons' 1996 achievements all the more remarkable.

After inexplicably missing the finals in the 12-team ARL competition in 1997, St. George's last season as a stand-alone entity ended with elimination from the first week of the inaugural NRL finals series at the hands of Canterbury in 1998. With strong connections to the Illawarra region—geographically and spiritually—St. George merged with the financially embattled Illawarra Steelers, becoming the premiership's first joint venture club in 1999. St. George was very much the senior partner in the St. George Illawarra Dragons from the outset, but it proved to be a smooth and successful transition, with both clubs retaining a strong identity in the premiership.

(see also Never Before, Never Again)

ILLAWARRA (1982-98) The Illawarra region is one of Australia's most prodigious Rugby League nurseries. Located south of Sydney and based around the industrial cities of Wollongong and Port Kembla, the area has produced Immortals Bob Fulton and Graeme Langlands, and revered internationals Kevin Schubert, Peter Dimond, Harry Wells, Michael Cronin, Craig Young, Steve Roach and Garry Jack. As part of the NSWRL's shift towards decentralisation during the 1980s, Illawarra and Canberra became the first premiership sides to be situated outside the Sydney metropolitan area in 1982. But the Steelers, so nicknamed after the steelworks that were the lifeblood of the region (and a lucrative sponsorship deal with BHP Steel), struggled for on-field success during their first decade. Under the tutelage of quality coaches Allan Fitzgibbon, Brian Smith and Terry Fearnley, and with representative players John Dorahy, Barry Jensen, Brian Hetherington and Alan McIndoe (the Steelers' first Australian representative) on its books, Illawarra remained a working-class side that struggled to achieve consistent results. After winning half of their games to finish two points adrift of the 1984 finals, the Steelers picked up consecutive wooden spoons in 1985-86.

The young club basked in a rare moment in the spotlight in 1989 when it progressed to the final of the midweek Panasonic Cup. Aided by short-term British imports Andy Gregory and Steve Hampson, Illawarra came within an ace of upsetting the star-studded Brisbane Broncos, eventually succumbing 22-20 in one of the most famous knockout competition matches in the game's history. But the reality for the Ron Hilditch-coached club was another Winfield Cup wooden spoon, netting just two wins while fellow '82 entrants the Raiders collected their first premiership.

The 1990s heralded a change, however, evolving from whipping boys to contenders on the back of a clutch of outstanding local talent. Robust goalkicking winger Rod Wishart, arguably the greatest player in the club's history, made his Origin debut in 1990 and broke into the Test side a year later. Dynamic centre Paul McGregor and scheming halfback John Simon joined Wishart in the NSW side in

1992—a watershed season for the Steelers under the coaching of Graham Murray. With talented youngsters Brett Rodwell, Neil Piccinelli, Ian Russell, John Cross and captain Dean Schifilliti complementing the aforementioned representative trio, and McIndoe providing the experience factor, Illawarra qualified for its maiden finals series. The Steelers finished the regular season in third place and stunned 'big brother' St. George 18-16 in their finals debut, before going down to Brisbane and the Dragons in consecutive weeks to miss out on a historic Grand Final berth.

Despite one-season stints from Test lock Bob Lindner in 1993 and former international Andrew Farrar in 1994, the Steelers narrowly missed the finals in the ensuing two seasons. Wishart and McGregor became the club's first Kangaroo tourists at the end of 1994, but 1995 was dominated by the Super League upheaval. After aligning with the ARL, the Steelers sacked coach Murray for meeting with Super League officials, and foundation mentor Allan Fitzgibbon took over the reins for the remainder of the season. Former Test fullback and Illawarra product Allan McMahon steered the club to another mid-table finish in 1996 and was replaced by Farrar the following season despite having two years to run on his contract. After finishing sixth in 1997's ARL-run Optus Cup, the Steelers were rolled by finals debutants Gold Coast in the minor qualifying final. Despite remaining competitive in the inaugural NRL season with young stars Trent Barrett, Craig Fitzgibbon and Luke Patten emerging, it became clear the club was going to struggle to survive financially as the NRL made moves towards scaling the number of teams in the premiership back to 14. The announcement that BHP would be terminating its long-running sponsorship deal with the Steelers ramped up the club's need to find a merger partner.

The Steelers were in contention for the finals until the final round of the NRL in 1998, but less than a month later they became part of Australian Rugby League's first joint venture when they helped form the St. George Illawarra Dragons. While the Steelers have been the junior partner in the merger, Illawarra has maintained a prominent identity. The Dragons play half of their matches at the Steelers' former home WIN Stadium in Wollongong, wearing predominantly red jumpers reminiscent of the Illawarra strip in matches at the ground. Illawarra has also supplied quality playing talent to the partnership, with Dragons Australian representatives Shaun Timmins, Trent Barrett, Jason Ryles, Luke Bailey, Matt Cooper, Ben Creagh, Ben Hornby, Dean Young and Brett Morris progressing through the region's junior ranks. Cooper, Creagh, Young and Morris featured in St. George Illawarra's breakthrough premiership in 2010 under Hornby's captaincy.

GOLD COAST (1988-98) The Gold Coast club had the makings of a successful Rugby League venture, but its 11-season premiership existence was a sorry tale of dreadful results on the paddock and off-field incompetence. The 'Internationals Syndicate,' which included former Australian Test representatives John Sattler, Peter Gallagher and Bob Hagan, was awarded the franchise to be based on the holiday strip, one of Australia's fastest-growing regions. Kangaroos legends Bob McCarthy (coach), Graeme Langlands (manager) and Ken Irvine (sprint coach) came on board for the Gold Coast-Tweed Giants maiden 1988 season.

The club's highest-profile signing was explosive Manly forward 'Rambo' Ron Gibbs, who was joined by veteran former Australian and Queensland centre Chris

Close, NSW representatives Neil Hunt and Tony Rampling, Penrith three-quarter Ben Gonzales, and pointscoring utility-back Mike Eden, a Rothmans medallist with Easts in 1983. Former Canterbury premiership-winning hooker Billy Johnstone was the club's inaugural captain. But the Giants struggled from the outset, finally recording their first win in round 10 of 1988—a euphoric 25-22 defeat of star-studded fellow debutants Brisbane—and finishing the year in 15th of 16 teams with just four victories and two draws. Seagulls Leagues Club purchased the Giants at the end of the year, while expectations soared with the signing of Test lock Bob Lindner, who became the club's first Origin representative when he turned out for Queensland during the 1989 series.

Although Lindner's solitary season with Gold Coast was disappointing (injury restricted him to 10 games), the Giants won seven and drew one of their 22 games to climb to a 13th-place finish. Prop Phil Daley, a 1986 Kangaroo, and former Queensland Origin centre Brett French linked with the club—rebranded as the Gold Coast Seagulls—for the 1990 season. But McCarthy was axed after another second-last finish and replaced by reserve grade mentor Malcolm Clift, who coached Canterbury to the 1974 Grand Final, for 1991.

Wally Lewis, arguably Queensland's greatest player, joined Gold Coast in 1991 after an acrimonious split with the Broncos. 'The King' led Queensland to series victory in his final year of Origin football and reclaimed his Australian spot for the first Test against New Zealand (before being dropped after the Kiwis' shock win), but the Seagulls won just two games and lost 13 straight to end the season, consequently collecting their first wooden spoon. Lewis took on the dual responsibility of captain-coach in 1992 (he remains the last player to captain-coach a first grade side) and his squad was bolstered by the arrival of Kangaroo backline star Dale Shearer, Kiwi Test prop Brent Todd, and Queensland Origin forwards Steve Jackson and Mike McLean. Gold Coast won six games in an improved campaign— including a 12-8 victory over defending premiers Penrith in the legendary Lewis' final match—but the Seagulls had two points stripped for fielding an illegal replacement in an early-season defeat of Illawarra, ultimately consigning the club to another wooden spoon (see Points Docked).

Remaining as the Seagulls' non-playing coach in 1993 and taking the coaching reins of the Queensland Origin side, Lewis endured a torrid season that garnered just one win and frequently found himself at odds with the club's board. Gold Coast consequently became the first club since Parramatta—wooden spooners from 1956-61—to finish last in three straight seasons. Struggling financially, the Seagulls appointed former Kangaroo forward and Canberra and Australian Test coach Don Furner to an administrator role late in 1993. Furner eventually assumed the chief executive position at the club. In personal highlights of a dismal year, Shearer represented Australia in the last of his 21 Tests, while he represented Queensland alongside Seagulls teammates Jackson and McLean.

Lewis parted company with the Seagulls at the end of 1993, while representative props Todd and Jackson retired. Former NSW, Manly and Easts prop John Harvey took over as coach and the club recruited veteran South Sydney halfback Craig Coleman. Despite finishing 15th, Gold Coast's 1994 season was a marked improvement, defeating defending champs Brisbane 25-12 (with Coleman and wily former St. George lock Peter Gill starring) and eventual premiers Canberra

8-4 among five wins for the season. Centre Adrian Vowles represented Queensland during the 1994 Origin series.

The premiership's expansion to 20 teams in 1995 decimated the Gold Coast's playing stocks—a host of Seagulls joined expansion clubs North Queensland (including Vowles) and South Queensland (most notably Terry Cook and then-appearance record holder Brett Horsnell), while promising goalkicking backrower/hooker Wayne Bartrim was snapped up by St. George. With 32-year-old skipper Coleman playing every match for the second straight season, the Seagulls performed creditably to finish 17th, while 18-year-old rookie Ben Ikin became the youngest-ever State of Origin player when he was selected for the Super League-depleted Maroons (before signing with Norths at the end of the year).

Eccentric businessman Jeff Muller purchased a controlling interest in the club and renamed it the Gold Coast Gladiators, but his overzealous interference in the running of football operations led to swift resignations from newly appointed first grade coach Graham Eadie, reserve grade coach Eric Grothe and CEO Mike Eden. Muller was eventually ousted by the ARL and the embattled Gold Coast club eventually took the field in 1996 as the Chargers.

Ironically, the off-field debacle heralded the club's most successful period. Phil Economidis was installed as coach and Kiwi Test utility back Dave Watson came on board as captain, while the modest roster was boosted by the acquisition of former Test prop Martin Bella. After an 18th-place finish in 1996, the Chargers qualified for the seven-team finals series in the 1997 ARL premiership with a club record 10 wins. Skippered by former Test three-quarter Graham Mackay, Gold Coast upset Illawarra 25-14 in its finals debut, before Sydney City ended the Chargers' run 32-10 a week later.

Outstanding hooker Jamie Goddard and backrower Jeremy Schloss were chosen to debut for Queensland, while Papua New Guinean pair, blockbusting winger Marcus Bai and five-eighth Thomas O'Reilly, represented Rest of the World in the Test against Australia. Economidis was a deserving winner of the ARL's Coach of the Year award, and other exceptional contributors included pint-sized livewire halfback Wes Patten, fullback Andrew King, goalkicking forward Brendan Hurst and his second-row partner Scott Sattler.

The Chargers rejected Super League club Hunter Mariners' merger bid, which would have brought Brett Kimmorley and Scott Hill among others to the proposed Gold Coast-based joint venture, opting to forge ahead into the inaugural NRL season alone. Gold Coast won just four games in 1998 and suffered a club record 62-6 loss to fledgling club Melbourne (featuring Kimmorley, Hill and former Chargers winger Bai) to finish 19th, ahead of wooden spooners Western Suburbs on for-and-against. After a disastrous season on the field and facing a bleak financial future off it, the club folded in December 1998. Gold Coast Rugby League supporters had eight years to wait before the advent of the Titans.

ADELAIDE (1997-98) Adelaide was part of the fledgling Super League competition's bold expansion focus, but the Rams suffered a premature death after just one season of the game's reunification under the NRL banner. Buoyed by local support of Winfield Cup matches staged in Adelaide during the early-1990s, the South Australian Rugby League aligned with the Super League movement.

The Adelaide Rams became the 10th and final club to be included in the rebel competition late in 1995. A court ruling against Super League prevented the breakaway competition from commencing in 1996, but the setback provided the Rams with an extra year to prepare for their shot at the big time. The Rugby League outpost attracted former Brisbane and Australian Test hooker Kerrod Walters, who was later installed as the club's first captain, and established first grade players Rod Maybon, Dean Schifillitti, Alan Cann and Kevin Campion, along with Papua New Guinea representatives Elias Paiyo and Bruce Mamando. Former St. George and Kangaroo firebrand backrower Rod Reddy was secured as Adelaide's first coach after initially being signed as Brian Smith's replacement at St. George for 1996.

The Rams performed admirably in their debut season in light of their isolation and modest playing roster. Adelaide's six wins and a draw from 18 matches—including a win over Grand finalists Cronulla and a final-round smashing of fifth-placed Penrith—was enough to stave off the wooden spoon. The Rams also won all three home matches against their British opponents in the World Club Challenge by handsome margins. Average crowds of over 15,000 at hallowed cricket venue Adelaide Oval helped the Rams survive the cull for the inaugural National Rugby League premiership.

But Adelaide endured a disastrous start to 1998. Reddy was dumped as coach after the Rams' return of one win in the opening nine rounds; he was replaced by former Canberra stalwart and Perth's 1997 coach Dean Lance. The Rams improved markedly after Lance's arrival, posting six wins in the space of 10 matches—including a club record 52-0 mauling of Balmain—to eventually wind up 17th of 20 teams. The Rams were boosted by the arrival of Kiwi Test forward Tony Iro and scheming halfback Noel Goldthorpe, while the mid-season signing of troubled Canberra utility-back Graham Appo proved extremely fruitful. Appo inked his name all over the Rams' record books with a series of impressive tryscoring and pointscoring efforts.

The club moved from Adelaide Oval to Hindmarsh Stadium midway through the year (and played one match in the Eyre Peninsula seaport city of Whyalla), but crowd numbers dropped to half of 1997's average. The NRL's pledge to cut the competition to 14 teams by 2000 under its rationalisation program, along with dwindling crowd support and a poor financial position, rendered the Rams' demise inevitable and the club was excluded from the 1999 competition. Canterbury took home games against Melbourne to Adelaide in 2010 and '11, while the NRL's recent push for expansion rekindled talk of a team being based in the South Australian capital once again, although the region appears to be well down the pecking order.

BALMAIN (1908-99) Balmain possesses one of the most successful and colourful Rugby League club histories, garnered from an uninterrupted 92 seasons in the premiership, before the rationalisation of the game led to a merger with Western Suburbs at the end of 1999. The inner-city Sydney club was one of the founding members of the competition, forming just two weeks after Glebe purportedly became the first Australian Rugby League club. The black-and-golds won 11 first grade titles—only Souths and St. George have won more in the code's history. Their foremost home ground, Leichhardt Oval, is one of Rugby League's most treasured venues, and lives on as one of the Wests Tigers' three home grounds.

After winning its way through to the premiership final in the competition's second season, 1909, Balmain forfeited the premiership to Souths. The club was protesting against the curtain-raiser status of the final, which was to be played prior to a Kangaroos vs. Wallabies fixture *(see Bizarre Matches)*. 'The Watersiders,' so-called because of the club's working-class association with the Harbour City's wharves, had to wait until 1915 to collect their maiden title. But they broke the duck in emphatic fashion under captain-coach Bill Kelly, a New Zealand dual international and 1914 Australian Test centre, becoming the first side to go through a season undefeated and the first club to claim premierships in all three grades in the same season. The Balmain side of the World War I-era and beyond produced one of the great dynasties in Rugby League history, winning further first grade titles in 1916-17 and 1919-20— only Souths denied the club six straight premierships by interrupting the streak in 1918. A quartet of legendary figures of the code's early decades spearheaded Balmain's unprecedented success—Jimmy Craig, Arthur 'Pony' Holloway, Charles 'Chook' Fraser and Reg 'Whip' Latta. Balmain also boasted esteemed Test representatives, centre Jack 'Junker' Robinson, five-eighth Albert 'Ricketty' Johnston and forward Bob Craig, a multi-talented former Wallaby who also excelled at soccer and swimming.

After winning the premiership again in 1924, Balmain endured a barren period, qualifying for the finals just once in the ensuing 11 seasons—during which time the club bid adieu to Birchgrove Oval and officially opened Leichhardt Oval in 1934. The Tigers resurfaced as a force in 1936, finishing runners-up to the all-conquering Easts side. Captained by the great tryscoring winger Sid Goodwin and featuring a young Frank Hyde in the centres, the Tigers captured their seventh premiership three years later, thrashing archrivals Souths 33-4 in the final. Balmain was the dominant club of the 1940s, winning three Grand Finals (1944, 1946-47) and finishing runner-up twice (1945, 1948). Prominent players that donned the black-and-gold strip during this period included two more wing wizards in Arthur Patton and Bobby Lulham, and all time greats Harry Bath and Pat Devery, shortly before the pair took up big-money offers to dazzle the crowds of England.

The Tigers were one of the foremost challengers to the dominant St. George sides of the 1950s and 1960s, going down in three deciders during the Dragons' run of 11 straight Grand Final victories (1956, 1964 and 1966). Featuring at fullback in all three of those matches—and captaining the Tigers in the latter two—was Keith 'Golden Boots' Barnes. The pointscoring maestro and Kangaroo captain ranks as one of the game's finest custodians, and is rated by many as the greatest Tiger. Ironically, Barnes retired a season prior to Balmain pulling off arguably the biggest upset in Grand Final history. After qualifying for the 1969 decider with a last-minute preliminary final victory over Manly *(see Finals Magic)*, the Tigers were rated rank outsiders against defending champions Souths, but triumphed in an 11-2 boilover thanks largely to the spoiling, 'go-slow' tactics deployed by crafty first-season coach Leo Nosworthy. The side was captained by Peter Provan, brother of the Dragons' 10-time premiership-winner Norm, and relied heavily on the brilliance of English half David Bolton. Future Immortal Arthur Beetson debuted for Australia in 1966 from the Tigers, but missed out on the Grand Final upset three years later through suspension. Balmain also became the first club side to defeat the Great Britain Lions, upsetting the tourists 9-8 in 1966.

343

That was to be Balmain's last premiership success, however, and a lean era ensued. The Tigers made the finals just once during the 1970s, while they finished with the wooden spoon in 1974 (for the first time in 63 years) and 1981. But Balmain enjoyed a renaissance under former Test coach Frank Stanton during the 1980s, with a crop of young internationals lighting up the competition and turning the club's on-field fortunes around. Wayne Pearce toured with the 1982 Kangaroos, while Garry Jack, Ben Elias, Steve Roach and Paul Sironen ventured to England and France with the 1986 version. British prodigy Garry Schofield starred in the Tigers' stirring 1985-87 finals drives, while Lions captain Ellery Hanley and Kiwi Test half Gary Freeman linked with the club the following season. The arrival of Warren Ryan as coach in 1988 honed a ruthless edge within the Balmain side, garnering a Grand Final berth on the back of a Hanley-inspired sudden-death charge (see Finals Magic). The Tigers' charmed run came to an end with a 24-12 defeat to Canterbury in the decider. Balmain lined up as favourites on Grand Final day a year later, but after leading Canberra 12-2 at halftime, the Tigers watched their lead evaporate and a try by Raiders winger John Ferguson with 90 seconds remaining forced the game into extra-time. The Raiders capitalised on their momentum and prevailed 19-14 after 100 minutes of what is generally regarded as the greatest Grand Final of them all.

Local hero Pearce retired after the Tigers bowed out of the 1990 finals, while former-Wallabies coach and radio personality Alan Jones succeeded Wests-bound Ryan. Jones' tenure was as controversial as it was fruitless, and the club's Grand Final side gradually disintegrated. Pearce, the prodigal son, was handed the coaching reins in 1994, but the toothless Tigers came last in skipper Ben Elias' farewell season. Balmain was battling financially and unable to attract quality players—brilliant fullback Tim Brasher was the club's only Australian international after 1994. The club was rebranded as the Sydney Tigers for the 1995-96 seasons, a marketing strategy designed to combat the changing demographics of the inner-city suburbs, before reverting to Balmain in 1997. Siding with the ARL during the Super League upheaval, and despite improved results on the field, the Tigers were on borrowed time as a stand-alone entity. After several clubs had been mooted as a potential merger partner, Balmain and fellow founding club Western Suburbs formed the Wests Tigers. The joint venture debuted in the 2000 NRL season. The two clubs shared working-class traditions and fanbases, while each was able to maintain a significant identity in the competition. Emerging from a trying initial few years, the Wests Tigers came from the clouds to snatch a memorable premiership in 2005, thus becoming the first joint venture to win the NRL title.

WESTERN SUBURBS (1908-99) Although 90 years in the premiership netted just four first grade titles—the last of them 47 seasons before its eventual merger with Balmain—Western Suburbs can lay claim to one of Rugby League's most intriguing club histories. Representing the tough, working-class district of Sydney's west, the club's narrative is equally rugged, while many of the game's luminaries have donned the black-and-white jersey. The foundation club was formed primarily by a group of disgruntled members of the Ashfield Rugby Union Club. Western Suburbs was caned 24-0 by Balmain in its first premiership match in 1908, a precursor to collecting the inaugural wooden spoon. Known as the Fruitpickers in the early years due to the abundance of orchards in the district, the club placed last in five of the following six seasons, but eventually climbed up the ladder, finishing as runners-up in 1918. 'Tedda' Courtney was a revered figure during Wests' formative years, joining from Norths and touring with the 1911-12 Kangaroos, while champion centre Herb Gilbert became the club's first Test captain in 1920. Courtney finally retired in 1924 at the age of 39, after a then-club record 161 games.

The arrival of the legendary Jim Craig as captain-coach in 1929 provided the impetus for Wests to break its premiership duck. Snaring the 1930 minor premiership, Wests recovered from a major semi-final loss to St. George to beat the same club 27-2 in the code's first official Grand Final. Another Grand Final appearance in 1932 (a 19-12 loss to Souths) was followed by the wooden spoon a season later, largely owing to the club's five-strong contingent that departed with the Kangaroos during the season. Wests' mercurial fullback Frank McMillan was chosen to captain-coach the 1933-34 Kangaroos squad, which also included the Magpies' incomparable five-eighth Vic Hey and powerhouse winger Alan Ridley. With its stars back onboard in 1934, Wests claimed its second premiership with a 15-12 final defeat of Easts, a club on the verge of a dynasty. McMillan's expert leadership and revolutionary fullback play established him of one of the club's greatest-ever players. He retired in 1935, while Hey departed for Toowoomba.

The Magpies produced their second Kangaroo Tour captain when centre Col Maxwell was chosen as skipper of the 1948-49 squad, ahead of incumbent captain-coach Len Smith in one of the most controversial and bewildering selections in representative history. While an injury-hampered Maxwell led the Kangaroos through Britain and France, Wests claimed the 1948 minor premiership, and celebrated its third title with a tense 8-5 Grand Final win over the Tigers. In the early-1950s, Keith Holman and Frank Stanmore formed one of the great club halves combinations of all time. 'Yappy' Holman, a tenacious competitor at halfback, became the first Western Suburbs player to appear in 200 first grade games, and played 35 Tests for Australia. Stanmore played 10 Tests at five-eighth in a five-season international career. The Magpies' fourth title came in 1952 (ironically, while the champion halves pairing was away with the 1952-53 Kangaroos), interrupting Souths' run of premierships courtesy of a 22-12 win over the Rabbitohs in the Grand Final. The victory was tainted by a highly contentious refereeing performance by George Bishop.

The Magpies became the first premiers to collect the wooden spoon the following season and spent two more seasons near the foot of the ladder. An aggressive recruitment drive during the middle stages of the decade captured the services of a host of Test players—which saw Wests dubbed 'The Millionaires'—and heralded one of the club's finest eras. The Magpies reached the Grand Final in 1958 and 1961-63, but finished on the wrong side of the ledger each time to the unstoppable St. George machine. Queenslanders Noel Kelly and Kel O'Shea, Dapto winger Peter Dimond and former Wallaby half Arthur Summons headlined the Magpies' outstanding imports during this period. Summons became the club's third Kangaroo skipper when he captain-coached the 1963-64 tourists.

A decade in the finals wilderness ensued for Wests following the 1963 Grand Final, before the club entered its famous/infamous 'Fibro' era. Spearheaded by Test halfback Tom Raudonikis, brilliant and brutal backrower Les Boyd, firebrand Australian Test forward John 'Dallas' Donnelly and talented fullback John Dorahy, the Magpies' sides of the late-1970s were equal parts tenacity, toughness, brutality and passion—with a liberal smattering of skill and flair thrown in for good measure. Raudonikis, in particular, embodied the club's fighting spirit, and turned out in a club record 201 first grade games. Arguably the dominant halfback of the 1970s, Raudonikis toured twice with the Kangaroos and made 29 Test appearances, including the 1973 Ashes-deciding third Test win as captain. Coach Roy Masters masterminded the siege mentality within Wests' squad shortly after his arrival in 1978—a method that yielded two preliminary final appearances in three seasons and inflamed a bitter rivalry with Manly's so-called 'Silvertails.'

Rival clubs later plundered the Magpies' playing ranks, with the nucleus of their side signing with big-spending Manly and Newtown. On-field results reflected the club's spiralling financial woes—the Magpies finished last in 1983 after qualifying for the previous season's finals, while their dire fiscal state saw them axed from the 1984 premiership by the NSWRL. But a court appeal resulted in Wests' reinstatement. Relocation to Campbelltown did little to stem the tide of wooden spoons, with the Magpies collecting another three last-place finishes before the end of the decade, but the acquisition of premiership-winning coach Warren Ryan and a clutch of his former Canterbury stars sparked a mini-revival in the early 1990s. Ex-Bulldogs David Gillespie, Paul Langmack, Andrew Farrar and Joe Thomas combined with Queensland Test backrower Bob Lindner and the rising talents of Jason Taylor and Jim Dymock to return the club to the finals in 1991 and '92 after a nine-year absence.

Prodigal son Raudonikis took over the coaching reins after Ryan's acrimonious departure late in 1994, and he steered the Langmack-skippered side to the 1996 finals, despite a distinct lack of star quality at his disposal. Aligning with the ARL during the game's split, the Magpies' fortunes faded after 1997. Woeful results and a worsening financial position dictated Western Suburbs was one of the favourites to be culled during the NRL's rationalisation of the game. The writing was on the wall, prompting Wests to launch a joint venture with Balmain after collecting consecutive wooden spoons in 1998-99. Although Tom Raudonikis lost out in the coaching stakes to Balmain mentor Wayne Pearce, and only seven Magpies turned out for Wests Tigers in 2000, the merger allowed the black-and-whites to retain an identity in the premiership. Wests Tigers won the 2005 NRL competition, with former Magpies Brett Hodgson and John Skandalis playing vital roles.

(see also From Millionaires to Fibros)

NORTH SYDNEY (1908-99) Despite boasting one of the great club sides of all time—the dual premiership-winning combination of 1921-22—North Sydney holds the dubious honour of the longest title drought in Australian Rugby League history. Norths failed to win another premiership before reluctantly merging with Manly at the end of 1999, while the club's history is a hapless narrative of missed opportunities and extended periods as the competition's whipping boys.

Situated in Sydney's North Shore, North Sydney was one of the eight foundation clubs to break away from rugby union and participate in the inaugural NSWRL premiership in 1908. Three members of the side that played in the club's first match (an 11-7 loss to South Sydney)—centre Jim Devereux, five-eighth Sid Deane and forward Denis 'Dinny' Lutge—went to England on the pioneering Kangaroo Tour at the end of the year, along with another Norths player, winger Andy Morton. Lutge was elected captain by the squad en route to England (but injury restricted him to just five games), Devereux was the top try-scorer on tour with 16, while Deane later captained Australia against England in 1914. Norths won six of its nine regular season games in 1908 to finish fourth, before losing the semi-final to Eastern Suburbs, 23-10. The club enjoyed little success during those pioneering years—Norths finished no higher than fifth in the ensuing 12 seasons, while it came last in 1915, 1917 and 1919.

Norths' fortunes transformed when the assembly of a team of extraordinary ability began in 1920. Brilliant winger Cec Blinkhorn returned to the club after a season at South Sydney, and he was joined by his Souths wing partner, the incomparable Harold Horder. Halfback genius Duncan Thompson, who played for Norths in 1916 before serving in World War I and making his Test debut from Ipswich in 1919, also rejoined the club in 1920. Coached by 1911-12 Kangaroos captain Chris McKivat, Norths swept to its first premiership in 1921 by going through a shortened regular season undefeated (outright minor premiers were declared champions between 1912 and 1925). Horder, Blinkhorn, Thompson, hooker Clarrie Ives, and centre pairing Herman Peters and Frank Rule were selected in the 1921-22 Kangaroo Tour squad, although Rule pulled out injured.

Playing its home games at North Sydney Oval—a venue equally admired for its quaint beauty and reviled for its concrete-like surface—the club secured back-to-back premierships in emphatic fashion. Norths finished the regular season tied at the top of the table with Glebe. The reigning premiers decimated the Dirty Reds 35-3 in the final at the Sydney Cricket Ground, with Rule, Blinkhorn and Horder bagging two tries apiece, while Horder landed seven goals.

But Norths' heavyweight status evaporated as quickly as it materialised. Horder and Blinkhorn returned to Souths at the end of 1923, while Thompson uprooted to Toowoomba following a controversial suspension handed down by the NSWRL for kicking during the same season, and the club quickly returned to the realm of the also-rans. Legendary internationals and subsequently revered coaches Frank Burge (1935) and Jimmy Craig (1936) guided North Sydney to consecutive finals appearances, with centre Arch Crippin, who played three Tests against Great Britain in 1936, and 1937-38 Kangaroo hooker Fred Nolan the club's standout players. But the reality was Norths finished the regular season no higher than fourth between 1926 and 1942, picking up another two wooden spoons along the way.

Former Newtown, Balmain and New South Wales centre Frank Hyde captain-coached Norths to its only Grand Final appearance in 1943. But in front of a then-record 60,992-strong SCG crowd, North Sydney was trounced 34-7 by the Frank Farrell-led Newtown side. The crushing defeat shattered the club's paper-thin confidence—after hovering mid-table over the next few seasons, Norths finished last in 1948 and 1950-51. Norths enjoyed a mini-revival with former Test centre Keith Middleton, Australian lock Peter Diversi and wonderful clubman hooker Norm Strong at the forefront, qualifying for the finals in three straight seasons (1952-54), but another Grand Final berth proved elusive. The brilliant, nomadic Brian Carlson joined Norths in 1957 and twice captained Australia against New Zealand during his six-year stay with the club. A mesmerising backline performer, Carlson toured with the 1959-60 Kangaroos, alongside clubmate Ken Irvine, who was just 19 at the time. Irvine became North Sydney's greatest player, and the most prolific try-scorer Australian Rugby League has ever known. He scored a premiership record

171 tries in 176 appearances for the Bears (he extended the mark to 212 after three seasons with Manly at the end of his career), and crossed for 33 tries in as many Test appearances for Australia, a mark which stood for 43 years until broken by Darren Lockyer in 2010. The elusive flyer's phenomenal strike-rate for Norths is made more remarkable by the club's lowly standing throughout most of his tenure.

Former St. George enforcer Billy Wilson and South African fullback Fred Griffiths arrived in 1963 and briefly turned the club's fortunes around. Griffiths captain-coached the Bears from 1963 to 1966 (topping the premiership's pointscoring charts in the first three seasons), guiding them to the finals in 1964 and 1965. Norths finished second on the ladder in the latter season, but lost the preliminary final to South Sydney, 14-9. Wilson became Norths' fourth (and Australia's oldest) Test captain in 1963. He assumed the position of non-playing coach in 1967, but came out of retirement to aid his injury-ravaged side, playing his last game at 40 years of age—a premiership record.

The late-1960s saw Norths return to the bottom half of the table, while Englishman Roy Francis' controversial coaching stint at the club (1969-70) encompassed the infamous 'walk-off' incident (see Bizarre Matches) and led to favourite son Irvine's departure to Manly at the end of the 1970 season. Aside from narrowly missing the 1974 finals, the Bears languished in the competition cellar throughout the 1970s, culminating in the club's last wooden spoon in 1979. Individual highlights came in the form of popular winger George Ambrum and clever five-eighth Tim Pickup debuting for Australia together against New Zealand in 1972. Former Manly coach Ron Willey steered the hapless Bears to the finals in 1982 (they were eliminated courtesy of consecutive defeats to the Sea Eagles and Easts), but was inexplicably shown the door by club secretary Ken McCaffery—a World Cup halfback while playing for Norths in 1957—for implementing a negative, 'defence-oriented' style of play. Inevitably, the Bears tumbled back down the ladder. Norths possessed some fine players, including 1982 Kangaroo tourist Don McKinnon (son of stalwart Norths prop of the 1930s and 1940s, and long-time club president Harry McKinnon), and Kiwi Test greats Mark Graham and Clayton Friend, but a fifth-place play-off loss in 1986 was the closest the Bears came to another finals appearance during the 1980s.

But the derision and long-running jokes at the club's expense subsided as the Bears established themselves as one of the premiership's powerhouses of the 1990s. The turnaround was built on the development of players such as club favourite Greg Florimo, who eventually broke Norm Strong's long-standing first grade appearances record; outstanding backrow trio David Fairleigh, Billy Moore and Gary Larson; scheming halfback and goalkicking maestro Jason Taylor; and dynamic fullback Matt Seers. The Bears qualified for the finals six times in eight seasons, but a drought-breaking premiership was tantalising out of reach Norths was eliminated at the preliminary final stage four times. Following an ill-fated attempt to relocate to the Central Coast—an area the club had strong traditional ties to—in 1999 that plunged the club into crippling debt, the Bears were left with no option but to form a merger with archrivals and North Shore neighbours Manly to retain an identity in the 2000 NRL competition. The Northern Eagles joint venture was doomed to failure and folded after just three seasons, with Norths' involvement having effectively ended a year earlier.

North Sydney continued to have a presence with teams in the now-defunct Premier League competition and as a current NSW Cup outfit, while NRL expansion hopeful the Central Coast Bears (with Florimo as chief executive and Fairleigh waiting in the wings to coach the proposed club) is effectively a Gosford-based reincarnation of the foundation club. The Bears still boast a massive supporter base, ever-hopeful for the return of the red and black jersey to the premiership scene.

(see also Heartbreak in Bears' Final Decade)

NORTHERN EAGLES (2000-02) The dismal failure of the Northern Eagles joint venture was one of the great disappointments of the NRL's rationalisation period. The peace achieved in forming a unified competition in 1998 dictated that there would be some bloodletting in the ensuing seasons, with the number of clubs to in the NRL to be cut to 14 by the 2000 season one of the criteria set down by the game's powerbrokers. Desperate to avoid the axe that claimed foundation club Souths, archrivals and neighbours North Sydney and Manly formed one of three mergers. It is the only one of the three not currently active in the NRL.

The Bears had banked their future on a move to the NSW Central Coast in 1999 to meet the NRL's dreaded performance criteria, but a failure to get the proposed new stadium at Gosford finished before the start of the season cruelled their season and placed Norths under even greater financial pressure. Despite the long and bitter rivalry between the two clubs, Manly agreed to amalgamate with North Sydney to form the Northern Eagles, with home games to be split between NorthPower Stadium at Gosford and the Sea Eagles' traditional home, Brookvale Oval.

The obvious problems of integrating the playing groups, administrations and boards of two headstrong clubs aside, the Eagles had a mouthwatering roster at their disposal for their inaugural 2000 season. Six Australian internationals (Geoff Toovey, Steve Menzies, Nik Kosef, Daniel Gartner, Adam Muir and Michael Buettner) and a further three Origin representatives (Jason Taylor, Jamie Goddard and Owen Cunningham) from Norths' and Manly's 1999 sides formed the basis of the new line-up. Manly coach and captain combination Peter Sharp and Geoff Toovey were installed in the roles for the fledgling joint venture club. But the talent did not transfer to results and the Northern Eagles could only muster nine wins in their debut season to finish 12th of 14 teams. The crowd figures for games in Gosford were a positive for the fledgling organisation, however, and the signing of gun halves Brett Kimmorley (Melbourne) and Ben Walker (Brisbane) provided the club with cause for optimism in 2001.

Although the Eagles' on-field performances improved in 2001, the club struggled for consistency, and a 10th-place finish was completely overshadowed by chaos behind the scenes. Financial problems and boardroom squabbling between North Sydney and Manly factions undermined the joint venture, which was officially dissolved late in the season after more funding was not forthcoming. Almost half of the playing staff deserted the Eagles—now effectively run by the Manly club—due to the uncertainty, including marquee signing Kimmorley. The undermanned Eagles were on course for an unlikely finals berth in 2002, but capitulated with a final-round 68-28 loss to Penrith to miss eighth spot by a single competition point.

All remnants of the disastrous merger were removed when the decision was made to revert to the name Manly-Warringah Sea Eagles and play exclusively out of Brookvale Oval from 2003. With the financial backing of property developer Max Delmege, astute coaching of Des Hasler and the emergence of several brilliant local juniors, Manly soon returned to premiership heavyweight status. The breakdown of the joint venture left North Sydney Bears fans without a club in the premiership for the first time since 1908, but hopeful of a return via a proposed team on the Central Coast that was pushing for admission to the NRL for 2015.

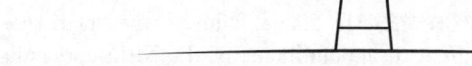

TEAM RIVALRIES AND LOCAL DERBIES

Few matches in Rugby League inflame the passions of players and supporters alike as much as a local derby or a clash between bitter rivals. The prospect of neighbourly bragging rights or a satisfying victory over an ardent enemy has produced countless memorable encounters and added an edge to every premiership season.

SOUTH SYDNEY vs. EASTERN SUBURBS / SYDNEY ROOSTERS

Only five kilometres separate Redfern and Bondi Junction, and the two Rugby League clubs that represent those distinctive locales have cultivated arguably the premiership's most keenly fought derby in a 103-year rivalry. The only two 1908 foundation clubs remaining in the NRL today, South Sydney and Eastern Suburbs contested the inaugural premiership final. Despite two tries by Easts winger Horrie Miller, Souths prevailed 14-12 to become Sydney's first premiers.

Easts defeated Souths 23-10 in the 1911 final to secure its first title on the back of a dominant performance by pioneering superstar Dally Messenger, who scored 20 of the Tricolours' points from two tries and seven goals. The rivals staged several high-powered classics as they established themselves as two of the most successful clubs of the competition's formative decades. Easts won an SCG final classic 15-12 in 1923, but Souths overwhelmed Easts in premiership deciders in 1928 and 1931 in the midst of a dynasty that yielded seven first grade titles in eight seasons.

Easts' nomination for the greatest club combination of all time—the phenomenal Dave Brown-led side of the mid-1930s—swamped Souths 19-3 in the 1935 final before winning the next two premierships in succession. Remarkably, despite periods of sustained dominance by both clubs since, the last finals clash between the Tricolours and the Rabbitohs was in 1938.

But the rivalry was no less fierce, and spiked in the early-1970s when the Roosters (along with Manly) pillaged the financially stricken Rabbitohs' playing stocks. Souths greats Ron Coote and Elwyn Walters, vital components of the club's last golden era that claimed four premierships in five seasons, both joined Eastern Suburbs and shared in the Roosters' 1974-75 premierships.

Despite the relative inconsistency of both sides, Souths dominated the rivalry during the 1980s, winning 15 of the 19 matches contested during the decade. But the Roosters' emergence as a competition heavyweight in the mid-1990s swung the rivalry pendulum their way, winning 13 consecutive derbies from 1995-2005—including a 62-0 demolition in 1996, a then-club record defeat for the Rabbitohs.

Souths broke the drought in a 17-16 thriller in the final round of 2005, and the arrival of Russell Crowe as club owner restored the rivalry to its position of arguably the most intense in the premiership. The clubs have faced off in the opening round of every NRL season since 2004, most notably in Rabbitohs' 52-12 drubbing of their most bitter opponent, featuring a Nathan Merritt hat-trick and Crowe's 'thumbs down' signal from the grandstand in reference to his move Gladiator.

In 203 derbies between the clubs to the end of 2011 (the most prolific head-to-head competition in premiership history), Souths won 106 to Easts/Sydney Roosters' 92, with five matches drawn.

SOUTH SYDNEY vs. ST. GEORGE / ST. GEORGE ILLAWARRA

Australian Rugby League's two most successful and famous clubs harbour an intense and eventful rivalry. South Sydney dominated 1921 premiership entrants St. George in the early years of competition between the sides, losing just four of the first 26 matches and overwhelming Saints in the premiership final in 1927, and semi-finals in 1928 and 1931. St. George exacted revenge in 1949, however, by knocking over minor premiers Souths in the semi-final and again in the Grand Final. The Dragons smashed the Rabbitohs 35-8 during the 1951 finals series but Souths still went on to claim the title, and thumped St. George 31-12 in the 1953 premiership final—the last before mandatory Grand Finals were introduced the following season. As the Dragons pieced together their record premiership-winning streak from 1956, they began to rule the rivalry with the Rabbitohs, winning 15 straight matches between the clubs from 1957 to 1964. A young, rejuvenated South Sydney outfit broke the drought by upsetting the nine-time premiers twice during the 1965 regular season, but St. George rebuffed the plucky Rabbitohs' challenge in the Grand Final, prevailing 12-8 in an epic decider played in front of a record Sydney Cricket Ground crowd.

Souths helped end Saints' world record 11-season Grand Final run in 1967 with a 13-8 semi-final victory over the minor premiers, before winning the decider against Canterbury, who eliminated the Dragons in the preliminary final. The Rabbitohs then despatched St. George in the 1968 preliminary final on the way to another title, and overcame the Dragons again in the 1971 Grand Final, 16-10, to claim their fourth premiership in five years. The Dragons ended Souths' premiership defence with a minor semi-final defeat in 1972, and halted the Rabbitohs' season at the same stage in 1980 and 1984, the latter season in a wild, brawling affair won 24-6 by St. George.

St. George dictated terms in the latter stages of the rivalry before its merger with Illawarra at the end of 1998—Souths emerged victorious just once over St. George during the 1990s. The Dragons finished the overall tally between the clubs with 92 wins to the Rabbitohs' 69, with two drawn. But Souths won the first clash with the St. George Illawarra joint venture, winning a thriller 25-24—fittingly, at the SCG. The clubs played three more matches at the hallowed venue from 2003-05, but the Rabbitohs could only boast four wins in their first 18 showdowns with the merged outfit. They produced victories to remember though, crushing the minor premiership-winning Dragons 41-6 in the penultimate round of 2009 and overhauling a 20-0 deficit to down the Saints, defending champs, 34-24 late in 2011.

South Sydney has played St. George or St. George Illawarra for the Charity Shield in every pre-season since 1982 (except the 2000-01 seasons, when the

Rabbitohs were excluded from the NRL). The Dragons have emerged victorious in 16 of the 29 matches, with Souths winning nine and four clashes ending in a draw. Interestingly, the Rabbitohs retained the Charity Shield after each of the four draws as the current holders.

ST. GEORGE vs. CRONULLA Southern Sydney clubs St. George and Cronulla forged one of the premiership's most fiercely contested local derbies. The Dragons, coming off 11 straight titles, immediately assumed the alpha male position in the neighbourly rivalry after the Sharks' 1967 promotion to the premiership (Cronulla previously fielded teams in the St. George district junior competitions). Saints won the first nine contests against the Sharks. The newcomers were captained by six-time St. George premiership-winning forward Monty Porter in their inaugural season, and coached by former Kangaroo hooker and Dragons great Ken Kearney in their first three seasons. Cronulla broke their duck in 1971, with a Dave Cotter hat-trick propelling the Sharks to a 19-15 upset of the eventual Grand Finalists. The Sharks rocketed to contender status two years later and made their finals debut with an 18-0 major preliminary semi shutout of the Dragons on their way to a Grand Final appearance. Two more St. George legends handled the Sharks' coaching reins during the 1970s; John Raper held the post in 1975-76, while Norm Provan guided the club to its second Grand Final appearance during his 1978-79 stint.

Cronulla won nine of 11 clashes with its Botany Bay-adjacent rivals between 1978 and 1983, and lost just two of the last eight derbies played before St. George's merger with Illawarra at the end of 1998 to close the gap established in the rivalry's early seasons. The ledger ended with St. George winning 31 and Cronulla 27 of 60 matches, with two drawn. But the intense competition continued to gather momentum following St. George Illawarra's 1999 debut. The minor premiership-winning Sharks defeated the star-studded Dragons twice during the regular season, but a brilliant three-try performance from Anthony Mundine spearheaded Saints' 24-8 preliminary final upset of Cronulla. The Sharks gained some retribution with a 40-24 victory over their archrivals at the semi-final stage in 2002, while the Dragons eliminated the team from Sutherland Shire with a hard-fought 28-22 qualifying final result in 2005. Cronulla held a one-win advantage over St. George Illawarra in 28 encounters at the end of 2011. Saints' WIN Jubilee Oval (formerly Kogarah Oval) and Cronulla's Toyota Stadium (originally known as Endeavour Field) are just 10 kilometres apart.

NORTH SYDNEY vs. MANLY With little more than 10 kilometres separating their respective home grounds, Sydney's North Shore clubs developed a bitter rivalry that was gradually dominated by Manly. The Bears and Sea Eagles eventually entered into an ill-conceived joint venture in 1999 that ultimately ended Norths' involvement in the premiership. North Sydney won the first two encounters between the neighbouring teams after Manly's 1947 inception, but Manly (who enlisted the services of Norths players such as future Test winger Johnny Bliss) quickly established itself as a premiership force, to the chagrin of long-suffering Norths. Norths thumped Manly 36-8 in a play-off for fourth place in 1952 and honours were relatively evenly shared during the 1950s and 1960s. The Sea Eagles won four premierships as the dominant team of the 1970s, claiming their maiden titles in 1972-73 after recruiting the Bears' legendary winger Ken Irvine in the twilight of his career.

The hapless Bears won just two of 20 games against their archrivals during the 1970s, while Manly prevailed 26-3 over Norths in the 1982 major preliminary semi-final—the Bears' first finals appearance in 17 years. Manly's subjugation of Norths was exacerbated by the Sea Eagles' poaching of several more high-profile players: star British import John Gray left Norths for Manly and the chance to play for a team in contention for a premiership, but suspension ruled him out of the Sea Eagles' 1978 Grand Final squad and he returned to the Bears in the early-1980s; stalwart Bears forward Bruce Walker also joined Manly in 1978, winning a Grand Final and a maiden Australia Test jumper in his first season at Brookvale; former Wallaby Mitchell Cox linked with the Sea Eagles after switching codes with Norths for four seasons; Cliff Lyons was brought to Sydney from the Riverina by Norths in 1985, but signed with Manly after just one season and became a Sea Eagles legend; and 1982 Kangaroo Don McKinnon—son of iconic Norths president Harry—joined Manly in 1988 after 183 games for the Bears.

With the Sea Eagles entrenched as the dominant partner of the rivalry, the dislike between the clubs intensified as Norths emerged as a title contender in the 1990s. Outspoken front-rower Martin Bella—who became a Test player while at Norths before defecting to Manly in 1990—famously remarked 'North Sydney is a very ordinary side—in fact a terrible side' in 1991. The Bears used the slur as motivation to upset Manly 28-16 in the major preliminary semi, the club's first finals win in 39 years. The clubs battled for North Harbour supremacy throughout the 1990s—Manly racked up twin 30-point thrashings in 1995, while the Bears reversed the trend with big wins in 1997 and '98. The Sea Eagles won the last encounter between the clubs, 28-22 in 1999. Manly won 64 of its 105 clashes against Norths, and the win ratio was exacerbated at Brookvale Oval; the Bears won just eight games at the Sea Eagles' fortress in 43 attempts.

The traditional enemies tentatively merged at the end of the year with the threat of expulsion from the rationalised NRL competition looming over stand-alone Sydney clubs. The Northern Eagles partnership was a disaster marked by back-room battles, financial struggles and poor on-field results. The Sea Eagles were effectively running the joint venture by 2002 and reverted to their original name the following season, while the Bears continue to push for readmission to the NRL with a proposed team on NSW's Central Coast.

CANTERBURY vs. PARRAMATTA The rivalry between the Bulldogs and Eels was fostered on a battle for premiership supremacy during the 1980s, and intensified by the events that transpired during the Super League war a decade later. The western Sydney foes did not meet in a finals match until 1975, when Parramatta eliminated Canterbury courtesy of a 6-5 minor preliminary semi victory. The Eels prevailed 22-15 in the corresponding match in 1978, but the Bulldogs rolled the blue-and-golds 20-14 in the following season's preliminary final.

Parramatta defeated Canterbury twice during the 1983 finals on its way to a third consecutive title; the Eels' 30-22 major preliminary semi win is best remembered for Eric Grothe's phenomenal individual try. Minor premiers Canterbury advanced to the Grand Final with a 16-8 major semi defeat of the Parramatta in 1984, and broke the Eels' premiership stranglehold with a tense 6-4 victory when the rivals met in the decider two weeks later. The Bulldogs crushed Parramatta 26-0 in the 1985 preliminary final en route to claiming back-to-back titles. Parramatta reversed the two-year trend the following season, hammering Canterbury 28-16 in the major semi and prevailing 4-2 as the Eels and Bulldogs played out the only try-less decider in Grand Final history. The Bulldogs equalled Parramatta as the most successful club of the 1980s with their fourth premiership of the decade in 1988—by which stage the Eels were at the beginning of a decade-long finals hiatus.

The Eels' slump reduced the intensity of their rivalry with the Bulldogs during the early-1990s, but the animosity soared to a crescendo when Super League hit in 1995. After initially signing with Super League—as their club had done—star Bulldogs quartet Jason Smith, Dean Pay, Jim Dymock and Jarrod McCracken reneged on their deals to link with the ARL and Parramatta. The Bulldogs stormed to a remarkable Grand Final victory at the end of the season (with Dymock winning the Clive Churchill Medal, alongside Smith and Pay), but the defections left the club severely depleted the following season, leading to veteran pivot Terry Lamb coming out of retirement. Canterbury outmuscled the Eels 22-4 in a 1996 grudge match, although only Kiwi centre McCracken turned out for Parramatta—Smith, Pay and Dymock were in Origin camp.

The Bulldogs staged a phenomenal comeback against the Eels in the 1998 preliminary final; down 18-2 with 11 minutes remaining, Canterbury rallied to a 32-20 extra-time victory in one of the great post-season matches. Two clubs with a passionate band of supporters, Parramatta vs. Canterbury encounters carry extra spice, which was never more evident than in the 2009 preliminary final showdown between the archenemies. The Eels triumphed 22-12 in another finals classic, played in front of 74,549 rabid fans—a premiership record crowd for a non-Grand Final. The overall tally between the two clubs stood at 68 wins to Canterbury and 57 to Parramatta with five drawn to the end of 2011.

PARRAMATTA vs. MANLY Parramatta and Manly entered the premiership together in 1947. While Manly took only a few seasons to become established as a force, playing in three Grand Finals in its first 13 seasons, the Eels languished near the bottom of the table and had collected nine wooden spoons by 1961. But as the Sea Eagles were dominating the 1970s, Parramatta finally arrived as a title contender and a ferocious club rivalry—built on a series of gripping and controversial matches—developed.

Results were evenly shared between the competition newcomers during the late-1940s, but Manly soon took control and won 22 of 25 matches against Parramatta between 1951 and 1963, and 17 of 20 between 1966 and 1975. The Eels defeated the Sea Eagles twice during the 1976 regular season and finished in second spot behind minor premiers Manly, before rolling their long-time tormentors again 23-17 in the major semi to advance through to their maiden Grand Final. The Sea Eagles regrouped to defy Parramatta 13-10 in a dramatic decider, collecting their third premiership in five seasons.

Minor premiers Parramatta fell agonisingly short of winning its first title in 1977, losing the Grand Final to St. George in a replay. In the 1978 finals against Manly, the Eels were on the wrong end of one of the most controversial refereeing performances in the game's history. Parramatta let a 10-point lead slip away in the minor semi showdown against Manly, and the combatants were forced into a replay after the scores were locked 13-all at fulltime. Notorious referee Greg Hartley sent Eels lock Ray Price and Sea Eagles hooker John Gray from the field in the replay, but several blatantly incorrect decisions conspired to propel Manly to a 17-11 victory. Sea Eagles halfback Steve Martin scored a try on the seventh tackle and Hartley allowed two other seven-tackle counts in favour of Manly, while the Eels were erroneously subjected to three short counts of five tackles. Parramatta's appeal to have the result annulled fell on deaf ears and Manly progressed to achieve an extraordinary premiership victory, winning the Grand Final against Cronulla in another replay.

The Eels vanquished their premiership hoodoo by defeating Newtown in the 1981 Grand Final, and Manly emerged as the biggest threat to the blue-and-golds' supremacy over the next two seasons. The Sea Eagles swamped minor premiers Parramatta 20-0 in the 1982 major semi, but the Eels turned the tables with a comfortable 21-8 victory in the Grand Final. Manly took out the minor premiership in 1983 and promptly advanced to the decider with a 19-10 major semi defeat of the Eels, before a carbon copy of the previous year's Grand Final unfolded—Parramatta cruised to an 18-6 win to claim a hat-trick of premierships.

Parramatta won another title in 1986, but the club's swift slide down the ladder in the latter part of the decade was encapsulated in a demoralising 64-12 defeat at the hands of rampant defending premiers Manly in 1988. Cliff Lyons and Dale Shearer each scored three tries, while Michael O'Connor amassed 24 points from a try and 10 goals in the shellacking. The Eels' status as minnows for much of the next decade saw their rivalry with perennial contenders Manly subside, but the club's resurgence in 1997 dredged up the long-held hostility.

Some of the most memorable grudge matches between the clubs in the last 15 years include: Parramatta's John Simon-inspired 17-10 defeat of runaway ARL competition leaders Manly in 1997; the Sea Eagles' 36-34 victory over the Eels in the inaugural golden point encounter in 2003; minor premiers Parramatta's 46-22 qualifying final elimination of eighth-placed Manly; the Sea Eagles building a 20-0 lead in an early-2010 clash with the Eels, only to be run down 24-20 on the back of a virtuoso display by Parramatta fullback Jarryd Hayne. Manly dominate the overall head to head between the two clubs with 78 wins to Parramatta's 44 and four drawn to the end of 2011—the Eels' second-worst winning percentage against all teams.

BRISBANE vs. GOLD COAST The battle of South East Queensland between the Brisbane Broncos and the Gold Coast Titans has developed into one of the NRL's most entertaining and close-fought derbies. Although the original incarnation of the Gold Coast club generally struggled against 'big brother' Brisbane, its two wins in 14 matches against the heavyweights rank among the most memorable wins in the minnow's 11-season existence. Both teams entered the NSWRL premiership in 1988—the Broncos won their first six games, while the Giants were winless in their opening nine matches. But Gold Coast pulled off a king-sized upset to claim its maiden win in first grade, knocking off the star-studded Broncos 25-22 at Seagulls Stadiuim in the inaugural derby. In 1994, three-time wooden spooners Gold Coast (at this stage known as the Seagulls) achieved arguably the finest victory in the club's history with a 25-12 boilover against two-time premiers Brisbane at Carrara Stadium. The matches attracted ground record crowds for the club's respective home venues.

The Chargers' demise at the end of 1998 put the Queensland derby on ice for almost a decade, but the advent of the Titans in 2007 provided the Broncos with a far more competitive rival neighbour. The Titans outmuscled the Broncos 28-16 in the first meeting between the clubs in 2007 and emerged victorious in a 26-24 classic early in 2008, while Darren Lockyer inspired Brisbane to thrilling golden point victories over Gold Coast in each season's return clash. The Titans made their finals debut in 2009 against the Broncos at Skilled Stadium, with Brisbane prevailing 40-32 in a 13-try epic. Derbies between the clubs drew average crowds of almost 42,000 at Suncorp Stadium and over 25,000 at Skilled Stadium during the Titans' first five seasons.

BRISBANE vs. NORTH QUEENSLAND Beating fellow Queenslanders the Broncos was seen as the Holy Grail for the struggling Cowboys in their formative seasons, but it took almost a decade for the Townsville-based club to topple the heavyweights. Brisbane was undefeated in its first 16 matches against North Queensland after the latter's 1995 premiership entry, piling on 50 or more points on four occasions and escaping with 20-all draws in Townsville in 1997 and 1999. But the Cowboys picked the perfect time to break their duck, shutting out the Broncos 10-0 in a gripping sudden-death semi-final in front of a sell-out Townsville crowd in 2004 (after the Broncos graciously proposed to move the showdown, originally scheduled for Sydney). The Sunshine State rivals met in the first round of the season at Suncorp in six of the ensuing seven seasons, staging several classic encounters. North Queensland carved out rousing wins in 2006 and '07, while Brisbane squeaked home in thrillers in 2009 and '10. Broncos skipper Darren Lockyer played his record-breaking 350th first grade match in a 34-16 defeat of the Cowboys at Dairy Farmers Stadium late in 2011. Brisbane still dominates the overall win tally, prevailing in 24 of 31 encounters with North Queensland.

BRISBANE vs. MELBOURNE The strong Broncos influence in the formation of the Storm ensured an intense rivalry from the Victorian club's 1998 inception. Brisbane's former Test centre Chris Johns was named as Melbourne's first chief executive, former Broncos and Super League CEO John Ribot was instrumental in setting up the franchise and all time great front-rower Glenn Lazarus left Brisbane to become foundation captain of the Storm. Brisbane prevailed 34-16 in the first meeting between the clubs in the second half of 1998, Melbourne's first loss by more than four points in an outstanding debut season, before eliminating the Storm during the finals 30-6.

The defending premiers crumbled to a club record 48-6 loss to Melbourne early in 1999. In 2005, the Storm became the first side to run 50 points past Brisbane in a match, racking up a stunning 50-4 scoreline to set a new biggest defeat record for the Broncos. Melbourne finished the regular season in sixth spot in 2004 and 2005, but produced qualifying final upsets of the third-placed Broncos at Suncorp Stadium in each season, 31-14 and 24-18 respectively.

Runaway minor premiers in 2006, the Storm entered their Grand Final showdown with Brisbane as strong favourites. But the wily Darren Lockyer-inspired Broncos nullified Melbourne's multi-faceted attacking arsenal to grind out a famous 15-8 victory. The hard-fought decider shifted the rivalry up another gear.

The Storm eliminated Brisbane from the finals in each of the next three seasons. Melbourne crushed an injury-ravaged Broncos outfit 40-0 at the qualifying final stage in 2007; Greg Inglis scored a last-minute try to snatch a drama-charged 16-14 semi-final victory at Suncorp Stadium in 2008 *(see Finals Magic)*; and the Storm despatched Brisbane 40-10 in a preliminary final showdown in 2009, with Inglis bagging a hat-trick.

Brisbane has recorded just four victories in its last 18 encounters with Melbourne to the end of 2011—a 28-15 win in 2005, the 2006 Grand Final, a 16-14 eclipse early in 2009 and a 36-14 boilover in the 2010 unveiling of the Storm's new home ground, AAMI Park. Melbourne leads the overall tally between the clubs with 18 wins to 11, with one match drawn—the only head-to-head ledger that the Broncos are on the negative side of.

MELBOURNE vs. MANLY Emerging as the two dominant clubs of the last five years, Melbourne and Manly developed a fierce and often violent competition. The rivalry began in earnest midway through 2007, when the Sea Eagles pipped the Storm 13-12 to snatch top spot on the ladder. But Melbourne surged to win the minor premiership and swept Manly (skippered by ex-Storm halfback Matt Orford) aside 34-8 in the Grand Final. The defending champs defeated Manly twice during the 2008 regular season, before the Sea Eagles rallied to crush their adversaries by a Grand Final record 40-0 scoreline to claim the premiership, with former Melbourne centre Steve Bell scoring the final try of the rout. Melbourne ended Manly's 2009 season courtesy of an emphatic 40-12 qualifying final victory—with Billy Slater bagging four tries—just three weeks after the Sea Eagles secured their maiden win at Olympic Park, 20-16. Manly won both regular season games in 2010 but the rivalry was overshadowed by Melbourne's salary cap drama, while the Sea Eagles only just scraped into the top-eight.

The Storm subdued Manly 18-6 on the opening weekend of 2011, but arguably the most explosive match of the NRL era awaited in the penultimate round. Test forwards Adam Blair (Melbourne) and Glenn Stewart (Manly) were despatched for 10 minutes after a melee, and were subsequently sent off after engaging in a wild punch-up on their way to the sin-bin. Blair's season (and his career with the Storm) ended with a five-match suspension, while Stewart returned for Manly's Grand Final triumph after the judiciary sidelined him for three weeks. Four more players from each side pleaded guilty after being cited for their respective roles in the brawling. Although it was lost amidst the drama, the Sea Eagles carved out an impressive 18-4 victory in the match dubbed 'Donnybrookvale,' the home side's seventh win in 10 matches against Melbourne at Brookvale Oval. The head-to-head count has Melbourne ahead 11 wins to Manly's 10 in 21 clashes.

EASTERN SUBURBS / SYDNEY ROOSTERS vs. CANTERBURY

Eastern Suburbs and Canterbury have engaged in many momentous and important matches in a 77-season rivalry between the clubs. In round six of Canterbury's 1935 debut season in the premiership, Easts slaughtered the newcomers 87-7 at the Sydney Sports Ground—the second-biggest winning margin in premiership history (St. George crushed hapless Cantebury 91-6 a week earlier to establish a still-standing record). The Tricolours defeated Canterbury 27-13 in the semi-final in 1936 on their way to the second of three consecutive premierships, but the Berries halted the run in 1938 with a 19-6 defeat of Easts in the premiership final to secure their maiden title in just their fourth season.

The rivals later used each other as springboards to drought-breaking seasons. Easts eliminated Canterbury in the 1960 minor semi on the way to a Grand Final appearance (losing to the mighty St. George side); it was the Tricolours' first finals win since claiming the 1945 premiership. The Berries repaid the favour with their first post-season victory in 20 years, despatching the Roosters during the 1967 finals on their way to the decider, where they went down to Souths. Easts won its first premiership in 29 years by defeating Canterbury 19-4 in the 1974 Grand Final, overturning the major semi result from two weeks earlier. The Bulldogs subsequently broke a 38-year title drought with an 18-4 victory over minor premiers Easts in the 1980 Grand Final.

The fierce competition subsided as the Roosters struggled for much of the ensuing 15 years, while the Bulldogs won four further Grand Finals. But the rivalry ramped up again in the late-1990s as the Roosters re-emerged as a premiership force. As the fourth- and fifth-placed teams respectively in 1999, Sydney City succumbed 12-8 to Canterbury in the inaugural finals match played under the controversial McIntyre System, before both sides were eliminated a week later.

When title favourites and runaway minor premiers the Bulldogs were stripped of 37 competition points late in the 2002 season due to salary cap breaches—effectively consigning the club to the wooden spoon—the Roosters swooped with nine straight victories to take out the premiership. The Bulldogs claimed that whoever won the 2002 Grand Final could not be considered true premiers, such was their dominance during the season before the penalty was issued (producing a 17-match winning streak, second only to the Roosters' 1975 side [19 wins] in premiership history). Meanwhile, the animosity was aggravated by niggly Sydney Roosters centre Justin Hodges allegedly phoning young Bulldogs five-eighth Braith Anasta to gloat about the Roosters' Grand Final triumph.

The Bulldogs won both highly anticipated regular season contests between the NRL heavyweights in 2003, but the Roosters prevailed 28-18 in a preliminary final showdown later in the season to reclaim bragging rights (before the Roosters were defeated by Penrith in the Grand Final). The Roosters and Bulldogs recorded a convincing win apiece in two regular season clashes in 2004, before finishing the minor premiership first and second respectively and winning their way through to the Grand Final. The Bulldogs recovered from a seven-point halftime deficit to pip the Roosters 16-13 in a gripping decider, but the debate regarding which club was the most dominant of the first half of the 2000s was never conclusively resolved.

The rivalry continued to bubble away despite the combatants failing to qualify for the finals in the same year in the ensuing seven seasons (the Bulldogs made the top-eight in 2006, '07 and '09; the Roosters in 2008 and 2010). Outspoken Test forward Willie Mason—the Clive Churchill Medallist in the Bulldogs' '04 Grand Final victory—quit the club at the end of 2007 and joined the Roosters, reuniting with premiership teammates Braith Anasta and Nate Myles at Bondi. A war of words erupted between Mason and Bulldogs superstar Sonny Billy Williams in the lead-up to the mouth-watering grudge match early in 2008, but Mason had the last laugh with two tries in the Roosters' 40 12 rout. The Roosters led the all time head-to-head ledger 78 wins to the Bulldogs' 75, with five drawn, at the end of 2011.

PARRAMATTA vs. PENRITH The battle for bragging rights in western Sydney has been waging between Parramatta and Penrith for 45 seasons. The clubs' home grounds are separated by a 35 kilometre trip down the M4 Western Motorway, but the Eels and Panthers have developed one of Sydney's keenest rivalries since Penrith's premiership debut in 1967. Parramatta dominated Penrith during the first two decades of competition between the sides, including an unbeaten run that stretched from 1975 to 1983 (see Bogey Teams). The long-suffering Panthers qualified for their maiden finals series in 1985, but were swamped 38-6 by the star-studded Eels in their post-season debut.

The rivalry has been remarkably even since Parramatta's period of dominance—a four-match streak is the longest either side has mustered since 1984. The Eels eliminated the Panthers at the semi-final stage of the 2000 NRL competition with a 28-10 victory, before winning the next three derbies—culminating in a 64-6 annihilation in the opening round of 2002, with Parramatta winger Luke Burt scoring a club record 28 points.

The most recent clash between the sides was arguably the most dramatic. In Parramatta great Nathan Hindmarsh's 300th first grade appearance for the club late in 2011, Penrith centre Michael Jennings scored a miraculous try after the fulltime siren and five-eighth Travis Burns' conversion sent the match into golden point at 22-all. Panthers halfback Luke Walsh slotted a field goal in the second period of extra-time to snatch a 23-22 victory over the shell-shocked Eels. Parramatta leads the head-to-head count comfortably, 51 wins to Penrith's 30, with one match drawn.

MANLY vs. WESTERN SUBURBS The rivalry between Western Suburbs and Manly centres on the wild and dramatic 'Fibros' v 'Silvertails' war of the late-1970s and early-1980s. Manly struggled against Wests after joining the premiership in 1947, losing the first eight matches between the clubs. But the Sea Eagles eliminated the Magpies on their way to Grand Final appearances in 1951 and 1959, and pieced together a 12-match winning streak against the black-and-whites from 1968-74. Wests scored a gripping 23-20 minor semi-final victory over Manly in 1974, but the rivalry exploded in the wake of a seemingly innocuous pre-season trial in the unlikely venue of Melbourne in 1978.

The teams travelled together to the Victorian capital for the 'Festival of Football,' the brainchild of VFL club Fitzroy. New Wests coach Roy Masters detected an air of superiority from the Sea Eagles and riled up his charges prior to the match, which descended into a violent and brawling contest. A bitter feud was born. Masters was the puppeteer of the conflict, dubbing his rugged working-class team the 'Fibros' (in reference to the inexpensive building material used in houses in less affluent areas) and gave the wealthy Manly club the derogatory 'Silvertails' moniker. The animosity boiled over in a match at Lidcombe Oval in 1978; rival enforcers John Donnelly (Wests) and Terry Randall (Manly) engaged in a savage brawl, while Sea Eagles winger Stephen Knight (a former Magpie) was sent off in Wests' 13-7 victory. But the Sea Eagles defeated their bitter enemies and minor premiers Wests 14-7 in the preliminary final later in the season on their way to an extraordinary premiership triumph. Manly was forced to play five finals games in 17 days, while the sudden-death run was set against the backdrop of a series of controversial refereeing displays by Greg Hartley, and the Magpies cried foul over several contentious decision that went against them in the preliminary final.

The extreme distaste between the two clubs was intensified at the end of 1979 when big-spending Manly lured Wests representative stars Les Boyd, John Dorahy and Ray Brown to the club. The Magpies defeated a Sea Eagles side containing Dorahy and Brown 19-4 in 1980, but Manly dominated the rivalry thereafter, losing just six of 34 matches between the sides before they both entered into mergers at the end of 1999. In 105 matches between the Sea Eagles and Magpies, Manly won 61 to Wests' 43, with one drawn. Manly and the Wests Tigers joint venture have developed a keen rivalry during the NRL era, but it does not compare to the ferocity and pure hatred exhibited by the 'Fibros' and 'Silvertails' of yesteryear.

BOGEY TEAMS

Throughout Rugby League history, certain clubs have proved an insurmountable proposition for rival teams during particular periods, often defying the general form guide to consistently produce upsets or bewildering head-to-head winning streaks. This chapter examines the most remarkable hoodoos and bogey teams of the premiership's 104 seasons.

SOUTH SYDNEY DOMINATE WESTS IN EARLY DECADES

Despite South Sydney's status as a dominant side of the premiership's formative seasons, relative minnows Western Suburbs' inability to compete with the men in myrtle and cardinal jumpers was extraordinary. Souths won the first 17 matches between the foundation clubs. The 'Fruitpickers'' woeful streak included a 67-0 loss in 1910—a margin that ranks as the Rabbitohs' biggest win and Wests' worst defeat—while they only finished less than eight points in arrears of their tormentors once. Wests broke through for a landmark 16-11 victory over Souths in 1917 and emerged victorious four of the next five times the teams faced off, before the Rabbitohs took control of the rivalry once again. From 1920 until 1929, Souths lost just one of 17 matches against Wests, including comprehensive semi-final defeats in 1927 and 1929.

BEARS GRILLED BY TIGERS

Foundation clubs North Sydney and Balmain faced off 175 times before merging with Manly and Wests respectively at the end of 1999. Norths scraped together just 59 wins against Balmain in 92 seasons—largely due to four periods of Tigers dominance over their northern adversaries. Balmain pieced together 11 consecutive victories over Norths between 1915 and 1920, claiming five premierships during that period. Norths won just seven of 36 encounters against Balmain from 1936 until 1952, while the Tigers lost only twice to the hapless Bears between 1960 and 1971. The Tigers renewed their control over the rivalry in 1986, winning 11 and drawing one of the next 14 matches against Norths. One of the heavyweight clubs of the 1990s, Norths gained some retribution for decades of torment by winning eight of the last nine clashes with the Tigers, including a 64-12 demolition in the final match between the clubs—the Bears' highest-ever score and the equal-highest score conceded in Balmain's history.

BALMAIN PROVES FORMIDABLE FINALS FOE FOR SOUTHS With 20 first grade titles on the honour board, South Sydney is the most successful club in premiership history. And the Rabbitohs have a post-season record to match, winning 60 per cent of their finals matches against all comers. But Souths has traditionally struggled against Balmain in September, winning just two of 10 finals games with its inner-city rivals. Balmain defeated Souths in narrow final victories to take out the 1916 and 1924 premierships, and hammered the Rabbitohs in the 1939 final. The Tigers accounted for the Rabbitohs again in the 1944 minor semi, before eclipsing the defending premiers in a high-scoring preliminary final classic in 1956 *(see Finals Magic)*. Souths belatedly broke the hoodoo with a 14-13 defeat of Balmain in the 1969 major semi, but the Tigers recovered to roll the minor premiers 11-2 two weeks later in a stunning Grand Final boilover. The Tigers thumped Souths in the 1986 minor semi, before the Rabbitohs gained some retribution with a 15-12 victory in the minor preliminary semi the following season. In the last finals match between the famous foundation clubs, Balmain upset minor premiers Souths 20-10 in the 1989 major semi. The disparity in finals results contradicts the overall record between the clubs— Souths won 95 games to Balmain's 80 victories, with three drawn—while Canberra (one win, two losses) is the only other club South Sydney has a win percentage of less than 50 per cent against in finals football.

NEWTOWN OWNED BY MIGHTY SAINTS Newtown defeated St. George in six straight matches during the mid-1950s, including finals victories that propelled the club into the 1954-55 Grand Finals. But the Dragons made the Bluebags their personal whipping boys as they established themselves as the most dominant club side of all time over the next decade. Newtown won just one of 34 matches against Saints between 1956 and 1972, despite remaining generally competitive during that 17-season period. Saints inflicted the worst defeat in Newtown's history in 1961, a 65-9 demolition at Kogarah Oval. The Bluebags' sole success was a 13-12 win late in the 1962 season that was vital to Newtown finishing second on the ladder— one competition point behind the Dragons. But the six-time premiers hammered Newtown 30-9 in the major semi a little over a month later, beginning a 21-match winning streak over the hapless inner-city club. Newtown made sure its drought-breaking victory in 1973 was memorable, defeating Saints in the only 1-0 scoreline in premiership history *(see Bizarre Matches)*. The rivals played out a drawn minor semi-final later that season, before Newtown advanced to the preliminary final with an 8-5 result in the replay. Newtown won just 45 of 129 matches against St. George from the Saints' 1921 entry into the premiership until Newtown's demise at the end of 1983—the club's worst winning percentage against any side. Remarkably, the Dragons won just two of nine finals matches against the Bluebags.

BALMAIN CONTROLS MANLY RIVALRY DURING THE 1960s

Manly and Balmain retained a keen and even rivalry during 53 seasons of competition between the two clubs—the Sea Eagles won 53 games to the Tigers' 51, with four drawn of 108 games. But Manly found the inner-city club an arduous opponent throughout the 1960s. The Tigers lost just one of 17 clashes with the Sea Eagles between 1961 and 1969, including an 8-5 triumph in the 1966 preliminary final. Manly, the previous year's runners-up, broke a 12-match winless streak against Balmain with a 14-11 win during the 1969 regular season. But the Tigers responded by ousting the Sea Eagles for a Grand Final spot two months later, scoring a last-minute try in a 15-14 preliminary final thriller (see Finals Magic).

EELS DOMINATE 'CHOCOLATE SOLDIERS' IN BATTLE OF THE WEST

Parramatta's emergence as a premiership force during the mid-1970s was to the detriment of the club's western Sydney rivals, the hapless Penrith Panthers. Disparagingly labelled the 'Chocolate Soldiers,' Penrith languished near the foot of the ladder throughout the 1970s and early-1980s. The Panthers failed to win a match against the Eels between 1975 and 1983—the only competition point they yielded in 18 encounters with Parramatta during the nine-season period was from a 19-all draw in 1980. Under the tutelage of Tim Sheens, Penrith took advantage of an Origin-depleted Parramatta side to break the drought in 1984, chalking up a 22-10 victory while five Eels stars were in camp with the NSW squad.

KNIGHTS STAMPEDED BY FELLOW '88 ENTRANTS

By the end of its third season, 1988 Winfield Cup entrants Newcastle had recorded a win every premiership side except Penrith and Brisbane. The Knights came close to rolling the heavyweight Panthers—finishing with a draw in 1990 and 1991—before defeating the defending premiers twice during 1992. But the Broncos, who also debuted in 1988, were a more difficult proposition. Brisbane won the first 10 matches between the clubs (at an average margin of almost 16 points) before the Knights finally broke through for an emphatic 24-10 victory in 1994. Despite achieving several momentous wins over the Broncos since that landmark success (including a 44-0 flogging in 2001, a then-record loss for Brisbane), the Knights have won just 12 of 37 matches between the clubs overall—their worst winning percentage against any side (32.43 per cent).

BUNNIES BY NAME AND NATURE

The Rabbitohs won their first two encounters with premiership newcomers Brisbane in 1988-89, before enduring a 17-year drought against the heavyweights from north of the border. Souths failed to record a victory in 16 straight games against the Broncos, suffering 50-point drubbings in 1993 and 1995. After escaping with a 34-all golden point draw in 2004, the Broncos finally succumbed to the Rabbitohs in 2006. Souths took advantage of an Origin-depleted Brisbane line-up to carve out a 34-14 win.

STORM HAUNTED BY WARRIORS

Despite winning more games than Melbourne in only the 2001-02 seasons, the Warriors have frequently troubled the Storm since the Victorian heavyweight's 1998 inception. Auckland was the first club to defeat Melbourne (16-12 in Auckland), putting a halt to the newcomers' four-match winning streak, while the Warriors were one of only two teams to leave Olympic Park with the competition points in 1998, courtesy of a miraculous after-the-bell 24-21 victory. Melbourne turned the tables with two wins over the Warriors in 1999, but lost the first match of its premiership defence in Auckland the following season, a defeat that paled into insignificance after the tragic death of team manager Michael Moore during the Storm's stay in Auckland. The rivals consequently play for the Michael Moore Trophy in honour of the popular Melbourne clubman. The Storm pummelled the Warriors 56-10 later in 2000 and recovered from an 18-point halftime deficit to draw 24-all in 2001, before New Zealand prevailed in both 2002 encounters.

But it was not until Melbourne emerged as the NRL's preeminent superpower in 2006 that the Warriors began to enjoye disproportionate success against the Storm. New Zealand, despite languishing out of finals contention in 2006, snapped the minor premiers' 11-match winning streak and inflicted the Storm's first Olympic Park defeat in 14 months with a heart-stopping 24-20 victory. In 2008, the Warriors pipped Melbourne 8-6 in Auckland, before becoming the first eighth-ranked side to topple the minor premiers in the first week of the finals under the McIntyre System, conjuring a stunning try at the death for an 18-15 upset. The Warriors bore the brunt of Melbourne's anger just days after the club had its 2007 and 2009 premierships stripped—copping a 40-0 hammering at Docklands—but grafted out a 13-6 win later in the year at Mt. Smart. After securing a famous 18-14 Anzac Day victory in 2011 to break Melbourne's 10-match winning run at AAMI Park, the Warriors produced arguably the finest performance in the club's 17-season history to roll the minor premiers 20-12 in the preliminary final later in the season.

New Zealand has recorded six wins (and one draw) in 14 matches against Melbourne since 2006, a head-to-head record against the Storm bettered only by powerhouse Manly (seven wins in 14 matches) during the same period. Only the Bulldogs (14 wins) have beaten Melbourne more times than the Warriors (13 wins) in the club's 14 seasons in the NRL.

DRAGONS GRAPPLE WITH RAIDERS HEX St. George Illawarra made Canberra its bunnies after making its NRL debut as a joint venture in 1999, winning five of the first six encounters between the clubs. But after recovering from a 13-point halftime deficit to snatch a 21-all draw with the Raiders in 2001, the Dragons suffered a bewildering run of outs against the team from the nation's capital over the ensuing decade. The Saints produced just one win in 13 matches (a 58-16 mauling in 2007) as the consistently underrated Raiders dined out on the perennial contenders, despite winning more games than the Dragons in only one season between 2002 and 2011. The Dragons' seven-match winning streak in 2009 was broken by a 24-12 loss to the Raiders, while Canberra emerged victorious in two clashes the following season as Saints claimed back-to-back minor premierships. The Raiders also produced a miraculous 24-19 victory in 2011 courtesy of a last-minute Josh Dugan try. The result was the Raiders' only victory in the last nine rounds of a disastrous year, while it extended the Dragons' winless streak at Canberra Stadium to 11 seasons. The Raiders (32.5 per cent) and Storm (26 per cent) are the only current NRL clubs that St. George Illawarra holds an all time win ratio of less than 45 per cent against.

MOMENTUM SHIFTS IN BRONCOS AND WARRIORS RIVALRY

Brisbane defeated Auckland in a 25-22 epic to mark the Warriors' 1995 premiership entry, and held a monopoly on matches between the clubs for the next five years. The Warriors came up empty in their first nine attempts against the perpetual heavyweights, plus a hard-fought World Club Challenge semi-final loss during the 1997 Super League season. 2001 was the turning point in the Warriors' history, and the club achieved a momentous victory soon after dropping the name Auckland in favour of New Zealand. A Stacey Jones field goal was the difference in the Warriors' 13-12 defeat of Brisbane, and they took advantage of the psychological breakthrough to win four straight matches against the Broncos during 2002-03, including some of the finest and most fondly remembered successes in the club's existence. Despite their disappointing form in 2005, the Warriors accounted for the Broncos twice, including a 30-18 result to snap the NRL front-runners' 10-match winning streak. New Zealand won the solitary clashes between the sides in the 2007 and 2008 seasons, before gaining a mental stranglehold over the Broncos during 2010. The Warriors inflicted a 48-12 defeat at Suncorp Stadium early in the year—with James Maloney scoring a club record-equalling 28 points—and effectively extinguished the Broncos' finals bid with a comprehensive 36-4 thrashing on a wet Auckland night in the penultimate round. The Broncos were not without success against the Warriors during this period, winning both regular season matches against New Zealand in 2004, 2006 and 2009. But the general perception was the Warriors were a side that consistently troubled Brisbane regardless of their position on the ladder. The Broncos recovered from the demoralising defeats of 2010 with twin Suncorp Stadium victories the following season—21-20 in a late-season classic, before crushing the highly fancied Warriors 40-10 in the qualifying final little over a month later.

MASTER COACH STRUGGLES IN BRONCOS vs. SAINTS RIVALRY

Wayne Bennett enjoyed overwhelming success against the Dragons for the majority of his record-breaking tenure as Brisbane coach, steering the club to its first two premierships with consecutive Grand Final victories over St. George in 1992-93. But St. George Illawarra emerged as a worrying bogey side for the Broncos a decade later, beating Bennett's charges in seven straight encounters from 2005 until the revered mentor's departure at the end of 2008—to the Dragons. Bennett guided Saints to a 25-12 victory over his former club in just his fourth match in charge of the joint venture, but that was to be one of only two wins he savoured against the Broncos in three seasons with the Dragons. Brisbane won five of the next six matches between the keen rivals, and ended St. George Illawarra's season with semi-final triumphs at Suncorp Stadium in 2009 and 2011. The latter result, a 13-12 golden point epic, concluded Bennett's highly successful stint with the Dragons ahead of his move to Newcastle in 2012.

WARRIORS SILENCE BULLDOGS' GROWL

Auckland's gutsy 20-6 victory over Canterbury in 1998—after having prop Jerry Seu Seu sent off in the first half—heralded a fruitful and highly eventful era for the Warriors against the perennial heavyweight Bulldogs. The Warriors won seven and drew two of the 11 clashes between the clubs to the end of 2003. Despite their dismal 1999 and

2000 campaigns, the Warriors had the wood over the Bulldogs during those two seasons, before staging a phenomenal comeback in 2001. The Bulldogs led 24-8 in Wellington, but three tries in the final 10 minutes salvaged an unfathomable draw for New Zealand. The Warriors thumped the Bulldogs 34-8 later in the season and were responsible for snapping the blue-and-whites' record 17-match winning streak in 2002. The adversaries claimed one win apiece during the 2003 regular season, but New Zealand's remarkable run against the Bulldogs peaked with a stunning 48-22 upset in the qualifying final (*see Finals Magic*). The Warriors averaged 27 points to the Bulldogs' 18 during the six-season period. The overall record between the clubs stands at 14 wins to Canterbury and 12 to the Warriors, with two games drawn.

CLUB COLOURS

Whether it is for fashion, tradition or necessity, the history and evolution of club colours and uniforms is explored in this chapter.

- Navy blue, red and white made up the Tricolours of Eastern Suburbs. The club played in a jersey consisting of blue, red and white bands from its inception until 1953, when the now-familiar predominantly blue jumper with a red and white 'V' was adopted. The bands have been intermittently revived by the Sydney Roosters during the 1990s and 2000s, while their away strip—which was worn in the 2002-03 Grand Finals—replaces the navy blue background with white. Due to a shortage of navy blue cotton during World War II, Easts sported a mainly sky blue jersey for a time, a design replicated for the Roosters' Heritage Round clashes in recent seasons.

- South Sydney inherited its famous club colours—officially recognised as cardinal red and myrtle green—from the South Sydney rugby union club. The Rabbitohs have worn the familiar hooped jersey design for the vast majority of their existence, first breaking with tradition in 1946-47 by taking the field in red 'V' on a green background, before reverting to the hoops. Souths incorporated white bands into its jersey during the early-1980s, bordering a solitary red hoop in the middle of a primarily green jersey. Although the club has tinkered with black strips and white outfits for away matches in the last decade, the red and green hoops remain South Sydney's most commonly used uniform. Currently, a black Rabbitoh logo and collar adorns the club's home strip, while a white Rabbitoh and collar is employed for away matches.

- Western Suburbs adopted the black and white of the Ashfield Rugby Union Club upon its inclusion in the inaugural 1908 premiership. Originally featuring a thick white band around the chest, Wests introduced its white 'V' on a black background jersey in the 1940s (the club also sported an all-black jersey during World War II due to shortages). The contrasting designs were alternated until the 'V' gained favour in the 1960s. A reverse away strip—black 'V' on a white background—was utilised sporadically during the 1980s and 1990s, while the 'magpie' colours feature in strips for selected Wests Tigers matches each season.

- Balmain's black and gold hoops—or 'tiger stripes'—was the club's staple strip from its 1908 inception until the black 'V' on a gold (closer to orange than the 'gold' of Australia's national sporting teams) background was introduced in the 1940s after a period of wearing all-gold jerseys due to World War II shortages. The thick 'V' soon morphed into two thinner black lines. The rebranding of the club as the Sydney Tigers during the mid-1990s saw a liberal smattering of white introduced to the jumper, while the original black and gold hoops made a comeback in Balmain's final years before its merger with Western Suburbs at the end of 1999. The hoops and 'V' designs have featured regularly as part of Wests Tigers' playing strip rotation.
- North Sydney's trademark colours of black and red featured in many uniform incarnations during the club's 92-season existence. Black and red hoops were the norm for most of Norths' first half-century, but a seemingly American-inspired strip of mainly red with black shoulders (and numbers on the front) was utilised in the 1960s. The strip worn in the infamous Ken Irvine 'walk-off' furore of 1970 (see Bizarre Matches) was predominantly white with black and red bands through the midriff. Hoops regained favour during the 1970s, while a red jersey with several black bands in a 'V' formation. The more modern Citibank-sponsored jersey of the 1990s featured red shoulders, black bottom and white middle with horizontal black lines.
- According to club lore, Newtown's royal blue jerseys were originally made from sacks died blue—hence the nickname 'Bluebags.' The club barely tinkered with the uniform of a blue jersey with a white collar and white shorts throughout its 76-season history, aside from adding white bands on the sleeves during the 1970s as the Newtown Jets attempted to jazz up their image.
- The Newcastle club that fielded a side in the 1908-09 premierships took the field in red and white hooped jerseys. The strip has been revived by the Knights for Heritage Round matches in recent years. The Knights club colours of red and blue have been manifested in a variety of jersey designs since 1988, including hoops, vertical stripes and 'V'-inspired motifs.
- Glebe's distinctive dark red jerseys spawned the nickname the 'Dirty Reds.' The club adopted new jumpers in 1913 that boasted chamois shoulders atop a predominantly dark red top.
- Royal blue and gold were Cumberland's colours of choice during the club's sole 1908 season. It was to be nearly four decades before the area boasted a first grade side again, and Parramatta adopted the same colours upon its 1947 entry. During the interim, University wore blue and gold throughout its 1920-37 premiership existence.
- The white jersey with a big red 'V' is synonymous with St. George, but the club played in red and white hoops (nicknamed 'blood and bandages') prior to the introduction of the 'V' in the late-1940s. The Dragons wore a hooped design reminiscent of an English club strip when they hosted the touring Lions in 1962, due to the similarity between the St. George and Great Britain jumpers. Saints revitalised the original hooped strip for World Sevens and Charity Shield fixtures during the 1990s, while St. George Illawarra has also intermittently sported the design during the last decade.
- Canterbury began life in 1935 with a blue and white hooped jersey, until the white jersey with blue 'V' and shoulders emerged in the 1960s. The 'V' design has

been the club's strip of choice for almost half a century, besides a brief period in the early-1970s when an English-style hooped jersey made a comeback, while heritage matches have seen the revival of the original strip from Canterbury's formative decades. Due to shortages during World War II, Canterbury wore maroon and blue jerseys for a period in the early-1940s.

- Manly-Warringah has sported maroon and white jerseys since its 1947 inception, encompassing a variety of designs in the club's 65-year history. During the late-1950s, Manly's jersey featured a large white Sea Eagle on the front with white stripes down the shoulders on a maroon background, before the predominantly maroon with thin white bands design emerged in the 1960s. The Sea Eagles introduced the latter in reverse colours in the 1970s, wearing maroon stripes on a white background in the 1976, 1978 and 1982-83 Grand Finals. The club's Pepsi-sponsored jerseys of the 1990s featured maroon shoulders and bottom, with white through the middle, while Manly's recent strip features the traditional thin bands.

- The Cronulla Sharks opted for the sky blue, black and white of the Cronulla Surf Live Saving Club upon their 1967 entry (after sporting a brown jersey with a gold 'V' while playing in Sydney's Second Division competition), originally favouring a 'V' design before switching to a thick white band outlined by black lines on a sky blue background for more than two decades.

- Penrith entered the competition in 1967 sporting a predominantly dark brown jersey with a large white 'V' encompassing the shoulders and collar, and a thinner brown 'V' (a departure from the royal blue and white strips previously worn by the club during its Second Division days). During the mid-1970s the Panthers took the field in soccer-style vertical stripes. A white jersey with brown shoulders and thin white stripes along the arms was Penrith's colour scheme of choice during the 1980s, a jersey that received its farewell in the 1990 Grand Final loss to Canberra, heralding the end of the 'Chocolate Soldiers' era. The club introduced black as its main colour the following season, with thin red, green and yellow bands through the middle, while the bottom half of the jersey was mostly white with thin black lines. A reverse, predominantly white jersey was also used regularly during the early-1990s. Generally employing a black home strip and white away strip throughout the late-1990s and 2000s, the Panthers have retained elements of red and green in the uniforms. Penrith has also experimented with several teale-dominated strips in the last decade. Several teams incorporate pink into their strips for the NRL's annual Women in League round, but the 'Pink' Panthers take it a step further, taking the field in bright pink outfits down to the shorts and socks.

- The Canberra Raiders have maintained a lime green jersey with small elements of white, gold and blue for virtually all of their 30-season existence. White outfits and black strips have been employed during the 2000s for away games and the Raiders sported a darker green strip for a period in the early-2000s, but lime green remains synonymous with the Canberra club.

- The Illawarra Steelers adopted the district's traditional colours of scarlet and white for their playing strip. The jerseys were predominantly red (or more specifically scarlet) with white bands on the sleeves, while a reverse strip was employed for away fixtures.

- The city of Brisbane's official colours, blue and gold, were deemed inappropriate for the premiership's first Queensland-based team—aside from the similarity to Parramatta's colours—and the state colours of maroon and white, with a liberal smattering of gold, were used for the Broncos' original uniform instead. White was largely eliminated from the club's home strip in the early-2000s, while the away strip—worn in the Broncos' 2006 Grand Final triumph—consisted of a white jersey with dark blue trim. Among the Broncos' more memorable jersey designs are the unique maroon, gold and white 'diamond' motif paraded in 1994, and a notorious aqua and blue jersey used on rare occasions in the 1990s and early-2000s, generally regarded as one of the ugliest strips in premiership history.

- The original incarnation of the Gold Coast club underwent a plethora of changes in every imaginable aspect during a calamitous 11-season existence, and its colour scheme was no exception. Entering the competition in 1988 as the Giants in a black, white and silver strip, Gold Coast's Seagulls era was defined by black, white and red jerseys, predominantly in hoop design. Rebranded as the Chargers in 1996, the club sported a garish aqua jersey with silver and purple stripes on the shoulders until its eventual demise at the end of 1998. The infinitely more professional Titans arrived in 2007 dressed in tasteful light blue, gold and white jerseys, representing the ocean and sand of the holiday strip's beaches.

- The Auckland Warriors' original strip combined the traditional blue and white of Auckland with a healthy dose of red and green. New owners and the rebranding of the club as the New Zealand Warriors prompted a change of colours. A predominantly black jersey with blue, white and red was used during 2001-02 —including the club's maiden Grand Final appearance in the latter season— while grey and black took over until the end of 2008. The Warriors adopted a predominantly black strip at home and reverse white strip for away games during 2009-11, before unveiling a black home jersey with white 'V' (reverse for away games) and red trim for the 2012 season. The Warriors are one of the NRL's foremost purveyors of heritage strips, playing in their original 1995 strip, a one-off dark blue Auckland representative strip, a New Zealand flag-inspired jersey, and a black strip with silver ferns on the chest similar to the rugby union All Blacks' outfit.

- The Cowboys combined the traditional navy blue of North Queensland representative sides with silver, gold and white. The club has stayed true to its original colours—albeit in a wide range of designs—and has unveiled an all-navy blue jersey for Heritage Round matches in recent seasons.

- The Perth-based Western Reds took the field in a black, red, yellow and white strip, consistent with the state colours of Western Australia, during the club's 1995-97 existence.

- The ill-fated South Queensland Crushers opted for an Aztec gold jersey with blue vertical stripes on one side, and a red collar—arbitrary colours with no regional significance, chosen instead by market researchers.

- The hastily assembled Melbourne Storm debuted in 1998 dressed in the combination of navy blue and white (Victoria's state colours), with purple (or mauve) and gold. The splash of gold—included to signify the lightning bolt of the Storm—was removed from the strip in 2005.

PETER STERLING picks up a teammate after the Eels' epic 4-2 Grand Final victory over Canterbury in 1986. The Parramatta halfback won the inaugural Clive Churchill Medal for his man-of-the-match performance in the decider.

MAL MENINGA (right) and **BRADLEY CLYDE** (left) flank coach **TIM SHEENS** after the Raiders' euphoric 19-14 extra-time Grand Final triumph over Balmain. Meninga captained the club's breakthrough victory, while 19-year-old lock Clyde won the Clive Churchill Medal for his performance in the decider.

MARK GEYER (left), the Panthers firebrand, is despatched to the sin-bin by referee **BILL HARRIGAN** (right), as captain **GREG ALEXANDER** looks on during this flashpoint in the 1991 Grand Final between Penrith and Canberra.

Balmain captain **WAYNE PEARCE** sums up the emptiness of a Grand Final defeat, after his side's 19-14 extra-time loss to Canberra in the 1989 decider at the Sydney Football Stadium. 'Junior' played 194 games for the Tigers and 19 Tests for Australia as one of the premier backrowers of the 1980s.

MICHAEL O'CONNOR, one of the great rugby union converts, on the fly for Manly in a 40-10 defeat of Parramatta in 1988. A breathtaking attacking talent, dual international O'Connor played 18 Tests for Australia and 19 Origins for NSW in a 10-season professional career.

'The King' **WALLY LEWIS** during his final State of Origin match—the 1991 decider —won 14-12 by Queensland. Lewis is regarded as Origin's greatest player, and captained the Maroons in 30 of his 31 appearances.

Canterbury captain **TERRY LAMB** in open spaces during a 1992 clash against Eastern Suburbs at Belmore Sports Ground. The mercurial five-eighth scored 164 tries in 349 games for Western Suburbs and the Bulldogs between 1980 and 1996.

Brisbane captain **ALLAN LANGER** reaches out for his second try in the Broncos'
28-8 Grand Final victory over St. George in 1992, despite the tackle of Saints prop
TONY PRIDDLE. Broncos hooker **KERROD WALTERS** demonstrates his delight, while
Dragons halfback **NOEL GOLDTHORPE** (right) sees the decider slipping away.

BRETT KENNY in full flight during one of his 17 State of Origin appearances for New South Wales (1982-87). The Parramatta five-eighth was one of the only players to get the better of Queensland's Wally Lewis at interstate level.

WHAT'S IN A NAME?

This chapter takes a look at the origins of club nicknames and name changes throughout Rugby League history.

- Legend has it that Newtown's first set of jerseys were made from old sugar bags and dyed blue, providing the foundation club with the nickname Bluebags that it would carry for almost seven decades. Under the coaching of Jack Gibson in 1973, the club was rebranded the Jets—suitable because of Newtown's proximity to Sydney Airport at Mascot, but also infinitely more marketable—and Newtown were known as such until the NSWRL excluded the club from the premiership at the end of 1983.

- Glebe—Australia's first Rugby League club—was affectionately known as the Dirty Reds during its 22-season existence. But the evocative moniker was due to Glebe's dark red jerseys rather than any untoward on-field antics undertaken by the club's players. Among the other short-lived clubs during the premiership's formative decades, Annandale was affectionately known as 'The Dales,' University was also referred to as Varsity or the 'Students,' and the 1908-09 Newcastle side was dubbed the 'Rebels.'

- Eastern Suburbs adopted the Roosters emblem in 1967. The Rooster is the unofficial national animal of France, and the French Rugby League touring teams were known as 'Les Chanticleers' (translating to 'the roosters') or 'Les Tricolores' due to their blue, red and white playing strip—similar to that of Easts. The Rooster has remained as the club's nickname for 45 years.

- The most popular school of thought regarding the origins of South Sydney's 'Rabbitohs' emblem is that many of the club's players sold skinned rabbits to earn extra money; this is commonly thought to have emerged during the Depression era, but it is possible that the practice—and subsequent moniker—began earlier. Another theory put forward is that Redfern Oval was formerly a cow paddock, pocked with potholes caused by rabbits, and 'rabbit-holes' was gradually modified into 'rabbitohs'—but that reasoning seems unlikely as Redfern Oval was not adopted as the club's home ground until 1948.

- Balmain's close association with the inner-city Sydney wharfs saw the club affectionately nicknamed the Watersiders during its formative years, while the black and gold striped jerseys naturally led to the Tiger link, which became the club's signature.

- Similarly, Western Suburbs were called the Fruitpickers during the early years of the premiership due to the abundance of rural properties in the club's catchment area. As Sydney's urban sprawl continued westward, the name eventually lost relevance and the Magpie emblem was an obvious match for the team's black and white uniforms. Wests became the first club to employ an animal as a club mascot, becoming known as the Magpies from 1928.

- North Sydney finally adopted an emblem in 1959, forming a partnership with local retailer Big Bear Supermarket, who supplied a man of the match award in exchange for a flag featuring a bear being flown about a kilometre down the road at North Sydney Oval. The association of North Sydney with the bear mascot flourished and the moniker stuck, but the intimidating imagery did not have the desired effect on the field. Despite winning the reserve grade and third grade competitions in 1959, the hapless Bears made the first grade finals just three times in the following 33 seasons. Norths were referred to as the Shoremen during the premiership's early decades due to the club's close proximity to Sydney's North Shore.

- According to tradition, Saint George was a Roman soldier in the third century AD who was venerated as a Christian martyr, and is the patron saint of England. He was immortalised in the tale of Saint George and the Dragon, and when the St. George district of Sydney had a Rugby League club admitted to the premiership in 1921, the Dragon Slayers seemed an appropriate nickname for the club (hence the silhouette of a horseman behind the dragon on the club's emblem). The moniker was shortened to the Dragons in the 1940s, which soon became a symbol for Rugby League supremacy as the club won 11 consecutive premierships form 1956-66.

- Canterbury-Bankstown entered the competition in 1935 and was nicknamed the 'Cantabs' during the club's formative seasons. Canterbury became affectionately known as the Berries—a moniker that stayed with the club for four decades. Canterbury adopted the more intimidating Bulldogs emblem in 1977, a change that was first suggested by *Rugby League Week* editor Geoff Prenter in 1975. In an attempt to attract a wider fan-base leading into the 1995 season, the club was renamed the Sydney Bulldogs; despite claiming a remarkable premiership, the club reverted to Canterbury the following year. The club became known as simply the Bulldogs in 2000 and carried on in that vein for a decade, before changing back to Canterbury-Bankstown Bulldogs once again in 2010.

- Two other clubs also changed names in 1995 to project a more metropolitan appeal. Balmain became the Sydney Tigers, while fellow foundation club Eastern Suburbs were rebranded as the Sydney City Roosters. The Tigers returned to the Balmain name after two seasons, while the Tricolours have been known as the Sydney Roosters since 2000.

- Originally known as Rose Hill, the western Sydney suburb was renamed Parramatta in 1791, derived from the Aboriginal term meaning 'head of waters' or 'the place where the eels lie down.' Renowned *Daily Mirror* journalist, the late Peter Frilingos suggested the Eels as an emblem for the Parramatta in the mid-1960s and the club took it on board.

- There remains conjecture over when Manly definitively adopted the Sea Eagles mascot. Some contest that the club was originally known as the Seagulls, before taking on the more intimidating Sea Eagle as an emblem during the 1950s. Others maintain that Manly was known as the Sea Eagles from the club's inception and the 'Seagulls' association was a misnomer from a journalist that stuck for several seasons.

- The 'Lions' was passed over as a potential emblem for fledgling Cronulla-Sutherland for its 1967 premiership entry, the club instead opting to be known as the Sharks to strengthen the link with the local surf lifesaving club. The club was simply known as the Sharks (with Cronulla in front of it) from 2000-02.

- The Brisbane Broncos and North Queensland Cowboys took on their emblems despite their lack of regional relevance and the fact they were quintessentially American—the Dallas Cowboys and Denver Broncos NFL franchises are two of the world's most instantly recognisable sporting teams. The nicknames were quickly accepted by fans, however, and have become synonymous with their respective areas. *Rugby League Week*'s John McCoy first publicly floated the name 'Brisbane Broncos' in the magazine early in 1987.

- Canberra, on the other hand, took on the Raiders name as a direct result of a connection with an American NFL team. The club's inaugural coach Don Furner had recently spent time in the US observing the operations at the Oakland Raiders franchise, prompting him to put the Raiders emblem forward for the Australian capital's rugby league side.

- Other clubs admitted to the premiership in the modern era adopted monikers closely linked to their locales, however. Illawarra became the Steelers as a nod to Wollongong's prominent steel works (and to court a lucrative sponsorship deal with BHP Steel), after supporters were originally asked to vote between the 'Lions' and the 'Steelies.' South Queensland entered the competition as the Crushers, representing the south-east Queensland region's prominent sugar cane production (referring to the crushing process to extract the sugar at the refinery).

- According to the history section of the Newcastle Knights' website, the club's nickname was chosen because Knights are men of steel, and Newcastle—a traditionally working-class community—was a steel town.

- The Auckland franchise entered the premiership in 1995 and became known as the Warriors as a result of a public naming competition. The 'Warrior' moniker was the overwhelming winner, projecting a staunch image and identifying with New Zealand's cultural heritage. Originally, the tongue on the Warrior emblem pointed to the right—believed to be bad luck according to Maori folklore. The club's disastrous first six seasons tend to support that theory, and the tongue was straightened when the Tainui Tribe became part-owners of the club in 1999.

- The original Gold Coast side that entered the Winfield Cup in 1988 underwent several name changes during 11 premiership seasons. Beginning life as the Gold Coast-Tweed Giants, the club became the Seagulls in 1990 and dropped Tweed from its name. The Seagulls were in dire financial straights leading into the 1996 season and were bought by eccentric businessman Jeff Muller, who rebranded the club the Gold Coast Gladiators. Muller was eventually ousted by the ARL before the start of the season, and the team took the field as the Chargers for three seasons before folding at the end of 1998. The Gold Coast franchise that entered the NRL in 2007 originally favoured the Dolphin as their emblem, but the move was blocked by Queensland Cup side Redcliffe Dolphins. A competition run jointly by the club and a Gold Coast radio station saw the Titans nickname beat out the Pirates and the Stingers.

- The Western Reds, who played in the 1995 and '96 ARL premierships, were rebranded as the Perth Reds for Super League's sole 1997 season, before folding at the end of the year.
- So unpopular was Newcastle-based Super League club the Hunter Mariners with the majority of Knights-loving, ARL-loyal Novocastrians, the local Maritime Union of Australia objected to the new franchise's use of the Mariner emblem. The maligned club performed admirably during the 1997 Super League season, but folded after the rebel organisation reconciled with the ARL.
- Melbourne was set to enter the inaugural NRL competition as the Mavericks—complete with a gunslinger logo holding a fistful of aces—before club officials had a change of heart due to concerns of the name sounding 'too American.' Going back to the drawing board, themes of 'power, lightning and storm' gave birth to the franchise's official handle, the Melbourne Storm.[16]

---

16 Ian Collis and Alan Whiticker, *A History Of Rugby League Clubs*. Sydney, 2006

CHAPTER 4
THE PLAYERS

Thousands of players have risen to the top level of Rugby League in Australia since the code's introduction in 1908. Many hundreds of players—for a variety of reasons—have carved their own indelible niche in the game's history. Rugby League's highest achievers, great leaders, record-breakers, colourful characters and notable figures are explored extensively in this section. The memorable individual performances that have enhanced the game's narrative are celebrated, while the players whose lives were tragically cut short are also remembered. The colour added to the game by cult figures, the fiery enforcers and embarrassing moments, features prominently in this section, along with Rugby League's standout rookies and the history of players switching codes.

THE CAPTAINS

There is no set recipe for becoming a successful Rugby League captain. Many different styles of skipper have made their mark throughout the code's history—from the enforcers that ruled with an iron fist, to the silent types that led the way with their on-field performances and leaders that inspired their charges to great deeds with stirring speeches and rousing rev-ups. Rugby League's most inspirational and successful captains are celebrated in the following pages.

DALLY MESSENGER Rugby League's first superstar, Dally Messenger was one of the preeminent captains of the game's pioneering seasons. Overlooked for the captaincy of the first Kangaroo tourists in 1908 (the players voted for the captain en route to England, selecting Norths' Dinny Lutge), Messenger led Australia in the first two Ashes Tests against England with Lutge sidelined due to injury. Messenger also skippered his country in the first Anglo-Australian Test played in Australia in 1910, before captain-coaching Eastern Suburbs to a hat-trick of premierships between 1911 and 1913.

ARTHUR HALLOWAY Brilliant pioneering halfback Arthur 'Pony' Halloway captained Balmain through one of the greatest club dynasties in the game's history. A rugby union defector, the diminutive Halloway toured with the Kangaroos in 1908-09 and 1911-12 before joining Easts and winning premierships in 1912 and 1913. He returned to Balmain in 1915 (after previously playing for the club in 1909-11), winning another five first grade titles (1915-17 and 1919-20)—the last four as captain-coach. Halloway captained Australia in three Tests against New Zealand in 1919 and later became one of the game's most celebrated coaches, guiding the great Eastern Suburbs combination to three straight titles from 1935 to 1937.

ALF BLAIR Five-eighth Alf 'Smacker' Blair ranks as one of the great club captains. He guided South Sydney's President's Cup side to a premiership in 1915, before making his first grade debut two years later and breaking into the NSW side in 1919. Blair played his only Test against Great Britain in Sydney in 1924 but his indelible mark was made as captain of one of the most dominant club combinations of all time. The clever pivot skippered Souths to titles in 1925-27 and 1929, captain-coaching the club in 1927. Blair left Souths at the end of 1930 to coach in New South Wales country. He later coached Wests in 1943, but died at the age of 48 a year after guiding the Rabbitohs to the 1944 semi-finals

JIM CRAIG 'Mr Versatile' Jim Craig's captaincy qualities blossomed after a mid-career move to Queensland. A member of the great Balmain premiership sides of 1915-17 and 1919-20, Craig toured with the 1921-22 Kangaroos before joining Ipswich in 1923. He skippered Queensland to a series victory over NSW in his first season north of the Tweed and captained Australia in the home Ashes series against Great

Britain in 1924 after leading Queensland to a 3-0 series whitewash of NSW and a historic victory over the touring Lions. Craig returned to Sydney in 1929 as captain-coach of Wests and guided the club to its first premiership the following season, retiring after the club's 27-2 defeat of St. George in the 1930 Grand Final He added to his legend by coaching Canterbury to its maiden premiership in 1938.

TOM GORMAN Revered centre Tom Gorman became Queensland's first Kangaroo Tour captain when he led the 1929-30 squad to England. Gorman first played for his state in 1921 and debuted for Australia in 1924, before guiding Brothers to a Brisbane premiership in 1926. He took over the Queensland captaincy in 1928 and led the Maroons to a series victory over NSW, resulting in Gorman's elevation to the Test captaincy for that year's home series against England. Gorman led the Kangaroos superbly the following season as Australia narrowly went down to England 2-1 in a four-Test series. His playing career came to end in 1930, but the 10-Test veteran was immortalised as Mal Meninga's centre partner in Queensland's Team of the Century in 2008.

DAVE BROWN Incomparable centre Dave Brown's phenomenal talent saw him bestowed with captaincy honours early in his career. After making his first grade debut with Easts in 1930, Brown broke into the NSW side the following season and was named state captain in 1932, aged just 19. Dubbed 'the Bradman of League' for his incredible tryscoring and pointscoring exploits, Brown became the youngest Australian Test skipper in history on the 1935 tour of New Zealand. Brown captained his country in the following season's home Ashes series, before leading Easts to premiership success in 1936. The genius three-quarter returned from a stint in England in 1939 to captain-coach the Tricolours, guiding the club to another title in 1940, although injury ruled him out of the final. Brown retired after Easts' Grand Final loss to St. George in 1941.

WALLY PRIGG A Newcastle legend, champion lock Wally Prigg played his entire career in the district and became the first player to tour three times with the Kangaroos. After touring England with the 1929-30 and 1933-34 squads, Prigg captained Australia for the first time against New Zealand in 1937 and made his record-breaking tour as skipper at the end of the season. Prigg led the Kangaroos in three Tests against England and was captain in Australia's first series against France on the tour. He retired with a then-record 19 Test appearances and was posthumously honoured during the ARL's 2008 Centenary season—Prigg was named as captain of the Newcastle Team of the Century (ahead of Clive Churchill), at lock in the NSW Country Team of the Century and on the bench in the NSW Team of the Century.

JACK RAYNER Tough prop Jack Rayner toured with the 1948-49 Kangaroos, but it is his role as an intimidating captain-coach in five premiership victories for Souths that cemented his place in the tapestry of Rugby League history. The Lismore product guided the Rabbitohs to their first title in 18 years in 1950, and was in charge as the club claimed further premiership glory in 1951 and 1953-55—a six-year unbroken title-winning run was foiled only by a controversial loss to Wests in the

1952 Grand Final, with several crucial decisions going against Souths in an infamous refereeing performance by George Bishop, who retired immediately after the match. Rayner retired from playing in 1957, coaching Parramatta without success for the following three seasons. He refused to acknowledge Bishop when they passed, as often occurred with both Maroubra residents.

CLIVE CHURCHILL Although Clive Churchill played most of his club career under the captaincy of Jack Rayner, the fullback nonpareil became a record-breaking Test skipper, leading Australia in 27 consecutive matches. Regarded by many as the greatest player in the game's history, 'The Little Master' captained his country for the first time in the 1950 home series against Great Britain—a famous 2-1 series victory that saw Australia reclaim the Ashes for the first time in 30 years. Churchill led the 1952-53 Kangaroos through Britain and France and in another home Ashes series triumph in 1954. After skippering Australia in an unsuccessful World Cup campaign in 1954 and a series loss against France the following season, Churchill was replaced as Test skipper by St. George's Ken Kearney in 1956. He toured with the 1956-57 Kangaroos (under Kearney's leadership) but was replaced by Newtown fullback Gordon Clifford after the first Ashes Test. Churchill captain-coached Souths in 1958, but left for Queensland and guided Norths to a Brisbane premiership as captain-coach in 1959. The beloved figure went on to a highly successful coaching career before being named as one of the original four Immortals in 1981. His Test appearances as captain remained a record until broken by Darren Lockyer in 2009.

KEN KEARNEY Ken 'Killer' Kearney was at the helm of St. George for the first half of the most dominant run in premiership history. The former Wallaby joined the Dragons in 1952 after a stint with Leeds and returned to England with the 1952-53 Kangaroos. Kearney captain-coached the Saints to consecutive preliminary final appearances in 1954-55, and despite being replaced by Norm Tipping as coach in 1956, he skippered the club to its first title in seven years before leading the 1956-57 Kangaroos to Britain and France (he captained Australia for the first time earlier in the year against the Kiwis). He was reinstated as St. George's captain-coach in 1957, a role that netted another four premierships in as many years, while he was in charge as non-playing coach when the Dragons swept to a sixth straight title in 1961 (injury ruled Kearney out of the Grand Final). Kearney later coached Parramatta, Wests and Cronulla.

DICK POOLE Dashing centre Dick Poole was one of the finest captains of his era. Poole debuted for Newtown in 1950 and captain-coached the Bluebags to the minor premiership and a narrow Grand Final loss to Souths in 1955 on the way to becoming a club legend. He skippered NSW in 1956 and toured with the Kangaroos at the end of the season (under Ken Kearney), before captain-coaching Australia to a historic undefeated World Cup victory in 1957. Wests recruited the respected backline star in 1959 and immediately installed him as captain, but after leading the Magpies to consecutive preliminary final appearances in 1959-60, Poole was forced into retirement due to recurring asthma during 1961. Poole later coached Newtown from 1966 to 1968.

KEITH BARNES One of Australia's finest fullbacks and goalkickers, Keith 'Golden Boots' Barnes also ranks amongst the code's most prolific captains. Barnes made his Test debut in 1957 and took over the captaincy during the 1959 series against the Kiwis, before being chosen as skipper of the 1959-60 Kangaroos. The rock-solid Balmain custodian led Australia in a narrow series loss to Great Britain and a 3-0 whitewash of France on the tour. Barnes skippered Australia in the drawn home series against France and in an unsuccessful World Cup campaign in 1960. After captaining his country in one last Test against Great Britain in 1962, he guided a young Tigers outfit to Grand Final losses at the hands of the mighty St. George side in 1964 and 1966 during the twilight of his career. Barnes' Test appearances as captain was second only to Clive Churchill at the time of his retirement, while his total of 14 (after World Cup appearances were given the same status as Tests in 2008) ranks Barnes as Australia's seventh-most prolific Test skipper.

NORM PROVAN Norm 'Sticks' Provan's status as an all time great was assured by 1962—the second-rower had played 18 Tests for Australia, toured with the 1956-57 Kangaroos and featured in the first six of St. George's record run of premierships. But he proved himself as one of the game's finest leaders towards the end of his career, captain-coaching the Saints to four more titles to extend the club's sequence to 10 Grand Final victories before retiring after the '65 decider.

ARTHUR SUMMONS Former Wallaby Arthur Summons switched codes to join Wests in 1960, breaking into the NSW and Australian sides the following season. He captained Australia to a famous 18-17 third Test victory over Great Britain in 1962 and led the Magpies in painstakingly close Grand Final losses to St. George in 1962 and '63. Summons' post-match embrace with Saints counterpart Norm Provan was immortalised in John O'Gready's photo 'The Gladiators', which has been used as the basis for the premiership trophy since 1982. The wily halfback captain-coached the 1963-64 Kangaroos—the first Australian side to claim the Ashes in England in over 50 years—and although he missed the Tests against Great Britain with injury, Summons skippered his country in two wins over France. Summons exited the premiership at the end of 1964 but later coached Australia against Great Britain in 1970.

IAN WALSH Eugowra legend Ian Walsh captained Western Division against the touring Lions in 1958 and made his Test debut the following season on the 1959-60 Kangaroo Tour. Enticed to Sydney by the all-conquering Dragons in 1962, Walsh skippered the 1963-64 Kangaroos to the first series victory in England in over half a century after injury ruled out tour captain Arthur Summons. Walsh led Australia in its retention of the Ashes in 1966, the same year he took over as captain-coach of St. George, guiding the club to its 11th consecutive premiership. He was at the helm again the following season but retired after the era-ending loss to Canterbury in the preliminary final. Coach of the Eels in 1971-72, Walsh's 10 Tests as captain ranked behind only Churchill and Barnes at the time of his retirement.

REG GASNIER St. George's plethora of experienced captaincy candidates precluded Reg Gasnier, regarded as the game's best-ever centre, from leading the

Dragons during their phenomenal run of 11 straight Grand Final victories. But the six-time premiership winner was an influential skipper at Test level who at 23 years and 28 days of age, became the youngest captain in Anglo-Australian Rugby League history when he led his country out against the touring Lions in the opening Ashes Test of 1962. He was replaced as skipper by Keith Barnes after the 31-12 loss, but captained Australia in one Test against South Africa in 1963 and two Tests of a home series victory over France in 1964. Following Saints teammate Ian Walsh's second tenure as Test skipper, Gasnier led Australia to a 3-0 series whitewash of New Zealand in 1967 and was chosen to captain-coach the Kangaroos to Britain and France at the end of the season. After leading the Kangaroos in the opening Ashes Test loss, injury hampered the remainder of Gasnier's tour and he retired after breaking down again on the French leg of the trip. Gasnier was one of the original Immortals named in 1981 and occupied a centre spot in Australia's Team of the Century announced in 2008.

JOHN SATTLER As a 24-year-old firebrand, John Sattler was a surprise choice to assume the South Sydney captaincy in 1967 from former Test five-eighth Jim Lisle but he carved out a magnificent record that ranks him alongside the all time great club captains and elevated him to the role of Test skipper. The celebrated Newcastle product ruled with an iron fist, leading the Rabbitohs to five straight Grand Finals (1967-71), collecting premierships in 1967, '68, '70 and '71. In arguably the bravest and certainly the most famous display of courage in Grand Final history, Sattler skippered Souths to a 23-12 victory over Manly in the 1970 decider, despite having his jaw badly broken in the opening six minutes by a savage blow from Sea Eagles prop John Bucknall *(see Courageous Performances)*. Sattler toured with the 1967-68 Kangaroos but played only minor matches in England and France before being handed the Australian captaincy for his Test debut against the Kiwis in 1969. He led his country in a drawn two-match series in New Zealand and captained Australia in the second Test of the home Ashes series in 1970, a disappointing 28-7 loss to the Lions at the SCG. After Souths' finals exit in 1972, Sattler moved to Queensland and skippered the state side against NSW and New Zealand Colts in 1973.

GRAEME LANGLANDS A young superstar in the last four of St. George's run of 11 straight Grand Final victories, Graeme Langlands became one of the most prominent captains of the 1970s. 'Changa' inherited the Dragons' captaincy from the great John Raper in 1970, leading the club to Grand Final appearances in 1971 and 1975, and as far as the preliminary final in 1970 and 1972. St. George went down 16-10 to Souths in a hard-fought 1971 decider, but it was Langlands' unfortunate 'white boots' Grand Final performance in 1975 that is so often recalled. Langlands carried a leg injury into the match (while wearing conspicuous white boots for promotional purposes) and a misdirected pain-killing injection at halftime rendered the fullback genius virtually useless in the second half as Easts ran out record 38-0 victors. He captained Australia for the first time in the first Ashes Test of 1970 and led his country in Tests against New Zealand in 1971-72, as well as the ultimately unsuccessful 1972 World Cup campaign. Langlands was chosen as captain-coach of the 1973 Kangaroos, skippering the tourists to victory in the first Test victory against Great Britain but a broken hand ruled him out of the remainder of the series. In 1974,

Langlands was dumped from the Test side altogether after captaining Australia to a lacklustre 12-6 win in the first Ashes encounter against the touring Lions, but was reinstated as fullback and captain for the decider after Australia's shock loss in the second Test. In one of the great performances by a Test captain, Langlands inspired Australia to an Ashes-retaining 22-18 victory with a 13-point haul from a try and five goals, and was famously carried shoulder-high from the SCG with the adoring crowd chanting 'Changa! Changa!' He captained Australia to four straight wins in the first half of the 1975 World Series, but the Grand Final injury ruled Langlands out of the second part of the tournament at season's end and he retired early in 1976. Inducted as an Immortal along with Wally Lewis in 1999, Langlands was named as a reserve in Australia's Team of the Century in 2008.

ARTHUR BEETSON The greatest ball-playing forward Rugby League has ever produced, Arthur Beetson's captaincy deeds with Easts, Australia and eventually Queensland provided a luminous adjunct to one of the game's most celebrated careers. Beetson replaced Ron Coote as the Roosters' captain in 1974 and led one of the great club combinations to back-to-back premierships under master coach Jack Gibson in 1974-75. The Roma product led Australia for the first time against France on the 1973 Kangaroo Tour, becoming the first Indigenous captain of an Australian national sporting team, and replaced Graeme Langlands as skipper for the second Test of the 1974 home Ashes series. Langlands returned after the 16-11 loss, but Beetson played a crucial role in the 22-18 victory in the decider. He captained Australia to World Series victory in 1975, but was at the centre of a selection storm when he was initially left out of Australia's squad for the 1977 World Cup. ARL President Kevin Humphreys refused to accept the selectors' team and Beetson was reinstated, but the Eastern Suburbs skipper pulled out of the first match in New Zealand upon hearing of the controversy. Beetson returned as captain-coach for the remainder of the World Series leading Australia to a 13-12 final victory over Great Britain in his last appearance for his country. Playing reserve grade for Parramatta in 1980, 35-year-old Beetson captained Queensland to a ground-breaking 20-10 triumph in the inaugural State of Origin match, inspiring his young and inexperienced charges. "Said he'd never seen us play before, but he believed in us," Wally Lewis—then a 20-year-old lock—said of Beetson's pre-match address, "and by the time we ran out, we felt 10-foot tall and bulletproof." 'Big Artie' was inducted as the seventh Immortal in 2002 and was named at prop in the Team of the Century in 2008. His death at the age of 66 in December 2011 drew an overwhelming outpouring of emotion and many tributes to one of Rugby League's great players and characters.

BOB FULTON Brilliant centre/five-eighth Bob Fulton was bestowed with weighty captaincy responsibilities at the tender age of 20, when, in just his third season of first grade, the Wollongong product captain-coached City against Country and led Manly to the 1968 Grand Final (a 13-9 loss to Souths). Hooker Fred Jones assumed the club captaincy and skippered the Sea Eagles to their first two premierships in 1972-73, but Fulton was restored to the role in 1974 and captained Manly to Grand Final glory in 1976. Fulton joined Easts in 1977 and skippered the club during a spirited finals campaign, before taking over the Test captaincy the following season. He led Australia to a series win against the Kiwis in 1978 and guided the Kangaroos to an Ashes series victory in England later that year, but his international career came to end after Australia suffered a 2-0 series loss to France. Named an Immortal in 1981, just two years after his retirement, Fulton carved out a career as one of the most prolific and successful club and Test coaches in the game's history. Fulton steered Manly to premierships in 1987 and 1996, while he coached Australia on two successful Kangaroo Tours (1990 and 1994) and to World Cup success in 1992 and 1995 during a 10-season reign in the national post.

STEVE EDGE Although representative honours largely eluded hooker Steve Edge during an admirable career, his record as a club captain elevates him to the top echelon of the game's skippers. A 24-year-old Edge inherited the St. George captaincy from retired legend Graeme Langlands in 1976 and led the club to a premiership the following season with victory over Parramatta in the first replay in Grand Final history. He won another title in 1979 under Craig Young's captaincy before joining the Eels and guiding the club to its first three premierships in 1981-83. Venerable Parramatta coach Jack Gibson installed Edge as captain ahead of a host of more vaunted teammates, including Test greats Ray Price and Mick Cronin. Edge retired after skippering the Eels to a narrow loss in the 1984 Grand Final.

MAX KRILICH Veteran Manly hooker Max Krilich's captaincy record makes for impressive reading. Krilich led the Sea Eagles to an incredible premiership victory in 1978, skippered NSW in five Origin matches in 1982-83 and captained the 1982 Kangaroos on an unbeaten tour of Great Britain and France—an unprecedented achievement that earned the tourists the tag of 'The Invincibles.' Krilich made his Test debut in 1978 and captained his country for the first time in a two-Test series win over the Kiwis in 1982, before leading Australia out in all six post-season Tests against Papua New Guinea, Great Britain and France.

STEVE MORTIMER Canterbury legend Steve Mortimer's rivalries with Tom Raudonikis and Peter Sterling restricted him to eight Test appearances, but the tenacious halfback's contributions as captain at club and Origin level rank him amongst the era's finest. The linchpin of the Bulldogs' 1980 premiership triumph under the captaincy of George Peponis, Mortimer took over as skipper during the run in to the 1984 finals after coach Warren Ryan had tried Chris Anderson and Terry Lamb earlier in the year. Despite a turbulent relationship with Ryan, Mortimer was inspirational in leading the Bulldogs to consecutive Grand Final victories in 1984-85, but gave up the captaincy during 1988—his last season before retiring. Mortimer inherited the NSW captaincy from Ray Price during the 1984 series and became the Blues' first series-winning skipper the following season before he, too, retired from representative football. With the 1985 series wrapped up after the opening matches, Mortimer stepped down ahead of the dead-rubber third encounter, his name securely entrenched in NSW Origin folklore.

WALLY LEWIS Team of the Century five-eighth Wally Lewis' achievements as captain at representative level are central to the legacy of one of Rugby League's greatest players and most polarising figures. Lewis assumed the Queensland captaincy at Origin level in 1981 and led the Maroons in 30 matches—an interstate record unlikely to ever be broken—including series victories in 1982-84, 1987-89 and 1991. State of Origin contests during the 1980s and early-1990s routinely hinged on Lewis' brilliance, reflected by his eight man of the match awards, with his tenacious leadership being the backbone of Queensland's overwhelming success. Lewis ousted Ray Price for the Test captaincy in 1984 and despite his vast unpopularity south of the Tweed, he became one of Australia's most successful and prolific captains. Leading Australia in 24 consecutive internationals, Lewis tasted defeat as captain just three times and guided his country on an unbeaten tour of Britain in France in 1986, to home Ashes series victories in 1984 and 1988, and World Cup final glory over New Zealand in 1988. He was controversially denied the opportunity to become the first player to captain two Kangaroo Tours when he was ruled out with injury in 1990, leaving him agonisingly short of Clive Churchill's Australian captaincy record. Battling his way back from a broken arm during the 1990 finals series, Lewis was ruled unfit to tour by Australian team doctor Nathan Gibbs. Lewis was the obvious choice as the Brisbane Broncos' inaugural skipper in 1988, but he was sensationally stripped of the captaincy in 1990, replaced by Gene Miles. He left the club to lead Gold Coast in 1991 and captain-coached the struggling club to another wooden spoon in his swansong 1992 season (no one has captain-coached a first grade side since). Lewis' often abrasive manner and domineering captaincy style drew regular criticism (particularly in New South Wales), but his extraordinary success at Origin and Test level is an unequivocal testament to his status as one of the great leaders.

WAYNE PEARCE Tireless backrower and Balmain great Wayne Pearce was a long-term Tigers captain and history-making Origin skipper. After starring on the 1982 Kangaroo Tour, 'Junior' took over the club captaincy the following season aged just 22 and led the Tigers to the finals in 1983 after a five-year absence. Pearce was installed as NSW skipper for the third Origin encounter in 1985 (after Steve Mortimer declared his representative retirement mid-series) and led the Blues to the first-ever series cleansweep in 1986. A frontline contender for the 1986 Kangaroos' vice-captaincy, Pearce was controversially ruled out of the tour with injury. He skippered Balmain in consecutive Grand Final defeats in 1988-89 before retiring at the end of an injury-plagued 1990 season.

MAL MENINGA Mal Meninga's captaincy feats elevated him into the stratosphere of Rugby League's all time greats. A dominant figure for Souths (Brisbane), Queensland and Australia during the 1980s, Meninga's career was at a crossroads after joining Canberra and breaking his arm four times in 1987-88. But the bulldozing centre courageously returned to the paddock in 1989, replacing Raiders stalwart Dean Lance as captain and leading the club to a maiden premiership with a famous extra-time defeat of Balmain in the Grand Final. Meninga skippered Australia for the first time in a 34-2 defeat of France during 1990 and after a second premiership success with the Raiders, he was named captain of the Kangaroos when Wally Lewis was controversially ruled unfit to tour. Following a successful Ashes campaign, Meninga retained the national captaincy despite Lewis' return for the first Test against the Kiwis in 1991. Meninga succeeded Lewis as Queensland skipper in 1992 but endured three straight series defeats in charge. The 34-year-old farewelled the game in spectacular style in 1994, leading the Raiders to an emphatic Grand Final victory over Canterbury and Australia to another Ashes series victory, simultaneously becoming the first player to tour with the Kangaroos four times and the first to captain two tours to England and France. Meninga's final match, a record 74-0 romp against France in Béizers, was his 24th Test as skipper.

LAURIE DALEY Regarded as the heir apparent to Canberra teammate Mal Meninga as Test skipper, the Super League split interfered with Laurie Daley's ascension to the national role, but he remains one of the most successful captains in Origin history. The Junee product was a genuine Rugby League prodigy, breaking into first grade in 1987 at 17, while he was still a teenager when he debuted for NSW and won a premiership in 1989. He became a Test regular and toured with the Kangaroos in 1990, and assumed the state captaincy in 1992 aged just 22. One of the game's foremost match-winners at five-eighth or centre, Daley led the Blues to three consecutive series victories (1992-94, ironically, with Meninga opposing as Queensland captain), while he deputised as Australian skipper for a suspended Meninga in the first Test of the 1993 series against the Kiwis. After touring with the Kangaroos as vice-captain at the end of 1994, the captaincy of Canberra and Australia appeared a mere formality, but Raiders coach Tim Sheens installed Ricky Stuart as club captain in 1995 and the Super League upheaval rubbed Daley out of the representative picture. Daley played in the 1996 Origin series under Brad Fittler, before leading Super League's Australian and NSW rep sides throughout 1997. He wrested the club captaincy from Stuart in 1998 and ousted Fittler as skipper of the first full-strength Test team in four years for the early-season clash with New Zealand. Daley also regained his position as NSW skipper in 1998, and although Fittler captained the Blues in the first two matches of the 1999 series, injury to the Roosters champion allowed Daley to skipper the Blues in his final Origin appearance—a 10-all draw in the series decider—before he retired at the end of 2000 as arguably Canberra's greatest-ever player.

TERRY LAMB Although he never captained at representative level, Terry Lamb's naming as skipper of Canterbury's best-ever line-up to mark the club's 70th anniversary in 2005—ahead of fellow premiership-winning captains George Peponis and Steve Mortimer—gives an indication of his influence as a leader. Briefly installed as skipper of the Bulldogs in his first season with the club (1984, after joining from Wests), Lamb won Grand Final with the club that same year and 1988, and toured with the 1986 Kangaroos. Lamb inherited the club captaincy in 1990 from Peter Tunks and was an inspiration to his younger teammates. The Canterbury pivot guided the Bulldogs to consecutive minor premierships in 1993-94, but a heavy knock in the first half of the 1994 Grand Final limited his impact in the 36-12 loss to Canberra. The 34-year-old was at the forefront of the Bulldogs' remarkable run from sixth spot to claim the last Winfield Cup in 1995 and although he retired after the Grand Final triumph over red-hot favourites Manly, Lamb returned to assist the depleted club under Simon Gillies' captaincy in 1996.

ALLAN LANGER Already established as Queensland's and Australia's No.1 halfback by the time the 1992 season rolled around, 25-year-old 'Alfie' Langer was installed as captain of the Broncos following the departure of veteran Gene Miles.

The role elevated Langer's performances to a new level—he won the Rothmans Medal in 1992 before leading Brisbane to a maiden premiership victory with a two-try, Churchill Medal-winning performance in the 28-8 Grand Final defeat of St. George. Langer guided the Broncos to another title in 1993, although setting a good example was probably not foremost in his thoughts when he crudely sang "St. George can't play" after the Broncos again downed the Dragons in the decider. He captained Queensland for the first time during the 1996 Origin series and skippered Queensland's Super League Tri-Series side the following season. After leading the Broncos to success in the Super League Grand Final and World Club Challenge final, Langer achieved an unprecedented captaincy treble in 1998. The diminutive No.7 became the first player to captain an Origin series win, a Grand Final victory and a Test series success in the same season. The two post-season defeats of New Zealand were Langer's first and only Tests as skipper of Australia, while his four premierships as captain rank him among the most successful club skippers in the game's history.

BRAD FITTLER The Super League war thrust Brad Fittler into multiple captaincy roles at an early age, but the former wild child blossomed into one of the best and most prolific skippers in Rugby League history. Fittler occasionally led the Panthers in the absence of Greg Alexander and John Cartwright during 1993-95, but the outbreak of the Super League war in 1995 catapulted Fittler into the NSW and Australian captaincy positions at just 23. Despite a disappointing 3-0 series loss to Queensland at his first attempt as skipper, Fittler's burgeoning maturity as a leader was on display in Australia's series victory over the Kiwis and the World Cup triumph in England at year's end. He retained the state captaincy in 1996 despite the return of the Super League contingent, but was ousted by Laurie Daley for the Origin and Test roles in 1998. Fittler was restored to both positions in 1999 and led NSW and Australia to emphatic Origin and World Cup victories in 2000. His final act as a representative captain was leading Australia to an Ashes series victory in England in 2001. His mark of 14 Origin matches as New South Wales captain remained a record until broken by Danny Buderus in 2008, while his 25 Tests as skipper ranks behind only Darren Lockyer and Clive Churchill. Fittler joined Sydney City in 1996 but played under Sean Garlick during his first season with the club, before taking over the following season and leading the Roosters to four Grand Finals in five years, including the 2002 premiership triumph. He retired in 2004 with a premiership record 216 first grade games as captain of Penrith and the Roosters (since broken by Nathan Cayless).

GEOFF TOOVEY The courageous Geoff Toovey led his club for nine seasons and skippered NSW and Australia at the peak of an outstanding career. Michael O'Connor's retirement elevated courageous halfback Geoff Toovey to the Manly captaincy in 1993, alternating with veteran Des Hasler before taking on the role solo in 1994 and going on to lead his state and country. The pint-sized halfback, renowned for his tenacious defence against much larger opponents, was a natural leader. He returned to Test and Origin level in 1995 after four- and five-year absences respectively, and guided the Sea Eagles to the minor premiership. Despite the shock loss to the Bulldogs in the Grand Final, Toovey emerged as the game's preeminent club captain and won the Clive Churchill Medal in Manly's 20-8 defeat of St. George in the 1996 decider. Injury to incumbent Brad Fittler allowed Toovey to captain Australia to a 52-6 win over Papua New Guinea at the end of 1996, before leading NSW to series victory in 1997. Toovey skippered Manly to a third successive Grand Final in 1997, a last-minute loss to the Knights. Although he had an increasingly tempestuous relationship with the game's referees, Toovey remained as captain of Manly until the club's merger with Norths at the end of 1999, and led the Northern Eagles joint venture for two seasons before retiring. The 13-Test and 15-Origin veteran took the field with the (c) next to his name in 190 of his 286 first grade appearances.

PAUL HARRAGON One of the modern era's true enforcers and a Knights foundation player, Paul 'Chief' Harragon became a Test and Origin regular in 1992. The intimidating prop assumed the Newcastle captaincy during 1995 and led the club to its first preliminary final, before skippering Australia in an 86-6 defeat of South Africa at the year-ending World Cup in England. Harragon was overlooked for the NSW captaincy in favour of Geoff Toovey when injury ruled Brad Fittler out in 1997, but he led the Knights to an epic Grand Final victory over Toovey's Sea Eagles later in the season. An inspirational and passionate leader, Harragon captained Country Origin in 1995 and 1997, but the latter years of his career were plagued by injury and he retired midway through 1999. Harragon was named in the Newcastle District Rugby League Team of the Century in 2008.

ANDREW JOHNS Team of the Century halfback Andrew Johns played under Knights elder statesmen Mark Sargent, Paul Harragon and Tony Butterfield for the first half of his club career with his unabashed larrikinism off the field possibly hindering his captaincy prospects early in his career. But Johns' leadership on the field saw him installed as Newcastle skipper in 2001, where he led the club to its second premiership in his first season in charge, collecting the Churchill Medal in the Knights' 30-24 upset of the Eels. Johns succeeded Brad Fittler as the captain of NSW and Australia in 2002. The role elevated his performances to another plane at Origin level, leading the Blues in the drawn 2002 series and to a 2-1 triumph in 2003 with a string of match-winning displays. Johns missed the 2004 series with injury before returning for an Origin swansong in 2005 under the captaincy of club-mate Danny Buderus. He led Australia in Test victories over Great Britain (2002) and New Zealand (2003), but Darren Lockyer had cemented the role as skipper by the time Johns returned to the national side from an injury layoff in 2005. Johns captained Newcastle 105 times before his injury-enforced retirement early in 2007.

DARREN LOCKYER A serious neck injury to Gorden Tallis thrust 24-year-old Darren Lockyer into the twin roles of captain of Brisbane and Queensland during 2001. Already lauded as one of the best fullbacks to play the game, Lockyer skippered the Maroons to an emphatic series victory with a man of the match display in the decider, before leading the injury-ravaged Broncos to a preliminary final, where they gallantly went down 24-16 to Parramatta. Tallis returned in 2002, but Lockyer was chosen to captain the severely depleted Kangaroos to Great Britain at the end of 2003, brilliantly guiding his country to a 3-0 series whitewash. He took over the state captaincy on a permanent basis the following season and the club leadership in 2005. Lockyer became just the second player (after Allan Langer in 1998) to skipper teams to Origin, premiership and Test series success in a watershed 2006 season. He surpassed Clive Churchill as Australia's most prolific Test skipper in 2009 and retired two years later with a total of 38 Tests in charge, while his record of captaining Queensland in 22 matches and six series victories (from eight series as skipper) is second only to Wally Lewis in Origin history. The talismanic Broncos skipper bowed out of premiership football after leading the club to the finals for the sixth time, kicking a golden point field goal (after sustaining a fractured cheekbone 10 minutes earlier when he collided with teammate Gerard Beale's knee) to down the Dragons during the 2011 finals in his last NRL match, his 166th as Brisbane captain.

CAMERON SMITH Melbourne coach Craig Bellamy devised a unique captaincy strategy in 2006 following the retirement of Robbie Kearns, rotating four skippers throughout the season. The quartet was made up of veterans David Kidwell, Matt Geyer and Scott Hill, and 22-year-old Queensland Origin hooker Cameron Smith. Despite not leading the side in the Storm's qualifying and preliminary final victories, Smith had the (c) next to his name for the Grand Final showdown against Brisbane—just the sixth time in 2006 he had skippered the side. The Broncos prevailed 15-8, but Smith made his Test debut in the year-ending Tri-Nations tournament and he assumed the club captaincy permanently after Bellamy scrapped the rotation policy midway through 2007. Smith guided Melbourne to a Grand Final victory over Manly and injury to Darren Lockyer catapulted Smith into the role of Test captain two weeks later—a record 58-0 demolition of the Kiwis—while Lockyer's ongoing knee problems saw Smith lead Australia in the Centenary Test win over New Zealand and Queensland to series victory in 2008. Suspension ruled Smith out of the '08 Grand Final loss to Manly and after guiding the club to another title with a 23-16 defeat of Parramatta in the 2009 decider, Melbourne's two premierships under Smith's captaincy were stripped following revelations of flagrant salary cap breaches. Smith's stoic leadership came to the fore during the Storm's soul-destroying 2010 season and he was magnificent in steering the club to the 2011 minor premiership. A dominant player with a level-headed temperament tailor-made for captaincy, Smith led Australia against Wales during the 2011 Four Nations tournament and shaped as the heir apparent to retiring legend Lockyer at Test and Origin level.

UNFORGETTABLE DEBUTS

Rugby League has witnessed some memorable and spectacular debuts at club and representative level. This chapter looks at the most unforgettable first games in the code's history.

VIV FARNSWORTH Newtown centre Viv Farnsworth showcased the talent that would see him become one half of Australia's first Test-playing brothers with a stunning first grade introduction in 1910. The rugby union convert scored a premiership record-equalling four tries in Newtown's 31-6 opening-round thrashing of Annandale. His older brother, former Wallaby Bill, also scored on debut in the victory. The brothers toured together with the 1911-12 Kangaroos to create an Australian Rugby League first, with Viv Farnsworth scoring two tries on Test debut in the first Ashes Test against England on the way to a historic series win. He was named as one of Australia's 100 Greatest Players in 2008 as part of the game's centenary celebrations.

DON MANSON South Sydney winger Don Manson set a phenomenal mark for a player on first grade debut by crossing for five tries in a 63-0 pasting of University in 1937. Manson's swag of tries equalled the Rabbitohs' club record for tries in a match and has never been matched by a player in their maiden premiership outing. The haul eclipsed the previous all time record for a player on first grade debut—four tries—held jointly by Easts' Johnno Stuntz (1908) and Newtown's Viv Farnsworth (1910), while Canterbury's Tony Nash (1942) and Gold Coast's Jordan Atkins (2008) have also crossed four times on debut since Manson's magical entrance. The feat is at long odds to be achieved again—just four players have scored five tries in a game since 1995. Manson went on to represent NSW and top the Sydney competition's tryscoring table in 1938, finishing in 1941 with career figures of 24 tries from 21 games for the Rabbitohs.

BOBBY BUGDEN St. George halfback Bobby Bugden was an integral part of the first half of the club's 11-year premiership run, winning six Grand Finals from 1956-61. Bugden was chosen to tour with the 1959-60 Kangaroos, but he played second-fiddle to Queenslander Barry Muir, who played all six Tests on tour. Bugden flourished when he was eventually picked to make his Test debut against France in 1960, however, scoring three tries in a 56-6 thrashing of the tourists at the Brisbane Exhibition Ground. He scored another try two weeks later at the SCG as Australia wrapped up the series, which was to be Budgen's only other Test appearance.

MICHAEL O'CONNOR Two seasons after switching codes, former Wallaby Michael O'Connor was chosen to make his Origin debut for NSW in 1985. He made an immediate impact, displaying the form that would see him become the Blues' most prolific try-scorer and point-scorer. O'Connor scored all of NSW's points in the series opener—two tries and five goals—in an 18-2 boilover at Lang Park. The win gave NSW the impetus to claim its maiden series triumph, while O'Connor went on to feature in another eight victories during the next six seasons.

ALLAN LANGER Pint-sized Ipswich halfback Allan Langer's selection as injured stalwart Mark Murray's replacement in the Queensland side for the 1987 series caused a minor uproar in the Sunshine State with coach Wayne Bennett and senior Maroons players among the doubters. There were question marks over the 20-year-old's defence, while Sydney-based halves Laurie Spina and Kevin Walters had outplayed Langer in a State of Origin trial. It has passed into interstate folklore that Queensland selector and former Ipswich Test prop Dud Beattie's plumping for Langer got him over the line, and Langer repaid the faith with interest. Although Queensland lost the first match of the series after a last-minute Mark McGaw try,

Langer's livewire display—complete with tenacious tackling—was a feature of the match. Langer would be the first-choice No.7 for the 'Canetoads' when available for the next 15 years—racking up an Origin record 34 appearances—and was named at halfback in Queensland's Team of the Century in 2008.

BRAD MACKAY Like fellow Dragon Bobby Bugden three decades earlier, the versatile Brad Mackay scored a hat-trick on Test debut against France. A NSW rep in 1989-90, Mackay was a late inclusion in place of the injured Brad Clyde for the one-off Test against the touring French side at Parkes in 1990. After grabbing the treble, Mackay starred on the ensuing Kangaroo Tour at the end of the year and finished his career with six tries from 12 Test appearances.

ANDREW JOHNS Newcastle legend Andrew Johns came off the bench in three first grade games for the Knights in 1993, but it was his run-on debut in the opening round of 1994 that projected his eventual elevation to the highest echelon of the game's greats. Johns scored 23 points—from two tries, seven goals and a field goal—in a 43-14 thrashing of Souths, smashing the club record for points in a match and the premiership record for most points in a starting debut. His performance was but a taste of what was to come—Johns spearheaded two premiership victories, won three Dally M Medals, broke the all time career pointscoring record and was named at halfback in the ARL Team of the Century. On international debut for Australia against South Africa in the 1995 World Cup, Johns equalled the world record for points in a Test with two tries and 11 goals for a haul of 30 points.

DARREN LOCKYER Brisbane fullback Darren Lockyer announced himself as a future superstar in 1997. He spearheaded the Broncos' resounding Super League premiership victory and starred for the Super League Australian outfit at the end of the season. The 21-year-old was selected on the bench to make his officially recognised Test debut in the 1998 Anzac Test against New Zealand—Australia's first full-strength side since 1994. Robbie O'Davis was preferred as starting fullback, but the Newcastle No.1 succumbed to injury after just nine minutes, thrusting Lockyer into the action. It was a debut to forget for the future superstar with Lockyer bustled into several errors leading directly to New Zealand tries as the underdog Kiwis scored a shock 22-16 result. It is a testament to Lockyer's champion qualities that he backed up for the Broncos two days later to produce a man of the match performance in a 60-6 massacre of Norths, before going on to become an all time Kangaroo great and record-breaking Test skipper over the next 13 years.

AMOS ROBERTS Indigenous speedster Amos Roberts broadcast his intentions in the NRL with his initial first grade performance, scoring a try and nine goals to tally 22 points—a premiership record for a player on debut (Andrew Johns scored 23 points in his run-on debut for Newcastle in 1994, but had made three interchange appearances the previous season). Roberts was outstanding on the wing in St. George-Illawarra's 54-0 demolition of the Warriors in 2000, and progressed to become one of the decade's most exciting outside backs. Scoring over 100 tries in nine years of NRL football, Roberts topped the competition's tryscoring charts in 2004 and represented City Origin for five successive seasons.

JUSTIN HODGES Justin Hodges endured the daddy of all horror Origin debuts in 2002. The 20-year-old Roosters centre was chosen on Queensland's wing for the second match of the series—one of six changes after the Maroons lost the opening encounter 32-4. Cleaning up an Andrew Johns grubber during the first half, Hodges threw a looping in-goal pass over Darren Lockyer's head, allowing NSW five-eighth Braith Anasta to pounce for the Blues' first try. Hodges covered another in-goal kick from Johns in the second half and legendary commentator Ray Warren summed it up best in his call of the match: "And will Hodges pass this time? I don't think... oh... I can't believe it! He's had another go at it!" Luke Ricketson dived on the loose ball for the Blues' second try. A despondent Hodges was hooked immediately by coach Wayne Bennett. Thankfully for the youngster, Queensland went on to win the match 26-18 to keep the series alive. Meanwhile, despite being dropped for the decider, Hodges bounced back to craft a long and decorated Origin career.

ISRAEL FOLAU It was 17-year-old Israel Folau's aim to play one first grade game for the Storm in 2007—he achieved that goal in spectacular fashion in round one and went on to carve out one of the greatest rookie seasons in the game's history. The giant teenage winger scored a magnificent double in an 18-16 defeat of the Tigers, demonstrating the aerial skills and power that became his trademarks. Folau won a premiership, broke the club tryscoring record and became Australia's youngest international in an incredible maiden season. He scored a double on Test debut against New Zealand in 2007 and was outstanding on Origin debut in a losing Queensland side the following season.

JARRYD HAYNE Parramatta prodigy Jarryd Hayne's 2007 debut for NSW played out as an extraordinary hero-to-villain narrative, but his first-half try is rightly remembered as one of the great individual tries. Picking the ball up on his toes after a miscued grubber by opposing winger Brent Tate as the halftime siren sounded, Hayne fended off Justin Hodges, tiptoed down the sidelined and kicked ahead just before being pushed into touch. The 19-year-old outpaced the Queensland chasers to finish the 50-metre special and set up an 18-6 lead at the break. But Hayne's night turned sour when he fielded a deep kick in his own quarter and, close to being forced into touch, flung a misdirected pass out of reach of his fullback Anthony Minichiello. Maroons skipper Darren Lockyer swept through to pick up the bouncing ball and run around behind the posts for the go-ahead score, with Queensland eventually getting home 25-18.

JORDAN ATKINS In the opening round of 2008, late-blooming Gold Coast winger Jordan Atkins became the first player in 66 years to score four tries on first grade debut. The 24-year-old's haul, which included a spectacular aerial effort, propelled the Titans to a 36 18 defeat of the North Queensland Cowboys to christen the club's brand new home, Skilled Stadium. Atkins' effort was the best since Tony Nash crossed four times on debut for Canterbury in 1942, while just three other players had previously scored four or more tries in their maiden first grade appearance. A succession of injuries restricted Atkins to just 28 games in three seasons with the Titans and he departed the holiday strip for Parramatta in 2011, where he played just 12 games.

DEAN WHARE Young Kiwi centre Dean Whare was promoted to Manly's first grade side to make his debut against North Queensland in the place of injured compatriot Steve Matai in round 12 of the 2010 season. The 20-year-old scored the first three tries of the match inside 25 minutes with his first three touches of the ball in the NRL, before setting up the Sea Eagles' fourth for winger Michael Robertson. Manly held off a fast-finishing home side to win 24-22, capping a truly memorable debut for Whare.

DYLAN FARRELL The 19-year-old South Sydney centre Dylan Farrell trumped Whare for the most spectacular debut of 2010. A game-day inclusion for the injury-stricken Rabbitohs' Round 22 clash with Wests Tigers, the Toyota Cup regular scored a powerful try in each half as Souths recovered from a 16-point deficit to force the game into extra-time. The game seemed destined for a draw, until Farrell backed up a Rhys Wesser bust in the dying seconds of golden point, completing his hat-trick and a miracle win for the desperate Rabbits. Farrell developed into one of Souths' backline stars in 2011.

UNLIKELY HEROES

Rugby League is a game built on heroic deeds and occasionally those heroics come from the unlikeliest of sources. Unheralded champions, improbable performances and astonishing plays, have earned these unlikely heroes a treasured place in the rich tapestry of Rugby League history.

LIN JOHNSON The most indelible moment of fullback Lin Johnson's career occurred in the 1942 Grand Final. Johnson first played for Canterbury in 1939, before representing New South Wales in two interstate matches while playing in Newcastle in 1940. He rejoined the Berries in 1941, and his accurate goalkicking and steady play at the back contributed to the club clinching the minor premiership the following season. Forced into a Grand Final showdown after losing the semi-final to St. George, Canterbury was locked at 9-all with the Dragons late in the decider, with Johnson landing three goals. He stepped up to take a penalty shot in the dying stages, but what would usually be a regulation attempt was complicated by the sodden Sydney Cricket Ground turf due to rainstorms earlier in the day (thousands of drenched supporters famously charged into the members and M.A. Noble stands during the reserve grade match to escape a downpour, with police unable to stop the horde). Johnson slipped as he approached the ball for the match-winning score, but he still managed to connect and it scraped over the crossbar for an 11-9 victory and Canterbury's second premiership. He finished his first grade career in 1946 with a total of 144 goals in 90 games.

DICK DUNN Goalkicking lock Dick Dunn became a finals hero for Easts in 1945, just a year after he was unwanted by the Tricolours after a dismal season saw the club finish second last with only four wins. A centre in the Tricolours' 1940 premiership victory, Dunn's career appeared to be on the scrapheap at the end of 1944. The local junior kept his spot, however, and played a brilliant hand in Easts' drive to supremacy in 1945. Dunn, who would play 134 games for Easts, scored a try and booted five goals in the minor premiers' semi-final defeat of Wests, before playing the game of his life in the premiership decider, scoring three tries and five goals for a 19-point haul to help subdue Balmain 22-18 and claim Eastern Suburbs' ninth title. Balmain led 10-5 at halftime and 18-17 with only eight minutes to play when Dunn, "with tears in his eyes" according to the *Telegraph*'s George Thatcher, begged captain Ray Stehr to allow him to shoot for goal after a penalty was awarded on the sideline close to halfway. Stehr declared the kick too far to land but eventually conceded, with Dunn justifying the captain's change of heart, landing the monstrous goal that put Easts in front. Dunn finished off the day with a try in the final minute after winning a scrum for the Tricolours with a giant clearing kick.

RON ROBERTS St. George winger Ron Roberts' name is synonymous with the series-winning try he scored for Australia in 1950 to break a 30-year Ashes drought. A bulldozing winger who scored 51 tries in 51 first grade games for the Dragons, Roberts was notorious for his poor ball-handling skills. But the 190cm winger, who had not played in the opening two Tests of the series, latched onto the one that mattered in the deciding Test against Great Britain in an SCG mudbath that was so wet 40 tons of sand was put onto the surface. With the match deadlocked at 2-all inside the final quarter, Australia produced a slick backline movement that defied some of the worst conditions international football has been played in, resulting in Roberts accepting a pass from centre Keith Middleton and sprinting 40 metres to score in the corner and secure the Ashes for Australia for the first time in 30 years. Lost in the euphoria of the victory was the fact that Roberts dropped the ball with the line open minutes later and would, in fact, never play another Test match. He had, nevertheless, delivered Australia its most coveted Rugby League prize and the try was voted the greatest moment in the game's history in a *Rugby League Week* poll during the 1980s.

STEVE JACKSON Hardworking Canberra prop Steve Jackson became ensconced in Grand Final folklore with one of the most incredible and memorable solo tries ever scored in a decider. Jackson sat on the bench for most of the epic 1989 Grand Final between Canberra and Balmain, but grabbed his moment of glory in extra-time after the Raiders had fought back from a 12-2 deficit to tie the game up 14-all with 90 seconds remaining. Chris O'Sullivan kicked a field goal to edge Canberra in front early in added time, and Jackson was trailing when Mal Meninga foiled a desperate Balmain counterattack deep inside Tigers territory as time ran out. Accepting the offload from his skipper, Jackson embarked on a bumping, weaving run from the quarter-line, leaving defenders strewn in his wake and carrying three over the line to seal the Raiders' maiden premiership 19-14. Jackson has been the star of thousands of replays since, and although he made nine Origin appearances for Queensland in subsequent stints with Wests and Gold Coast, scoring the winning try on debut in the third game of the 1990 series, he left the most indelible mark of his career by planting the ball over the tryline at the SFS on the last Sunday of September, 1989.

GARY COYNE Tireless backrower Gary Coyne was an unsung hero of Canberra's 1989-90 premiership victories, despite debuting for Queensland in 1989 and narrowly missing selection for the 1990 Kangaroo Tour. But in 1991, in a high-scoring finals classic against Manly, Coyne emerged as the improbable star. Coyne produced a memorable haul of four tries to equal the premiership record for most tries in a finals match and propel the Raiders to a stirring 34-26 victory. Coyne's overall record boasted just 28 four-pointers in 159 games for Canberra, while he failed to score in 11 Origins and two Test appearances. He was rewarded with selection for Australia's tour of Papua New Guinea following the Raiders' Grand Final loss to Penrith.

PAUL OSBORNE A late replacement in Canberra's side for the 1994 decider against Canterbury in the place of the suspended John Lomax, ball-playing prop Paul Osborne became a Grand Final hero for the ages with a brilliant cameo. Osborne played just 10 regular season games in 1994, stuck behind Kiwi Test front-rowers Lomax and Quentin Pongia, and was set to take up a deal in England before the Australian season finished. But he delayed his departure to provide depth in Tim Sheens' squad for the Raiders' finals campaign and received his opportunity on the biggest stage of all when Lomax was suspended after being marched for a high tackle on North Sydney lock Billy Moore in the preliminary final. Sensational Osborne offloads produced the opening two tries for David Furner and Ken Nagas in the opening 16 minutes as Canberra hammered the Bulldogs 36-12 in a one-sided Grand Final. Osborne decided to retire after the match (aged just 28), benefitting from his new-found popularity in the nation's capital by embarking on a career in ACT politics, before a controversial two-year stint as Parramatta's CEO came to an end in 2011.

CRAIG SMITH Melbourne winger Craig Smith was the unwitting, unconscious hero of the Storm's Grand Final victory over St. George Illawarra in 1999. A first grade regular with 110 points in the club's debut 1998 season, Smith was out of favour the following year and spent the entire regular season turning out for feeder club Norths in Brisbane before receiving a shock call-up to first grade during the finals series, replacing Ben Anderson, son of coach Chris, after senior players demanded the five-eighth's sacking. Smith came into the Melbourne side on the flank, with New South Wales Origin winger Matt Geyer moving to pivot. Smith made the most of his opportunity, kicking four goals against the Bulldogs and three goals against Parramatta in consecutive two-point, sudden-death victories to steer Melbourne into the decider. Smith booted three goals and produced a crucial try-saving tackle on Anthony Mundine as the Storm clawed back from a 14-point halftime deficit, and looked set to level the scores with four minutes remaining when he caught a Brett Kimmorley cross-kick in the St. George Illawarra in-goal. But as he returned to the turf, Smith was collected in a high tackle by Saints three-quarter Jamie Ainscough that forced the ball loose. Video referee Chris Ward agonised over the decision as Smith lay unconscious on the Stadium Australia turf, eventually awarding Melbourne a penalty try and a remarkable premiership in the club's second season in the NRL. In a sad post-script to the premiership win, the accidental hero retired from the game at just 26 years of age, rejecting an offer from the Storm to play on after losing his zest for the game during an unhappy year of weekly travel from

Melbourne to Brisbane. He will, however, be long remembered for his involvement in one of the most extraordinary Grand Final incidents ever seen.

CHRIS HICKS Underrated winger Chris Hicks was a reluctant goalkicker for Penrith, filling in on occasion for injured sharpshooter Ryan Girdler. Going into the Panthers' Round 16 clash with Parramatta in 2000, Hicks had a career strike-rate of just 55 per cent, including a dismal two goals from seven attempts a fortnight earlier against the Knights. Consequently, Hicks' confidence was ebbing low when he was called upon to line up a 40-metre penalty goal attempt to break a 14-all deadlock on fulltime. But he stepped up and nailed the kick, becoming the archetypal reluctant hero. Incredibly, Hicks reprised his match-winning role with the boot two weeks later in a phenomenal comeback against the Tigers. Penrith fought back from a 23-point deficit midway through the second half, with Hicks landing a pressure conversion from the sideline to seal a remarkable 32-31 triumph. Hicks played 194 first grade games for Penrith and Manly, joining Warrington after scoring a try in the Sea Eagles' Grand Final loss to Melbourne in 2007. He was lured back to the NRL by Parramatta in 2011, where he played seven games before retiring. In no season did Hicks kick at better than 70 per cent, finishing his career with a 57.93 per cent strike-rate.

SCOTT SATTLER Workmanlike backrower Scott Sattler spent much of his career in the shadow of his father, famed South Sydney and Kangaroo tough guy John Sattler. The captain of four Grand Final-winning sides between 1967 and 1971, Sattler senior is predominantly remembered for playing almost all of the 1970 decider against Manly with a badly broken jaw. But Scott Sattler also played himself into Grand Final folklore as a 31-year-old in 2003 while packing down for the Penrith Panthers. The decider against the Roosters was evenly poised at 6-all when, in the 55th minute, Roosters winger Todd Byrne streaked away down the touchline from his own quarter with not one Panther in front of him. But the veteran Sattler, not renowned for his speed and at huge odds to catch the winger, hared across the sodden field to cut Byrne down and bundle him into touch in one of Rugby League's most famous tackles. The momentum swung Penrith's way after the tackle and the underdogs went on to win the premiership 18-6, with Sattler lauded as the hero in his final game as a Panther. The Queensland Origin rep finished his career with a season at the Wests Tigers in 2004.

BRETT FINCH Tenacious and often maligned half Brett Finch was an 11th-hour inclusion for the Blues in the 2006 series opener, becoming a State of Origin hero in the process. First-choice No.7 Craig Gower was injured at training a day before the opening match of the series and legendary Newcastle halfback Andrew Johns turned down an invitation to replace him, having retired from representative football after the Trans-Tasman Test three weeks earlier. After considering a myriad of options for the key role, selectors opted for Finch, who took the field in the conspicuous No.20 jumper. Finch experienced a dream game in his first NSW appearance since his debut match in 2004. He backed up a long movement to score the opening try of the match in the first half, before kicking a 35-metre field goal with less than two minutes on the clock to break a 16-all deadlock. Finch's kick was later honoured with the inaugural Peter Frilingos Memorial Award at the Dally Ms for Headline Moment of the Year.

ADAM MOGG 'Adam who?' was many people's reaction to the news Canberra utility back Adam Mogg had been selected for the injury-ravaged Maroons during the 2006 Origin series. Mogg starred in the Queensland Cup before joining Parramatta in 2002 at the age of 24 and was a solid performer for the Raiders after heading to the nation's capital two years later, but even his most ardent supporters would have been shocked to learn he had replaced injured star Greg Inglis for Origin two. The lanky flyer experienced a dream debut, however, scoring a memorable double in Queensland's 30-6 victory at Suncorp Stadium to keep the series alive. Retained for the decider, Mogg scored the opening try in spectacular fashion, planting the ball in the corner while falling backwards in mid-air after latching onto a cross-field kick. Queensland went on to win the dramatic decider 16-14 to start a record series-winning streak, with Mogg one of the heroes. He left the Raiders at the end of 2006 for a successful Super League stint, before returning for a swansong with the club midway through 2010.

MICHAEL ROBERTSON In a team of backline superstars, underrated winger Michael Robertson was the standout in Manly's record 40-0 grand final thrashing of Melbourne in 2008. Electrifying fullback Brett Stewart, rookie winger David Williams and rep veteran Jamie Lyon had earned most of the plaudits during the season, but Robertson outshone the trio to become just the second player in 47 years to score a hat-trick of tries in a decider. The ultra-consistent flyer also set up departing Manly great Steve Menzies for a late try, capping an excellent performance that was unlucky to not be rewarded with the Churchill Medal and World Cup selection for Australia. At one stage Robertson held the NRL active consecutive games record with 139 and played in Manly's 2011 triumph before moving to Super League club Harlequins.

ONE-GAME WONDERS

There are a variety of reasons behind a player making just one appearance at club, state or international level. The most notable, laudable and regrettable are recalled below.

BENNY WEARING Despite being regarded as one of the 1920s' truly outstanding players, South Sydney winger Benny Wearing was continually overlooked for Test duty. A club legend with a Souths record 144 tries and then-record 836 points in 173 games, Wearing represented NSW 12 times before finally winning an Australian cap in 1928. After missing out on the first two Test sides against England, Wearing scored two tries and kicked three goals in the 21-14 third Test victory—Australia's only success of the series. England captain Jonty Parkin remarked after the match: "Where art thou been hiding yon winger?" But he was again left out when the following year's Kangaroo Tour squad was named.

Nevertheless, Wearing was recognised as one of the 100 greatest players of all time during the ARL's Centenary celebrations in 2008. Selectors' repeated snubbing of Wearing—regarded by some historians as Australia's greatest winger—has been a constant source of disbelief for more than eight decades.

COL MAXWELL Wests centre Col Maxwell was an unwitting player in the biggest selection controversy in the game's history *(see Bolters and Unlucky Omissions—Len Smith)*. In 1948 Maxwell debuted for NSW and was a non-playing reserve for Australia's series with the Kiwis, but a dramatic loss of form saw him finish the year in reserve grade. Incumbent Test captain Len Smith was considered a certainty to lead the 1948-49 Kangaroos, but in what at the time appeared a politically and religiously motivated move, Smith was infamously left out of the squad, while Maxwell was a shock selection as captain-coach. Maxwell was hampered by injury throughout the tour, and played the only Test match of his career as skipper in Australia's 16-7 loss to Great Britain in the second Ashes encounter at Station Road, Swinton.

ALLAN McKEAN Rock-steady fullback Allan McKean, the one-time holder of the Roosters' career pointscoring record, was chosen for his one and only Test during the 1970 Ashes series. Injury had claimed skipper Graeme Langlands in the first encounter and Australian selectors gave McKean the call-up for the deciding third Test. McKean starred on debut with seven goals, but it was not enough to prevent a 21-17 defeat. The Tricolours custodian was the competition's leading point-scorer in 1972 but never received another representative opportunity, while Australia has not lost an Ashes series since.

JOHN RHEINBERGER Although his two appearances technically rule him ineligible for one-game wonder status, Roosters centre John Rheinberger made his only first grade start in the 1975 Grand Final. A member of the inaugural Australian Schoolboys squad in 1972, the youngster came on as a replacement in one match during the 1975 season, before being called up to replace Mark Harris, who broke his leg in the preliminary final. Rheinberger did his job in Easts' 38-0 demolition of St. George, but broke his shoulder early in 1976 and did not play another first grade game. He went on to have a successful career in indoor cricket.

GREG SMITH American Greg Smith is undoubtedly the most notable and notorious one-game wonder of the NRL era, and perhaps in premiership history. Smith arrived at Newcastle in 1999 amid much hype, claiming to have been a former NFL player with the Philadelphia Eagles. Knights coach Warren Ryan fast-tracked Smith into first grade for the round three clash with Canterbury—with disastrous results. After taking his place on the wing, it all went pear-shaped for Smith. Newcastle led 24-4 with half an hour of the match remaining, but on the back of two lamentable Smith errors and some Rod Silva magic, the Bulldogs came back to snatch a 28-26 victory. Newcastle's loss was generally regarded as the 'choke' of the season, while Smith was promptly dropped from first grade and departed the club. It was later revealed Smith had never played in the NFL and he quickly earned Rugby League curiosity status.

DAVID PEACHEY Despite being one of the most gifted fullbacks of his generation, Cronulla great David Peachey has just one NSW State of Origin jumper and one Super League Test guernsey to show for a thrilling 14-season career. A brilliant start to the 1997 Super League season saw Peachey selected for the rebel organisation's Anzac Test against the Kiwis early in the year, but his position was usurped for the post-season internationals by a 20-year-old Darren Lockyer, who was preparing to launch himself into the realm of the all time great custodians. Despite winning consecutive Dally M Fullback of the Year awards in 1999-2000, Peachey only made one Origin appearance for the Blues. Melbourne No.1 Robbie Ross kept Peachey out of the side in 1999, while injury ruled him out of the final two clashes in 2000 after he scored a vital try in the series opener.

ALWYN SIMPSON In 2007 Brisbane winger Alwyn Simpson became the first player since Parramatta livewire Dennis Moran a decade earlier to make his first grade debut in a finals match. Injury had ravaged the defending premier during the second half of the season and Simpson was selected on the end of a reshuffled backline to take on Melbourne in the qualifying final. Simpson, who was formerly contracted to the Raiders, experienced a torrid afternoon as his opposing winger Steve Turner crossed for three tries in a 40-0 drubbing. The Storm went on to emphatically claim the premiership, while Simpson was destined to slip out of NRL contention, instead plying his trade for the Redcliffe Dolphins in the Queensland Cup.

STATE OF ORIGIN

Queensland's selectors have long been regarded as being more loyal than their New South Wales counterparts, evidenced by the fact that the Blues have used 70 more players in 32 seasons of Origin football. It is also backed up by the number of players that have made just one appearance in the Origin cauldron—NSW's figure is more than double that of Queensland's. The Blues have 48 players with only one match to their name—although 2010-11 debutants Jamal Idris, Josh Dugan, Will Hopoate, Keith Galloway and Michael Gordon are likely to add to their tally, while Terry Campese, Steve Turner and James McManus are still prominent NRL players capable of forcing their way into the future squads. North of the border only 20 players have been given just one chance to prove themselves in the Maroon jumper. Just five of those have been in the last decade and, importantly, only Matt Ballin (a 2010 debutant who is a highly rated understudy to hooker Cameron Smith), David Stagg (who remains in the Origin mix) and Antonio Kaufusi have not made it past their debut match since Queensland's remarkable series-winning streak began in 2006.

In 1995, when Super League-aligned players were ruled ineligible, NSW used three different players on the right wing during the series—and it was to be each player's lone Origin appearance. Steady Manly veteran Craig Hancock played in the Blues' shock loss in the opening match before injury ruled him out of the remainder of the series. He was replaced by Sea Eagles teammate John Hopoate. The volatile rookie was dumped after Queensland's series-sealing victory at the MCG, allowing North Sydney speedster David Hall to come into the side for the third encounter, also won by the Maroons.

Injury has often played a role in a player being consigned to one-match wonder status at Origin level. Such was the case for NSW's Illawarra centre Brett Rodwell, who injured his knee scoring a try in the Blues' 20-12 loss to Queensland in the second match of the 1995 series, and for the Maroons' Antonio Kaufusi in 2007. Others, unfortunately, have never been given the chance after a horror debut—the most pertinent example being Moree winger Phil Duke, who was involved in an infamous in-goal gaffe during his only Origin appearance for NSW in 1982 (*see Minties Moments*).

Michael Buettner, Hazem El Masri, Antonio Kaufusi and Dean Young are the only players to have played just one Test match and made a solitary Origin appearance. North Sydney centre Buettner was rewarded for a breakthrough year in 1996 with selection for Australia's post-season Test against Papua New Guinea, before coming off the bench in the Blues' 18-12 loss to Queensland in the dead-rubber third encounter of the 1997 series. El Masri, chosen on the wing in the 2000s' Team of the Decade by David Middleton's *Rugby League Annual* in 2009, was largely ignored by rep selectors during his stellar career. A Lebanon international, El Masri played his only Test in the green-and-gold at the end of 2002, kicking four goals in Australia's 32-24 defeat of the Kiwis in Wellington. He had to wait until 2007 to win a sky-blue jumper—and like Buettner, it was for a dead-rubber encounter. But El Masri proved pivotal in NSW's 18-4 victory to avoid a cleansweep, scoring a crucial try and kicking three goals. Kaufusi benefitted from his role in the front-row for the NRL's newest superpower, making his Test debut for Australia shortly after playing in Melbourne's Grand Final loss to Brisbane. The dynamic prop came off the bench in the Kangaroos' 33-10 thrashing of Great Britain at Suncorp Stadium, but suffered a season-ending knee injury in his first Origin match, as an interchange in the first match of the 2007 series. Failing to rediscover his best form for the Storm, Kaufusi headed north for a disappointing stint with North Queensland, before transferring to Newcastle midway through 2010. Kaufusi played three Tests for Tonga at the 2008 World Cup. St George Illawarra hooker/backrower Dean Young made belated Test and Origin debuts in 2010 and 2011 respectively on the back of his role in the Dragons' premiership victory in 2010.

INDIVIDUAL RIVALRIES

Rugby League is a team game, with success achieved by a group of players combining to collectively outplay their opposition. But one-on-one rivalries have provided fascinating sidelights throughout the game's timeline. Some of the game's most heated on-field rivals and other pairs who simply had a healthy, long-running competition for representative positions are profiled in this chapter.

CHRIS McKIVAT AND ARTHUR HALLOWAY Small in stature but giants of Rugby League's pioneering era, Chris McKivat and 'Pony' Halloway jousted for the game's premier halfback mantle. Halloway made the jump from rugby union to play for Glebe in the inaugural 1908 premiership season and toured with the 1908-09 Kangaroos before joining Balmain, while McKivat switched from the amateur code in 1910 to Glebe. The brilliant duo teamed up in the halves for NSW during the 1910 interstate series—McKivat at five-eighth and Halloway at scrum half but McKivat was chosen as Australia's halfback for the subsequent home Test series against England. McKivat skippered the 1911-12 Australasian Kangaroos and led the side to a historic Test series victory over England, with Halloway as his halfback deputy. Halloway joined Easts and was a linchpin in consecutive first-past-the-post premiership victories in 1912-13—ahead of McKivat's second-placed Glebe side in the former year. Halloway played all three home Tests against England in 1914, while McKivat retired at the end of the year. Returning to Balmain in 1915, Halloway won five more premierships (1915-17 and 1919-20) and toured New Zealand with the Australian side in 1919. Both men achieved spectacular results in the coaching sphere after their playing days finished—McKivat with the mighty Norths sides of the early-1920s, Halloway predominantly with Easts in the 1930s and 1940s. The keen rivals were both named in the ARL's 100 Greatest Players of the Century in 2008.

RAY STEHR AND JACK ARKWRIGHT Australian enforcer Ray Stehr and English tough nut Jack Arkwright were the participants in one of Ashes Rugby League's most infamous and brutal individual clashes. The fiery props clashed for the first time on the 1936 Lions tour of Australia. Warrington stalwart Arkwright notoriously received his marching orders twice in an early tour game against Southern Division—called back onto the field by local captain Jack Kingston after the first send-off, Arkwright returned only to be despatched again for punching Kingston. After missing England's first Test loss, Arkwright returned to help the tourists level the series 12-7. Stehr, who was sent off in the opening encounter, clashed ferociously with Arkwright in the deciding Test at the SCG. According to the most reliable accounts of the match, Arkwright floored Stehr with a vicious punch during a brawl in back-play, but referee Lal Deane sent both men from the field. Stehr consequently became the first and only player to be sent off twice in an Ashes series, while England settled to retain the Ashes with another 12-7 victory. The firebrands faced off one more time, in the first Test of the 1937-38 Kangaroo Tour, a tense 5-4 win to Arkwright's England side at Headingley. Two colourful characters of a bygone era, Stehr and Arkwright settled their differences from the SCG Test with a friendly chat off the field, while the Eastern Suburbs great later gave several different versions of the incident that saw the pair marched—ranging from Stehr taking a dive to being the innocent victim of thuggery.

NOEL KELLY AND IAN WALSH Ipswich product Noel Kelly and Eugowra great Ian Walsh wrestled for the Test hooker position at the close of the 1950s and throughout the 1960s, becoming two of Rugby League's most revered rakes in the process. Kelly made his Test debut during the 1959 series against New Zealand, before both players won selection for the year-ending Kangaroo Tour. Walsh played all six Tests on tour, but Kelly and Billy Rayner shared the hooking duties during the 1960 home series against France. Kelly held the spot throughout the 1960 World Cup and headed to Sydney to join Wests the following season, but Walsh reclaimed the Australian No.12 jumper in 1961 before signing with St. George in 1962. The illustrious pair went head-to-head in the 1962-63 Grand Finals, with Walsh's Saints emerging victorious in two gripping deciders. After both were selected for the 1963-64

Kangaroo Tour, Walsh skippered Australia to a historic Ashes series victory in the absence of tour captain-coach Arthur Summons, while Kelly starred alongside him at prop. Walsh captained Australia in the first Test against France in Sydney in 1964 but suffered a season-ending elbow injury, allowing Kelly to slot in at hooker for the remaining two Tests. After leading his country in a drawn series against the Kiwis in 1965, Walsh finished his Test career as skipper of a thrilling home Ashes series victory in 1966 (again with Kelly at prop) and captain-coached the Dragons to the last of their 11 straight premierships. He stepped down from rep football the following season and retired after Saints' run came to end in the 1967 preliminary final, allowing Kelly to take over as Test rake in becoming the first hooker/prop to make three Kangaroo Tours. Kelly was a surprise choice as hooker in the ARL's Team of the Century in 2008—given that he played a significant portion of his career at prop—while Walsh was considered one of the unluckiest players to be overlooked.

WALLY LEWIS AND BRETT KENNY Two of the finest five-eighths of all time, Wally Lewis and Brett Kenny, faced off for the first time in the 1982 State of Origin Origin decider, with Lewis scoring the winning try and claiming man of the match honours in leading Queensland to a 10-5 win. Lewis was named as vice-captain of the Kangaroo Tour squad at the end of the season, but he was deposed by Kenny as first-choice five-eighth. Kenny linked with Eels teammate Peter Sterling in the halves, wearing the No.6 in five of the six Tests on tour (he started at centre in the first Test against France, with Lewis inside him at pivot). Lewis regained his spot the following season and assumed the national captaincy in 1984, while Kenny played the remaining 11 Tests of his international career in the centres with Lewis as skipper. Recognised as two of the world's greatest players (Lewis won the inaugural Golden Boot in 1985, followed by Kenny in 1986), the brilliant rivals waged many great battles at interstate level. Kenny won eight of the 12 matches he started at five-eighth for NSW opposite Lewis (the Maroons maestro only lost 13 games in a 31-match Origin career), including the Blues' initial series successes in 1985-86. Kenny and Lewis did not clash at club level until after the Broncos' 1988 arrival into the premiership. 'The King' emerged victorious on each of three occasions they opposed each other at five-eighth—once for Brisbane in 1989 and in lowly Gold Coast's upset wins over Parramatta in 1991 and 1992.

WALLY LEWIS AND OLSEN FILIPAINA Australian captain Wally Lewis was widely regarded as Rugby League's finest player in the mid-1980s, but an Eastern Suburbs reserve grader challenged his supremacy at international level in 1985. Olsen Filipaina was a New Zealand Test regular from 1977—predominantly in the centres—and was chosen to mark Lewis at five-eighth in the three-match series against Australia. The rampaging Samoan had struggled to maintain a first grade spot during stints with Balmain and the Roosters but saved the most memorable performances of his career for the hard-fought Trans-Tasman battles. Lewis got Australia out of jail in the opening two Tests, firing pinpoint long passes that resulted in last-gasp match-winners for winger John Ribot on each occasion. But Filipaina's outstanding displays in both games were rewarded with consecutive man of the match awards—a tribute that surely irked 'The King', arguably the most competitive player of his generation. Filipaina scored a try and kicked four goals in the 26-20 first Test loss, while he steam-rolled defenders at will in the 10-6 second Test defeat. In the dead-rubber third Test at Carlaw Park, Filipaina outplayed the ARL Team of the Century five-eighth as New Zealand powered to an emphatic 18-0 boilover. While Australia won the 1985 series on the back of Lewis' brilliance and the skipper inspired the green-and-golds to a comprehensive series whitewash over Filipaina and the Kiwis in 1986, Filipaina's career-defining series opposite Lewis holds a cherished place in New Zealand's Rugby League folklore.

PETER STERLING AND STEVE MORTIMER Canterbury legend Steve Mortimer and Parramatta maestro Peter Sterling were both named in the ARL's 100 Greatest Players in 2008—more than two decades after they staged a lengthy battle for the mantle of the game's best halfback. Mortimer made his Test debut in the 1981 home series against France, but Sterling claimed the NSW jumper for the one-off Origin clash. 'Turvey' displaced 'Sterlo' for the 1982 interstate series and went away on the Kangaroo Tour as Australia's first-choice halfback after featuring in two mid-season Test victories over the Kiwis. The mercurial Sterling usurped his position on tour, however, and Mortimer was consigned to playing with the midweek second-stringers while Sterling became an Ashes hero. Sterling returned as NSW's No.7 for the first two matches of the 1983 series, before Mortimer ousted Sterling for the dead-rubber third Origin clash. Mortimer was also bestowed with the state captaincy and was named man of the match in the 22-12 victory. After skippering the Bulldogs to a 6-4 Grand Final victory over Sterling's Eels, Mortimer retained the halfback spot and the captaincy for the start of the 1985 Origin series. His inspirational leadership was central to the Blues' maiden series victory. Despite the pair's contrasting styles—Mortimer was a tenacious competitor, brilliant cover defender and incisive runner, while Sterling was the cool-headed, consummate ball-on-a-string playmaker—Mortimer's career is often framed in the context of his rivalry with Sterling. The illustrious linchpins duelled once again in the 1986 Grand Final. Mortimer gallantly captained the Bulldogs to a dramatic 4-2 loss, while Sterling won the inaugural Clive Churchill Medal as man of the match. Mortimer's place amongst the best halfbacks of all time is unquestioned, and he boasts a 12-11 win-loss ratio over Sterling, but Sterling is generally regarded as the best No.7 of the era.

BEN ELIAS AND MARIO FENECH Few rivalries in premiership history compare in intensity to that of dummy-half combatants Ben Elias and Mario Fenech. Brilliant Balmain playmaker and serial niggler Ben Elias and fiery, ultra-competitive Souths rake Fenech genuinely did not care for each other. The pair routinely traded verbal barbs and regularly came to blows, most infamously as respective captains in the 1986 minor semi-final. Just after halftime of the spiteful encounter, Fenech was sent off for gouging in a scrum and Balmain swept to a 36-11 victory and a preliminary final berth. Embarking on an off-season stint with Bradford Northern at the end of the year, Fenech faced the uncomfortable scenario of taking on the touring Kangaroos—with Elias at hooker. Fenech's (Malta) and Elias' (Lebanon) Mediterranean heritage added another facet to the fierce competition. Fenech exacted some revenge by skippering the Rabbitohs to a minor preliminary semi win over the Tigers in 1987, before displacing incumbent NSW hooker Elias for the 1989 Origin series. But a broken hand cost Fenech a certain Australian debut, while

Elias helped navigate the Tigers past minor premiers Souths in the major semi later in the season. The on-field rivalry tapered off after Fenech joined Norths in 1991 and moved permanently to prop—Elias in the mean time was an Ashes hero with the 1990 Kangaroos and retired in 1994 with 19 Origin appearances—but the hostility remained. Reunited on *The Footy Show* more than a decade after the pair retired, the lingering animosity was clearly evident. Perennial fall-guy Fenech attempted to extend the olive branch, but the ever-antagonistic Elias made a sincere conciliation impossible.

BEN ELIAS AND STEVE WALTERS As the head-to-head clashes between Elias and Fenech became less frequent, another equally ferocious dislike developed between the Balmain linchpin and Canberra rake Steve Walters. The pair jousted at club level during the late 1980s—Elias outpointed Walters in the Tigers' minor semi victory in 1988, before Walters emerged triumphant in the Raiders' Grand Final win over Balmain the following season—but the rivalry manifested itself most passionately at Origin level. During the infamous Wally Lewis-Mark Geyer push-and-shove in the 1991 series, NSW captain Elias and Queensland No.9 Walters grappled in the SFS mud. After the Maroons' series success that year, Walters dethroned incumbent Elias in the Test side and remained Australia's first-choice rake until the Super League war turned the rep scene upside down in 1995. Elias revelled in three consecutive Origin series victories against Walters before retiring in 1994, but Walters produced this classic line during another scuffle at interstate level: "Take it easy on me Benny, I've got a Test to play next week."

ALLAN LANGER AND RICKY STUART Respective halfbacks for premiership giants Brisbane and Canberra, Allan Langer and Ricky Stuart waged many classic battles at Origin level and grappled for the Test No.7 jumper for the first half of the 1990s. Ex-Wallaby Stuart made his first grade debut off the bench in the Raiders' 36-16 thrashing of incumbent Queensland halfback Langer's Broncos in 1988. Langer made his Test debut later in the season and the pair did not clash again until the 1990 Origin series as Stuart broke into the Blues' side. Stuart helped NSW reclaim the Origin crown for the first time since 1986, while the Blues won four of the five series (1990-94) in which Stuart and Langer occupied the lead playmaking roles, although the match tally was just eight wins to six in favour of the Canberra maestro. Langer played 24 Tests to Stuart's nine and kept his rival out of the Australian side for most of their careers, but he relinquished the No.7 jumper to Stuart on consecutive Kangaroo Tours (1990 and 1994) after first Test defeats at Wembley. Stuart went on to become an Ashes hero on both occasions, engineering an injury-time try for a last-gasp win in the second Test at Old Trafford in 1990 and spearheading the 1994 series victory as the architect of comfortable second and third Test wins. Boasting contrasting styles—Langer was the instinctive game-breaker, while Stuart was the scheming puppeteer—the combatants waged many memorable battles at club level. Stuart emerged victorious in his only two showdowns with Langer in finals football, while in regular season matches the series finished 5-5.

PAUL HARRAGON AND MARK CARROLL No on-field rivalry was more explosive during the 1990s than that of front-row enforcers Paul Harragon and Mark

Carroll. Foundation Knight Harragon opposed Carroll during the latter's stints with Penrith and Souths, but it was not until Carroll's move to Manly in 1994 that the animosity escalated. The most memorable regular season showdown came in 1995 in front of a bumper Marathon Stadium crowd. The twin towers traded verbal jousts and massive hits in a bruising duel that saw Harragon knocked unconscious after he launched himself at a charging Carroll, while the Newcastle skipper was later sent to the sin bin when his temper boiled over. The pair locked horns several times in the 1997 Grand Final, coming to blows during the first half, while Harragon's aggressive approach earned multiple cautions. But Harragon took the spoils as captain of the Knights' last-gasp victory—the last time the rivals squared off and the first time in eight matches Carroll had lost to Harragon as a Sea Eagle. Teammates for NSW in five Origin matches, Carroll deposed Harragon from Australia's starting side for the 1995 Test series against New Zealand, while Harragon's Country Origin side defeated Carroll's City Origin line-up three times in four clashes.

WENDELL SAILOR AND ADAM MACDOUGALL Two of the game's most blockbusting and charismatic wingers of the NRL era forged a fierce, entertaining rivalry in the late-1990s and early-2000s. Their wing battle was one of the highlights of the 1998 Origin series—Sailor opened the scoring for Queensland in game two after Allan Langer put a kick in behind MacDougall, but the Newcastle winger hit back with a try of his own as NSW levelled the series 26-10. MacDougall's 22-week ban for testing positive to a controlled substance (a prescribed medication taken for a damaged pituitary gland) following the Blues' series loss only served to ramp up the incessant sledging between the pair. Sailor's man of the match performance in the drawn 1999 Origin decider opposite MacDougall saw the Maroons retain the shield, but MacDougall secured bragging rights in 2000. He scored a brilliant double in the Knights' 20-14 loss to Brisbane (stripping the ball from Sailor and running 70 metres to score his second) and crossed for three tries in his two matches against Sailor in NSW's emphatic Origin series whitewash. The rivals teamed up for Australia's victorious World Cup campaign at the end of the year before squaring off in interstate battle for the final time in 2001. Sailor's Maroons carved out an upset series victory but MacDougall replaced the rugby union-bound Broncos flyer on Australia's wing for the end-of-year Ashes series. The increasingly friendly rivalry was afforded a memorable finale in 2009 following Sailor's return to the NRL with the Dragons. Sailor scored two tries as the Saints opened up a 14-6 halftime lead and celebrated enthusiastically in front of Knights centre MacDougall. But he hobbled off with a hamstring injury during the second half and MacDougall scored the try that ultimately proved the difference in Newcastle's 24-18 win, earning 'Mad Dog' the rights to the last verbal jab post-match.

ANDREW JOHNS AND BRETT KIMMORLEY As Andrew Johns began to establish himself as a representative star and Newcastle's linchpin during the mid-1990s, Brett Kimmorley was steering the Knights' reserve grade side around of a weekend (including a premiership victory in 1995). Kimmorley made his first grade starting debut in 1995 in the absence of an injured Johns, but with no way past him for a regular spot, 'Noddy' joined hometown Super League club Hunter Mariners in 1997. Kimmorley represented Super League Australia in a breakthrough year and emerged as a genuine contender to Johns' halfback throne, despite Newcastle's 1997 Grand Final hero developing a reputation as potentially the best No.7 of all time. Kimmorley claimed the spoils in the first showdown against his former club-mate in 1998, propelling NRL newcomers Melbourne to a 32-16 victory over the Knights and scoring an 80-metre intercept try from a Johns pass. But Johns outpointed his younger rival in the corresponding match the following season, producing a man of the match display in a gripping 27-26 win. Kimmorley won the Churchill Medal in Melbourne's epic 1999 Grand Final victory and replaced the sidelined Johns to make his Test debut in the year-ending Tri-Nations tournament. Johns was forced to make his representative comeback via the bench during the 2000 Origin series as Kimmorley occupied the No.7 jersey throughout a 3-0 whitewash, and played at hooker during Australia's World Cup campaign to accommodate the Storm playmaker. But Johns reconfirmed his status as the game's number-one halfback—and player—in 2001 by captaining the Knights to another title and starring in Australia's Ashes series triumph. After Johns led Newcastle to a 52-8 thrashing of Kimmorley's Sharks early in 2002, the Cronulla playmaker enjoyed one of his finest hours in the return clash later in the season. He scored a club record 28 points and earned a rare '10' rating from *Rugby League Week* in Cronulla's 64-14 demolition job on Johns' Knights. But Kimmorley's representative appointments from that point came only when Johns was unavailable (which, admittedly, was often—Kimmorley finished his career with 20 Test appearances) prior to the latter's retirement in 2007. Johns was named halfback in the ARL's Team of the Century in 2008, while Kimmorley became the first No.7 to play 300 first grade games during a fine late-career stint with the Bulldogs.

ROBBIE FARAH AND MICHAEL ENNIS A current-day Elias-Fenech rivalry developed between Tigers hooker Robbie Farah and Bulldogs rake Michael Ennis in the late-2000s—two top-shelf No.9s with a genuine distaste for each other. They first packed down in the front-row opposite each other in 2008, with then-Bronco Ennis accusing Farah of throwing a head-butt after a scrum blow-up during a gripping 19-18 defeat of the Tigers. The pair emerged as the overwhelming favourites to occupy the NSW No.9 jumper vacated by long-term skipper Danny Buderus for the 2009 series and the much-hyped round eight showdown between new Bulldog Ennis and Tigers captain Farah did not disappoint. The dummy-half combatants dominated a thrilling match, staging one of the great individual contests. Ennis claimed three Dally M points after steering the Bulldogs to a 22-20 victory, while Farah was the Tigers' standout and picked up two votes. Farah pegged bragging rights back when he captained City Origin to a 40-18 win over a Country line-up featuring Ennis just five days later, sealing a debut NSW berth. But after the Blues crumbled in the opening two matches of the series, Ennis replaced Farah for the dead-rubber third encounter and helped NSW to a face-saving 28-16 upset. Both players recorded top-10 finishes in the Dally M count, while Farah pipped Ennis for a spot in Australia's Four Nations squad as Cameron Smith's understudy. Despite consecutive top-four finishes by the Tigers in 2010-11 while the Bulldogs floundered, Ennis rebuffed Farah's challenge to retain the NSW role, although Farah was preferred in Australia's Four Nations squad in both seasons (albeit with club coach Tim Sheens at the helm).

BILLY SLATER AND JARRYD HAYNE The battle between brilliant custodians Billy Slater and Jarryd Hayne for the label of Rugby League's best fullback elevated the pair's performances to another plane. Storm flyer Slater finally discovered the consistency to cement the Australian and Queensland No.1 jumpers in 2008, claiming the Golden Boot as the world's best player. Hayne only settled in as Eels fullback midway through 2009, three years after a memorable debut season in 2006, but hit an unbelievable vein of form—including a man of the match performance in an 18-16 upset of Slater's Melbourne side—that netted the Dally M Player of the Year Award and propelled Parramatta into the Grand Final. But in the face of intense pressure for his Test spot, Slater's Churchill Medal-winning performance opposite Hayne provided the impetus for Melbourne's 23-16 defeat of the Eels in the decider. Opposing fullbacks in the previous year's World Cup semi-final—Slater for Australia and Hayne for Fiji—the rivals teamed up during the 2009 Four Nations tournament, with Hayne slotting in on the wing. The competition between the No.1 counterparts turned ugly in a Grand Final rematch in 2010. With revelations of Melbourne's salary cap rorting still fresh, the match was played in a tense atmosphere that boiled over when the opposing fullbacks came to grips. Hayne nudged Slater with a slight but deliberate head-butt and was put on report, before Slater's temper got the better of him minutes later and he was sin-binned for punching Hayne in the back of the head. Hayne was exonerated on the striking charge and the pair faced off at Origin level 12 days later, with Slater having the last laugh as Queensland powered to a series whitewash. While Slater's scintillating form in 2011 promoted him to the stratosphere of the best fullbacks in the game's history, Hayne produced his best only in patches and dropped out of the Test side.

TRAGIC FIGURES

The Rugby League players who lost their lives far too young and men whose careers were cut short by catastrophic injury or illness are gone from our great game, but they are by no means forgotten.

ALBERT BASKERVILLE Few people were more determined or influential in making Rugby League a success in Australasia than Albert Henry Baskerville. The driving force behind organising the New Zealand 'All Golds' tour to Britain in 1907-08, Baskerville scored a try in the first Rugby League Test against Australia in Sydney in May, 1908, during a 10-match tour en route home to New Zealand. But Baskerville caught pneumonia following the 11-10 victory and died during the team's trip by boat to Brisbane, denying him the opportunity to witness the rise of Rugby League that his tireless efforts were so vital to. Future Australian touring sides to New Zealand visited Baskerville's gravesite, paying tribute to one of the game's most significant pioneers.[17]

---

17   Malcolm Andrews, *The A-Z Of Rugby League*. Auckland, 1995

JACK HOLMES Five-eighth Jack Holmes made his first grade debut with Wests in 1926 before joining Newtown the following season. A shrewd five-eighth, Holmes toured with the 1929-30 Kangaroos and played 12 games on tour, but was kept out of the Test side by NSW Country legend Eric Weissel. He represented NSW during the 1929 and 1930 interstate series, but a leg wound incurred from a first grade game at the SCG during 1931 eventually led to his death. Holmes contracted septicaemia from bacteria in the soil and the illness tragically cut short the talented pivot's life at the age of 25.[18]

RAY MORRIS Talented three-quarter Ray Morris became the first [and only] player selected for Australia from the University club, but tragically died en route to England with the 1933-34 Kangaroos. Morris scored 24 tries from 36 games in six seasons with Wests, before joining University in 1933 and representing NSW for the third successive season. Morris was selected for the Kangaroo Tour at the end of the year but developed an ear infection onboard the ship sailing to Malta. He was hospitalised in Malta and, with his teammates having to sail on without him, passed away two days later.

CHARLES BROOMHAM In April 1938, North Sydney reserve grade winger Charles Broomham died from an internal haemorrhage after receiving a knock against South Sydney at the Sydney Cricket Ground.[19] Broomham was just 19 years old. His father Ernest played two first grade games for Norths in 1910, while his uncle Albert Broomham was a pioneering North Sydney star, representing Australia in five Tests and touring with the 1911-12 Kangaroos.

BOBBY LULHAM One of the code's greatest tryscoring wingers, Balmain star Bobby Lulham had his career ruined by an alleged accidental poisoning that was at the centre of a sensational court case in the 1950s. Lulham scored an incredible 85 tries in 87 games—including a club record 28 in 1947—and toured with the 1948-49 Kangaroos, playing three Tests. But after being hospitalised during the 1953 season, Lulham was found to have been a victim of thallium poisoning. Lulham's mother-in-law Veronica Monty was arrested, but was later found not guilty of attempted murder, contending that the chocolate drink she had poisoned was intended for herself. It was revealed during the court case that Lulham and Monty had been engaged in an affair after she moved in with her daughter and son-in-law, following the separation from her husband. The case captivated the public, and in the aftermath. both marriages ended in divorce, while Lulham never played top grade football again.

DON AMOS Valued Balmain clubman Don Amos appeared in 25 matches for the Tigers between 1957 and 1961 but tragedy struck for the young prop when he embarked on a post-season trip to Brisbane with the club at the conclusion of 1961 competition. Amos collapsed and died from a brain haemorrhage during a match

---

18 Sean Fagan, *Rugby League Week: 30 Greatest Players Of The Last 30 Years 1978-2008.* Sydney, 2008

19 Ian Heads and David Middleton, *A Centenary Of Rugby League.* Sydney, 2008

against Brisbane Norths having played in Balmain's finals matches against Manly and Wests just one month earlier.

GEORGE PIPER Veteran ex-Balmain prop George Piper died in 1968 while contracted to Penrith. Piper made his first grade debut for the Tigers in 1960 and played in the club's loss to St. George in the 1964 Grand Final, racking up 77 first grade appearances in black and gold. He signed on as a foundation Panther in 1967 and played 25 games in two seasons for the fledgling club, scoring two tries in the Wills pre-season final victory over Newtown in 1968. On September 22 that year—just a day after the Sydney Grand Final—Piper died of head injuries following a late-night altercation outside a Balmain nightclub, robbing the game of one of its great characters.

APISAI TOGA One of the first Pacific Islanders to make a sizeable impression on the premiership, Fijian forward Apisai Toga played 65 games for the Dragons between 1968 and 1972 (including five finals matches in 1969-70 and 1972). A Fiji rugby union international, Toga also played with English club Rochdale in the 1960s, and was a rugged and popular clubman at St. George. Sadly, Toga passed away from tetanus poisoning during the 1973 pre-season, contracting the illness from a coral injury suffered while on a trip back home to Fiji.[20] His brother Inosi remained at the club for two more seasons.

GEOFF STARLING Exciting centre Geoff Starling appeared destined for a long career at the top when he became Australia's youngest-ever representative aged 18 years and 178 days in 1971 but his career was ruined by a mystery illness three years later. After touring New Zealand with the Australian side in 1971, the Balmain prodigy made his Test debut in 1972 and won selection in the World Cup squad at the end of the year. Starling excelled on the 1973 Kangaroo Tour, but his career was put on hold after being struck down by an energy-sapping illness in 1974. He was hospitalised and subsequent comeback attempts had to be aborted with Starling eventually diagnosed—years later—with Addison's disease, a rare endocrine disorder wherein the adrenal glands produce insufficient steroid hormones. After many years he overcame the disease that robbed Rugby League of one of its brightest talents.

KEVIN YOW YEH Brilliant Aboriginal centre Kevin Yow Yeh was signed by Balmain along with Redcliffe teammate Arthur Beetson at the end of 1965 with Yow Yeh playing on the wing in the Tigers' 1966 Grand Final loss. The talented three-quarter finished with 41 games over two seasons for the club, deciding to leave at the end of 1967, unable to adapt to life in the city and tormented by racial vilification that was prevalent in 1960s Australia. Yow Yeh battled alcoholism for the remainder of his life and he died in custody at Mackay Jail in 1975. His great-nephew Jharal Yow Yeh burst onto the NRL scene as an exciting winger with the Broncos in 2009, representing the Indigenous All-Stars and breaking into the Kangaroo and Queensland sides over the next two seasons.

---

20 Alan Whiticker and Glen Hudson, *The Encyclopedia Of Rugby League Players*. Sydney, 2007

JOHN FARRAGHER Gilgandra product John Farragher made his first grade debut with Penrith in 1978 but in just his seventh appearance in the top flight, against Newtown at Henson Park, tragedy struck. The rugged forward was left a quadriplegic after a scrum collapsed. The Panthers struck an award in his honour—the John Farragher Award for Courage.

PAUL HAYWARD Respected as a tough, resourceful five-eighth for Newtown in 79 matches between 1973 and 1978, Paul Hayward was good enough to tour New Zealand with a Combined Sydney side in 1976. But after becoming involved with a drug trafficking syndicate responsible for importing heroin from Thailand to Australia, Hayward spent a decade in a hellish Bangkok prison. Famously interviewed by *Rugby League Week*'s Neil Cadigan for an award-winning and highly controversial article in 1985, Hayward was finally released and returned to Australia in 1989. Hayward contracted the HIV virus during his jail term and died of a heroin overdose in 1992.

GARRY DOWLING One of the premiership's finest custodians of the 1970s, Garry Dowling played 113 first grade games for Canterbury and featured in the club's 1974 Grand Final loss to the Roosters. He debuted for NSW in 1975 before switching to Parramatta for a fine two-season stint in 1979, making a belated Test debut against New Zealand in 1980. Dowling played one last season for the Magpies in 1981 and represented the Blues in that year's one-off Origin clash. He moved to the Gold Coast at the end of the year but was tragically killed in a terrible car accident returning from a game in Beaudesert in March, 1983.

JOHN DONNELLY Affectionately known as 'Dallas,' John Donnelly was a larger-than-life character—a genuine cult figure for the Western Suburbs club during the Magpies' 1970s resurgence. His larrikinism often overshadowed his footballing talent, but the burly firebrand second-rower represented Australia in the 1975 World Series and in a Test against New Zealand in 1978. Two suspensions for foul play that each exceeded three months only added to the legend of 'Dallas,' and the lovable rogue accepted the captain-coach position with Byron Bay at the conclusion of his professional career. But Donnelly, a lifelong epilepsy sufferer, drowned during the 1986 pre-season after having a seizure while swimming in the surf off Byron Bay. The outpouring of grief in his home town of Gunnedah, and the Rugby League community as a whole, was testament to the effect 'Dallas' had on those he crossed paths with.

GEOFF SELBY Promising lock Geoff Selby played 99 first grade games for Illawarra and St. George, before his life was tragically cut short during the 1989 pre-season. The St. George junior was lured to the Steelers in 1984 by coach Brian Smith, his former teacher at James Cook High, and played 38 games in two seasons in Wollongong. Selby returned to the Dragons in 1986, cementing his place at the back of the scrum during three impressive seasons and spending the 1986-87 off-season with English club Salford. The 23-year-old died in a car accident on February 13, 1989. St. George Illawarra present the Geoff Selby Memorial Award (the coach's award to a first grade player) each year in his memory.

BEN ALEXANDER The death of Ben Alexander, aged just 20, devastated the Penrith club. The younger brother of Panther great Greg, utility Ben played 37 games for the Panthers between 1990 and 1992. After attending a function to honour the previous year's premiership winning side on June 21, 1992, Alexander was tragically killed in a car accident. The disaster shocked the Rugby League community and ripped the heart out of the Panthers. Although not as gifted as his illustrious sibling, Alexander was an extremely important and popular member of the club and his death sparked an outpouring of emotion throughout the district.

JAMES MATTHEWS James Matthews spent several seasons with Illawarra before joining the Roosters in 1992. The move paid immediate dividends for the talented three-quarter—he played 15 matches and was Easts' top point-scorer, while also earning selection for City Firsts. But Matthews died in a car crash on Christmas Eve, 1992—the second promising young player to be claimed in a road accident that year. He is honoured each year by the Roosters with the presentation of the James Matthews Clubman of the Year award.

ADAM RITSON Giant prop Adam Ritson was one of the game's most exciting front-row prospects of the 1990s, but his career was cut short after the discovery of a brain cyst. Thrust into first grade at Cronulla by coach Arthur Beetson at just 16 years and 303 days—the fourth youngest player in premiership history at the time—Ritson's size and ball skills saw him earmarked as a future international. He represented City Origin in 1995 and his ARL allegiances resulted in a move to Parramatta the following season. A victim of high shots throughout his short career, Ritson was knocked out by an ugly high tackle by Canberra firebrand John Lomax in 1996, leading to the discovery of a cyst after undergoing a precautionary scan. Ritson was fortunate to survive but eventually regained his health after a succession of operations, although sadly, he would never play Rugby League again.

PETER JACKSON A brilliant centre or five-eighth in a decorated career for Brisbane Souths, Canberra, Brisbane Broncos, North Sydney, Queensland and Australia, Peter Jackson was one of Rugby League's great characters of the modern era—the archetypal Aussie larrikin. A veteran of nine Tests and 17 Origin appearances, a neurological disorder curtailed his career, forcing his retirement in 1993 after guiding the Bears' reserve grade side to a premiership. A mooted return to the field for the Bulldogs—for whom he was on the coaching staff—was shelved in 1995, and Jackson took his own life two years later after a long battle with depression. The passing of the game's much-loved clown prince was mourned by the entire Rugby League world.

TAI SAVEA Sonny Fai's death in 2009 evoked sad memories of fellow Junior Kiwi representative Tai Savea, who also drowned in New Zealand. In an eerie coincidence, Savea drowned while fishing in the Port Waikato River in the central North Island in January, 1999, almost exactly 10 years prior to Fai's tragic passing. Both men were 20 years of age. Savea, a gifted junior, had just signed to play with NRL club Balmain at the time of his death.

DAVID BUKO Talented fullback David Buko was a long-serving Papua New Guinean international and played in Western Suburbs' last-ever match in 1999. Buko represented Papua New Guinea's Northern Zone against the touring Australian side as a teenager in 1991, kicking three goals against Mal Meninga's star-studded side. He was part of the Kumuls' 1995 and 2000 World Cup squads, scoring tries against France and Tonga at the 2000 tournament on the way to a quarter final appearance. Buko also lined up against the Kangaroos in a pre-tournament Test match. But after signing a deal with French club Limoux for the 2002 season, Buko died of typhoid fever in Goroka, Papua New Guinea, in January of 2002, aged just 29.

SONNY FAI New Zealand Warriors centre/backrower Sonny Fai had the Rugby League world at his feet before he tragically drowned on January 4, 2009, at Te Henga (Bethells Beach), Auckland. Fai died after rescuing his brother and cousin, who had been swept away in a rip at the surf beach. The 20-year-old's heroic death had a devastating impact on the Warriors and the Rugby League fraternity. Fai was one of 2008's outstanding rookies, scoring five tries in 15 games with a stunning combination of size, power and pace. He was chosen in Samoa's and New Zealand's World Cup train-on squads at the end of the season, destined for international honours and NRL stardom in 2009. As a tribute to their fallen brother, Fai's profile remained in the NRL media guide for 2009 and the Warriors' jersey for the season bore his signature—honouring a humble and popular young man, and a footballer of limitless potential.

SAM FAUST The passing of former North Queensland second-rower Sam Faust from leukaemia in 2011 saddened the Rugby League world. The Proserpine native was a star junior and spent several seasons with St. George-Illawarra, but was unable to break into first grade. Returning to Queensland, 22-year-old Faust made his NRL debut in 2007 with the Cowboys, cementing a backrow spot during the club's charge to a preliminary final berth. After making 13 appearances in his debut season, Faust played another 10 games in 2008 before being diagnosed with acute myeloid leukaemia a year later. Faust's brave battle with the illness came to end in Townsville in May 2011, drawing a flood of tributes from the North Queensland community and the Rugby League fraternity.

THE UTILITY PLAYERS

The 'utility' tag has historically entailed 'jack of all trades, master of none' connotations—a solid player capable of occupying several positions, but none of them to an elite standard. But versatility has become an invaluable commodity in the modern era, and Rugby League's utility players have become a vital cog in many a premiership-winning squad or representative line-up.

JIM CRAIG One of the most iconic and influential figures of Rugby League's formative decades, Jim Craig won four premierships with Balmain (1915-17 and

1919-20) and captain-coached Western Suburbs to its maiden title in 1930. He played seven Tests against England between 1921 and 1928, was inducted into the ARL Hall of Fame in 2005 and was named as a reserve in Queensland's Team of the Century in 2008. But another lasting impression of Craig is his status as the game's first great utility, as his nickname 'Mr. Versatile' attests. Capable of playing in any position on the field, Craig made his Test debut as a centre on the 1921-22 Kangaroo Tour. He captained Australia in the 1924 home series against the Old Enemy—from halfback in the first Test and at centre in the remaining two encounters. Craig's final international series was in 1928, playing fullback and centre against the touring Englishmen. He even played hooker for New South Wales on a tour to New Zealand in 1922, back in the days when scrums were a contest and only the fearless packed down in the front row, while he filled in at lock and on the wing at club level.

GREG HAWICK South Sydney star Greg Hawick was arguably the finest utility of the 1950s. Emerging as a lock, Hawick played five-eighth in the Rabbitohs' 1950 premiership-winning side—his first season in top grade. Hawick was a centre in Souths' victory in the first mandatory Grand Final in 1954, and played nine Tests between 1952 and 1958—three at five-eighth, three at halfback, two in the centres and one at lock. In 2006, Hawick was named at pivot in the Team of the 1950s.

DES HASLER Manly great Des Hasler's biography was entitled *The Utility Player*—a fair indicator to his unparalleled versatility. But Hasler was no spare-parts competitor. One of the best halfbacks of the 1980s, Hasler successfully switched to the backrow in the early-1990s and was a premiership-winning hooker in the twilight of his career, while he was also capable of filling any position in the backline. A Penrith junior, Hasler joined the Sea Eagles in 1984 and made his Test debut at halfback the following season. Hasler's versatility was crucial to his selection for the 1986 and 1990 Kangaroo Tours, and to his selection on the bench for nine of his 12 appearances for Australia. The super-fit Hasler started half of his 12 Origins for NSW on the bench and made starts at halfback, five-eighth and lock. He won two Grand Finals with Manly, in 1987 wearing the No.7 and 1996 as a hooker, while he was named Dally M Lock of the Year in 1991. Hasler was the prototype for recent utilities such as Shaun Berrigan and Craig Wing that have been so vital to modern-day teams.

JOHN PLATH Initially a disadvantage in securing a top grade berth with Brisbane, John Plath's versatility saw him win a Grand Final in his 10th first grade game and become a crucial element of the glamour club's success during the 1990s. Plath was predominantly a half early in his career, making his debut in 1990, although his path was blocked by the incomparable pairing of Allan Langer and Kevin Walters. But he forged a spot on the bench late in 1992—just in time to celebrate in the Broncos' maiden premiership victory. The tenacious Plath was a permanent member of the first-choice squad for the next six seasons, coming off the bench in three more Grand Final triumphs. He made 99 of his 149 first grade appearances from the bench, but exhibited his adaptability with starts at centre, five-eighth, halfback, hooker and lock without missing a beat.

STEVE GEORGALLIS An underrated veteran of 206 games in a 12-season first grade career, Steve Georgallis was one of the most versatile players of the 1990s. Georgallis was graded as a half by Eastern Suburbs, making his first grade debut in 1989 but he is best remembered as a mainstay for Western Suburbs from 1993 until their demise at the end of the decade, and as an integral member of the inaugural Wests Tigers squad in 2000. Georgallis played most of his football at halfback, five-eighth and lock, but also spent time at fullback, centre, hooker and off the bench.

JASON CROKER One of the most durable players to ever strap on a boot, Canberra stalwart Jason Croker was also one of the most adaptable, starting in every position on the field except halfback and hooker in 318 first grade appearances for the club. Croker burst onto the scene as a winger for the star-studded Raiders in 1991, before making a sensational transition to lock in 1993. He made his Origin debut for New South Wales off the bench and scored nine tries in a five-match period from the back of the Canberra scrum. After playing most of the 1994 season on the wing or at five-eighth while Laurie Daley battled injury, Croker switched to the second-row late in the year, scoring his 22nd try of the season in Canberra's Grand Final thrashing of Canterbury, equalling the club record. He was desperately unlucky to miss out on Kangaroo Tour selection that year—Croker's versatility would have made him an ideal tourist—but he persevered and returned to the NSW Origin side two years later after replacing retired skipper Mal Meninga in the centres at club level in 1995. Reverting to a five-eighth/lock role in 1998, Croker finally cracked the Australian side for the 2000 World Cup after two NRL seasons predominantly playing in the backrow. Croker came off the bench in a warm-up Test against Papua New Guinea and three World Cup matches, and scored two tries against Russia after starting on the wing. The ageless utility proved his value to the club by playing 2002 in the centres and 2003 at five-eighth, before rounding out his career with three seasons in the backrow. Croker departed the NRL at the end of 2006 in sixth place on the premiership's all time appearance list with a Canberra-record 120 tries to his name. He reprised his utility role in three seasons with Super League side Catalans, finally retiring at the end of 2009 aged 36.

DANIEL WAGON Brisbane-born Daniel Wagon began his first grade career in 1997 as a handy outside back for St. George, but his versatility saw him play over 200 matches for Parramatta. He proved a superb Mr. Fix-it for the Eels, frequently switching between centre, five-eighth and lock after joining the club in 1999, and made his Origin debut for Queensland in the No.6 jumper, featuring in all three games of the Maroons' 2001 series success. After playing lock in the Eels' Grand Final loss to Newcastle, he was chosen for Australia's shortened Kangaroo Tour in 2001, but did not play a match. Wagon was ever-dependable at club level playing predominantly in the backrow in 2002-03, at five-eighth in 2004 and and in the centres in 2005, before reverting primarily to the backrow until his retirement in 2008.

SHAUN BERRIGAN Shaun Berrigan was a spectacular success in every position he tried his hand at and deserves to be recognised as the finest utility the game has produced in the past two decades. After debuting for Brisbane in 1999, Berrigan came off the bench in the Grand Final victory over the Sydney Roosters a year later and appeared destined for an Origin debut in 2001 following a great start to the year at halfback, but injury cut him down until the late rounds of the season. He moved to five-eighth to accommodate the return of Allan Langer in 2002, and partnered the Broncos champion in the halves for Queensland. Berrigan reverted to halfback after Langer's retirement and also assumed the Maroons' No.7 spot in 2003. A switch to the centres in 2004 paid immediate dividends for Berrigan, who made his Test debut off the bench that year against the Kiwis, and although injury ruled him out of the Origin series, he played six post-season Tests in the centres, including the Tri-Nations final thrashing of Great Britain. He was the NRL regular season equal-top try-scorer with 19 in 2005 and played in the centres for Queensland, but lost his spot in the Australian side, with St. George Illawarra duo Mark Gasnier and Matt Cooper preferred for the Tri-Nations tour. The next chapter of Berrigan's positional rollercoaster came when Wayne Bennett switched him to hooker late in the 2006 season. The move coincided with the Broncos' form reversal that took the club all the way to a Grand Final upset of Melbourne, with Berrigan taking out the Churchill Medal in the No.9. He reclaimed a Test spot in Australia's victorious Tri-Nations side at the end of the year as a bench utility, a role he filled in Queensland's 2006-07 series-winning teams. Berrigan departed the NRL at the end of 2007 for Super League side Hull, where he played predominantly hooker and halfback, but returned with the Warriors as a 32-year-old in 2011. He featured at centre, hooker and as an interchange for the Warriors (although injury ruled him out of the club's Grand Final charge) before linking with Canberra in 2012.

CRAIG WING Craig Wing's supreme athleticism saw him start in every position in first grade except prop and second-row, while his versatility was the key to a fine representative career that yielded 16 Tests for Australia and 12 Origin appearances for New South Wales. In his 1998 debut season for Souths, he played at halfback, five-eighth, lock, centre and wing, showing an astonishing amount of versatility for a rookie. He was a sensation at fullback early in 1999 for the Rabbitohs, but was used primarily as an interchange after joining the Sydney Roosters in 2000, coming off the bench in the Grand Final loss to Brisbane. Adrian Lam's departure eventually resulted in Wing taking over the halfback role inside Brad Fittler late in 2001, and that combination took the club to the 2002 premiership. Brett Finch arrived in 2003 and the multipurpose Wing slotted into hooker—a move that earned a maiden Origin guernsey off the bench for NSW in 2003. He played 10 games in all for the Blues from 2003 to 2006, all as an interchange. Wing developed into one of the NRL's elite hookers, but played most of 2005 in the No.6 after Fittler's retirement left the Roosters short in the halves. His two-season return to Souths at the end of 2007 was largely interrupted by injury, but his time on the field was valuable at hooker, lock or in the halves, and he earned a recall to the NSW bench after an absence of three years in 2009. Wing started 10 Tests on the bench, one at five-eighth and two at hooker, while he played all three Ashes Tests on the 2003 Kangaroo Tour in the centres following an injury crisis within the inexperienced squad.

CASEY McGUIRE Underrated Caloundra junior Casey McGuire played the same role for Brisbane in the 2000s that John Plath occupied so well in the 1990s—

a magnificent trouble-shooter off the bench capable of filling any position on the park. An Australian Schoolboys centre in 1997, McGuire joined Parramatta and played five-eighth in the President's Cup Grand Final loss to Canterbury in 1998, before reverting to fullback for Parramatta's First Division Grand Final victory and for the Junior Kangaroos in 1999. He joined the Broncos and played a chunk of the season as starting five-eighth in 2002 before playing predominantly off the bench in 2003. An injury to Brett Seymour saw McGuire step into the halfback spot for the second half of 2004 and his versatility was rewarded with a place on Queensland's bench for two matches in 2005. McGuire, who also played centre and lock on occasion, filled in at hooker for the Broncos regularly in 2005-06 and left the club after playing a handy role as an interchange in Brisbane's Grand Final defeat of the Storm in 2006. He linked with Super League club Catalans, switching between hooker and the halves, before doing likewise in an impressive return to the Eels in 2011.

KURT GIDLEY Simultaneously one of the game's best fullbacks and halfbacks, Newcastle skipper Kurt Gidley developed into the resident bench utility for NSW and Australia. Gidley played centre and halfback in 2002—his first full season in first grade—before slotting into injured fullback Robbie O'Davis' spot for the finals. He flitted between the centres and pivot during 2003 before taking over as the Knights' chief playmaker at halfback late in the year and for most of 2004 as Andrew Johns battled successive injury problems. Gidley had his own injury woes in 2005 but spent the following season as Johns' halves partner at five-eighth. A permanent switch to fullback was the catalyst for Gidley's selection on the bench for his Origin and Test debuts in 2007. He retained those spots in 2008, frequently coming off the bench for a spell at dummy-half, before taking over the fullback spot and the captaincy for NSW in 2009. A Test start against France followed at the end of the year, but he was ousted from the Blues' No.1 jersey by Eels superstar Jarryd Hayne during the 2010 series—although, unusually, he retained the captaincy for one match from the bench. Reverting to his customary interchange utility role for NSW, Gidley was replaced as skipper by Trent Barrett for the third encounter of the 2010 series, before Paul Gallen assumed the post in 2011. Settled at fullback at club level, Gidley's spark was intermittently used at hooker and in the halves for Newcastle as one of the NRL's most influential skippers. The arrival of Test fullback Darius Boyd at the Knights in 2012 forecasted a fixed return to the halves for Gidley.

LANCE HOHAIA New Zealand Test star Lance Hohaia bounced around the Warriors' team line-up sheet throughout his career. Hohaia burst onto the scene as a brilliant rookie at five-eighth in 2002, before dropping back to the bench during the Warriors' charge to the Grand Final. He also made his Test debut as a pivot in 2002 and looked set for a long career in the halves. But Hohaia lost his spot in the national side, making a return at hooker three years later in a Tri-Nations defeat of Australia in 2005 after spending much of the NRL season in the No.9 jumper. The diminutive utility played most of his first grade football during the next two injury-interrupted seasons in the centres or off the bench, but found a niche in 2008 as the injured Wade McKinnon's replacement at fullback—a position he filled outstandingly for New Zealand at the World Cup, scoring one try and being awarded a penalty try in the boilover defeat of Australia in the final. McKinnon's return in 2009 saw Hohaia mix starts at five-eighth, centre and hooker as well as starring off the bench, but his sizzling form at the back in 2010 forced McKinnon to join the Tigers mid-season. Hohaia was a walk-up start for the Kiwis' No.1 jersey in the two seasons after his World Cup heroics and featured in the Four Nations final victory at the end of 2010. Kevin Locke's emergence as one of the NRL's most brilliant young fullbacks resulted in another move for Hohaia in 2011, but the veteran was superb off the bench for the majority of the season and starred as starting hooker in the Warriors' remarkable run to the Grand Final. Hohaia joined St. Helens in 2012.

LUKE LEWIS Luke Lewis rose to prominence as a teenage winger for Penrith in 2002, but developed into an elite backrower and one of the NRL's most versatile players. He was part of the Panthers' Grand Final-winning side in 2003 and won selection for that year's Kangaroo Tour, although he did not play a Test—coach Chris Anderson controversially called in veteran Darren Smith from St. Helens for the third Ashes encounter when injuries hit the squad, leaving a fit Lewis sitting in the grandstand. Making his Origin debut in 2004, Lewis played two games on the wing and one at centre for the victorious Blues, but disappeared into the representative wilderness for the next four seasons (although he retained a centre spot in the City Origin side). He played almost exclusively in the outside backs, with the occasional cameo at five-eighth, until 2008, when he starred for the Panthers as the biggest halfback in the NRL. Mixing appearances at five-eighth and lock in 2009, Lewis won an Origin recall as a super-sub for the first match of the series, but injury kept him out of the remaining two clashes. Lewis returned to make his Test debut off the bench in the Four Nations tournament and started in the second-row against England in the final, a position he retained for the mid-season Test against NZ in 2010—despite playing pivot at club level in the weeks leading up to selection. He reverted to lock for the rest of the NRL season—the Panthers' best year since 2004— and promptly claimed the 2010 Dally M Lock of the Year award. Lewis became a permanent second-row fixture in the Test side in 2010-11.

CHRIS FLANNERY Chris Flannery's uncanny ability to adapt to different positions on a week-to-week basis allowed him to start in every position except prop and hooker during his seven seasons with the Sydney Roosters. After debuting for the club in 2000, the Cowra-born and Sunshine Coast-raised Flannery split his duties between fullback and wing in 2001, with cameos in the centres and at halfback. Flannery became a genuine Mr. Fix-it in 2002, playing in a new spot virtually every week—in 21 appearances he played in the same position in consecutive weeks just five times. He played the first two matches of the Roosters' finals campaign at fullback before dropping back to the bench for the Grand Final victory over New Zealand. After coming off the bench in the 2003-04 Grand Final losses, Flannery's versatile talents were frequently required at five-eighth in 2005, before he settled in the backrow for most of 2006—probably his best-suited position. Flannery played predominantly backrow for St. Helens after joining the Super League club in 2007, with the occasional stint in the centres. In 10 Origin appearances for Queensland, Flannery came off the bench six times, started at lock in three games and stood in for injured skipper Darren Lockyer at five-eighth for one match, in 2004.

SWITCHING POSITIONS

Some of Rugby League's biggest names started their careers in very different roles to the ones they eventually mastered and achieved greatness with. Others changed at the height of their powers for the balance of their team, because of the game's changing structure or because of their evolution as a player. For some it added another glorious chapter to an already decorated career, while for others it proved career-defining.

ARTHUR BEETSON The greatest ball-playing forward in the game's history began his career in the backline. Future Immortal Arthur Beetson was graded as a centre for Redcliffe as a teenager, where he partnered Kevin Yow Yeh. But Beetson's burly physique, sublime ball skills and offloading ability saw him swiftly moved into the pack. Beetson, along with Yow Yeh, was signed by Balmain in 1966. Australian jumpers, premierships with Eastern Suburbs and the Queensland captaincy for the inaugural State of Origin match in 1980 followed with Beetson named as one of the props in the ARL Team of the Century in 2008.

BILLY SMITH Recognised as one of Rugby League's finest halfbacks, tenacious Dragon Billy Smith also started his senior football in the centres. The St. George junior made his first grade debut in 1961 and partnered Reg Gasnier in the centres in three straight Grand Final victories (1963-65). But it was at halfback that Smith made an impact at representative level, making his Test debut in the No.7 in 1964 by playing all three matches of Australia's home series whitewash against France. He made the spot his own in the Red V from 1966 onwards, winning another Grand Final that year, and was named at halfback in the Team of the 1960s. Smith, renowned for his toughness and determination, Smith finished with 18 Tests to his credit and played in two losing Grand Finals for the Saints (1971 and 1975) before retiring in 1977. He was included in the ARL's Top 100 Players as part of the Centenary celebrations in 2008, and was named as the seventh best halfback of all time in Alan Whiticker and Ian Collis' book *The Top 10 of Rugby League* two years later.

KEN MADDISON Ken Maddison was a long-serving centre for St. George, partnering the Immortal Reg Gasnier in the 1966 Grand Final—the last of the Dragons' sequence of 11 premierships. He left the club after losing the 1971 decider to Souths, joining neighbours Cronulla and switching to the backrow. The move paid almost immediate dividends. Maddison became the first forward to win the Rothmans Medal in 1973 and helped the Sharks to their maiden Grand Final appearance that year, before winning selection in the Kangaroo Tour squad at the end of the year. Maddison played four Tests on tour against Great Britain and France, scoring three tries. He debuted for New South Wales the following season and retired in 1975.

PAUL SAIT The remarkable depth of backrow talent during South Sydney's last great era initially prevented Paul Sait from forging a regular place in the top grade. Sait debuted for the Rabbitohs in 1968 and sat on the bench for the Grand Final loss to Balmain a year later, but found first grade permanency as an aggressive centre in 1970. He featured in the backline in Souths' Grand Final victory over Manly, but debuted for Australia against the Kiwis in the backrow at the season-ending World Cup, before reverting to the centres for the win over Great Britain in the final. Sait remained in the centres for the one-off Test against New Zealand in 1971 and for Souths in another Grand Final triumph against the Dragons later that season, but legendary lock Ron Coote's departure to Easts at the end of the year opened the door for Sait to finally take up residency in the Rabbitohs' backrow from 1972. He went on to play lock for Australia at the 1972 World Cup, in four Tests on the 1973 Kangaroo Tour and two Tests against the touring Lions in 1974, before winding up his international career at the 1975 World Cup. Sait retired in 1978 after 16 Tests for his country and 165 games as a South Sydney great, and was named in 'best-ever' Rabbitohs line-ups in 2002 and 2004—both times as a centre.

STEVE MORRIS 'Slippery' Steve Morris was the last player to be selected for Australia from a country side, chosen at halfback for the first Test against New Zealand in 1978 from Dapto. He joined St. George the following season and developed into one of the game's best young No.7s. Morris was adjudged man of the match opposing Steve Mortimer in the Dragons' 1979 Grand Final defeat of the Bulldogs. But St. George mentor Roy Masters chose to utilise Morris' speed and elusiveness on the flank midway through 1983 and he ranked amongst the decade's finest wingers. He was twice named Dally M Winger of the Year—once with St. George (1984) and again after joining Easts (1987)—and played two games on the flank for New South Wales. The diminutive flyer finished his first grade career in 1990 with 122 tries to his name, while his twin sons, Brett and Josh, became international outside backs in 2009.

JOHN RIBOT A Queensland representative in the mid-1970s, John Ribot shifted to Sydney with Newtown in 1978 and equalled the premiership record for most tries by a forward in a debut season, touching down 12 times in 17 games. The robust backrower represented NSW before grappling with injury in 1979, but his career gained a second wind after being shifted to the wing by Western Suburbs coach Roy Masters in 1980. He represented Queensland in eight Origin matches on the flank, and scored nine tries in as many Test appearances between 1981 and 1985. His highlights in the Australian jersey included touring with the 1982 Kangaroos and scoring match-winning tries in consecutive Tests in the 1985 series against the Kiwis. A fast and powerful presence on the wing, Ribot also appeared in Grand Final losses for Manly in 1982-83 before returning home to play for Redcliffe. Ribot became better known after retirement, as the inaugural CEO of the Broncos and Melbourne, as well as being a central figure in the Super League movement.

ROBBIE McCORMACK Foundation Newcastle Knight Robbie McCormack featured at five-eighth during the club's 1988 debut season. But the arrival of Canterbury pivot Michael Hagan in 1989 saw McCormack bounce around the team sheet over the next three seasons, playing centre and lock with the occasional appearance in the halves as he endeavoured to find a niche in the Knights' squad. McCormack's stocks skyrocketed after slotting into hooker early in 1992, however. His outstanding early-season form was rewarded with selection on the bench for his maiden Country Origin and New South Wales appearances. McCormack was replaced by Penrith's Steve Carter following the Blues' 14-6 win in the series opener, but his inventive dummy-half play was vital to Newcastle qualifying for its maiden finals series at the end of the season. He replaced injured NSW rake Ben Elias for the second Origin encounter of 1993 and represented Country in 1993 and 1994. McCormack was the highest-profile Knights player to defect to Super League hometown rivals the Hunter Mariners in 1997. He led the club in its World Club Challenge loss to Brisbane, before joining Wigan and rounding off a fine career with an English Super League title in 1998.

GEOFF TOOVEY The 1995 World Cup and the 1996 State of Origin series were precursors to long-time Manly halfback and captain Geoff Toovey making a permanent move to hooker at club level. The Australian and New South Wales brains trusts gambled on a Toovey-Andrew Johns halfback-hooker combination—and it paid off handsomely in both instances. Johns wore the No.9 jumper and packed into the scrums, but Toovey predominantly played the role of dummy-half, with Johns at first receiver. Australia won the aforementioned World Cup, while the Blues swept the 1996 Origin series 3-0. Toovey, one of the toughest and most courageous men to play the game despite his diminutive frame, was a Churchill Medal winner as skipper and halfback in the Sea Eagles' 1996 Grand Final triumph. He also captained Australia in the No.7 at the end of that season, and ranks alongside Allan Langer, Ricky Stuart and Johns as one of the decade's best halfbacks. But Toovey switched to hooker permanently for Manly in 1999, remaining at dummy-half as skipper of Manly and Northern Eagles before retiring at the end of 2001. He was named Dally M Hooker of the Year in 1999 and played eight Origin matches between 1997 and 2000 in the No.9.

LUKE RICKETSON Luke Ricketson played five Tests for Australia and made 10 Origin appearances for NSW as a backrower, meanwhile turning out a record 301 times in first grade for the Roosters. But Ricketson played all but a couple of his first 50 premiership matches as a wing or centre. A robust runner with a solid defensive game and adequate speed for the outside backs, Ricketson debuted in 1991 and had his first start in a game on the wing the following season before being switched to the backrow by new coach Phil Gould in 1995. He was a key man in the pack for the next decade, playing in three Grand Finals (including the 2002 premiership triumph) and succeeding Brad Fittler as the Roosters' captain in 2005—Ricketson's last season before retiring.

JASON HETHERINGTON Ipswich junior Jason Hetherington was groomed as the successor to two of the game's greatest five-eighths, but eventually developed into a Test and Origin hooker of immense class. Signed by Gold Coast with a view to assuming Wally Lewis' No.6 jumper, the Rockhampton product made 15 appearances in 1993 at pivot, centre and off the bench. He was lured to

Canterbury in 1994 as a potential long-term replacement for captain Terry Lamb, but cemented a spot at hooker in the second half of his debut year at Canterbury. Hetherington thrived in his adopted position, scoring a try in the loss to Canberra in the 1994 Grand Final, and was a key figure in the Bulldogs' incredible charge to the premiership the following season—with the ageless Lamb still at five-eighth. A powerful defender and creative dummy-half, Hetherington played eight Origin matches for Queensland and appeared in two Tests for Australia between 1998 and 2000.

RUBEN WIKI Kiwi powerhouse Ruben Wiki emerged in 1994 as Mal Meninga's equally robust centre partner at the Raiders, scoring 15 tries in 25 matches on his way to a Grand Final victory lap in his first full season of first grade. He made his Test debut for New Zealand on the 1994 tour of Papua New Guinea and was a backline mainstay for Canberra and the Kiwis until 1999, when Meninga, who was now coach of the Raiders, decided to utilise Wiki's size and strength in the pack. The transition was seamless. New Zealand's selectors agreed, switching Wiki to lock for the 2000 World Cup. Wiki was one of the Raiders' most consistent forwards—predominantly used as a backrower—before a successful four-season homecoming to the Warriors in 2005 as a fearsome prop. He racked up a world record number of Tests for the Kiwis (54), retiring from international football at the end of 2006, and from the NRL at the end of 2008 after 312 games.

MATT ADAMSON Parramatta junior Matt Adamson debuted for the Eels in 1991 and spent several seasons struggling to cement a spot in Penrith's first grade squad as a lanky fullback/winger. But Panthers coach Royce Simmons changed the trajectory of Adamson's career in 1996 by switching him to the second-row. The following season Adamson played all five of Super League Australia's Test matches against New Zealand and Great Britain, starting three of them in the backrow. Adamson was consistently one of the Panthers' best players and broke into the New South Wales Origin side for two matches in 2001, but joined English club Leeds at the end of the season. He spent three seasons as an engine-room mainstay for the Rhinos before joining Canberra for one final season in the NRL in 2005.

DARREN LOCKYER After establishing himself as a superstar in the No.1 jumper during Brisbane's 1997 Super League premiership season, Darren Lockyer cemented his status as one of the all time great fullbacks. A winner of three premierships and a Churchill Medal by 2000 before becoming a victorious Queensland skipper a year later, Lockyer assumed the Test captaincy in 2003 and guided the injury-hit Kangaroos to a spectacular 3-0 Ashes series whitewash of Great Britain, culminating in Lockyer being awarded the Golden Boot. But at the behest of Brisbane super-coach Wayne Bennett, Lockyer switched to five-eighth the following season. Lockyer had been earmarked as a gifted pivot earlier in his career and quickly became recognised as the game's premier No.6 in 2004, assuming the five-eighth role in the Queensland and Kangaroo sides. Under pressure after a difficult 2005 season, Lockyer experienced one of the greatest individual seasons in the game's history in 2006 and was awarded his second Golden Boot award. Of all Lockyer's magnificent achievements and records, arguably the strongest indicator of his greatness as a player is his ability to have dominated two very different positions for long periods of time—he was the undisputed best fullback in the game for six seasons and was the premier five-eighth after the switch until his retirement at the end of 2011. He has won three positional Dally M awards each at fullback and five-eighth, while Alan Whiticker and Ian Collis named Lockyer as the third-greatest custodian and fourth-greatest pivot (and 10th-greatest Australian player) of all time in their 2010 book *The Top 10 of Rugby League*.

COOPER CRONK The loss of Matt Orford to Manly at the end of 2005 was viewed as a bitter blow for Melbourne supporters. But they needn't have worried. One of the modern era's best halfbacks was already on their books—he just hadn't played there yet. Cooper Cronk came into first grade in 2004 and forged a permanent spot in the top-17 for his uncanny versatility, able to cover every position in the backline, as well as hooker and lock. Cronk played all 27 matches in the Storm's watershed 2006 season as Orford's replacement at halfback, including the Grand Final loss to Brisbane, and made his Test debut at halfback in 2007 after playing a key role in Melbourne's defeat of Manly in the decider. He captained Melbourne to Grand Final defeat in 2008 in the absence of Cameron Smith, before winning a second Grand Final and representing Australia again in 2009. Cronk's status as the number two halfback in the game behind Johnathan Thurston was assured by 2010, and he stuck with the Storm through the gut-wrenching salary cap scandal that saw the premierships he had been so vital to stripped from the club. Now a bona fide No.7, Cronk's versatility landed him a belated Origin debut as an interchange for Queensland in 2010. Cronk cemented the bench utility role at Origin and Test level the following season and shaped as retired great Darren Lockyer's halves replacement at Test level from 2012.

THE GREAT FIVE-EIGHTH DEBATE St George coach Nathan Brown and Melbourne mentor Craig Bellamy raised a few eyebrows at the beginning of 2007 with their respective announcements that two of the NRL's elite centres would be moving to five-eighth. Mark Gasnier was to replace Wigan-bound Trent Barrett in the No.6 for St. George-Illawarra, while the game's newest superstar Greg Inglis was earmarked to fill the gap left by Scott Hill at Melbourne. In both instances, the switches were met with scepticism and disdain by fans and critics alike. Gasnier had played pivot for New South Wales in an unsuccessful gamble as the Blues relinquished the Origin crown in 2006. The decision was taken out of Brown's hands for most of the season as Gasnier succumbed to injury in the 2007 pre-season, but he handed the 13-Test centre the No.6 jumper for his round 19 return. The experiment was aborted after four games—Gasnier returned to the centres for the Dragons before the end of the season, and for NSW in 2008. The biggest drawback of Inglis' move closer to the scrum was the effect it would have on his peerless running game that set the NRL alight from centre, wing and fullback in 2006. But Bellamy persisted with the switch throughout 2007, despite Inglis remaining on the flank for Queensland and Australia. The coach's greatest vindication came in the Grand Final, with Inglis terrorising Manly in a two-try, Churchill Medal-winning performance in the 34-8 triumph. Inglis scored 17 tries (including three hat-tricks) in 2008 and was adjudged Dally M Five-eighth of the Year, but the arrival of Brett Finch at the Storm early in 2009 allowed Inglis to revert back to his more natural role in the centres.

Injury to Darren Lockyer left Queensland without a recognised five-eighth for the 2008 Origin series, but the obvious choice for a replacement was in-form Gold Coast No.7 Scott Prince, who was considered unlucky to miss out on Australia's Centenary Test squad a few weeks earlier. But selectors sprung a surprise by selecting incumbent fullback Karmichael Hunt in the No.6, raising eyebrows and sparking debate across the state. Hunt was typically courageous and his non-traditional pivot display in the 18-10 loss to the Blues was marked by bone-crunching defence and full-throttle charges. Prince received the call-up to partner Johnathan Thurston in the halves for the remaining two matches that saw Queensland win a third consecutive Origin crown, while Hunt was selected on the bench but eventually started both games at fullback.

New Parramatta coach Daniel Anderson employed a similar tactic in 2009 with star outside back Jarryd Hayne. Installed at five-eighth for the opening rounds of the season, Hayne struggled to adjust to his new role in a disastrous start to the season for the Eels that saw halfback Brett Finch depart for Melbourne. Meanwhile, Hayne was relieved of the pivot duties after just four games. It is now part of the game's folklore that Hayne moved to fullback for the rest of 2009 and embarked on one of the most spectacular runs of form seen in premiership history, carrying Parramatta to the Grand Final and taking out the Dally M Player of the Year award. Anderson's successor, Kiwi Test coach Stephen Kearney, moved Hayne to pivot again for the second half of the Eels' disappointing 2011 season, with mixed results.

THE IRONMEN

Injuries are a regrettable but an inevitable facet of Rugby League. The following players, however, avoided the injury curse sufficiently to set towering appearance records and piece together extraordinary streaks of consecutive matches.

FIRST GRADE

MOST APPEARANCES

355—Darren Lockyer 1995-2011 (Brisbane)
Darren Lockyer became the first player in the game's history to play 350 first grade games in 2011, the Brisbane legend's final season.

349—Terry Lamb 1980-1996 (Wests, Canterbury)
Terry Lamb passed the hallowed 300-game mark in 1994—becoming just the second player to do so—and held the all time first grade appearance record for 15 years.

349—Steve Menzies 1993-2008 (Manly, Northern Eagles)
Evergreen backrower Steve Menzies equalled Lamb's record with his final appearance for Manly—the 2008 Grand Final victory. Incredibly, Menzies played 76 Super League games to the end of 2011 and signed another one-year deal with Catalans for 2012.

336—Brad Fittler 1989-2004 (Penrith, Roosters)
The only man to play 200 games for one club and bring up a century of appearances with another, Fittler became the first player to captain 200 first grade games. He retired after the 2004 Grand Final behind only Lamb on the all time appearance list.

332—Cliff Lyons 1985-1999 (Norths, Manly)
Lyons became just the second player to register 300 appearances for one club when he answered an SOS from the Sea Eagles to come out of retirement in 1999. The mercurial five-eighth is the only Indigenous member of the 300-game club.

328—Andrew Ettingshausen 1983-2000 (Cronulla)
Sharks legend Andrew Ettingshausen was the first player to appear in 300 first grade games for one club, achieving the mark in 1999. His single-club record stood until broken by Darren Lockyer in 2010.

325—Geoff Gerard 1974-89 (Parramatta, Manly, Penrith)
Former Kangaroo forward Geoff Gerard was recognised as the first player to break the 300-game barrier in 1989. But an anomaly in Penrith's record-keeping—the club previously did not recognise replacement appearances—meant Gerard's career appearance total remained at 303 in most publications, until updated in the game's official statistics in 2006.

318—Jason Croker 1991-2006 (Canberra)
Ultra-versatile Raiders stalwart Jason Croker broke Laurie Daley's club appearance record in 2003 and became the fourth player to amass 300 games for one club, after Ettingshausen, Lyons and Luke Ricketson (Sydney Roosters).

317—Hazem El Masri 1996-2009 (Canterbury)
The highest point-scorer in premiership history, Hazem El Masri eclipsed Steve Mortimer's long-standing Bulldogs appearance record in 2008 and became the sixth player to reach the 300-game mark with one club the following season, just a fortnight after Lockyer achieved the feat with Brisbane.

315—Paul Langmack 1983-1999 (Canterbury, Wests, Sydney Roosters)
A three-time premiership-winner with the Bulldogs and a 1986 Kangaroo tourist, ball-playing lock Paul Langmack became just the third player to make 300 first grade appearances in 1997. Langmack topped a century of matches with Canterbury and Wests.

315—Luke Priddis 1997-2010 (Canberra, Brisbane, Penrith, St. George Illawarra)
Durable hooker Luke Priddis eclipsed the 300-barrier in 2010. A Grand Final-winner with Brisbane and Penrith, the former Test and Origin rake played more than half of his career total with the Panthers (162).

MOST CONSECUTIVE APPEARANCES

194—Jason Taylor 1992-2000 (Wests, Norths, Northern Eagles)
Scheming halfback and pointscoring wizard Jason Taylor was maligned for most of his career for perceived defensive frailties, but the No.7 linchpin defied the detractors to become the most durable player in first grade history. Taylor broke Roy Fisher's long-standing consecutive games record in 1998 as captain of the Bears. Remarkably, Taylor's run was not broken as a result of injury—he was dropped by Northern Eagles coach Peter Sharp during the joint venture's dismal debut season.

He retired after the Eels' 2001 Grand Final loss as the most experienced first grade halfback of all time.

174—Hazem El Masri 1999-2005 (Bulldogs)

Celebrated Bulldogs winger Hazem El Masri's bid to break Taylor's record was foiled by a knee injury that ended his 2005 season. El Masri began his streak early in 1999, accumulating 90 tries and 1,434 points during his unbroken run.

147—Richard Swain 1997-2003 (Hunter, Melbourne, Brisbane)

Journeyman hooker Richard Swain combined a phenomenal work-rate with extraordinary durability. Debuting for the Mariners in 1997, Swain played in Melbourne's first 132 games, sharing in the 1999 premiership success and becoming the first player to amass 1,000 tackles in a season. Swain, a veteran of 19 Tests for New Zealand, extended his run of appearances until he was sidelined by an ankle injury midway through a one-off season with the Broncos in 2003, before linking with Hull.

147—Brett Kimmorley 1997-2003 (Hunter, Melbourne, Northern Eagles, Cronulla)

Gifted playmaker Brett Kimmorley spread his unbroken run of 147 first grade games over stints with four clubs. Linking with the fledgling Storm in 1998 after the Mariners' demise, Kimmorley starred in the club's 1999 premiership victory and made his Test and Origin debuts before signing with Northern Eagles. After playing every game of a disappointing 2001 season for the joint venture, Kimmorley joined Cronulla, where his streak was snapped courtesy of a fractured jaw during 2003.

146—Luke Douglas 2006-11 (Cronulla)

Yamba prop Luke Douglas has not missed a game since making his first grade debut in the Sharks' opening match of the 2006 season. Douglas' astonishing feat of playing every game in his first six seasons—in spite of the rigours of front-row warfare in the NRL—has kept him in the running to break Jason Taylor's all time record. He defied an MCL knee injury sustained against Melbourne in 2011—initially predicted to keep him out for four to six weeks—to take his place in the Sharks line-up against Brisbane just five days later. The representative hopeful joined the Titans in 2012.

143—Roy Fisher 1954-62 (Parramatta)

The original first grade ironman, Parramatta prop Roy Fisher's record of 143 consecutive first grade games stretched over nine seasons and stood for 36 years. In a cruel irony, the resilient front-rower's run came to end in 1962 and he missed the Eels' maiden finals appearance later in the season. Fisher joined North Sydney the following year.

139—Michael Robertson 2006-11 (Manly)

A durable and underrated winger, Michael Robertson joined the Sea Eagles from Canberra in 2006 and racked up 139 straight games for the club. Robertson became a Grand Final hero with a hat-trick in Manly's 2008 romp over Melbourne, and played every minute of every game since debuting for the Sea Eagles in round two of the 2006 season, until a knee injury ended his astonishing streak in 2011 (ironically, on the same weekend as Luke Douglas suffered his MCL injury above). He departed the NRL with a second premiership ring before signing with English club Harlequins.

STATE OF ORIGIN *Note: The figures below exclude residency-based interstate matches played between 1908 and 1981.*

MOST APPEARANCES

36—Darren Lockyer 1998-2011 (QLD)

Long-serving captain Darren Lockyer broke Allan Langer's Origin appearance record in 2011—his farewell series before retiring at the end of the season. Lockyer appeared in every series between 1998 and 2011, except for 2008, which he missed through a recurring knee injury. He also played two Super League Tri-Series matches for Queensland in 1997.

34—Allan Langer 1987-2002 (QLD)

Halfback genius Allan Langer's Origin career spanned an unprecedented 16 series, while his appearance record stood for nine years. The perennial match-winner could have reached an insurmountable total had the Super League war and a two-year hiatus from early-1999 not intervened.

32—Mal Meninga 1980-1994 (QLD)

Maroons skipper Mal Meninga eclipsed Wally Lewis' appearance record in his last interstate game, the 1994 decider. Meninga was the last survivor from the inaugural State of Origin clash in 1980 to retire, while his six non-Origin appearances for Queensland gives Meninga an all time interstate record of 38 matches.

31—Wally Lewis 1980-91 (QLD)

'The King' Wally Lewis appeared in 31 of the first 33 State of Origin matches, casting a giant influence over the interstate series that is unlikely to ever be seen again. His appearance record stood for three seasons, while his appearances as captain record (30) is likely to stand the test of time.

31—Brad Fittler 1990-2004 (NSW)

Inspirational Blues skipper Brad Fittler broke Andrew Ettingshausen's NSW appearance record in 2001, retiring from representative football at the end of the year. After two seasons away from Origin, Fittler heeded his state's call in 2004 and extended his record with a two-match comeback.

30—Petero Civoniceva 2001-11 (QLD)

Unrelenting prop Petero Civoniceva became the first forward to make 30 Origin appearances in 2011. Civoniceva missed just three games in 11 seasons as a cornerstone of the Maroons' pack.

28—Steve Price 1998-2009 (QLD)

Bulldogs and Warriors prop Steve Price seemed to get better with age, playing in all but one match of Queensland's 2006-09 series victories and breaking Bob Lindner's record for most Origin appearances for a forward in 2009.

27—Andrew Ettingshausen 1987-2008 (NSW)

Brilliant and versatile back Andrew Ettingshausen became NSW's most-capped Origin player by eclipsing Michael O'Connor's previous mark of 19 in 1994. He held the record for seven years, while the current crop of players' lack of Origin experience ensures he will remain in second spot until at least 2016.

26—Dale Shearer 1985-1996 (QLD)

Enigmatic utility back Dale Shearer finished a memorable career behind only Meninga, Lewis and Langer on the all time Origin appearance list, while he remained the equal-top try-scorer in Origin history 15 years after his final game for the Maroons.

25—Bob Lindner 1984-93 (QLD)

Magnificent backrower Bob Lindner broke long-time Queensland teammate Paul Vautin's Origin record for most appearances by a forward in his swansong 1993 series. Lindner's mark stood for 16 years until broken by Price.

MOST CONSECUTIVE APPEARANCES

24—Gary Larson 1991-98 (QLD)

Maroons workhorse Gary Larson played every match from making his debut in the opening match of the 1991 series to the end of the 1998 series, when he was 31. The North Sydney stalwart shared in three series victories.

21—Wally Lewis 1980-87 (QLD)

State of Origin's undisputed greatest player, Wally Lewis featured in the ground-breaking concept's first 21 encounters, captaining his state in all but the inaugural 1980 clash. Lewis missed just two matches during the first 12 seasons of Origin football—one in 1988 and the other in 1990—and was the key figure in seven series triumphs.

21—Shane Webcke 1998-2004 (QLD)

Brisbane great Shane Webcke established himself as arguably Queensland's greatest Origin front-rower while playing 21 straight games from his 1998 debut until his representative retirement at the end of 2004. Webcke featured in the Maroons' 1998 and 2001 series wins and was installed as captain for one match of his farewell series in the absence of Darren Lockyer.

21—Danny Buderus 2002-08 (NSW)

Lion-hearted hooker Danny Buderus made 21 appearances in a row after debuting in the 2002 series-opener. His last 15 appearance were as captain—a NSW record—before his departure to Super League at the end of 2008. Buderus starred in the Blues' 2003-05 series wins.

21—Petero Civoniceva 2002-09 (QLD)

After missing the second game of 2002 series with injury, Queensland front-row warhorse Petero Civoniceva strung together 21 consecutive appearances until injury forced his exclusion from game three of the 2009 series.

21—Johnathan Thurston 2005-11 (QLD)

Halfback superstar Johnathan Thurston has not missed a game for Queensland since making his Origin debut in 2005. He is the only player to feature in every match of the Maroons' record-breaking six-series winning streak and will equal Gary Larson's Origin record if he plays all three matches of the 2012 series.

20—Paul Harragon 1992-98 (NSW)

In a fascinating footnote to an injury-riddled career, Knights enforcer Paul Harragon set a long-standing record of 20 consecutive appearances for NSW. Harragon played every match from making his debut in 1992 until he was ruled out of the 1998 decider with injury, despite missing 42 club matches for the Knights during the same period.

AUSTRALIAN TEST AND WORLD CUP MATCHES *Note: In 2008, the Australian Rugby League decreed World Cup and World Series matches played from 1950 would be given the same status as Test matches in all international appearance lists.*

MOST APPEARANCES

59—Darren Lockyer 1998-2011

Record-breaking skipper Darren Lockyer became the first Australian to make 50 appearances in 2009 and broke Kiwi great Ruben Wiki's world record in 2011. Lockyer's 13-year Test career-span is matched only by pioneering legend 'Sandy' Pearce (1908-21).

46—Mal Meninga 1982-94

Despite four broken arms in two seasons limiting his international outings in the late-1980s, powerhouse centre Mal Meninga set an Australian appearance record that stood for 15 years. The only player to tour four times with the Kangaroos, Meninga broke Reg Gasnier's long-standing Test appearance mark (36) in 1992.

45—Graeme Langlands 1963-75

Virtuoso fullback and centre Graeme Langlands' record for combined Test and World Cup matches mark stood for almost two decades, while his 12-year international career-span is one of the longest in history.

45—Petero Civoniceva 2001-11

Petero Civoniceva became Australia's most-capped forward with his 40th international appearance in the 2009 Four Nations final, overtaking Immortal Johnny Raper.

40—Brad Fittler 1991-2001

The youngest Kangaroo tourist of all time, Brad Fittler appeared in more Tests than any other player during the 1990s. He featured in three Ashes series victories and skippered two World Cup triumphs during a decorated career.

39—Reg Gasnier 1959-67

Immortal centre Reg Gasnier held the record for most Test appearances (36) for 25 years after eclipsing Clive Churchill's mark during the 1967 series against the Kiwis.

39—John Raper 1959-68

Legendary Saints lock Johnny Raper boasted the record for most Test appearances by an Australian forward for more than four decades after his retirement.

37—Clive Churchill 1948-56

Clive Churchill became Australia's most-capped Test player in one of Rugby League's greatest careers, holding the record for 11 years.

35—Bob Fulton 1968-78

Electrifying centre/five-eighth Bob Fulton played a record 15 World Cup and World Series matches, as well as 20 Tests. His international swansong was as captain of the 1978 Kangaroos.

35—Keith Holman 1950-58

Australia's most-capped halfback of all time, Keith 'Yappy' Holman's record of 14 Ashes Test appearances stood for 34 years before eventually being broken by Meninga.

MOST CONSECUTIVE APPEARANCES

35—Clive Churchill 1948-55

After making his debut against New Zealand in 1948, Immortal Clive Churchill played every Test until missing the 1956 series against the Kiwis. Churchill famously played 99 representative matches straight before being incongruously left out of the Sydney team to take on France in 1955.

31—Ken Kearney 1952-58

Ken Kearney's 31 international appearances all came consecutively following his debut in the third Test against Great Britain on the 1952-53 Kangaroo Tour. His remarkable run included two further Ashes series and two World Cups.

27—Wally Lewis 1983-89

After wresting the Test five-eighth spot permanently from brilliant Parramatta pivot Brett Kenny in 1983, Wally Lewis played every international to the end of the decade. A broken arm halted his run in 1990 and ultimately cost him a third Kangaroo Tour.

24—Bob Fulton 1970-75

Bob Fulton's unbroken run of 24 international appearances extended from the third Ashes Test of 1970 until the halfway point of the 1975 World Series tournament.

24—Petero Civoniceva 2004-08

Front-row workhorse Petero Civoniceva played every match of Australia's 2004-06 Tri-Nations campaigns before his streak of 24 consecutive Tests came to an end when he was rested in the pool stage of the 2008 World Cup.

23—Michael Cronin 1975-82

Record-breaking point-scorer Mick Cronin played his last 23 internationals consecutively, a run that stretched from the 1975 World Series until his representative retirement prior to the 1982 Kangaroo Tour.

21—Garry Jack 1984-88

Courageous Balmain fullback Garry Jack made his Australian debut in the opening Ashes Test in 1984 and played his last international match in the 1988 World Cup final victory, appearing in every Test in between, including all five Tests on the 1986 Kangaroo Tour.

20—Mal Meninga 1989-92

Following his horror injury run, Mal Meninga embarked on a streak of 20 consecutive internationals that stretched from the 1989 Test series in New Zealand until suspension ruled him out of the first Test against the Kiwis in 1993.

19—Reg Gasnier 1959-62

The incomparable Reg Gasnier played the first 19 Tests of his vintage career in the green-and-gold consecutively. His streak was broken when injury ruled him out of the third Ashes Test of 1962.

18—Danny Buderus 2001-04

Courageous hooker Danny Buderus' supreme durability at representative level saw him amass 18 straight Test appearances from his 2001 debut against New Zealand. Injury ruled Buderus out of the one-off Test against New Zealand in 2005.

18—Anthony Minichiello 2003-05

After receiving his maiden international call-up against New Zealand in 2003, Sydney Roosters fullback Anthony Minichiello was a standout performer in the green-and-gold for three seasons. He played in 18 straight Tests and won consecutive Harry Sunderland Medals in 2004-05 for his brilliant efforts in Australia's Tri-Nations campaigns.

THE CONVERTS

Rugby League's origins are entwined with the working class rebellion against rugby union's amateur ideals. But while the birth of Rugby League (or the Northern Union, as it was initially known as) in England in 1895 was almost strictly regionally based, the success of a semi-professional code in Australia swung on proponents of Rugby League enticing the best and highest-profile rugby union talent available in those formative seasons. The promise of compensation for lost earnings through injuries and leave taken from work to play saw many prominent union players join the rebel movement.

THE PIONEERS New Zealand's 'All Golds'—the first professional rugby team from the southern hemisphere—contained eight former All Blacks and played three matches against a New South Wales side made up entirely of disgruntled rugby union players, before touring Britain. The defection of Australia's finest rugby player of the time, 'Dally' Messenger, sealed Rugby League's eventual success. The rugby union Test representative toured with the 'All Golds' as a guest player and dominated the early seasons of Rugby League in Australia. Messenger toured with the pioneering 1908-09 Kangaroos and captain-coached Easts to Sydney premierships in 1911-13. A peerless exponent of almost every facet of the game in the early years of the fledgling code, Messenger's legacy looms large over Rugby League's century-old history in Australia.

Dinny Lutge and Alex Burdon played in the inaugural rugby union Test against New Zealand in 1903 before joining the mass exodus to Rugby League in 1907. Injury suffered by Burdon was one of the catalysts for the push for Rugby League in Australia and subsequent compensation for players. Both players toured with the 1908-09 Kangaroos, Lutge as captain. Another nine former rugby union internationals debuted for the Australian Rugby League side during the 1908 series against New Zealand or on the first Kangaroo Tour, including well-travelled forward Bill Hardcastle. Hardcastle represented New Zealand on a rugby union tour of Australia in 1897 and moved across the Tasman the following season, playing for Australia against the touring British Isles team in 1899. He played in the 1903 Test against his former countrymen, before switching codes and winning selection for Australia from Ipswich. Hardcastle joined Sydney club Glebe in 1909.

A clutch of influential converts emerged during the ensuing seasons. Pioneering luminaries Chris McKivat, Charlie 'Boxer' Russell, Bob Craig, Paddy McCue and Herb Gilbert toured with the 1911-12 Kangaroos after earlier representing the Wallabies. McKivat was named as skipper of the squad that eventually claimed the Ashes and is regarded as one of Australia's greatest ever halfbacks—along with Gilbert, he was named in the ARL's 100 Greatest Players in 2008.

Bill Farnsworth initially resisted overtures to switch codes in 1907, but he eventually joined Newtown along with brother Viv and made his Rugby League Test debut in 1910 against England. Touring with the 1911-12 Kangaroos, Bill and Viv Farnsworth became Australia's first Test-playing brothers.

Tourists with the 1905-06 'Originals' All Blacks side to Britain, George Gillett and Arthur 'Boller' Francis were invited to tour with the 1911-12 Kangaroos after defecting to League—their presence on the tour, along with fellow Kiwis Charles Savory and Francis Woodward, resulted in the squad being commonly referred to as the 'Australasian' Kangaroos.

Another New Zealander, goalkicking centre Karl Ifwersen, was a convert of the rarest breed—after playing seven Tests for the New Zealand Rugby League team between 1913 and 1920, he joined rugby union's ranks and represented the All Blacks in one Test against South Africa in 1921, taking advantage of an amnesty that allowed World War I servicemen to return the amateur code. Ifwersen was the only League-first dual international from a major Test-playing nation until former Great Britain tyro Barrie-Jon Mather represented England at the 1999 Rugby Union World Cup. Ned Hughes played four Tests for the All Blacks in 1907-08, but was suspended by the NZRU in 1909 for playing in a benefit match under Rugby League rules. Hughes swapped codes and played a Test for New Zealand against the touring British side in 1910. Reinstated to rugby union after serving in World War I, Hughes became the oldest-ever All Black, playing two Tests against South Africa in 1921 aged 40.

CONVERT DROUGHT LASTS THREE DECADES Rugby League dwarfed rugby union in popularity by the 1920s as the amateur code struggled to overcome the effects of ceasing competition during World War I. With comparatively little union talent to choose from (the Queensland Rugby Union dissolved during the war and did not regroup until 1928), Rugby League clubs consequently did not benefit from any notable converts during the 1920s.

In contrast with the situation in Australia, several prominent All Blacks switched codes between the wars. Two legendary members of the 1924-25 'Invincibles' All Blacks tour to the British Isles, France and Canada joined Rugby League's ranks in the 1930s. Revered centre Bert Cooke represented the Kiwis in five Tests between 1932 and 1935, while fullback George Nepia, regarded as one of the greatest All Blacks of all time, kicked two goals in his only Rugby League Test appearance— the Kiwis' 16-15 defeat of Australia at Carlaw Park in 1937. 1946 All Black halfback Jimmy Haig became New Zealand's last dual international for more than 40 years. Haig made his Kiwis debut on the 1947-48 tour of Britain and France, going on to play 21 Tests, including nine as captain.

Doug McLean Jr was Australia's only dual international of the period between 1919 and 1952. The son of the pioneering dual international of the same name, Doug McLean Jr played 10 Tests for the Wallabies before switching codes and playing two Tests on the 1937-38 Kangaroo Tour. He was a prominent member of a famous Queensland rugby union family, which produced three generations of Wallaby representatives.

Len Smith, a premiership-winner with Newtown and the Australian captain-coach who was at the centre of the 1948-49 Kangaroos selection controversy, was robbed of dual international status by World War II. A promising rugby union star in the 1930s, Smith was selected for the Wallabies' tour of Britain in 1939, but war was declared upon their arrival and the squad returned home without playing a game. Smith switched to Rugby League after serving in the Australian Army.

RUGBY LEAGUE'S GOLDEN AGE GRACED BY BRILLIANT CONVERTS

Centre Trevor Allan captained the Wallabies before starring during the 1950s with English Rugby League club Leigh. He returned to Australia and captain-coached Norths later in the decade. Seven-Test Wallaby hooker Ken Kearney defected from rugby union to Leeds in 1948 before becoming one of the most influential figures in Australia's Rugby League history. Kearney played 31 Tests and, as captain-coach, was the driving force behind the first half of St. George's world record sequence of 11 premierships.

Rupert Mudge and Tony Paskins went directly from Sydney club rugby union to English Rugby League club Workington Town, winning a Challenge Cup together in 1953 before joining Easts. Paskins represented NSW and later captain-coached Manly. Wallaby lock Rex Mossop was lured into changing codes by English club Leigh, where he enjoyed Challenge Cup success alongside Allan. Mossop joined Manly and played nine Tests, touring with the 1959-60 Kangaroos as vice-captain. He achieved even greater fame in a long and colourful Rugby League broadcasting career. Legendary Welsh dual international Lewis Jones moved to Australia in the twilight of his career to captain-coach Wentworthville to Second Division success in the mid-1960s.

Arthur Summons played 10 Tests for the Wallabies at first five-eighth in the late 1950s before becoming one of the great Rugby League halves with Wests. He skippered the Magpies in the 1962 and '63 Grand Final losses to the mighty St. George side and led the 1963-64 Kangaroos to Britain and France among nine Test appearances. Wallaby back Jim Lisle enjoyed a meteoric rise to dual international status in 1962, receiving a call-up to the NSW side after just one first grade game with Souths before making his Test debut in the third Ashes encounter. Lisle played six Tests and toured with Summons' 1963-64 Kangaroos. He skippered Souths in the 1965 Grand Final loss to St. George before winning a premiership with the Rabbitohs two years later.

Brisbane product Kevin Ryan was a five-Test Wallaby at No.8 prior to building a reputation as one of Rugby League's most feared forwards. Ryan debuted for St. George in 1960 and became a dual international on the 1963-64 Kangaroo Tour with two Test appearances against France. Ryan featured in seven straight Grand Final victories for the Dragons (1960-66) before orchestrating the end of the club's world record premiership run as captain-coach of Canterbury in 1967.

Two players who represented Australia in three sports made the transition from union to League during the 1960s. Dick Thornett went to the 1960 Rome Olympics with the Australian water polo team before representing the Wallabies alongside older brother John in 1961-62. He switched codes with the Eels in 1963 and toured with the Kangaroos at the end of the year with another older sibling, all time great fullback Ken. The ball-playing forward played 11 Rugby League Tests in a decade-long professional career. Wing speedster Michael Cleary joined Souths after representing the Wallabies in 1961, but retained his amateur status to allow him to take his place in Australia's 1962 Commonwealth Games team as a sprinter.[21] Cleary also made the first of eight Rugby League Test appearances in 1962 and toured with the Kangaroos the following season. A Grand Final-winner with Souths in 1967-68 and 1970, Cleary finished an outstanding career with 93 tries from 153 games for the Rabbitohs and Roosters.

Superb attacking centre Bob Honan played two Tests in union and League, switching codes in 1967 and winning premierships with Souths in 1968 and 1970-71. Teenage Wallaby representative Phil Hawthorne went on to play 21 rugby union Tests before St. George lured the brilliant fly-half to the professional game in 1968. An outstanding field goal exponent, Hawthorne played the entire 1970 Ashes series at five-eighth and captained his country in the deciding third Test loss, his last appearance for Australia.

Several South African rugby union converts made a sizeable impact on the 13-a-side game during the 1950s and 1960s. Fred Griffiths, Len Killeen and Col Greenwood were the most notable South African imports to Australian clubs, while Tom Van Vollenhoven and Wilf Rosenberg became legends of the British game (*see South Africans Make their Mark*).

CONVERT DIAMONDS FOR ROOSTERS AND EELS, DUST FOR PANTHERS

PANTHERS Eastern Suburbs received tremendous value from a trio of converts in the 1970s. Goal-kicking first five-eighth John Ballesty played nine Tests for the Wallabies before linking with the Tricolours in 1970. He won *Rugby League Week*'s Player of the Year award in 1972 and starred as Easts qualified for that season's Grand Final. Wallaby centre John Brass, who played 12 union Tests, made the switch in 1969 and played all three Tests of Australia's home series against Great Britain in 1970. He was crucial to Easts' drought-breaking premiership-winning sides of 1974-75 and skippered Australia in a World Series match against New Zealand in the latter season. An accomplished goalkicker, Brass scored 715 points in 143 games for the Roosters. Joining the list of Wallaby No.10s to defect, 21-year-old Russell Fairfax joined Eastern Suburbs in 1974 after a dazzling eight-Test rugby union career. Fairfax was an immediate success, representing NSW and winning a Grand Final in his first season. Injuries stymied his progress and he was fated to never achieve dual international status. He retired in 1981 after 119 games for Easts and Souths, later embarking on a disastrous coaching stint with the Roosters in 1989 90 that ended with his sacking before the 1990 season was out in light of the club's woeful results, before a long and successful career in the media. Easts dipped into the rugby union ranks again in the late-1970s, snaring classy flyhalf Ken Wright, a veteran of nine Tests for the Wallabies. Wright scored the Roosters' only points in the 1980 Grand Final, kicking two goals in the 18-4 loss to Canterbury, before linking with Souths in 1982. He alternated between five-eighth, centre and wing during a five-season, 58-game first grade game career.

Three-quarter Stephen Knight became a dual international in his first Rugby League season after joining Wests in 1972, playing two games in Australia's World Cup campaign. The six-Test Wallaby scored 49 tries in 142 games for Wests, Balmain and Manly, winning a premiership with the Sea Eagles in 1978. Geoff Richardson

---

21 Alan Whiticker and Glen Hudson, *The Encyclopedia Of Rugby League Players*. Sydney, 2007

played nine Tests in the Wallabies' No.10 jumper in the early 1970s before signing with Wests in Brisbane and representing Australia in two Ashes Tests in 1974. The wily five-eighth also played six games for Queensland. Wallaby captain Peter Sullivan shocked the rugby union fraternity by joining St. George in 1974, becoming the first Australian rugby union skipper since Trevor Allan to switch codes, but the 13-Test flanker made just one first grade appearance in the Red V.

Outstanding flanker Ray Price made eight Test appearances for the Wallabies before joining Parramatta in 1977 and becoming an all time Rugby League great. The inspirational lock-forward enjoyed a 22-Test career for Australia—encompassing two Kangaroo Tours—and was a vital component of the Parramatta machine that won four premierships in the 1980s, bowing out from the game as captain in the club's dramatic 4-2 victory over Canterbury in the 1986 Grand Final. Price was included in the ARL's 100 Greatest Players as part of the 2008 Centenary celebrations, one of only three post-World War II dual internationals to be included, along with Ken Kearney and Arthur Summons.

Big spending cellar-dwellers Penrith made an ambitious, but ultimately fruitless, foray into recruiting rugby union talent during the 1970s and 1980s. A scouting mission to South Africa saw Peter Swanson and Keith Howie turn out in first grade in 1973-74, with limited success (see South Africans Make their Mark). Manawatu prop Kent Lambert, a veteran of 11 Tests in the All Blacks' front-row, switched to Rugby League on the principles that originally gave birth to the code. Publicly lamenting the financial constraints placed on amateur union players, Lambert joined the Panthers in 1978, but a string of injuries restricted him to one first grade appearance. Unperturbed, the Panthers had another crack in 1983 by luring 10-Test Wallaby prop Tony D'Arcy to the club. Perhaps due to the unsuited body shape of rugby union props to Rugby League forward play, D'Arcy's switch was also a failure and he did not progress past the lower grades.

O'CONNOR AND STUART HEADLINE 1980s CONVERTS Few defections hit the ARU harder than dazzling 13-Test Wallaby centre Michael O'Connor's switch to St. George in 1983. O'Connor agonised over the decision, but established himself as one of the great attacking players in Rugby League history in a decade-long professional career. A mesmerising ball-runner at centre or wing, O'Connor set a host of pointscoring and tryscoring records at representative level in 19 Origins for NSW and 18 Test appearances, and starred in Manly's 1987 Grand Final victory. O'Connor retired in 1992 after three season as Sea Eagles captain, and was selected in best-ever club line-ups in 1990 and 2006. He was picked in top-100 players of all time lists in Rugby League Week (1992) and Daily Telegraph (2000), but was a surprise omission from the ARL's 100 Greatest Players of the Century in 2008.

Fellow rugby union prodigy Tony Melrose joined the Rugby League ranks three years prior to O'Connor's code jump. Melrose captained the revered 1977-78 Australian Schoolboys side that featured O'Connor, the Ella brothers and Wally Lewis on a tour of England. He played six Tests for the Wallabies before signing with the Eels as a 20-year-old. After missing out on the club's maiden Grand Final victory in 1981, Melrose linked with Souths and immediately won NSW selection. The versatile back later turned out for Manly and Easts, proving a fine goalkicker and one of the game's foremost field goal exponents.

Flyhalf Mitchell Cox, whose father Brian and brother Phillip also represented the Wallabies, played two rugby union Tests on Australia's tour of Britain in 1981, before jumping across to Rugby League with North Sydney in 1982. He made 94 first grade appearances for Norths and Manly in six seasons as a clever five-eighth.

Another unlucky ARL Top 100 exclusion, influential No.7 Ricky Stuart, joined the Raiders in 1988 after touring Argentina with the Wallabies the previous season. He won Canberra's player of the year award in his debut season and was the architect of the club's 1989, 1990 and 1994 premiership successes. Stuart was an Ashes hero on consecutive Kangaroo Tours, displacing the great Allan Langer during the 1990 and 1994 series, while he steered NSW to four Origin series victories over Queensland in five attempts opposite Langer. A ruthless competitor, Stuart's peerless passing and kicking game netted a plethora of individual awards during a 243-game first grade career, including the 1990 Churchill Medal and a rare Rothmans Medal-Dally M Medal double in a brilliant 1993 season. Stuart finished his career in 2000 after two seasons with the Bulldogs, before embarking on a highly successful coaching career, which included a premiership with the Roosters in 2002, an Origin series victory in 2005 and three years in charge of the Kangaroos.

James Grant (five rugby union Tests) and Andrew Leeds (14 Tests) made successful code switches in 1989. Grant joined Balmain, scoring the opening try of the 1989 extra-time Grand Final loss and racking up 30 tries in 65 games for the Tigers before late-career stints with Hull and the Western Reds. Leeds was a rock-steady fullback and a superb goalkicker in an 11-season career with the Eels, Panthers and Magpies, accumulating 875 points in 177 games.

But the decade provided its share of rugby union flops. Star centre Brett Papworth played 15 Tests for his country before his much-hyped arrival at the Roosters in 1988. Papworth's League experiment was cruelled by bad luck however—he played just six first grade games amid a horror run of injuries. Centre Matt Burke scored 15 tries in 23 Tests and starred at the 1987 World Cup before joining the Sea Eagles for an encouraging two-season stint. He linked with Easts in 1990 along with brother Brad—a 1988 Wallabies tourist as Nick Farr-Jones' halfback understudy—but the pair enjoyed little success at the club. Like Papworth, Brad Burke was eventually reinstated to rugby union, while Matt Burke's League career ended with a fruitless stint at Balmain. The Burke brothers are the sons of Manly Grand Final halfback and 1959-60 Kangaroo tourist Peter Burke.

KIWI INVASION In 1989, Kurt Sherlock became New Zealand's first dual international since Jimmy Haig more than four decades earlier. An All Black tourist to Argentina in 1985 (no Tests) and a mainstay of the all-conquering Auckland provincial side's midfield, Sherlock signed with Easts in 1987 and played four Tests for the Kiwis in 1989, touring with the national side to Britain and France. Sherlock was a handy utility and excellent goalkicker in 88 games for the Roosters. Wellington loose forward and Tongan international Emosi Koloto also made the switch in the late-1980s, joining English powerhouse Widnes and representing the Kiwis in five Tests in 1991, including the 24-8 upset of Australia in Melbourne.

The floodgates opened in the early-1990s, with established All Blacks and frustrated second-stringers alike defecting to Australian and English Rugby League clubs. Manly and ex-Kiwi coach Graham Lowe was a conspicuous observer at the

1990 All Black trials. Only weeks later he trumpeted the signing of precociously talented fullback Matthew Ridge for the Sea Eagles (he also almost nabbed Zinzan Brooke, who later pulled out of a deal with the club and went on to become one of the great All Black forwards). Ridge toured the British Isles and Canada with the All Blacks in 1989 but the Aucklander was stuck behind the world's best fullback, John Gallagher, for the Test spot. Much to Ridge's chagrin, Gallagher shocked the union fraternity by defecting shortly afterwards to Leeds, where he achieved only moderate success. Ridge nevertheless was one of the all time great converts. With the help of several countrymen, Ridge revolutionised goalkicking in the Australian premiership and was one of the 1990s' most courageous and valuable fullbacks. Ridge scored 1,331 points in 159 games for Manly and Auckland, winning a premiership with the Sea Eagles in 1996 and playing 25 Tests as arguably New Zealand's best-ever No.1.

Following the immediate success of Ridge's switch, Winfield Cup clubs ravaged New Zealand's rugby union ranks. Norths signed Wellington winger Paul Simonsson and Waikato fullback Daryl Halligan for the 1991 season. Simonsson scored seven tries in two minor matches for the All Blacks on a tour of Japan in 1987, but played just three first grade games with the Bears. Halligan, meanwhile, became the highest point-scorer in premiership history. Continually overlooked for All Black selection despite the defection of Ridge and Gallagher, Halligan topped the competition's pointscoring in his first four seasons with the Bears and Bulldogs, winning a Grand Final with the latter in 1995. A winger for virtually all of his Rugby League career, Halligan's turtle-like pace was tempered by a magnificent positional sense and he was the first player to break the 2,000-points barrier in first grade. The 19-Test Kiwi retired in 2000 after 230 first grade games and 2,034 points, including 80 tries.

Two former All Blacks achieved legend status with English giants Wigan during the 1990s. Frano Botica, a seven-Test All Black but fly-half understudy to the great Grant Fox, joined the Riversiders in 1990 and was a pointscoring phenomenon, becoming the fastest player to 1,000 points in English Rugby League history (93 games) and representing the Kiwis in seven Tests. Botica joined Wigan mentor John Monie during the Auckland Warriors' 1995 debut season, but a terrible leg injury ended his stint after just five games. He returned to the 15-a-side code after it became professional, eventually returning to NZ provincial side North Harbour. Powerhouse All Black winger Va'aiga Tuigamala, a veteran of 19 Tests, was a Wigan crowd favourite after signing with the club in 1993. Tuigamala represented Western Samoa at the 1995 World Cup before switching back to union and starring for Samoa in 23 Tests.

Leeds also lured devastating centre Craig Innes to Rugby League in 1991. The 17-Test All Black excelled with the English club and joined the Western Reds in 1995, before starring in Manly's premiership charge the following season. Only Innes' ARL affiliations denied him the opportunity to play Test Rugby League with New Zealand, but he represented Rest of the World in a Test against Australia in 1997. After scoring a try in Manly's 1997 Grand Final loss to Newcastle, Innes returned to rugby union and played at Super 12 level until 2001.

All Black midfield-back John Schuster, also a Western Samoa union international, joined Newcastle in 1991. A devastating ball-runner, Schuster set several modest pointscoring records with the Knights and played in the club's maiden finals campaign in 1992 before joining English side Halifax for several seasons and representing Samoa. Bay of Plenty fullback Eion Crossan, another fringe All Black, linked with the Rabbitohs in 1992. A maligned figure due to perceived defensive weaknesses, Crossan scored 324 points in 45 games for Souths and Cronulla. Wellington flanker and New Zealand Maori rep Gavin Hill was a handy goalkicking forward for the Bulldogs in 1992-93, representing the Kiwis in five Tests before signing on as a foundation Warrior. But Hill played just 14 games in two seasons with Auckland and eventually returned to union, playing in Ireland and Canada before moving into the coaching ranks in New Zealand.

Besides Botica and Hill, the Warriors recruited three more high-profile union stars during their fledgling seasons. All Blacks legend John Kirwan—30 and a veteran of 63 Tests and a then-record 35 tries—was a surprise success story for the Warriors in 1995-96. The grandson of former Kiwis centre Jack Kirwan, a 1920s union convert, 'JK' was the club's top try-scorer in 1996. Flamboyant utility-back Marc Ellis, who scored 11 tries in eight All Blacks Tests (including a record six against Japan at the 1995 World Cup), spent two colourful seasons with the Warriors and represented the Kiwis in five Tests, before returning to provincial rugby union in 1998. Auckland flanker Mark Carter was less successful, playing just eight games for the Warriors in 1996, but he regained his All Blacks jumper after rejoining union the following season.

John Timu sacrificed a certain All Blacks spot at the 1995 rugby union World Cup to sign with the Bulldogs. He won a premiership and became a dual international in his first Rugby League season, playing in the Centenary Rugby League World Cup in England instead. The 26-Test All Black spent three seasons with the Bulldogs and played nine Tests for the Kiwis, before rounding out his career with the London Broncos. Timu debuted for the All Blacks on the 1989 tour of the British Isles and Canada—all told, eight members of that squad eventually switched to Rugby League.

Former Auckland and All Blacks fullback Shane Howarth spent the 1996 season under Graham Lowe at the Cowboys before controversially representing Wales in rugby union. Aggressive forwards Gordon Falcon (Penrith) and Matua Parkinson (Canterbury), and goalkicking fullback Simon Forrest (Souths) also spent low-profile stints in the Australian premiership before returning to the 15-a-side game in New Zealand.

AUSTRALIAN CONVERT TALENT DRIES UP Towering backrower Scott Gourley—the son of former St. George Grand Final-winner Robin Gourley (himself an ex-union player in Ireland)—signed with the Dragons in 1990 after playing five Tests for the Wallabies in the late 1980s. Gourley became a dual international in 1991 when he toured PNG with the Australian Rugby League side, represented NSW in 1993 and played in three Grand Final losses for the Saints. He rounded out a fine 173-game career with two seasons at the Roosters.

Former Wallabies coach and high-profile radio personality Alan Jones took over the reins at Balmain in 1991 for a colourful—but ultimately unsuccessful—three-season stint. Jones recruited former Wallaby and Ireland rugby union international Brian Smith, who Jones controversially installed as the Tigers' No.7 ahead of Kiwi captain Gary Freeman. Smith represented City Origin in 1992 but his career stalled soon afterward and he joined the Roosters for a fruitless one-season stay in 1994—ironically as Freeman's replacement.

Wallaby backline stars David Campese, Tim Horan and Jason Little were frequently rumoured to be in the sights of Rugby League clubs, but the only current Australian internationals to make the switch during the 1990s were two-metre lock Garrick Morgan (son of former Manly and Australian Test forward John 'Pogo' Morgan) and centre Anthony Herbert, both much-hyped recruits for the South Queensland Crushers' 1995 debut season. But each convert appeared in just two matches for the Crushers, while Morgan returned to the Wallabies' fold the following season.

Three former Welsh rugby union Test players—all of whom became dual internationals by representing Great Britain and Wales in Rugby League—ventured to Australia during the first half of the 1990s. Jonathan Davies, a great of both codes, starred for Canterbury in 1991 and was a foundation Cowboy; centre John Devereux spent 1993 with Manly; and winger Allan Bateman turned out in five finals matches in two seasons with Cronulla. Davies and Bateman later returned to union and Test rugby. "It's the first time I've been cold for seven years. I was never cold playing Rugby League," Davies remarked of his 15-a-side comeback.

Fijian winger Noa Nadruku played 13 rugby union Tests for his country before being snapped up by the Canberra Raiders following some standout performances for Fiji at the Rugby League World Sevens in 1993. Nadruku was a sensation, topping the premiership's tryscoring table in 1993 and 1996, and winning a Grand Final with Canberra in 1994. He became a dual international in 1994 and retired in 1999 after 131 games and 90 tries for the Raiders and Cowboys. Fellow Fiji 1991 World Cup squad members Fili Seru (South Queensland, Illawarra) and Kaleveti Naisoro (Parramatta) failed to live up to the hype created by Nadruku, but both became dual internationals. Springbok forward Tiaan Strauss spent two seasons with Cronulla, playing 14 first grade games, but switched back to union and represented the Wallabies after fulfilling residential requirements.

Perhaps rugby union's greatest gift to Rugby League in the 1990s was Australian Under-21s rep Ben Kennedy, who joined the Raiders and won the Norwich Rising Star award in 1996. An aggressive and inspirational backrower, Kennedy played 16 Tests for Australia and 13 Origins for NSW, and was a driving force behind the Knights' 2001 premiership success. Despite spending just two seasons with Manly in the twilight of his career, Kennedy was named in the club's best-ever line-up in 2006.

Junior All Black Tasesa Lavea was recruited by Melbourne in 1999 and the talented utility-back won the 2000 Dally M Rookie of the Year award before playing four Tests for the Kiwis. But after a disappointing stint with Northern Eagles, Lavea returned to union in 2003, playing for the Blues and Chiefs in Super Rugby and representing Samoa at the 2011 World Cup.

THE TIDE TURNS Rugby union's move to professionalism in 1995 offered formerly amateur players similar riches to what was on offer in Rugby League. The tap of union talent defecting to League had been effectively switched off and gradually the trend began to reverse. Broncos winger Willie Carne was the first high-profile Rugby League player to defect to union. After 10 Tests for Australia, 12 Origins for Queensland and two premierships, Carne joined Super 12 franchise

Queensland Reds 1997. But he struggled to make the transition and parted ways with union at the end of the season.

Enigmatic Roosters fullback/five-eighth Andrew Walker and Brisbane hitman Peter Ryan were the next notable NRL players to swap codes, making the move in 2000 with Super 12 side ACT Brumbies. Indigenous star Walker, a brilliant match-winner on his day, became Australia's first dual international to represent in Rugby League first—he played one League Test against PNG in 1996 and turned out in seven Tests for the Wallabies in 2000-01.

Former Queensland Origin forward Ryan, a two-time Grand Final-winner with the Broncos, became the first player to claim a Rugby League premiership and a Super 12 title after helping the Brumbies defeat Coastal Sharks in 2001, alongside Walker. Walker later returned to the NRL with Manly in 2004 but received a two-year ban for recreational drug use before resurfacing with Queensland Reds in 2007. His colourful career ended with a record of 145 first grade Rugby League appearances (600 points) and 56 Super Rugby games (263 points).

Queensland and Kangaroos wingers Mat Rogers, Wendell Sailor and Lote Tuqiri joined the worrying exodus to union in the ensuing seasons. Rogers and Sailor defected in 2002 and Tuqiri a season later—the trio made up the Wallabies' back-three in the 2003 World Cup final, an extra-time loss to England. Rogers played 45 Tests to the end of 2006, Sailor represented in 37 Tests before receiving a two-year ban for cocaine use, while Tuqiri scored 30 tries in 67 Tests before his tenure with the Waratahs also ended in acrimonious circumstances in 2009. All three returned to Rugby League with great success: Rogers signed on as a foundation Titan and was one of the fledgling club's best before retiring at the end of 2010, while a comeback in 2011 was aborted after one game due to a broken foot; Sailor added an impressive and colourful postscript to his career with an 18-month stint at the Dragons; and Tuqiri joined the Wests Tigers in 2010, scoring 18 tries and reclaiming a Kangaroos jumper in a spectacular comeback season.

Tryscoring freak and Kangaroos winger Nathan Blacklock quit the NRL in 2002 and signed up with the Waratahs, but his Super Rugby stint lasted just five games and he returned to finish his career at St. George Illawarra with a career total of 121 tries in 142 games. Former Newcastle and Northern Eagles winger Lenny Beckett, a veteran of 59 first grade games, crossed over to play for the Brumbies in 2003.

Former Raiders captain and Queensland Origin fullback Clinton Schifcofske switched codes at the end of 2006, starring for Queensland Reds and Irish club Ulster, before a Rugby League comeback with Welsh Super League club Celtic Crusaders. Roosters centre Ryan Cross, an Australian Schoolboys rep in union and the son of flamboyant Eastern Suburbs and Balmain winger Paul, also made the jump in 2007 with Perth-based Western Force, eventually attaining Wallabies selection.

Despite becoming a dual international in his first season in union, Timana Tahu's foray into 15-a-side rugby was generally an unhappy experience. The five-Test Kangaroo returned to the NRL with the Eels in 2010, immediately winning a place in the NSW Origin side, although he walked out of camp following racist remarks made by assistant coach and former Knights teammate Andrew Johns, while off-field problems and injury ended stints with the Eels and Panthers respectively. He signed with Newcastle—where he won a premiership in 2001—for the 2012 season.

Premiership-winning Penrith skipper and Australian Test halfback Craig Gower became the first of three high-profile NRL internationals to switch to French rugby union in 2008. Gower signed with Bayonne and won Test selection with Italy, making his debut against the Wallabies in 2009. Kiwi superstar Sonny Bill Williams controversially walked out on the Bulldogs mid-season in 2008 despite being just 18 months into a five-year contract, joining Toulon before becoming New Zealand's second League-first dual international (after Karl Ifwersen) with an All Blacks debut in 2010. Williams starred for Super 15 side Canterbury Crusaders and helped the All Blacks to a belated World Cup final victory in 2011 and despite constant speculation about an NRL return, he signed with Super 15 club Waikato Chiefs for 2012. Gun Dragons centre Mark Gasnier sacrificed certain selection in Australia's 2008 World Cup squad to sign with Stade Francais, but returned less than two years later to help St. George Illawarra to the 2010 NRL title before winning back a NSW Origin jumper and retiring at the end of 2011.

Raiders (165 games) and Harlequins (72 games) livewire Mark McLinden joined the Queensland Reds in 2009, while incoming Super 15 side Melbourne Rebels dipped into the NRL's reservoir of talent for their 2011 entry, recruiting powerhouse ex-Warriors and Knights winger Cooper Vuna and promising Saints forward Jarrod Saffy. Former Penrith and Kangaroos winger Luke Rooney, who joined French union club Toulon at the end of 2008, also came on board for the Rebels' debut season. Brilliant Roosters and Rabbitohs utility Craig Wing—a veteran of 256 first grade games, 12 Origins and 16 Tests—signed a lucrative deal in Japanese rugby union for 2010. Controversial forward Willie Mason spent a brief stint in French rugby in 2011 after yet another acrimonious split with a Rugby League club, this time Super League franchise Hull KR.

Several low-profile converts' achievements in rugby union far outstripped their accomplishments in Rugby League. Duncan McRae, a fringe first grader for Souths and Canterbury between 1993 and 1998, was a star fly-half for the Waratahs after switching codes in 1999; eight-game Rabbitoh Brett Sheehan played three Tests for the Wallabies; and rookie Broncos half Berrick Barnes' code switch in 2006 garnered 37 Test appearances and two World Cup campaigns to the end of 2011. Flanker Rocky Elsom won a Jersey Flegg premiership with the Bulldogs in 2001 before joining the Waratahs and playing 75 Tests for the Wallabies, captaining his country in 2010-11.

Several Great Britain Rugby League stars also joined the exodus—Barrie-Jon Mather, Jason Robinson, Andy Farrell and Chris Ashton played Test rugby union for England, while popular former Knights winger Brian Carney represented Ireland in the 15-a-side game. Kiwi Test players Henry Paul, Lesley Vainikolo and Shontayne Hape also broke into the England rugby union side after switching codes, qualifying on residential grounds after lengthy Super League careers.

The occurrence of established rugby union players switching to the NRL during this period was minimal. Five-Test All Black halfback Mark Robinson had a brief stint with the Warriors in 2003 en route to English union club Northampton, while Waratahs centre Sam Harris played 64 games in the backrow for Manly and Wests Tigers—representing City Origin in 2004—before returning to Super Rugby. Australian Schoolboys rugby union rep Cooper Cronk decided on a future in Rugby League, which saw him become a representative star and one of the NRL's dominant players with Melbourne.

BRAD THORN Towering forward Brad Thorn is arguably the most remarkable convert in Rugby League/rugby union history. Dunedin-born Thorn harboured a desire to become an All Black at an early age, but moved to Australia as a youngster and debuted for the Broncos in 1994. Origin honours with Queensland followed two years later and he played three Tests for Australia in 1998. After savouring his third premiership with Brisbane in 2000, Thorn returned to New Zealand with the Canterbury Crusaders in 2001. Thorn turned down his maiden All Blacks berth after winning selection in 2001 and sat out the 2002 season due to his uncertainty about his commitment to the 15-a-side code, but made his debut in the famous jersey in 2003 and played in the year-ending World Cup.

He made an NRL comeback with the Broncos at the age of 30 in 2005 and secured an immediate return to the Queensland side to extend his total Origin appearances to 11, before partaking in his fourth Grand Final victory lap the following season. After 200 first grade games for Brisbane, Thorn again switched to rugby union, winning a Super Rugby title with the Crusaders in 2008 (after final defeats in 2003-04) and taking his total of Super Rugby appearances to 77. He slotted straight back into the national side and became a mainstay of the All Blacks' pack at lock. Thorn was a key member of the All Blacks' World Cup-winning side in 2011—the 8-7 defeat of France in the Final was his 59th Test appearance. The 37-year-old signed a deal to play Japanese rugby union in 2012.

AFL THREAT EMERGES The Broncos felt the brunt of the AFL's expansion to 18 teams in 2011-12. The Gold Coast Suns signed brilliant fullback Karmichael Hunt—a veteran of 11 Tests and 10 Origins at just 22 years old—on a reported $3 million, three-year deal during 2009. A year later, Greater Western Sydney lured electrifying three-quarter Israel Folau with an estimated $6 million, four-year contract. The overblown salaries were largely panned as publicity stunts by the wider AFL community. Hunt played 16 games in the bottom-placed Suns' debut 2010 season, given a pass mark by the majority of critics, while Folau's AFL debut would come courtesy of the GWS Giants' 2012 entry to the premiership.

Rugby League and Australian Rules football have a brief but colourful history of code-swappers. Ray Smith was a centre in Fortitude Valley's Brisbane premiership victory in 1970 before heading to Melbourne and playing 104 games for Essendon and Melbourne over the ensuing seven seasons.[22] Greg Brentnall turned down a career in the VFL to pursue Rugby League, winning a premiership with Canterbury and playing 13 Tests for Australia. Former Origin forward and Magpies enforcer Bob Cooper played Australian Rules during his 15-month suspension from the premiership in 1983 before a short-lived comeback with North Sydney. Adrian Barich played 47 games as a midfielder for West Coast Eagles before joining fledgling Perth-based ARL club Western Reds, although he did not feature in first grade. Brilliant Warriors halfback Shaun Johnson and Storm winger Matt Duffie represented the New Zealand Falcons—the national AFL representative team— before excelling in the NRL. Duffie made his Kiwis Test debut in 2011, while Johnson steered the Warriors to that season's Grand Final.

---

22 Jim Main and Russell Holmesby, *The Encyclopedia Of League Footballers*. Melbourne, 1992

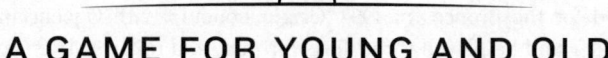

A GAME FOR YOUNG AND OLD

Subscribing to the maxim that age is just a number, the youngest and oldest players in the game's history are featured in this chapter.

ADELAIDE

YOUNGEST: LUKE WILLIAMSON—18 YEARS AND 292 DAYS IN 1997

Luke Williamson was one of the 1997 Super League season's brightest young talents, making his debut for Adelaide as an 18-year-old goalkicking centre. He carved out a 218-game first grade career (scoring 609 points) with subsequent stints at Canberra, the Northern Eagles and Manly, developing into an extremely versatile competitor capable of playing five-eighth, backrow and hooker. Williamson played lock in the Manly's 2007 Grand Final loss to Melbourne, but joined Super League club Harlequins after being left out of the Sea Eagles' squad for the 2008 decider victory.

OLDEST: WAYNE SIMONDS—31 YEARS AND 304 DAYS IN 1998

Journeyman winger Wayne Simonds wound up an 11-season first grade career with two seasons in Adelaide. After six seasons with Western Suburbs, Simonds had stints with Parramatta and South Queensland before joining the fledgling Rams in 1997. Simonds retired with 131 appearances to his name.

BALMAIN

YOUNGEST: CHARLES 'CHOOK' FRASER—17 YEARS AND 214 DAYS IN 1910

Just 17 when he debuted for Balmain in 1910, Charles Fraser was a late inclusion in the 1911-12 Kangaroo Tour squad and set a record that stood for almost 96 years when he made his Test debut at 18 years and 301 days old. A member of six premiership-winning sides with Balmain, Fraser was vice-captain of the 1921-22 Kangaroos before retiring in 1926. Israel Folau finally broke Fraser's Test record by 107 days in 2007, just months before the pioneering great was named as one of the Australia's 100 Greatest Players during the 2008 Centenary celebrations.

OLDEST: ROBERT CRAIG—37 YEARS AND 364 DAYS IN 1919

Recognised as one of Australia's greatest all-round sportsmen, champion swimmer and Wallaby representative Bob Craig toured with the 1911-12 Kangaroos and eventually finished a decade-long career with Balmain two days shy of his 38th birthday in 1919.

BRISBANE

YOUNGEST: KARMICHAEL HUNT—17 YEARS AND 118 DAYS IN 2004

Broncos coach Wayne Bennett sprung an opening round surprise when he chose the youngest player in club history at fullback to replace Test skipper Darren Lockyer, who switched to five-eighth at the start of 2004. Hunt starred from the outset—

he was courted by his native New Zealand after just a handful of NRL appearances but pledged his allegiance to Queensland and Australia—and became the first 17-year-old to score four tries in a premiership match. His haul against Souths equalled Brisbane's club record and he went on to collect Dally M Rookie of the Year honours. The brave and brilliant custodian made his Test and Origin debuts aged 19 in 2006, developing into one of the decade's outstanding players prior to switching codes with AFL expansion side Gold Coast at the end of 2009. Hunt's record beat Justin Hodges' previous mark, set in 2000, by 230 days.

OLDEST: DARREN SMITH—36 YEARS AND 264 DAYS IN 2005
Returning to the aid of the injury-hit Broncos after stints in England and the Queensland Cup, veteran centre/backrower Darren Smith played 16 games in 2005. Already in the record books as the third-oldest Test player and the fifth-oldest Origin player in history (fourth and seventh respectively by the end of 2011), Smith bowed out in the club's finals exit to the Tigers at almost twice the age of teammate Hunt.

CANBERRA

YOUNGEST: TODD PAYTEN—17 YEARS AND 198 DAYS IN 1996
One of the youngest forwards to debut in the modern era, Todd Payten was rushed into the Raiders' first grade squad in 1996 while still attending Erindale College. Payten came off the bench in two late-season fixtures before representing Australian Schoolboys at the end of the season. After seven years with the Raiders, Payten spent 2003 with the Sydney Roosters and won a premiership in 2005 during an eight-year stay with the Tigers. Capable of playing at prop and in the backrow, Payten retired at the end of 2011 after 259 first grade appearances.

OLDEST: JOHN FERGUSON—36 YEARS AND 70 DAYS
NSW's oldest State of Origin representative, evergreen winger 'Chicka' Ferguson retired at the age of 36 in the wake of Canberra's 1990 Grand Final victory. The former Test flyer scored a try in the Raiders' 18-14 defeat of Penrith.

CANTERBURY

YOUNGEST: BRETT DALLAS—17 YEARS AND 245 DAYS IN 1992
Red-headed speedster Brett Dallas played three matches as a 17-year-old during the Bulldogs' 1992 campaign, scoring a try in each appearance. He became the first 18-year-old to represent Queensland at Origin level the following season and established himself as one of the game's finest finishers for Canterbury and Norths, earning six Test caps and 10 Origin jerseys before starring in Super League with English giant Wigan.

OLDEST: ROY KIRKALDY—38 YEARS AND 149 DAYS IN 1948
Revered Berries rake Roy Kirkaldy was the second-oldest player in premiership history when he took the field for his 147th and final game for Canterbury in 1948 (Kirkaldy and 'Tedda' Courtney were subsequently passed by Billy Wilson). Lauded as 'the prince of hookers' during his career, Kirkaldy's mark is 121 days ahead of long-time Canterbury front-row companion Henry Porter's, who played his last first grade game three weeks earlier. The pair sit third and fourth respectively on the all time list of the oldest players in first grade history.

CRONULLA

YOUNGEST: ADAM RITSON—16 YEARS AND 303 DAYS IN 1993

Giant front-row prodigy Adam Ritson became the youngest first grade prop in 57 years—and the fourth-youngest debutant in premiership history—when he came off the bench for the Sharks against Illawarra in 1993. He represented Australian Schoolboys in the same season from De La Salle College, the school that produced Cronulla legend Andrew Ettinghausen, who debuted for the club as a 17-year-old in 1983. Ritson was still just 18 when he represented City Origin in 1995, but the discovery of a brain cyst after joining Parramatta cut his career short the following season *(see Tragic Figures)*.

OLDEST: LES DAVIDSON—36 YEARS AND 304 DAYS IN 1998

Former Kangaroo foward Les Davidson was a 31-year-old teammate of debutant Ritson in 1993 and continued as a hard-man of the Sharks' pack for another five seasons. A veteran of five Origins for NSW and four Tests during the 1980s while at Souths, Davidson played in Cronulla's Super League Grand Final loss to the Broncos in 1997 and retired at the end of the following season after 242 first grade appearances.

GLEBE

YOUNGEST: FRANK BURGE—16 YEARS AND 258 DAYS IN 1911

Team of the Century member Frank Burge was a giant of the code's early decades and towers over the history of the Glebe club. Burge debuted for the Dirty Reds three-and-a-half months shy of his 17th birthday in 1911—a premiership record that stood until 1929, two years after the all time great forward and freakish tryscoring talent retired.

Note: No records available for oldest Glebe player.

GOLD COAST

YOUNGEST: JORDAN RANKIN—16 YEARS AND 238 DAYS

Gold Coast's Jordan Rankin became the youngest back in the history of the premiership in 2008. The 16-year-old half came off the bench in the Titans' late-season loss to the Knights. After biding his time with the club's Under-20s side, Rankin eventually returned to the first grade side in 2011 at fullback—still aged just 19. Half prodigy Andrew Dunemann was the original incarnation of the Gold Coast's youngest player, coming off the bench to make his debut in 1993 aged 18 years and 44 days. Dunemann went on to play 251 Australian first grade and English Super League games for Gold Coast, North Queensland, South Sydney, Canberra, Halifax, Leeds and Salford City before retiring in 2007.

OLDEST: MAT ROGERS 35 YEARS AND 157 DAYS

Dual international Mat Rogers returned to Rugby League as a 31 year old foundation Titan in 2007, finally calling it a day after the club's preliminary final exit in 2010. The former Cronulla, Queensland and Australian flyer came out of retirement to assist the Titans during a disastrous 2011 campaign, but the veteran's comeback last just one game due to injury. Rogers' mark eclipsed the oldest Gold Coast player record set by former Test winger Larry Corowa, who came out of retirement for the Seagulls in 1991 and played his final game aged 34 years and 335 days.

HUNTER MARINERS

YOUNGEST: SCOTT HILL—19 YEARS AND 276 DAYS IN 1997

Precocious five-eighth Scott Hill made his first grade debut for Canterbury in 1996 before joining the fledgling Hunter Mariners for the club's sole 1997 Super League season. The teenage pivot was one of the Mariners' best performers, before joining Melbourne in 1998. Hill played 12 Tests for Australia and five Origins for NSW—primarily as a lock—and departed for English club Harlequins following the Storm's 2006 Grand Final loss to Brisbane.

OLDEST: ROBBIE McCORMACK—32 YEARS AND 314 DAYS IN 1997

Former New South Wales Origin hooker Robbie McCormack was the highest-profile Newcastle Knights defector to Super League hometown rivals Hunter Mariners for their 1997 debut. A foundation Knight with 154 appearances to his name (second only to Marc Glanville in club history at the time), McCormack's experience was vital to the Mariners' moderately successful sole season, and he skippered the club in its World Club Challenge final loss to Brisbane. McCormack joined English powerhouse Wigan and won a Super League Grand Final in 1998 before hanging up the boots.

ILLAWARRA

YOUNGEST: JASON MOON—17 YEARS AND 111 DAYS IN 1984

Winger Jason Moon was handed arguably the most ominous task in the game for his first grade debut—marking powerhouse Parramatta winger Eric Grothe at the peak of his powers. Grothe scored a try in the Eels' 26-6 win over the Steelers, but Moon impressed during his rookie season with four tries in seven games. He joined Souths in 1986 for a three-season stint before returning to Illawarra in 1989.

OLDEST: BRIAN HETHERINGTON—34 YEARS AND 212 DAYS IN 1988

A NSW Origin debutant at the age of 30 in 1984, former Newtown centre Brian Hetherington was one of the fledgling Steelers' standout foundation players, turning out in 144 games during seven seasons with the club. Hetherington played his second and final game for the Blues aged 32 in 1986 and retired two years later as Illawarra's oldest player.

MANLY

YOUNGEST: GRAHAM EADIE—17 YEARS AND 186 DAYS IN 1971

Woy Woy product Graham 'Wombat' Eadie debuted for the Sea Eagles in 1971 and took over the fullback spot from club great Bob Batty permanently the following season. Eadie was still just 18 when he featured in Manly's maiden Grand Final victory in 1972 and made his Test debut a day before his 20th birthday on the 1973 Kangaroo Tour on the way to becoming one of the code's greatest custodians. A winner of four premierships with Manly, Eadie retired in 1983 with a then-premiership record 1,917 career points.

OLDEST: CLIFF LYONS—37 YEARS AND 313 DAYS IN 1999

Something of a late-bloomer, master ball-playing five-eighth Cliff Lyons made his first grade debut for Norths in 1985 aged 23 and frequently defied Father Time during an illustrious career. He joined Manly the following season and eventually made his Test debut at the age of 29 on the 1990 Kangaroo Tour. Lyons was 32 when he won his second Dally M Medal in 1994 and 34 when he celebrated a second premiership in 1996. A reluctant retiree, Lyons heeded an SOS to rejoin the struggling Sea Eagles in 1999 and played his final match less than two months short of his 38th birthday. Lyons' 332 first grade games ranked second in premiership history at the time.

MELBOURNE

YOUNGEST: ISRAEL FOLAU—17 YEARS 347 DAYS IN 2007

Israel Folau exploded onto the NRL landscape in the opening round of 2007, scoring two tries against the Tigers as a 17-year-old debutant. The giant three-quarter broke the club tryscoring record and won a Grand Final during an extraordinary rookie year, before becoming the youngest Australian Test representative in history at 18 years and 194 days in the post-season showdown against the Kiwis. Folau debuted for Queensland in 2008 aged 19 years and 47 days—the fourth-youngest Origin player ever—and was still just 21 when he switched codes to play with AFL newcomers GWS Giants at the end of 2010.

OLDEST: JOHN LOMAX—34 YEARS AND 60 DAYS IN 2000

Wainuiomata prop John Lomax was 27 when he made his first grade and Test debuts for Canberra and New Zealand respectively, but quickly became an engine-room cornerstone for club and country. He missed the Raiders' 1994 Grand Final victory through suspension and subsequent seasons with Canberra and North Queensland were plagued by injury and judiciary appearances. A veteran of 16 Tests (three as captain) for the Kiwis, the enforcer played three games for defending premiers Melbourne in 2000.

NEWCASTLE

YOUNGEST: OWEN CRAIGIE—17 YEARS AND 81 DAYS IN 1995

The only player to represent Australian Schoolboys in three consecutive seasons (1994-96), Newcastle prodigy Owen Craigie was plucked from obscurity by Knights coach Malcolm Reilly in 1995 to debut less than three months after his 17th birthday. Craigie eventually cemented a first grade centre spot in 1997 and was integral to the club's maiden premiership victory that season despite being just 19. A dazzling individual talent that fit squarely into the 'enigmatic' category, Craigie failed to live up to his enormous potential in subsequent stints with Wests Tigers and Souths, departing the NRL after 153 first grade appearances and retiring after spending the 2005 season with English club Widnes.

OLDEST: ADAM MACDOUGALL—36 YEARS AND 126 DAYS IN 2011

A teenage first grade debutant with the Roosters in 1995, Adam MacDougall developed into one of the game's most damaging three-quarters after joining Newcastle, winning two premierships and playing 11 Origins and 11 Tests between 1997 and 2001. The second half of his career was plagued by injury (he played just 195 games in 17 first grade seasons), but he returned to Newcastle impressively in 2007 following a three-year stint with Souths. The only player in the 2011 premiership whose first grade career predated Darren Lockyer's, MacDougall retired at the end of the year as the Knights' most prolific try-scorer with 87 four-pointers.

NEWTOWN

YOUNGEST: ARTHUR HODGINS—17 YEARS AND 201 DAYS IN 1939

Arthur Hodgins debuted as a 17-year-old for the Bluebags in 1939, scoring five tries in his rookie season, but he was unable to cement a position in subsequent years and played the last of his 15 first grade appearances with the club in 1943.

OLDEST: HERB NARVO—36 YEARS AND 268 DAYS IN 1949

One of the finest forwards of his era and an Australian heavyweight boxing champ, Newtown enforcer Herb Narvo debuted for the Bluebags in 1937, sandwiching stints with Norths in Newcastle, St. George, and country sides Cootamundra and Camden in between his final appearance for the club in 1949. Narvo toured with the 1937-38 Kangaroos and represented NSW for the last time at the age of 32 in 1945, retiring four years later as the Bluebags' oldest-ever player. He was named as one of Australia's 100 Greatest Players during the game's 2008 Centenary season.

NEW ZEALAND

YOUNGEST: COOPER VUNA—17 YEARS AND 47 DAYS IN 2004

Nuggety winger Cooper Vuna became the youngest non-Australian to appear in the premiership when he came off the bench against Parramatta in 2004, less than two months after his 17th birthday. A regular first grade spot with the Warriors eluded him in subsequent seasons, but his career flourished after joining Newcastle in 2007. Still just 19 when he played his first game for the Knights, Vuna represented Tonga at the 2008 World Cup and scored 35 tries in 54 games for Newcastle before joining fledgling Super 15 rugby union franchise Melbourne Rebels in 2011.

OLDEST: RUBEN WIKI—35 YEARS AND 250 DAYS IN 2008

The first overseas player to bring up 300 premiership games and the first player in history to appear in 50 Tests, Kiwi legend Ruben Wiki brought down the curtain on a 16-season first grade career with the Warriors in 2008. A premiership-winning centre with Canberra in 1994, Wiki later moved into the forwards *(see Switching Positions)* and finished with 224 appearances in lime green before returning home to round out his career in Auckland. The 35-year-old Wiki bowed out after the Warriors' preliminary final loss to Manly.

NORTHERN EAGLES

YOUNGEST: MARK O'MELEY—18 YEARS AND 260 DAYS IN 2000

Front-row prodigy Mark O'Meley made his first grade debut for North Sydney as a 17-year-old in the opening round of 1999. He set a youngest player record in Northern Eagles' first match the following season that would not be broken in the ill-fated joint venture's three-season existence. O'Meley made his NSW debut shortly after turning 20 in 2001 and racked up 10 Origin and 15 Test appearances to the end of 2006. The mobile enforcer won a premiership with the Bulldogs in 2004 and ended his 201-game NRL career with Sydney Roosters in 2009, joining Super League club Hull FC.

OLDEST: OWEN CUNNINGHAM—33 YEARS AND 188 DAYS IN 2000

Former Manly stalwart Owen Cunningham played every game of the merged Northern Eagles' maiden 2000 season. Cunningham was in his 11th season of first grade with the Sea Eagles when he made his Origin debut for Queensland in 1996 as a 29-year-old. A specialist backrower capable of filling in at prop or hooker, Cunningham spent 1997-98 with North Queensland before returning to Manly in 1999. One of the Northern Eagles' most reliable performers in a disappointing debut season, Cunningham retired at the end of 2000 after 276 first grade games—10th in premiership history at the time.

NORTH QUEENSLAND

YOUNGEST: JASON TAUMALOLO—17 YEARS AND 81 DAYS IN 2010

Despite his tender years, 110kg Kiwi wrecking ball Jason Taumalolo entered the NRL late in 2010 as one of the competition's biggest forwards. After biding his time in the Toyota Cup for most of 2011, Taumalolo earned rousing plaudits for a series of destructive late-season performances for the Cowboys' first grade side.

OLDEST: JASON SMITH—35 YEARS AND 186 GAMES IN 2007

In many ways the antithesis of the modern, professional footballer—a smoker, drinker and notoriously lazy trainer—brilliant backrower/five-eighth Jason Smith nevertheless experienced a career of rare longevity. An 18-year-old debutant for Canterbury in 1990, Smith broke into Queensland's Origin side and toured with the Kangaroos in 1994, before winning a premiership with the Bulldogs in 1995. The mesmerising ball-player starred in five seasons with Parramatta and a four-year Super League stint with Hull before returning to the NRL in 2006. A veteran of 16 Tests and 16 Origins, Smith spent a season each with the Raiders and Cowboys, showing he had lost little of his playmaking class. The 35-year-old retired at the end of 2007 as one of just four players in premiership history to boast a career span of 18 seasons or more. He was still one year and 78 days younger than brother Darren's retirement age with the Broncos two seasons earlier.

NORTH SYDNEY

YOUNGEST: STAN RIDGWAY—16 YEARS AND 363 DAYS IN 1932

Stan Ridgway played 85 games in a first grade career with the Bears that spanned 13 seasons. He debuted in 1932 three days before turning 17 and remains just one of seven 16-year-olds to appear in first grade. Ridgway played fullback in Norths' 1943 Grand Final loss to Newtown—the Bears' only appearance in a decider—and was the club's equal-top goalkicker with 19 in 1944, his final season in first grade.

OLDEST: BILLY WILSON—40 YEARS AND 5 DAYS IN 1967

'Captain Blood' Billy Wilson is the only player in the history of the premiership to appear in first grade at the age of 40. The rugged forward debuted for St. George in 1948 and went on to win six premierships with the Dragons, captaining the side's Grand Final victory in 1961 before joining Norths at the end of the following season. A member of the 1959-60 Kangaroo Tour squad, Wilson became Australia's second-oldest Test player and the oldest Test captain in history when he led the green-and-golds out against New Zealand aged 36 years and 23 days in 1963. Wilson retired after four seasons with Norths and took over the coaching reins in 1967 but returned to the playing field to assist his injury-ravaged squad. He consequently broke Wests forward 'Tedda' Courtney's all time record and trudged out for his last game five days after his 40th birthday. Wilson's cameo extended his premiership record career span to 20 seasons, a mark that still stands.

PARRAMATTA

YOUNGEST: DANNY MAMO—17 YEARS AND 81 DAYS IN 1989

Danny Mamo filled some of the biggest boots in the game to make his first grade debut in the final round of 1989. The 17-year-old wore the Eels' No.7 jumper in the place of injured superstar Peter Sterling in the club's 24-14 loss to a 12-man Newcastle outfit. Mamo's only other first grade appearance was off the bench for Manly early in the 1993 season.

OLDEST: VIC HEY—36 YEARS AND 170 DAYS IN 1949

Five-eighth great Vic Hey's reputation as a legend of the game in Australia and England was already secured by the time he took on the Eels' captain-coach role in 1948, the club's second season in the premiership. Hey retired from playing the following season (injuries restricted him to just 10 games in two years), but he remained as Parramatta's coach until 1953.

PENRITH

YOUNGEST: NATHAN BARNES—17 YEARS AND 32 DAYS IN 1992

Schoolboy winger Nathan Barnes debuted for defending premiers Penrith just one month after his 17th birthday. Barnes was chosen on the flank for the Panthers' final two matches in 1992—the same season he represented Australian Schoolboys—and went on to fruitful stints with Newcastle and Parramatta, before finishing his career with Canberra in 2000.

OLDEST: PETERO CIVONICEVA—35 YEARS AND 134 DAYS IN 2011

Stalwart prop and captain Petero Civoniceva broke the previous record of club legend Greg Alexander (34 years and 177 days) during 2011. The veteran of 45 Tests and 30 Origins departed at the end of the season to rejoin Brisbane, where he will become the oldest Broncos player of all time if he carries on beyond the 2012 NRL season.

ST. GEORGE

YOUNGEST: LANCE THOMPSON—17 YEARS AND 128 DAYS IN 1995

Flame-haired backrower Lance Thompson was thrown into the first grade cauldron at 17, debuting off the bench against Cronulla in 1995. He cemented a permanent berth in Saints' squad the following season and played in the club's Grand Final loss to Manly aged 18, and in St. George Illawarra's heartbreaking defeat to Melbourne in the 1999 decider. Thompson represented City Origin five times in the 2000s but left the Dragons after a contract dispute at the end of 2005, finishing his 239-game career with three seasons for the Sharks.

OLDEST: KEN KEARNEY—37 YEARS AND 59 DAYS IN 1961

Ex-Wallaby Ken 'Killer' Kearney starred with English club Leeds before becoming a central figure in the great St. George sides of the 1950s and 1960s. Kearney captained Grand Final-winning sides in 1956-60 and coached the club to premierships in 1957-61. A Kangaroo tourist in 1952-53 and 1956-57 (the latter as captain-coach), Kearney played the last of his 25 Tests in 1958 aged 34 and played his final first grade game in 1961 two months after his 37th birthday.

ST. GEORGE ILLAWARRA

YOUNGEST: CHASE STANLEY—17 YEARS AND 296 DAYS IN 2007

As a 17-year-old Kiwi three-quarter, Chase Stanley made a tryscoring first grade debut for the Dragons against Newcastle in the second round of 2007. An outstanding rookie season was rewarded with selection on New Zealand's tour of Great Britain and France, and Stanley crossed for a double on Test debut aged just 18 years and 163 days—31 days younger than Israel Folau when he broke the Australian record just weeks earlier (Dennis Williams holds the New Zealand Test record for youngest player, debuting at five-eighth against Great Britain in 1971 on his 18th birthday).

OLDEST: WENDELL SAILOR—35 YEARS AND 65 DAYS IN 2009

Larger-than-life Broncos great Wendell Sailor returned to the NRL with the Dragons in 2008 after five seasons in rugby union and a two-year recreational drug ban. The dual international added a memorable postscript to his 17-season professional career with 17 tries in 33 games for the Saints, finally hanging up the boots after the club's finals exit against Brisbane in 2009 at the age of 35.

SOUTH QUEENSLAND

YOUNGEST: SCOTT LAWSON—18 YEARS AND 240 DAYS IN 1995

Winger Scott Lawson was blooded late in the Crushers' debut season, scoring a try in his maiden first grade match, a plucky 25-18 loss to eventual premiers the Bulldogs. It was the Queensland Under-19s representative's only appearance in 1995, while he played just three first grade games the following season. Lawson celebrated in the short-lived club's only premiership success, scoring two tries in South Queensland's 1996 President's Cup Grand Final victory.

OLDEST: MARIO FENECH—33 YEARS AND 240 DAYS IN 1995

Veteran hooker/prop Mario Fenech was recruited as South Queensland's inaugural captain. A passionate and wholehearted performer in 14 previous seasons with Souths and Norths, Fenech made just 11 appearances for the Crushers and was replaced as skipper by Trevor Gillmeister after just two rounds. The former NSW Origin rake retired at the end of 1995 with 274 first grade appearances (fourth in premiership history at the time) before embarking on a long career in the Rugby League media.

SOUTH SYDNEY

YOUNGEST: PAUL MELLOR—16 YEARS AND 313 DAYS IN 1991

Tall winger Paul Mellor became the fourth-youngest first grade player in premiership history and the youngest in 55 years when he came off the bench for the Rabbitohs against Gold Coast in 1991. Mellor scored 90 tries in 221 games for Souths, Canterbury and Cronulla in a first grade career that was punctuated by a two season stint with English club Castleford, retiring after the Rabbitohs' finals loss to Manly in 2007. Mellor joined the refereeing ranks and officiated as a video referee during the 2011 NRL season.

OLDEST: JACK RAYNER—36 YEARS AND 93 DAYS IN 1957

A vital figure in the South Sydney story, tough prop Jack Rayner skippered the Rabbitohs to five premierships during the 1950s. Rayner toured with the 1948-49

Kangaroos, and although further Test honours eluded him, he ranks as one of the code's most revered figures. He played his 194th and final game in the myrtle-and-cardinal jumper in 1957 at the age of 36.

EASTERN SUBURBS / SYDNEY ROOSTERS

YOUNGEST: RAY STEHR—16 YEARS AND 85 DAYS IN 1929

Ray Stehr was one of the giant figures of the pre-World War II era, carving out a highly successful and colourful career as a front-row enforcer after making his first grade debut in 1929 at the inconceivably young age of 16 years and 85 days, a premiership record which still stands more than 80 years later. Stehr toured with the 1933-34 and 1937-38 Kangaroos, winning three premierships with Easts in between (1935-37). He skippered the Tricolours to further premierships in 1940 and 1945, before retiring in 1946 and turning his hand to coaching.

OLDEST: SANDY PEARCE—38 YEARS AND 25 DAYS IN 1921

NSW Team of the Century hooker Sandy Pearce set a new mark for the oldest first grade player in the premiership's short history when he retired in 1921 after 157 games for Eastern Suburbs. One of Rugby League's pioneering greats, Pearce toured with the Kangaroos in 1908-09 and 1921-22, setting a record for the oldest Australian Test representative at 38 years and 158 days that is yet to be bettered.

WESTERN REDS

YOUNGEST: JOHN WILSHERE—19 YEARS AND 69 DAYS IN 1997

John Wilshere debuted during the ill-fated Reds' 1997 Super League season, featuring on the wing in the club's final four matches before folding. Like many of his Perth-based teammates, Wilshere joined Melbourne in 1998, but made just one NRL appearance. He resurfaced to play 10 games for St. George Illawarra in 2003. A versatile backline performer, Wilshere was a long-serving Papua New Guinean international and played for English Super League clubs Warrington, Leigh and Salford City before retiring in 2009.

OLDEST: MICHAEL POTTER—32 YEARS AND 340 DAYS IN 1996

Much-admired fullback Michael Potter was one of Reds' highest-profile signings for their 1995 premiership debut. A dual Dally M Player of the Year with Canterbury (1984) and St. George (1991), Potter was a New South Wales Origin representative and a veteran of four Grand Finals (winning premierships in 1984 and '85 with the Bulldogs). Potter made 21 appearances in two seasons with the fledgling Reds, hanging up the boots after a final-round loss to his former club the Dragons in 1996.

WESTERN SUBURBS

YOUNGEST: JACK ARNOLD—16 YEARS AND 220 DAYS IN 1936

The second-youngest debutant in premiership history, tough front-rower Jack Arnold left Wests to play 114 games in a 12-season career with Easts. Arnold was sent off in the Tricolours' Grand Final loss to St. George in 1941, but won a premiership with the club in 1945.

OLDEST: 'TEDDA' COURTNEY—39 YEARS AND 311 DAYS IN 1924

Esteemed Rugby League pioneer Tedda Courtney went on the first two Kangaroo

Tours and held the premiership record for oldest first grade player for 44 years. Courtney turned out for Newtown and Norths in the competition's formative seasons before become a Wests stalwart. A veteran of 11 Tests, Courtney eclipsed former Australian teammate Sandy Pearce's first grade mark in 1923 and retired the following season, playing his final game less than two months short of his 40th birthday.

WESTS TIGERS
YOUNGEST: CHRIS LAWRENCE—17 YEARS AND 283 DAYS IN 2006
Schoolboy three-quarter Chris Lawrence scored a memorable try on debut in the Tigers' 20-6 upset of the Broncos at Suncorp Stadium in 2006. He scored 16 tries in 18 games as an 18-year-old in 2007 and developed into one of the game's most dangerous centres before breaking into the national squad in 2010, helping the Kangaroos regain the Four Nations crown the following season.

OLDEST: JOHN SKANDALIS—34 YEARS AND 73 DAYS IN 2010
Highly respected prop John Skandalis came out of short retirement to play for the Tigers in 2010 as a 34-year-old. Part of the Tigers' 2005 premiership-winning side, Skandalis played five late-season games to extend his club appearance record to 185 games.

Note: No records available for players from Cumberland, Newcastle (1908-09), Annandale or University.

STATE OF ORIGIN
YOUNGEST:
Ben Ikin (Queensland)—18 years and 83 days in 1995
The biggest shock in a team stacked with bolters as the Super League upheaval decimated the Maroons' playing stocks in 1995, Gold Coast rookie Ben Ikin broke Brad Fittler's Origin record by 31 days and played a key role off the bench in a 3-0 series boilover. Ikin played 17 Origins and two Tests, winning a premiership with Brisbane in 2000 after earlier starring with North Sydney.

Brad Fittler (New South Wales)—18 years and 114 days in 1990
A Rugby League prodigy in every sense of the term, Brad Fittler played in two finals matches for Penrith as a 17-year-old in 1989, before smashing Origin's youngest player record the following season. Fittler played in a Grand Final at 18 later in 1990 and was subsequently chosen as the youngest Kangaroo tourist in history. He took over the NSW and Test captaincy at just 22 in 1995 on his way to becoming one of the game's all time greats.

Brett Dallas (Queensland)—18 years and 225 days in 1993 *(see Canterbury above)*

William Hopoate (New South Wales)—19 years and 37 days in 2011
Earmarked as a future superstar as a schoolboy, Will Hopoate debuted for Manly a month after turning 18 in 2010 and won an Origin call-up the following season, scoring a wonderful try in the Blues' 18-8 victory. Hopoate starred in the Sea Eagles' Grand Final triumph at the end of the season before embarking on a two-year Mormon mission.

Israel Folau (Queensland)—19 years and 47 days in 2008 *(see Melbourne above)*

OLDEST:

Allan Langer (Queensland)—35 years and 331 days in 2002
Brilliant halfback Allan Langer's Origin career spanned a record 16 seasons and he broke inaugural captain Arthur Beetson's oldest player record by turning out in the 2002 series, winning the man of the match award in his final game just a month shy of his 36th birthday. Langer set a new club mark when he played his final match for the Broncos aged 36 years and 60 days, a record that was broken by Darren Smith three years later.

Arthur Beetson (Queensland)—35 years and 168 days in 1980
Immortal front-rower Arthur Beetson was in the twilight of an incomparable career when he led Queensland out in the first Origin clash in 1980, guiding the Maroons to a 20-10 victory that kick-started an interstate Rugby League revolution.

Steve Price (Queensland)—35 years and 125 days in 2009
Workhorse prop Steve Price hit his peak in his 30s and was still in tremendous form when he played Test and Origin football at 35 in 2009. The former Bulldogs stalwart and Warriors skipper was poised to break the Origin record the following season, but a foot injury forced him into retirement.

Petero Civoniceva (Queensland)—35 years and 75 days in 2011 *(see Penrith above)*

John Ferguson (New South Wales)—34 years and 348 days in 1989 *(see Canberra above)*

AUSTRALIAN TEST PLAYERS

YOUNGEST:

Israel Folau—18 years and 194 days in 2007 *(see Melbourne above)*

Charles Fraser—18 years and 301 days in 1911 *(see Balmain above)*

Kerry Boustead—18 years and 316 days in 1978
Diminutive Innisfail winger Kerry Boustead became the youngest Test player in 67 years when he debuted against New Zealand in 1978, just 15 days short of 'Chook' Fraser's then-record. Boustead went on to become one of the game's greatest-ever wingers.

Dugald McGregor—19 years and 5 days in 1909
Bundaberg fullback Dugald McGregor had just turned 19 when he debuted against the Kiwis in 1909. His only other Test appearance was against England in the following year's Ashes series, while he represented Queensland four times in 1910-11.

Ian Schubert—19 years and 35 days in 1975
Easts fullback Ian Schubert was a teenage rookie sensation in 1975, starring in the Roosters' emphatic Grand Final win before winning selection in Australia's World Series squad. Schubert later toured with the 1978 and 1982 Kangaroos.

OLDEST:

Sandy Pearce—38 years and 158 days in 1922 *(see Eastern Suburbs / Sydney Roosters above)*

Billy Wilson—36 years and 23 days in 1963 *(see North Sydney above)*

Steve Price—35 years and 57 days in 2009 *(see State of Origin above)*

Petero Civoniceva—35 years and 15 days in 2011 *(see Penrith above)*

Darren Smith—34 years and 349 days in 2003 *(see Brisbane above)*

COURAGEOUS PERFORMANCES

Few occurrences in Rugby League stir up supporters' emotions as much as a player defying injury to remain on the field, or an undermanned team digging deep to pull off an unlikely victory.

THE RORKE'S DRIFT TEST The Battle of Rorke's Drift was the successful defence of the Rorke's Drift mission station by 150 British soldiers against an onslaught of 3,000-4,000 Zulu warriors in 1879, during the Anglo-Zulu War in South Africa. The labelling of a 10-man England side's 14-6 defeat of Australia at the SCG in 1914 as 'The Rorke's Drift Test' provides an indication of the tourists' heroic effort. Ahead 9-0 at halftime of the deciding third Test, England lost winger Frank Williams, centre Billy Hall and forward Douglas Clark to injury. With no replacements allowed under the rules of the day, England was forced to stoically defend the lead with a three-man disadvantage, but sealed a series victory that has become enshrined in the history of Anglo-Australian Rugby League with a try to forward Albert Johnson.

ARTHUR PATTON The disregard for self-preservation displayed by Balmain winger Arthur Patton in the 1948 final remains one of the most awe-inspiring acts of courage in premiership history. Patton broke his leg just prior to halftime as his side trailed St. George 2-0. But with no replacements allowed in Rugby League until the 1960s, Patton returned to the field with the limb heavily strapped and played out the match in severe pain. The Tigers defended grimly to hang on for a 13-12 victory despite a raft of injury problems, with Patton the undisputed hero of a phenomenally brave team display. The injury ended the prolific try-scorer's career, while Balmain went down 8-5 to Wests in the Grand Final a week later.

CLIVE CHURCHILL A broken wrist suffered against Manly in the penultimate round of 1955 ruled Clive Churchill out of Souths' Grand Final triumph, but the legendary fullback's gutsy decision to play on in the match is regarded as the pivotal moment in the Rabbitohs' unlikely charge from the bottom of the table to their fifth premiership in six years. Churchill broke his wrist in the opening minutes of the clash against third-placed Manly, requiring a pain-killing injection to dull the intense pain, while team medics famously fashioned a makeshift splint from the cardboard cover of an exercise book. With Souths trailing 7-4 in the dying moments, Churchill put lock Les 'Chicka' Cowie away to score the equaliser, and was charged with the responsibility of taking the after-the-bell conversion attempt from the sideline. Churchill guided one of the great pressure kicks through the posts to secure a dramatic 9-7 victory. While he didn't play again in 1955, Churchill's heroics kept the Rabbitohs' tenuous finals bid on track and inspired the club to arguably its greatest title success.

ALAN PRESCOTT St. Helens great Alan Prescott is predominantly remembered by Australian Rugby League supporters for his valiant display as captain in the second Ashes Test in 1958 at the Brisbane Exhibition Ground. The veteran prop was at the helm of a team under siege following the Lions' 25-8 first Test defeat, but led Great Britain to a famous 25-18 turnaround in the second encounter despite breaking his arm in the opening minutes. The tourists lost halfback Dave Bolton in the first half and Prescott refused to leave his team two players short, declining a pain-killing injection and defying medical advice to stay on the field until fulltime. Prescott reportedly remarked to coach Jim Brough, 'I'll play till I drop', while the injury was later revealed to be a compound fracture of the radius bone.[23] Great Britain's against-the-odds triumph is fondly recalled in the annals of Rugby League history as 'Prescott's Test' and the Lions won the Ashes in Australia for the first time in 12 years with a 40-17 thumping in the SCG decider, minus their injured skipper. The Brisbane Test was to be the last of Prescott's 31 appearances for Great Britain.

JOHN SATTLER South Sydney captain John Sattler's bravery in playing out the 1970 Grand Final with a badly smashed jaw is one of the most well-known and oft-recalled acts of courage in the game's history. The front-row enforcer had his jaw fractured in three places and several teeth knocked out following a savage attack by Manly counterpart John Bucknall after just six minutes of the SCG decider. But Sattler fought through the excruciating pain to lead his side to a 23-12 victory—the Rabbitohs' third premiership in four years. "It wasn't about trying to be a hero," Sattler humbly recalled of his famous display. "It was just something that had to be done. It was a Grand Final and nothing was going to stop me."[24] Despite the severity of the damage to his jaw, the skipper remained out on the Sydney Cricket Ground until well after the match, accepting the premiership trophy while attempting to hide the injury to remain in contention for Australia's World Cup squad to tour England (he would have been a frontrunner to captain the side). It was to no avail as Sattler was hospitalised for two weeks after the match and had his jaw wired for three months, but his heroics became embedded in the fabric of Rugby League folklore for eternity. The John Sattler Award, rewarding players for displays of courage on the Rugby League field, was struck in 2001 in honour of the Souths great's career-defining performance.

STEVE EDMED No-frills Balmain front-rower Steve Edmed evoked memories of Sattler's Grand Final heroism when he played on with a fractured jaw early in the 1989 season. A reserve in the Tigers' Grand Final loss to Canterbury the previous season, Edmed played on for 30 minutes after suffering the injury before being replaced in a controversial encounter with Newcastle. The 21-year-old's brave effort helped inspire Balmain to a 22-20 victory over a 12-man Knights outfit. Edmed started at prop in the extra-time Grand Final loss to Canberra at the end of the season and later joined North Queensland at the height of the Super League war after 136 games for the Tigers. He won the Cowboys' player of the year award in 1996 before linking with English club Sheffield Eagles.

---

23 Alan Whiticker and Ian Collis, *Rugby League Test Matches In Australia*. ABC Books, 1994
24 David Sygall, "Why NRL Players Win The Mind War Over Pain", *Sydney Morning Herald*, 11 April 2010

INJURY-RAVAGED MAROONS HANG ON FOR BRAVE VICTORY

Queensland overcame a crippling injury toll to seal the 1989 Origin series with a 16-12 victory in the second interstate encounter, a performance so gallant that the Sydney faithful could not even muster their customary jeering of Wally Lewis' men. Halfback Allan Langer (broken leg), centre Mal Meninga (fractured cheekbone) and second-rower Paul Vautin (suspected fractured elbow) all succumbed to match-ending injuries at or before halftime, while a shoulder injury to winger Michael Hancock left the Maroons with no reserves during the final quarter. Tony Currie and Trevor Gillmeister stayed on the field despite being concussed, while an injured ankle was not enough to force Sam Backo out of proceedings. Lock Bob Lindner, who injured his leg early in the match, was carried from the field with four minutes remaining, forcing Queensland to desperately defend a four-point lead with 12 men. The Maroons' stoic effort drew comparisons to the 'Rorke's Drift Test' 75 years earlier, but the NSW fans' deferential silence was perhaps the greatest compliment of all.

TREVOR GILLMEISTER The 31-year-old Queensland skipper Trevor Gillmeister had already led the Maroons to a phenomenal against-the-odds series triumph with victories in the opening two Origin clashes against the Blues in 1995. But the veteran nevertheless climbed out of a hospital bed in the lead-up to the dead-rubber game three encounter to inspire his inexperienced charges to a 3-0 cleansweep. The second-row hitman overcame a blood disorder and a consequent spell on a drip to make his 21st appearance for Queensland, guiding the team of misfits to a 24-16 success before returning to hospital. 'The Axe' became the oldest forward to debut at Test level when he was selected in Australia's first Test squad in the subsequent series against the Kiwis.

ANDREW JOHNS Newcastle's 1997 campaign hinged on the influence of brilliant No.7 Andrew Johns, and a rib injury suffered during his match-winning display in the first week of the finals against Parramatta threatened the Knights' compelling premiership bid. He missed the following week's loss to minor premiers Manly, but took the field for the preliminary final showdown with Norths. A misguided pain-killing needle at halftime left Johns with a punctured lung, and despite the Knights clinching a maiden Grand Final berth after Matthew Johns piloted over a late field goal, Andrew's prospects of playing in the decider hung in the balance after a spell in hospital. Despite Manly and Australian team doctor Nathan Gibbs' claims that Johns risked death by playing with a punctured lung adding more drama to the linchpin's quest to play, Johns fronted up for the most important match in the club's history. In obvious discomfort (he attempted to leave the field at one stage, but was ordered to return by coach Malcolm Reilly), Johns' inspirational play kept Newcastle in the match, before he produced the blindside burst that set up Darren Albert's winning try in the dying seconds.

JACK ELSEGOOD Sydney Roosters winger Jack Elsegood overcame the anguish of the sudden death of his father just days earlier to play an inspirational hand in a stirring come-from-behind victory over the Raiders in 1999. Elsegood's brave decision to front up for the mid-season clash at the SFS was rewarded with a first half try, but the undermanned Roosters seemed destined for defeat when they trailed 22-12 midway through the second half. But skipper Brad Fittler dragged the Roosters back into the contest and sent Elsegood over for his second try to level the scores, before interchange Julian Bailey crashed over for the match-winner in the 75th minute. The emotion-charged victory saw the Roosters retain top spot on the NRL table, while former Dally M Rookie of the Year Elsegood was lauded for his gutsy display.

SHANE WEBCKE A modern-day purveyor of the old world Rugby League values of courage and disregard for personal protection, Broncos warhorse Shane Webcke twice defied serious injury to take the field in big matches. Webcke broke his arm in round 24 of Brisbane's dominant 2000 season, but returned after just five weeks to take his place in the preliminary final defeat of Parramatta and the Grand Final victory over the Roosters, refusing to shirk his duties as the cornerstone of the Broncos' pack despite carrying a still-healing injury. Four years later, Webcke underwent an arthroscopy on a recurring knee injury after the Broncos' qualifying final loss to Melbourne, but still managed to front up for the sudden-death semi-final against the Cowboys a week later. With his reputation as one of his generation's most resilient competitors assured, Webcke retired after Brisbane's 2006 Grand Final defeat of Melbourne.

JASON CROKER The valour shown by the Raiders, and in particular veteran Jason Croker, in an extraordinary victory over the Roosters stood out like a beacon in Canberra's otherwise disappointing 2001 season. A devastating run of injuries in the Bruce Stadium clash left the Raiders with an empty bench five minutes into the second half, by which stage the home side trailed the previous year's grand finalists 22-10. But the undermanned Raiders surged home to record a 32-22 victory and no player better demonstrated the side's courage than Croker. After rolling his ankle early in the match, Croker damaged his knee to the extent that he was subsequently ruled out for the season with a ruptured cruciate ligament and torn medial ligament, but soldiered on to the end of the match. Croker's heroic display earned the former Test and Origin utility the inaugural John Sattler Award celebrating courage on the Rugby League field.

PRESTON CAMPBELL One of the modern era's most diminutive players, livewire Titan Preston Campbell ranks amongst the bravest to play the game. The pint-sized fullback's toughness was emphatically illustrated when he played 43 minutes of a 2008 derby against the Brisbane Broncos with a broken jaw. Campbell suffered a knock late in the first half at Suncorp Stadium, but played a starring role in Gold Coast's gallant golden point loss with his customary attacking brilliance and wholehearted defence. After scoring the Titans' first try prior to receiving his injury, Campbell finished the match with three line breaks, a try assist and 162 metres from 14 runs in the 25-21 late-season defeat. The painful break ended Campbell's season two games early, but cemented his reputation as one of the NRL's most courageous competitors.

DARREN LOCKYER The Rugby League world held its collective breath late in the 2011 semi-final between archrivals Brisbane and St. George Illawarra when

Darren Lockyer was felled by friendly fire with eight minutes remaining. Airborne Brisbane fullback Gerard Beale's knee collided with Lockyer's face, leaving the Broncos' skipper in a distressed state on the Suncorp Stadium turf. Escalating the dramatic turn of events, the Dragons scored a 78th minute try to level the scores and send the sudden-death encounter into golden point extra-time while Lockyer— playing in his final season—struggled to regain his bearings. But the mercurial five-eighth produced yet another clutch play in his last appearance in the NRL stepping up to land the match-winning field goal under pressure in the second minute of added time, despite carrying what was later revealed to be a depressed fracture of the cheekbone. After the euphoria of his epic Suncorp Stadium farewell subsided, Lockyer eventually made the agonising decision to pull out of the following week's preliminary final, effectively ending his club career as the inexperienced Broncos were eliminated with a 26-14 loss to Manly. The Test captain recovered in time to lead Australia's successful Four Nations campaign in England.

THE TRY-SCORERS

MOST FIRST GRADE TRIES

212—Ken Irvine
180—Steve Menzies
165—Andrew Ettingshausen
164—Terry Lamb
159—Matt Sing

159—Hazem El Masri
152—Harold Horder
147—Bob Fulton
146—Frank Burge
144—Benny Wearing

MOST TRIES IN A SEASON

38—Dave Brown (1935)
34—Ray Preston (1954)
29—Les Brennan (1954)
28—Bobby Lulham (1947)
28—Johnny Graves (1951)

27—Rod O'Loan (1935)
27—Norm Jacobson (1948)
27—Phil Blake (1983)
27—Nathan Blacklock (2001)
26—Tommy Ryan (1957)

MOST TRIES IN A MATCH

8—Frank Burge (1920)
7—Rod O'Loan (1935)
6—Frank Burge (1916)
6—Dave Brown (1935)

6—Dave Brown (1935)
6—Alan Ridley (1936)
6—Jack Lindwall (1947)
6—Jack Troy (1950)

HORDER AND BLINKHORN Harold Horder and Cec Blinkhorn are generally regarded as the greatest club wing pairing in the game's history. The figures emphatically back up that claim. Horder began his career with Souths in 1912, Blinkhorn with Norths two years later. The duo combined for the first time at Souths in 1919, before both shifted to Norths the following season and became an integral part of one of the great club line-ups—the 1921-22 premiership-winning North Sydney side. The illustrious twosome finished their careers together with a season for the Rabbitohs in 1924.

Blinkhorn scored 86 tries in 115 games, while Horder finished with a phenomenal 152 tries in 138 games—his total of tries was a premiership record until broken by Ken Irvine in 1969, but his strike-rate remains unparalleled in the game's history. Horder was the competition's leading try-scorer three times (1913-14, 1917) and finished second on two occasions (1918 and 1921), while Blinkhorn topped the premiership in 1922. His 20 tries could not be bettered as a North Sydney club record by even legendary Bears winger Irvine, remaining until Michael Buettner crossed 21 times in 1998.

Horder scored seven hat-tricks, four bags of four tries, plus two South Sydney record five-try hauls during his stellar career. Blinkhorn netted five hat-tricks and crossed for a Bears' record five tries against Annandale in 1920. At representative level, Horder scored a mindboggling 23 tries in nine games for NSW, and scored 11 tries from 13 Tests for Australia. He scored 35 tries in 25 games on the 1921-22 Kangaroo Tour—surpassed only by Blinkhorn's 39 touchdowns in 29 games on the same tour, an all time Kangaroos record.

BENNY WEARING Although South Sydney legend Benny Wearing has just one Test appearance next to his name, the 1920s and 1930s star is rated one of the code's greatest-ever wingers. Remarkably, Wearing finished in the premiership's top-five try-scorers in all 13 of his seasons in first grade except the last (1933). Wearing topped the competition in 1925-27 and finished second in 1921, 1923, 1928 and 1930-31. With 144 tries from 172 games, Wearing is the most prolific try-scorer in South Sydney's history—39 touchdowns ahead of his nearest rival—and is still amongst the top-10 try-scorers in premiership history almost 80 years after his retirement. Wearing scored 15 tries in 21 matches for NSW and bagged a double in his only appearance for Australia, the third Ashes Test of 1928.

TRICOLOURS DYNASTY PRODUCES TRYSCORING MARVELS

Eastern Suburbs' magnificent side that won premierships in 1935-37 and 1940 ranks as one of the all time great teams, and produced devastating try-scorers to match. Centre Dave Brown, arguably the finest player of the era, and wingers Fred Tottey and Rod O'Loan were the main benefactors of the Tricolours' dominance, scoring a combined 246 tries from 253 games for Easts. The trio took out the premiership's top three tryscoring positions in the 1935 and 1936 seasons, scoring extraordinary totals of 84 and 60 tries respectively.

Captain of the 1940 premiership side, Brown scored 93 tries in 94 games, including a premiership record 38 tries in 1935, which incorporated two hauls of six tries. He was the competition's third top-try-scorer in 1936, while at representative level he crossed for seven tries in nine Tests and 11 tries in 21 appearances for NSW.

O'Loan began his career with University, but went on to forge a fine tenure with Easts that netted 76 tries in 83 games, including touchdowns in the Roosters' 1935, 1936 and 1940 premiership final successes. The dashing flanker scored seven tries against his former club in 1935—the second-most tries in a match in premiership history—and another four against University the following season, the only two times he scored more than a brace of tries in a game. He was the competition's third top-try-scorer in 1933 with the Students and finished second in the premiership in 1935 and 1936 with Easts. His 27 tries in 1935 is the equal-sixth all time highest try total in a season.

Tottey scored 77 tries in just 76 games for Easts, topping the premiership with 25 tries in 1936 and with a more modest 10 touchdowns in 1937. Tottey scored four hat-tricks and claimed two hauls of four tries, while he crossed the tryline in a record 15 consecutive matches bridging 1935 and 1936. After scoring a double in the 1936 premiership final, Tottey scored three tries in three matches for NSW in 1937.

ALAN RIDLEY Powerhouse winger Alan Ridley was the tryscoring force behind heavyweights Western Suburbs during the 1930s. A Country and NSW rep as a teenager from Canberra, Ridley toured with the 1929-30 Kangaroos and scored 11 tries in just seven tour games. Ridley joined defending premiers Wests in 1931 and scored 12 tries in his first season, before topping the premiership with 18 tries in 1932—a record that stood unmatched at the club for 62 years. He toured again with the 1933-34 Kangaroos and top-scored with 25 tries from 27 matches. Ridley's double against Easts in the premiership final helped Wests to their second premiership in 1934, while his last tryscoring effort for the club was a record six-try haul against Newtown in 1936, giving him the enviable record of 64 tries in 64 games. Although he scored just once in five Tests, Ridley scored a phenomenal 25 tries in just 19 appearances for NSW.

JACK LINDWALL Arguably the game's finest tryscoring exponent of the 1940s, winger/centre Jack Lindwall became the first try centurion in St. George's history, scoring 110 tries in just 133 games for the Dragons. The brother of Australian cricket great and St. George teammate Ray Lindwall, Jack was the competition's top try-scorer in 1940, 1942 and 1946. Injury ruled him out of the club's inaugural premiership success in 1941 and World War II stymied his representative aspirations, but in 1947 Lindwall became the last player to score six tries in a first grade match, achieving the club record mark against Manly. Lindwall also bagged six hat-tricks and two hauls of four tries during an admirable career.

GOLDEN ERA OF BALMAIN WINGERS The now-defunct Balmain Tigers had a penchant for producing brilliant tryscoring wingers during the 1930s and 1940s; the careers of the top three try-scorers in the club's 92-season history fit into a magical 21-year period. Sid Goodwin debuted for the club in 1933 and his tryscoring feats at premiership and representative level were dazzling. He represented Australia in the 1935 series against New Zealand—scoring two tries—and holds the record for most tries in an interstate match, with a haul of six for NSW against Queensland in 1939. Goodwin also captained the club to the premiership that year and scored 86 tries in 118 games in a decade with the club. He moved on to Newtown, scoring 42 tries in 41 games and winning another title in 1943.

Port Kembla speedster Arthur Patton emerged in 1937 and set a record for the club that would not be bettered—95 tries in 117 matches. Although World War II hampered his rep ambitions, Patton skippered Balmain to the 1944 title with a victory over Goodwin's Newtown in the Grand Final.

Bobby Lulham scored a season record 28 tries for the Tigers in 1947—his first year with the club—and toured with the Kangaroos a year later. Arguably the best of the trio, Lulham scored 85 tries in as many matches for Balmain, but his career ended abruptly when he became embroiled in a sensational domestic dispute case in 1953 *(see Tragic Figures)*.

Goodwin, Patton and Lulham each posted a club record five tries in a match during their careers—a feat matched by just one other Tiger, British five-eighth Dave Topliss against Newtown in 1977. Goodwin and Patton each scored five hat-tricks and one haul of four tries, while Lulham scored a remarkable six hat-tricks and bagged four touchdowns twice during his seven seasons with Balmain. The trio scored a combined 266 tries from 320 matches in the black-and-gold.

JOHNNY GRAVES Newcastle winger Johnny 'Whacka' Graves was a tryscoring sensation in six seasons with South Sydney, scoring 79 tries in just 77 games—one of only four players (with Harold Horder, Reg Gasnier and Fred Tottey) to score 50 first grade tries and finish with a record of better than one per game. He scored a then-club record 28 tries in 1951 (Les Brennan surpassed the mark with 29 in 1954), including a Grand Final record four tries in the 42-14 thrashing of Manly and three regular season hat-tricks. The eccentric flyer scored a total of eight hat-tricks in his career, and crossed for an equal-club record five tries against Easts in 1949. Graves scored nine tries in as many appearances for New South Wales, five tries in seven Tests for Australia, and was the equal-top try-scorer (with Queenslander Jack Horrigan) on the 1948-49 Kangaroo Tour with 16 in 20 games.

KEN IRVINE Ken Irvine is quite simply the greatest try-scorer Rugby League in Australia has ever known. The dazzling winger sits atop the list of all time premiership try-scorers with 212 from 236 games—32 tries clear of the nearest player—despite playing most of his career with the hapless North Sydney Bears. Crossing for at least 13 tries in each of his 15 full seasons in first grade, Irvine was the leading try-scorer in the premiership in 1959 (his first full season), 1966 and 1969-70, while he finished second in 1960-61, 1963 and 1967. The Team of the Century winger collected nine hat-tricks and seven bags of four tries during his glittering career, which finally reaped the premiership success it deserved when he switched to Manly for his final two seasons (1972-73).

Equally devastating on the representative stage, Irvine scored an interstate record 34 tries in just 30 matches for NSW. He also scored a staggering 33 Test tries in as many appearances for Australia, a record which stood until 2010. Irvine was the top try-scorer on the 1963-64 Kangaroo Tour with 29 tries from 28 games, while he totalled 54 tries on three trips to Britain and France (he also toured in 1959-60 and 1967). The incomparable winger passed away in 1990 at the age of 50 after losing his battle with leukaemia.

DRAGONS WING PAIRING AMONG THE GREATS Elite wingers Johnny King and Eddie Lumsden were a vital component of St. George's record 11 consecutive premierships between 1956 and 1966. Barnstorming right winger Lumsden played in nine of those Grand Final victories, scoring eight tries, while left flank speedster King played in the last seven. King scored in six consecutive

Grand Finals (1960-65), including a double against Easts in 1960. After starting his career at Manly, Lumsden finished with 136 tries from 166 matches in the Red V, second only in Dragons' history to King, who amassed 143 tries in 195 appearances. Both flyers topped the premiership try table twice during the Saints' reign—Lumsden in 1958 and 1962, King in 1961 and 1965. King netted six hat-tricks and two hauls of four tries during his career, while Lumsden grabbed an astounding 14 career hat-tricks (including two in Grand Finals).

PUFF THE MAGIC DRAGON The only man to challenge King and Lumsden in the tryscoring stakes for the great St. George sides of the 1950s and 1960s was Immortal centre Reg Gasnier. Although injury robbed the game of one of its finest exponents at just 28 years of age, Gasnier scored 127 tries in only 129 games. He was the premiership's top try-scorer in 1960, 1963 and 1964, and collected 10 hat-tricks and four bags of four tries in an incomparable career. Gasnier's tryscoring form was equally devastating at representative level: he scored 13 tries in 16 appearances for NSW and 28 tries in 39 Tests for Australia (third in all time Test tryscoring). Such is his colossal standing within the game's history, Gasnier's tryscoring potency is rarely examined when his greatness is discussed.

IAN MOIR Lightning-quick winger Ian Moir's 105 tries in 118 games is third in South Sydney club history, while he added 14 tries in 28 games for Wests at the end of his career. Moir was the competition's leading try-scorer in 1953 with 23, including a hat-trick in the premiership final defeat of the Dragons. He finished third in 1954 with 21 tries and equal-first in 1955 with 18, scoring in twin Grand Final defeats of Newtown in each of those seasons. Moir was equal-second in the 1956 premiership, before scoring a club record-equalling five tries against Parramatta in 1957. He finished his career with two hauls of four tries and seven hat-tricks to his name. The brilliant flankman scored 11 tries in 10 appearances for NSW, nine tries in 12 Tests for Australia (including a hat-trick against New Zealand in 1959) and was the top try-scorer on the 1956-57 Kangaroo Tour with 13.

BOB FULTON When the Immortal five-eighth/centre Bob Fulton retired in 1979, he sat behind only legendary wingers Ken Irvine and Harold Horder on the all time premiership try-scorers table. He scored a then-record 129 tries for Manly in 219 games, before finishing his career with 18 tries in 50 games for Easts. Fulton was the competition's leading try-scorer in 1972-73 and 1976—Manly's first three premiership-winning seasons. His brilliant double in the brutal 1973 Grand Final victory over Cronulla rates as one of the great performances in a decider. Proving he had not lost his tryscoring touch after joining the Roosters, Fulton was second in the 1977 premiership with 14 tries, just shy of his 30th birthday. Fulton was the top try-scorer on the 1973 Kangaroo Tour, with 20 from just 14 games, and was equal-first as captain on the 1978 Tour. He scored 25 tries in 35 Tests in the green-and-gold, the fourth-highest total of all time, while he scored 14 tries in 16 interstate appearances for NSW.

TERRY LAMB Wests and Canterbury five-eighth Terry Lamb built a tryscoring reputation on being the game's best support player. Lamb's strike-rate slowed as he entered the veteran stage of his career, but he still retired as the second-most prolific try-scorer in premiership history, amassing 164 tries in a record 349 games. He was the competition's top try-scorer in 1984 and 1987, and finished second in 1985. The evergreen No.6 bagged five hat-tricks as one of the Bulldogs' greatest-ever players and scored a career-best four tries against his former club the Magpies in 1987. Some 15 years after his retirement, Lamb still sits in fourth spot on the all time tryscoring list. Lamb's crowning achievement at representative level was playing all 20 matches on the 1986 Kangaroo Tour—where he was the squad's top try-scorer with 19 touchdowns.

THE GREAT TRYSCORING FORWARDS Rugby League has produced several prolific try-scorers from the engine room, but three players tower above their forward pack contemporaries—Frank Burge, Bob McCarthy and Steve Menzies. The trio are the only forwards to have topped a century of tries in first grade (Jason Croker and Darren Smith played a significant portion of the careers in the backline), and rank among the most dangerous try-poachers in the code's rich narrative.

Glebe legend Frank Burge was a marvel. He racked up an astonishing 137 tries in 148 games for the Dirty Reds between 1911 and 1926, and added another nine touchdowns in a solitary season for St. George in 1927. Burge set a premiership record with 20 tries in 1915, before extending it to 22 tries the following season and 24 in 1918. The record stood until bettered by Easts' Dave Brown in 1935, but another premiership mark set by Burge remains unbeaten to the present day—and shows no signs of being broken. Already the premiership record holder with six tries against Norths in 1916, Burge crossed eight times against University in 1920. No player has scored six tries in one game since 1950 and just four men have achieved five touchdowns in the past 17 seasons. All told, Burge topped the premiership's season tryscoring on four occasions. Burge was equally potent at representative level. He scored 15 tries in 18 games for NSW and finished the 1921-22 Kangaroo Tour with an incredible 33 tries from 23 appearances.

South Sydney great Bob McCarthy was a revolutionary figure in the late 1960s. The introduction of the four-tackle rule saw McCarthy, a magnificent tight defender, develop into a wide-running backrow forward the likes of which had never been seen. McCarthy was integral to four premiership victories for the Rabbitohs and scored 100 tries in a club record 211 games, while he added 19 touchdowns in 40 games in a late-career stint for Canterbury. His most famous try was a long-range intercept to spearhead Souths' 12-10 victory over Canterbury in the 1967 Grand Final. McCarthy, a veteran of 15 Tests, scored three hat-tricks during his career and topped 10 tries in a season of six occasions, but his lasting legacy is as a ground-breaking second-rower—one of the best of all time.

In 2004 Steve Menzies broke Burge's 77-year old mark for first grade tries by a forward and retired four seasons later as the second-highest try-scorer in the game's history. The second-rower spectacularly hit the premiership scene in 1994, instantly forming a deadly combination with Manly's master playmaker Cliff Lyons and scoring 16 tries. Menzies made the Kangaroo Tour squad at the end of his rookie season and crossed for seven tries in 11 minor matches. He was the premiership's top try-scorer in 1995 with 22, becoming the first forward to head the competition since Newtown lock Charles 'Chicka' Cahill in 1945, and scored a tournament-high six tries at the season-ending World Cup. Menzies finished second in the competition in 1996 and third in 1998, crossing 20 times in each season. His uncanny knack of finding holes in the defensive line netted five hat-tricks and two hauls of four tries among his 180 career touchdowns for Manly and the Northern Eagles, while he bagged 12 tries in 15 Tests for Australia between 1995 and 2006.

THE MODERN DAY TRY-POACHERS

- Brisbane's Steve Renouf was the most potent tryscoring centre since the great Reg Gasnier, and arguably the finest attacking exponent to play in the position since the Immortal Saint. In 11 seasons, Renouf scored an extraordinary 142 tries in 183 games for the Broncos. He scored at least 12 tries a season between 1991 and 1998, and topped the club's tryscoring lists five times and was second three times. He set a Brisbane record with 23 tries in 1994 (equalled by Darren Smith in 1998), and in 1991 became the first Brisbane player to score four tries in a game—a record he matched four more times before another player from the club achieved the mark. Renouf also bagged six hat-tricks at first grade level. Injuries and the Super League upheaval limited his representative opportunities, but Renouf still managed 11 tries in 10 Tests for Australia. Renouf has been seemingly overlooked by historians and experts when the greatest centres in the game's history are discussed, but he was named as one of the 10 best centres of all time in Alan Whiticker and Ian Collis' book *The Top 10 of Rugby League*.

- Nathan Blacklock's 121 tries in 142 first grade games puts him in elite company in any era—but he would be near the top of the tree if statistics specified how many tries were spectacular solo efforts. The gifted Dragons match-winner was the NRL's top try-scorer in three consecutive seasons (1999-2001), a feat achieved by only two other players in the Australian game's history—Easts' Gordon Wright (1919-21) and South Sydney legend Benny Wearing (1925-27). Blacklock scored eight hat-tricks between 1999 and 2003, but was continually overlooked by representative selectors. The Aboriginal flyer could not force his way into the NSW side, while he played just two Tests for Australia, despite scoring a double on debut against Papua New Guinea in 2001.

- Nigel Vagana became the first New Zealander to top the premiership's tryscoring table in 2002, and is the only overseas player to score more than 100 career tries. He ranks as the 13th-highest try-scorer of all time with 140 touchdowns from 240 games for the Warriors, Bulldogs, Sharks and Rabbitohs. He was most potent at the Bulldogs (61 tries in 76 games), where he headed the NRL in 2002 (23 tries) and finished third in 2003 (22 tries). On one charmed night against Souths early in 2002, Vagana became the first player in eight years to score five tries in a premiership match, equalling the Bulldogs' club record. Vagana claimed seven career hat-tricks and is also the Kiwis' most prolific Test try-scorer, collecting 19 in 37 appearances.

- Fijian rugby union international Noa Nadruku became a 13-a-side phenomenon in 1993. Recruited by the Raiders after starring for Fiji in the pre-season World Sevens competition, Nadruku was the premiership's top try-scorer with 22 tries from 21 games, including hat-tricks against Souths and Wests and in a finals loss to Brisbane. Nadruku scored 73 tries from 92 games in five thrilling seasons in the nation's capital and topped the premiership again in 1996 with 21 touchdowns from as many games. Nadruku finished with five career hat-tricks and touched down four times against the Crushers in 1996. While a subsequent stint with the Cowboys was not as fruitful (17 tries in 37 games), Nadruku ranks as one of the 1990s' great entertainers and tryscoring exponents.

- Matt Sing scored 159 tries in 275 first grade games for Penrith, the Roosters and North Queensland, retiring at the end of 2006 as the equal-fourth most prolific try-scorer in premiership history. Sing accumulated 14 tries for the Panthers and 72 for the Roosters, but his strike-rate accelerated dramatically after joining the Cowboys in 2002. He scored the first hat-trick of his career in 2003 and picked up five more trebles over the next three seasons to finish his tenure in Townsville with 73 tries from 104 games. Sing was the club's top try-scorer in 2002 (16 tries), 2003 (21) and 2006 (13). While his tryscoring frequency did not translate to representative level (24 Origins and 14 Tests for five tries in each arena), Sing equalled the Origin record for tries in a match with a hat-trick for Queensland in the third match of the 2003 series.

- Hazem El Masri is best known as the player who set new standards in goalkicking and pointscoring excellence in the modern era, but he was also a deadly try merchant. The Bulldogs great scored a club record 159 tries in 317 games—equal-fifth on the all time premiership register. El Masri scored four tries in a match on two occasions and notched seven hat-tricks in a celebrated career, while he was the Bulldogs' top try-scorer on four occasions.

- Andrew Ettingshausen retired in 2000 as the second-most prolific try-scorer in premiership history behind Ken Irvine (he has since been overtaken by Steve Menzies). 'ET' crossed for 165 tries in 328 games for Cronulla, equalling the club season record of 17 tries in 1988, before extending it to 18 in 1994. He was in the premiership's top-five try-scorers in each of those seasons and in 1989. Ettingshausen bagged four hat-tricks and two hauls of five tries in one of the modern era's great careers. Ettingshausen was the top try-scorer on consecutive Kangaroo Tours (1990 and 1994) and scored 14 times in 25 Test appearances.

- Phil Blake burst onto the scene as a dynamic halfback for Manly in 1982, scoring nine tries in 12 games, before scoring 27 tries in just 23 games for the Sea Eagles the following season—a premiership record for tries in a season by a No.7 and the sixth-equal highest season total by any player. Also the equal-top try-scorer in the 1985 premiership, Blake finished a nomadic career with 138 tries in 262 games, which placed him in the top-10 try-scorers at the time of his retirement in 1997. Blake has the distinction of scoring the first-ever four-point try in 1983, and the first try in the Warriors' history in 1995.

- Larger-than-life winger Wendell Sailor was a tryscoring machine on the flank for Brisbane, crossing for 110 tries in 189 games. He scored a career-best 18 tries in 1998, 2000 and 2001 and collected six hat-tricks and a finals record-equalling four tries against the Dragons in 2001. Returning to the NRL in 2008 with St. George Illawarra (after a five-year rugby union stint followed by a two-year recreational drug suspension), Sailor scored 17 tries in 33 games over two seasons, including a hat-trick against Parramatta. Sailor scored 17 tries in 16 Test appearances for Australia, including an equal-Test record four against Russia at the 2000 World Cup, where he was the tournament's top try-scorer with ten.

- Brett Mullins was one of the most exciting attacking fullbacks in the game's history, scoring 122 tries in 209 first grade appearances for Canberra and the Roosters. Second in the 1994 premiership with a club record-equalling 22 tries, Mullins became the first player to bring up a century of tries for Canberra in 2000, before ending his career with 17 tries and a premiership for the Roosters in 2002. Mullins also scored five tries in as many Tests for Australia and four touchdowns in five Origin matches for the Blues.

- Although his NRL career was interrupted by seven years in rugby union, Lote Tuqiri is one of the finest try exponents of Rugby League's modern age. Tuqiri scored 56 tries in 99 games for the Broncos and was the club's top try-scorer in 2000, 2001 and 2002. His hat-trick for Queensland in 2002 and five tries for the series equalled Origin records, while he scored five tries in four Tests in 2001. Tuqiri returned to the NRL in spectacular fashion with 18 tries for Wests Tigers in 2010 and a recall to the Australian Test line-up.

- The most prolific try-scorer in North Queensland's history, Matt Bowen brought up a century of first grade tries in 2009 in just his 180th game. The will-o'-the-wisp fullback was the NRL's top try-scorer in 2005 (21 tries) and 2007 (22). He has nabbed two first grade hat-tricks, while also scoring four tries in 10 Origin appearances for Queensland.

- Billy Slater scored a double in Melbourne's preliminary final thrashing of Brisbane in 2009 to pass 100 career tries in just his 155th NRL game. Slater boasts four hat-tricks in Storm colours and crossed for a career-best four tries in a qualifying final against Manly, also in 2009. His excellent strike-rate translates to representative level, where he has scored 11 tries in 17 Origins for Queensland and 18 tries in 17 Tests for Australia. He passed Matt Geyer's club record for career tries early in 2011.

- Timana Tahu brought up a century of NRL tries just weeks prior to his switch to rugby union at the end of 2007, a move that lasted just two seasons before he rejoined Parramatta. He cracked the ton in only 139 games. Tahu was particularly potent for Newcastle, where he racked up 82 tries in 97 matches and finished second in the NRL tryscoring race in 2000 and 2002, before joining the Eels in 2005. His stats at representative level are outstanding—five tries in as many Tests for Australia and eight tries in 12 Origin matches for the Blues.

- Despite turning out for generally poorly performed South Sydney and Cronulla sides throughout his career, Nathan Merritt became a try centurion in his 156th game late in 2010. Merritt was the NRL's leading try-scorer in 2006 despite his Rabbitohs coming last, while he finished fifth in 2009 and eighth in 2010, even though Souths missed the finals in both years. He topped the premiership again in 2011 (equal with Canterbury's Ben Barba) with a career-high 23 tries, also bagging the first haul of five tries in an NRL match for eight years in a 56-6 mauling of Parramatta from fullback and backing up with a hat-trick against Canberra just six days later. After returning from a fruitless two-season stint with the Sharks at the end of 2005, Merritt has been Souths' top try-scorer in each of the last six seasons, while he also topped the club's try table in 2003. He moved past Ian Moir into second on Souths' all time tryscoring charts in 2011 and has record holder Benny Wearing in his sights.

- When Rhys Wesser scored 25 tries during Penrith's 2003 title-winning season, he smashed the Panthers' club record for tries in a season and the all time premiership mark for tries in a season by a fullback. The Indigenous speed machine had set the club record at 19 just one season earlier and scored his 100th try in 2006 after just 138 games—one of the quickest ascensions to the try centurions club in the modern era. Wesser left the Panthers at the end of 2008 as the club's most prolific try-scorer (113), scoring 16 tries in three seasons for Souths.

- Israel Folau's senior Rugby League career lasted just four seasons—two each for Melbourne and Brisbane—before he switched to the AFL at the end of 2010. But the youngster proved himself as one of the most consistent try-scorers in the NRL during that time, leaving the code with 73 tries in 91 matches. Debuting as a 17-year old in 2007, Folau scored 21 tries to finish the regular season as the competition's leading try-scorer and break the Storm's season record. Folau was the Broncos' top try-scorer in both seasons he spent with the club, crossing for 17 tries in 19 games in 2009 and amassing 20 touchdowns from as many games in 2010, finishing just one short of the NRL's best in the latter year. At rep level he crossed seven times in eight Origin matches for Queensland and scored six tries in eight Test appearances.

- Giant Kiwi Manu Vatuvei transformed himself from one of the most maligned players in the NRL into the most feared winger in the world—and one of the game's finest try-scorers. Vatuvei broke the Warriors' club record for most career tries in 2010 with his 78th touchdown in just his 113th appearance. After being dropped from first grade in 2007, Vatuvei scored 16 tries in 2008 (17 games), 13 tries in 2009 (19 games) and 20 tries in 2010 (19 games). Vatuvei is set to become the first Warrior to rack up a century of tries after adding another 12 in 2011. As well as scoring four NRL hat-tricks in the past four seasons, Vatuvei counts a haul of four for New Zealand against England during the 2008 World Cup among 13 Test tries from 19 appearances.

- Manly fullback Brett Stewart has developed an astonishing tryscoring frequency since becoming a first grade regular in 2004, particularly at the Sea Eagles' home ground, Brookvale Oval. To the end of 2011, the flying custodian had scored 113 tries from 138 games. But Stewart has been even more potent at Brookvale, scoring a phenomenal 62 tries in 63 games, including five of his six career hat-tricks.

- Amos Roberts was one of the 2000s' foremost tryscoring exponents, crossing for 106 tries in 177 games for St. George Illawarra, Penrith and the Roosters. He posted 29 tries in 65 games for the Dragons, but his try-poaching exploits went into overdrive after joining the Panthers in 2004. Roberts topped the premiership with 23 tries in as many games, including a four-try haul in his second match for the club, against New Zealand. Roberts scored 17 tries in 2005 and 18 in 2006 for the Roosters—eighth and fourth-equal in the premiership respectively. Finishing his NRL career in 2008 after posting 54 tries in 89 appearances for the Tricolours, Roberts was equally prolific for Super League powerhouse Wigan in 2009-10.

TRY-SCORERS FAST FACTS

- Just three players have posted 50 tries with two premiership clubs. Harold Horder (102 for Souths, 50 for Norths), Matt Sing (72 for the Roosters, 73 for North

Queensland) and Darren Smith (53 for the Bulldogs, 62 for Brisbane) have reached the milestone for multiple teams.

■ Twin brothers Brett and Josh Morris were the NRL's top-two leading try-scorers in 2009. Dragons winger Brett topped the premiership with 25 tries in 24 games, while Bulldogs centre Josh finished second with 22 tries in 21 games. Both are well on the way to scoring a century of first grade tries, which would emulate the feat of their father, diminutive halfback-cum-winger Steve, who scored 122 tries in an admirable career with St. George and Eastern Suburbs.

■ Mullins and his father, powerhouse Eastern Suburbs winger Bill, are the only father-son combination to score a century of first grade tries each. Bill Mullins scored a Roosters club record 104 tries in 190 games between 1968 and 1978, while Brett finished with 122 touchdowns from 209 games for Canberra and the Roosters.

■ One of the most astounding tryscoring coincidences of all time involves Cronulla great Andrew Ettingshausen. 'ET' bagged five tries in the final round of 1989 against Illawarra—and five years later to the day, scored another five against Souths on the last weekend of the 1994 regular season.

■ Canberra fullback Brett Mullins scored 11 tries in three matches during his breakthrough 1994 season. He followed up a hat-trick against Cronulla with four-try hauls in back-to-back matches against Souths and Newcastle. Two of his tries against the Knights were spellbinding length-of-the-field efforts, and Mullins went on to win a premiership and tour with the Kangaroos that year.

■ A St. George player topped the premiership's tryscoring table in all but two years of the Dragons' record-breaking run of 11 premierships between 1956 and 1966. Tommy Ryan (1956-57), Eddie Lumsden (1958 and 1961), Reg Gasnier (1960 and 1963-64) and Johnny King (1961 and 1965) each finished as the top try-scorer on multiple occasions during the club's dominant period. North Sydney legend Ken Irvine was the only player to wrest the tryscoring title from the Saints, heading off Dragons Brian Messiter in 1959 and King in 1966, despite the Bears missing the finals in each year.

■ Dave Brown's premiership record haul of 38 tries in 1935 can largely be accredited to an extraordinary late-season flurry of touchdowns. In the last five rounds, Brown scored 22 tries—six against both Canterbury and Balmain, four against University and Norths, and a double against Souths.

■ Newtown flankmen Ray Preston and Kevin Considine hold the record for most tries in season by a club wing combination. In 1954, Preston crossed the stripe 34 times, the second-highest season total of all time, while Considine scored 21 tries for a combined total of 55 tries. Remarkably, South Sydney wing duo Les Brennan (29 tries) and Ian Moir (21) combined for 50 tries in the same year as the Bluebags wingers' feat. Other impressive wing pairings include: Easts' Rod O'Loan and Fred Tottey (46 tries in 1935 and 45 tries in 1936); Saints pairing Tommy Ryan and Eddie Lumsden (44 tries in 1957); Brisbane's Lote Tuqiri and Wendell Sailor (39 tries in 2001 and 36 in 2000); Bears combination Cec Blinkhorn and Harold Horder (37 tries in 1922); St. George greats King and Lumsden (37 tries in 1962); Newcastle duo Akuila Uate and Cooper Vuna (37 tries in 2009); and Penrith's two Lukes, Lewis and Rooney (35 tries in 2003).

- Brisbane's crack backline cashed in during the club's dominant 1998 season. Darren Lockyer scored 19 tries; wingers Wendell Sailor and Michael Hancock crossed for 18 and 10 tries respectively; centre pairing Darren Smith (23) and Steve Renouf (20) scored 43 tries collectively and were both in the top three try-scorers in the NRL; and halfback Allan Langer bagged 10 tries—exactly 100 tries between six players.

- Seven players jointly hold the Australian Test record for most tries in a match: John Ribot, Dale Shearer, Michael O'Connor, Brett Dallas, Gorden Tallis, Mat Rogers and Wendell Sailor each crossed four times in a Test between 1982 and 2000. But the world record belongs to Kiwi great and Roosters stalwart Hugh McGahan—the backrower plunged over for an incredible six tries in just his third Test, a 60-20 drubbing of Papua New Guinea in 1983. Emphasising McGahan's feat is the fact the 1988 joint Golden Boot winner scored just 20 tries in 117 first grade games for Easts.

- Darren Lockyer became Australia's greatest Test try-scorer in 2010, crossing for his 34th try against Papua New Guinea during the Four Nations to break Ken Irvine's 43-year old record. Lockyer broke the record in his 52nd Test, however, while Irvine collected 33 tries in as many Test appearances. Current players with a realistic chance of challenging Lockyer's new mark include Greg Inglis (20 tries in 18 Tests), Billy Slater (18 tries in 17 Tests) and Brett Morris (11 tries in 10 Tests).

- Inglis equalled Dale Shearer as State of Origin's greatest try-scorer in 2011, notching his 12th try in just 15 matches for the Maroons (fellow Queenslander Shearer achieved his total in 26 appearances). Michael O'Connor is the most prolific NSW Origin try-scorer with 11 touchdowns from 19 matches. Current Queensland fullback Billy Slater boasts 11 tries from 17 matches, while Jarryd Hayne is the best-placed NSW player to launch an assault on the record, nabbing seven tries in 13 appearances since 2007.

CLUB TRY-SCORERS

Adelaide: Graham Appo—12 in 14 games (1998)

Annandale: J. Bain—16 in 61 games (1915-20)

Balmain: Arthur Patton—95 in 117 games (1937-48)

Brisbane: Steve Renouf—142 in 183 games (1989-99)

Canberra: Jason Croker—120 in 318 games (1991-2006)

Canterbury: Hazem El Masri—159 in 317 games (1996-2009)

Cronulla: Andrew Ettingshausen—165 in 328 games (1983-2000)

Cumberland: Edward Bellamy—2 in 5 games (1908)

Glebe: Frank Burge—137 in 138 games (1911-26)

Gold Coast (1988-98): Danny Peacock—28 in 67 games (1991-95)

Gold Coast Titans: Mat Rogers—32 in 77 games (2007-11)
and Anthony Laffranchi—32 in 102 games (2007-11)

Hunter Mariners: Nick Zisti—9 in 17 games (1997)

Illawarra: Rod Wishart—68 in 154 games (1989-98)

Manly: Steve Menzies—151 in 280 games (1993-2008)

Melbourne: Billy Slater—124 in 203 games (2003-11)

Newcastle (1908-09): Bill 'Jerry' Bailey—18 in 17 games (1908-09)

Newcastle Knights: Adam MacDougall—87 in 158 games (1997-2011)

Newtown: Ray Preston—109 in 113 games (1949-56)

New Zealand Warriors: Manu Vautvei—90 in 132 games (2004-11)

Northern Eagles: Brendon Reeves—30 in 66 games (2000-02)

North Queensland: Matthew Bowen—111 in 225 games (2001-11)

North Sydney: Ken Irvine—171 in 176 games (1958-70)*

Parramatta: Luke Burt—117 in 244 games (1999-2011)

Penrith: Rhys Wesser—113 in 177 games (1998-2008)

St. George: Johnny King—143 in 191 games (1960-71)

St. George Illawarra: Matt Cooper—116 in 220 games (2000-11)

South Queensland: Jason Hudson—11 in 39 games (1996-97)

South Sydney: Benny Wearing—144 in 172 games (1921-33)

Sydney Roosters/Eastern Suburbs: Anthony Minichiello—107 in 227 games (2000-11)

University: Ernest 'Sammy' Ogg—24 in 116 games (1924-33)

Western Reds: Chris Ryan—21 in 58 games (1995-97)

Western Suburbs: Peter Dimond—84 in 155 games (1958-67)

Wests Tigers: Benji Marshall—66 in 155 games (2003-11).

Premiership record for a single club

THE POINT-SCORERS

MOST FIRST GRADE POINTS

2,418—Hazem El Masri

2,176—Andrew Johns

2,107—Jason Taylor

2,034—Daryl Halligan

1,971—Mick Cronin

1,917—Graham Eadie

1,841—Eric Simms

1,690—Ryan Girdler

1,659—Luke Burt

1,604—Clinton Schifcofske

1,604—Craig Fitzgibbon

MOST POINTS IN A SEASON

342—Hazem El Masri (2004)

308—Brett Hodgson (2005)

296—Hazem El Masri (2006)

294—Hazem El Masri (2003)

284—Ivan Cleary (1998)

282—Mick Cronin (1978)

279—Mick Cronin (1982)

279—Ben Walker (2001)

279—Andrew Johns (2001)

272—Darren Lockyer (1998)

MOST POINTS IN A MATCH

45—Dave Brown (1935)

38—Dave Brown (1935)

38—Mal Meninga (1990)

36—Les Griffin (1935)

36—Jack Lindwall (1947)

36—Terry Campese (2008)

34—Matt Geyer (1999)

34—Andrew Johns (2001)

34—Hazem El Masri (2006)

32—Frank Burge (1920)

32—Dave Brown (1935)

THE GREAT POINTSCORING FORWARDS

- Second-rower Bernie Purcell, who played his only Test in the famous 1950 Ashes decider and toured with the 1956-57 Kangaroos, was the code's first great pointscoring forward. He started his career with a season for Wests in 1948 before scoring a South Sydney record 1,126 points during 12 seasons for the Rabbitohs (later eclipsed by Eric Simms). Purcell finished in the premiership's top-four point-scorers in 1950 and 1954-56, scoring a career-high 19 points against Canterbury in 1955. He was the first player to accumulate 500 first grade goals. With a grand total of 1,152 points, his standing as the most prolific pointscoring forward went unchallenged for 40 years after his retirement.

- Goalkicking backrower David Furner surpassed Purcell as the game's highest pointscoring forward in 2000—the Canberra great's final season in the premiership. Furner played 200 games for the Raiders in nine seasons and scored a club record 1,218 points. He topped 100 points in seven consecutive seasons, finishing second in the competition in 1993, fourth in 1994 and third in 1995 (with a career-high 198 points). Furner's 10 goals against Parramatta in 1993 remains an equal-club record mark.

- Workhorse backrower Craig Fitzgibbon built a reputation as one of the NRL's finest goalkickers during a stellar career. He topped 100 points in each of his 10 seasons with the Roosters, beating Allan McKean's club record by more than 500 points to finish with 1,454 when he retired at the end of 2009. Adding points he scored at the beginning of his career with Illawarra and St George Illawarra, Fitzgibbon passed Furner's pointscoring mark for a forward in 2006, while his career total of 1,604 points places him in the top 10 point-scorers in the history of the premiership. Fitzgibbon scored a career-best 196 points in 2001, is the fourth-most prolific scorer in Grand Final history (32) and has scored the sixth-most points in finals matches (132). He scored 90 points in 18 Tests for Australia—equal-13th with Brian Carlson on the all time register.

- Aggressive, underrated match-winner Wayne Bartrim is the third-highest pointscoring forward of all time (1,158). The hooker/lock set a host of modest records with the now-defunct Gold Coast Seagulls: most points (224); most points in a season (124 in 1994); and most points in a match (20, vs. Balmain in 1994). Bartrim joined the Dragons in 1995 and topped 100 points in all seven of his seasons with St. George and St. George Illawarra. He finished third in the 1996 pointscoring race with 176 points, a premiership record for a lock-forward, and fourth in the 1997 ARL competition. A brilliant clutch goalkicker *(see Goalkicking Feats)*, Bartrim scored a career-best 22 points against Souths in 1997. Pointscoring is just another string to the bow of decorated Melbourne captain Cameron Smith.

The only career hooker to top 1,000 first grade points, Smith's 192 points in 2007 represents the highest season total by a rake in the game's history. The left-footed goalkicker has scored more points than any player for the Storm and was the NRL's second-top point-scorer in 2008, third in 2007, equal-fourth in 2011 and fifth in 2006. Passing 1,000 career points was a rare highlight for Smith during Melbourne's gut-wrenching 2010 season.

■ Harry Bath holds the record for most points in a season by a forward, scoring 225 points as a second-rower for St. George in 1958. Bath, who spent most of his career achieving legendary status in England, also set a new mark for most points in a season by a prop with 205 in 1959, his last season of first grade. He is the only forward to exceed 200 points in a season, while his eight goals and 16 points in the 1957 Grand Final against Manly remain records for a decider.

DALLY MESSENGER Australian Rugby League's first superstar was also the game's first great point-scorer. Pioneering legend Dally Messenger scored 381 points in just 48 games for Eastern Suburbs from 1908 to 1913—his total included three hauls of 18 points and 20 points in the semi-final against Souths in 1911 on the way to the Tricolours' first premiership. Messenger's season aggregate of 148 points in 1911 stood as a premiership record for 11 years. His feats at representative level set the standard for all other point-scorers to follow: Messenger top-scored on the 1908-09 Kangaroo Tour with 155 points; and he scored 232 points in 25 appearances for NSW, including 32 points (four tries, 10 goals) against Queensland in 1911—an interstate record that was eventually equalled by Ryan Girdler 89 years later. Pointscoring ran in the Messenger family—Dally's pointscoring record for Easts was broken by younger brother Wally, who amassed 624 points in 98 games.

THE 'BRADMAN OF LEAGUE' Brilliant centre Dave Brown's mammoth pointscoring achievements and masterful application of every aspect of the game saw him dubbed 'The Bradman of League' in reference to the most celebrated of all cricketers, Sir Donald Bradman. Brown scored 667 points in 94 games for Eastern Suburbs, but his efforts in 1935 produced premiership records that are unlikely to be bettered. Brown's 38 tries in just 15 matches and 45 points (from five tries and 15 goals) against Canterbury set records still unsurpassed 76 years later. For good measure, Brown scored 38 points later in the season in the return clash with Canterbury— the second-highest match total in history. Brown's hauls of 32 and 26 points— against Balmain and Norths respectively—in 1935 take up the next two lines on the Tricolours' points in a match honour board. His total of 244 points in that phenomenal season stood as a premiership record for 34 years and a club record until 1983. Brown had earlier topped the competition in points in 1934 and finished third in 1936.

Brown scored 73 points in just nine Tests for Australia and 124 points in 21 interstate games for NSW, but it was his exploits on the 1933-34 Kangaroo Tour that left an indelible mark on the record books. He amassed 285 points in 32 matches, smashing the previous record of 155 (in 31 matches) set by Dally Messenger on the first tour in 1908-09. Noel Pidding's 228 points in 1952-53 is the next-highest Kangaroo Tour total, while the scrapping of full-scale tours since the mid-1990s ensures Brown's mark will stand forever—although there was a good chance of that being the case anyway.

KEITH BARNES Widely considered the greatest player in Balmain's history and one of the best fullbacks of all time, Keith 'Golden Boots' Barnes was the first player to reach the milestone of 1,500 points in first grade. Barnes was the premiership's second top-point-scorer in 1956 and 1963 and finished third in 1958 and 1966, gathering 1,519 points in 194 appearances for the Tigers. He scored a club record-equalling 22 points against Norths in 1960 and posted 117 points in 17 Test appearances for Australia. The rock-steady custodian scored 202 points as captain of the 1959-60 Kangaroos.

RON ROWLES Wollongong winger Ron Rowles ranks among the all time great point-scorers thanks to his phenomenal strike-rate—Rowles accumulated 842 points in just 81 games, at the unmatched average of 10.4 points per game. Joining Manly in 1950, Rowles set a new premiership benchmark by topping the competition's pointscoring in the ensuing four seasons. Rowles set a new club record with 220 points in 1951 and extended it with 221 points in 1954—his last season in Sydney— including a 30-point haul against Canterbury, which remains a Manly record. His points in a season club record stood for 21 years. Rowles' son Peter scored 346 points in 56 games for Wests and Newtown, 1977-80.

ERIC SIMMS South Sydney fullback Eric Simms smashed Keith Barnes' premiership record for career points, amassing 1,841 points in 206 games for the Rabbitohs. Simms was the competition's top point-scorer from 1967 to 1970 and finished second in 1971 and 1972. He is only player to top 200 points in a season for Souths (which he did each year from 1967-70) and his 265 points in 1969 beat the all time mark of 244 posted by Easts' Dave Brown 34 years earlier. Simms was over 300 points clear of his nearest rival in all time scoring when he retired at the end of 1975, while he gathered 87 points in eight Tests for Australia, leading the scoring at the 1968 and 1970 World Cups.

GRAEME LANGLANDS The Immortal Graeme 'Changa' Langlands finished behind only Eric Simms in the history of premiership pointscoring when he retired in 1976, becoming just the third player to pass 1,500 first grade points. Langlands finished with 1,554 points in 227 games as a St. George legend, finishing atop the competition in 1971 and 1973 and in the top-four in 1963, 1965-66, 1969 and 1972. He scored a career-best 27 points (three tries, nine goals) in a match against Parramatta at the SCG in 1964—a premiership record for a finals match that stood for 41 years. Langlands was the top point-scorer in Australian Test and World Cup history at the time of his retirement, scoring 206 points in 45 appearances, and has scored more points than any other player on Kangaroo Tours—a total of 374 points garnered from the 1963-64, 1967 and 1973 tours, the latter as captain.

GRAHAM EADIE Rated alongside the finest fullbacks of all time, Manly great Graham 'Wombat' Eadie went on to become the game's most prolific point-scorer. Eadie eclipsed Eric Simms' career pointscoring record by collecting 226 points in 1983, his final year in the premiership and the fourth time in his career he had posted more than 200 points in a season. He finished with 1,917 points in 237 games for the Sea Eagles and was the premiership's top point-scorer in 1974, 1975 and 1976 (including a then-club record 242 points in 1975). Eadie scored 28 points in a match against Penrith in 1973 and 27 points against Souths in 1975. Playing during the same era as Mick Cronin—the man who eventually beat his premiership record—limited Eadie's pointscoring opportunities at rep level, but he still managed 45 points in 20 Test appearances for Australia, including 17 in a World Cup fixture against France in 1975.

MICK CRONIN Outstanding centre Mick Cronin set new standards for pointscoring excellence in the 1970s and 1980s. The Gerringong product debuted for Australia in 1973 but resisted overtures to come to Sydney until 1977, when he joined Parramatta and scored a premiership record 1,971 points over just 10 seasons. He was the premiership's top point-scorer in 1977 and bettered Rabbitoh Eric Simms' all time mark by scoring 282 points the following season for the Eels. Combining that record total with points accrued for City, NSW and Australia, Cronin scored 547 points in 1978—a world record for a calendar year.

Cronin topped the competition again in 1979, 1982 (with 279 points, then the second-highest season total of all time) and 1985, the season he passed Graham Eadie's premiership record mark for career points. 'The Crow' scored a then-club record 26 points against Newtown in 1978, before bettering the mark with 27 points against Norths the following season and Canberra in 1982.

Cronin's 201 points in Test matches was a record for Australia that was overtaken by Mal Meninga, but a record-keeping change in 2008 that saw World Cup games given the same status as Tests elevated Cronin back to the top of the tree with 309 points. Named as one of Australia's 100 greatest-ever players in 2008, Cronin top-scored on the 1973 and 1978 Kangaroo Tours and at the 1975 and 1977 World Cups.

LIKE FATHER, LIKE SON The late Steve Rogers, one of the finest players of the 1970s and 1980s at centre,five-eighth and lock, and dual international son Mat, equally versatile throughout the backline, were both outstanding accumulators of points. Arguably Cronulla's greatest-ever player, Steve Rogers was the premiership's leading point-scorer in 1981 and holds the club record with a career total of 1,253 points. Mat Rogers was second in the 1997 Super League and 2000 NRL pointscoring stakes, and departed for rugby union after seven seasons and 1,112 points for the Sharks. Steve's two seasons with St. George netted 121 points, taking his career total to 1,374—incredibly just 14 points ahead of his son's career tally. Mat returned to the NRL with four seasons and 248 for the Titans prior to his retirement in 2010. Steve set a Cronulla record with 26 points in a match in 1977, equalled by Mat 23 years later, while Rogers junior set a new club season record with 212 points in 2000—18 points superior to his father's best effort in 1981 (both records were surpassed by Brett Kimmorley in 2002). Mat Rogers is the eighth-highest point-scorer in Australian Test history with 168 points from just 11 Tests, including 34 points against Fiji, 26 points against Papua New Guinea and 24 points against the Kiwis during the 2000 season.

MAL MENINGA The pure numbers of Mal Meninga's record-breaking career are almost as huge as the man himself. The Team of the Century centre holds a myriad of appearance records, but is also a colossus in the pointscoring record books. Meninga is the highest point-scorer in Origin history, scoring 161 points in

32 appearances for Queensland. He was recognised as the most prolific point-scorer in Test history until 2008, when World Cup matches were given the same status as Test matches by Rugby League authorities, but his total of 278 points ranks behind only Mick Cronin. Meninga's 304 points on a record four Kangaroo Tours is second only to Graeme Langlands' 374 points in tour history.

Meninga scored a then-club record 864 points in premiership football for Canberra between 1986 and 1994, despite relinquishing the goalkicking duties to David Furner in 1992 and having the 1987-88 seasons decimated by four broken arm injuries. He topped the 1990 competition with 212 points, including 38 points (from five tries and nine goals) against the Roosters—the equal-second highest match total in premiership history and the best first grade effort since 1935.

MICHAEL O'CONNOR Former Wallaby international Michael O'Connor scored 985 points in a decade-long career with St. George and Manly, but his most spectacular pointscoring achievements occurred at representative level. O'Connor was the competition's fifth-top point-scorer in 1985 with the Dragons and in 1987 after switching to the Sea Eagles, before scoring a career-best 202 points in 1988—second in the premiership. He set an Origin record on debut, scoring all 18 of the Blues' points in the first match of the 1985 series, a match record which stood for 15 years. The gifted centre/winger scored a NSW Origin record 129 points in 19 appearances, while his 198 points for Australia places him as the seventh-top Test point-scorer. O'Connor top-scored on the 1986 Kangaroo Tour with 190 from just 14 matches; his 22 points against Great Britain at Old Trafford on that tour is an Anglo-Australian Test record; and the 30 points he scored against Papua New Guinea in 1988 stood as a world record for eight years.

DARYL HALLIGAN Kiwi rugby union convert Daryl Halligan was a ruthless accumulator of points, averaging over 200 points a season in a decade-long career that saw him become the first player to pass the 2,000 point barrier. Joining Norths in 1991, Halligan topped the premiership with a club record 196 points in his debut season. He led the competition again in 1992 and 1993 as a Bear, and again in 1994 after joining Canterbury, scoring a club record 270 points. Halligan finished second to fellow New Zealander Matthew Ridge in 1995, and third in the 1997 Super League season and 1998-99 NRL seasons. The valuable, steady winger passed Mick Cronin's all time mark during 2000 and eclipsed the 2,000-point milestone a few weeks before his retirement, finishing with 2,034 points from 230 appearances. Halligan set a new Canterbury record with 28 points in a match against Gold Coast in 1998 and repeated the dose with 28 against Wests in 1999. The man known as 'Chook' scored 125 points in 19 Tests for New Zealand—behind only Ridge, Stacey Jones and Des White in Kiwi Test history.

JASON TAYLOR Halfback sharpshooter Jason Taylor became the greatest point-scorer in premiership history in 2001. Taylor was third in the premiership behind Daryl Halligan and Matthew Ridge with 170 points for Wests in 1991, and again behind the Kiwi pair in 1994 while beating Halligan's North Sydney record with 217 points. He bettered that mark as he topped the 1996 premiership with 238 points (breaking a five-year Kiwi stranglehold on the pointscoring title) and the 1997 ARL competition with 242 points. The scheming No.7 became the first player to pass 1,000 points for the Bears in 1998, while he soared past 2,000 points and Daryl Halligan's premiership record with a career-best 265 points for Parramatta in 2001—his last season in the NRL. Taylor scored a North Sydney record-equalling 26 points in a match twice, while he matched that for the Eels against Wests Tigers in 2001. His total of 2,107 points in 276 games stood as the premiership record for five years.

MATTHEW RIDGE Injury hampered much of Kiwi sharpshooter Matthew Ridge's career, but the former All Black retired at the end of 1999 as the 11th-top point-scorer of all time, amassing 1,331 points in just 159 games. The courageous Manly and Auckland fullback immediately stamped himself as a goalkicking marvel after switching codes, finishing second to countryman and fellow code-swapper Daryl Halligan in the 1991 pointscoring race—his first full season in the premiership. He was behind only Halligan again in 1994, scoring 234 points, but topped the competition in 1995 with a Manly record 257 points. Ridge scored 26 points against Canberra in 1991, 25 points against St. George in 1994 and 28 points against the Western Reds in 1995, before equalling Ron Rowles' club record with 30 points against the Magpies in 1996. He became just the third player to score 1,000 points for the Sea Eagles in 1996, leaving the club to score 238 points in three injury and suspension-tinged seasons with the Warriors. Ridge garnered a New Zealand Test record 168 points in 25 appearances between 1990 and 1998.

RYAN GIRDLER Penrith great Ryan Girdler owns a host of pointscoring records with the Panthers, but marks he set at representative level in 2000 are even more likely to stand the test of time. After starting his career with Illawarra, Girdler joined Penrith in 1993 and topped Super League's pointscoring table in 1997 with a club record 197 points. He bettered that mark with 229 points in 1999 (second in the NRL), and he scored a club record 28 points in a match in 1999 and 2002 (both records were surpassed by Michael Gordon in 2010). Girdler's 1,572 points remains a Panthers record, while his career total of 1,690 places him eighth in premiership history. In 2002 Girdler became the third player in history to accumulate 100 tries and 1000 points in a career, and the first to tally 100 tries and 500 goals.

Girdler benefitted spectacularly from the Blues' dominance in the 2000 Origin series. He smashed records for most points, goals and tries in an Origin series, while his 32-point haul from three tries and 10 goals set unthinkable new marks for points and goals in a match, and equalled the record for tries in a match. Later that year, Girdler scored a world record 46 points (three tries, 17 goals) in a 110-4 World Cup thrashing of minnows Russia.

ANDREW JOHNS Rated by many as the best player in the game's history, Team of the Century halfback and three-time Dally M winner Andrew Johns added the distinction of being the game's most prolific point-scorer to his long list of glittering achievements. Johns scored 2,176 points in 249 games on the way to becoming a Newcastle legend, passing Jason Taylor's premiership record career total in 2006. He finished on top of the premiership's pointscoring table just once, equal with Ben Walker on 279 points in 2001, while he finished in the top-five in 1995, 1999, 2000, 2002 and 2006. His 34-point haul against Canberra in 2001 is the seventh-equal highest match total in premiership history, while he owns the top eight Newcastle match and season points records outright. At rep level, Johns contributed 94 points in 23 Origin matches for NSW—second only to Michael O'Connor—and scored 226 points in 26 Tests for Australia (third-equal of all time). Johns equalled O'Connor's Test world record for most points on debut with 30 points against South Africa at the 1995 World Cup and bettered it with 32 points against Fiji in 1996.

'EL MAGIC' Despite Daryl Halligan's presence preventing him from taking on the goalkicking duties at the Bulldogs until his sixth season in first grade, evergreen winger Hazem El Masri was the greatest point-scorer in premiership history by the time he retired in 2009. El Masri assumed Halligan's kicking role with aplomb in 2001, equalling his predecessor's club record of 270 points (third in the NRL). He topped the NRL in 2002 with 254 points, and again in 2003 with a premiership record 294 points. The Lebanese flyer, affectionately dubbed 'El Magic,' smashed his own record with a phenomenal 342 points in 2004, helped by a then-finals series record 54 points as the Bulldogs surged to the title. El Masri was the NRL's premier point-scorer a record six times, winning the race again in 2006-07 and 2009. He accumulated 296 points in 2006, behind only his record 2004 haul and Brett Hodgson's 2005 total of 308 points in premiership history. The Bulldogs club great passed Andrew Johns' all time career pointscoring record early in 2009, El Masri's last season in the NRL, and extended the mark to 2,418 points.

El Masri's 34 points against Wests Tigers in 2006 is a Canterbury club record, while he bagged more than 20 points in a match on 10 further occasions. Recognised as an equally impressive ambassador for Rugby League as he was a player, El Masri also ranks fourth in all time finals scoring, with 142 points from just 18 matches.

MODERN-DAY POINTSCORING MACHINES

- Rod Wishart holds every pointscoring record available with the Steelers and finished his career with 1,092 points after one final season with St. George-Illawarra in 1999. The powerful winger ranks 10th on the all time Test point-scorers list (138 in 17 Tests), while he was the top point-scorer on the 1994 Kangaroo Tour, scoring 174 points at a record average of almost 16 points per game.

- Clinton Schifcofske set every club pointscoring record on offer during the South Queensland Crushers' brief existence, before topping 100 points in nine consecutive seasons for Parramatta and Canberra. One of the NRL's top-five point-scorers in 2001, 2003 and 2006, Schifcofske became just the second player to pass 1,000 points for the Raiders during the latter season. His 245 points in 2001 and 222 points in 2003 are the top-two highest season aggregates by a Canberra player, while Schifcofske's career total of 1,604 points ranks him equal-10th in premiership history.

- Luke Burt's total of 1,659 points to the end of 2011 places him behind only Mick Cronin in Parramatta club history. The ever-reliable winger has scored a club record 28 points in a match on two occasions—against Penrith in 2002 and Canberra in 2005—and topped 200 points in a season twice. Burt's 214 points in 2005 and 217 points in 2009 placed him second and third respectively on the NRL pointscoring table, while he also finished in the top-five in 2007-08 and 2011.

In 2009 he became just the seventh player to score 100 tries and 1,000 points in first grade, while he became only the third player to amass 100 tries and 500 goals the following season. Burt moved into the top-10 point-scorers in 2011.

- It would surprise most that Matt Orford ranks amongst the top-15 point-scorers in premiership history, accumulating exactly 1500 points in 10 NRL seasons prior to an ill-fated comeback with Canberra in 2011. A Dally medallist and Grand Final-winning captain with Manly in 2008, Orford left Melbourne at the end of 2005 with a club record 877 points (since eclipsed by Cameron Smith). Orford scored a career-high 216 points in 2001, while he finished as one of the NRL's top-five point-scorers in 2003 and 2008.

- Future Warriors and Panthers coach Ivan Cleary's 1,363 points from just 186 games places him in the premiership's top-20 point-scorers. Cleary was in the competition's top-five in 1993 despite playing just 13 games, scoring 126 points for Manly. Jason Taylor handled the goalkicking during Cleary's two seasons with Norths, but the classy fullback or centre scored 722 points in four seasons with the Sydney Roosters—at the time behind only Allan McKean in club history. Cleary was second behind Taylor in the 1996 and 1997 (ARL) pointscoring races, and amassed a premiership record 284 points in 1998, eclipsing Mick Cronin's 20-year-old mark. Joining the Warriors in 2000, Cleary scored a club record 173 points in 2001 and extended the benchmark to 242 points in 2002 (fourth in the NRL), including a club record-equalling 28 points against Northern Eagles.

- Brett Hodgson passed a rare milestone in 2005 when he became just the second player to score 300 points in a season. He finished the year with a colossal 308 points for Wests Tigers, including a finals record 30 points in the qualifying final thrashing of North Queensland. His finals total of 58 points bettered Hazem El Masri's mark set just 12 months earlier. The lightweight fullback scored 1,289 points in 12 seasons with the Magpies, Eels and Tigers, despite not being the first-choice goalkicker for much of the first half of his career. He departed the Tigers with a then-club record 786 points in just five seasons. Hodgson scored 220 points for Super League club Huddersfield on the way to winning the 2009 Man of Steel award.

- Johnathan Thurston became the Cowboys' all time top scorer in 2011, finishing the year with 969 points, and is quickly closing in on long-standing representative records. After scoring an equal-club record 24 points in a match twice in 2006, Thurston was the NRL's second-top point-scorer in 2007 (196 points) and fourth in 2009 (202 points). In just 22 Tests he has moved into equal-third on the all time Test pointscoring list with 226 points, while he stands behind only Mal Meninga and Michael O'Connor in Origin history, with 118 points in 21 appearances. Thurston was the top scorer at the 2008 World Cup with 50 points in just four matches.

POINTSCORING FAST FACTS

- Daryl Halligan (Norths and Bulldogs) and Matt Orford (Melbourne and Manly) are the only players in premiership history to score 500 points for two clubs. Veteran centre Ron Giteau holds the unique distinction of scoring 300 points for three different clubs, passing the mark with Wests, Easts and Canberra between 1974 and 1986.

- Canberra pivot Terry Campese was unwittingly robbed of an indelible place in the record books near the end of a 74-12 annihilation of Penrith in 2008. Campese had dominated the match, scoring four tries and 10 goals, and was in sight of Mal Meninga's club record of 38 points in a match. But captain Alan Tongue, unaware of Campese's imminent honour, gave the last conversion attempt of the match to rookie halfback Marc Herbert, leaving Campese two points short. It would have also put Campese alongside Meninga and Dave Brown as the scorer of the second-highest points total in a match in the history of the premiership. Nevertheless, Campese's 36-point haul ranks equal-fourth of all time, and is the best effort in a match since Meninga's mauling of Eastern Suburbs in 1990.

- Les Griffin was the first player to score 36 points in a match, collecting two tries and 15 goals in St. George's premiership record hammering of Canterbury in 1935 to pass Frank Burge's mark of 32 points set for Glebe against University in 1920. But Griffin's new Sydney competition record stood for just one week—Dave Brown scored 45 points the following Saturday, also against the hapless Berries.

- Manly winger Ron Rowles played just five seasons of premiership football, but set new standards for pointscoring excellence when he topped the competition in four consecutive seasons (1951-54)—a feat that has been equalled by just two other players. South Sydney pointscoring machine Eric Simms won the pointscoring race from 1967 to 1970, while Kiwi sharpshooter Daryl Halligan ruled the pointscoring roost from 1991 to 1994 playing for Norths and Canterbury. Balmain great Charles 'Chook' Fraser (1915-17), North Sydney's South African fullback Fred Griffiths (1963-65), Manly custodian Graham Eadie (1974-76), Parramatta legend Mick Cronin (1977-79) and Bulldogs winger Hazem El Masri (2002-04) each topped the premiership three years in a row.

- El Masri—the greatest point-scorer in premiership history—has won more pointscoring titles than any other player, topping the competition six times (2002-04, 2006-07, 2009). Tommy Kirk headed the premiership on five occasions, once with Canterbury (1938) and four times with Newtown (1940, 1943-44 and 1946), while Mick Cronin was also top point-scorer five times during his decade with the Eels (1977-79, 1982, 1985).

CLUB POINT-SCORERS

Adelaide: Graham Appo—116 in 14 games (1998)

Annandale: Ray Norman—84 in 46 games (1910-13)

Balmain: Keith Barnes—1,519 in 194 games (1955-68)

Brisbane: Darren Lockyer—1,191 in 355 games (1995-2011)

Canberra: David Furner—1,218 in 200 games (1992-2000)

Canterbury: Hazem El Masri—2,418 in 317 games (1996-2011)

Cronulla: Steve Rogers—1,253 in 202 games (1973-85)

Cumberland: H. Bloomfield—19 in 8 games (1908)

Glebe: Frank Burge—509 in 138 games (1911-26)

Gold Coast (1988-98): Brendan Hurst—285 in 74 games (1994-97)

Gold Coast Titans: Scott Prince—581 in 102 games (2007-11)

Hunter Mariners: Nick Zisti—76 in 17 games (1997)

Illawarra: Rod Wishart—1,044 in 154 games (1989-98)

Manly: Graham Eadie—1,917 in 237 games (1971-83)

Melbourne: Cameron Smith—1,168 in 213 games (2002-11)

Newcastle (1908-09): Stan Carpenter—80 in 19 games (1908-09).

Newcastle Knights: Andrew Johns—2,176 in 249 games (1994-2007)

Newtown: Ken Wilson—1,001 in 150 games (1971-83)

New Zealand Warriors: Stacey Jones—674 in 261 games (1995-2009)

Northern Eagles: Ben Walker—279 in 26 games (2001)

North Queensland: Johnathan Thurston—969 in 144 games (2005-11)

North Sydney: Jason Taylor—1,274 in 147 games (1994-99)

Parramatta: Michael Cronin—1,971 in 216 games (1977-86)

Penrith: Ryan Girdler—1,572 in 204 games (1993-2004)

St. George: Graeme Langland—1,554 in 227 games (1963-76)

St. George Illawarra: Jamie Soward—822 in 108 games (2007-11)

South Queensland: Clinton Schifcofske—108 in 23 games (1996-97)

South Sydney: Eric Simms—1,841 in 206 games (1965-75)

Sydney Roosters/Eastern Suburbs: Craig Fitzgibbon—1,454 in 228 games (2000-09)

University: Tom McInerney—178 in 53 games (1930-35)

Western Reds: Chris Ryan—210 in 58 games (1995-97)

Western Suburbs: Bill Keato—776 in 119 games (1938-50)

Wests Tigers: Benji Marshall—840 in 155 games (2003-11)

Premiership record for a single club

GOALKICKING FEATS

MOST FIRST GRADE GOALS

942—Jason Taylor

917—Andrew Johns

891—Hazem El Masri

865—Mick Cronin

855—Daryl Halligan

847—Graham Eadie

803—Eric Simms

742—Keith Barnes

718—Craig Fitzgibbon

652—Clinton Schifcofske

MOST GOALS IN A SEASON

139—Hazem El Masri (2004)

129—Hazem El Masri (2003)

124—Brett Hodgson (2005)

123—Mick Cronin (1982)

117—Mick Cronin (1978)

116—Ivan Cleary (1998)

116—Daryl Halligan (1998)

116—Jason Taylor (2001)

114—Hazem El Masri (2006)

112—Eric Simms (1969)

MOST GOALS IN A MATCH

15—Les Griffin (1935)

15—Dave Brown (1935)

14—Graham Eadie (1973)

12—Les Mead (1935)

12—Graham Eadie (1975)

12—Ivan Cleary (2002)

BEST SEASON GOALKICKING PERCENTAGES

93.4%—Michael Gordon (57 from 61 in 2009)

92.5%—Michael Witt (62 from 67 in 2007)

91.6%—Ryan Girdler (76 from 83 in 1997)

87.1%—Daryl Halligan (88 from 101 in 2000)

86.6%—Daryl Halligan (116 from 134 in 1998)

DALLY M'S GREAT GOALS Herbert Henry 'Dally' Messenger was the game's first superstar—a player so dexterous and consummate at every aspect of Rugby League he was simply dubbed 'The Master'. He was the first great goalkicker, kicking 62 goals in 1911—which stood as a premiership record until broken by Dave Brown 24 years later—including two magnificent goals to help Eastern Suburbs to their first title. Messenger landed a penalty goal from beyond the halfway line to open the scoring in the final against minor premiers Glebe and the Tricolours went on to win 22-9. In the 'challenge' final rematch against the Dirty Reds, Messenger piloted a sideline conversion with 13 minutes remaining to give his side the lead for the first time, 9-8. Easts hung on to win its maiden premiership 11-8.

RUSSELL SECURES NEWTOWN'S FIRST PREMIERSHIP

Charles 'Boxer' Russell kicked the most famous and dramatic goal of the premiership's pioneering seasons. Defending premiers South Sydney led minor premiers Newtown 4-0 at halftime of the 1910 final on the back of two penalty goals to former Kangaroo Jim Davis. Russell pegged a goal back for Newtown to trail by just two, and with time almost up Souths fullback Howard Hallett cleared with a kick off his own line. Newtown centre Albert Hawkes claimed a 'mark'—under the rules of the day, if an opposing player's kick was caught on the full, a 'mark' could be called and a shot at goal awarded. Russell lined up the kick from wide out on the halfway line and steered his towering attempt between the posts to lock up the scores. As minor premiers, Newtown needed only a draw to take out its maiden title, presenting Russell with a treasured place in goalkicking folklore.

'THE LITTLE MASTER' KICK-STARTS 'MIRACLE OF '55'

Immortal South Sydney fullback Clive Churchill landed arguably the most famous goal in premiership football in 1955. The Rabbitohs, defending premiers, were anchored to the bottom of the ladder at the halfway mark of the competition, but strung six sudden-death wins together to remain in contention before their title hopes threatened to come unstuck against Manly. After breaking his arm in the first half against Manly, Churchill returned for the second half with a splint made from an exercise book cover. Trailing 7-4 in the dying stages, Souths scored through champion lock Les Cowie to tie up the match. Churchill stepped up and nailed the match-winning conversion from the sideline with his arm dangling loosely by his side. The Rabbitohs went on to take out the premiership—the Grand Final victory over Newtown was their 11th-straight win—without Churchill, but his inspired goal was integral to the team's remarkable success, since dubbed 'The Miracle of '55'.

'GOLDEN BOOTS' Balmain fullback legend Keith Barnes' goalkicking prowess earned him the nickname 'Golden Boots'. The Welsh-born Wollongong junior kicked 90 goals for the Tigers in 1956—a club record that stood until Balmain's merger with Wests at the end of 1999. He was the third player to kick 500 premiership goals, after Bernie Purcell and Ron Willey, and finished with 742 in a wonderful career—139 goals clear of Willey's former premiership record. Barnes equalled Frank Driese's club record with 11 goals against Norths in 1960—the same year he famously kicked the Tigers to a 19-15 victory over superpowers St. George with a penalty from his own half and another from the sideline. He was chaired shoulder-high from Leichhardt again in 1966 after booting Balmain to a 22-17 victory against Manly in 1966 with seven second half goals, after the Tigers had trailed 15-2 at halftime. Barnes kicked 59 goals in 17 Tests, including 10 against France in 1960—an Australian record that stood for 35 years.

IRVINE'S LITTLE HELPER Ken Irvine, Australian Rugby League's greatest try-scorer, kicked the most celebrated goal in Test history in 1962. Australia had already lost the home series to Great Britain with losses in the first two Tests, but was desperate for a face-saving victory in the third encounter at the SCG. Irvine's second try in the dying stages pegged Australia back to a one-point deficit—and it was left to the North Sydney legend, who rarely kicked at club or representative level, to win the match with a sideline conversion. He admitted to the referee Darcy Lawler that he was at long odds to pilot the kick over, to which Lawler agreed and responded by suggesting Irvine adjust the positioning of the ball. The advice did the trick—Irvine refocused and nailed the conversion to snatch a famous 18-17 triumph for Australia.

ERIC SIMMS Indigenous fullback/winger Eric Simms was the most potent field goal exponent the game had ever seen, but also kicked a then-premiership record 803 goals for the Rabbitohs between 1965 and 1975. He kicked 112 goals in 1969—another unprecedented total—and landed 16 goals in six Grand Final appearances. Simms booted 39 goals in eight Test appearances (all at World Cups), including 25 goals in four games as Australia claimed the 1968 World Cup.

'THE CROW' Test centre Michael Cronin resisted offers to leave Gerringong and come to the Sydney premiership for several seasons. But when he finally agreed to join Parramatta in 1977, he set new standards for pointscoring and goalkicking excellence over the ensuing decade. Cronin broke South Sydney great Eric Simms' premiership record with 117 goals in 1978 on his way to 282 points (another all time record), before bettering it with 123 goals in 1982—a mark that stood for 21 years. He also set a world record by kicking 26 consecutive goals in 1978 which stood until the late-1990s. For all Cronin's magnificent goalkicking prowess, it is regrettably two misses that stand out in the Parramatta legend's career—a conversion that went astray late in the drawn 1977 Grand Final against St. George (the Eels lost the replay 22-0), and a missed penalty goal in the dying stages of the 6-4 loss to Canterbury in the 1984 decider. But his radar-like kicking (in the traditional front-on, toe-poking style) won many more matches for the Eels, including his farewell from the game—he kicked two goals in Parramatta's 4-2 defeat of the Bulldogs in the try-less 1986 Grand Final that saw Cronin and Ray Price bow out as premiership winners. Cronin is also the only the player to kick over a century of Test goals with 141 from 33 appearances, 42 goals clear of Mal Meninga.

O'CONNOR LANDS ORIGIN'S GREATEST GOAL It is one of State of Origin's most replayed and enduring images: Michael O'Connor bending a sensational sideline conversion through the posts in pouring rain at the Sydney Football Stadium. Needing to win the second match of 1991 to keep the series alive, the Blues had just levelled the scores with a Mark McGaw try in the corner in the dying stages of one interstate football's most dramatic and fierce contests. Up stepped O'Connor, who had missed a kick from a similar spot late in the 6-4 series-opening loss at Lang Park. Despite the atrocious conditions, O'Connor curled this one around magnificently, dropping it over the bar to clinch an epic 14-12 victory. O'Connor kicked 311 goals at club level for St. George and Manly, while his 42 goals are a NSW Origin record and he sits seventh in Australian Test history with 65 goals.

LEEDS HAUNTS TIGERS WITH BUZZER-BEATERS Wallaby Andrew Leeds switched codes in 1989 to join Parramatta, and was one of the most reliable fullbacks of the 1990s for the Eels, Panthers and Magpies and a fine goalkicker to boot. Leeds kicked 363 goals in a decade-long Rugby League career, including two on-the-bell penalties to snatch victory from Balmain in consecutive seasons. The Eels trailed Balmain 15-14 in a 1991 clash at Parramatta Stadium, until a controversial last-minute penalty went against the Tigers. Leeds, coming off the bench, duly slotted the goal to grab the competition points. He trumped that effort in 1992 playing for defending premiers Penrith, landing a towering penalty from halfway after the fulltime siren to again sink the Tigers, 14-12.

RIDGE AND HALLIGAN LEAD KIWI INVASION The immediate success of former All Black fullback Matthew Ridge—and his radar-like boot—at Manly in 1990 sparked a swarm of talent scouts to pillage New Zealand's rugby union ranks for expert kickers. Over the next two seasons North Sydney recruited Waikato fullback Daryl Halligan; Bay of Plenty custodian Eion Crossan linked with Souths; devastating All Black inside-centre John Schuster was enticed to Newcastle; Wellington forward Gavin Hill signed with the Bulldogs; and former All Black five-eighth Frano Botica became a superboot with English powerhouse Wigan.

But it was Ridge and Halligan that had the biggest impact on the Australian competition, almost single-handedly changing the notion that an expert goalkicker was a luxury and not a necessity. Ridge's superb six-from-seven on debut against Cronulla in 1990 caused a sensation and Halligan rivalled him as the game's No.1 sharpshooter after joining the Bears in 1991. Despite a horror one-from-five effort in Norths' heartbreaking 16-14 loss to Penrith in the major semi in his debut season,

Halligan topped the pointscoring table in each of his first four seasons. Both players clocked 100 goals in a season for the first time in 1994 after Halligan's move to Canterbury, while Ridge eclipsed the hallowed mark again in 1995 as he snatched his compatriot's pointscoring crown.

Ridge finished with a career strike-rate of just over 80 per cent in a 10-season career with Manly and the Warriors, including two hauls of 11 in a match for the Sea Ealges, while he also kicked a New Zealand record 71 goals in Test matches. Halligan, meanwhile, got better with age—he kicked a career-high 116 goals in 1998 at the incredible average of 86.6 per cent, before retiring in 2000 with his best season average of 87.1 per cent. The steady winger also landed 10 goals in a match on three occasions. Halligan kicked his most famous goal in the Bulldogs' phenomenal comeback against Parramatta in the 1998 preliminary final. Down 18-2 with 11 minutes to play, Halligan landed a sideline conversion to cut the deficit to six points and drilled another high-pressure conversion down the middle from near touch to tie up the scoreboard. The Bulldogs went on to win 32-20 in extra-time. Halligan also broke Mick Cronin's long-standing premiership record by kicking 30 consecutive goals without a miss in 1998.

NOVICE STEALS RARE WIN FOR SEAGULLS Gold Coast fullback Alan Kempnich's only attempt at goal in first grade was a memorable one. The lowly Seagulls' 1994 match against Newcastle was Kempnich's second first grade match—and his first in four years. But after regular goalkicker Wayne Bartrim exhausted himself scoring a late, long-range try to tie the game up at 10-all, Kempnich was called upon to win the match. Kempnich drilled the sideline conversion attempt to secure one of the club's five wins of 1994. He played just four more first grade games and was not required to kick for goal again, finishing his modest first grade career with a flawless kicking record.

JASON TAYLOR Goalkicking in the 1990s was dominated by New Zealand rugby union converts Halligan and Ridge, but flying the flag for Australian goalkickers was halfback Jason Taylor, who went on to become the most prolific kicker of all time. Taylor began his career at Wests and emerged as a genuine match-winner with the boot before joining Norths in 1994. He kicked 108 goals in 1996 at a magnificent 83.7 per cent conversion rate and equalled that season total for the Bears in 1998. Taylor finished his career in 2001 with a season at Parramatta, and a career-high 116 goals at over 80 per cent. The scheming No.7's colossal career total of 942 goals was 77 clear of the previous record set by goalkicking legend Mick Cronin. Taylor kicked a North Sydney record-equalling 10 goals against Balmain in 1999 and equalled Cronin's Parramatta record with 11 goals against the Tigers in 2001.

BARTRIM A THORN IN THE RAIDERS' SIDE Dragons hooker/lock Wayne Bartrim proved himself as a genuine clutch goalkicker with two stunning match-winners during the 1990s—both times at the expense of Canberra. Bartrim had already scored one of the great individual tries in the first half of the 1996 quarter-final against the Raiders, but his prodigious talents were required to win the sudden-death match in the dying minutes. Saints winger Mark Bell crossed in the corner to lock the game up 14-all, and Bartrim's towering conversion attempt swung in to drop over the bar, keeping the Dragons' season alive. Bartrim repeated the dose early in the merged St. George-Illawarra outfit's debut season. Winless heading into the third round of 1999, the under pressure Dragons came back from a 14-0 deficit to level the scores with a last-minute Rod Wishart try. With the echoes of the fulltime siren ringing in his ears, Bartrim coolly slotted the conversion from out wide to seal the joint-venture's maiden victory. One of the highest pointscoring forwards of all time, Bartrim kicked 489 goals in a 232-game career.

'EL MAGIC' Despite assuming the goalkicking duties from the premiership's greatest-ever point-scorer and arguably the finest goalkicker of all time, Bulldogs winger Hazem El Masri bettered the achievements of his illustrious predecessor. El Masri stepped into the breach created by revered Kiwi Daryl Halligan's retirement at the end of 2000. He topped the NRL's pointscoring table for the first time in 2002 with 254 points—including 103 goals—and produced one of the great conversions to cap an astonishing Bulldogs comeback at Newcastle. The Dogs had fought back from 19-0 down to trail 21-20 with a last-minute try in the corner. Contending with a swirling breeze, the sun in his eyes and the baying pro-Knights crowd, El Masri curled the ball between the posts magnificently to secure a famous after-the-bell victory. His goalkicking exploits over the next few seasons placed him on a trajectory to being rated the best ever; El Masri landed a premiership record 129 goals in 2003, and bettered the mark by 10 goals the following season as the Bulldogs took out the title (kicking at well over 80 per cent in each season). He equalled Bradford's Kiwi star Henry Paul's world record with 35 consecutive goals without a miss for the Bulldogs in 2003 (including a club record 11 from 11 against Souths), and kicked another 31 straight for Lebanon and the Bulldogs at the end of 2003 and beginning of 2004. But perhaps his finest exhibition came in a final-round defeat of Penrith in 2006, when he goaled five from five in blustery winds and driving rain. El Masri finished his career with an astonishing strikerate of just under 82 per cent.

Note: Incredibly, just hours after El Masri equalled Paul's world record, Batley goalkicker Barry Eaton finished a run of consecutive goals in the National League (England) competition at 38 to take ownership of the record.

'JOEY' JOHNS Andrew Johns' reputation as the game's finest clutch player of recent times was not restricted to his expertise in general play. The Newcastle No.7 thrived on pressure and brilliant goalkicking was another feature of his match-winning kitbag. Johns kicked 917 goals for Newcastle (second in first grade history), 37 Origin goals for NSW (second in Blues' history) and 89 goals in Test matches (fourth-highest of all time for Australia). But he kicked arguably his greatest goal during the 2003 NRL season against St. George Illawarra. The Knights scored a last-minute try in the corner to lock the game up at 28-all, before Johns—backing up 48 hours after leading NSW to an Origin victory—stepped up and faded a brilliant conversion between the uprights after the siren.

RYAN GIRDLER Ryan Girdler became the first player to break the 90 per cent barrier in a season of goalkicking at premiership level. Girdler, rated a solid goalkicker in his previous five seasons with Illawarra and Penrith, hit a phenomenal vein of form during the Panthers' 1997 Super League season. The centre kicked 76 goals at an unprecedented 91.6 per cent, including a run of eight premiership games without a miss (a break in the competition for the World Club Challenge pool games denied Girdler a world record). The sharpshooter's next-best season performance was 46 goals at 80.7 per cent in 2004, his final season, while he kicked a club record-equalling 10 goals against Northern Eagles in 2000. Girdler kicked an Origin record 10 goals in New South Wales' 56-16 thrashing of Queensland in game three of the 2000 series to give him 16 for the series—another record tally. At the end of the year, Girdler broke the world record with a phenomenal haul of 17 goals in Australia's 110-4 thrashing of Russia at the 2000 World Cup, beating Mat Rogers' Australian record of 13 goals against Papua New Guinea set less than a month earlier.

DRAGONS NO.9S THWART BRONCOS St. George Illawarra pipped Brisbane in memorable Suncorp Stadium clashes in 2003 and 2006, with hookers Mark Riddell and Aaron Gorrell slotting booming goals to secure last-gasp victories. Darren Lockyer had put the Broncos 25-24 ahead late in the last-round match in 2003, but man of the match Riddell stepped up to boot a 41-metre penalty on fulltime to snatch victory. Three seasons later, the Origin-weary Broncos were set to record a momentous win over the Saints, until rookie winger Brett Morris crossed in the last minute to level the scores at 16-all. Left-footed rake Gorrell displayed nerves of steel to pilot the conversion from the sideline to break Brisbane hearts once again. Riddell and Gorrell kicked 198 and 94 goals for the Dragons respectively, both at respectable 70 per cent-plus success rates.

ICE-COOL GIDLEY Newcastle linchpin Kurt Gidley assumed the goalkicking duties for the Knights upon the retirement of Andrew Johns early in 2007. He quickly developed into one of the NRL's finest pressure kickers, landing two memorable conversions in the space of five weeks in 2010. The Newcastle captain slotted a sideline conversion in stormy conditions to steal a 6-4 win at the death of a dour round 15 clash with Parramatta—his first attempt of the night. Five rounds later he kicked a conversion from a similar position in Townsville with two minutes on the clock, sending the Knights' match with the Cowboys into golden point. Newcastle went down in extra-time, but Gidley's status amongst the game's best clutch goalkickers was assured.

JOHNATHAN THURSTON Champion halfback Johnathan Thurston's distinctive and incredibly effective goalkicking style is but another string on a crowded bow. The Cowboys superstar's right-to-left swing on his kicks from the tee appears to defy physics, but the phenomenal arc he produces has yielded scores of sideline conversions since 2005. Thurston's career goalkicking average in first grade is just below the 80 per cent mark, while in 2010 he kicked at a career-high 86 per cent with 43 goals from 50 attempts—including 25 in succession to start the season. He boasts an 80 per cent average in the pressure-cooker Origin arena, landing 52 goals from 65 attempts, while he is closing in on Mal Meninga's record of 69 goals. Thurston needs just five goals to become only the second player (after Mick Cronin) to kick 100 Test goals. The tenacious No.7 became a YouTube sensation in 2011 when he curled a shot at goal from the corner-post through the sticks at Kangaroos training.

POINTSCORING FAST FACTS

- The only two occasions 15 goals have been kicked by an individual in one match occurred in the space of a week in 1935—both against hapless premiership debutants Canterbury. NSW rep Les Griffin booted 15 goals in St. George's premiership record 91-6 thrashing of Canterbury, and pointscoring legend Dave Brown equalled the mark seven days later as Easts put the cleaners through the competition's newest team 87-7. Canterbury was subjected to another goalkicking master-class in the final round of 1935 as Wests halfback Les Mead booted 12 goals in a 65-11 drubbing.

- Manly's superlative fullback Graham Eadie is the only player to kick more than 12 goals in a match since 1935, landing 14 in a 70-7 mauling of Penrith in 1973. He booted 12 goals against Souths two seasons later, becoming the only player with two hauls of 12 goals or more to his name. The Sea Eagles legend held the premiership record for career goals, passing Eric Simms' mark in 1983, before Mick Cronin overtook him in 1985. Eadie kicked 100 goals or more in a season twice and 99 in his final season.

- Warriors fullback Ivan Cleary became the first player in 27 years to land 12 goals in first grade match when he kicked 12 goals from as many attempts in New Zealand's 68-10 thrashing of the hapless Northern Eagles early in 2002. No other player has managed 12 goals since Cleary's flawless afternoon in Auckland.

- Forward legend Harry Bath became the first player to kick 100 goals in a season in the twilight of his illustrious career. After booting eight goals in the Dragons' 1957 Grand Final victory—a record that still stands—Bath landed 108 goals as St. George cruised to another premiership in 1958, a mark that remains as a premiership record for a forward. Bath, who spent most of his career in England, kicked 240 goals in three seasons for the Saints.

- 1950s great Greg Hawick set an interstate record in 1957 when he booted 15 goals in NSW's 69-5 demolition of Queensland in Sydney. Only an intermittent goalkicker at club and representative level, Hawick's effort topped the previous record of Queensland's Dan O'Connor, who landed 12 in the Maroons' 45-8 victory over NSW in 1940.

FIELD GOAL EXPONENTS

The field goal, achieved by drop-kicking the ball in general play through the opposition's goal posts, has been a popular nuance of the game of Rugby League since the code's early days. Originally worth two points, field goals were lumped in with conversions and penalty goals in the scoring column until the mid-1960s, when they began to be recorded separately. But an explosion of field goal sharp-shooters during the back end of the decade saw the scoring play reduced to one point, effective from 1971.

South Sydney pointscoring machine Eric Simms and Easts goalkicker Kevin Ashley each landed 12 field goals in 1967, followed by Manly's future Immortal

Bob Fulton, with nine. Simms stepped it up a notch the following season with a phenomenal haul of 29 field goals, including three in a match on six occasions; champion St. George five-eighth Phil Hawthorne, a former Wallaby and future Australian Rugby League skipper, slotted 18 in his first season in the 13-a-side code, including four in a match against Balmain; Manly pair Fulton and Dennis Ward collected 14 field goals apiece; and Wests field goal merchant Barry Glasgow put 13 between the posts in 1968.

Glasgow equalled Simms' record of 29 field goals in 1969, while the Rabbitohs fullback set a mark to stand the test of time with five in a match against Penrith among his total of 19 for the season. Hawthorne was the field goal king in 1970 with 25, including field goals in six consecutive matches, but Simms left an indelible mark once again. He landed four field goals in Souths' 23-12 defeat of Manly in the Grand Final to take his season total to 20—one ahead of Fulton, who landed two field goals in the decider for the beaten Sea Eagles.

The burgeoning overreliance on the field goal as a scoring option prompted the game's authorities to reduce its value to one point in 1971. It had the desired effect: just 22 field goals were kicked in the first season following the rule change—down from a colossal 159 in 1970. Simms kicked just six of his premiership record 86 career field goals in the one-point era; likewise, Fulton's 58 career field goals included just 11 one-pointers; Hawthorne, who landed the first-ever one-pointer in a reserve grade game against Balmain, kicked only one field goal in 1971; and Glasgow landed just one field goal in three seasons for Norths after slotting 44 in the same period of time for the Magpies.

The field goal has endured as an integral part of Rugby League, however, providing the game with some of its most memorable moments. It remains the ultimate deadlock-breaker and has taken on extra importance since the advent of golden point extra-time in 2003, while modern-day field goal specialists such as Darren Lockyer and Chris Sandow are as important to their respective teams as Simms, Fulton, Hawthorne and Glasgow were four decades ago.

MOST PREMIERSHIP FIELD GOALS (SINCE 1964)

86—Eric Simms (1965-75)	44—Terry Lamb (1980-96)
58—Bob Fulton (1966-79)	35—Jason Taylor (1990-2001)
56—Phil Hawthorne (1968-72)	33—Ken Wilson (1971-83)
45—Barry Glasgow (1967-73)	33—Ben Elias (1982-94)
45—Neil Baker (1981-89)	30—Dennis Ward (1964-72)
44—Billy Smith (1963-76)	30—Tony Melrose (1980-89)

FIELD GOAL EXPONENTS OF THE ONE-POINT ERA

■ Ken Wilson was the man responsible for the only 1-0 scoreline in premiership history, kicking a field goal in Newtown's 1973 defeat of St. George *(see Bizarre Matches)*, and was one of the code's most accurate field goal sharpshooters over the ensuing decade. He landed 33 field goals for Newtown and Penrith between 1971 and 1983. Fittingly, Wilson kicked a field goal in his—and the Jets'—last premiership match, a 9-6 defeat of Canberra.

- One of the finest field goal merchants of the late-1960s, St. George great Billy Smith continued to plunder field goals after their value was halved. The Kangaroo halfback kicked 23 of his 44 career field goals when they were worth a solitary point, topping the premiership's field goal scorers in 1971 and 1973. Smith landed two field goals in a match on eight occasions, and three in a match twice—including a treble in the Dragons' 15-12 preliminary final defeat of Manly in 1971.

- Bulldogs legend Terry Lamb, a prolific try-scorer and point-scorer, was also one of the game's foremost field goal exponents during a record-breaking career. He kicked 44 one-pointers in 17 seasons with Wests and Canterbury, including a career-high 10 for the Bulldogs in 1986—he landed three in one match against Easts and another two in the preliminary final defeat of Balmain. Lamb potted a vital field goal in the 17-4 upset of Manly in the 1995 Grand Final, but it was an ill-timed one-pointer against Newcastle in 1992 that unfortunately ranks as the most memorable of his career. The Canterbury skipper—believing the scores were locked 10-all—snapped a late field goal in his side's 12-11 loss (see Minties Moments).

- Utility-back Neil Baker was the king of the field goal during the 1980s, potting 45 one-pointers in six seasons for Souths and Penrith. He kicked a phenomenal 20 in 1986—the highest season total in the one-point field goal era—which included three in a match against Canberra to lift the Rabbitohs to a 10-8 victory. Baker also bagged three in a 15-10 victory for Penrith over Norths in 1988.

- Former Wallaby Tony Melrose's rugby union background aided him in becoming one of the most potent field goal merchants of the 1980s. The versatile back bagged 30 field goals in 179 games for Parramatta, Souths, Manly and Easts. He kicked a career-high eight one-pointers in 1983 for the Rabbitohs, including two in a match in consecutive wins over Newtown and Canberra. In 1987 for the Roosters, Melrose landed two field goals in a 12-all draw with Balmain—one off each foot—and backed it up the following week with a booming 40-metre effort in the final minute to snatch a 15-14 victory from Penrith.

- Brilliant Balmain rake Ben Elias was one of the first 'halfback' style hookers and, accordingly, kicked 33 field goals during his career for the Tigers. Elias had a penchant for kicking one-pointers in big games: he kicked two field goals in a midweek playoff defeat of Norths and a key field goal in a 29-22 victory over Manly in the minor preliminary semi a week later; he landed a vital field goal in a 9-2 disposal of Cronulla in the 1988 preliminary final; and the wily rake kicked two field goals as man of the match in NSW's 27-12 victory in the 1994 Origin decider—his last match in a decorated career for the Blues.

- Ricky Stuart was a master of every facet of kicking the oval ball, and booting field goals was no exception. The dual international landed 27 one-pointers in a distinguished career with Canberra and Canterbury. Stuart kicked two field goals in a first grade match twice, including a 14-8 finals victory over Brisbane in 1995, and nailed one in Australia's 23-4 victory in the deciding Ashes Test of 1994.

- One of the sweetest strikers of the ball the game has seen, Jason Taylor landed 35 field goals during a career that saw him become the game's greatest point-scorer. Taylor's highest total in a season was seven, in 1994, which included field goals to twice sink defending premiers Brisbane—in an 11-10 regular season victory, and a memorable 30-metre effort to bundle the Broncos out of the finals 15-14 in the minor semi. Three years later, Taylor landed three field goals in an extra-time finals loss to the Roosters.

- Star Indigenous halfback John Simon was one of the 1990s' finest field goal exponents, kicking 23 in a 230-game, five-club career. Simon landed 13 in the 1997-98 seasons for Parramatta, including three in a 17-10 triumph over heavyweights Manly in 1997. He struck field goals in three consecutive weeks twice during his career, and landed a one-pointer for NSW that proved the difference in a series-sealing 15-14 defeat of Queensland in 1997.

- As arguably the greatest all-round player in Australian Rugby League's first century, it is no surprise Andrew Johns was among the best field goalkickers of his generation. Johns accumulated 22 one-pointers at club level for Newcastle and an Origin record four field goals for NSW.

- One of the greatest champions of the modern game, Darren Lockyer has had a knack of kicking crucial field goals throughout his career. Lockyer kicked 17 one-pointers for the Broncos up to the end of 2010, including a last-minute field goal in a 9-8 defeat of the Roosters to keep Brisbane's season alive; a late field goal to sink the Bulldogs in 2005; a field goal in the dying minutes of the 2006 Grand Final to seal a 15-8 upset of Melbourne; and a booming golden point effort to down the Titans 19-18—the ball bounced off each upright before dropping over the bar. Lockyer nailed a towering one-pointer came in the third match of the 2010 Origin series, an angled attempt from 46 metres out in Queensland's 23-18 victory. But the most memorable field goal of his career promises to be his last— just minutes after suffering a fractured cheekbone that would end his Broncos career, a bandaged Lockyer stepped up and kicked a golden point field goal to sink the Dragons in the 2011 semi-final, his last act in a Brisbane jumper and at Suncorp Stadium.

- Braith Anasta also possesses the uncanny ability to land the field goals that matter. The oft-maligned pivot's field goal was the difference in City Origin's 17-16 defeat of Country in 2003 and he landed 10 one-pointers in five seasons for the Bulldogs, including two in a semi-final defeat of Melbourne in 2003. But two field goals following his mid-career switch to the Roosters stand out even brighter— a 38-metre beauty in a 31-all draw with the Warriors in 2007; and one of the all time great field goals in the 2010 finals, after the siren to force the Roosters' match against the Tigers into extra-time *(see Finals Magic)*.

- Dynamic South Sydney halfback Chris Sandow has developed into arguably the NRL's foremost purveyor of field goal kicking since debuting in 2008. After kicking a crucial one-pointer on first grade debut in a 35-28 upset of the Warriors, Sandow capped an extraordinary comeback with a late field goal for a 29-28 victory over the Cowboys in just his third game on the way to rookie of the year honours. The Indigenous star landed seven field goals in 2011, including one of the best of all time from 49 metres out in golden point to down the Roosters 21-20. Sandow took his match-winning wares to Parramatta on a lucrative contract in 2012.

- St. George-Illawarra linchpin Jamie Soward has plundered field goals with monotonous regularity in recent seasons, piloting 16 one-pointers between the posts in 75 games since 2009. But none were more important than his deadlock-breaking strike late in the 2009 preliminary final against the Wests Tigers, steering the Dragons into the decider and ultimately premiership glory with a 13-12 victory. Soward projected his field goal prowess at age-group level, landing two field goals—including the match-winner from 40 metres out in extra-time—in the Roosters' 14-13 Jersey Flegg Grand Final defeat of Cronulla in 2004.

NOTABLE FIELD GOALS

- Dally Messenger was Australian Rugby League's first superstar, and some of his kicking deeds from the game's formative years have passed into folklore. One such field goal occurred for Eastern Suburbs against Glebe in 1911, when Messenger ran towards the sideline near halfway and launched a massive drop-kick in the opposite direction to which he was running, thus landing the most famous field goal of the premiership's early years.

- Crafty British half Dave Bolton kicked two field goals in consecutive weeks to help Balmain to an unlikely premiership in 1969. Bolton landed two in the Tigers' heart-stopping win over Manly in the preliminary final, before collecting another brace of field goals in the king-sized upset of Souths in the Grand Final. He kicked 21 field goals in 78 games for the Tigers during the two-point era.

- Andrew Farrar's only field goal in a decade-long stint with Canterbury was an important one—it proved the difference in the Bulldogs' 7-6 victory over St. George in the 1985 Grand Final. The rugged centre's kick put Canterbury ahead 7-0 and allowed his side to hold off a late rally by the Dragons.

- Former Kangaroo second-rower John Muggleton kicked one of the great regular season field goals for Parramatta in 1987. Playing in the centres, Muggleton had already contributed six goals as the Eels and Dragons entered the final minute locked at 20-all. Muggleton drilled an incredible 42-metre field goal in the shadows of the siren to clinch victory. It was Muggleton's first one-pointer in first grade—he kicked the only other field goal of his career three weeks later in a win over Wests.

- Opposing skippers and gun playmakers Peter Sterling and Michael Hagan embarked on an enthralling field goal duel in a 12-all draw between Parramatta and Newcastle in 1990. The Knights trailed 8-0 at halftime but fought back to level, and took the lead for the first time when Hagan potted the first field goal of his career. The Eels snatched the lead back 10-9 with a penalty goal and Sterling extended it with a one-pointer. A Newcastle penalty goal tied the scores again at 11-all, before Hagan and then Sterling landed their second field goals respectively for a fulltime deadlock. All time great Sterling kicked seven of his 15 career field goals during that 1990 season, while Hagan landed just one other one-pointer in a 185-game career.

- Greg Alexander's 38-metre gem in 1991 is arguably the greatest Grand Final field goal ever kicked. The Panthers trailed for most of the decider against Canberra, before squaring the match at 12-all with 10 minutes remaining. Alexander put Penrith in front in the 74th minute with a swinging drop-kick and the Panthers went on to win 19-12. 'Brandy' landed 14 one-pointers in a stellar career that saw him become Penrith's favourite son.

- Halfback genius Allan Langer kicked one of Origin football's greatest field goals for Queensland in 1992. Despite not having landed a one-pointer in five seasons of first grade with Brisbane, Langer slotted a late field goal in game two at Lang Park to sink the Blues 5-4 and keep the series alive. The following season, Langer kicked a vital deadlock-breaker in the Broncos' preliminary final defeat of Canterbury.

- Shaun Timmins landed just one field goal in 210 first grade games—for Illawarra in 1996—but kicked a famous one-pointer to win Origin's first golden point encounter. The scores were tied 8-all at fulltime in the first match of the 2004 series, before the makeshift NSW five-eighth unloaded with a 37-metre special in the third minute of extra-time.

- Rookie halfback Trent Hodkinson kicked Manly to victory against Souths in 2010 by landing two field goals in the final three minutes. The Rabbitohs overturned a 24-13 deficit to lead by a point in the dying minutes, but Hodkinson levelled the scores with three minutes on the clock. The boom No.7 repeated the effort with just over a minute to play to seal a thrilling 26-25 win. Incredibly, another field goal double for his new club Canterbury in 2011 snatched a golden point victory over Parramatta. Hodkinson knocked one over to level the scores at 7-all with two minutes remaining, before slotting a sensational 42-metre effort seven minutes into extra-time for the win.

- Just two days after Darren Lockyer's booming field goal for Queensland *(see above)*, Tigers genius Benji Marshall nailed a towering one-pointer from halfway against the Titans in 2010. Marshall landed the stunning long-range shot—just the third field goal of his career—on the stroke of halftime for a 9-8 lead. The kick ultimately proved the difference in a tense 15-14 win, and provided one of the true highlights of the 2010 NRL season *(see also Finals Magic, Golden Point and Bizarre Matches)*.

MID-SEASON SWITCHES

The increasingly regular practice of players changing clubs during the season has produced some fascinating sidelights and remarkable reversals of fortune.

JOHN ELIAS Colourful journeyman forward John Elias made an art form of switching clubs mid-season more than a decade before it became commonplace. A former Rabbitoh, Elias started 1986 with the Bulldogs but ended the year with Wests. Elias was later dumped by Easts in 1989, only to be snapped up by Balmain, playing against the Roosters in his first match in the black-and-gold. Balmain would become the most permanent home of a controversial career, but he departed halfway through 1994 to return to South Sydney for the remainder of the year.

ROD SILVA Big-stepping, free-running fullback Rod Silva created history in 1995 by becoming the first player to change clubs mid-season and win a premiership. Silva debuted for the Roosters in 1988 and was a standout during a fruitless period for the club. But he switched to the Bulldogs midway through 1995 after signing a Super League contract and being dumped to reserve grade by Roosters coach Phil Gould, making his first appearance for his new club in round 11. He quickly cemented the No.1 jersey and was integral to the Bulldogs' unlikely charge to the title. Silva scored a hat-trick in the final-round pummelling of the Cowboys, laid on a vital four-pointer to captain Terry Lamb in the preliminary final defeat of Canberra and scored the match-sealing try in the 17-4 Grand Final upset of Manly. Silva went on to score 56 tries in 100 games for the Bulldogs and spearheaded another remarkable finals run in 1998.

GRAHAM APPO Graham Appo's career was at a crossroads after being punted by Canberra early in 1998 for repeated off-field indiscretions, but the utility-back landed on his feet by joining the Adelaide Rams and setting a host of club records. Appo scored 12 tries and 116 points in 14 appearances for the battling Rams—adding the four tries he scored earlier in the year for Canberra, Appo finished among the NRL's top-10 point-scorers and try-scorers. Adelaide folded at the end of the season, leading Appo to unproductive stints with the Roosters and Cowboys, but his name will forever dominate the Rams' record books. He set marks for most tries in a season and total tries for the club (12); most tries in a match (three, vs. Gold Coast); most points in a season and total points for the club (116); most points in a match (20 [twice] vs. Gold Coast and Balmain); and most goals in a match (eight, vs. Balmain). Appo joined Super League club Huddersfield in 2001 and later enjoyed a successful stint with Warrington, scoring 23 tries and 216 points in the 2003 season.

CHRIS WALKER Electrifying three-quarter Chris Walker was a high-profile recruit for South Sydney in 2003, a six-game Queensland Origin rep boasting 40 tries from 67 first grade games for the Broncos. But after an unhappy start at the Rabbitohs, Walker was granted a release after just five appearances, despite having two seasons to run on his big-money contract. Walker joined the Roosters for the remainder of 2003, scoring 10 tries in 14 games (including a try off the bench against Souths in his third game), and played in the club's Grand Final loss to Penrith. He scored a try in the Roosters' loss to the Bulldogs in the 2004 decider, before subsequent stints with Melbourne, Gold Coast and Catalans, and an eventual return to the NRL with Parramatta in 2011.

LUKE MACDOUGALL The brother of former Kangaroo Adam 'Mad Dog' MacDougall, fellow three-quarter Luke MacDougall was consequently known as 'Mad Pup' and undertook two mid-season switches during his career. After debuting for the Sharks in 2002, MacDougall linked with South Sydney midway through 2003, scoring seven tries in nine games (including a last-round touchdown against the Sharks). He played a further three seasons with the Rabbitohs before signing with St George Illawarra at the end of 2006, but jumped ship again during 2007, this time joining his illustrious sibling at Newcastle. After an injury-riddled run, MacDougall resurfaced with Melbourne in 2010 before defecting to rugby union and then returning to the NRL with Canterbury in 2012.

JAMIE SOWARD A genuine match-winner at halfback or five-eighth, Jamie Soward had failed to deliver on his potential since breaking into first grade in 2005 with the Sydney Roosters. The club consequently granted him a mid-season release during 2007. Just six days after helping the Roosters to a 13-12 defeat of Cronulla, Soward kicked a decisive field goal to seal St. George Illawarra's 11-4 upset of Brisbane. Soward quickly became the Dragons' linchpin and key playmaker as the club claimed back-to-back minor premierships in 2009-10, before taking out a long-awaited title in the latter season. The quicksilver No.6 kicked six goals in the 32-8 Grand Final defeat of the Roosters and debuted for NSW the following season.

CLINT NEWTON Newcastle supporters were outraged with club officials when popular stalwart Clint Newton departed midway through 2007, citing differences with new coach Brian Smith. Newton had failed to gain an assurance from Smith that he would be retained by the Knights in 2008 and was subsequently granted an immediate release to join Melbourne. He had made his representative debut for Country Origin earlier in the season, but just a month later was suiting up for the Storm. Newton slotted seamlessly into the well-oiled Melbourne machine and the robust backrower picked up a premiership ring at the end of the season. He scored a try in the Storm's 34-8 thrashing of Manly in the Grand Final, becoming just the second player in history (after Rod Silva) to win a title after changing clubs mid-season. Newton headed to Super League in 2008 and became a permanent fixture for Hull KR before being lured back to the NRL in 2012 by Penrith.

SONNY BILL WILLIAMS A mid-season switch to French rugby union caused a massive stir in 2008. Bulldogs star and Kiwi international Sonny Bill Williams walked out on the embattled club to link with Toulon in arguably the year's biggest controversy. Williams became one of the most vilified figures in Australia, but he excelled in his new code, returning to New Zealand in 2010 and winning selection for the All Blacks.

MARK GASNIER Champion centre Mark Gasnier's defection to French rugby union a few months after Williams at the end of 2008 caused much consternation within Rugby League circles. One of the NRL's biggest stars with a surname as famous as any in the code, Gasnier had been used as a focal point of the advertising for the year-ending Centenary World Cup. Gasnier played two seasons for Stade Francais, before rejoining the Dragons midway through the 2010 NRL season. After blasting out the cobwebs with a few early appearances off the bench, the 29-year-old showed glimpses of his form of yesteryear and scored the opening try in St. George Illawarra's breakthrough Grand Final victory over the Roosters. Gasnier made a return to the representative arena with NSW in 2011 but retired at the end of the year.

BRETT FINCH Former New South Wales halfback Brett Finch was Parramatta's No.1 playmaker during 2007-08, but the Eels' dismal start to the 2009 NRL season under new coach Daniel Anderson brought matters to a head. Finch was granted a release after just four rounds and was playing for Melbourne before the end of April. Five-eighth had been a problem spot for Melbourne since Scott Hill left the club at the end of 2006, and Finch's mature displays outside halfback Cooper Cronk added another dimension to the Storm's armoury. After losing consecutive Grand Finals with the Roosters in 2003-04, Finch finally received a premiership ring following

Melbourne's 2009 Grand Final victory—ironically, against Parramatta. It turned sour the following season when the club's 2007 and 2009 premierships were stripped for salary cap breaches, while Melbourne was also forced to play for nothing in 2010. But Finch continued to produce typically wholehearted displays throughout a torturous season, despite being part of an inevitable player purge that saw him sign with Wigan for 2011.

NATHAN FIEN Former Queensland Origin rep Nathan Fien had been a tenacious, versatile contributor in over 100 games for the Warriors, controversially becoming a Kiwi international (he made his Test debut in 2006 on the basis of have a New Zealand-born grandmother, but it turned out it was in fact his great-grandmother and he was dropped from the squad [see Points Docked], before qualifying on residential grounds in 2008) and helping the club to the finals in 2007-08. But coach Ivan Cleary and the Warriors decided Fien was surplus to requirements two months into the 2009 season and released the feisty utility. Undeterred, St. George Illawarra eagerly recruited Fien for the remainder of the season—new Dragons coach Wayne Bennett had previously been involved with Fien at Origin level in 2001 and during the Kiwis' 2008 World Cup campaign. Fien slotted into St. George-Illawarra's squad and was a key component of the club's charge to a maiden minor premiership. Despite breaking his leg in the opening round of 2010, Fien returned late in the year and was a valuable bench weapon, scoring the last try in the Dragons' Grand Final victory over the Roosters. Fien also scored the epic match-winner in New Zealand's Four Nations final triumph at the end of the year.

SHANE TRONC A veteran of 125 games in six seasons with North Queensland, giant front-rower Shane Tronc took up a deal with Wakefield Trinity for the 2010 Super League season. But Tronc and his wife were unable to settle into English life and he played just 11 games before returning to Australia. Incredibly, Tronc suited up for his first game for the Broncos just 12 days after his last game for the Wildcats and only hours after flying back from England. The skilful prop quickly cemented a starting spot in Brisbane's pack and played all 18 remaining matches of the 2010 NRL season.

RYAN TANDY Burly prop Ryan Tandy switched clubs midway through his first season in the NRL, joining South Sydney after starting the year with St George Illawarra. Following a stint with Wests Tigers and three matches for Ireland at the 2008 World Cup, Tandy joined Melbourne, breaking into first grade late in 2009 and coming off the bench in the Storm's Grand Final win over Parramatta. The premiership was stripped the following season for salary cap breaches and Tandy left for Canterbury mid-season—a mutually beneficial arrangement that allowed Melbourne to ease some cap pressure. Tandy quickly cemented a starting front-row spot for Canterbury, but became embroiled in a betting scandal late in the season, painted as the main protagonist in a plunge on the 'first scoring play' option in a match against North Queensland. He was arrested and charged early in 2011, and despite maintaining his innocence, Tandy was understandably stood down by the Bulldogs. A court found Tandy guilty of the fixing charges later in the year.

STEVE MICHAELS Formerly one of Brisbane's hottest outside-back prospects, Steve Michaels' bewildering loss of form and confidence in the second half of 2009 eventually saw him dropped from first grade. Michaels slipped down the club's backline pecking order and was granted a release to join the neighbouring Gold Coast after making just one appearance in the first half of 2010 for the Broncos. After biding his time behind a talented batch of Titans centres, injuries gave Michaels a chance in round 20 and he held a starting spot for the remainder of the season. Michaels played in both of the Titans' finals matches, while his former club missed the playoffs for the first time since 1991.

THE JOURNEYMEN

The era of the salary cap has rendered the one-club player a rare commodity, giving birth to a generation of transient players moving from club to club, or city to city, to chase contracts. Some of the players slapped with the 'journeyman' tag are high-profile stars constantly in demand from several clubs, but most are second-tier players forced to take their opportunities, wherever they may arise.

HERB GILBERT One of the game's early stars, 1911-12 Kangaroo tourist Herb Gilbert was one of the few players in Rugby League's formative years to appear for more than two clubs. The residential restrictions in place at the time—stating that a player must live in the district of the team he played for—limited the now-common practice of players switching regularly from club to club. The former Wallaby developed into one of Rugby League's finest centres after changing codes to play with South Sydney in 1911. After becoming a dual international in his first season, Gilbert left Sydney at the end of 1912 to play for English club Hull, captaining the club to Challenge Cup success in 1914. Gilbert returned to play another year for Souths in 1915, before spending a solitary season with Eastern Suburbs prior to joining Western Suburbs in 1917. His four seasons with Wests were marked by a return to the Australian Test team. Gilbert retired after captaining St. George during their 1921 entry into the premiership.

ROY LISTON Like Gilbert, Roy Liston played for four different clubs during the stringent residential rule era. Liston first appeared in first grade in 1920, playing 12 games in Annandale's final season. A handy goalkicker, Liston spent three seasons in Balmain colours (1921-22 and 1924) with a season for Glebe (1923) sandwiched in between. Liston finished his first grade career with a stint for Western Suburbs in the late-1920s.

PHIL BLAKE One of the most prolific try-scorers in the game's history, mercurial utility-back Phil Blake spread his 262 first grade appearances over stints with six clubs. Blake burst onto the scene as a brilliant halfback with Manly in 1982, playing in two Grand Finals and setting a premiership record for tries in a season by a halfback in 1983. After five seasons at Brookvale, Blake joined Souths for four years, winning the Dally M Five-eighth of the Year award and New South Wales selection in 1989 as the Rabbitohs took out the minor premiership. Disappointing one-season stints with Norths and Canberra in the early-1990s followed, but he made another Grand Final appearance with St. George in 1993. Blake linked with the Auckland Warriors for their inaugural premiership season in 1995, scoring their first try and the club's first haul of four tries among 14 for the season from 17 games. Blake retired at the end of 1997 after three seasons in Auckland, before eventually moving into rugby union coaching and joining the Wallabies' set-up in 2010.

LES CLEAL Although Les Cleal only played one season of premiership football, he fits the 'journeyman' mould. The brother of fearsome Kangaroo second-rower Noel Cleal, Les played 14 games alongside his brother at the Roosters in 1982. But he played with a dozen other clubs during his career—predominantly in country NSW—where he achieved unparalleled success. His other foray into professional football was an off-season stint with English club Widnes in 1986-87.

JOHN ELIAS Infamous backrower John Elias turned out for five premiership clubs, began and finished his first grade career with Souths and played for two clubs in the same season three times. Notorious for his life on the wrong side of the law, depicted in his explosive autobiography *Sin Bin*, released in 2010, Elias was graded by Newtown but made his first grade debut for the Rabbitohs in 1984. After a stint in France and a premiership in the Brisbane competition under Wayne Bennett at Souths Magpies in 1985, Elias linked with his junior club Canterbury in 1986. But he was released mid-season and joined Wests until the end of 1987. Elias experienced a fruitless period after moving to Easts and was dumped midway through 1989, only to be picked up by Balmain. He played the following three seasons with the Tigers to bring up 100 first grade games, but left at the end of 1992 and played the following season with Metropolitan Cup side Guildford. Elias rejoined the Tigers in 1994 to play under Wayne Pearce, but departed mid-season and finished the year—and his first grade career—with South Sydney. The colourful character later coached the Lebanon national side and in French club Rugby League, but became embroiled in the betting scandal emanating from an NRL match between Canterbury and North Queensland late in 2010.

GRAHAM MACKAY A Test and Origin representative, blockbusting winger Graham Mackay appeared for six Australian sides and three UK Super League clubs during a 15-year professional career. Mackay debuted for Wests in 1988 and spent three seasons with the Magpies, but his career took off when he was picked by Penrith in the controversial player draft. He won a Grand Final with the Panthers in 1991, debuted for NSW the following season and scored two tries against Papua New Guinea in his only Test appearance later in 1992. Mackay followed his Penrith mentor Phil Gould to the Roosters in 1995 but lasted just one season before heading north to play with the South Queensland Crushers. He captained the Gold Coast Chargers to their maiden finals appearance in the 1997 ARL competition and spent a modest season with Manly in 1999. Heading to England, Mackay was named in the Super League Dream Team with Leeds and represented Scotland at the World Cup in 2000, won a Grand Final with Bradford in 2001 and retired after a fruitful season with Hull in 2002.

KEVIN AND TONY IRO Kevin and Tony Iro rank amongst New Zealand's finest footballing brothers. Devastating centre Kevin played the first of 34 Tests for the Kiwis in 1987, while winger-cum-backrower Tony debuted a year later, going on to play 25 Tests. Both had similarly colourful, globetrotting careers. The Aucklanders both played under Graham Lowe for the all-conquering Wigan side during the late 1980s, before following Lowe to Manly—Tony in 1990 and Kevin a year later. Kevin returned to England after two seasons and joined Leeds, while Tony stayed with Manly until he linked with Eastern Suburbs in 1994. The pair reunited at the Hunter Mariners in 1997, but they headed in opposite directions after the club folded at the end of the year—Kevin went east, returning home to play for the Warriors, while Tony ventured west, adding experience and class to the Adelaide Rams' squad. Kevin moved back to England again in 1999 and spent three seasons with St. Helens, winning Super League Grand Finals in 1999 and 2000. Tony retired after a quality season for South Sydney in 1999 and eventually moved into coaching as an assistant to Ivan Cleary with the Warriors and as part of the Kiwis' Test set-up.

DARRIEN DOHERTY Perhaps the lowest-profile of the journeymen profiled in this chapter, Darrien Doherty is the equal-most prolific collector of clubs in premiership history—the hardworking backrower turned out for seven clubs during an 11-season first grade career. Doherty debuted for Penrith in 1990, before cracking the top grade again with Western Suburbs in 1993-94. He joined the Bulldogs for 1995, but experienced his best year with Illawarra the following season, playing a career-high 20 matches. Doherty was part of the Hunter Mariners' squad in the Newcastle-based club's only season, starting in the World Club Challenge final loss to Brisbane. He spent 1998 with Adelaide before the Rams, too, folded. His last club was North Queensland, with whom he spent the 1999 and 2000 seasons, retiring with a total of 67 first grade games to his credit.

SCOTT WILSON Utility-back Scott Wilson's career was as widespread as it was colourful and controversial. He debuted as an illegal replacement for Souths in 1988 *(see Points Docked)* and was sacked by the Rabbitohs in 1990 after testing positive to recreational drugs. After two seasons of varying success with North Sydney, Wilson joined Canterbury in 1993 and cemented the club's fullback spot, starting in the No.1 jersey in the 1994 Grand Final against Canberra. But after a difficult day in the decider in a well-beaten side, Wilson linked with the lowly Gold Coast Seagulls in 1995. His fortunes improved when he headed to Perth to join the Western Reds and he won representative honours during Super League NSW's Tri-Series campaign in 1997. The Reds' demise at the end of the year saw Wilson traipse back across the continent to play for North Queensland in 1998, but he was released and finished the season back at Canterbury.

DAVE WATSON Talented Kiwi utility-back Dave Watson played 15 Tests for New Zealand during a nomadic career in England, appearing for Hull KR, Halifax and Bradford Northern over five northern winters. Watson split his international appearances between fullback, wing, centre and five-eighth, playing his last Test against Great Britain in 1993. He then embarked on a four-season stay in the Australian premiership—with four different clubs! Watson was impressive in a nine-game stint for Cronulla in 1994, before playing two late-season matches for Balmain in 1995. He was superb at fullback for the Gold Coast Chargers in 1996 and was a regular five-eighth for the soon-to-be-axed South Queensland Crushers in 1997. Watson finished his professional career with two seasons for Super League club Sheffield Eagles, playing his part in one of the biggest Challenge Cup upsets of all time—the Eagles' 17-8 upset of Wigan in the 1998 final at Wembley.

KEVIN CAMPION A versatile, tough-as-nails forward, Kevin Campion's first grade career spanned almost 250 games, three states and two countries. Debuting in 1993, Campion spent his formative seasons with Gold Coast before joining St. George in 1996 and playing a Grand Final in his only season with the club. Campion joined Adelaide for the 1997 Super League season, but enjoyed his greatest success during a three-season stint with the Broncos, winning premierships in 1998 and 2000. After representing Ireland at the 2000 World Cup, Campion linked with the Warriors and played four Origin matches for Queensland, while also becoming part of a select group of players to turn out in Grand Finals for three different clubs in 2002 (a feat previously achieved by Phil Sigsworth, Glenn Lazarus and Anthony Mundine, and only Joe Galuvao since). Best suited to the backrow, Campion was synonymous with having his head split open as his career wore on, and the bandaged warrior retired at the end of 2004 after two seasons with North Queensland.

TYRAN SMITH Eight-Test Kiwi Tyran Smith played first grade for an equal-record seven premiership clubs. Beginning his career as a lanky winger for Souths in 1993, Smith developed into a skilful, dynamic lock over the following three seasons in Rabbitohs' colours. Signing with Super League, Smith began the 1997 season with North Queensland and represented New Zealand in the Anzac Test and Tri-Series, but ended the year with the Hunter Mariners, partnering fellow 'most clubs' record-holder Darrien Doherty in the backrow in Hunter's World Club Challenge final loss to Brisbane. He returned to his birthplace of Auckland to play for the Warriors in 1998, before joining Balmain in 1999 and winning the Wests Tigers' player of the year going in the merged outfit's inaugural season a year later. After playing his last Test for New Zealand in 2000 and representing New Zealand Maori at the World Cup, Smith left the Tigers at the end of 2001 for the nation's capital. Smith played some of the best football of his career in a four-season stint with Canberra, retiring at the end of 2005 after 188 first grade appearances.

TIM MADDISON Burly forward Tim Maddison, the son of 1973 Kangaroo Ken, started and finished his career with Newcastle, playing for four clubs in between. Maddison debuted for the Knights in 1993 but struggled to break into the club's star-studded first grade pack, joining the Sydney City Roosters after captaining the Knights to a reserve grade premiership in 1995. He played finals football for Sydney City before being one of Hunter's most consistent players during the 1997 Super League season. Three mixed years with Cronulla preceded a two-season stint with North Queensland, where he brought up his 100th first grade appearance before being sent off and slapped with a 10-week striking suspension for a sickening late shot on Roosters halfback Justin Holbrook in 2002. Maddison's return to Newcastle in 2003 garnered just two first grade games.

BRETT KIMMORLEY Evergreen halfback Brett Kimmorley does not fit the typical journeyman profile—he played 20 Tests for Australia, 10 Origins for NSW and was the focal point of his club side for the bulk of his career. Kimmorley won a reserve grade premiership and made his top grade debut for Newcastle in 1995 but, stuck behind Andrew Johns as the Knights' first-choice No.7, he joined Hunter for their 1997 Super League season and represented the rebel organisation's Australian representative side. He followed several teammates to the fledgling Melbourne Storm in 1998 after the Mariners folded and become a superstar of the NRL. A Churchill medallist in Melbourne's 1999 Grand Final victory, Kimmorley made his Test debut at the end of the year and played Origin for the first time the following season. He was a high-priced recruit for the Northern Eagles in 2001 but left after only one season, linking with his former Storm coach Chris Anderson at Cronulla. After a rocky start, Kimmorley set several pointscoring records with the Sharks and played 140 games for the club between 2002 and 2008. He guided the Sharks to a preliminary final berth in his first and last seasons with the club, before doing the same in his first year with the Bulldogs in 2009—his sixth premiership club. Kimmorley retired at the end of 2010 after becoming the first halfback to bring up 300 first grade appearances.

JOHN CARLAW Consistent centre John Carlaw won a reserve grade title with Newcastle in 1995, but had to wait until 1997 to debut in first grade—with hometown Super League rivals Hunter Mariners. Carlaw joined several ex-Mariners at the Storm in 1998 and played finals football, but linked with Balmain in 1999. He was one of West Tigers' best during 2000-01 before joining the New Zealand Warriors. His late try in the preliminary final against Cronulla propelled the Auckland-based club into the 2002 Grand Final, but he struggled to hold down a first grade spot in 2003. Carlaw joined his sixth premiership club in 2004, making 15 appearances for St. George Illawarra in his only season with the merged entity. Carlaw finished his eight-season first grade career with 48 tries in 151 games.

JOE GALUVAO Auckland-born Joe Galuvao earned his first grade spurs with the Warriors as an outside back, but moved on to play in Grand Finals for three different clubs as a quality forward. He debuted in 1998 and played 27 games for Auckland before representing Samoa at the 2000 World Cup. Joining lowly Penrith in 2002, Galuvao was a major factor in the club's remarkable surge to the 2003 premiership, forming a devastating second-row combination with fellow Kiwi-Samoan Tony Puletua. Galuvao turned out in four Tests for New Zealand in 2003-04. He linked with Souths in 2006, but was released with a year to run on his contract and advised to join the ministry by high-profile club owner Russell Crowe following a personally disappointing 2007 campaign. Parramatta snapped up his services, however, and Galuvao provided tremendous service in two seasons with the Eels, scoring a vital try in the 2009 preliminary final defeat of the Bulldogs before coming off the bench in the Grand Final loss to Melbourne. A mainstay of Manly's pack in 2010-11, Galuvao stepped into the breach created by injured prop and co-captain Jason King in the latter season. The 33-year-old collected his second premiership ring after the Sea Eagles' 24-10 defeat of his first NRL club in the 2011 decider, and signed on to remain at Brookvale in 2012—extending his career at least five years past Crowe's short-sighted recommendation.

CHRIS WALKER An undeniable game-breaker, controversial three-quarter Chris Walker played six Origin matches for Queensland early in his career, but was unable to settle after leaving the Brisbane Broncos as a 22-year-old. Walker scored 40 tries in four seasons with Brisbane before joining Souths in 2003, but walked out on a rich deal at the club after playing just five matches. He switched to the Sydney Roosters and played in the 2003-04 Grand Finals, but was released by the club in 2005. The erratic centre/winger spent an uninspiring 2006 season with the Melbourne Storm before rejuvenating his career somewhat with the fledgling Gold Coast Titans in 2007. Walker scored the club's first try, but injury ruined much of 2007-08 before he bounced back with a strong 2009 season, playing in the club's maiden finals series. Unable to secure a contract for 2010, Walker joined several expat Australians at Super League club Catalans for one season before Parramatta threw him a lifeline for 2011. Walker made just five appearances for the Eels and retired at the end of the season with 81 tries in 151 NRL games to his name.

DAVID KIDWELL Christchurch-born centre/backrower David Kidwell travelled all the way to South Australia for a first grade start, spending 1997-98 with the Adelaide Rams. A move to Parramatta in 1999 kick-started his career and he made the first of 25 Test appearances for New Zealand while playing for the Eels. After a disappointing 2000 season, Kidwell joined Super League side Warrington in 2001, before returning to the NRL early in 2002. Kidwell made 19 appearances for the Sydney Roosters, but dropped out of the first grade squad during the finals series and missed out on a Grand Final victory. He proved to be a quality buy for Melbourne from 2003, playing over 100 first grade games in four seasons, but he was recruited by the big-spending Rabbitohs and departed the Storm after the 2006 Grand Final loss to Brisbane. Kidwell experienced three injury-interrupted seasons for Souths and retired at the end of 2009 to concentrate on coaching, guiding the club's Toyota Cup side to the 2010 Grand Final before rejoining the Storm as part of Craig Bellamy's staff in 2011.

CULT HEROES

The qualities that garner cult hero status in Rugby League are fundamentally indefinable—the game's supporters latch onto certain players at a rate that does not necessarily correlate with their on-field ability (just two of the players listed below have played Test football for Australia). Wild hair, an explosive or flamboyant playing style, or an unusual name are just some of the traits that have turned first grade footballers into cult figures, with their popularity often transcending parochial club support. The game experienced a boom of cult heroes in the 1980s and the characters spawned during that era are among the most fondly recalled players of all time. Interestingly, 14 of the 15 cult heroes celebrated below are either front-rowers or wingers (the exception being giant second-rower Ron Gibbs), suggesting powerhouses and speedsters have a sizeable head start in becoming a fan favourite—as long as their hair also fits the bill.

GEOFF ROBINSON A veteran of over 200 grade games for Canterbury (including 139 in first grade), Geoff Robinson was nicknamed 'The Wild Colonial Boy' due to his long dark hair and bushranger beard. In contrast to the style of the Canterbury 'Entertainers' of the early-1980s, Robinson's kamikaze style of football played more of a role in gaining cult status with Bulldogs fans than his trademark appearance. The bruising prop debuted in the blue-and-white in 1977 and later became famous as the player who broke down the 'Parramatta Wall' *(see Signature Moves)*. 'Robbo' was one of the premiership's most feared forwards during the late-1970s and early-1980s, winning Grand Finals under Ted Glossop in 1980 and Warren Ryan in 1984, before bowing out after Canterbury's loss in the 1986 decider. Ignored by rep selectors throughout his career, the unassuming Robinson thoroughly embodied the spirit of the cult hero.

ZIGGY NISZCZOT Setting a record for most Zs in a name, sporting a moustache and high-octane wing-play was a perfect recipe for cult hero status for Newcastle product Ziggy Niszczot. He joined South Sydney in 1980 and scored two tries on his Origin debut for New South Wales in 1982. Assuming the club captaincy—unusual for a winger—Niszczot led the Rabbitohs to the 1984 finals after a three-season absence, before leaving the Sydney premiership at the end of the year with a record of 39 tries in 114 games as a Redfern crowd favourite.

KERRY HEMSLEY Fearless Balmain forward Kerry Hemsley also perfectly captured the essence of the cult hero. Instantly recognisable with his long hair and beard, Hemsley may not have reaped the same representative rewards as fellow Tigers forwards Steve Roach, Paul Sironen and Wayne Pearce, but he was equally popular with club supporters. Hemsley was one of premiership's true enforcers, playing 135 games in the black-and-gold from 1980 to 1988 and winning a Challenge Cup final at Wembley in 1985 for Wigan alongside Brett Kenny and John Ferguson. He played in the Tigers' gallant loss to Canterbury in the 1988 Grand Final before finishing his career in England. Hemsley proved time had not diminished his appeal when he was given a standing ovation while he rode around Leichhardt Oval on his trademark Harley Davidson during a tribute to former club greats before a Wests Tigers match two decades later.

RON GIBBS 'Rambo' Ronnie Gibbs burst into the consciousness of Australian Rugby League fans after joining Manly in 1986. Originally a centre from Newcastle, Gibbs had a limited impact in three seasons with Easts. But he was a sensation after switching to the forwards under Bob Fulton at Manly with an explosive running game and punishing defence. Easily identified by his giant stature and trademark headgear, Gibbs earned the ire of the previously adoring Sea Eagles fans after news broke in 1987 that he had signed with the fledgling Gold Coast-Tweed Giants for their premiership debut the following season. But his contributions on the field for Manly continued to flourish—his chip-and-chase try against Canterbury late in 1987 was one of the most memorable tries of the decade and he featured in the club's Grand Final victory at the end of the season. His career wound down with disappointing stints for Gold Coast and Wests, but the most enduring image of Gibbs is as a human missile cult hero dressed in maroon and white.

TERRY REGAN Playing just 78 first grade games in six seasons for Balmain, Easts and Canberra, fearless prop/second-rower Terry Regan ranked as one of the players opposition sides least liked to come up against during the 1980s. An aggressive, punishing defender, Regan rose to prominence playing for Cessnock under coach Gary Johns, the father of Newcastle greats Andrew and Matthew Johns. He represented Country Firsts and won the NSW Country Player of the Year award in 1981, earning himself a contract with Balmain for the following season—and an instant cult following in Sydney. After one season with the Tigers that netted 19 first grade appearances and a reserve grade premiership, Regan joined Eastern Suburbs but frequently found himself in hot water with officials for his take-no-prisoners tackling approach. He was a popular, if intermittent, member of the Raiders' line-up after shifting to the nation's capital in 1985 and played his final first grade match off the bench in Canberra's 18-8 loss to Manly in the 1987 Grand Final. The uncompromising forward finished his professional career with a season for English club Hull.

JOE KILROY 'Smokin' Joe Kilroy was one-of-a-kind on the Brisbane Rugby League scene in the 1980s. Man of the match in Brisbane Norths' defeat of Souths in the 1980 BRL Grand Final, Kilroy was a proud motorcycle club member, joining Brothers in 1984 with a Harley Davidson chopper as his sign-on fee. Kilroy's image as something of an outlaw garnered the versatile back a substantial cult following, as did his trademark handlebar moustache. But he displayed the on-field class to warrant the fanfare. The Aboriginal speedster was also extremely popular with Queensland's Indigenous youth. An electrifying performer best suited to wing or fullback, Kilroy was voted the best fullback in the world by British scribes in the early-1980s and toured Papua New Guinea and Britain with a Queensland representative side in 1983, but Origin selection eluded him for much of his career. Kilroy spent an off-season with English club Halifax and was a foundation Bronco, scoring a try in the club's 1988 premiership debut thrashing of Manly. He belatedly made his Origin debut on the wing later that season. Kilroy played in the first and third matches of Queensland's series cleansweep, crossing for a try in the latter encounter, but was jailed in 1989 on drugs-related charges. The enigmatic flyer returned to play one last match for the Broncos in 1991.

ADRIAN TOOLE An unlikely cult hero, no-frills front-rower Adrian Toole was nevertheless an overwhelming crowd favourite in 130 games for the Bears. A Norths junior, Toole debuted in 1985 but did not become a permanent fixture in first grade until 1988. The crowd's low-pitched call of 'Tooooooooolllle' rung out over North Sydney Oval each time the reliable prop carted the ball up during the late-1980s and early-1990s. Toole played 69 consecutive first grade games between 1990 and 1992, including all three matches of the Bears' heartbreaking 1991 finals campaign. He retired after coming off the bench in Norths' 20-10 loss to Newcastle during the 1995 finals.

HITRO OKESENE Despite playing just 22 first grade games for the Auckland Warriors from 1995 to 1997, prop/hooker Hitro Okesene is an oft-remembered figure by supporters from the club's formative years. Nicknamed 'Nitro Glycerine' for his explosive playing style as much as the obvious similarity to his name, Okesene made his Test debut for the Kiwis in 1994 after starring for Counties-Manakau in the New Zealand domestic competition. Short for a prop, the nuggety Okesene was an instant hit with Warriors fans during the club's 1995 debut season. With his long hair flailing as he pulled off a ferocious tackle or made a trademark, head-down charge into opposition defences, Okesene played 17 first grade games and won selection in New Zealand's 1995 World Cup squad. He came off the bench in both pool games and the extra-time semi-final loss to Australia, but was relegated at club level, playing in twin reserve grade Grand Final losses in 1996-97. An import for Carlisle in the late-1980s and early-1990s, Okesene's nomadic career continued with stints for Hull, Featherstone and Workington Town between 1998 and 2003.

MARK TOOKEY Burly front-rower Mark Tookey was a custom-made cult hero. Debuting with the South Queensland Crushers in 1996, the sight of Tookey launching his ample frame into opposition defences became a crowd-pleasing feature of the late-1990s and early-2000s during subsequent stints with Parramatta and the Warriors. Similar to the crowd tribute that was afforded to Bears fan-favourite Adrian Toole, the rumbling call of 'Toooooookks' could be heard when the goateed Tookey came into the action. He played 40 games in two seasons with the Eels, including all five of the club's finals appearances in 1998-99, before joining the Warriors in 2000. The robust prop was not engineered for long spells on the field, fitting squarely into the impact player category, but he emerged as a key figure in the Auckland-based club's historic charge to a maiden Grand Final appearance in 2002. Tookey departed the NRL in 2004 after 125 first grade games and finished his professional career with Super League stints for Castleford and London.

MARCUS BAI An absolute legend in his homeland of Papua New Guinea, powerful winger Marcus Bai was one of the most popular and recognisable figures during the Melbourne Storm's formative years. Bai debuted for the Kumuls at the 1995 World Cup before making his first grade debut for the Gold Coast Chargers in 1997—the same year he represented Rest of the World in a Test against Australia. But he genuinely rose to prominence the following season, playing all 27 matches in the Storm's debut season and scoring 14 tries (including a dazzling hat-trick against heavyweights Newcastle) to be named Dally M Winger of the Year. The overwhelming crowd favourite featured in Melbourne's Grand Final victory in 1999 and left the club at the end of 2003 with a club record 70 tries from 144 games. The northern end of Olympic Park was unofficially dubbed the 'Marcus Bai Stand' by a fanatical throng of supporters, a tradition that has carried over into Melbourne's new home ground AAMI Stadium. Bai proved equally popular in Britain, scoring 26 tries in his first season with Leeds on the way to Grand Final victory in the 2004 Super League competition. He retired after spending the 2006 season with Bradford, boasting a record of 126 tries in 243 Australian first grade and European Super League games.

WILLIE MASON A 196cm, 115kg wrecking ball of polarity for most of his career, outspoken Test forward Willie Mason began his first grade tenure as one of the NRL's most popular cult favourites. The massive afro hairstyle that sat atop Mason's equally huge frame encouraged a sea of imitators in the crowd at Bulldogs games during the early-2000s. Mason rose to prominence during the club's record-breaking 2002 season that unravelled after revelations of salary cap breaches (see Points Docked). His unstoppable charges with the ball and monstering defence inspired commentating luminary Ray Warren's memorable line: "I bet every club wishes it had a Willie this big." Mason made his Test debut at the end of 2002 and was an automatic selection for Australian and NSW teams for several seasons, finishing with 24 Tests and 13 Origin appearances to his credit. But as his wardrobe of representative jumpers multiplied, so did his candid and controversial comments in the media, eroding Mason's formerly sky-high popularity. He left the Bulldogs and then the Roosters in acrimonious circumstances, before spending one season for North Queensland after every other club baulked at signing the divisive enforcer. Mason departed for the European Super League at the end of 2010, but his stint with Hull KR also ended prematurely on bad terms.

MATT PETERSEN Steady winger Matt Petersen's main claim to cult hero status was a memorable hairstyle. Nicknamed 'Sideshow Bob' for his uncanny follicular resemblance to the homicidal character from cartoon TV show The Simpsons, Petersen became a crowd favourite during stints with the Cowboys, Eels and Titans. He scored an impressive 54 tries in 94 games between 2002 and 2008, and was Parramatta's top try-scorer in 2003 and 2004 with 14 in each season. Petersen sported an unusual pedigree—another common trait for cult figures. Born in Western Australia, Petersen played for the United States against Australia in Philadelphia following the Kangaroos' 2004 Tri-Nations campaign (see Stars and Stripes), qualifying through his American father.

DAVID WILLIAMS Few players have risen to cult hero status as swiftly as Sea Eagles winger David Williams. Making his NRL debut in 2008, Williams' bushy beard quickly saw him dubbed 'The Wolfman' by fans, but he backed up the adoration with a sensational rookie season on the flank. Williams scored 14 tries in 20 games, including a touchdown in Manly's 40-0 Grand Final defeat of Melbourne, and rivalled departing club legend Steve Menzies in the popularity stakes. His meteoric rise continued with selection in Australia's World Cup squad at the end of the season. Williams scored a hat-trick on Test debut against Papua New Guinea and crossed again in the Kangaroos' shock loss to the Kiwis in the World Cup final. But after representing NSW in 2009, his career was stymied for more than two years by a series of injuries.

FUIFUI MOIMOI Jarryd Hayne provided the brilliance, but the muscle behind Parramatta's incredible charge from the NRL cellar to the 2009 Grand Final came from Kiwi cult hero prop Fuifui Moimoi. Shown the door at Souths without playing a first grade game, Tongan-born Moimoi joined the Eels in 2004, finally cementing a permanent top grade berth in 2007. After playing two internationals for Tonga in 2006, the stocky front-rower made his New Zealand Test debut in 2007 during the Kiwis' disastrous post-season international schedule. On top of his bullish, defence-scattering charges and ferocious tackling, Moimoi possessed several cult hero traits: an unusual name; a uniquely shy off-field demeanour; and trademark hairstyles ranging from the traditional afro to coloured dreads. Moimoi's form skyrocketed at the same rate as his adoring fanbase during the Eels' late-season charge in 2009. He turned 30 in Grand Final week and celebrated with one of the modern era's most memorable individual tries late in the decider against Melbourne—the bulldozing touchdown pegged his side back into the match before the gallant Eels went down 23-16. Moimoi won a recall to the Kiwis' squad for the 2009 Four Nations campaign, and despite patchy NRL form in 2010, he brought up 100 first grade appearances for the Eels. He remains an overwhelming crowd favourite at Parramatta Stadium, while Eels teammate Shane Shackleton's parody of Moimoi on *The Footy Show* has further enhanced the enforcer's profile.

GEORGE ROSE Tipping the scales at 115kg, burly George Rose is a tailor-made front-row cult hero. Rose debuted for the Roosters in 2004 but a move to Manly in 2006 kick-started his first grade career. The Bathurst junior missed all of 2008 with injury—ruling him out of the Sea Eagles' premiership success—but he returned better than ever the following season. Although far from an 80-minute player, Rose's high-impact charges and refined ball skills have made him a beloved figure at Brookvale. Rose represented the Indigenous All-Stars in the inaugural clash with the NRL All-Stars in 2010 and retained his spot in 2011 and 2012, with the larger-than-life character sporting a star shaved into the side of his head. He won a belated premiership ring in Manly's 2011 Grand Final triumph over the Warriors.

MINTIES MOMENTS

The popular lolly Minties, originating in Australia in the 1920s, became synonymous with promotional cartoons and later television ads depicting mishaps or unfortunate events, accompanied by the immortal slogan "It's moments like these you need Minties." During the 1980s and 1990s, many of these ads featured a montage of calamitous sporting moments, similar to the gaffes illustrated in this chapter. But it is doubtful a bag of Minties would have consoled these unfortunate individuals.

STEVE MAVIN Perhaps the most infamous finals performance of all time belongs to flamboyant South Sydney three-quarter Steve Mavin. After enjoying a fine rookie season in 1987 in the centres, Mavin was switched to the wing late in the year and experienced a minor semi-final nightmare on the flank against Canberra. The Raiders terrorised Mavin with a pinpoint kicking game and scored three tries down his wing after just 16 minutes, at which point he was hooked by coach George Piggins. A distraught Mavin had left the ground by the time Canberra finished the scoring blitz at 46-12. Mavin went on to chalk up over a century of first grade games with Souths and Canterbury, but his career is unfortunately measured against one ill-fated September afternoon at the SCG.

Commentary—Rex Mossop: "Mavin's world has fallen about him at the moment. Have a look at him, the poor lad."

NEVILLE GLOVER A dropped ball in a Grand Final has somewhat unfairly tainted Parramatta winger Neville Glover's career—it is the predominant memory his name evokes despite the fact he scored 59 tries in 130 first grade games and represented Australia in 1978. With the Eels in search of their maiden premiership and trailing Manly 11-10 in the 1976 decider, an unmarked Glover spilled a pass with the tryline and Grand Final hero status beckoning. Sea Eagles sharpshooter Graham Eadie kicked a fourth penalty two minutes later to clinch a 13-10 win.

MAX MANNIX Speedy winger Max Mannix played 24 games for Canterbury and Illawarra, but his name is synonymous with one unfortunate blunder. A mid-season 1984 match between heavyweights Canterbury and St. George was evenly poised at 8-4 in favour of the Bulldogs when Canterbury fullback Mick Potter sliced through. Potter's pass found Mannix—playing in his second first grade game—who set off on a thrilling 60-metre run to the tryline, outpacing the cover defence. But as Mannix dived and stretched out his arms to score, the ball flew out of his hands. Luckily for the rookie, the Bulldogs clung to their four-point lead, but footage of the incident is invariably wheeled out when memorable gaffes are mentioned.

Commentary—Ray Warren: "And it's a try... oh he's dropped it! Oh how embarrassing!"

NATHAN MERRITT Mercurial tryscoring South Sydney winger Nathan Merritt missed out on a four-pointer in the opening round of 2010 against archrivals the Roosters in embarrassing circumstances. After retrieving a kick in his own in-goal, Merritt broke through the first line of defence and set sail for the tryline with only open pasture in front of him. Few players in the NRL would have been capable of reining in the Rabbitohs flyer and the closest chaser was a determined Nate Myles, a backrower. Nevertheless, Merritt looked up at the giant screen to check his progress and the ball popped out of his grasp, denying him a 101-metre try. Merritt still managed to score both of Souths' tries in a 36-10 loss, but his howler was replayed countless times in the days the followed—and is likely to be for many seasons to come.

Commentary—Ray Warren: "Oh it's not Max Mannix is it?"

MARTIN KENNEDY Roosters tyro Martin Kennedy trumped Merritt for the most cringe-worthy bungle of 2010 just a fortnight later. Trailing 22-0 early in their round three clash with the Bulldogs, the Bondi boys finally got on the board just before the half-hour mark. But any hopes of a miracle comeback were dashed from the ensuing kick-off. Roosters halfback Mitchell Pearce collected the ball on his own tryline and popped a regulation pass to his charging front-rower Kennedy, but the young Queenslander tripped and the ball ricocheted off his head. Canterbury pivot Ben Roberts scooped up the loose ball and shifted it to centre Josh Morris, who evaded three defenders—including Kennedy—to dot down for the third of his four tries in the 60-14 walloping.

Commentary—Phil Gould: "If it wasn't so tragic it would be funny."

RUSSELL RICHARDSON With Cronulla comfortably leading the Hunter Mariners during a 1997 Super League fixture, Sharks centre sensation Russell Richardson looked set to put the icing on the cake with a length-of-the-field runaway try. But after doing all the hard work, Richardson's lackadaisical approach to planting the football resulted in the youngster dropping it over the line to seal his place in the Rugby League hall of infamy.

LUKE PHILLIPS Valuable Roosters custodian Luke Phillips produced one of the most lamentable howlers witnessed in an NRL finals match. With his side trailing Parramatta 10-8 just after halftime in the 2000 qualifying final, Phillips spilled a deep kick by the Eels. But instead of cleaning up the loose ball, he ran past the ball in exasperation, expecting a scrum to be packed. Eels centre David Vaealiki played to the whistle and toed the ball through to score an easy try, setting the underdogs on the path to a 32-8 boilover. Phillips bounced back to play a brilliant hand in the Roosters' Grand Final loss to Brisbane three weeks later, and won a premiership with the club in 2002.

BRETT FINCH A bold attempt to push for a late victory backfired horribly for 19-year-old Canberra halfback Brett Finch against the Knights in 2001. The enthralling round eight clash was locked at 20-all in the dying stages and the Raiders were awarded a restart on their own 20-metre line. Finch opted to kick the ball downfield towards the sideline—bouncing the ball into touch would give his side a scrum feed in handy field position, and the opportunity to work the ball into position for a last-minute field goal attempt. But the youngster put the ball into touch on the full—by less than a metre—giving the Knights a gift penalty in front of Canberra's posts. Andrew Johns duly slotted the penalty goal for a 22-20 victory, leaving an inconsolable Finch slumped on the Canberra Stadium turf.

JASON BULGARELLI One of the closest-fought finals matches of the NRL era to date was played out between Canberra and New Zealand in 2003. The Raiders and Warriors had struggled for 20 minutes of the second half to break a 16-all deadlock and save their respective seasons, and with five minutes to go it seemed certain the Green Machine were headed for a preliminary final berth. Canberra half Mark McLinden threaded through a grubber and robust centre Jason Bulgarelli only had to claim the bouncing ball, which sat up for him on the Warriors' tryline. But just as finals survival beckoned, the ball rebounded out of Bulgarelli's hands. New Zealand worked the ball to the other end of the park for Stacey Jones to kick the Warriors to a famous victory with a late field goal.

BRETT HODGSON Despite performing admirably for NSW in two series (2002 and 2006), courageous fullback Brett Hodgson's career in the Blue jumper is chiefly remembered for his role as the fall guy in two indelible Origin moments. After being rag-dolled over the touchline by Gorden Tallis in the drawn third match of the 2002 series, Hodgson fired a misdirected pass out of dummy-half near his own line with NSW ahead by four points in the late stages of the 2006 decider. Queensland skipper Darren Lockyer swooped on the loose ball to score under the posts and clinch the match and series 16-14—starting in motion an unprecedented series-winning streak for the Maroons. Tallis' tackle and Lockyer's try are two of the most replayed sequences every year at Origin time.

PHIL DUKE AND PHIL SIGSWORTH NSW debutant winger Duke (see One Game Wonders) and fullback Sigsworth conjured one of Origin's most infamous gaffes in the deciding match of the 1982 series. With Queensland holding a slender 5-3 lead, Sigsworth popped a dicey pass to an unsuspecting Duke behind his own tryline when confronted by a menacing Maroons chasing party. Duke fumbled the ill-conceived pass, allowing Wally Lewis to pounce on the ball for the series-winning try. Sigsworth went on to achieve further infamy as the last player to be sent off in a Grand Final (for Canterbury in 1986), while Duke, one of only three players chosen for NSW while playing for a country club, is now synonymous with the in-goal bungle. Duke was awarded the Blues' only try earlier in the match but, ironically, video replays showed he had stepped into touch and fumbled the ball over the line.
Commentary—Rex Mossop: "That's a terrifying bit of football from a New South Wales point of view."

JUSTIN HODGES Evoking memories of Duke and Sigsworth, Justin Hodges endured the most notorious debut in Origin history in 2002 with two misdirected in-goal passes that led to NSW tries. The Sydney Roosters centre sent a pass flying over former Brisbane teammate Darren Lockyer's head for Blues five-eighth Braith Anasta to score in the first half, before sending another poorly executed in-goal pass, grubbering past Lockyer in the second stanza, allowing NSW lock Luke Ricketson to pounce (see Unforgettable Debuts). Queensland hung on for a series-levelling 26-18 victory—with a dejected Hodges watching on from the bench after being hooked by coach Wayne Bennett.
Commentary—Ray Warren: "And will Hodges pass this time? I don't think... oh... I can't believe it! He's had another go at it!"

TERRY LAMB Canterbury legend Terry Lamb kicked the most poorly timed field goal of all time late in a 1992 clash with Newcastle. He struck the ball sweetly from 40 metres out and it went straight down the middle—the only problem was the Bulldogs were two points behind at the time. A sheepish Lamb admitted after the match he thought the scores were tied, with his clanger allowing the Knights to hang on for a 12-11 win.

ANDREW GEE Veteran Brisbane prop and Queensland Origin stalwart Andrew Gee cost the Broncos at least one competition point on a technicality in a 1996 match against the Roosters. The two sides had staged a Monday night classic and, with the scores locked at 10-all in the final minute, Gee took a 20-metre tap after the ball had rolled dead. But he incorrectly brought his foot up to meet the ball in his hands (instead of executing a mandatory tap with the ball on the ground), drawing a penalty in front of the posts. Sydney City centre Ivan Cleary slotted the simple goal after the fulltime siren to secure a 12-10 victory over the shattered Broncos. The rule regarding tap restarts has since been changed—an amendment that is surely of scant consolation to Gee and the Broncos.

WADE MCKINNON'S TRY Parramatta held a tenuous 16-14 lead against St. George Illawarra in a 2005 regular season grudge match when Dragons skipper Trent Barrett kicked downfield from near halfway. Barrett over-reacted to a perceived late and high shot from PJ Marsh, grabbing the Eels hooker by the throat before unleashing several punches, attracting a swarm of players from both sides. Meanwhile, Parramatta fullback Wade McKinnon fielded the kick and evaded the few defenders not involved in the melee to score a bizarre 80-metre try untouched. The video referee concluded that Marsh did not hit Barrett high and the try was subsequently awarded. The evenly poised match suddenly swung Parramatta's way with the home side eventually running out 40-14 winners, while Barrett copped a one-match suspension for striking.

ADAM O'NEILL A late-comer to Rugby League, South Sydney winger Adam O'Neill quickly gained a reputation as a fiery customer. The son of former Test cricketer Norm O'Neill, he did not play the game until his late teens, but made enough of an impact at Souths to represent City Firsts and the President's XIII in 1988. But his short fuse cost the Rabbitohs a competition point later that season. With Souths tied 12-all with Cronulla at the SFS in the dying minutes, O'Neill was held on his own 20-metre line before reacting wildly to the tackle of Cronulla prop Craig Dimond. O'Neill was penalised and Sharks winger Sean Watson calmly slotted the penalty goal after fulltime to win the match.
Commentary—Rex Mossop: "Now there is a stupid action."

JOHNATHAN THURSTON North Queensland captain Johnathan Thurston had the opportunity to clinch a much-needed win for the floundering club against Cronulla in round 16, 2010. The Cowboys had given up an 18-0 lead for the match to head into golden point with the scores tied 19-all at fulltime. Thurston, who earlier in the season landed his first 25 shots at goal in a row, duffed a simple 30-metre penalty shot from in front during the extra period that would have ended the game. Cronulla captain Trent Barrett subsequently slotted a field goal, consigning the home side to a heartbreaking loss.
Commentary—Mark Braybrook: "Thurston to win the game... he has missed it! Can you believe it?"

MARK LEVY The Panthers made the leap from perennial cellar-dwellers to finals contenders in 1984, but were left to rue a lost opportunity against eventual premier Canterbury that could have earned them a maiden post-season appearance. Nearing the end of a thrilling round 20 contest, rookie Greg Alexander pegged Penrith back to 22-20 behind with a determined try. Penrith fullback Mark Levy had the chance to draw the match with a conversion attempt slightly to the left of the posts, but he shanked the simple shot into the right-hand upright. The one competition point that went begging would have been enough to put the Panthers into a play-off for fifth spot.

Commentary—Ray Warren: "Oh he's missed it! Oh my goodness, how could you do it?"

DARREN LOCKYER Darren Lockyer's extraordinary farewell season—which included another Origin series victory for Queensland and a semi-final golden point field goal in his last match for the Broncos—was winding down to a fitting conclusion in the 2011 Four Nations final. The legendary skipper scored the Kangaroos' fifth try with a clever kick-and-chase in the dying minutes at Elland Road to round out an emphatic victory over England. He was handed the conversion attempt—which was adjacent to the uprights—after the fulltime siren. But Lockyer, the highest point-scorer in Broncos history, sprayed the seemingly unmissable kick in the final act of one of the great careers. Lockyer could only shake his head and offer a wry grin after the gaffe.

Commentary—Mike Stephenson: "He'll never live it down if he fluffs this ... ohhh hahahaha!" **Eddie Hemmings:** "You hexed him!"

DON FOX A section containing tragic goalkicking misses would not be complete without mentioning versatile Great Britain international, and Featherstone and Wakefield great Don Fox. In the 1968 'Watersplash' Challenge Cup final against Leeds, Wakefield scored a try under the posts with the last play of the game to trail 11-10. Fox was left with the simplest of conversion attempts to win English club football's biggest prize, but infamously skewed it wide in the quagmire conditions. Legendary English commentator Eddie Waring summed up the thoughts of millions with his reaction: "He's a poor lad." In a cruel irony, Fox had already been adjudged the winner of the Lance Todd Trophy for man of the match—little consolation for the devastated goalkicker.

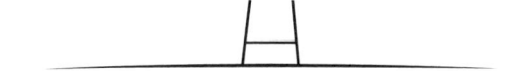

ENFORCERS, FIREBRANDS AND HITMEN

Rugby League's tough guys have been an integral part of the game's story. No players can stir the emotions of admiration and hatred in supporters to the extent the men whose playing style bend—and often break—the laws of the game can. The code's toughest, fiercest, feared and notorious characters are profiled on the following pages.

RAY STEHR A pre-World War II Rugby League icon, Eastern Suburbs stalwart Ray Stehr was a merciless front-row competitor in an 18-year career that began in 1929 as a 16-year-old. Stehr's heavy-handed approach to forward play was a crucial element in the dominant Easts sides of the mid-1930s, while he captained the club to premierships in 1940 and 1945. He was a punishing defender and renowned pugilist, and a significant portion of the enforcer's legend can be attributed to his deeds during Ashes combat for Australia. Stehr's clashes with the British forwards on consecutive Kangaroo Tours in 1933-34 and 1937-38 have passed into folklore refusing to take a backward step against the likes of Jack Arkwright and Martin Hodgson, and showing incredible stamina to play 26 of the 37 tour games on the 1933-34 tour. He is also the only player to be sent off twice during an Anglo-Australian series. Stehr was marched in the first and third Tests of the 1936 home series against the touring England side. In retirement, the 11-Test veteran took on the game's establishment in his roles as coach, administrator and commentator with the same ferocity as he did his on-field opponents during an illustrious playing career.

HERB NARVO Newcastle product Herb Narvo's boxing prowess commanded respect from his Rugby League opponents, but the Newtown great was also one of the game's finest forwards of the 1930s and 1940s. A tough but fair front-row enforcer, Narvo was a late addition to the 1937-38 Kangaroos squad at the end of his first season with the Bluebags. His hard running and powerful defence were features of the tour. World War II dictated Narvo would not represent Australia again, but he played 11 interstate matches for NSW between 1938 and 1945, scoring 10 tries. Following his vital role in Newtown's Grand Final thrashing of Norths in 1943 (the club's last premiership), Narvo claimed the Australian heavyweight boxing title in 1945. Narvo captain-coached St. George to the Grand Final in 1946 and retired after a brief return to Newtown in 1949 as one of his generation's most respected players. He was named in the NSW Country Team of the Century in 2008.

FRANK FARRELL Fearsome prop Frank 'Bumper' Farrell ruled the football fields of Sydney with an iron fist during the 1940s. A ruthless adversary, Farrell feasted on opponents with a mixture of power, aggression and brutality, and was the dominant front-rower of his era. Farrell captained Newtown to its last premiership in 1943 (and in a controversial Grand Final loss to Balmain the following season), before captain-coaching the Bluebags in 1946-51 and setting an unmatched club mark of 204 first grade appearances. World War II prevented Farrell from making his Test debut until 1946, while his achievements are often overshadowed by his implication as the perpetrator in the infamous Bill McRitchie ear-biting incident. St. George prop McRitchie reeled out of scrum in a 1945 clash with Newtown, sporting a severed ear that required months of hospital treatment to repair. McRitchie fingered Farrell as the culprit, but the Newtown hardman was exonerated and the allegations were never proven nor admitted, the rival props taking the truth to their graves. Farrell's prowess as an enforcer came in handy in a long and fruitful career as a well-known policeman, taking on Sydney's seedy underworld in typically fearless fashion. He was named Newtown's Clubman of the Century in 2008.

DUNCAN HALL Intimidating prop Duncan Hall was the only member of the ARL's Team of the Century unveiled in 2008 that did not play in the Sydney premiership. The Rockhampton forward played 23 Tests and toured with the 1948-49 and 1952-53 Kangaroos during stints in Brisbane and Toowoomba. Hall refused to take a backward step on the Rugby League field—regardless of his opponent's reputation—and was a formidable competitor in four Ashes series. He was relentlessly baited by the English forwards and subsequently sent off during the 1952 series. An exceedingly popular character, Hall was a prominent identity in Brisbane for many years after his retirement and managed Australia's World Series-winning side in 1977.

NOEL KELLY "Fifteen send-offs and 16 broken noses" begins the chapter depicting Noel Kelly in Tony Adams' book *Hitmen*. While the figures provided by 'Ned' Kelly may or may not be accurate, there is no doubt the legendary hooker/ prop's brutal style of play made them entirely possible. An Ipswich product, Kelly played over a century of games for Wests in the Sydney premiership and became part of a select band of players to tour Britain and France three times with the Kangaroos—in 1959-60, 1963-64 and 1967. Kelly was an irresistible blend of larrikin and firebrand—illustrated by his refusal to leave the field on a tour match in France despite being ordered off twice—and ranks as one of the era's most irreverent and best-loved characters. But his place among the all time great forwards is also assured. Kelly was named at hooker in the Queensland and Australian Teams of the Century in 2008, while he is also regarded in the top echelon of Rugby League props.

BRIAN HAMBLY A backrow mainstay of the national side during the 1950s, Brian Hambly played 21 Tests for Australia and toured with the 1959-60 and 1963-64 Kangaroos. 'Grumpy' Hambly was an uncompromising character, receiving his marching orders for punching in the third Test of the 1963 Ashes series. Hambly began his career with Souths in 1956 prior to a stint in Wagga that garnered his first Kangaroos call-up. The tough and versatile forward joined Parramatta in 1961 and was the muscle behind the club's belated rise to a maiden finals berth the following season. Hambly finished an often underrated career in 1967 as captain-coach of the Eels and was honoured in 2008 as one of the ARL's 100 Greatest Players.

BRIAN CLAY St. George five-eighth Brian 'Poppa' Clay ranks amongst the most feared and effective defenders of the post-World War II era. After partnering Dick Poole in Newtown's 1954-55 Grand Final defeats to Souths, Clay became an integral figure in the Dragons' world record sequence of premierships, featuring in eight Grand Final wins (1957-61 and 1964-66). Clay missed the 1962 Grand Final with injury, while he played in the club's reserve grade premiership victory in 1963 as he recovered from a broken arm. An astute playmaking pivot, Clay's bone-shattering defence was his trademark. The tough pivot featured in Australia's 1957 World Cup triumph before playing five Tests on the 1959-60 Kangaroo Tour. He retired in 1967 and shares the premiership record for most Grand Final appearances with long-time Saints teammate Norm Provan.

BILLY WILSON St. George and Norths enforcer Billy Wilson's nickname 'Captain Blood' stemmed from the countless times he was cut open on the field, but his gung-ho approach to Rugby League forward play no doubt expelled plenty of claret from opposing players during a career of unmatched longevity. Debuting for Saints in 1948, Wilson was sent off (along with Souths centre Martin Gallagher) for fighting in the club's 1953 final loss, but went on to feature in six Grand Final victories (1956 and

1958-62). After captaining the club to a 22-0 thumping of Wests in the 1961 decider, Wilson was sent off in the following year's Grand Final for decking Magpies forward Jim Cody in an act of retribution after Saints skipper Norm Provan had been forced from the field in the first half. Fortunately for the fiery Wilson, the 12-man Dragons hung on to win the 1962 premiership 9-6. The 1959-60 Kangaroo retired after the match, but resurfaced to captain North Sydney, later becoming the oldest player in premiership history and extending his career-span to a record 20 seasons.

KEVIN RYAN Rugged Wallabies forward Kevin Ryan switched codes in 1960 and became one of the most feared defenders in Rugby League history, as the nickname 'Kandos'—the small NSW town famous for cement production—testifies. He developed a calculated and devastating defensive technique that added yet another facet to the St. George machine. Also a talented boxer, which solidified his intimidation factor, Ryan featured in the Dragons' 1960-66 Grand Final victories, before masterminding the end of the club's record run by captain-coaching Canterbury to a famous defeat of Saints in the 1967 preliminary final. Ryan's only Test appearances came in the 1964 home series against France.

JOHN SATTLER Revered South Sydney captain John Sattler dished out more than his share of punishment—legal and otherwise—on the football field, but it was his bravery in playing out the 1970 Grand Final with a badly broken jaw that has enshrined his name into Rugby League history. Sattler arrived at Souths from Newcastle in 1963 and the fiery front-rower's early career was marred by a spate of send-offs. Though a surprise choice to assume the Rabbitohs' captaincy in 1967, he went on to lead the club to four Grand Final victories. A Kangaroo tourist in 1967, Sattler captained Australia in the second Ashes Test against England in 1970, while his legend has continued to flourish almost four decades after his retirement.

GEORGE PIGGINS Tenacious hooker George Piggins' association with South Sydney is embedded in the club's proud history. He made his first grade debut in 1967 but was kept in the lower grades for several years by Test rake Elwyn Walters. Resisting overtures to join rival clubs, Piggins remained with Souths and was rewarded with a Grand Final victory in 1971 in the absence of the injured Walters. He finally claimed the hooking role for himself in 1974 (after Walters joined Easts) and represented Australia during the 1975 World Series. A rugged and fiery competitor, Piggins' head-butting duel with Manly's British lock Malcolm Reilly at the SCG in 1973 and his defence scattering try against Wests in 1976 are two of the decade's enduring images. Piggins was equally pugnacious during a successful term as Rabbitohs coach (1986-90) and as the ring-leader of the club's passionate fight for readmission to the NRL after being expelled at the end of 1999.

JOHN O'NEILL John 'Lurch' O'Neill's ruthless approach to tackling and ball-running rendered him one of the true gladiators of a brutal era. Playing eight Grand Finals in nine years (1965, 1967-73) for Souths and Manly, O'Neill collected six premierships and represented Australia in 10 Tests during the 1970s. The 1973 Kangaroo tourist was no stranger to the judiciary and suspensions cost the front-row enforcer representative jumpers on more than one occasion. Sent off many times for violent play, O'Neill also asked no quarter, accepting callous punishment from the opposition as just a part of Rugby League. O'Neill returned to Souths in 1975 after his fruitful Manly stint, retiring the following season and coaching the club in 1977.

BOB O'REILLY Despite his burly frame and penchant for taking on opposition forward packs head-first, ball-playing enforcer Bob 'The Bear' O'Reilly became the most durable player the premiership had ever seen. The Parramatta junior debuted for the Eels in 1967 and featured in Australia's 1970 and 1972 World Cup campaigns, before starring on the 1973 Kangaroo Tour. He overcame a mid-career slump at Penrith by resurrecting his career at Easts in the late-1970s, while his toughness and guile played a key role in the Eels' maiden Grand Final triumph in 1981. Injury forced the 33-year-old's retirement the following season after a then-record 284 first grade games.

ARTHUR BEETSON 'Artie' Beetson's attacking dynamism and ball-playing brilliance are the foremost qualities that garnered premierships, Test jumpers, Immortal status and selection at prop in Australia's Team of the Century. But Beetson certainly did not shirk the tough stuff, simultaneously embodying the enforcer role at club and representative level. Regarded as something of a hothead early in his career, Beetson was sent off in the 1969 major semi and missed Balmain's Grand Final victory. He gradually learned to harness his temper, but Beetson's aggression was still a vital cog in his armoury as he led Easts to titles in 1974-75. A constant thorn in the side of international teams during a 28-Test career, Beetson's inspirational role as Queensland's skipper in the inaugural State of Origin match in 1980—which included punching NSW centre and Parramatta teammate Mick Cronin—helped instil the fierce interstate rivalry which exists today.

MALCOLM REILLY Great Britain lock Malcolm Reilly's compelling mix of brilliance and brutality set him on a path to Rugby League greatness. Reilly was the driving force behind Great Britain's 1970 Ashes success, prompting Manly to shell out a massive transfer fee to bring him to Sydney the following season. A magnificent ball-player and punishing defender, Reilly's ruthless edge was vital to the Sea Eagles' breakthrough premierships in 1972-73. Reilly's take-no-prisoners style meant send-offs were common during his five-season stint in Australia, before he returned home to become a Castleford legend. He later restored Great Britain's international credibility during seven years as Test coach and guided the Knights to their maiden title in 1997.

JIM MILLS Welsh rugby union forward Jim Mills brought his aggressive talents to North Sydney, playing 37 games in three seasons for the Bears before becoming a Wales and Great Britain international in the mid-1970s. A Widnes legend, Mills was infamously banned for stomping New Zealand forward John Greengrass during Wales' 25-24 win over the Kiwis in the 1975 World Series.

TOM RAUDONIKIS One of the great halfbacks, Tommy Raudonikis played with the ferocity of a front-row firebrand. A veteran of 29 Tests for Australia and two Kangaroo Tours (1973 and 1978), Raudonikis typified the Western Suburbs spirit during the 1970s, racking up over 200 games for the club. The terrier-like Raudonikis was hell-bent on playing over the top of his opposing No.7 every time he took the field—regularly employing roughhouse tactics to get the job done (he was sent off during the 1978 Ashes series). He drew criticism and a fine from the NSWRL after revealing himself as the 'Phantom Biter,' taking a chunk out of rival Manly half John Gibbs in a 1976 clash, but remained one of the competition's finest competitors and captained Newtown to a gallant 20-11 loss in the 1981 Grand Final. A unique and much-loved Rugby League character, Raudonikis imparted his old-world wisdom during a long and eventful coaching career which included stints with Ipswich, Wests and the NSW Origin side.

TERRY RANDALL When the subject of Rugby League's most punishing defenders is raised, Manly backrower Terry Randall's name is invariably one of the first names mentioned. Certainly, dozens of battered opponents from the 1970s and 1980s would put the 1973 Kangaroo tourist and veteran of 11 Tests at the top of the list. Randall combined perfect technique with unbridled aggression to become the most feared tackler of a tough era, featuring in Manly's four premiership-winning sides the 1970s.

CHARLIE FRITH Roma product Charlie Frith's premiership games played to fear instilled ratio was off the charts. One of the most brutal defenders of all time, Frith played 47 games in three seasons with Souths (1979-81), featuring in the Rabbitohs' 1980 finals campaign. Frith's pulverising hit on Magpies forward Bill Cloughessy in 1979 is one of the most regularly recalled tackles of the era. The unassuming front-rower returned to Queensland in 1982.

ROD REDDY Backrow enforcer Rod Reddy was one of Rugby League's dominant forwards of the 1970s and 1980s. Twice a Kangaroo tourist (1978 and 1982), the 'Rockhampton Rocket' mixed powerful and astute ball-running with aggressive defence. His renegade performance for St. George in the 1977 Grand Final replay attracted several cautions, but he remained on the field and was integral to the Dragons' 22-0 drubbing of Parramatta. He won another title with the club in 1979 before starring for Queensland in the inaugural State of Origin encounter in 1980 and finishing his career with Illawarra in 1985.

STEVE KNEEN Hothead Cronulla second-rower Steve Kneen represented Australia, but later received two of the heaviest suspensions in premiership history during the NSWRL's crusade to eradicate foul play from the game during the early-1980s. Kneen played in the 1978 Grand Final and replay for the Sharks, earning selection for the subsequent Kangaroo Tour. He received a 15-week suspension for a high tackle and tackling a player without the ball in 1981, and was slapped with a whopping 12-month ban the following season, effectively ending his tenure at Cronulla after 86 games. An Illawarra junior, Kneen attempted a comeback with the Steelers in 1984 but a hamstring injury forced his retirement.

JOHN DONNELLY Gunnedah product John 'Dallas' Donnelly's untamed playing style epitomised the 'Fibro' spirit adopted by Wests during the late-1970s and early-1980s. An exceedingly popular cult figure, Donnelly represented Australia in 1975 and 1978, but his career was regularly interrupted by send-offs, judiciary appearances and lengthy bans as he became a poster boy for judiciary chairman Jim Comans' clean-up of the game in the 1980s. Donnelly tragically drowned in Byron Bay in 1986 after having an epileptic fit while swimming *(see Tragic Figures)*.

STEVE BOWDEN Newtown tough-guy prop Steve Bowden is predominantly remembered for his role in the Jets' wild minor semi-final victory over Manly in 1981. Bowden was sent off following an all-in brawl and his consequent savage punch-up with the Sea Eagles' Kiwi prop Mark Broadhurst, immortalised by a famous photo of Bowden unleashing a savage uppercut. The resultant suspension cost Bowden a Grand Final appearance. Earlier in the season, Bowden was sin-binned for fighting in the one-off Origin clash, his only appearance for NSW.

BOB COOPER Towering backrower Bob Cooper was an integral member of the Magpies' wild pack of forwards during the club's colourful 'Fibro' era, matching strides with notorious firebrand teammates 'Dallas' Donnelly and Les Boyd. Cooper represented NSW in the inaugural State of Origin match in 1980, but a send-off and 15-month suspension for viciously breaking Steelers winger Lee Pomfret's nose and cheekbone during a brawl in 1982 stopped his career in its tracks. A comeback with North Sydney in 1984 was short-lived due to injury.

LES BOYD Supremely talented second-rower Les Boyd's career was ultimately brought undone by two lengthy suspensions. Aggressive and dynamic, Boyd typified the fire-and-brimstone approach of Wests in the late-1970s. Despite his early career being peppered with suspensions, he was chosen in the 1978 Kangaroo Tour squad and ventured to England and France again four years later after joining Manly. Boyd is the most recent Australian to be sent off in an Ashes Test, receiving his marching orders for kicking during the 1982 series. He was banned for 12 months after smashing Queensland forward Daryl Brohman's jaw in the 1983 Origin series-opener, and his Australian premiership career was effectively ended four matches into his comeback the following season. Boyd was rubbed out for 15 months for gouging Canterbury hooker Billy Johnstone. A Harry Sunderland Trophy-winning performance in Warrington's 1986 Premiership Final victory over Halifax provided a bright footnote to Boyd's controversial career.

CRAIG YOUNG Craig Young was St. George's forward pack anchor for more than a decade. Debuting for the Dragons in 1977, the 21-year-old won a premiership in his first season as the club downed Parramatta in a historic Grand Final replay. He captained Saints to another title in 1979 and led the side in the 1985 decider defeat to Canterbury, retiring in 1988 with 234 games in the Red-V to his credit—second-equal in club history. The rugged and imposing prop starred on consecutive Kangaroo Tours (1978 and 1982) among 20 Test appearances for his country, roughing up English, New Zealand and French forwards with the same vigour as he did his premiership rivals.

RON HILDITCH Hooker/prop Ron Hilditch menaced opposition ball-runners during a 156-game career with Parramatta. His reputation as one of the premiership's hardest forwards was sealed when he manned the apex of the Eels' infamous 'Flying Wedge' in the 1976 Grand Final loss to Manly (*see Signature Moves*). A 1978 Kangaroo tourist, Hilditch played three Tests for Australia and provided the intimidation factor in Parramatta's long-overdue maiden premiership victory in 1981. Hilditch later coached Illawarra (1989-90) and Parramatta (1993-96).

MARK BUGDEN Aggressive hooker Mark Bugden scored the Bulldogs' only try in their 6-4 victory over Parramatta in the 1984 Grand Final, but is equally remembered for a brutal tackle that effectively ended the great Steve Rogers' career. Bugden's reckless tackle in the opening round of 1985 shattered the Cronulla legend's jaw and resulted in legal action and a 14-week suspension. He played in the 4-2 loss to the Eels opposite brother Geoff in the 1986 decider, before coming off the bench in Canterbury's 1988 Grand Final win and finishing his career with an uneventful stint at Parramatta.

KEVIN TAMATI Star Widnes and Warrington import Kevin Tamati did not venture to play in the Sydney premiership during an illustrious career, meaning the 22-Test Kiwi will be remembered in Australia principally for his sideline stoush with rival prop Greg Dowling in the Trans-Tasman Test at Lang Park in 1985. Tamati and Australian front-rower Dowling were despatched to the sin-bin during the hard-fought encounter and tempers boiled over as the pair headed for the tunnel, resulting in an infamous brawl metres away from a baying crowd. The Kiwi enforcer claimed a unanimous points decision in the oft-replayed melee, but his hard-man reputation in England was built on punishing defence and rugged front-row play rather than fisticuffs.

PETER KELLY Fiery front-rower Peter Kelly was the muscle behind Warren Ryan's 'Dogs of War' during the mid-1980s. After debuting for Newtown in 1982, Kelly won Grand Finals with Canterbury in 1984-85 and established a reputation as one of the premiership's toughest props. He infamously ironed out Souths winger Ross Harrington in the first tackle of the 1986 Anzac Day clash at the SCG, receiving his marching orders after just 16 seconds. Kelly joined Penrith and belatedly won a NSW call-up, receiving a two-match suspension for striking Mal Meninga in his second state appearance. Injury forced Kelly into retirement during 1990.

STEVE ROACH A fiery and dynamic prop, Steve Roach frequently found himself on the wrong side of officialdom, but his game-breaking ability and aggression class the Balmain enforcer as one of the most valuable forwards of the 1980s. A veteran of 17 Origins for NSW, 19 Tests for Australia and two Kangaroo Tours (1986 and 1990), Roach was equally known for his volatile on-field temperament as his undoubted ability. He was cited for a head-butt in a fiery finals win over Souths in 1986 and was suspended from the following week's preliminary final. Sent off for another head-butt in the final round of 1988 against Penrith, Roach was exonerated on that charge but was banned for four weeks on a high tackle citing and missed the Tigers' Grand Final assault, despite a brazen attempt to serve out the suspension in England. Roach was outed for another four weeks and fined heavily in 1990 after infamously patting the head of referee Eddie Ward and abusing a touch judge on his way to the sin-bin. One of the modern era's true characters, Roach retired in 1992.

CHRIS MORTIMER Chris Mortimer was a cast-iron presence in the centres alongside brothers Steve and Peter in three Grand Final victories for Canterbury during the 1980s, before featuring at five-eighth and in the backrow in the twilight of his career at Penrith. 'Louie' Mortimer toured with the 1986 Kangaroos and made nine Origin appearances for the Blues. A robust runner and punishing defender, Mortimer's toughness was illustrated when he famously pulled out two steel pins from a broken thumb to participate in the Panthers' 1989 finals campaign.[25] He retired after the club's 1990 Grand Final loss.

DAVID GILLESPIE David 'Cement' Gillespie is the most celebrated defender of the modern era. Faultless timing and technique, combined with power and aggression made opposition ball-runners' lives a misery during Gillespie's 14-season career. A vital member of Canterbury's relentless forward packs that won premierships in 1985 and 1988, Gillespie took his rib-rattling talents to Wests and later Manly, where he finished his career with three straight Grand Final appearances. Gillespie held a mortgage on *Rugby League Week*'s Players' Poll's most hurtful tackler category during the Poll's first seven years in existence. He was rated the game's foremost hitman from 1986 to 1992, before being pipped by one vote by Trevor Gillmeister in 1993. Gillespie rated third in 1994, but the 31-year-old returned to the top of the premiership's hardest hitters list in 1995. The unassuming enforcer, who ended champion halfback Peter Sterling's career with a powerful tackle in 1992, played 19 Tests for Australia and 15 Origins for NSW between 1986 and 1995.

PAUL SIRONEN A menacing proposition in attack and defence, Balmain man-mountain Paul Sironen was one of the most effective and damaging forwards of the 1980s and 1990s. A three-time Kangaroo tourist (1986, 1990 and 1994), the second-rower played 23 Tests in a nine-year international career—including two World Cup final victories—while his seek-and-destroy mission on Great Britain talisman Ellery Hanley was integral to Australia's 14-0 shutout in the 1990 Ashes decider. Sironen featured in four series victories among 14 Origin appearances for NSW. He played in the Tigers' 1988-89 Grand Final losses, finishing one of the great tries in a decider with a rampaging run in the latter year. Clocking in at a fear-inducing 195cm and 115kg, Sironen retired in 1998 with a club record 246 first grade appearances alongside his name, and was named in the Team of the 1990s in 2003.

BRAD IZZARD Penrith great Brad Izzard's hitman reputation was sealed by one earth-shattering tackle at Leichhardt Oval in 1988. The burly, versatile back launched himself at Ben Elias, hitting the Balmain hooker across the chest and barrelling him sideways through mid-air in the decade's most memorable tackle. A teenage NSW Origin rep in 1982, Izzard was an integral member of the Panthers' rise to heavyweight status, culminating in a maiden premiership in 1991.

---

25 Neil Cadigan, *Rugby League Yarns: 100 Great Stories From 100 Great Years*. Sydney, 2008

GLENN LAZARUS NSW Team of the Century prop Glenn Lazarus' reputation as an enforcer was built on relentless displays of front-row excellence rather than heavy-handed tactics. A big, mobile forward, Lazarus was dubbed 'The Brick with Eyes' early in his career, but his peerless go-forward, monstering defence and underrated ball skills saw him become the best of his generation. The only player to win premierships with three clubs (Canberra, Brisbane and Melbourne), Lazarus played 21 Tests and 19 Origins in a decorated career. He was named as one of the ARL's 100 Greatest Players in 2008.

BRENDON TUUTA Kiwi backrower Brendon Tuuta was recruited by the Magpies in 1989 and made his Test debut a few months later against Australia. He was swiftly dubbed 'The Baby-faced Assassin' by the media following a series of unsavoury incidents in New Zealand's 26-6 loss in Christchurch. Tuuta is predominantly remembered for that infamous display by the majority of Australian fans and pundits, but after leaving Wests at the end of 1990 he carved out a successful career in England, played in the Western Reds' 1995 debut season and finished with 16 Test appearances.

TREVOR GILLMEISTER Trevor 'The Axe' Gillmeister's apt nickname clearly illustrates his expertise in taking down much larger opponents. Small in stature but powerful and endowed with perfect technique, Gillmeister picked up the moniker after joining Easts in 1986 (the same nickname given to club great Barry Reilly in the 1970s). The Brisbane Norths junior linked with the Broncos in 1991 and helped the club to back-to-back premierships. He broke David Gillespie's seven-year stranglehold on the Players' Poll's hardest tackler gong, topping the category in 1993, while he ranked second in 1992 and fourth in 1994. The unassuming hitman enhanced his rib-rattling reputation in 22 Origin appearances for the Maroons—a crunching tackle on NSW enforcer Paul Harragon is replayed regularly—and captained his state to a remarkable 3-0 series whitewash as a 31-year-old in 1995. 'Gilly' subsequently became Australia's oldest Test debutant forward, before retiring at the end of 1996 as skipper of the South Queensland Crushers. He later joined the Titans' coaching staff and is a long-serving assistant with the Queensland Origin side.

LES DAVIDSON Souths and Cronulla forward Les Davidson ranked among the most intimidating enforcers in the game during the 1980s and 1990s. Davidson toured with the 1986 Kangaroos, and made his NSW debut and was named Dally M Players' Player of the Year the following season. His peers voted him the competition's second most hurtful tackler in *RLW*'s Players' Poll in 1987, while he polled third in 1988-89. He added much-needed starch to the Sharks' pack after joining the club in 1991 and made his only Grand Final appearance in the 1997 Super League decider, retiring at the end of 1998 after 242 first grade games.

MARK GEYER One of the most notoriously hot-headed players in the game's history, Penrith firebrand Mark Geyer wreaked havoc throughout the late-1980s and 1990s. Geyer debuted for the Panthers in 1986 and received his first heavy suspension in the last round of 1988, but was chosen to make his Origin debut the following season. Rating second in the Players' Poll's most hurtful tackler category in 1989 and 1991, Geyer toured with the 1990 Kangaroos. He overcame a five-week suspension after an infamous performance for NSW during the 1991 Origin series to play two Tests against the Kiwis and star in the Panthers' maiden premiership win—despite being sin-binned for dissent in the 19-12 Grand Final victory over Canberra. The turmoil surrounding teammate and close friend Ben Alexander's death and a 10-week ban for testing positive to marijuana ended his tenure at Penrith in 1992, while his stint at Balmain ended prematurely and acrimoniously in 1993. Geyer resurrected his career with the fledgling Western Reds but copped a four-week ban for a reckless high tackle in 1995, sat out six weeks on three counts of misconduct from a game in 1996, and was slammed with a contentious 10-week suspension in 1997 on reckless high tackle and gouging charges. Following the Reds' demise, Geyer finished his career with a heart-warming and suspension-free three-season homecoming at Penrith.

IAN ROBERTS Statuesque forward Ian Roberts displayed a blatant disregard for self-preservation throughout a wonderful career that garnered 13 Tests and nine Origin appearances. Roberts' full-throttle approach for Souths, Manly and North Queensland contributed to many injury-enforced stints on the sideline, but he was among the most feared and respected enforcers of his era. Balmain fullback Garry Jack infamously took Roberts to court for beating him to a bloody pulp in a 1991 match while Roberts was with Manly, while a controversial tackle that knocked Queensland debutant Jason Smith unconscious in a 1994 Origin match escaped censure. Even taking into account his on-field heroics, Roberts' most courageous act was becoming the first openly gay Rugby League player.

PETER JOHNSTON Headgeared hitman Peter Johnston may not have reaped any representative rewards during a nine-season first grade career with Parramatta, Souths and Illawarra, but he caused plenty of anxiety amongst the premiership's ball-runners between 1989 and 1997. Despite his low profile, Johnston rated in the competition's top three most hurtful tacklers in *RLW*'s Players' Poll in 1993 and 1995-97, topping the poll in 1996.

JARROD McCRACKEN A fearsome competitor in the centres and later as a backrower, Kiwi firebrand Jarrod McCracken was no stranger to the judiciary during a decade-long premiership career. McCracken burst onto the first grade and Test scenes with Canterbury and New Zealand in 1991, but was slapped with an eight-match ban for biting near the end of the season. The ruthless defender was suspended again in 1993, before switching to Parramatta in 1996 and spending a five-match stretch on the sidelines for a dangerous throw two years later. Installed as Wests Tigers' inaugural captain, the 22-Test veteran's career was ended in 2000 when he was on the receiving end of a spear tackle by Melbourne duo Stephen Kearney and Marcus Bai.

MARTIN MASELLA Balmain front-rower Martin Masella quickly developed a reputation as a heavy hitter after debuting in 1991, ranking fourth in the hardest tackler category in the 1993 *RLW* Players' Poll. Masella was sent off and suspended for four weeks for a high tackle against Brisbane in 1994, before joining Illawarra the following season and getting sent off again for ironing out Broncos winger Willie Carne in an ugly tackle. He was slapped with a hefty 10-match ban on an intentional high tackle charge. Masella joined Souths in 1996 and was sent off for illegal use of the elbow against the Steelers, but was exonerated by the judiciary. Departing Australia at the end of that season, Masella spent five seasons in the English Super League and captained Tonga at the 2000 World Cup.

PAUL HARRAGON Newcastle great Paul Harragon was arguably the 1990s' foremost enforcer. His peers rated him the game's second hardest hitter in *RLW*'s Players' Poll in 1992, before he topped the category in 1994. Famous for his battles with fiery Manly prop Mark Carroll at club level *(see Individual Rivalries)*, Harragon epitomised the brutal physical encounters that prevailed in interstate football during 20 consecutive appearances for the Blues. Harragon's brawl with Queensland front-rower Martin Bella during the 1993 series is some of Origin football's best-known footage. His fearless approach resulted in a myriad of injury problems throughout his career, but Harragon still represented Australia in 17 Tests and captained the Knights to the club's maiden premiership in 1997.

DEAN PAY A highly respected and skilful forward, Canterbury and Parramatta enforcer Dean Pay routinely rattled ribcages throughout the 1990s. The Dubbo product debuted for NSW and toured with the Kangaroos in 1994, before winning a premiership with the Bulldogs the following season. Pay later co-captained the Eels and was rated as one of the game's top four hardest hitters in the 1996 and 1998-99 Players' Polls. His representative resumé boasts 12 Origin and 10 Test appearances.

JOHN LOMAX Intimidating Wellington (New Zealand) prop John Lomax's tackling technique sailed close to the wind throughout his career, costing him a Grand Final appearance and many stints on the sideline. Lomax was sent off for a high tackle in Canberra's 1994 preliminary final defeat of Norths and was subsequently rubbed out of the decider. He was sent off and suspended for four weeks for a reckless high tackle in a fiery 1996 clash with the Dragons and, three matches into his comeback, was marched again and outed for six weeks for another reckless high tackle against Parramatta. The latter incident led to the discovery of a cyst on the brain of Eels prop Adam Ritson *(see Tragic Figures)*. Lomax joined Raiders coach Tim Sheens at North Queensland in 1997, but he copped a three-match ban in his first season in Townsville, while a high tackle in the last round of 1998 saw him miss New Zealand's post-season Tests against Australia. A veteran of 15 Tests, Lomax captained his country in 1995 and eventually finished his NRL career with Melbourne in 2000 aged 34.

QUENTIN PONGIA Like fellow Kiwi and Canberra bookend Lomax, Canterbury (New Zealand) product Quentin Pongia's judiciary record often overshadowed his tremendous footballing ability. He was slapped with a four-match ban for a high tackle during his 1993 debut season with the Raiders, before celebrating in the club's Grand Final triumph the following season. A three-game high tackle suspension followed in 1995 and he spent six weeks on the sideline after being sent off in a spiteful encounter with St. George in 1996. Just three matches into his return, Pongia was cited and suspended for six weeks on a head-butting charge. The imposing 35-Test Kiwi received another four-week ban early in the 1997 Super League season and joined the Auckland Warriors at the end of the year. The judiciary appearances flowed, however, with Pongia suspended for four weeks in just his second game for Auckland. Pongia linked with the Sydney Roosters in 1999 but his bid to stay suspension-free for just the second season in his career was foiled by a two-game ban late in the year. Far from reformed, Pongia was outed for seven matches for a reckless high tackle early in 2000 and his tenure at the club ended with a two-match suspension late in 2001. After a brief stint with St George in 2003, Pongia finished his career with two seasons for English giant Wigan.

GORDEN TALLIS St. George and Brisbane second-rower Gorden Tallis is arguably the most feared and destructive forward the modern era has produced. A Test and Origin skipper, Tallis' defence-scattering charges and brutal defence were his trademarks. Tallis was overwhelming rated the game's hardest hitter in the 2000 Players' Poll, while he ranked second in 1999 and 2001-02, and he polled in the top-two of the 'Who wouldn't you pick a fight with?' category from 1998 to 2004. Memorable one-on-one stoushes with Wigan prop Terry O'Connor in 1997 and Panthers tyro Ben Ross in 2003 highlighted Tallis' pugilistic ability, while he became just the second player in Origin history to be sent off (for dissent in the 2000 series-opener). Tallis relied heavily on aggression and emotion in a decorated career that garnered three premierships with the Broncos, 13 Tests for Australia and 17 Origins for Queensland.

JOHN HOPOATE Few players have longer judiciary rap-sheets than John Hopoate, while the notorious Manly winger's is easily the most bizarre. An Origin and Test debutant in an award-winning 1995 rookie year, Hopoate was swiftly labelled as an aggressive, niggly player with an uncontainable penchant for trash-talking. Hopoate was sent off for dissent and suspended for two games in the opening round of 1998, beginning a long line of misdemeanours. After joining Wests Tigers, Hopoate infamously was found to have inserted his finger into the backsides of several opposition players in 2001, attracting a 12-match contrary conduct ban. The Northern Eagles threw Hopoate a lifeline after he was sacked by the Tigers, and although his form was outstanding for the joint venture club and later Manly, he eventually courted trouble again. Hopoate's 2004 season ended prematurely due to a nine-match ban for making threatening and derogatory remarks to an official, before his NRL career was extinguished two matches into his 2005 comeback with a 17-match suspension for a sickening elbow to the head of Cronulla forward Keith Galloway. Equally controversial away from the field, Hopoate's behaviour detracted from a fantastic ability to play Rugby League.

PETER RYAN Brisbane backrower Peter Ryan was one of the most punishing defenders of the 1990s, rattling the ribcages of countless opponents in 147 first grade games. Ryan played two matches for Queensland in 1998, the same season a late elbow on Melbourne halfback Brett Kimmorley cost him a Grand Final appearance. He topped the Players' Poll's hardest hitter category in 1998-99. The rangy forward took his hard-hitting talents to rugby union in 2000.

SOLOMON HAUMONO Tongan wrecking-ball Solomon Haumono ranked amongst the 1990s' most destructive forwards, coming off the bench in Manly's 1995 Grand Final loss and representing Tonga at the World Cup as a teenager. Haumono terrorised opponents during the Bulldogs' 1997 Super League season, crunching Broncos winger Michael Hancock in one of the decade's biggest hits, breaking Steve Renouf's jaw (he was cleared of any foul play) and skittling several Cronulla defenders in one of the modern era's great individual tries. He topped the hardest hitter category of the 1997 Players' Poll but controversially walked out on Canterbury the following season, before eventually returning to the Sea Eagles after stints with Balmain and St. George, finishing his NRL career in 2004. Even Haumono's mother Lavinia running onto the field to aid her injured son in two separate matches during his time with the Bulldogs—in a televised Super League game in 1997 and an early-season clash with Gold Coast at Belmore—could not diminish his fearsome image.

SHANE WEBCKE All time great prop Shane Webcke's toughness *(see Courageous Performances)* marks him as one of the most respected and admired competitors of the modern era. Webcke made 25 Test and 21 Origin appearances, while his bullish charges and granite-like defence were vital components of four Brisbane premierships (1997-98, 2000 and 2006). The Darling Downs product won three consecutive Dally M Prop of the Year gongs in 2000-02 and was named the *Official Rugby League Annual*'s Team of the Year in 1998-2003.

PETERO CIVONICEVA The most-capped Australian Test and Origin forward of all time, front-row warhorse Petero Civoniceva commanded his opponents' respect from the outset of a magnificent career. Rated the game's hardest hitter in 2003 and second in 2011 according to *RLW*'s Players' Poll, Civoniceva also got the nod as the NRL's best prop four years running (2007-10). The Fiji-born Redcliffe junior's defensive style occasionally sailed close to the wind, but he has remained relatively unscathed by the judiciary.

CRAIG SMITH Twelve-Test Kiwi Craig Smith was a robust, aggressive prop, but his tackling and running techniques saw him front the judiciary with monotonous regularity. While playing for Illawarra, Smith incurred a three-match ban in 1997 and a seven-week holiday in 1998 on high tackle citings. He nevertheless secured a contract with St. George-Illawarra, but was outed for four games for dropping his knees in a tackle in just his second appearance for the joint venture. After two more high tackle bans in 2000, Smith was suspended an incredible four times in 2001 despite being installed as captain of the Dragons—twice for raising his knees while running the ball, and twin six-match penalties for a careless high tackle and a striking charge. Smith joined Wigan for three fruitful seasons before returning to the NRL with Newcastle (he was forced to serve out the remainder of his last 2001 suspension in the early rounds of 2005) and escaped censure from the judiciary in two impressive years as a Knight.

KEVIN CAMPION Notorious for shedding blood on the football field, Kevin Campion may have had tissue paper skin but his shoulders were like granite. After stints with Gold Coast, St. George and Adelaide, Campion won two premierships with Brisbane. He was a popular import for the Warriors, where he famously knocked down former Broncos teammate and noted hard-man Shane Webcke with a fierce punch in 2002—consequently winning that year's 'Which player would you not pick a fight with?' category in the Players' Poll—and represented Queensland before finishing an admirable career with the Cowboys.

ADRIAN MORLEY English firebrand Adrian Morley ranks as one of the premiership's best-ever imports from the Old Dart, playing seven seasons for the Roosters and winning an NRL title in 2002. But Morley, rated the game's second-hardest hitter in the 2003 Players' Poll, was the competition's most regular visitor to the judiciary. He was rubbed out for a total of 26 weeks from 11 separate suspensions, including a send-off and seven-match ban that prematurely ended his NRL tenure late in 2006. Proving a fiery customer during an international career that eventually saw become the most-capped Great Britain and England player of all time, Morley was infamously sent off for a high tackle on Australian rival Robbie Kearns in the opening seconds of the 2003 Ashes series.

RUBEN WIKI A rampaging centre in Canberra's 1994 premiership-winning side, Kiwi legend Ruben Wiki later became one of the NRL's most intimidating figures after moving into the pack. Joining the Warriors in 2005, Wiki was ranked second in the Players' Poll's hardest hitter category the following season. The respected Auckland-born hard-man set a world record of 54 Test appearances and became the first overseas player to break the 300 first grade game barrier.

JOSH STUART Aggressive North Sydney prop Josh Stuart was one of the premiership's most promising young front-rowers during the 1990s, representing City Origin in 1997, but a sickening high tackle on Newcastle backrower Troy Fletcher halted his progress the following season. Stuart received a whopping 12-match ban and he made just 37 first grade appearances in three subsequent seasons with the Bears and Northern Eagles.

DANNY WILLIAMS A versatile and aggressive competitor in 12 seasons for Norths and Melbourne, Danny Williams came off the bench in 155 of his 212 first grade appearances and featured in the Storm's 1999 Grand Final victory. Williams represented Ireland at the 2000 World Cup, but his NRL career came to an abrupt halt in 2004 following his savage king-hit on Tigers forward Mark O'Neill and subsequent 18-week suspension. He rounded out a colourful career with two Super League seasons for London/Harlequins.

TONIE CARROLL After bursting into first grade as a hard-running outside back in 1996, Tonie Carroll carved out a reputation as one of the hardest and most pure tacklers of the modern era before retiring in 2009. A representative anomaly, Carroll played 18 Origins for Queensland, seven Tests for Australia and five Tests for New Zealand between 1998 and 2007, while he celebrated in four premiership victories with the Broncos. The barrel-chested lock became a 'minder' for oft-targeted five-eighth superstar Darren Lockyer at club and Origin level, topping the hardest hitter category of *RLW*'s Players' Poll in 2006-07 and ranking third in 2008.

MATT RUA Rangy Melbourne backrower Matt Rua ruled the hitman roost during the early 2000s. Part of the Storm's 1999 premiership-winning side, Rua was rated the NRL's third biggest hitter in the 2000 Players' Poll, before emphatically topping the category in 2001-02. Rua's bone-rattling defence often drew attention away from his ability with the ball in hand, but the Auckland-born forward represented New Zealand in 11 Tests between 1999 and 2001.

SONNY BILL WILLIAMS Sonny Bill Williams' devastating shoulder-charge prowled the Bulldogs' defensive line for five seasons. A remarkable all-round talent, Williams reeled off scores of memorable bell-ringers in 73 appearances for the Bulldogs and seven Tests for New Zealand. The Kiwi star ranked third in the Players' Poll hardest hitter category in 2006 and second in 2007, before topping the Poll in 2008. He controversially walked out on the club and the NRL during 2008 to play rugby union where, ironically, shoulder-charges are illegal.

STEVE MATAI Manly centre Steve Matai is undoubtedly one of the most intimidating backline defenders of the modern era. The 10-Test Kiwi's aggressive style has regularly resulted in judiciary-enforced stints on the sideline, however. He was sent off in New Zealand's record 58-0 loss to Australia in 2007 for a savage high tackle on Mark Gasnier, also earning a two-match ban. After minor suspensions in 2008 and 2009, Matai was rubbed out for seven games following a reckless high tackle charge in the final round of 2010. A fine attacking centre and one of the NRL's foremost purveyors of niggle, Matai was a key member of the Sea Eagles' 2008 and 2011 premiership sides, and has been a regular in the Players' Poll hardest hitter category.

NIGEL PLUM Wagga junior Nigel Plum is the epitome of the low-profile hitman, but his NRL peers certainly know who he is. Plum debuted for the Sydney Roosters in 2005, but only became a first grade regular after joining Canberra three years later. He topped *RLW*'s Players' Poll's hardest hitter category in 2009, and despite moving to Penrith and spending virtually all of the following season sidelined with injury, Plum finished just one vote behind Sam Burgess in the 2010 Poll. Plum returned to regular football with a career-high 20 games in 2011 and was a resounding choice as the game's hardest hitter.

SAM BURGESS Dynamic English forward Sam Burgess made an unquestionable impact in the NRL after arriving at Souths in 2010. A teenage Test debutant with Great Britain in 2007, Burgess took out the Players' Poll hardest hitter honour in his first season with the Rabbitohs, rattling off some of the year's biggest bell-ringers. The 112kg tyro spent most of his sophomore NRL season in the stands injured.

SIGNATURE MOVES

This chapter pays homage to the great innovators of Rugby League play and the individuals that have become synonymous with a trademark manoeuvre. Some inspired a horde of copycats and others prompted officialdom to alter the rules, while a select few were too tricky or too crazy to replicate.

THE GIDLEY FLICK Silkily skilled Newcastle centre Matthew Gidley's trademark piece of play was so distinctive it has become part of the Rugby League commentating vernacular. A veteran of 17 Tests for Australia, 11 Origin matches for NSW and 221 games for the Knights, one of the most lethal components of his attacking armoury was the 'Gidley Flick.' Able to get on the outside of his rival centre with monotonous regularity, Gidley would draw the opposition winger off his line and slip a one-handed flick pass to his supporting winger to score down a narrow corridor. Gidley's sleight of hand was particularly profitable for Timana Tahu at both club and representative level, but several Newcastle wingers benefitted from his brilliant offloads. The 'Gidley Flick' is a must-have in the modern-day centre's arsenal, but broadcasters invariably give a nod to the patented move's creator when it is produced.

'BOMBER' PEARD The up-and-under kick has been utilised since the game's inception, but no-one truly turned the bomb into an art form until Easts and Parramatta five-eighth John Peard began terrorising opposition fullbacks in the mid-1970s. Hours upon hours of practice allowed Peard, who consequently picked up the nickname 'Bomber,' to land his high kicks on a sixpence. In those days, catching a kick defensively in the in-goal area did not entitle a team to a 20-metre restart, and Peard's relentless aerial assault was seen to devastating effect in four consecutive Grand Finals with the Roosters (1974-75) and Eels (1976-77). The rule was changed in the mid-1980s to negate the overuse of the bomb to trap opposing fullbacks behind the tryline.

PARRAMATTA INNOVATIN' IN THE 70s The Eels emerged as one of the code's superpowers in the mid-1970s, and employed some revolutionary set moves (of questionable legality) to gain a competitive edge over Manly, St. George, Wests and the other heavyweights of the era. Under the tutelage of coach Terry Fearnley, Parramatta's most infamous forward set-pieces were undoubtedly the 'Parramatta Wall' and the 'Flying Wedge.'

The 'Parramatta Wall' involved several Eels forwards lining up side by side with their backs to the defence from a tap-kick, with the opposing side unable to see the whereabouts of the ball, thus keeping them guessing as to who would break away with the ball or pass it to a trailing runner. Canterbury hitman Geoff Robinson is known as the man who broke down the 'Parramatta Wall' after he launched himself at the congregation of conspiring Eels forwards and sent blue-and-gold jerseys skittling, but the club persisted with the move well into the 1980s.

The 'Flying Wedge' holds an indelible place in the fabric of Grand Final history. Borrowed by Fearnley from the rugby union forwards' playbook, it involved the pack charging towards the defence in a scrum formation, with the ball-carrier at the apex of the wedge. Fearnley introduced the fear-inducing (for both sides) manoeuvre to his team in the lead-up to the 1976 decider, and with the Eels trailing Manly by three points late in the decider, the 'Flying Wedge' play was called. Hooker/prop hard-man Ron Hilditch had the dubious honour of holding onto the pill. Confounding the Manly players and spectators alike, the Parramatta engine room trundled its way towards the Sea Eagles' tryline. But fearless Manly fullback Graham Eadie put his body on the line to deny Hilditch the match-levelling try—legend has it Hilditch's eyes were over the tryline, with Eadie holding the ball up inches short. The Grand Final ended with Manly victorious 13-10.

DALLY'S TRICK OUTLAWED Dally Messenger, Australia's first Rugby League superstar, was the earliest player to inspire a rule change. The Kangaroo pioneer and Eastern Suburbs legend would run to the defensive line and throw the football over would-be tacklers, before running through and regathering the ball on the full—like a chip and chase minus the kick. The manoeuvre was outlawed while the game was still in its infancy.

BLAKE PERFECTS CHIP AND CHASE There are few sights in Rugby League as thrilling as a perfectly executed chip-and-chase—a short kick over the defensive line and regather—and no player employed the move with greater regularity or fluidity than the mercurial Phil Blake. Rookie of the year in 1982, the will-o'-the-wisp utility scored 138 first grade tries in a 16-season career with Manly, Souths, Norths, Canberra, St. George and Auckland. A significant chunk of that total can be credited to his masterful use of the chip-and-chase. Blake scored the first ever four-point premiership try in the opening match of the 1983 season for Manly, fittingly from a sensational kick and regather that is regarded as one of the great individual tries.

Fellow journeyman half Scott Gale also thoroughly deserves a mention when celebrating the chip-and-chase. Beginning his career with Wests and Easts, Gale rocketed to prominence as a brilliant game-breaker with Balmain from 1985, scoring some of the decade's most scintillating individual tries—with a little help from his magical chip-and-chase, of course. Gale wound down with stints for Norths and Canberra, but tragically, he died in 2004 following a long battle with Motor Neurone Disease.

JOHNS BOYS GO BANANAS Now an essential part of any self-respecting playmaker's kitbag, the banana-kick was unleashed in its physics-defying glory by Andrew and Matthew Johns in the late-1990s. Employed by dropping the ball onto the outside edge of the boot horizontally, the kick is characterised by its banana-shaped trajectory and a late, swinging dip that has become the stuff of nightmares for defending fullbacks and wingers. Newcastle's brilliant brothers were the original purveyors of the banana kick—an innovation enthusiastically replicated by their playmaking contemporaries and followers alike.

THE INTERCEPT KINGS The intercept is ingrained within the history of Rugby League—it is the ultimate run-against-play moment, requiring expert anticipation and luck in equal quantities. Bob McCarthy's intercept of Canterbury hooker Col Brown's pass to score a try from his own quarter was the pivotal moment of Souths' 12-10 premiership victory in 1967, and is one of the most famous of all Grand Final tries. Queensland's Matt Bowen latched onto a pass from New South Wales halfback Brett Kimmorley to win the 2005 series opener with a golden point try, while Kiwi centre Shaun Kenny-Dowall did likewise for the Roosters in a 2010 finals epic against the Tigers, seizing a misguided pass from Liam Fulton and running 60 metres to score in the 100th minute.

But few players compare to three intercept poachers whose careers overlapped during the modern era—Brett Kenny, Sean Hoppe and Ryan Girdler. Parramatta centre/five-eighth Kenny, an all time great of the game, can credit dozens of try assists for his club record 110 touchdowns to hapless opposition players. Hoppe was a potent try-scorer for Canberra, Norths and the Warriors, and represented the Kiwis in 34 Tests. The intercept was a key part of his attacking arsenal. He snatched a match-turning try from an ill-conceived Dale Shearer pass in New Zealand's shock 14-all draw with Australia in 1993, and grabbed two intercept tries in one match for the Warriors against South Queensland in 1995. But it was Girdler, as a match-winning centre for Penrith, who most vividly revived memories of the legendary Kenny. Girdler terrorised opposition ball distributors to collect 109 premiership tries—just one short of Kenny's tally—and collected intercept tries at all levels, but never more importantly than in the Panthers' 28-18 qualifying final defeat of Brisbane in 2003.

BATTEN CAUSES ASHER HEADACHES British three-quarter Billy Batten was a giant of the code during its formative decades, representing England and Great Britain between 1908 and 1921. Batten was synonymous with a tactic that saw him hurdle defenders, known as the 'Batten Leap.' Against an Australasian side in Sydney, 1910, Batten came up against Kiwi winger Opai Asher. The former New Zealand Maori captain anticipated Batten's trick and leapt in unison with the British legend, but collected a knee in the head for his foresight and required stitches in a head wound. The move was eventually outlawed.

GRAY FIRST OF THE 'ROUND-THE-CORNER' KICKERS Nowadays every goalkicker in the NRL kicks the ball using the instep of his boot, but it was not until British hooker John Gray joined North Sydney in 1975 that the 'round-the-corner' style was introduced to the Australian game. Based on the technique used for kicking a soccer ball, the new method provided far greater accuracy. Gray, a 1974 Lions tourist, kicked almost 300 goals in 138 games for Norths and Manly. While most kickers persevered with the front-on style for many years after Gray's revolutionary introduction, 'round-the-corner' kickers became the norm by the early-1990s. Mal Meninga (Canberra) and Terry Matterson (Brisbane), who retired in 1994 and 1995 respectively, were the last of the toe-pokers.

THE BIG-STEPPING ROOKIES OF 2004 The 2004 NRL season produced a clutch of multi-talented youngsters that would go on to dominate the competition for years to come. Benji Marshall, who made an auspicious entrance into first grade with the Tigers in 2003, and 2004 debutants Karmichael Hunt and Sonny Bill Williams, set the competition alight with some dazzling displays—highlighted by unavoidably eye-catching sidesteps. The Kiwi-born trio employed a remarkably similar style—leaping into mid-air as they approached the defensive line, before unleashing a giant step of either foot that left opposing players frequently clutching at air.

The move produced countless line breaks for the freakishly talented teenagers, and sparked a copycat craze not seen in Australian schoolyards since Shane

Warne made leg-spin bowling fashionable in the mid-1990s. Within two seasons Hunt had ditched the sidestep and became synonymous with his full-throttle kick-return charges into the defensive line from fullback, before switching to the AFL at the end of 2009, while Williams switched to rugby union after just 73 games with the Bulldogs and represented the All Blacks after a stint in France. He was more closely associated with defence-scattering charges and a lethal offload during a 13-a-side career that also garnered seven Test appearances for the Kiwis. Marshall's unbelievable footwork and sleight of hand was integral to Wests Tigers' 2005 premiership success, and he continued to be a linchpin for the club and as captain of the New Zealand Test side into the next decade, winning the 2010 Golden Boot.

ROOKIES AND THE SECOND-YEAR SYNDROME

The dreaded 'second-year syndrome' has been a much-debated phenomenon in Rugby League throughout the modern era. Some pundits declare it a myth, while others contend it is almost inevitable: an outstanding rookie struggling with form and confidence in his second season in first grade. While star youngsters are predictably targeted by opposition teams in their sophomore year—whereas they may have slipped under the radar as a rookie—some players' form slides over the past 30 years have been beyond explanation.

1980 Twenty-year-old lock Jim Leis was named the inaugural Dally M Rookie of the Year in 1980 after an outstanding debut season for Wests, winning selection for New South Wales in the first State of Origin match and scoring eight tries in 21 games (including four in just his second match in first grade, against Penrith). But Leis played only 12 games in a disappointing 1981 season and failed to score a try. Leis' Magpies teammate Terry Lamb backed up a superb debut year in 1980 with an equally impressive 1981 season, despite the club's slide down the ladder, on his way to becoming an all time great with Canterbury and amassing a record-breaking 349 first grade appearances.

1981 Dally M Rookie of the Year Jeff Masterman became part of a select band of players to represent Australia in their maiden first grade season. The Roosters hooker played two Tests against France in 1981 and helped his club to the minor premiership. Masterman was a key man again for Easts again in 1982 as the club qualified for another preliminary final, but did not play for his country again.

1982 Phil Blake exploded onto the scene in the second half of 1982, scoring nine tries and featuring at halfback in Manly's Grand Final loss on the way to winning the Dally M Rookie of the Year gong. He was even better in 1983, scoring 27 tries in 23 games—a premiership record for a No.7. But predictions of future Test jumpers proved wide of the mark—one game for City Origin in 1988 and an appearance off the bench for NSW in 1989 was the extent of his representative career.

1983 Indigenous winger David Liddiard was a standout for Dally M Rookie honours in 1983, playing all 27 of Parramatta's matches and scoring 12 tries on the way to a debut-season premiership. But he backed up with just 14 games in 1984 and was shunted to the bench for the Eels' finals campaign. Subsequent stints with Penrith, Parramatta again, and Manly paled in comparison to his rookie year heroics. Fellow 1983 debutant, teenage lock Paul Langmack, went on to establish himself in the Bulldogs' much-vaunted pack and win a Grand Final in 1984.

1984 There was no case of the second-year blues for brilliant Penrith teenager Greg Alexander. The 1984 Dally M Rookie of the Year continued his meteoric rise the following season by taking out the Dally M Player of the Year prize— a feat unmatched in the award's history. Alexander scored 13 tries and 192 points— third and fourth in the competition respectively—as he spearheaded the club's drive to a maiden finals appearance.

1985 Dally M Rookie of the Year Steve Linnane was 1985's top try-scorer with 17 in 26 games. The young Dragons half also played in a Grand Final in his first year, but struggled in 1986, scoring just two tries. He failed to live up to his potential with St. George and later Newcastle.

1986 Towering backrower Paul Sironen was chosen for the 1986 Kangaroo Tour after clinching the Dally M Rookie of the Year award, but could not make the NSW or Australian sides in a somewhat disappointing 1987 season. Sironen eventually debuted for the Blues in 1989 and toured twice more with the Kangaroos as one of the modern era's most destructive forwards.

1987 Cronulla's goalkicking backrower Alan Wilson dispelled the second-year syndrome theory by representing NSW in 1988 after taking out the previous season's Dally M Rookie award. Wilson also scored 171 points for the minor premiership-winning Sharks in 1988 and was one of the club's best until departing at the end of 1991.

1988 Cameron Blair won the Dally M Rookie of the Year Award in 1988 and enjoyed a superb follow-up season with the battling Magpies in 1989, playing in every match. The underrated Blair was a tireless performer in a decade-long career with Wests, Parramatta, the Western Reds and Adelaide.

1989 In a bumper year for rookies Tim Brasher played in a Grand Final for Balmain aged 18, Penrith schoolboy Brad Fittler took the competition by storm late in the year and Souths hooker Jim Serdaris carried off the Dally M honour. Brasher produced a worthy follow-up season, scoring 12 tries and topping a century of points before eventually debuting for NSW and Australia in 1992, while Fittler became the youngest-ever NSW and Kangaroo Tour representative respectively in 1990. Serdaris, however, struggled to have the same impact in 1990, playing most of the season off the bench for the wooden-spoon Rabbitohs. He bounced back in subsequent stints with Canterbury, Wests and Manly however, touring with the 1994 Kangaroos.

1990 North Sydney half Jason Martin became one of the most celebrated rookies of the modern era in 1990, and was considered unlucky to miss out on a Kangaroo Tour spot. He performed admirably in 1991 as the Bears qualified for the finals, but his form tapered off after joining Newcastle. Fellow 1990 debutant Jason Taylor quickly became a linchpin for the Magpies in 1991, scoring 170 points.

1991 Diminutive Balmain half Will Robinson was the 1991 Dally M Rookie of the Year, scoring nine tries in 11 games, and backed up in 1992 with another 11 touchdowns. His career failed to reach similar heights with Souths and Illawarra and he departed for the UK Super League in 1999. Brisbane's 1991 Rookie of the Year Julian O'Neill was a key component of the club's maiden premiership side at fullback in 1992 and was unlucky to miss out on a World Cup berth with the Australian side.

1992 One of the most prominent case-in-points supporting the second-year syndrome is Newcastle halfback Matthew Rodwell, the Dally M Rookie of the Year and inaugural Norwich Rising Star in 1992. Touted as a future international, Rodwell was overshadowed by rookie Matthew Johns in 1993, and by 1994 the Johns brothers had a mortgage on halves spots at the club. Rodwell resurrected his career with stints at the Reds, Dragons and Panthers, but never reached the heights his rookie season projected.

1993 Just about every critic in the game had Manly's Jack Elsegood, the 1993 Dally M Rookie of the Year and Norwich Rising Star, pencilled in as a 1994 Kangaroo Tour certainty 12 months before the squad was to set off for England and France, such was the regular brilliance the winger produced during his debut season. But his confidence appeared to take a battering in his 1994 after receiving a couple of nasty high shots, and he eventually lost his first grade spot before the end of the season after weeks of indifferent form. Elsegood provided good value in later seasons with the Roosters, but did not scale the representative heights. Matthew Johns followed up an outstanding debut season in 1993 by forming one of the game's most lethal halves combinations with younger brother Andrew in 1994.

1994 The 1994 premiership produced an incredible crop of youngsters that were hell-bent on shattering the second-year syndrome model that befell Rodwell and Elsegood. The season's standout rookies included Dally M Rookie of the Year Steve Menzies, Norwich Rising Star Matt Seers, Andrew Johns, Matt Sing, Paul Green, Adrian Lam, Anthony Mundine and Richie Barnett. In 1995 Menzies (a Kangaroo the previous season), Johns and Sing played Origin and were part of Australia's World Cup squad; Seers represented NSW; Paul Green won the Rothmans Medal and steered the Sharks to their first finals appearance in six years; Lam starred for Queensland and captained Papua New Guinea; Mundine proved himself as one of the game's most exciting match-winners for St. George; and Barnett excelled on the wing for Cronulla and for the Kiwis at the World Cup.

1995 Norwich Rising Star John Hopoate continued to be a menacing presence on the flank for Manly in his second season, scoring 11 tries and featuring in the Sea Eagles' Grand Final victory. Dally M Rookie of the Year Mat Rogers also showed no signs of second-year syndrome in 1996, accumulating 150 points for the Sharks as they charged to the preliminary final. Fellow 1995 rookies Darren Lockyer, Stacey Jones, Craig Greenhill and David Peachey carried their debut season form into 1996 and each player had achieved representative honours by 1997.

1996 The season's outstanding rookies were backrowers Ben Kennedy (Norwich Rising Star), Glenn Morrison (Dally M Rookie of the Year), Dean Treister and Damian Kennedy. Ben Kennedy was magnificent for the Raiders in 1997, scoring 15 tries in 18 games, while Balmain's Morrison won selection for City Origin. Treister was a key part of Cronulla's Super League Grand Final side, but Damian Kennedy, a robust ball-runner for Wests as the club qualified for the 1996 finals, had a limited impact for the Magpies in 1997.

1997 ARL Rookie of the Year Scott Cram was relegated to the bench for Illawarra in 1998, before heading to Super League club London in 1999. Fellow Steeler Trent Barrett, denied the rookie gong after being suspended, played for NSW in 1997—his first full season in first grade—and backed up his limitless potential in 1998 by equalling the premiership record for most tries in a season by a five-eighth (18). Papua New Guinea winger Marcus Bai followed up his excellent debut season with Gold Coast by starring for the fledgling Storm in 1998. The pick of Super League's 1997 rookies—Tony Puletua, Luke Priddis, Michael De Vere and Russell Richardson—backed up superbly in 1998, continuing the form that would eventually see them become internationals.

1998 Diminutive Canberra utility-back Mark McLinden took the NRL by storm in 1998 and was duly named Dally M Rookie of the Year. Despite closer scrutiny from rivals the following season, McLinden was one of the Raiders' most dangerous attacking weapons, although he was frequently shunted around the backline. Canberra teammate Lesley Vainikolo terrorised opposing wingers in his debut year and was similarly explosive in 1999. Fellow winger Brett Howland scored 13 tries for the Sharks in 1998 and backed it up with 18 in 1999. Manly's twin 1998 outside back discoveries Albert Torrens and Alf Duncan had contrasting fortunes in their sophomore seasons—Torrens was the Sea Eagles' top try-scorer while Duncan made just four appearances. Teenage Steelers fullback Luke Patten beat a hot field of contenders to nail down the St. George Illawarra No.1 jumper and play in the 1999 Grand Final.

1999 Parramatta forward Michael Vella was named 1999's Dally M Rookie of the Year (despite playing eight games in 1998), representing NSW and Australia. He retained his rep spots in 2000, playing three matches at the World Cup. Eels teammate and 1999 debutant Luke Burt suffered a mild case of second-year syndrome, struggling to maintain a starting spot amidst a host of outstanding outside-back talent at the club. Second-year player Lote Tuqiri exploded in 2000, scoring 18 tries and winning a Grand Final with the Broncos, before captaining Fiji at the World Cup aged just 21.

2000 Dally M Rookie of the Year Tasesa Lavea debuted for New Zealand at the end of his first NRL season and was selected at five-eighth against France mid-season in 2001, but his form for Melbourne lacked the same spark. Lavea switched to rugby union following a dismal stint with the Northern Eagles in 2002. Winger Pat Richards' 2001 season was largely interrupted by injury after bursting onto the scene with the youthful Eels side that strode to the preliminary final in 2000.

2001 Braith Anasta thumbed his nose at the second-year syndrome by making his Origin debut for the Blues in 2002. The 2001 Dally M Rookie of the Year was also one of the key figures in the Bulldogs' record winning streak in 2002, but became a focal point for derision following the club's salary cap scandal that rocked the NRL late in the season. Matt Bowen, Michael Crocker and Mark Riddell all backed up standout rookie seasons with even better form in 2002.

2002 After crossing for 13 tries in his debut year, 2002 Dally M Rookie of the Year Matt Utai proved he was no flash in the pan by collecting 21 touchdowns in 2003. Brent Tate and Luke Lewis kicked on in similar fashion—Lewis won a premiership with Penrith and both toured with the Kangaroos—but Warriors half and 2002 Kiwi Test debutant Lance Hohaia's impact in 2003 was muted by injury.

2003 Melbourne No.1 Billy Slater was a certainty for the 2003 Dally M Rookie of the Year gong before the awards were cancelled, and he was even more devastating in 2004. He wrote himself into Origin folklore with a memorable try in game two and scored 14 tries for Melbourne. Injury restricted Dragons halfback Brett Firman to one game in 2004 after a superb debut season and his career never recovered.

2004 The 2004 season produced another remarkable crop of new faces, headed by Dally M Rookie of the Year Karmichael Hunt. The Brisbane fullback—along with fellow 2004 discoveries Anthony Tupou, Sonny Bill Williams and Frank Pritchard—went on to have a stellar 2005 season. All four were internationals by the end of 2006. New St. George-Illawarra halfback Mathew Head had a forgettable second season, however, suffering a season-ending injury midway through the year to miss the Dragons' finals charge.

2005 One of the most celebrated recent cases of second-year syndrome beset Parramatta halfback Tim Smith. A runaway winner of the Dally M Rookie award, Smith was a shadow of the 2005 version the following season, before leaving the club in acrimonious circumstances in 2008. Broncos winger Leon Bott suffered an equally unhappy 2006, playing just one game after scoring 13 tries in 2005. Greg Inglis bucked the trend, however—the 2005 rookie was lauded as potentially one of the best players ever after an incredible 2006 season.

2006 Jarryd Hayne's brilliant Dally M Rookie award-winning 2006 season led to Origin and Test debuts in 2007. Second-year syndrome hit a year late with Hayne struggling throughout an indifferent 2008, but he bounced back to win the Dally M Player of the Year award and the RLIF Player of the Year award in 2009. Brett Morris played just two games in his second season after a stellar 2006 rookie year, while Darius Boyd maintained his solid form for the Broncos.

2007 Israel Folau enjoyed arguably the greatest debut season in history in 2007—he broke Melbourne's tryscoring record, won a Grand Final and became Australia's youngest-ever Test player in a two-try debut against New Zealand. He was equally dominant in 2008, becoming a permanent fixture on the flank for Queensland and Australia. Sydney Roosters halfback Mitchell Pearce debuted for NSW in his second season, but Parramatta outside back Krisnan Inu failed to rediscover the magic of his 2007 rookie year and has been branded with the 'enigmatic' label ever since.

2008 The batch of rookies that entered the NRL in 2008 provided some fuel for devotees of the second-year syndrome theory. Dally M Rookie of the Year Chris Sandow was a hit-and-miss proposition for Souths in 2009, despite playing all but one game. Manly winger David Williams became a cult figure, Grand Final winner and international in his rookie season, but had a woeful Origin debut in 2009 and was less effective at club level, while his 2010 campaign was ruined by injury.

2009 Dreadlocked 2009 Dally M Rookie of the Year Jamal Idris debuted for NSW in 2010. Despite being inexplicably dropped after one game for the Blues, he was awesome for the misfiring Bulldogs, proving equally explosive in the centres and during a late-season stint in the backrow. Parramatta half Daniel Mortimer was one of the stars of Parramatta's surge to the Grand Final in 2009, but could not handle the extra responsibility thrust upon him in a difficult second season. He was tried in the No.7 jumper on several occasions—with little success—and was briefly dropped from first grade late in the year. Mortimer made just nine first grade appearances in 2011 and joined the Roosters at the end of the year in an attempt to revive his flagging fortunes. Canberra fullback Josh Dugan showed no signs of second-year jitters by becoming one of the game's hottest properties in 2010, while teammate Jarrod Croker was similarly outstanding after a superb rookie year in 2009. Warriors winger/fullback Kevin Locke gave further indication of his sublime match-winning talent in 2010 after an impressive NRL introduction the previous season.

2010 Versatile Brisbane backrower Matt Gillett soared to the Dally M Rookie honours with 12 tries (an equal premiership record for a first-season forward) and a dazzling array of skills. After a spluttering, injury-hampered start to 2011, Gillett was one of the Broncos' trumps during their admirable charge to the preliminary final and he was unlucky to miss out on Kangaroos selection. Trent Hodkinson, outstanding in his debut season for Manly in 2010, initially struggled after joining the Bulldogs in 2011, but enjoyed a form revival late in the season. Lightweight Cronulla fullback Nathan Gardner emphasised the courage and blistering pace that marked his 2010 rookie season with a fine follow-up year while Storm winger Matt Duffie made a tryscoring Test debut for the Kiwis in 2011 after providing a rare highlight during Melbourne's gut-wrenching 2010 campaign with an excellent debut year.

While the second-year syndrome theory appears to hold some weight—Matthew Rodwell, Jack Elsegood and Tim Smith are pertinent examples—the overwhelming majority of the game's outstanding rookies kick on to have an equally impressive follow-up year. Similarly, a disappointing sophomore year does not necessarily spell disaster for a young player's career—Rodwell and Elsegood resurrected their careers with other clubs, while Paul Sironen and Jim Serdaris represented Australia with distinction after sub-par second seasons. The heat will be on 2011 Dally M Rookie of the Year, Manly premiership-winning halfback and Kangaroos bolter Daly Cherry-Evans, powerhouse Cowboys second-rower Tariq Sims, Broncos centre and English international Jack Reed and boom Warriors halfback Shaun Johnson to sidestep the second-year syndrome and produce identical form in 2012.

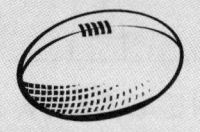

CHAPTER 5

AWARDS AND HONOURS

Many individual awards have been instigated to recognise Rugby League's outstanding performers at club and representative level each season, while the game's luminaries have been retrospectively honoured with the naming of best-ever line-ups and 'greatest players' lists throughout the modern era. The Rothmans Medal became the premiership's first official player of the year award in 1968, while the Dally M Medal—which was struck in 1980—has been the Australian game's highest individual honour since 1998. The Golden Boot has recognised the best player in world Rugby League since 1984 and the Clive Churchill Medal has been the coveted honour awarded to the best player in each year's Grand Final since 1986. Publications such as *Rugby League Week* (which initiated the Immortals concept) and David Middleton's *Official Rugby League Annual* have also paid tribute to the game's best. Australian Rugby League's 2008 Centenary season provided a forum for the naming of the 100 Greatest Players of all time and several Team of the Century line-ups.

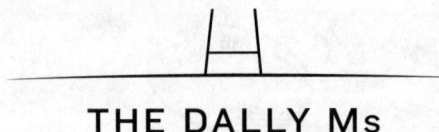

THE DALLY Ms

The Dally M Awards were established by News Limited's the *Daily Mirror* newspaper (now the *Daily Telegraph*) in 1980. Named in the honour of Australian Rugby League's first superstar, the great Henry Herbert 'Dally' Messenger, the Dally M Medal is based on a 3-2-1 points voting system on each match in the premiership's regular season by members of the media. Besides the prestigious Dally M Medal—which has been recognised as the official player of the year award since 1998—the year's outstanding rookie, coach, captain and representative player of the year are also honoured, along with the best player in each position. Voting is open for the public to view until Round 16 of the premiership, after which voting is made secret until the glamorous Dally M Awards night during the finals series. Only twice since 1980 has there been no Dally M presentation—in 1997 when two rival competitions were played, and in 2003, when a dispute between the Rugby League Players' Association and the NRL led to a boycott of the awards.

DALLY M PLAYER OF THE YEAR Andrew Johns is the only player to have taken out the game's greatest individual honour three times (1998, 1999 and 2002). Suspension cost the Newcastle legend the award in 2001 (won by Preston Campbell). He also went tantalisingly close to winning a fourth in 2005, finishing one point behind Johnathan Thurston, despite playing just 16 games for the last-placed Knights. Johns polled a phenomenal 28 points from a possible 36 in his final 12 matches.

Thurston claimed the award in 2005 and 2007, before finishing second behind Jarryd Hayne in 2009. Parramatta No.7 Peter Sterling won the award in consecutive years (1986-87), as did Cronulla ball-playing backrower Gavin Miller (1988-89). The only other players with two Dally M Medals on their mantelpiece are Manly wizard Cliff Lyons (1990 and 1994), and fullback Michael Potter (1984 and 1991), the only player to win with two different clubs (Canterbury and St. George respectively).

Terry Lamb won the award with Western Suburbs in 1983, and finished second three times (1984, 1987 and 1992) and third once (1986) during a celebrated career with the Canterbury. Eastern Suburbs stalwart Kevin Hastings ranks as perhaps the unluckiest player to miss out on the top honour—he finished second in each of the first three years the Dally M Medal was awarded (1980-82).

Wests Tigers hooker Robbie Farah finished second by a solitary point in 2007 and 2010, while Craig Gower can also consider himself unlucky—he was leading the Dally M count in 2003 going into the last round before the awards were cancelled. Melbourne fullback Billy Slater was denied a Dally M victory in 2008 by a one-match suspension late in the season, but atoned by topping the count in 2011. Slater pipped Benji Marshall, who finished fourth in 2010, for the 2011 gong.

Souths five-eighth Robert 'Rocky' Laurie, the inaugural winner in 1980, is perhaps the least-heralded player to take out the honour—Laurie, Preston Campbell and Matt

Orford are the only Medal-winners that did not play Origin or Test football during their careers. Meanwhile, former Kiwi captain Gary Freeman is the only overseas player to win the Dally M (with Easts in 1992). Just four players have won the Dally M Medal and a premiership in the same season—Ray Price (1982), Michael Potter (1984), Peter Sterling (1986) and Matt Orford (2008).

Todd Carney's victory in 2010 ranks as arguably the most remarkable story of any Dally M winner. Sacked by Canberra during 2008, and deregistered by the NRL and denied a UK visa to take up a Super League deal in 2009 following a string of alcohol-related offences, Carney spent a season in Atherton, North Queensland. He played bush football and worked fulltime in a pub throughout 2009, before the Sydney Roosters threw him a lifeline the following season. The brilliant playmaker responded with a series of match-winning displays, firstly in the unfamiliar fullback spot, then at five-eighth. Carney spearheaded the Roosters' push to the Grand Final a year after finishing with the wooden spoon, and his triumph in the Dally M Medal count was a popular one.

Predictably, halfbacks have dominated the award, with 13 of the 30 Dally M Player of the Year awards going to No.7s. Five-eighths have collected seven, fullbacks four, and second-rowers, locks and hookers two each. No centre, winger or prop has taken out the gong to date.

DALLY M PLAYER OF THE YEAR

1980 Robert Laurie (South Sydney)

1981 Steve Rogers (Cronulla)

1982 Ray Price (Parramatta)

1983 Terry Lamb (Western Suburbs)

1984 Michael Potter (Canterbury)

1985 Greg Alexander (Penrith)

1986 Peter Sterling (Parramatta)

1987 Peter Sterling (Parramatta)

1988 Gavin Miller (Cronulla)

1989 Gavin Miller (Cronulla)

1990 Cliff Lyons (Manly)

1991 Michael Potter (St. George)

1992 Gary Freeman (Eastern Suburbs)

1993 Ricky Stuart (Canberra)

1994 Cliff Lyons (Manly)

1995 Laurie Daley (Canberra)

1996 Allan Langer (Brisbane)

1997 Award not presented

1998 Andrew Johns (Newcastle)

1999 Andrew Johns (Newcastle)

2000 Trent Barrett (St. George Illawarra)

2001 Preston Campbell (Cronulla)

2002 Andrew Johns (Newcastle)

2003 Award not presented

2004 Danny Buderus (Newcastle)

2005 Johnathan Thurston (North Queensland)

2006 Cameron Smith (Melbourne)

2007 Johnathan Thurston (North Queensland)

2008 Matt Orford (Manly)

2009 Jarryd Hayne (Parramatta)

2010 Todd Carney (Sydney Roosters)

2011 Billy Slater (Melbourne)

POSITIONAL AWARDS

MOST WINS BY POSITION

Fullback: 3 Garry Jack (Balmain), Gary Belcher (Canberra), Michael Potter (Canterbury and St. George), Darren Lockyer (Brisbane); 2 Greg Brentnall (Canterbury), David Peachey (Cronulla), Billy Slater (Melbourne).

Winger: 3 Nathan Blacklock (St. George-Illawarra); 2 John Ribot (Wests and Manly), Steve Morris (Easts), John Ferguson (Easts and Canberra), Noa Nadruku (Canberra), Akuila Uate (Newcastle).

Centre: 3 Michael Cronin (Parramatta), Steve Ella (Parramatta), Michael O'Connor (St. George and Manly); 2 Mal Meninga (Canberra), Brad Fittler (Penrith), Andrew Ettingshausen (Cronulla), Ryan Girdler (Penrith), Nigel Vagana (Bulldogs), Mark Gasnier (St. George-Illawarra), Jamie Lyon (Manly).

Five-eighth: 7 Terry Lamb (Western Suburbs and Canterbury); 3 Brad Fittler (Sydney Roosters), Darren Lockyer (Brisbane); 2 Cliff Lyons (Manly), Laurie Daley (Canberra).

Halfback: 4 Peter Sterling (Parramatta); 3 Kevin Hastings (Easts), Greg Alexander (Penrith), Allan Langer (Brisbane), Andrew Johns (Newcastle), Johnathan Thurston (North Queensland).

Prop: 3 Steve Roach (Balmain), Ian Roberts (Souths and Manly), Shane Webcke (Brisbane); 2 Craig Young (St. George).

Hooker: 3 Ben Elias (Balmain), Steve Walters (Canberra), Danny Buderus (Newcastle), Cameron Smith (Melbourne); 2 Mal Cochrane (Manly), Kerrod Walters (Brisbane), Jim Serdaris (Western Suburbs and Manly), Robbie Farah (Wests Tigers).

Second-Rower: 5 Nathan Hindmarsh (Parramatta); 3 Steve Menzies (Manly); 2 Mark Graham (Norths), Noel Cleal (Manly), Gavin Miller (Cronulla), John Cartwright (Penrith), Anthony Watmough (Manly), Sam Thaiday (Brisbane).

Lock: 5 Ray Price (Parramatta); 3 Jim Dymock (Canterbury and Parramatta); 2 Wayne Pearce (Balmain), Bradley Clyde (Canberra), Ben Kennedy (Manly).

Terry Lamb's seven Five-eighth of the Year awards is a clear record for any position, while Darren Lockyer and Brad Fittler won six positional awards apiece. Lockyer collected three fullback and three five-eighth awards, and Fittler is the only player to win awards in three different positions—five-eighth (three times), centre (twice) and lock (once).

Ray Price's five consecutive Lock of the Year awards between 1982 and 1986 is an outright record. Nathan Blacklock (1999-2001), Michael O'Connor (1986-88), Terry Lamb (1991-93), Kevin Hastings (1980-82), Shane Webcke (2000-02), Danny Buderus (2002, 2004-05)*, and Nathan Hindmarsh (2004-06) have each won awards in their respective positions three years in a row.

There was no Dally M presentation in 2003.

CAPTAIN OF THE YEAR Steve Price is the only three-time winner of the Captain of the Year gong. The ageless prop won the award in 2002, 2004 (both Bulldogs) and 2007 (Warriors). Cronulla's David Hatch (1985 and 1988) and Canberra great Mal Meninga (1991 and 1994) are the only other players to be recognised as the game's best skipper on two occasions.

ROOKIE OF THE YEAR The Dally M Rookie of the Year has only been recognised as the game's official rookie award since 1998, but has been a much sough-after prize by the game's new breed each year since its 1980 inception. The premiership's official rookie award from 1992-96 was the Norwich Rising Star Award—Matthew Rodwell (1992) and Jack Elsegood (1993) are the only players to collect both awards. Fourteen recipients of the Dally M Rookie of the Year Award have achieved international status with Australia or New Zealand, while a further three have played State of Origin football. (*For a full breakdown of the fate of each year's outstanding rookies, see Rookies and the Second-Year Syndrome*).

REPRESENTATIVE PLAYER OF THE YEAR The player adjudged to have made the greatest contribution on the domestic representative scene has been honoured on the Dally M Awards night, with the exception of 1995 and 1996. Queensland and Australian stars Wally Lewis, Allan Langer, Darren Lockyer, Greg Inglis and Cameron Smith have each won the Representative Player of the Year Award twice.

COACH OF THE YEAR Tim Sheens and Craig Bellamy are the only club mentors to win three Coach of the Year Dally M awards. Remarkably, Sheens achieved the honour with three different clubs—Penrith in 1984, Canberra in 1990 and the Wests Tigers in 2005. Melbourne's Bellamy is the only coach to claim back-to-back gongs (2006-07), before becoming a deserving recipient of the award for the third time in 2011. Roy Masters (Wests and St. George), Bob Fulton (Easts and Manly), George Piggins (Souths), Wayne Bennett (Canberra and Brisbane), Chris Anderson (Canterbury and Melbourne), John Lang (Cronulla) and Brian Smith (Parramatta and Sydney Roosters) have each been named twice.

PLAYERS' PLAYER OF THE YEAR Voted on by the competition's players, the Players' Player of the Year was awarded between 1983 and 1996. Terry Lamb received the ultimate compliment from his peers three times (1984, 1986 and 1995), while Bradley Clyde (1989 and 1994) and Allan Langer (1991 and 1992) won the award twice. Gavin Miller (1988) and Ricky Stuart (1993) are the only men to win the Dally M Player of the Year and Players' Player of the Year awards in the same season.

THE CLUBS Parramatta, Cronulla and Newcastle can lay claim to having produced the most Dally M Player of the Year winners with four apiece, while Manly boasts three medallists. The Eels and Sea Eagles have produced a record four Rookie of the Year recipients, followed by Balmain and the Bulldogs with three each.

Manly players have collected the most positional awards (32), two ahead of Parramatta. Canberra and Canterbury have produced 24 positional award recipients apiece. Brisbane players have won 23 positional awards, despite not entering the premiership until the Dally M Awards' ninth season.

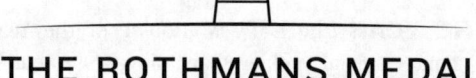

THE ROTHMANS MEDAL

The Rothmans Medal was the premiership's official player of the year award from its inception in 1968 until 1996, when a ban on tobacco company sponsorship in Australia saw the award discontinued. The medal was presented to the season's best-and-fairest player, voted on a 3-2-1 basis for each premiership match by the game's referees.

Second-year Cronulla halfback Terry Hughes was a surprise winner of the inaugural Rothmans Medal, pipping St. George lock and future Immortal Johnny Raper by a point. Hughes' victory started a charmed run for Cronulla players winning the award, in particular the club's No.7s. Hughes was the first of six Sharks to claim the award in its 29 years, including fellow halfbacks Barry Russell (1988) and Paul Green (1995).

True to form with individual awards, halves dominated the Rothmans Medal— 12 halfbacks and four five-eighths received the honour. Five backrowers won the award, all time greats Mick Cronin and Steve Rogers were the only centres to win, while Graham Eadie and Greg Brentnall flew the flag for the fullbacks. Newtown's Geoff Bugden and Newcastle enforcer Mark Sargent were surprise prop winners, and Manly rake Mal Cochrane was the only hooker to claim the best-and-fairest award, leaving wing as the only position not represented on the honour roll.

South Sydney pivot Denis Pittard and Parramatta champions Cronin and Peter Sterling were the only dual winners of the Rothmans Medal. Pittard was victorious in two of the Medal's first four seasons (1969 and 1971); Cronin won the award in consecutive seasons (1977-78, his first two seasons in Sydney), while Sterling was adjudged the season's standout in 1987 and 1990. Parramatta forwards Ray Higgs (1976) and Ray Price (1979) bookended Cronin's victories to put the Eels alongside Cronulla as the club with the most Rothmans Medal victories. Easts and Canterbury produced the next most winners with three apiece.

Despite a number of tight finishes, the only tie in Rothmans Medal history occurred in 1989. Genius ball-playing backrower Gavin Miller added to Cronulla's tally, sharing the honour with hard-working Knights prop Sargent.

Miller and Peter Sterling are the only two players to collect the Rothmans Medal and the Dally M Player of the Year award in the same year during the 17 seasons the two gongs ran concurrently. Sterling achieved the feat in 1987, two years before Miller.

North Sydney second-rower David Fairleigh accumulated the highest number of points by any winner—33 in 1994—two points ahead of rookie sensation Steve Menzies. The Manly tryscoring freak's total would have been enough to win the award in 25 of the previous 26 seasons. But the 1994 Rothmans Medal was shrouded in controversy, with an alleged results leak sparking a betting plunge in the lead-up to the awards. Fairleigh finished second behind Bears team-mate Jason Taylor in the 1996 Rothmans Medal count, the final year the award was run.

Only three Rothmans Medal winners coupled the game's highest individual honour with a premiership victory. Pittard went on to win the 1971 Grand Final with Souths; Terry Lamb claimed a premiership in his first season with Canterbury after taking out the Medal in 1984; and Allan Langer captained Brisbane to its maiden Grand Final triumph in 1992 just weeks after winning the Rothmans Medal, becoming the only player to win Rugby League's official player of the year award (Rothmans Medal and later the Dally M Medal) and the Clive Churchill Medal in the same season.

The 1991 awards night was the most comical in the 29 years of the Rothmans Medal, and caused event organisers undoubtedly the most consternation. Mercurial but painfully shy Canterbury halfback Ewan McGrady ousted Allan Langer by two points, but the Indigenous match-winner was nowhere to be seen at Sydney's Hilton Hotel. McGrady dodged attempts by club officials to transport him to the ceremony, and it took the lengthy persuasion of Bulldogs team-mate Matthew Ryan and a police escort to coax him to turn up and accept the award—an hour after the scheduled presentation time.

ROTHMANS MEDAL WINNERS

1968 Terry Hughes (Cronulla)

1969 Denis Pittard (South Sydney)

1970 Kevin Junee (Eastern Suburbs)

1971 Denis Pittard (South Sydney)

1972 Tom Raudonikis (Western Suburbs)

1973 Ken Maddison (Cronulla)

1974 Graham Eadie (Manly)

1975 Steve Rogers (Cronulla)

1976 Ray Higgs (Parramatta)

1977 Michael Cronin (Parramatta)

1978 Michael Cronin (Parramatta)

1979 Ray Price (Parramatta)

1980 Geoff Bugden (Newtown)

1981 Kevin Hastings (Eastern Suburbs)

1982 Greg Brentnall (Canterbury)

1983 Mike Eden (Eastern Suburbs)

1984 Terry Lamb (Canterbury)

1985 Wayne Pearce (Balmain)

1986 Mal Cochrane (Manly)

1987 Peter Sterling (Parramatta)

1988 Barry Russell (Cronulla)

1989 Gavin Miller (Cronulla) and Mark Sargent (Newcastle)

1990 Peter Sterling (Parramatta)

1991 Ewan McGrady (Canterbury)

1992 Allan Langer (Brisbane)

1993 Ricky Stuart (Canberra)

1994 David Fairleigh (North Sydney)

1995 Paul Green (Cronulla)

1996 Jason Taylor (North Sydney)

THE CLIVE
CHURCHILL MEDAL

The Clive Churchill Medal—awarded to the best player in the Grand Final since 1986—is one of the most coveted individual honours in Rugby League. Named after legendary South Sydney fullback and Australian captain Clive Churchill, who passed away in 1985, the award is voted on by the Australian Test selectors. While several established internationals have won the Medal, it has often provided the impetus for stars on the rise to claim an Australian jersey for the first time and has invariably seen the winner's career rocket to a higher level.

1986 PETER STERLING (PARRAMATTA) By the time Sterling played his masterful hand in the only try-less decider in the game's history—Parramatta's dramatic 4-2 eclipse of Canterbury—he was already established as one of Australia's greatest-ever halfbacks. After the Grand Final, Sterling was duly selected for his second Kangaroo tour, where he played a leading hand in another series cleansweep of Great Britain as vice-captain. He skippered New South Wales for the first time and became the first player to achieve the Rothmans Medal-Dally M Player of the Year double in 1987.

1987 CLIFF LYONS (MANLY) One of the greatest ball-players in Rugby League history, Lyons scored the first try in Manly's 18-8 defeat of Canberra in the last Grand Final played at the SCG, and was dynamic throughout the convincing win. Lyons had made his NSW debut earlier in the season and played two further Origins in 1988. While he had to wait until 1990 to play for Australia (establishing himself as an Ashes hero in the process), Lyons' Churchill Medal display saw him become recognised as a genuine match-winner and temporarily shed the enigmatic tag. He was regularly ignored by rep selectors during the 1990s, however, despite winning the Dally M Medal in 1990 and 1994.

1988 PAUL DUNN (CANTERBURY) Skilful prop Paul Dunn had a Kangaroo Tour and seven Tests to his name before his robust performance in the Canterbury's 24-12 victory over Balmain in the 1988 Grand Final, but had played just one Test, against Papua New Guinea, since 1986. Dunn was selected in Australia's side for the World Cup final following his Churchill Medal-winning performance, while he was rewarded with his first Origin start in 1989 after one appearance as a reserve in 1988.

1989 BRADLEY CLYDE (CANBERRA) The 19-year-old lock's tireless display in the greatest Grand Final of them all—Canberra's 19-14 extra-time classic against Balmain—added to Clyde's skyrocketing reputation. He had returned as 'Player of the Tour' after Australia's mid-season trip to New Zealand earlier in the year. While he was plagued by injury for much of his career, Clyde became one of the great backrowers and was an automatic selection for Australia and NSW for the next five years.

1990 RICKY STUART (CANBERRA) Former Wallaby rugby union international Ricky Stuart played a vital role as conductor of the Canberra's second premiership victory in the 18-14 defeat of Penrith in the 1990 decider. The brilliant No.7 won his first Australian call-up as a member of the 1990 Kangaroo Tour squad hours after the Grand Final. After playing five-eighth in the first Test loss to Great Britain at Wembley, he displaced Brisbane and Queensland rival Allan Langer at halfback and it was Stuart's injury-time bust to send Mal Meninga over for a try that saved the Ashes at Old Trafford.

1991 BRADLEY CLYDE (CANBERRA) Clyde became the first (and, to date, only) player to win the Churchill Medal twice, while he was also the first player to claim the award while playing on a losing side—his Canberra side succumbed 19-12 to Penrith. He was an automatic selection for Australia's post-season tour to Papua New Guinea and was installed as vice-captain of the squad at just 21 years of age.

1992 ALLAN LANGER (BRISBANE) Incomparable Brisbane halfback and captain Allan Langer was one of the game's elite players when his dominant two-try performance in the 28-8 Grand Final thrashing of the Dragons delivered the Broncos their first premiership. Langer went on to spearhead Australia's 10-6 victory in the 1992 World Cup final over Great Britain at Wembley, and established himself as Queensland's greatest-ever halfback and a legend of the game over the ensuing decade.

1993 BRAD MACKAY (ST. GEORGE) Mackay's energetic Grand Final effort saw him become the second player to win the Churchill Medal from a losing side, with St. George going down 14-6 to Brisbane in a dour decider. A Test and Origin regular, the versatile Mackay played all three matches for NSW in 1994 and the one-off Test against France, although he missed out on Kangaroo selection at the end of the year.

1994 DAVID FURNER (CANBERRA) Second-rower David Furner scored the first try and kicked four goals in Canberra's 36-12 demolition of Canterbury in the 1994 Grand Final. His Churchill Medal win was followed by selection for the Kangaroo tour squad that night—the 23-year-old's maiden international call-up. Furner forced his way into the squad for the first Test against Great Britain and scored 56 points in nine tour appearances.

1995 JIM DYMOCK (SYDNEY BULLDOGS) Despite being one of four Bulldogs to renege on Super League contracts to sign with the ARL and Parramatta, ball-playing lock Dymock played a pivotal role in the club's remarkable charge to the Grand Final and subsequent 17-4 boilover against red-hot favourites Manly in the decider. Initially chosen for Tonga, Dymock went to England as part of Australia's 1995 World Cup squad. He played in four matches at the tournament and debuted for NSW the following season.

1996 GEOFF TOOVEY (MANLY) The courageous Toovey defied a fractured eye socket to captain his Manly side to Grand Final victory over St. George, 20-8. A Test regular during the mid-1990s, Toovey captained Australia for the first time against Papua New Guinea a week after being awarded the Clive Churchill Medal for another typically gutsy display.

1997 ROBBIE O'DAVIS (NEWCASTLE) Newcastle custodian O'Davis was a standout choice for the Clive Churchill Medal following his dazzling two-try display in the Knights' dramatic 22-16 triumph in the 1997 ARL Grand Final. An Australian representative during the fractured Super League years but behind Tim Brasher in the Test pecking order, O'Davis was chosen at fullback for the 1998 Anzac Test—the first full-strength Australian team since 1994. He held off a challenge from Brisbane's Darren Lockyer (who debuted off the bench in the match), but was banned later in the year after testing positive to steroids.

1998 GORDEN TALLIS (BRISBANE) The 'Raging Bull' was a reluctant recipient of the Medal after Brisbane's superb team effort swamped Canterbury 38-12 in the decider. The rampaging second-rower deflected praise onto his teammates for the win, but was chosen to make his Test debut two weeks after the Grand Final, scoring two tries in a 30-12 defeat of New Zealand. Tallis became a Test and Origin captain in the early-2000s.

1999 BRETT KIMMORLEY (MELBOURNE) Kimmorley was the linchpin of the Melbourne side that scored a dramatic 20-18 upset of St. George Illawarra in the 1999 Grand Final, putting up the cross-field kick that resulted in a penalty try to unconscious winger Craig Smith to win the match. Ultra-talented but trapped behind greats Andrew Johns and Allan Langer in the representative stakes to that point in his career, Kimmorley made his Test debut during Australia's end-of-season Tri-Nations campaign, playing all three Tests as the green-and-golds won the inaugural tournament.

2000 DARREN LOCKYER (BRISBANE) Well on his way to becoming a all time great, Brisbane fullback Lockyer was an obvious choice for the Medal after his side's 14-6 defeat of the Roosters, displaying many of the traits that made Clive Churchill a Rugby League Immortal. Lockyer went on to star in Australia's emphatic 2000 World Cup success and captained Queensland to victory in the 2001 Origin series, before becoming a record-breaking Test skipper over the following decade.

2001 ANDREW JOHNS (NEWCASTLE) Widely regarded as the game's No.1 player and potentially the best ever, Andrew Johns orchestrated Newcastle's 30-24 upset of runaway minor premiers Parramatta with a first half ambush. Johns was also the key figure in Australia's retention of the Ashes in England at the end of 2001 and succeeded Brad Fittler as Test skipper the following season.

2002 CRAIG FITZGIBBON (SYDNEY ROOSTERS) Playing in the third Grand Final of his relatively young career, Craig Fitzgibbon scored a try and kicked five goals as the Sydney Roosters subdued the New Zealand Warriors 30-8 in the

Grand Final. Yet to break into representative football, the backrower was chosen to debut for Australia in the one-off Test against New Zealand following the decider, the first of 18 appearances for his country. Fitzgibbon broke into the NSW side for the first time in 2003 and starred in three consecutive series wins.

2003 LUKE PRIDDIS (PENRITH) Evergreen hooker Luke Priddis was magnificent in Penrith's 18-6 victory over favourites and defending premiers the Sydney Roosters in the 2003 Grand Final, scoring a try and setting up another two for winger Luke Rooney. A Super League international with the Canberra in 1997 and NSW's hooker in the 2001 series while playing for Brisbane, Priddis was unlucky to miss out on the 2003 Kangaroo Tour squad. Priddis did, however, play his one and only Test a little over 18 months later against New Zealand in 2005.

2004 WILLIE MASON (BULLDOGS) Controversial forward Willie Mason's damaging running and bruising defence was a catalyst for the Bulldogs' 2004 Grand Final victory over archrivals the Sydney Roosters. Mason regained his Test spot during the 2004 Tri-Nations after missing out on the Test side to play New Zealand earlier in the year, starring in Australia's defeat of Great Britain in the final and retaining first-choice status until 2008.

2005 SCOTT PRINCE (WESTS TIGERS) After several luckless seasons plagued by injury, brilliant halfback Scott Prince emerged to captain the effervescent Wests Tigers to the premiership with a superb display in the 30-16 Grand Final win over the Cowboys. Prince made his Queensland debut in 2004 but was displaced by Johnathan Thurston in 2005. But Prince's points decision over his North Queensland counterpart Thurston in the decider saw him chosen for Australia's Tri-Nations campaign, where he made his Test debut against Great Britain.

2006 SHAUN BERRIGAN (BRISBANE) One of the most versatile players of the modern era, Shaun Berrigan was honoured with the Churchill Medal after his performance as Brisbane's hooker in the 15-8 upset of Melbourne. Berrigan embarked on a one-man mission to contain Storm danger man Greg Inglis and was lethal with the ball out of dummy-half. A former Test centre, Berrigan regained a spot in the Australian side during the 2006 Tri-Nations series after the Grand Final as an interchange utility. Broncos captain Darren Lockyer was unlucky not to win his second Clive Churchill Medal for his virtuoso display in the decider, laying on both of his side's tries and kicking a match-sealing field goal.

2007 GREG INGLIS (MELBOURNE) Melbourne coach Craig Bellamy had endured a season of criticism for moving Greg Inglis to five-eighth after the young superstar had previously flourished at centre, wing and fullback. But Inglis' dominant two-try exhibition in the Storm's 34-8 disposal of Manly in the Grand Final thwarted the detractors. With captain Darren Lockyer occupying the No.6 jumper in the Queensland and Australian sides, Inglis has been an automatic choice in the centres since (and eventually returned there at club level), but won the Dally M Five-eighth of the Year award in 2008 before reverting to the three-quarter line in 2009.

2008 BRENT KITE (MANLY) It is unusual for a prop to carry off man of the match honours in a 40-0 victory, but such was Manly prop Brent Kite's powerful performance in the 2008 Grand Final belting of Melbourne, few were surprised at his naming as Clive Churchill Medallist. A Test regular from 2006, Kite played in all five matches of Australia's World Cup campaign at the end of the season.

2009 BILLY SLATER (MELBOURNE) Melbourne fullback Billy Slater had launched himself into the top echelon of the NRL's stars before his Churchill Medal-winning display helped the Storm beat Parramatta 23-16 in the 2009 Grand Final. The reigning Golden Boot and RLIF Player of the Year had become one of the first players picked in the Test side and rebuffed the challenge of Eels superstar Jarryd Hayne before scoring three tries in Australia's Four Nations final defeat of England at the end of 2009. Storm halfback Cooper Cronk was magnificent in the decider and must have gone close to snaring the best on ground honour, but had to be content with a recall to the Kangaroos squad for the inaugural Four Nations tournament.

2010 DARIUS BOYD (ST. GEORGE ILLAWARRA) St. George Illawarra fullback Darius Boyd capped a superb season, in which he finished third in the Dally M Medal count, with a man of the match display in the Dragons' drought-breaking defeat of the Sydney Roosters in the 2010 decider. Boyd lost his Australian wing spot in 2009, but was recalled by Kangaroo selectors for the Four Nations tournament less than 24 hours after collecting the Churchill Medal and was named fullback of the year at the RLIF awards.

2011 GLENN STEWART (MANLY) Dynamic Manly lock Glenn Stewart's Churchill Medal-winning performance in Manly's 24-10 defeat of the New Zealand Warriors is one of the most remarkable stories in the award's 26-season history. Suspended for his role in an infamous sideline brawl with Melbourne forward Adam Blair in the penultimate round of the regular season, Stewart was sidelined for the first two matches of his side's finals campaign, making his return in the decider. In a brilliant all-round performance, Stewart had a leading hand in two tries and scored a crucial four-pointer himself, despite not having played for a month. He was selected in Australia's Four Nations squad the following day—his first national call-up since the 2009 mid-season Test against New Zealand but he later withdrew, citing personal reasons.

While it should come as no surprise that winning the Churchill Medal has led to higher honours, as it symbolises a player's ability to rise on the biggest occasion, the strike-rate is remarkable. Seven uncapped players made an immediate Test debut, while the remaining two who had not represented Australia, did so within three years. Five players earned a recall to the national side at the next available opportunity, two captained Australia for the first time within a season, two more were chosen as vice-captain on tours directly following the Grand Final and the remaining eight retained their positions in the Australian Test side.

THE GOLDEN BOOT

Seminal British Rugby League publication *Open Rugby*, in conjunction with sportswear giant Adidas, instigated the Golden Boot award—bestowed on the player adjudged as the world's best—during the mid-1980s. The award lapsed in the early 1990s after Adidas withdrew its sponsorship, before enjoying a renaissance in 1999 when *Open Rugby* became *Rugby League World* magazine. Performances in the Test arena have traditionally been the main criterion for the Golden Boot, although club and domestic representative form has played an increasingly bigger role. Australia's dominance of the modern era is echoed by Kangaroos claiming 15 of the 19 Golden Boot awards, compared to three Kiwis and two British players (the 1988 award was shared). As the Australian and British seasons ran during opposite times of the year, the Golden Boot was initially awarded at the conclusion of the British season (mid-year), with Australian players' efforts from the previous year taken into consideration. The award's pre-1990 winners were initially recognised for the year they collected the Golden Boot (not for the year of their performances) but this was retrospectively changed by *Rugby League World* in 2010. The European Super League's shift to the Northern Hemisphere summer (in alignment with the Australian Rugby League winter) saw the Golden Boot awarded at the end of each year after its reinstatement in the late-1990s.

1984 WALLY LEWIS 'The King' Wally Lewis was the dominant player of the 1980s, but was at the absolute peak of his powers in 1984—and an obvious choice as the inaugural Golden Boot recipient. His dazzling list of achievements in 1984 included: leading the Combined Brisbane representative side to glory as player of the series in the mid-week Panasonic Cup which included every club in the NSWRL premiership; captaining Queensland to a third successive State of Origin series victory and winning two man of the match awards; taking over as Australian skipper and leading his country to an emphatic 3-0 home Ashes series defeat of Great Britain; and guiding his new club Wynnum-Manly to victory in the Queensland State League and Brisbane premiership.

1985 BRETT KENNY The only player to challenge Wally Lewis as the game's dominant five-eighth during the 1980s, naturally gifted Parramatta great Brett Kenny was a worthy winner of the 1985 Golden Boot. Kenny played a vital role opposite Lewis in NSW's maiden series victory in '85. Kenny's form at club level that year was typically exemplary despite injuries restricting him to 14 appearances, but it is likely his performance for Wigan in the 1985 Challenge Cup final had the biggest impact on the British judges of the Golden Boot award. He scored a dazzling solo try and laid on two more in arguably the greatest Wembley decider of them all, becoming the first Australian to win the Lance Todd Trophy for man of the match.

1986 GARRY JACK Courageous fullback Garry Jack maintained Australia's stranglehold on the Golden Boot award with his superb performances for Balmain, NSW and Australia in 1986. Jack was vital to the Blues' Origin series cleansweep in 1986 and was inspirational in Balmain's charge from a play-off for fifth spot to the preliminary final. He was awarded the Dally M Fullback of the Year award in 1986, starred for Australia in a 3-0 demolition of New Zealand and was in superlative form for the Kangaroos on the unbeaten tour of Papua New Guinea, Great Britain and France, scoring eight tries in five Tests.

1987 PETER STERLING AND HUGH McGAHAN On the only occasion the award has been shared, Parramatta, NSW and Australian halfback Peter Sterling and Eastern Suburbs and New Zealand backrower Hugh McGahan were named joint winners of the 1987 Golden Boot. Although Parramatta missed the finals for the first time in seven years in 1987, Sterling enjoyed arguably his best year form-wise at club level. The peerless No.7 became the first player to win the Dally M Medal and the Rothmans Medal in the same season. He starred in NSW's series loss to Queensland, winning two man of the match awards—on the losing side in the second encounter and as skipper in the historic fourth match in California. Sterling was Australia's halfback in a shock 13-6 loss to the Kiwis, who were captained by McGahan. The rangy forward was inspirational in the Lang Park upset, and was equally devastating for the Roosters during 1987. He was adjudged best second-rower at the Dally M awards and skippered Easts to the preliminary final—the club's first post-season appearance since 1982.

1988 ELLERY HANLEY Ellery Hanley's dominant performances in both hemispheres in 1988 saw 'The Black Pearl' become the first British winner of the Golden Boot award. He skippered the Lions' tour to Papua New Guinea, Australia and New Zealand, which included a spirited 2-1 series loss to Australia and Great Britain's first Test victory over the green-and-golds in a decade. Hanley stayed on in Australia after the tour to play out the season for Balmain. A dominant presence at lock or five-eighth, Hanley was untouchable in the centres for the Tigers, carrying the club from a play-off for fifth-place all the way to the Grand Final with a series of sensational individual displays. On the British domestic scene, Hanley captained Wigan to the glory in the Challenge Cup final.

1989 MAL MENINGA Mal Meninga's courageous effort to overcome four broken arm injuries in 1987-88 to win the Golden Boot for his efforts in 1989 is perhaps the most remarkable story in the award's history. Playing in his first Origin match since 1986, Meninga scored two tries for Queensland in the 1989 series opener and helped the Maroons retain the shield with victory in the second encounter. Meninga toured New Zealand with the Australian side and played all three Tests in the series cleansweep, including a superb display in the uncustomary position of second-row in the third clash. But the pinnacle of Meninga's renaissance—and indeed his career—was skippering the Raiders to their maiden premiership. After taking over the club captaincy midway through the season, Meninga was a tower of strength in Canberra's tightrope ride through the finals, culminating in an epic extra-time victory over Balmain in the Grand Final.

1990 GARRY SCHOFIELD Great Britain five-eighth Garry Schofield was scheduled to receive the Golden Boot for his performances in 1990, but Adidas pulled its sponsorship and the awards ceremony never took place. *Rugby League World* retrospectively announced Schofield as the 1990 Golden Boot winner in 2011. Schofield was at his mercurial best for Leeds and starred in the Lions' Test series victory on their tour of New Zealand. The pivot was magnificent in Great Britain's brave 2-1 Ashes series loss to the 1990 Kangaroos.

1999 ANDREW JOHNS After the award's nine-year hiatus, Andrew Johns was rewarded for a marvellous season with the 1999 Golden Boot. With the NRL and Super League seasons running concurrently, the Golden Boot was awarded at the end of the year for the first time, and Johns' virtuoso displays for Newcastle, NSW and Australia in 1999 rendered him a worthy recipient. Although his Knights were eliminated in the first week of the NRL finals, Johns won the Dally M Player of the Year and *Rugby League Week* Player of the Year awards for the second season in a row. Johns played all three matches for the Blues in the drawn Origin series and helped Australia to victory in the mid-season Test against New Zealand, before injury kept him out of the season-ending Tri-Nations series. The Golden Boot confirmed Johns' burgeoning status as the game's premier player, and potentially the best of all time.

2000 BRAD FITTLER Brad Fittler went within one victory of achieving a remarkable captaincy treble in 2000. He skippered NSW to a resounding series cleansweep over Queensland to claim the Origin crown for the first time since 1997, and finished the year by captaining Australia to World Cup glory in England, becoming the first player to lead teams to victory in two World Cup finals. The only title that eluded Fittler was the NRL premiership. The Sydney Roosters captain and match-winning five-eighth spearheaded the club's drive to the Grand Final, where they were overwhelmed 14-6 by Brisbane. But Fittler's masterful displays at club, state and international level were justly recognised with the 2000 Golden Boot award.

2001 ANDREW JOHNS Andrew Johns became the first dual winner of the Golden Boot award in 2001—suitable recognition of another season of rare quality from the Newcastle halfback. He missed the Origin series with injury, but starred in Australia's 28-10 mid-season victory over the Kiwis and was untouchable at club level. Suspension ruled Johns ineligible for a third Dally M gong, but he led the Knights brilliantly in the Grand Final upset of Parramatta where the skipper was awarded the Clive Churchill Medal for his devastating performance. Johns was undoubtedly the key to Australia's retention of the Ashes in England. After Great Britain sprung a major upset by downing the Kangaroos in the first Test, Johns responded with a 20-point haul from two tries and six goals in a 40-12 second Test victory, and was similarly influential in the decider.

2002 STACEY JONES Mercurial New Zealand Warriors halfback Stacey Jones became just the second Kiwi winner of the Golden Boot award in 2002. Jones assumed the club captaincy when regular skipper Monty Betham succumbed to a season-ending injury after just two matches. He led the Warriors with aplomb, turning in regular match-winning displays, despite the added responsibility of skippering the side. Jones guided the Warriors to a maiden minor premiership and into their first Grand Final. Although he could not prevent a 30-8 defeat to the ruthless Sydney Roosters in the decider, Jones scored one of the most memorable Grand Final tries of all time with a sizzling 40-metre solo effort. Less than a week later, Jones captained the Kiwis in a gallant 32-24 loss to Australia in Wellington, before leading his country in a drawn away series against Great Britain. The Golden Boot was the perfect recognition for the diminutive No.7's giant impact on the code in 2002.

2003 DARREN LOCKYER Inspirational fullback Darren Lockyer's performances reached an even higher plane in 2003, garnering the Golden Boot award for the world's standout player. Although a late-season fadeout consigned Lockyer's Broncos to eighth spot and an early finals exit, the custodian produced a string of inspirational performances. Lockyer took on the burden of being Brisbane's chief playmaker following Allan Langer's retirement at the end of 2002—a responsibility he assumed with trademark composure and class. He was Queensland's best in a 2-1 series loss to NSW, while an injury to Andrew Johns saw Lockyer installed as Australian captain for the Kangaroo Tour at year's end. Leading an inexperienced Australian side after a myriad of stars pulled out with injury, Lockyer contributed three phenomenal displays as the Kangaroos got out of jail in each Test to win the series 3-0. Lockyer scored a try in the dying moments to win the first Test and produced two brilliant touches that led to a try on fulltime to Luke Ricketson that won the third Test and sealed a memorable cleansweep.

2004 ANDY FARRELL Wigan and Great Britain captain Andy Farrell became just the third British player and the second forward to win the Golden Boot in 2004. Farrell scored 239 points in taking the Warriors to the penultimate weekend of the Super League competition and was named at prop in the Super League Dream Team, but illustrated his versatility by captaining Great Britain from the second-row. Farrell was superb for hosts Great Britain in the season-ending Tri-Nations tournament. He led by example as the home side twice defeated New Zealand and scored a rare victory over Australia, beating the world champions 24-12 at Farrell's home ground in Wigan. Although Great Britain was blitzed 44-4 by Australia in the final, Farrell's contribution for his country could not be denied. The Golden Boot award was a fitting send-off for Farrell—he joined rugby union club Saracens the following season and became a dual international by representing England at Test level.

2005 ANTHONY MINICHIELLO Anthony Minichiello's ultra-consistent performances at all levels of the game earned the fullback Golden Boot honours in 2005. Although his Sydney Roosters missed the finals for the first time in a decade, Minichiello was a shining light, scoring 14 tries in 22 games and enhancing his status as one of the game's safest custodians. He starred in NSW's 2-1 Origin series victory, crossing for a vital double as the Blues kept the series alive with a 32-22 victory in the second encounter. Minichiello was named man of the match in the decider and collected the Wally Lewis Medal as player of the series. The season ended in disappointment for 'The Count' as the Kangaroos crashed to their first series loss since 1978 in the Tri-Nations, but Minichiello's form never wavered and he was awarded the Harry Sunderland Medal as Australia's standout player for the second year in a row.

2006 DARREN LOCKYER Winning two Golden Boot awards is a massive achievement, but to win them playing in two different positions is on another level. After getting the gong in his last season as a fullback in 2003, Darren Lockyer became just the second dual winner of the Golden Boot by collecting the award in his adopted position of five-eighth in 2006. Lockyer captained Brisbane to the NRL title, Queensland to the Origin crown and Australia to Tri-Nations success in a season of unprecedented achievement. Under pressure following the Maroons' series-opening loss, Lockyer was named man of the match in game two and scored a memorable match-winning try in the decider, winning the Wally Lewis Medal in the process. Lockyer also bore the brunt of criticism of the Broncos' recent fadeouts, but was named Dally M Five-eighth of the Year and produced a series of magnificent performance as the club charged to the Grand Final. He laid on both Brisbane tries and kicked the title-sealing field goal in the 15-8 upset of Melbourne in the decider. Capping an extraordinary year, Lockyer scored a golden point try as Australia regained the Tri-Nations crown with a pulsating extra-time victory over New Zealand in the final. The Golden Boot award provided yet another accolade for the champion No.6.

2007 CAMERON SMITH Cameron Smith celebrated leading Melbourne to Grand Final glory and captaining Australia for the first time by becoming the first hooker to take out the Golden Boot. The Storm No.9 played a leading hand in Queensland's retention of the Origin shield and was awarded the Wally Lewis Medal for player of the series and the Ron McAuliffe Medal for Queensland's players' player of the series. Smith's magnificent form at club level saw the 2006 Dally M winner finish third in the 2007 count, before skippering Melbourne to an emphatic 34-8 defeat of Manly in the Grand Final. The goalkicking rake's 192 points was third-highest in the NRL and a premiership record for a hooker. Two weeks after the NRL decider, Smith captained an Australian side (with Darren Lockyer sidelined due to injury) containing eight Test rookies to a record 58-0 demolition of the Kiwis in Wellington.

2008 BILLY SLATER After searing onto the NRL scene in 2003, Billy Slater finally broke into the Australian side in 2008. Slater's electrifying form for Melbourne, Queensland and Australia made his naming as the Golden Boot winner a mere formality. The fullback was selected to debut in May's Centenary Test against New Zealand after a sensational start to the NRL season, and scored the winning try in the Maroons' 16-10 victory in the deciding Origin clash. A late-season suspension cost him victory in the Dally M Medal, instead finishing second-equal with his

Storm skipper Cameron Smith and settling for the Fullback of the Year gong. Slater's majestic World Cup campaign, in which he scored a tournament-high seven tries, ended on a sour note after he gifted New Zealand a crucial try in Australia's 34-20 loss in the final, but a deserved Golden Boot award provided some solace for the fullback ace.

2009 GREG INGLIS Greg Inglis cemented his status as one of the great big-match players in spearheading Melbourne, Queensland and Australia's 2009 successes. Equal parts graceful and forceful, Inglis terrorised NSW yet again in Queensland's fourth consecutive series victory and was duly awarded the Wally Lewis Medal and Ron McAuliffe Medal, before picking up his second Dally M Representative Player of the Year award in succession. He scored 16 tries in a stellar season for Melbourne, including a hat-trick in the preliminary final mauling of Brisbane, and scored a freakish try and kicked a decisive field goal in the 23-16 Grand Final triumph over Parramatta. Inglis was unstoppable during Australia's Four Nations tournament campaign and won the Harry Sunderland Medal for his breathtaking efforts. The Golden Boot award was a fitting finale to a year of rich achievement for the man widely regarded as the game's best player.

2010 BENJI MARSHALL Undeniably gifted but injury-prone earlier in his career, Wests Tigers five-eighth and New Zealand skipper Benji Marshall finally produced a season of consistent quality from start to finish in 2010. Marshall played all 27 club matches and scored a career-high 203 points as the Tigers returned to finals for the first time since winning the 2005 premiership, and produced a highlights reel bursting at the seams with bewildering sleight of hand, dazzling tries and ball-on-a-string kicking. Marshall finished fourth in the Dally M Medal count and provided one of the NRL season's most memorable moments by landing a 50-metre field goal that ultimately proved the difference in a victory over the Titans. Although the Tigers' season finished agonisingly one game short of the Grand Final, Marshall capped a marvellous year by skippering the Kiwis to an epic 16-12 victory over Australia in the Four Nations final. Marshall had his full range of ball-playing trickery on display as he laid on all three of New Zealand's tries, handling twice brilliantly in the last-gasp try to Nathan Fien that delivered the silverware to the Kiwis. His ascension to the mantle as arguably the game's premier match-winner was supported by his naming as the Golden Boot winner for 2010—just the third time a New Zealander had taken out the honour.

2011 BILLY SLATER Melbourne superstar Billy Slater capped his maiden Dally M Medal victory and his undisputed rise to the top echelon of Australia's greatest fullbacks with a second Golden Boot award. Typically brilliant at Test and Origin level—he scored a blistering try in the mid-season Test against New Zealand and crossed for the match-winner in Queensland's series-opening victory—it was Slater's consistent attacking class and bravery at the back for the Storm that garnered the most glowing plaudits in 2011. He was integral to Melbourne's capture of the minor premiership following the salary cap scandal of 2010, and earned comparisons with the likes of Clive Churchill for his remarkable all-round displays.

MIDDLETON'S
PLAYERS OF THE YEAR

David Middleton is widely credited with sparking a renewed interest in the preservation of the game's history during the 1980s. A former reporter with *Rugby League Week*, Middleton has compiled the *Official Rugby League Annual* since 1987, released the seminal *A Centenary of Rugby League 1908-2008* with Ian Heads, and is regarded as one of the foremost historians and statisticians in the code. While not receiving the fanfare of awards such the Dally Ms, Middleton's naming of the top five players of the year and the team of the year in each *Annual* is eagerly anticipated by Rugby League buffs—a prestigious nod to the season's best from one of the game's leading authorities.

Unsurprisingly, Andrew Johns featured in Middleton's top five players of the year on a record seven occasions, just clear of Darren Lockyer with six nominations. Allan Langer was named among the game's best quintet five times, Cameron Smith was named four times in the space of six seasons, while a host of players have received the honour three times: Brad Fittler, Mal Meninga, Bradley Clyde, Gorden Tallis, Nathan Hindmarsh, Ben Kennedy and Billy Slater. Johns was also named in a record five consecutive seasons (1998-2002), again one ahead of Lockyer, who was named four times in a row (2001-04).

Fittler was named in the team of the year more times than any other player, and is the only player to make the team in three different positions. He was picked at five-eighth four times, in the centres once and at lock on five occasions for a total of 10 selections. Lockyer's five appearances at fullback and three at five-eighth for a total of eight is next best, while Johns' seven nominations at halfback and Nathan Hindmarsh's naming in the second-row seven times is the most for a single position, just ahead of front-row greats Glenn Lazarus and Shane Webcke with six.

Webcke has appeared in the team of the year in the most consecutive years—all six of his nominations came in successive seasons (1998-2003). Fittler (1993-97), Johns (1998-2002), Lockyer (2000-04) and hookers Steve Walters (1991-95) and Danny Buderus (2001-05) were each named in the team of the year five times in a row.

Halfbacks Allan Langer and Brett Kimmorley were both kept out of the team of the year twice despite being named in the top five players of the year. Middleton opted for Geoff Toovey in 1996 and Andrew Johns in 1998 ahead of Langer, while Johns was chosen ahead of Kimmorley in 1999 and 2000. Other top five players of the year to miss team of the year selection include: Greg Alexander, Ewan McGrady and Gary Freeman (all kept out by Langer); and Preston Campbell, Brent Sherwin, Stacey Jones and Johnathan Thurston (all ousted by Johns). The only non-halfbacks to be picked in the top five players and miss out on team of the year honours are fullbacks Rhys Wesser (2003), Kurt Gidley (2008) and Billy Slater (2009), bumped by Lockyer, Slater and Jarryd Hayne respectively.

To mark the *Official Rugby League Annual*'s 25th season in 2011, Middleton named a team based on his player and team of the year selections.

Fullback: Darren Lockyer

Wings: Rod Wishart and Michael Hancock

Centres: Steve Renouf and Jamie Lyon

Five-eighth: Brad Fittler

Halfback: Andrew Johns

Props: Glenn Lazarus and Shane Webcke

Hooker: Cameron Smith

Second-rowers: Nathan Hindmarsh and Paul Sironen

Lock: Bradley Clyde

John Ferguson, Willie Carne and Michael Hancock could not be split with three wing appearances each, one behind Rod Wishart, but Hancock's achievements earned him the nod. Steve Walters, Danny Buderus and Cameron Smith were tied on five positional nominations apiece, but Smith got the nod on account of being named as one of the top five players of the year four times (Walters was named twice and Buderus once). Bradley Clyde and Paul Gallen were each named at lock in the team of the year four times, but Clyde's three nominations in the top five players of the year got the Canberra great over the line. Walters, Buderus and prop Steve Price were unluckiest players to miss out after being named in the team of the year five times. Nevertheless, it is a formidable line-up that proudly represents the best of the past quarter century.

OFFICIAL RUGBY LEAGUE ANNUAL PLAYERS OF THE YEAR

Greg Alexander (1991)

Marcus Bai (1998)

Gary Belcher (1989, 1990)

Matt Bowen (2007)

Darius Boyd (2010)

Tim Brasher (1996)

Danny Buderus (2004)

Preston Campbell (2001)

Todd Carney (2010)

Nathan Cayless (2001)

Daly Cherry-Evans (2011)

Petero Civoniceva (2006)

Bradley Clyde (1989, 1991, 1994)

Mark Coyne (1993)

Laurie Daley (1995, 1996)

Ben Elias (1988)

Brad Fittler (1995, 1997, 2002)

Greg Florimo (1994)

Israel Folau (2007)

Gary Freeman (1992)

Paul Gallen (2011)

Daniel Gartner (1996)

Kurt Gidley (2008)

Ryan Girdler (2000)

Craig Gower (2003)

Ben Hannant (2009)

Paul Harragon (1997)

Jarryd Hayne (2009)

Nathan Hindmarsh (2000, 2004, 2006)

Greg Inglis (2009)

Garry Jack (1988)

Andrew Johns (1995, 1998, 1999, 2000, 2001, 2002, 2006)

Stacey Jones (2002)

Ben Kennedy (2001, 2005, 2006)

Shaun Kenny-Dowall (2010)

Brett Kimmorley (1999, 2000)

Allan Langer (1988, 1991, 1992, 1996, 1998)

Gary Larson (1995)

Glenn Lazarus (1990, 1992)

Wally Lewis (1988)

Darren Lockyer (1998, 2001, 2002, 2003, 2004, 2006)

Cliff Lyons (1990)

Brad Mackay (1993)

Benji Marshall (2010, 2011)

Hugh McGahan (1987)

Ewan McGrady (1991)

Mal Meninga (1989, 1990, 1991)

Steve Menzies (1995)

Gavin Miller (1988, 1989)

Anthony Minichiello (2005)

Fuifui Moimoi (2009)

Adrian Morley (2003)

Brett Mullins (1994)

Michael O'Connor (1987)

Robbie O'Davis (1997)

Mark O'Meley (2004)

Dean Pay (1994)

David Peachey (1999)

Wayne Pearce (1987)

Steve Price (2004, 2007)

Scott Prince (2005)

Steve Renouf (1992)

Mat Rogers (1999)

Dale Shearer (1987)

Brent Sherwin (2002)

David Shillington (2010)

John Simon (1997)

Billy Slater (2008, 2009, 2011)

Cameron Smith (2006, 2007, 2008, 2011)

Peter Sterling (1987, 1990)

Glenn Stewart (2008)

Ricky Stuart (1993, 1994)

Gorden Tallis (1998, 1999, 2000)

Johnathan Thurston (2005, 2007)

Geoff Toovey (1996, 1997)

Manu Vatuvei (2008)

Kerrod Walters (1989, 1993)

Steve Walters (1992, 1993)

Rhys Wesser (2003)

Craig Wing (2003)

RUGBY LEAGUE WEEK'S AWARDS AND HONOURS

Rugby League Week magazine made its newsstand debut in April 1970, and defied the cynics who predicted its swift demise to become the code's preeminent publication. Affectionately referred to as 'The Bible,' *RLW* has been a weekly staple for Rugby League lovers for 42 seasons and is ingrained in the constitution of the game's modern era. *RLW* has run a prestigious Player of the Year award since its inception, and run several contests that have contributed to Rugby League's story and honoured many of the game's greats.

RLW PLAYER OF THE YEAR *Rugby League Week's* Player of the Year award is the longest-running annual individual prize in the history of Australian Rugby League. Established in 1970, the gong is the ultimate reward for consistency, based on the magazine's exclusive player rating system for every match of the season—out of five from 1970-76, and out of 10 since 1977. Cronulla captain-coach and former Great Britain halfback Tommy Bishop was the inaugural winner of the award in 1970. Fellow No.7s, Easts' Kevin Hastings (1980-82), Parramatta general Peter Sterling (1984 and 1986-87) and Newcastle maestro Andrew Johns (1998-99 and 2002) each claimed the honour a record three times. Hastings' hat-trick came in the same seasons he finished as runner-up in the Dally M Medal on three consecutive occasions. Eels backrowers Ray Price (1979 and 1985) and Nathan Hindmarsh (2004 and 2006) collected the award on two occasions.

Parramatta trio Ray Higgs (1976), Mick Cronin (1977) and Price (1979), Hastings (1981), Sterling (1987), Sharks second-rower Gavin Miller (1989) and Canterbury halfback Ewan McGrady were each named *RLW* Player of the Year in the same season they claimed the Rothmans Medal. Sterling (1987) and Miller (1989) are the only players to win the *RLW* Player of the Year/Rothmans Medal/Dally M Medal treble in the same year, while Sterling also picked up the *RLW*/Dally M double in 1986. Other winners of the *RLW* honour and the Dally M in the same season are Cliff Lyons (1994), Laurie Daley (1995), Allan Langer (1996), Johnathan Thurston (2007, joint winner of the *RLW* award with North Queensland teammate Matt Bowen) and Jarryd Hayne (2009), while Andrew Johns won his record three Dally M Medals in the years he was named *RLW's* best. Sydney City linchpin Brad Fittler won the *RLW* Player of the Year award and the Provan-Summons Medal (the ARL competition's official player of the year prize) in 1997.

1970 Tommy Bishop (Cronulla)

1971 Bob Grant (Souths)

1972 John Ballesty (Easts)

1973 Johnny Mayes (Manly)

1974 Arthur Beetson (Easts)

1975 Bob Fulton (Manly)

1976 Ray Higgs (Parramatta)

1977 Michael Cronin (Parramatta)

1978 Geoff Gerard (Parramatta)

1979 Ray Price (Parramatta)

1980 Kevin Hastings (Easts)

1981 Kevin Hastings (Easts)

1982 Kevin Hastings (Easts)

1983 Phil Sigsworth (Manly)

1984 Peter Sterling (Parramatta)

1985 Ray Price (Parramatta)

1986 Peter Sterling (Parramatta)

1987 Peter Sterling (Parramatta)

1988 Ben Elias (Balmain)

1989 Gavin Miller (Cronulla)

1990 Mal Meninga (Canberra)

1991 Ewan McGrady (Canterbury)

1992 Paul Langmack (Wests)

1993 Steve Walters (Canberra)

1994 Cliff Lyons (Manly)

1995 Laurie Daley (Canberra)

1996 Allan Langer (Brisbane)

1997 Brad Fittler (Sydney City)

1998 Andrew Johns (Newcastle)

1999 Andrew Johns (Newcastle)

2000 Brett Kimmorley (Melbourne)

2001 Shane Webcke (Brisbane)

2002 Andrew Johns (Newcastle)

2003 Steve Price (Canterbury)

2004 Nathan Hindmarsh (Parramatta)

2005 Luke Bailey (St. George Illawarra)

2006 Nathan Hindmarsh (Parramatta)

2007 Matt Bowen (North Queensland) and
Johnathan Thurston (North Queensland)

2008 Billy Slater (Melbourne)

2009 Jarryd Hayne (Parramatta)

2010 Paul Gallen (Cronulla)

2011 Corey Parker (Brisbane)

Halfbacks have taken out the award 16 times; five-eighths, locks and second-rowers on five occasions; props four times; centres and fullback three times; and hookers twice. Wing is the only position not represented by a *RLW* Player of the Year award winner. Fourteen different clubs boast *RLW* Player of the Year award recipients. Parramatta is easily the most prolific club with 11 winners, followed by the Roosters (six) and Manly (four). The *RLW* Player of the Year went on to enjoy Grand Final glory in three of the first five seasons the award was run—Souths halfback Bob Grant (1971), Manly No.7 Johnny Mayes (1973) and Easts captain Arthur Beetson (1974). But only Sterling (1986) and Canberra skipper Mal Meninga (1990) have won a premiership in the same season as taking out the honour since.

THE IMMORTALS *Rugby League Week* instigated a contest in 1981 that would become part of the game's fabric, introducing a term that grew into a symbol of true Rugby League greatness. The selection of the four best post-World War II players—the 'Immortals'—was the beginning of a fantastic tradition. South Sydney fullback and unparalleled Australian captain of the 1940s and 1950s Clive Churchill was an automatic choice, regarded by many as the greatest player of all time. Two stars of the dominant St. George sides of the 1950s and 1960s, centre Reg Gasnier and lock Johnny Raper, also had undeniable claims to Immortal status. The duo's achievements at club, state and international level saw them become viewed as the best ever in their respective positions. The last spot in the Immortal quartet belonged to champion five-eighth or centre Bob Fulton, a brilliant individual talent and tremendous leader in a decorated career for Manly, Easts, New South Wales and Australia.

Amid much excitement and speculation, *RLW* announced it would name the fifth Immortal in 1999. The verdict came in and two players could not be split—St. George fullback/centre Graeme Langlands and Queensland five-eighth Wally Lewis were both elevated to Immortal status. Langlands, who was rumoured to be very close to selection in 1981, and Lewis carved out careers as magnificent match-winners and revered captains. The pair looked at home in the exalted company of the four original Immortals. The masterful ball-playing prop Arthur Beetson was named as the seventh Immortal in 2003, a fitting tribute to a player whose contribution to the game as a unique and influential figure was immense.

Who should be the next Immortal is a popular subject of debate for Rugby League fans and experts alike. Recently retired greats Andrew Johns and Darren Lockyer have their supporters, while the tag would not look out of place bestowed upon the likes of Mal Meninga, Peter Sterling and Norm Provan. The eighth Immortal will be named in 2012.

THE HALL OF FAME To commemorate 75 years of Rugby League in Australia, *RLW* named the greatest team in the game's history in 1982. The judges were playing greats Frank Hyde (also a legendary commentator), Herman Peters, Herb Steinohrt, Dick Dunn and Jack Reardon (who later became a highly respected journalist), revered Rugby League scribes Tom Goodman and George Crawford, and long-time administrator Alex Mackie—a panel of experts with a collective experience numbering in the hundreds of years.

Six players that were later named in the ARL's Team of the Century in 2008—Churchill, Gasnier, Irvine, Hall, Provan and Raper—were named in the Hall of Fame Team (Messenger was named on the bench in the Team of the Century). Dally Messenger the only player not seen in action by the judges—was picked over fellow Easts great Dave Brown and St. George fullback/centre Graeme Langlands. The legendary Harold Horder was chosen ahead of Brian Bevan; Vic Hey ousted Bob Fulton for the five-eighth spot; Duncan Thompson was named at halfback over Keith Holman and Billy Smith; pioneer Sandy Pearce was chosen at hooker, denying the claims of the likes of Ian Walsh and Noel Kelly; and Souths second-rower George Treweek earned a place ahead of another Rabbitohs legend, Ron Coote.

The surprise inclusion was revered Queensland and Kangaroos prop of the 1920s and 1930s Mick Madsen, who earned the judges' nod ahead of future Team of the Century front-rower Arthur Beetson.

Fullback: Clive Churchill

Wing: Harold Horder

Centre: Dally Messenger

Centre: Reg Gasnier

Wing: Ken Irvine

Five-eighth: Vic Hey

Halfback: Duncan Thompson

Prop: Duncan Hall

Hooker: Sandy Pearce

Prop: Mick Madsen

Second-row: George Treweek

Second-row: Norm Provan

Lock: John Raper

THE MASTERS *RLW* marked 15 years in circulation by soliciting a panel of experts to select a team of the best players from 1970-85. Former Kangaroos player and coach Frank Stanton, the Immortal Reg Gasnier, then-Australian Test coach Terry Fearnley, and legendary journalists Alan Clarkson and Jack Reardon, who was also an outstanding centre and toured with the 1937-38 Kangaroos, were charged with selecting the team. The judges' decisions in assembling the crack line-up were almost unanimous.

St. George champions Langlands and Smith were chosen despite retiring in 1976 and 1977 respectively, ousting Manly custodian Graham Eadie and Wests halfback Tom Raudonikis, whose illustrious careers fit snugly into the 15-year timeframe. Contemporary stars Steve Mortimer and Peter Sterling also had claims to the No.7. As he would be in the ARL Team of the Century in 2008, Ron Coote was bumped to the second-row to accommodate a brilliant lock, with Parramatta great Ray Price getting the nod. The panellists resisted the temptation to move Bob Fulton to centre and pick burgeoning all time great Wally Lewis at pivot, keeping the magnificent 14-Test centre pairing of Cronin and Rogers together. Manly rake Max Krilich was chosen ahead of Elwyn Walters and George Peponis.

The group of Rugby League luminaries assembled for a team photo bedecked in green and gold, and in a touching moment, they spontaneously chose the incomparable 'Changa' Langlands to sit in the centre of the front row as captain. The Masters 1970-85:

Fullback: Graeme Langlands

Wing: Kerry Boustead

Centre: Mick Cronin

Centre: Steve Rogers

Wing: Eric Grothe

Five-eighth: Bob Fulton

Halfback: Billy Smith

Prop: John O'Neill

Hooker: Max Krilich

Prop: Arthur Beetson

Second-row: Ron Coote

Second-row: Bob McCarthy

Lock: Ray Price

THE PLAYERS' POLL *Rugby League Week* introduced the Rugby League Players' Poll in 1986, canvassing the opinions of 100 of the game's top players on their peers and the game's hottest topics. An anonymous survey, the annual Players' Poll consistently produces fascinating insights and surprising results, becoming arguably the magazine's most anticipated issue each season. The vote for the premiership's best or most valuable player has seen some of the modern era's greatest exponents given the ultimate nod by their colleagues. Early winners of the category included Brett Kenny, Peter Sterling and Wally Lewis. Canberra champions Laurie Daley (1991 and 1995) and Bradley Clyde (1992 and 1994) were named the game's best player twice, while Daley also polled second three times. Brad Fittler topped the category three years running (1996-98), before polling second in the ensuing two seasons to Andrew Johns, who was honoured by his peers for five straight seasons from 1999-2003 (including a record 81 per cent of the vote in 2001). After two injury-plagued seasons, Johns was named the game's most valuable player again in 2006. Darren Lockyer polled as the best player in the NRL in 2004 and '05 after finishing second to Johns in three consecutive seasons, and was runner-up again in 2007 to Johnathan Thurston. The North Queensland linchpin rated at the top of the best player category again in 2009 and 2011, while he finished second in 2008 and 2010. Melbourne's Greg Inglis (2008) and Billy Slater (2010) pipped Thurston for the honour.

- **Fullbacks:** Gary Belcher and Darren Lockyer were each named the game's best custodian five times, followed by Billy Slater (four times) and Anthony Minichiello (three times).
- **Wingers:** Wendell Sailor polled as the top winger six times, while Michael Hancock and Eric Grothe Jr. achieved the honour three times.
- **Centres:** Mal Meninga was chosen as the best centre five times, followed by Greg Inglis (four times) and Steve Renouf (three times).
- **Five-eighths:** Darren Lockyer was named the game's outstanding pivot in eight straight seasons (2004-11) after switching from fullback. Laurie Daley ranked as the best five-eighth seven times, and Brad Fittler on four occasions (Fittler was named as both the best five-eighth and best lock in 1998).
- **Halfback:** Andrew Johns polled as the NRL's best halfback seven times, with Allan Langer (six times) and Johnathan Thurston (five) not far behind.
- **Locks:** Bradley Clyde was named best lock a record seven times, with Fittler's and Scott Hill's three poll-topping seasons the next best effort.

- **Second-rowers:** Gorden Tallis' peers chose him as the game's best second-rower five times, while Nathan Hindmarsh topped the poll on three occasions.
- **Props:** Shane Webcke polled as the best prop a colossal eight times, followed by fellow Brisbane bookends Glenn Lazarus (five times) and Petero Civoniceva (four).
- **Hooker:** Steve Walters was named the best No.9 in seven consecutive seasons (1991-97), while Danny Buderus (2001-06) and Cameron Smith (2007-11) also dominated the category.

In the most comprehensive results in the positional categories in the poll's history, Clyde netted 96 per cent of the best lock vote in 1992, 94 per cent of the players polled named Belcher as the best fullback in 1990, Smith attracted 92 per cent of the best hooker vote in 2011, and Lockyer was named best five-eighth in 2007 with 91 per cent of the vote. Canterbury, Wests and Manly prop David Gillespie was named the competition's most hurtful defender in the first seven seasons the poll was run, before being knocked off his perch by Brisbane hitman Trevor Gillmeister in 1993.

AWARDS MISCELLANY

E.E. CHRISTENSEN'S PLAYER OF THE YEAR Ernie Christensen ranks as one of the giants of Rugby League journalism and Australian sportswriting in general, most prominently with Sydney's *The Sun* newspaper during the 1960s and 1970s. Christensen edited the official *NSWRL Year Book* from 1946-77 and chose the New South Wales Player of the Year, who appeared on the cover of the annual publication. Easts and Australian Test winger Lionel Cooper was the inaugural winner of the award based on performances at club and representative level in 1946, before joining Huddersfield at the end of the season and becoming a luminary of the English club scene. Balmain's brilliant winger Bobby Lulham won the award in 1947, while Newtown centre Len Smith—Australia's captain-coach against New Zealand during the season—was named the NSW Player of the Year in 1948 despite his notorious non-selection in that year's Kangaroo Tour squad.

Souths and Easts lock Ron Coote was bestowed with the honour a record four times (1968-69, 1974 and 1976). Future Immortals Clive Churchill (1949-50 and 1952) and Reg Gasnier (1959, 1961 and 1964), and Wests' wonderful halfback Keith Holman (1951, 1956 and 1958) were named Player of the Year in three seasons, while Johnny Raper (1960 and 1964), Graeme Langlands (1970-71) and Bob Fulton (1972-73) collected the gong twice. Parramatta centre Mick Cronin won the last award in 1977—the Test centre's first season in Sydney. The award was shared just once, when Gasnier and Raper were named joint winners in 1964. Manly prop Roy Bull, the 1954 winner, is the only player to collect Christensen's award playing for a team that failed to make the finals. The Rugby League and Australian sporting fraternity was shocked and saddened to hear of Christensen's death shortly after he returned from covering the 1980 Moscow Olympics.

1946 **Lionel Cooper** (Easts)

1947 **Bobby Lulham** (Balmain)

1948 **Len Smith** (Newtown)

1949 **Clive Churchill** (Souths)

1950 **Clive Churchill** (Souths)

1951 **Keith Holman** (Wests)

1952 **Clive Churchill** (Souths)

1953 **Jack Rayner** (Souths)

1954 **Roy Bull** (Manly)

1955 **Ken Kearney** (St. George)

1956 **Keith Holman** (Westerns)

1957 **Norm Provan** (St. George)

1958 **Keith Holman** (Wests)

1959 **Reg Gasnier** (St. George)

1960 **Johnny Raper** (St. George)

1961 **Reg Gasnier** (St. George)

1962 **Arthur Summons** (Wests)

1963 **Ian Walsh** (St. George)

1964 **Johnny Raper** (St. George) and **Reg Gasnier** (St. George)

1965 **Ken Thornett** (Parramatta)

1966 **Billy Smith** (St. George)

1967 **Les Johns** (Canterbury)

1968 **Ron Coote** (Souths)

1969 **Ron Coote** (Souths)

1970 **Graeme Langlands** (St. George)

1971 **Graeme Langlands** (St. George)

1972 **Bob Fulton** (Manly)

1973 **Bob Fulton** (Manly)

1974 **Ron Coote** (Easts)

1975 **Arthur Beetson** (Easts)

1976 **Ron Coote** (Easts)

1977 **Michael Cronin** (Parramatta)

THE HARRY SUNDERLAND MEDAL The Australian Rugby League inaugurated the Harry Sunderland Medal in 1964 in memoriam of one of the code's great administrators and entrepreneurs. Sunderland was integral to the establishment of Rugby League in Queensland and France (as well as ambitious attempts to get the game up and running in Victoria and the United State), and managed three Kangaroo Tours (1929-30, 1933-34 and 1937-38). Following his death in Manchester, England, in 1964, a Medal was struck in his honour and awarded to the best Australian player in home Test series. Johnny Raper was the first winner of the Harry Sunderland Medal for his efforts in the 1964 series against France. St. George halfback Billy Smith collected the award in consecutive years after being the standout Australian player in series against Great Britain (1966) and New Zealand (1967). The Medal was solely awarded during home Ashes series during the next 25 years; Ron Coote received the honour in 1970 and 1974, Ray Price was adjudged the best Australian player in the 1979 series, Wayne Pearce won the Medal after Australia's whitewash of the touring Lions in 1984, captain Wally Lewis was a worthy winner following the 2-1 series victory in 1988, and Bradley Clyde was the Harry Sunderland medallist in 1992, the last time an Ashes series has been played in Australia.

The award was discontinued as traditional international tours and Test series became a thing of the past, but the Harry Sunderland Medal was reinstated in 2004 for the best Australian player in international tournaments at home and abroad. Fullback Anthony Minichiello won the Medal in 2004 and '05 for his brilliant performances in back-to-back Tri-Nations tournaments in England, while Petero Civoniceva received the award after the 2006 Tri-Nations played in Australia and New Zealand. Skipper Darren Lockyer collected the gong in the wake of Australia's unsuccessful World Cup campaign in 2008; Greg Inglis won the award after the Kangaroos won the inaugural Four Nations tournament in 2009 in England and France; and lock Paul Gallen deservedly took out the Medal after the 2010 Four Nations in Australia and New Zealand and the 2011 tournament in England.

THE KEN STEPHEN MEDAL Ken Stephen's brief first grade career with Balmain and Souths which included an appearance for New South Wales in 1948 was cut short by injury, but he made a lasting contribution as an administrator, succeeding Harold Matthews as NSWRL secretary in 1967. The Ken Stephen Medal was struck in his honour following his death at the age of 62 in 1988, and awarded annually for services to Rugby League and the community. Wayne Pearce was the inaugural recipient in 1988, while some of the game's greats have collected the award for their selfless efforts off the field, including Peter Sterling, Paul Harragon, Andrew Ettingshausen, Hazem El Masri, Ruben Wiki and Nathan Hindmarsh. In a departure from the usual practice of bestowing the Medal on an individual player, the 2001 Ken Stephen Medal was awarded to the Parramatta club. Many Indigenous players have been recognised with the Ken Stephen Medal for their tireless work within their communities, including Ricky Walford, Nathan Blacklock, David Peachey, Dean Widders, Preston Campbell and Sam Thaiday.

THE PROVAN-SUMMONS MEDAL The Provan-Summons Medal named after St. George second-rower Norm Provan and Wests halfback Arthur Summons, the subjects of the famous 'Gladiators' photograph taken of the mud-caked rival captains after the 1963 Grand Final who have also adorned the premiership's various trophies since 1982 was inaugurated in 1997 for the best player in the ARL competition during the game's split after a ban on tobacco advertising brought an end to the Rothmans Medal. Voted on by the Rugby League media, the 1997 Nokia Provan-Summons Medal was won by Sydney City captain Brad Fittler, ahead of halfbacks John Simon (Parramatta) and Jason Taylor (North Sydney). Newcastle fullback Robbie O'Davis and Eels pivot Jason Bell rounded out the top-five, while pint-sized Gold Coast No.7 Wes Patten was a bolter in sixth spot. Across the divide, Canberra skipper Laurie Daley won Super League's Player of the Year award, the Telstra Medal.

After the establishment of the National Rugby League in 1998 and the subsequent elevation of the Dally M Medal to the premiership's official player of the year award mantle, the Provan-Summons Medal became a people's choice award announced at the Dally M Awards night. Andrew Johns was the public's vote as winner of the award for five straight seasons (1998-2002), while it was not awarded in 2003 due to the cancellation of the Dally Ms. Darren Lockyer became the only Queenslander to collect the gong in 2004, before Parramatta backrower Nathan Hindmarsh held a mortgage on the Medal for the following four seasons. St. George Illawarra pivot Jamie Soward won the award in 2009, and Roosters No.6 Todd Carney picked up the Dally M/Provan-Summons Medal double in 2010 before veteran Hindmarsh regained the honour in 2011.

LAURIE DALEY (left) and **BRAD FITTLER**, two of Australian Rugby League's great five-eighths and captains, after the Sydney Roosters' 38-10 semi-final defeat of Canberra in 2000. The loss signalled the end of Daley's 244-game career with the Raiders, while Fittler retired in 2004 after 336 first grade appearances.

STACEY JONES, New Zealand Warriors captain, steps around Sydney Roosters counterpart **BRAD FITTLER** on the way to one of the great Grand Final tries in 2002. The Warriors eventually went down 30-8 in their maiden appearance in a decider, while brilliant halfback Jones claimed the Golden Boot award as the best player in world Rugby League at the end of the year.

ANDREW JOHNS, Newcastle halfback and captain—arguably the greatest player of all time, taking the ball to the line for the Knights against the Cronulla Sharks in 2006, his last full season before a neck injury forced his premature retirement.

DARREN LOCKYER evades the tackle of New Zealand's **STACEY JONES** at Auckland's Mt. Smart Stadium in the Kangaroos' 30-18 tournament-opening victory in the 2006 Tri-Nations. Lockyer skippered his country in 38 of his 59 Test appearances, scoring 35 tries—all record tallies.

SAM RAPIRA (left) and captain **NATHAN CAYLESS** congratulate **JEREMY SMITH** after Smith scores New Zealand's first try in the 2008 World Cup final against Australia at Suncorp Stadium. The Kiwis staged a famous 34-20 victory to claim their first World Cup triumph, simultaneously breaking Australia's 36-year stranglehold on the 'world champions' tag.

BILLY SLATER (left), the Melbourne fullback, celebrates his try in the Storm's 23-16 Grand Final victory over Parramatta in 2009 with winger **STEVE TURNER.** The club's 2007 and 2009 titles were stripped six months later after revelations of extensive salary cap breaches.

THE RLIF AWARDS The Rugby League International Federation instigated a series of awards in 2008 to honour the official International Player of the Year, the International Rookie of the Year, Coach of the Year, the best player in each position, and Referee of the Year. Melbourne, Queensland and Australian fullback Billy Slater was named the International Player of the Year in 2008 and 2011 to complement the Golden Boot Awards he won in each season, while the brilliant No.1 also won the Dally M Medal in 2011 to claim a unique treble. Dally M medallists Jarryd Hayne (2009) and Todd Carney (2010) also doubled up their awards tally by being named International Player of the Year. Israel Folau was the inaugural International Rookie of the Year, followed by English youngsters Ryan Hall (2009) and Sam Tomkins (2010), and Brisbane winger Jharal Yow Yeh (2011). The Coach of the Year gong from 2008-11 went to the premiership-winning NRL mentor in each season. Multiple positional award winners include Wests Tigers and New Zealand five-eighth Benji Marshall (2009-11), Melbourne and Australian hooker Cameron Smith (2008-09 and 2011), Leeds, Wests Tigers and England second-rower Gareth Ellis (2008-10), Gold Coast and Australian halfback Scott Prince (2008 and 2010), fullback Slater (2008 and 2011), and Melbourne and Australian superstar Greg Inglis (2008 [five-eighth] and 2009 [centre]). Australians have won 25 of the 36 positional awards (note: Ellis tied with Gold Coast and Australian second-rower Anthony Laffranchi in 2008) available in the first four years of the RLIF Awards, including expat Wigan winger Pat Richards. Kiwi captain Marshall was the only non-Australian to win a positional award in 2011.

AUSTRALIAN AWARD-WINNERS IN ENGLAND The Man of Steel Award is the premier individual prize in British Rugby League, given to the outstanding player of each Northern Hemisphere season. The award began in 1977 and was originally voted on by the members of the Rugby League press. The players themselves have chosen the winner since 2008. Gavin Miller was the first Australian to receive the honour, being named the Man of Steel in the 1985-86 season while playing for Hull Kingston Rovers. Cronulla stalwart Miller won the 1989 Rothmans Medal, thus becoming the first and only winner of the official player of the year award in Australia and England. Easts three-quarter and New Zealand Test veteran Dean Bell, who later became the Auckland Warriors' inaugural captain, won the Man of Steel Award in 1992 as skipper of the all-conquering Wigan side. Adrian Vowles, a former Gold Coast and North Queensland centre/five-eighth who represented Queensland in one Origin match, collected the gong in 1999 en route to becoming a Castleford great. Former Parramatta and Australian Test centre Jamie Lyon's exceptional 2005 season with St. Helens was rewarded with the Man of Steel Award, before he returned to Australia and premiership success with Manly. Inspirational former NSW and Wests Tigers fullback Brett Hodgson won the Man of Steel in his first season for Huddersfield. Hodgson's 2005 Grand Final teammate, winger Pat Richards has become revered figure at Wigan, and was named 2010's Man of Steel after topping the Super League competition with 32 tries and a record 434 points on his way to a premiership with the Warriors.

New Zealand-born Rangi Chase played in the NRL with Wests Tigers and St. George Illawarra, before joining Castleford in 2009 and representing New Zealand

Maori in 2010. He won the Man of Steel Award after a magnificent 2011 season and controversially debuted for England in the Four Nations tournament, qualifying on residential grounds. Pat Richards and Chase are the only players to date to collect the Man of Steel/Albert Goldthorpe Medal double. The Albert Goldthorpe Medal was established as a media-voted award for the season's best player in 2008 after the Man of Steel became a players' player award. Junee product and former Canberra halfback Michael Dobson won the Albert Goldthorpe Medal in 2009 after joining Hull KR. Albert Goldthorpe was the Northern Union's first superstar, becoming a Hunslet legend between the code's formation in 1895 and 1910.

Parramatta great Brett Kenny became the first Australian winner of the Lance Todd Trophy named in honour of the 1907-08 New Zealand 'All Golds' and Wigan star, who became a well-known administrator and radio announcer in 1985 as man of the match in the Challenge Cup final. Kenny's Wigan side defeated Hull (whose linchpin was his Eels teammate Peter Sterling) 28-24 in one of the great Cup finals. Veteran fullback and Australian Test great Graham Eadie claimed the Lance Todd Trophy in Halifax's victory over St. Helens in the 1987 Final. Michael Monaghan, a tenacious halfback or hooker in 126 games for Canberra and Manly, won the 2009 Lance Todd Trophy during a long and fruitful stint for Warrington. New Zealanders Dean Bell (1993), Robbie Paul (1996), Henry Paul (2000) and former Melbourne stalwart Jeff Lima (2011) have also had their names engraved on the Lance Todd Trophy.

Famed Australian administrator Harry Sunderland (*see above*) was honoured for his contribution to the game in England with the inauguration in 1965 of the Harry Sunderland Trophy for the man of the match in the premiership final, and from 1996, the Super League Grand Final. Former Test fullback and Wests, Manly and Illawarra star John Dorahy became the first Australian recipient of the Trophy for his performance in Hull KR's premiership final victory over Castleford in 1984. Dorahy's former Magpies and Sea Eagles teammate, firebrand second-rower Les Boyd, claimed the honour for Warrington in 1986. Former Souths, Illawarra and Canterbury halfback Greg Mackey, a veteran of 145 first grade games in Australia, won the Harry Sunderland Trophy in 1991 while playing for Hull FC. Ex-Balmain outside-back Michael Withers is the only Australian winner of the prize in the Super League era, collecting the Trophy after Bradford's 37-6 victory over Wigan in the 2001 Grand Final. Kiwi recipients include Wigan duo Sam Panapa (1994) and Thomas Leuluai (2010), and Bradford's Henry Paul (1999).

TEAMS OF THE CENTURY

The dawning of the Australian Rugby League's Centenary season in 2008 provided the forum for several prestigious 'Team of the Century' selections to be named throughout the year. The incredible talent that graced the Rugby League fields of Australia in the code's first 100 years was not only reflected in the quality of the teams chosen, but also in the calibre of the players that missed out.

TEAM OF THE CENTURY

Fullback: Clive Churchill

Winger: Ken Irvine

Centre: Reg Gasnier

Centre: Mal Meninga

Winger: Brian Bevan

Five-eighth: Wally Lewis

Halfback: Andrew Johns

Lock: Johnny Raper

Second-row: Ron Coote

Second-row: Norm Provan

Prop: Duncan Hall

Hooker: Noel Kelly

Prop: Arthur Beetson

Reserve: Graeme Langlands

Reserve: Dally Messenger

Reserve: Frank Burge

Reserve: Bob Fulton

A group of former Rugby League greats and historians gathered in 2008 for the arduous task of selecting a team of the best players in the Australian game's history. The ARL Team of the Century possessed a phenomenal array of talent and achievement but, almost inevitably, its announcement on April 17 sparked widespread conjecture and barroom debate.

The wing selection of Brian Bevan, the tryscoring phenomenon who played virtually his entire career in England, was controversial in light of the claims of Australian Test greats Harold Horder, Brian Carlson and Eric Grothe. Many thought Graeme Langlands, a centre early in his career but later one of the greatest fullbacks of all time, should have been picked ahead of record-breaking Kangaroo skipper Mal Meninga. Immortal centre/five-eighth Bob Fulton, pioneering legend Dally Messenger and dominant figure of the 1930s Dave Brown—arguably the best player to miss out on the squad altogether—were also edged by Meninga.

There was a school of thought that Newcastle genius Andrew Johns' revelations of many years of recreational drug abuse in 2007 should have ruled him out of contention for the Team of the Century, but his astounding match-winning ability was impossible for the selection panel to resist. Duncan Thompson, a legend of the code's early decades, 35-Test Wests great Keith Holman, Parramatta linchpin Peter Sterling and Brisbane champion Allan Langer were the other contenders for the halfback spot.

But arguably the most contentious selection was Noel Kelly at hooker in an all-Queensland front-row. Undoubtedly one of the greatest-ever Australian forwards and one of a select band of players to tour with the Kangaroos three times, Kelly played much of his career at prop. St. George legend Ian Walsh captained Australia 10 times in a 25-Test career during the 1950s and 1960s (many times with Kelly at prop), while pioneer Sandy Pearce and modern great Steve Walters also had strong claims to the hooking spot in the Team of the Century.

The Team of the Century pandered heavily to Australian Rugby League's golden era of the 1950s and 1960s—just five of the 17 players selected did not feature during that 20-year period. Reserves Messenger and Frank Burge were the only pre-World War II players to win selection, while Meninga, Johns and the incomparable Wally Lewis were the only inclusions whose heyday was post-1980.

Few would deny Jack Gibson's naming as coach of the century. A revolutionary coaching figure, Gibson won five premierships with Easts and Parramatta, moulding two of the all time great club combinations. Gibson passed away three weeks after the team was named, just hours before the Centenary Test against New Zealand at the SCG.

NSW TEAM OF THE CENTURY

Fullback: Clive Churchill

Winger: Ken Irvine

Centre: Reg Gasnier

Centre: Graeme Langlands

Winger: Dally Messenger

Five-eighth: Bob Fulton

Halfback: Andrew Johns

Prop: Glenn Lazarus

Hooker: Sandy Pearce

Prop: Frank Burge

Second-row: Norm Provan

Second-row: Ron Coote

Lock: John Raper

Reserve: Wally Prigg

Reserve: Dave Brown

Reserve: Steve Rogers

Reserve: Roy Bull

The seven NSW members of the ARL Team of the Century's starting side were retained in their respective positions for the state Team of the Century, named on May 19 of the game's centenary season. The four reserves in the ARL's best-ever side—Dally Messenger, Graeme Langlands, Bob Fulton and Frank Burge— all claimed starting spots in the NSW Team of the Century.

The other two additions were dual Kangaroo tourists Sandy Pearce (1908-09 and 1921-22) and Glenn Lazarus (1990 and 1994) in the front-row. Pre-World War II legends Wally Prigg and Dave Brown, 25-Test Manly prop Roy Bull and Cronulla's three-time Kangaroo Steve Rogers were honoured with reserve spots.

The NSW Team of the Century paid homage to the game's first four decades, with five pre-war players selected. The 1950s and 1960s were again strongly represented, while Rogers, Lazarus and halfback Andrew Johns were the only modern greats selected.

QRL TEAM OF THE CENTURY

Fullback: Darren Lockyer

Winger: Cecil Aynsley

Centre: Tom Gorman

Centre: Mal Meninga

Winger: Dennis Flannery

Five-eighth: Wally Lewis

Halfback: Allan Langer

Prop: Mick Madsen

Hooker: Noel Kelly

Prop: Duncan Hall

Second-row: Brian Davies

Second-row: Arthur Beetson

Lock: Bob Lindner

Reserve: Jim Craig

Reserve: Duncan Thompson

Reserve: Gene Miles

Reserve: Herb Steinohrt

Coach: Wayne Bennett

The Queensland Team of the Century was announced on the eve of the second State of Origin clash of the 2008 series at Suncorp Stadium. The team paid tribute to several stars of Rugby League's first half-century who played their entire careers in the Sunshine State, while seven State of Origin representatives won selection. ARL Team of the Century members Mal Meninga, Wally Lewis, Noel Kelly and Duncan Hall were selected in the same positions in Queensland's best-ever line-up, while Arthur Beetson was shifted to the second-row to accommodate Mick Madsen, a veteran of nine Tests for Australia and 34 matches for the Maroons in the 1920s and 1930s.

Despite switching to five-eighth in 2004, Darren Lockyer, the only current player selected, was picked at fullback, where he starred for Queensland at Origin level between 1998 and 2003. Queensland's first Kangaroo skipper Tom Gorman (1929-30) was a popular choice to partner Meninga in the centres, nudging out Origin stars Gene Miles and Steve Renouf. Test wingers Cecil Aynsley (four Tests from 1924-28) and Dennis Flannery (15 Tests from 1950-57), who, like Gorman, never ventured to play in the Sydney premiership, were somewhat surprising selections on the flanks ahead of modern masters Kerry Boustead, Michael Hancock and Wendell Sailor.

Brilliant Brisbane captain Allan Langer beat Duncan Thompson and Barry Muir for the halfback spot, while Noel Kelly resisted the challenge of Ipswich junior and Canberra rake Steve Walters. Dan Dempsey, Vic Armbruster and Herb Steinohrt (who was picked in the reserves) were unlucky forward pack omissions, but the credentials of the selected six cannot be questioned. The fact that Harry Bath played most of his career in England and Sydney is surely the only factor that kept the Brisbane Souths junior out of Queensland's best-ever 17.

In contrast to the Australian and NSW Teams of the Century, the Queensland side contained six players who dominated during the 1980s or after, while six players came from the pre-World War II era. Wayne Bennett, the former Test winger who coached in the Brisbane competition and at Origin level with distinction before guiding the Broncos to six premierships, was an obvious choice as coach, ahead of the legendary Bob Bax.

CRL TEAM OF THE CENTURY

Fullback: Clive Churchill

Winger: Brian Carlson

Centre: Michael Cronin

Centre: Graeme Langlands

Winger: Eddie Lumsden

Five-eighth: Bob Fulton

Halfback: Andrew Johns

Prop: Glenn Lazarus

Hooker: Ian Walsh

Prop: Steve Roach

Second-row: Herb Narvo

Second-row: Bradley Clyde

Lock: Wally Prigg

Emphasising the rich vein of talent that country areas in New South Wales have produced throughout Australian Rugby League history, the NSW Country Team of the Century featured four ARL and six NSW Team of the Century members. The remaining seven inclusions were strong contenders for NSW's best-ever side.

The plentiful Rugby League heartlands of Newcastle and Illawarra were well-represented. Six players—Clive Churchill, Brian Carlson, Eddie Lumsden, Andrew Johns, Herb Narvo and Wally Prigg—hailed from the Hunter Valley, while Mick Cronin, Bob Fulton, Graeme Langlands and Steve Roach came from the Illawarra region. Canberra Raiders stars Bradley Clyde (Belconnen) and Glenn Lazarus (Queanbeyan) represented the ACT and south-eastern NSW area. Hooker Ian Walsh shot to stardom from the most isolated background of any Team of the Century member, debuting for Australia in 1959 from the small town of Condobolin in NSW's Central West.

Riverina legend Eric Weissel, Gilgandra product and St. George great Johnny King, Junee's brilliant future Kangaroo Laurie Daley, Illawarra juniors Kevin Schubert and Craig Young, and Newcastle Team of the Century members Paul Harragon, Danny Buderus, Les Johns and Johnny Graves were among the best players to miss out on selection in the Country Team of the Century.

INDIGENOUS TEAM OF THE CENTURY

Fullback: Eric Simms

Winger: Lionel Morgan

Centre: Steve Renouf

Centre: Greg Inglis

Winger: Dale Shearer

Five-eighth: Laurie Daley

Halfback: Johnathan Thurston

Prop: Sam Backo

Hooker: Mal Cochrane

Prop: Arthur Beetson

Second-row: Gorden Tallis

Second-row: Sam Thaiday

Lock: Cliff Lyons

Reserve: George Green

Reserve: Wally McArthur

Reserve: Frank Fisher

Reserve: John Ferguson

The naming of the Indigenous Team of the Century in August, 2008, recognised several pioneering Indigenous Rugby League players along with a plethora of modern greats.

George Green—generally regarded as the first Aboriginal player to appear in the premiership, although his heritage has been a source of conjecture for historians (see Indigenous Rugby League) represented NSW in 1910 and was part of the Bears' renowned 1921-22 title-winning sides; Frank Fisher, the grandfather of athletics great Cathy Freeman, was a Queensland country legend of the 1930s; and Wally McArthur gained a Rugby League grounding in South Australia and Western Australia before starring in England. All three trailblazers were honoured with spots on the bench.

Wynnum-Manly winger Lionel Morgan, who became the first Indigenous Australian representative when he was selected for the 1960 World Cup, edged out modern wing greats Larry Corowa, John 'Chicka' Ferguson (who was selected on the bench), Wendell Sailor, Matt Sing and Nathan Blacklock.

Former NSW and Australian captain Laurie Daley's Indigenous heritage was not widely known before his selection in the Team of the Century, but he bumped master ball-playing pivot Cliff Lyons to lock. Superstar Greg Inglis was selected after just three full seasons of first grade ahead of Queensland teammate Justin Hodges and 1980s Test three-quarter Tony Currie, while South Sydney pointscoring machine Eric Simms was chosen at fullback, denying the claims of modern stars Matt Bowen and Preston Campbell.

THE 100 GREATEST PLAYERS

The Australian Rugby League unveiled its highly anticipated 100 Greatest Players to mark the game's centenary in 2008, a glowing tribute to best players of all time that inevitably sparked endless debate. But the ambitious task had been undertaken twice before—by *Rugby League Week* in 1992 and by the *Daily Telegraph* in 2000, with specially convened panels of selectors charged with the arduous task of narrowing down the plethora of great Rugby League players to the top 100.

South Sydney fullback legend Clive Churchill was the No.1 choice in the 1992 and 2000 lists. In order, Johnny Raper, Reg Gasnier, Dally Messenger and Graeme Langlands rounded out the top five in 1992, and again in 2000, with Langlands and Raper swapping positions. Bob Fulton ranked sixth and Wally Lewis seventh in the *RLW* poll, while the five-eighth greats traded positions in the *Telegraph*'s list. Vic Hey and Dave Brown, legends of the 1930s, were named as the eighth and ninth best Australian players respectively in 1992 and 2000. Halfback Duncan Thompson placed 10th in 1992, before slipping to 19th in 2000; tryscoring genius and fellow North Sydney great Ken Irvine moved up from 15th in 1992 to finish in the top 10 in 2000.

A handful of then-current players made the *RLW* and *Telegraph* top 100 lists. Lewis (No.7), Peter Sterling (No.11) and Michael O'Connor (No.51) were in their last seasons in 1992, while Mal Meninga (No.13) and Brett Kenny (No.27) were nearing the end of their decorated careers. The quintet of modern luminaries held similar positions in the 2000 poll. Bradley Clyde (No.33), Laurie Daley (No.50) and Allan Langer (No.80) were approaching their prime in 1992; Clyde dropped to 58th in 2000, while Daley moved up to 36th and Langer was elevated to 22nd place. Still playing in 2000, Brad Fittler (No.24), Andrew Ettingshausen (No.50) and Andrew Johns (No.82) were additions to the *Telegraph* top 100, as were recently retired modern stars Terry Lamb (No.65), Steve Walters (No.81), Garry Jack (No.89), Steve Roach (No.90), Paul Sironen (No.96), Gene Miles (No.98) and Glenn Lazarus (No.100). Of the aforementioned players, only O'Connor and Balmain pair Jack and Sironen missed selection in the ARL's 100 Greatest Players in 2008.

The ARL's top 100 was selected by a voting college consisting of Australian players, coaches, administrators, media representatives and historians that was established in 2002 to induct players into the Hall of Fame. All 36 inductees to the Hall of Fame to the end of 2007 (three players from the pre- and post-World War II eras were inducted each season) were automatic selections in the ARL's 100 Greatest Players. The decision was made to ensure an even allocation of players from the pre- and post-war eras, leaving the judges with 41 post-war and 23 pre-war players to add to the Hall of Fame contingent. Somewhat disappointingly, the automatic selections pre-empted a ranking of the top 100 players which had been a feature of the *RLW* and *Telegraph* lists.

Brisbane, Queensland and Australian captain Darren Lockyer was the only current player named in the ARL's 100 Greatest Players; Steve Menzies, Cameron Smith, Johnathan Thurston, Danny Buderus, Petero Civoniceva and Nathan Hindmarsh were considered the unluckiest of the players whose careers were still active to miss out—although Smith and Thurston would almost certainly be guaranteed a place in any future top 100 lists.

Broncos prop Shane Webcke, a 2006 retiree, was the only modern great besides Lockyer that did not feature in the previous top 100 lists to be named in the ARL's 100 Greatest Players, with Gorden Tallis and Ricky Stuart arguably the most notable omissions. The selection stipulations catapulted pioneering greats 'Tedda' Courtney, Bill Cann and Dan Frawley, and stars of the 1920s and 1930s Dan Dempsey, Viv Thicknesse and Andy Norval into the venerated list after being omitted in the 1992 and 2000 polls, while 1960s luminaries Arthur Summons, John Sattler and Johnny King joined the ARL's 100 Greatest Players despite being left out of the previous lists. Easts centre and 1921-22 Kangaroos captain Les Cubitt, and Queensland and Kangaroos prop of the 1960s Peter Gallagher were chosen in the ARL's 100 Greatest Players after originally being selected in 1992 but missing out in 2000.

Eleven inclusions of the 1992 and 2000 lists were victims of the desire to achieve an even spread of pre- and post-war players in the ARL's 100 Greatest Players. Ian Moir (No.49 in 1992 and No.44 in 2000), Les 'Chicka' Cowie (No.49 and 51), Michael O'Connor (No.51 and 60), Lionel Cooper (No.48 and 62), Jack Rayner (No.71 and 73), Bob 'Bear' O'Reilly (No.62 and 77), Dick Thornett (No.78 and 84), Peter Dimond (No.79 and 85), Kevin Schubert (No.82 and 87), Wally O'Connell (No.90 and 91) and Frank Stanmore (No.91 and 92) were omitted from the ARL's list after being chosen in the *RLW* and *Telegraph* polls.

Of the ARL's 100 Greatest Players, 72 were born in New Souths Wales, while the list contained 22 Queensland-born players. Two were born in Victoria and one in each of South Australia and Western Australia. Keith Barnes (Port Talbot, Wales) and Bob Fulton (Warrington, England) were the only players born overseas. Only two players had not represented Australia—wing wizard Brian Bevan and revered forward Harry Bath built their legends on the fields of English club Rugby League; Bath enjoyed five magnificent seasons in Australia for Balmain and St. George, but Bevan played just seven first grade games for Easts before becoming the greatest try-scorer the code has ever known with Warrington.

Eastern Suburbs/Sydney Roosters was the best-represented club in the ARL's 100 Greatest Players with 21 players selected, followed by St. George (15), South Sydney and Western Suburbs (14 each). Centres dominated the list with 24 selected in the top 100, while just six hookers were chosen. Regardless of the contentious selection criteria and the phenomenal players that were unfortunate to miss out, the ARL's 100 Greatest Players is an honour roll of extraordinary talent and immense contribution to the history of Rugby League in Australia.

RLW Top 100 (1991)	Telegraph Top 100 (2000)	ARL 100 Greatest (2008)*
1. Clive Churchill	Clive Churchill	Clive Churchill
2. John Raper	Graeme Langlands	Graeme Langlands
3. Reg Gasnier	Reg Gasnier	Reg Gasnier
4. Dally Messenger	Dally Messenger	Dally Messenger
5. Graeme Langlands	John Raper	John Raper
6. Bob Fulton	Wally Lewis	Wally Lewis
7. Wally Lewis	Bob Fulton	Bob Fulton
8. Vic Hey	Vic Hey	Vic Hey
9. Dave Brown	Dave Brown	Dave Brown
10. Duncan Thompson	Ken Irvine	Ken Irvine
11. Peter Sterling	Brian Carlson	Brian Carlson
12. Harold Horder	Harold Horder	Harold Horder
13. Mal Meninga	Brian Bevan	Brian Bevan
14. Brian Carlson	Peter Sterling	Peter Sterling
15. Ken Irvine	Mal Meninga	Mal Meninga
16. Arthur Beetson	Frank Burge	Frank Burge
17. Frank Burge	Wally Prigg	Wally Prigg
18. Wally Prigg	Arthur Beetson	Arthur Beetson
19. Keith Holman	Duncan Thompson	Duncan Thompson
20. Joe 'Chimpy' Busch	Ron Coote	Ron Coote
21. Tom Gorman	Keith Holman	Keith Holman
22. Brian Bevan	Allan Langer	Allan Langer
23. Ron Coote	Michael Cronin	Michael Cronin
24. Ian Walsh	Brad Fittler	Brad Fittler
25. Duncan Hall	Ian Walsh	Ian Walsh
26. Norm Provan	Duncan Hall	Duncan Hall
27. Brett Kenny	Graham Eadie	Graham Eadie
28. Herb Narvo	Steve Rogers	Steve Rogers
29. Ken Thornett	Tom Gorman	Tom Gorman
30. Harry Bath	Eric Weissel	Eric Weissel
31. Steve Rogers	Brett Kenny	Brett Kenny
32. Eric Weissel	Norm Provan	Norm Provan
33. Bradley Clyde	Chris McKivat	Chris McKivat
34. Jimmy Craig	Sid 'Sandy' Pearce	Sid 'Sandy' Pearce

35. George Treweek	Joe 'Chimpy' Busch	Joe 'Chimpy' Busch
36. Graham Eadie	Laurie Daley	Laurie Daley
37. Bob McCarthy	Bob McCarthy	Bob McCarthy
38. Michael Cronin	Les Johns	Les Johns
39. Les Johns	Jimmy Craig	Jimmy Craig
40. Howard Hallett	Brian Davies	Brian Davies
41. Brian Davies	George Treweek	George Treweek
42. Chris McKivat	Sid 'Joe' Pearce	Sid 'Joe' Pearce
43. Sid 'Sandy' Pearce	Ken Thornett	Ken Thornett
44. Cec Blinkhorn	Ian Moir	Johnny King
45. Sid 'Joe' Pearce	Herb Narvo	Herb Narvo
46. Billy Smith	Harry Bath	Harry Bath
47. Les Cowie	Harry Wells	Harry Wells
48. Lionel Cooper	Charles 'Chook' Fraser	Charles 'Chook' Fraser
49. Ian Moir	Les Cowie	John Sattler
50. Laurie Daley	Andrew Ettingshausen	Andrew Ettingshausen
51. Michael O'Connor	Howard Hallett	Howard Hallett
52. Charles 'Chook' Fraser	Billy Smith	Billy Smith
53. Ray Price	Barry Muir	Barry Muir
54. Eric Grothe	Noel Kelly	Noel Kelly
55. Barry Muir	Ray Price	Ray Price
56. Herb Steinohrt	Keith Barnes	Keith Barnes
57. Harry Wells	Tom Raudonikis	Tom Raudonikis
58. Arthur Clues	Bradley Clyde	Bradley Clyde
59. Noel Kelly	Cec Blinkhorn	Cec Blinkhorn
60. Arthur 'Pony' Halloway	Michael O'Connor	Darren Lockyer
61. 'Mick' Madsen	Eric Grothe	Eric Grothe
62. Bob O'Reilly	Lionel Cooper	Arthur Summons
63. Tom Raudonikis	Roy Bull	Roy Bull
64. Albert Rosenfeld	Ken Kearney	Ken Kearney
65. Roy Bull	Terry Lamb	Terry Lamb
66. Ray Stehr	Ray Stehr	Ray Stehr
67. Keith Barnes	Brian Clay	Brian Clay
68. Brian Clay	Kerry Boustead	Kerry Boustead
69. Eddie Lumsden	Arthur Clues	Arthur Clues
70. Herb Gilbert	Kel O'Shea	Kel O'Shea
71. Jack Rayner	Arthur 'Pony' Halloway	Arthur 'Pony' Halloway

72. Kel O'Shea	Eddie Lumsden	Eddie Lumsden
73. Steve Mortimer	Jack Rayner	Bill Cann
74. Brian Hambly	Herb Steinohrt	Herb Steinohrt
75. Ken Kearney	Brian Hambly	Brian Hambly
76. Frank McMillan	Herb Gilbert	Herb Gilbert
77. John O'Neill	Bob O'Reilly	Shane Webcke
78. Dick Thornett	Steve Mortimer	Steve Mortimer
79. Peter Dimond	'Mick' Madsen	'Mick' Madsen
80. Allan Langer	Viv Farnsworth	Viv Farnsworth
81. Ernie Norman	Steve Walters	Steve Walters
82. Kevin Schubert	Andrew Johns	Andrew Johns
83. Kerry Boustead	Albert Rosenfeld	Albert Rosenfeld
84. Viv Farnsworth	Dick Thornett	Viv Thicknesse
85. Vic Armbruster	Peter Dimond	'Tedda' Courtney
86. Pat Devery	Jack Beaton	Jack Beaton
87. Kevin Ryan	Kevin Schubert	Benny Wearing
88. Benny Wearing	Vic Armbruster	Vic Armbruster
89. Jack Beaton	Garry Jack	Dan Dempsey
90. Wally O'Connell	Steve Roach	Steve Roach
91. Frank Stanmore	Wally O'Connell	Dan Frawley
92. Bob Lindner	Frank Stanmore	Andy Norval
93. Dick Poole	John O'Neill	John O'Neill
94. Les Cubitt	Frank McMillan	Frank McMillan
95. Billy Wilson	Ernie Norman	Ernie Norman
96. Rod Reddy	Paul Sironen	Les Cubitt
97. Jack 'Bluey' Watkins	Wayne Pearce	Wayne Pearce
98. Peter Gallagher	Gene Miles	Gene Miles
99. Wayne Pearce	Kevin Ryan	Peter Gallagher
100. Jack Reardon	Glenn Lazarus	Glenn Lazarus

The ARL's 100 Greatest Players was not named in a numbered order

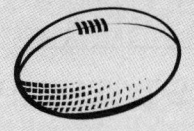

CHAPTER 6

THE REPRESENTATIVE SCENE

Domestic representative matches and rivalries hold a cherished place in the story of Australian Rugby League. The code's preeminent state sides—New South Wales and Queensland—have waged on-field war since 1908, Rugby League's inaugural season in Australia. Interstate football was solely played under a residency-based selection format until 1980, when State of Origin made its debut and revolutionised representative Rugby League in Australia. The history of pre-Origin interstate competition is profiled in this section, along with a detailed season-by-season account of State of Origin's 32 years. The rivalry between NSW's Country and City representative sides is also delved into, along with the most memorable, controversial and surprising selection occurrences in the code's history.

INTERSTATE RIVALRY

Interstate Rugby League competition between New South Wales and Queensland was initiated during the code's first season in Australia. While Queensland enjoyed prosperous periods against its southern rivals, New South Wales was the dominant force in interstate football for the bulk of the 72 seasons prior to the advent of State of Origin in 1980. New South Wales defeated Queensland 43-0 at Sydney's Agricultural Ground in the inaugural interstate match in 1908. South Sydney winger Tommy Anderson scored four tries in the drubbing, while Dally Messenger kicked eight goals. The Queensland side featured prominent pioneering figures Mick Dore, Mick Bolewski, Bill Heidke, Bill Hardcastle and Jack Fihelly. An all-new NSW line-up recorded a 12-3 victory in the second and final match of the series.

The first three-match series was played in Brisbane in 1910, with NSW winning all three clashes at the Brisbane Cricket Ground by comfortable margins. The interstate series moved back to Sydney in 1911, but Queensland was comprehensively outclassed in another 3-0 whitewash. NSW scored 15 tries in a 65-9 victory in the first encounter; Messenger scored 32 points from four tries and 10 goals—a mark unmatched at interstate level until equalled by NSW centre Ryan Girdler in a State of Origin match 89 years later. Messenger finished the series with 75 points (including nine tries) after 49-0 and 32-8 thrashings in the ensuing two clashes.

Queensland was again crushed 65-9 in 1912—although, mercifully, Messenger's scoring was restricted to 23 points—with NSW forwards Frank Burge and Bill Cann scoring three tries each. Interstate competition was suspended from 1916-18 due to World War I, but NSW resumed its domination with a 4-0 series victory in 1919. The Maroons finally broke their duck in a one-off clash in 1922 courtesy of a 25-9 triumph at the Sydney Sports Ground. Captained by forward Norm Potter, the Queensland side featured fellow 1921-22 Kangaroo tourist E.S. 'Nigger' Brown, future Kangaroos captain Tom Gorman and former Test winger Bill Paten, while the victory triggered the state's greatest period of dominance prior to State of Origin's introduction in 1980.

Led by Test star and Balmain great Jimmy Craig, who had moved to Ipswich, Queensland won both interstate clashes in 1923, and swept the 1924 series 3-0 after all time great halfback Duncan Thompson returned to his home state from North Sydney (Thompson quit the Sydney premiership after receiving a hotly disputed suspension for kicking in 1923). Queensland won two of the three interstate matches played in Sydney in 1925, before winning both matches in Brisbane staged later in the season. NSW's 1927 series victory was bookended by Queensland triumphs in 1926 and 1928, with Maroons forward pack luminaries Mick Madsen (who amassed a pre-Origin interstate record 36 appearances), Vic Armbruster, Dan Dempsey and Herb Steinohrt emerging. Queensland racked up its biggest-ever win in 1926—a 38-0 mauling at Brisbane's Exhibition Ground.

Queensland captured further series wins over NSW in 1931 and '32, but success was intermittent for the northerners from that point. The Maroons' only series victory in the subsequent 18 seasons was a 3-1 result in 1940, while they drew four-match series in 1934 and 1939. Balmain winger Sid Goodwin scored an interstate record six tries for NSW in a 54-13 victory in 1939, while fullback Dan O'Connor kicked a Queensland record 12 goals in a 45-8 drubbing of the Blues during the 1940 series. NSW boasted the likes of Newcastle's three-time Kangaroo lock Wally Prigg, a veteran of a record 34 appearances for the Blues, and pointscoring machine Dave Brown (who scored 117 points in 19 interstate matches) during the 1930s. Queensland's mainstays were Madsen, Jack Reardon and Les Heidke, son of pioneer Bill and a veteran of 35 interstate appearances in the maroon jersey.

After winning just three of 24 games from 1941-50 (interstate football was put on hold from 1942-44 due to World War II), Queensland prevailed in the 1951 series 2-1. Captain Duncan Hall, a future ARL Team of the Century prop, was joined in the forward pack by fellow Test greats Harold 'Mick' Crocker and Brian Davies, complemented by burgeoning backline stars Ken McCaffery, Dennis Flannery and Noel Hazzard. NSW's international-laden line-up was captained by Clive Churchill and featured Keith Holman, Frank Stanmore, Johnny Graves and Les Cowie. But NSW routinely dominated the decade, and demolished Queensland by a record 69-5 in 1957, with Greg Hawick kicking 15 goals to set a mark unlikely to be broken.

Queensland enjoyed another fruitful period in the late-1950s and early-1960s. Churchill left South Sydney at the end of 1958 following a pay dispute and joined Brisbane Norths. Although injury prevented Churchill from representing Queensland in the 1959 series (he donned the maroon jumper against New Zealand), the veteran of 27 interstate matches for NSW coached Queensland to a memorable 3-1 series victory. Captain Bob Banks was partnered in the halves by 25-Test halfback Barry Muir, while the pack included second-rower Elton Rasmussen and a front-row of Dud Beattie, Noel Kelly and Gary Parcell—an engine-room quartet on the verge of impressive Test careers.

The 1959 and 1960 series were drawn two games apiece, but the purple patch marked the beginning of a bleak era at representative level for the Maroons. The materialisation of 'star scalpers' had reached epidemic proportions. Sydney premiership clubs and NSW country clubs lured scores of Queensland's most talented players south. It was not a new phenomenon—Brisbane Souths junior Harry Bath joined Balmain in 1946 before crafting his legend in England, while champion backrower Kel O'Shea linked with Western Suburbs Magpies from Ayr in 1956—but the trend accelerated in the 1960s, despite the QRL's introduction of transfer fees. Parramatta lured Toowoomba's Kangaroo centre Ron Boden in 1960; the Magpies captured the signature of Test front-rower Kelly in 1961; Rasmussen joined St. George in 1962; Brisbane Souths' Test second-rower Mick Veivers linked with Manly in 1965; and Redcliffe pair Arthur Beetson and Kevin Yow Yeh joined Balmain in 1966.

Queensland won just four of 64 matches against NSW from 1962 until the residency-based interstate format was discontinued at the end of 1981. The Maroons won a match in each of the 1967 and '68 series with steadfast Test players such as Peter Gallagher, Denis Manteit and John Gleeson forming the core of the state squad, but the drain continued with the departure of the likes of John McDonald (Manly) and Lionel Williamson (Newtown). Crowds for the interstate fixtures (particularly in Sydney) began to wane as Queensland became less competitive, while the

QRL became increasingly frustrated by its representative side being dominated by a NSW line-up featuring Sunshine State products Beetson, Rod Reddy, Ray Higgs and Kerry Boustead.

Through the foresight and tireless campaigning of the QRL and in particular its president, Ron 'The Senator' McAuliffe, the 'State of Origin' concept—which would allow the Maroons to select Queensland-bred players based in Sydney—gained legs in the late-1970s. NSWRL and ARL President Kevin Humphreys was receptive to the idea and the Sydney premiership clubs voted overwhelmingly in favour of the new format. The first two interstate clashes of 1980 were played under the residency-based selection rules, with NSW winning comfortably 35-3 and 17-7, before a State of Origin fixture was staged in Brisbane in July.

The concept had its sceptics from the public, the media, and those within the game, but Queensland—captained by veteran prop Arthur Beetson (who was playing with Parramatta) and supported by Sydney-based stars Boustead, Reddy, John Lang and Rod Morris—triumphed 20-10 in the inaugural clash to start an interstate football revolution. The 1981 Origin match was also a one-off encounter preceded by two residency-based interstate clashes won easily by NSW (with Beetson, who had returned to play for Redcliffe, in the Queensland line-up). But Beetson-coached Queensland's stirring 22-15 victory in the Origin clash was a precursor to a three-match Origin series replacing the residency-based format permanently from 1982.

State of Origin has become regarded as arguably the highest-quality Rugby League contest in the world, and a highlight of the Australian sporting calendar. Queensland and NSW have each enjoyed multiple periods of dominance, while the passion and ferocity State of Origin evokes from players and supporters alike has transformed interstate Rugby League.

(see also State of Origin)

INTERSTATE RECORDS 1908-81 (NON-STATE OF ORIGIN)

BIGGEST WINS

New South Wales—69-5 at the Sydney Cricket Ground, 1957

Queensland—38-0 at the Brisbane Exhibition Ground, 1926

MOST APPEARANCES

Mick Madsen (Qld) 36, Les Heidke (Qld) 35, Wally Prigg (NSW) 34, Herb Steinohrt (Qld) 34, Graeme Langlands (NSW) 33, Ray Stehr (NSW) 30, Brian Davies (Qld) 31, Sid 'Joe' Pearce (NSW) 30

MOST TRIES

Ken Irvine (NSW) 28, Harold Horder (NSW) 23, Keith Holman (NSW) 21, Eddie 'Babe' Collins (Qld) 19, Graeme Langlands (NSW) 19, Noel Pidding (NSW) 17, Dennis Flannery (Qld) 16, Bob Fulton (NSW) 14

MOST TRIES IN A MATCH

New South Wales—Sid Goodwin 6 in 1939, Harold Horder 5 in 1915

Queensland—Alan Smith 4 in 1979

MOST POINTS

Noel Pidding (NSW) 169, Les Johns (NSW) 169, Michael Cronin (NSW) 142, Graeme Langlands (NSW) 137, Dave Brown (NSW) 117, Dan O'Connor (Qld) 112

MOST POINTS IN A MATCH

New South Wales—Dally Messenger 32 (four tries, 10 goals) in 1910, Greg Hawick 30 (15 goals) in 1957

Queensland—Dan O'Connor 24 (12 goals) in 1940

STATE OF ORIGIN

State of Origin is the battle for interstate Rugby League supremacy between New South Wales and Queensland. First staged in 1980, Origin has built a reputation as the toughest, most ferocious and highest-quality contest in the code. Prior to 1980, interstate teams were selected based on where a player resided, robbing Queensland of many players who had been lured to the Sydney premiership. Queensland was rarely competitive in the 1970s and public interest waned, sparking support for the State of Origin concept, where players were selected based on where they played their first senior football.

QRL President Ron McAuliffe was the foremost purveyor of the concept, tired of seeing the Queensland representative side routinely thrashed by a NSW side containing stars from the Sunshine State, and inspired by a 'State of Origin' AFL match between premiership stronghold Victoria and the rich breeding ground of Western Australia. McAuliffe and his NSWRL and ARL counterpart Kevin Humphreys secured the approval of the majority of the Sydney premiership clubs, allowing the concept to debut in 1980.

The inaugural Origin clash was played at Lang Park as a one-off match, with two residency-based interstate matches having already been won comfortably by NSW. Queensland, led by all time great forward Arthur Beetson and featuring several Sydney-based stars, upset the Blues 20-10 and the Origin legend was born. Queensland won another one-off Origin clash in 1981, and a three-game State of Origin series was initiated in 1982, supplanting the residency-based format permanently.

The Maroons dominated the first decade of Origin. Ironically, Queensland's success in the early series was thanks largely to the incomparable skipper and Valleys/Wynnum-Manly five-eighth Wally Lewis and a loyal band of Brisbane-based stars. NSW enjoyed a fruitful two-year period in the mid-1980s prior to a barren end to the decade, before seizing the interstate ascendancy during the 1990s under coach Phil Gould, with inspirational captains Laurie Daley and Brad Fittler steering the ship. The Blues also had the upper hand during the first half of the 2000s with Andrew Johns, Danny Buderus and Anthony Minichiello at their peak, before Queensland won an unprecedented six consecutive series from 2006. With former Queensland great Mal Meninga as coach, record-breaking champion Darren

Lockyer as captain and a host of burgeoning superstars, the Maroons moulded the greatest side in Origin history.

The State of Origin arena had hosted 93 games from 1980 until the end of 2011, with Queensland's recent dominance opening up a 49 wins to 42 lead, with two matches drawn. Likewise, the Maroons have won 16 series to NSW's 12 after trailing the Blues by two series at the end of 2005. Queensland has scored 1,542 points to NSW's 1,474, and has scored 269 tries—just 18 more than the Blues. The parity of these figures illustrates the even, hard-fought nature of Origin football, ensuring the series between the Queensland 'Canetoads' and the 'Cockroaches' from New South Wales will remain the marquee event on the Australian Rugby League calendar.

1980 QUEENSLAND WON 20-10 (ONE-OFF STATE OF ORIGIN MATCH) Queensland, coached by former international John McDonald, named seven Sydney-based players for the inaugural State of Origin clash at Lang Park, including the front-row trio of captain Arthur Beetson, John Lang and Rod Morris, halves pairing Greg Oliphant and Alan Smith, firebrand backrower Rod Reddy and star winger Kerry Boustead. Lang, Morris, Reddy and Boustead represented NSW in the residency-based matches against Queensland staged earlier in the season. Queensland centre Mal Meninga opened the scoring with two penalty goals, before NSW winger Greg Brentnall crossed for Origin's first try. Boustead responded with the Maroons' first try after superb lead-up work from centre Chris Close to set up a 9-5 halftime advantage. Meninga continued slotting penalties in the second half—finishing the match with seven goals from as many attempts (still a Queensland Origin record)—while man of the match Close scored a rampaging individual try to extend Queensland's lead to 13 points. NSW skipper Tom Raudonikis crashed over under the posts to reduce the deficit, but Meninga goaled again to seal a 20-10 triumph. Beetson was inspirational as captain with the 35-year-old playing a vital hand in both Queensland tries, while his aggressive approach in giving no quarter to his NSW opponents—including his Parramatta teammates (Beetson famously whacked the Eels' esteemed Test centre Mick Cronin)—sealed State of Origin's future and is integral to its legacy. The delirious 33,210-strong Lang Park throng lapped up the comprehensive victory in one of the most important nights in Australian Rugby League history.

1981 QUEENSLAND WON 22-15 (ONE-OFF STATE OF ORIGIN MATCH) Queensland called upon the services of just four Sydney-based players for the one-off clash in 1981—Rod Morris, Paul McCabe, Paul Khan and Mitch Brennan—but the Maroons' stunning 22-15 comeback victory at Lang Park was central to the future establishment of State of Origin as the principal interstate Rugby League format. Queensland was coached by Arthur Beetson, who was kept out of the playing line-up with injury. NSW, captained by Steve Rogers, opened up a 15-0 lead after a blockbusting double to winger Eric Grothe either side of a Mick Cronin try. Queensland flanker Brad Backer scored before halftime to put the home side on the scoreboard, while skipper Wally Lewis scored a brilliant try after the break, Chris Close (who again claimed man of the match honours) scored from dummy-half after unleashing an infamous back-hander on NSW defender Grothe, and Mal Meninga was awarded a penalty try. Ferocious defence and brawling featured throughout the match—rival props Morris and Steve Bowden were sin-binned for fighting—sealing State of Origin's reputation as Australia's fiercest Rugby League rivalry and contradicting the sceptics that suggested it would not be 'fair dinkum.'

1982 QUEENSLAND WON SERIES 2-1 Frank Stanton was installed as NSW coach for the first three-match Origin series, replacing 1980-81 coach Ted Glossop. The Blues captured their maiden Origin victory in game one, with Souths winger Ziggy Niszczot crossing for a double and Penrith's teenage debutant Brad Izzard scoring the match-sealing try in a 20-16 result for the Max Krilich-led NSW side. Future Queensland greats Paul Vautin and Gene Miles debuted in the series-opener, while Mal Meninga was announced as man of the match in a losing side after setting up both Maroons tries and kicking five goals.

Queensland fought back to take out the series with two tight victories. Miles scored the first try of the second game, before a dazzling 50-metre effort by Izzard saw the Blues trail just 5-3 at halftime. Second half tries to John Ribot and Vautin propelled Queensland to an 11-7 win. Rod Morris was named man of the match. The Sydney Cricket Ground decider—the first Origin match played outside of Brisbane—swung on a diabolical in-goal mix-up between NSW fullback Phil Sigsworth and debutant Moree winger Phil Duke, the first Origin player to be selected from a country club. Queensland led 5-3 after 15 minutes of the second half when Wally Lewis sent a searching kick behind the NSW tryline. Sigsworth popped an ill-conceived pass to Duke, who scored the Blues' only try in the first half, but the winger fumbled it and Lewis raced through to pounce on the loose ball. The Maroons held on to win 10-5, while skipper Lewis was adjudged man of the match, setting the tone for a decade of interstate dominance from the brilliant five-eighth.

1983 QUEENSLAND WON SERIES 2-1 Ted Glossop returned as NSW coach in 1983, but the Canterbury mentor still had no answer to Wally Lewis' match-winning genius. The Queensland captain scored two tries to set up an 18-6 halftime lead in the opener of the 1983 series, while halfback Mark Murray's try five minutes from fulltime clinched a 24-12 result. But the Maroons' victory was overshadowed by NSW hothead Les Boyd's savage elbow on Daryl Brohman, breaking the Queensland prop's jaw. The injury cost Brohman the chance to make his Test debut against New Zealand, while Boyd was rubbed out for 12 months by the judiciary. Brohman never played for Australia.

Max Krilich was ruled out of game two with injury and was replaced as captain by lock Ray Price, who was joined in the NSW side by seven Parramatta teammates (including six Eels in the backline). The new-look Blues won 10-6 at a muddy SCG, with a Steve Ella try the only points of the second half following a 6-all deadlock at the break. Eels halfback Peter Sterling was named man of the match after the dour struggle.

NSW's chances of wresting interstate supremacy from Queensland were skittled in the first half of the Lang Park decider. Krilich returned as captain, while Price and Sterling were ruled out with injury, and the Maroons capitalised on their opponents' discontinuity by scorching to a 21-0 halftime lead. Queensland extended the advantage to 33-0 after 50 minutes and 37-6 with 15 minutes remaining. Steve

Mortimer sparked a spirited NSW fightback, with veteran winger Chris Anderson claiming the first Origin hat-trick to peg the Blues back to a 15-point deficit. Gene Miles crossed for the last try of the match for a final scoreline of 43-22, while Lewis collected his second man of the match award of the series.

1984 QUEENSLAND WON SERIES 2-1 NSW crashed to a third straight series defeat courtesy of convincing losses in the opening two matches in 1984. The Blues, with coach Frank Stanton again at the helm, were outclassed 29-12 in the series-opener at Lang Park. Queensland scored six tries to NSW's one, including a hat-trick to winger Kerry Boustead. Game two was played on an SCG quagmire, and the 0-0 halftime scoreline reflected the atrocious conditions. But the Maroons found the decisive score in the 57th minute; a Wally Lewis chip kick ricocheted off the NSW crossbar and hulking prop Greg Dowling defied the wet weather to scoop the ball off his toes and plunge over for a famous try. Gene Miles' four-pointer from dummy-half wrapped up the match and the series 14-2. Lewis was named man of the match for the third consecutive Origin match and the fifth time in six interstate clashes.

Blues captain Ray Price retired from representative football prior to game three and was replaced as skipper by Canterbury halfback Steve Mortimer, while NSW named six debutants for the dead-rubber clash. St. George centre Brian Johnston crossed for two tries in his first Origin appearance, while destructive Manly backrower Noel Cleal scored a vital four-pointer in NSW's face-saving 22-12 victory. Captain Mortimer, whose brother Chris debuted in the centres, was named man of the match. Arthur Beetson—such a central figure in Origin's formative years—celebrated in his third consecutive series triumph as coach.

1985 NEW SOUTH WALES WON SERIES 2-1 Arthur Beetson stepped down as coach and was replaced by former Queensland representative and Easts (Brisbane) stalwart Des Morris, while Terry Fearnley was installed as coach of NSW. Former Wallaby Michael O'Connor made a spectacular debut for the Blues in the 1985 series-opener, scoring all of his team's points from two tries and five goals (an Origin record points haul that would stand for 15 years) in NSW's emphatic 18-2 victory at Lang Park. Parramatta second-rower Peter Wynn won the man of the match award.

The Blues finally broke Queensland's stranglehold on the State of Origin crown courtesy of a 21-14 win at the SCG in game two. In a fluctuating contest, NSW took a 12-8 lead into halftime after Queensland had scored the opening try. A try to replacement forward Ian French put the Maroons 14-12 in front heading into the final quarter of the match, but O'Connor landed a penalty and a field goal to edge the Blues ahead. Gifted five-eighth Brett Kenny sealed the result with a superb solo try in the dying minutes. Captain Steve Mortimer's emotional reaction to the triumph—first raising his fists in the air, before sinking to his knees and kissing the SCG turf—displayed a mixture of relief and ecstasy, and ranks as one of Origin's most memorable images. Despite the historic loss, Maroons skipper Wally Lewis won yet another man of the match award.

Mortimer retired from representative football after the victory; Balmain lock Wayne Pearce assumed the captaincy, while Manly's Des Hasler made his state debut at halfback in the dead-rubber game three. Queensland flyer Dale Shearer, who debuted in the series-opener, scored two tries as the Maroons restored pride with a 20-6 result. Backrower Wally Fullerton-Smith collected man of the match honours.

1986 NEW SOUTH WALES WON SERIES 3-0 Veteran mentor Ron Willey assumed the NSW coaching reins in 1986 and guided the Blues to the first-ever Origin series cleansweep opposite new Queensland coach Wayne Bennett. NSW led the series-opener 12-2 during the first half, but the Maroons rallied with three tries to hit the front just after halftime. Tries to man of the match Royce Simmons and Andrew Farrar restored NSW to the lead and the Blues opened their defence of the Origin crown with a 22-16 victory.

Queensland dropped fullback Colin Scott, a veteran of 14 Origins, for game two and named Canberra's Gary Belcher to debut. But the Blues wrapped up a second straight series victory with a 24-20 result at the SCG after the scores were locked 12-all at halftime. NSW displayed greater poise to prevail in a close-fought contest, and halfback Peter Sterling was a deserving man of the match.

The Blues achieved the unprecedented series whitewash with a dramatic 18-16 win in the third game at Lang Park. Queensland scored four tries to NSW's three in the first half, but the Maroons failed to land a conversion and the scores were tied 16-all as the combatants headed for the sheds. A controversial penalty from referee Kevin Roberts against Wally Lewis with eight minutes remaining allowed Michael O'Connor to slot his fourth goal to snatch victory, despite desperate last-ditch attempts by Queensland to grab a match-winning try. The 3-0 result belied the even nature of the series which, ironically, was the closest to date.

1987 QUEENSLAND WON SERIES 2-1 (FOURTH MATCH STAGED BUT NOT INCLUDED IN SERIES RESULT) Pre-series debate focussed on Queensland's selection of diminutive Ipswich halfback Allan Langer in the place of injured 15-match veteran Mark Murray, ignoring the claims of Eastern Suburbs No.7 Laurie Spina and Canberra's Kevin Walters. But despite concerns over his size and supposed defensive frailties, Langer produced an outstanding debut in the 1987 series-opener, featuring trademark livewire attack and tenacious tackling. It was not enough to prevent a NSW victory at the death, however, with Cronulla duo and Blues debutants Andrew Ettingshausen and Mark McGaw combining, before McGaw somehow planted his hand on the ball amid a swarm of players after it had been toed through to the Queensland in-goal. The last-minute try broke a 16-all deadlock after the Blues had led 10-6 at halftime, and ranks as one of the most dramatic finishes in Origin history. Capping a memorable night for the debuting contingent, South Sydney forward Les Davidson was named man of the match in his first Origin following the 20-16 triumph.

Queensland squared the series and secured its first victory under Wayne Bennett with a 12-6 outcome in game two. In atrocious conditions at the SCG, the Maroons trailed 6-4 at halftime, but tries to prop Greg Dowling and winger Colin Scott propelled them to a gritty series-saving win. The 42,048-strong Sydney crowd was a record turnout for an Origin match until the interstate showpiece was taken to the Melbourne Cricket Ground in 1994, while Blues skipper Peter Sterling became the first NSW player to be named man of the match on a losing side.

The score favoured Queensland 10-8 at halftime of the decider after tries to Bob Lindner and Dale Shearer, and the scoreboard remained unchanged at the end of a frantic second half despite end-to-end action as both states strained for the decisive try. The Maroons regained the State of Origin shield with the gripping victory after two years of Blue reign, while Langer—a controversial selection just six weeks earlier—claimed game three man of the match honours. An exhibition State of Origin match was played in the United States at the conclusion of the series, with Peter Sterling captaining the Blues to a 30-18 victory and winning another man of the match award in front of 12,349 curious fans at Veterans Stadium in Long Beach, California. The promotional fixture was not included as part of the 1987 series, but the players' appearance and scoring records are included in official Origin statistics.

1988 QUEENSLAND WON SERIES 3-0 New Brisbane Broncos coach Wayne Bennett remained at the helm for Queensland and steered the Maroons to their first series whitewash, while the 1988 instalment of Origin was a gruelling introduction to representative coaching for John Peard, who replaced Ron Willey as NSW mentor. Queensland was without 'The King' Wally Lewis for the first time after injury ruled the influential captain out of game one, the first Origin played at Rugby League's new headquarters, the Sydney Football Stadium. Peter Jackson slotted into five-eighth for the Maroons, while Paul Vautin became just Queensland's third Origin captain. The heir to Lewis' throne, Allan Langer, inspired Queensland to a 26-18 victory in the series-opener, scoring two tries in a man of the match display. The Maroons led 12-6 at halftime before racing away to 26-6 inside the final quarter; two late tries added a semblance of respectability to the scoreboard for the Blues.

Lewis returned for the second game and Queensland wrapped up a successful defence of the Origin shield, prevailing 16-6 in a dramatic night at Lang Park. NSW held a slender 6-4 lead when Maroons hooker Greg Conescu and Blues prop Phil Daley were sin-binned for 10 minutes after engaging in a scuffle just before the hour mark, while Lewis was despatched for five minutes for arguing with referee Mick Stone. In one of Origin's most infamous moments, beer cans rained onto the field from the irate Lang Park crowd, briefly halting play. NSW backrower Steve Folkes was sin-binned—reducing both sides to 11 players—and the Maroons regrouped, with bustling prop Sam Backo barging over from dummy-half and Langer sealing the result with a try from close range.

NSW endured a disjointed build-up to game three when halves Peter Sterling and Terry Lamb were ruled out with injury (replaced by Manly duo Cliff Lyons and Des Hasler), while Phil Daley was booted from the squad after leaving camp to visit his pregnant wife. In an uncharacteristically free-flowing Origin contest, the dead-rubber was locked at 18-all at halftime. But Queensland put an exclamation point on the series triumph in the second half, powering away to a 38-22 victory. Backo scored two tries to pick up his second straight man of the match award, while Langer scored his fourth try of the series to cap a wonderful campaign and clinch his maiden Australian Test call-up.

1989 QUEENSLAND WON SERIES 3-0 The 1989 series marked the return of Arthur Beetson as Queensland coach, while the great Jack Gibson—coach of the Beetson-led Easts premiership sides of 1974-75—took the reins for NSW. Cronulla's ball-playing backrower Gavin Miller replaced Peter Sterling, who had retired from representative duty, as captain. The most courageous team performance in Origin history was bookended by comprehensive drubbings as the Maroons secured another 3-0 series cleansweep. Queensland soared to a seven-tries-to-one, 36-6 thrashing of a NSW side featuring eight debutants in the series-opener at Lang Park. Brisbane winger Michael Hancock scored two tries on debut, while Mal Meninga—playing his first Origin match since 1986 after four broken arm injuries curtailed his 1987-88 seasons—crossed for a double and kicked four goals for a then-Queensland record 16 points. Prop Martin Bella was named man of the match.

Queensland overcame a crippling injury toll in game two to hold on for a famous 16-12 triumph at the SFS. The scores were tied 6-all at halftime, by which stage the Maroons had lost Meninga, Allan Langer and Paul Vautin to match-ending injuries. Hancock was forced from the field in the second half, leaving an empty interchange bench. Concussed pair Tony Currie and Trevor Gillmeister remained on the field, while Sam Backo defied an ankle injury. Man of the match Wally Lewis scored one of the great Origin tries with an arcing, dummying solo run from 30 metres out to open up a 16-6 lead, but Bob Lindner finally succumbed to a leg injury and was carried off with four minutes on the clock, leaving Queensland to grimly defend a 16-12 lead with 12 men. The Sydney crowd's silence after the match—rather than customary jeering of the Queenslanders—was a glowing tribute to a phenomenally brave team effort.

Meninga, Langer and Lindner were ruled out of game three at Lang Park, but Queensland nevertheless carved out an emphatic 36-16 victory over the hapless Blues. The Maroons trailed 12-8 at halftime, before blitzing the visitors with six second half tries. Hooker Kerrod Walters, who debuted in the series-opener after displacing 20-game veteran Greg Conescu, capped a brilliant series by scoring a try and laying on three more in a man of the match display, while Dale Shearer picked up a double. Gibson blooded several players that would be integral to NSW's success in the early 1990s, including Laurie Daley, Bradley Clyde, Glenn Lazarus, Paul Sironen, John Cartwright and Brad Mackay. Broncos Chris Johns and Terry Matterson became the first Queensland-based players to represent NSW.

1990 NEW SOUTH WALES WON SERIES 2-1 Supercoach Jack Gibson steered NSW to its first series victory since 1986 with a hard-fought, low-scoring 2-1 result. Wally Lewis was ruled out of the SFS series-opener with injury with Michael Hagan coming into the side at five-eighth and Paul Vautin deputising as captain for the second time. Steve Walters made his debut at hooker in the place of his injured brother Kerrod. Led by hooker Ben Elias and featuring debutants Ricky Stuart, Rod Wishart and Ian Roberts, the Blues built a 6-0 lead at the break on the back of a miraculous Mark McGaw try, before grinding out an 8-0 victory in a dour second stanza. Elias was named man of the match.

State of Origin broke new ground when game two of the 1990 series was staged at Melbourne's Olympic Park, drawing a 25,800-strong crowd. Lewis and Kerrod Walters returned for Queensland, while Vautin was dropped, bringing a stellar 22-match Origin career to an end. Man of the match Stuart scored an intercept try from inside NSW's quarter to set up a 6-0 halftime advantage, but a try to Queensland winger Les Kiss and a superb Mal Meninga conversion locked up the scores with 10 minutes remaining. Wishart kicked the Blues to an 8-6 lead after a contentious penalty against Allan Langer, before Brad Mackay sealed the series victory with an intercept try in the dying stages to finish the scoring at 12-6. Brad Fittler made his debut off the bench, aged just 18 years and 114 days—a then-Origin record and a still-standing mark for NSW.

Queensland avoided a series whitewash with a 14-10 win at Lang Park in game three. After a lengthy 10-all stalemate, Maroons interchange forward Steve Jackson—best known for his extra-time try in Canberra's 1989 Grand Final triumph—plunged over for the match-winner on Origin debut from an Allan Langer pass.

1991 QUEENSLAND WON SERIES 2-1 In the most controversial coaching appointment in State of Origin history, Manly coach and former New Zealand Test mentor Graham Lowe was named Queensland boss in 1991. Lowe previously coached Brisbane Norths to a BRL premiership in 1980, providing him with a tenuous link to Queenslander status. Canberra coach Tim Sheens took over from Gibson at the helm of the NSW side. A Mal Meninga penalty was the only score of the first half of game one at Lang Park. Still smarting from his controversial exclusion from the 1990 Kangaroo Tour (he failed a team medical due to an arm injury), Queensland captain Lewis produced the crucial play with a searching run and deft inside ball for Meninga to power over for the first try of the match. NSW centre Laurie Daley scored a brilliant kick-and-chase try in the corner in the dying minutes to peg the score back to 6-4, but Michael O'Connor's conversion attempt was off the mark. Meninga restarted as the siren sounded, prompting a jubilant Lowe to head out onto the field. But the kick-off went dead on the full and the Blues were awarded a penalty on halfway with time up. Fullback Greg Alexander's 50-metre penalty goal fell short and Queensland took a 1-0 series lead as Lewis was adjudged man of the match for the eighth and final time.

Game two, played in driving rain at the SFS, ranks as arguably the most explosive Origin encounter of all time. NSW led 8-6 at the end of a fiery first half, with a brawl erupting as the halftime siren sounded after Mark Geyer's heavy-handed tackle on Queensland hooker Steve Walters. The shouting match and push-and-shove between Geyer and Lewis as the pair was being addressed by referee David Manson—and again as the combatants headed for the dressing-rooms—is ingrained in the Origin story. Geyer sparked another melee in the second half with an ugly high tackle with a cocked elbow on lanky Queensland fullback Paul Hauff (for which he later received a five-week suspension). The Maroons grabbed a 12-8 lead through a Dale Shearer try, before Mark McGaw crashed over in the corner from a long Ricky Stuart pass to draw NSW level. O'Connor stepped up to curl a spine-tingling conversion between the posts from the sideline in one of the great goalkicking moments in Rugby League history, snatching a 14-12 victory and forcing a hotly anticipated decider. Steve Walters was named man of the match despite Queensland's loss.

NSW winger Chris Johns scored the opening try of game three from a superb grubber by five-eighth Brad Fittler, but Queensland held an 8-4 halftime lead after a well-deserved try to young custodian Hauff and a four-pointer against the run of play to Michael Hancock after Ricky Stuart was unable to contain an Allan Langer chip-kick. The Blues hit the front 12-8 in the second half following a touchdown to

Michael O'Connor, who had his nose broken by Meninga during the first half, and a fortuitous runaway try to Des Hasler from a deflected kick. The nerve-wracking decider swung Queensland's way inside the final quarter after a helter-skelter passing movement eventually provided Shearer with enough space to slice through the NSW defence for the equaliser. Meninga slotted the tricky conversion attempt to edge the Maroons in front 14-12. With little more than 10 minutes remaining, the announcement came over the PA system that Wally Lewis—Queensland's greatest player—would be retiring from Origin football after the match. Fittingly, the Maroons hung on for a pulsating victory to send the inspirational skipper out a winner. Martin Bella collected man of the match honours despite his second half sin-binning, while Kiwi Lowe sealed his place in Queensland Origin folklore after the closest—and arguably the best—interstate series on record.

1992 NEW SOUTH WALES WON SERIES 2-1 Phil Gould, coach of defending premiers Penrith, replaced Tim Sheens in 1992 and singlehandedly dismissed the notion that State of Origin passion was the sole domain of the Queenslanders. He appointed 22-year-old five-eighth Laurie Daley as skipper, and the Blues responded immediately with a hard-fought 14-6 victory in the series-opener at the SFS. NSW scored early through Bradley Clyde, but an Allan Langer try from close range saw the combatants head to the sheds with the score at 6-all. Blues interchange forward Craig Salvatori crashed over beside the posts to seal victory with 15 minutes remaining, while former skipper Ben Elias was named man of the match.

Queensland achieved its first win of the post-Lewis era with a gripping 5-4 result at Lang Park in game two. Maroons lock Billy Moore scored a memorable four-pointer on debut, while two penalties to NSW winger Rod Wishart set up another halftime deadlock. Langer broke the second half impasse with a superbly taken field goal inside the final two minutes. Remarkably, Langer had played 82 first grade games for Brisbane without kicking a field goal. It was a valiant win for the Mal Meninga-led Maroons, who played 10 minutes of the first half with just 11 men after five-eighth Peter Jackson and prop Martin Bella were despatched to the sin bin for dissent by referee Bill Harrigan. Veteran Queensland lock Bob Lindner claimed man of the match honours.

NSW reclaimed the Origin shield with an ultimately comfortable 16-4 game three win in Sydney—the Blues' first victory in a decider in five attempts. Blues No.7 and man of the match Ricky Stuart dummied his way over for the only try of the first half, while Laurie Daley and Paul McGregor combined to conjure a spectacular try for Andrew Ettingshausen 14 minutes into the second half, and John Cartwright burrowed over from dummy-half shortly afterward. The 1992 series marked the beginning of long and fruitful Origin careers for Blues tyros McGregor, Paul Harragon and Tim Brasher. The 2-1 series loss marked the end of Graham Lowe's colourful two-year tenure as Maroons coach.

1993 NEW SOUTH WALES WON SERIES 2-1 The great Wally Lewis returned to the Queensland set-up as coach in 1993. NSW built a 12-2 halftime lead in the series-opener at Lang Park with tries to Rod Wishart and man of the match Ricky Stuart, but the Maroons pegged their way back to four points in arrears with two second half tries. Queensland was unable to find the equaliser despite a wealth of possession and the Blues took a 1-0 series lead courtesy of the gritty 14-10 result.

NSW wrapped up the series with a 16-12 game two victory in an Origin classic at the SFS. A try to captain Mal Meninga gave Queensland a 6-0 lead at the break, but Maroons fullback Dale Shearer bombed a certain four-pointer by losing the ball over the line and winger Willie Carne had another disallowed by a controversial offside call. Three tries propelled the Blues to a 10-point advantage in the second stanza, before Queensland pivot Kevin Walters crossed to set up a grandstand finish. In a match packed with end-to-end excitement, the Blues' victory was sealed when a long Meninga break in the dying seconds was shut down. NSW fullback Tim Brasher was named man of the match.

Queensland restored pride in the game three dead-rubber, overturning a six-point halftime deficit to send retiring backrow great Bob Lindner out with an emphatic 24-12 victory. Lindner scored a farewell try, while Carne bagged a double and Shearer was named man of the match. The game featured a memorable stoush between rival props Martin Bella and Paul Harragon after a first half scrum erupted with hookers Steve Walters and Ben Elias throwing punches. The brawling foursome was ordered to the sin bin by referee Greg McCallum, while Harragon claimed a unanimous points decision in his showdown with Bella.

1994 NEW SOUTH WALES WON SERIES 2-1 Queensland took a stunning series lead with the greatest at-the-death try in the history of Australian Rugby League in game one at the SFS. The Blues were comfortable at 12-4 after a fortuitous Brad Mackay try heading into the final 10 minutes, but quick passing allowed man of the match Willie Carne to score in the 76th minute. The Maroons played the ball on their own 40-metre line inside the last two minutes and enacted the movement that is burned into Origin folklore. The ball swept the width of the field through long passes from halves Allan Langer and Kevin Walters, and a looping pass from Carne to Steve Renouf. The dazzling centre found space up the sideline, tearing past halfway and finding winger Michael Hancock in support on the inside. Hancock offloaded in the tackle to Darren Smith, who drew NSW winger Graham Mackay and passed to Langer. The No.7 flung a desperate pass to a stampeding Mal Meninga and the captain found Mark Coyne on his outside. Coyne, faced with the sideline and the converging Blues defence, stepped inside and planted the ball over the tryline, despite the desperate cover of Brad Fittler, Ricky Stuart and Ben Elias. A stunned hush gripped the SFS crowd as the Queensland players, coaches and pockets of supporters went berserk. Commentating legend Ray Warren famously summed up Queensland's back-from-the-dead effort: "That's not a try, that's a miracle!"

NSW levelled the series in front of an 87,161-strong crowd—a then-record for a Rugby League match in Australia—at the Melbourne Cricket Ground. Unyielding defence and tries to Glenn Lazarus and Paul McGregor were the catalysts for the Blues' 14-0 shutout, while Paul Harragon collected man of the match honours. Retiring Maroons captain Meninga broke his coach and long-time teammate Wally Lewis' record by making his 32nd Origin appearance in the decider at Lang Park, but his farewell was spoiled by a comprehensive 27-12 loss to the Blues. A brilliant individual try to skipper Laurie Daley and intercept four-pointers to Canberra teammates Bradley Clyde and Brett Mullins set up an imposing 18-6 halftime lead.

Also playing in his final interstate match, veteran NSW hooker Ben Elias kicked two field goals in the second half of a man of the match performance. NSW had secured three straight series victories for the first time in State of Origin history, while Phil Gould's status as the Blues' best-ever coach was assured. Queensland counterpart Lewis stepped down after two unsuccessful series in charge. Meninga was the last of the combatants from the inaugural Origin clash in 1980 to retire.

1995 QUEENSLAND WON SERIES 3-0 The outbreak of the Super League war in 1995 threw the State of Origin series into disarray. The ARL blacklisted Super League-aligned players from selection, which ruled out Brisbane's contingent of Queensland stars (with the exception of prop Gavin Allen), including Allan Langer, Kevin Walters, Steve Renouf, Wendell Sailor, Willie Carne, Michael Hancock, Darren Smith, Andrew Gee and Julian O'Neill. Canberra hooker Steve Walters and St. George tyro Gorden Tallis were also ineligible after signing with the rebel outfit. NSW's stocks were similarly depleted—Raiders quartet Laurie Daley, Ricky Stuart, Bradley Clyde and Brett Mullins, Broncos prop Glenn Lazarus, Manly forward Ian Roberts and veteran Cronulla centre Andrew Ettingshausen had sided with Super League. But with a far greater pool of talent to draw from, the Blues approached the 1995 series as the most overwhelming favourites in Origin history.

Broncos coach Wayne Bennett was due to return to the Origin arena in 1995, but his commitment to the rebel cause resulted in former Maroons backrower and two-game skipper Paul Vautin stepping in as coach. But Queensland's ragtag squad of fringe first graders and representative rookies—mixed with a handful of experienced Origin players and captained by veteran second-rower Trevor Gillmeister—caused the most extraordinary boilover in Origin history by winning all three matches. A supreme defensive effort paved the way for a 2-0 victory in the series-opener at the SFS, with a penalty goal to debutant Queensland hooker Wayne Bartrim the only scoring play of the match. Time and again unheralded rookies such as winger Matt Sing produced massive try-saving plays to keep the star-studded Blues scoreless and seal a euphoric victory. Workhorse forward Gary Larson was a deserving man of the match.

The Maroons clinched an improbable series victory in game two at the MCG, which was marked by a wild all-in brawl in the opening minutes. Ahead 8-2 at halftime, Queensland led by just two points in the dying stages and the Blues appeared certain to snatch victory. But a forward pass called against skipper Brad Fittler as fullback Tim Brasher crashed over foiled NSW's hopes of levelling the series. Lightning-quick winger Brett Dallas scored a memorable runaway try on fulltime to cap Queensland's 20-12 triumph. Five-eighth Jason Smith, who was drafted into the Maroons' squad for the second game after reneging on a Super League contract to sign with the ARL, was adjudged man of the match.

A 40,189-strong Suncorp Stadium crowd turned out for the dead-rubber clash to show their appreciation for their unlikely heroes, and the Maroons responded with a magnificent 24-16 victory. Livewire Sydney City Roosters halfback Adrian Lam capped a brilliant series with the man of the match award, while 18-year-old interchange Ben Ikin—who became Origin's youngest-ever player when he was picked for the series-opener after just four first grade games for the Gold Coast Seagulls—scored the match-sealing try. Skipper Gillmeister famously climbed out of a hospital bed, where he was on an intravenous drip, to take his place in the match (*see Courageous Performances*). Queensland's astonishing series whitewash ranks as one of the great State of Origin stories, and provided a bright point in a painfully divisive year for the code. Queensland rookies Lam, Sing, Ikin and Robbie O'Davis crafted long and illustrious careers in the Maroon jersey, while NSW blooded future Origin greats Andrew Johns and Steve Menzies, and welcomed Geoff Toovey back to the Blues fold after a five-year absence.

1996 NEW SOUTH WALES WON SERIES 3-0 Phil Gould's NSW side gained the ultimate retribution for the humiliating series loss of 12 months earlier with a resounding series cleansweep in 1996. Super League players returned as the warring factions reached an uneasy stalemate for the winter, but Queensland's rebel stars were unable to prevent a lacklustre 14-6 loss in the series-opener at Suncorp Stadium. Maroons captain Gillmeister was dumped, with Allan Langer installed as skipper for game two, but the Blues wrapped up the series 18-6 in Sydney. Steve Renouf opened the scoring for Queensland, but NSW led 8-6 at halftime and a second half double to Blues winger Brett Mullins sealed the convincing result.

NSW charged to a 15-2 lead in the dead-rubber game three after Mullins scored another try, Andrew Ettingshausen finished off a mesmerising run by Andrew Johns, and captain Brad Fittler landed a booming long-range field goal. Queensland rallied with a try to Mark Coyne and a slashing Brett Dallas touchdown to trail by a point, but Coyne was ruled offside inside the final minute after he dived on a Langer kick under NSW's posts. The Blues' selectors' experiment with club No.7s Geoff Toovey and Andrew Johns as a halfback/hooker combination (first used in the previous season's World Cup) was a masterstroke—Toovey was man of the match in the series-opener, while Johns collected the gong in game two. Interchange backrower Steve Menzies was man of the match in game three.

The Blues achieved a unique feat by retaining the same squad of 17 players throughout the entire series; just six were Super League-aligned players, while 11 were ARL-loyal. Queensland used 24 players during the series, split evenly between Super League and ARL players (including five of the Maroons' 1995 Origin rookies).

1997 NEW SOUTH WALES WON SERIES 2-1 New South Wales assumed comfortable favouritism again with the advent of the Super League premiership and consequent drain of the talent pool for State of Origin. But what transpired was one of the tightest series on record. Wests coach Tom Raudonikis—NSW's inaugural Origin captain—took the reins from Phil Gould, who stood down from his post after four series wins in five years. The Blues led 8-0 at halftime of the series-opener at Suncorp Stadium, before new Queensland skipper Adrian Lam put his side on the board with less than 15 minutes remaining with a super individual try. NSW held out late Maroons attacking raids to prevail 8-6. Geoff Toovey, named skipper in the injury-enforced absence of Brad Fittler, was the man of the match.

Dazzling first half performances by man of the match Paul McGregor and Jim Dymock propelled NSW to a 14-0 lead in game two at the MCG, but two quick Queensland tries cut the Blues' halftime lead to four points. Brett Dallas crossed for the only try of the second half to level the scores shortly after the break, before Blues halfback John Simon—playing his first Origin match in five years—landed a superb angled field goal to edge NSW in front with 11 minutes remaining. Queensland interchange Julian O'Neill, who was called into the Maroons' squad after being punted by Super League club Perth Reds and joining Souths mid-season, had a chance to snatch victory inside the final five minutes. But his long-range penalty goal attempt dropped agonisingly under the crossbar. NSW's 15-14 victory sealed the series and was its fifth straight win—an Origin record for the Blues. Raudonikis came under fire for leaving hooker Aaron Raper unused on the Blues' bench. Raper was destined never to represent NSW in an Origin match.

Queensland scored a morale-boosting 18-12 win in the dead-rubber at the SFS. Maroons five-eighth Ben Ikin's scything 40-metre try and a wild brawl in the first half (triggered by NSW coach Raudonikis' infamous 'Cattledog' call) were notable highlights of an entertaining contest. Opposing hookers Andrew Johns and Jamie Goddard were sin-binned after a memorable and lengthy one-on-one stoush that left Johns battered and bloodied. The Maroons used 12 of their 1995 heroes during the close-fought series, which brought an end to 'Fatty' Vautin's eventful three-year tenure as Queensland coach.

1998 QUEENSLAND WON SERIES 2-1 Although the first year of the newly formed National Rugby League commenced in 1998 to bring a fractured three years to an end, many of the wounds inflicted by the Super League war remained fresh. For that reason, the State of Origin series shaped as arguably the most important to date. It was hoped that the best the game had to offer would aid the healing of the game's divisions and bring back dissident fans that had abandoned Rugby League. The hierarchy could hardly have hoped for a better start, with Queensland and NSW staging an epic game one encounter at the SFS.

A see-sawing classic was eventually decided in the final minute. Queensland trailed 13-6 at halftime, before surging to an 18-13 lead. The Blues rallied with two tries and appeared to have the match wrapped up at 23-18 inside the final two minutes. The Maroons' last possession began a metre out from their own line. Five-eighth Kevin Walters rolled the dice by kicking downfield and the gamble paid off when interchange Ben Ikin displayed blistering pace to win the race to the ball near halfway. Queensland worked the ball into NSW's quarter in the ensuing two plays as the defence scrambled, and slick passing allowed Tonie Carroll to cross the tryline with just 45 seconds remaining. Fellow debutant Darren Lockyer's conversion after the siren gave Queensland a heart-stopping 24-23 result in a chilling reminder for the Blues of Mark Coyne's try at the same venue in the series-opener four years earlier. Seven NSW players from that 1994 clash received a double-dose of heartache with a first-hand view of Carroll's match-winner. Captain Allan Langer was at his elusive, majestic best, and was a standout man of the match.

The Blues bounced back emphatically in the second clash, running out convincing 26-10 winners at Suncorp Stadium on the back of a barnstorming performance from man of the match prop Rodney Howe, superb direction from Brad Fittler and captain Laurie Daley, and classy finishing by Paul McGregor. But NSW's preparations for the decider were thrown into turmoil. Howe was suspended after testing positive to steroids, before a series of injuries beset the squad. A ruthless Queensland outfit capitalised, surging to a comfortable 19-4 victory. Kevin Walters' opening try and a runaway Ikin four-pointer after tremendous lead-up work by firebrand backrower

Gorden Tallis laid the platform for the triumph. Langer was again sensational, sealing the win with a fine solo try, while first-year Origin prop and man of the match Shane Webcke was unstoppable. The match marked the end of Raudonikis' tenure as NSW coach, but was a triumph for Queensland mentor Wayne Bennett, coaching his state for the first time in a decade.

1999 SERIES DRAWN 1-ALL Both states appointed new coaches for the 1999 instalment of Origin. Former Maroons halfback Mark Murray assumed the post vacated by Wayne Bennett, but it was Balmain boss Wayne Pearce's novel approach to team bonding as the Blues' new coach that garnered the pre-series headlines. Keen to steer away from the booze culture associated with Origin camps, Pearce took his NSW charges horseriding in country NSW. But the move backfired abhorrently. Key forwards Bradley Clyde and Robbie Kearns fell from their mounts, suffering injuries that kept them out of the entire series and prompted talk of legal action from their respective clubs. NSW scored the only try of the first clash—via the instinctive Anthony Mundine, one of nine debutants in the Blues' squad—but Mat Rogers' boot won the night in his first Origin appearance for Queensland; the Cronulla winger's four goals and late field goal clinched a 9-8 win to open the Maroons' shield defence. Queensland hooker Jason Hetherington was named man of the match.

Kevin Walters was awarded the Queensland captaincy after injury ruled Adrian Lam out of the second encounter. Fighting to keep the series alive, the Blues began game two with a remarkable try to Robbie Ross inside the first 60 seconds. Centre Ryan Girdler made a bust from inside NSW's half and sent the supporting fullback on a 40-metre run to the line. The match was considerably tighter for the ensuing 79 minutes, but NSW held on for a 12-8 victory. Blues legend Laurie Daley was superb in his final appearance for NSW in Sydney, scoring his side's other try and inspiring his teammates in attack and defence to collect man of the match honours. The 88,336-strong Stadium Australia crowd broke the Origin attendance record set at the MCG in 1994.

Daley was handed the captaincy for his Origin farewell after Test skipper Brad Fittler pulled out of game three with injury. The conclusion to the hard-fought series was something of an anti-climax—a 10-all draw in driving rain at Suncorp Stadium. But the tied result did nothing to dampen the Maroons' celebrations, after the drawn series saw them retain the trophy as the previous year's winners. The Adrian Lam-skippered 'Canetoads' had a chance to take a late lead with a field goal, but instead chose to wind down the clock and play for a draw. Wendell Sailor was a standout man of the match choice, a rarity for a winger in State of Origin football, particularly in such a grinding, dour contest.

2000 NEW SOUTH WALES WON SERIES 3-0 The 2000 series began with one of the most controversial and explosive finishes seen in Origin's three decades. The Maroons held a tenuous 16-12 lead late in the match after a magnificent double from captain Adrian Lam, while powerhouse winger and eventual man of the match Adam MacDougall had crossed twice for the Blues. NSW equalised inside the final 10 minutes through a Ryan Girdler try from a sweeping movement, after what appeared to be two blatant knock-ons in the lead-up seen by everyone at the ground except referee Bill Harrigan. Queensland's firebrand second-rower and forward spearhead Gorden Tallis confronted Harrigan, and was sent from the field after allegedly calling the official "a fucking cheat". Debutant NSW fullback David Peachey crossed for the 77th-minute match-winner.

The maelstrom that followed the Blues' 20-16 win was all but forgotten in the wake of two more comprehensive NSW victories, however. A flurry of second-half tries to the Blues in game two—after Queensland led 4-0 at halftime—resulted in a 28-10 victory and series glory for the first time in three years. Fullback Tim Brasher was adjudged man of the match after coming into the side for the injured Peachey, while Andrew Johns played a brilliant hand off the bench in his return from injury, with Brett Kimmorley starring at halfback in the five-tries-to-two triumph. But few would have predicted the landslide that unfolded in the dead-rubber third match. Queensland was blown off the park 56-16 as NSW rewrote almost every Origin record on offer. Man of the match Ryan Girdler scored an incredible 32 points from three tries (also an equal Origin record) and 10 goals, equalling Dally Messenger's interstate record set in 1911. NSW's other centre, Newcastle's Matt Gidley, crossed for a double in the nine-try rout, while the Maroons' humiliation was compounded by the Blues' use of elaborate try-celebrations during the second half. The one-sided series prompted some sections of the Rugby League fraternity to doubt the future of State of Origin.

2001 QUEENSLAND WON SERIES 2-1 After the embarrassment of the previous season, the 2001 series shaped as the most important in Queensland's Origin history. The Maroons called on Wayne Bennett to lift the state side out of the mire, and picked a squad for the series-opener that was even more inexperienced than the Super League-ravaged 1995 side. A total of 10 players made their debuts for Queensland, and the youngsters responded magnificently. Carl Webb, John Buttigieg, John Doyle and Chris Walker all scored great tries in their first taste of Origin as Queensland powered to a shock 34-16 win. New captain Gorden Tallis was at his destructive best in a man of the match display and Darren Lockyer was a constant threat from fullback.

A serious neck injury robbed Queensland of its skipper for the second clash, while the Blues made some crucial changes to their line-up. Trent Barrett came in at halfback and claimed man of the match honours as the Blues bounced back with a 26-8 series-levelling victory. Debutant prop Mark O'Meley terrorised the Queensland defence and laid on a memorable try for captain Brad Fittler.

Bennett produced the most sensational—and one of the most successful—selection ruse in representative Rugby League history for the third match. Lacking penetration in the halves, Queensland called upon favourite son Allan Langer—34 years old and playing for Warrington after retiring from the NRL early in 1999. Langer was marvellous in the decider, laying on several tries, scoring one himself, and generally creating havoc for the Blues' defence. Stand-in captain Lockyer was named man-of-the-match, scoring two tries and a Queensland record-equalling 16 points, while Paul Bowman and Chris Walker also picked up doubles. The eight-tries-to-two, 40-14 thrashing was sweet revenge for the Maroons after the horrors of 2000, and represented a rejuvenation of the Origin concept after rumblings that the interstate series was on the wane. It was also a crowning achievement for Langer, but a sad end for what was scheduled to be NSW great and appearance record-holder Fittler's farewell match. 'Freddy' would get his chance at a fairytale finish in 2004, while Langer returned a year later to add another remarkable chapter to his Origin story.

2002 SERIES DRAWN 1-ALL Queensland picked one of the biggest packs in Origin history in game one, but was blitzed by a youthful and mobile NSW side containing eight debutants. Blues skipper Andrew Johns was at his dominant best, toying with the defence in tandem with first-gamers Danny Buderus and Brett Hodgson. Pace-laden three-quarters Jamie Lyon and Timana Tahu scored tries on debut, while Hodgson notched a memorable runaway 90-metre four-pointer. Behind 21-4 at the break, the Maroons stemmed the tide somewhat in the second half to eventually lose 32-4, but had their work cut out to save the series in the return clash in Brisbane. Gorden Tallis continued his long-running battle with referee Bill Harrigan, who sent the Queensland skipper to the sin bin in the series-opener.

The Maroons were heavily criticised in the wake of the Sydney debacle and made several changes, including the naming of three Origin rookies. For one of them, game two descended into a nightmare. Winger Justin Hodges gifted two tries to NSW with wayward passes in his own in-goal, and was hooked by coach Wayne Bennett. But Queensland rallied, and in a see-sawing contest, prevailed 26-18. Two pieces of brilliance from man of the match centre Chris McKenna provided winger Lote Tuqiri with two tries and set the home side up with an 8-6 halftime lead. Chiselled backrower Dane Carlaw—who former Maroons prop Greg Dowling publicly declared "looks like Tarzan, but plays like Jane" after the series-opener—scored in the second half to extend Queensland's lead to 12 points before the Blues rallied. The result was not sealed until the final minute when Lote Tuqiri completed a hat-trick to equal the Origin record, while his ensuing conversion gave him a Queensland record 18 points.

The result set up an enthralling decider, and the bitter rivals produced one of the great game three matches. NSW led 12-8 at halftime, but the match swung wildly during a frantic second half, neither side able to gain the ascendancy for long periods. Darren Lockyer was controversially denied a try inside the final 10 minutes by the video referee that would have sealed victory, before NSW winger Jason Moodie grabbed his second try to put the Blues in front 18-14 with three minutes on the clock. Queensland appeared beaten, until 35-year-old man of the match Allan Langer hit backrower Dane Carlaw with a long pass with less than a minute to play. Carlaw charged through a gap on the halfway line and powered through the tackle of fullback Brett Hodgson to level the scores. Tuqiri missed the angled conversion, but it did not matter to Queensland—as they did in 1999, the Maroons retained the trophy after a drawn decider as the previous year's winner. The result reignited debate about the merits of extra-time in Origin football, of which NSW coach Phil Gould was understandably an enthusiastic proponent. In a sour aftermath unbefitting of such an epic contest, Tallis gestured to NSW fans holding up a derogatory sign about Tallis' mother. The incident polarised opinion and detracted attention from the quality of the contest. Tallis earlier rag-dolled lightweight Hodgson over the sideline in one of Origin's most replayed sequences.

2003 NEW SOUTH WALES WON SERIES 2-1 Pre-series media attention focussed on disquiet in the NSW camp between skipper Andrew Johns and coach Phil Gould. Whether the supposed rift was hot air or a cunning ploy from Gould, it worked to the Blues' advantage as Johns asserted himself as the arguably the most dominant Origin player since Wally Lewis with a five-star display in a 25-12 game one victory. Johns scored a try, kicked four goals and a field goal as the physical Blues side overpowered Queensland. Debutant fullback Anthony Minichiello scored two tries, while interchange forward Luke Bailey was menacing and claimed man of the match honours. The Maroons scored first through Darren Lockyer, but lost Justin Hodges and Paul Bowman to injury, and ran out of steam in the second half.

Their hopes of forcing a decider were skittled in the first half of the second encounter. NSW charged to a 17-0 lead at the break as Queensland turned in one of the most lacklustre displays in its Origin history. The relentless Blues took out the match and the series courtesy of the 27-4 result. Bailey was almost unstoppable once again, while the incomparable Johns was named man of the match. The Maroons resisted the urge to make wholesale changes for the dead-rubber third game, but blooded debutants Cameron Smith and Josh Hannay and shocked the new Origin shield-holders with a 36-6 thrashing, equalling Queensland's biggest-ever win. Evergreen winger Matt Sing scored three of his side's seven tries, and was a popular man of the match. It was a bittersweet end to the series for NSW and captain Johns, who raised the shield to an unappreciative Suncorp Stadium crowd, while it provided the Maroons with significant hope for a reversal of fortune in 2004.

2004 NEW SOUTH WALES WON SERIES 2-1 After game three draws saw Queensland retain the Origin crown in 1999 and 2002, NSW benefitted from the introduction of extra-time in Origin matches with 9-8 golden point triumph in the series-opener at Telstra Stadium. The Blues' preparation had been less than ideal, with Anthony Minichiello and debutant Mark Gasnier stood down from the side after an obscene phone message was left on a woman's phone during a drunken team 'bonding' session. Minichiello's suspension handed Ben Hornby his maiden Origin jumper, while the Blues also blooded five new faces to Queensland's four newcomers. One of Queensland's debutants, Scott Prince, scored the only points of the first half with a clever try, but NSW hit back through a Shaun Timmins try and built an 8-4 lead. Prince put his stamp on the game again by brilliantly setting up Brent Tate for the leveller. Deadlocked 8-all after 80 minutes, Blues five-eighth and man of the match Timmins slotted a booming 37-metre field goal in the third minute of the extra period. Timmins' only other top-level field goal was with Illawarra eight seasons earlier.

Brilliant young Melbourne fullback Billy Slater, selected on the wing for his first series in the Maroon jersey, stole the limelight in game two. Two Timana Tahu tries—both laid on by Newcastle teammate Matt Gidley—set up a 12-6 halftime lead for NSW, who had recalled Brad Fittler due to a halves injury crisis. But a try to debutant centre Willie Tonga narrowed the deficit to two points. Slater then trailed a Darren Lockyer grubber on halfway, gathered the ball and changed direction to kick over Anthony Minichiello's head, before outsprinting the recalled NSW fullback to collect his double and one of the most famous of all Origin tries. Queensland extended the lead to 20-12 with a Dane Carlaw four-pointer, and grimly hung on for a 22-18 win to keep the series alive.

NSW recalled Gasnier for the decider, promoted his St. George Illawarra centre partner Matt Cooper to debut, and selected the previously injured Trent Barrett at halfback. Each change paid off; Gasnier gained redemption with a fine double, and Barrett scored a try and combined brilliantly with Fittler. 'Freddy,' who extended his NSW appearance record to 31 games, scored a fairytale intercept try to finally cap a stellar Origin career with another series victory after the disappointment of '01. Queensland, in its first series under Knights mentor Michael Hagan, took an 8-6 lead midway through the first half, but were eventually outgunned 36-14. Blues backrower Craig Fitzgibbon was named man of the match and the series, adding 10 goals to his tireless efforts in attack and defence. The series was a triumph for departing coach Gould after the pre-series tribulations, and for promoted skipper Danny Buderus.

2005 NEW SOUTH WALES WON SERIES 2-1 The Sydney Roosters' 2002 premiership-winning coach Ricky Stuart followed in his mentor Phil Gould's footsteps by taking on the NSW coaching job, and guided the Blues to series victory in his maiden campaign. Queensland named three debutants, including halfback Johnathan Thurston, for a classic opening encounter in Brisbane. In front of a ground record 52,484-strong crowd at Suncorp Stadium, the Maroons built a 19-0 lead after two converted tries, and three penalty goals to Cameron Smith. But NSW erased the Maroons' advantage with four tries in a remarkable 19 minute-period to lead 20-19 inside the final 10 minutes. The opening Origin went into golden-point for the second year in a row after Thurston piloted over the wobbliest of field goals from close range two minutes from fulltime. In the 84th minute, quicksilver Queensland interchange Matt Bowen plucked a pass from Blues halfback Brett Kimmorley out of the air on the NSW 40-metre line to race away for the match-winner. Tireless prop Steve Price was named man of the match, while the Blues were 1-0 down and facing their first series defeat since 2001.

Enter Andrew Johns. After missing most of the previous two seasons with a succession of injuries, the No.7 maestro drew further comparisons with Wally Lewis by turning in one of the most dominant displays ever seen in State of Origin in the return clash. The Blues trailed 12-8 at halftime, but with the series on the line, man of the match Johns exploded and laid on four second half tries to mastermind a 32-22 victory.

The scene was set for a wonderful decider, but the resultant game three contest was a fizzer, with Johns again instrumental in NSW's 32-10 victory. The Blues led 32-0 after Matt King crossed for his third try with 15 minutes remaining, before the home side added a hint of respectability to the scoreline with two late tries. King's heroics saw him named the inaugural Brad Fittler medallist as NSW players' player of the series, while Cameron Smith was awarded the counterpart Queensland gong, the Ron McAuliffe Medal. Blues fullback Anthony Minichiello was man of the match in game three and was also honoured with the Wally Lewis Medal as official player of the series. NSW's achievement of three series victories in a row equalled the efforts of Queensland's 1987-89 side and the Phil Gould-coached Blues of 1992-94.

2006 QUEENSLAND WON SERIES 2-1 Queensland took a punt on Maroons legend Mal Meninga to coach his state for the 2006 series; the all time great centre had not coached since his difficult five-season stint with the Raiders came to an end in 2001. North Queensland Cowboys mentor Graham Murray took over from Ricky Stuart, who stepped down from the NSW role to become Test coach. Brett Finch was the hero of the opening Origin encounter for NSW. Finch was a late inclusion at halfback and the fourth-choice No.7 after a succession of halfbacks pulled out with injury. Wearing the No.20, Finch finished off a long-range try in the first half before kicking a wonderful 35-metre field goal in the dying minutes to break a 16-all deadlock and win the match. NSW led 14-0 at halftime on the back of man of the match Willie Mason's rampaging performance, but a Darren Lockyer-inspired Queensland rallied with two tries to teenage winger Greg Inglis. Fellow debutant Steve Bell crossed in the corner, and Johnathan Thurston landed a brilliant conversion to level the scores with three minutes remaining. Finch's heroics earned the Peter Frilingos Memorial Headline Moment of the Year at the Dally M Awards.

Lambasted in the media—including the likes of Phil Gould calling for captain Lockyer to be dumped—the injury-hit Maroons bounced back spectacularly in the second match. Queensland called upon two of the biggest bolters in Origin history: Canberra winger Adam Mogg, and Cowboys backrower Jacob Lillyman, just 19 games into his NRL career. But the Maroons were sublime, with Mogg scoring a dream double on debut. Test custodian Karmichael Hunt justified his Origin debut call-up for the Maroons in the place of Matt Bowen, while Lockyer was at his talismanic best in a man of the match display. The 30-6 pasting kept the series alive, setting up an intriguing decider in Melbourne.

Queensland faced more injury problems, and was forced to recall Clinton Schifcofske, Rhys Wesser and Josh Hannay for sidelined backline stars Hunt, Bell and Justin Hodges. A tense first half finished at 4-all, with Mogg producing a spectacular aerial try for Queensland and hulking winger Eric Grothe racing 95 metres to score for the Blues. NSW skipped ahead 14-4 on the back of two extremely controversial video referee decisions—a bewildering no-try ruling against Queensland allowed the Blues to sweep downfield and score, before a clear Brett Hodgson knock-on was overlooked for Grothe's second. But the Maroons held their nerve. Thurston sent man of the match Brent Tate on a thrilling 70-metre run to the line, and with five minutes remaining man of the series Darren Lockyer swooped on a loose Hodgson pass in front of the NSW posts to score an unforgettable series-winning try. The result sent the pro-Queensland crowd and the players alike into raptures, and gave the team from north of the border their first series victory for five years.

2007 QUEENSLAND WON SERIES 2-1 Queensland stamped itself as the dominant state in Australian Rugby League with its first back-to-back series victories since the 1980s. With virtually a full contingent to choose from after their courageous—but injury-plagued—series win a year earlier, the Maroons fielded a star-studded side and staged yet another stirring Origin comeback in the opening encounter. Greg Inglis opened the scoring, but NSW led 18-6 at the break, thanks to a brilliant try on the stroke of halftime to 19-year-old debutant winger Jarryd Hayne.

The Parramatta speedster scored a kick-and-chase try to rival Billy Slater's effort from 2004, and stunned the packed Suncorp Stadium crowd. But Inglis' second try and a rare four-pointer to workhorse prop Steve Price levelled the scores. Hayne became the archetypal hero-turned-villain when he flung an ill-fated pass back infield to his fullback Anthony Minichiello inside the NSW quarter, which was snapped up by Darren Lockyer in an ugly case of déjà vu for the Blues. Johnathan Thurston capped a man of the match performance by closing out the 25-18 win with a field goal.

The Maroons overcame an eight-year hoodoo to become the first Queensland side since 1995 to wrap an Origin series up inside two games. The Maroons were yet to register a win in 12 matches at Sydney's Telstra Stadium, but outlasted NSW 10-6 in a classic, grinding Origin battle. The scores were tied 6-all at halftime, and the combatants were eventually separated by a Steve Bell try from a Thurston grubber with little more than 15 minutes remaining. Queensland's defence withstood wave after wave of desperate Blues attack, but the engine-room, led by Price, Petero Civoniceva, man of the match Cameron Smith and Dallas Johnson, who racked up over 60 tackles, got the Maroons over the line.

The result in game three may have been reversed, with NSW winning 18-4 in Brisbane, but Queensland received ample plaudits for a gallant performance. Johnson was knocked unconscious in the first tackle of the game, but later returned, Brent Tate left the field with a season-ending knee injury, and Nate Myles played on with a serious shoulder concern. The 6-4 halftime scoreline remained until the 73rd minute, when the Maroons were unable to withstand another attacking raid and Matt King crossed for NSW. Veteran winger Hazem El Masri, making a belated NSW debut at the age of 31, sealed the win with a late try to add to his three goals. Blues five-eighth Greg Bird was named man-of-the-match, but the hard-earned spoils belonged to Queensland.

2008 QUEENSLAND WON SERIES 2-1 Melbourne's burgeoning 'supercoach' Craig Bellamy replaced Graham Murray as NSW's coach. Meanwhile, Queensland was on a mission to match NSW's 2003-05 series three-peat despite missing injured captain Darren Lockyer for the series. But the Maroons began in uninspiring fashion, going down 18-10 to a methodical NSW outfit, who blooded four Origin rookies. The eight-point margin did not do justice to the level of the Blues' dominance. NSW opened up a 14-0 lead courtesy of an early double to debutant winger Anthony Quinn, and wrapped up the result in the second half through interchange forward Anthony Laffranchi, who was also playing his first game in the sky blue. Behind 18-4, Queensland produced some belated attacking flair, but it was not enough to snatch victory. NSW halfback Peter Wallace was superb on debut, playing with the control and poise of an Origin veteran. His kicking game frequently hemmed in Queensland's dangerous back-three, his running game caused problems, and he was unlucky to miss out on man of the match honours, which went to Greg Bird for the second consecutive Origin match.

Written off after the lacklustre game one performance, Queensland blew NSW off Suncorp Stadium with a record-equalling 30-0 pummelling. Greg Inglis, who copped a barrage of criticism for a quiet first-up game, was at his breathtaking best, setting up two long-range tries for debutant winger Darius Boyd. The Blues were never in the hunt, while 19-year-old Israel Folau scored his second try of the series and Johnathan Thurston kicked seven from seven, matching coach Meninga's performance from the inaugural Origin in 1980. The result was a personal vindication for Scott Prince, who had been a controversial omission from the Queensland side for the first encounter before winning a recall at five-eighth.

But Prince's involvement was thwarted by a broken arm in the first half of the decider. The setback failed to stymie Queensland's attack, however, with Israel Folau scoring two spectacular aerial tries. NSW rallied to lead 10-8 at halftime, before a Thurston penalty goal set up a lengthy stalemate. Thurston had stepped into the role of sole playmaker with typical aplomb, and produced the series-winning play in the 68th minute, using his trademark 'show-and-go' to break the NSW line and put Billy Slater on a path to the tryline. It was Queensland's first hat-trick of series wins since 1987-89. Folau was named man of the match, Petero Civoniceva the Ron McAuliffe medallist and Thurston the Wally Lewis medallist. Courageous NSW captain Danny Buderus, bound for Super League and playing his 21st consecutive Origin and 15th as captain (both NSW records), was a deserved Brad Fittler Medal winner.

2009 QUEENSLAND WON SERIES 2-1 NSW named seven debutants for the 2009 series-opener at Melbourne's Etihad Stadium, and appeared to get off to a flying start after winger Jarryd Hayne touched down following a scorching 40-metre run. But after countless replays, video referee Bill Harrigan ruled Hayne had stepped on the sideline and denied the try, sparking vigorous debate in the commentary box and in the media post-match. Queensland compounded the Blues' frustration with three tries in the space of nine minutes to build an 18-2 lead. Centre Greg Inglis scored his second try soon after halftime, but NSW produced a spirited comeback to trail by just six points with 12 minutes remaining. Inglis sent winger Darius Boyd over in the corner on fulltime, however, icing a 28-18 victory for the Maroons. Halfback Johnathan Thurston scored a try and kicked four goals in a man of the match display.

A succession of calamitous NSW errors allowed Queensland to shoot out to an 18-0 lead after just 23 minutes in the second game in Sydney, but Hayne pegged the Blues back into the contest with two first half tries—including a 90-metre intercept effort. The Maroons were hampered by a stomach virus that hit the squad in the lead-up to the match, while Inglis was forced off the field with concussion after a high tackle by recalled veteran NSW five-eighth Trent Barrett (he later received a two-match suspension), and several Queensland forwards picked up injuries. A try to debutant winger David Williams slashed Queensland's lead to four points with 18 minutes on the clock, but the undermanned Maroons held firm and sealed the series 24-14 after a late try to hooker Cameron Smith. The courageous performance under duress drew comparisons with Queensland's famous 16-12 victory in game two of the 1989 series. The triumph, in which backrower Sam Thaiday was named man of the match, marked an Origin record four straight series victories for Mal Meninga's Queensland side.

NSW made nine changes to its side for the dead-rubber clash at Suncorp Stadium and restored some pride with a 28-16 victory in one of the most explosive interstate clashes of the decade. Queensland's workhorse lock Dallas Johnson opened the scoring with his first Origin try, but the Blues led 14-6 at halftime after the first of backrower Ben Creagh's two tries, and an eight-point try awarded after Thurston struck David Williams with his boot as the winger touched down. Justin Hodges and Billy Slater scored to reduce the Blues' advantage to 20-16, but Creagh's double secured the result. Trent Waterhouse became the first NSW player sent off in Origin football for being third man in to a toe-to-toe stoush between teammate Brett White and Queensland prop Steve Price in the 79th minute. The fiery atmosphere reached fever pitch in the remaining few seconds as the Maroons launched a bomb from the ensuing penalty and barrelled NSW fullback Kurt Gidley, sparking another brawl. Thaiday and Creagh were despatched to the sin-bin, while Darren Lockyer lifted the Origin shield once again after the dust finally settled.

2010 QUEENSLAND WON SERIES 3-0 Queensland extended its Origin domination to five straight series and achieved the only feat that had eluded the Maroons during their record streak—a series whitewash. The 28-24 scoreline in the series-opener in Sydney belied Queensland's control. Halfback Johnathan Thurston was unstoppable, laying on all five of the Maroons' tries with a masterful passing and kicking game, while he produced a one-on-one steal to send Sam Thaiday away for his side's final four-pointer. Two late tries to the outclassed Blues added some respectability to the scoreboard.

The NSW squad was engulfed in a maelstrom in the lead-up to game two. Centre Timana Tahu walked out of camp following racist remarks made by assistant coach and former playing legend Andrew Johns about Queensland's Indigenous centre Greg Inglis. The Maroons feasted on the besieged Blues in Brisbane, with Inglis scoring the opening try and Israel Folau—a controversial selection in the Queensland side after the announcement he would switching to the AFL at the end of the year—bagging a double. Skipper Darren Lockyer, who considered retiring from representative football at the start of the season before opting to play on, was named man of the match. Queensland was on track for a record victory, before a late try to Blues prop Brett White made the final score 34-6.

Trent Barrett replaced Kurt Gidley as NSW captain for the dead-rubber encounter at Stadium Australia (Gidley had skippered the Blues starting on the bench in game two), but the Blues trailed 13-6 at halftime after tries to Queensland winger Darius Boyd and second-rower Nate Myles, and a remarkable 46-metre field goal by Lockyer. NSW finally displayed some grit in the second half and captured the lead for the first time in the series when lock Greg Bird dotted down with 11 minutes remaining. But the Blues imploded in the closing stages; man of the match Billy Slater blazed over after NSW hooker Michael Ennis conceded a silly penalty, and Thurston's conversion put Queensland a point in front. A try in shadows of fulltime to centre Willie Tonga stretched the final score to 23-18 and confirmed the Maroons' first series whitewash in 15 years.

2011 QUEENSLAND WON SERIES 2-1 Craig Bellamy relinquished the coaching role and Ricky Stuart—NSW's last series-winning coach—returned, hell-bent on restoring pride and passion to the blue jersey. Queensland dominated the first half of game one at Suncorp Stadium, but led just 6-0 at halftime after a supreme defensive effort by the new-look Blues, who blooded five Origin rookies. Debutant winger Jharal Yow Yeh increased the Maroons' lead to 10 points shortly after halftime, but NSW snatched a shock 12-10 lead with 11 minutes remaining courtesy of brilliant tries to halfback Mitchell Pearce and centre Michael Jennings in the space of five minutes. The Maroons held their nerve to conjure a 72nd-minute match-winner, with Billy Slater brilliantly finishing off a set move involving the old firm of Johnathan Thurston and Darren Lockyer to secure a nail-biting 16-12 victory.

Stuart made three injury-enforced changes to his backline for game two at Stadium Australia, while he put a broom through the NSW forward pack after the Blues' front-row contingent's lacklustre performance in the series-opener. Captain and backrow regular Paul Gallen was a shock selection at prop, but he responded with one of the great individual displays seen at Origin level. The Cronulla workhorse played 80 minutes, making 27 runs for 211 metres and racking up 31 tackles in a performance that earned a rare '10' in *Rugby League Week*'s exclusive player ratings—the first ever awarded for an Origin match. The Blues trailed 8-6 at halftime, but a sensational try to 19-year-old debutant William Hopoate and a late four-pointer to recalled fullback Anthony Minichiello—making his first Origin appearance in four years after a wretched run with injury—clinched a richly deserved 18-8 triumph.

The great Darren Lockyer's Origin farewell added another element to a feverishly anticipated decider at Suncorp Stadium. Extending his record to 36 Origin appearances, Lockyer was magnificent as Queensland effectively extinguished the Blues' compelling bid for a drought-breaking series victory in the opening 33 minutes, scorching to a 24-0 lead. Two tries late in the first half raised faint hopes of a NSW revival, but Greg Inglis' second try—which saw the centre equal Dale Shearer's Origin record of 12 tries—put the game and the series to bed. The Blues pegged the final score back to 34-24 with two tries in the dying minutes. Captain-in-waiting Cameron Smith picked up his second man of the match award for the series after also claiming the honour in game one, while Lockyer lifted the Origin shield for the sixth and final time (after previous series wins as skipper in 2001, 2006-07 and 2009-10) and Queensland stretched its domination to six consecutive series victories.

MEN OF THE MATCH

- Wally Lewis' undisputed standing as the greatest-ever State of Origin player is supported by the brilliant Queensland five-eighth's eight man of the match awards in 31 appearances—twice as many gongs as any other player. NSW halfbacks Peter Sterling and Andrew Johns, and Maroons No.7 Allan Langer each boast four man of the match awards, while fellow Origin greats Ben Elias, Ricky Stuart, Darren Lockyer, Cameron Smith and Johnathan Thurston have achieved the honour three times.

- Lewis is the only player to be named man of the match in three consecutive Origins, claiming the award in the final match of the 1983 series and the first two matches of the 1984 series. He also was adjudged best on ground in the 1983 series opener, meaning he is the only player to win two man of the match awards in a series twice.

- Chris Close was named man of the match in the first two Origin matches—the one-off clashes in 1980 and 1981. Close and intimidating Blues forward Les Davidson (Game one, 1987) are the only players to be adjudged man of the match on Origin debut.

- Robust prop Sam Backo is the only player besides Lewis to win consecutive awards in the same series, claiming the honour for powerhouse performances in the final two matches of Queensland's 1988 series whitewash. Greg Bird is the most recent player to win consecutive man of the match awards—he spearheaded NSW victories from five-eighth in the third match of the 2007 series and the 2008 series-opener. Peter Sterling, who was named man of the match in the second and fourth matches in 1987, is the only NSW player to win two awards in the same series, while Queensland hooker Cameron Smith won man of the match awards in the 2011 series-opener and decider.

- Four players have been named man of the match from a losing side—Queenslanders Mal Meninga (Game one, 1982), Wally Lewis (Game three, 1985) and Steve Walters (Game two, 1991), and NSW's Peter Sterling (Game two, 1987).
- NSW forwards Steve Menzies (Game three, 1996) and Luke Bailey (Game one, 2003) are the only players to win the man of the match award after starting on the bench.
- Wally Lewis (Game three of 1983 and 1984) and Allan Langer (Game three of 1987 and 2002) are the only award recipients in multiple series deciders. Langer (Game three, 2002) and Blues hooker Ben Elias (Game three, 1994) are the only players to be named man of the match in their final Origin appearance.
- Unsurprisingly, 22 halfbacks and 16 five-eighths have won man of the match awards. Perhaps less predictably, props are the next best represented, with 10 awards going to front-rowers. Hookers and second-rowers have won nine times each, followed by centres with eight. Fullbacks and wingers have each claimed six awards, while just two recipients have been lock-forwards.

THE CAPTAINS

- Queensland used 12 skippers in the first 32 seasons of State of Origin, compared to 17 NSW captains. Intriguingly, in the 1980s just three players captained Queensland, while eight skippered the Blues. But in the 1990s Queensland had seven captains, in contrast to NSW's four. Since 2000, Queensland has employed five captains and NSW six skippers.
- Queensland and NSW have used two different captains in the same series six times apiece. The Blues used two skippers in four of the first six three-match series, but did so just twice after 1988; all six series that Queensland employed multiple skippers occurred after 1987.
- The incomparable Wally Lewis set an Origin captaincy record that is unlikely to be bettered—he led Queensland in 30 of his 31 appearances. The only match he did not have the (c) next to his name was in the inaugural match in 1980, when fellow Immortal Arthur Beetson famously skippered the Maroons to a 20-10 boilover. Queensland won 18 of 30 matches and seven of 10 series with Lewis in charge.
- Darren Lockyer led Queensland in 22 of his record 36 Origin appearances, winning 14 matches and six of eight series at the helm. Mal Meninga (nine matches) is the next most prolific Maroons captain.
- Danny Buderus became NSW's most prolific captain with his 15th and final appearance in charge in 2008, eclipsing Brad Fittler's mark of 14 matches between 1995 and 2001. Fittler made a two-game Origin comeback in 2004 under Buderus' captaincy.
- NSW greats Laurie Daley (13 matches) and Wayne Pearce (10) are the only other players whose appearances as captain top double figures.

- Newcastle players led the Blues in 26 consecutive games between 2002 and 2010. Andrew Johns captained NSW in 2002 and '03, Danny Buderus took over in 2004 and skippered the Blues until his representative retirement in 2008, before Kurt Gidley was handed the reins for 2009 and the first two matches of the 2010 series.
- Gidley is the only captain to start an Origin match on the bench. He wore the No.14 in the second match of the 2009 series and took the field late in the first half. Following that game, he became the first Origin player to be replaced as captain while still retaining a spot in the squad, with Trent Barrett named as skipper for the third match. Queensland captains Paul Vautin (1990) and Trevor Gillmeister (1996) are the only incumbent captains to be dropped during a series. The backrow stalwarts lost their places after skippering the Maroons to series-opening losses, and neither player represented Queensland again.
- NSW has been captained by a forward 49 times in 93 Origin matches, while a member of the pack has led Queensland on just 15 occasions. Hooker Danny Buderus is the most prolific forward leader with 15 matches as captain, followed by tireless backrower Wayne Pearce, who skippered the Blues in 10 matches. Gorden Tallis' six appearances as captain is the most by a Queensland forward.

THE COACHES

- Queensland has used 10 coaches in 32 seasons of Origin football, while NSW has employed 13 different mentors.
- NSW's Phil Gould and Queensland's Mal Meninga are the most successful coaches in Origin history with six series wins. Gould won series in 1992-94, 1996 and 2003-04, and lost just one—in 1995. His Blues side drew the 2002 series. No other Blues coach has won more than one series at the helm. Mal Meninga's six consecutive Origin series wins as coach since taking on the role ranks as arguably the finest coaching achievement in interstate football. Meninga has won 13 of his 18 matches in charge and guided Queensland to an unprecedented six series triumphs from 2006-11. Arthur Beetson (1982-84 and 1989) and Wayne Bennett (1987-88, 1998 and 2001) have won four series apiece as coach, while Beetson also coached the one-off victory in 1981. Bennett is Queensland's longest-serving coach with seven series in charge, a record that is set to be equalled by Meninga in 2012.
- Six former Queensland Origin representatives have later coached the Maroons, compared to just three Blues players that have done the same for NSW. Inaugural NSW captain Tom Raudonikis became the first former Blues player to coach his state in 1997, by which stage Origin greats Arthur Beetson, Wally Lewis and Paul Vautin had already coached Queensland. Mark Murray, Michael Hagan and Mal Meninga have also played for and coached Queensland, while Wayne Pearce and Ricky Stuart have represented NSW in both capacities.

FATHERS AND SONS

- John Lang and Martin Lang: The first-ever father-and-son pair to appear at State of Origin level. John Lang, a 1973 Kangaroo tourist, was Queensland's hooker in the first Origin match in 1980, while fearless prop Martin played eight games for the Maroons between 1998 and 2000.

- Steve Rogers and Mat Rogers: A veteran of 24 Tests as one of the finest players of the 1970s and '80s, Steve Rogers played in the first four Origin matches in the centres for NSW, captaining the Blues in 1981. Son Mat, raised on the Gold Coast, debuted for Queensland in 1999 and played five matches in the maroon jersey before switching to rugby union and becoming a dual international.
- Eric Grothe and Eric Grothe Jr.: Two of the biggest, most fearsome wingers to run out for NSW at Origin level, Eric Grothe played nine matches for the Blues between 1981 and 1986, while his son of the same name played all three matches of the 2006 series. Eric Grothe Jr. was originally selected for NSW in 2000 after just 14 NRL games, but was forced to withdraw due to injury.
- Wayne Pearce and Mitchell Pearce: Highly respected backrower Wayne Pearce ranks as a NSW great, captaining the Blues to the first series cleansweep in Origin history in 1986 among 15 wholehearted appearances. Son Mitchell debuted for NSW aged just 19 in 2008 at halfback and had made six Origin appearances by the end of 2011.
- Steve Morris and Brett and Josh Morris: 'Slippery' Steve Morris, who played one match in each of the 1984 and 1986 series for NSW, is the only Origin player to produce two sons that have made it to Origin level. Josh made his debut for the Blues in 2009, while twin brother Brett broke into the state side in 2010.
- Craig Young and Dean Young: St. George front-row great Craig Young played in the inaugural Origin contest in 1980 and represented New South Wales five times. Hooker/backrower Dean made a belated debut for the Blues in the 2011 series-opener—he was previously 18th man for NSW in 2006.
- John Hopoate and William Hopoate: Notorious Manly winger John Hopoate was selected in NSW's side for game two of the Super League-depleted 1995 series, after just 20 first grade appearances for the Sea Eagles. His son, the even more talented and infinitely better behaved William, debuted for the Blues as a 19-year-old in game two of the 2011 series after only 15 NRL games for Manly. John was dropped after NSW's series-sealing 20-12 loss in his debut and never represented at Origin level again, while Will was injured after scoring a vital try in the Blues' 18-8 upset on Origin debut and missed the decider, before leaving the NRL at the end of 2011 to embark on a two-year Mormon mission.

BROTHERS

- Steve Mortimer and Chris Mortimer: Steve Mortimer made his Origin debut for NSW in 1982 and was joined in a blue jumper by brother Chris in 1984, becoming the first siblings to appear in an Origin match together. Both played in nine matches, with Steve's last match occurring in 1985 as NSW's first series-winning captain, while Chris finished as a 30-year-old in 1989.
- Graeme Wynn and Peter Wynn: Graeme Wynn made his only Origin appearance in the inaugural 1980 clash. Brother Peter shared his debut with Chris Mortimer in 1984 to simultaneously become the first two sets of Origin-playing brothers. Peter Wynn played in the Blues' maiden series victory in 1985.
- Brett French and Ian French: The French brothers became the first siblings to represent Queensland at Origin level. Centre Brett debuted in 1984 and played five matches for the Maroons, while second-rower Ian debuted a year later and made nine appearances.

They were denied the opportunity to appear in an Origin match together when they were both unused replacements in the first match of the 1985 series.

- Kerrod Walters, Kevin Walters and Steve Walters: The only set of three brothers to play Origin football, the Walters clan tallied 40 appearances for Queensland between them. Twins Kerrod and Kevin debuted in 1989, while elder brother Steve filled in for an injured Kerrod to make his debut in 1990. Suspension ruled Kerrod out of the 1991 series-opener and Steve never looked back, becoming one of the all time great hookers and playing 14 Origin matches. Kevin played 20 matches for the Maroons, captaining his beloved state for one match in 1999, his last Origin series. Kevin and Steve hold the record for the most appearances together by a set of brothers with 12. The last of Kerrod's six appearances came in 1994 when he deputised for the injured Steve in game two.

- Darren Smith and Jason Smith: Versatile brothers Darren and Jason Smith played a combined 38 Origin matches for Queensland. Darren debuted in 1992 and, ironically, came off the bench for his injured brother when Jason was knocked unconscious on debut in 1994. Darren played the last of 22 matches in 2002, while Jason made 16 appearances from 1994-2000. The Smith brothers appeared together in the same match on nine occasions.

- Matthew Johns and Andrew Johns: The only siblings to debut together and to play in the halves together at Origin level, Newcastle's Johns brothers first played for the Blues in 1995. Matthew, the elder of the pair, made four appearances for NSW, while Andrew became arguably the Blues' greatest-ever player in 23 matches, including six games as skipper in 2002-03.

- Mark Geyer and Matt Geyer: Firebrand second-rower Mark Geyer had a controversial three-game career for the Blues between 1989 and 1991, while younger brother Matt scored two tries in three games on the wing for NSW during the 1999 series.

- Matt Gidley and Kurt Gidley: Classy centre Matt Gidley played 11 Origin matches for NSW between 2000 and 2004. Utility Kurt followed in his older brother's footsteps when he made his debut for the Blues in 2007, and captained his state in 2009-10.

- Brett Stewart and Glenn Stewart: Quicksilver fullback Brett Stewart played five matches for NSW in 2007-08 and his older brother, backrower and Manly teammate Glenn, made three appearances from 2009-11.

- Josh Morris and Brett Morris: The Morris boys are the only twins to represent NSW at Origin level. Josh played two matches in 2009, with Brett debuting a year later.

SENT OFF

- Despite the high-intensity, physical nature of State of Origin football and the passion it evokes often spilling over into violence, just three players have been sent off in the first 31 seasons of Origin. Queensland forward Craig Greenhill, playing in just his second Origin match, became the first player sent off in game two of the 1996 series. Greenhill was marched by referee David Manson for an ugly high tackle on Blues enforcer Paul Harragon, for which he was later suspended for four matches.

- Maroons firebrand Gorden Tallis became the second player sent off in Origin football when he gave controversial whistleblower Bill Harrigan a massive spray late in the opening game of the 2000 series. Tallis allegedly called Harrigan a "fucking cheat" after the referee missed two apparent knock-ons before awarding a crucial NSW try. He was found guilty of contrary conduct at the judiciary but was not suspended.

- The first Blues player to be sent off in Origin was Penrith backrower Trent Waterhouse, in the dying minutes of the spiteful dead-rubber game three of the 2009 series at Suncorp Stadium. Waterhouse was unfortunate—he ran in to intervene in a toe-to-toe fight between rival props Brett White and Steve Price, arriving a moment after White had landed the knockout blow on Queensland great Price. Waterhouse was sent off for contrary conduct, but was later exonerated at the judiciary.

LONGEVITY

The following players' Origin careers spanned more than a decade:

Allan Langer (Qld)—15 years and 24 days (game one, 1987 to game three, 2002)

Brad Fittler (NSW)—14 years and 39 days (game two, 1990 to game three, 2004)

Mal Meninga (Qld)—13 years and 352 days (game one, 1980 to game three, 1994)

Darren Lockyer (Qld)—13 years and 45 days (game one, 1998 to game three, 2011)

Andrew Gee (Qld)—13 years and 26 days (game two, 1990 to game two, 2003)

Trent Barrett (NSW)—13 years and 12 days (game three, 1997 to game three, 2010)

Wally Lewis (Qld)—11 years and 347 days (game one, 1980 to game three, 1991)

Steve Price (Qld)—11 years and 54 days (game one, 1998 to game three, 2009)

Steve Menzies (NSW)—11 years and 51 days (game one, 1995 to game three, 2006)

Dale Shearer (Qld)—11 years and 20 days (game one, 1985 to game three, 1996)

Andrew Ettingshausen (NSW)—11 years and 3 days (game one, 1987 to game two, 1998)

Petero Civoniceva (Qld)—10 years and 61 days* (game one, 2001 to game three, 2011)

Andrew Johns (NSW)—10 years and 52 days (game one, 1995 to game three, 2005)

Matt Sing (Qld)—10 years and 52 days (game one, 1995 to game three, 2005)

Brett Kimmorley (NSW)—10 years and 37 days (game one, 2000 to game two, 2010)

Laurie Daley (NSW)—10 years and 31 days (game one, 1989 to game three, 1999)

Geoff Toovey (NSW)—10 years and 29 days (game one, 1990 to game three, 2000)

Kevin Walters (Qld)—10 years and 23 days (game two, 1989 to game three, 1999)

Glenn Lazarus (NSW)—10 years and 3 days (game one, 1989 to game one, 1999)

LONG TIME BETWEEN APPEARANCES

The following players experienced at least three full series in between Origin appearances.

- **Brad Izzard (NSW)—8 years and 355 days (game three, 1982 to game three, 1991):** Izzard debuted as a teenager, playing all three matches in 1982, but the Penrith stalwart was not selected again until the 1991 decider.
- **Greg Florimo (NSW)—6 years and 328 days (game three, 1988 to game one, 1995):** Versatile North Sydney great Florimo debuted off the bench in the 1988 dead-rubber. He won a recall almost seven years later after touring with the 1994 Kangaroos.
- **Josh Perry (NSW)—6 years and 34 days (game one, 2003 to game three, 2009):** Newcastle prop Perry was dropped after his debut in the 2003 series-opener.

But he enjoyed a career renaissance at Manly, representing Australia at the 2008 World Cup and breaking back into the NSW side the following season.

- **John Simon (NSW)—5 years and 36 days (game one, 1992 to game two, 1997):** Illawarra halfback Simon deputised for the injured Ricky Stuart in the 1992 series-opener. He kicked a decisive field goal in his next Origin appearance more than five years later after joining Parramatta.
- **Geoff Toovey (NSW)—5 years and 34 days (game one, 1990 to game three, 1995):** Manly No.7 Toovey debuted off the bench as a 20-year-old in 1990, but the presence of Ricky Stuart blocked his path for five years. He won a recall during the Super League-affected 1995 series and missed just two games in the following five series.
- **Trent Waterhouse (NSW)—5 years and 29 days (game two, 2004 to game three, 2009):** Backrower Waterhouse broke into the Blues' squad on the back of Penrith's 2003 premiership triumph, but was unsighted at Origin level for more than five years. He was unluckily sent off in his first match back in the sky blue jersey, before playing two games in the 2010 series.
- **Brad Thorn (Qld)—4 years and 352 days (game three, 2000 to game one, 2005):** Thorn's first stint in rugby union was the cause of his Origin hiatus, but the Broncos giant came back into the Queensland side at the first available opportunity after returning to the NRL in 2005.
- **Willie Tonga (Qld)—4 years and 352 days (game three, 2004 to game two, 2009):** Bulldog Tonga was a centre sensation in 2004, displacing Justin Hodges in the Queensland side. Due to injuries and indifferent form, Tonga did not return to the Origin arena until joining the Cowboys in 2009, ironically replacing an injured Hodges.
- **PJ Marsh (Qld)—4 years and 331 days (game two, 2003 to game one, 2008):** Marsh appeared set for a long stint as Queensland hooker, but a career-threatening neck injury sustained playing for the Warriors allowed young Melbourne rake Cameron Smith an opportunity. After resurrecting his career with Parramatta and Brisbane, Marsh was a shock inclusion on the bench for the 2008 series-opener.
- **Luke Lewis (NSW)—4 years and 331 days (game three, 2004 to game one, 2009):** Penrith's Lewis starred in the Blues' 2004 series victory as a young three-quarter, but resurfaced as a backrower in 2009 and was an automatic selection when available in the 2010-11 series.
- **Jason Croker (NSW)—4 years and 323 days (game three, 1996 to game one, 2001):** Ultra-versatile Canberra stalwart Croker played in all three matches of the Blues' 1996 series whitewash. He won a recall at lock for the 2001 series-opener, the last of his five Origin appearances.
- **Trent Barrett (NSW)—4 years and 30 days (game one, 2005 to game two, 2009):** Dragons captain Barrett joined English club Wigan at the end of 2006. He returned to the NRL with Cronulla after two Super League seasons and won an Origin recall at the age of 31 in 2009, before captaining NSW in one match the following season.
- **Anthony Watmough (NSW)—4 years and 30 days (game one, 2005 to game two, 2009):** Manly backrower Watmough spent several seasons in the representative wilderness after making his NSW debut in 2005, but has been an Origin regular since his recall during the 2009 series.
- **Anthony Minichiello (NSW)—4 years and 23 days (game one, 2007 to game two, 2011):** A star of NSW's 2003-05 series successes, fullback Minichiello endured a

wretched run with injuries. He was recalled at the age of 31 during the 2011 series in the place of the injured Josh Dugan.

- **Kerrod Walters (Qld)—3 years and 360 days (game three, 1990 to game two, 1994):** Suspension saw Broncos hooker Walters give up his Queensland jersey to elder brother Steve. Kerrod's last Origin appearance was as a replacement for the injured Steve during the 1994 series.
- **Gorden Tallis (Qld)—3 years and 350 days (game three, 1994 to game two, 1998):** St. George tyro Tallis played two matches for the Maroons in 1994, but his Super League allegiance excluded him from Origin contention in 1995 and 1997, while he sat out the 1996 season as he waited to join the Broncos.
- **Trent Barrett (NSW)—3 years and 350 days (game three, 1997 to game two, 2001):** Illawarra five-eighth Barrett made his Origin debut as a 19-year-old in the 1997 dead-rubber, but had to wait almost four years for another opportunity due to the presence of Brad Fittler and Laurie Daley.
- **Scott Prince (Qld)—3 years and 340 days (game three, 2004 to game two, 2008):** Wests Tigers halfback Prince had a fine debut series for Queensland in 2004, but was usurped by Johnathan Thurston the following season. Injury to Darren Lockyer gave Prince an opportunity during the 2008 series.
- **Andrew Gee (Qld)—3 years and 337 days (game three, 1998 to game one, 2002):** After playing in Queensland's 1998 series victory, Broncos veteran Gee left the NRL at the end of 1999 to spend two seasons with Super League club Warrington. Gee was recalled to the Maroons' squad at the age of 32 after returning to Brisbane in 2002.
- **Darren Smith (Qld)—3 years and 336 days (game three, 1994 to game one, 1998):** The Super League war interrupted Darren Smith's Origin career, but he returned to the Queensland side in 1998 and played another 15 matches for the Maroons.
- **Brett Hodgson (NSW)—3 years and 332 days (game three, 2002 to game one, 2006):** Brilliant for the Blues in the drawn 2002 series, Hodgson was kept out of the NSW side for three series by Roosters fullback Anthony Minichiello. The Tigers custodian won a recall in 2006 with Minichiello sidelined due to injury.
- **Jamie Lyon (NSW)—3 years and 311 days (game three, 2003 to game one, 2007):** Parramatta centre Lyon starred for NSW in the 2002-03 series, but walked out on the Eels and the NRL at the beginning of 2004. After spending the 2005-06 seasons with Super League side St. Helens, Lyon returned to Australia with Manly and was immediately recalled to the NSW line-up.
- **Brett French (Qld)—3 years and 305 days (game three, 1984 to game one, 1988):** Wynnum centre Brent French played two matches for Queensland during the 1984 series, before earning a recall on the bench for all three matches of the Maroons' 1988 series whitewash while playing for North Sydney.

CLUB REPRESENTATION

The Brisbane Broncos are the pacesetters of Origin representation—the club has produced 54 players (48 for Queensland, six for NSW). Manly is the next most prolific club with 46 Origin representatives, including a NSW record 33 players. The North Queensland Cowboys have produced the second-highest number of Queensland representatives with 16, while Parramatta has provided 27 players to NSW teams—

second only to the Sea Eagles—and six to Queensland line-ups. Canterbury has produced a total of 36 Origin representatives—25 for NSW and 11 for Queensland.

Manly set an Origin record by providing nine players to game one of the 1983 series (six for NSW, three for Queensland), while a NSW record eight players were picked from Parramatta for game two of the same series. But the all time record was toppled by the Broncos, who provided 11 players to an Origin match on five occasions between 2001 and 2003 (twice with 11 Queensland players, twice with 10 and once with nine). An impressive total of 10 Melbourne players ran out for game two of the 2008 series—six for Queensland and four for NSW.

THE AWARDS

Originally awarded to Queensland's best and fairest player from 1992-2003, the Wally Lewis Medal became the overall award for the best player in each year's Origin series in 2004. The Ron McAuliffe Medal was initiated in 2004 for Queensland's players' player of the series, while NSW's players' player has been honoured with the Brad Fittler Medal since 2005.

THE WALLY LEWIS MEDAL (for official player of the State of Origin series)

- **2004 Craig Fitzgibbon (NSW):** The workhorse second-rower was inspirational in the Blues' 2-1 series victory and was man of the match in the decider.
- **2005 Anthony Minichiello (NSW):** The Roosters fullback lifted his performances to another level in 2005, winning man of the match honours in NSW's 32-10 decider victory.
- **2006 Darren Lockyer (Qld):** Under-fire after Queensland's series-opening loss, the captain was man of the match in game two and scored the series-winning try in the decider.
- **2007 Cameron Smith (Qld):** Cemented his standing as the game's premier hooker with his brilliant control at dummy-half. Smith was man of the match in the series-sealing game two victory.
- **2008 Johnathan Thurston (Qld):** The linchpin halfback stepped up in the absence of Lockyer and laid on the series-winning try for Billy Slater in the decider.
- **2009 Greg Inglis (Qld):** Emphasised his status as the preeminent attacking weapon in Rugby League with a double in the series-opener and another try as Queensland sealed the series in game two.
- **2010 Billy Slater (Qld):** Scored the winning try and was named man of the match in game three to seal Queensland's first series whitewash in 15 years.
- **2011 Cameron Smith (Qld):** Man of the match awards in games one and three saw the ultra-consistent hooker become the first player to secure two Wally Lewis Medals.

THE WALLY LEWIS MEDAL (for Queensland best and fairest player)

1992—Allan Langer	**1996**—Allan Langer
1993—Bob Lindner	**1997**—Robbie O'Davis
1994—Billy Moore	**1998**—Allan Langer
1995—Gary Larson	**1999**—Jason Hetherington

2000—Darren Smith

2001—Darren Lockyer

2002—Shane Webcke

2003—Darren Lockyer

THE RON McAULIFFE MEDAL (for Queensland players' player)

2004—Steve Price

2005—Cameron Smith

2006—Darren Lockyer

2007—Cameron Smith

2008—Petero Civoniceva

2009—Greg Inglis

2010—Sam Thaiday

2011—Petero Civoniceva

THE BRAD FITTLER MEDAL (for NSW players' player)

2005—Matt King

2006—Steve Menzies

2007—Jarryd Hayne

2008—Danny Buderus

2009—Jarryd Hayne

2010—Kurt Gidley

(2011 winner was not announced)

Biggest Wins: New South Wales—56-16 at Stadium Australia, 2000; 32-4 at Stadium Australia, 2002; 27-4 at Telstra Stadium, 2003. Queensland—36-6 at Lang Park, 1989; 36-6 at Suncorp Stadium, 2003; 30-0 at Suncorp Stadium, 2008

Most Appearances: Darren Lockyer (Qld) 36, Allan Langer (Qld) 34, Mal Meninga (Qld) 32, Brad Fittler (NSW) 31, Wally Lewis (Qld) 31, Petero Civoniceva (Qld) 30, Steve Price (Qld) 28, Andrew Ettingshausen (NSW) 27

Most Tries: Greg Inglis (Qld) 12, Dale Shearer (Qld) 12, Michael O'Connor (NSW) 11, Billy Slater (Qld) 11, Allan Langer (Qld) 10, Darren Lockyer (Qld) 9, Brad Fittler (NSW) 8, Anthony Minichiello (NSW) 8, Timana Tahu (NSW) 8

Most Points: Mal Meninga (Qld) 161, Michael O'Connor (NSW) 129, Johnathan Thurston (Qld) 118, Andrew Johns (NSW) 94, Ryan Girdler (NSW) 82, Darren Lockyer (NSW) 82, Dale Shearer (Qld) 66, Rod Wishart (NSW) 66

Most Tries in a Series: New South Wales—Ryan Girdler 5 in 2000. Queensland—Lote Tuqiri 5 in 2002

Most Points in a Series: New South Wales—Ryan Girdler 52 in 2000. Queensland—Darren Lockyer 34 in 2001

Most Tries in a Match: New South Wales—Chris Anderson 3 in 1983, Ryan Girdler 3 in 2000, Matt King 3 in 2005. Queensland—Kerry Boustead 3 in 1984, Lote Tuqiri 3 in 2002, Matt Sing 3 in 2003

Most Points in a Match: New South Wales—Ryan Girdler 32 (three tries, 10 goals) in 2000. Queensland—Lote Tuqiri 18 (three tries, three goals) in 2002

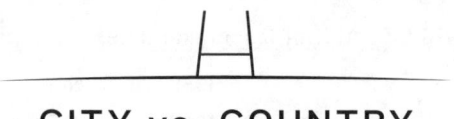

CITY vs. COUNTRY

A New South Wales Country representative side first took on the best from the Sydney premiership in 1928. Captained by legendary Riverina five-eighth Eric

Weissel, Country Firsts defeated City Firsts (who boasted South Sydney greats Benny Wearing, George Treweek and Eddie Root) 35-34 at the Sydney Cricket Ground. The upset result was a springboard to Test debuts for Weissel, Cootamundra lock Jack Kingston and Gundagai winger Eric Freestone in the subsequent home Ashes series between Australia and England.

With the great Jimmy Craig as skipper, City Firsts recorded its first win over Country in 1929—a 16-5 success at the Sydney Sports Ground. Weissel led Country to a 36-25 victory against a star-studded City side in 1930; Country's line-up contained 1929-30 Kangaroos, lock Wally Prigg and winger Bill Shankland. The annual City v Country matches were intermittently played as a two-match series during the 1930s and 1940s, and Country Firsts' next success against City came with two wins in 1937. Prigg captained Country to a 20-12 victory in the first encounter, before Bombala three-quarter Bert Williams (who toured with the 1937-38 Kangaroos at the end of the year) led the bush boys to a 15-5 result in the second clash. Williams was partnered in the centres by a 19-year-old Col Maxwell, who later joined Wests and was controversially chosen to captain the 1948-49 Kangaroos.

After Country's 14-11 victory in 1942, City was unbeaten in the annual contests for more than a decade. The matches began to draw crowds in excess of 50,000 at the SCG during the 1940s and 1950s, while the City v Country clash was played outside of Sydney for the first time in 1948, with a City side containing Test greats Clive Churchill, Frank Stanmore, Jack Holland, Noel Mulligan and Les Cowie prevailing 6-5 at the Wollongong Showground. The Country line-up featured five-eighth Johnny Hawke and 18-year-old winger Bobby Dimond, who both toured with the Kangaroos at the end of the year. Hawke later scored three tries in City Firsts' 51-13 defeat of Country in 1950 after moving to St. George.

Country Firsts broke an 11-year drought with a famous 28-27 victory at the SCG in 1953. Future all time great backs Brian Carlson and Harry Wells, Kurri Kurri Test pivot Rees Duncan and a pack including current or future international forwards Don Schofield, Charlie Gill, Ernie Hammerton and Bryan Orrock spearheaded the win over the Churchill-led all-star City squad.

Under the leadership of inspirational captain Tony Paskins, a former Wallaby who starred on the Rugby League fields of Britain before returning to Australia with Easts, Country scored back-to-back victories over City in 1961-62. Wollongong fullback Graeme Langlands (who was a late call-up for injured Newcastle custodian Les Johns) starred in the 18-8 win in 1962 and represented NSW in the subsequent interstate series, before joining St. George the following season and becoming an Immortal of the game.

Carlson—who scored four tries in City's 55-14 victory in 1958—coached Country Firsts to a 16-12 win against City Firsts (captain-coached by a 19-year-old Bob Fulton) in 1967, but public interest began to wane and Sydney crowds dwindled during the 1970s as City continued to dominate its rural rivals. Country's only success during the 1970s was a 19-9 boilover in 1975. Coached by former dual international and 1963-64 Kangaroos captain-coach Arthur Summons, and captained by former South Sydney Test prop Jim Morgan, the Country side featured 1973 Kangaroo Mick Cronin and future internationals Greg Brentnall and Terry Fahey in the backline. But it was to be Country Firsts' last success against City under the traditional format.

City Firsts thrashed Country by a record 55-2 scoreline in 1980, with fullback Graham Eadie scoring four tries and Cronin kicking 11 goals. The annual clash was staged in Canberra in 1981—the first time in 33 years it had been played outside Sydney—and ventured to Newcastle in 1982-83 and 1985-86. To alleviate the one-sided nature of the contests, the authorities allowed Country Firsts to select country-born players from 1984; Parramatta halfback Peter Sterling captained Country to a 38-12 loss in the first match played under the new format (ironically, with Wagga great Steve Mortimer wearing the No.7 for City). Canterbury halfback Mortimer captained a Country side featuring his brother Chris, Balmain prop Steve Roach and Manly second-rower Noel Cleal to a hard-fought 18-12 defeat to City in 1985, but a convincing 34-18 loss in 1986 prompted another revamp.

The match became a Place of Origin contest in 1987, with Country Origin and City Origin picking teams based on where players had made their debut in senior football. Bulldogs coach Warren Ryan was installed as coach of Country Origin, while Sterling captained a side containing premiership stars Cleal, Garry Jack, Chris Mortimer, Andrew Farrar and Peter Kelly. City Origin, led by Balmain captain Wayne Pearce and featuring Michael O'Connor, Eric Grothe, Brett Kenny and Terry Lamb, prevailed 30-22 in the inaugural Origin clash at Parramatta Stadium. A City Firsts side made up of NSW first grade players played Country Firsts, containing only country-based players, in the curtain-raiser.

City Origin won the first five Place of Origin contests, including a 28-26 thriller in 1990, as the match increasingly became regarded as a trial for the NSW State of Origin side. Country Origin broke through for its maiden victory in 1992, with the Laurie Daley-led side scoring an emotion-charged 17-10 victory. Mick Cronin was coach of the Country line-up. After a dour 7-0 win by City in 1993, Country emerged victorious again in 1994, smashing the city side 22-2. A last-minute try to Newcastle Knights backrower Adam Muir snatched a thrilling 18-16 victory for Country Origin in 1996, while Paul Harragon captained Country to a 17-4 win in 1997. The match was played in either Newcastle or Wollongong from 1994-97.

The representative fixture was discontinued in 1998 following the formation of the National Rugby League, before the concept was reinvigorated in 2001 with the match to be staged in NSW country centres. The Brett Kimmorley-led Country Origin side racked up an emphatic 42-10 victory against City Origin in Bathurst in 2001. City recorded its first win since 1995 with a 26-16 success in Gosford in 2002. Bizarrely, City and Country selectors both picked Parramatta backrower Andrew Ryan (a Dubbo junior) for the match. Ryan eventually took his place on the Country bench after an hour of deliberation between the rival selectors.

Subsequent matches were played in Lismore, Dubbo, Coffs Harbour, Wollongong, Orange, Port Macquarie and Albury, but the fixture's place on the representative calendar was routinely a topic of debate each season. Players selected in the Australian side for the early-season Test against New Zealand were exempt from the City-Country match, which became pigeonholed primarily as a NSW trial (becoming problematic when Test players were left out of the Blues' squad after being excluded from the City-Country clash), while it was played on the same night as the Trans-Tasman Test from 2009-11.

Each year fresh calls came for the match to be dumped. But players involved in the City-Country clashes insisted they wanted the event to remain a part of the

Rugby League landscape, relishing the chance to represent their community as well as pushing their chances for higher representative honours. The Country Origin players' jubilation after Knights winger Akuila Uate scored a try on the bell to steal an 18-12 victory in 2011—and Uate's subsequent selection to make his debut for NSW—was a testament to the value of the contest, both as a genuine representative match and as a State of Origin trial. The City-Country match was moved to a standalone representative weekend in 2012, to be played in Mudgee two days after the trans-Tasman Test match, with no NRL matches scheduled.

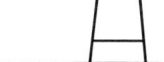

BOLTERS, CONTROVERSIAL SELECTIONS AND SHOCK OMISSIONS

Few events capture the Rugby League public's imagination more than a selection 'bolter'—a player who comes from the clouds to win representative selection. Meanwhile, a player considered a certainty only to be snubbed by selectors is a guaranteed recipe for a media storm and supporter backlash.

THE LEN SMITH CONTROVERSY Newtown centre Len Smith was the victim of the greatest selection controversy in the game's history. Smith captain-coached Australia's series victory over New Zealand during 1948, but was inexplicably left out of the Kangaroo Tour squad at the end of the season. For many years, a popular theory among experts and historians is that selectors' decision was religiously motivated—Smith was Catholic while the majority of the selectors were Masons.

Kangaroos five-eighth Wally O'Connell, who captained an Ashes Test on the 1948-49 tour, revealed the reason he believed Smith was omitted in his 2005 autobiography *In Defence*. O'Connell asserted that NSW coach and former Balmain player and coach Norm 'Latchem' Robinson, who was one of the selectors, wanted the Kangaroos coaching post. Smith was subsequently not chosen as one of the four centres in the squad—despite having no desire to coach the side, thus making Robinson's campaign against him essentially pointless. Smith's Newtown club attempted to seek reasoning for his exclusion from the NSWRL, but were denied, despite ARL Chairman Harry 'Jersey' Flegg maintaining that the board was as dumbfounded as the public.[26]

Robinson was ultimately overlooked for the coaching position. Col Maxwell was the shock replacement as captain-coach of the squad, despite being a non-playing reserve in the Test series earlier in the season and struggling for form at club level with Wests—a bizarre selection that none of the proposed reasons for Smith's omission can explain. The injustice led to Smith's retirement from the game at the end of the season and left a blot on the careers of the conspirators. Smith was named as 1948's Player of the Year in the E.E. Christensen-edited NSWRL *Official Yearbook*,

---

26 Ian Heads and David Middleton, *A Centenary Of Rugby League 1908-2008*. Sydney, 2008

but severed his ties with the code and politely declined NSWRL General Manager John Quayle's offer to begin the healing process in 1990.

The furore and confusion following Smith's omission overshadowed another surprise exclusion—Canterbury front-rower Eddie Burns. One of the finest props of the era whose rep career was hindered by World War II *(see The Best to not Represent)*, Burns was adjudged man-of-the-match in two appearances for NSW earlier in the season, but his name was also left off the list.

TEST INJUSTICE FOR DARCY HENRY The truth behind one of the great selection mysteries was finally revealed in an interview in the *Canberra Times* in 2004, retold in Neil Cadigan's book *Rugby League Yarns*, released in 2008. Ex-Easts five-eighth Darcy Henry made his Test debut from Forbes in the first Test victory over France in 1955. Unlucky to be dropped for the second encounter, which Australia lost, Henry won a recall for the decider. He was picked out of position in the centres, controversially replacing the great Harry Wells. Henry injured his back playing for Forbes the weekend prior to the third Test, but was passed fit and suited up to take the field. But when the side ran onto the Sydney Cricket Ground, debutant Dick Poole was in Henry's place, wearing the No.14 jersey. Many theories were put forward as to why Henry was left out at such a late stage, but none were confirmed or denied by Henry as he did not want to jeopardise his future representative chances. After Henry's death in 2004, his wife revealed the truth in an interview with Robert Messenger: captain Clive Churchill had told Henry in the changing rooms that he would have him switch places with selected pivot Graham Laird once the team took the field. After hearing of Churchill's plans, irate coach Vic Hey told the Australian selectors, who came into the changing rooms and dumped Henry from the team, accusing him of hiding his injuries from management. An inquiry found the selectors innocent of any wrongdoing, but all three were off the panel by 1956, Hey was replaced as coach and NSWRL secretary S. George Ball, who headed the inquiry, also lost his post. Henry played one more Test, scoring a try at five-eighth in a 31-14 victory over New Zealand at the SCG in 1956.

LISLE'S RAPID RISE Former Wallaby representative Jim Lisle made the quickest ascension to international honours in Australian Rugby League history when he switched codes in 1962. Lisle was picked to debut for City, NSW and Australia after just one match for South Sydney. His career was chequered by injury, but the five-eighth still toured with the 1963-64 Kangaroos, captained the Rabbitohs in their 1965 Grand Final loss and won a premiership with the club in 1967.

FUTURE GREATS LEFT AT HOME The 1967-68 Kangaroo Tour squad announcement was notable for more than reports several players had been told they were already in the squad well before it was made public. There was widespread disbelief at the omission of young superstars Bob Fulton, Bob McCarthy and Arthur Beetson. Manly centre/five-eighth Fulton was quickly gaining a reputation as one of the premiership's outstanding players in 1967 and made his debut for NSW, while McCarthy was thought to be a certainty, even before his decisive long-range intercept try in Souths' Grand Final defeat of Canterbury. Beetson had already debuted for Australia against Great Britain in 1966, but his exclusion was contributed to by his sending-off in a Kangaroo selection trial. Fulton and Beetson were both selected in the 1968 World Cup squad and later captained Australia, before being named as Immortals of the game in retirement. McCarthy had to wait until 1969 to make his international debut, but also skippered his country and is recognised as one of the greatest backrowers of all time.

TEST LEGEND DUMPED—THEN REINSTATED Despite superbly leading NSW to two victories over Queensland in 1977, future Immortal forward Arthur Beetson was inexplicably left out of Australia's subsequent midyear tour squad to New Zealand by the national selectors. The disbelieving ARL took the extraordinary step of refusing to accept the team without Beetson and demanded the selectors add him to the tour party. But upon hearing of the furore, Beetson pulled out of the squad and Queenslander Greg Veivers led the Australian side across the Tasman. Beetson regained his green-and-gold jersey at the end of the season and guided Australia to victory in the World Series tournament—the great prop's last international football campaign.

CONTROVERSIAL INJURY CALLS RULE OUT 'JUNIOR' AND 'THE KING' The two most contentious medicals in Australian Rugby League history occurred in the lead-up to consecutive Kangaroo Tours—Wayne Pearce in 1986 and Wally Lewis in 1990. Balmain and NSW captain Pearce suffered a knee injury late in 1986 to seemingly ruin his tour prospects, but he underwent an operation and a gruelling rehabilitation program to remain in contention. A certain selection if fit, Pearce failed the medical after purportedly tripping in a divot while running. The ARL doctors mistook the stumble for his knee giving way. Four years later, long-serving Test captain and future Immortal Wally Lewis was ruled unfit due to a broken arm that had kept him out for most of the 1990 premiership. Lewis made a comeback in Brisbane's preliminary final loss to Canberra, but was controversially ruled out by Dr. Nathan Gibbs. He would have become the first player to captain two Kangaroo Tours (after leading the 1986 side), an honour which instead went to his 1990 replacement Mal Meninga, who also skippered the 1994 squad.

'FREDDY' AND 'SPUD' THE 1990 BOLTERS Even Brad Fittler's mum would have been reluctant to declare the Penrith teenager a Kangaroo Tour chance at the start of the season. The precociously talented centre/five-eighth had played just four games prior to 1990, but after debuting for NSW and scoring a try in the Panthers' Grand Final loss to Canberra, Fittler found himself on board a flight to England as the youngest-ever Kangaroo tourist. North Sydney's Dally M Rookie of the Year Jason Martin was unlucky not to land a halves spot in the squad, but Fittler's slashing finals form and versatility were irresistible.

Meanwhile, Mark Carroll bucked the school of thought that a player had to be in a performing team to win representative selection. Carroll joined defending minor premiers South Sydney in 1990 after being blooded at Penrith, but the Rabbitohs finished as woeful wooden spooners. Nonetheless, Carroll's wholehearted displays were recognised by the Australian selectors when he was chosen to debut in the one-off Test against France at Parkes midway through the season, despite not being picked for the NSW Origin side. Carroll's consistent form for the struggling Rabbitohs garnered a tour spot at the end of the year.

Canberra's two-time premiership-winning No.9 Steve Walters, arguably the finest hooker of the modern era, was perhaps the unluckiest omission from the 1990 squad. His younger brother Kerrod and NSW captain Ben Elias were chosen as the team's rakes, while Kerrod's twin, five-eighth Kevin, also toured.

GODDEN COMES FROM THE CLOUDS Newcastle fullback Brad Godden ranks as one of the biggest bolters for the Australian side in the modern era. Godden stormed into contention with a series of confident displays in the Knights' charge to their maiden finals appearance in 1992. He beat Brisbane's premiership-winning custodian Julian O'Neill and St. George veteran Michael Potter for the second fullback spot for the World Cup final tour to England. Godden made his debut in a minor tour game, while Tim Brasher wore the No.1 in the 10-6 final victory. It was to be Godden's last representative appointment, and he struggled to assert himself in first grade in subsequent seasons with Newcastle and Hunter.

SAINTS' 'ROO TOUR STREAK ENDS IN 1994 The proud St. George club had supplied at least one player to every Kangaroo Tour party since entering the competition in 1921. But that record came to an abrupt end when the Dragons' green-and-gold contenders paid the price for the club's abysmal 1994 season. Brad Mackay was regarded as one of the unluckiest omissions from the squad. A 1990 tourist and Origin and Test regular, Mackay featured for NSW and played in the one-off home Test against France during 1994. North Sydney veteran and Australian debutant Greg Florimo claimed his spot as the squad's utility player—a position Canterbury lock Jim Dymock and versatile Raider Jason Croker were also unlucky to miss out on after the pair played in the Grand Final.

St. George centre Mark Coyne was also unfortunate to be overlooked after scoring a memorable match-winning try for Queensland in his fourth Origin series. The last centre spot behind automatic selections Mal Meninga, Steve Renouf and Paul McGregor went to Manly's Terry Hill, despite rumours he was carrying an injury. Hill made just nine appearances on tour—his club association with national coach Bob Fulton may have secured him a seat on the plane to England. Destructive backrower Gorden Tallis was another Saint with strong claims to a tour berth after debuting for Queensland earlier in the season, but fellow youngsters Steve Menzies and David Furner got the nod after featuring in the finals series.

Canberra's long-striding winger Ken Nagas was arguably the unluckiest not to tour in 1994 after making his Origin debut for NSW and scoring two slashing tries in the Raiders' Grand Final victory. Instead, the third specialist winger spot went to fellow greenhorn Wendell Sailor. Dymock, Croker, Coyne and Tallis eventually fulfilled their Test ambitions, but Nagas had to settle for a Super League Australia guernsey in 1997.

VETERAN SMITH RECEIVES CONTROVERSIAL CALL-UP In one of the most bizarre selections in Australian Test history, 34-year-old centre/backrower Darren Smith became the first England-based player to represent Australia. The 2003 Kangaroos encountered several injury problems during the end-of-year Ashes series in England, but despite having a fit Luke Lewis in the squad for the dead-rubber third Test, coach Chris Anderson drafted in Smith, who had spent the season with Super League club St. Helens. The selection caused much consternation back in Australia, but Smith nonetheless made his first international appearance since 1999, becoming the third-oldest Australian Test player of all time in the 18-12 win over Great Britain. Lewis eventually made his Test debut six years later during the 2009 Four Nations tournament.

BRITISH-BASED LYON PICKED IN AUSTRALIAN SQUAD Three years after Smith's left-field selection, another St. Helens player was controversially picked for Australia. Jamie Lyon spent the 2005-06 seasons with Saints after infamously walking out on Parramatta, and was one of Super League's brightest stars, winning the 2005 Man of Steel Award. A veteran of five Tests from 2001 to 2003, Lyon returned home at the end of his second season abroad to take up a deal with Manly, and was promptly picked in Australia's squad for the 2006 Tri-Nations. The dangerous centre made just one appearance during the tournament, in a 23-12 loss to Great Britain, before playing in the 2007 mid-season Test against the Kiwis and returning to the NSW side. Lyon was criticised in subsequent seasons for requesting exemption from representative selection. A premiership-winning captain with the Sea Eagles in 2011, Lyon last played Test and Origin football in 2010.

NRL NOVICE DEBUTS FOR KIWIS Even the most ardent of New Zealand Rugby League supporters would have been puzzled at the selection of unheralded Parramatta player Krisnan Inu at fullback for the 2007 mid-season Test against Australia. Inu had played just one first grade game for Parramatta—at centre—before being chosen to wear the No.1 jersey for his country against the world's best. But Inu was the Kiwis' standout performer in a disappointing 30-6 loss at Suncorp Stadium, displaying ample courage and poise. He went on to become one of the NRL season's finest discoveries with the Eels, scoring 12 tries in 20 matches and goalkicking superbly before retaining his Test spot for the return clash against Australia in Wellington at the end of the year. Pigeonholed as an enigmatic player in subsequent seasons, Inu joined the New Zealand Warriors in 2011 and featured in the club's stirring finals charge. He was recalled to the Kiwis' squad after a three-year absence for the Four Nations tournament at the end of the year, but pulled out with injury.

COWBOYS LIVEWIRE OVERLOOKED AGAIN One of the great attacking players of the modern era, superlative North Queensland fullback Matt Bowen was accustomed to representative rejection, making eight of his 10 Origin appearances for Queensland off the bench and playing just one Test for Australia—against minnows France in 2004. Admittedly, Bowen starred in an era swarming with sensational No.1s, but Bowen was favoured to win the fullback spot for the post-season Test against the Kiwis in 2007 with regular Kangaroos Anthony Minichiello and Karmichael Hunt unavailable through injury. Manly's Grand Final fullback Brett Stewart was chosen to debut instead, however, despite Bowen's sizzling form that saw him top the NRL's tryscoring table for the second time and poll fourth in the Dally M Medal count. Bowen's latest snubbing prompted equally diminutive former Kangaroos Kerry Boustead and Allan Langer to offer their Test jumpers back to the ARL in protest.

ORIGIN BOLTERS Three players have been selected for the Blues from NSW country centres—Moree winger Phil Duke, Cootamundra product Paul Field and North Newcastle clubman Rex Wright. Duke was involved in an infamous in-goal incident in his only Origin appearance, the 1982 series decider *(see One-Game Wonders and Minties Moments)*. Field played second-row in the final two matches of NSW's unsuccessful 1983 campaign, while Wright played hooker in a 29-12 series-opening loss in 1984 before being replaced by Royce Simmons for the following encounter. Duke later had a brief stint with Western Suburbs, while Wright spent three seasons with North Sydney.

Brad Fittler became the youngest-ever Origin player in 1990 (a title taken by Ben Ikin five years later) when he debuted for Jack Gibson's New South Wales side at the age of 18 years and 114 days—despite having just 12 first grade games for Penrith under his belt. Fittler came off the bench in the Blues' series-sealing 12-6 win at Melbourne's Olympic Park, and went on to become his state's most-capped Origin player.

Queensland's 1995 side contained several bolters, but rather out of necessity than irresistible form. With Super League players ruled ineligible by the ARL, the Maroons were forced to call on nine debutants, including veteran South Queensland Crushers Terry Cook and Craig Teevan, unheralded Sydney City Roosters halfback Adrian Lam, and young outside backs Matt Sing and Danny Moore. But the biggest bolter was undoubtedly Ben Ikin, an 18-year-old utility-back with the Gold Coast Seagulls with just four first grade games to his credit, and to this day the youngest player in Origin history. To the bolters' respective credit, they featured in the entire series and only Cook and Teevan failed to play in a subsequent series, while Queensland staged a stunning 3-0 series cleansweep.

Following a 3-0 hiding at the hands of NSW in the 2000 series, Queensland, under Wayne Bennett, opted for a youth policy in 2001. Unheralded Cowboys John Buttigieg and John Doyle, and Brisbane tyros Carl Webb, Chris Walker, Lote Tuqiri and Brad Meyers were chosen to debut in the opening encounter (along with the more experienced Kevin Campion, Petero Civoniceva, Chris Beattie, and Daniel Wagon). Buttigieg, Doyle, Webb and Walker each scored in the 34-16 boilover, while Meyers' and Tuqiri's outstanding performances in the series were rewarded with Australian jumpers following Queensland's 2-1 victory.

Adam Mogg would have gone down as arguably the biggest Origin bolter of all time—had he not been joined on debut for the injury-ravaged Maroons by little-known Cowboys forward Jacob Lillyman for the second match of the 2006 series. Rangy outside-back Mogg famously went on to star with three tries in two matches *(see Unlikely Heroes)*, but it was Lillyman—a veteran of just 19 NRL games—whose selection really left fans scratching their heads. Lillyman went on to play for Queensland in the subsequent two Origin series before joining the Warriors and earning a recall for Queensland in 2011.

Newcastle's 20-year-old half Jarrod Mullen was chosen as the man to wear the contentious NSW No.7 jersey for the 2007 series opener. Mullen, with only 31 NRL appearances to his credit, beat the challenges of Manly captain Matt Orford and former Blues Brett Kimmorley, Craig Gower and Brett Finch. The Novocastrian had a palatable debut in a 25-18 loss, but missed the rest of the series with injury and was replaced by Kimmorley, while he is yet to play for NSW again.

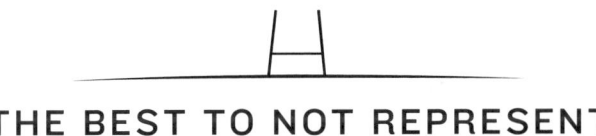

THE BEST TO NOT REPRESENT

Australian Rugby League history is peppered with players who, for a variety of reasons, were denied the opportunity to represent their state or country despite outstanding club careers. Competition for positions, ill-timed injury, international wars, signing to play in England or simply being out of favour with selectors has conspired to prevent these elite competitors from donning representative jumpers.

RAY MARKHAM Newcastle product Ray Markham was lured to Britain on the prompting of British great Stanley Brogden, who opposed the young winger on the 1932 Lions tour of Australia. Brogden's Huddersfield club brought Markham to England, where he became one of the finest wingers of the era. Spending his career abroad cost Markham the chance to represent Australia, but that concession allowed him to become a phenomenal try-scorer with one of Britain's premier clubs. Markham scored over 300 tries for Huddersfield, winning a Challenge Cup in 1933 against Warrington opposite fellow Australian three-quarter Bill Shankland.

WAR DENIES CANTERBURY FRONT-ROW TRIO Props Eddie Burns and Henry Porter, and hooker Roy Kirkaldy are together recognised as arguably the greatest club front-row combination in premiership history. Playing a combined 501 first grade games for Canterbury, the trio was integral to the club's first two premierships in 1938 and 1942. But the embargo on international football during World War II prevented almost certain Australian Test jumpers for the three Berries. Porter and Kirkaldy played 12 and 10 matches respectively for NSW between 1935 and 1941, while Burns was unlucky to be left out of the 1948-49 Kangaroos squad after belatedly debuting for his state in 1948.

ARTHUR PATTON The greatest try-scorer in the history of the Balmain club (see *The Try-scorers*), Arthur Patton's representative career was also curtailed by World War II. Patton scored 95 tries in 117 games for the Tigers between 1941 and 1948 and captained the club to a premiership victory in 1944. Interstate matches were halted between 1942 and 1944 because of the war and Patton's 1945 season was wrecked by injury, combining to deny the wing speedster the chance to represent NSW.

FRANK HYDE Best known for his role as a legendary Rugby League commentator, Frank Hyde was one of the World War II-era's finest centres. Hyde debuted for NSW in 1938 and captained his state the following season, before playing a major role in Balmain's Grand Final win in 1939. Joining North Sydney in 1942, Hyde captain-coached the Bears to their only Grand Final appearance (a 34-7 loss to his former club Newtown in 1943) and retired a year later. The war kyboshed Hyde's ambitions of representing Australia, but he went on to become one of the most recognisable figures in the game as a much-loved part of the Rugby League media.

ERIC HARRIS Dubbed 'The Toowoomba Ghost' by adoring Leeds fans, electrifying winger Eric Harris rates as one of the finest Australian imports to play English club football. Harris scored almost 400 tries and won two Challenge Cup finals with Leeds during the 1930s. The outbreak of World War II saw him return home, but it also thwarted his chances of playing for Australia. Harris played for Brisbane Wests and resumed his representation of Queensland, featuring against New South Wales in 1941.

BRIAN BEVAN Brian Bevan is regarded as the greatest winger in the history of British Rugby League. The skinny flyer made a handful of unremarkable appearances for Easts before heading to England in 1946 to become a legend with over 800 tries in two decades of brilliance. Bevan played out his professional career in England, denying Australian audiences the opportunity to witness the peerless try-scorer in action, and preventing Bevan from pulling on the green-and-gold jumper. Despite not representing Australia, Bevan was chosen in the Australian Team of the Century as part of the game's Centenary celebrations in 2008.

HARRY BATH Magnificent forward Harry Bath is routinely referred to as one of the best players to have never represented Australia. A Brisbane Souths junior, Bath played for Queensland and NSW early in his career and won two Grand Finals with Balmain in 1946-47. Injuries sidelined Bath from Test selection during those seasons, and he forewent certain selection in the 1948-49 Kangaroo Tour squad by signing to play in England. He became a legend of the British game. Bath captained Warrington to Challenge Cup glory against in front of a then-world record crowd of 102,569 in 1954, before returning to Australia and winning three premierships in as many seasons with St. George. Despite his status as one of the premiership's dominant forwards, Bath's advancing years counted against him at the selection table and he retired at the end of 1959 after missing selection for the Kangaroo Tour.

BOB BATTY Playing in the golden era of Australian fullbacks thwarted Manly stalwart Bob Batty's representative ambitions. Batty debuted for the Sea Eagles in 1959 and played 196 games for the club until his retirement at the end of 1971, scoring 1,174 points—both then-club records. But state and national call-ups eluded the reliable custodian during an admirable career while all time greats Keith Barnes, Les Johns, Ken Thornett and Graeme Langlands presided over the NSW and Australian fullback spots.

BILL MULLINS Powerful winger Bill Mullins' aspirations of representing Australia were repeatedly cruelled by injury. The father of Canberra and Kangaroo fullback of the 1990s Brett Mullins, Bill won two premierships with Easts in 1974-75 and became the first player in club history to score 100 first grade tries. But Mullins broke his jaw in a World Cup selection trial in 1970; he represented NSW in 1971 before injury ruled him out of contention for Australia's tour of New Zealand; and broke his jaw again in 1973 to miss his chance to tour Great Britain and France with the Kangaroos.

JOHN HARVEY One of the finest front-rowers of the 1970s, firebrand forward John Harvey featured in Manly's 1976 and 1978 premiership triumphs. Harvey was a non-playing reserve for Australia against New Zealand during the 1978 Test series, but turned down the opportunity to tour with the Kangaroos at the end of the season, citing family reasons. He joined Easts in 1979 and shared in the club's Grand Final disappointment in 1980. Finishing his professional career with the Sea Eagles in 1984, Harvey later enjoyed considerable success in country club football and coached the struggling Gold Coast first grade side in 1994 and '95.

KEVIN HASTINGS Named on the bench in the Eastern Suburbs/Sydney Roosters Team of the Century, Kevin Hastings was a wonderful competitor in a then-record 228 games for the club and ranks as one of the finest halfbacks to miss out on an Australian jersey. Hastings won the Rothmans Medal in 1981, collected three consecutive *Rugby League Week* Player of the Year awards (1980-82) and finished second in the Dally M Medal count in each of those seasons. But Tom Raudonikis occupied the Test No.7 spot early in Hastings' career, while the emergence of all time great halfbacks Steve Mortimer and Peter Sterling kept him in the shadows during the 1980s. Hastings recorded a solitary appearance as a reserve for NSW in 1983.

CRAIG COLEMAN The presence of Mortimer and Sterling also curtailed the representative aspirations of tenacious, scheming South Sydney halfback Craig Coleman. One of just three players to top 200 appearances for the Rabbitohs, Coleman attained selection for City Firsts during a commendable career, but was placed behind Mortimer, Sterling and youngsters Des Hasler, Greg Alexander, Ricky Stuart and Allan Langer in the queue for Origin and Test jumpers.

THE HUGHES BROTHERS Graeme, Garry and Mark Hughes were one of the finest band of footballing brothers, winning a premiership together for Canterbury in 1980, remarkably, playing alongside Steve, Chris and Peter Mortimer. But while Steve and Chris Mortimer played for Australia and Peter Mortimer represented NSW against Great Britain, the Hughes boys could muster just one interstate appearance between them—backrower Graeme played for the Blues in 1975. Garry was a brilliant thinker and skilful five-eighth, while Mark was a valuable centre/lock for a decade with the Bulldogs, but neither could break into the state side.

PETER KELLY One of the premier front-row enforcers of the 1980s, Peter Kelly was desperately unlucky to miss out on an Australian jumper. The firebrand prop began his career at Newtown, before winning premierships in 1984-85 with the

Bulldogs (he was adjudged best on ground in the 1984 decider). Kelly played twice for Country Origin after joining Penrith in 1988 and belatedly made his debut for NSW under Jack Gibson in 1989. But national selectors preferred Steve Roach, Craig Young, Greg Dowling, Dave Brown, Paul Dunn, Sam Backo, Phil Daley, Martin Bella and fellow Bulldogs bookend Peter Tunks during Kelly's heyday.

MICHAEL POTTER Despite becoming the first dual winner of the Dally M Player of the Year award, collecting the honour with Canterbury in 1984 and St. George in 1991, Michael Potter was only selected once for NSW. Potter played his lone Origin as a 20-year-old in 1984 and won back-to-back premierships with the Bulldogs in 1984-85 before joining the Dragons in 1989. He represented Country Origin three times from 1990-1992, but was controversially omitted from the 1992 World Cup squad after playing in the Saints' Grand Final loss and being named the game's best fullback at the Dally Ms for the second consecutive season. NSW No.1 Tim Brasher and Newcastle bolter Brad Godden were preferred to the veteran Potter.

MARIO FENECH Nicknamed 'Test Match' by teammates for his passionate, intense approach to games, the great irony of South Sydney enforcer Mario Fenech's career is that he never received the opportunity to represent Australia. One of the finest hookers of the 1980s, Fenech was overlooked for a Test spot for Ben Elias, Royce Simmons and Greg Conescu. The inspirational Rabbitohs captain's best chance came in 1989 when he finally debuted for NSW. Fenech played the first two matches of the series, but was injured and ruled out of the third clash and Australia's subsequent tour to New Zealand. His replacement for the Blues in the third encounter, David Trewhella, and new Queensland rake Kerrod Walters occupied the hooking spots on tour. Despite unwaveringly wholehearted performances as a prop for Norths in the early-1990s, Fenech was fated to never represent his state again, or his country.

CRAIG INNES All Black Craig Innes, who played 13 Tests in the union game, became one the top centres in world Rugby League following his code switch in 1992. After starring for English club Leeds for three years, Innes joined the Western Reds during the club's 1995 premiership debut, but found his greatest success in the 13-man code after joining Manly in 1996. Innes was a dominant presence in the three-quarter line, forming the competition's most dangerous centre pairing with Terry Hill. He scored the first try of the Sea Eagles' 1996 Grand Final defeat of St. George and crossed again in the last-minute loss to Newcastle in the decider a year later. But Innes' allegiance to the ARL ruled him out of certain selection for the Super League-aligned New Zealand Test side. He did technically become a dual international, however, representing Rest of the World against Australia in 1997. Innes' return to rugby union with Super 12 side Auckland Blues in 1998 coincided with Manly's slide down the NRL ladder.

THE SUPER LEAGUE 'INTERNATIONALS' Thirty players represented Super League's Australian 'Test' side during five internationals against New Zealand and Great Britain in 1997. While the matches are included as Tests in the official records of New Zealand and Great Britain, they are not recognised as Tests by Australia as they were not sanctioned by the ARL. Of the 30 Super League internationals, 10 were already fully fledged Australian Test players—all touring with the 1994 Kangaroos. Another 13 made their ARL-sanctioned Test debuts between 1998 and 2005, including modern greats Darren Lockyer, Shane Webcke, Gorden Tallis and Brett Kimmorley. But future Australian selection eluded the remaining seven Super League internationals—Matt Adamson, Paul Green, Craig Greenhill, Solomon Haumono, Ken Nagas, Julian O'Neill and David Peachey—who were destined to carry an asterisk next to their names in the Test registry. Haumono was the only one of the seven that did not achieve State of Origin selection.

ANTHONY MUNDINE Anthony Mundine's abrasive demeanour on and off the field and regular brash comments in the media sphere made him an easy target for detractors, but there is no denying his status as one of the outstanding individual talents of the 1990s. But the brilliant St. George five-eighth's representative ambitions were not aided by playing in an era opposite revered figures in the No.6 such as Brad Fittler, Laurie Daley (who Mundine infamously claimed was 'running on old legs'), Matthew Johns and Kevin Walters. The extent of Mundine's representative career was three appearances off the bench for the Blues in 1999, while national selection eluded him. Mundine publicly slated selectors of the NSW and Australian sides, citing prejudice against his Aboriginal heritage as a reason for his non-selection. He walked out on St. George Illawarra early in 2000 to pursue a career in boxing, where his motor-mouthed media outbursts were better suited.

MATT ORFORD Premiership-winning skipper and Dally M medallist Matt Orford was desperately unlucky not to represent New South Wales (or Australia, for that matter) given that the Blues used eight different halfback options during his career. One of the 2000s' dominant No.7s with Melbourne and Manly, Orford played for City in 2001, 2004 and 2006. He was hardest-done by in 2006, when injury ruled original selection Craig Gower out of the opening Origin encounter. But despite outstanding form in his first season for Manly that earned him a top-five finish in the Dally Ms, Orford was overlooked for Brett Finch. The Sydney Roosters half was the match-winner in game one (*see Unlikely Heroes*), but was dropped after a heavy loss in the return clash, whereupon Gower returned to the NSW line-up. Orford's ultra-consistent form persisted over the next three seasons in which he won the 2008 Dally M Medal and Manly reached consecutive Grand Finals, winning the premiership in 2008 under his captaincy. But young guns Jarrod Mullen, Peter Wallace and Mitchell Pearce and veteran Brett Kimmorley were preferred to the Sea Eagles general at the NSW selection table.

LUKE DAVICO Injuries frequently interrupted a potential Origin call-up for front-rower Luke Davico during a decade-long career with Canberra. Davico, one of the NRL's toughest and most consistent bookends, was sidelined for extended mid-season periods during 1998, 1999, 2001, 2002 and 2004, denying him the chance to press for NSW selection.

ALAN TONGUE As versatile as he was valuable to Canberra, Alan Tongue is arguably the best player not to have represented NSW during the Maroons' era of

Origin dominance that began in 2006. The Raiders skipper combined an impeccable work ethic with superb defence and underrated ball-playing ability, and was capable of producing a match-turning play from the backrow, dummy-half or the halves. Tongue would have been an ideal bench utility option in representative football, a role that was occupied by Kurt Gidley and Craig Wing for NSW from 2003. The flame-haired utility made a tryscoring debut for Country Origin at lock in 2009, before retiring at the end of 2011.

PRESTON CAMPBELL One of just three Dally M medallists to not play Origin or Test football during their careers (Robert Laurie and Matt Orford are the other two), courageous half/fullback Preston Campbell was continually overlooked by rep selectors during the 2000s. Campbell won his Dally M after a brilliant 2001 season at halfback for Cronulla and was unlucky to be left out of the Kangaroo squad to tour England at the end of the year. Following his excellent contribution to Penrith's premiership triumph at five-eighth in 2003, Campbell debuted for Country Origin in 2005 and retained the bench utility spot for the next two seasons. But despite his versatility and several inspirational seasons at fullback after joining the fledgling Titans in 2007, Campbell could not break into the NSW side, perhaps considered too small for the rigours of Origin at 76kg.

CHRIS HEIGHINGTON Busy and dynamic Wests Tigers backrower Chris Heighington is one of the best players to be repeatedly overlooked for Test and Origin duty in recent seasons. A powerful runner and tireless defender, Heighington's continual omission from NSW sides has been perplexing given Queensland's Origin dominance since 2006. The 2005 premiership-winner finished 11th-equal in the 2008 Dally M count and was considered unlucky to miss out on Australia's World Cup squad. He also polled well as the Tigers returned to the finals in 2010, but could not force his way into the Four Nations squad at the end of the year. His representative honours in Australia were restricted to one game for Country Origin in 2008 and appearances for the Prime Minister's XIII against Papua New Guinea in 2008 and 2009. Heighington was sounded out about representing England (he qualifies through his English-born father) and looked set to jump ship in 2010, but opted to keep his NSW and Kangaroo dream alive for one more season. Despite winning a recall to the Country Origin side in 2011, the valuable forward switched allegiances and featured at lock in three Tests for England during the Four Nations tournament at the end of the year.

NATHAN MERRITT Like fellow Indigenous winger Nathan Blacklock before him, several seasons of brilliant tryscoring form has not been enough to earn South Sydney's Nathan Merritt a NSW or Australian guernsey. Merritt represented the Prime Ministers' XIII against Papua New Guinea and was named in the Kangaroos' Tri-Nations train-on squad in 2006 after topping the NRL's tryscoring table for the last-placed Rabbitohs, but further honours have so far eluded the flyer. He scored 58 tries in the ensuing four NRL seasons, and the South Sydney hierarchy's frustration at Merritt's continued snubbing boiled over in 2010 when he was overlooked by NSW selectors for the dead-rubber third encounter in favour of Penrith pointscoring machine Michael Gordon.

RYAN CROSS A veteran of three Grand Finals during a nine-season career with the Roosters, Ryan Cross ranks as one of the finest centres to miss out on playing Origin football. Cross played for City Origin in 2004-05, scoring two tries on debut, but could not convince selectors he was ready for the next step, despite scoring 85 tries in 143 first grade games. A dual international at junior level in Rugby League and rugby union, Cross switched back to the 15-man code in 2007 and played eight Tests for the Wallabies.

LUKE PATTEN Bulldogs stalwart Luke Patten experienced the misfortune of playing in a period of remarkable fullback talent. Patten's compelling representative claims were frustrated at Origin level by NSW custodians Brett Hodgson, Anthony Minichiello, Brett Stewart, Kurt Gidley and Jarryd Hayne, while Queensland No.1s Darren Lockyer, Matt Bowen, Karmichael Hunt and Billy Slater also stood in the way of a Kangaroos call-up. Debuting for Illawarra in 1998 before playing in a Grand Final for the Dragons and winning a premiership during a celebrated decade with the Bulldogs, Patten represented Country Origin in 2002, 2004 and 2009. The closest he came to higher honours was in 2009, when he joined the NSW squad as 18th man for the third match of the series. A veteran of 281 first grade games, including 225 for the Bulldogs, Patten's status as one of the modern era's finest club fullbacks is unquestioned.

CHAPTER 7

RUGBY LEAGUE AROUND THE WORLD

The century-plus rivalries between Australia and its two greatest competitors—Great Britain and New Zealand—are comprehensively covered in this section. The great Ashes battles, trans-Tasman competition and tours are recalled in the following pages, as well as the British and New Zealand players to make an impact in the Australian premiership, and the Australian and Kiwi stars that have graced the fields of Britain. The history of the World Cup and World Club Challenge competitions are detailed comprehensively, along with the representative combinations that have seen players from different nations come together. An overview of the Rugby League histories of France, Papua New Guinea, the United States and South Africa—and the contribution of each country's players and national sides to the Australian Rugby League narrative—also features in this section.

ANTIPODEANS ACHIEVE LEGEND STATUS IN THE OLD DART

Australian and New Zealand players have had a profound influence on British Rugby League since the advent of the code in the Antipodes in 1907-08. The lure of greater money and opportunities has attracted players to the Northern Hemisphere for more than 100 years.

Six players from the New Zealand 'All Golds,' who in 1907 became the first Rugby League side to tour Britain, returned to play for English clubs. The most notable of the Kiwi expatriates was Lance Todd. The centre played in one Challenge Cup and four championship finals for Wigan, but later found fame as a commentator with the BBC. Todd died in a car accident returning home from calling a match in 1942, and in 1946 an award for the man of the match in the Challenge Cup final was struck in his memory. The Lance Todd Trophy is one of British Rugby League's most coveted individual honours.

Charlie Seeling is regarded as one the finest loose forwards to don the All Black jersey. Representing New Zealand in 11 rugby union Tests, Seeling toured Europe with the famed 1905 'Originals' and returned to England in 1910 after accepting Wigan's substantial offer to switch codes. Seeling played in three championship final losses and two Challenge Cup final defeats for the cherry-and-whites in a stellar 13-year professional career. His son, Charlie Seeling Jr., played for Warrington and Wigan in a career that spanned more than two decades. He appeared in two Challenge Cup final defeats for 'The Wire' in 1928 and 1933.

Ten members of the trailblazing 1908-09 Kangaroo Tour squad went on to play English club football, including tryscoring marvel Albert Rosenfeld. The diminutive winger played two seasons for Eastern Suburbs and four Tests for Australia before joining Huddersfield (where he combined with former New Zealand All Gold Edgar Wrigley) and becoming a legend of the British game. In the 1911-12 season, Rosenfeld scored an unprecedented 78 tries, and extended his record with an incredible 80 tries in 1913-14, a mark that still stands. A Challenge Cup and championship final winner in 1913 and 1915, Rosenfeld scored 388 tries for Huddersfield's 'Team of all Talents.' He was an original inductee to the British Rugby League Hall of Fame in 1988 and was named as one of Australia's 100 Greatest Players to mark the Centenary of the game in 2008.

Other pioneering players to feature prominently for British clubs include North Sydney winger Jim Devereux, the top try-scorer on the 1908-09 Kangaroo Tour, who won a Challenge Cup final with Hull in 1914 after competing in losing sides in 1910 and '11. Fellow 1908-09 tourists Sid Deane and George Anlezark played in Oldham's Challenge Cup runner-up side of 1912, while 1911-12 Kangaroo Tour star Herb Gilbert became the first Australian to captain a British side to Challenge Cup success alongside Devereux at Hull in 1914. Australia's first Test representative brothers, Bill and Viv Farnsworth, joined Oldham in 1913. The Northern Union imposed a ban on

British clubs signing Australian and New Zealand players in 1913, unless the player had lived in England for two years.

Australia and New Zealand also put transfer bans in place to stem the drain of their best playing talent to the Mother Country, but this was lifted in 1927 at the insistence of British clubs, and a golden era of imports ensued. Leeds was particularly aggressive in luring Australian talent. The Yorkshire club's 1932 Challenge Cup-winning side contained former University winger Frank O'Rourke, who went on to score over a century of tries for Leeds, and 'The Toowoomba Ghost' Eric Harris. The electrifying Harris scored almost 400 tries in a decade-long career on the flank for Leeds, including a club record 64 tries in the 1935-36 season, and also starred in the club's 1936 Challenge Cup success. Famous 1929-30 Kangaroo halfback Joe 'Chimpy' Busch spent four seasons with the club in the early-1930s and Vic Hey, rated among the top echelon of Australia's greatest five-eighths, was one of the brightest stars of the British game during World War II, featuring in Challenge Cup victories in 1941 and 1942 for Leeds before subsequent stints with Dewsbury and Hunslet.

Ray Markham won a Challenge Cup for Huddersfield in 1933 and scored 264 tries in 269 games for the club, including nine in a match against Featherstone Rovers; former Test halfback Hec Gee won a championship with Wigan in 1933-34 to start a decade-long association with the club; and Warrington benefitted from the services of 1929-30 Kangaroo winger Bill Shankland and all time great centre Dave Brown. Shankland skippered 'The Wire' to Challenge Cup final defeats in 1933 and 1936, while Brown transferred his remarkable pointscoring exploits to Britain in the late-1930s. The 1937-38 Kangaroos experienced the depth of talent that had left Australia's shores—they lost a tour match 8-6 to a Warrington side containing Brown and Shankland, before Hey and Harris spearheaded Leeds' 21-8 defeat of the Australian side.

But it was a less-likely Australian that became Warrington's greatest import after World War II. Fragile-looking winger Brian Bevan became the most prolific try-scorer in Rugby League history and arguably the best-ever overseas player to feature on the British club scene. Bevan joined Warrington on the recommendation of Shankland, and went on to amass 796 tries in 695 games and 18 years for 'The Wire' and Blackpool-Borough, and in matches for Other Nationalities and various representative combinations—300 more than his nearest rival, Welsh powerhouse Billy Boston. Although he never played for his country, Bevan was contentiously named in the Australian Team of the Century in 2008, ahead of Souths and Norths 'Wonder Winger' Harold Horder. He won Challenge Cup titles with Warrington in 1950 and 1954 and championship-winning sides in 1948 and 1954-55. Bevan and Albert Rosenfeld are the only Australian inductees to the British Rugby League Hall of Fame.

Bevan was joined in the 1950 and 1954 Challenge Cup sides by another Australian and a rival for the best-ever import label: legendary forward Harry Bath. 'The Old Fox' famously kicked Warrington to victory as captain in front of a world record crowd of 102,569 at Odsal Stadium in the 1954 final replay, and played over 300 matches for the club. Former Wallaby Ken Kearney starred with Leeds in the late 1940s and early 1950s and, with Bath, formed the nucleus of the St. George pack that started a run of 11 consecutive premierships in Sydney. The experience and skills, particularly in defence, that players such as Bath and Kearney took home from Britain is credited as a crucial element of Australia's ascension to world Rugby League supremacy in the 1950s and 1960s, while Hey coached Australia to a drought-breaking Ashes series win in 1950.

Many more players lit up the British game in the post-war period, despite the British Rugby League Council imposing another ban on the transfer of players between Australian and English clubs. Second-rower Arthur Clues, a three-Test Australian representative in 1946, linked with Leeds and played in the club's 1947 Challenge Cup final loss. Revered as one of Leeds' finest players for his tough and skilful play, and as arguably the best forward in Britain during the 1950s, Clues joined Hunslet to round out a career which garnered 14 appearances for Other Nationalities. He was named as one of the ARL's 100 Greatest Players in 2008, despite playing just four top-flight seasons in Australia.

One of the brightest periods in Huddersfield's history was substantially contributed to by a triumvirate of Australian stars—Lionel Cooper, Pat Devery and Johnny Hunter. The trio spearheaded Huddersfield to a championship in 1949 and Challenge Cup success in 1953. Former Easts player Hunter was a classy fullback, ex-Balmain and Australian Test representative Devery was one of the great five-eighths and a prolific point-scorer, but it was Cooper who had the most devastating impact. An Australian teammate of Clues and Devery in 1946, Cooper scored 432 tries for Huddersfield, including 71 tries in the 1951-52 season and a record 10 tries in a match against Keighley. The powerful winger played 14 times for Other Nationalities and also captained the esteemed representative combination.

Several players went straight from the Australian rugby union ranks to English club football. Tony Paskins and Rupert Mudge won a Challenge Cup with Workington Town in 1953 and were on the losing side in the 1955 final, while Wallaby internationals Trevor Allan and Rex Mossop were valuable acquisitions for Leigh. Mudge and Paskins returned to Australia to play for Easts (Paskins went on to represent NSW), Allan turned out for Norths, and Mossop became an respected dual international with Manly and later an iconic Rugby League media identity before passing away in 2011.

Cec Mountford, a five-eighth from Blackball on the West Coast of New Zealand's South Island, became a superstar for Wigan in the 1940s and 1950s. He won Challenge Cups with the club in 1948 and 1951 and championships in 1947 and 1950. Mountford became the first overseas player to win the Lance Todd Trophy after he skippered Wigan to Wembley success in 1951. In a historic day for New Zealand Rugby League, Mountford played opposite his brother and fellow West Coast great, six-Test New Zealand lock Ken, in Wigan's 10-8 loss to the touring 1947-48 Kiwis. He enhanced his reputation with a glittering period as coach of Warrington before returning to impart his vast knowledge in New Zealand, coaching the Kiwis from 1979-82 and receiving an MBE in 1990 for his services to Rugby League.

The introduction of poker machines to the Leagues clubs of Sydney sides reversed the player flow, with many British players instead coming to Australia during the 1960s and 1970s *(see British Invasion)*. Fewer Australian stars ventured to the British competition during this period, with Canterbury's Test winger Chris Anderson a notable exception. He starred for Widnes in the 1974-75 off-season, and was flown back for the Challenge Cup final in 1975, which Widnes duly won. Anderson returned to English football after he retired from the Sydney premiership, captain-coaching Halifax to Challenge Cup victory in 1987. He had persuaded former Kangaroo teammate and all time great Manly fullback Graham Eadie out of retirement to play for Halifax in what proved to be a masterstroke: Eadie won the Lance Todd Trophy in the 19-18 Wembley triumph.

The lifting of transfer bans in the early-1980s resulted in a wave of Australian stars venturing to England for the Sydney and Brisbane premiership off-seasons. Mal Meninga has been afforded icon status at St. Helens ever since scoring 28 tries in 31 games for the Saints in 1984-85; the Immortal Wally Lewis turned out for Wakefield Trinity; John Dorahy won the Harry Sunderland Memorial Trophy as man of the match in the 1984 premiership final for Hull Kingston Rovers (Dorahy also later captain-coached Halifax at the conclusion his Australian premiership career), an honour bestowed on two-time Kangaroo forward Les Boyd for Warrington two years later; Gavin Miller became the first overseas winner of the Man of Steel award for English club player of the year while starring for Hull KR in 1985-86; and Michael O'Connor and Paul Vautin featured in the St. Helens side that went down in the 1989 Challenge Cup final.

The southern hemisphere flavour during the 1980s was never more prevalent than in the 1985 Challenge Cup final between Wigan and Hull, regarded as the greatest Wembley final of all time. Brett Kenny became the first Australian winner of the Lance Todd Trophy after a magnificent display in Wigan's 28-24 triumph, supported by mercurial Australian winger John Ferguson and Kiwi Test great Graeme West. Kenny's Parramatta halves partner Peter Sterling was magnificent for the beaten Hull side, alongside 1982 Kangaroo John Muggleton and outstanding Kiwi backline quartet Gary Kemble, James Leuluai, Dane O'Hara and Fred Ah Kuoi.

If anything, New Zealanders were more prominent than their Australian counterparts in British Rugby League during the 1980s and early-1990s. Intimidating prop Kevin Tamati won a Challenge Cup final with Widnes in 1984 (with cousin and fellow Kiwi international Howie Tamati in the losing Wigan side) and a premiership final with Warrington in 1986, while long-serving Cronulla forward and 27-Test Kiwi Kurt Sorensen guided Widnes to back-to-back premierships in the late-1980s.

Coached by former New Zealand Test mentor Graham Lowe, Wigan embarked on a period of unprecedented success, with a number of his countrymen at the forefront. Dean Bell, brothers Kevin and Tony Iro and Adrian Shelford featured at the beginning of a run of eight consecutive Challenge Cup final victories that began in 1988. With former Parramatta premiership-winning coach John Monie taking over when Lowe moved to Manly, the success continued unabated. Bell assumed the captaincy, winning the Man of Steel award in 1992 and the Lance Todd Trophy in 1993. Bell's compatriots Sam Panapa, pointscoring wizard Frano Botica, Va'aiga Tuigamala (like Botica, a former All Black), and former Australian Test representatives Gene Miles and Andrew Farrar starred in the cherry and white jersey during the early-1990s.

The introduction of Super League saw the British season moved to the northern hemisphere summer in 1996, thus coinciding with the Australian Rugby League season and eliminating the opportunity for off-season sojourns with British clubs. But the temptation of the British pound and the chance to experience a different part of the world enticed many Australian and New Zealand players to link with UK Super League sides.

New Zealand's Paul brothers, Henry and Robbie, were genuine superstars of the British game. Robbie, the younger of the two, became the first player to score three tries in a Wembley Cup final in 1996, winning the Lance Todd Trophy despite his Bradford side going down 40-32 to St. Helens. Henry, earlier a linchpin with Wigan, joined Bradford and took out the Harry Sunderland Memorial Trophy for man of the match in the 1999 Super League Grand Final and the Lance Todd Trophy in the Bulls' 2000 Challenge Cup final defeat of Leeds.

Astute hooker Michael Monaghan is the only Australian winner of the Lance Todd Trophy since Graham Eadie claimed the award in 1987, taking out the honour following Warrington's 2009 Challenge Cup final defeat of Huddersfield. Michael Withers, a utility back who achieved only modest success in Australia, became a superstar for Bradford and is the only Australian winner of the Harry Sunderland Memorial Trophy during the Super League era, taking it out in 2001. Veteran Kiwi Test halfback Thomas Leuluai joined the list of New Zealand winners of the Harry Sunderland Memorial Trophy playing for Wigan in 2010, while former Melbourne and New Zealand Test prop Jeff Lima collected the Lance Todd Trophy after Wigan's 2011 Challenge Cup success.

Four of the finest Australian imports to Super League have won the Man of Steel award for player of the year. Former Queensland Origin representative Adrian Vowles won in 1999 on the way to becoming a Castleford great; Australian Test centre Jamie Lyon received the gong in 2005 during a mid-career stint with St. Helens in 2005; Wests Tigers premiership-winner Brett Hodgson won it as captain of Huddersfield in 2009; and his former Tigers teammate Pat Richards collected the award in 2010 after a record-breaking season on the wing for Wigan.

A run-down of the Australian and New Zealand players to dominate for Super League clubs is worthy of another chapter, such is the volume and impact of stars from Down Under on the British competition: Adrian Lam, Trent Barrett and Brett Dallas are regarded as some of the finest players to wear the cherry and white of Wigan; blockbusting Kiwi winger Lesley Vainikolo scored 135 tries in 136 matches for Bradford; fleet-footed wingers Darren Albert and Scott Donald were even more prolific try-scorers in Super League than they had been in the NRL; and Matt Gidley became recognised as one of Super League's best centres in the twilight of his career with St. Helens.

Australian and New Zealand players to have topped the Super League tryscoring charts include Nigel Vagana, Dennis Moran (twice), Lesley Vainikolo (twice), Justin Murphy, Brent Webb and Pat Richards, while Richards has finished as Super League's top point-scorer three times (2008-10). Meanwhile, a representative fixture pitting England against the Exiles—a team made up of Super League-based overseas players—was established in 2011 (see International Stars Unite). Led by Leeds and ex-Newcastle and Australian Test hooker Danny Buderus, the Exiles won the inaugural clash 16-12.

The steady flow of players from Australia to Super League has emerged as a perennial bugbear for the NRL over the past decade. Despite overseas quotas being imposed on Super League clubs, scores of players—both veterans in the twilight of their careers and younger players in their prime—take the big-money offers available in the European competition. The prevalence of Australian and Kiwi players has also been pinpointed as a contributing factor to Great Britain's and England's recent poor showings in the international arena. But as long as the demand and funds remain, the rich history of Antipodean players starring on the fields of Britain will inevitably continue.

CROSSING THE DITCH

New Zealanders currently represent a sizeable chunk of most National Rugby League clubs' playing rosters. There has been a Kiwi presence in every Grand Final since 1993, while a number of stars from the Shaky Isles rank among the world's finest individual talents. But it took many decades for players from Australia's easterly neighbours to make a major impact in the Sydney premiership.

Several Kiwis ventured to British club football following the advent of Rugby League in New Zealand and the subsequent 'All Golds' tour to the Mother Country in 1907-08—most notably Lance Todd and former All Black Charlie Seeling—and the national side was a formidable opponent for Australia and England (later Great Britain). The first New Zealanders to play in the Sydney premiership were members of the trailblazing 1908 Maori side that toured Australia—Peter Moko (nine games for Glebe in 1909) and Punga 'Glen' Pakere (five games for North Sydney in 1910). The captain of a Maori squad that toured Australia in 1922, Huatahi Turoa Brown Paki, played 15 games for St. George in 1923.

Wellington prop Con Sullivan toured Australia with the Kiwis in 1909 and played in one Test, before migrating across the Tasman and joining North Sydney in 1910. Sullivan became the second player to represent New Zealand and Australia in Rugby League (after the great Dally Messenger, who guested for the 1907-08 'All Golds' before playing in Australia's maiden Test series against the Kiwis in 1908) in 1910. He toured with the 1911-12 Kangaroos and played the last of five Tests for Australia in 1914, while amassing 72 appearances for Norths. His son, five-eighth Bob, also played Test football for Australia in 1954, and was a stalwart North Sydney player (122 games) before a long tenure as president of the Bears.

Bill Kelly, a former All Black who toured Australia with the Kiwis in 1912 and 1913, was lured across the Tasman by Balmain in 1914. He became the third player to represent New Zealand and Australia in Rugby League (a feat which has been replicated only by Tonie Carroll since, 89 years later) in his first season in Sydney, playing in the centres in one Test for Australia against the touring England side. He captain-coached Balmain to its maiden first grade title in 1915—the first time a premiership club had gone through a season undefeated. Kelly became a revered coaching figure after his retirement as a player in stints with University, Newtown, Balmain (including another premiership win in 1939), St. George and Canterbury. Fittingly, Australia and New Zealand compete for the Bill Kelly Cup in the mid-season Test.

Wellington rugby union centre George Martin, a professional artist, moved to Sydney in 1952 to further his career, and subsequently joined North Sydney. He scored 44 tries in 72 games during four seasons with the club, representing City

Firsts against Country and NSW against the touring American All-Stars in 1953. But the New Zealand Rugby League prevented their 'amateur' players from crossing the Tasman to play in Australia for several decades, finally easing that stance in the 1960s—provided the sought-after player had given satisfactory service to the game in New Zealand.

Lock Rex Percy, a veteran of nine Tests and two Kiwi tours to Australia in 1956 and 1959, joined Balmain in 1961 and spent three seasons at Leichhardt before heading to the country and captain-coaching in Parkes and Yass. The Kiwis' success on the international stage in the early part of the decade—including a 2-0 home series defeat of Great Britain in 1962—piqued the interest of clubs in Australia. Manly signed New Zealand Team of the Century hooker Jock Butterfield and 11-Test forward Trevor Kilkelly in 1964, but both players had modest seasons. Butterfield, a veteran of 36 Tests, played only nine games, while Kilkelly appeared in six games in the Sea Eagles' disappointing campaign.

New Zealand Team of the Century lock and 22-Test Kiwi Mel Cooke accepted a player-coach role with Canberra in 1965 and skippered the Monaro representative side against the touring Lions the following season. The brilliant loose forward also won selection for NSW Country, featuring in a 32-2 loss to City in 1965. Another backrower in New Zealand's Team of the Century, 18-Test Kiwi Ron Ackland, finished an admirable career with stints for Goulburn and Inverell in country New South Wales.

Many more Kiwi greats bolstered the line-ups of country clubs in NSW and Queensland—predominantly in captain-coach roles—including former Test captain Graham Kennedy (Wagga Kangaroos), Team of the Century five-eighth George Menzies (Harden), 28-Test utility-back Cyril Eastlake (Narromine, Goulburn), 18-Test prop Robert Orchard (Redcliffe, Mount Isa, Mackay, Cairns) and 22-Test centre Bill Sorenson (Glen Innes). Further loosening of the NZRL's transfer regulations ramped up the flow of players to Sydney, with Bill Schultz spending three seasons with Eastern Suburbs in the late-1960s, although the former Test hooker struggled to cement a regular first grade berth.

Playing professionally overseas meant the end of the international careers of departing New Zealand players, but that did not deter several Kiwi representatives joining Sydney clubs in their prime during the early 1970s. Tough forward Oscar Danielson, the first Samoan-born player to join an Australian club, played five Tests for New Zealand before linking with Newtown for a three-season stint beginning in 1970. Fearsome prop Bill Noonan cut his Kiwi career short after just two Tests to join Canterbury in 1970, where he became the first New Zealander to appear in a Grand Final. He was part of the Berries' side that went down to Easts in the 1974 decider, and went on to play 161 games for the club in nine seasons, before joining Newtown in 1979.

Canterbury also acquired the services of goalkicking prop Henry Tatana and centre Bernie Lowther in 1972 following New Zealand's stunning 24-3 defeat of Australia the previous season. Tatana, who kicked six decisive goals in the Test upset, was second in the premiership's pointscoring race in 1973 with 159—the second-highest total in club history at the time. He topped a century of points again in 1974 but was dropped from first grade late in 1974 and missed out on a Grand Final appearance. Lowther was similarly unlucky. He was the club's top try-scorer in 1973 with 13 (equal-fourth in the premiership) and scored four tries in a match against Penrith in 1974, but was relegated before the finals.

Both players left the club, with Lowther proving a handy buy for Souths over the next two seasons, while Tatana topped the scoring for St. George in 1975 and '76. Tatana's reliable kicking helped the Dragons to finals victories over Manly and Easts in 1975, but he became the second Kiwi to suffer Grand Final defeat when the Roosters hammered the Graeme Langlands-led Saints 38-0 in the decider. Tatana departed following St. George's finals exit in 1976, having scored 547 points in five seasons in the premiership.

Penrith delved into New Zealand's rugby union ranks in 1978, luring highly rated Manawatu prop Kent Lambert to the club. Lambert, an 11-Test All Black, had publicly bemoaned the financial hardships suffered by the then-amateur code's players and signed with the Panthers. He penned a three-year contract, but a severe run of injuries limited him to just one first grade appearance.

More successful were Auckland's Rugby League Test brothers, Dane and Kurt Sorensen, who joined Cronulla in the late-1970s. Dane crossed over in 1977 but suspension ruled him out of the following year's Grand Final, before Kurt linked with the club in 1979. In a mutually beneficial move, the NZRL allowed overseas-based players to continue representing the national side, and the intimidating forwards carved out illustrious international careers for the Kiwis. Dane Sorensen played a then-record 216 first grade games for the Sharks, while Kurt finished his career with a successful stint in England after 118 games in Cronulla colours.

The trickle of New Zealand players to the Sydney premiership became a torrent in the early-1980s. Powerful five-eighth Olsen Filipaina, who later outpointed Wally Lewis at Test level in 1985, linked with Balmain in 1980. But he was unable to replicate his international form on a consistent basis and left the Tigers after five patchy seasons, before spending much of his time in subsequent stints with Easts and Norths in reserve grade. Filipaina captained Ryde-Eastwood to a premiership in the inaugural Metropolitan Cup in 1990 at the age of 33. Tough-as-teak Papanui prop Mark Broadhurst gave excellent service to Manly and Illawarra in 68 first grade appearances, but Kiwi greats James Leuluai (Manly) and Fred Ah Kuoi (Norths) struggled to adapt and found greater success in English club football.

But the Bears and Roosters benefitted handsomely from a host of successful Kiwi imports during the 1980s. Powerful second-rower Mark Graham's contribution in eight years with the club saw him chosen in the Bears' Team of the Century in 2006. A long-serving Kiwi captain, Graham won a premiership with Brisbane Norths under his former Otahuhu (Auckland) club coach Graham Lowe in 1980 before linking with the Bears and winning the Dally M Second-rower of the Year award in 1981 and '82. He was named New Zealand's Player of the Century in 2009 and appeared in 147 games for North Sydney. Tenacious half Clayton Friend, who played a vital role in New Zealand's euphoric Test victories over Australia in 1985 and 1991, played four seasons of first grade for the Bears and finished third in the 1987 Dally M Medal count.

Kiwi Test regulars Gary Prohm, robust three-quarter Dean Bell and ultra-talented lock Hugh McGahan joined Easts in 1985. McGahan was the most influential signing, captaining the Kiwis while playing for the Roosters and taking over the club captaincy in the late-1980s. The Auckland product skippered Easts to the finals in 1987 and was subsequently named as joint winner of the Golden Boot with Parramatta halfback Peter Sterling. McGahan was temporarily installed as captain-coach after the mid-season sacking of Russell Fairfax in 1990, before retiring at the end of 1991 with 118 first grade games and 32 Tests (and a then-record 16 Test tries) to his credit. Former All Black Kurt Sherlock became just the second post-World War II dual international and was a valuable utility-back over six seasons with the Roosters, racking up 88 appearances and 235 points.

Darrell Williams became the first Kiwi to win an Australian premiership in 1987, featuring in the centres in Manly's 18-8 Grand Final victory over Canberra. In the Raiders side that day was New Zealand Test prop Brent Todd, who won titles with the Green Machine in 1989-90 and lost another Grand Final against Penrith in 1991, before wrapping up his career with Gold Coast. The tenacious Gary Freeman was Balmain's halfback in the club's twin Grand Final losses in 1988-89. After falling out with new Balmain coach Alan Jones in 1991, Freeman moved to Easts and became the first overseas player to win the Dally M Medal in 1992. A veteran of a then-record 45 Tests for New Zealand, Freeman was a valuable No.7 in subsequent stints with the Panthers and Eels, retiring in 1996 with a total of 151 first grade appearances.

Newcastle dipped heavily into New Zealand's reservoir of talent for its 1988 entry into the premiership. Sam Stewart was the club's first captain, while current or future Test representatives James Goulding, Tea Ropati, Adrian Shelford and Tony Kemp also turned out for the Knights in their inaugural season. Kemp's return to Newcastle in 1989 was initially blocked by the NZRL but the centre/five-eighth eventually spent six seasons in blue and red, and played for the South Queensland Crushers in their 1995 debut season, while also amassing 25 Test appearances.

A vigorous raid on New Zealand's rugby union ranks in the early 1990s resulted in several All Blacks and provincial players switching codes. The recruitment drive simultaneously elevated the importance of a quality goalkicker within a first grade side's make-up. Amateur recruits Matthew Ridge (Manly), Daryl Halligan (Norths), Eion Crossan (Souths), John Schuster (Newcastle) and Gavin Hill (Canterbury) emerged as genuine match-winners with the boot for Australian Rugby League clubs.

Ridge, enticed to Australia by Manly's Kiwi coach Graham Lowe in 1990, was joined at Brookvale by the game-breaking Iro brothers, Kevin and Tony, and Adrian Shelford (the trio had played under Lowe at Wigan). Ridge was one of the decade's finest fullbacks, winning a premiership with Manly, setting a host of pointscoring records and captaining his country before heading home to finish his career with the Super League-aligned Auckland Warriors. Halligan became the first player in premiership history to pass 2000 first grade points in a decorated career with Norths and Canterbury that garnered a premiership in 1995 and 19 Test appearances.

Initially a lower grade player at North Sydney, Jarrod McCracken quickly gained a reputation as fiery, game-breaking centre after being recruited by the Bulldogs from Port Macquarie in the early-1990s. A 22-Test Kiwi rep between 1991 and 1999 (and the son of 1960s New Zealand Test winger Ken), McCracken controversially joined the Eels in 1996 and developed into an intimidating second-rower. He co-captained Parramatta in 1998 and '99 and was the inaugural skipper of the Wests Tigers during their 2000 debut season.

Northcote winger Sean Hoppe was a sensation for the Raiders in 1992-93 but was axed from the club after he signed to join the Warriors for their 1995 debut season. He signed a one-year deal with Norths and scored 15 tries in 1994, while his ex-Canberra teammates Ruben Wiki and Quentin Pongia played a crucial role in the Raiders' Grand Final victory. Pongia's front-row partner John Lomax suffered the same fate as compatriot Dane Sorensen 17 years earlier when suspension ruled him out of the decider. Lomax and Pongia, though outstanding props, had careers littered with suspension and injury, but Wiki became one of the all time great Kiwi imports. An ironman in 225 appearances for Canberra, Wiki eventually joinied the Warriors (where he originally signed a contract to play in 1995 before backing out of the deal) in 2005 and became the first overseas player to make 300 first grade appearances.

McCracken, Halligan and Kiwi Test winger Jason Williams were in Canterbury's losing Grand Final side in 1994, but the latter two tasted title success the following season, alongside former All Black John Timu (McCracken was demoted from first grade after signing with the ARL during the 1995 Super League war) in the club's 17-4 boilover against Manly in the 1995 decider. Ridge was in the Manly side that went down to the Bulldogs in 1995, but combined with another ex-All Black, devastating centre Craig Innes, in the Sea Eagles' 1996 triumph.

The Auckland Warriors' 1995 entry into the premiership enticed several Australian-based Kiwi players back to New Zealand, including Hoppe, Hill, Gene Ngamu and Western Suburbs' Kiwi international Stephen Kearney. The skilful and intimidating second-rower joined Melbourne in 1999 and was a vital component of the Storm's premiership-winning side in his first season. He left the NRL at the end of 2005 with 264 first grade games and 43 Tests under his belt. Kearney built a reputation as a future NRL mentor as Craig Bellamy's assistant at the Storm and took over the New Zealand Test role (guiding the Kiwis to a World Cup final triumph in 2008), which led to a first grade head coach position with Parramatta in 2011.

Despite the homeward pull of the Warriors, New Zealand players remained integral to Australian clubs throughout the 1990s. Inspirational lock Tawera Nikau helped Cronulla to the 1997 Super League Grand Final before joining Kearney and fellow New Zealanders Matt Rua and Richard Swain in Melbourne's 1999 Grand Final celebrations. Despite spending just two seasons with the Storm, one of the grandstands at the club's Olympic Park home was renamed 'The Tawera Nikau Stand' in 2005. Richie Barnett, Nikau's teammate at Cronulla, was an outstanding backline player for the Sharks and the Sydney Roosters and captained New Zealand in 11 of his 26 Test appearances.

Formidable but suspension-prone prop Craig Smith debuted with Souths in 1995 before joining Illawarra and representing Queensland and Rest of the World in 1997 under the ambiguous representative rules of the Super League war years. He debuted for the Kiwis the following year in the first of 12 Test appearances and was part of St. George Illawarra's losing Grand Final side in 1999. Another valuable front-rower, 16-Test Kiwi Jason Lowrie, played 160 games for the Roosters, Balmain and the Wests Tigers, and was renowned for taking 139 first grade appearances to score his first try. Prop Terry Hermansson played 150 first grade games for the Rabbitohs, Roosters and Warriors from 1993-2000.

Although Nathan Cayless was born in Sydney, he identified with his New Zealand parentage and represented the Kiwis 39 times, captaining the Kiwis to a historic World Cup final victory in 2008. Installed as Parramatta captain as a 21-year-old, Cayless became the first player to captain one club in 200 first grade games before retiring in 2010. His brother Jason won a premiership with the Roosters in 2002 and played 10 Tests for the Kiwis.

Powerhouse winger Lesley Vainikolo (Canberra) and classy centre Willie Talau (Canterbury) managed to slip through the Warriors' net to debut during the 1998 NRL season, with Talau forming a superb right-side combination with Halligan in a Bulldogs side that powered to the Grand Final. Talau represented New Zealand in 13 Tests and played 101 games for Canterbury before joining St. Helens in 2004, while Vainikolo left to dominate the European Super League after four seasons with the Raiders. He scored 14 tries in as many Test appearances for the Kiwis.

Explosive forward Tony Puletua made his debut for Penrith in 1997 and was a mainstay of the Panthers' pack, before forming one of the modern era's best second-row combinations with former Warrior Joe Gulavao as the club won the 2003 premiership. Puletua linked with St. Helens at the end of 2008 after 211 games for Penrith, while Galuvao had subsequent stints with Souths and Parramatta, playing in the Eels' 2009 Grand Final loss, before winning another NRL title with Manly as a 33-year-old in his 212th first grade appearance.

Nigel Vagana began his first grade career with the Warriors but was a tryscoring sensation at the Bulldogs, topping the premiership in 2002 with a club record 23 touchdowns. Subsequent stints with the Sharks and Rabbitohs took his career tally to 140 tries and the devastating centre remains the only overseas player to break the 100-try barrier.

Three young New Zealand-born players—Benji Marshall, Sonny Bill Williams and Karmichael Hunt—took the NRL by storm in 2004, although Brisbane Broncos fullback Hunt pledged his allegiance to Australia and represented Queensland and the Kangaroos with distinction. 'SBW' was the complete package: sublimely skilled, fast, and strong, he was one of the game's biggest hitters, best offload exponents and most damaging ball-runners. The centre/backrower was part of the Bulldogs' premiership-winning side in his debut season, alongside fellow Kiwis Matt Utai and future South Sydney captain and Test skipper Roy Asoatasi. But Williams infamously walked out on the club in 2008 to play rugby union in France, before becoming an All Black in 2010. Meanwhile, Asotasi was at one stage recognised as the world's best prop and 2002 Dally M Rookie of the Year Utai scored 71 tries in 127 games for the Bulldogs before joining the Tigers in 2011 after a season in the NRL wilderness.

Marshall, the only one of the aforementioned superstar trio to remain in Rugby League after Hunt's 2010 switch to the AFL, stamped himself as one of the decade's most dazzling individual talents. The Wests Tigers' unheralded squad, which contained New Zealanders Paul Whatuira (previously a premiership-winner at Penrith) and Dene Halatau, rode Marshall's brilliance all the way to Grand Final glory in 2005. The mercurial pivot emerged through several injury-riddled seasons to star in the Kiwis' 2008 World Cup triumph and take over the New Zealand captaincy in 2009. He became arguably the game's premier match-winner in 2010 after spearheading the Tigers' return to the finals and the Kiwis' stunning upset of Australia in the Four Nations final to collect the Golden Boot. Marshall finished second to Billy Slater in the 2011 Dally M Medal count after another sublime season.

Melbourne's champion side of the late-2000s, which has been sullied by revelations of salary cap breaches that resulted in the stripping of two premierships, contained a strong Kiwi influence. Forwards David Kidwell (a 25-Test Kiwi who played over 200 games for five NRL clubs), Jeremy Smith, Adam Blair and Sika Manu each played a key role in the Storm's on-field dominance during this period. After switching to St. George Illawarra in 2009, Smith was one of seven New Zealand Test players in the 2010 Grand Final. Jason Nightingale and former Warrior Nathan Fien accompanied Smith on the Saints' victory lap, while young stars Sam Perrett, Shaun Kenny-Dowall, Frank-Paul Nuuausala and Jared Waerea-Hargreaves were in the Roosters side that went down 32-8.

New Zealand's brazen challenge to Australia's world Rugby League supremacy—which included the Kiwis' upset of the Kangaroos in the 2008 World Cup and 2010 Four Nations finals—was exacerbated by the Warriors' memorable charge to a second Grand Final appearance in 2011. The gallant Warriors were beaten 24-10 by a Manly side featuring Kiwi stars Galuvao, budding superstar five-eighth Keiran Foran and centre enforcer Steve Matai. The Warriors' Under-20s outfit took out their second straight title, while feeder side the Auckland Vulcans also qualified for the NSW Cup decider in a monumental year of achievement for the club.

Many other Kiwis have had a massive impact on the NRL with Australian clubs in the last decade—Frank Pritchard at Penrith and Canterbury, Bronco and Bulldog Greg Eastwood, Tigers bulldozer Taniela Tuiaki (the 2009 Dally M Winger of the Year whose career was subsequently cut short by a shocking leg injury), former Cowboys captain Paul Rauhihi, among scores of New Zealand stars—ensuring that there will continue to be a sizeable presence in the NRL outside of the Warriors. Australians joke (or complain) about the hordes of New Zealanders in general that move across the Tasman, and that influx is also reflected in the proportion of Kiwis starring in the NRL. From the humble beginnings when the Kiwis in the premiership could be counted on one hand, there is now at least a handful of New Zealanders at every NRL club—and the competition is all the more richer for it. According to information available in the 2012 NRL Season Guide, 55 of the 375 players in the NRL clubs' top-25 squads (excluding the Warriors) were born in New Zealand—a figure representing 14.67 per cent of Australian-based players in the premiership.

TRANS-TASMAN RIVALRY

Although Rugby League was established in New Zealand prior to the new code hitting Australia—the first matches played in Australia were between the touring New Zealand 'All Golds' (en route to a trailblazing tour of Britain) and a team of New South Wales rugby union defectors in 1907—Australia almost immediately assumed the 'big brother' role in the 13-a-side rivalry between the Antipodes neighbours. Ashes series between England or Great Britain and Australia were the marquee clashes in international football until the late-1990s, when the Kiwis muscled their way into the No.2 spot in the Test pecking order. But trans-Tasman competition has provided many highlights to the rich history of Test football in Rugby League's 104 years—arguably peaking with the Kiwis' bold bid for international dominance in recent seasons.

NEW ZEALAND WINS FIRST SERIES The New Zealand 'All Golds', featuring Australian star Dally Messenger, toured Britain in 1907-08 and upset England in the first Rugby League Test series. On their way home from the gruelling tour, the match-hardened New Zealanders stopped in Australia for the first trans-Tasman Test series. With Messenger playing for Australia against his former teammates, alongside luminaries of the code's formative years such as Albert Rosenfeld, Jim Devereux, Sid 'Sandy' Pearce and captain Arthur Hennessy, the Kiwis emerged triumphant 2-1 in a hard-fought series. Hubert Turtill skippered New Zealand to an 11-10 victory in Sydney, before the Conrad Byrne-led Kiwis emphatically wrapped up the series in Brisbane 24-12. Australia restored pride in the third encounter by coming from behind to record its first Test win 14-9. The revered Albert Baskerville—organiser of the tour, a tireless founding father of Rugby League in New Zealand and a vital figure in cementing the game's future in Britain and Australia—scored a try in the first Test but died from pneumonia in Brisbane prior to the second Test *(see Tragic Figures)*. Baskerville's body was taken back to New Zealand and his resting place was a regular stop for subsequent Australian touring sides.

New Zealand won the first Test of the 1909 series, 19-11 in Sydney, but Larry 'Jersey' O'Malley and Bob Graves led Australia to victories in the second and third Tests respectively. Brisbane Norths centre Charlie Woodhead scored two tries in each of the 10-5 and 25-5 wins that saw Australia claim its first Test series success. New Zealand toured Australia in subsequent seasons but did not play any official Tests, while New South Wales intermittently toured New Zealand. Four New Zealand players—Arthur 'Bolla' Francis, George Gillett, Charles Savory and Frank Wooward—were invited to tour with the 1911-12 'Australasian' Kangaroos. Francis top-scored for the tourists with 125 points, and was the only New Zealander to appear in a Test on tour. World War I then curtailed trans-Tasman Rugby League competition until 1919.

WONDER WINGER TORMENTS KIWIS The great Australian wing three-quarter Harold Horder was a constant thorn in the side of New Zealand during the four-Test series in 1919. Horder began the series with a brace of tries in the 44-21 first Test thrashing at Wellington, and backed that up by scoring all of Australia's points in the 26-10 loss a week later in Christchurch, collecting two tries and two goals. In the third encounter in Auckland, Horder crossed for another double and slotted five goals in a 34-23 victory, before scoring a hat-trick of tries and a goal as Australia secured the series with a 32-2 fourth Test victory, also in Auckland. Horder's haul from the series: nine tries and eight goals for 43 points. He added five tries from two minor matches, but the title of top try-scorer for the tour went to Easts centre Les Cubitt, who amassed an incredible 24 tries in eight games.

New Zealand embarked on tours to Australia in 1921, 1925 and 1930, but did not play any Tests, instead taking on NSW and Queensland representative sides. The Kiwis proved they could be a formidable force on the world stage, however, defeating the touring England side 2-1 in the 1924 Test series. Australia and New Zealand both sought an invitation to send a touring team to Britain in the 1926-27 northern winter, and the British authorities chose the Kiwis. But New Zealand was comprehensively outplayed 3-0 by England in the Test series during a disastrous tour. Trans-Tasman Tests finally resumed in 1935.

ALL BLACK LEGENDS INSPIRE 1930s VICTORIES Prominent eight-Test former All Black Bert Cooke switched codes in 1932 and captained New Zealand to a 22-14 victory in the first trans-Tasman Rugby League Test staged in 16 years in 1935. Cooke led the team from fullback in the Carlaw Park boilover against the Dave Brown-captained Australian side, with winger Lou Brown scoring three tries for the Kiwis. Dave Brown skippered Australia to handsome victories in the ensuing two Tests to take the series 2-1.

George Nepia, an All Black teammate of Cooke's on the New Zealand 'Invincibles' Northern Hemisphere tour in 1924-25, switched to Rugby League in 1935 with London club Streatham and Mitcham. Regarded as one of the greatest players in rugby union history, Nepia returned to New Zealand in 1937 and became a dual international. After kicking four goals in New Zealand Maori's 16-5 defeat of Australia, he landed two vital goals in the Kiwi Test side's 16-15 triumph against the Wally Prigg-led Australians at Carlaw Park to square the two-Test series.

World War II halted Test Rugby League for several years, but trans-Tasman competition resumed in the late-1940s. Test series in Australia (1948) and New Zealand (1949) were each drawn 1-all.

KIWIS HOLD UPPER HAND IN EARLY-1950s Australia and New Zealand both recorded historic Test series victories over the touring Great Britain side in 1950, building anticipation for the next instalment of trans-Tasman rivalry. But Australia was dominated by one of the finest New Zealand sides of all time in the ensuing two series. After comfortably winning the first Test of the 1952 series 25-13 at the Sydney Cricket Ground, Australia lost by a record margin in the second encounter in Brisbane. Kiwi fullback Des White kicked 11 goals in the 49-25 thrashing, and another five as New Zealand took out its first series since 1908 with a 19-9 win in the third Test in Sydney. Desperate to atone in the New Zealand-hosted series the following season, Australia was humbled 25-5 in Christchurch and pipped 12-11 in Wellington, before saving face with an 18-16 victory in Auckland. The consecutive series victories featured Kiwi luminaries Tom Baxter, Cyril Eastlake, George Menzies, and captains Jimmy Haig (the last New Zealand dual international for more than 40 years) and Travers Hardwick.

Australia restored order with a comprehensive 3-0 series whitewash of the Kiwis in 1956, bookended by emphatic victories over New Zealand in the 1954 and 1957 World Cups. Maitland winger Don 'Bandy' Adams scored five tries in the 1956 series, including a hat-trick in the 31-14 third Test victory.

NEW ZEALAND THRASHED IN BRISBANE After losing the first Test of the 1959 series in Sydney 9-8, New Zealand headed to Brisbane eager to keep the series alive. But the Kiwis did not count on the lethal left-side combination of legendary St. George centre Reg Gasnier and flying South Sydney winger Ian Moir. The pair was untouchable, scoring three tries apiece, while fullback Keith Barnes added seven goals in the 38-10 series-clinching demolition. New Zealand gained some consolation with a 28-12 victory in the third Test at the SCG.

New Zealand and Australia drew two-Test series 1-all in 1961 and 1965, while Australia won a three-match series 2-1 in 1963. But the Kiwis were awarded the Courtney Goodwill Trophy in 1965 as the nation with the best Test winning percentage over the previous five-year period, thanks largely to a 2-0 series triumph over Great Britain in 1962. Australia did not claim the Courtney Goodwill Trophy until 1975, but nevertheless swamped New Zealand 3-0 in the 1967 Test series.

SIMMS REVELS IN WORLD CUP THRASHINGS South Sydney pointscoring machine Eric Simms feasted on the Kiwis in consecutive World Cups. The sharpshooter landed six goals and two field goals in Australia's 31-14 victory over New Zealand at Lang Park in the 1968 tournament, among 28 goals and field goals he landed in Australia's successful four-match campaign. On the way to claiming a famous World Cup victory in Britain in 1970, Australia swept aside the Kiwis 47-11 at Wigan's Central Park. Father John Cootes grabbed two of the Ron Coote-captained green-and-golds' nine tries. Simms also crossed for a try, and slotted nine goals and a field goal for a personal haul of 23 points—an Australian record for a Test or World Cup match at the time.

KIWIS SPRING UPSET AT CARLAW PARK New Zealand won just one Test against Australia during the 1970s—but it was a victory to remember. A starstudded Australian side ventured across the Tasman to play a one-off Test in 1971 at New Zealand's spiritual home of Rugby League, Carlaw Park. But the Graeme Langlands-captained side, which included fellow greats of the era Bob Fulton, Bob McCarthy, John Sattler and Bob O'Reilly, was ambushed by the unheralded Kiwis 24-3. The home side scored four tries to one, with bruising front-rower Henry Tatana adding six goals. Tatana was snapped up by Canterbury in 1972 and scored more than 500 points for the Canterbury and St. George.

The Carlaw Park aberration preceded a period of unmatched trans-Tasman dominance. Australia won the following 14 Tests against New Zealand—by an average margin of 17 points. The streak included comprehensive 3-0 series cleansweeps in 1972 and 1978.

LANG PARK A HAPPY HUNTING GROUND FOR THE KIWIS After 12 winless years against the mighty Australian side, New Zealand found success during the 1980s at an unlikely venue—the hallowed turf of Lang Park in Brisbane. Under inspirational former Otahuhu and Brisbane Norths coach Graham Lowe, New Zealand produced a boilover for the ages in 1983. The Graeme West-captained Kiwis employed roughhouse tactics to get the upper hand on their big-name rivals, carving out a stirring 19-12 upset. The match featured a brilliant try to Joe Ropati after a Dean Bell bust, and a crunching try-saver on Mal Meninga by debutant Kiwi fullback Nicky Wright. Four years late at the same ground, New Zealand, containing five players making just their second Test appearance, conjured another seven-point victory. Australia was ambushed in its only international of 1987 and succumbed 13-6 after a scoreless second half. Unheralded Kiwi coach Tony 'Tank' Gordon revelled in the victory, spearheaded by little-known New Zealand-based youngsters Kevin Iro, Gary Mercer and Ross Taylor, along with experienced campaigners Dean Bell and skipper Hugh McGahan.

RIBOT BREAKS KIWI HEARTS TWICE BEFORE THIRD TEST BOILOVER Two years after their breakthrough victory at Lang Park, New

Zealand proved the gap was closing in international football during an epic three-Test series against Australia in 1985. But Graham Lowe's New Zealand side was forced to swallow gut-wrenching losses in the opening two encounters. Powerful Queensland winger John Ribot crossed for his second try in the dying stages of the first Test at Lang Park to seal a 26-20 victory for the green-and-golds, and he repeated the dose less than two weeks later at Auckland's Carlaw Park, finishing off a long-range movement featuring Wally Lewis and Garry Jack in the final seconds to wrap up the series 10-6. The Kiwis dusted themselves off for the third clash and triumphed 18-0 at Carlaw Park on one of New Zealand Rugby League's greatest-ever days. Livewire replacement half Clayton Friend scored two tries and giant pivot Olsen Filipaina—who was named man of the match in losing sides in the opening two Tests—dominated the great Lewis. But the match is remembered in Australian circles for a split in the ranks caused by interstate differences. NSW had won its first State of Origin series in 1985 under national coach Terry Fearnley and the bitter rivalry spilled over on the tour of New Zealand. Four Queensland players—Chris Close, Mark Murray, Greg Conescu and Greg Dowling—were dropped from the Australian side before the third Test after featuring in the opening two successes.

Australia had it easier in the 1986 series with a 3-0 whitewash. Brett Kenny scored five tries in the series, while Wally Lewis, Garry Jack and Michael O'Connor ran roughshod over New Zealand, who went on to suffer a maiden Test loss in Papua New Guinea later in the year in Graham Lowe's last match as national coach.

WILY AUSTRALIANS AMBUSH KIWIS AT EDEN PARK Australia successfully pulled the wool over New Zealand's eyes by talking up the Kiwis as favourites for the 1988 World Cup final in Auckland. Optimism was sky-high for the match, played in front of a New Zealand Rugby League record crowd of 47,363 at the famed rugby union venue Eden Park, in the wake of the Kiwis' Lang Park upset the previous season. But the Kiwis were overawed by the occasion and the weight of expectation, bumbling their way to a 21-0 halftime deficit courtesy of a spate of errors and penalties. Australian captain Wally Lewis was forced off with a broken arm at halftime, but another try just after the break effectively wrapped up the World Cup for the visitors. Tries to the Iro brothers, Tony and Kevin, added respectability to a 25-12 final scoreline. Brisbane Broncos halfback Allan Langer was adjudged man of the match for his two-try display, while Gavin Miller and Dale Shearer also crossed for Australia.

Australia emphasised its position as the alpha male in trans-Tasman international Rugby League on its 1989 tour of New Zealand. Despite a shock 24-22 loss to the Auckland provincial side, Australia won the Test series convincingly 3-0. The first encounter—a 26-6 victory to the tourists—is best-remembered for the heavy-handed tactics of young Kiwi backrower Brendon Tuuta, who was subsequently dubbed 'the Baby-faced Assassin' by the appalled Australian media in the wake of a spate of high tackles and cheap shots. The Kiwis embarked on a disastrous tour of Great Britain and France at the end of the year (which, among other catastrophes, saw winger David Ewe sent home for off-field misbehaviour), while Bob Bailey—brother of legendary 29-Test Kiwi centre Roger—took over from 'Tank' Gordon as national coach in 1990. Australia prevailed 24-6 in a one-off Test in atrocious conditions at Wellington's Athletic Park in 1990.

RAMPANT KIWIS END 'THE KING'S' TEST CAREER New Zealand entered the 1991 Test series, hosted by the world champion Australians, as rank outsiders. The Kiwis' underdog status was heightened by the selection of captain Gary Freeman from Balmain's reserve grade side and Clayton Friend from the Metropolitan Cup. But, in the first Test in Australia played outside NSW or Queensland, New Zealand caused one of international football's biggest boilovers with a 24-8 victory at Melbourne's Olympic Park. The green-and-golds led 8-2 following a tight and tense opening half, but they were powerless to halt a Kiwi attacking assault in the second stanza. Jarrod McCracken and Richie Blackmore scored memorable tries to snatch the lead, before replacement Clayton Friend and intimidating lock Tawera Nikau capped one of the New Zealand's finest victories with four-pointers. The match proved to be the last of the incomparable Wally Lewis' Test career—'The King' was dropped following the shock loss, along with Dale Shearer, Steve Roach and debutant Paul Hauff. Australia denied New Zealand its first series victory since the 1950s however, handing out 44-0 (a then-record victory) and 40-12 thrashings in the second and third Tests respectively.

STAND-IN SKIPPER SAVES AUSTRALIA Australia entered the first Test of the 1993 series against New Zealand without its suspended captain Mal Meninga, and almost tasted defeat in a series-opener for the third time in four years. After losing to Great Britain at Wembley in 1990 and New Zealand in Melbourne the following season, it took Meninga's replacement as skipper, Canberra teammate Laurie Daley, to snatch a face-saving late draw for Australia at Mt. Smart Stadium. The green-and-golds led early, but two opportunist tries to Kiwi winger Sean Hoppe set up a 14-7 advantage. The reply from hooker Steve Walters reduced the deficit to one point at the break—the precursor to a gripping defensive slugfest in the second half. With no score in the first 36 minutes of the second period, the Kiwis were on the verge of a gallant victory, until Daley stepped up to tie the game 14-all with his second field goal. With Meninga back at the helm, Australia took out the series with a win 16-8 win in farcical circumstances in Palmerston North when members of the crowd refused to return the balls and the players were forced to stand in freezing conditions while a new one was pumped up, *(see Bizarre Matches)* and a comfortable 16-4 result at Lang Park.

KIWIS THRIVE UNDER 'HAPPY FRANK' The New Zealand Rugby League side was at one of its lowest ebbs following the Kiwis' disastrous tour of Great Britain and France at the end of 1993. The year began promisingly enough—the national team drew 14-all with Australia in the first Test before going down in the final two encounters in spirited displays, while the impending introduction of the Auckland Warriors to the Australian premiership saw the game's popularity reach an all time high in the Shaky Isles.

The Kiwis were confident of victory abroad after a drawn series against the Lions at home in 1992, but were comprehensively outplayed on foreign soil, losing the three Tests 17-0, 29-12 and 29-10—New Zealand's first 3-0 series loss to Great Britain in 23 years. Captain Gary Freeman was dropped before the third encounter and replaced by 21-year-old Western Suburbs second-rower Stephen Kearney. Results were more satisfactory on the French leg of the tour, but the trip ended on a sour note when Kearney and St. George winger Jason Donnelly were injured when a hotel balcony collapsed. Former Test hooker Howie Tamati's two-year stint as Kiwi coach inevitably came to an end after the tour.

Tamati's replacement was affable and passionate Cantabrian Frank Endacott. A handy Christchurch club player and Junior Kiwis representative, Endacott devoted three decades of his life to grassroots Rugby League in the region. He achieved great success as coach of the Canterbury provincial side in the early-1990s and guided the Junior Kiwis and New Zealand Residents representative squads on successful overseas tours. Endacott was appointed coach of the national team in 1994 and remained at the helm for seven seasons, ushering in an era of unprecedented consistency, and garnering respect from traditional international powerhouses Australia and Great Britain.

New Zealand's 1994 playing schedule consisted of a two-Test tour of Papua New Guinea at the end of the season. The Kiwis won both Tests and three tour matches comfortably to prepare for a busy 1995. Meanwhile, Endacott was installed as the fledgling Warriors' reserve grade coach.

A win and a draw against France at home and a disappointing 3-0 away series defeat against Australia during 1995 did not augur well for the ensuing World Cup tournament in England, but Endacott's Kiwis came within inches of knocking Australia out of the tournament. Endacott kick-started the international career of future Kiwi legend Stacey Jones by selecting the 19-year-old at halfback ahead of veteran Freeman for the tournament-opener against Tonga, which required two late tries and a Matthew Ridge field goal for New Zealand to get out of jail 25-24.

The Kiwis cruised through to a semi-final showdown with Australia after putting Papua New Guinea away 22-6 in their other pool match. Despite missing a host of Super League-aligned stars, Australia went into the match as strong favourites, and supported that billing by surging to a 20-6 lead in the second half. But New Zealand roared back into the contest and levelled the scores with a late try to Kevin Iro. Agonisingly, Ridge's sideline conversion attempt and long-range, left-footed field goal shot on fulltime both shaded the upright and the match went into extra-time. Australia booked a spot in the final with two tries in the added period for a 30-20 win, leaving the Kiwis to lament an opportunity lost.

The ongoing Super League saga skittled a proposed series between New Zealand and Australia in 1996, but the Kiwis produced stunning results against the touring Kumuls and Lions at the end of the season. After routing Papua New Guinea 62-8 and 64-0, New Zealand claimed its first series win over Great Britain since 1984 with an emphatic 3-0 cleansweep.

Endacott guided the Warriors' reserve grade side to the 1996 Grand Final (going down 14-12 to Cronulla) and was thrust into the first grade role in the place of John Monie midway through the 1997 Super League season. The Warriors enjoyed a late-season resurgence under Endacott that culminated in a gallant semi-final defeat to the Broncos in the World Club Challenge competition.

Although not given Test match status by Australian authorities, New Zealand (who awarded caps to its players) played two matches against Super League Australia in 1997. New Zealand performed creditably in a 34-22 loss to Australia in the Anzac Day Test, before causing a major boilover with a crushing 30-12 victory a week after the Super League Grand Final. Stacey Jones and Syd Eru each scored doubles, while

Matthew Ridge and Logan Swann were inspirational as the rampant Kiwis set North Harbour Stadium alight in New Zealand's first victory over an Australian side since 1991. Darren Lockyer made his debut in a green and gold jersey in the loss, starring in a sublime two-try performance.

Despite the nature of the win, the Kiwis were expected to be cannon fodder for Australia in the early-season Bill Kelly Cup Test at the same venue in 1998. But Australia's first full-strength line-up since 1994 was stunned by a ferocious New Zealand performance. Australia raced to a 12-2 lead in the first half, but the Kiwis bustled replacement fullback Darren Lockyer into several errors that led to tries (*see Unforgettable Debuts*) and snatched an 18-12 advantage. Kevin Iro played a memorable role off the bench and his second try wrapped up a momentous 22-16 triumph. The mercurial Paul brothers, Henry at hooker and Robbie at five-eighth, were outstanding for the victors, while skipper Matthew Ridge played a characteristically authoritative role.

The Kiwis were overwhelmed by the Brisbane-dominated Australian side in the remaining two Tests—the Broncos provided an all time record nine players to the second Test side—which were played after the completion of the NRL season. But the Kiwis finished the year with a fleeting, history-making tour of Great Britain. New Zealand wrapped up the series with victories in the first two Tests, while the third was drawn. It was the Kiwis' first series victory in Britain since 1971 and the first time a New Zealand side had gone through a series on British soil unbeaten.

A Graham Lowe-led consortium ousted Endacott from the Warriors coaching post at the end of 1998, but 'Happy Frank' curbed his disappointment by channelling his coaching energy solely into the national side in 1999—with exceptional results. The first Test of the year saw a gallant New Zealand go down 20-14 to Australia in Sydney. Both sides scored three tries in a gripping encounter, but the superior goalkicking of Australian winger Mat Rogers proved the difference, with Kiwi hooker Henry Paul landing just one goal. But the Paul brothers reprised their early-season Test role of 12 months earlier with another brilliant double-act, and almost spearheaded another international upset as the Kiwis pushed Australia until the final whistle.

That effort steeled New Zealand for the end-of-year Tri-Nations tournament, and a scintillating first half performance set up another triumph over the powerful Australian side in the series-opener in Auckland. Stacey Jones was at his effervescent best, setting up four first half tries to steer the Kiwis to a 24-4 halftime lead. New Zealand held off the resurgent Kangaroos in the second half to win 24-22. It was the first time since 1952-53 that New Zealand had beaten a full-strength Australian Test team in consecutive years.

New Zealand booked a rematch with Australia in the final with a 26-4 thumping of Great Britain, but Australia edged out the Kiwis 20-18 in one of the great trans-Tasman Test matches. Australia led 14-10 after an even first half, before the Kiwis snatched their first lead inside the final 10 minutes with a try to Nigel Vagana. A wonderful team try to Wendell Sailor appeared to seal New Zealand's fate, but the men in black and white recovered to launch one last attacking raid. Henry Paul put in a kick on fulltime, which was claimed by Logan Swann after a mad scramble. Swann claimed a try, but the video referee ruled the backrower was held up, handing Australia the spoils. The narrow loss denied the Kiwis their first series win over Australia in 46 years, while it kept the world champions' streak of series wins against all-comers—that stretched back to 1978—intact.

Endacott accepted the head coaching position at heavyweight Super League club Wigan Warriors at the end of 1999, but the lowest point of his reign as Kiwi coach came months later in the 2000 Bill Kelly Cup Test. Struggling for cohesion after a disjointed build-up, New Zealand was taken to the cleaners 52-0 by a ruthless Kangaroos side. Australia ran nine tries past the woeful Kiwis outfit, while Mat Rogers scored a trans-Tasman record 24 points. The Kiwis' preparation for the year-ending World Cup appeared to be in tatters, but Endacott rallied his charges to give the tournament an almighty shake.

Led by inspirational captain and fullback Richie Barnett, the Kiwis swept aside their pool group opposition, crushing Lebanon 64-0, the Cook Islands 84-10 and Wales 58-18. France was next in the firing line, decimated 54-6 at the quarter-final stage, before host nation England was sent packing at the hands of the ruthless New Zealanders in the semi-final by a humiliating 49-6 scoreline.

New Zealand approached the final with confidence after Australia was given a fright by Wales in the other semi-final, and the Kiwis pushed the star-studded Australian side all the way, trailing just 18-12 after 67 minutes. But the individual brilliance of the Kangaroos came to the fore, running in four late tries for an emphatic 40-12 victory—a scoreline that flattered Australia and belied the Kiwis' stoic effort. Endacott stepped down from the national post after the tournament and was replaced by Gary Freeman in 2001.

Endacott led Wigan to the 2000 and 2001 Super League Grand Finals—both of which the Warriors lost—and received a first-hand lesson in the fickle realities of coaching in England when he was shown the door at the end of 2001. But his legacy as the Kiwis' longest-serving national coach should not be undersold. New Zealand forcefully asserted itself as the strongest contender to Australia's crown as the nNo.1 international side, remaining unbeaten in eight matches against Great Britain and England under Endacott. He broke down the epithet of the 'Australian supermen' that for so long plagued New Zealand's ability to regularly challenge the green-and-golds.

The transformation of the late-1990s was a catalyst for New Zealand's stunning successes against Australia that followed over the next decade, which saw the Kiwis defeat the Kangaroos in the Tri-Nations, World Cup and Four Nations finals in the space of five years. Endacott instilled a belief amongst his players that New Zealand was no longer 'little brother' to the overbearing Australian side, but a worthy adversary capable of rolling the world's best—an ethos the next generation of Kiwi stars put into practice on the international stage.

Australia won one-off Tests against New Zealand in 2001 and 2002, before smashing the Kiwis 48-6 in a mid-season encounter in 2003. But New Zealand carved out a 30-16 boilover in Auckland against the Kangaroos, who were en route to England, with elusive centre Clinton Toopi scoring three tries. Australia was lucky to escape with a 16-all draw against a New Zealand line-up inspired by rookie backrower Sonny Bill Williams in the opening match of the 2004 Tri-Nations, but prevailed 32-12 in the rematch a week later, while the Kiwis faded to miss the final of the tournament. New Zealand Warriors NRL coach Daniel Anderson became the first Australian to coach the Kiwi Test side, guiding the national squad from 2003-05.

KIWI BOILOVER ENDS 27-YEAR REIGN Despite defeating Australia in the 2005 Tri-Nations opener 38-28 in a Sydney thriller—with Clinton Toopi scoring a hat-trick for the second time against the Kangaroos—New Zealand went into the final at Elland Road, Leeds, as rank underdogs. The Kiwis—coached by Auckland's Brian 'Bluey' McClennan—were humbled 38-12 by Great Britain in their final preliminary game, while Australia coasted through to the final on the back of three straight wins (including a Darren Lockyer-inspired 28-26 victory against New Zealand in Auckland). But New Zealand inflicted Australia's first defeat in an international series since 1978 with an emphatic 24-0 shutout. Veteran Stacey Jones, who came out of international retirement to play in the Tri-Nations tournament, pulled the strings for the rampant Kiwis, while 19-year-old winger Manu Vatuvei scored a powerful double. The stunning result also represented New Zealand's first series victory over Australia since 1953.

AUSTRALIA RECLAIM TITLE IN TITANIC FINAL The Kangaroos gained revenge for their shock loss to the Kiwis a year earlier with a nail-biting victory in the 2006 Tri-Nations final in Sydney. Australia took a 10-6 lead into the break after both sides scored a first half try, but New Zealand drew level when imposing centre Iosia Soliola crashed over. Opposing halfbacks Johnathan Thurston and Stacey Jones traded penalty goals in a tense closing half hour and the final became the first golden point Test when field goal attempts by the brilliant No.7s went astray. Thurston was denied the match-winning try by the video referee in extra-time, but after 87 pulsating minutes the Kangaroos linchpin made a break and sent skipper Darren Lockyer over to score under the posts—Australia's first try for 76 minutes— to reassert their international supremacy. The match was widely acclaimed as one of the all time great Test matches.

GREENHORN KANGAROOS TEACH KIWIS A LESSON Following the results of the previous two seasons, the Kiwis would have fancied their chances in 2007's post-season trans-Tasman Test after injuries wreaked havoc on Australia's selection contingent. Eight players debuted for the green-and-golds at Wellington's Westpac Stadium two weeks after the NRL Grand Final, including Storm winger Israel Folau, who became Australia's youngest-ever Test representative. Folau scored two tries and fellow debutants Jarryd Hayne, Brett Stewart and man of the match Greg Bird also got on the scoresheet, while Greg Inglis bagged a hat-trick in the record 58-0 massacre. New Zealand's cause was not aided by the first half send-off of firebrand Manly centre Steve Matai for a reckless high tackle on Mark Gasnier. The Kiwis were also sporting six first-timers—including two players named Jeremy Smith—but there was no cause for celebration as the debacle in the nation's capital set the tone for a disastrous tour of England and France that resulted in the sacking of coach Gary Kemble after just one season in charge.

The Kangaroos scored a convincing 28-12 victory over the Kiwis in the Centenary Test at the SCG in 2008—marking 100 years of Test football between the neighbouring nations—highlighted by a freakish act of athleticism by Greg Inglis in the lead-up to Mark Gasnier's first half try. Australia wore sky blue and maroon hooped jerseys (representative of the NSW and Queensland state colours) in a throwback to the strip worn by Test sides until 1928. The match carried sombre overtones following the news recently named ARL Coach of the Century Jack Gibson had passed away hours before kick-off. Former New Zealand backrower and captain Stephen Kearney assumed the national coaching post prior to the Test.

WORLD CUP SHOCK Australia blitzed the competition during the 2008 World Cup pool stage, hammering New Zealand 30-6 in the tournament-opener and subjecting England to a 52-4 demolition, and consequently entered the final rematch with the Kiwis as red-hot favourites. The showdown in front of 50,559 fans at Suncorp Stadium was going to script when the Kangaroos leapt ahead 10-0, but New Zealand struck back with tries to Jeremy Smith and Jerome Ropati to take a 12-10 lead. Darren Lockyer's brilliant second try saw the hosts head to the break 16-12 in front. Diminutive Kiwi fullback Lance Hohaia snatched back the lead with a determined try, before his Kangaroos counterpart Billy Slater infamously threw a wild pass as he was going into touch near his own tryline. The wayward pass was scooped up by New Zealand five-eighth Benji Marshall to score in the corner. Australia coolly hit back minutes later through Greg Inglis to reduce the deficit to two points, before another disaster beset the defending world champions. Hohaia was awarded a penalty try by the video referee after Australian winger Joel Monaghan tackled him without the ball with just 10 minutes remaining, sending the solid Kiwi contingent in the crowd into raptures. Adam Blair scored an opportunist try to seal one of the great Test upsets over the dumbstruck Kangaroos. It was New Zealand's first World Cup triumph and the first time since 1972 a country other than Australia had collected the silverware in a World Cup tournament. Legendary Brisbane coach and former Australian Test mentor Wayne Bennett assisted Stephen Kearney in the victorious Kiwis' preparation for the tournament and celebrated with the team on the field after the final. Australian coach Ricky Stuart was forced to resign in the aftermath of the shock loss after berating referee Ashley Klein in the team hotel.

Australia escaped with a late 20-all draw against New Zealand in the opening match of the inaugural Four Nations tournament in England in 2009. The Kiwis looked to have sealed another upset, but Cameron Smith scored in the dying minutes and Johnathan Thurston's conversion secured the tied result. Defending world champions New Zealand crumbled against England to miss the final, while the Kangaroos powered to an emphatic tournament triumph by trouncing the hosts.

KIWIS ADD FOUR NATIONS TROPHY TO SILVERWARE COLLECTION New Zealand revived painful World Cup memories for Australia with a cliff-hanger victory over the Kangaroos in the 2010 Four Nations final, again at Suncorp Stadium. The Kangaroos opened the scoring in the third minute when Kiwi fullback Lance Hohaia failed to clean up a grubber, allowing Brent Tate to pounce for an easy try. Replays showed winger Brett Morris had gone into touch two plays earlier and the try should not have been awarded, while Tate succumbed to a knee injury before halftime in a poignant dressing-room scene, requiring a reconstruction for the third time in his career. Sydney Roosters centre Shaun Kenny-Dowall put New Zealand on the board just before the break with a beautifully timed—but dubiously forward—pass from captain Benji Marshall. Tempers flared on halftime, sparking a spirited push-and-shove and setting the tone for a fiery second period.

Australia grabbed a 12-6 lead when Paul Gallen and Greg Bird combined to put Billy Slater into space. The superstar fullback beat the tackle of Hohaia to score heading into the final quarter. But when Slater was forced back into the in-goal with less than 10 minutes remaining, it provided the opportunity for Marshall to thread a glorious grubber through for winger Jason Nightingale to score and reduce the deficit to two points. Marshall's conversion agonisingly cannoned off the upright, and despite Slater coughing up a simple bomb in front of his posts to conjure images of his World Cup nightmare, the Kangaroos appeared set to hold on for a 12-10 win. But Marshall rolled the dice with two minutes on the clock. As he had for Kenny-Dowall's try, the livewire five-eighth ran the ball on the last, putting 'SKD' on the outside of his opposite Willie Tonga. Kenny-Dowall offloaded for Nightingale, who tiptoed down the sideline and flung a one-handed speculator infield. The pass deflected off Darren Lockyer for Marshall to pick up the scraps, before the Kiwi skipper popped a no-look pass over his head in the tackle of Cooper Cronk. Halfback Nathan Fien collected the loose ball to score unopposed. New Zealand celebrated in scenes eerily reminiscent of the World Cup final two years earlier.

The Kiwis performed poorly again in the England-hosted 2011 Four Nations tournament, failing to make the final and forgoing the opportunity to capitalise on their burgeoning status as a realistic contender to Australia's No.1 mantle. Meanwhile, Australia has won every mid-season Bill Kelly Cup Test against New Zealand since the shock loss in 1998, and the overall head-to-head count stood at 90 wins to Australia to New Zealand's 29 with three drawn at the end of 2011. But the Kiwis' recent victories in the World Cup and Four Nations finals have reinvigorated Test football, and fanned the flames of a passionate sporting rivalry.

BRITISH INVASION

In Rugby League's first half-century, Australian fans, clubs and administrators became accustomed to seeing many of their finest players lured to the Northern Hemisphere. England's fields were treated to the best years of the careers of luminaries such as Harry Bath, Brian Bevan, Lionel Cooper and Arthur Clues. Welsh rugby union convert and British Rugby League Test great Ben Gronow, a giant goalkicking forward for the revered Huddersfield side of the 1910s, was something of an anomaly in spending the 1926 season as captain-coach of central west New South Wales club Grenfell. But the tide began to turn with the advent of poker machines in licensed leagues clubs in the 1960s, finally providing Sydney's teams with a cash cow capable of competing with Britain's big-spending clubs.

The flow of playing talent from Australia to England was stemmed to a trickle, and a steady trail of British players began to venture Down Under, peaking with the import heyday of the 1970s. Barrow's 27-Test veteran Phil Jackson was the first notable player to be enticed to Australia, signing with NSW country club Goulburn Workers in 1960. Parramatta was the pacesetting Sydney club for luring British players—Mike Jackson joined the Eels in 1962 and fellow three-quarter Derek Hallas become the first Great Britain representative to play in the Sydney premiership when he linked with the club a season later. Jackson played 48 games and Hallas 44 in three seasons each with Parramatta, with the pair helping the Eels to the preliminary final in 1963. Featherstone Rovers half Ivor Lingard joined Jackson and Hallas at Parramatta in 1964, becoming the first British player to chalk up 100 first grade games in Sydney and featuring in the Eels' 1964-65 finals campaigns. Fred Pickup joined Manly in 1964 before spending three seasons with Parramatta from 1966.

Two Great Britain legends also hit Australia's shores in 1964. Welsh dual international and pointscoring phenomenon Lewis Jones signed on as Wentworthville's captain-coach in the twilight of his career, guiding the western Sydney club to great success in the Second Division competition. Champion backrower Dick Huddart, a Lions tourist to Australia in 1958 and 1962, became the first British player to win a Sydney premiership after St. George handed over a massive transfer fee for the St. Helens great. Injury prevented Huddart from taking part in the Dragons' 1964-65 Grand Final triumphs, but he scored a try in the emphatic 23-4 defeat of Balmain in 1966—the last of the club's world record 11 successive premierships. Huddart played 78 games in the Red V before departing at the end of 1968.

The Ashes second-rower Nat Silcock—the son of the 1930s English great of the same name—linked with Easts in 1964 via a stint in the Newcastle competition. The veteran was installed as captain-coach of the Tricolours and led the club to a ninth-place finish in his only season in Sydney.

Brilliant five-eighth Dave Bolton, a 23-Test veteran and two-time Lions tourist, was in the Balmain side that lost the 1966 decider, but was pivotal to arguably the greatest Grand Final upset of all time three years later. Bolton kicked two field goals and directed traffic superbly as the Tigers' stop-start tactics propelled them to an 11-2 boilover against defending premiers South Sydney. Bolton retired after 78 games for the Tigers and later coached Parramatta in 1973-74, before assisting Tim Sheens at Penrith in the 1980s.

Former Great Britain Test forward Merv Hicks was part of the Canterbury side that ended Huddart's Dragons' run in the 1967 preliminary final, but tasted Grand Final defeat a week later, 12-10 to Souths. The prop played 97 games in a seven-season premiership career with Canterbury and Norths, and was captain-coach of the Bears in 1971-72. Hicks took over the coaching from another former Great Britain international, Roy Francis, who spent two colourful seasons with Norths and quelled the infamous 'walk-off' sensation against Canterbury in 1970 *(see Bizarre Matches)*.

The Sydney premiership was inundated with British stars during the 1970s, but Manly and Cronulla were the foremost benefactors from the influx of imports. Brilliant and brutal lock Malcolm Reilly joined the Sea Eagles in 1971 after starring in Great Britain's Ashes victory in Australia the previous season. Manly forked out a massive transfer fee to Castleford for Reilly's services, but he paid the club back with interest, providing the hard edge the Sea Eagles needed to finally break through for a maiden premiership in 1972 with a Grand Final victory over Easts. Reilly helped the club to a second title a year later despite leaving the field injured during the 10-7 defeat of Cronulla in the wild 1973 decider.

Reilly left the club after the 1975 season, but returned to Australia 20 years later to coach the Newcastle Knights for four highly successful years, which included a historic first premiership for the club in 1997—ironically after defeating Manly in the Grand Final, who had Reilly's former teammate Bob Fulton at the helm. He was named in the Manly's best-ever team and the premiership's Team of the 1970s in 2006. Fellow Great Britain Test forwards Phil Lowe and Steve Norton, and Castleford and future international halfback Gary Stephens, joined the Sea Eagles in the mid-1970s and shared in the club's 1976 Grand Final win over Parramatta, with Lowe scoring Manly's only try.

Opposing Reilly in the 1973 decider were three British players—Tommy Bishop, Cliff Watson and Bob Wear. Fiery halfback Bishop, in particular, was integral to the young Cronulla club's relatively rapid rise to contender status. He joined the Sharks in 1969 and took over as captain-coach the following season. Bishop, who later coached North Sydney and the Sharks, and intimidating forward Watson were named in Cronulla's 'Dream Team' in 2006, while winger Wear scored 29 tries in 104 matches for the club. Magnificent five-eighth Roger Millward, regarded as the player most responsible for Great Britain winning the Ashes in Australia in 1970, spent a season with the John Raper-coached Sharks in 1976.

Ken Batty (St. George, 1971) and Brian Lockwood (Canterbury, 1974) also played in losing Grand Finals during the decade, but a clutch of British players turning out for the competition's lesser lights had a far greater impact. Hooker John Gray was a superb buy for Norths (who hosted vicious Welsh forward Jim Mills from 1970-72), joining the club in 1975 and winning an award for player of the series after the Bears reached the final of the midweek Amco Cup. He introduced the 'round-the-corner' goalkicking style to Australia and scored 141 points in 1977 before joining neighbours and archrivals Manly, for whom suspension ruled him out of the Grand Final in 1978. Gray rejoined Norths in 1981 and finished his Australian career with 613 points.

Penrith handed over massive transfer fees for rake Mike Stephenson (Dewsbury) and backrower Bill Ashurst (Wigan) in 1974. Stephenson and Ashurst were polar opposites and famously did not get along, but both provided considerable value to the hapless Panthers. Stephenson, a valuable toiler at hooker, displayed professionalism and leadership, and took over as captain-coach in 1975 (he resigned from the role midway through the year, partly due to his difficult relationship with Ashurst). Tempestuous ball-playing backrower Ashurst was a brilliant individual talent—creative, dynamic and a superb goalkicker. But discipline problems on and off the field soured his stint with Penrith, and he eventually walked out on the club prior to the start of the 1977 premiership season.

Wakefield Trinity five-eighth Dave Topliss also played for the Panthers in 1976, but he had far more success in a one-year stay at Leichhardt the following season. Topliss equalled the Balmain club record with five tries in a late-season clash with Newtown, before starring with a try and a field goal in the club's finals upset of Manly. Highly rated Great Britain forward Doug Laughton had a less fruitful time Down Under—after giving up the captaincy of the Lions tour to Australia to join Canterbury in 1974, he lasted just five games and left mid-season after losing the first grade captaincy, while the club went on to make the Grand Final. The Berries pursued English talent with relentless vigour in the 1970s, also procuring the services of former Great Britain Test three-quarter Alan Burwell and future internationals Eric Hughes and Mick Adams.

The stream of British talent coming to Australia dried up in the early-1980s, coinciding with the Great Britain Test side's lowest ebb. But a bevy of Test players descended on the premiership in 1985 for the English off-season. Internationals Kevin Beardsmore (Canberra), Brian Noble (Cronulla), Andy Goodway (Manly) and Henderson Gill (Souths) produced uninspiring stints, but youngsters Garry Schofield and Lee Crooks proved refreshing exceptions for Balmain and Wests respectively.

Schofield turned 20 during his stay in 1985, in which he scored 11 tries from 17 appearances. He was even more potent after returning to Leichhardt in 1986—the elusive centre scored a hat-trick in the final round against Souths to deny the Rabbitohs the minor premiership and propel the Tigers into a fifth-place playoff. Schofield starred in Balmain's charge to the preliminary final, incredibly scoring another three tries as the black-and-golds eliminated Souths in the minor semi-final. He finished the year equal-first on the competition's tryscoring table with 13, despite not playing his first match until round nine. Schofield helped the Tigers to the finals again in a brief stint the following season, and played nine matches for strugglers Wests in 1989. Fittingly, Schofield scored three tries in his final premiership match—the Magpies' 34-4 drubbing of Norths—before causing Australia's Test team headaches during the first half of the 1990s.

Crooks, who became Great Britain's youngest-ever Test forward in 1982, was superb for the battling Magpies in 1985-86, topping the pointscoring in his first season for the club. He played alongside Schofield at Balmain in 1987, another of six English players to turn out in Tigers colours during the second half of the 1980s. Five-eighth Tony Myler played 12 games for Balmain in 1986 and came off the bench in both of the club's finals matches, centre Daryl Powell played four games in 1988 and returned to play for Gold Coast in 1991, while goalkicking centre Andy Currier and brilliant utility Shaun Edwards played in the Tigers' heartbreaking 1989 Grand Final defeat to Canberra. Currier was the competition's equal-top point-scorer with 146 (including an equal team-high 10 tries) despite playing just 16 games, before returning for a less eventful spell in 1990.

But the British Tiger who had the most spellbinding impact was Ellery Hanley. Arriving with three rounds of the regular season remaining, Hanley turned the 1988 premiership on its head. Starring in the centres, Hanley spearheaded Balmain's remarkable drive to the Grand Final with tries in the playoff victory over Penrith and finals boilovers against Manly, Canberra and Cronulla. He was forced off the field in the decider against Canterbury after a Terry Lamb tackle left him dazed, and the Tigers subsequently went down 24-12. Hanley was the star attraction at Wests during a 13-game stint alongside Schofield in 1989 and returned to the Tigers as a 35-year-old in 1996, playing 26 games in two seasons.

Front-rower Kevin Ward became the first British player in more than a decade to win a premiership in Australia. He was forced to return to England after playing 10 regular season games for Manly in 1987, but he was so highly regarded that the Sea Eagles flew him back for the Grand Final. Many fine judges believe Ward should have won the Clive Churchill Medal for his towering display in the 18-8 defeat of Canberra in the decider.

Gifted utility-back Joe Lydon spent two successful off-seasons with Easts. A brilliant, crucial solo try in the final round against Cronulla helped seal a top-three spot for the Roosters in 1987, and he was on the flank in the Tricolours' defeat of Canberra in the major preliminary semi and the loss to the Raiders in the preliminary final a fortnight later. He linked with the club again in 1989, and was joined by wing sensation Martin Offiah. The tryscoring machine dotted down in his first match, a 12-10 victory over a Magpies outfit featuring Hanley, Schofield and 16-Test Great Britain prop Kelvin Skerrett, finishing the year with nine tries in 12 games. He scored 11 tries in 14 games for St. George in 1991, but a return to the Roosters in 1993 lasted less than an hour after he dislocated his shoulder in his first appearance.

Andy Gregory and Steve Hampson added class to wooden spooners Illawarra's line-up in 1989—both were sensational in the Steelers' gripping 22-20 loss to the star-studded Broncos in the midweek Panasonic Cup final. Hugh Waddell and Bernard Dwyer had less colourful stays at Manly in 1989, but Paul Bishop was Cronulla's halfback in its finals campaign. Bishop later became one of a large contingent that turned out for the Gold Coast during the battling club's formative seasons, including Powell, Graham Steadman, Paul Dixon (who earlier played for Canterbury), Gary Divorty and Gary Charlton.

Besides the Gold Coast's recruits, British imports were scarce in the early-1990s, but the Bulldogs received tremendous value from backline stars Jonathan Davies and Garry Connolly. Welsh genius Davies scored 100 points for Canterbury in 1991, including 18 points in a mesmerising final-round display against Cronulla. The Bulldogs trailed 16-0, but two individual tries and five goals to Davies helped snatch a 26-16 win and a fifth-place playoff berth. Connolly arrived at Belmore midway through 1993 and played 15 games, including both of the club's finals appearances. Fellow Test backs John Devereux (Manly) and John Bentley (Balmain) also embarked on Australian sojourns in the first half of the 1990s.

The 1995 season heralded the admission of four new clubs—and a new demand for playing talent from England. A 32-year-old Davies was a marquee signing for the fledgling North Queensland Cowboys; Daio Powell played one match for the Perth-based Western Reds while Barrie-Jon Mather spent three seasons with the club; halfback Mike Ford steered around debutants the South Queensland Crushers, where he was joined by winger/fullback St. John Ellis; and the Auckland Warriors enlisted the services of modern Test forward greats Andy Platt and Dennis Betts for two and three seasons respectively.

The signings of Chris Joynt (Newcastle), Lee Jackson (Souths) and Phil Clarke (Roosters) gave the 1995 premiership extra British flavour, while Dean Sampson and Vince Fawcett turned out for lowly Parramatta. But Clarke, one of Great Britain's finest Test players of the 1990s and a stalwart of the all-conquering Wigan side, suffered a broken neck in just the second round of the 1996 season, prematurely ending his career. Clever hooker Lee Jackson moved to Newcastle in 1996 and played 58 games in three seasons for the Knights, coming off the bench in the club's 1997 Grand Final triumph over Manly.

Front-rower Harvey Howard debuted for the Roosters in 1993, before returning in 1996 to play four seasons for the Magpies. He featured in the club's last finals match, a loss to Cronulla in 1996, and was in Wests' last-ever team in the final round of 1999. The veteran prop secured a contract with the Broncos for 2000 and benefitted from a broken arm suffered by Petero Civoniceva. Howard was promoted to the first grade side on the eve of the finals and came off the bench in the 14-6 Grand Final defeat of the Roosters, two days shy of his 32nd birthday.

Fiery forward Adrian Morley arrived at the Roosters in 2001 and became one of the greatest-ever British imports. Despite frequently finding himself on the wrong side of the judiciary (he was outed for 26 weeks from 11 separate suspensions), he played 113 games before a seven-week suspension for kneeing ended his tenure with the club prematurely towards the end of 2006. He was integral to the Roosters' 2002 premiership success and anchored the club's pack in the 2003-04 Grand Finals. Morley was named as one of David Middleton's Top Five Players of 2003 in his *Official Rugby League Annual*.

Forwards Ian Sibbit and Keith Mason had a limited impact at Melbourne in the early-2000s, while goalkicking halfback Chris Thorman experienced a difficult time taking on the poisoned chalice of the Parramatta No.7 jersey in 2004. But Irish winger Brian Carney, a superstar for Great Britain and Wigan, had a charmed stint in Australia. He was one of the Gold Coast Titans' first high-profile signings for their 2007 entry to the NRL, and opted to spend 2006 with Newcastle. Carney was a sensation, scoring 16 tries in 26 games (including a hat-trick against Canberra) and becoming the first player from Britain or Ireland to win a Dally M positional award. But in a major blow for the Titans, Carney returned home during the 2007 pre-season, citing personal and family reasons. The NRL debutants did have the services of one British player though—Leeds fullback Richie Mathers spent the season as Preston Campbell's understudy in 2007.

Mark Edmondson and Jordan Tansey joined the Roosters for brief stints during the 2000s, before a new wave of British stars hit the NRL at the close of the decade. Veteran forward Gareth Ellis proved to be an excellent buy, winning Wests Tigers' Player of the Year award in three straight seasons from 2009-11, and receiving plaudits as one of the world's best backrowers. Ellis was joined at the Tigers by backrow tyro Mark Flanagan in 2010.

Giant young forward Sam Burgess exploded onto the international scene for England in 2009, and his signing was a major coup for Souths in 2010. The buzz created by his impending NRL debut saw him drafted into the fan-selected NRL All Stars team in the 2010 pre-season, while he was an imposing presence throughout the season for the Rabbitohs. The club snapped up Burgess' teenage brother George for 2011 (playing predominantly for NSW feeder cup side Norths), while another brother Luke joined Souths midway through that season to alleviate the forward injury crisis that had claimed Sam early in the year.

Gareth Widdop scored the winning try for Melbourne in the 2009 Toyota Cup Grand Final as a fullback, before breaking into first grade during the club's tumultuous 2010 season and debuting for England at just 21 years of age. He slotted seamlessly into the Storm's vacant five-eighth spot in 2011. England's recent poor showings on the international stage has sparked calls for more players to make the voyage to Australia and gain valuable NRL experience, ensuring the rich and colourful story of British players in the Australian premiership will continue. World-class St. Helens prop and Test veteran James Graham joined Canterbury in 2012, while several other British stars have professed their desire to prove themselves in the world's toughest competition.

KANGAROOS, LIONS AND THE ASHES

Anglo-Australian Tests took little time to assume the status of the greatest contest in world Rugby League. Kangaroo Tours ranked as career highlights for Australian players, while Lions tours Down Under were awaited with feverish excitement in the 'colony' and met with massive Test crowds. England and later Great Britain dominated the first four decades of Ashes warfare, before Australia achieved a drought-breaking success in 1950 and gradually began to acquire the upper hand in the intense rivalry over the ensuing 30 years. Australia has dominated Great Britain and England in international Rugby League post-1980, dropping just five Ashes Tests in the last nine series contested. But there has been no shortage of memorable moments and classic matches to maintain the magic of Anglo-Australian Rugby League competition. The discontinuation of full-scale Kangaroo Tours to Britain and France and Lions tours to Australia has effectively ground the battle for the Ashes to a halt since 2003—a shame, given the quality of Ashes showdowns through the decades.

1908-09 THE PIONEERS With the inaugural Sydney premiership season still underway, NSWRL secretary James J. Giltinan led a hardy group of 35 players to England for a gruelling 45-match tour. The first 'Kangaroos' made the voyage on the RMS Macedonia. The seven-month tour was one of many hardships—a cotton mill strike in England contributed to disappointing gate-takings and the tour was consequently a financial disaster; the harshest England winter in years frequently subjected the Australian side to arduous playing and living conditions; and the team won just 17 of their matches. But the Kangaroos inaugurated a marvellous tradition of touring to the 'Home Country' that would stand as the pinnacle for Australian Rugby League players for almost 90 years, while the hard-fought Test series against England laid the foundations for the fierce Anglo-Australian Rugby League rivalry.

North Sydney forward 'Dinny' Lutge was elected captain by the squad en route to England, but played just five matches on tour (no Tests) due to a leg injury. The Kangaroos prevailed 20-6 over Mid Rhonda in their first match, at Tonypandy, and remained undefeated until a 10-3 loss to Warrington in the seventh fixture of the tour. The first Anglo-Australian Test ended in a thrilling 22-all draw in front of just 2,000 supporters at Park Oval in London—the match was short-sightedly scheduled at the same time as popular soccer and rugby union clashes. England (also known as Northern Union) led 14-5 at halftime, but three tries to Norths winger Jim Devereux pegged Australia—playing in blue and maroon hooped jerseys to represent New South Wales and Queensland—back to level by fulltime. Captain Dally Messenger, the undoubted star of the tour, kicked five goals and inspired Australia's comeback with his customary attacking brilliance.

Messenger scored a try and a goal in the injury-hit Kangaroos' 15-5 loss in the second Test at St. James' Park in Newcastle (observed by a bumper crowd of 22,000), with England captain James Lomas crossing for a try and landing two goals. Glebe forward Alex Burdon led Australia in the absence of Messenger in the third Test, a tense 6-5 victory to England. Revered pioneering Easts winger Dan Frawley scored Australia's try, but England halfback Johnny Thomas and winger George Tyson crossed to give the hosts a narrow series win.

Devereux was the Kangaroos' top try-scorer with 17, while Messenger's 155 points remained a record until the 1933-34 Kangaroo Tour. Easts forward Larry 'Jersey' O'Malley displayed remarkable endurance to play a record 35 matches on tour. Other standouts of the trailblazing journey including winger Albert Rosenfeld, halfback Arthur 'Pony' Halloway, hooker Sid 'Sandy' Pearce and pivot Sid Deane. Giltinan, one of Australian Rugby League's founding fathers who had taken the full financial responsibility for the tour by borrowing £2,000, was unceremoniously dumped from his post as NSWRL secretary after the deficit the Kangaroos incurred (the Northern Union had to sponsor the squad's voyage back to Australia). But his contribution and ambition was integral to one of the game's great institutions.

1910 LIONS TOUR—ENGLAND'S FIRST TOUR England—known until the 1950 tour as the Northern Union—made its first tour to Australia and New Zealand in 1910, led by centre Jim Lomas and boasting champions of the era such as winger Billy Batten. England won the two official Tests on tour against Australia. A hat-trick from prop-forward Bill Jukes spearheaded England's 27-20 victory at the Royal Agricultural Ground in Sydney in the first Anglo-Australian Test played in Australia, while captain Dally Messenger scored a try and kicked four goals. Queenslander Bill Heidke led Australia in the second Test staged at the Brisbane Exhibition Ground two weeks later, but England overturned an 11-10 halftime deficit to prevail 22-17. England winger Jim Leytham scored four tries—an unmatched haul in Anglo-Australia Test Rugby League—while England forward George Ruddick earned the dubious distinction of being the first player sent off in an Anglo-Australian Test.

England played two internationals against an Australasian line-up (containing New Zealanders Albert 'Opai' Asher and Riki Papakura), with the first clash drawn 13-all and Australasia claiming the second 32-15. England was also defeated by a combined New South Wales and Queensland 'Kangaroos' representative side, but comprehensively outplayed New Zealand in a one-off Test in Wellington, 52-20. Confusion reigned for several decades over which matches constituted Tests during the tour, but Australia eventually relented and aligned its Test records with Britain's.

1911-12 THE 'AUSTRALASIAN' KANGAROOS Four New Zealand players were invited to tour England—Arthur 'Bolla' Francis, Charles Savory, Frank Woodward and George Gillett—and the 1911-12 tourists were subsequently dubbed the 'Australasian' Kangaroos. Glebe halfback Chris McKivat was elected captain onboard the RMS Orvieto, with Newtown forward and fellow dual international Paddy McCue chosen as his vice-captain. The second Kangaroos achieved remarkable success, losing just five matches on tour and winning the Test series— a feat Australia would not achieve in England for another 52 years.

Australia prevailed 19-10 in the first Test at Newcastle. Five-eighth Viv Farnsworth scored two tries, complemented by further touchdowns to second-time Kangaroo forward Bill Cann, magnificent South Sydney fullback Howard Hallett playing in the centres and front-rower Francis. Viv Farnsworth moved to centre for the second Test, with brother Bill slotting in as pivot—thus becoming the first set of Australian brothers to appear in a Test together (and the last until Ken and Dick Thornett in 1963). The second Test, played in Edinburgh, Scotland, was drawn 11-all. Two tries to all time great England centre Harold Wagstaff and a three-pointer to captain James Lomas was cancelled out by Australian tries to winger Dan Frawley (who was also on his second tour), skipper McKivat and winger Charles 'Boxer' Russell. Australia secured a historic Test series victory—reportedly the first Anglo-Australian Rugby League series to be referred to as 'the Ashes'—courtesy of an emphatic 33-8 triumph at Birmingham. Leading just 11-8 at halftime, a second half blitz by the Kangaroos spearheaded the amazing nine-tries-to-two win; Frawley, McCue, McKivat and Norths winger Tom Berecry (playing in his only Test) scored two tries apiece.

New Zealander Francis top-scored for the Kangaroos with 125 points. Dual international centre Herb Gilbert led the squad with 20 tries, closely followed by Viv Farnsworth (19) and Frawley (18). The Kangaroos also featured Arthur 'Pony' Halloway for the second time (although McKivat kept him out of the Tests) and the great utility-back Charles 'Chook' Fraser, who at 18 years and 301 days set a mark as Australia's youngest Test player that stood until beaten by Israel Folau 96 years later.

1914 LIONS TOUR—'RORKES DRIFT' TEST SECURES ASHES FOR ENGLAND The 1914 Anglo-Australian Test series was played in a whirlwind eight-day period, culminating in a heroic victory for the weary and injury-hit Northern Union tourists. Captained by legendary centre Harold Wagstaff, England won the first Test 23-5 with a double to winger Stan Moorhouse proving critical. Just two days later in the first Test between the nations at the Sydney Cricket Ground, the Sid Deane-led Australians levelled the series 12-7 on the back of tries to Frank Burge and Charles 'Chook' Fraser, while Dally Messenger added three goals.

The combatants returned to the SCG for the decider—a Test forever immortalised as the 'Rorke's Drift Test' (see Courageous Performances). England led 9-0 at halftime but suffered a succession of injuries (no replacements were allowed) and was forced to bravely defend the advantage with just 10 men, eventually holding on for a famous 14-9 triumph. The tourists racked up a record 101-0 defeat of South Australia, while they pipped New Zealand 16-13 in the sole Test against the Kiwis in Auckland.

1920 LIONS TOUR—ANGLO-AUSTRALIAN TESTS RESUME The World War I-enforced embargo on Anglo-Australian Test Rugby League ended with England's tour to Australia in 1920. The Lions were again led by Harold Wagstaff and featured magnificent future Hall of Fame halfback Jonty Parkin, Welsh dual international forward Ben Gronow and veteran forward Douglas Clark, who was also on his second tour Down Under. Australia won the first Test in Brisbane 8-4, despite a heavily disrupted build-up. After two players pulled out with injury, Souths pivot Alf 'Smacker' Blair and Balmain centre Jack 'Junker' Robinson were called into the squad and transported from Sydney—but floods prevented the duo from reaching Brisbane in time. As a result, Queensland-based players Nev Broadfoot and Harry Fewin were drafted in to make their only Test appearances. Frank Burge and Charles Fraser scored Australia's tries—as they did in the second Test of 1914—and the great winger Harold Horder kicked a goal.

Centre Herb Gilbert assumed the captaincy from five-eighth Albert 'Ricketty' Johnston, and Australia secured its first series victory at home against England courtesy of a five-tries-to-two, 21-8 result in the second Test at the SCG. England salvaged a 23-13 victory in the third Test, in which Queensland forward Bill Richards became the first Australian player sent off in an Ashes Test (on a tripping charge), before sweeping the series against New Zealand 3-0.

1921-22 KANGAROO TOUR—KANGAROOS TURN PROFIT AND HEADS WITH BRILLIANT PERFORMERS

The first Kangaroo Tour in a decade (due to World War I) was the first to record a profit—the squad returned home £6,000 in the black, a princely sum in the 1920s. Although the closely fought Test series was lost 2-1, the Kangaroos' spellbinding individual performers ensure the tour retains a cherished place in Rugby League folklore. Les Cubitt was chosen as captain, although a knee injury restricted the marvellous Easts centre to four minor tour matches, while the Kangaroos were again technically an Australasian squad due to the selection of New Zealand fullback Bert Laing (his selection was controversial, and said to be purely to justify the 'Australasian' tag—he played just 10 minor games on tour).

Skippered by tour vice-captain Charles 'Chook' Fraser, the Kangaroos led the first Test at Leeds 5-3 at halftime on the back of a try to Norths winger Cec Blinkhorn and a goal to Jim Craig, the versatile all time great who was playing in the centres. But a try from a charge-down snatched a 6-5 win for the hosts. Blinkhorn scored two tries, while fellow winger and clubmate Harold Horder also crossed in Australia's resounding 16-2 second Test victory in Hull. The Kangaroos' bid for series victory was thwarted in the decider when captain Fraser was carried off with a broken leg. The Harold Wagstaff-led England side prevailed 6-0 in a gruelling third Test on a snow-covered pitch at Salford.

Blinkhorn scored a Kangaroos record 39 tries in 29 games (including nine in a 92-7 thrashing of Bramley—another record); Horder—regarded by many as Australia's greatest winger—bagged 35 tries in 25 games, and added 11 goals to be the squad's top point-scorer with 127. Glebe's remarkable tryscoring forward Frank Burge crossed for 33 tries in only 23 games. The revered halfback Duncan Thompson kicked a tour-high 49 goals, but his 107 points was fourth-highest for the Kangaroos due to the extraordinary tryscoring exploits of the magnificent trio. The Kangaroos won 27 of their 36 matches on tour, despite Cubitt (who was rumoured to be injured before the squad set off for England), Edwin 'Nigger' Brown, Jack 'Bluey' Watkins and Bert Gray all undergoing knee surgery in England. Young St. George centre George Carstairs narrowly avoided becoming the first and only Kangaroo sent home after damage was done onboard the ship during a drinking session one day out from San Francisco, en route to England. But Carstairs' teammates intervened when management was set to send him back to Australia, and he went on to play 17 matches, including two Tests.

1924 LIONS TOUR—PARKIN'S LIONS RETAIN THE ASHES

Jonty Parkin captained the 1924 Lions squad, which contained fellow second-time tourist Ben Gronow and gave Australia its first glimpse of all time great goalkicking fullback Jim Sullivan. Parkin, whose superb leadership was vital to England's series win, scored two tries and Sullivan landed five goals in England's resounding

22-3 victory in the first Test against Jim Craig's Australian side at the SCG. England wrapped up the series with a tense 5-3 victory in the second Test at the same venue; Parkin scored the Lions' try, while a Sullivan goal proved the difference after Queensland winger Cec Aynsley scored Australia's only try for the second successive match.

Australia avoided a series cleansweep with a 21-11 win in the third Test at the Brisbane Exhibition Ground. Queenslanders Vic Armbruster and Bill Paten delighted the home crowd with tries, while replacement forward Arthur Oxford also crossed in his final Test appearance. New Zealand upset Great Britain 2-1 in the Test series during the Lions' subsequent trip across the Tasman—a result not aided by Parkin's and Sullivan's quarantining after contracting diphtheria, before the star duo returned to inspire a third Test win.

1928 LIONS TOUR—ENGLAND PREVAIL IN TIGHT ASHES SERIES The first-ever three-time Lions tourist, Jonty Parkin emulated Harold Wagstaff by leading his second Northern Union tour of Australia and New Zealand, but bettered the revered centre's record by leading England to a second Ashes Test series victory abroad. Queensland centre Tom Gorman captained Australia in all three matches. England won the first Test 15-12 in Brisbane and secured the Ashes 8-0 in the return clash at a mud-filled SCG, with famed St. Helens winger Alf Ellaby—playing in his first Test series—scoring a try in each victory, among 20 he scored on tour. Easts halfback Joe 'Chimpy' Busch, who would become entrenched in Ashes history 18 months later, made his Australian debut in the second Test.

Australia called upon the 'People's Champion,' South Sydney's magnificent winger Benny Wearing, to make his debut in the dead-rubber third Test. Wearing was frequently overlooked for Test duty, but responded to his belated selection with two tries and three goals in Australia's 21-14 victory. It was to be Wearing's only appearance for his country. England became the first recipient of the grand Ashes trophy—an urn donated by the City Tattersalls Club in Sydney. England gained revenge for its series loss to New Zealand in 1924 by coming from one Test down to beat the Kiwis 2-1.

1929-30 KANGAROO TOUR—'CHIMPY' BUSCH'S NO-TRY FORCES HISTORIC FOURTH TEST The Kangaroos made a belated return to Britain after the proposed 1926-27 tour was scuppered by the English authorities' decision to invite the New Zealand Kiwis to tour. The 1929-30 Kangaroos were the first to be captained by a Queenslander—the great centre Tom Gorman—but the tour will forever remembered for a disallowed try against Australian halfback Joe 'Chimpy' Busch in the scoreless draw in the third Test at Swinton that denied an Ashes series victory.

Easts winger Bill Shankland crossed for two tries and Temora pivot Eric Weissel scored a try and five goals in Australia's astounding seven-tries-to-two, 31-8 defeat of England in the first Test at Hull's Craven Park. Shankland scored again in the second Test, but the Jonty Parkin-led England side levelled the series with a 9-3 result, forcing a decider that has become ensconced in Ashes folklore. Played at Station Road on January 4 1930, the third Test was locked at nil-all when Busch dived over in the corner in the tackle of England lock Fred Butters with mere minutes remaining before fulltime. But touch judge Albert Webster ruled Busch—and not Butters—had taken out the corner post, ruling against a series-winning try. Referee Bob Robinson famously remarked: 'Fair try Australia—but I am overruled.' The general consensus—one vehemently backed by Busch himself—was that the halfback touched down well inside the corner post. The contentious draw led to the staging of an unprecedented (and unscheduled) fourth Test at Rochdale to decide the Ashes. Winger Stanley Smith scored the only points of the match with a second half try, securing the Ashes trophy for England, captained by celebrated fullback Jim Sullivan.

The Kangaroos won 24 and drew two of their 35 matches in Britain. Weissel, the NSW country legend, top-scored with 127 points. Shankland, who later carved out a marvellous career in English club football, led the tourists with 24 tries, one ahead of Bundaberg winger Bill Spencer.

1932 LIONS TOUR—CAPTAIN SULLIVAN TRIUMPHS ON THIRD TOUR

Fullback Jim Sullivan returned for his third Northern Union tour of Australia and New Zealand as skipper of a Lions squad containing prolific try-scorer Alf Ellaby, burgeoning centre great Stanley Brogden, and forward luminaries Nat Silcock, Martin Hodgson and Joe Thompson, who became the first British forward to make three tours. England won the opening Test 8-6 in front a 70,204-stong crowd at the SCG after a scoreless second half. Ellaby and centre Artie Atkinson scored England's tries, while Australia's points consisted of three goals by Riverina pivot Eric Weissel, who was playing in the uncustomary position of centre. Sullivan missed a goal from in front of the posts during the match, before having a wonderful penalty goal disallowed because English forward Martin Hodgson was offside when the kick was taken, but the bizarre misses fortunately did not have bearing on the close-fought result.

The Herb Steinohrt-captained Australian side squared the series with a 15-6 success in the second Test at the Brisbane Cricket Ground. Ipswich halfback Hec Gee and Weissel, who moved back to five-eighth for the match, masterminded Australia's victory. Gee scored a try in each half—the second set up by a long break by Weissel, who was carrying an ankle injury—and laid on the other for winger Joe Wilson, another Ipswich product. The victory is regarded as Australia's 'Rorke's Drift' Ashes victory, after several players soldiered on with serious injuries in an effort reminiscent of England's win in the third Test of 1914.

Australia was on target for its first Ashes series victory in 12 years after building a 9-0 lead in the first half of the third Test, but a second half hat-trick to winger Stanley Smith and a try to Brogden secured an 18-13 win for the Lions. Sullivan's triumphant tourists swept the Kiwis 3-0 in New Zealand.

1933-34 KANGAROO TOUR—DAVE BROWN'S TOUR Captained by the

mercurial Western Suburbs fullback Frank McMillan, the 1933-34 Kangaroos lost the Ashes series in a 3-0 whitewash and endured tragedy en route to Britain, but the tour will be fondly remembered for the exploits of 'the Bradman of League,' incomparable Easts centre Dave Brown. Three-quarter Ray Morris—the only player selected for Australia from the University club—developed an ear infection after the Kangaroos left for Britain, and died in hospital after disembarking in Malta (*see Tragic Figures*).

In a repeat of the controversial Test at Station Road on the 1929-30 tour, the opening Test at the same venue finished try-less. But England captain Jim Sullivan kicked two goals to lift the home side to a 4-0 victory. Brown scored a try and a goal in the second Test at Headingley in Leeds, but another two goals to Sullivan and winger Jack Woods' try sealed the series for England 7-5. The third Test—back at Station Road—was a more free-flowing contest, although England prevailed 19-16 to complete the cleansweep. Brown and Sullivan kicked five goals apiece, but England's three tries outstripped Australian touchdowns to five-eighth Vic Hey and lock Wally Prigg. Rugby League history was created on New Year's Eve, 1933, when Australia and England—largely thanks to the lobbying of Kangaroos manager Harry Sunderland—staged an international in France. On a frozen pitch in Paris, Australia romped to a thrilling 63-13 victory, with Dave Brown scoring 27 points in a match that was crucial to the eventual establishment of the code in France.

Brown scored an extraordinary 285 points on tour (from 19 tries and 114 goals) to smash Dally Messenger's 1908-09 mark by 130 points, which was never remotely challenged as a Kangaroos record. Remarkably, Brown was not a recognised goalkicker before the tour, but he went on to become one of Rugby League's greatest point-scorers. He was second on the squad's tryscoring lists, behind only powerhouse Wests winger Alan Ridley, who crossed 25 times in just 27 appearances. The Kangaroos won 27 of their 37 matches.

1936 LIONS TOUR—STEHR SENT OFF TWICE AS ENGLAND'S ASHES DOMINANCE CONTINUES Dual international fullback Jim Brough captained the Lions after Jim Sullivan withdrew from what would have been a record-breaking fourth tour for family reasons. Brough was ruled out of the first Test with injury and centre Artie Atkinson led England onto the SCG, but Australia won the opening encounter at home for the first time since 1920. Captain Dave Brown, the superlative Eastern Suburbs centre, was at the peak of his powers after a mind-boggling season of achievement in 1935, and scored two tries and four goals in Australia's 24-8 victory. Australian prop Ray Stehr was sent off with British counterpart Nat Silcock, who was an unfortunate victim of mistaken identity—Stehr had clashed with backrow enforcer Martin Hodgson in a scrum, but referee Lal Deane marched Silcock in error.

Brough returned for the second Test in Brisbane and a double to winger Alan Edwards helped England to a 12-7 series-levelling victory. Centre Gus Risman, who led the Lions to Australia a decade later, was named captain for the decider after Brough again pulled out with injury. Meanwhile, Australian selectors opted to carry three props in the front-row and drop hooker Percy Fairall—a surprising decision that proved crucial in the context of the match, as all time great Queensland prop Mick Madsen was dominated in the scrums in his hooking debut. Stehr was sent off again, this time after being decked by England prop John Arkwright, who was also dismissed. England retained the Ashes trophy with another 12-7 result, building a 12-2 lead in the second half before a dazzling run by Australian lock Wally Prigg set up brilliant pivot Vic Hey for a try late in the match. England defeated New Zealand 2-0 in the subsequent two-Test series.

1937-38 KANGAROO TOUR—ASHES SUCCESS ELUDES WALLY PRIGG'S KANGAROOS Newcastle lock Wally Prigg became the first player to embark on three Kangaroo Tours and was honoured with the captaincy of the 1937-38 squad. Hit by injuries and the player drain to English club football, the tourists were among the least successful to leave Australia's shores. Key forward Sid 'Joe' Pearce broke his leg in the second Test against New Zealand en route to England (his place was taken in the squad by future great Herb Narvo), while the quality of unavailable players was emphasised by tour match losses to Warrington (containing Dave Brown and Bill Shankland) and Leeds (featuring Vic Hey and Eric Harris).

England won the first Test 5-4, but the match could have resulted in an Australian victory had Prigg given Easts centre Jack Beaton the opportunity to attempt a long-range penalty goal late in the game—the skipper instead opted to push for a try and the game was lost. The Gus Risman-led hosts wrapped up their retention of the Ashes with a comprehensive 13-3 result in the second Test. The Kangaroos salvaged some credibility by reversing the scoreline in the third encounter, downing England 13-3 in Huddersfield with tries to Narvo, Queensland five-eighth Jack Reardon and Andy Norval, the great Easts lock who was playing out of position on the wing.

With a disappointing record of 13 wins and a draw in 25 matches in Britain, the Kangaroos set off on a trailblazing trek of France, winning nine of their 10 matches—including both Test matches. Beaton was the tourists' top point-scorer with 124, while Prigg became the first forward to lead the tryscoring stakes on a Kangaroo Tour, scoring 13 to finish equal with Reardon.

1946 LIONS TOUR—THE INDOMITABLES Welsh legend Gus Risman led the first post-World War II touring team—nicknamed 'The Indomitables' after the aircraft-carrier that transported the squad from England—to Great Britain's first unbeaten series victory in Australia. A brilliant long-range try to Test debutant winger Lionel Cooper (who, along with five-eighth Pat Devery, left to play in England at the end of the year) secured an 8-all draw for the hosts in the first Test at the SCG. The Lions battled on with 12 men after centre Jack Kitching was sent off during the first half. Great Britain prevailed 14-5 in the second encounter in Brisbane (after the Australian side had to be snuck into Lang Park via a back gate due to the throng of supporters desperate to get into the sold out venue) despite hooker Joe Egan being dismissed late in the contest, before wrapping up a 2-0 series triumph 20-7 back in Sydney. Centres Joe Jorgensen and Ron Bailey captained the inexperienced Australian side during the series, while the tourists featured British legends such as Egan, prop Ken Gee and fullback Ernest Ward, who kicked 17 goals in a 94-0 defeat of Southern Districts in Mackay. The Lions lost tour games to NSW South Coast, Newcastle and Queensland, while New Zealand upset Great Britain 13-8 in a subsequent one-off Test in Auckland.

1948-49 KANGAROO TOUR—SELECTION CONTROVERSY OVERSHADOWS FIRST POST-WAR TOUR The announcement of the 1948-49 Kangaroo Tour squad was met with disbelief and bewilderment by all and sundry—the 28-strong side was missing incumbent Australian captain-coach Len Smith. The Newtown centre's exclusion—apparently due to the greedy ambitions of a selector—remains one of the darkest episodes in Australian Rugby League history *(see Bolters, Controversial*

Selections and Shock Omissions). Wests centre Col Maxwell was the surprise choice to captain-coach the tourists, an inexperienced bunch that lost the Test series against Great Britain in a convincing 3-0 whitewash.

Easts five-eighth Wally O'Connell captained Australia in the injury-enforced absence of Maxwell as Great Britain prevailed 23-21 in a magnificent first Test at Headingley. The Kangaroos trailed 17-6 with little more than a quarter of the match remaining before launching a stunning comeback. Souths fullback Clive Churchill, playing in his second Test, came up just short of the tryline in the dying seconds to allow the Ernest Ward-led hosts to hold on. But Great Britain was far superior in the remaining Tests, winning 16-7 at Station Road and sealing the cleansweep with an emphatic 23-9 victory at Bradford's Odsal Stadium. Maxwell returned as skipper for the second Test, before Queensland forward Bill Tyquin led Australia in the third encounter. The Kangaroos won the Test series 2-0 on the French leg of the tour.

Although outclassed by Great Britain, the Kangaroos featured many players that would feature prominently in the halcyon successes of the 1950s. Churchill, hooker Kevin Schubert and forwards Duncan Hall, Jack 'Dutchy' Holland and Fred de Belin later featured in Australia's 1950 Ashes triumph. Tempestuous winger Johnny 'Wacka' Graves was the Kangaroos' top point-scorer with 118, while he shared top try-scorer honours with Queensland centre Jack Horrigan on 16 touchdowns.

1950 LIONS TOUR—AUSTRALIA BREAKS ASHES DROUGHT Great Britain's visit to Australia in 1950 represents one of the most significant milestones in Australia's Rugby League history as the Clive Churchill-led green-and-golds secured the prized Ashes trophy for the first time in 30 years. Captained by Ernest Ward, Great Britain won the first Test at a muddy SCG 6-4, with Lions winger Jack Hilton's two tries outdoing Australian counterpart Noel Pidding's two goals. Australia rallied in Brisbane, building a 7-3 lead before Great Britain halfback Tommy Bradshaw and prop Ken Gee were sent off during the second half, allowing the home side to stretch out for a 15-3 victory with two late tries.

The decider in Sydney was played on a SCG quagmire, with 40 tonnes of river sand spread on the pitch to alleviate the deluge that had transformed the famed venue into a swimming pool. Skippers Churchill and Ward traded penalty goals for a 2-all halftime scoreline, before St. George winger Ron Roberts etched his name into Rugby League folklore with 14 minutes of the series remaining. The conditions limited free-flowing attack, but Australia pieced together a sweeping backline movement and 19-year-old centre Keith Middleton drew Hilton to put Roberts in the clear. The tall flanker powered 40 yards to the Sheridan Stand corner to score the most famous try in the Australian game's history. The hosts defended their 5-2 lead grimly to break Great Britain's three-decade stranglehold on the Ashes in arguably the greatest moment of Australia's 104-year Rugby League narrative. The 'Old Enemy' was finally vanquished. The relatively young Australian side featured the Western Suburbs scrumbase combination of Keith Holman and Frank Stanmore, each playing in their first Test series, while Churchill was magnificent in his first series as captain.

The Lions racked up more than 80 points three times in tour matches, but lost to Queensland and Southern Division, while New Zealand scored a 2-0 series victory over the weary tourists.

1952-53 KANGAROO TOUR—CHURCHILL'S KANGAROOS RELINQUISH

ASHES Inspirational fullback and captain-coach Clive Churchill led a Kangaroos squad to England given little chance of retaining the Ashes in the wake of a dismal series loss to New Zealand earlier in the year. The wily Great Britain line-up—led by five-eighth Willie Horne—won back the cherished prize inside two Tests, but Australia fared better than expected and achieved an emphatic third Test victory.

Horne kicked five goals in Great Britain's 19-6 victory in the opening Test at Headingley, while Australia was kept try-less. Doubles to three-quarters Doug Greenall and Frank Castle provided the impetus for a series-sealing 21-5 result in the second encounter at Station Road, with Newtown centre Col Geelan's try little more than a consolation score for Australia. Pride was restored following a second half scoring spree in the third Test. The Kangaroos led 9-7 at halftime, before piling on four tries for a 27-7 final score. Tommy Ryan scored two tries and his fellow St. George winger Noel Pidding bagged a try and six goals, while vice-captain Duncan Hall became the first player sent off in an Anglo-Australian Test in England after an in-goal incident with British centre Ernest Ward.

Despite being lambasted as 'the weakest team to represent Australia abroad' prior to their departure, the Kangaroos lost just one match in Britain outside the Test series (an early tour game against St. Helens), while the squad contained all time greats Churchill, Hall, Keith Holman, Brian Carlson, Ken Kearney, Brian Davies, Harry Wells and Roy Bull. But France, still glowing from 'Les Chanticleers' famous 1951 series triumph in Australia, continued to have the wood on Australia with a 2-1 Test series victory. Pidding top-scored with 228 points—second only to Dave Brown's 1933-34 total—and the casual genius Carlson scored 29 tries in just 19 games, a total bettered only by the famed 1921-22 trio of Blinkhorn, Horder and Burge.

1954 LIONS TOUR—ABANDONED INTERNATIONAL OVERSHADOWS

AUSTRALIA'S ASHES TRIUMPH Clive Churchill became the first player to captain Australia in three series against Great Britain, leading his country to another Ashes triumph on home soil in a high-scoring Test series. Australia romped home in the first Test at the SCG, building on a 10-5 halftime lead to power away by a then-record 37-12. Centre Ken McCaffery scored two tries, while winger Noel Pidding set an unprecedented mark with 19 points from a try and eight goals.

But Pidding was trumped by Welsh dual international fullback and pointscoring wizard Lewis Jones in the second Test in Brisbane. Jones kicked an Ashes record 10 goals for a 20-point haul in the Lions' series-levelling 38-21 victory. Winger Billy Boston, just 19 years of age, scored two tries in the convincing win, and racked up a Lions record 36 touchdowns in just 18 tour games. The magnificent Brian Carlson netted a double for the beaten hosts.

The tour descended into disgrace in the lead-up to the third Test; after 54 brawling minutes of the Lions' match against New South Wales, referee Aub Oxford walked off the SCG after being unable to stem the violence and thuggery *(see Bizarre Matches)*. Great Britain selected several forwards in the backline and was accused of trying to injure NSW's Test stars before the decider. But thankfully, the third Test at the SCG was played in the spirit in which Rugby League is intended, and the rivals produced a thrilling conclusion to the series. Great Britain led 8-0 early, before Australia recovered to build a 15-8 advantage just after halftime. The combatants traded tries, with Lions captain and five-eighth Dickie Williams scoring his second touchdown seven minutes from fulltime, but it was not enough to retain the Ashes as Australia held on for a 20-16 result.

The Lions defeated New Zealand 2-1 in the subsequent Test series, while Lewis Jones finished with 278 points from just 21 tour matches.

1956-57 KANGAROO TOUR—DIFFICULT TOUR FOR KEARNEY-LED

KANGAROOS Hooker Ken Kearney was controversially selected to captain-coach the Kangaroos after leading St. George to the first of its 11 consecutive premierships, chosen ahead of Clive Churchill. The disappointing tour, in which Australia lost nine of its 19 games in Britain, also brought down the curtain on the glittering Test career of 'The Little Master.'

Great Britain, led by prop Alan Prescott, won the opening Test 21-10; powerhouse Welsh winger Billy Boston scored two tries in the convincing victory. Churchill was dropped from the Test side for Newtown custodian Gordon 'Punchy' Clifford, who kicked five goals as Australia regrouped to take out the second Test 22-7. Halves Bob Banks and Keith Holman, and props Brian Davies and Roy Bull scored tries in the stunning turnaround. But hopes of a drought-breaking series victory in England were dashed by Great Britain's emphatic five-tries-to-nil, 19-0 shutout at Station Road.

Churchill played one final Test for Australia—the 15-8 first Test victory over France—but Clifford, who top-scored for the Kangaroos with 94 points, returned as Australia completed a 3-0 series whitewash. Speedy winger Ian Moir was the squad's top try-scorer with 13, ahead of Queensland flanker Dennis Flannery (12) and Maitland flyer Don 'Bandy' Adams (11).

1958 LIONS TOUR—COURAGEOUS CAPTAIN INSPIRES GREAT BRITAIN

ASHES VICTORY The brave performance of Lions captain Alan Prescott to remain on the field with a broken arm was the catalyst for a stirring series-saving win in the second Test against Australia, and a precursor to a record-breaking victory in the decider. Australia, captained by Queensland forward Brian Davies, surged to a convincing 25-8 result in the series-opener at the SCG after leading 18-0 at halftime. The 1957 World Cup champions firmed in favouritism to reclaim the Ashes with a Test to spare in Brisbane, but despite Prescott's injury in the opening minutes, Great Britain led 10-2 at the break and powered to a 25-18 upset. The front-rower's bravery was immortalised, with the Test henceforth referred to as 'Prescott's Test' *(see Courageous Performances)*.

Without injured skipper Prescott for the decider, Great Britain was captained by five-eighth Phil Jackson at the SCG. Leading just 14-12 at halftime, the Lions embarked on a scoring blitz in the second term and when the dust settled, Great Britain had kept possession of the Ashes with a stunning 40-17 result. Winger Mike Sullivan scored three tries in the rampage, and finished the tour with a Lions record 38 tries—aided by a seven-try haul in a match against Western Australia played after the New Zealand leg of the tour. The Test series against the Kiwis was drawn 1-all, while a 24-all draw against Western Division was the only one of 25 minor tour games the triumphant Lions did not win. Besides the veteran Prescott, Great Britain's engine-room contingent contained revered forwards Vince Karalius, Dick Huddart and Brian McTigue.

1959-60 KANGAROO TOUR—BARNES' KANGAROOS CLOSE TO ASHES SUCCESS AS GREATS EMERGE

Balmain fullback Keith Barnes captained the 1959-60 Kangaroos on a memorable tour of Britain and France, leading a squad bursting with future legends of Rugby League. Reg Gasnier, Johnny Raper, Ken Irvine and Noel Kelly—a quartet that was named in the ARL's Team of the Century almost half a century later—each made the first of three Kangaroo Tours. Clive Churchill ventured on his fourth Kangaroo Tour, this time as non-playing coach.

Gasnier scored a dazzling hat-trick in his maiden Ashes Test, while centre partner Harry Wells also crossed and Barnes landed five goals as Australia carved out a 22-14 victory in the first Test—the Kangaroos' first win in an Ashes series-opener in England since the 1929-30 tour. Two tries to Brian Carlson propelled Australia to a 10-6 lead early in the second half, before Carlson (deputising for Barnes, who had pulled a hamstring) thudded a penalty attempt into the upright. Great Britain lock Johnny Whitely scored 16 minutes from fulltime and Neil Fox's conversion put the hosts in front 11-10—which is where the score remained as a famous series victory slipped from the Kangaroos' grasp. Fox scored a try and kicked six goals in Great Britain's 18-12 success in the deciding third Test. A flash of Gasnier brilliance to send Carlson away for a try was a rare attacking highlight in a dour contest.

The Kangaroos swept France in the Test series 3-0 before making a groundbreaking trip to Italy, winning internationals 37-15 and 67-22. Barnstorming St. George winger Eddie Lumsden scored 25 tries, followed by Gasnier (20), Carlson (19) and Irvine (17). The phenomenal goalkicking of Barnes netted 202 points (from 101 goals)—the fourth-highest total in Kangaroos history.

1962 LIONS TOUR—IRVINE'S FAMOUS GOAL THWARTS CLEANSWEEP FOR BRILLIANT TOURISTS

The great centre Eric Ashton led arguably the finest Lions tourists to Australia in 1962. The squad featured prodigious pointscoring centre Neil Fox, the ever-prolific tryscoring winger Billy Boston (who was controversially excluded from the 1958 squad), veteran lock Derek Turner, and returning Lions stars Alex Murphy, Dick Huddart, Brian McTigue and Mike Sullivan. Ashton and Sullivan scored two tries apiece in Great Britain's emphatic 31-12 first Test victory. Reg Gasnier became Australia's youngest Ashes captain in the loss, before Keith Barnes was reinstated as skipper for the second Test—a superb series-winning 17-10 victory for the Lions, despite losing halfback Murphy with an ankle injury during the second half. Boston scored a double for Great Britain.

The dead-rubber third Test witnessed one of the most thrilling and eventful encounters in Ashes history. Sullivan was sent off for throwing a punch at opposing winger Ken Irvine, while Turner was marched along with Australian prop Dud Beattie. Needing to leave the field due to a dislocated shoulder, Beattie famously goaded Turner into fighting him, and the pair was despatched by referee Darcy Lawler. Despite being down to 11 men, Great Britain led 17-11 inside the final quarter. But Irvine kept Australia in touch with a penalty goal, before flashing over in the corner for his second try in the dying minutes (from a dubious pass by Wests forward Bill Carson). In an oft-recounted yarn, the legendary winger—only a stopgap goalkicking option—landed the touchline conversion after Lawler suggested adjusting the positioning of the ball, snatching an epic 18-17 victory on fulltime.

665

The Lions again succumbed to Newcastle and Southern Division on tour, but they smashed the all-conquering St. George side—on the verge of their seventh straight premiership—33-5. New Zealand thumped Great Britain 19-0 and 27-8 in an upset 2-0 series victory.

1963-64 KANGAROO TOUR—TRIUMPHANT KANGAROOS RETURN WITH THE ASHES

Dominant performances in the first two Tests against Great Britain secured a euphoric Ashes series victory for the 1963-64 Kangaroos—the first all-Australian team to win a Test series in England (the 1911-12 Kangaroos also contained New Zealand players). Wests' dual international half Arthur Summons was chosen to captain-coach the squad, but injury ruled him out of the Tests against Great Britain. St. George hooker Ian Walsh had the honour of leading the Australian team out during the Ashes series.

Reg Gasnier repeated his feat of four years earlier by racing over for three tries in Australia's 28-2 victory in the first Test at London's Wembley Stadium. His centre partner and St. George teammate Graeme Langlands scored a try and kicked five goals, while winger Ken Irvine and fullback Ken Thornett also crossed against Eric Ashton's shell-shocked Great Britain side. But an even more emphatic result awaited the hosts in the second Test at Station Road. In what became known as 'the Swinton Massacre,' the Kangaroos produced arguably the greatest performance in Australia's Test history. The 50-12 destruction smashed records for biggest win and highest score in an Ashes Test, while Irvine scored three tries, Gasnier and winger Peter Dimond scored two each, and Langland amassed an Ashes record-equalling 20 points from two tries and seven goals. But the undoubted star was lock Johnny Raper. 'Chook,' in the top bracket of Rugby League's greatest players, played his finest hand of an incomparable career in the Test. He sliced through the Great Britain defence at will to have a hand in nine of Australia's 12 tries, and tackled with trademark tenacity and precision.

Great Britain won a rough-and-tumble third Test 16-5 after Australian halfback Barry Muir and forward enforcer Brian Hambly, along with British counterpart Cliff Watson, were sent off by 'The Sergeant Major,' referee Eric Clay. The Kangaroos finished with 10 men after Irvine was carried off with injury. Summons returned in the second Test against France to lead Australia to a 2-1 series victory, after the Kangaroos had lost the first encounter. Langlands scored 207 points—the third-highest total in Kangaroos history—while Irvine topped the tryscoring charts with 29 in 28 appearances.

1966 LIONS TOUR—LUCKLESS LIONS NARROWLY DEFEATED IN EPIC ASHES SERIES

A new breed of Lions tourists ventured to Australia in 1966 after the experienced campaigners of four years earlier, including tenacious halfback Tommy Bishop, brilliant five-eighth Alan Hardisty and front-row enforcer Cliff Watson. Harry Poole was the tour captain, but was ruled out of the Ashes series with injury and prop Brian Edgar led Great Britain against Australia. The Lions overturned an 8-7 halftime deficit to win the opening Test 17-13, with a sensational individual try by lightweight pivot Hardisty the highlight. The Ian Walsh-captained home side levelled the series 6-4 in the first try-less Test since the 1933-34 Kangaroo Tour, after Lions second-rower Bill Ramsey was sent off on a kicking charge early in the second half.

Arthur Beetson made his Test debut in the second-row in a tantalising decider at the SCG. The Queensland-bred, Balmain tyro spearheaded Australia's 8-2 halftime lead, throwing an overhead pass for Ken Irvine to score the opening try, before busting the defensive line and kicking ahead for Johnny King to score. The burly forward was replaced at halftime due to injury—spawning the derisive tag 'Half a Game Artie'—but Beetson's cameo ranks as one of the most memorable in Australia's Test history. Another kicking send-off—this time against Lions hard-man Watson (who became just the second player after Australian prop Ray Stehr to be sent off twice in Ashes Tests)—left Great Britain a man short for most of the second half, but Hardisty scored an intercept try and was awarded the first-ever Ashes penalty try for the tourists to trail just 16-14. Irvine's third try sealed Australia's retention of the Ashes, 19-14 over the plucky Lions.

The Lions suffered eight losses in minor tour matches in Australia, including a 9-8 defeat to Balmain (the first suffered by Great Britain against a club side), but scored a drought-breaking 5-2 win over Newcastle and won the Test series in New Zealand 2-0.

1967-68 KANGAROO TOUR—BOWLER HAT HIGHLIGHTS CONTROVERSIAL ASHES-WINNING TOUR

The Kangaroo Tour was embroiled in a storm before the team jetted to Britain, following revelations several members of the squad had privately been told they had been selected well before the team was announced. Australia returned with the Ashes after its third straight series victory against Great Britain and won consecutive series in England for the first time, but player misbehaviour away from the frosty playing fields and a winless Test series against France marred the Reg Gasnier captain-coached 1967-68 Kangaroos' achievements.

A new-look Great Britain line-up posted a 16-11 win in the first Test at Headingley, after the scores were locked 7-all at halftime. Five-eighth Roger Millward, playing in just his second Test, scored a try and kicked three goals, while Graeme Langlands scored all of Australia's points with a try and four goals. Langlands repeated those numbers in the second Test, and further tries to lock Ron Coote and winger Johnny King propelled Australia to a 17-11 victory after another halftime stalemate (2-all). The series-levelling win was particularly stoic considering injury ruled Gasnier and Johnny Raper out of the side; Queensland prop Peter Gallagher captained Australia in the second Test, before Raper returned to lead his country for the first time in the decider at Swinton—the scene of his heroics four years earlier. Tries to Coote, King and replacement Tony Branson provided the impetus for the Kangaroos' 11-3 triumph.

But reports of extensive damage to the team's hotel and the infamous 'Man in the Bowler Hat' controversy overshadowed the series victory. A member of the squad allegedly ventured out into the streets near the Ilkley Moor Hotel wearing nothing but a bowler hat, which consequently became the most famous clothing accessory in Rugby League history. Raper was pinpointed as the likely culprit and played up to the insinuations in the ensuing decades, but prop Dennis Manteit confessed to being the nude stroller in 1988. The less light-hearted matter of the damages resulted in players receiving fines after the tourists returned to Australia, while attitudes failed to improve on the French leg of the tour. France won the series 2-0 after the first Test was drawn. Langlands was the top point-scorer for the second straight

Kangaroo Tour with 101, and Newtown centre Brian 'Chicka' Moore led the squad with 10 tries. Gasnier made a comeback from his broken leg injury in Avignon, but eventually limped off in the last act of a career of indescribable quality, dripping with spectacular achievement.

1970 LIONS TOUR—LIONS RECOVER FROM FIRST TEST THRASHING TO TAKE ASHES Led by 31-year-old centre Frank Myler, the 1970 Lions achieved a remarkable Ashes series victory—Great Britain's last—despite crashing 37-15 to Australia in the first Test in Brisbane. Winger Johnny King and prop Jim Morgan scored two tries apiece, while captain Graeme Langlands kicked nine goals in the drubbing. A broken thumb ruled Langlands out of the remainder of the Ashes, and Great Britain levelled the series with an emphatic 28-7 victory over a John Sattler-captained Australian side in the second Test. Despite having centre Syd Hynes sent off in the 56th minute, the Lions continued to build on their 11-2 halftime lead. Five-eighth Roger Millward scored two tries and kicked six goals and a field goal for an Ashes record-equalling 20 points in one of Ashes Rugby League's most majestic individual displays.

Five-eighth Phil Hawthorne was installed as Australia's captain for the decider, but seven goals from debutant fullback Allan McKean was not enough to prevent a 21-17 victory as Great Britain outscored the hosts five tries to one. The triumphant squad returned as the most successful Lions tourists in history—the first Test defeat was their only loss. The 1970 Lions also set a remarkable record with all 26 squad members appearing in at least one Test in Australia or New Zealand. Millward and fellow 22-year-old Malcolm Reilly, a skilful and merciless lock who returned to play for Manly the following season, were the undisputed stars of the tour, while the likes of Cliff Watson provided vital experience.

1973 KANGAROO TOUR—CHANGA'S KANGAROOS TRIUMPH IN FIRST OF THE SHORTENED TOURS Graeme Langlands was named captain-coach for his third Kangaroo Tour of Britain and France—a streamlined expedition consisting of just 19 matches. It was the first Kangaroo Tour in six years, with a glut of World Cup tournaments filling the interim. Eager for revenge after relinquishing the Ashes at home in 1970 and losing the 1972 World Cup to Great Britain in a controversial final, Australia got off to a rocky start with a 21-12 loss in the first Test. Two second half tries to Great Britain backrower Phil Lowe, who won a premiership with Manly three years later, provided the impetus for the impressive result.

Langlands pulled out of the second Test with injury, but second-rower Bob McCarthy led the Kangaroos to a resolute 14-6 series-levelling win in howling winds at Headingley. McCarthy scored the only try of the match, while Langlands' replacement at fullback, debutant Graham Eadie (one day shy of his 20th birthday), defied the conditions to kick five goals. The Kangaroos again overcame adverse weather and injuries to carve out another brave triumph in the decider. Tenacious Wests halfback Tom Raudonikis captained Australia after McCarthy pulled out with injury, while the pitch at Wilderspool in Warrington was frozen. Despite the treacherous and unfamiliar conditions, Australia powered to a 12-2 halftime lead and held Great Britain off to regain the Ashes 15-5. Backrower Ken Maddison scored two tries in a career-defining performance, while five-eighth Bob Fulton and centre Geoff Starling also bagged three-pointers.

The Kangaroos, who were again pilloried for their off-field antics, comfortably accounted for France in the two-Test series (with Raudonikis and Arthur Beetson captaining a Test each) and lost just two games on tour—the first Test against Great Britain and a match against St. Helens. Bob Fulton's 20 tries from 14 matches was more than double his closest teammate, while young Gerringong centre Mick Cronin scored a tour-high 77 points. Langlands scored 66 points to take his Kangaroo Tour career tally to a record 374 points.

1974 LIONS TOUR—WRITTEN-OFF LIONS CHALLENGE AUSTRALIA IN HARD-FOUGHT ASHES SERIES
The heyday of British players starring in the Sydney premiership robbed the Lions of many talented players for the 1974 tour, and consequently the squad was tipped to struggle in the Ashes series. But Great Britain showed plenty of resolve throughout the tour, and went down to Australia by only 12-6 in the first Test. Queensland winger Warren Orr scored the only try of the match. Captain-coach Graeme Langlands was dropped as fullback from the second Test squad (although he remained as coach) for Graham Eadie. Arthur Beetson was installed as captain, but Australia suffered a shock 16-11 defeat at the SCG.

Langlands was reinstated for the deciding third Test and the match was a personal triumph for the great 'Changa.' Great Britain led 11-10 at halftime, but Langlands scored a brilliant try in the second half and kicked Australia to a 17-16 lead with a penalty goal. Ron Coote's try—converted by Langlands—sealed a 22-18 victory and the Ashes. The skipper passed 100 points in Ashes Tests during the match, and was chaired from the field by his teammates with the adoring SCG crowd chanting 'Changa! Changa!' Clever British hooker John Gray kicked six goals for the gallant tourists, who went on to record a 2-1 series victory in New Zealand.

1978 KANGAROO TOUR—ASHES SUCCESS BEFORE FRENCH SHOCK FOR FULTON'S KANGAROOS
Veteran five-eighth Bob Fulton was chosen to captain the Kangaroos in his international farewell, while a non-playing coach was selected for the team for the first time since the 1959-60 Kangaroo Tour. Fulton's former Manly mentor Frank Stanton assumed the Australian coaching post. The 1978 model was an experienced squad—despite the withdrawal of experienced stars such as Terry Randall for personal reasons, and a number of other notable selection omissions—with eight members of the 1973 squad returning for a second tour.

Rival halfbacks Tom Raudonikis and Steve Nash were sent off in the first Test at Wigan's Central Park for fighting, before Fulton's influence secured a 15-9 victory for Australia. The skipper scored a try, created another for 19-year-old winger Kerry Boustead and slotted a field goal after the scores were tied 6-all in a try-less first half. Captained by five-eighth Roger Millward, Great Britain's ageing but crafty side squared the series with an 18-14 success in the second Test. A bumper crowd in excess of 30,000 swarmed into Headingley for the third Test, but the decider was a fizzer—Australia dominated from the outset to construct a 19-0 halftime lead, and coasted to an eventual 23-4 win.

Widnes defeated the Kangaroos 11-10—the last time a club side has beaten Australia—in the tourists' only non-Test defeat of the British leg of the tour.

But France capitalised on a complacent Australian side and dubious local refereeing to win the Test series 2-0 in a stunning upset. The Kangaroos also succumbed to Les Espoirs, a French Colts line-up. Fulton and Balmain fullback/centre Allan McMahon finished as equal-top try-scorers with nine, while Parramatta centre Mick Cronin topped the pointscoring charts for the second successive Kangaroo Tour with 142.

1979 LIONS TOUR—LIONS SET RECORDS FOR ALL THE WRONG REASONS

The 1979 Lions marked the commencement of Great Britain Rugby League's sharp decline that lasted for almost a decade. Australia, captained by Canterbury hooker George Peponis, won an Ashes series 3-0 for the first time against a Great Britain side—an ageing squad dubbed 'Dad's Army' by the press—that was hopelessly outclassed. The tourists were swamped 35-0—an Ashes-record loss on Australian soil—in the first Test at Lang Park. Winger Kerry Boustead and man of the match Ray Price scored two tries each, while Mick Cronin equalled British legend Lewis Jones' Ashes record with 10 goals.

Tour captain Doug Laughton was ruled out of the remainder of the tour with injury following the first Test, but the Lions, led by prop George Nicholls, showed greater resolve in the second encounter. Cronin starred again with 18 points from two tries and six goals as Australia prevailed 24-16 at the SCG. The dead-rubber third encounter drew the smallest crowd for an Ashes Test in Australia, just 16,844, who witnessed the home side wrap up the historic whitewash 28-2. Cronin kicked eight goals for a world record total of 54 points for the series (beating Jones' mark of 48 set against France in 1956). The despondent Lions salvaged some pride with a 2-1 series victory in New Zealand.

1982 KANGAROO TOUR—THE INVINCIBLES

The 1982 Kangaroos etched their names into history by embarking on the first-ever unbeaten tour of Britain and France, winning all 23 matches (including a Test in Papua New Guinea en route to England) to be forever known as 'The Invincibles.' Captained by veteran Manly hooker Max Krilich and coached by Frank Stanton, the tourists became the first side in Test history to inflict a 3-0 series defeat on England or Great Britain on British soil and the first to go through a series unbeaten since the 'Australasian' Kangaroos of 1911-12. The Australian Test side was brimming with class from numbers one to 13, and deservedly rank as one of the greatest international combinations of all time. Such was the superstar calibre of the squad, vice-captain Wally Lewis was forced to play off the bench, unable to break up the Parramatta's young premiership-winning halves combination of Brett Kenny and Peter Sterling.

The Kangaroos' 40-4 trouncing of Great Britain in the first Test at Hull sounded an ominous warning for the remainder of the series, and they rounded out a spectacular series cleansweep with 27-6 and 32-8 thrashings at Wigan and Leeds respectively. Australia's backline was unstoppable: Eric Grothe scored tries in each of the first two Tests before injury ruled him out of the third; the centre combination of veteran Steve Rogers and newcomer Mal Meninga flourished, with Meninga collecting 48 points (two tries, 21 goals) for the series; and Kenny and Sterling—21 and 22 years old respectively—toyed with the British defence. Australia's forward contingent was no less dominant, with Balmain's Wayne Pearce establishing himself as a new star on the international scene and Les Boyd producing some of his best football at Test level, despite being sent off at Wigan.

Australia won the two Tests in France 15-4 and 23-9. Meninga top-scored with 166 points, while Manly and Queensland winger John Ribot was the top try-scorer on tour with 25 touchdowns. Parramatta three-quarters Steve Ella—who scored seven tries against French club Villeneuve, an equal-Kangaroo record—and Eric Grothe scored 21 tries each.

1984 LIONS TOUR—DISMAL LIONS SWAMPED The 1984 Lions were the worst on record, suffering 3-0 series cleansweeps against Australia and New Zealand. Great Britain was swamped 25-8 in the first Test in Sydney, a fiery clash that saw replacement forward David Hobbs sent off for a high tackle on Australian hooker Greg Conescu. Wally Lewis opened the scoring with a typically magnificent try, while subsequent second half tries to Ray Price, Kerry Boustead and Mark Murray highlighted the Lions' defensive ineptness. Great Britain was similarly outclassed in the second Test, 18-6 in Brisbane, before an improved showing back at the SCG. The Lions scored the first try, a brilliant solo effort to a young Ellery Hanley playing on the wing. But a trademark try to powerhouse winger Eric Grothe propelled Australia to an 8-7 lead just before halftime and fractured the Lions' brittle resolve. Second half touchdowns to Greg Conescu and Garry Jack sealed the 20-7 result and the whitewash.

Bradford Northern hooker Brian Noble, just 23 years of age, captained the squad after original choice Trevor Skerrett withdrew due to injury. Noble subsequently became Great Britain's youngest Ashes skipper.

1986 KANGAROO TOUR—THE UNBEATABLES The 1986 Kangaroos had plenty to live up to after the record-breaking exploits of four years earlier, but they lost nothing in comparison and were tagged 'The Unbeatables' after another flawless tour. There were several changes from the 1982 side—Peter Sterling and Brett Kenny (playing in the centres) were the only players to retain a starting spot in the 1986 Ashes series—but the new version was equally dominant. The Wally Lewis-captained side crushed Great Britain 38-16 in front of a 50,000-strong crowd at Old Trafford, with Gene Miles and Michael O'Connor each collecting hat-tricks. O'Connor added five goals for an Ashes-record 22-point haul. Australia's attacking brilliance was again at the forefront in the 34-4 second Test thrashing that wrapped up the series. Garry Jack scored two of the Kangaroos' six tries, becoming the first fullback to score a double in Ashes history. The hard-fought third Test represented Great Britain's best performance against Australia since its second Test victory over the Kangaroos at Bradford in 1978. Australia defeated a gallant Great Britain side 24-15 at Wigan's Central Park, with the hosts displaying promising signs for the future. A feature of the series was brilliant long-range tries scored by the British backs. Joe Lydon's try in the first Test was a classic, while Garry Schofield scored a magnificent double in the third encounter to give him four for the series.

Australia exposed France's dwindling stocks with 44-2 and 52-0 (including an Australian Test record-equalling four tries to winger Dale Shearer) drubbings in the two-Test series. O'Connor scored 44 points (four tries, 14 goals) in the Ashes series and 36 points (four tries, 10 goals) in the series against France to finish as the tour's top point-scorer with 190. Canterbury five-eighth Terry Lamb achieved the remarkable feat of playing in all 20 matches in Britain in France, coming off the bench in all five Tests and topping the squad's tryscoring charts with 19.

1988 LIONS TOUR—LIONS SHOW SPIRIT DOWN UNDER Expectations for the 1988 Lions were low following four consecutive 3-0 Ashes series defeats stretching back to 1979. The prospects of being competitive against the mighty Australian side appeared slim after the tourists crashed to heavy defeats against Northern Divsion (36-12) and Manly (30-0) in their first three matches. But in the first Test in Sydney— the maiden Test played at the Sydney Football Stadium and the 100th Anglo-Australian Test—Great Britain produced a big-hearted display, before eventually succumbing 17-6. A try to brilliant captain Ellery Hanley provided the Lions with a shock 6-0 halftime lead, but the star quality of the Australians eventually wore them down. Halfback Peter Sterling laid on tries for Sam Backo and Peter Jackson, before Jackson's second touchdown sealed the hard-fought result.

Great Britain's shabby display in the return clash at Lang Park belied its first Test improvement, with poor defence and ill-discipline the standout themes of a 34-14 loss. Led by another superb display from man of the match skipper Wally Lewis, Australia scored six tries in a polished performance. British pride was restored in the third Test, however, with a 26-12 boilover back in Sydney. After opening up a 10-0 halftime advantage, the Lions went on with job with three second half tries. Flamboyant winger Henderson Gill scored a magical double tries, while backrower Mike Gregory's match-sealing try, set up by man of the match Andy Gregory in a movement that covered 90 metres, typified the renewed spirit in the British side. It was Great Britain's first victory over Australia in a decade and the Lions' first on Australian soil since 1974. Burly Australian prop Sam Backo scored a try in each of the three Tests.

The Lions drew the two-Test series against New Zealand 1-all, with the 12-10 loss in the second encounter in Auckland costing Great Britain a berth in the World Cup final at the end of the year.

1990 KANGAROO TOUR—RICKY SAVES THE ASHES Mal Meninga was chosen to captain the Bob Fulton-coached Kangaroos after Wally Lewis was controversially ruled out after failing a medical on his broken arm injury, denying Lewis' bid to become the first player to skipper two Kangaroo Tours. Endeavouring to become the third consecutive tourists to go through Britain and France undefeated, the Kangaroos began the 1990 tour strongly, thrashing the cream of Britain's club sides. But a 37-match winning streak on British soil came unstuck in the first Test at Wembley. A penalty-riddled first half saw the combatants change ends at 2-all, but the second half glimmered with attacking sparkle. Great Britain winger Paul Eastwood scored a double, the beneficiary of inspired lead-up work by captain Ellery Hanley and Garry Schofield, while Mark McGaw scored a classic solo try for Australia. With a record crowd for a Test in Great Britain (52,274) vigorously cheering their heroes on, the hosts held on for a 19-12 victory—Australia's first loss in England since 1978.

Australia had not lost an Ashes series since 1970, but it took a villain-to-hero performance from Test rookie Ricky Stuart at Old Trafford to level the series and realise arguably the greatest escape in Test match history. The Kangaroos led a gripping match 10-6 midway through the second half following a four-pointer to Cliff Lyons that ranks among the best tries ever scored in an international, passing through 14 sets of hands before Andrew Ettingshausen's centring kick sat up for the mercurial Manly pivot to score. But Canberra linchpin Stuart, who replaced Allan Langer as halfback among seven starting line-up changes after the Wembley loss, allowed Great Britain to equalise with a long pass that was intercepted by replacement winger Paul Loughlin, who ran 50 metres to score. With the clock deep into injury time and the Kangaroos hemmed inside their half, Stuart produced the ultimate redemption play when he dummied and broke into the clear on his own quarter-line. Stuart scampered 70 metres and with the Great Britain defence converging, Mal Meninga loomed in support, bustling British defenders aside, to take a short ball from Stuart and crash over for the unforgettable match-winner.

Great Britain was left to rue the lost opportunity to take the Ashes with a Test to spare. Australia returned home with the trophy after a 14-0 shutout at Elland Road. Giant second-rower Paul Sironen was the standout performer of a supreme defensive effort, comprehensively negating the brilliance of Great Britain skipper Ellery Hanley. It was the first time Great Britain had been held scoreless by Australia on home soil since the 0-0 draw against Australia at Swinton in 1930. Greg Alexander was the tour's top point-scorer with 156—aided by a total 36 points in the 60-4 and 34-10 Test thrashings of France—and Andrew Ettinghausen led the squad with 15 tries, one ahead of Alexander.

1992 LIONS TOUR—AUSSIES RETAIN ASHES DESPITE MELBOURNE SHOCK

The outlook for Great Britain's 1992 Ashes challenge was grim—the Lions narrowly beat Papua New Guinea en route to Australia, and inspirational captain Ellery Hanley lasted just nine minutes of his only appearance of the tour against Newcastle, breaking down with injury. Pre-series predictions of an Australian rout seemed on track when the green-and-golds swept the Lions aside 22-6 in the first Test in front of a 40,141-strong crowd at the SFS with captain Mal Meninga crossing for two tries. But in one of Ashes history's most stunning turnarounds, Great Britain thumped Australia 33-10 at Melbourne's Princes Park in the second Test—the first time the two nations had met in the Victorian capital. The Lions were simply electrifying. New captain Garry Schofield was especially majestic, scoring a brilliant solo try and kicking a field goal. The 23-point thrashing equalled the 1958 Lions' 40-17 victory in Sydney as Australia's biggest defeat against Great Britain.

A man of the match performance from Meninga in a gripping decider helped secure the Ashes with a 16-10 third Test win at Lang Park. The captain scored a try and kicked three goals, while Canberra teammate Laurie Daley crossed for Australia's other four-pointer. The Lions drew a thrilling two-Test series against New Zealand 1-all, going down 15-14 after a late Daryl Halligan field goal, before levelling the series 19-16 in the second encounter.

1994 KANGAROO TOUR—BIG MAL'S LAST STAND

Retiring centre great Mal Meninga, already the Australia Test appearance record holder, became the first player to tour four times with the Kangaroos and the first player to captain two Kangaroo Tours. Nine of the 1990 tourists returned to Britain and France, while

Bradley Clyde and Ian Roberts—who were ruled out of the 1990 tour with injury—were selected for their maiden trip. The Test series of the 1994 Kangaroo Tour started exactly as it had been four years earlier—with a shock loss to Great Britain in the first Test at Wembley. Down to 12 men after Shaun Edwards became the first captain to be sent off in an Ashes Test for an ugly high tackle on Bradley Clyde, Great Britain famously held on for an 8-4 upset on the back of a brilliant individual try from Welsh fullback Jonathan Davies.

Coach Bob Fulton responded by making several changes, including dropping debutant winger Wendell Sailor for Rod Wishart and in another repeat of the 1990 Tour, bringing in Ricky Stuart for Allan Langer at halfback. The result was a commanding 38-8 demolition at Old Trafford, with greyhound fullback Brett Mullins scoring a double and Wishart kicking seven goals. As it had in the corresponding match of the 1990 series, Australia's defence in the decider at Elland Road was the key to retaining the Ashes. Great Britain was held try-less, suffocated out of the game by the Kangaroos, who scored two tries in the last 10 minutes to record an emphatic 23-4 victory.

Australia racked up a record 74-0 scoreline in the one-off Test against France, including a 26-point haul by Rod Wishart (one try, 11 goals) to equal Greg Alexander's Franco-Australian Test record set in the first Test of the 1990 series. Wishart was the tour's top point-scorer with 174 in just 11 games, at a Kangaroos record 15.82 points per game. Andrew Ettingshausen became just the second player (after his 1990 and 1994 Kangaroos coach Bob Fulton) to lead a Kangaroo squad's tryscoring charts twice, crossing 15 times in 11 games.

2001 KANGAROO TOUR—THE SERIES THAT ALMOST WASN'T The first Ashes series and Kangaroo Tour for seven years was almost cancelled due to the worldwide unease caused by the terrorist attack on New York's World Trade Centre on September 11, 2001. The ARL initially cancelled the tour after several players voiced their concern over travelling to England, but the decision was reversed following public condemnation and pressure from English officials. A shortened tour was rescheduled, with all minor matches abandoned and the three Tests to be played on consecutive weekends. Brisbane prop Shane Webcke was the only player from the initial squad to stand by his original decision not to tour.

Great Britain continued a remarkable run by defeating Australia in the first Test on home soil for the third straight series. Game-breaking five-eighth Paul Sculthorpe mesmerised the lethargic Kangaroos with two tries and two field goals to spearhead a 20-12 upset. Facing the prospect of becoming the first Australian side to lose the Ashes in 31 years, the Chris Anderson-coached Kangaroos responded with a dominant display in the second Test. Andrew Johns scored 20 points from two tries and six goals and Darren Lockyer ran riot from fullback as Australia swept to a 40-0 lead before the hour mark. Great Britain scored two late consolation tries for a 40-12 final score. Despite a spirited effort in the decider, Great Britain was unable to wrest the Ashes from Australia, who outlasted the dogged hosts to record a 28-8 victory in captain Brad Fittler's final international appearance.

2003 KANGAROO TOUR—LOCKYER'S PATCHED-UP KANGAROOS CLINCH WHITEWASH Darren Lockyer's record-breaking run as national captain began in 2003, with the Kangaroos facing monumental odds to maintain Australia's 33-year stranglehold on the Ashes. A bevy of frontline contenders were unavailable for the tour due to injury, including seven players from Australia's mid-season defeat of New Zealand. A 30-16 defeat to the Kiwis in Auckland en route to England intensified scrutiny of the depleted squad. But the Kangaroos, coached by Chris Anderson, recorded the first Ashes whitewash since 1986 with victories in three remarkable cliff-hangers. With his side trailing 18-16 six minutes from fulltime in the first Test at Wigan, Lockyer ran the ball on the last tackle to put makeshift centre Craig Wing into space and backed up to score the match-winner. Great Britain competed bravely after having forward enforcer Adrian Morley sent off for a high tackle on Robbie Kearns in the first tackle of the match, but a double to popular Irish winger Brian Carney was not enough to prevent a 22-18 loss.

The Kangaroos wrapped up the series with a superb comeback victory in the second encounter at Hull. Great Britain rattled the tourists with three first half tries to lead 20-8, but tries either side of halftime to Craig Fitzgibbon and Brett Kimmorley reeled the margin back in to two points. Fitzgibbon levelled the scores with a penalty goal with 10 minutes to go and Kimmorley kicked the decisive field goal five minutes later, before Fitzgibbon iced the 23-20 win with another penalty goal in the dying moments. Although the Ashes were safely in their keeping, the Kangaroos were not finished breaking British hearts. Australia's third Test victory at Huddersfield was the most extraordinary of the series, with talismanic skipper Lockyer again the architect. Down 12-6 with four minutes on the clock, Australia drew level when Lockyer sent Brisbane teammate Michael De Vere in to score in the corner and Fitzgibbon coolly converted. In his last game at fullback before switching to five-eighth in 2004, Lockyer then received an awkward pass on the last tackle, 40 metres out from his own line going into the final minute. He made a break and unloaded a desperate pass away which was picked up by Craig Wing, who linked with halfback Kimmorley. After a 20-metre run, Kimmorley found Lockyer backing up and the captain brilliantly fired a pass to lock Luke Ricketson to score his second try, snatching an unbelievable 18-12 win. The 2003 series is the last time the Ashes have been contested to date.

OLD ENEMY, NEW FORMATS The era of fulltime professionalism eventually heralded the demise of the full scale Kangaroo Tour, a four-yearly expedition to England and France with the Australian national team that routinely ranked as a career highlight for those fortunate enough to be chosen. The last of the conventional Kangroo Tours was undertaken in 1994. But the advent of the Super League competition in the UK, which saw the domestic competition moved to the Northern Hemisphere summer, made an extended tour by a national side impractical, as Kangaroo Tour schedules were largely made up of clashes against club sides. But the demise of the Kangaroo Tour did not diminish the intense rivalry between Australia and Great Britain/England, despite the Ashes being contested just twice since 1994. World Cups and international tournaments have provided the stage for Anglo-Australian Rugby League combat to continue unabated.

1997 SUPER LEAGUE AUSTRALIA IN ENGLAND Super League sent an Australian representative side to play a full-strength Great Britain line-up in England at the end of the divided 1997 season. Although the matches are not recognised as Tests by the Australian Rugby League, the three-match series produced some entertaining football—and some anxious moments for an Australian side eager to prove Super League was superior to the ARL competition. A hat-trick by Australian captain Laurie Daley spearheaded a convincing 38-14 victory for the visitors in the first encounter, but Great Britain levelled the series with a 20-12 upset in the second Test. The boilover was largely due to poor discipline on the part of the Australians, and in particular sin-binned second-rower Gorden Tallis—the match finished two tries apiece but Andy Farrell kicked six goals for the home side. A dominant first half performance wrapped up the series for Australia in the third Test, building a formidable 25-2 lead at the break before coasting to a 37-20 final score.

1999 TRI-NATIONS IN AUSTRALIA The inaugural Tri-Nations tournament between Great Britain, New Zealand and Australia—contested in the latter two countries—was a disaster for the Poms. Australia, a week after a shock loss to the Kiwis, hammered the Lions 42-6 in the first Test between a full-strength Australian side and Great Britain since the 1994 Ashes decider at Elland Road. Fullback Darren Lockyer starred with two tries against the experienced tourists, while Wendell Sailor scored a memorable 80-metre touchdown. Great Britain exited the competition with another comprehensive loss to the Kiwis, who in turn narrowly went down to Australia in the final.

2002 ONE-OFF TEST IN AUSTRALIA The one-off Test at Sydney's Aussie Stadium proved to be one of the darkest hours in Britain's proud Rugby League history. The Lions were routed 64-10 by a rampant Australian side. Scott Hill and Darren Lockyer crossed for doubles among the hosts' 11 touchdowns, 10 of which were converted by Andrew Johns to equal the Anglo-Australian Test record held jointly by Welsh wizard Lewis Jones and Parramatta great Mick Cronin.

2004 TRI-NATIONS IN ENGLAND Great Britain entered the first England-based Tri-Nations tournament confident of knocking Wayne Bennett-coached Australia off its perch, particularly after the close nature of the 2003 Ashes series. Great Britain lost all three matches by narrow margins in 2003, but there was more heartbreak in store for the hosts' first match of the 2004 tournament. Trailing 8-4 at halftime, Australia scored to set up a lengthy stalemate, before Penrith winger Luke Rooney scored his second try in the final minute, planting the ball just inside the corner post to snatch a 12-8 win.

Buoyed by a 10-point win over the Kiwis a week later, Great Britain scored its first victory over Australia since the 1994 Kangaroo Tour (Australia lost to England at the 1995 World Cup). Great Britain scored three first half tries to open up an 18-6 lead at the break, but was forced to defend its lead grimly in the second half when Kangaroo prop Mark O'Meley scored shortly after the resumption. Despite a wealth of possession to the Australian side, Great Britain's lionhearted defence refused to submit, and a stoic 24-12 victory was sealed when Leeds centre Keith Senior snaffled an intercept try in the dying minutes.

Great Britain's ambitions of inflicting Australia's first Test series loss since 1978 was obliterated in the final at Elland Road by arguably the most dominant 40-minute performance in international football history. Captain Darren Lockyer was the chief architect as Australia ran in six first half tries to lead 38-0 at the break. Described by Immortal former Kangaroo captain and coach Bob Fulton as the most dominant individual performance in the history of the game, Lockyer tormented Great Britain with a perfect exhibition of every facet of Rugby League attack. There was some respite for Great Britain in the second half as Australia eased off the pedal, but the 44-4 final scoreline represented its biggest-ever loss on home soil—eclipsing the famous 50-12 'Swinton Massacre' of 1963.

2005 TRI-NATIONS IN ENGLAND Perhaps rocked by the nature of the defeat in the final of the previous year's Tri-Nations, Great Britain experienced a tournament to forget at the end of 2005. The hosts went down to New Zealand 42-26 in their opening match, before crashing 20-6 to Australia a week later. Great Britain was well in contention until late in the match, played in miserable conditions at Wigan, before two tries in the final five minutes wrapped up the Kangaroos' win built on iron-clad defence. St. George Illawarra centre Matt Cooper finished with two tries.

Great Britain kept its chances of making the final alive with a comprehensive 38-12 thrashing of the Kiwis at Huddersfield, but Australia bundled the home side out of the tournament with a four-tries-to-two, 26-14 defeat at Hull—despite having five-eighth Trent Barrett twice sent to the sin-bin. Newcastle hooker Danny Buderus captained Australia in the absence of the injured Darren Lockyer. New Zealand's win over Australia in the tournament-opener saw the Kiwis finish ahead of Great Britain on the points table, and the underdogs recorded a momentous 24-0 triumph over the Kangaroos in the final—Australia's first Test series defeat since 1978.

2006 TRI-NATIONS IN AUSTRALIA Two losses to New Zealand ruined Great Britain's chances of qualifying for the 2006 Tri-Nations final, but the Lions' first victory against the green-and-golds in Australia in 14 years offered some consolation. In a fiery Sydney Football Stadium clash, controversial Australian forward Willie Mason floored highly regarded Great Britain prop Stuart Fielden with a devastating punch early on, but it was the visitors who took the ascendancy when the two sides settled to play football. The scores were locked 6-all at the break and 12-all during the second half. Great Britain exhibited greater staying power, however, with tries to Lee Gilmour and Gareth Raynor, and a late field goal to mercurial halfback Sean Long rounding off a superb 23-12 defeat of their arch-enemies. Long returned home early from the tour in acrimonious circumstances, missing the return clash with Australia in Brisbane, won comfortably 33-10 by the home side and capped off by a sparkling long-range try to Brent Tate after the fulltime siren.

2009 FOUR NATIONS IN ENGLAND With Great Britain opting to permanently split into separate nations for international Rugby League (which previously occurred only at selected World Cups and European championships), England and France hosted the inaugural Four Nations tournament in 2009, joined by Australia and New Zealand. A repeat of the World Cup debacle from the previous season loomed for England when it trailed Australia 26-0 at halftime in Wigan. Five first half tries to Australia, including a long-range effort finished off by Darren Lockyer to lift the skipper to level with Ken Irvine as Australia's most prolific Test try-scorer (33),

677

virtually wrapped up the match. But England rallied in the second stanza, led by the British game's bright new hope: giant forward Sam Burgess. The soon-to-be South Sydney Rabbitoh powered over for England's first try and was a constant threat, before late tries to Wests Tigers backrower Gareth Ellis and centre Lee Smith gave the home side a brief sniff of victory. The scoring ended 26-16, but England enjoyed renewed hope that the gap was closing between the two nations.

England qualified for final rematch against Australia at Elland Road after defeating world champions New Zealand. Another king-sized upset was on the cards when a rampant Burgess propelled England to a 16-14 lead with half an hour to play. Burgess scored two tries, but a six-try blitz by Australia wrenched the final from the hosts' grasp in emphatic fashion. Billy Slater claimed a second half hat-trick, while the tournament's top try-scorer, Brett Morris, finished with a double. The 46-16 final score belied England's wholehearted effort, but was also a testament to the attacking brilliance of the Australian side, who partially buried the memories of their World Cup final defeat of 12 months earlier. Darren Lockyer became the first Australian player to rack up 50 Test appearances, while veteran prop Petero Civoniceva passed Johnny Raper as Australia's most-capped forward in his 40th Test appearance.

2010 FOUR NATIONS IN AUSTRALIA England's Four Nations expedition was another campaign to forget, missing the final after opening the tournament with convincing losses to New Zealand and Australia. Taking on the Kangaroos in Melbourne, England started promisingly, hitting back after Luke Lewis opened the scoring to take an 8-6 lead with a try to Sam Burgess and a penalty goal. But a bevy of handling errors and a couple of dubious video referee decisions cruelled England's chances of an upset. Trailing 26-8 at halftime, the visitors scored the first try of the second stanza but poor ball control at a wet AAMI Park prevented a genuine comeback threat and Australia cruised to a 34-14 victory en route to the final. Lewis finished with a double in the six-tries-to-two win, but the Kangaroos again fell to New Zealand in a final at Suncorp Stadium, 16-12 to the Benji Marshall-inspired Kiwis.

2011 FOUR NATIONS IN ENGLAND Following a comfortable tournament-opening 26-12 victory over defending champions New Zealand in Warrington, Australia booked a spot in the Elland Road final with a 36-20 success against hosts England in its last preliminary match. The Kangaroos led 12-8 at halftime and scored six tries in the win, while burly winger Ryan Hall scored a spectacular first half double for England. But the result was soured for Australia by the broken collarbone injury suffered by superstar fullback Billy Slater in attempting to stop Hall's second try. He was replaced by St. George Illawarra custodian Darius Boyd for the final, while Brisbane's Jharal Yow Yeh took Boyd's place on the wing.

England swamped a dismal New Zealand outfit 28-6 to leapfrog the Kiwis into the final, while Australia warmed up for the decider with a 56-14 demolition of tournament minnows Wales. The final followed a remarkably similar script to the 2009 decider at the same venue. A contentious penalty try awarded to Leeds star Hall after a high tackle by Kangaroos halfback Johnathan Thurston pegged England back to 6-all in the first half. England put Australia under pressure early in the second half, before the composed visitors streaked away for a convincing victory. Thurston, who had been rated next to no chance of playing by coach Tim Sheens after sustaining a groin injury, spearheaded the Kangaroos' triumph by scoring a try and setting up touchdowns to Paul Gallen and Greg Inglis for a 26-8 lead. His conversion of Inglis' try hoisted him to level with Andrew Johns as Australia's third-top Test point-scorer on 226.

Retiring legend Darren Lockyer, extending his world record to 59 Test appearances in his last game of Rugby League, scored a fairytale kick-and-chase try in the dying moments (his 35th Test try, another record). But, in the last act of an incomparable career, Lockyer implausibly duffed the celebratory conversion attempt (*see Minties Moments*). The 30-8 victory was nevertheless a fitting farewell to the game for the record-breaking captain.

FRENCH RESISTANCE

The establishment of Rugby League in France was a gradual process. Rugby union was strong in the European nation in the early part of the 20th century, while under-the-table payments to 'amateur' players rendered Rugby League's obvious drawcard—financial compensation—largely redundant to French union players. The 1921-22 Kangaroos' attempts to stage a match in France were thwarted by rugby union officials. But the boycott of France as a rugby union Test opponent by England, Wales, Scotland and Ireland due to France's contravening of the amateur ethos opened the door for Rugby League during the 1930s.

Harry Sunderland, manager of the 1933-34 Kangaroos, was instrumental in setting up the first Rugby League match in France—an international exhibition clash between Australia and England in Paris. Australia prevailed 63-13 in a sparkling demonstration of attacking football, while the phenomenal centre Dave Brown scored 27 points and was chaired off the ground by the enamoured French crowd. A foothold for the code in France had been established. Former France rugby union star Jean Galia, who was also heavily involved in the staging of the exhibition match, assembled a team to tour England in 1934 and helped launch a domestic club competition.

France hosted the Wally Prigg-led 1937-38 Kangaroos in a two-Test series, with Australia emerging victorious 35-6 in Paris and 16-11 in Toulouse. After a maiden victory over England in 1939, World War II crippled Rugby League's progress in France. The Nazi Germany-aligned Vichy Government banned Rugby League in France in 1941, deeming the sport's officialdom sympathetic to the Allies' cause. Nazi supporters burned down the French Rugby League's headquarters, while all of its assets were handed over to the French Rugby Union—an injustice that the French Rugby League is yet to be compensated for.

The code slowly regrouped after the war. France featured in the European Championship and played Tests against New Zealand for the first time, securing a 1-all series result against the touring 1947-48 Kiwis. Queensland forward Bill Tyquin captained the 1948-49 Kangaroos to a hard-fought 2-0 series win in France—a precursor to the first French tour Down Under.

Les Chanticleers—as touring French teams became known—ventured to Australia and New Zealand in 1951, and the squad's deeds are entrenched in international Rugby League folklore. France's unpredictable and unorthodox attacking flair propelled the tourists to a shock 2-1 series victory. Fullback Puig-Aubert kicked seven goals in the 26-15 first Test victory at the SCG, before the Clive Churchill-led Australians squared the series 23-11 in Brisbane—a spiteful clash that prompted the Australian Board of Control to issue a stern warning to both sides in the lead-up to the decider. The third Test attracted an extraordinary 67,009-strong SCG crowd, who witnessed a stunning 35-14 French victory. Puig-Aubert slotted another seven goals, while halfback Jo Crespo raced over for three tries. The series defeat was a harsh reality check for the Australian side that regained the Ashes from Great Britain for the first time in three decades just 12 months earlier.

The French side contained the revered second-row pairing of Elie Brousse and Edouard Ponsinet—regarded by Rugby League historian George Crawford as the best combination of all time—and brilliant lightweight centre/five-eighth Jacques Merquey. But the undoubted star was the captain and cavalier genius Puig-Aubert. Notoriously casual in his approach to the game—reportedly smoking cigarettes while playing—Puig-Aubert's ability was beyond repute. He kicked 18 goals from as many attempts during the 1951 series and outplayed the incomparable Churchill, while also amassing 221 points on tour.

Churchill's 1952-53 Kangaroos were again thwarted; France recovered from a first Test loss to carve out a 2-1 series success. France hosted the inaugural World Cup in 1954 (finishing runners-up to Great Britain), before touring Australia again in 1955. Australian halfback Keith Holman scored two tries in a 20-8 first Test defeat of the visitors, who were without the injured Puig-Aubert's services for the series. But the spontaneous and often volatile French side overhauled a 12-point deficit to brilliantly snatch a 29-28 victory in the second Test in Brisbane. Captain Merquey scored two tries, while wonderful pivot Gilbert Benausse landed six vital goals. France toughed out an 8-5 triumph in the decider to secure a third successive series victory over Australia, in what was to be Churchill's last series as Australian captain.

Ken Kearney led the 1956-57 Kangaroos to an emphatic 3-0 series whitewash of hosts France (despite a 25-2 penalty count against them in the third Test as farcical French refereeing plunged to new depths), and Keith Barnes' 1959-60 tourists repeated the dose three years later. But remarkably, Australia was still unable to secure a series victory against France at home in 1960. Following an 8-all draw in the first Test, Australia swamped France 56-6 in the second encounter; Ken Irvine and debutant halfback Bobby Bugden scored hat-tricks, while captain Barnes slotted 10 goals. However, despite having centre Bernard Fabre sent off with 10 minutes remaining (bizarrely, Fabre refused to walk and had to be coaxed from the field by coach Jean Duhau), France held on for a 7-5 third Test victory. France scored just one try in the series, but somehow snatched a 1-all series draw.

France also claimed the first Test 8-5 from the Ashes-winning 1963-64 Kangaroos, before Australia won the ensuing two clashes. But France's stocks deteriorated momentarily—Australia refused to host a World Cup competition in 1965 after Les Chanticleers' dismal performances in a 3-0 series loss against the green-and-golds in 1964. Ever the enigmas of international Rugby League, however, France defeated the 1967-68 Kangaroos 2-0 in a home series (after the first Test was drawn) and qualified for the final of the 1968 World Cup in Australia, going down to the hosts 20-2 at the SCG.

But the French Test side struggled throughout the 1970s; they were convincingly beaten by the 1973 Kangaroos, while their only Southern Hemisphere tour was for a disappointing 1977 World Cup campaign in New Zealand and Australia. After just four wins in its last 31 Tests, France staged another bewildering boilover against Australia. In a series marked by diabolical local refereeing (a trademark of tours to France down the years), Bob Fulton's 1978 Kangaroos were defeated 13-10 and 11-10 in the two-Test series. Australia would not be beaten in a Test series or international tournament again for 27 years.

France won the 1980-81 European Championship with victories over England and Wales, but Les Chanticleers' Southern Hemisphere tour in 1981—their first full-scale tour in 16 years—was a disaster, conceding heavy defeats in 2-0 series losses to New Zealand and Australia. Although France was able to jag the odd win against Great Britain, it was no match for the touring Kangaroos and Kiwis sides during the 1980s, while the national side did not venture to Australia again until 1990.

Tas Baitieri, a veteran of 55 first grade games for Penrith and Canterbury from 1978-85, starred in French club Rugby League and took over as coach of the national side in the mid-1980s. His tenure was brief after becoming a victim of internal politics, but Baitieri maintained his involvement with Rugby League in the country and managed France's 2000 World Cup squad. His son, talented forward Jason, made his Test debut for France in 2010 and joined Super League club Les Catalans the following season.

No longer billed as a big enough drawcard to play in Sydney or Brisbane, France's one-off Test against Australia in 1990 was played in the New South Wales country centre of Parkes. Australia prevailed 34-2 on a freezing night, with debutant Brad Mackay scoring three tries. France hosted the Kangaroos at the end of the year and was pummelled 60-4 by the rampant tourists in the first Test—highlighted by Greg Alexander's 26-point haul—before a markedly better performance in a 34-10 loss in the second encounter.

French Rugby League was ebbing low and the 1994 season was almost a carbon copy of four years earlier—with a 29-22 loss to Papua New Guinea in Port Moresby en route to Australia thrown in for good measure. Australia trounced France 58-0 at Parramatta Stadium, while the Kangaroos amassed a record 74-0 scoreline against the struggling nation in Béziers at the end of the year, which doubled as retiring captain Mal Meninga's final Test.

Captained by halfback Patrick Entat—one of only a few French players of an elite standard during the first half of the 1990s—France endured a miserable campaign at the 1995 World Cup, losing its pool games heavily to Wales and Samoa. France was subsequently brushed by Australia and New Zealand in international scheduling, but fared better in the 2000 tournament with former veteran Test five-eighth Gilles Dumas as coach, winning pool games against Tonga and South Africa before suffering a 54-6 loss to the Kiwis at the quarter-final stage.

France's 2000 squad featured Warrington forward Jérôme Guisset, who made four NRL appearances off the bench for Canberra in 1999. Guisset amassed 272 Super League games in 11 seasons for Warrington, Wigan and Catalans. He captained a French Selection against the 2003 Kangaroos, represented France against Australia in 2005 and skippered his country's 2008 World Cup campaign.

In the jet-stream of the Super League revolution, Paris St. Germain formed in late-1995 and the fledgling club featured in the first two UK Super League seasons. After winning just three games in 1996, Paris St. Germain enlisted the services of former Western Reds coach Peter Mulholland for 1997, but he lasted just half a season and was replaced by ex-Great Britain international Andy Goodway. Despite improved results in the second half of the year, the club drew poor crowds and dissolved after narrowly missing relegation for the second successive season. Paris St. Germain's playing roster was bolstered by prominent Australian imports such as 1990 Dally M Rookie of the Year Jason Martin, two-time Dally M Lock of the Year Ian Russell, backrower Wayne Sing (all three joined from the North Queensland Cowboys), ex-St. George prop Tony Priddle and former Manly hooker David O'Donnell, along with New Zealanders David Lomax and Phil Bergman.

Based in Perpignan in the south of France, Catalans Dragons joined the European Super League in 2006, and has been augmented by a strong Australian and New Zealand influence since their inception. Former Newcastle and St. George mentor David Waite was the club's foundation coach, before being replaced midway through 2006 by dual Dally M-winning fullback Michael Potter. Brisbane great Kevin Walters succeeded Potter in 2009 for a two-season stint, and former Wests Tigers and Parramatta forward Trent Robinson took the reins in 2011.

Former Bulldogs and Warriors winger Justin Murphy scored 26 tries for Catalans in the 2006 Super League season, while Kiwi legend Stacey Jones was the club's linchpin as it surged to the 2007 Challenge Cup final—the first played at the new Wembley Stadium—with a line-up boasting ex-Canberra stalwart and Test player Jason Croker, Queensland Origin hero Adam Mogg, Kiwi Test forward Alex Chan and former St. George Illawarra fullback Clint Greenshields. Casey McGuire and Greg Bird captained the club in subsequent seasons, while Manly great and Test veteran Steve Menzies joined the French club in 2011. Catalans qualified for the Super League finals in 2009 and 2011. The club provides a tremendous pathway to professional Rugby League for young French talent.

France's Test team faced New Zealand and Australia in 2004 (both sides were in England for the Tri-Nations tournament) and almost caused two massive boilovers. After narrowly going down to the Kiwis 24-20 in Carcassonne, France staged a stirring comeback in its first Test against Australia since 1994, trailing just 34-30 in Toulouse with seven minutes remaining. But Australian captain Darren Lockyer sparked a late flurry of tries for a 52-30 final score.

Former Parramatta premiership-winning coach, and Wigan and Auckland mentor John Monie became France's Test coach in 2005, guiding the team to a 44-12 loss to Australia in Perpignan in his first year in charge. Monie took a French squad containing Australians Justin Murphy, former Wests Tigers centre John Wilson, former Cronulla and Souths fullback Jared Taylor and ex-Newcastle halfback James Wynne (after the quartet fulfilled residential qualifications) to the 2008 World Cup in Australia. France defeated Scotland in its first pool game, but was convincingly beaten by Fiji and Samoa.

France, with former firebrand Great Britain Test halfback Bobbie Goulding as coach, participated in the inaugural Four Nations tournament in 2009 with Greenshields and Auckland-born brothers Kane and Andrew Bentley bolstering the squad. After performing creditably in a 34-12 loss to England, France was swamped 62-12 by New Zealand and 42-4 by Australia, with debutant Penrith centre Michael Jennings crossing for a hat-trick. A loss to Wales in the 2010 European Cup denied France a place in the 2011 Four Nations tournament. The heady days of the 1950s were a distant memory, but the success of Catalans Dragons in Super League and the Test side's increased activity in recent seasons has ensured a significant French presence on the Rugby League landscape.

THE KUMULS

Papua New Guinea—Australia's closest geographical neighbour—is the only country in the world which claims Rugby League as its national sport. The code has a vibrant history in the nation, while the Papua New Guinean population's fanaticism for the game and its players is unparalleled. The game slowly became established in Papua New Guinea from 1949, when two teams were established in Port Moresby. The competition in the capital gradually expanded, while the game spread to populous areas such as Rabaul, Lae and Goroka.

Papua New Guinea was admitted as the fifth country to the International Board of Rugby League in 1974, the year before the nation gained its independence from Australia. Papua New Guinea played its first international against Great Britain at Lloyd Robson Oval in Port Moresby in 1975, going down 40-12 in a spirited performance, and also hosted the Pacific Cup (New Zealand Maori defeated Papua New Guinea in the final). France made its first daunting trip to the Melanesian island group in 1977 and failed to adapt to the conditions, succumbing 37-6 to the Papua New Guinean side. New Zealand visited in 1978 and was forced to work hard for a 30-21 victory, with Olsen Filipaina scoring a hat-trick for the Kiwis.

Papua New Guinea—nicknamed the Kumuls (translating to bird of paradise in Tok Pisin, the nation's official language)—embarked on a trailblazing tour of Britain and France in 1979. The Kumuls lost two hard-fought Test matches against France 16-9 and 15-2, while they won three of eight minor tour matches, including a 23-9 defeat of English county Cumbria. France and Papua New Guinea resumed the rivalry during Les Chanticleers Southern Hemisphere tour in 1981; the one-off Test match ended in a 13-all draw.

After a 56-5 loss to New Zealand in 1982, Papua New Guinea encountered Australia for the first time in Port Moresby. The Kangaroos were en route to an unbeaten tour of Britain and France, and defeated Papua New Guinea 38-2, with winger John Ribot crossing for an Australian Test record four tries. The Kumuls' first trip to New Zealand resulted in a 60-20 loss at Carlaw Park and a world record six tries to Kiwi backrower Hugh McGahan, but the Papua New Guinea side displayed plenty of mettle in holding the touring Great Britain Lions to 38-20 in 1984.

Papua New Guinea's reputation as the toughest destination in world Rugby League to visit was cemented following the Kiwis' 1986 tour. The sweltering conditions, high altitude, rock-hard playing fields, questionable refereeing and overzealous local crowds (which necessitated police escorts to and from the ground, while tear gas often had to be dispensed during games to disperse the baying supporters) drove touring teams to distraction. New Zealand prevailed 36-26 in the first Test in Goroka, but Papua New Guinea upset the weary Kiwis 24-22 in the second encounter in Port Moresby. Winger Dane O'Hara was denied a match-winning try on fulltime by Australian referee Kevin Roberts, who the Kiwis claimed was acting in self-preservation—the rabid crowd would have reportedly torn Lloyd Robson Oval apart had the try been awarded.[27] But no one could refute the wholehearted Kumuls' deservedness of a historic victory.

The Kangaroos again travelled to Britain and France via Papua New Guinea at the end of the 1986, defeating the Kumuls 62-12. Kumuls centre Bal Numapo, who later represented Rest of the World against Great Britain in 1988, scored both of the local side's tries.

Captained by Numapo, the Kumuls toured Britain and France for the second time in 1987, but were subdued 42-0 by Great Britain and 21-4 by France in one-off Test clashes. A 42-22 home loss to the touring Lions, a 66-14 defeat to New Zealand in Auckland and a 70-8 thrashing at the hands of Australia (including a then-world record 30-point haul to Michael O'Connor) in the New South Wales country centre of Wagga Wagga followed in 1988.

Wingers Dairi Kovae and Arnold Krewanty broke new ground in the late-1980s by playing for Australian premiership clubs. Kovae came off the bench in two matches for North Sydney in 1988, before joining Newcastle the following season and making eight appearances. He was joined at the Knights by Krewanty, who played two first grade games in 1989. Numapo spent 1989 with Canterbury, but did not break into first grade.

Papua New Guinea achieved another euphoric milestone in 1990, claiming its maiden Test win over Great Britain at Goroka. The Lions had to endure extreme heat, riots and tear gas from police to restore order in the crowd, but the Arebo Taumaku-captained Kumuls' 20-18 triumph ranks as one of the high points in Papua New Guinea's Rugby League history.

After narrow losses to New Zealand (1990) and France (1991) at home, Papua New Guinea hosted a tour by Australia in 1991, prompting unprecedented hysteria in the nation. Australia comfortably won the Tests 58-2 and 40-6, while the world champions prevailed in three spirited minor tour matches. Unfortunately, that tour is the last visit the Australian side has made to Papua New Guinea.

The Kumuls' Test performances followed a familiar pattern—another Northern Hemisphere tour at the end of 1991 garnered heavy defeats to Wales, Great Britain and France, while New Zealand swamped the minnows 66-10 in Auckland in 1992. But Papua New Guinea was a formidable proposition at home. Two tries in the final eight minutes by Lions winger Martin Offiah salvaged a 20-14 victory for Great Britain in Port Moresby in 1992.

In arguably Papua New Guinea's finest hour on the international Rugby League stage, the Kumuls held Australia to a 36-14 scoreline in Townsville in 1992. Coach John Wagambie claimed a moral victory after the match, while tongues were

---

27   John Coffey and Bernie Wood, *The Kiwis: 100 Years Of International Rugby League.* Auckland, 2007

wagging about livewire halfback Aquila Emil, who produced a dazzling chip-and-chase try. Emil became one of the first players signed by the North Queensland Cowboys for the fledgling club's 1995 entry to the premiership, although he was released from the deal before the Cowboys' debut. He later was heavily involved with schoolboy Rugby League in Papua New Guinea. Sadly, Emil was shot and killed in Port Moresby in 2010.

Emil and five-eighth Tusky Karu were the stars of the Port Moresby Vipers side that reached the cup quarter-finals stage of the 1993 World Sevens tournament. The Vipers previously entered a team in the midweek Panasonic Cup competitions from 1986-89, playing against Australian premiership sides, and played full seasons in the Queensland Cup competition in 1996 and 1997.

After a 29-22 victory over France in Port Moresby in 1994, the Kumuls hosted New Zealand in a two-Test series, going down in respectable 28-12 and 30-16 losses. Papua New Guinea's new Test linchpin was halfback Adrian Lam, who joined the Eastern Suburbs Roosters in 1994 from Brisbane Wests. Lam became Papua New Guinea's greatest player. He was one of the premiership's dominant halfbacks of the 1990s, partnering Brad Fittler in the Roosters' halves and playing in a Grand Final in 2000 before joining Wigan, where he starred for four seasons and won a Challenge Cup final in 2002. Lam was selected as Queensland's Origin halfback in 1995 after the Super League war decimated the Maroons' playing pool, captaining the state in eight of his 14 Origin appearances from 1995-2000. Retaining his Kumuls status despite representing Queensland due to the hazy qualification rules during the Super League years, Lam skippered Papua New Guinea at the 1995 and 2000 World Cups, while he racked up 253 top-flight appearances in Australia and England.

Stanley Gene made his Test debut in the 1994 defeat of France, scoring a try and kicking a field goal, before carving out a career that saw him rival Lam as Papua New Guinea's finest Rugby League export. Primarily a five-eighth but versatile and rock-solid enough to play in the forwards, Gene made 179 Super League appearances with Hull FC, Huddersfield, Bradford and Hull KR from 2000-09. Mystery has surrounded Goroka-born Gene's actual age throughout his career, but he starred for the Kumuls at the 2008 World Cup at the generally accepted age of 34.

Papua New Guinea performed admirably at the 1995 World Cup in England with Lam and Gene steering the side, securing a 28-all draw with Tonga before being beaten 22-6 by New Zealand. The Kumuls squad was bolstered by Canberra forwards David Westley and Bruce Mammando. Westley won a Grand Final with the Raiders in 1994 and made 143 first grade appearances for Canberra, Parramatta and the Northern Eagles, while Mammando played 32 games for Canberra, Adelaide and North Queensland.

Rugged and clever hooker Elias Paiyo represented the Kumuls at the 1995 and 2000 World Cups and spent the 1997 season with Adelaide, making six first grade appearances. Fullback David Buko featured in Papua New Guinea's 1995 campaign and later played for Western Suburbs in 1999 before representing his country at the 2000 World Cup, but died of typhoid poisoning in Goroka, early in 2002 (see Tragic Figures).

Winger Marcus Bai also debuted at the 1995 tournament and enjoyed a highly impressive rookie season with the Gold Coast Chargers in 1997, before garnering national hero status during seven seasons with Melbourne that featured a Grand

Final victory in 1999 and 70 tries in 144 games. The blockbusting 1998 Dally M Winger of the Year won a Super League title with Leeds in 2005 (scoring 26 tries in 29 games) and retired after two fruitful seasons with Bradford.

The PNGRL aligned with Super League during the game's 1995 upheaval and Bob Bennett—brother of the venerable Brisbane coach Wayne—assumed the national coaching post. A full-strength Kumuls team narrowly lost 32-30 to Great Britain in 1996, but Papua New Guinea was without Lam for two lopsided Test defeats to New Zealand. The Roosters halfback skippered an ARL-aligned Papua New Guinea side (dubbed the Palais) in a 52-6 loss to Australia while the Kumuls were on tour in New Zealand. Lam gave the Palais a 6-0 lead in the Port Moresby-hosted clash by scoring the opening try, but the home side was eventually overwhelmed by the Geoff Toovey-led Australians.

Promising five-eighth Thomas O'Reilly played in the Palais side and made 34 appearances for the Chargers in 1997-98, before representing the Kumuls at the 2000 World Cup and spending two seasons with English Super League club Warrington (2001-02).

Papua New Guinea was swamped 82-0 by Australia in Townsville in a warm-up to the 2000 World Cup, with a rampaging Gorden Tallis scoring an Australian record-equalling four tries. But the Kumuls won all three pool games at the tournament against France, South Africa and Tonga to qualify for the quarter-finals, where they were eliminated 22-8 by Wales. Headlined by professional stars Lam, Gene, Bai and Mammando, the Kumuls' squad was predominantly made up of players from Queensland and New South Wales second-tier competitions, and contained a handful of Papua New Guinea-based players. Former Perth Reds and Melbourne outside back John Wilshere was a key member of the side; he later had a season with St. George Illawarra, before playing 105 Super League games for Warrington, Leigh and Salford City.

The Kumuls were defeated 54-12 by Australia in Port Moresby in 2001, but endured something of a Test hiatus until qualification for the 2008 World Cup began. Papua New Guinea representative sides hosted the Junior Kangaroos in 2004-05, and an Australian Prime Minister's XIII at the end of each season from 2006, while Lam took over as coach of the Kumuls. He led Papua New Guinea into the 2008 World Cup with a squad captained by Wilshere and containing Gene, Canberra and Queensland State of Origin backrower Neville Costigan (who was born in Rabaul), Penrith hookers Paul Aiton and Keith Peters, and Gold Coast Titans speedster David Moore (who subsequently changed his name to David Mead after the tournament).

The Kumuls were gallant in a 32-22 loss to England in Townsville—which has been something of a spiritual home for the Papua New Guinea team in Australia—while they performed wholeheartedly in convincing losses to New Zealand and Australia. Papua New Guinea won the Pacific Cup in 2009 to qualify for the 2010 Four Nations tournament. Coached by Gene and captained by Aiton, who had joined Cronulla, the Kumuls played well in losses to England and Australia, but were swamped 74-12 by New Zealand.

An Origin regular and a premiership-winner with the Dragons before joining Newcastle in 2011, Costigan's plea to concurrently represent Queensland and Papua New Guinea (as Lam had done a decade earlier) was rejected by the ARL. Port Moresby-born Mead appeared to be the best-equipped player to follow in the footsteps of Lam and Bai as an elite NRL player, scoring 16 tries for the last-placed Titans in 2011, while James Segeyaro's 2011 rookie season with North Queensland had many predicting a big future for the nuggetty and dynamic hooker.

A bid to enter a Papua New Guinea-based team in the NRL was launched in 2008. The ambitious bid is well-organised, enthusiastic and boasts high-level support (including backing from the Brisbane Broncos), as well as receiving encouragement from NRL CEO David Gallop. The proposed team appears to be down the pecking order for admission to the premiership in 2015, when two clubs are scheduled to join the NRL competition, with infrastructure and Papua New Guinea's proximity to Australia's main centres potential hurdles for the bid. But with plenty of passion and money being poured into Papua New Guinea's national sport, the future appears bright for the world's fourth-ranked Rugby League-playing nation.

STARS AND STRIPES

Several attempts have been made to establish Rugby League in the crowded American sporting market over the last 60 years. Despite the code's inherent marketability, Rugby League remains a minnow sport in the United States. But the contribution of Americans holds a cherished, albeit minor, place in the history of the game in Australia. Meanwhile, the tireless efforts of United States Rugby League enthusiasts and expat Australians have led to a burgeoning domestic competition and an increased presence on the international stage.

The Rugby League News reported in 1932 that English and Australian administrators were making official moves to 'popularise the game in America.'[28] Harry Sunderland was the first prominent figure to spread the Rugby League gospel to the United States. A renowned administrator and expansionist, Sunderland was integral to the development of Rugby League in Queensland as secretary and financial guarantor in its formative years. His attempt to launch Rugby League as a major sport in Victoria in the 1920s was unsuccessful, but he went on to manage three Kangaroo tours and was integral to the establishment of the sport in France by setting up an exhibition match between Australia and England in 1933.

But plans to establish Rugby League in the United States were Sunderland's most ambitious yet. It was through Sunderland's endeavours that the American All-Stars ventured on a trailblazing tour of Australia and New Zealand in 1953, under the guidance of flamboyant manager-player Mike Dimitro, a talented all-round sportsman. Dimitro assembled a team of gridiron players to tour Down Under, where the All-Stars were met by Balmain stalwart player, coach and administrator Norm 'Latchem' Robinson, and former Test player and referee George Bishop, to teach the squad the finer points of Rugby League.

Plenty of hype surrounded the tour, but the All-Stars were generally a disappointment, despite defeating Monaro and Southern Division 34-25 in their

---

28 Ian Heads and David Middleton, *A Centenary Of Rugby League In Australia*. Sydney, 2008

opening match. Resplendent in their gridiron-style red, white and blue uniforms (with stars on the shoulders), the All-Stars were greeted by a phenomenal 65,453-strong Sydney Cricket Ground crowd for the second match of the tour, a 52-25 loss to Sydney. The American side toured regional and country centres throughout New South Wales and Queensland, but could only muster two more wins, against Newcastle and Ipswich, and draws with Far North Queensland and Wide Bay. Queensland-based stars Ken McCaffery, Brian Davies, Harold 'Mick' Crocker and Alan Hornery—all of whom represented Australia in 1953—bolstered their line-up in a match against NSW late in the tour, but the All-Stars' record of 13 losses in 18 games supported the claims of Australian detractors—the most vocal of which was former Test prop Ray Stehr—that the tour was a farce.

The All-Stars won three of their eight matches in New Zealand, against Taranaki, Northland and South Auckland. Despite the American team's lack of success on tour, Australian officials persisted in their drive to build a profile for Rugby League in the United States, staging two exhibitions games in California between Australia and New Zealand following the 1954 World Cup in France. Australia won both matches in front of modest crowds and the experiment was a financial flop. USA was comfortably beaten by France in an international in 1954, while Dimitro's bid for the United States to host a World Cup tournament in the 1960s was unsuccessful after receiving little support from the major Rugby League-playing nations.

An offshoot of the All-Stars tour was Parramatta's signing of winger Al E. Kirkland for the 1956 season. Kirkland played all 18 games for the last-placed Eels, crossing for four tries. He was not the first American-born player to feature in the premiership, however. Charlie Peoples, who hailed from Montana, was a foundation player for the University club. He played all 13 games for the Students in 1920 and scored two tries.

But neither player could match the fanfare that met Newtown's NFL recruit Manfred Moore, a Super Bowl winner with the Oakland Raiders in 1977. The African-American California native set Henson Park alight when he soared to catch a bomb and score a try in his debut for the Jets, a 17-10 victory over Wests in the opening round of the 1977 premiership. He famously spiralled a football gridiron style over the King George V Stand at Henson Park to whip up further hysteria amongst the Newtown faithful. But Moore played just five games on the wing for Newtown and returned to the States after suffering a head injury.

Rugby League underwent a mini-revival in the U.S. in the late-1980s. After an American national side played the inaugural international against northern neighbours Canada in 1987, won by the Canadians, California hosted a promotional State of Origin match between NSW and Queensland. The Blues defeated the Maroons (who earlier won the annual three-match series in Australia) 30-18 in front of 12,349 fans at Veterans Stadium, Long Beach. NSW captain Peter Sterling was named man of the match in the five-tries-to-three victory. While the match is officially recognised in State of Origin statistics, it is not considered part of the 1987 series.

Another Rugby League exhibition match was staged in 1989, between heavyweight English clubs Wigan and Warrington in Wisconsin, Milwaukee. The most significant development since the All-Stars tour occurred in 1992. A United States team was invited to play in the pre-season World Sevens tournament in Sydney, and despite failing to win a game in the 1993-94 tournaments, the Patriots proved to be one of the most popular and colourful teams. Playing in an American flag-inspired jersey, USA reached the 'plate' final of the 1995 tournament, going down to Tonga after recording wins over Italy and Russia. Following the 1994 competition, USA played a 13-a-side game against Metropolitan Cup champs St. Mary's, but was comprehensively beaten to the tune of 44-4.

St. George's 1991 end-of-season trip to Hawaii had a long-lasting impact on Rugby League in the United States. Halfback David Niu met his future wife on the holiday and moved to Philadelphia. He was a key figure in establishing a domestic competition in America and played for the national side—variously nicknamed the Patriots and the Tomahawks—between 1994 and 2006. Niu also represented the United States Eagles at the 1999 rugby union World Cup, but his heart remained in Rugby League and he took over as coach of the Tomahawks after his retirement as a player, while also serving in high-ranking administrative posts for the American National Rugby League.

International matches against Canada and Russia in 1993-94 were a precursor for USA's entry into the Emerging Nations World Cup in 1995. As a warm-up for the tournament, the United States hosted Wales in a two-international series in Philadelphia. Both matches were won convincingly by the visitors—92-4 and 66-10— with young Welsh stars Keiron Cunningham and Iestyn Harris running riot. The Patriots were defeated in all three pool games against Cook Islands, Scotland and Russia at the Emerging Nations World Cup.

USA also fielded teams in both the Australian Rugby League's World Sevens tournaments and Super League's World Nines tournaments in 1996 and '97. A semi-professional domestic competition began in the late 1990s, beginning with four teams and expanding to 11 teams by 2010, and the USA national side dominated Canada in regular internationals. But USA's quest to participate in the 2000 World Cup in England was halted by a heavy loss to Lebanon.

The USA Tomahawks, as they were now known, ventured to Australia to play South Sydney as a warm-up for the 2000 Emerging Nations World Cup. Souths won 82-12 in front of 20,535 fans at Redfern Oval in a match that doubled as a forum to push for the Rabbitohs' reinstatement to the NRL. After a crushing 110-0 loss to England in another warm-up match, the Tomahawks defeated Morocco in a play-off for third place in the Emerging Nations tournament.

The NRL had a brief but memorable encounter with an American player in 1998 when Greg Smith turned out in one match for Newcastle. Smith claimed to be a former NFL player with the Philadelphia Eagles and was fast-tracked into the Knights' line-up, but he turned in a notorious error-riddled display as Newcastle was run down by Canterbury and was later revealed as a fraud—he had never played in the NFL *(see One Game Wonders)*. South Carolina-born Clint Newton, the son of former top Australian golfer Jack Newton, debuted for the Knights in 2001. A robust backrower, Newton played over 100 games for Newcastle, represented NSW Country Origin and won a Grand Final with Melbourne in 2007 *(see Mid-Season Switches)*. Former Taranaki (New Zealand) rugby union player Andrew Suniula played his first Test for the United States in the 15-a-side game in 2008, before joining defending premiers Manly in 2009 and playing four first grade games on the wing. He returned to rugby union and represented the United States at the 2011 World Cup. One of the biggest coups achieved by an American Rugby League side came in the shape of the

Aston Bulls' signing of versatile former Parramatta veteran and Queensland Origin representative Daniel Wagon in 2010.

The most important international match played in the United States to date was in 2004, when the Kangaroos played the Tomahawks in Philadelphia en route back to Australia after their successful Tri-Nations campaign in England. The match was expected to be a cakewalk for the star-studded Australian side, but the Tomahawks stunned the travel-weary world champions to lead 24-6 at halftime. Bolstered by NRL players Matt Petersen and Brandon Costin (who both qualified for the United States team through family links), the Tomahawks were eventually overrun 36-24 by the fatigued Kangaroos, with North Queensland fullback Matt Bowen scoring a hat-trick.

South Sydney owner and Hollywood actor Russell Crowe set up an exhibition match between the Rabbitohs and Super League champions Leeds prior to the 2008 NRL season. The contest was played in front of a 12,500-strong crowd in Jacksonville, Florida. The Rhinos emerged victorious 26-24 after Souths fought back from 26-0 down at halftime.

Veteran Parramatta winger Petersen, ex-Cronulla and Castleford utility-back Ryan McGoldrick, and the versatile David Myles (who played 117 NRL games for the Gold Coast Chargers, New Zealand Warriors, North Queensland and the Gold Coast Titans) represented USA in 2007 in the Tomahawks' unsuccessful bid to qualify for the following year's World Cup in Australia. The Tomahawks lost 42-10 to the Nigel Vagana-led Samoan side in the final qualifying match. Halfback Damian O'Malveney, raised in the NSW country town of Canowindra, was named player of the tournament in the USA's victory at the 2010 Atlantic Cup (the Tomahawks were coached by AMNRL chief executive Niu). But the bulk of the Tomahawks' squads have been drawn from the burgeoning domestic club competition.

Matthew Elliott, boasting a decade of NRL head coaching experience with Canberra and Penrith, assumed the position of United States coach in 2011. He guided the Tomahawks—featuring Petersen, McGoldrick, Myles and brothers Junior and Joseph Paulo—to victories over South Africa and Jamaica to qualify for a historic maiden World Cup berth for the 2013 tournament in Britain. Junior Paulo played 17 games for Parramatta in 2007-08, while fellow forward Joseph debuted for Penrith in 2008 and represented Samoa at the World Cup before joining the Eels midway through 2011.

The north-east coast has traditionally been the heartland of Rugby League in the United States, but recent expansion has seen a team from Jacksonville, Florida, established. Six teams that competed in the American National Rugby League (AMNRL) competition split from the AMNRL including Jacksonville, plus a club from Rhode Island, and two teams based in Boston to contest the inaugural USA Rugby League (USARL) National Championship in 2011. The Philadelphia Fight defeated the New Haven Warriors 28-26 in the first USARL Grand Final, while several West Coast-based development clubs have been founded.

The experience of expat Australian players and coaches, the enthusiasm of the American players, and the passion and expertise of administrators such as David Niu will go a long way towards achieving the twin goals of a truly professional, national club competition and a prominent national representative side. The maiden appearance of the Tomahawks at a World Cup in 2013 shapes as the most significant milestone of the United States' 60-year Rugby League history.

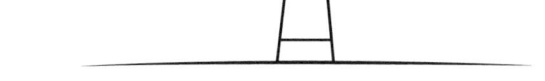

SOUTH AFRICANS MAKE THEIR MARK

Rugby League in South Africa is dwarfed by soccer and rugby union in the popularity stakes, but several players from the Rainbow Nation—predominantly rugby union converts—have excelled in the 13-a-side game in Australia and England. Tom Van Vollenhoven, Wilf Rosenberg and Fred Griffiths were the three most prominent South African footballers to switch codes and star on the English club scene in the late-1950s.

Van Vollenhoven's deeds on the wing for St. Helens rendered him a giant of British Rugby League. A highly regarded Springbok international, Van Vollenhoven scored an astonishing 392 tries in 409 games for the Saints, including a club record 62 in the 1958-59 season. Arguably his finest day was the 1959 championship final, scoring a hat-trick in the triumph over Hunslet. He was inducted into the Rugby League Hall of Fame in 2000.

Fellow rugby union international Rosenberg was also an extremely potent wingman, scoring over a century of tries in stints for Leeds, where he won the Challenge Cup in 1961, and Hull. Although Griffiths did not break into the national side, he was a talented exponent of the then-amateur game, and spent five fruitful seasons with Wigan after switching codes. The brilliant fullback scored over 1500 points in the cherry and white jumper, winning a Challenge Cup and a championship title. Griffiths was lured to Australia to captain-coach North Sydney in 1963 and proved to be one of the era's finest overseas imports. He scored 590 points in four seasons, topping the premiership in 1963, '64 and '65, including a club record 177 points in the latter season—a mark that stood for 26 years. The maligned Bears flourished under his leadership. After a much-improved fifth-place finish in 1963, the club qualified for the finals for the first time in a decade in 1964, and reached the preliminary final in 1965. He left Norths after the 1966 season to captain-coach successfully in country New South Wales and remained in Australia until his death in 2000 at the age of 65, in Perth.

Griffiths was the star attraction in South African Rugby League's boldest expedition—the national side's 1963 tour of Australia and New Zealand. The tour was regarded as a failure from a results perspective; South Africa won just three of 10 minor matches and was hammered 34-6 and 54-21 in the Test matches against an Australian side featuring five future Team of the Century members. But the tourists, coached by legendary Eastern Suburbs and Australian Test centre of the 1930s Dave Brown, caused a major boilover when they defeated New Zealand 4-3 in the one-off Test at Auckland's Carlaw Park. Former Springbok and Wakefield Trinity centre Alan Skene, who was based in Australia for a one-season stint with South Sydney, was one of the tourists' best performers, while two more stars of the Sydney premiership were seconded to the squad for the New Zealand leg of the tour—revered Cape Town-born Canterbury hooker Fred Anderson and Newtown forward Graham Wilson, who was chosen for the Kangaroo Tour at the end of the year.

South Africa faded off the international scene for almost 30 years following the trailblazing tour, but another member of the squad made a substantial impression on the Sydney competition. Versatile Springbok Test back Col Greenwood switched codes to play with Wakefield Trinity and scored two tries in South Africa's second Test loss at the SCG. He joined Griffiths at North Sydney in 1964 and played 77 games in five seasons. Greenwood was installed as captain-coach of the club in 1968, but poor results saw him replaced before season's end, and he concluded his professional career with Canterbury in 1969.

Len Kileen, another South African rugby union player to star in England before being lured to Sydney, challenges Griffiths as the finest player from the Rainbow Nation to take the field Down Under. The outstanding goalkicker scored over 1000 points for St. Helens and won the Lance Todd Trophy in the Saints' 1966 Challenge Cup final victory. Venturing to Australia with Balmain in 1967, Killeen set a new club record with 207 points in 1969, the year he became the first South African to play in a Sydney premiership-winning side. Killeen kicked four goals in the last-minute preliminary final defeat of Manly and two more in the Tigers' 11-2 upset of Souths in the Grand Final. He left the club at the end of 1971 with a total of 664 points, before rounding out his tenure in Sydney with a modest season for Penrith.

Two more of South Africa's outstanding amateur players switched codes to star in the English competition before heading to Australia in the late-1960s. Rugged forward Louis Neumann was a prominent performer in a stint with Leeds and linked with Eastern Suburbs in 1967. He made 74 appearances in five seasons for the Tricolours, and continued the remarkable strike-rate of South African captain-coaches in Sydney when he took over from Jack Gibson for a season in 1969. Trevor Lake upheld the fine tradition of South African wingers in England with his tryscoring exploits on the flank for Wigan, but his two-season sojourn in Australia with the powerful St. George Dragons was dogged by injury. Lake was instrumental in the formation of the SARL and the push that eventually saw South Africa invited to participate in the World Sevens in the early-1990s.

Penrith officials embarked on a trailblazing trip to South Africa in 1972 in search of playing talent and returned with two rising rugby union stars. Peter Swanson, a non-Test playing Springbok tourist, and Keith Howie turned out for the Panthers in 1973 and 1974, but failed to make a genuine impact. North Sydney visited the republic for a two-match promotional tour 20 years later. The Bears thrashed the Cape Town Coasters and a South African national side by identical scores—48-6—and an impressive crowd of almost 7,000 attended the latter clash, played at the iconic rugby union venue Ellis Park in Johannesburg.

The Western Reds also ventured to South Africa in 1994 as part of their preparation for entry into the following year's ARL premiership, clocking up 184 points and conceding just six in three games, including a 36-6 defeat of the national team. The Queensland Residents representative side followed the trend by touring the Republic in 1994 and achieved similarly lopsided results on a three-match tour.

The next notable South African convert to play in the Australian premiership was 15-Test Springbok Tiaan Strauss. He joined Cronulla in 1996 but had a limited impact in two seasons with the club and switched back to rugby union, turning out in 11 Tests for the Wallabies after fulfilling residential qualifications. Robust St. George-Illawarra forward Jarrod Saffy was born in Johannesburg and came to Australia as a teenager, while the Sydney Roosters recruited rugby union outside back JP Du Plesis, who played for the Tricolours' Toyota Cup side in 2010. But both players were snapped up by the fledgling Melbourne Rebels Super 15 franchise for their inaugural 2011 season, reversing a 50-year-old trend of South African rugby union players switching codes.

After narrowly going down in two internationals against the Commonwealth of Independent States (CIS) in 1992, South Africa fielded a team in the 1993-95 World Sevens tournaments in Sydney. South Africa sent teams to the 1995 and 2000 World Cups, both staged in England, but were hopelessly outclassed at both tournaments. Its 1995 campaign included an 86-6 thrashing at the hands of Australia, while its best result at the 2000 competition was a 16-0 loss to PNG. Hard-working Canberra Raiders back-rower Sean Rutgerson and former Canterbury, Souths and Illawarra rake Sean Skelton featured for the Rhinos at the 2000 tournament. The SARL, for whom Tom Van Vollenhoven is president, landed a major coup in 2010 by securing former Great Britain skipper Garry Schofield as part of the national side's coaching set-up, although the relationship was short-lived. South Africa's quest to qualify for the 2013 World Cup was ultimately unsuccessful, but a burgeoning domestic Rugby League competition bodes well for the future of the sport in the Republic.

WORLD CUPS

Rugby League's four powerhouse nations—Australia, Great Britain, New Zealand and France—began staging World Cup competitions during the 1950s. After many years of persistent lobbying, the establishment of the International Board of Rugby League in Bordeaux in 1948, and a succession of shelved plans, a satisfactory arrangement for all countries was reached and the inaugural tournament finally came to fruition in France in 1954. Thirteen Rugby League World Cups have been staged; Australia has won nine, Great Britain three and New Zealand one. A dearth of genuinely competitive countries, and frequent tampering with the format and time between each tournament has prevented the Rugby League World Cup from achieving the prestige of the FIFA or Rugby Union World Cups. But the tournaments—and the classic matches they have produced—have added a colourful sidebar to international Rugby League history, and remain an important tool in the development of the code around the world.

1954 WORLD CUP IN FRANCE The inaugural World Cup tournament was appropriately staged in France—French officials had been the foremost advocates of the need for a series showcasing Rugby League's Test-playing nations for many years. The French Rugby League was eager for a money-spinning tournament to help recoup the losses suffered during World War II, when Nazi sympathisers seized its assets and gave them to the rugby union establishment. France, Great Britain, Australia and New Zealand assembled for the World Cup in late-October, 1954. Despite a comprehensive 34-15 defeat of New Zealand in Marseille (with Brisbane

Wests centre Alex Watson scoring three tries), the Clive Churchill-led Australian side missed the final after succumbing 28-13 to Great Britain and 15-5 to the hosts. The Kiwis finished winless at the bottom of the table, while Great Britain and France were unbeaten after the round-robin stage following a 13-all draw between the sides in Toulouse. The first World Cup final was played at Paris' Parc des Prince with a 30,368-strong crowd in attendance. Five-eighth Gordon Brown scored two tries as the Dave Valentine-captained Great Britain side became the first official world champions courtesy of a 16-12 victory over France.

1957 WORLD CUP IN AUSTRALIA Australia hosted the second World Cup three years after the original instalment, and the green-and-golds—captain-coached by Newtown centre Dick Poole—were crowned world champions after finishing the round-robin stage undefeated. After accounting for New Zealand 25-5 in the tournament-opener in Brisbane, Australia beat Great Britain in a seven-tries-to-nil 31-6 drubbing and thumped France 26-9, with Brian Carlson scoring 17 points from a try and seven goals. Great Britain, France and New Zealand won one match apiece, while the hosts' clear-cut dominance dictated there would be no final played (a final was only played in the first three World Cups if two teams were tied at the top of the table). The Australian squad took the loss to injury of star trio, fullback Keith Barnes and halves Keith Holman and Greg Hawick, after the first match in their stride. Carlson, Ken McCaffery and Brian 'Poppa' Clay stepped into the breach seamlessly to play vital roles in Australia's maiden World Cup triumph, while the success was a crowning achievement in the career of the highly respected Poole.

1960 WORLD CUP IN ENGLAND The inventors of Rugby League hosted the World Cup for the first time in 1960, while Great Britain became the first two-time winners of the tournament by defeating New Zealand, France and Australia. Keith Barnes captain-coached the Australian side, who opened the tournament with a 13-12 victory over France. Brian Carlson starred in Australia's next-up 21-15 success against the Kiwis, scoring three tries and three goals from the wing after deputising for Barnes at fullback against France. The round-robin fixture between previously unbeaten Great Britain and Australia at Odsal Stadium was effectively a play-off to decide the World Cup. Australia struggled with the heavy conditions and went down 10-3; wingers Billy Boston and Mike Sullivan scored for Great Britain, while Carlson scored Australia's lone try.

1968 WORLD CUP IN AUSTRALIA AND NEW ZEALAND A compulsory final was instigated for the 1968 World Cup tournament, co-hosted by Australia and New Zealand. With former St. George teammates Johnny Raper and Harry Bath as the captain and coach combination, Australia assumed tournament favouritism with a 25-10 defeat of the Bev Risman-led Great Britain line-up to open the tournament at the Sydney Cricket Ground. France beat New Zealand 15-10 in Auckland, and the co-hosts' chances of reaching the final received a crushing blow with a 31-12 loss to Australia in Brisbane. France scored a 7-2 upset over Great Britain in Auckland to effectively seal a spot in the final, before being subjected to a 37-4 thrashing at Lang Park by Australia, with Bob Fulton and Innisfail winger Lionel Williamson each scoring two tries. Winger Clive Sullivan scored a hat-trick in Great

Britain's 38-14 consolation victory over New Zealand—bizarrely played in Sydney—in the battle of the also-rans. Williamson bagged another double in Australia's emphatic 20-2 defeat of France in the final at the SCG. The radar-like boot of South Sydney fullback Eric Simms was a feature of the tournament: the Indigenous star kicked eight goals against Great Britain, landed six goals and kicked two field goals against New Zealand, piloted over five goals and three field goals in the round-robin defeat of France, and added four goals in the final to finish with 56 points.

1970 WORLD CUP IN ENGLAND The Ron Coote-led Australian side scraped into the 1970 World Cup final—regarded as one of the most brutal and violent matches in international Rugby League history—on for-and-against. Australia opened the tournament with a 47-11 demolition of New Zealand, highlighted by fullback Eric Simms' 23 point haul—a then-Australian record for a World Cup or Test match. But the green-and-golds had to face hosts Great Britain just three days later, and Billy Smith captained Australia to an 11-4 loss at Headingley. Father John Cootes scored two tries but could not prevent a 17-15 loss to France in Australia's last preliminary match. Australia's superior for and against to France and the Kiwis booked a spot in the final against unbeaten Great Britain. In what became known as 'The Battle of Leeds,' Australia prevailed 12-7 in a savage encounter, with Cootes and Lionel Williamson scoring tries. English referee Fred Lindop struggled to maintain control as the final was marred by brawling and vicious off-the-ball incidents. Another wild melee in the dying minutes resulted in Billy Smith and Great Britain centre Syd Hynes receiving their marching orders. Inevitably, sensationalist headlines from the aghast British press denouncing the violent encounter followed, but the result was a triumph for skipper Ron Coote and coach Harry Bath, and sweet revenge for Australia after a home Ashes series loss earlier in the season.

1972 WORLD CUP IN FRANCE Australia and Great Britain played out another highly contentious World Cup final just two years after 'The Battle of Leeds.' A Bob Fulton hat-trick was not enough for Australia to overcome Great Britain in Perpignan in the preliminary rounds. The 27-21 loss put the acid on captain Graeme Langlands and coach Harry Bath, but the Australian side responded with a tight 9-5 defeat of New Zealand. Australia's first two round-robin matches were marked by bizarre calls by French officials: Great Britain was awarded a 'seven-point try' by referee Claude Teisseire after a late challenge by Australian second-rower John Elford on try-scorer John Atkinson—despite the rules of the time not offering the extra penalty kick at goal as an option; and Ray Branighan was denied a try in the victory over the Kiwis after French touch judge Jo Biou changed his call to the referee from a forward pass being thrown (which he was advised touch judges were not permitted to adjudicate on) to Branighan stepping into touch. After lengthy deliberation between referee Mick Naughton, Biou and French officials, the three-pointer was disallowed.

Great Britain five-eighth John Holmes scored a then-World Cup record 26 points (from two tries and 10 goals) as New Zealand was subjected to a 53-19 humiliation, and Australia thrashed hosts France 31-9, with Easts centre Mark Harris and Souths lock Paul Sait scoring two tries apiece, to set up an intriguing final between the bitter rivals. A dismal crowd of 4,321 turned out at Lyon's Stade Municipal de Garland for the final, which was overshadowed by another refereeing blunder. Australian front-row enforcer John O'Neill scored the opening try from a superb solo burst, before Langlands had a spectacular touchdown disallowed by referee Georges Jameau. The skipper raced after a high kick by halfback Denis Ward and caught it at full stretch in the in-goal, but Jameau incorrectly ruled Langlands offside (Langlands claims Jameau later apologised to him after viewing a television replay). British captain and wing speedster Clive Sullivan scored a memorable 90-metre try to level the scores 5-all before halftime. Ward made a break to send Arthur Beetson over for try in the second half, but Great Britain hooker Mike Stephenson's converted try consigned the final to extra-time. No change was made to the 10-all scoreline in the additional 20 minutes and Great Britain was handed the World Cup due to its superior record in the preliminary matches.

1975 WORLD SERIES PLAYED IN FIVE COUNTRIES The 1975 version of the tournament to decide the best Rugby League nation in the world saw Great Britain split into England and Wales, while the format consisted of the teams playing each other twice in a home-and-away series spread over eight months. England, Wales and France played the first set of matches in March, before the Northern Hemisphere squads ventured Down Under in June. Mick Cronin scored two tries and kicked six goals and captain-coach Graeme Langlands also bagged a double in Australia's first match, a 36-8 destruction of New Zealand in Brisbane. The Gerringong sharpshooter landed nine goals in the 30-13 defeat of Wales, while three-quarters Bob Fulton and Mark Harris each scored a brace of tries as Australia subdued France 26-6. In a quirky coincidence, Australia and Great Britain played out a 10-all draw at the SCG—an identical scoreline to the 1972 World Cup final.

The World Series shifted focus to Britain and France at the conclusion of the Sydney premiership in September. Arthur Beetson assumed the Australian captaincy, while the injured Langlands remained as coach—the superstar duo opposed each other as skippers in the Grand Final as Beetson's Easts side decimated Langlands' St. George line-up 38-0. Australia comfortably accounted for New Zealand 24-8 in Auckland en route to Britain, where an Ian Schubert hat-trick spearheaded an 18-6 defeat of Wales in Swansea. After the green-and-golds dismantled France 41-2, 19-year-old Schubert scored another treble against England. But the goalkicking of England fullback George Fairbairn propelled England to a 16-13 victory. Australia finished top of the table, however, with its six wins and a draw from eight games edging England's five wins and two draws. With no provisions for a final to be played, Australia was crowned world champions—much to the chagrin of the England side, who were the only nation to beat every other team during the series.

1977 WORLD CUP IN AUSTRALIA AND NEW ZEALAND The original World Cup format was restored in 1977, while England and Wales competed as Great Britain. Australia's campaign encountered controversy before it began after selectors bewilderingly omitted Arthur Beetson. The incredulous ARL Board refused to accept the squad without the revered ball-playing forward included, and he was swiftly added. But upon hearing of the unrest, Beetson pulled out of the team and Queensland front-rower Greg Veivers captained Australia—with Parramatta mentor Terry Fearnley as coach—to a convincing 27-12 win over New Zealand in the tournament-opener at Auckland's Carlaw Park. Beetson returned for the remainder of the tournament and skippered his country to a 21-9 victory over France in Sydney and a 19-5 success against Great Britain at Lang Park (with Manly fullback Graham Eadie scoring two tries in each match) as Australia finished unbeaten at the top of the table. The final rematch against the Roger Millward-led Great Britain side—played in front of a disappointing SCG crowd of 24,457—was a considerably closer affair. In what was to be the last match of a distinguished international career, Beetson led Australia to a 13-12 victory to retain world champion status.

1985-88 WORLD CUP PLAYED IN FIVE COUNTRIES After a lengthy break, the World Cup format underwent another revamp in the mid-1980s. The competing nations were Australia, New Zealand, Great Britain, France and, for the first time, Papua New Guinea. The teams played each other twice in home and away fixtures scheduled over four years (1985-88), with one-off Tests and the final match of Test series doubling as fixtures for World Cup points. France was forced to abandon its Southern Hemisphere tour, forfeiting World Cup tournament Tests to Australia, New Zealand and Papua New Guinea to finish at the bottom of the table. The Kumuls' only victory was a historic 24-22 upset of New Zealand in Port Moresby. Australia lost two Tests—to New Zealand at Carlaw Park in 1985, and to Great Britain at the Sydney Football Stadium in 1988—and finished top of the table. The other spot in the final came down to the third Test of the Lions' tour to New Zealand in 1988—Gary Freeman scored two tries as the Dean Bell-captained Kiwis grinded out a 12-10 victory in Christchurch. Auckland's hallowed rugby union venue Eden Park was chosen to host the final between New Zealand and Australia in November 1988, and the hosts were rated a strong chance of winning their first World Cup after upsetting perennial powerhouses Australia at Lang Park in 1987. But Australia stunned the Kiwis—and the expectant 47,363-strong home crowd—with a first half blitz. Captain Wally Lewis left the field with a broken arm at halftime, by which stage Australia already had the Cup wrapped up 21-0. Man of the match Allan Langer finished with two tries, while New Zealand scored a pair of consolation four-pointers for a 25-12 final score. The triumph was 1986 Kangaroos coach Don Furner's last match in charge of the national side.

1989-92 WORLD CUP PLAYED IN FIVE COUNTRIES The next World Cup was an identical four-year series of home and away matches. Australia won all eight of its World Cup-allotted Test matches between 1989 and 1992, while Great Britain and New Zealand finished equal-second on five wins. Great Britain advanced to the October 1992 final on account of its superior for and against record. A Rugby League record crowd for an international match of 73,361 packed London's Wembley Stadium for a gripping final between the bitter Anglo-Australian rivals. Centre Garry Schofield captained Great Britain—despite the presence of Ellery Hanley at lock—and the hosts led 6-4 at halftime courtesy of three penalty goals to halfback Deryck Fox. Australian skipper Mal Meninga landed two first half penalties, the second after a vicious elbow from British hooker Martin Dermott that fractured five-eighth Brad Fittler's cheekbone. Fittler valiantly battled on and played brilliantly, but the crucial moment came deep into the second half when Brisbane pivot Kevin

Walters (who was injected from the bench) fired a beautiful pass for debutant centre Steve Renouf to sprint 20 metres and score in the corner. Meninga's sideline conversion made it 10-6—a lead Australia doggedly defended until fulltime to retain the World Cup.

1995 WORLD CUP IN GREAT BRITAIN The 1995 World Cup was staged to celebrate Rugby League's centenary in Britain. The tournament was expanded to 10 teams, with Great Britain splitting into England Wales, and Tonga, Fiji, Western Samoa and South Africa joining the traditional Test-playing nations. The teams were split into three pools, with Australia and England grouped together in a four-team pool, from which the top two teams would progress to the semi-finals. The top team from each of the remaining three-team pools also advanced to the semi-final stage.

But Australia's defence of the world champion tag was rattled by the Super League upheaval that engulfed the code earlier in the season. Australia sent a side consisting entirely of ARL-aligned players to the 1995 World Cup, leaving behind Super League stars and Test regulars Laurie Daley, Allan Langer, Steve Renouf, Bradley Clyde, Steve Walters and Glenn Lazarus. Knockers of the under-strength squad were provided with ample ammunition when the Brad Fittler-captained side fell 20-16 to England in the tournament-opener at Wembley. Australia led 6-4 at halftime, but England snaffled the lead 16-10 after a diabolical error from Manly winger John Hopoate that resulted in a try to Wigan flyer Jason Robinson. Paul Newlove's intercept try extended England's lead and the hosts held on for a 20-16 victory. It was Australia's third loss in four clashes at Wembley during the 1990s. Newcastle prop Paul Harragon captained Australia to an 86-6 thrashing of South Africa, in which Andrew Johns scored a Test record-equalling 30 points in his green-and-gold debut, while Hopoate crossed for a hat-trick. Queensland wingers Brett Dallas and Robbie O'Davis each claimed three tries as Australia dismantled Fiji 66-0 in its other pool game.

New Zealand booked a semi-final date with Australia after topping its pool. But the Kiwis were given an almighty fright by Tonga; New Zealand trailed by 12 points late in the second half, but scored two tries and a field goal to avoid an embarrassing early exit from the tournament. Wales, captained by dual international maestro Jonathan Davies, topped the other pool to advance to the semi-finals, but succumbed 25-10 to England.

Australia booked a rematch with England after surviving an extra-time thriller against the Kiwis in the semi-final. Trailing 20-6 in the second half, New Zealand piled on three tries to level the scores and almost steal a miraculous victory, but Australia prevailed 30-20 in extra-time. Australia led the final 10-4 over the Dennis Betts-captained England side at halftime in front of 66,540 supporters at Wembley, but Newlove again proved troublesome for the visitors, scoring a determined try to cut the deficit to two points. Australia secured its fifth straight World Cup trophy when fullback Tim Brasher pounced on a grubber kick from his captain to score the final try of a 16-8 triumph. Emphasising the international inexperience of the Australian side, Brasher and Fittler were the only survivors of the 1992 World Cup victory at the same venue. Andrew Johns was named man of the match and player of the tournament—the beginning of a decade of torment for the Poms at the hands of the champion halfback, although Johns played most of the tournament wearing the

No.9 *(see Switching Positions)*. Manly coach Bob Fulton had steered Australia to World Cup glory for the second time after overseeing his country's victory in 1992.

2000 WORLD CUP IN UNITED KINGDOM AND FRANCE The 2000 instalment of the World Cup expanded its participation again, this time to 16 teams. The added sides were Ireland, Scotland, Cook Islands, Lebanon, Russia and New Zealand Maori. The tournament followed the Rugby Union World Cup model of four pools of four teams, with the top two qualifiers from each pool advancing to the quarter-finals.

Australia and co-hosts England were paired in the same pool. In a dour tournament-opener at hallowed rugby union venue Twickenham, Australia prevailed 22-2 over England after holding a six-point advantage at halftime. Wendell Sailor scored two tries for the Brad Fittler-led Kangaroos. Australia hammered Fiji—captained by 22-year-old Brisbane winger Lote Tuqiri—by 66-8, with winger Mat Rogers amassing a World Cup record 34 points from four tries and nine goals. Centre Ryan Girdler trumped Rogers' effort with 46 points (three tries, 17 goals) in Australia's 110-4 dismemberment of Russia, while Sailor bagged four tries. New Zealand dominated Group 2, swamping a Lebanon side featuring Canterbury winger Hazem El Masri 64-0 in freezing conditions in Gloucester, before Melbourne's Dally M Rookie of the Year Tasesa Lavea scored 30 points (two tries, 12 goals) in the Kiwis' 84-10 rout of the Kevin Iro-led Cook Islands. Wales finished second in the group to qualify for the quarter-finals.

Unbeaten in the pool games, the Adrian Lam-captained Papua New Guinea side advanced from Group 3 along with France. Ireland, featuring NRL stars Luke Ricketson, Kevin Campion and David Barnhill, and a host of seasoned Great Britain internationals, topped Group 4, while Samoa also qualified for the quarter-finals. Sydney Roosters backrower Bryan Fletcher scored three tries in Australia's 66-10 pummelling of Samoa in its quarter-final. New Zealand, England and Wales joined Australia in the semi-finals. England exited the tournament courtesy of a humiliating 49-6 defeat to the Kiwis. But Wales pushed Australia in the other semi-final, charging to a shock 20-8 lead after 30 minutes on the back of Super League stars Iestyn Harris, Keiron Cunningham and Lee Briers. The Kangaroos did not seal victory until well into the final quarter, running in a string of late tries to finish the scoring at 46-22. Captain Brad Fittler and fullback Darren Lockyer scored two tries each in the shaky win. New Zealand proved stern competition for Australia in the final, trailing just 18-12 with 13 minutes remaining. But the Kangaroos eventually broke the Kiwis' resolve and powered away to a 40-12 triumph. Wendell Sailor scored a double to take his total to a tournament-high 10 tries. Chris Anderson was coach of the Australian side, while Fittler became the first skipper since Arthur Beetson (1975 and 1977) to lead two successful World Cup campaigns.

2008 WORLD CUP IN AUSTRALIA The 2008 World Cup was staged as the jewel in the crown of Australian Rugby League's Centenary season. 10 teams competed in the tournament, which sported a bizarre format. Group A consisted of heavyweights Australia, New Zealand and England, along with the competitive Papua New Guinea, with the top three teams qualifying for the semi-finals. France, Scotland and Fiji made up Group B, while Tonga, Samoa and Ireland squared off in

Group C. The top team in each of Groups B and C advanced to a qualifying match for the last semi-final spot.

The Darren Lockyer-led hosts opened their campaign with an emphatic 30-6 defeat of New Zealand at the Sydney Football Stadium, and they finished the pool stage with a 46-6 thrashing of the Kumuls in Townsville. England's performance at the 2008 World Cup ranks as one of the most dismal chapters in Rugby League history for the inventors of the code. There were danger signs for England in a scratchy 32-22 win over Papua New Guinea in its opening match, but even the most pessimistic supporter would not have predicted the humiliation inflicted by the ruthless Kangaroos in Melbourne a week later. Australia's attack was breathtaking, at times making English defenders look like schoolboys. Hometown heroes Billy Slater and Greg Inglis scored three tries apiece, while international rookie backrower Anthony Laffranchi bagged a double. England's 52-4 drubbing was matched only by the caning dished out by the British press, who suggested the team should return home after the embarrassing loss. England showed greater heart in consecutive losses to New Zealand in its final pool match and the semi-final. Barnstorming winger Manu Vatuvei scored four tries in the Kiwis' 36-24 pool victory over England, before a Jerome Ropati double helped propel New Zealand into the final with a 32-22 success in the semi-final against the hapless Poms.

A Jarryd Hayne-inspired Fiji side defeated Ireland 30-14 in the qualifying final (with 21-year-old Newcastle winger Akuila Uate scoring two tries) to win the right to take on Australia in the semi-final. Halfback Johnathan Thurston scored 24 points (three tries, six goals) and Slater scored another hat-trick as Australia crushed the Bati 52-0 to advance to the final. Red-hot favourites to retain the World Cup in the Suncorp Stadium showdown against New Zealand, the Kangaroos raced out to a 10-0 lead before being reeled in by the plucky Kiwis. Australia led 16-12 at halftime after man of the match Lockyer's second try, but New Zealand secured one of the all time great international upsets in an extraordinary second half. A Slater howler handed Kiwi five-eighth Benji Marshall a crucial four-pointer and a penalty try to fullback Lance Hohaia extended the underdogs' advantage. New Zealand finished the euphoric triumph—its maiden World Cup success—as 34-20 victors over the shell-shocked Kangaroos, who had not lost a World Cup tournament since 1972.

THE WORLD CLUB CHALLENGE

A championship match between the premiers of the Australian competition and the British club champions has been staged intermittently and in various incarnations since 1976.

1976—EASTERN SUBURBS 25 DEFEATED ST. HELENS 2 AT THE SYDNEY CRICKET GROUND

Easts' premiership-winning side of 1974-75 was established as one of the great club combinations of all time, and hosted Challenge Cup and English premiership victors St. Helens during the 1976 Australian winter. The Arthur Beetson-led Roosters swamped the Saints in the long-awaited encounter, however, scoring five tries to one in a fizzer. The lopsided result stymied interest in the continuation of the concept. The under-conditioned St. Helens side had gone down 21-16 to Queensland prior to the clash with Easts, and subsequently lost 20-13 to Auckland at Carlaw Park after the Australian leg of the trip. Eager to push their claims as the world's best team (despite the fact Queensland and Auckland were representative line-ups), the Roosters challenged the other two sides that had beaten the Saints. Queensland declined, but Auckland accepted the offer and Easts defeated New Zealand's premier provincial side 26-22 at Carlaw Park.

1987—WIGAN 8 DEFEATED MANLY 2 AT CENTRAL PARK, WIGAN The World Club Challenge concept was revived more than a decade later, with Manly venturing to England after defeating Canberra in the 1987 Grand Final. Ellery Hanley captained a star-studded Wigan side, including modern British greats Shaun Edwards, Andy Gregory and Joe Lydon, to a try-less 8-2 victory in front of a bumper home crowd. The Sea Eagles' chances were hampered by the dismissal of backrower Ron Gibbs, who was playing in his last game for the club before joining the fledgling Gold Coast-Tweed Giants in 1988. Gibbs was sent off for a late tackle on Lydon, while Manly five-eighth Cliff Lyons spent 10 minutes in the sin-bin. Fullback Dale Shearer starred in the visitors' loss.

1989—WIDNES 30 DEFEATED CANBERRA 18 AT OLD TRAFFORD, MANCHESTER A showdown between the Australian and English champions was not scheduled for 1988, but returned a year later, with Widnes subduing the Canberra Raiders, who had secured their maiden premiership a fortnight earlier with an extra-time Grand Final victory over Balmain. Widnes was captained by New Zealand Test forward Kurt Sorenson and featured British stars Martin Offiah, Jonathan Davies, Alan Tait and Andy Currier (who played in the Tigers' Grand Final loss during an off-season stint in Australia). After trailing 12-0 early, Widnes rallied to win 30-18 with a second half blitz. Wing speedster Offiah scored two tries.

1991—WIGAN 21 DEFEATED PENRITH 4 AT ANFIELD STADIUM, LIVERPOOL After another two-year gap, Penrith made the trip to England after securing its maiden first grade title with Grand Final victory against Canberra. Panthers centre Brad Fittler was on Australia's tour of Papua New Guinea, while Mark Geyer was also unavailable due to a passport mix-up. The under-strength Panthers were outclassed 21-4 by the all-conquering Wigan outfit at famed Liverpool soccer venue Anfield Stadium, despite scoring the first try through winger Darren Willis from a superb cross-field kick by skipper Greg Alexander. New Zealand international Sam Panapa scored a fine individual try for Wigan, before Shaun Edwards snaffled an intercept and sent winger David Myers in for the match-sealer. Frano Botica kicked six goals for the 'Riversiders.'

1992—BRISBANE 22 DEFEATED WIGAN 8 AT CENTRAL PARK, WIGAN The Brisbane Broncos became the first Australian side to win a World Club Challenge in England with an emphatic 14-point victory over the powerful Wigan side, five weeks after claiming their first premiership with a 28-8 Grand Final thrashing of St. George.

Featuring six players from Australia's 10-6 defeat of Great Britain at Wembley a week earlier, the Broncos scored four tries to one in a fiery clash marked by several wild brawls. Test winger Michael Hancock crossed for a double, while fullback Julian O'Neill and hooker Kerrod Walters also notched tries for the victors.

1994—WIGAN 20 DEFEATED BRISBANE 14 AT STADIUM AUSTRALIA, BRISBANE

A 54,220-strong crowd packed Brisbane's Stadium Australia during the 1994 Australian winter to see two-time premiers the Broncos host Wigan, the English champions of the previous five seasons. Wigan raced to an 18-4 lead on the back of an opportunist try to backrower Dennis Betts, a 50-metre effort by centre Barrie-Jon Mather and a blistering four-pointer to winger Jason Robinson, before holding off a late Broncos comeback to prevail 20-14.

1997—SUPER LEAGUE'S WORLD CLUB CHALLENGE

The rebel Super League organisation's most ambitious venture of its sole season in operation in Australia was the ill-fated World Club Challenge tournament, pitting the 10 Australian Super League clubs against the European Super League's 11 clubs. The teams were split into two pools—Pool A contained the top six ranked clubs from each competition, while the remainder made up Pool B—and played in a home and away series scheduled during two four-week breaks in the premiership season.

Lopsided scorelines marred the competition from the outset and crowds rapidly dropped off. European clubs won just eight of the 60 pool matches staged; some of the more embarrassing results included:

- Canberra winger Ken Nagas scoring six of the Raiders' 13 tries in a 70-6 demolition of Halifax at Bruce Stadium.
- After defeating Canterbury in the opening round, English heavyweight Wigan was thumped 34-0 by Brisbane and 56-22 by Canberra.
- Halifax being humiliated 58-6 by Canterbury and then obliterated 76-0 by the Broncos, who scored 15 tries.
- Lowly Australian side Adelaide racking up 126 points to just 30 conceded in the three matches of the English leg of its tournament against Salford, Leeds and Oldham.
- Premiership strugglers the Auckland Warriors decimating English powerhouses Bradford 64-14 and St. Helens 70-6 on their English leg of the tournament.

The WCC finals were played at the conclusion of the Super League premierships in each hemisphere. The three top Australian Pool A teams and the top Australian Pool B side qualified for the quarter-finals, facing off against the top four European Pool A teams (St. Helens, the fourth-ranked Pool A side, defeated the top European Pool B side Paris St. Germain in a play-off for the last quarter-final spot). The Australian clubs won all four quarter-finals: Auckland thrashed Bradford again, 62-14; Steve Renouf scored five tries in Brisbane's 66-12 thrashing of St. Helens; the Hunter Mariners rolled Wigan 22-18; and Cronulla comfortably accounted for London 40-16.

The Broncos overcame the Warriors 22-16 in a high-quality semi-final, while Hunter booked the other spot in the final with a 22-18 upset of Super League Grand finalists Cronulla. Darren Smith scored a hat-trick as Brisbane added the World Club Challenge to its Super League premiership with a 36-12 defeat of the Mariners in Auckland, bringing a costly and ill-fated tournament to a close. Penrith's Ryan Girdler topped the tournament's pointscoring table with 118, followed by Warriors captain Matthew Ridge with 102. Renouf was the top try-scorer with 13 touchdowns, while Girdler, Nagas and Broncos winger Wendell Sailor each bagged 11 tries.

2000—MELBOURNE 44 DEFEATED ST. HELENS 6 AT JJB STADIUM, WIGAN The World Club Challenge returned in 2000, with the reigning National Rugby League and Super League champions squaring off in England early in the following year—a format that has been retained for 13 straight seasons. Melbourne swamped St. Helens in the wake of the club's euphoric Grand Final success against St. George Illawarra in 1999. Scott Hill and Robbie Ross scored two tries apiece for the Storm, who were captained by Robbie Kearns following the retirement of Glenn Lazarus.

2001—ST. HELENS 20 DEFEATED BRISBANE 18 AT REEBOK STADIUM, BOLTON St. Helens atoned for its demoralising defeat in the previous season's WCC with a comeback victory over the NRL's 2000 premiers Brisbane. The Broncos led 12-6 at halftime, but were overrun by a Sean Long-inspired Saints outfit.

2002—BRADFORD 41 DEFEATED NEWCASTLE 26 AT MCALPINE STADIUM, HUDDERSFIELD A two-try performance from Newcastle captain Andrew Johns was not enough to prevent a comprehensive defeat to Super League champions Bradford for the 2001 NRL premiers. New Zealand Test star Robbie Paul and former Balmain three-quarter Michael Withers scored try-doubles, while Paul Deacon kicked eight goals. Highly rated British hooker James Lowes was named man of the match.

2003—SYDNEY ROOSTERS 38 DEFEATED ST. HELENS 0 AT REEBOK STADIUM, BOLTON In a rematch between the two clubs that squared off in the inaugural World Club Challenge in 1976, the Roosters again emerged victorious in emphatic fashion. The shell-shocked Saints—containing former Australian stars Darren Smith, Darren Britt and Darren Albert, and British Test players Sean Long, Paul Sculthorpe and Martin Gleeson—had no answer for the ruthless NRL premiers. In a unique double, 2002 Clive Churchill Medallist Craig Fitzgibbon was named man of the match in the WCC match, kicking nine goals.

2004—BRADFORD 22 DEFEATED PENRITH 4 AT MCALPINE STADIUM, HUDDERSFIELD The Bradford Bulls, missing five stars from their 2003 Super League Grand Final victory, comfortably accounted for NRL premiers Penrith. Leading 16-0 at halftime, the Jamie Peacock-led Bulls ground out the win in a dour second half to secure the club's second WCC title in three years.

2005—LEEDS 39 DEFEATED BULLDOGS 32 AT ELLAND ROAD, LEEDS In arguably the finest WCC encounter to date, Leeds withstood a stirring Bulldogs comeback to prevail 39-32. The Rhinos leapt out to a 26-6 halftime lead, but a Sonny Bill Williams-inspired second half charge pegged the Bulldogs back to within six points. A field goal by Leeds captain Kevin Sinfield sealed the result with three minutes remaining, while his halves partner Danny McGuire was named man of the match. Hazem El Masri crossed for two tries and kicked four goals for the Bulldogs.

2006—BRADFORD 30 DEFEATED WESTS TIGERS 10 AT GALPHARM STADIUM, HUDDERSFIELD Bradford equalled Wigan as the most successful World Club Challenge side with the club's third victory, a comprehensive 20-point defeat of 2005 NRL premiers the Wests Tigers, who were missing star five-eighth Benji Marshall with injury and Wigan-bound winger Pat Richards. Former Melbourne winger Marcus Bai and man of the match, prop Stuart Fielden, scored two tries each for the Bulls.

2007—ST. HELENS 18 DEFEATED BRISBANE 14 AT REEBOK STADIUM, BOLTON St. Helens repeated its effort of six years earlier by pipping Brisbane in the WCC. The 2006 NRL premiers surrendered a 14-6 lead to go down by four points. Winger Ade Gardner scored two tries for the Saints, while Paul Sculthorpe—one of four survivors from the 2001 victory with Sean Long, Keiron Cunningham and Paul Wellens—was named man of the match.

2008—LEEDS 11 DEFEATED MELBOURNE 4 AT ELLAND ROAD, LEEDS Leeds claimed its second WCC triumph in four years with a grinding victory over Melbourne in terrible conditions at Elland Road. Rhinos captain Kevin Sinfield was named man of the match, kicking three goals and a field goal, while former NRL speedster Scott Donald scored the home side's only try. Storm captain Cameron Smith and star centre Greg Inglis were absent from the visitors' line-up.

2009—MANLY 28 DEFEATED LEEDS 20 AT ELLAND ROAD, LEEDS Manly broke the five-season British stranglehold on the World Club Challenge crown with an impressive 28-20 defeat of defending WCC champions Leeds. The Sea Eagles led 12-4 at halftime, before putting the game to bed with three tries in the space of five minutes directly after the break. The Rhinos scored three late tries to add a semblance of respectability to the scoreboard. Devastating backrower Anthony Watmough was named man of the match after a stunning two-try display, while quicksilver fullback Brett Stewart also bagged a double.

2010—MELBOURNE 18 DEFEATED LEEDS 10 AT ELLAND ROAD, LEEDS Inclement weather again plagued Melbourne's second trip to Elland Road in three years, but the Storm reversed the result of 2009 with a superb second half display to prevail 18-10. With seven changes to their Grand Final line-up, the Storm were held to 4-all at the end of a try-less first half, but touchdowns to wingers Luke MacDougall and Anthony Quinn lifted the visitors to victory.

2011—ST. GEORGE ILLAWARRA 21 DEFEATED WIGAN 15 AT DW STADIUM, WIGAN St. George Illawarra added another trophy to a bulging cabinet that included the NRL premiership and the J.J. Giltinan Shield as minor premiers with a gritty six-point victory over Super League champs Wigan. The Dragons were coached by assistant Steve Price after Wayne Bennett remained in Australia for family reasons, but the Saints were typically clinical after recovering from a 15-14 halftime deficit. Man of the match Brett Morris scored two tries for the Dragons, while former Newcastle centre George Carmont crossed for a double for Wigan.

2012—LEEDS 26 DEFEATED MANLY 12 AT HEADINGLY, LEEDS Leeds compensated for twin defeats in the 2009-10 WCC fixtures with an emphatic 14-point defeat of NRL premiers Manly. The Sea Eagles, rocked by a horror off-season that saw coach Des Hasler leave the club just a month after the Grand Final, were scratchy against a committed Rhinos outfit. Leeds winger Ryan Hall scored two tries, including a 95-metre intercept effort in the first half.

Each year brings fresh calls for an overhaul of the World Club Challenge format. The inherent disadvantage to Australian clubs travelling every year while in the midst of a gruelling pre-season has hampered the WCC's credibility as a genuine gauge of the world's best club. Taking the game to Australia and other locations around the world has been frequently mooted, while more recently suggestions for a tournament involving multiple clubs have gathered momentum. Super League's diabolical tournament in 1997 has proved a deterrent for similar ventures coming to fruition, but the desire for a definitive answer to who is the best club in world Rugby League will ensure the push continues.

INTERNATIONAL STARS UNITE

Some of Rugby League's greatest names have featured in combined representative sides consisting of players from multiple nations, playing matches against national sides, county teams and other representative line-ups.

ANTIPODEANS ASSIST LIONS IN CURTAIN-RAISER The first Test between Australia and the touring Lions in 1910 in Sydney was preceded by a curtain-raiser pitting the remaining members of the England squad against a Newcastle representative side. Unable to field a full team, four Australians and one New Zealander were drafted in to bolster the England line-up for the encounter with the Novocastrians. Wingers Jim Devereux and Dan Frawley (1908-09 Kangaroos who had joined Warrington), Hull's Andy Morton (another pioneering Australian tourist), Souths forward Alby 'Son' Burge (later one of a famous band of Glebe Rugby League brothers) and 1907-08 New Zealand All Gold tourist Conrad Byrne helped England to a 24-8 victory over Newcastle. The Lions won the first Anglo-Australia Test played on Australian soil later that day, 27-20.

REST OF THE WORLD The first two matches played by a Rest of the World selection were staged at the end of the 1957 and 1960 World Cups, due to a final not being required to decide the winner of the tournament in either year. Following Australia's maiden World Cup success in 1957, Dick Poole led a formidable green-and-gold line-up to a 20-11 victory over a Rest of the World combination made up of players from France, Great Britain and New Zealand in front of a 30,675-strong Sydney Cricket Ground crowd. French centre Jacques Merquey skippered the Rest of the World line-up, which featured British luminaries Lewis Jones and Eric Ashton, French five-eighth Gilbert Benausse and veteran Kiwi prop Cliff Johnson.

Great Britain claimed the 1960 World Cup and Ashton captained the victorious side to a 33-27 victory over Rest of the World at Odsal Stadium, Bradford. Ashton, revered halfback Alex Murphy and five-eighth Frank Myler each scored two tries, while New Zealand pivot George Menzies crossed for a hat-trick for Rest of the World. Australian players in the Rest of the World side included centre Ron Boden, halfback Barry Muir and forwards Brian Hambly, Dud Beattie and Billy Rayner. Johnson captained the combined XIII as the only survivor from the 1957 Rest of the World line-up. The 1960 version contained four Frenchmen, and Kiwi greats Tom Hadfield and Cyril Eastlake. A disappointing crowd of less than 4,000 turned out for the match.

The Rest of the World concept was dusted off in 1988 to commemorate Australia's Bicentenary. The Wally Lewis-led Australian side defeated Rest of the World 22-10 at the Sydney Football Stadium, with Mark McGaw scoring two tries in his international debut. But the result was overshadowed by Mal Meninga's fourth broken arm injury in the space of two seasons. The match would be the only appearance in an Australian jersey for winger Alan McIndoe, who became Illawarra's first international. The Rest of the World side was captained by tough New Zealand second-rower Mark Graham and featured compatriots Kevin Iro and Dean Bell. Ellery Hanley, Andy Gregory and Kevin Ward headlined the Great Britain contingent, while Dairi Kovae (Papua New Guinea) and Jean-Philippe Pougeau (France) were their respective nations' only representatives.

Great Britain took on a Rest of the World selection later in 1988 to mark the opening of the British Rugby League Hall of Fame. Hanley led a Test-strength Great Britain side to a 30-28 victory at Headingley, Leeds. Graham was again named skipper of Rest of the World, a squad this time dominated by Australian stars, including Allan Langer, Steve Ella, Michael O'Connor, Dale Shearer, Gavin Miller, Noel Cleal, Sam Backo and Cliff Lyons (the only Australian player in the side yet to make his international debut). The line-up contained two French players and two Papua New Guineans, while Graham was joined by fellow Kiwis Kurt Sorenson and Peter Brown.

The last match staged against a Rest of the World side was in the fractured 1997 season. Australia, with little competitive international opposition during the Super League years, awarded full Test caps for the 28-8 victory over Rest of the World at Suncorp Stadium. Restricted to choosing ARL-aligned players, the Rest of the World side contained British stars Jason Robinson, Gary Connolly, Lee Jackson and Harvey Howard; Manly's former All Black Craig Innes and fellow New Zealanders Jarrod McCracken, Jason Lowrie, Terry Hermansson and Craig Smith (who represented Queensland in the Origin series just weeks earlier); and was captained by halfback and Queensland and Papua New Guinea skipper Adrian Lam, who was joined in the side by two fellow Kumuls, Gold Coast Chargers pair Thomas O'Reilly and Marcus Bai. Newcastle and former Great Britain mentor Malcolm Reilly coached the Rest of the World outfit, who led the Brad Fittler-captained Australia side 8-6 at halftime. Fullback Tim Brasher scored two tries in Australia's 20-point victory, while prop Paul Harragon was named man of the match.

GREAT BRITAIN/FRANCE vs. NEW ZEALAND A week after the Australia-hosted 1957 World Cup concluded, European rivals Great Britain and

France joined forces and ventured across the Tasman to take on New Zealand. The exhibition match was a thrilling encounter, won 37-31 by the combined XIII in front of 15,000 supporters at Auckland's hallowed Carlaw Park. British centre Eric Ashton scored a phenomenal five tries and five goals (for 25 points), while his famed French centre partner Jacques Merquey—one of five players from France in the side—also found his way onto the scorers sheet. The Kiwis fought back from a 19-2 halftime deficit, with winger Tom Hadfield notching a hat-trick and hooker Jock Butterfield scoring two tries for the Cliff Johnson-led New Zealand side.

DOMINION XIII A team labelled the Dominion XIII played internationals against fledgling Rugby League nation France in 1936 and 1937. The team featured prominent British-based Australian and New Zealand players; former Kangaroos winger Bill Shankland, former Australian Test halfback Hec Gee, former Kiwi Test forward Len Mason, legendary former All Black fullback George Nepia and Charlie Seeling Jr.—son of the former All Black and Wigan forward of the same name—competed in the combination's 8-5 loss in Paris in 1936. Shankland, Mason, Nepia and Seeling were joined by former Kangaroos centre Cec Fifield and Newcastle product and Huddersfield wing great Ray Markham for the 6-3 victory over France in Toulouse in 1937.

BRITISH EMPIRE XIII A British Empire XIII, made up of British players and Australian players based at English clubs, played three internationals. The British Empire—featuring legendary Australian five-eighth Vic Hey, former Australian Test halfback Hec Gee and famed Leeds winger Eric 'the Toowoomba Ghost' Harris—defeated France 15-0 in 1937, while France reversed the result with a 23-10 victory in 1949 against a British Empire XIII side containing Lionel Cooper, Tony Paskins, Pat Devery and Harry Bath. The 1951-52 New Zealand Kiwis side faced off against the British Empire XIII combination in a tour match in London. The British Empire prevailed 26-2, with former Australian Test winger and Huddersfield legend Cooper crossing for three tries, while compatriots Brian Bevan and Trevor Allan also scored. The selection also contained Australian forward luminaries Bath and Arthur Clues, and British greats Alan Prescott and Ernest Ward.

OTHER NATIONALITIES Other Nationalities, made up of Australian, New Zealand and South African players from English club sides, competed in the International Championship (also known as the European Championship) against England, Wales and France between 1949 and 1955. The inaugural Other Nationalities side contained Australian stars Brian Bevan, Harry Bath, Lionel Cooper, Ken Kearney, Pat Devery and Tony Paskins. Arthur Clues and Trevor Allan also represented Other Nationalities in subsequent seasons. Other Nationalities won 12 of its 17 International Championship matches, and won the round-robin tournament in the 1952-53 and 1955-56 seasons.

England had previously played 'friendly' internationals against Other Nationalities selections made up of players from Scotland and Wales between 1904 and 1933. The only Other Nationalities match to be played in Australia was staged in 1964, against Sydney Colts as a curtain-raiser to the third Test between Australia and France at the SCG. Other Nationalities was captained by South African and

North Sydney fullback Fred Griffiths, and featured Welsh legend Lewis Jones, who was playing with Wentworthville in Sydney's Second Division, and English players who were signed to Sydney premiership clubs, including Dick Huddart (St. George), Nat Silcock (Easts) and Parramatta trio Derek Hallas, Mike Jackson and Ivor Lingard. Manly rake and New Zealand Team of the Century hooker Jock Butterfield was the only Kiwi representative in the side, which also contained two members of the French touring squad. Sydney Colts were captained by North Sydney five-eighth Len Diett, and boasted future Australian internationals Ron Coote, Kevin Junee, Nick Yakich and Ron Saddler, and burgeoning first grade stars Bob Batty and Arthur Branighan. The Colts prevailed 25-16, with Manly winger Yakich scoring two tries.

An England-based Other Nationalities team took on the touring Kiwis in 1965 (New Zealand prevailed 15-7), while the combination also fielded a side in County Championships against Lancashire, Yorkshire and Cumbria in 1974 and '75.

OCEANIA vs. EUROPE A match between an Oceania representative side—made up of Australian, New Zealand and Papua New Guinean players—and Europe, containing French and British players, was staged in 1984 to mark 50 years since the establishment of Rugby League in France. The Oceania squad was captained by Wally Lewis and contained eight Australian stars—Lewis, Mal Meninga, Gene Miles, Kerry Boustead, Steve Mortimer, Ray Price, Wayne Pearce and Brad Tessman. The Kiwi contingent featured Mark Graham, Dean Bell, Hugh McGahan and cousins Kevin and Howie Tamati. Two Papua New Guinea players—David Noifa and Ekon Togila—were selected on the bench. The Europe side consisted of 10 Frenchmen, including captain Joel Roosebrouck, and six British players, headlined by brilliant centre Ellery Hanley, who scored Europe's only try in the 54-4 thrashing at Stade de la Cipalle Velodrome in Paris. Tessman, Miles and McGahan each crossed for doubles in the 11-tries-to-one mismatch.

THE ANZACS A combined Australian and New Zealand team played a representative side from the English county of Cumbria at Derwent Park, Workington, during the 2004 Tri-Nations series. The Anzacs line-up was made up of players from the Australian and New Zealand Tri-Nations squads, and bolstered by a bench containing European Super League-based Australians Ben Roarty and Chris Nero, and New Zealanders Henry Fa'afili and Lusi Sione. The Anzacs—wearing jerseys that were split down the middle, half-Kangaroo (green and gold) and half-Kiwi (black and white)—were coached by Melbourne mentor Craig Bellamy and former Kiwi Test great James Leuluai. Captain Brett Kimmorley kicked nine goals and was named man of the match in the 64-12 romp, while Bulldogs prop Mark O'Meley scored a hat-trick and Kiwi centre Shontayne Hape picked up a double. The Cumbria side was led by former England international fullback Gary Broadbent and featured future Great Britain Test winger Ade Gardner.

THE EXILES The inaugural match between the England national side and the Exiles, a team made up of Super League players hailing from overseas, was staged in 2011. It was marketed as the first international Origin match and played at Headingley in Leeds. The Exiles were coached by former Leeds and New Zealand Test mentor Brian McClennan, and boasted former Kangaroos Danny Buderus (who was named captain), Mark O'Meley and Craig Fitzgibbon, and fellow Australian stars Brett Hodgson, Pat Richards and Glenn Morrison. Kiwi Test representatives Thomas Leuluai, Sia Soliola, Francis Meli, Tony Puletua, Louis Anderson, David Fa'alogo and David Faiumu were also selected, along with Samoan internationals George Carmont and Kylie Leuluai, and Tongan representative Willie Manu. Former St. George Illawarra and Wests Tigers player Rangi Chase, a New Zealand Maori representative in 2010, played five-eighth for the Exiles before controversially winning selection in England's 2011 Four Nations squad on residential grounds.

England was denied the services of NRL stars including Wests Tigers' Gareth Ellis and Melbourne's Gareth Widdop after their respective clubs refused to release them for the match. The Exiles led an otherwise Test-strength England side 10-6 at halftime, before England appeared to have secured victory with a 69th-minute intercept try to Wigan star Joel Tomkins. But former Newcastle Knights centre Carmont crossed inside the final minute to snatch a 16-12 win for the Exiles.

A two-match series between England and the Exiles was announced for 2012, with former New Zealand Warriors, St. Helens and Parramatta coach Daniel Anderson named to take charge of the squad of expats.

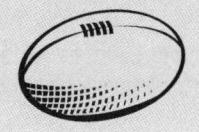

CHAPTER 8

THE TOP 50 PLAYERS OF ALL TIME

The selection of any 'best-ever' list of Rugby League players is an arduous undertaking, unmistakably self-indulgent and destined to elude widespread agreement. But it was an inherently fascinating and rewarding process—despite the hours spent agonising over the credentials of the game's greatest exponents from 104 seasons of competition.

Naturally, the most difficult aspect is leaving out players altogether. The calibre of stars not included in this list is staggering. How could the influential halfbacks Chris McKivat, 'Pony' Halloway, 'Chimpy' Busch, Billy Smith, Tom Raudonikis and Steve Mortimer be excluded? But then, who would they replace? The great Queensland forwards of past eras, Herb Steinohrt, Vic Armbruster and Brian Davies were tough to overlook, as were New South Wales counterparts Sid 'Joe' Pearce, Ray Price and Bradley Clyde.

The major diversion from similar lists that have been compiled in the past is the exclusion of Team of the Century winger Brian Bevan—this is on account of him having spent virtually his entire career in England. Placing the NRL's current stars among the pantheon of retired legends is also tricky—no doubt the estimation of Billy Slater will have soared again after another season, but this list is reflective of where they stood as of the end of 2011.

The criterion for inclusion was not hard and fast; but longevity, accomplishments at club and representative level, individual achievements and—above all—the ability to influence the outcome of a match all held significant sway. This list is intended as a tribute to Rugby League's finest. If nothing else, I hope it sparks vigorous debate, along with an appreciation of the men that have graced the Rugby League fields of Australia since 1908.

I ANDREW JOHNS (B. 1974)

- **Newcastle (1994-2007):** 249 games—80 tries, 917 goals, 22 field goals (2,176 points)
- **New South Wales (1995-2005):** 23 Origins—4 tries, 37 goals, 4 field goals (94 points)
- **Australia (1995-2006):** 26 Tests—12 tries, 89 goals (226 points)

Newcastle halfback Andrew Johns is the most complete player in Australian Rugby League history—a supreme match-winner. His prodigious talent was apparent from the moment he cemented the Knights' No.7 jumper in 1994, accelerating toward representative honours and spearheading a euphoric maiden premiership for the club in 1997. Johns' form in the late-1990s prompted calls that he may be the best halfback the game had seen; that accolade was almost a fait accompli a few short years later, and debate shifted to whether he was the best player of all time. 'Joey' won a record three Dally M Medals, two Golden Boot awards and collected the Clive Churchill Medal in captaining Newcastle to the title in 2001. Johns is regarded as arguably New South Wales' greatest Origin player; he was inspirational as captain in the 2002-03 series, while his performances in 2005 rank among the finest individual displays the game has witnessed. He was typically brilliant at Test level during a period when Australia was particularly dominant. Johns' masterful passing and kicking game, robust and determined running game, brilliant goalkicking and superb defensive capabilities were honed by incredible dedication and a fierce competitive streak. Revelations in 2007 that Johns had been battled drug and alcohol problems and bipolar disorder throughout his career were condemned in some quarters, but in many respects they made his list of achievements all the more remarkable—a tortured genius of sorts. Johns was named at halfback in the ARL Team of the Century in 2008, setting a new benchmark for all No.7s to aspire to.

2 CLIVE CHURCHILL (B. 1927 D. 1985)

- **South Sydney (1947-58):** 157 games—13 tries, 75 goals, 2 field goals (193 points)
- **New South Wales (1948-57):** 27 matches—4 tries, 16 goals, 2 field goals (48 points)
- **Australia (1948-56):** 37 Tests—10 goals (20 points)

Clive Churchill's name is invariably the first put forward when the subject of Rugby League's greatest player comes up for debate. The Newcastle fullback went to South Sydney in 1947 and became the greatest Rabbitoh—the pivotal figure in the club's golden age that garnered five premierships in six seasons (1950-51 and 1953-55). As Australian captain, Churchill led Rugby League in this country into a new era. He was the undisputed star and linchpin of the green-and-golds' series victory over the touring Lions in 1950, breaking Great Britain's 30-year-old stranglehold on the Ashes. Churchill was captain in 27 of his 37 Test appearances, captain-coaching the 1952-53 Kangaroo Tour squad and leading Australia to another home Ashes series triumph in 1954. Small in stature, Churchill played like a goliath. He was courageous, intensely competitive and perfected every facet of attack and defence. Churchill redefined fullback play, emulating the pioneering running fullbacks Charles 'Chook' Fraser and Frank McMillan, and taking it to a new level—Churchill was the catalyst for modern fullbacks becoming among the most dangerous attacking players in Rugby League. His performance against Manly during Souths' unbeaten run in the 'Miracle of '55'—remaining on the field after breaking his arm to set up the levelling try and kick the match-winning conversion from the touchline—was Churchill's most famous day in myrtle and cardinal, and summed up his greatest qualities. Many of Rugby League's pioneering players and administrators—including Dally Messenger and 'Jersey' Flegg—declared Churchill the best player they ever saw. He was named at fullback in the ARL Team of the Century; came in at No.1 in *Rugby League Week* (1992) and *Daily Telegraph* (2000) top 100 lists voted on by panels of experts; and was one of the four original Immortals—glowing acknowledgements of the greatness of the man they called 'The Little Master.'

3 WALLY LEWIS (B. 1959)

- **Brisbane, Gold Coast (1988-92):** 80 games—26 tries, 12 goals, 2 field goals (132 points)
- **Queensland (1979-91)*:** 35 matches—7 tries, 1 goal, 2 field goals (30 points)
- **Australia (1981-91):** 34 Tests—11 tries, 2 field goals (45 points)

The 1980s belonged to Wally Lewis, a brilliant, bold and abrasive Queenslander. An extraordinarily polarising figure, the five-eighth's status as one of the Rugby League's most gifted match-winners and greatest competitors cannot be argued. Lewis' legacy is steeped in his performances at Origin level, captaining Queensland in 30 of his 31 appearances, winning seven of the first 10 series against NSW and claiming eight man of the match awards. The spectre of Lewis looms over Origin football two decades after his retirement—still by far the most dominant player the concept has witnessed. He assumed the Test captaincy in 1984 and led Australia in 24 Tests, encompassing the unbeaten 1986 Kangaroo Tour and a World Cup final victory in 1988. Lewis' lack of success in the NSWRL premiership is the only accomplishment missing in his phenomenal career. He was the inaugural skipper and marquee player for the fledgling Brisbane Broncos, but was stripped of the captaincy after two seasons and ousted from the club a year later, finishing his career with two seasons for the struggling Gold Coast. But Lewis dominated the domestic Brisbane competition, the BRL, winning premierships with Valleys (1979) and Wynnum-Manly (1984 and '86). His 1984 season is regarded as one of the most dominant by an individual—premiership success with the Seagulls, and captaining the Brisbane representative side to victory in the Panasonic Cup, leading Queensland to an Origin series triumph, and skippering Australia in the 3-0 home series whitewash of Great Britain. Lewis was the recipient of the inaugural Golden Boot award following his season of unbridled achievement. The ARL Team of the Century five-eighth's reputation as Queensland's greatest-ever player is rarely questioned, as his nickname—'The King'—would suggest.

4 REG GASNIER (B. 1939)

- **St. George (1959-67):** 125 games—127 tries, 20 goals (421 points)
- **New South Wales (1959-67):** 16 matches—13 tries, 3 goals (45 points)
- **Australia (1959-67):** 39 Tests—28 tries (84 points)

St. George champion Reg Gasnier was the next in the line of great Australian centres after pioneering superstar Dally Messenger and 1930s phenomenon Dave Brown—but 'Puff the Magic Dragon' arguably exceeded the deeds and the ability of the Easts legends. Gasnier's unparalleled attacking brilliance saw him chosen as one of the four original Immortals in 1981, while he was named in the ARL Team of the Century in 2008. A three-time winner of E.E. Christensen's NSW Player of the Year honour, the St. George junior made his first grade debut in 1959. Gasnier missed the Grand Final with injury in that season, but won six subsequent premierships with the all-conquering Dragons, scoring three tries in the 1960 Grand Final. His first grade career garnered an incredible 127 tries in 125 games—a strike-rate among try centurions bettered only by Harold Horder—and he topped the premiership on three occasions. Gasnier scored 28 tries in 39 Tests, including Ashes hat-tricks on the 1959-60 and 1963-64 Kangaroo Tours. His incredible tryscoring potency was despite his reputation as a wholly unselfish centre and a tremendous provider for his wingers. Blessed with blinding pace and acceleration, he was a superbly balanced runner—Gasnier in full stride was as close to beauty as Rugby League came. He became Australia's youngest Ashes captain in 1962 and was chosen to captain-coach the 1967-68 Kangaroos—his third tour to Britain and France. But Gasnier broke his leg in the first Test loss to Great Britain, and although Australia retained the Ashes, he broke down again in his comeback game in France. Gasnier retired after the tour aged just 28—a cruel way for one of the game's most admired and gifted players to exit. But the premature departure did little to diminish his aura—the name 'Gasnier' still evokes sparkling memories of Rugby League genius for the ages.

5 DARREN LOCKYER (B. 1977)

- **Brisbane (1995-2011):** 355 games—123 tries, 341 goals, 21 field goals (1,195 points)
- **Queensland (1998-2011):** 36 Origins—9 tries, 22 goals, two field goals (84 points)
- **Australia (1998-2011):** 59 Tests—35 tries, 31 goals, 2 field goals (204 points)

The bare figures of Darren Lockyer's career are destined to amaze Rugby League followers for generations to come. Records for most appearances in first grade, State of Origin and Test football—and unprecedented marks for most appearances as captain, most tries and longest career-span for Australia—are a testament to the modern day legend's durability and longevity. But the numbers tell only part of the story of Lockyer's unsurpassed consistency and match-winning brilliance. The Roma product's place among Australia's finest fullbacks of all time was assured in 2003 after he spearheaded the Kangaroos' incredible 3-0 Ashes cleansweep of Great Britain in his first series as skipper and was awarded the Golden Boot. He shifted to five-eighth the following season—a selfless move for the benefit of his Brisbane club side—and became one of the best-ever pivots. Lockyer won a second Golden Boot in 2006 after captaining the Broncos, Queensland and Australia to stunning successes in one of the most extraordinary seasons by an individual in the code's history. His gliding, incisive running and playmaking class were features of his tenure at fullback—the position he was named in when Queensland's Team of the Century was announced in 2008—while he developed into one of the greatest ball-players and cool-headed match-winners of all time after his transition to the No.6. Lockyer can lay claim to being the greatest clutch player Rugby League has ever known. As his career wore on, Lockyer produced match-deciding plays in the dying minutes and seconds with incredible regularity. Lockyer possessed remarkable toughness, while he invariably responded to criticism with a man of the match performance.

6 JOHNNY RAPER (B. 1939)

- **Newtown, St. George (1957-69):** 215 games—57 tries, 4 field goals (179 points)
- **New South Wales (1959-70):** 24 matches—5 tries (15 points)
- **Australia (1959-68):** 39 Tests—11 tries (33 points)

Johnny Raper's mantle as Australia's greatest lock-forward has never been questioned nor challenged, while there are many respected judges—including the doyen of Rugby League callers Frank Hyde—that assert the man known affectionately as 'Chook' is the best player the game has produced. His textbook defence—complete with trademark brilliant cover tackling—was without peer, while his instinctive skill in attack was equally awe-inspiring. Raper's fitness and dedication to training was as legendary as his penchant for partying; Rugby League has never had a more distinctive or loved character. He began his career with Newtown, but was lured to St. George and won eight straight premierships with the club (1959-66); Raper captain-coached the Dragons for two seasons after their world record run ended and his contribution was recognised when the Men of League named him St. George's greatest-ever clubman as part of the centenary celebrations in 2008. He was named the *Sun Herald*'s Best and Fairest three times and E.E. Chistensen's NSW Player of the Year twice. Raper made his Test debut in 1959 against New Zealand and was an automatic selection until he bowed out of representative football as captain of the 1968 World Cup triumph. He toured three times with the Kangaroos, producing his most famous performance in the 'Swinton Massacre' that secured the Ashes for Australia on English soil for the first time in over half a century on the 1963-64 tour, while he captained Australia to victory in the deciding third Test on the 1967-68 tour. Lock in the ARL Team of the Century and one of the four original Immortals, Raper was one of a kind—as Frank Hyde said: 'When Johnny Raper was born, they not only destroyed the mould, they pulped it.'

7 DAVE BROWN (B. 1913 D. 1974)

- **Eastern Suburbs (1930-41):** 94 games—93 tries, 194 goals (667 points)
- **New South Wales (1931-36):** 19 matches—9 tries, 45 goals (117 points)
- **Australia (1933-36):** 9 Tests—7 tries, 26 goals (73 points)

'The Bradman of League' handle is fair indicator of the astonishing feats of the Easts and Kangaroos centre phenomenon of the 1930s, Dave Brown. An uncontainable attacking force, Brown debuted for Eastern Suburbs at the age of 16 in 1930, and was the overwhelming star of the 1933-34 Kangaroo Tour, setting a record to stand the test of time with 285 points in 32 matches. Brown became Australia's youngest-ever Test captain against New Zealand (22 years and 177 days) in 1935 and led his country in the Ashes series against the touring Lions in 1936. As captain of the first two premierships of the Easts dynasty that won three straight titles from 1935-37, Brown set a host of almost inconceivable records in the 1935 season—his 45 points in a match and 38 tries in a season have never been remotely challenged, while his 244 points stood as a record season total for 34 years. He joined English club Warrington at the end of 1936 for a luminous four-season stint, but returned to finish his career as captain-coach of the Tricolours, overseeing another premiership in 1940 and retiring a year later. Brown played down his remarkable pointscoring exploits as a by-product of playing in a champion team, but that sentiment was typical of his trademark modesty—the records are a tangible marker of a footballing genius of the highest order. He was a glaring omission from the ARL Team of the Century in 2008, but was chosen as a reserve in the NSW Team of the Century.

8 BOB FULTON (B. 1947)

- **Manly, Eastern Suburbs (1966-79):** 263 games—147 tries, 26 goals, 58 field goals (510 points)

- **New South Wales (1967-68):** 17 matches—14 tries (42 points)
- **Australia (1968-78):** 35 Tests—25 tries, 6 field goals (82 points)

Equally brilliant at centre or five-eighth, Rugby League has produced few more dazzling individual talents than Bob Fulton. A tenacious, unrelenting competitor, Fulton's acceleration and evasiveness marked him as one of the game's foremost attacking threats during the 1960s and 1970s. Born in Warrington but raised in Wollongong, Fulton debuted for Manly as a teenager in 1966, and captained the Sea Eagles from five-eighth in a gallant Grand Final loss against Souths in 1968, aged just 20. 'Bozo' starred in Manly's breakthrough premiership successes in 1972-73 (under the captaincy of Fred Jones), scoring a mesmerising double in the brutal '73 decider that ranks as one of the great individual performances in a Grand Final. Fulton resumed as skipper and led the Sea Eagles to victory in the 1976 Grand Final, his last match for the club before finishing his career at Easts. A shock omission from the 1967-68 Kangaroo Tour squad, Fulton was the top try-scorer on the 1973 and 1978 tours to Britain and France—the latter as captain in his international swansong. His total of 25 Test tries ranks fourth on the all time list, while he is still the eighth-highest try-scorer in premiership history. Fulton's naming as one of the four original Immortals in 1981 reflects his standing in the game, while he was selected as a reserve in the ARL Team of the Century, and at five-eighth in the NSW and NSW Country Teams of the Century.

9 GRAEME LANGLANDS (B. 1941)

- **St. George (1963-76):** 227 games—86 tries, 648 goals (1,554 points)
- **New South Wales (1962-75):** 33 matches—19 tries, 40 goals (137 points)
- **Australia (1963-75):** 45 Tests—20 tries, 73 goals (206 points)

Graeme 'Changa' Langlands placed fifth in *Rugby League Week*'s Top 100 poll in 1992 and second in the *Daily Telegraph*'s Top 100 in 2000—a glowing appraisal of one of the game's most accomplished, decorated and admired players. Langlands arrived at St. George—a club that had just secured its seventh straight premiership—from Wollongong in 1963. He won four titles in his first four seasons in Sydney (firstly in the centres and then in his preferred fullback spot) and was the last playing remnant of the Dragons' world record run, retiring early in 1976 after six seasons as captain with his name elevated alongside Gasnier and Raper in the pantheon of the club's greats. Fiercely competitive, courageous and regularly brilliant, 'Changa' toured three times with the Kangaroos (1963-64, 1967-68 and 1973)—the third tour as captain-coach. A prolific accumulator of points, Langlands' phenomenal on-field deeds overshadowed any story numbers could tell. The freakish tries and extraordinary play he produced were forerunners to modern superstars such as Billy Slater. There were disappointments in his wonderful career—the notorious 'White Boots' 1975 Grand Final is the best-known—but the multitude of match-winning performances far outweigh those aberrations. The shining highlight of his 45-Test career was undoubtedly the 1974 Ashes decider at the SCG; the 32-year-old captain was chaired from the field with the crowd chanting his name after a wonderful display in the 22-18 triumph—a fitting tribute for the great 'Changa.' He was named as an Immortal in 1999, and while Clive Churchill occupied the fullback spot in the Team of the Century selections in 2008, Langlands was chosen as a reserve in the ARL, and centre in the NSW and NSW Country line-ups.

10 DALLY MESSENGER (B. 1883 D. 1959)

- **Eastern Suburbs (1908-13):** 48 games—21 tries, 157 goals, 2 field goals (381 points)
- **New South Wales (1908-12):** 6 matches—10 tries, 43 goals (116 points)
- **Australia (1908-14):** 7 Tests—4 tries, 16 goals (44 points)
- **New Zealand (1908):** 2 Tests—1 try, 3 goals (9 points)

Herbert Henry 'Dally' Messenger was Rugby League's first superstar, a glorious exponent of every facet of the game, whose status and fame was almost greater than the code itself during its formative seasons. The preeminent rugby union player of his time, Messenger's defection was one of the most significant precursors to the breakaway Rugby League movement's eventual success. Messenger toured Britain as a guest with the trailblazing New Zealand 'All Golds' in 1907-08, and was the undeniable star again on the pioneering 1908-09 Kangaroo Tour, top-scoring with 155 points. He captained Australia in Tests against England on the tour and at home in 1910, but declined the opportunity to tour with the 1911-12 Kangaroos. Messenger captained Eastern Suburbs to a hat-trick of premierships from 1911-13, retiring after the third triumph. A masterful attacking player and a goalkicker extraordinaire, Messenger's deeds with the boot and with ball in hand are entwined within Rugby League folklore. He was named as a reserve in the ARL Team of the Century and on the wing in the NSW Team of the Century in 2008—100 years after he spearheaded the fledgling code. Admirers exhausted every possible accolade and metaphor in describing his footballing genius, but Messenger's most common soubriquet sums him up best—'The Master.'

11 FRANK BURGE (B. 1894 D. 1958)

- **Glebe, St. George (1911-27):** 154 games—146 tries, 49 goals (536 points)
- **New South Wales (1912-26):** 6 matches—7 tries, 5 goals (31 points)
- **Australia (1914-22):** 13 Tests—7 tries, 7 goals (35 points)

Australia's greatest tryscoring forward and one of the most destructive ball-runners the game has produced, Frank Burge stands over the history of the extinct Glebe club like a colossus. Burge's strike-rate of 137 tries in 138 matches for the Dirty Reds dwarfs that of even the most prolific modern-day wingers and fullbacks. A first grade debutant at just 16 in 1911, Burge topped the competition's tryscoring table three times during the 1910s and scored a premiership record eight tries in a match against University in 1920 (he also added four goals for a then-record 32 points). Big, powerful and blindingly fast, 'Chunky' Burge scored 33 tries in just 23 matches on the 1921-22 Kangaroo Tour. He was unable to deliver a premiership for Glebe—runners-up finishes in 1911-12, 1915 and 1922 was the closest the club came to a title—but his influence was underlined during a one-season stint as captain-coach of St. George. The 32-year-old led the previous season's wooden spooners to their maiden appearance in a premiership final, where they were defeated by South Sydney. A player ahead of his time, Burge's dedication to training and fitness—combined with the obvious advantage of natural ability—gave him a giant head-start over his rivals. Burge was named as a reserve in the ARL's Team of the Century and at prop in NSW's Team of the Century (despite playing predominantly in the backrow) during the 2008 Centenary celebrations, but he was unquestionably the greatest forward Australia produced during the code's first half-century.

12 ALLAN LANGER (B. 1966)

- **Brisbane (1988-2002):** 258 games—100 tries, 8 goals, 6 field goals (422 points)
- **Queensland (1987-2002):** 34 Origins—10 tries, 1 field goal (41 points)
- **Australia (1988-98):** 24 Tests—5 tries (20 points)

Allan Langer can lay claim to being the No.1 player of the 1990s. The diminutive Brisbane halfback was capable of turning a match by himself—and did so with phenomenal regularity. 'Alfie' was the undisputed linchpin as captain of the Broncos' 1992-93 and 1997-98 premiership successes, winning the Rothmans Medal and the Clive Churchill Medal in the club's maiden title-winning season. He won the Dally M Medal in 1996, finished third in 1988 and 1994, and was named Dally M Players' Player in 1991 and '92, while collecting five Broncos player of the year gongs. Impossible to contain, Langer's tricky footwork, fantastic all-round kicking game and brilliant playmaking instincts marked him as the most dangerous attacking player of the decade. He is the only player in premiership history to score 100 tries at halfback. Being displaced by his great rival Ricky Stuart on consecutive Kangaroo Tours (1990 and 1994) after first Test losses to Great Britain were glaring and rare disappointments in a charmed career, but he bounced back on each occasion to re-establish himself as the game's best No.7, and captained Australia to victory over New Zealand in 1998. Langer's deeds in a then-record 34 matches for the Maroons place him in the top bracket of players in Origin history, while he was named at halfback in Queensland's Team of the Century.

13 HAROLD HORDER (B. 1894 D. 1978)

- **South Sydney, North Sydney (1912-24):** 136 games—152 tries, 150 goals (756 points)
- **New South Wales (1915-24):** 9 matches—23 tries, 18 goals (105 points)
- **Australia (1914-24):** 13 Tests—11 tries, 10 goals (53 points)

Harold Horder, the 'Wonder Winger' of the 1910s and 1920s, rates as the most devastating try-scorer in Australian Rugby League history. His strike-rate of 152 tries in 136 first grade games—102 in just 86 games for Souths and 50 in as many appearances for Norths—dwarfs all of the game's great try-poachers. Horder's try on debut in myrtle and cardinal has passed into folklore—a 90-metre effort in which he beat a swarm of Glebe defenders, giving supporters but a glimpse of what they could expect for the following 12 seasons. He starred in South Sydney premierships in 1914 and 1918, before joining North Sydney and featuring in the club's celebrated line-up that won back-to-back titles in 1921-22. After making his Test debut against England in 1914, Horder was unstoppable in Australia's first series following World War I, scoring nine tries in four Tests against New Zealand in 1919. Horder delighted the crowds of England on the 1921-22 Kangaroo Tour, crossing for 35 tries in just 25 matches. The undisputed star of his era, he was lightning quick with mesmerising footwork and a deceptive swerve, setting an unattainable benchmark for wingers through the generations to follow. Horder was arguably the most controversial omission from the ARL and NSW Teams of the Century in 2008—Brian Bevan, who spent virtually his entire career in England, was named in the Australian side, while centre Dally Messenger was moved to the flank in the state line-up. But Horder retains a strong base of pundits that rank him at the top of the tree in the pantheon of Australia's wingers.

14 VIC HEY (B. 1912 D. 1995)

- **Western Suburbs, Parramatta (1933-49):** 37 games -21 tries, 1 goal (65 points)
- **New South Wales (1933-35):** 11 matches—9 tries (27 points)
- **Queensland (1936):** 3 matches—0 points
- **Australia (1933-36):** 6 Tests—2 tries (6 points)

One of the most influential figures in Australia's Rugby League history, Vic Hey's status as the game's best-ever five-eighth went unchallenged until the emergence of Bob Fulton and Wally Lewis several decades later. He toured with the 1933-34 Kangaroos as a 20-year-old after just one season of first grade with Western Suburbs, and returned to spearhead the previous season's wooden spooners' drive to a premiership triumph in 1934. Hey moved to Queensland for a season in 1936, guiding Toowoomba to its first Bulimba Cup success in eight years, representing the state side against NSW and playing all three Tests against the touring Lions—two at centre and one at pivot. Leeds lured Hey to England in 1937 and he became one of great Australian imports during a decade with the club. His class underpinned Leeds' Challenge Cup victories in 1941 and '42, before heading back to Australia and captain-coaching the young Parramatta club. Stocky and powerful, Hey was a punishing defender and a dazzling ball-runner, while he possessed tremendous hands—the hallmark of all the great five-eighths. Hey's expertise in every facet of the game was integral to Australia's euphoric Ashes series wins in 1950 and '54 as a shrewd coach.

15 ARTHUR BEETSON (B. 1945 D. 2011)

- **Balmain, Eastern Suburbs, Parramatta (1966-80):** 221 games—24 tries, 1 field goal (73 points).
- **New South Wales (1966-77):** 17 matches—3 tries (9 points)
- **Queensland (1980-81)*:** 3 matches—0 points.
- **Australia (1966-77):** 28 Tests—1 try (3 points)

A master ball-player and one of the greatest attacking forwards Rugby League has ever known, Arthur Beetson's vast list of achievements in the game is matched only by his phenomenal natural ability and magnetic personality. The Roma product arrived at Balmain in 1966 via Redcliffe, switching from centre to the pack and producing one of the most famous Test debuts of all time in his first season with the Tigers. Beetson laid on two first half tries with brilliant pieces of attacking skill to spearhead Australia's Ashes-winning third Test victory against Great Britain. The burly forward battled criticisms of being lazy for much of his career and garnered a reputation as a hothead (he missed Balmain's 1969 Grand Final win with suspension), but he quashed those jibes after being handed the captaincy at Easts and magnificently leading the Roosters to emphatic premiership victories in 1974-75. Inconceivably skilful and fast for a big man, Beetson was a cornerstone of much of Australia's success during the 1970s, starring in Ashes series triumphs on the 1973 Kangaroo Tour and in 1974 at home, before captaining his country to World Series and World Cup success in 1975 and 1977 respectively. Beetson's role as the 35-year-old skipper of Queensland's inaugural State of Origin side in 1980 provided a glorious addendum to his magnificent legacy. Named as the seventh Immortal in 2003, Beetson was honoured with selection at prop in the ARL Team of the Century and the Indigenous Team of the Century, and in the second-row in the Queensland Team of the Century in 2008, while he was previously chosen in the front-row in best-ever Balmain and Eastern Suburbs combinations.

16 MAL MENINGA (B. 1960)

- **Canberra (1986-94):** 166 games—74 tries, 283 goals, 2 field goals (864 points)
- **Queensland (1979-94)*:** 38 matches—9 tries, 78 goals (188 points)
- **Australia (1982-94):** 46 Tests—21 tries, 99 goals (278 points)

ARL Team of the Century centre Mal Meninga's list of achievements is almost as colossal as his giant frame that terrorised defenders throughout a 17-year top-level career. A teenage sensation with Brisbane Souths in the late-1970s, Meninga won BRL Grand Finals in 1981 and 1985 before joining Canberra and captaining the club to premiership success in 1989-90 and 1994. He is the only player to make four Kangaroo Tours and captain two squads to Great Britain and France, while his Test appearances and points totals were record marks at the time of his retirement. Meninga is the highest point-scorer in Origin history, with 161 in a then-record 32 appearances for Queensland. A large part of his legendary legacy stems from his comeback from four broken arm injuries that derailed his 1987-88 seasons, winning the Golden Boot and leading the Raiders to their historic maiden Grand Final triumph in 1989. A destructive runner with express pace in the first half of his career, Meninga developed into a skilful, first-rate ball distributor as he progressed. He tormented Great Britain in five Ashes series, but never more importantly than in his towering displays as captain in the hard-fought 1992 campaign at home. Meninga was named at centre in the Teams of the 1980s and 1990s, as well as the Australian and Queensland Teams of the Century. His contribution to the Raiders was recognised by his selection as Canberra's greatest clubman by the Men of League in 2008.

17 BRAD FITTLER (B. 1972)

- **Penrith, Sydney Roosters (1989-2004):** 336 games—122 tries, 14 goals, 10 field goals (526 points)
- **New South Wales (1990-2004):** 31 Origins—8 tries, 2 field goals (34 points)
- **Australia (1990-2001):** 38 Tests—17 tries, 1 goal, 1 field goal (71 points)

A schoolboy phenomenon and a self-confessed larrikin, Brad Fittler developed into one of the modern era's great leaders and dominant match-winners. The Penrith junior debuted for the Panthers aged just 17 in 1989—a little over 12 months later he had become the youngest State of Origin player, scored a try in Penrith's maiden Grand Final (an 18-14 loss to Canberra) and won selection as the youngest-ever Kangaroo tourist. Fittler was integral to the Panthers' breakthrough premiership success in 1991 and was an automatic Test selection when he embarked on his second Kangaroo Tour in 1994. Pitched into the dual role of NSW and Australian captain at 23 after the Super League war broke out, Fittler became one of the most prolific representative skippers of all time, leading the Blues in a then-record 14 matches (including 3-0 series victories in 1996 and 2000) and Australia to World Cup triumphs in 1995 and 2000 among 25 Tests as captain. He joined the Sydney Roosters and led the club to four Grand Finals—winning the 2002 NRL title—in becoming the first player to skipper 200 first grade games. Fittler was the complete package: a powerful ball-runner with a superb all-round kicking game and a majestic passing ability, he possessed a devastating step off either foot that left countless defenders grasping at air. He played predominantly in the centres early in his career, and extensively at lock during the mid-to-late-1990s, but was best suited to five-eighth, where he was named in the Team of the 1990s and the Penrith and Eastern Suburbs/ Sydney Roosters Teams of the Century. Fittler is the only player to win Dally M awards in three different positions, while he collected the Provan-Summons Medal as the ARL competition's player of the year in 1997 and the Golden Boot in 2000.

18 BRIAN CARLSON (B. 1933 D. 1987)

- **North Sydney (1957-62):** 72 games—31 tries, 211 goals (515 points)
- **New South Wales (1952-59):** 10 matches—8 tries, 13 goals (50 points)
- **Queensland (1957):** 4 matches—2 tries, 1 goal (8 points)
- **Australia (1952-61):** 23 Tests—16 tries, 21 goals (90 points)

Brian Carlson was a tremendously versatile backline player and an attacking genius, possessing a cavalier brilliance that rendered him one of the dominant players of the 1950s. His famously casual approach to the game was offset by an extraordinary natural ability and awe-inspiring instincts. The North Newcastle prodigy toured with the 1952-53 Kangaroos as a 19-year-old and scored an incredible 29 tries in just 19 games, earning plaudits as the greatest wing prospect since Harold Horder. Carlson featured in Australia's 1954 Ashes series victory, before switching to fullback during the 1957 World Cup after injury claimed Keith Barnes—and duly won player of the tournament honours in Australia's historic success. Joining North Sydney, Carlson's multifaceted talents were utilised at fullback, centre and wing as needs dictated, excelling in all three positions. He captained Australia in a Test against New Zealand in 1959, toured with the 1959-60 Kangaroos and amassed another 19 tries, and captain-coached his country on a tour of New Zealand in 1961 which proved to be his international swansong. Carlson's total of 16 tries in Test and World Cup matches was a record at the time, but his magnificent on-field deeds extend far beyond mere statistics. He was named in the Newcastle District's Team of the Century on the wing and the NSW Country Team of the Century in the centres in 2008, while he was chosen at fullback in North Sydney's Team of the Century in 2006—supporting Noel Kelly's assertion that Carlson was 'the greatest all-rounder the game ever saw.'

19 PETER STERLING (B. 1960)

- **Parramatta (1978-92):** 227 games—48 tries, 1 goal, 15 field goals (190 points)
- **New South Wales (1981-88):** 13 Origins—0 points
- **Australia (1982-88):** 18 Tests—4 tries, 1 field goal (16 points)

Parramatta halfback Peter Sterling blossomed under the tutelage of Jack Gibson after the master coach's arrival at the club in 1981, developing into one of Australia's greatest halfbacks—a superb organiser, a peerless playmaker with finely tuned passing and kicking skills, and a supreme competitor. Among a galaxy of stars at the Eels, 'Sterlo' was the key to the club's premiership successes of 1981-83 and 1986. Sterling tormented Great Britain on the unbeaten 1982 and 1986 Kangaroo Tours (the latter as vice-captain) and featured in home Ashes series triumphs in 1984 and 1988, frequently thwarting the Test aspirations of his great rival, the brilliant Canterbury No.7 Steve Mortimer. Born in Toowoomba but a Wagga junior, Sterling played 13 matches for NSW in the Origin cauldron, starring in the 1986 series whitewash and captaining the Blues in a narrow series loss in 1987. The plethora of individual awards Sterling collected is indicative of his consistency and class—two Rothmans Medals (1987 and 1990), two Dally M Medals (1986-87) and three *Rugby League Week* Player of the Year awards (1984 and 1986-87), while he was named the inaugural Clive Churchill medallist after Parramatta's epic 4-2 win in the 1986 Grand Final. A recurring shoulder injury hampered the latter part of his career and forced his premature retirement early in 1992, by which stage his status as one of the game's legends was assured—Sterling placed 11th in *Rugby League Week*'s top 100 players of all time later that year, and 14th in a similar poll run by the *Daily Telegraph* in 2000.

20 KEN IRVINE (B. 1940 D. 1990)

- **North Sydney, Manly (1958-73):** 236 games—212 tries, 70 tries, 1 field goal (778 points)
- **New South Wales (1959-67):** 25 matches—28 tries, 4 goals (92 points)
- **Australia (1959-67):** 33 Tests—33 tries, 11 goals (121 points)

The most prolific try-scorer in premiership history despite playing 13 of his 16 seasons at battling North Sydney, Ken Irvine found the line with unprecedented regularity at representative level and is one of Australian Rugby League's most revered figures. Irvine is the greatest player Norths produced, scoring 171 tries from 176 games and topping the competition in three seasons, before joining Manly in the twilight of his career and achieving long overdue club success with Grand Final victories in 1972 and '73, extending his record mark to 212 tries. Blindingly fast (he ran as a professional sprinter for a time) and elusive, Irvine toured three times with the Kangaroos—the first time as a 19-year-old with the 1959-60 squad. 'Mongo' Irvine boasted the extraordinary record of 33 tries in 33 Tests (a mark that stood until broken by Darren Lockyer in his 52nd Test in 2010), including Ashes hat-tricks during the 1963 and 1966 series successes, while his 28 tries remains a record for interstate matches. Irvine died at the age of 50 in 1990 after a long and private battle with leukaemia, robbing Rugby League of one of its most adored figures and truly majestic players. He was named on the wing in the ARL and NSW Teams of the Century in 2008.

21 DUNCAN THOMPSON (B. 1895 D. 1980)

- **North Sydney (1916-23):** 58 games—10 tries, 46 goals (128 points)
- **Queensland (1915-25):** 11 matches—18 goals (36 points)
- **New South Wales (1922):** 1 match—0 points
- **Australia (1919-24):** 9 Tests—1 try, 4 goals (11 points).

Duncan Thompson was ranked 10th when a panel of experts convened to pick the 100 greatest players of all time for *Rugby League Week* in 1992—the highest-placing halfback. Doubtlessly, he was the finest exponent of the position in the pre-World War II era. Thompson first represented Queensland from Ipswich in 1915, before spending the following season with North Sydney, and was shot in the lung while in France serving in World War I. Despite the injury, he debuted for Australia in 1919 and rejoined North Sydney in 1920. Fast, nimble and a brilliant creator of play, Thompson was the linchpin of Norths' phenomenal dual premiership-winning combination of 1921-22, captaining the side in the latter season. He starred on the 1921-22 Kangaroo Tour, but his Sydney career ended abruptly when he was sent off and suspended for kicking an opponent (a charge the cleanskin vehemently denied).

Thompson vowed never to play in the Sydney premiership again and returned to his native Queensland. Adding another glorious chapter to his career, Thompson was a catalyst for Queensland's continued domination of NSW in the 1924-25 interstate series and for the all-conquering performances of the Toowoomba representative side, the famed 'Galloping Clydesdales'. The 'Downs Fox' was an attacking genius and one of Australian Rugby League's most influential players.

22 BILLY SLATER (B. 1983)

- **Melbourne (2003-11):** 203 games—124 tries (496 points)
- **Queensland (2004-11):** 17 Origins—11 tries (44 points)
- **Australia (2008-11):** 17 Tests—18 tries (72 points)

The trajectory of exceptional Melbourne fullback Billy Slater's career suggests he will be an automatic top 10 selection in future 'greatest players' lists. A rookie sensation for the Storm in 2003, Slater scored one of State of Origin's greatest tries in just his second appearance for Queensland in 2004. The Innisfail product was unquestionably one of the NRL's most exciting attacking talents, boasting explosive speed and wonderful tryscoring instincts, but he was also erratic and inconsistent. The 2008 season proved a turning point: he made his Test debut, cemented the Queensland No.1 jersey and had confirmed his status as the game's undisputed best fullback by the end of the year. A one-match suspension cost him the Dally M Medal, but he was named the Golden Boot winner and the inaugural RLIF Player of the Year. Slater won the Clive Churchill Medal after Melbourne's 2009 Grand Final victory—and within two years he was challenging 'The Little Master's' mantle as Rugby League's best-ever custodian. His freakish deeds in attack and defence, peerless positional play, burgeoning ball-playing skills and unflagging support play had rendered him the complete package. An unwavering match-winner at club and representative level throughout the Storm's harrowing 2010 salary cap drama, Slater won a belated Dally M Medal in 2011 and claimed the Golden Boot-RLIF Player of the Year double for the second time as his performances reached an unprecedented level.

23 WALLY PRIGG (B. 1908 D. 1980)

- **New South Wales (1929-39):** 34 matches—12 tries (36 points)
- **Australia (1929-38):** 19 Tests—4 tries (12 points)

The greatest lock-forward of the 1930s, Wally Prigg's longevity was matched only by the quality of his play. Prigg revolutionised the lock role, combining typically tireless and stiff defence with a creative passing game—the first of the 'second five-eighth' style locks. He was also a dangerous runner and a superb support player. The Newcastle champion played his entire career in the region and became the first player to embark on three Kangaroo Tours, captaining the 1937-38 squad (the only player based in a country centre to do so). His brilliant performance in the 10-3 third Test victory against England was perhaps his most famous, earning plaudits from the British press, before scoring a try in each of the two Tests in the historic series against France—the last of his then-record 19 appearances for Australia. Distinctive with his curly red hair protruding from his headgear, Prigg played a record 34 interstate matches for NSW. His legacy as 'Newcastle's favourite son' was honoured by his naming as captain of the Newcastle Team of the Century in 2008 ahead of Clive Churchill, while he was also named at lock in the NSW Country Team of the Century and as a reserve in the NSW Team of the Century.

24 KEITH HOLMAN (B. 1925 D. 2011)

- **Western Suburbs (1949-61):** 200 games—70 tries, 83 goals (376 points)
- **New South Wales (1950-58):** 25 matches—21 tries, two goals (67 points)
- **Australia (1950-58):** 35 Tests—14 tries, 6 goals (54 points)

Dubbo product Keith Holman was twice turned away by South Sydney as a junior on account of being too small, but found a home with Western Suburbs, becoming the club's greatest player and one of Australia most distinguished halfbacks. The Victorian-born No.7 made his debut for Australia in the drought-breaking Ashes series victory in 1950 and toured with the 1952-53 and 1956-57 Kangaroos. 'Yappy' Holman played a then-record 14 Ashes Tests, while his total of 32 Tests for Australia was second only to Clive Churchill at the time. He missed the Magpies' 1952 Grand Final victory while he was away with the Kangaroos, but he formed a magnificent partnership with five-eighth Frank Stanmore at club and representative level, and his mark of 200 first grade games for the club was bettered only by fellow Test halfback Tom Raudonikis. Holman played in Grand Final losses to St. George in 1956 and 1961—the last match of his career. His insatiable passion for Rugby League was legendary, while he took halfback play in a new direction with his tenacious and aggressive defence to complement the traditional attacking role. Holman was named E.E. Christensen's NSW Player of the Year in 1951, 1956 and 1958, while he won a record four *Sun Herald* Best and Fairest awards (1950-51, 1956 and 1958).

25 LAURIE DALEY (B. 1969)

- **Canberra (1987-2000):** 244 games—87 tries, 44 goals, 9 field goals (445 points)
- **New South Wales (1989-99):** 23 Origins—6 tries, 1 goal (25 points)
- **Australia (1990-98):** 21 Tests—11 tries, 2 field goals (46 points)

Laurie Daley combined breathtaking flashes of individual brilliance and an intense competitive streak to become one of the modern era's most dominant match-winners. A 17-year-old first grade debutant with Canberra in 1987, the Junee product starred in the Raiders' 1989-90 premiership victories at centre, but his devastating running game and playmaking instincts saw him become the heir apparent to Wally Lewis as the game's dominant five-eighth, wearing the No.6 in the 1994 Grand Final triumph. Daley toured with the 1990 and 1994 Kangaroos (the latter as vice-captain), and assumed the NSW Origin captaincy at just 22 in 1992, spearheading three straight series victories for the Blues. The Super League war prevented him from beginning a long tenure as Test skipper, but his performances at club level remained as dazzling as ever, winning the Dally M Medal in 1995 and the Super League Player of the Year Award in 1997. Daley assumed the Test and Origin captaincy after the game reunited in 1998, and retired from representative football the following season as arguably NSW's greatest Origin player. Fiercely determined and a strong defender, Daley was blessed with exquisite hands. Despite suffering a number of serious injuries, Daley was durable competitor and played a then-record 244 games for the Raiders, while the statue erected of him outside Canberra Stadium is a fitting tribute to the player regarded by many as the club's finest.

26 RON COOTE (B. 1944)

- **South Sydney, Eastern Suburbs (1964-78):** 257 games—87 tries (261 points)
- **New South Wales (1965-75):** 13 matches—6 tries (18 points)
- **Australia (1967-75):** 23 Tests—13 tries (39 points)

Ron Coote's selection in the second-row in the ARL's Team of the Century is perhaps the most pertinent illustration of his greatness. St. George's Johnny Raper was an automatic choice at lock, but the long-striding Coote—Raper's contemporary and successor—was too good to leave out of the side. A devastating ball-runner and the only cover defender in the game's history that can compare to Raper, Coote played eight of his first nine Tests in the second-row before assuming the lock position for Australia in 1970, the year he captained Australia to a World Cup triumph. Coote's influence can be measured by his extraordinary Grand Final record—from 1965-75, Coote featured in nine deciders (behind only Norm Provan and Brian Clay in premiership history). He won premierships with Souths in 1967-68 and 1970-71 before joining Easts, captaining the Roosters to a Grand Final defeat in 1972, and starring in back-to-back title triumphs in 1974-75. Awarded the Harry Sunderland Medal for his performances in the 1970 and 1974 Ashes series, Coote was named Player of the Year in E.E. Christensen's *Official Rugby League Yearbook* a record four times (1968-69, 1974 and 1976). Coote's ability to find the tryline is often overlooked, but with 13 tries he is the most prolific tryscoring forward in Australia's Test history, despite a self-imposed representative hiatus from 1971-73.

27 IAN WALSH (B. 1933)
- **St. George (1962-67):** 94 games—4 tries (12 points)
- **New South Wales (1959-66):** 17 matches—1 try (3 points)
- **Australia (1959-66):** 25 Tests—0 points

Ian Walsh is a strong contender for the mantle of Australia's greatest hooker, while his place among Rugby League's finest captains is even more assured. He was selected for the 1959-60 Kangaroo Tour from the central west NSW country town of Eugowra, playing all six Tests against Great Britain and France. Walsh was shrewdly lured to Sydney by six-time premiers St. George in 1962 and represented Australia against the touring Lions, before captaining his country to a historic Ashes series victory on the 1963-64 Kangaroo Tour in the absence of injured captain-coach Arthur Summons. He assumed the Dragons' captain-coach role from retired great Norm Provan in 1966 and led the club to the last of its 11 straight premierships, just months after skippering Australia's home series triumph over Great Britain in a stunning season of achievement for the hooker. Walsh retired after the Saints' run ended in the 1967 preliminary final. The man known as 'Abdul' was a tremendous all-round hooker—a voracious ball-winner when scrums were still a contest, a slick dummy-half and a tough defender. Walsh was named as hooker in the Team of the 1960s and the NSW Country Team of the Century, while he was one of the unluckiest omissions from the ARL Team of the Century—the hooker spot went instead to Noel Kelly, a hooker-prop and regular Test teammate of Walsh's.

28 TOM GORMAN (B. 1901 D. 1978)
- **Queensland (1921-30):** 27 matches—6 tries (18 points)
- **Australia (1924-30):** 10 Tests—0 points

Tom Gorman's treasured place in Australian Rugby League history was solidified when he became the first Queenslander to captain a Kangaroo Tour, leading the 1929-30 squad to Britain and through the famous 'Chimpy' Busch 'no try' Ashes series. But 'Gentleman Tom' had already crafted a legacy as arguably the finest centre of the 1920s. Gorman was an integral part of Toowoomba's 'Galloping

Clydesdales' line-up that defeated all-comers during the mid-1920s and was a mainstay of the Queensland backline during a period of Maroons dominance unmatched in the pre-Origin era. He made his Test debut against the touring Lions in 1924 and captained Australia in all three Tests of the hard-fought series loss to the 1928 England tourists. A stylish and elusive attacking centre, players and pundits in both hemispheres marvelled at his class. Gorman was chosen to partner Mal Meninga in the centres in Queensland's Team of the Century named in 2008.

29 JIMMY CRAIG (B. 1895 D. 1959)

- **Balmain, University, Western Suburbs (1915-30):** 93 games—28 tries, 108 goals (310 points)
- **Queensland (1923-28):** 18 matches—8 tries, 29 goals (82 points)
- **New South Wales (1929):** 2 matches—3 goals (6 points)
- **Australia (1921-28):** 7 Tests—6 goals (12 points)

Jimmy Craig's status as an all time great is predominantly built around his supreme versatility. But such is Craig's immense talent, he would have ranked among the best ever in his position had he stayed in one spot. Craig was integral to the Balmain side that won five premierships in six seasons (1915-17 and 1919-20), predominantly in the three-quarter line. He made his Test debut at centre on the 1921-22 Kangaroo Tour and spent a season with University before moving north in 1923, becoming one of the most influential players in the history of Queensland Rugby League. Craig skippered Queensland to interstate series victories in 1923-24 and featured in further triumphs over NSW in 1925-26 and 1928, starring at fullback, centre or in the halves. He captained Australia in the 1924 home Ashes series loss to Great Britain and finished his Test career by playing all three matches when the Lions toured again in 1928. Craig played Tests at centre, fullback and halfback. Returning to Sydney as captain-coach of Wests in 1929, Craig led the club to its maiden premiership as a 35-year-old halfback in 1930—a triumphant finish to a truly unique playing career. A wonderful all-round attacking player, Craig was rated by no less a judge than Dally Messenger as the finest player he ever saw. A reserve spot in Queensland's Team of the Century named in 2008 was a fine tribute to the game's first great utility.

30 DUNCAN HALL (B. 1925—D. 2011)

- **Queensland (1948-55):** 19 matches—8 tries (24 points)
- **Australia (1948-55):** 23 Tests—9 tries (27 points)

Inimitably tough and skilful, front-row enforcer Duncan Hall was one of five Queenslanders picked in the ARL's Team of the Century in 2008—but was the only one to not feature in the NSWRL premiership. His outstanding performances in 23 Tests for Australia swayed the judges to include Hall, whose nomadic career featured stints in Rockhampton, Home Hill, Toowoomba, and Brisbane with Valleys and Wests. Hall made his Test debut against New Zealand in 1948 and toured with the Kangaroos at the end of the year. He proved a frequent thorn in side of British Test teams, clashing with some of the great forwards in home Ashes series triumphs in 1950 and 1954, and on the 1952-53 Kangaroo Tour. Never taking a backward step in the face of provocation or intimidation, Hall was sent off in the spiteful third Test of 1952. A tremendous scrummager and expert of tight forward play, he was also a prolific try-scorer for a prop, crossing for nine Test tries. Hall's selection in the ARL and Queensland Teams of the Century was due recognition for the outstanding front-row forward from one of the game's toughest eras.

31 BRETT KENNY (B. 1961)

- **Parramatta (1980-93):** 265 games—110 tries (440 points)
- **New South Wales (1982-87):** 17 Origins—2 tries (8 points)
- **Australia (1982-87):** 17 Tests—10 tries (36 points)

Brett Kenny's breathtaking natural ability carried him to the loftiest of Rugby League's heights. A graceful ball-runner possessing blinding acceleration and unparalleled anticipation, Kenny was the consummate big-match performer. The five-eighth scored two tries in each of Parramatta's 1981-83 Grand Final victories, and had another two disallowed in the Eels' triumph in the try-less decider of 1986. Kenny kept vice-captain Wally Lewis out of the Test side on the 1982 Kangaroo Tour, while his instinctive brilliance was utilised at centre for Australia in subsequent seasons. One of NSW's finest Origin players, Kenny won eight of the 12 games he directly opposed Lewis at five-eighth, and won the 1985 Golden Boot as world Rugby League's outstanding individual. Kenny's phenomenal strike-rate of snaffling opposition passes garnered the title of the 'intercept king,' and he retired in 1993 with then-club record totals of 265 games and 110 tries.

32 NORM PROVAN (B. 1932)

- **St. George (1951-65):** 256 games—63 tries, 1 goal (191 points)
- **New South Wales (1954-61):** 20 matches—4 tries (12 points)
- **Australia (1954-60):** 18 Tests—8 tries (24 points)

Norm Provan's phenomenal Grand Final record alone is an obvious sign of the towering second-rower's influence. 'Sticks' featured in 10 consecutive premiership victories for the mighty St. George side, beginning with the 1956 Grand Final that started the club's world record run and culminating in a triumphant exit from the game after the pulsating 1965 decider against Souths played in front of a record SCG crowd. Provan captain-coached the Dragons from 1962-65, prolonging the legacy of revered club leader Ken Kearney. An imposing physical presence, Provan's powerful ball-running and tough defence were his on-field trademarks. His Test career began in the 1954 Ashes triumph on home soil, before touring with the 1956-57 Kangaroos, featuring in the World Cup-winning campaign in 1957 and grappling with the British forwards again in 1958. Provan's selection as a second-rower in the ARL Team of the Century in 2008 secured his rightful place as one of Australia's greatest forwards.

33 HARRY BATH (B. 1924 D. 2008)

- **Balmain, St. George (1946-59):** 90 games—21 tries, 240 goals (543 points)
- **Queensland (1945):** 2 matches—1 try (3 points)
- **New South Wales (1946-47):** 3 matches—2 tries (6 points)

Referred to as the 'greatest forward never to play for Australia' for more than half a century, it is doubtful whether any player has been as revered or achieved more success without starring in the rigours of Test football than the 'Old Fox.' The Brisbane Souths junior won a premiership and represented Queensland in 1945, before heading to Sydney and winning back-to-back Grand Finals with Balmain in 1946-47, representing NSW in each season. Only a knee injury prevented him from representing Australia against the touring Lions. Bath was lured to from Australia's shores by English club Barrow and became a legend of the British game with Warrington, celebrating Challenge Cup success in 1950 and 1954 along with the status as one of the best-ever Australian imports. He returned home at the age of 32 in 1957, joining defending premiers St. George and helping the club to three more Grand Final victories before retiring at the end of 1959. Bath's experience and guile garnered from the fields of England provided yet another facet to the unstoppable Saints machine's amoury. A prolific point-scorer on the British club scene, Bath set a Sydney premiership record for most points in a season by a forward (225), while his eight goals in the 1957 decider remains a Grand Final record. Bath's feat of winning five Grand Finals in his only five seasons in the premiership is unmatched.

34 CAMERON SMITH (B. 1983)
- **Melbourne (2002-11):** 216 games—31 tries, 530 goals (1,184 points)
- **Queensland (2003-11):** 24 Origins—4 tries, 15 goals (46 points)
- **Australia (2006-11):** 28 Tests—6 tries, 23 goals (70 points)

Cameron Smith is a contender for the title of the most dominant player of the NRL era and has arguably usurped Steve Walters and Danny Buderus as the greatest of the modern hookers. An effective and tireless defender, incredibly durable, a superb organiser from dummy-half and a wonderful kicker—both in general play and from the tee—Smith possesses the playmaking class of the game's top halves. The Logan Brothers junior has developed into the consummate leader since joining Melbourne in 2002, and is the heir apparent to the Australian and Queensland captaincy in the wake of Darren Lockyer's retirement. Smith has collected a plethora of individual awards: he won the Dally M Medal in 2006 and finished in the top-three in 2007-08; he was the 2007 Golden Boot recipient; and won the Wally Lewis Medal as the player of the State of Origin series in 2007 and 2011. The personification of consistency, Smith's contribution to the recent dominance of Melbourne, Queensland and Australia has been colossal.

35 STEVE ROGERS (B. 1953 D. 2006)
- **Cronulla, St. George (1973-85):** 231 games—90 tries, 543 goals, 10 field goals (1,374 points)
- **New South Wales (1973-82):** 19 matches—7 tries, 6 goals (33 points)
- **Australia (1975-83):** 24 Tests—12 tries, 4 goals (45 points)

Steve Rogers' selection as a reserve in the NSW Team of the Century is a glowing endorsement of his status as one of Rugby League's brightest stars of the 1970s and early-1980s. He debuted for Cronulla, played in a Grand Final and toured with the Kangaroos in 1973 as an 18-year-old, and won the coveted Rothmans Medal in 1975. Rogers toured twice more with the Kangaroos (1978 and 1982), forming one of the greatest centre partnerships with Mick Cronin during a 24-Test career and captaining his country against France in 1981. An incisive ball-runner with brilliant speed, footwork and balance, and a copybook defender, it was at centre that 'Sludge' shone on the representative scene. But he proved his versatility and playmaking class by winning the Dally M Medal in 1981 while playing at lock for the Sharks. Named Cronulla's greatest clubman by the Men of League during the 2008 Centenary celebrations, Rogers fell agonisingly short of winning an elusive premiership during a two-season stint at St. George.

36 HERB NARVO (B. 1912 D. 1958)

- **Newtown, St. George (1937-49):** 61 games—18 tries, 15 goals (84 points)
- **New South Wales (1937-45):** 11 matches—10 tries (30 points)
- **Australia (1937-38):** 4 Tests—2 tries (6 points)

Herb Narvo led a nomadic Rugby League existence, but left a legacy as one of the toughest forwards Australia has produced and one of the foremost players of the 1930s and 1940s. The Newcastle product joined Newtown in 1937 and toured with the Kangaroos at the end of the season after injury claimed Easts forward Sid 'Joe' Pearce. Narvo was a star of the tour, featuring in four Tests. He returned to Newcastle for several seasons, while World War II curtailed his Test career. But Narvo came back to Newtown in 1943 and provided the muscle in the Bluebags' last premiership triumph. A punishing defender and a fearsome ball-runner, Narvo was a genuine enforcer but a scrupulously clean and fair player. Narvo mixed first grade football with a professional boxing career in the first half of the 1940s, and won the Australian heavyweight title in 1945. He was lured to St. George as captain-coach in 1946 and guided the club to the minor premiership and a Grand Final appearance (a 13-12 loss to Balmain), before stints in NSW Country and late-career homecomings at Newtown and Newcastle Norths. Narvo was named as a second-rower in the Newtown, Newcastle District and NSW Country Teams of the Century in 2008.

37 JOHNATHAN THURSTON (B. 1983)

- **Canterbury, North Queensland (2002-11):** 176 games—63 tries, 386 goals, 3 field goals (1,027 points)
- **Queensland (2005-11):** 21 Origins—3 tries, 52 goals, 2 field goals (118 points)
- **Australia (2006-11):** 22 Tests—9 tries, 95 goals (226 points)

North Queensland halfback Johnathan Thurston has emerged as one of the NRL era's great individual talents. After playing a bit-part role in the Bulldogs' 2004 premiership victory, Thurston joined the Cowboys and spearheaded the club's drive to a maiden Grand Final appearance (a 30-16 loss to the Wests Tigers) in 2005. He won the Dally M Medal that year, before becoming part of a select band of players to win the award twice in 2007, while he finished second in 2009 and garnered a top-five placing in 2006 and 2011. An intrepid competitor, Thurston boasts brilliant playmaking instincts, superb sleight of hand, a penetrative running game and a consummate all-round kicking game. Thurston has been the first-choice Australian No.7 since Andrew Johns' representative retirement in 2006, while he has made 21 consecutive Origin appearances for Queensland since making his debut in 2005 and has been the linchpin of the Maroons' run of six straight series victories. The Souths-Sunnybank (Brisbane) junior was named at halfback in the Indigenous Team of the Century in 2008.

38 MICHAEL CRONIN (B. 1951)

- **Parramatta (1977-86):** 216 games—75 tries, 865 goals, 2 field goals (1,971 points)
- **New South Wales (1973-83)*:** 25 matches—7 tries, 81 goals (183 points)
- **Australia (1973-82):** 33 Tests—9 tries, 141 goals (309 points)

Michael Cronin's greatness is a two-pronged phenomenon—he was a magnificent presence at centre setting up his supports, and he was a point-scorer the likes of which Australian Rugby League had never seen. The Gerringong great had already toured with the 1973 Kangaroos and made 12 Test appearances before Parramatta finally lured him to Sydney in 1977. He won back-to-back Rothmans Medals in his first two seasons for the Eels, and broke the premiership record for points in a season with 282 (a mark that stood for 20 years) among 547 points in games at all levels— a world record for a calendar year. Veteran Cronin was a steadying influence in the dazzling young Parramatta backline that won four premierships (1981-83 and 1986), retiring in triumph with great mate Ray Price after the 1986 Grand Final. Cronin's career pointscoring total of 1,971 remained a record for 14 years. He toured with the Kangaroos again in 1978 before retiring from representative football prior to the 1982 tour with 309 Test points to his name—a record total unsurpassed three decades later. Cronin's popularity and importance in Parramatta's narrative was emphasised by his naming as the Eels' greatest clubman by the Men of League in 2008, while he was named in the centres in the NSW Country Team of the Century.

39 ERIC WEISSEL (B. 1903 D. 1972)

- **New South Wales (1929-32):** 5 matches—7 goals (14 points)
- **Australia (1928-32):** 8 Tests—1 try, 15 goals (33 points)

A legendary Rugby League figure in the Riverina region, Eric Weissel ranks as one of the two greatest players (with Newcastle's Wally Prigg) to play their entire career in country NSW. Weissel played 18 seasons with Riverina clubs and dominated the famed Maher Cup competition. His international career consisted of eight Tests against England in three hard-fought Ashes series; he earned an incredible plaudit from legendary England halfback and captain Jonty Parkin, who proclaimed Weissel was the best player he ever saw. A fine goalkicker, Weissel top-scored with 127 points on the 1929-30 Kangaroo Tour, while his brilliant long run on an injured ankle to set up a try for halfback Hec Gee during the 1932 series has passed into Ashes folklore. Widely described as the complete five-eighth, the Cootamundra-born Weissel captained Country Firsts to upset victories of City Firsts in 1928 and 1930.

40 GRAHAM EADIE (B. 1953)

- **Manly (1971-83):** 237 games—71 tries, 847 goals, 3 field goals (1,917 points)
- **New South Wales (1974-80)*:** 13 matches—3 tries, 8 goals (25 points)
- **Australia (1973-79):** 20 Tests—7 Tests, 12 goals (45 points)

Woy Woy product Graham Eadie debuted for Manly as a 17-year-old in 1971; by the time he was 20, Eadie had won two Grand Finals and made his Test debut on the 1973 Kangaroo Tour. A 95kg powerhouse, 'Wombat' built a reputation as one of the most damaging fullbacks Rugby League has produced—and one of the best. Eadie played in four Grand Final victories for the Sea Eagles, with his magnificent performance in the 1978 Grand Final replay paving the way for a 16-0 triumph. He replaced injured captain-coach Graeme Langlands at fullback during the 1973 Ashes series and was Australia's first-choice No.1 from 1975 until the end of the decade, playing 20 Tests. Eadie's goalkicking prowess and powerful ball-running earned him a then-premiership record 1,917 points by the time he retired after Manly's 1983 Grand Final loss (the record was eclipsed two years later by Mick Cronin). In a wonderful postscript to his career, Eadie was lured out of retirement by former Test teammate Chris Anderson to play for Halifax and won the Lance Todd Trophy as man of the match in the club's 1987 Challenge Cup final victory.

41 KEN THORNETT (B. 1937)

- **Parramatta (1962-71):** 129 games—17 tries, 6 field goals (63 points)
- **New South Wales (1963-64):** 2 matches—0 points
- **Australia (1963-64):** 12 Tests—6 tries (18 points)

Ken Thornett's nickname—'The Mayor of Parramatta'—gives a fair indication of the brilliant fullback's impact on his club. A rugby union convert, Thornett arrived at Parramatta via English club Leeds in 1962. After six straight wooden spoons, the Eels qualified for their maiden finals series on the back of Thornett's magnificent performances. He spearheaded the club's top-four finishes in the following three seasons, including 1965 as captain-coach. Thornett, a dangerous attacking No.1 and impregnable in defence or under the high ball, had a brief but memorable spell in the international limelight. He played 12 Tests in the space of 13 months and toured with the 1963-64 Kangaroos alongside brother Dick, a former Wallaby and a teammate at Parramatta. Thornett starred in Australia's resounding Ashes triumph over Great Britain—the first series win on British soil in 52 years. He left Parramatta for Coonabarabran at the end of 1968, but made a triumphant return in 1971 to revive the Eels' flagging fortunes, captaining the club to a finals appearance.

42 GEORGE TREWEEK (B. 1905 D. 1991)

- **South Sydney (1926-34):** 118 games—37 tries (117 points)
- **New South Wales (1927-33):** 18 matches—8 tries (24 points)
- **Australia (1928-30):** 7 Tests—1 try (3 points)

When *Rugby League Week* assembled a panel of experts to select a 'best-ever' team in 1982 to mark 75 years of Rugby League in Australia, South Sydney great George Treweek was chosen in the second-row alongside Norm Provan; many fine judges that were fortunate enough to see the tall, destructive ball-runner attest that he was the greatest second-row forward the game has seen. An integral part of the Souths dynasty that dominated the premiership in the late-1920s and early-1930s, Treweek shared in title victories in 1926-28 and 1932-33, captaining the side in 1933 (he was on tour with the Kangaroos and missed the club's 1929 final victory). Treweek played seven Tests against England in the 1928 home Ashes series and on the 1929-30 Kangaroo Tour, but business commitments curtailed his representative career thereafter. Chosen in best-ever South Sydney teams in 2002 and 2004, Treweek's legacy as one of Rugby League's greatest attacking forwards remains strong.

43 KEITH BARNES (B. 1934)

- **Balmain (1955-68):** 194 games—11 tries, 742 goals, 1 field goal (1,519 points)
- **New South Wales (1956-63):** 11 matches—4 tries, 49 goals (110 points)
- **Australia (1957-66):** 17 Tests—59 goals (118 points)

Invariably, discussion about Keith Barnes' wonderful career turns to his outstanding goalkicking ability—he was a phenomenal match-winner with the boot—but he was also a courageous, skilful and unflappable fullback, and one of Rugby League's finest captains. The Welsh-born Barnes debuted for Australia during the 1957 World Cup, before captaining the 1959-60 Kangaroos to Britain and France, top-scoring for the squad with 202 points. Barnes led his country in 10 of his 17 Test appearances, a captaincy mark second only to Clive Churchill at the time. He captained Balmain in the 1964 and '66 Grand Final losses to St. George, before retiring in 1968 with a then-premiership record 1,519 points to his name. Ironically,

Balmain claimed its last premiership a year later, but Barnes was rightly recognised as the greatest Tiger of them all—the Men of League named him as Balmain's greatest clubman as part of the 2008 Centenary celebrations.

44 BOB McCARTHY (B. 1944)

- **South Sydney, Canterbury (1963-78):** 251 games—119 tries, 1 field goal (358 points)
- **New South Wales (1969-75):** 11 matches—7 tries (21 points)
- **Australia (1969-74):** 15 Tests—7 tries, 1 field goal (22 points)

South Sydney great Bob McCarthy was revolutionary figure—the first of the wide-running second-row forwards. McCarthy's combination of speed, power and size saw him become one of the game's most dangerous attacking weapons in the 1960s. Playing in five Grand Finals for the Rabbitohs, McCarthy won premierships in 1967 and 1970-71, scoring a famous intercept try in the 12-10 defeat of Canterbury in the 1967 decider. McCarthy was a shock omission from the subsequent Kangaroo Tour squad, but he went on to play 15 Tests and captained Australia in the series-saving second Test victory against Great Britain on the 1973 Kangaroo Tour. The powerhouse backrower became the first forward since the legendary Frank Burge to score 100 career tries in 1975, before having a two-season stint with Canterbury and captaining the club to the finals in 1976. McCarthy returned to finish his illustrious career with Souths in 1978 and was named in best-ever club line-ups in 2002 and 2004.

45 SID 'SANDY' PEARCE (B. 1883 D. 1930)

- **Eastern Suburbs (1908-21):** 157 games—5 tries (15 points)
- **New South Wales (1910-20):** 6 matches—1 try (3 points)
- **Australia (1908-21):** 14 Tests—0 points

A giant of the pioneering era, Sid 'Sandy' Pearce was the greatest of the pre-World War II hookers and ranks as one of the most durable players in Rugby League history. Pearce was one of the rugby union defectors that played against the New Zealand 'All Golds' in 1907, becoming a foundation Easts player in the inaugural premiership season and touring with the 1908-09 Kangaroos. He was a key component of the Tricolours' 1911-13 premiership-winning dynasty and played all three Tests against the touring Lions in 1914 and 1920. Tough, uncompromising and an exceedingly popular character within the Rugby League fraternity, Pearce became the first Sydney player to amass 150 first grade appearances and toured with the 1921-22 Kangaroos at the age of 38, playing in the first two Tests against England before a broken leg ruled him out of the remainder of the tour. Pearce's Test career-span has been matched only by Darren Lockyer in 104 seasons of Rugby League in Australia. 'The Prince of Hookers' passed away prematurely in 1930, while his son Sid 'Joe' Pearce was one of the finest forwards of the decade and represented Australia in 13 Tests—the first father-son combination in Australian Test history. He was named at hooker in the NSW Team of the Century in 2008.

46 LES JOHNS (B. 1942)

- **Canterbury (1963-71):** 103 games—14 tries, 233 goals, 19 field goals (545 points)
- **New South Wales (1962-69):** 15 matches—5 tries, 74 goals, 3 field goals (169 points)
- **Australia (1963-69):** 14 Tests—2 tries, 30 goals (66 points)

A shining example of Les Johns' brilliance was his selection at fullback in the Team of the 1960s—a decade that featured fellow all time great custodians Graeme

Langlands, Keith Barnes and Ken Thornett. The golden-haired Newcastle champion arrived at Canterbury in 1963 and toured with the Kangaroos at the end of the year, but played the role of understudy to Test fullback Thornett. Johns played in Australia's Ashes-deciding third Test victory in 1966 and toured with the 1967-68 Kangaroos after helping Canterbury to a Grand Final appearance. He forced Langlands to centre and played all six Tests in Britain and France. Johns' career was frequently hampered by injury, but he possessed superb defence to complement a array of attacking attributes and was an outstanding goalkicker. His standing at Canterbury is emphasised by his selection at fullback in best-ever club combinations in 1985 and 2005.

47 BENJI MARSHALL (B. 1985)

- **Wests Tigers (2003-11):** 155 games—66 tries, 285 goals, 6 field goals (840 points)
- **New Zealand (2005-11):** 23 Tests—5 tries, 33 goals (86 points)

Benji Marshall debuted for the Wests Tigers as a precocious 18-year-old schoolboy in 2003, showing glimpses of the mesmerising footwork and ball-playing wizardry that would electrify the NRL in the ensuing years. The five-eighth's audacious flick pass for Pat Richards to score in the Grand Final was the iconic moment of the unheralded Tigers' 2005 premiership, but it is just one in a long line of spellbinding moments Marshall has conjured in his career to date. A succession of injuries threatened to derail his rise, but he played a vital role New Zealand's World Cup victory in 2008 and has proved extremely durable in recent seasons. Marshall came of age in 2010, winning the Golden Boot award after captaining the Kiwis to Four Nations glory with a majestic individual display in the final victory against Australia. His form at club level soared to new levels of virtuosity and consistency, finishing fourth in the 2010 Dally M Medal count and second in 2011. Marshall's eventual place among the all time greats is dependent on his longevity, but on the score of skill and match-winning brilliance, he already rates as one of the best the game has produced.

48 RICKY STUART (B. 1957)

- **Canberra, Canterbury (1988-2000):** 243 games—41 tries, 7 goals, 27 field goals (205 points)
- **New South Wales (1990-94):** 14 Origins—3 tries (12 points)
- **Australia (1990-94):** 9 Tests—1 try (4 points)

Largely overlooked in the pantheon of Australia's greatest halfbacks, Canberra linchpin Ricky Stuart was a notable omission from the ARL's 100 Greatest Players in 2008. But the tenacious, scheming No.7 rivalled Allan Langer and Raiders teammate Laurie Daley as the most influential player in the first half of the 1990s. Stuart's radar-like long and short kicking game, sleight of hand and pinpoint passing ability had few peers during his prime. The former Wallaby was integral to Canberra's maiden title success in 1989, finished second in the Dally Ms and won the Clive Churchill Medal after the club's 1990 Grand Final victory, and was at the absolute peak of his powers during the Raiders' resounding 1994 premiership charge. Stuart collected the rare Rothmans Medal-Dally M Medal double in 1993, but the Raiders' title bid fell to pieces after their key playmaker broke his ankle in the penultimate round. Langer kept him out of the Test line-up for the most part and ensured he never played an international on home soil, but Stuart's legacy to the Australian jersey is as an Ashes hero on consecutive Kangaroo Tours. Stuart replaced Langer after first Test losses to Great Britain in 1990 and 1994, steering Australia to series victories on each tour—most famously by setting up an injury-time try for Mal Meninga in the 14-10 second Test victory at Old Trafford in 1990. Stuart thrived in the Origin arena, playing opposite Langer in all 14 of his NSW appearances and spearheading four Blues series triumphs in five years from 1990-94.

49 CHARLES FRASER (B. 1893 D. 1981)

- **Balmain (1910-26):** 185 games—54 tries, 165 goals (492 points)
- **New South Wales (1915-21):** 5 matches—2 tries, 4 goals (14 points)
- **Australia (1911-22):** 11 Tests—2 tries, 1 field goal (8 points)

Charles 'Chook' Fraser's longevity and versatility mark him as a special player of Australian Rugby League's formative decades. Fraser was chosen to tour with the 1911-12 'Australasian' Kangaroos, and made his Test debut at fullback in the first encounter England aged 18 years and 301 days—retaining the record as Australia's youngest Test player for 97 years. He played two Tests at five-eighth against the touring England side in 1914, before playing a vital role in the Balmain dynasty's run of five premierships in six seasons from 1915-20. 'Chook' scored a memorable try from pivot in the first Test victory against England in 1920 and reverted to fullback as Australia secured its last Ashes series win for 30 years, while he captained his country in all three Tests on the 1921-22 Kangaroo Tour in the absence of injured skipper Les Cubitt. The Balmain legend captain-coached the club to the 1924 premiership and finished two years later with a club record of 185 games that stood for more than four decades. The diminutive and inventive 'Chook' Fraser was capable of playing anywhere in the backline, and was named at centre in Balmain's Team of the Century in 2000.

50 GLENN LAZARUS (B. 1965)

- **Canberra, Brisbane, Melbourne (1987-1999):** 254 games—21 tries, 1 goal (86 points)
- **New South Wales (1989-99):** 19 Origins—2 tries (8 points)
- **Australia (1990-99):** 21 Tests—1 try (4 points)

Glenn Lazarus was the dominant front-rower of the 1990s and the prototype for the modern-day prop—big, mobile and a rock-solid defender, with a liberal dash of skill to top it off. The Queanbeyan product is the only player in premiership history to win Grand Finals with three different clubs. Making this unique achievement all the more remarkable is the fact Lazarus was the engine-room cornerstone for the maiden title triumphs of Canberra, Brisbane and Melbourne. He won back-to-back premierships with the Raiders in 1989-90, provided the forward grunt the Broncos required to break through for their first titles in 1992-93, and was the 33-year-old captain of the Storm's incredible 1999 Grand Final victory in just the club's second season. Lazarus was equally dominant at representative level, starring on the 1990 and 1994 Kangaroo Tours and laying the forward platform for NSW Origin series victories in 1990, 1992-94 and 1996.

Notes: Club statistics available for NSWRL, ARL, Super League and NRL premierships only. Statistics for New South Wales and Queensland representation are for interstate and State of Origin matches only.

*Indicates the player represented in both residency-based and State of Origin interstate matches.

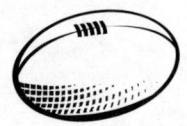

BIBLIOGRAPHY

BOOKS

Malcolm Andrews, *The ABC Of Rugby League*. ABC Books, Sydney, 2006

Geoff Armstrong (editor), *Wayne Pearce Presents: The Greatest Game*. Ironbark Press, Sydney, 1991

Neil Cadigan, *Rugby League Yarns: 100 Great Stories From 100 Great Year*, Dolphin Press, Sydney, 2008

Ray Chesterton, *100 Years Of Rugby League*. Hachette, Sydney, 2007

John Coffey and Bernie Wood, *The Kiwis: 100 Years Of International Rugby League*, Hachette Livre, Auckland, 2007

Ian Collis and Alan Whiticker, *Rugby League Test Matches In Australia*, ABC Books, Sydney, 1994

Ian Collis and Alan Whiticker, *The History Of Rugby League Clubs*. New Holland, Sydney, 2004

Ian Collis and Alan Whiticker, *The Top 10 Of Rugby League*, New Holland, Sydney, 2010

Michael Croke and Peter Jackson, *Whatd'yareckon!* Ironbark Press, Sydney, 1992

Helen Elward and Graeme Langlands, *State Of Origin: Gods Of The Ground*. Best Legenz, Australia, 2003

Sean Fagan, *The Rugby Rebellion: The Divide Of League And Union*. Sean Fagan, 2005

Sean Fagan and Dally Messenger III, *The Master: The Life And Times Of Dally Messenger, Australia's First Sporting Superstar*. Hachette Livre, Sydney, 2007

Jack Gallaway, *Brisbane Broncos: The Team To Beat*. University of Queensland Press, Brisbane, 2001

Steve Haddan, *The Finals: 100 Year Of National Rugby League Finals* (Third Edition). S. Haddan, Brisbane, 2008

Liam Hauser, *State Of Origin: 30 Years 1980-2008*. Rockpool Publishing, Sydney, 2010

Ian Heads, *True Blue: The Story Of The NSW Rugby League*. Ironbark Press, Sydney, 1992

Ian Heads and David Middleton, *A Centenary Of Rugby League 1908-2008: The Definitive Story Of The Game In Australia*. Pan Macmillan, Sydney, 2008

Max and Reet Howell, *The Greatest Game Under The Sun: The History Of Rugby League In Queensland*. Leon Bedington, Brisbane, 1989

Max and Reet Howell, *State Of Origin: The First Twelve Years*. Herron Publications, Brisbane, 1992

Gary Lester, *The Story Of Australian Rugby League*. Lester-Townsend Publishing, Sydney, 1988

Jim Main and Russell Holmseby, *The Encyclopedia Of League Footballers: Every AFL/VFL Player Since 1897*. Wilkinson Books, Melbourne, 1992

Roy Masters, *Bad Boys.* Random House, Sydney, 2006

John Maynard, *Aboriginal Stars Of The Turf: Jockeys Of Australian Racing History.* Aboriginal Studies Press, Canberra, 2002

David Middleton (editor), *Rugby League Week: 25 Sensational Years.* HarperSports, Sydney, 1995

Jack Pollard, *Rugby League The Australian Way.* Landsdowne Press, NSW, 1981

Jack Pollard, *Rugby League Legends.* The Book Company, Sydney, 1996

Bernie Pramberg, Paul Malone, Mike Colman and Barry Dick, *Broncos: 20 Fabulous Years.* Playwright Publishing, Sydney, 2007

Colin Tatz, *Obstacle Race: Aborigines In Sport.* University of New South Wales, 1995

Alan Whiticker, *Grand Finals Of The New South Wales Rugby League.* Gary Allen, Sydney, 1992

Alan Whiticker and Glen Hudson, *The Encyclopedia Of Rugby League Players.* Gary Allen, Sydney, 2007

ANNUALS AND YEARBOOKS

David Middleton's *Official Rugby League Yearbooks* (published by Lester-Townsend Publishing, 1988-91; Playwright Publishing, 1992; Ironbark Press, 1993; Pan Macmillan, 1994; HarperSports, 1995-2003; Lothian Press, 2004; News Magazines, 2004-2011)

Bernie Wood's *New Zealand Rugby League Annual* (published in Auckland by the New Zealand Rugby League, 1976-2003)

NEWSPAPERS, MAGAZINES AND PERIODICALS

Big League

Big League Annual

Bronco Magazine

Courier Mail

Daily Telegraph

National Rugby League Official Season Guide

Rugby League News

Rugby League Review

Rugby League Week

Rugby League Week: 40 Years 1970-2009

Rugby League Week: State of Origin— 25 Years Of Passion

Sunday Mail

Sunday Telegraph

Super League Official Magazine

Sydney Morning Herald

WEBSITES

www.allblacks.com

www.centenaryofrugbyleague.com.au

www.eraofthebiff.com

www.espnscrum.com

www.nrl.com

www.nrlstats.com

www.rleague.com

www.rugbyleagueproject.com

www.stats.rleague.com

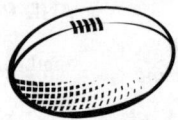

ACKNOWLEDGEMENTS

I am incredibly indebted to Nick Tedeschi, firstly for putting my original manuscript forward for publication, then for his months of industrious effort as editor of the book. Nick, thank you for your enthusiasm, guidance, suggestions, corrections and eagle-eyed editing. Working with such a passionate and knowledgeable Rugby League fanatic and a fantastic editor has been an absolute pleasure, and helped the book immeasurably. A huge thank you to Geoff Slattery for having the belief and vision to bring this project to fruition—your confidence in my original manuscript has seen it develop into something more ambitious than I could have imagined and I am infinitely grateful. And thanks to the entire team at Slattery Media Group for your tireless efforts and wonderful work in bringing this project together. Helen Alexander and Bronwyn Wilkie deserve a special mention—you made an unfamiliar and hectic process an incredibly smooth and enjoyable one for me.

Thanks to Alana, Kimily and Gemma for convincing me way back in our Dundas Street flat in 2006 that writing a book was a realistic goal—awesome pep talk. Massive thanks to Tim Butters, Mike Duncan, and Jo and Dean Bell for the constant encouragement from day one. Cam and Rich, your feedback and support from the book's early days was a huge help. Bryn, thanks for your professional services early on and your encouragement throughout.

Mizz and Dan, thanks for keeping me company as the earliest chapters came together at Camp Street, and for your support as the book progressed. Alice, I don't think anyone has been as enthusiastic as you about my writing—your support has been amazing. Huge thanks to all of my friends and family in Australia, New Zealand and further abroad—in particular the Brisbane crew—your kind words of encouragement have been overwhelming and incredibly humbling.

A special thank you to the team at Imprint Graphics in Whangarei, New Zealand— Mum's husband Phil Whitfield, Murray Inder (a true craftsman), Christine Robson and Jasmine Horton—for so generously printing off the original incarnation of the book in 2011.

Ian Heads, thank you for your assistance and guidance during the last few weeks of the process—to receive help and feedback from someone I've looked up to for so long has been a real thrill. Thanks to Brad Fittler for generously giving up your time to become involved in the book; having one of the all time greats and one of my personal favourites onboard has been something I'll never forget. A sincere thanks to Bob Howitt, Neil Cadigan, Terry Williams, Lyle Beaton, Ian Hauser, Glen Dwyer from the Newtown RLFC, Michael Hillier from the QRL, Terry Liberopoulos from

Rugby League Review, and especially Frank Endacott for the advice and help you have given me.

An enormous thanks to Christy and Big Russ for your constant support and enthusiasm, and for the care packages as the deadline loomed. Mum, words can't express how much I appreciate your unwavering support and encouragement through all these years; Dad, thanks for introducing me to Rugby League and helping instil my passion for the game—this book was written with you in mind.

The biggest thanks of all time goes to my soon-to-be wife Ruth. Your support and encouragement, hours of proof-reading, and extraordinary patience has been amazing. I love you.

And lastly, thanks to all of the players, officials, writers, media and fans that have made—and continue to make—Rugby League such a great game, inspiring me to write this book.

BIOGRAPHIES

Will Evans was born in Southport, Queensland, in 1981. He was brought up in Tutukaka and Queenstown in New Zealand, where his obsession with Rugby League began. After graduating from the University of Otago in 2006 with a Bachelor of Arts in History, Will returned to Australia to live in Brisbane. Will writes for *Rugby League Review* and website *Back Page Lead. A Short History of Rugby League in Australia* is his first book.

Nick Tedeschi was born in Cowra, New South Wales, in 1981 and fell in love with Rugby League at a young age. Nick studied Arts/Commerce at ANU and after working as a political advisor and a bookmaker, Nick became a sportswriter. Nick is the owner/managing editor of website *Making The Nut*, the Rugby League editor of website *Back Page Lead* and the author of *The Punters' Guide to the 2012 NRL Season*, published by The Slattery Media Group (2012).

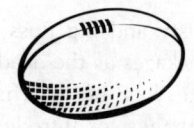

INDEX